EVIDENCE

ASPEN CASEBOOK SERIES

EVIDENCE

A Structured Approach

Fourth Edition

David P. Leonard
Late Professor of Law and William M. Rains Fellow
Loyola Law School, Los Angeles

Victor J. Gold
William H. Hannon Professor of Law and Dean Emeritus
Loyola Law School, Los Angeles

Gary C. Williams
Professor of Law and Johnnie L. Cochran, Jr. Chair in Civil Rights
Loyola Law School, Los Angeles

Wolters Kluwer

Published by Wolters Kluwer in New York.

Wolters Kluwer Legal & Regulatory US serves customers worldwide with CCH, Aspen Publishers, and Kluwer Law International products. (www.WKLegaledu.com)

To contact Customer Service, e-mail customer.service@wolterskluwer.com, call 1-800-234-1660, fax 1-800-901-9075, or mail correspondence to:

> Wolters Kluwer
> Attn: Order Department
> PO Box 990
> Frederick, MD 21705

Printed in the United States of America.

1 2 3 4 5 6 7 8 9 0

ISBN 978-1-4548-6310-6

Library of Congress Cataloging-in-Publication Data

Names: Leonard, David P., author. | Gold, Victor J., 1950- author. |
    Williams, Gary C. (Lawyer), author.
Title: Evidence : a structured approach / David P. Leonard, Late Professor of
    Law and William M. Rains Fellow Loyola Law School, Los Angeles; Victor J.
    Gold, William H. Hannon Professor of Law and Dean Emeritus, Loyola Law
    School, Los Angeles; Gary C. Williams, Professor of Law and Johnnie L.
    Cochran, Jr. Chair in Civil Rights, Loyola Law School, Los Angeles.
Description: Fourth edition | New York : Wolters Kluwer, 2016. | Series:
    Aspen casebook series | Includes index.
Identifiers: LCCN 2016012937 | ISBN 9781454863106
Subjects: LCSH: Evidence (Law) — United States. | LCGFT: Casebooks.
Classification: LCC KF8935 .L458 2016 | DDC 347.73/6 — dc23
LC record available at http://lccn.loc.gov/2016012937

About Wolters Kluwer Legal & Regulatory US

Wolters Kluwer Legal & Regulatory US delivers expert content and solutions in the areas of law, corporate compliance, health compliance, reimbursement, and legal education. Its practical solutions help customers successfully navigate the demands of a changing environment to drive their daily activities, enhance decision quality and inspire confident outcomes.

Serving customers worldwide, its legal and regulatory portfolio includes products under the Aspen Publishers, CCH Incorporated, Kluwer Law International, ftwilliam.com and MediRegs names. They are regarded as exceptional and trusted resources for general legal and practice-specific knowledge, compliance and risk management, dynamic workflow solutions, and expert commentary.

SUMMARY OF CONTENTS

CONTENTS

PREFACE TO THE FOURTH EDITION

In this edition we have added a section at the end of each chapter entitled Assessments, consisting of five multiple-choice questions and an analysis of the answers. This new feature provides the student with an opportunity to assess the extent to which he or she has mastered the material in each chapter. Many questions also require that the student recall matters covered in preceding chapters, thus providing an opportunity to see the relationships between the different parts of evidence law. The analysis following the questions gives a detailed explanation of why each alternative answer is correct or incorrect. It also gives the student tips on how to analyze multiple-choice questions, an important skill to acquire before taking the Multistate Bar Examination.

We also have streamlined and clarified the materials contained in the Third Edition while maintaining our basic approach, which emphasizes the use of explanatory text and concise examples and deemphasizes cases. For more detail about our method, please refer to the Preface to the First Edition, which immediately follows.

This edition goes to press over five years after the passing of one of the original authors, Professor David P. Leonard. His name remains on this edition because it continues to reflect the clarity of his thought and writing, his gentle humor, and his love of teaching.

Victor J. Gold
Gary C. Williams

January 2016

PREFACE TO THE FIRST EDITION

The goal of *Evidence: A Structured Approach* is to make it easier both to teach and to learn evidence law, while keeping the subject intellectually challenging. The book facilitates teaching because its unique format complements the way most evidence professors already teach. The book facilitates learning because its format encourages preparation by focusing students' attention on the specific questions to be posed during class. As a result, basic doctrine can be covered quickly and efficiently, leaving more classroom time for analysis. The format employs what we call a "structured approach" to Socratic teaching.

A Structured Approach

Virtually every section of the book begins with one of the Federal Rules of Evidence or a part of one of the rules. The rule is followed by text that explains the rule's background, rationale, and content. This text provides numerous examples to ensure that students understand the law. Transcript exercises, diagrams, charts, and other materials supplement the explanatory text. We include an edited version of a case if it illustrates the rule effectively or provides important additional law. Working together, these features free the professor from the need to take extensive class time to describe the law and thus leave more time to focus on application and analysis.

Although we include many of the seminal cases in evidence law, these cases are provided only as supplements to the rules and explanatory text. Cases are intended to be neither the main source of information about the rules nor the principal focus of classroom discussion. Instead, the centerpiece of each section is a feature entitled Questions for Classroom Discussion. Most of these questions are short hypotheticals, each of which explores a limited aspect of the rule in question. The hypotheticals logically build upon preceding questions until the rule is fully explicated. As the title of this feature implies, these are the very questions the professor will pose during classroom discussion. The book thereby lends itself to Socratic teaching while providing a clear structure and direction for the classroom dialogue.

Because the format of the book encourages students to prepare for class, it makes teaching less frustrating and more fun. It also allows more class time to be devoted to issues of special interest to the professor. And because the Questions for Classroom Discussion are narrowly drawn and are preceded by an explanation of the law, students who prepare for class are in an excellent position to understand the questions and analyze them properly. In addition, students who use laptop computers in class may download the questions from our website before class, for a head start on class notes (https://my.lls.edu/evidence structuredapproach). Students appreciate this approach because it saves time and allows them to focus on what is important.

Emphasis on the Federal Rules

Traditional casebooks often complicate teaching and learning evidence law. This is because judicial opinions usually include facts and issues that are not pertinent to evidence law and sometimes even get that law wrong. Cases rarely facilitate the professor's systematic effort to build students' understanding of an evidence rule because judicial opinions simply are not written with that purpose in mind. As a result, students using a traditional casebook may have difficulty determining the meaning of a case and which aspects of a case will be the focus of the professor's attention. Students are often surprised by the professor's questions and discouraged from devoting significant effort to class preparation. Unprepared students are not ready to participate or think when they come to class. Because they are confused about the law when they arrive, they think the purpose of attending class is to transcribe what the professor says about the law.

Law students have to learn to teach themselves the law. But written rules, not cases, are the primary source of evidence law today. Students figure this out very early in the evidence course, which leads them to pay little attention to cases. As a result, classroom discussion of the details of the cases can be frustrating and unproductive. By focusing discussion on the rules, this book encourages preparation, making classroom discussion much more satisfying for students and teachers alike.

In focusing on the Federal Rules of Evidence, we seek not only to teach the particulars of each individual rule, but also to demonstrate that the Rules comprise a mostly coherent system of interrelated parts, many of which may be pertinent to the admissibility of just a single item of evidence. Again, our format is well adapted to conveying this message. As you review the Questions for Classroom Discussion in a given section, you will encounter questions that return to rules previously covered or anticipate issues developed in a subsequent chapter. The pedagogical intent is both to show the interrelationships among different rules and to reinforce earlier lessons.

Organization

Two aspects of our book's organization are important to note. First, Chapter 1 addresses rules governing the principal sources of evidence: witnesses and documents. Most evidence textbooks address these rules toward the end. As a consequence, many of the rules are covered in haste during the last days of the semester, or simply are not covered at all. We *begin* with these rules because they acquaint students with the basic nature of proof and the trial process, they are fairly simple and ease students into the subject of evidence law, and they provide an important foundation for understanding more complex doctrines to follow, such as hearsay.

Second, having established the basics of relevance analysis in Chapter 2, we immediately proceed to hearsay in Chapter 3. We address this subject as early as possible because it is the most difficult material in the course. In our experience, the more time students have to think about hearsay, the better they will come to understand it. We then immediately return in Chapter 4 to the relevance rules.

Teaching and Leaning Hearsay

As the most difficult material in the course, the hearsay coverage is the most crucial chapter in any evidence textbook. We have found that the most effective way to teach and learn hearsay is through as many short practice hypotheticals as possible. Our format, centered around the Questions for Classroom Discussion feature, is well adapted to this approach, Accordingly, the hearsay chapter features a very large number of short hypotheticals that illustrate virtually every angle of the definition of hearsay and the important hearsay exceptions and exemptions.

The Importance of Technology

Aside from providing students with some of the seminal cases in evidence law, we have chosen a number of cases that illustrate how courts are interpreting the rules to address problems posed by modern technological innovations. Special attention is given to authentication, hearsay, and best evidence problems raised by evidence in various digital formats. We also focus on the latest controversies concerning the admissibility of scientific and other expert evidence, including recent amendments to the opinion evidence rules.

Real Life

The gap between most textbooks and the real-life practice of law is immense. We aim to narrow that gap in several ways. For example, this book contains many transcripts illustrating how a given issue typically is presented in court. We also include cases selected to show how race and gender questions pose special issues under the Federal Rules of Evidence. It is important to show that, although those rules on their face appear race and gender neutral, in real life the application of the rules can implicate race and gender issues in surprising ways.

Thanks

Many people have helped in the creation of this book. We would like to thank the William M. Rains Foundation for its support, and our colleagues at Loyola Law School for their encouragement and advice. Professors Laurie Levenson and Gary Williams were especially helpful. Law students Joohan Song (Class of 2004) and Sabrina Cao-Garcia (Class of 2005) provided valuable assistance. Finally, special recognition goes to our evidence professor and mentor, Kenneth W. Graham, Jr., who — with wit and brilliance — taught us how to read. This book is dedicated to him.

David P. Leonard
Victor J. Gold

March 2004

ACKNOWLEDGMENTS

Foer, Jonathan Safran. "Introduction" in *The Diary of Petr Ginz: 1941-1942*, ed. Chava Pressburger, 28-29. Grove/Atlantic. Copyright © 2007 Jonathan Safran Foer. Reprinted by permission of Grove/Atlantic, Inc.

Kaye, David H. *Science in Evidence*. Anderson Publishing. Copyright © 1997 David H. Kaye. Reprinted by permission.

Lewinsky, Monica S. "Tell Mama All About It? Not Without a Lawyer: Parents and Children Shouldn't Be Required to Testify Against Each Other", *Los Angeles Times*, May 11, 2003 at M5. Copyright © 2003 Monica S. Lewinsky. Reprinted by permission.

Myers, Richard E., II. "Detector Dogs and Probable Cause", 14 *George Mason Law Review*, 1, 13-15. Copyright © 2006 George Mason Law Review. Reprinted by permission.

EVIDENCE

CHAPTER
1

The Process of Proof

A. THE TRIAL: AN OVERVIEW

1. Introduction

A trial involves the telling of a story. But a good writer would never tell a story the way the law conducts a trial. People who know what happened are not allowed simply to tell the story in the way they see fit. Instead, lawyers often rudely interrupt a witness's narrative to argue about arcane legal issues. At the end of these arguments the judge might instruct the witness not to talk about certain things or to talk about them in one way but not another, all without ever explaining why. The lawyers further control the telling of the story by deciding what questions to ask. These questions rarely allow the witness to explain things the way she would like and often fail to tell the jurors what they want to know. After the witness responds to one lawyer's questions, the other lawyer typically attacks her answers and sometimes even her character. To put it simply, testifying can be a frustrating, intimidating, and even humiliating experience.

Consider what one physician who had been called to testify as an expert on a number of occasions had to say about the experience:

> Physicians are sometimes hesitant to testify in a court of law because it's not a very pleasant experience to be called upon as a so-called expert witness. . . . I've been humiliated and demoralized and I've been accused of having second-rate training and of being less than intelligent, and that's not a very pleasant experience. I've always felt that when I've appeared as an expert witness that I was performing a service. . . .
>
> And some physicians look at what happens in the courtroom as simply a big chess game played by people who make up their own rules, speak their own language. And wonder under those circumstances how possibly a court could have the audacity to make scientific decisions in that kind of a setting. And so, many physicians have decided after going through this once or twice, that to hell with them. . . . The decisions that are going to be made aren't going to be made on the basis of medicine anyway. It's going to be some sort of arbitrary decision made by people who listen to words that can only be spoken under rules that nobody but a lawyer understands.[1]

---

1. Comments of Derek Sharvelle, M.D., to David Leonard's Torts class, Indiana University School of Law — Indianapolis (1981).

1

Lawyers and law students steeped in the traditions of the adversary system might be quick to dismiss this critique on the ground it reflects the typical layperson's ignorance of that system. But this reaction fails to pay sufficient attention to the essence of the critique. The physician assumes that the goal of a trial should be to get at the truth and that trial procedures should be similar to the procedures used by scientists to uncover the truth. In the most popular view of the scientific method,[2] the inquiry begins with an idea — a hypothesis — and proceeds by the accumulation of evidence to test the validity of that hypothesis as an accurate description of a phenomenon. Acting as both gatherers and evaluators of information, scientists refine their ideas until they believe they have achieved an accurate description and understanding of nature — as good an approximation of "truth" as possible. The inquiry will proceed for as long as it takes to achieve that goal. In fact, it never ends.

Why don't we use this method in a trial? Certainly, an important goal of the trial is to discover the "truth." But two points distinguish the judicial from the scientific search for truth. *First*, the justice system is time-constrained in a way that science is not. The trial must reach a result within a reasonably limited period of time. This necessarily restricts the amount of evidence that can be heard as well as the degree of certainty in the accuracy of the result. Once a result has been reached, it is essentially final. Aside from rare adjustments justified by serious errors committed during the trial, factual findings are not subject to further contention. "Truth" in a trial, therefore, is a relative concept. "Truth" in science — at least as an ultimate goal — is more absolute.[3]

Second, a trial serves goals other than the truth. Among these goals are maintaining peace and social order by providing a formal setting in which to engage in conflict, resolving those conflicts, achieving "justice," and testing the viability and scope of specific rules of law. Achieving these goals is sometimes consistent with the goal of determining truth, but at times the goals conflict. For example, we will see that evidentiary privileges often prevent the fact-finder from obtaining information crucial to the discovery of truth. But privileges exist both to encourage candor in certain relationships and to respect the privacy of the parties in those relationships. A client will not confide in her lawyer unless the client is convinced that what she says will be kept confidential under the attorney-client privilege. When a privilege applies, it does so because candor and privacy outweigh the goal of truth-determination. A trial, therefore, is a complex creature that does not lend itself to the pure "scientific" inquiry.

The adversary system and the rules of evidence are the mechanisms we use to strike the complex balance between truth and the competing goals of the trial

---

2. This view is usually associated with Karl Popper. *See, e.g.,* Karl R. Popper, Conjectures and Refutations: The Growth of Scientific Knowledge (5th ed. 1989). One adherent of Popper's view explains:

> The law frames questions in adversarial terms, and lawyers see problems as best resolved by controlled argument. In contrast, the scientific method is (ideally) not adversarial, but cooperative, and scientists usually find answers in the slow accumulation of evidence from many sources.

Marcia Angell, Science on Trial: The Clash of Medical Evidence and the Law in the Breast Implant Case 28-29 (1996).

3. Even scientific study often does not purport to reveal absolute truth. Rather, science often states its findings in terms of probabilities. In this limited sense, the scientific and legal processes are similar. The search never ends.

process. The adversary system relies on the parties, through their attorneys, to determine what evidence to present. In most other nations throughout the world, the judge is an active participant in the trial, frequently interrogating witnesses and directing the presentation of evidence. In U.S. courts, the judge is largely passive. Typically, it is only when the parties call on the court to rule on objections to evidence that the court becomes involved in the fray. And even then the court's role is merely to rule on the objection, give any necessary instructions, and sit back until the next objection is lodged. We assume, rightly or wrongly, that justice will be done and a reasonable approximation of the truth arrived at through a system in which each side presents its own version of the story.

But even though the adversaries decide what evidence to present, the evidence rules that control the presentation are usually essential to getting at the truth. The objective of a trial attorney is to win, not to reveal the truth. In fact, attorneys have considerable opportunity to use trial tactics that conceal the truth. Attorneys sometimes try to confuse or distract the fact-finder, take undue advantage of the inexperience or incompetence of opposing counsel, and unfairly prejudice the adverse party by revealing irrelevant but damaging facts that might inflame the passions of the fact-finder. The evidence rules provide judges with the means to control these abuses. Because evidence rules govern everything from the phrasing of questions to the form and substance of testimony, opportunities to object are presented frequently throughout a trial.

The result is a system that typically does not produce a simple, coherent story of the facts in a case. Instead, in our system, the parties are motivated to control the evidence, trying always to reveal and emphasize whatever is favorable to their positions while invoking the evidence rules in an effort to prevent disclosure of, or divert attention from, conflicting evidence. Proceedings are frequently interrupted by objections and legal argument, moving awkwardly and fitfully toward their eventual conclusion. It is no wonder that the physician quoted above, who thought he was performing a public service by testifying, was humiliated and angered by the experience.

As we will see, the evidence rules are designed to do more than simply control what the lawyers can do inside a courtroom. Rules of evidence can also promote and serve the law's substantive goals by influencing the behavior of non-lawyers outside the courtroom. For example, one goal of tort law is to encourage people to engage in conduct that will avoid accidents. Imagine a case in which a plaintiff claims he was injured by falling because defendant's stairway was slippery. After the accident, defendant considers installing a surfacing on the stairs that would make them slip-proof, thereby avoiding future accidents. If defendant repairs the stairs in this manner, evidence of his work certainly would be relevant to show that the stairs were unsafe when plaintiff fell. But if defendant knew that this evidence could be admitted at trial for such a purpose, he might be dissuaded from fixing the stairs. In other words, he might decide to leave the stairs alone, and risk future accidents, in order to avoid hurting his cause in the pending suit. Accordingly, the law typically makes evidence of repairs inadmissible so as to encourage behavior that will avoid future accidents.

Evidence rules are also designed to promote other important values. For example, our legal tradition has long assumed that those charged with crimes should be judged according to their behavior on the occasion in question, and not by their general character as evidenced by their other misdeeds or their bad reputation. The rules of evidence support this value by limiting the use of what is called character evidence. Indeed, the rules explicitly instruct the trial judge to keep in mind the values of the system and the goals of the trial. Federal Rule of Evidence 102, for example, provides:

> These rules should be construed so as to administer every proceeding fairly, eliminate unjustifiable expense and delay, and promote the development of evidence law, to the end of ascertaining the truth and securing a just determination.

Sometimes it is necessary to balance one or more of these goals against the others and, often, it will be unclear how that balance should be struck. The rules of evidence will provide at least the framework for constructing arguments concerning the direction in which the scales of justice should tip.

Further Reading: Jerome Frank, Courts on Trial ch. 6 (1950); Stephan Landsman, *A Brief Survey of the Development of the Adversary System*, 44 Ohio St. L.J. (1983).

2.   What Is "Evidence"?

It might seem strange that most evidence codes do not attempt to define *evidence*. Maybe this is because it is assumed that those who need to know what evidence is—judges and lawyers—have a pretty good idea without a formal definition. At the same time, however, we cannot understand the scope and application of evidence rules without at least attempting to define what is, and what is not, evidence.

Unlike the Federal Rules of Evidence, the California Evidence Code does attempt to define *evidence*. Section 140 provides:

> "Evidence" means testimony, writings, material objects, or other things presented to the senses that are offered to prove the existence or nonexistence of a fact.

This definition is notable as much for what it does not contain as for what it does. Consider what you know about those "things" that take place in a courtroom that can be perceived with the senses. You know that witnesses are called to recount the facts by responding to questions posed by lawyers and that sometimes those questions even suggest facts. In addition to what the witness says, her facial expressions, tone of voice, and other aspects of demeanor may also be evident. An observer can also perceive the reactions of others sitting in the courtroom.[4] You also know that lawyers often present "exhibits," and that these exhibits can take many forms, from the purported murder weapon to an

---

4. A good illustration is this famous joke: A defendant was on trial for murder. There was lots of incriminating evidence but the defense could point to the fact that the victim's body was never found. In his closing statement, defense counsel said to the jury, "My client is innocent. In one minute the alleged victim is going to walk into this courtroom. The jurors stared expectantly at the courtroom door. Nothing happened. The defendant's attorney then said, "I don't really know where the victim is, but the fact that you all looked at the door means you believe there is a reasonable doubt as to guilt." The jury then retired to deliberate and returned to the courtroom just a few minutes later to pronounce a guilty verdict. Questioning the jury afterwards, the defense counsel said in an exasperated tone, "You must have had some doubt. I saw you all stare at the door." The jury foreman replied, "Yes, we looked. But your client didn't."

illustrative chart prepared either before trial or during the testimony of a witness. The judge will sometimes make statements about what is taking place in the courtroom. Finally, the lawyers will make arguments and other statements to the judge and the jury.

Are all these things evidence? Under the definition quoted above, it is difficult to tell. Certainly, the testimony of witnesses qualifies, as do exhibits admitted by the court. But are facial expressions or body language evidence? Are statements made by the judge or the lawyers evidence?

One way to approach the question is to ask why we want to know what constitutes evidence. For a novelist or a filmmaker, all the things just mentioned are evidence because they contribute to the telling of the story. They supply richness and texture to a book or film. In many ways, they are as essential to understanding the story as the words spoken or the documents presented. The same is true for a trial. As part of our effort to attach meaning to testimony, we notice the witness's tone of voice and consider what the attorneys argue about that meaning. There is, in other words, a big difference between the straight-faced, serious-toned statement, "I didn't rob the bank," and the same words spoken while squirming and without looking the questioner in the eye.

As we will see, the evidence rules do not treat as evidence facial expressions, body language, tone of voice, arguments, statements by the judge, or the like. The evidence rules are directed only to the words spoken by witnesses and the tangible evidence shown to the fact-finder. It could hardly be any other way. Any effort to control how jurors treat things like facial expressions is not likely to work.

3.   The Rules of Evidence

Until the last third of the twentieth century, virtually all evidence rules were a product of common law. Many scholars favored codification and worked on a project to develop what came to be called the Model Code of Evidence. John Henry Wigmore, who more than anyone deserves the title of "parent" of U.S. evidence law, opposed that effort (though he grudgingly drafted his own version of a detailed evidence code). But the twentieth century was marked by an inexorable movement toward uniformity in procedural rules, and the movement eventually caught up with evidence law. A few states, including California, adopted evidence codes in the 1960s. Finally, in 1975 Congress enacted the Federal Rules of Evidence to govern trials in federal courts.

The Federal Rules of Evidence do not form a *code* in the usual sense of that term. Normally, we think of a code as a comprehensive set of detailed rules. The Internal Revenue Code and the Uniform Commercial Code are good examples.[5] The Federal Rules of Evidence are different in that they are neither lengthy nor comprehensive in coverage. The entire set of rules can be fit into a short pamphlet. A number of areas of evidence law are not covered by the rules and are left to judicial development. Even where rules govern particular areas, they are often written in general, rather than specific, language. As a result,

---

5. Sometimes the codes themselves are supplemented by even further detailed bodies of rules. The Treasury Regulations accompanying the Internal Revenue Code are one example.

federal evidence law requires a great deal of interpretation, and many rules explicitly call upon the trial judge to exercise discretion.

Despite their lack of comprehensiveness, the Federal Rules of Evidence began a virtual landslide of evidence law codification. Today all but a few states have codified their evidence rules, and more than 40 states have adopted a version of the Federal Rules for use in state courts. Less than a handful of states still cling to the common law of evidence, and it is probably only a matter of time before they, too, opt for codification.

The Federal Rules are not revolutionary, nor were they meant to be. In all but a few areas, the rules adopted the existing common law. At the same time, however, the Federal Rules employ a more flexible approach to evidence than had been the case previously. Whereas the common law had maintained some rather stringent exclusionary rules and adhered to certain strict conventions, the Federal Rules generally take a more relaxed approach, entrusting the trial judge with the responsibility "to administer every proceeding fairly, eliminate unjustifiable expense and delay, and promote the development of evidence law, to the end of ascertaining the truth and securing a just determination." (Rule 102.) And there is a decided bias in favor of admissibility, the theory being that the more evidence admitted, the more likely these goals can be achieved.

In the decades since enactment, however, Congress has come to see the Federal Rules of Evidence as a means to promote substantive policies and to resolve issues not previously thought to be within the arid domain of evidence law. Amendments to the rules have sought to protect rape victims, discourage litigation based on questionable scientific claims, and promote convictions of repeat sex offenders, to name but a few. The pace of amendment has increased with the passage of time.

Because of the enormous influence of the Federal Rules, we will focus on these rules. Here and there, however, we contrast the Federal Rules with the practice in particular states.

Why will we focus on the Federal Rules when students expect to be practicing law in state courts? There are four reasons for this. *First,* as already indicated, the vast majority of states follow the Federal Rules closely, and both interpretations of and amendments to the Federal Rules exert a continuing influence on state law. Thus, the evidence law in your state is not likely to deviate much, if at all, from the federal law. *Second,* and perhaps more important, this is an introductory course in the law of evidence. Our job is to help you become acquainted with the types of problems addressed by evidence rules, and the ways in which those problems generally have been handled. When you complete this course, you will have a basic understanding of all significant evidence issues that arise in every U.S. jurisdiction. Armed with the knowledge you gain from this introductory course, you will be able to identify an evidence issue arising in any U.S. court, and you will have a good idea how the rules generally tend to deal with that issue. The only thing you will then need to do is determine whether the jurisdiction in which you practice treats that problem in some unusual way. Because most evidence law is now codified, it should be easy to make that determination. *Third,* by focusing most of our attention on one codification of evidence law, we are better able to develop an understanding of evidence law as a system, and not just a series of unconnected rules. *Fourth,* evidence questions on the Multistate Bar Examination are based on the Federal Rules of Evidence.

Studying the Federal Rules therefore helps you prepare for the bar examination in your state.

Finally, bear in mind that the rules of evidence are subject to the overarching principles of constitutional law. If the application of a particular rule will violate a constitutional right of a party or witness, the evidence rule must give way. Though we do not attempt a comprehensive review of such situations, we look at one aspect of the problem when we study the hearsay rule in Chapter 3.

Further Reading (Codification): 21 Charles A. Wright & Kenneth W. Graham, Jr., Federal Practice and Procedure: Evidence §§ 5001-5006 (1977); Stephan Landsman, *Of Mushrooms and Nullifiers: Rules of Evidence and the American Jury*, 21 St. Louis U. Pub. L. Rev. 65 (2002); Glen Weissenberger, *Evidence Myopia: The Failure to See the Federal Rules of Evidence as a Codification of the Common Law*, 40 Wm. & Mary L. Rev. 1539 (1999).

Further Reading (Interpretation): Edward R. Becker & Aviva Orenstein, *The Federal Rules of Evidence After Sixteen Years — The Effect of "Plain Meaning" Jurisprudence, the Need for an Advisory Committee on the Rules of Evidence, and Suggestions for Selective Revision of the Rules*, 60 Geo. Wash. L. Rev. 857 (1992); Randolph N. Jonakait, *The Supreme Court, Plain Meaning, and the Changed Rules of Evidence*, 68 Tex. L. Rev. 745 (1990); Eileen A. Scallen, *Classical Rhetoric, Practical Reasoning, and the Law of Evidence*, 44 Am. U. L. Rev. 101 (1995); Andrew E. Taslitz, *Interpretive Method and the Federal Rules of Evidence: A Call for a Politically Realistic Hermeneutics*, 32 Harv. J. on Legis. 329 (1995).

4.   *The Stages of the Trial*

A trial is an unwieldy event, lasting anywhere from an hour or two to weeks or months. Even short trials consume large amounts of resources. If the vast majority of cases did not settle without the need for trial, our system of justice would collapse because there would not be enough judges, court employees, or courtrooms to handle the burden. Fortunately, at least 90 percent of all civil and criminal cases settle. For those that do not settle, the typical trial consists of about a dozen stages.

Evidence law affects the way lawyers plan their cases long before the trial begins. Even though the rules of evidence have little application to proceedings prior to trial, thoughtful lawyers keep the rules in mind throughout the pretrial process and even before commencing an action. This is because the admissibility of evidence is a crucial factor in estimating the likely outcome of a trial and in evaluating the prospects for settlement.[6] While some inadmissible evidence helps to lead to the production of admissible evidence, counsel knows that if the case goes to trial, inadmissible evidence will then be useless. At every pretrial point, therefore, attorneys must keep in mind not only what facts they must

---

6. One important difference between civil and criminal trials is the degree of pretrial discovery available to the parties. In civil trials, pretrial discovery is extensive. Skillful counsel seldom enter a trial without a very good idea of the evidence on which the opponent will rely; much of the evidence, in fact, will have been made available by the opponent pursuant to discovery requests. This is not generally true in criminal trials, for which discovery is considerably more limited.

prove to prevail, but how they are going to go about proving those facts. Moreover, attorneys must also consider how to ensure that certain evidence will *not* be
admissible at trial. Thus, every time an attorney speaks to her client, she must
keep in mind what the evidence laws require to protect that communication
under the attorney-client privilege.

a. Pretrial Motions

In some trials, the court makes evidentiary rulings even before the jury is sworn
and any testimony is heard. On the eve or even the day of trial the attorneys are
likely to meet with the judge at what may be called a pretrial hearing or pretrial
conference. At that meeting, the parties might try one last time to settle and,
failing that, attempt to agree on other matters, including the issues to be tried
and the admissibility of evidence. If the attorneys cannot resolve all the evidence
issues by agreement, they may then make motions that ask the judge to resolve
the outstanding issues.[7] Usually called motions *in limine,* these motions attempt
to resolve important issues outside the hearing of the jury, thus avoiding the
possibility that the jury will hear questionable evidence before the court rules on
its admissibility. In criminal cases, such motions often involve constitutional
questions such as the admissibility of the defendant's confession, or the legality
of a search and seizure or an arrest. But many pretrial motions concern admissibility under the rules of evidence. When a party knows that the opponent is
very likely to offer certain evidence, and the party believes the evidence is objectionable, obtaining a pretrial ruling will both prevent the jury from being prejudiced through exposure to inadmissible evidence and help the attorney plan
for the trial. In fact, pretrial rulings on admissibility might get settlement negotiations restarted because those rulings give the attorneys grounds to recalculate
their prospects of winning at trial.

   In theory, parties can obtain pretrial rulings on any type of evidentiary issue.
In practice, however, the court will often decline to make a pretrial ruling
because admissibility might depend on the context in which the evidence is
actually offered at trial. Consider two examples. First, suppose the plaintiff in
a personal injury action plans to call a witness to testify that, a few hours after the
accident, someone who had seen the accident told the witness that the defendant's car had run a red light and struck the plaintiff's car. If defendant's attorney makes a pretrial motion to exclude this evidence on the grounds that it is
inadmissible hearsay, the court will likely grant the motion. As we see when we
study the hearsay rule (see Chapter 3), the evidence is clearly hearsay if offered
to prove that the defendant's car ran the red light, and as long as there is no
dispute about the context in which the person made the statement to the
witness, no exception will apply that would make the evidence admissible.
The court will not need to wait until trial to make that ruling.

---

   7. A motion is a request directed to the judge for an order or ruling. For example, the defendant
in a criminal prosecution might make a motion asking that the court rule that evidence concerning
the defendant's prior criminal history will be inadmissible at trial, and order the prosecution to not
allude to that history during the questioning of witnesses.

Suppose, however, that in a murder prosecution the defendant asks the court to make a pretrial ruling that certain gruesome photographs of the victim's body taken during an autopsy will not be admissible. The admissibility of such evidence might be highly dependent on the context. If, for example, the defendant claims self-defense and the photographs show entry wounds in the victim's back, the photographs might carry substantial value in suggesting that the victim was retreating when she was shot. The gruesome photos also might undercut a claim of self-defense by showing the use of force beyond what was necessary to repel an attack by the victim. Before trial, the court might not be in a position to assess the importance of the evidence because the court likely will not know what other evidence will be admitted on these issues. In addition, before trial the court probably will not have a good idea of the effect the evidence is likely to have on the sensibilities of the jurors. In such a case, the court is unlikely to issue the pretrial ruling. This means that the defendant will need to raise the question during trial.

Pretrial motions therefore present an important opportunity to shape what issues are presented to the jury and to resolve certain conflicts before they arise. Effective use of pretrial conferences and motions can lead to smoother, more efficient trials.

b.   Jury Selection

The right to jury trial is deeply embedded in U.S. jurisprudence. The Sixth Amendment to the United States Constitution guarantees criminal defendants the right to a trial by jury. In a civil case, the Seventh Amendment preserves the right to jury trial "in Suits at common law, where the value in controversy shall exceed twenty dollars." The right can, of course, be waived. But when the parties assert their jury trial right, it is necessary to select individuals to serve on the jury. Different jurisdictions maintain different rules regarding the number of jurors required for particular types of trials, the sources from which the names of prospective jurors may be drawn, and the methods for actually selecting the persons who will hear the case.

In all states, jury selection occurs through "voir dire," a process of questioning prospective jurors. In many states, the trial judge asks all the questions, though the parties may suggest questions they wish the court to pose. In a few states, the lawyers are permitted to put their questions to prospective jurors directly. Lawyers will listen to the jurors' answers to these questions to decide whether to "challenge" any particular prospective juror. Challenges can be "for cause," meaning that the juror's answers reveal disqualifying information such as familiarity with the facts of the case or the parties, possible bias in favor of or against the parties or their causes, or an unwillingness to follow the law. Typically, each side will also have the right to use a specified number of "peremptory challenges," which may be exercised without showing cause. Often, a lawyer exercises peremptory challenges to eliminate prospective jurors who might tend to favor or oppose certain types of claims, even if the lawyer cannot demonstrate to the court that the prospective juror harbors such bias in a manner sufficient to be excused for cause.

When the required number of jurors has been chosen, perhaps along with a few alternates in the event one or more jurors must be excused during the trial, the court will swear in the jury and begin the main part of the trial.

c. Preliminary Jury Instructions

At the beginning of the trial it is customary for the court to give a number of preliminary instructions to the jury. The court is likely to inform the jurors that they must decide all questions of fact; that they must not allow themselves to be influenced by sympathy, prejudice, or passion; that they are forbidden to make any independent investigation; that statements of counsel are not evidence (unless counsel are reciting the terms of a stipulation to which the parties have agreed); that they must not speculate about how a witness might have answered a question to which the court sustained an objection, and that they must disregard any evidence the court struck from the record; and that they must not speculate about the presence or absence of insurance covering any party. In addition, the court is likely to admonish the jurors to keep an open mind throughout the trial, to avoid any discussion of the case with other jurors until it is time to deliberate, and to forgo all contacts about the case outside the courtroom until the matter is completed. In criminal cases, in addition to the above instructions, the court might also instruct the jurors not to be influenced by the fact that the defendant has been arrested for the crime, charged with the crime, or brought to trial.

d. Opening Statements

At this point, the judge's active role is largely suspended and the parties, through their attorneys, take over the trial. The first step is opening statements. The plaintiff (in a civil action) or the prosecution (in a criminal case) will usually go first. Note that the term used is opening *statement*, not opening *argument*. This is because, in theory at least, this presentation is not an argument. Rather than advocating a particular position, counsel's job at this point is to present the fact-finder with a brief roadmap of the case she will present on her client's behalf. Counsel will likely explain the nature of the case, name some of the witnesses she intends to call, explain the nature of the testimony the witnesses will give, and, perhaps most important, state what she expects the evidence to prove. This is a time for the attorneys to be careful about what they promise the jury, for the jury is just as likely to remember promises broken as promises kept.

After the plaintiff or prosecution has made its opening statement, the defendant has an opportunity to make its own opening statement. Defense counsel may give her opening statement immediately after the plaintiff or prosecution has concluded its opening statement or may choose to wait until plaintiff or prosecution has presented its entire case-in-chief. The defense has at least two distinct advantages at the opening statement stage of the trial. *First*, the plaintiff's or prosecution's opening statement may help the defense make decisions about the evidence it should offer. If, for example, the defense had expected the plaintiff or prosecution to contest a certain issue, and the opponent's opening statement makes clear that the matter will not be contested, the defense may point out that fact in its own opening statement and indicate that it will either forgo calling its own witnesses on the point or significantly limit the evidence it will offer. *Second*, if the defense postpones its opening statement until the plaintiff or prosecution has presented its case-in-chief, the defense has the opportunity to remind the fact-finder of promises the opponent made that it was unable to keep.

Many experienced trial lawyers believe that the opening statement is the most important part of the trial because it provides the opportunity to influence how the trier of fact will evaluate all that comes later. The party that is best able to set the tone, flow, and agenda for the trial has the best chance of prevailing in the end.

e. Presentation of Evidence and Limiting Instructions

The parties now present their evidence. Evidence comes in several forms, most notably direct and cross-examination of witnesses and the presentation of documents, real and demonstrative evidence in the form of exhibits.[8] In addition, the parties will notify the fact-finder of the substance of any stipulations they have reached.

Witness testimony begins with direct examination by the party that called the witness. This is followed by cross-examination, which provides an opportunity for the opponent to question the witness, usually with the objective of casting doubt on the witness's direct examination testimony specifically or her credibility in general. In most courts, the party who called the witness then has an opportunity to conduct a redirect examination, and sometimes the opponent may follow with a recross-examination.

As we discuss in Chapter 6, the direct examination of a witness usually proceeds with questions that allow the witness, rather than the attorney, to tell the story. These questions can range from reasonably open-ended inquiries requiring the witness to describe an event or condition, to very narrow questions, requiring perhaps only a one-word answer. The use of questions calling for a long narrative response ("tell us everything that happened") is objectionable. So-called leading questions are usually also objectionable on direct examination. A leading question is a question that suggests the answer ("Isn't it true you ran the red light?").

On cross-examination, it is usually the lawyer, not the witness, who tells the story. The lawyer accomplishes this by asking leading questions, which are usually permitted on cross-examination. The point of leading questions is to carefully control the witness, who typically is either aligned with the opponent or at least has something to say that helps the opponent. All trial lawyers have heard stories about the lawyer who lost control by asking "one too many" questions on cross-examination, or who gave the witness an opportunity to explain her way out of what seemed to be an inescapable trap.

In the course of the presentation of evidence, the parties will often argue points of evidence law, seeking the court's rulings on objections and motions to strike. Usually, these arguments take place in front of the jury because the objectionable questions or testimony come in the course of witness examination. To prevent jury confusion or prejudice, counsel sometimes will argue these matters close to the bench, in soft tones audible to the judge and court reporter but not the jury. At other times, the court will have the jury removed from the

---

8. "Demonstrative evidence" refers to a chart, diagram, or a courtroom reenactment of an event that illustrates the testimony of a witness. "Real evidence" refers to a tangible item, such as a weapon or plastic baggie of drugs, that is relevant in its own right.

courtroom to permit more lengthy argument or consideration of particularly prejudicial matters.

After ruling on an evidentiary objection or motion, it is sometimes necessary for the court to instruct the jury about the evidence. Such "limiting" or "cautionary" instructions can be given in several types of situations. If the court sustains an objection to a question, the court might instruct the jury to disregard any inference that might be drawn from the question itself. If the court grants a motion to strike the witness's answer to a question, it is likely to instruct the jury to disregard the answer. Most jurors probably make a good faith effort to follow the judge's instructions. However, lawyers know that jurors are not always successful in this endeavor. In particular, it is difficult for jurors, who are only human, to disregard evidence they have heard and that the judge subsequently rules inadmissible. For this reason, lawyers sometimes try to allude to evidence in front of the jury even when they think it is likely that the judge may ultimately rule it inadmissible. This can violate ethical rules, especially where it is clear that the evidence is inadmissible. To protect against this maneuver, a sharp lawyer will make a pretrial motion to establish that the evidence is inadmissible.

Some instructions are governed generally by Federal Rule of Evidence 105. That rule, titled "Limited Admissibility," provides:

> If the court admits evidence that is admissible against a party or for a purpose — but not against another party or for another purpose — the court, on timely request, must restrict the evidence to its proper scope and instruct the jury accordingly.

As its wording shows, Rule 105 applies in two types of situations. First, it applies where some evidence is admissible against one party but not another. For example, in Chapter 3, we learn that the hearsay rule does not exclude a party's own statement when offered against that party. We call such statements "opposing party statements." For example, suppose plaintiff is injured when a vehicle collides with another car. Plaintiff, a passenger in one of the cars, sues both drivers. At trial, plaintiff may offer into evidence the statement of one of the defendants made at the accident scene. That statement will be an opposing party statement and admissible against the defendant who made that statement, but may be inadmissible hearsay if offered against the other defendant. If the court admits the statement against the defendant who made it, the other defendant's attorney may ask the court to instruct the jury that it should not consider the statement as evidence against her client. Because this is an appropriate situation for a limiting instruction, and because the party has requested the instruction, Rule 105 requires the court to give it. Even in the absence of a request, the court may still issue the instruction.

The second situation covered by Rule 105 is one in which evidence is admissible for one purpose but not another. Suppose that in a negligence action against her landlord following a fall on a common stairway, plaintiff wishes to offer evidence that a week before the accident, another tenant told the landlord that one of the stairs was broken. This evidence is logically relevant to prove two things: that the stair was broken and that the landlord was put on notice that a stair was broken. We will learn that the hearsay rule forbids the use of that statement to prove that the stair was actually broken, but that the statement will be admissible to prove that the landlord was on notice of the problem.

If the court admits the statement to prove notice, the landlord's counsel is likely to request a limiting instruction informing the jury that it may use the statement only for that purpose and not to infer that the stairway was actually defective.

Of course, jurors are not always able or willing to engage in the mental hair-splitting required by such instructions. If the danger that the jury will ignore the court's instructions seems too great, the court may determine that the evidence should be excluded entirely. But such a situation is not common; for the most part, courts continue to take on faith that juries will understand and abide by the terms of limiting instructions. Even the Supreme Court has taken this position, stating in Weeks v. Angelone, 528 U.S. 225, 234 (2000), that there is a "presumption" that juries follow the court's instructions. Nevertheless, when the issue is important, counsel should be prepared to argue that the court should not rely on a limiting instruction, but instead should exclude the evidence.

Suppose, for example, that Defendant is charged with murder. Defendant testifies, denying any involvement in the crime. The prosecution has evidence that Defendant has a prior conviction for an unrelated murder. This evidence is logically relevant to prove two things: (1) Defendant is a violent person and, thus, may have committed the murder; and (2) Defendant is a law breaker and, thus, may have been willing to break the law again by committing perjury on the witness stand. We will see in Chapter 6 that a witness's prior conviction of a serious crime sometimes is admissible to attack the credibility of that witness, which is a process called impeachment. We will learn in Chapter 4, however, that evidence of a defendant's prior bad act usually is inadmissible to prove that she is the type of person who would commit the crime for which she is charged. In our hypothetical, if the prosecution wishes to impeach Defendant by offering evidence of Defendant's prior conviction (the second purpose noted above), Defendant at least is entitled to a limiting instruction under Rule 105. That instruction will tell the jury that it may consider the conviction evidence only insofar as it bears on Defendant's honesty when she testified about the crime. But Defendant likely will argue that the court should exclude the evidence entirely because of the danger that the jury will misuse the evidence by using it to infer that defendant is a violent person and, therefore, committed the murder. The argument might go as follows (Def is Defendant and Pros is Prosecution):[9]

Def: Your Honor, may we approach?[10]

By the Court: Yes.

    Def: Your Honor, Defendant is charged with murder. The prior conviction is for the same type of crime. It is simply not going to be possible for the jury to distinguish between considering the prior offense for impeachment purposes and considering it to prove my client's guilt of the murder for which she is charged. Under the circumstances, the probative value of the evidence for its permissible purpose is overwhelmed by the danger of misuse, and we ask that the court exclude it entirely.

---

9. We will assume that the matter was not resolved in a pretrial motion, or "motion *in limine.*"

10. By "approach," defense counsel is asking if she and the prosecutor may stand next to the judge's bench so that they may argue in hushed tones that the judge and court reporter can hear but the jury cannot.

    Pros: Your Honor, Rule 609(a)(1) expressly permits us to use a prior conviction to impeach if its probative value exceeds the danger of unfair prejudice. We think it's entirely reasonable to assume that a person who has been convicted of murder will lie when she faces another murder charge. Moreover, Defendant is entitled to a limiting instruction, and we have no reason to believe that the jury will not follow it.

    Def: We understand that a limiting instruction is the usual remedy, Your Honor, but how can the jury be expected to abide by this instruction in this situation? Once a murderer, always a murderer, is what the jury will think. And that's not permissible.

By the Court: Motion denied. I'll issue a limiting instruction when the evidence is admitted.

Further Reading: Reed Hastie et al., Inside the Jury (1983); Joe S. Cecil et al., *Citizen Comprehension of Difficult Issues: Lessons from Civil Jury Trials*, 40 Am. U. L. Rev. 727 (1991); Mason Ladd, *Objections, Motions and Foundation Testimony*, 43 Cornell L.Q. 543 (1958); Joel D. Lieberman & Bruce D. Sales, *What Social Science Teaches Us About the Jury Instruction Process*, 3 Psych. Pub. Pol'y & L. 589 (1997); Peter Meijes Tiersma, *Reforming the Language of Jury Instructions*, 22 Hofstra L. Rev. 37 (1993); Note, *The Limiting Instruction — Its Effectiveness and Effect*, 51 Minn. L. Rev. 264 (1966).

The presentation of evidence takes place in several stages, described briefly below.

i.   Plaintiff's or Prosecution's Case-in-Chief

The plaintiff or the prosecution presents its affirmative case first. The prosecution in a criminal case, and plaintiff in virtually every civil action, bears the burden of producing sufficient evidence to establish every element of its prima facie case. (We discuss burdens of proof in Chapter 9.) At the close of that party's case-in-chief, it is not unusual for the defendant to ask the court to dismiss the case on the ground that the opponent has not met its burden. In a civil jury trial, such a request normally comes in the form of a motion for directed verdict. In a criminal trial, the defendant will move for acquittal. The task of the prosecution or plaintiff is therefore to present sufficient evidence of each element of the prima facie case to *justify* a fact-finder in awarding a verdict in its favor. We emphasize the word *justify* because at this stage of the trial, the issue is not whether a verdict in favor of the plaintiff or prosecution would be required, but only whether there is sufficient evidence to allow the trial to continue. To put it another way, when faced with a motion for directed verdict at the close of the plaintiff's or prosecution's case-in-chief, the court must ask itself whether, if the jury rendered a verdict for that party based on the evidence admitted so far, the court would be obliged to grant defendant a new trial or even enter a judgment notwithstanding the verdict. If the court's answer to that question is yes, it should grant the defendant's motion to avoid the time and expense of a prolonged trial.

ii. Defendant's Case-in-Chief

At the close of the plaintiff's or prosecution's case-in-chief, and after the court has disposed of any motions, it is the defendant's turn to present its case-in-chief. If defendant has asserted an affirmative defense,[11] the defendant usually has the burden of producing sufficient evidence to survive a motion by the plaintiff or prosecution to dispose of the defense as a matter of law. The question such a motion poses for the court is precisely the same as in dealing with a defense motion at the close of the plaintiff's case-in-chief. This is true even in a criminal case. For example, if the defendant asserts self-defense but fails to offer sufficient evidence to permit a rational fact-finder to determine that the elements of that defense are present, the court may refuse to instruct the jury to consider that defense. (In a criminal case, the defendant's Sixth Amendment right to jury trial prevents the court from directing a verdict for the prosecution.)

In addition to offering evidence to support any applicable defenses, it is almost always wise for defendant to offer any evidence it has that undermine the elements of the opponent's prima facie case. This is especially true in civil actions, where the burden of persuasion usually favors the defendant only slightly. Even in criminal cases, where the prosecution's burden of persuasion is considerably more formidable, a defendant who possesses exculpatory evidence is almost always advised to offer that evidence.

iii. Plaintiff's or Prosecution's Rebuttal Case and Defendant's Surrebuttal

After the defense has presented its case-in-chief, the plaintiff or prosecution usually has an opportunity to respond by presenting evidence rebutting the defense presentation. This is fair, as defendant had an opportunity to rebut the plaintiff's or prosecution's case-in-chief. The normal rule is that the rebuttal case is limited to the issues raised by the defendant's case-in-chief. In the interests of justice, however, the court may waive that rule.

Sometimes, the plaintiff or prosecution will withhold certain witnesses or other evidence in anticipation of the rebuttal. Although this is permitted, the decision can be risky, particularly if the court decides to place narrow restrictions on the subject matter of the rebuttal.

If the court deems it appropriate, it may grant defendant an opportunity for surrebuttal. Defendant's request to present evidence at this point is more likely to succeed if the court has permitted the plaintiff or prosecution to go beyond the scope of the defendant's case-in-chief during its rebuttal case.

f. Motions After the Presentation of Evidence

All evidence having been presented, either party may now ask the court to decide all or part of the case "as a matter of law." Defendant in a civil action, for example, might ask for a directed verdict as to all or some claims, arguing

---

11. An affirmative defense is the defendant's assertion of facts and arguments that, if true, will defeat the plaintiff's or prosecution's claim, even if all the allegations in the complaint are true.

that no rational jury could find the facts necessary to support plaintiff's claims based on the evidence presented. A criminal defendant might ask the court to dismiss one or more charges. In a civil case, plaintiff might make similar motions as to certain affirmative defenses. In more unusual circumstances, it might even be appropriate for the court to direct a verdict in favor of the party that had the burden of persuasion as to that matter. The court usually will deny such motions on the ground that the party against whom each motion has been brought has presented sufficient evidence to *justify* a verdict in its favor. The effect of such a ruling is to give the jury, if there is one, the power to render a verdict in the case.

g. Closing Arguments

At this point, each party's attorney is given a chance to explain how all of the pieces of the puzzle fit together in a way to compel victory for her client. Usually, the party with the burden of persuasion as to the affirmative claims (normally the plaintiff or prosecution) will argue first, followed by the opponent. The party that went first then has an opportunity to give a rebuttal argument.

Effective attorneys use closing argument to do much more than summarize the evidence. Because a rational fact-finder often can draw different conclusions from the same evidence, a good closing argument shows the fact-finder why it should adopt a particular version of the story and reject others. It explains why, of all possible ways to view the evidence, the story favored by that side is most plausible. In making a closing argument, counsel may not state facts or suggest inferences unsupported by evidence in the record. But she may explain why certain evidence should be viewed more favorably than other evidence, why certain witnesses are more credible or less credible than others, and why certain inferences from the evidence are more justified than others. Counsel's task is to appeal to the fact-finder's life experiences and common sense, leading the fact-finder to conclusions that support her client while rejecting those suggested by the opponent. Closing argument represents counsel's last opportunity to influence the fact-finder before it begins deliberating.

h. Jury Instructions

Juries decide the facts while the judge decides the law. This means that, before submitting the case to the jury for deliberation, the court must instruct the jury about the law it should apply to those facts. Because these instructions serve the critical function of informing the jury of the facts it must find in order to render a verdict for either party, counsel usually will supply the court with suggested instructions. As might be expected, the parties often differ about how the court should instruct the jury, and it is the court's job to determine the applicable legal standards and choose the instructions that best state those standards. Of course, neither the court nor the parties must draft these instructions from scratch. There are many books containing "pattern" jury instructions, most of which will have been tested through the litigation process and found to describe the law accurately. Courts prefer such instructions because they are less likely to raise an issue for appeal than are instructions written on the spot for the individual case. At the same time, the court and counsel are not bound by instructions that can be found in books. Sometimes, an issue arises in a unique way, or an unusual issue carries such central importance to the case that a custom-written instruction does a better job of notifying the jury of the applicable law than does a canned instruction.

i. Jury Deliberation and Verdict

The case is now in the hands of the jury. Jurors will be asked to render one of two types of verdicts. A general verdict simply declares who wins and, where applicable, the remedy. A special verdict answers a series of specific questions posed by the court on a special form. The court then uses the jury's written responses to determine the precise verdict. Jury deliberations are, of course, secret. As we discuss later in this chapter, the circumstances in which a jury's verdict may be attacked are very limited and failure to understand or follow the court's instructions is rarely one of those circumstances.

During deliberations, the court usually will allow jurors to examine exhibits that were admitted into evidence.[12] In addition, should jurors wish to review specific testimony of witnesses, the court usually will oblige by calling the jurors, parties, and counsel back to the courtroom and having the court reporter read that testimony from the record. Jurors are not permitted to review the transcript in the jury room, however. Sometimes jurors will ask the court to clarify its instructions in some respect. The court will sometimes do so, but often will choose instead to re-read the same instructions, preferring to avoid the possibility of creating an issue for appeal on the chance that a clarifying instruction mischaracterizes the law.

When the jury reaches its verdict, the jurors will return to the courtroom and read the verdict in the presence of the parties and counsel. (In some courtrooms, the judge or clerk reads the verdict.) On request, the court will "poll" the jurors to verify that the verdict represents the views of each of them. At this point, the court will usually thank and excuse the jury.

j. Post-trial Motions and Entry of Judgment

After the jury verdict has been read, it is common for the losing party to ask the court to set aside the verdict and either grant a new trial or enter judgment notwithstanding the verdict (JNOV). In criminal cases, these options are not available to the prosecution. In some civil cases, the losing party may move for remittitur, a demand that the prevailing party either accept a lower damage award or be forced to retry the case. Somewhat less commonly, a prevailing party unhappy with the level of damages may ask the court for additur, which is a demand that the losing party pay a higher damage award or suffer retrial.

---

12. As we will learn, however, not all items shown to the jury in the courtroom may be examined by the jury during deliberations.

After ruling on any post-trial motions, the court will enter judgment on the verdict. Unlike the verdict itself, the judgment is an appealable order. Any party except the government in criminal cases may appeal the judgment.[13]

B. APPELLATE REVIEW OF EVIDENTIARY ISSUES

> ### FED. R. EVID. 103.   RULINGS ON EVIDENCE

(a) Preserving a Claim of Error. A party may claim error in a ruling to admit or exclude evidence only if the error affects a substantial right of the party and:

    (1) if the ruling admits evidence, a party, on the record:

        (A) timely objects or moves to strike; and

        (B) states the specific ground, unless it was apparent from the context;
or

    (2) if the ruling excludes evidence, a party informs the court of its substance by an offer of proof, unless the substance was apparent from the context.

(b) Not Needing to Renew an Objection or Offer of Proof. Once the court rules definitively on the record — either before or at trial — a party need not renew an objection or offer of proof to preserve a claim of error for appeal.

(c) Court's Statement about the Ruling; Directing an Offer of Proof. The court may make any statement about the character or form of the evidence, the objection made, and the ruling. The court may direct that an offer of proof be made in question-and-answer form.

(d) Preventing the Jury from Hearing Inadmissible Evidence. To the extent practicable, the court must conduct a jury trial so that inadmissible evidence is not suggested to the jury by any means.

(e) Taking Notice of Plain Error. A court may take notice of a plain error affecting a substantial right, even if the claim of error was not properly preserved.

Discussion

The successful appeal of an alleged evidentiary error is a three-step process. *First*, the party must preserve the issue for appeal. This usually means obtaining a clear ruling from the trial court and making certain that the record is sufficiently complete to allow for effective review. *Second*, the party must persuade the appellate court that the trial court committed an error in the admission or exclusion of evidence. *Third*, the party also must convince the appellate court that the error affected a substantial right of that party. Courts sometimes use different language to describe this third step, describing the error as "prejudicial" or "not

---

13. In some jurisdictions, the government is allowed to "appeal" an acquittal. The purpose of the appeal will not be to overturn the acquittal, but to seek a legal ruling about any possible errors that might have occurred during the trial. The result of the appeal, therefore, does not affect the acquittal.

harmless." An appellate court will only reverse a judgment if it holds both that the trial court erred and that the error affected a substantial right of the party.

As implied by the first requirement, not every evidentiary error the trial court may have committed may be reviewed on appeal. Generally speaking, an appellate court will not review an aggrieved party's assertion of evidentiary error unless the party has properly made a record of that error. Rule 103(a) establishes that, if the party's claim is that the court erroneously *admitted* evidence, the party must have made a timely objection to the evidence on the record and, usually, stated the specific ground for the objection. (Example: "Objection, hearsay.") The requirement that the ground for objection be stated with specificity is relaxed if that ground is apparent from the context. An objection is timely if it is stated as soon as the basis for the objection is clear. Optimally, objections should be made after a question is asked and before the answer is given because, once jurors have heard the answer, it may be difficult for them to disregard it even if instructed by the judge to do so. If the ground for objection is not clear until the answer is given, or if the objecting party simply cannot state the objection faster than the witness can answer, the court usually will conclude that a motion to strike the answer to be timely if it is made immediately after the answer is given.

If a party claims that the court erroneously *excluded* evidence, the party must have made an "offer of proof." An offer of proof can take several forms, but the goal is always the same: to make a record of what the substance of the excluded evidence would have been. (Example: Outside the presence of the jury, or out of the jury's hearing, counsel states, "If permitted to answer the question, the witness would have stated that the bystander told her the light for Main Street traffic turned red just before the collision.") The requirement of making a formal offer of proof does not apply if the substance of the excluded evidence is apparent from the context.

There are two main reasons to require making a record of evidence rulings. First, the process of making the record gives the trial court a full opportunity to assess its own ruling. Thus, the trial judge might realize she is wrong and correct herself before committing an error that might warrant an appeal. Second, unless the record clearly reflects the nature of the evidence involved and the evidentiary issue, the appellate court has no effective way to determine whether the trial court in fact committed error and, if it did, whether that error affected a "substantial right." Thus, the appellate court typically will not review a judgment on the ground of alleged evidentiary error in the absence of a proper record.

An exception to the requirement of making a record is the doctrine of "plain error." Rule 103(e) states that if the court committed "plain error," an appellate court will review the issue even if the party did not make a record for appeal. An error is "plain" if it is so obvious that a formal objection should not be necessary to alert the trial court to the problem. For example, suppose that during the prosecution's case-in-chief in a murder case, a witness testifies that defendant is a member of a political movement dedicated to the violent overthrow of the U.S. government and repeal of the amendments to the Constitution banning slavery and giving women the right to vote. Assuming defendant's obnoxious political beliefs have nothing to do with the murder in question, the evidence is irrelevant and might seriously prejudice the jury against him. Even if defendant's counsel fails to object, the trial transcript will reveal the error quite clearly. An appellate court will review the matter and reverse if it finds that the error affected a substantial right of the defendant.

What does it mean to say that the error must affect a "substantial right"? Unfortunately, the courts do not give a clear answer. Certainly, an appeals court will reverse if it concludes that the error substantially swayed the jury in rendering its verdict or had a material effect on that verdict. Thus, erroneous exclusion of evidence might affect a substantial right of the offering party if the evidence went to a crucial issue. Conversely, if the error was purely technical in nature or likely did not affect the jury's deliberations or the outcome of the case, the court will deem the error "harmless." For example, an appellate court will rarely reverse a trial judge's erroneous admission or exclusion of evidence that went to an undisputed or marginal issue.[14]

EXAMPLES: Preserving Evidentiary Issues for Review

Following are several examples of making the record. Each example takes place during the trial of a negligence action arising from an automobile accident. "P" refers to Plaintiff's counsel, and "D" to Defendant's counsel.

1. During her case-in-chief, Plaintiff has called John, an eyewitness, to testify about the relevant events. At one point during John's testimony, the following exchange takes place:

> *P:* Shortly after the collision, did you speak with the passenger in Defendant's car about what had happened?
>
> *John:* Yes.
>
> *P:* Please tell the court what the passenger told you.
>
> *D:* Objection. Calls for hearsay.
>
> *By the Court:* Objection overruled. The witness may answer the question.
>
> *John:* I asked him what happened, and he said the white car ran the light.

In this example, Defendant's attorney has made a specific objection at the appropriate time, which is before the witness has had an opportunity to answer the question. Had the witness answered the question before the attorney had an opportunity to object, the proper procedure would have been to make a "motion to strike" the testimony. In either case, counsel must be specific, and Defendant has satisfied that requirement by stating that hearsay is the basis of the objection or motion to strike. Defendant has properly preserved the issue for appeal.

2. Later in John's testimony, the following exchange takes place:

> *D:* Objection, hearsay. Plaintiff has not established that this is admissible as a business record. Plaintiff is not a qualified witness.
>
> *P:* Did you speak with any bystanders?
>
> *John:* Yes.
>
> *P:* With whom did you speak?

---

14. Even most constitutional errors can be harmless, though the standard the court must apply is whether a constitutional error was harmless beyond a reasonable doubt. For non-constitutional errors, the level of certainty the court must have has not been settled definitively.

John:	I spoke to a lady who had been standing at the corner since before the accident. I think she was waiting for a bus.
P.	When did this conversation take place?
John:	Maybe a minute after the crash. I only talked with Defendant for a few seconds, and then I went back to the sidewalk and started talking with the lady.
P.	What was the conversation about?
John:	We talked about what we'd seen — about the crash.
P.	What did the lady tell you?
D:	Objection. Calls for hearsay.
P.	Your Honor, this is admissible as a present sense impression. *By the Court:* Objection sustained.
P.	Your Honor, may the jury be excused while I make an offer of proof?
By the Court:	The bailiff will please escort the jury out of the courtroom.
P.	John, please tell the court what the woman said.
John:	She said the Mustang — that's the car Defendant was driving — ran the red light and hit the other car.
P.	Did the woman make this statement in response to a question you asked?
John:	No. In fact, I was going to ask her what she saw, but before I had a chance, she just blurted it out. I think her exact words were "Did you see that Mustang run the light and hit the other car."
P.	Your Honor, I believe we have laid the foundation for admission of the statement under Rule 803(1), the present sense impression exception.
D:	Your Honor, too much time had passed. The woman obviously had an opportunity to deliberate before speaking. That undermines the reliability of the statement.
By the Court:	My ruling stands. The objection is sustained.

In this example, the aggrieved party is the one who offered the evidence (the proponent). As we have noted, when the court's ruling excludes evidence and the proponent believes the ruling is erroneous, the proponent must make a record of the reasons why it was error to exclude the evidence as well as of what the evidence would have been if the court had allowed the proponent to present it. This offer of proof gives the appellate court a basis to review not only whether the trial court erred, but also whether the error affected a substantial right.

3. Plaintiff now takes the stand. After testifying about the accident, Plaintiff's counsel shows Plaintiff a document marked Plaintiff's Exhibit B. Plaintiff identifies the document as the itemized bill she received from the automobile repair shop for the repair of the damage her car sustained in the collision. The document is stamped "PAID." Plaintiff testifies that she received the document from the repair shop's cashier. Plaintiff's counsel offers the admission of the document into evidence. At that point, the following exchange takes place:

D:	Objection, hearsay. Plaintiff has not established that this is admissible as a business record. Plaintiff is not a qualified witness.

P: Your Honor, Plaintiff has established each foundational fact required by Rule 803(6). To the extent the witness lacks knowledge of the shop's record-keeping system, the document speaks for itself. It bears the name of the repair shop, as well as its logo. The foundation is quite sufficient.

By the Court: Counsel, in the absence of a witness familiar with the business, you have not established the necessary foundation for the business records exception. Objection sustained.

P: Your Honor, the repair shop is no longer in business, and we have been unable to locate its former owner or manager. Under the circumstances, holding the document inadmissible places us in a difficult position with respect to proof of damages.

D: Your Honor, perhaps counsel should have thought about that problem earlier. Unless she can demonstrate that the document is admissible under the rules of evidence, our objection stands.

By the Court: Defendant's counsel is correct. The ruling stands.

P: Your Honor, we ask that the clerk place the document, which has been marked Plaintiff's Exhibit B, into the record so that it may be reviewed on appeal if necessary.

By the Court: The clerk will place Plaintiff's Exhibit B into the record.

In this example, it is once again the proponent who has lost the evidentiary issue. To determine the correctness of the trial court's ruling, and to decide whether any error was prejudicial to Plaintiff's case, it will be necessary for the appellate court to view the questioned document. "Making the record" in this situation required Plaintiff to place the document into the court's file, so that it will become a part of the record forwarded to the appellate court. The jury, of course, will not see the document because it has not been admitted into evidence.

How much deference should appellate courts show to trial courts' evidentiary rulings? Appellate courts often answer this question with a simple generalization such as, "we review alleged evidentiary errors under an abuse of discretion standard." This means that appellate courts give great deference to the evidentiary rulings of trial judges. There are good reasons for this. Trial courts must make most evidentiary rulings "on the fly," with little time for reflection. This means that mistakes are inevitable in almost every case. The justice system would grind to a halt if every mistaken evidentiary ruling required reversal and retrial. Thus, it is often said that parties are entitled to a fair trial, not a perfect trial. Where, then, do the appellate courts draw the line between deference and abuse of discretion? To understand where that line is drawn we must take a closer look at the structure of the rules and the roles of trial and appellate judges.

As we will see, some rules of evidence are flexible, giving the trial judge room to exercise discretion in their application. Other rules establish a fixed standard of admissibility. The best example of the former is Rule 403, which states that a trial court "may" exclude relevant evidence if the court finds that the probative value of the evidence is substantially outweighed by concerns such as unfair prejudice, confusion, delay, and waste of time. Rather than establish a fixed standard for admissibility, this rule explicitly calls for the court to balance, a highly subjective process dependent on the unique facts and circumstances of each situation. And even after balancing, Rule 403 states only that the court "may" exclude the evidence where the balance strongly tips against probative value. Similarly, Rule 611 empowers the trial court to exercise control over the mode and order of interrogation of witnesses, scope of cross-examination, and use of leading questions. As with Rule 403, the judge's power under Rule 611 is broad, and the validity of its exercise depends heavily on the precise context in which the ruling is required. Many other rules, or parts of rules, also give the trial court flexibility in dealing with objections.

These rules give the trial court flexibility because a trial court is in a better position to evaluate the relevant factors than is an appellate court. For example, the determination whether particular evidence is unfairly prejudicial under Rule 403 cannot be made in the abstract, nor is it possible in most cases to determine the real danger of prejudice from the cold record that the appellate court has before it. The trial judge is in a better position to evaluate not only the abstract probative value and danger of unfair prejudice, but how *this* jury, in *this* trial, is likely to be affected.[15] Much of this is intuitive and might depend on the court's ability to read facial expressions, body language, and other factors that are not reflected in the written record. Accordingly, only if the appellate court concludes that the trial court "abused" its discretion — a difficult standard for any aggrieved party to meet — would it be appropriate to hold that the trial court erred.

Other rules establish fixed standards for admissibility. Most of these are rules excluding evidence. For example, Rule 402 provides that irrelevant evidence is inadmissible. Rule 804 provides that the hearsay exceptions it creates only apply if the declarant is "unavailable." Rules like these do not give the trial court discretion. They represent a determination that certain evidence, under particular circumstances, is either admissible or inadmissible. Such rules typically do not require any case-by-case judgment that depends on factors that might not be clear from an appellate record. As such, the trial court is in no better position than an appellate court to evaluate admissibility, making deference to the trial court unnecessary. (Remember that the finding of error does not necessarily mean the appellate court will reverse. Reversal is only required if the error is prejudicial.) A more appropriate standard of review for alleged errors based on this type of rule is "de novo" review, or review for "error of law."

Effective appellate counsel must be prepared both to bring to the court's attention the need for different standards of review depending on the type of rule involved, and to demonstrate to the court why it should reverse a judgment for evidentiary error.

Further Reading: David P. Leonard, *Appellate Review of Evidentiary Rulings,* 70 N.C. L. Rev. 1155 (1992); Stephen A. Saltzburg, *Offers of Proof: The Basic Requirement,* 17 Crim. Just. 50 (2002); Stephen A. Saltzburg, *The Harm of Harmless Error,* 59 Va. L. Rev. 988 (1973); Girardeau A. Spann, *Functional Analysis of the Plain Error Rule,* 71 Geo. L.J. 945 (1983); Edson R. Sunderland, *The Problem of Appellate Review,* 5 Tex. L. Rev. 126 (1927).

---

15. We discuss the meanings of "probative value" and "unfair prejudice" in Chapter 2.

Questions for Classroom Discussion

1. Action for personal injuries suffered in an automobile accident. Plaintiff's attorney asks a witness, "What did Plaintiff tell the police when they arrived at the scene?" Defendant's counsel loudly states, "Objection!" The court overrules the objection. The witness then answers, "Plaintiff said Defendant ran the red light." Assume the testimony was inadmissible hearsay. On appeal Defendant's counsel argues that admission of the testimony over her objection was error. How should the appellate court rule?

2. Same case. Plaintiff's attorney asks the witness, "What did Plaintiff tell the police when they arrived at the scene?" Defendant's counsel states, "Objection, hearsay!" The court sustains the objection. Plaintiff's counsel then asks, "OK, then what did Plaintiff tell the paramedics when they arrived?" Defendant's counsel states, "Objection!" The court overrules the objection and allows the witness to answer. The witness testifies, "Plaintiff said Defendant ran the red light." Assume the testimony was inadmissible hearsay. On appeal Defendant's counsel argues that admission of the testimony over her objection was error. How should the appellate court rule?

3. Same case. Plaintiff's attorney asks the witness, "Did Defendant run the red light?" The witness quickly answers, "I didn't see what happened, but I heard Plaintiff tell the police that Defendant ran the red light." What should Defendant's counsel do now? Is it too late?

4. Same case. Plaintiff's attorney calls the plaintiff to testify and asks, "Who had the red light?" Before Plaintiff can answer, Defendant's counsel objects on the ground of hearsay and the court sustains the objection. Plaintiff's counsel has no evidence other than Plaintiff's testimony to prove who had the red light, which is the crucial issue in the case. Assuming the trial court was wrong to sustain the objection, what must Plaintiff's counsel do to preserve the issue for appeal?

5. Prosecution for murder. A rule (studied in Chapter 4) forbids the prosecution in a murder case from presenting evidence during its case-in-chief of Defendant's character for violent behavior. If Defendant objects to such evidence, and the trial court overrules the objection, is the court's decision subject to "abuse of discretion" review on appeal?

6. Same case. The prosecution offers evidence during its case-in-chief of Defendant's character for violent behavior. Defense counsel does not object, the evidence is admitted, and Defendant is convicted. Assuming the evidence was inadmissible under the rules, what must

---

Defendant's counsel argue on appeal in response to the claim that the failure to object at trial means the error cannot be considered on appeal?

7. If an appellate court finds that a trial court committed error in the admission or exclusion of evidence, will the appellate court necessarily reverse the judgment of the trial court? Why not reverse whenever the trial court errs? Wouldn't a reversal make the court more careful in issuing its evidentiary rulings?

C.   SOURCES OF EVIDENCE AND THE NATURE OF PROOF

1.   *Introduction*

Trials mostly consist of fights over facts. Evidence law regulates proof of facts. But where does evidence come from? In this section, we address some basic rules that describe the permissible sources of evidence and other forms of proof.

The most common way to prove a fact is by introducing evidence. Evidence comes from two sources. The most common source is witnesses. By "witness" we mean a natural person who testifies in court. The second source of evidence consists of writings and other tangible items, sometimes called "real evidence." Some rules apply to both sources of evidence while other rules apply to one source or the other. Subsection 2 considers various rules regulating witness testimony and subsection 3 discusses rules pertinent to writings and real evidence.

Facts sometimes may be proved without resort to evidence.[16] For example, the law sometimes permits courts to assume the existence of facts even without supporting evidence when those facts are well known and indisputable. The process of recognizing these facts is called judicial notice. The rule regulating this process is analyzed in subsection 4.

In the vast majority of cases, it is necessary to present evidence to prove a fact. This means that proving a fact is difficult when there is little or no evidence. Even when there is ample evidence on a given fact, proving that fact is often complicated because the evidence is in conflict. The law regulating burdens of proof guides the resolution of cases in which the evidence is lacking or in conflict. Burdens of proof are introduced in subsection 5 and covered in detail in Chapter 9.

Finally, other laws permit or even compel the trier of fact to assume the existence of one fact based on proof of a different fact or set of facts. The devices that effectuate these laws are called presumptions. We introduce the subject of presumptions in subsection 5 of this chapter and cover that subject in detail in Chapter 9.

---

16. Recall the definition of *evidence* presented in section A.2 above.

2. *Witnesses: The Requirements of Competency, Personal Knowledge, and Oath or Affirmation*

a. "Competent to Be a Witness"

FED. R. EVID. 601.   COMPETENCY TO TESTIFY IN GENERAL

Every person is competent to be a witness unless these rules provide otherwise. But in a civil case, state law governs the witness's competency regarding a claim or defense for which state law supplies the rule of decision.

Discussion

Most evidence rules deal with a "what" question: What can the trier of fact hear or see? The law of witness competency addresses a "who" question: Who is qualified to testify as a witness? Thus, the focus of competency law is the witness, not what the witness has to say.

Rule 601 establishes that, except as otherwise provided in other rules, "every person is competent to be a witness." This rule makes obsolete an enormous amount of old law that disqualified many different categories of people from testifying. For example, early common law disqualified witnesses with mental defects or substance abuse problems, children, parties and their spouses, felons, and people who failed to follow certain mainstream religious beliefs. Rule 601 abolishes all of this law.

But while most people are competent to testify, competency does not equate with credibility. In fact, many of the old bases for disqualifying witnesses are now permissible grounds for attacking witness credibility. For example, at common law, a person generally was not considered competent to testify as a witness unless the court found that she possessed the capacity to perceive, recollect, and communicate accurately, and unless the court found that she understood the obligation to testify truthfully.[17] Rule 601 abolishes these grounds for disqualifying a witness, but the rule does not prevent the cross-examiner from attacking the witness's credibility by inquiring into these matters.

Even Rule 601 acknowledges that there are limits on who is competent. The first sentence of the provision makes it clear that other rules may carve out exceptions to the general principle of witness competency. We will see that other rules still make two categories of people incompetent to testify: the trial judge and the members of the jury. We consider those exceptions in detail below.

Another limitation on the effect of the first sentence of Rule 601 is the provision regarding state law contained in the second sentence of that rule. This sentence says that state law sometimes controls the competency of a witness testifying in federal court. This is important because many states still recognize some of the old limits on witness competency. For example, the Ohio version of Rule 601 states, "Every person is competent to be a witness except . . . [t]hose of unsound mind, and children under ten years of age, who appear incapable of

---

17. The study of hearsay in Chapter 3 and witness impeachment in Chapter 6 demonstrate the central importance of inquiry into perception, recollection, communicative abilities, and sincerity.

receiving just impressions of the facts and transactions respecting which they are examined, or of relating them truly." A few states also have statutory versions of something known as the Dead Man's Act. Most versions of the Dead Man's Act make incompetent a party-witness proposing to testify about a conversation or other transaction with a person now deceased when that testimony is offered against the estate of the deceased. The purpose of such laws is to protect estates from fraudulent claims by prohibiting a claimant from putting words in the mouth of a deceased person, who cannot deny or respond.

The state law provision in Rule 601 requires the application of state competency law when three conditions are satisfied:

1. the issue arises in a civil action or proceeding;
2. it concerns an element of a claim or defense; and
3. the claim or defense is one as to which state law supplies the applicable substantive rule.

This is an application of what is called the Erie doctrine, which is discussed in most law school courses in Civil Procedure. In most cases, the state law provision of Rule 601 makes state competency law control in civil actions brought in federal court under diversity jurisdiction.

Further Reading: 27 Charles Alan Wright & Victor J. Gold, Federal Practice and Procedure 2d §§ 6001-6012 (2007); John E.B. Meyers, *The Testimonial Competency of Children*, 25 J. Fam. L. 287 (1986-1987); Victoria Talwar et al., *Children's Conceptual Knowledge of Lying and Its Relation to Their Actual Behaviors: Implications for Court Competence Examinations*, 26 Law & Hum. Behav. 395-415 (2002); Symposium, *Children as Victims and Witnesses in the Criminal Trial Process*, 65 Law & Contemp. Probs. 1-255 (2002) (Robert P. Mosteller, Special Editor).

Questions for Classroom Discussion

1. A three-year-old child says she saw the incident in question and promises to tell "what really happened and not make up something." She then gives a coherent description of the incident. Is the witness competent?

2. Same case. Assuming the witness is competent and her testimony is admitted against your client, does Rule 601 preclude you from attacking her credibility? What would you argue to the jury about her credibility?

3. A witness is an atheist and states she does not believe she will be punished by God if she lies. Is the witness competent?

4. Why do you think the common law disqualified from testifying witnesses such as children and atheists? What assumption does Rule 601 seem to make about the ability of jurors to evaluate the credibility of witnesses?

(continued)

5. Does evidence of a witness's atheism suggest she is not a credible witness? If so, is the evidence admissible to attack her credibility? Read Rule 610.

6. Civil action brought in a federal district court in Ohio under diversity jurisdiction. Plaintiff calls a three-year-old child to testify. What law must the court apply to determine if the child is competent to testify?

b. Competency of Judge, Jurors, and Attorneys

FED. R. EVID. 605.   JUDGE'S COMPETENCY AS A WITNESS

The presiding judge may not testify as a witness at the trial. A party need not object to preserve the issue.

FED. R. EVID. 606.   JUROR'S COMPETENCY AS A WITNESS

(a) At the Trial. A juror may not testify as a witness before the other jurors at the trial. If a juror is called to testify, the court must give a party an opportunity to object outside the jury's presence.

(b) During an Inquiry into the Validity of a Verdict or Indictment.

(1) *Prohibited Testimony or Other Evidence.* During an inquiry into the validity of a verdict or indictment, a juror may not testify about any statement made or incident that occurred during the jury's deliberations; the effect of anything on that juror's or another juror's vote; or any juror's mental processes concerning the verdict or indictment. The court may not receive a juror's affidavit or evidence of a juror's statement on these matters.

(2) *Exceptions.* A juror may testify about whether:

(A) extraneous prejudicial information was improperly brought to the jury's attention;

(B) an outside influence was improperly brought to bear on any juror; or

(C) a mistake was made in entering the verdict on the verdict form.

Discussion

Recall that Rule 601 states that every person is competent to be a witness "unless these rules provide otherwise." The Federal Rules of Evidence provide few exceptions. One is contained in Rule 605 and two are found in Rule 606.

Rule 605 disqualifies a judge from testifying in a trial over which she presides. This is not because judges are untrustworthy. Rather, it is precisely because such a witness may seem so credible to a jury that her testimony is problematic. Because the presiding judge occupies a position of great authority, what she says from the witness stand may have more influence on the jury than it should. Further, opposing counsel may be reluctant to cross-examine the judge or object to her testimony for fear of giving offense. Combining the roles of judge and witness in the same person not only prevents that person from properly fulfilling the role of witness, it also prevents her from properly functioning as a judge. If a judge has important testimony to give in a case, this means she cannot be an impartial arbiter of the facts. Indeed, a judge is typically disqualified from presiding over a case in which she might be called as a witness. Once a judge has been disqualified, Rule 605 presents no obstacle to that judge testifying as a witness in a trial over which a different judge presides.

For similar reasons, Rule 606(a) disqualifies a member of the jury from testifying as a witness in the trial of the case in which the juror is sitting. Obviously, if a juror has personal knowledge of the facts of a case, that juror cannot be an impartial arbiter of those facts. For this same reason, a prospective juror typically will be excused from serving on the jury when pretrial questioning reveals she has knowledge of the facts in the case.

No evidence rule makes attorneys incompetent to testify in proceedings in which they also occupy the role of advocate. However, the rules of professional ethics prohibit an attorney from accepting employment in most cases in which it is obvious at the outset that the attorney will be called as a witness. Where it is not obvious at the outset, related ethics rules usually require that the attorney withdraw if it later becomes clear she will be called to testify. Many courts will exercise their discretionary powers under Rules 403 and 611 to preclude an attorney from testifying in violation of these rules because juries might be confused by the blurring of boundaries between the roles of witness and advocate.

Questions for Classroom Discussion

1. Recall that Rule 103(a)(1) provides that the right to appeal for error based on erroneous admission of evidence usually is waived in the absence of a timely objection. Normally, an objection is timely if it is made as soon as the evidence is offered. Notice that Rule 606(a) provides, "the court must give an adverse party an opportunity to object outside the jury's presence." This creates an exception to Rule 103(a)(1), permitting a valid objection to be stated much later than usually required: namely, when the juror has finished testifying and the entire jury has been excused from the courtroom. Why does Rule 606(a) create such an exception?

2. Notice that when the judge testifies, Rule 605 creates an even more complete exception to Rule 103(a)(1), stating "A party need not object to preserve the issue." Why does Rule 605 create such an exception?

Rule 606(b) recognizes a third exception to Rule 601 that applies in only a limited procedural context: "an inquiry into the validity of a verdict or indictment." For example, this provision applies in a hearing on a motion for new trial page 30   1. The Process of Proof

based on a claim that a jury's verdict is invalid because of some sort of jury misconduct. Rule 606(b) provides that jurors are incompetent to testify in that hearing as to what happened during deliberations or what mental processes and emotions played a role in their decision.

Without a rule like this, our system of trial by jury might become so inefficient as to be impossible to maintain. It would become routine for lawyers on the losing end of a verdict to search for one disgruntled juror who was willing to describe some irregularity in deliberations. Given that jurors are not experts in the requirements of the law, there probably is some jury confusion or irregularity in many, if not most, cases. Thus, if jurors were freely permitted to testify as to such problems, few verdicts would ever be final and the jury system would collapse. By making jurors incompetent to give such testimony, Rule 606(b) takes the same approach toward jury decision making as a gourmet takes toward sausage-making — it is better not to know how the result is produced.

The rule recognizes limited exceptions, permitting a juror to testify concerning the presence of "extraneous prejudicial information" and "outside influence." A third exception permits a juror to testify that a mistake was made in entering the verdict onto the verdict form.

The jury receives "extraneous prejudicial information" when it learns about the facts of the case from some source other than admitted evidence, such as a newspaper, television, or radio report. "Outside influence" refers to external pressures on the jury such as bribes or threats. These narrow exceptions mean that Rule 606(b) bars juror testimony concerning irregularities in jury decision making when they are internal to the jury, such as juror mistakes about the law or the facts. The third exception in Rule 606(b) applies in the rare case where the jury made a mechanical error in writing its verdict on a verdict form. It is clear that this exception covers only a recording error and does not extend to other types of juror mistake or misconduct.

There are good reasons to preclude jurors from testifying about what happens during deliberations. Two important goals served by the rule are the achievement of finality and insulation of jurors from harassment by losing counsel. But achieving these goals sometimes comes at a high price, requiring that we turn a blind eye toward egregious jury misconduct.

TANNER v. UNITED STATES

483 U.S. 107 (1987)

[Defendants were convicted of fraud. They brought a motion for a new trial on the ground that, after the trial was over, one of the jurors informed a defense attorney that several of the jurors consumed alcohol during lunch breaks, causing them to sleep through the afternoon sessions of the trial. Investigators interviewed another juror who stated he "felt like . . . the jury was on one big party." He claimed that four jurors consumed between them "a pitcher to three pitchers" of beer during various recesses. He also stated that on several occasions he observed two jurors having one or two mixed drinks during the lunch recess, and one other juror, who was also the foreperson, having a liter of wine on each of three occasions. The juror also stated that he and three other jurors smoked marijuana quite regularly during the trial and that one juror ingested cocaine five times and another two or three times. One juror sold a quarter pound of marijuana to another juror during the trial, and took marijuana, cocaine, and drug paraphernalia into the courthouse. The juror noted that some of the jurors were falling asleep during the trial, and that one of the jurors described himself as "flying."]

Justice O'CONNOR delivered the opinion of the Court.

There is little doubt that postverdict investigation into juror misconduct would in some instances lead to the invalidation of verdicts reached after irresponsible or improper juror behavior. It is not at all clear, however, that the jury system could survive such efforts to perfect it. Allegations of juror misconduct, incompetency, or inattentiveness, raised for the first time days, weeks, or months after the verdict, seriously disrupt the finality of the process. . . . Moreover, full and frank discussion in the jury room, jurors' willingness to return an unpopular verdict, and the community's trust in a system that relies on the decisions of laypeople would all be undermined by a barrage of postverdict scrutiny of juror conduct. . . .

[P]etitioners argue that substance abuse constitutes an improper "outside influence" about which jurors may testify under Rule 606(b). In our view the language of the Rule cannot easily be stretched to cover this circumstance. However severe their effect and improper their use, drugs or alcohol voluntarily ingested by a juror seems no more an "outside influence" than a virus, poorly prepared food, or a lack of sleep. . . .

[L]ong-recognized and very substantial concerns support the protection of jury deliberations from intrusive inquiry. Petitioners' Sixth Amendment interests in an unimpaired jury, on the other hand, are protected by several aspects of the trial process. The suitability of an individual for the responsibility of jury service, of course, is examined during voir dire. Moreover, during the trial the jury is observable by the court, by counsel, and by court personnel. . . . Moreover, jurors are observable by each other, and may report inappropriate juror behavior to the court before they render a verdict. . . . Finally, after the trial a party may seek to impeach the verdict by nonjuror evidence of misconduct. . . . Indeed, in this case the District Court held an evidentiary hearing giving petitioners ample opportunity to produce nonjuror evidence supporting their allegations.

In light of these other sources of protection of petitioners' right to a competent jury, we conclude that the District Court did not err in deciding, based on the inadmissibility of juror testimony and the clear insufficiency of the nonjuror evidence offered by petitioners, that an additional postverdict evidentiary hearing was unnecessary.

[Justice MARSHALL dissented, and was joined by Justices BRENNAN, BLACKMUN, and STEVENS.]

Are there Limits to Tanner?

In a unanimous opinion written by Associate Justice Sotomayor, the United States Supreme Court recently ruled that Federal Rule of Evidence 606(b) makes a juror incompetent to testify that another member of the jury lied during voir dire when that testimony is offered in support of a motion for a new trial. Warger v. Shauers, 135 S. Ct. 521 (2014).

Warger was a negligence action brought to recover for injuries suffered in a motor vehicle accident. During voir dire, plaintiff's counsel asked prospective jurors if there was any reason they would be unable to be fair and impartial. The prospective juror who later became jury foreperson answered no. The jury eventually returned a defense verdict. Plaintiff's subsequent motion for a new trial asserted that the jury foreperson lied during voir dire. Plaintiff submitted in support of that motion a juror's affidavit that, during deliberations, the jury foreperson stated that her daughter once had been at fault in an auto accident and that, had she been sued, her life would have been ruined. The District Court denied defendant's motion for a new trial, holding that the affidavit was barred by Federal Rule of Evidence 606(b). The Eighth Circuit affirmed and the Supreme Court granted certiorari.

The facts in *Warger* present a good example of the mischief that might ensue without a law like Rule 606(b). As in *Warger*, virtually every potential juror in virtually every case is asked the generic question, "Is there any reason why you might be unable to be fair and impartial?" Of course, only those who answer "no" are selected to serve on the jury. But every trial lawyer takes that answer with a grain of salt. Every juror has biases. In fact, lawyers strive during jury selection to impanel jurors who are favorably biased. Few verdicts would survive if statements made during deliberations were admissible to support a motion for new trial on the ground jurors lied during voir dire in response to the generic question about being fair and impartial.

The Supreme Court in *Warger* read Federal Rule 606(b) as barring juror testimony regarding statements or other matters occurring during deliberations. The Court noted that this approach is limited only by the few exceptions in the rule, including the exception permitting juror testimony showing that extraneous prejudicial information was brought to the jury's attention. As for that exception, the Court concluded that information can be deemed "extraneous" only if it derives from a source external to the jury. Such external matters include publicity and information specifically related to the case before the jury, but do not include the general body of life experience that jurors bring into the jury room. The evidence in question, concluded the Court, was internal since it may have informed the foreperson's general views about negligence liability for car crashes, but did not involve specific facts regarding the case at bar. In so reasoning, the Supreme Court's decision in *Warger* is consistent with its 1987 opinion in Tanner v. United States.

The Court in *Warger* also relied upon *Tanner* for its conclusion that excluding evidence a juror lied during voir dire does not render Rule 606(b) unconstitutional. Of course, the Sixth Amendment guarantees a right to trial before a jury that is both impartial and mentally competent. That right is undermined when jurors lie about being impartial or are intoxicated during trial. But the Court in both *Warger* and *Tanner* held that this right was sufficiently protected under the facts of those cases because Rule 606(b) precludes only one type of evidence — juror testimony attacking the validity of a verdict. The provision does not preclude testimony from jurors before a verdict is rendered or testimony from non-jurors even after a verdict.

But this reasoning suggests there may be limits to *Warger* and *Tanner*. For example, what if there is no evidence of juror bias that emerges prior to a verdict, the only evidence that emerges thereafter comes from statements made by a juror during deliberations, and no one other than a juror heard those statements made? And what if those statements are compelling evidence that a juror intentionally lied during voir dire to conceal a bias like racial animus toward the defendant in a criminal prosecution? The Supreme Court acknowledged in the final footnote in *Warger* that such a case might produce a different result: "There may be cases of juror bias so extreme that, almost by definition, the jury trial right has been abridged. If and when such a case arises, the Court can consider whether the usual safeguards are or are not sufficient to protect the integrity of the process."

Further Reading: 27 Charles Alan Wright & Victor J. Gold, Federal Practice and Procedure 2d §§ 6061-6077 (2007); Mark Cammack, *The Jurisprudence of Jury Trials: The No Impeachment Rule and the Conditions for Legitimate Decisionmaking*, 64 U. Colo. L. Rev. 57 (1993); Shari Seidman Diamond & Neil Vidmar, *Jury Room Ruminations on Forbidden Topics*, 87 Va. L. Rev. 1857 (2001); John H. Mansfield, *Jury Notice*, 74 Geo. L.J. 395 (1985).

Questions for Classroom Discussion

1. Defendant is convicted after a jury trial. Defendant makes a motion for new trial on the ground of jury misconduct and calls the courtroom bailiff to testify that jurors were drinking alcohol and doing drugs whenever he entered the jury room during deliberations. Is the bailiff's testimony barred by Rule 606(b)?

2. Defendant is convicted after a jury trial. Defendant makes a motion for new trial on the ground of jury misconduct and calls a juror to testify that the jury decided the case by flipping a coin. Is the juror's testimony barred by Rule 606(b)?

3. Defendant, an African American, is convicted of murder and sentenced to death. Defendant makes a motion for new trial and calls a juror to testify that, during deliberations, several jurors made remarks disparaging African Americans and one said, "It doesn't matter if he committed the murder or not, we should execute them all." In a hearing on a motion to overturn the conviction, is the juror's testimony barred by Rule 606(b)? If it is, what other argument might Defendant make?

4. Negligence action by Plaintiff against Defendant after Defendant allegedly ran Plaintiff down as Plaintiff crossed the street in a crosswalk late one night. Defendant claims she was not the one whose car struck Plaintiff. To identify Defendant's car as the one that hit Plaintiff, Plaintiff calls Witness, who testifies that she was standing approximately 200 feet from the point of impact, and that the car that hit Plaintiff was a 1995 Acura Integra. Other evidence shows that Defendant owns a 1995 Acura Integra. After a jury verdict for Defendant, Plaintiff's attorney learns that one of the jurors is a

(continued)

car buff and, during deliberations, said that "there's no way to tell the difference between a 1995 Integra and a 1996, 1997, 1998, 1999, 2000, or 2001 Integra from 200 feet in the dead of night." Plaintiff moves for a new trial on the ground that the juror employed improper personal knowledge outside the record and offers the testimony of another member of the jury to prove what was said during deliberations. How should the court rule on the competency of the juror to testify?

5. Same case as Question 4. The jury reached a verdict for Plaintiff and recorded on the verdict form their decision to award Plaintiff $1,000,000 in compensatory damages. A juror subsequently writes a letter to Plaintiff's counsel expressing her belief that the jury made a mistake in calculating the damage award because it incorrectly assumed that Plaintiff would not have to pay attorneys' fees out of the judgment. Plaintiff makes a motion for a new trial and argues that the juror's letter is admissible under the exception in Rule 606(b)(3) for mistakes in entering the verdict onto the verdict form. How should the court rule?

c. The Competency of a Witness Whose Recollection Has Been Refreshed Through Hypnosis

Some scientific studies indicate that hypnosis can be used to restore memory of experiences repressed due to their unpleasant nature or simply forgotten in the passage of time. A few scientists have attempted to explain these results in light of a theory of memory that contends that, like a video camera, the brain permanently records all the information it receives from the body's senses. Under this theory, memory failure is just an inability to retrieve or "play back" that information, and hypnosis becomes a method to eliminate the retrieval problems.

Because of the apparent promise of this theory of memory, some law enforcement agencies have come to use hypnosis to aid witnesses in recalling details of crimes and related events. Hypnosis of eyewitnesses was credited with uncovering the crucial leads in a California case involving the kidnapping of 26 children from a school bus and in another case involving the murder of a cellist at the Metropolitan Opera in New York City.

It is probably safe to say that the failures have received somewhat less attention in the press. In fact, some empirical studies indicate that hypnosis is not an effective means of restoring memory. Nevertheless, the use of hypnosis in criminal investigations continues and even courts generally critical of hypnosis concede it is sometimes a useful investigative tool.

The use of hypnosis in criminal investigations raises a difficult evidence question. The issue usually has been framed in terms of questioning the competency of an individual who has been hypnotized to assist a criminal investigation when that same individual is later called to testify at trial for the prosecution. The issue is not whether a witness can be hypnotized in court and then examined while hypnotized — no judge would permit this. Rather, the issue is whether a witness who, prior to trial, was hypnotized in connection with the events at issue is later competent to testify at trial. Competency is questioned on the ground that the "recollections" produced by hypnosis frequently are unreliable products of the hypnotic experience rather than the events supposedly recalled. A number of prominent scientific authorities contend that the reliability of a witness's subsequent testimony may be significantly undermined by hypnosis. They assert that reliability may be diminished by the effects of *suggestion, confabulation,* and *overconfidence.*

All theories of hypnosis agree that it is fundamentally a process of suggestion: The subject falls into a hypnotic state by following the suggestions of the hypnotist. The subject remains extremely susceptible to the hypnotist's suggestions throughout the session. In fact, suggestions made to the subject during hypnosis influence the subject's behavior and beliefs even after the subject emerges from a hypnotic state. The awakened subject usually has no recollection that suggestions were ever made. Thus, suggestions made to a witness under hypnosis concerning the existence of alleged facts or events will tend to convince the witness that these suggested facts or events were real. When the witness testifies, she may believe that hypnosis refreshed her recollection as to matters she perceived when in fact she is only repeating suggestions implanted during hypnosis. This is not only a problem in those instances when an unscrupulous or incompetent hypnotist intentionally suggests the existence of incriminating facts. Hypnosis can implant suggestions unintentionally through unconscious verbal and nonverbal cues transmitted to the witness. Not even the hypnotist, whose unintended suggestions may have inspired the testimony, can distinguish real from implanted recollection.

A subject under hypnosis usually has a compelling desire to please the hypnotist. As a result, if the subject knows the hypnotist is seeking to refresh recollection and uncover additional facts or details concerning an event, the subject rarely will admit to an inability to recall the information sought. She may fill the gaps in her actual memory concerning the event with details drawn from other experiences or even pure fantasy. After the hypnosis has ended, the subject is commonly unable to distinguish between memory based on actual perception and details invented during the session. This process, called *confabulation,* may be common in witnesses who have been hypnotized by the police in connection with a criminal investigation because such witnesses will almost always know that the hypnotist's objective is to discover new facts concerning the case. As in the case of recollection implanted by suggestion, the hypnotist and his subject are typically unable to distinguish confabulation from true recollection.

The typical subject emerges from hypnosis convinced that her "recollections" are accurate. Uncertainties concerning facts remembered prior to hypnosis are washed away. New facts revealed for the first time while under hypnosis are steadfastly believed, notwithstanding the complete absence of such recollections prior to hypnosis and the danger that the new facts may be the product of confabulation or suggestion. This overconfidence may itself be the product of suggestion; the hypnotist commonly tells the subject that she will recall true facts while under hypnosis and remember all those facts upon awakening. Even if the hypnotist avoids making such suggestions explicitly, the subject's own expectations as to the nature and effect of hypnosis and the effort by the police to place the subject under hypnosis may suggest enough about the powers of hypnosis to engender overconfidence. Even after the session ends, the subject's confidence may increase with each retelling of the story first told under hypnosis.

The responses of the courts to these reliability problems have varied greatly. Four general approaches have emerged concerning the competency of a witness whose recollection was allegedly refreshed through hypnosis.

The witness is per se competent.   Some courts take the position that the use of hypnosis to refresh recollection does not render the witness incompetent. Instead, the jury is asked to evaluate credibility in light of the effects of hypnosis as demonstrated by cross-examination of the witness, expert testimony, and instructions from the court.

The witness is per se incompetent.   On the opposite extreme, several state courts have held that a witness who has undergone hypnosis for the purpose of refreshing recollection is, subsequently, per se incompetent to testify as to any subject discussed while under hypnosis. Many more courts adopt what might be called a modified per se incompetent approach: The witness is incompetent to testify except as to those matters the witness recalled prior to hypnosis. The theory behind permitting the witness to testify as to such matters is that this testimony is less likely to be the product of suggestion or confabulation than is testimony concerning facts recalled for the first time under hypnosis.

The witness is competent if safeguards are employed.   Under this middle-of-the-road position, courts permit the witness to testify if procedures were followed during the hypnosis session to guard against suggestion and confabulation. The required safeguards vary from one jurisdiction to another. Among the procedures commonly required are (1) a psychiatrist or psychologist experienced with hypnosis and not regularly employed by the police conducts the session, (2) the session is recorded, (3) before hypnosis, a detailed record is created of the witness's then-existing recollection, and (4) only the hypnotist and the subject are present during the session.

The witness is competent if, on balance, circumstances suggest reliability.   This final approach makes witness competency depend on a review of all the circumstances having a bearing on the reliability of the witness's post-hypnosis recollections.

PEOPLE v. SHIRLEY

723 P.2d 1354 (Cal. 1982)

[After a trial, defendant was found guilty of sexual assault. Defendant testified that the sexual acts were consensual. The complaining witness had been drinking at the time of the alleged crimes, and, on the eve of trial, she was hypnotized by a deputy district attorney for the purpose of "filling the gaps" in her story. The trial court denied defendant's pretrial motion to exclude all of the witness's testimony resulting from hypnosis, and the witness was allowed to testify to a number of matters that she did not recall prior to hypnosis. A psychiatrist with extensive training in hypnosis was called by the defense as an expert witness. He testified that hypnosis is not a reliable method for determining the truth and that most psychiatrists agreed. The prosecution neither discredited the witness's opinion on cross-examination, nor called any expert witness of its own.]

Mosk, J.

In accord with recent and persuasive case law and the overwhelming consensus of expert opinion, we conclude that the testimony of such a witness should not be admitted in the courts of California. . . .

The professional literature . . . demonstrates beyond any doubt that at the present time the use of hypnosis to restore the memory of a potential witness is not generally accepted as reliable by the relevant scientific community. Indeed, representative groups within that community are on record as expressly opposing this technique for many of the foregoing reasons, particularly when it is employed by law enforcement hypnotists. In these circumstances it is obvious that the Frye test of admissibility has not been satisfied. We therefore hold . . . that the testimony of a witness who has undergone hypnosis for the purpose of restoring his memory of the events in issue is inadmissible as to all matters relating to those events, from the time of the hypnotic session forward. It follows that the trial court erred in denying defendant's motion to exclude Catherine's testimony.

We do not undertake to foreclose the continued use of hypnosis by the police for purely investigative purposes. We recognize that on occasions in the past a subject has apparently been helped by hypnosis to remember a verifiable fact — such as a license plate number — that the police previously did not know and were then able to use as a "lead" for further investigation of the crime. It is neither appropriate nor necessary for us to enter the debate as to the need for this investigative technique, or its reliability. We reiterate, however, that for the reasons stated above any person who has been hypnotized for investigative purposes will not be allowed to testify as a witness to the events that were the subject of the hypnotic session. Evidence discovered by such an investigation, of course, is not ipso facto rendered inadmissible by the prior hypnosis.

CAL. EVID. CODE § 795. TESTIMONY OF HYPNOSIS SUBJECT; ADMISSIBILITY; CONDITIONS

(a) The testimony of a witness is not inadmissible in a criminal proceeding by reason of the fact that the witness has previously undergone hypnosis for the purpose of recalling events that are the subject of the witness's testimony, if all of the following conditions are met:

(1) The testimony is limited to those matters that the witness recalled and related prior to the hypnosis.

(2) The substance of the prehypnotic memory was preserved in a writing, audio recording, or video recording prior to the hypnosis.

(3) The hypnosis was conducted in accordance with all of the following procedures:

(A) A written record was made prior to hypnosis documenting the subject's description of the event, and information that was provided to the hypnotist concerning the subject matter of the hypnosis.

(B) The subject gave informed consent to the hypnosis.

(C) The hypnosis session, including the pre- and post-hypnosis interviews, was video recorded for subsequent review.

(D) The hypnosis was performed by a licensed medical doctor, psychologist, licensed clinical social worker, or a licensed marriage and family therapist experienced in the use of hypnosis and independent of and not in the presence of law enforcement, the prosecution, or the defense.

(4) Prior to admission of the testimony, the court holds a hearing pursuant to Section 402 at which the proponent of the evidence proves by clear and convincing evidence that the hypnosis did not so affect the witness as to render the witness's prehypnosis recollection unreliable or to substantially impair the ability to cross-examine the witness concerning the witness's prehypnosis recollection. At the hearing, each side shall have the right to present expert testimony and to cross-examine witnesses.

(b) Nothing in this section shall be construed to limit the ability of a party to attack the credibility of a witness who has undergone hypnosis, or to limit other legal grounds to admit or exclude the testimony of that witness.

Questions for Classroom Discussion

1. Would the witness in People v. Shirley have been competent to testify if Federal Rule of Evidence 601 applied? In a civil action arising under diversity jurisdiction brought in federal district court in California, is a witness competent under Rule 601 to testify if her recollection had been refreshed through hypnosis?

2. The court in People v. Shirley stated that it did not "foreclose the continued use of hypnosis by the police for purely investigative purposes." Can you see why the decision might still discourage police from using hypnosis in an investigation? What are the disadvantages of this?

3. Evidence Code § 795 was enacted in response to People v. Shirley. Why do you think the legislature did this?

4. In an earlier set of discussion questions, you considered the assumptions Rule 601 makes about the ability of jurors to evaluate witness credibility. Make an argument that those assumptions are not valid in the case of a witness whose recollection has been refreshed through hypnosis and, therefore, limits on such a witness's competency are justified.

The decision in People v. Shirley might be justified on the ground that unreliable evidence should not be admitted when the jury may have difficulty weighing reliability problems. As we will see, many rules that exclude evidence are based on the same premise. But, as the following case makes clear, when exculpatory evidence is excluded in a criminal prosecution, constitutional rights might trump the reliability concerns of evidence law.

ROCK v. ARKANSAS
483 U.S. 44 (1987)

[Defendant was charged with manslaughter for shooting her husband. To refresh her memory as to the precise details of the shooting, she twice underwent hypnosis at the suggestion of her defense attorney. After the hypnosis, she recalled exculpatory details. The state courts ruled that no hypnotically refreshed testimony could be admitted, limiting defendant to a reiteration of the statements she made prior to hypnosis.]

BLACKMUN, J., delivered the opinion of the Court, in which BRENNAN, MARSHALL, POWELL, and STEVENS, JJ., joined.

The issue presented in this case is whether Arkansas' evidentiary rule prohibiting the admission of hypnotically refreshed testimony violated petitioner's constitutional right to testify on her own behalf as a defendant in a criminal case.

Petitioner's claim that her testimony was impermissibly excluded is bottomed on her constitutional right to testify in her own defense. At this point in the development of our adversary system, it cannot be doubted that a defendant in a criminal case has the right to take the witness stand and to testify in his or her own defense. This, of course, is a change from the historic common-law view, which was that all parties to litigation, including criminal defendants, were disqualified from testifying because of their interest in the outcome of the trial. *See generally* 2 J. Wigmore, Evidence §§ 576, 579 (J. Chadbourn rev. 1979). The principal rationale for this rule was the possible untrustworthiness of a party's testimony. Under the common law, the practice did develop of permitting criminal defendants to tell their side of the story, but they were limited to making an unsworn statement that could not be elicited through direct examination by counsel and was not subject to cross-examination.

The right to testify on one's own behalf at a criminal trial has sources in several provisions of the Constitution. It is one of the rights that "are essential to due process of law in a fair adversary process." Faretta v. California, 422 U.S. 806, 819, n.15, 95 S. Ct. 2525, 2533 n.15, 45 L. Ed. 2d 562 (1975). The necessary ingredients of the Fourteenth Amendment's guarantee that no one shall be deprived of liberty without due process of law include a right to be heard and to offer testimony:

> A person's right to reasonable notice of a charge against him, and an opportunity to be heard in his defense — a right to his day in court — are basic in our system of jurisprudence; and these rights include, as a minimum, a right to examine the witnesses against him, to offer testimony, and to be represented by counsel.

In re Oliver, 333 U.S. 257, 273, 68 S. Ct. 499, 507, 92 L. Ed. 682 (1948).

The right to testify is also found in the Compulsory Process Clause of the Sixth Amendment, which grants a defendant the right to call "witnesses in his favor," a right that is guaranteed in the criminal courts of the States by the Fourteenth Amendment. Washington v. Texas, 388 U.S. 14, 17-19, 87 S. Ct. 1920, 1922-1923, 18 L. Ed. 2d 1019 (1967). Logically included in the accused's right to call witnesses whose testimony is "material and favorable to his defense," United States v. Valenzuela-Bernal, 458 U.S. 858, 867, 102 S. Ct. 3440, 3446, 73 L. Ed. 2d 1193 (1982), is a right to testify himself, should he decide it is in his favor to do so. In fact, the most important witness for the defense in many criminal cases is the defendant himself. There is no justification today for a rule that denies an accused the opportunity to offer his own testimony. Like the truthfulness of other witnesses, the defendant's veracity, which was the concern behind the original common-law rule, can be tested adequately by cross-examination.

Even more fundamental to a personal defense than the right of self-representation, which was found to be "necessarily implied by the structure of the Amendment," *ibid.*, is an accused's right to present his own version of events in his own words. A defendant's opportunity to conduct his own defense by calling witnesses is incomplete if he may not present himself as a witness. . . .

The question now before the Court is whether a criminal defendant's right to testify may be restricted by a state rule that excludes her posthypnosis testimony. . . .

Just as a State may not apply an arbitrary rule of competence to exclude a material defense witness from taking the stand, it also may not apply a rule of evidence that permits a witness to take the stand, but arbitrarily excludes material portions of his testimony. In Chambers v. Mississippi, 410 U.S. 284, 93 S. Ct. 1038, 35 L. Ed. 2d 297 (1973), the Court invalidated a State's hearsay rule on the ground that it abridged the defendant's right to "present witnesses in his own defense." *Id.*, at 302, 93 S. Ct., at 1049. Chambers was tried for a murder to which another person repeatedly had confessed in the presence of acquaintances. The State's hearsay rule, coupled with a "voucher" rule that did not allow the defendant to cross-examine the confessed murderer directly, prevented Chambers from introducing testimony concerning these confessions, which were critical to his defense. This Court reversed the judgment of conviction, holding that when a state rule of evidence conflicts with the right to present witnesses, the rule may "not be applied mechanically to defeat the ends of justice," but must meet the fundamental standards of due process. *Ibid.* In the Court's view, the State in *Chambers* did not demonstrate that the hearsay testimony in that case, which bore "assurances of trustworthiness" including corroboration by other evidence, would be unreliable, and thus the defendant should have been able to introduce the exculpatory testimony.

Of course, the right to present relevant testimony is not without limitation. The right "may, in appropriate cases, bow to accommodate other legitimate interests in the criminal trial process." *Id.*, at 295, 93 S. Ct., at 1046. But restrictions of a defendant's right to testify may not be arbitrary or disproportionate to the purposes they are designed to serve. In applying its evidentiary rules a State must evaluate whether the interests served by a rule justify the limitation imposed on the defendant's constitutional right to testify.

The Arkansas rule enunciated by the state courts does not allow a trial court to consider whether posthypnosis testimony may be admissible in a particular case; it is a per se rule prohibiting the admission at trial of any defendant's hypnotically refreshed testimony on the ground that such testimony is always unreliable. Thus, in Arkansas, an accused's testimony is limited to matters that he or she can prove were remembered before hypnosis. This rule operates to the detriment of any defendant who undergoes hypnosis, without regard to the reasons for it, the circumstances under which it took place, or any independent verification of the information it produced.

In this case, the application of that rule had a significant adverse effect on petitioner's ability to testify. It virtually prevented her from describing any of the events that occurred on the day of the shooting, despite corroboration of many of those events by other witnesses. Even more importantly, under the court's rule petitioner was not permitted to describe the actual shooting except in the words contained in Doctor Back's notes. The expert's description of the gun's tendency to misfire would have taken on greater significance if the jury had heard petitioner testify that she did not have her finger on the trigger and that the gun went off when her husband hit her arm. In establishing its per se rule, the Arkansas Supreme Court simply followed the approach taken by a number of States that have decided that hypnotically enhanced testimony should be excluded at trial on the ground that it tends to be unreliable. Other States that have adopted an exclusionary rule, however, have done so for the testimony of witnesses, not for the testimony of a defendant. The Arkansas Supreme Court failed to perform the constitutional analysis that is necessary when a defendant's right to testify is at stake. . . .

We are not now prepared to endorse without qualifications the use of hypnosis as an investigative tool; scientific understanding of the phenomenon and of the means to control the effects of hypnosis is still in its infancy. Arkansas, however, has not justified the exclusion of all of a defendant's testimony that the defendant is unable to prove to be the product of prehypnosis memory. A State's legitimate interest in barring unreliable evidence does not extend to per se exclusions that may be reliable in an individual case. Wholesale inadmissibility of a defendant's testimony is an arbitrary restriction on the right to testify in the absence of clear evidence by the State repudiating the validity of all posthypnosis recollections. The State would be well within its powers if it established guidelines to aid trial courts in the evaluation of posthypnosis testimony and it may be able to show that testimony in a particular case is so unreliable that exclusion is justified. But it has not shown that hypnotically enhanced testimony is always so untrustworthy and so immune to the traditional means of evaluating credibility that it should disable a defendant from presenting her version of the events for which she is on trial.

In this case, the defective condition of the gun corroborated the details petitioner remembered about the shooting. The tape recordings provided some means to evaluate the hypnosis and the trial judge concluded that Doctor Back did not suggest responses with leading questions. Those circumstances present an argument for admissibility of petitioner's testimony in this particular case, an argument that must be considered by the trial court. Arkansas' per se rule excluding all posthypnosis testimony infringes impermissibly on the right of a defendant to testify on his own behalf.

Rehnquist, C.J., filed a dissenting opinion, in which White, O'Connor, and Scalia, JJ., joined.

Questions for Classroom Discussion

1. Assume the defendant in *Rock* was hypnotized by a therapist who lacked training in hypnosis, was paid by defense counsel, and kept no record of the procedures employed. According to *Rock*, does a

(continued)

> state law excluding hypnotically refreshed recollection produced under such circumstances necessarily violate the Constitution?
>
> 2. Does *Rock* mean that an accused has a constitutional right to present the hypnotically refreshed testimony of a witness other than the defendant when that testimony is crucial?

d. The "Personal Knowledge" Requirement

FED. R. EVID. 602.   NEED FOR PERSONAL KNOWLEDGE

A witness may testify to a matter only if evidence is introduced sufficient to support a finding that the witness has personal knowledge of the matter. Evidence to prove personal knowledge may consist of the witness's own testimony. This rule does not apply to a witness's expert testimony under Rule 703.

Discussion

Rule 602 provides that a witness may testify to a fact only if she has personal knowledge of it. A witness can have personal knowledge of facts only if she perceived those facts with one or more of her senses. The idea can be expressed in this simple equation: $FP = FT$, where "FP" refers to the facts perceived and "FT" refers to the facts to which the witness will be permitted to testify. If the facts to which the witness proposes to testify are not facts she perceived, the witness's testimony is rejected.

Sensory perception is just the first part of what Rule 602 demands of a witness. Implicit in the concept of "knowledge" is the notion that a witness also must be able to comprehend, remember, and communicate what she perceived. Rule 602 expresses the common sense notion that, absent one or more of these capacities, a witness has nothing of value to contribute to the process of fact-finding.

This does not mean that a witness's knowledge must be perfect. Rule 602 only requires that there be evidence "sufficient to support a finding" of personal knowledge. This is not a demanding standard. A witness has personal knowledge as long as a reasonable juror could conclude that the witness perceived, comprehends, remembers, and can communicate the facts. As long as this minimal standard is satisfied, doubts about the extent of the witness's knowledge do not make her testimony inadmissible. Instead, evidence concerning the extent of the witness's knowledge is itself admissible so the trier of fact can determine what weight to give her testimony.

There are many ways to prove that a witness has personal knowledge. The most common way is to show that the witness was at the scene of an event, establish that the witness was in a position to observe, hear, or otherwise perceive the event with one or more of her senses, and then ask the witness to testify as to what she perceived. To illustrate, assume Plaintiff sues Defendant for personal injuries, claiming that Defendant drove a red Chevy into her as she crossed the street. Defendant admits he was at the scene in his red Chevy, but claims that he stopped for Plaintiff and that another car struck her. Plaintiff calls Witness to establish that Defendant's car struck Plaintiff.

P: Where were you at 3:15 on the afternoon of July 1?

W: I was walking on the sidewalk on Main Street.

P: Which side of Main Street were you on?

W: I was on the south side.

P: Which direction were you walking?

W: East.

P: What street were you approaching?

W: First Street.

P: Did you have a clear view of the cars moving west along Main Street for about a block ahead of you?

W: Pretty much. My view was limited a little bit because of a tree on the sidewalk between me and the street, but I could see quite well.

D: Objection, Your Honor. The witness lacks personal knowledge.

P: Your Honor, even if the witness's view was obscured to some extent, there is adequate evidence of personal knowledge.

By the Court: Objection overruled.

P: As you were walking at that time, which way were you looking?

W: I was looking ahead of me, straight ahead.

P: Did you observe anything unusual as you approached First Street?

W: Yes. I saw a car hit a pedestrian.

P: Please describe the car.

W: It was a red Chevy.

P: Which way was the red Chevy moving?

W: It was moving west, toward me.

P: About how far from you was the red Chevy when it hit the pedestrian?

W: I would guess it was about 50 feet ahead of me.

P: Did you see the pedestrian before the collision?

W: Yes. She was in a group of people I saw walking across the street at First and Main.

P: Do you remember what the pedestrian looked like?

W: Yes.

P: Please describe the pedestrian.

W: The pedestrian was a woman, medium height, with long straight brown hair.

P: Do you see that woman in the courtroom today?

W: Yes. She's sitting next to you, on your left.

P: Your Honor, may the record reflect that the witness has indicated the Plaintiff?

By the Court: The record will reflect that the witness has pointed to the Plaintiff.

P: From what direction was the pedestrian coming?

> *W:* She was coming from my side of the street, the south side of Main Street.
>
> *P.* Did you hear a sound at the time you saw the red Chevy strike the pedestrian?
>
> *W:* Yes. I heard a thump, and then I saw the pedestrian fall.

In this example, Plaintiff's lawyer has carefully established that Witness was in a position to observe the collision, that she was paying attention at the relevant time, and that she saw and heard the collision. This shows that each detail to which Witness testifies is based on personal knowledge. The court correctly overruled Defendant's objection because a witness need not have a perfect view of an event to have personal knowledge of it. Problems with perception usually bear upon witness credibility—how much weight her testimony should receive—not the admissibility of her testimony. This does not mean, of course, that the court has concluded that Witness saw what she claims to have seen. It only means that Plaintiff has laid an adequate foundation to permit the jury to consider Witness's testimony. Defendant's lawyer will have an opportunity to cross-examine Witness and try to attack the accuracy of her observations.

Note that in the example, Plaintiff's lawyer demonstrated the personal knowledge before Witness testified to the crucial facts. The rule does not require this. All Rule 602 says is that there must be evidence sufficient to support a finding of personal knowledge; it does not require that the evidence showing personal knowledge be offered before the witness begins to testify to the facts in question. Thus, it would have been permissible to ask the witness first to describe the collision itself, and then to show that the witness was in a position to see the accident and, thus, had personal knowledge of the details to which she testified. Though such a method of questioning the witness might elicit an objection from the opponent, the court will usually overrule the objection if the party who called the witness represents that she will establish the witness's personal knowledge within a short time.

The requirement that a witness must have personal knowledge is part of the foundation on which much of the rest of evidence law is built. As we learn in Chapter 7, Rule 701 establishes that a lay witness often is prohibited from giving opinion testimony. This very proposition is implicit in the assumption underlying Rule 602 that a lay witness's testimony normally should be limited to describing her perceptions, as opposed to her opinions and conclusions. We will see that, even where Rule 701 permits lay opinion testimony, it still must be based on perception. Rule 802, the hearsay rule, sometimes prevents a witness from repeating in court what someone said out of court. Like Rule 602, the hearsay rule is based in part on concern for the reliability of testimony unsupported by the witness's firsthand observation.

The last sentence of Rule 602 expressly recognizes one narrow exception to the personal knowledge requirement—Rule 703 sometimes permits an expert witness to testify based on facts she did not perceive with her own senses. We study that exception in Chapter 7.

Further Reading: 27 Charles Alan Wright & Victor J. Gold, Federal Practice and Procedure 2d §§ 6021-6028 (2007); Ronald Raitt, *Personal Knowledge Under the Federal Rules of Evidence: A Three Legged Stool,* 18 Rutgers L.J. 591 (1987).

Questions for Classroom Discussion

1. Prosecution of Defendant for the murder of Joe. Defendant denies committing the crime. A prosecution witness testifies he saw a person resembling Defendant shoot Joe, but the witness admits he did not have his glasses on, his view was obstructed by a tree, and the sun was in his eyes. Does the witness have personal knowledge of the shooter's appearance? What standard of proof applies to the question?

2. Same case. A prosecution witness testifies, "Defendant shot Joe." After further questioning, the witness admits he did not see the shooting but a police officer told him Defendant was the perpetrator. Does the witness have personal knowledge?

3. Same case. A prosecution witness testifies, "The police officer told me, 'Defendant shot Joe.'" Does the witness have personal knowledge? If so, is there any other reason why we might not want to admit this testimony?

4. Same case. A prosecution witness testifies he had a dream that Defendant shot Joe. Does the witness have personal knowledge?

5. Same case. A prosecution witness testifies that, before the crime was committed, Defendant told the witness, "I had a dream that I shot Joe." Does the witness have personal knowledge? Is the testimony relevant?

6. Prosecution for bank robbery. A prosecution witness testifies he overheard a conversation between Defendant and an alleged accomplice just before the crime was committed. The witness says that the conversation was in a foreign language he does not understand. The witness then offers to testify that he believes Defendant was talking about robbing the bank. Does the witness have personal knowledge?

7. Personal injury action arising from an automobile accident. Plaintiff calls the emergency room doctor to testify about Plaintiff's injuries. The doctor states that she does not remember, but offers to read to the jury the notes she made at the time in the hospital's records. Does the witness have personal knowledge?

8. Prosecution for election fraud in which Defendant is alleged to have cast votes in the name of elderly patients living in a nursing home. The prosecution alleges the patients could not have been capable of casting the votes themselves. The prosecutor puts one of the patients on the witness stand and asks a series of questions. In response, the patient only stares blankly at the ceiling. Does the patient have personal knowledge? If not, is the patient even a witness subject to Rule 602? If he is not a witness, does he serve some other function in the trial?

e. The "Oath or Affirmation" Requirement

**FED. R. EVID. 603.   OATH OR AFFIRMATION TO
TESTIFY TRUTHFULLY**

Before testifying, a witness must give an oath or affirmation to testify truth-fully. It must be in a form designed to impress that duty on the witness's conscience.

Discussion

Even if a witness is competent to testify, she must first take an oath or affirm that she will tell the truth. Rule 603 expressly recognizes one reason for this require-ment — "to impress that duty on the witness's conscience." There is also a second reason: A witness commits perjury only if she lies while testifying after an oath or affirmation to tell the truth. Thus, Rule 603 ensures that the predicate for a perjury prosecution is established.

Both an oath and an affirmation are promises to tell the truth. In the case of an oath, the witness invokes God in connection with her promise. The witness affirming to tell the truth makes a promise to do so but without invoking God. Notice that Rule 603 does not require that the oath or affirmation in fact awaken the witness's conscience. Rather, the provision only requires a ceremony designed to stimulate truthfulness. Thus, an insincere witness may testify so long as she "goes through the motions" of oath or affirmation. But questions concerning the witness's sincerity may be raised on cross-examination, as we see in Chapter 6.

Questions for Classroom Discussion

1. Prosecution of Defendant for perjury. Previously, Defendant had been a defense witness in the criminal trial of Jane. The prosecution alleges that Defendant lied when she testified that she and Jane were together in another state when the crime was committed. Prior to taking the stand in Jane's trial, Defendant had refused to take an "oath," claiming that she was an atheist. The court allowed her simply to state that she would testify "honestly." May Jane be tried for perjury?

2. At the trial of an auto accident case, Plaintiff calls Witness to testify about the accident. Witness refuses to take an "oath" before testi-fying, and also refuses to affirm that she will tell the truth. Defendant objects to Witness testifying. How should the court rule?

3.   *Real Evidence: Authentication and the Best Evidence Rule*

a.   Introduction: Tangible Evidence

Evidence can be something you hold in your hand. A photograph, a weapon, a bloody garment, a model of the accident site — all these differ from witness testimony in that they are tangible and their primary impact in the courtroom usually is visual or sometimes even tactile. And because psychologists say that humans process information that is received visually more easily than information received audibly, tangible evidence often has a powerful impact. This is why evidence law employs rules to ensure that these items move the jury toward the truth, not away from it.

Before we consider those rules, it is necessary to learn some terms. There are two types of tangible evidence. *Real evidence* usually refers to an item that was directly involved in the very events that are at issue in the case. In a homicide prosecution, the murder weapon, the victim's clothing, and the note luring the victim to the scene of the crime are all examples of real evidence. Once real evidence has been admitted, the jury can examine it and, usually, that evidence may be present in the jury room during deliberations. *Demonstrative evidence* refers to an item that merely illustrates testimony, such as a diagram of the details of the murder scene as described by eyewitnesses. The diagram may be prepared before trial or even during the trial as the witnesses are testifying. Such a diagram is not real evidence because it was not directly involved in the events at issue — it was not even in existence at the time the crime was committed. Demonstrative evidence can be used only if the testimony it illustrates is admissible and the demonstrative evidence accurately reflects that testimony. Some courts refuse to permit the jury to take demonstrative evidence to the jury room during deliberations on the theory that this would give undue emphasis to the testimony it illustrates.

It is sometimes said that demonstrative evidence is not really "evidence" since it usually is manufactured for trial and can have no probative force beyond that of the testimony it illustrates. Whether or not demonstrative evidence can be considered evidence, it is clear that evidence law regulates the use of both real and demonstrative evidence. As we see in the next chapter, both forms of tangible evidence can raise issues under Rule 403 because the jury may overweigh their evidentiary value. In the next section, we learn that real and demonstrative evidence must satisfy the requirement of authentication.

b.   Authentication

FED. R. EVID. 901.   AUTHENTICATING OR IDENTIFYING EVIDENCE

(a) **In General.** To satisfy the requirement of authenticating or identifying an item of evidence, the proponent must produce evidence sufficient to support a finding that the item is what the proponent claims it is.

(b) Examples. The following are examples only—not a complete list—of evidence that satisfies the requirement:

(1) *Testimony of a Witness with Knowledge.* Testimony that an item is what it is claimed to be.

(2) *Nonexpert Opinion about Handwriting.* A nonexpert's opinion that handwriting is genuine, based on a familiarity with it that was not acquired for the current litigation.

(3) *Comparison by an Expert Witness or the Trier of Fact.* A comparison with an authenticated specimen by an expert witness or the trier of fact.

(4) *Distinctive Characteristics and the Like.* The appearance, contents, substance, internal patterns, or other distinctive characteristics of the item, taken together with all the circumstances.

(5) *Opinion about a Voice.* An opinion identifying a person's voice—whether heard firsthand or through mechanical or electronic transmission or recording—based on hearing the voice at any time under circumstances that connect it with the alleged speaker.

(6) *Evidence about a Telephone Conversation.* For a telephone conversation, evidence that a call was made to the number assigned at the time to:

(A) a particular person, if circumstances, including self-identification, show that the person answering was the one called; or

(B) a particular business, if the call was made to a business and the call related to business reasonably transacted over the telephone.

(7) *Evidence about Public Records.* Evidence that:

(A) a record is from the public office where items of this kind are kept; or

(B) a document was lawfully recorded or filed in a public office.

(8) *Evidence about Ancient Documents or Data Compilations.* For a document or data compilation, evidence that it:

(A) is in a condition that creates no suspicion about its authenticity;

(B) was in a place where, if authentic, it would likely be; and

(C) is at least 20 years old when offered.

(9) *Evidence about a Process or System.* Evidence describing a process or system and showing that it produces an accurate result.

(10) *Methods Provided by a Statute or Rule.* Any method of authentication or identification allowed by a federal statute or a rule prescribed by the Supreme Court.

i. Introduction

Authentication[18] refers to the process of proving that an item of evidence is what its proponent claims it to be. The authentication requirement of Rule 901 works something like the personal knowledge requirement of Rule 602. Both are foundational requirements that must be met in order to establish that the evidence is worth considering.

---

18. There is a slight difference in the meanings of authentication and identification, but the difference is of no consequence in the application of Rule 901. The text refers only to authentication to save space and avoid unnecessary complexities.

Rule 901(a) recognizes three general principles. First, evidence must be authenticated "in order to have it admitted." Second, evidence is authenticated by showing that the "item is what the proponent claims it is." Finally, the showing must be "sufficient to support a finding."

By stating that evidence must be authenticated in order for it to be admitted, Rule 901(a) gives a trial court authority to exclude evidence when this requirement is not satisfied. Whether that requirement is satisfied is an issue decided by the court under Rule 104(b), which we discuss in Chapter 2. Even after the court determines that an item is authenticated and admissible, evidence contesting authenticity also remains admissible. This is because the jury has the power to determine what weight to give evidence in light of questions concerning its authenticity. In fact, the jury may conclude that the evidence is not what its proponent claims it to be and, accordingly, should be disregarded completely even though it was admitted.

It is important to understand what Rule 901(a) means when it says that authentication is accomplished by proving that the item "is what the proponent claims it is." This means that the party offering the evidence, by deciding what she offers it to prove, can control what will be required to authenticate it. For example, the prosecution in a murder case might offer a gun owned by the defendant into evidence under one of two theories: It is either the gun actually used in the homicide or it is a gun that looks like the weapon used in the homicide. The prosecution might offer the gun just to prove the latter fact, for example, if the only authentication evidence available is the testimony of a witness who saw the gun used in the homicide but can only testify that the defendant's gun "looks like" the gun she saw at the crime scene. A witness might give such testimony if there are many similar appearing guns of the same make and model. While the prosecution would like the witness to testify that the gun is the very weapon used in the homicide, the defendant's gun is still relevant even if the witness can only say that it "looks like" the weapon used in the crime.

This suggests that there is a significant limitation on the power of a party offering tangible evidence to decide what she "claims" that evidence to be: A party's claims about an item of evidence must be consistent with establishing that the item is relevant. Relevance is a concept we discuss in detail in Chapter 2. But for purposes of the current discussion, you can assume that evidence is relevant if it logically tells us something about the issues in the case. Thus, if there is no witness available to testify that the gun is the one used in the homicide or even just looks like the gun used, the prosecution may only be able to prove that the item is, indeed, a gun. But if the prosecution only shows that the item is a gun without also showing a connection to the crime, the evidence probably should be excluded on the ground it is irrelevant.

The third general principle established by Rule 901(a) is that the proponent of evidence has the burden of proving its authenticity and that this burden is sustained by evidence "sufficient to support a finding." This is the same standard we discussed in connection with the personal knowledge requirement. As we have seen, it is not a demanding standard. It means that the judge should admit the evidence unless the proof on authenticity is so weak that no reasonable juror could consider the evidence to be what its proponent claims it to be.

Questions for Classroom Discussion

1. Action for breach of contract. Defendant denies accepting Plaintiff's offer to make a contract. Plaintiff produces a signed letter that reads, "I accept your offer." For this letter to be relevant, what must Plaintiff claim this letter to be?

2. Same case. What does Plaintiff have to prove to authenticate the letter?

3. What are some ways to authenticate a signature under Rule 901(b)?

4. Same case. Plaintiff offers the testimony of a handwriting expert that he has compared the signature on the letter in question with other signatures shown to be that of Defendant and that, in the expert's opinion, the letter in question is signed by Defendant. Defendant offers the testimony of another handwriting expert who comes to the opposite conclusion. Assume that the judge finds both experts to be qualified and believes their opinions are equally convincing. Should the judge admit the letter?

5. Same case. If the judge admits the letter, is the jury bound to conclude that the letter is signed by Defendant?

Subdivision (b) of Rule 901 lists examples of evidence that will satisfy the authentication requirement. The provision makes clear that these are "examples only — not a complete list." This means that evidence may be authenticated in ways other than those specifically listed. Rule 901(b) is illustrative rather than inclusive because the variety of circumstances that might raise authentication problems and the number of ways in which authentication might be demonstrated are too great to enumerate.

Rule 901(b)(1) describes the most common way an item of evidence is authenticated: The party offering the item calls a witness with personal knowledge of the item to testify that the item is what the offering party claims it to be. There are unlimited variations of circumstances under which a witness may acquire the degree of perception-based knowledge sufficient to authenticate evidence under Rule 901(b)(1). However, a limited number of situations occur with regularity. In the case of a physical object such as a weapon, a witness can authenticate the object if she perceived it under any circumstances that permit the witness to establish its relevance. In the case of a document, a witness can authenticate it if she wrote it, signed it, used it, or saw others do so. A conversation may be authenticated by a participant or listener.

Of the many regularly occurring examples of authentication problems under Rule 901(b)(1), two commonly raise complex issues: (1) What facts must a witness have personal knowledge of to authenticate a photograph? (2) When is it necessary to establish knowledge based on a series of perceptions that form a chain of custody?

ii. Authentication of Photographs

Recall the formula that determines if a witness has personal knowledge sufficient to testify: $FP = FT$, where "FP" refers to the facts perceived and "FT" refers to the facts to which the witness proposes to testify. This formula is important in problems concerning the authentication of photographs because the resolution of those problems often depends on determining who has the personal knowledge needed to provide authenticating testimony. The alternatives usually are the photographer or an eyewitness to the events at issue in the case.

The personal knowledge required to authenticate a photograph varies depending on what the party offering the photograph claims it to be. For example, assume the government in a prosecution for the theft of a valuable painting from an art gallery offers into evidence a photograph taken by a police investigator shortly after the crime occurred, for the purpose of revealing the likely appearance of the gallery at the time it was robbed. The prosecution intends to use the photograph during the testimony of an eyewitness to the crime so that the witness can refer to the photograph to show where certain events associated with the crime took place. This meets the definition of *demonstrative evidence* because it does not consist of the real objects or events at issue but merely illustrates a witness's testimony about them. Thus, any witness who observed the gallery at the time of the robbery could authenticate the photograph by testifying that it is a "fair and accurate depiction" of the gallery at that time. The photographer, who only came to the scene after the robbery, could not provide this authenticating testimony because he did not view the scene at the relevant moment. The testimony of a person who observed the gallery at the time of the robbery might proceed as follows (Pros stands for Prosecutor, and W stands for Witness):

Pros: Where were you at 2:00 in the afternoon on September 1 of last year?

W: I was in the art museum.

Pros: What part of the museum were you in?

W: I was in the Old Masters gallery.

Pros: Is the Old Masters gallery a single room?

W: Yes.

Pros: I'd like to direct your attention to the photograph marked State's Exhibit 4, which is set up on the easel to your left. Are you able to tell the court what it depicts?

W: It's a photograph of the Old Masters gallery.

Pros: Does the photograph fairly and accurately depict the location of furniture and other items in the Old Masters gallery as you saw it at 2:00 in the afternoon on September 1 of last year?

W: Yes. It looks exactly the way I remember it on that day.

At this point, the witness has adequately authenticated the photograph. She may now use it to illustrate her testimony.

Suppose instead that the government offers a photograph taken on his phone by a witness to the robbery, while the robbery was in progress. In that situation, any witness who observed the robbery can authenticate the photograph by testifying that it is a fair and accurate depiction of that event. But in this instance the photographer also can authenticate the photograph by testifying to a different fact — that the exhibit is a photograph of the robbery itself. Unlike other witnesses to the robbery, the photographer is not limited to testifying that the photograph is a "fair and accurate depiction" of the robbery because he has personal knowledge of exactly what he photographed. In that case the photograph is called *real evidence* because it is offered as evidence of the actual events in question and not merely as an illustration of a witness's testimony concerning those events. The photographer's testimony would simply be as follows:

> *Pros:* Where were you at 2:00 in the afternoon on September 1 of last year?
>
> *W:* I was in the art museum.
>
> *Pros:* Where in the art museum were you located?
>
> *W:* I was in the Old Masters gallery.
>
> *Pros:* Why were you there?
>
> *W:* I went to the museum that day to take a photograph of one of the Rembrandts in that gallery.
>
> *Pros:* Did you observe anything unusual while you were in the Old Masters gallery?
>
> *W:* Yes. I saw someone remove a small painting from the wall and run off with it.
>
> *Pros:* Did you do anything when you saw this event take place?
>
> *W:* Yes. I took a photograph on my cellphone as the thief was running from the room.
>
> *Pros:* Directing your attention to State's Exhibit 5, which is on the easel to your left, do you recognize it?
>
> *W:* Yes. It is an enlargement of the photograph I just testified about.
>
> *Pros:* To your knowledge, has the photograph been altered in any way, other than by enlarging it?
>
> *W:* No.

The photographer's testimony is sufficient to authenticate the photograph as a depiction of the robbery itself.

Finally, if the stolen art was itself a unique, one-of-a-kind photograph, any witness who observed what was stolen has sufficient knowledge to authenticate that photograph by testifying that it is the very item taken during the robbery. This is another example of real evidence. Of course, photographs also can be authenticated under Rule 901(b) by means other than the testimony of a witness with knowledge.

Questions for Classroom Discussion

1. Suit for injuries suffered in an auto accident. Plaintiff shows an eyewitness a photo of the intersection taken by a photographer one year before the accident. Plaintiff asks the witness, "Does this

photo fairly and accurately depict what the intersection looked like at the time of the accident?" The witness answers in the affirmative. Defendant objects, claiming only the photographer can authenticate the photo. How should the court rule?

2. Same case. This time Plaintiff asks, "Is this a photo of the intersection?" Defendant objects on the ground the witness cannot authenticate the photo. How should the court rule?

iii. Authentication by Chain of Custody

When an item of evidence has a unique appearance or character, often a single witness can authenticate that item based on seeing it just once before testifying. Establishing the subsequent history of the item is not essential because the item's unique appearance permits the witness to testify that it is the very item previously perceived and that it does not appear altered in any material way.

But sometimes more than a single perception by one witness is required to authenticate an item of evidence. This is the case if no single witness can uniquely identify the item because it is indistinguishable from other items with a similar appearance. A vial of blood, a plastic bag containing drugs, or a modern handgun all have a generic appearance characteristic of many similar items. This means that a witness who once observed an item of this sort in connection with the events at issue might be able to testify only that an exhibit presented at trial "looks like" the item previously perceived. However, that witness may be unable to state that it is the very item in question. Thus, when the relevance of such an exhibit depends on showing it is a specific item rather than a generic example, something called a "chain of custody" is necessary to establish that it is the same item previously perceived. A chain of custody also may be required when the item is unique but is still susceptible to alteration in ways that might be difficult to detect, as in the case of a digital recording or sounds or images.

In proving a chain of custody, the proponent of an item of evidence shows that it was continuously in the safekeeping of one or more specific persons beginning with the event that connects that evidence to the case and continuing until the moment the evidence was brought to court and marked for identification. All witnesses in the chain testify to the circumstances under which they took custody of the item, the efforts they made to safeguard it, what if any changes appear in the item since they last had custody, and the circumstances under which they surrendered custody. Laying the foundation for a chain of custody may require calling as witnesses several people who had possession of the item to testify that, while it was in their custody, the item was not altered in any significant respect or switched with some similar-appearing item. This foundation then permits the inference that the evidence offered is the very item associated with the events at issue in the case. Perceptions and personal knowledge are central to this foundation. In fact, the process might be described more accurately as establishing a chain of perceptions.

Questions for Classroom Discussion

1. Prosecution for cocaine possession. The prosecutor seeks the admission of a bag of white powder, claiming it is the same bag Officer Smith found on Defendant. In the following transcript, does the court make the proper rulings? As the transcript begins, Officer Smith is on the stand and has already testified that he found a bag of white powder in Defendant's pocket. Are the rulings of the court correct?

> *Pros:* Officer, I show you now what has been marked State's Exhibit A. Do you recognize it?
>
> *Smith:* It looks just like the baggie of white powder I found in Defendant's pocket.
>
> *Pros:* Can you tell if it is the same baggie?
>
> *Smith:* Well, I can't be sure because I have seen many baggies filled with white powder and they all look pretty much alike.
>
> *Pros:* Does Exhibit A differ in appearance in any respect from the baggie you found in Defendant's pocket?
>
> *Smith:* No.
>
> *Pros:* Your Honor, we offer Exhibit A.
>
> *Def:* Objection, insufficient foundation.
>
> *By the Court:* Sustained.
>
> *Pros:* Officer, after you found the baggie of white powder in Defendant's pocket, what did you do with it?
>
> *Smith:* When I returned to headquarters I turned the baggie over to the custodian of the evidence room, Sergeant Jones.
>
> *Pros:* No further questions.
>
> *Def:* No questions, Your Honor.

2. [The prosecution then calls its next witness, Officer Jones. The transcript picks up after Jones has testified that he is the custodian of the evidence room at police headquarters and that Officer Smith turned over to him a bag containing white powder on the date in question.]

> *Pros:* What did you do with the baggie after Smith gave it to you.
>
> *Jones:* I placed it in an evidence bag and wrote on the bag the case number Smith gave me. The evidence bag is a large, thick plastic bag we use to store items of this nature. It can be sealed in a way that shows if it has been tampered with.
>
> *Pros:* What did you do with the evidence bag?
>
> *Jones:* I sealed it and then placed the bag in an evidence locker and then locked it with a key.
>
> *Pros:* Who has access to that locker?

Jones:	Me. I have the only key.
Pros:	When was the next time you saw that evidence bag?
Jones:	This morning. I unlocked the locker and brought the bag to court. I opened the evidence bag and handed the baggie of white powder to you. I then saw you take it to the clerk and saw that it was marked Exhibit A.
Pros:	Before you opened the evidence bag this morning, did you notice any signs that it had been previously opened or tampered with in any way?
Jones:	No.
Pros:	The State offers Exhibit A into evidence.
Def:	Your honor, may I take the witness on voir dire?
By the Court:	Proceed.
Def:	Officer Jones, isn't it true that right after Smith handed you the baggie, you got a phone call?
Jones:	Yes.
Def:	And when the phone rang you set the baggie down on the table behind you?
Jones:	Correct.
Def:	So during the entire phone conversation the baggie was not in your sight, right?
Jones:	That is true.
Def:	Nothing further. Objection, insufficient foundation.
Pros:	May I ask three questions, Your Honor?
By the Court:	Of course.
Pros:	Officer Jones, how long did the phone call last?
Jones:	One minute, at most.
Pros:	And was anyone else in the evidence room at that time?
Jones:	No, I was alone.
Pros:	And when you finished your phone conversation and returned your attention to the baggie, did you notice anything that suggested someone might have tampered with it?
Jones:	No. It was in exactly the same place and same condition as it was when I placed it on the table behind me.
Pros:	Thank you. The State offers Exhibit A.
By the Court:	The objection is overruled. Exhibit A will be received in evidence.

3. Same case. Officer Smith (the arresting officer) admits he absent-mindedly left the baggie of white powder in the men's room of the bus station overnight. When he returned the next morning, he

(continued)

found a baggie on the counter in approximately the position in which he left a baggie the previous night. Is the baggie admissible?

4. Murder prosecution. The victim was found with a jewel-encrusted, gold dagger stuck in his heart. The prosecutor shows a dagger to the investigating officer, who testifies, "That's the dagger I found stuck in the victim." Has the dagger been authenticated, or will it be necessary for the prosecution to establish a chain of custody?

5. Murder prosecution. The victim was shot and found with a smoking gun next to his body. The gun is identical to thousands of similar guns in circulation. The investigating officer testifies that, when he found the gun at the scene of the crime, he etched his initials in the barrel. He then examines a gun handed to him by the prosecutor and says, "That's the gun I found next to the victim—it has my initials on the barrel." Has the gun been authenticated, or do we need a chain of custody?

iv. *Examples of Authentication Under Rule 901(b) — Problems Posed by New Technologies*

Recall that Rule 901(b) lists examples of evidence that will satisfy the authentication requirement, but that these are "examples only—not a complete list." Flexibility in how evidence may be authenticated is a particularly important feature of the provision because modern technology now permits communications and other types of evidence to be generated in forms the drafters of the evidence rules could not have anticipated at the time the list in subdivision (b) was compiled over 40 years ago. Consider the problems posed by the following two cases.

UNITED STATES v. SIMPSON
152 F.3d 1241 (10th Cir. 1998)

[Defendant appealed his conviction for receiving child pornography on the ground that a computer printout of the alleged Internet chat room exchange between defendant and an FBI agent should not have been admitted because it was not authenticated by a showing it was in defendant's handwriting or voice.]

Stephen H. ANDERSON, Circuit Judge.
    At trial, the government's evidence was almost entirely circumstantial. Agent Rehman testified that he had a "conversation" under the assumed name of "FlaHawk" in a chat room called "Kidsexpics" with an individual identified as "Stavron" who said that his name was "B. Simpson" and who gave a street address and e-mail address. Other witnesses testified that both the street and e-mail addresses belonged to the Defendant, Bill Simpson. Agent Rehman and the individual discussed several items of child pornography in lurid detail

and the individual identifying himself as B. Simpson indicated that he possessed many images of child pornography. The two also made a deal that the individual would send Rehman a check for $30 and a floppy disk containing numerous pornographic images of children under age 13 and in return, Rehman would send a video tape containing sexual interactions between a twelve-year-old girl and a sixteen year-old boy. A printout of this conversation was admitted as evidence and published to the jury. Agent Rehman testified that through a series of e-mails from the given e-mail address, the individual backed out of the deal because he was afraid of using the U.S. mail, so nothing was ever sent. Agent Rehman also was qualified as an expert witness on computer terms and usages and testified about the process of transferring files over the Internet.

Detective Johnson testified that he had verified that a Bill Simpson lived at the street address given to Agent Rehman and prepared an affidavit for a search warrant of that address. Detective Johnson and other officers executed the warrant and seized many things, including a computer, disks, and several papers located near the computer. The papers contained the name "FlaHawk" and the name, street address, and e-mail address that Agent Rehman had given the individual in the chat room. . . .

The prosecution recalled Agent Rehman, who was then accepted by the court as an expert on the use of computers and investigating child exploitation and pornography. He testified how many of the individuals who use computers to view child pornography name the files and organize them on their computers. He also went through the list of directories on the seized computer's hard drive and explained what the directory names could mean. Agent Rehman then explained that in his experience the fact that the dates differed on the file transfer protocol ("ftp") log and on the files found on the seized computer is not uncommon because people downloading through the Internet typically receive copies of files they already have, so they then delete the duplicates. He also testified that his experience has shown that a child pornography file with a complex name generally contains the same image no matter where he has found them on the Internet, and he expressed his opinion that the files downloaded through the Internet at a site in Boston were the same as the ones located on the seized computer.

Next, Jeff Bewley, the Server Administrator for an Internet service provider testified that the ftp log found on the seized computer indicated a transfer of files named "doit007.jpg" and "kk-a0021.jpg" from an Internet site located in Boston. He also indicated that files would not be transferred via the Internet accidentally—in other words, the user would know that he or she was getting a file, although they might not know what the file contained. . . .

Simpson next argues that the trial court erred in admitting Plaintiff's Exhibit 11, which is a computer printout of the alleged chat room discussion between Simpson and Detective Rehman, because the government could not identify that the statements attributed to Simpson were in his handwriting, his writing style, or his voice pursuant to Fed. R. Evid. 901(b)(2)-(5). Therefore, argues Simpson, the evidence was not authenticated and should not have been admitted. The specific examples of authentication referred to by Simpson are merely illustrative, however, and are not intended as an exclusive enumeration of allowable methods of authentication. See Fed. R. Evid. 901(b). Rather, all that is ultimately required is "evidence sufficient to support a finding that the matter in question is what its proponent claims." Fed. R. Evid. 901(a).

The evidence introduced at trial clearly satisfies this standard. In the printout of the chat room discussion, the individual using the identity "Stavron" gave Detective Rehman his name as B. Simpson and his correct street address. The discussion and subsequent e-mail exchanges indicated an e-mail address which belonged to Simpson. And the pages found near the computer in Simpson's home and introduced as evidence as Plaintiff's Exhibit 6 contain a notation of the name, street address, e-mail address, and telephone number that Detective Rehman gave to the individual in the chat room. Based on this evidence, the exhibit was properly authenticated and admitted as evidence.

Question for Classroom Discussion

In *Simpson*, could the printout of the alleged chat room discussion have been authenticated under one of the specific subdivisions of Rule 901(b)? Which one?

UNITED STATES v. JACKSON
208 F.3d 633 (7th Cir. 2000)

Terence T. EVANS, Circuit Judge.

This case is about a tragic waste of talent. Angela Jackson probably would be sitting in a comfortable law firm today—instead of doing time in a federal penitentiary—if she had devoted as much energy to her legal studies as she did trying to rip off the United Parcel Service in a bizarre and elaborate scheme that included sending hate mail to a number of prominent African-Americans. Her activities led to a bevy of federal charges, and a jury found her guilty on every count in the indictment. Today, her appeal is up for consideration.

In 1996–1997 Jackson (a young African-American woman) was enrolled at the William Mitchell College of Law in St. Paul, Minnesota. She previously lived in Chicago for several years while working and attending the Chicago-Kent law school. In the fall of 1996 Jackson and a friend incorporated a business that planned to sell prints and paintings depicting African-American culture. She purchased several prints from Chicago artist Bayo Iribhogbe for a total of $2,000. She then sent Iribhogbe four United Parcel Service mailers preaddressed to her St. Paul address and on which she had written in bold letters "Kwanzaa," an African-American holiday. Iribhogbe packed his artwork in the mailers and sent them off.

UPS delivered the packages to Jackson's St. Paul apartment building on December 4, 1996. The UPS driver, the apartment building's receptionist, and the apartment building's concierge who handed the packages directly to Jackson all testified that there were four packages and that none were damaged or defaced. Jackson, however, reported to UPS that she had received only three packages and that all were damaged and contained racial epithets. Though she had paid only $2,000 for the artwork, though her company had received no orders for the art, and though Iribhogbe never previously sold a single print for more than $15, Jackson filed a $572,000 claim with UPS. When UPS balked,

Jackson faxed letters to various African-American officials, claiming that "racist elements" within UPS were responsible for defacing her packages and for refusing to compensate her.

That evidence alone might well have been enough to convict Jackson of the fraud charges that were ultimately filed against her, but there was much more. Much more. On December 3, 1996, a search of federal cases and statutes for the words "united," "parcel," "service," "damaged," and "packages" in the same paragraph was done on the LEXIS-NEXIS research service on Jackson's computer under the LEXIS password of Jacqueline Whittmon. Whittmon testified that when she worked in the Chicago-Kent law library she gave Jackson her password, that she never used her LEXIS password after leaving her position at Chicago-Kent in the spring of 1996, that Jackson called her from Minnesota in the fall of that year to ask if her LEXIS password still was activated, and that she never gave her password to anyone else. Also gleaned from Jackson's computer was evidence that it was used in November of 1996 to search the Internet for "white supremacy" organizations and to visit the web sites for the "Euro-American Student Union" and the "Storm Front," two such groups.

On November 25, 1996, seven letter packs were placed in a UPS mailing box in Chicago that were addressed to three African-American members of Congress, two African-American newspapers in Washington, D.C., the NAACP, and the Rainbow Coalition. The Euro-American Student Union's address was listed as the return address. The packages never were delivered because the UPS driver noticed racial slurs on the outside of the items and turned them over to his supervisor. UPS opened the packages and inside found racially offensive materials under the UPS logo. On that day, Jackson made a withdrawal from an ATM machine located next to the UPS drop box. A piece of paper with the UPS billing identification number for these packages later was found in Jackson's apartment and Jackson initially gave that number when she called UPS in December to complain about her allegedly defaced packages. . . .

In June 1998 the government filed a motion alleging that Jackson had created false email correspondence on May 20, 1998, that attempted to frame David Stennett, the head of the Euro-American Student Union, for the hate mail. Evidence at the trial showed that Jackson subsequently tried to create an alibi by altering and falsifying records to make it appear that she was being treated at Meharry Medical Clinic in Tennessee on May 20, 1998, when she actually was treated there on other dates. . . .

Jackson appeals her conviction on the eight fraud counts involving UPS on the grounds that Judge Norgle excluded admissible evidence. . . .

Jackson's defense is that she didn't do it—in other words, the original four packages sent to her actually were damaged and defaced by UPS and the hate mail really was sent by white supremacists. She says her defense was stymied, however, by Judge Norgle's refusal to allow Stennett to testify and the judge's refusal to admit postings from the web sites of the white supremacy groups. We review the exclusion of evidence for abuse of discretion.

[The court discussed the trial court's conclusion that defendant's evidence concerning the alleged content of white supremacist web sites was inadmissible on various grounds.]

Even if we are wrong about the web postings being unfairly prejudicial, irrelevant, and hearsay, Judge Norgle still was justified in excluding the evidence because it lacked authentication. *See* Fed. R. Evid. 901. Jackson needed to show that the web postings in which the white supremacist groups took responsibility for the racist mailings actually were posted by the groups, as opposed to being slipped onto the groups' web sites by Jackson herself, who was a skilled computer user. . . . Jackson was unable to show that these postings were authentic.

Questions for Classroom Discussion

1. In *Jackson*, assume that the defense offered a printout of a white supremacist web site that contained a statement taking responsibility for the racist mailings the prosecutor alleged had been sent by Defendant. A defense witness testifies she typed the correct Internet address of the white supremacist web site and made the printout, which was an accurate copy of the content of the web site. Would the court be correct in concluding that this was insufficient to authenticate the web site or the printout because Defendant was a skilled computer user who could have "slipped" the statement into the web site?

2. To prove that the Lexis-Nexis search described in *Jackson* was conducted from Defendant's computer, assume that the prosecution offered into evidence a printout from the computer records of Lexis-Nexis that contained the words searched, the time of the search, the password employed to conduct the search, and a series of numbers that identifies the computer from which the search was conducted. Assume that searches through Lexis-Nexis are completely automated and that no human at that company participates in the processing of a search. How could the prosecutor authenticate this document? What sections of Rule 901(b) are pertinent?

---

v. Self-Authentication

FED. R. EVID. 902.   EVIDENCE THAT IS SELF-AUTHENTICATING

The following items of evidence are self-authenticating; they require no extrinsic evidence of authenticity in order to be admitted:

(1) *Domestic Public Documents That Are Sealed and Signed.* A document that bears:

(A) a seal purporting to be that of the United States; any state, district, commonwealth, territory, or insular possession of the United States; the former Panama Canal Zone; the Trust Territory of the Pacific Islands; a political subdivision of any of these entities; or a department, agency, or officer of any entity named above; and

(B) a signature purporting to be an execution or attestation.

(2) *Domestic Public Documents That Are Not Sealed but Are Signed and Certified.* A document that bears no seal if:

(A) it bears the signature of an officer or employee of an entity named in Rule 902(1)(A); and

(B) another public officer who has a seal and official duties within that same entity certifies under seal — or its equivalent — that the signer has the official capacity and that the signature is genuine.

(3) *Foreign Public Documents.* A document that purports to be signed or attested by a person who is authorized by a foreign country's law to do so. The document must be accompanied by a final certification that certifies the genuineness of the signature and official position of the signer or attester — or of any foreign official whose certificate of genuineness relates to the signature or attestation or is in a chain of certificates of genuineness relating to the signature or attestation. The certification may be made by a secretary of a United States embassy or legation; by a consul general, vice consul, or consular agent of the United States; or by a diplomatic or consular official of the foreign country assigned or accredited to the United States. If all parties have been given a reasonable opportunity to investigate the document's authenticity and accuracy, the court may, for good cause, either:

(A) order that it be treated as presumptively authentic without final certification; or

(B) allow it to be evidenced by an attested summary with or without final certification.

(4) *Certified Copies of Public Records.* A copy of an official record — or a copy of a document that was recorded or filed in a public office as authorized by law — if the copy is certified as correct by:

(A) the custodian or another person authorized to make the certification; or

(B) a certificate that complies with Rule 902(1), (2), or (3), a federal statute, or a rule prescribed by the Supreme Court.

(5) *Official Publications.* A book, pamphlet, or other publication purporting to be issued by a public authority.

(6) *Newspapers and Periodicals.* Printed material purporting to be a newspaper or periodical.

(7) *Trade Inscriptions and the Like.* An inscription, sign, tag, or label purporting to have been affixed in the course of business and indicating origin, ownership, or control.

(8) *Acknowledged Documents.* A document accompanied by a certificate of acknowledgment that is lawfully executed by a notary public or another officer who is authorized to take acknowledgments.

(9) *Commercial Paper and Related Documents.* Commercial paper, a signature on it, and related documents, to the extent allowed by general commercial law.

(10) *Presumptions Under a Federal Statute.* A signature, document, or anything else that a federal statute declares to be presumptively or prima facie genuine or authentic.

(11) *Certified Domestic Records of a Regularly Conducted Activity.* The original or a copy of a domestic record that meets the requirements of Rule 803(6)(A)-(C), as shown by a certification of the custodian or another qualified person that complies with a federal statute or a rule prescribed by the Supreme Court. Before the trial or hearing, the proponent must give an adverse party reasonable written notice of the intent to offer the record — and must make the record and certification available for inspection — so that the party has a fair opportunity to challenge them.

(12) *Certified Foreign Records of a Regularly Conducted Activity.* In a civil case, the original or a copy of a foreign record that meets the requirements of Rule 902(11), modified as follows: the certification, rather than complying with a federal statute or Supreme Court rule, must be signed in a manner that, if falsely made, would subject the maker to a criminal penalty in the country where the certification is signed. The proponent must also meet the notice requirements of Rule 902(11).

Discussion

Rule 902 identifies 12 categories of items with respect to which "they require no extrinsic evidence of authenticity in order to be admitted." The term *extrinsic evidence* in this context means any evidence other than the item of evidence in question. For example, assume that the plaintiff in a defamation action against The New York Times offers into evidence the front page of a newspaper on which the allegedly defamatory statements are printed. Plaintiff alleges that the evidence is an edition of The New York Times. Testimony from the editor of the newspaper that the item is, indeed, a copy of The New York Times is extrinsic evidence of that fact. Rule 902(6) makes clear that such evidence is not necessary. The exhibit, which reads "New York Times" across the top of the page, authenticates itself.

Thus, the authentication requirement of Rule 901(a) can be satisfied by self-authentication under Rule 902. Of course, only a limited number of items are self-authenticating under that rule. If an item is not self-authenticating under Rule 902, it may still be authenticated by extrinsic evidence under Rule 901(b). But if an item is neither self-authenticating under Rule 902 nor authenticated under Rule 901(b), it is inadmissible.

Even if the authentication requirement is satisfied, however, the item is not necessarily admissible. Admissibility issues other than authenticity may still be raised under the evidence rules or the Constitution. For example, a document that is self-authenticating under Rule 902 may still be inadmissible hearsay or excludable under the "best evidence rule," which we consider after the following questions.

Further Reading: 31 Charles Alan Wright & Victor J. Gold, Federal Practice and Procedure §§ 7101-7143 (2000); Kenneth S. Broun, *Authentication and Contents of Writings*, 1969 Law & Soc. Ord. 611; Charles E. Carr, *Voices, Texts, and Technology: Evidence Law Confronts Tapes and Their Transcriptions*, 35 St. Louis U. L.J. 289 (1991); Paul C. Gianelli, *Chain of Custody and the Handling of Real Evidence*, 20 Am. Crim. L. Rev. 527 (1983); Christine A. Guilshan, *A Picture Is Worth a Thousand Lies: Electronic Imaging and the Future of the Admissibility of Photographs into Evidence*, 18 Rutgers Computer & Tech. L.J. 365 (1992); Mark A. Johnson, Comment, *Computer Printouts as Evidence: Stricter Foundation or Presumption of Reliability*, 75 Marq. L. Rev. 439 (1992); Rudolph J. Peritz, *Computer Data and Reliability: A Call for Authentication Under the Federal Rules of Evidence*, 80 Nw. U. L. Rev. 956 (1986); John W. Strong, *Liberalizing the Authentication of Private Writings*, 52 Cornell L.Q. 284 (1967).

Questions for Classroom Discussion

1. Will contest. Defendant offers into evidence a document entitled "Last Will and Testament" that purports to bear the signature of the testator. The signature is not notarized. Plaintiff objects on the ground that the document has not been authenticated. Defendant argues the document is self-authenticating since it appears to be what Defendant claims it to be — testator's will. How should the court rule?

2. Plaintiff alleges that he was injured when he drank a bottle of Whoopsie Cola in which there was a piece of broken glass. Defendant Whoopsie denies it was one of its bottles. Plaintiff offers into evidence the bottle in question, which is imprinted with the words "Whoopsie Cola." To authenticate the bottle, does Plaintiff need the testimony of someone who knows that this specific bottle was produced by Defendant?

3. Prosecution of Alice for murder. The prosecution offers into evidence a newspaper that carried an article about the crime the day after it was committed. The article quotes the investigating police officer as stating, "Alice committed the murder." Does the prosecutor need to call the newspaper reporter to authenticate the newspaper? Is there any other problem with admitting the evidence?

---

c. The Best Evidence Rule

i. The Basic Rule

> **FED. R. EVID. 1001.   DEFINITIONS THAT APPLY TO THIS ARTICLE**

In this article:

(a) A "writing" consists of letters, words, numbers, or their equivalent set down in any form.

(b) A "recording" consists of letters, words, numbers, or their equivalent recorded in any manner.

(c) A "photograph" means a photographic image or its equivalent stored in any form.

(d) An "original" of a writing or recording means the writing or recording itself or any counterpart intended to have the same effect by the person who executed or issued it. For electronically stored information, "original" means any printout — or other output readable by sight — if it accurately reflects the information. An "original" of a photograph includes the negative or a print from it.

(e) A "duplicate" means a counterpart produced by a mechanical, photographic, chemical, electronic, or other equivalent process or technique that accurately reproduces the original.

FED. R. EVID. 1002.   REQUIREMENT OF ORIGINAL

An original writing, recording, or photograph is required in order to prove its content unless these rules or a federal statute provides otherwise.

Discussion

The best evidence doctrine, the heart of which is Rule 1002, provides a safeguard against unreliable evidence concerning the contents of a writing, recording, or photograph. The doctrine does this by stating in Rule 1002 a preference for the so-called best evidence of those contents: the original. This concern for reliability is justified because the precise content of items such as writings is frequently the central issue in a case. Because rights under written instruments frequently turn on a single word or phrase, even minor mistakes concerning their contents can be dangerous.

But we will see that other provisions, especially Rules 1003 and 1004, provide ample room for admitting secondary evidence of the contents of an original, such as duplicates or witness testimony. This recognizes that the reliability of secondary evidence frequently is high while the exclusion of that evidence, because it is not the "best" evidence, can sometimes present the greater danger to accurate fact-finding.

The scope of the best evidence doctrine as defined in Rule 1002 is limited in two important ways. First, the doctrine does not apply to evidence about tangible items other than writings, recordings, and photographs. This is true notwithstanding the fact that witness testimony concerning the characteristics of other forms of tangible evidence is often inaccurate. For example, an automobile employed in the commission of a crime or tort has many characteristics that might be crucial in identifying it, such as its color or manufacturer. A witness might misperceive these details or the details might entirely escape the witness's notice, especially if the witness had limited time in which to perceive. Yet evidence concerning the characteristics of an automobile is generally not considered to be within the coverage of the best evidence doctrine because an automobile is not a writing, recording, or photograph. While limiting the scope of the best evidence rule to evidence about writings, recordings, and photographs excludes from the coverage of that rule many items of physical evidence, note that the definitions of writings, recordings, and photographs in Rule 1001 are broad. For example, a "writing" consists of "letters, words, numbers, or their equivalent *set down in any form.*" This definition is broad enough to cover any collection of data in a tangible format, such as computer disks, thumb drives, CDs, or any other medium that currently exists (or might be invented) to store digital data.

The best evidence doctrine also is limited in that it does not apply to all evidence concerning writings, recordings, and photographs. Rule 1002 establishes that the doctrine applies only to evidence offered *to prove the contents* of such items. For example, evidence that a document simply was written or that a photograph was taken raises no issue under Rule 1002. On the other hand, Rule

1002 typically will apply in cases in which the contents of a legal instrument are in dispute. For example, in an action for breach of contract alleging the seller delivered goods late, testimony that the written contract called for delivery on a specific date is evidence offered to prove the content of a writing. Similarly, Rule 1002 applies whenever a fact at issue in the case is revealed by the contents of a writing or photograph. Thus, in a prosecution for bank robbery, testimony that defendant signed a statement in which he confessed to robbing the bank raises an issue under Rule 1002.

Many students are misled by the title, "best evidence doctrine," and think it applies whenever the evidence being offered to prove a particular fact is not the "best" evidence available to prove that fact. As we have just seen, the scope of the rule is much narrower.

Questions for Classroom Discussion

1. Prosecution for theft of a briefcase and its contents owned by Victoria. The arresting officer testifies that when Defendant, Sam, was arrested he had a briefcase in his car. The defense objects under Rule 1002 on the ground the briefcase itself should have been offered. How should the court rule?

2. Same case except the officer testifies that when Defendant was arrested he had a briefcase in his car and that in the briefcase was a business card with Victoria's name on it. The defense objects under Rule 1002. How should the court rule?

3. Same case except the officer testifies that a surveillance video taken in the store where the robbery occurred shows Defendant pointing a gun at Victoria. The defense objects under Rule 1002. How should the court rule?

4. Action for personal injuries. A doctor testifies that an x-ray revealed Plaintiff suffered a broken arm. The defense objects under Rule 1002. How should the court rule?

5. Same case. The doctor testifies that, in her opinion, Plaintiff is unable to work. She bases this opinion on her review of Plaintiff's x-ray. The defense objects under Rule 1002. How should the court rule?

6. Action for infringement of computer trade secrets. Plaintiff offers into evidence a printout of its software source code that was created from the disk on which the software resides. The printout is offered so it can be compared line for line with a printout of Defendant's software. Defendant objects under Rule 1002 to the admissibility of the printout of Plaintiff's software. How should the court rule?

7. Prosecution for murder. Defendant's conviction was reversed on appeal and he is being retried. The prosecution's eyewitness, Joe,

(continued)

testified against Defendant at the first trial but is unavailable at the retrial. The prosecutor calls Sally, who heard Joe testify at the first trial, and asks, "What did Joe say when asked who shot the victim?" Sally responds, "Joe said Defendant was the shooter." Is the testimony objectionable under Rule 1002 because Joe's answer is in a written transcript?

8. Same case. Assume Sally was not present at the first trial. She testifies, "The transcript says that Joe identified Defendant as the murderer." Is the testimony objectionable under Rule 1002?

9. Same case. Assume again that Sally was not present at the first trial. She testifies, "Defendant is the murderer." Defense counsel knows that Sally did not see the crime committed and is basing her testimony on reading the transcript of the first trial. What is the proper objection to Sally's testimony?

ii. Exceptions to the Best Evidence Rule

FED. R. EVID. 1003.   ADMISSIBILITY OF DUPLICATES

A duplicate is admissible to the same extent as the original unless a genuine question is raised about the original's authenticity or the circumstances make it unfair to admit the duplicate.

FED. R. EVID. 1004.   ADMISSIBILITY OF OTHER EVIDENCE OF CONTENT

An original is not required and other evidence of the content of a writing, recording, or photograph is admissible if:

(a) all the originals are lost or destroyed, and not by the proponent acting in bad faith;

(b) an original cannot be obtained by any available judicial process;

(c) the party against whom the original would be offered had control of the original; was at that time put on notice, by pleadings or otherwise, that the original would be a subject of proof at the trial or hearing; and fails to produce it at the trial or hearing; or

(d) the writing, recording, or photograph is not closely related to a controlling issue.

FED. R. EVID. 1006.   SUMMARIES

The proponent may use a summary, chart, or calculation to prove the content of voluminous writings, recordings, or photographs that cannot be conveniently examined in court. The proponent must make the originals or duplicates available for examination or copying, or both, by other parties at a reasonable time or place. And the court may order the proponent to produce them in court.

Discussion

Rules 1003, 1004, and 1006 recognize that an original is not always the only way to prove the contents of a writing, recording, or photograph. Secondary evidence of contents, such as copies of the original or testimony, often also will be admissible. This is because secondary evidence usually does not present a significant danger of inaccuracy. Modern forms of copying are far more accurate than methods employed in earlier times that were more susceptible to human error. In addition, modern discovery rules usually empower parties to compel the production of originals, thereby reducing the danger that the introduction at trial of inaccurate secondary evidence will go unchallenged.

Accordingly, while Rule 1002 requires proof of the contents of a writing, recording, or photograph to be in the form of an original, Rule 1001(3) defines "original" broadly. And Rule 1002 requires the original, "unless these rules or a federal statute provides otherwise." The most important exception is contained in Rule 1003, which usually permits the admission of "duplicates." The term *duplicates* is also broadly defined by Rule 1001(4).

Rule 1004 permits the admission of other secondary evidence, such as witness testimony, where the dangers of mistake, fraud, and omission are mitigated by various factors. Other evidence rules and various specific statutes outside the Federal Rules of Evidence also establish exceptions to Rule 1002. Ultimately, the provisions of Article X permit the courts great flexibility to admit secondary evidence of the contents of a writing, recording, or photograph, reflecting the judgment that excluding such evidence often will retard, not promote, accurate fact-finding.

Further Reading: 31 Charles Alan Wright & Victor J. Gold, Federal Practice and Procedure §§ 7161-8064 (2000); Edward W. Cleary & John W. Strong, *The Best Evidence Rule: An Evaluation in Context*, 51 Iowa L. Rev. 825 (1966); Dale A. Nance, *The Best Evidence Principle*, 73 Iowa L. Rev. 227 (1988).

Questions for Classroom Discussion

1. Action for breach of contract. Plaintiff offers a photocopy of the contract. Is this an original? If not, is it still admissible?

2. Same case. Plaintiff offers a handwritten copy of the contract. Is it admissible?

3. Same case. Defendant claims his alleged signature on the contract is a forgery. Is the photocopy admissible?

4. Prosecution for treason. A prosecution witness testifies to the contents of a note in which Defendant outlined details of his plan to sell military secrets to a foreign government. Defendant ate the note when the FBI kicked in his door. Is this testimony concerning the contents of the note admissible?

(continued)

> **5.** Same case. Defendant offers to testify that the note simply listed the groceries he intended to pick up at the market. Is this testimony admissible?

Illustrating the best evidence rule.   Application of the best evidence rule is relatively straightforward. Assume Plaintiff sues Defendant for negligence following an automobile accident. At trial, to prove the nature and extent of the damage to her car, Plaintiff calls Mechanic to the stand. After establishing that Mechanic worked on Plaintiff's car, the following takes place. "Pl" indicates Plaintiff's counsel; "Def" indicates Defendant's counsel.

Pl: Please describe the nature of the damage to Plaintiff's car.

Mechanic: The car suffered serious damage to the rear. The bumper was destroyed, as were the taillights. The trunk was smashed and the back window was broken.

Pl: Were you able to repair these parts?

Mechanic: No. I had to replace all the parts I just mentioned.

Pl: What was the total labor and materials cost for that work?

Mechanic: I don't remember off the top of my head, but I have a photocopy of the invoice at my shop, and I looked at it before I came down here. I jotted down the total. It was . . .

Def: Objection, Your Honor. The witness is not testifying from personal knowledge, but from the contents of a writing. This violates Rule 1002.

By the Court: Objection sustained. Counsel, you'll have to bring in the invoice.

Pl: I understand, Your Honor. My client does not have the actual invoice, but he does have a photocopy, and I would like to show that document to the witness. It has been marked for identification as Plaintiff's "A."

By the Court: Go ahead, counsel.

Pl: Let the record show that I have provided Defendant's counsel with a copy of this document. Mechanic, do you recognize this document?

Mechanic: Yes. It's a copy of the invoice I sent to your client for the work done on the car.

Pl: Do you always provide customers with such a document?

Mechanic: Yes.

Pl: Do you use the same form for all work?

Mechanic: Yes. This is our standard form.

Pl: Who prepares the invoice?

Mechanic: My secretary prepares it from information supplied by the mechanic who does the actual work. I then review the invoice and we send it to the customer.

Pl: Your Honor, we move the admission of Plaintiff's Exhibit "A."

By the Court: The document will be marked as admitted into evidence.

Pl: Please look at the document and tell the court what the total cost of the work was, including labor and materials.

> *Def:*   Objection. This is not the original writing.
>
> *Pl:*   Your Honor, this is a photocopy. A photocopy qualifies as a duplicate under Rule 1001(4). And under Rule 1003, it is admissible to the same extent as the original unless a genuine question has been raised about the authenticity of the original. No such question has been raised.
>
> *By the Court:*   Objection overruled. The witness may read the total from the document.
>
> *Mechanic:*   The total for the work, including labor and materials, was $4,512.34.
>
> *Pl:*   No further questions.

In this example, Plaintiff's counsel successfully satisfied the requirements of the best evidence rule after it became clear that the witness did not have personal knowledge of the information sought. The source of proof was a photocopy of the invoice. Since the invoice is a "writing" and Plaintiff was seeking to prove its contents, the best evidence rule applied. A photocopy of the invoice is a "duplicate" and is admissible to the same extent as the original. Thus, the court's ruling was correct. Note, as well, that it was necessary to show that the invoice qualified as a business record. This is because the invoice constituted hearsay. In Chapter 3, we discuss the hearsay rule and its exceptions, including the exception for "regularly conducted activity," which includes businesses.

Suppose that in this example, a fire had destroyed Mechanic's shop and all of his records, including the photocopy of the invoice. Assume as well that Defendant's counsel had asked Plaintiff to produce the invoice during discovery, that Plaintiff had done so, and that Defendant failed to bring the invoice to court after Plaintiff notified Defendant that she intended to use it to prove the damage to the car. In that case, Rule 1004(3) would allow Plaintiff to offer secondary evidence to prove the contents of the writing (the invoice). That evidence could consist of a number of things, including Plaintiff's testimony from memory about what the invoice said.

4. Judicial Notice

FED. R. EVID. 201.   JUDICIAL NOTICE OF ADJUDICATIVE FACTS

(a) **Scope.** This rule governs judicial notice of an adjudicative fact only, not a legislative fact.

(b) **Kinds of Facts That May Be Judicially Noticed.** The court may judicially notice a fact that is not subject to reasonable dispute because it:

(1) is generally known within the court's territorial jurisdiction; or

(2) can be accurately and readily determined from sources whose accuracy cannot reasonably be questioned.

(c) **Taking Notice.** At any stage of the proceeding, the court:

(1) may take judicial notice on its own; or

(2) must take judicial notice if a party requests it and the court is supplied with the necessary information.

(d) **Opportunity to Be Heard.** On timely request, a party is entitled to be heard on the propriety of taking judicial notice and the nature of the noticed fact. If the court takes judicial notice before notifying a party, the party, on request, is still entitled to be heard.

(e) **Instructing the Jury.** In a civil case, the court must instruct the jury to accept the noticed fact as conclusive. In a criminal case, the court must instruct the jury that it may or may not accept the noticed fact as conclusive.

a. Adjudicative Facts

Some facts that are indisputable can be established quickly and easily without the need for the presentation of evidence. This saves time and largely eliminates the possibility that one or the other party will offer testimony that distorts those facts. The process by which this is accomplished is called judicial notice. Judicial notice is appropriate under the following circumstances:

1. The fact at issue is one that is a matter of general knowledge or can be established conclusively by consulting reliable sources; and
2. The party seeking to establish the fact presents those sources to the court; and
3. The opponent is given an opportunity to contest the propriety of the court's taking notice of the fact.

Federal Rule 201 regulates the taking of judicial notice of "adjudicative facts." Adjudicative facts are facts normally left to the jury to determine in its deliberations at the end of the case. As one authority states, these are "facts about the particular event which gave rise to the lawsuit and . . . [that help] explain who did what, when, where, how, and with what motive and intent." 2 McCormick on Evidence § 328, at 369 (5th ed. John W. Strong ed. 1999). Adjudicative facts need not be ultimate facts (facts necessary to the success of a charge, claim, or defense); they include any facts along the chain of reasoning leading to those ultimate facts. Usually, adjudicative facts must be the subject of formal proof, whether by witness testimony, real evidence, documentary evidence, or some combination of these tools. If the requirements of Rule 201 are satisfied, a party wishing to establish a particular adjudicative fact may dispense with these formal methods of proof.

For example, assume a case in which Plaintiff sues Defendant for negligence after Plaintiff is run down while crossing the street. Plaintiff claims Defendant struck Plaintiff while driving Defendant's 2005 Mercedes. Defendant owns a 2005 Mercedes but denies driving the car that struck Plaintiff. To prove that another person was responsible, Defendant calls Witness, a pedestrian who was near the intersection at the time of the accident. Witness testifies that Plaintiff was struck by a 2000 Ford Thunderbird. After cross-examining Witness, Plaintiff asks the court to take judicial notice of the fact that the Ford Motor Company did not manufacture a Thunderbird model from 1998 to 2001. To establish this fact, Plaintiff presents the court with a Ford Motor Company official publication that describes the history of the Thunderbird, and states that the company discontinued production of the Thunderbird after model year 1997, and that the company did not introduce the model again until model year 2002.

The fact that there was no 2000 Thunderbird would be offered to "impeach" Witness by casting doubt on the accuracy of Witness's identification of the car that struck Plaintiff. How would Plaintiff establish that there was no such thing as a 2000 Thunderbird if the court could not take judicial notice? Plaintiff could offer the Ford publication itself into evidence but this might require an authenticating witness, presumably a Ford employee. Even if such a witness was not required, the document might be hearsay. Alternatively, Plaintiff could call an expert witness familiar with the Thunderbird line of automobiles to testify that Ford did not manufacture a 2000 Thunderbird. Any witness called by Plaintiff would be subject to cross-examination.

But common sense suggests we should not make Plaintiff or the court take this time and make this effort. If the Ford publication is authoritative, it would make more sense for the court simply to examine the publication and declare the fact to be true, assuming Defendant is unable to raise any objection that calls into question the accuracy of the publication. This procedure is not only efficient, it poses little, if any, risk since the possibility that such a publication would be wrong about the fact in question is negligible.

The doctrine of judicial notice follows this common sense reasoning. As codified in Federal Rule 201(b), to be subject to judicial notice, a fact must "not [be] subject to reasonable dispute" in that it is either (1) generally known in the court's jurisdiction or (2) capable of being determined by consulting authoritative sources. Our example is of the second type. The question of whether Ford manufactured a 2000 model Thunderbird is subject to accurate determination by consulting an authoritative source.

A second example illustrates a fact that is not subject to reasonable dispute because it is generally known in the jurisdiction. Assume Plaintiff and Defendant are involved in a contract dispute concerning Defendant's failure to deliver certain goods by September 13, 2001, the date the contract requires delivery. Defendant claims timely delivery was made impossible by the grounding of all aircraft for a period of several days following the terrorist attacks of September 11, 2001. Defendant asks the court to take judicial notice that all aircraft were grounded for several days after September 11, 2001. The court may do so because this is a fact that was "generally known" within the trial court's territorial jurisdiction.

Some facts can be established with relative ease but do not qualify for judicial notice. That a traffic signal at a certain intersection was not operating during a particular period of time probably can be established without great difficulty, but it is unlikely to be a fact "generally known" within the trial court's territorial jurisdiction or one that is recorded in an undisputable source. The same would be true of the question whether there was a series of potholes on a particular street on a particular date.

Rule 201 describes not only *what* facts are subject to judicial notice but also *how* a court takes judicial notice. The rule establishes that a court *may* take judicial notice whether requested to do so or not. It further provides that if the party wishing the court to take judicial notice supplies the court with the information necessary to do so, the court *must* take judicial notice. The rule also preserves the right of the adverse party to be heard as to the propriety of taking notice.

Subsection (c) makes clear that judicial notice may be taken at any time in a proceeding. This means any time during a trial, or even after the completion of the trial. Judicial notice may be taken even on appeal. This is an exception to the general rule that the parties cannot supplement on appeal the factual record established at trial. Thus, under this general rule no new evidence may be introduced on appeal and no evidence may be referred to unless it was admitted at trial. The judicial notice exception to this rule is important because it permits a party who has failed to prove an essential fact at trial to establish that fact on appeal. The exception, however, is limited to facts that may be judicially noticed, namely, facts not subject to reasonable dispute.

Subsection (e) shows the power of the judicial notice doctrine. When the court in a civil action takes judicial notice of a fact, it must inform the jury that the fact is established conclusively. This rule is designed to protect the integrity of the truth determination process. If a fact is not reasonably subject to dispute, neither adverse parties (through proof or argument) nor the jury (through its own deliberations) should deny that fact once the parties have been heard on the matter and the court has taken judicial notice. An instruction to the jury that the fact is established conclusively might not work in every case, but it is designed to impress on the jury the impropriety of treating the fact differently.

In criminal cases, a different rule applies. Subsection (e) states that in criminal cases, "the court must instruct the jury that it may or may not accept the noticed fact as conclusive." This does not mean that a court may not take judicial notice in criminal cases. On the contrary, this is done routinely. But the taking of notice may not be deemed final or conclusive, and the court is obligated to inform the jury of that fact. Why the difference between civil and criminal cases? Consider the following opinion.

RAE v. STATE

884 P.2d 163 (Alaska Ct. App. 1994)

Michael L. Rae was tried before a jury on charges of second-degree criminal mischief, reckless driving, driving while license revoked (DWLR), and failure to stop at the direction of a police officer. On the criminal mischief charge the jury convicted Rae of the lesser-included offense of third-degree criminal mischief. Rae was convicted as charged on the other three counts. . . .

Rae also claims plain error in the trial court's taking of conclusive judicial notice of one of the elements of DWLR. During the presentation of the state's case, the prosecutor asked the court to take judicial notice of the fact that Rae's driver's license had been revoked at the time of the offenses alleged in this case. Rae did not object to the prosecutor's proposal. The court told the jury:

> I'm going to advise you that the court has taken judicial notice based upon records of the Division of Motor Vehicles that as of September 12, 1992, the Alaska operator's license of Michael L. Rae was suspended or revoked. The court will advise you in an instruction which we will give you at the end of the case of that judicial notice.

At the close of the trial, again without objection from Rae, the court instructed the jury:

> I may take judicial notice of facts or events which are matters of common knowledge. When I declare that the court will take judicial notice of some fact or event, you must accept my declaration as evidence and regard as conclusively proved the fact or event which I have judicially noticed.

The state concedes that the court's instruction regarding judicial notice constitutes reversible error. The concession is well taken. The taking of conclusive judicial notice of an element of a criminal charge violates Alaska Evidence Rule 203(c), and deprives the defendant of his right to be convicted only upon a jury's finding of proof beyond a reasonable doubt of every element of the offense. This is reversible error without regard either to whether there was an objection from the defense, or to whether the defendant suffered any prejudice other than having had his guilt adjudged by the wrong entity.

The judgment of conviction against Rae is REVERSED.

———————————————

Why doesn't the law compel the jury to accept judicially noticed facts in a criminal case? Wouldn't the jury in these cases be committing factual error if it failed to find that a defendant's driver's license had been revoked when public records clearly showed that it had been? Almost certainly, the answer is that any contrary finding would be inaccurate. But accuracy is not the only concern of the law. As the court in *Rae* noted, the right to trial by jury includes at least the right to have the jury decide each fact essential to proof of the crime. The value of the right to jury trial should not be minimized. In our system of representative government, jury service is the most direct way in which citizens can express their views about the validity of the laws. During the Vietnam War, for example, some juries that refused to convict men who avoided the draft or who burned their draft cards were not rendering verdicts in line with the facts. The principle that permits a jury to engage in this conduct is an important feature of our system of justice. A similar principle supports the notion that the jury in a criminal case is not required to accept as conclusive a judicially noticed fact.

Would it be less destructive of the right to jury trial to compel a jury to accept as conclusive a judicially noticed fact that is not itself essential to proof of the crime, but is merely circumstantial evidence of an element of the crime? Rule 201(e) does not distinguish between facts essential to the crime and facts that merely provide evidence that leads to proof of essential facts. In a criminal case, the court may take judicial notice, but may not instruct the jury that such notice is conclusive. Instead, it must instruct the jury that the jury may find, but is not required to find, that the noticed fact is true.

Illustrating judicial notice of adjudicative facts.   Assume Plaintiff sues Defendant for negligence following a nighttime collision between Defendant's car and Plaintiff's bicycle. The car struck Plaintiff from behind. Plaintiff admits she was wearing dark clothing, but claims Defendant should have seen her because the roadway was lit that night with bright moonlight. At trial, Defendant seeks to prove that the moon was not visible that evening. The colloquy might proceed as follows. "Pl" indicates Plaintiff's counsel; "Def" indicates Defendant's counsel.

> *Def:*   I would ask the court to take judicial notice that on the evening in question, the moon was not visible because that night was a new moon, which cannot be seen.
>
> *Pl:*   Objection, Your Honor. My opponent has not presented any data showing this to have been the case.
>
> *Def:*   May I approach?

By the Court: You may.

         Def: I have handed the bailiff a copy of a nationally circulated almanac for the year in which this accident took place. The court will find a yellow tag on the page showing the phases of the moon during the relevant month. The date on which the accident took place is denoted a new moon.

By the Court: Any objection?

          Pl: May I see the almanac, Your Honor?

By the Court: Will the bailiff please show counsel the book?

          Pl: Thank you, Your Honor. I withdraw the objection.

By the Court: The court will take judicial notice that there was no visible moon on the night in question.

         Def: Would the court please instruct the jury accordingly?

By the Court: The jury is instructed that there was no visible moon on the night in question. You must take that fact as true.

In this example, Defendant has done all that is necessary to require the court to take judicial notice. Under Rule 201(b), a fact may be judicially noticed if it is "not subject to reasonable dispute because it . . . can be accurately and readily determined from sources whose accuracy cannot reasonably be questioned." Because the phases of the moon can be proven by the simple expedient of consulting an almanac, the fact qualifies for judicial notice. In addition, because Defendant has supplied the court with the almanac, the requirements of Rule 201(c) have been satisfied and the court must take judicial notice. Plaintiff has been given an opportunity to be heard pursuant to Rule 201(d), and the court has instructed the jury according to the requirements of Rule 201(e).

b. Judicial Notice of Law

As we have already stated, Rule 201 addresses only judicial notice of adjudicative facts (facts concerning the event that gave rise to the lawsuit). Because "the law" is not an adjudicative fact, the rule does not regulate the courts' power to take judicial notice of law. It might seem strange to ask whether a court may take "judicial notice" of the law, but the issue can be very real. Suppose, for example, that Plaintiff sues Defendant for negligence after Defendant's dog bit Plaintiff while in a city park in another state.[19] Defendant admits that the dog was off leash when it bit Plaintiff, but claims that a city ordinance permitted owners to walk their dogs in city parks without a leash. To determine whether Defendant was negligent, it would be crucial to know whether Defendant's contention concerning the municipal law of the city is accurate.

If a court may take judicial notice of adjudicative facts, why should there be any question about its power to take judicial notice of the municipal law of a city within another state? If Defendant produces a certified copy of the ordinance at issue, why should the court hesitate to take judicial notice? There are at least two reasons. *First*, cities are notoriously bad at keeping accurate and

---

19. We assume that a strict liability claim would fail because the dog had always been friendly to strangers and Defendant had no reason to suspect that the dog would bite anyone.

up-to-date codifications of their ordinances. What appears to be a perfectly legitimate version of the ordinance might in fact be outdated, or the ordinance might have been repealed. Cities simply do not have the resources to update their codes as often as do states or the federal government (though even those entities sometimes lag in updating their codes). So what might appear to be a valid ordinance might actually be invalid. *Second,* the precise meaning of the ordinance might not be as clear as its wording suggests. Perhaps the city or the courts have supplied a non-intuitive reading of the ordinance, a reading that would not occur to a judge in another state perusing its language for the first time.

To a lesser degree, these issues concern all law, including federal law, the law of other states, municipal law within the state where the case is being tried, and even the law of the same state. And indeed, courts have long hesitated to take judicial notice of the law. At the same time, all would agree that it is the task of the court, not of the jury, to decide what the law is. In doing so, courts follow several conventions, which may be summarized generally as follows:

1. *Law of same state (domestic law).* Courts regularly take judicial notice of so-called domestic law. To provide the court with the necessary information, the parties will brief the court on the law, whether orally or in writing. Often the court will conduct its own legal research to determine the law. Occasionally, the court will listen to expert legal testimony, subject, of course, to examination and cross-examination by the parties.
2. *Federal law.* The same standards apply to any controlling federal law.
3. *Law of other states.* Many states have adopted the Uniform Judicial Notice of Foreign Law Act, which requires every court in an adopting state to take notice of the statutory and common law of every other state, at least when certain procedural requirements are satisfied. More recently, states have begun adopting the Uniform Interstate and International Procedure Act, which broadens the provisions of the earlier uniform law.
4. *Law of foreign nations.* At common law, the law of foreign nations was treated as a fact to be decided by jury. The Uniform Judicial Notice of Foreign Law Act made foreign law a matter for the court to decide, although not by judicial notice. The more recent Uniform Interstate and International Procedure Act allows the court to take judicial notice of the law of foreign nations, subject to certain requirements.
5. *Municipal law.* The common law reluctance to take judicial notice of municipal law, whether of the same state or of sister states, continues. Normal means of pleading and proof are usually required to determine municipal law.

c. Judicial Notice of Legislative Facts

When politicians say that they favor the appointment of "strict constructionist" judges who will only interpret the law and not make new law, they are either being disingenuous or do not understand the U.S legal system. Everyone familiar with our system knows that much of our law is "common law," which, by definition, is judicially made and constantly refined. In addition, statutes have gaps that must be filled and ambiguities that need to be interpreted. Sometimes the gaps and ambiguities are large, requiring the court to engage in rather extensive lawmaking. Sometimes the gaps can be filled and the ambiguities resolved in whole or part by broader principles standing behind the law general or the subject legislation in particular. In either event, it is the court's obligation to exercise its judgment and interpretive power to decide the applicable rules, and doing so often involves some lawmaking.

When a court engages in its lawmaking function, it must make certain assumptions about the world in which the law operates. Those assumptions are factual in nature and provide the social, political, and public policy foundations for legal rules. These facts are commonly called "legislative facts." As the Advisory Committee to the Federal Rules of Evidence wrote, "[l]egislative facts . . . are those which have relevance to legal reasoning and the lawmaking process, whether in the formulation of a legal principle or ruling by a judge or court or in the enactment of a legislative body." Fed. R. Evid. 201 Advisory Committee's Note. While Rule 201 regulates judicial notice of adjudicative facts, there is no rule regulating judicial notice of legislative facts.

Examples of legislative facts are legion. When the Supreme Court decided, in Brown v. Board of Education, 347 U.S. 483 (1954), that racially segregated schools are inherently unequal even when provided with equal resources, the Court was making a determination of legislative fact. When the Supreme Court held in Roe v. Wade, 410 U.S. 113 (1973), that the states had only limited power to control abortion, the Court relied on its view of medical, social, and other data. A state court faced with deciding the legitimacy of certain social or economic regulations must make similar decisions. These are the types of decisions judges of every political persuasion must make, and do make, on a daily basis.

Courts must be permitted to take judicial notice of legislative facts. But the standards by which judicial notice may be taken of legislative facts must be quite different than those applicable to adjudicative facts. This is because, unlike the adjudicative facts of which courts may take judicial notice, legislative facts by their very nature are not indisputable. On the contrary, they are often controversial. When issues of this type arise, the parties will brief the issue, expert witnesses will sometimes be called (at the trial court level), and the court will make a decision. Appellate review serves as a check on the findings of the lower courts, and it is not uncommon to see reversals based precisely on what the appellate court considers to be error in the trial court's identification or application of matters of policy, supported by its view of the relevant legislative facts.

Because of the nature of legislative facts, the law of evidence has no special role to play in regulating judicial notice of such facts. Normal processes of proof apply, and all general rules governing the presentation of evidence apply the same way here as they do in other situations.

Further Reading: Arthur John Keeffe et al., *Sense and Nonsense About Judicial Notice*, 2 Stan. L. Rev. 664 (1950); Robert E. Keeton, *Legislative Facts and Similar Things: Deciding Disputed Premise Facts*, 73 Minn. L. Rev. 1 (1978); Charles T. McCormick, *Judicial Notice*, 5 Vand. L. Rev. 296 (1952); Edmund M. Morgan, *Judicial Notice*, 57 Harv. L. Rev. 269 (1944).

Questions for Classroom Discussion

1. Prosecution of Defendant for robbing a convenience store. Defendant claims she was in church attending Sunday services when the robbery took place. The prosecutor asks the court to take judicial notice that the date of the robbery fell on a Wednesday, not a Sunday, and provides the court with a Sierra Club calendar. May the court take judicial notice?

2. Same facts as in Question 1. The prosecutor asks the court to instruct the jury that it must accept as conclusive that the day on which the robbery occurred was a Wednesday. Defendant objects. How should the court rule?

3. Defendant appeals a judgment for Plaintiff in a negligence action arising from an accident in which Defendant's car struck Plaintiff. At trial, Plaintiff alleged that Defendant was going 50 miles per hour in a school zone, where the speed limit is 25 miles per hour. Defendant's appeal is based on Plaintiff's failure to offer evidence at trial to prove the accident was in a school zone. Plaintiff provides the appellate court with a copy of a city ordinance declaring the block in question to be a school zone. Defendant does not deny the truth of this fact, but claims that it would be improper for the court to take judicial notice on appeal. How should the court rule?

4. Negligence action by Plaintiff against Defendant arising from an automobile collision. To prove Defendant was driving intoxicated, Plaintiff calls a police officer who testifies that she conducted a breathalyzer test on Defendant five minutes after the collision, and that it revealed that Defendant's blood-alcohol content was .16 percent, twice the legal limit. The officer testifies that she calibrated the device earlier on the same day. After the jury renders a verdict for Plaintiff, Defendant moves for a new trial on the ground that Plaintiff failed to demonstrate that a breathalyzer can measure blood-alcohol content accurately. Plaintiff asks the court to take judicial notice that a breathalyzer accurately measures the concentration of alcohol in blood when properly calibrated. How should the court rule?

5. Personal injury action by Plaintiff against Defendant arising from the head-on collision after Defendant's car crossed the center line. Plaintiff claims this occurred because Defendant was not paying attention. Defendant claims her car suddenly ran through a deep puddle, causing her to lose control. Defendant asks the court to take judicial notice that a large puddle often forms at the accident site. The judge is personally aware that this is true. Should the court take judicial notice?

(continued)

---

6. Prosecution of Defendant for murder. Defendant claims self-defense. The prosecution calls Witness, Defendant's 15-year-old child, to testify to a conversation Defendant had with Witness shortly after the crime. Defendant objects, asking the trial court to recognize a parent-child privilege. There is no statutory parent-child privilege, though the jurisdiction allows its courts to develop the law of privileges as those courts think appropriate. The court decides to create a parent-child privilege on the ground it would encourage communication between parents and children. Accordingly, the court sustains Defendant's objection. The prosecution argues that the court's rationale involved a question of fact that is not beyond reasonable dispute, making the court's action inappropriate. Did the court act within its authority?

---

5.   Burdens of Proof and Presumptions: An Introduction

It is a bit misleading to call burdens of proof and presumptions a "source of proof" because they do not add any evidence that does not already exist. Rather, these are procedural devices that establish preferences for or against particular parties and in favor of or against the existence of specific facts. Thus, they affect the way in which the fact-finder is supposed to view the evidence.

The power of burdens and presumptions should not be underestimated because they can, and frequently do, have a fundamental effect on the outcome of cases. Exactly how that is true is explored in depth in Chapter 9. For the present, we set forth only the most basic information so that you may begin to understand how these mechanisms affect the process of proving facts.

Burdens of proof establish preferences in favor of or against particular parties depending on the evidence that has been or can be produced. There are two very different types of burden of proof. The first, which we will call the "burden of persuasion," is established by the substantive law. It determines two things. *First,* the burden of persuasion describes the amount of proof that must exist for a fact to be deemed proven. One of the most famous of these descriptions, applicable in a criminal case, is "beyond a reasonable doubt." *Second,* allocation of the burden of persuasion identifies the party who must lose if the burden is not satisfied. In a typical criminal case, for example, the prosecution bears the burden or persuasion. This means that if the jury is not persuaded of the defendant's guilt beyond a reasonable doubt, the jury must acquit.

The second type of burden of proof is sometimes called the "burden of production." At every point in a case, one or the other of the parties has the responsibility to offer evidence in support of its position. The party bearing that responsibility at any given time is said to have the burden of production. The identity of the party who has the burden of production is important when a party seeks to have the judge decide the case without a trial or, if the trial has begun, decide the case without submitting it to the jury. When a motion to decide the outcome of the case is made, the court must determine whether the party who has the burden of production has offered enough evidence to allow the case to move forward. If the party has done so, the court will deny the motion. If that party has not done so, the court will grant the motion and terminate the case or the part of the case to which the motion was addressed.

Presumptions are also procedural devices, and they establish preferences in favor of or against the existence of certain facts. Their purpose, in a nutshell, is to *require* the fact-finder to accept that certain facts are true if it finds that other facts are true.

At the close of a trial, the fact-finder will usually be allowed to employ everyday reasoning to decide the facts of a case. Sometimes, however, the law does not allow the fact-finder to use everyday reasoning, but instead creates a presumption. A presumption is a conclusion of fact that the law *requires* the fact-finder to draw from another fact or group of facts. For example, the law in many jurisdictions recognizes that, if a letter has been stamped and placed in a proper mailbox, it should be presumed that the letter was received. Thus, unlike an inference, which is permissive, a presumption is conclusive. If certain facts exist, the presumption will *require* that a particular fact be found to exist. But to say that a presumption requires a particular finding of fact does not mean that this will always be true. True presumptions are *rebuttable*, meaning that under some circumstances, their effect can be overcome. In Chapter 9, we discuss in detail how that can be done.

Assessments

1. Defendant was prosecuted and convicted of murder after a jury trial. Defendant made a motion for a new trial on the ground of jury misconduct. In support of his motion, he offered the testimony of a member of the jury, who stated, "During deliberations I read in a newspaper that defendant had a previous conviction for a violent assault, which was something we never heard during the trial." The best objection to this testimony is:
   a. The witness is not competent to testify under Rule 606(b)
   b. The witness lacks personal knowledge of the violent assault
   c. The testimony violates the best evidence rule
   d. The newspaper was never authenticated

2. Civil tort action arising out of an automobile collision. The suit is brought in federal district court in California under diversity jurisdiction. Plaintiff was a passenger in one of the vehicles and suffered severe injuries, including brain damage and resulting memory loss. He was hypnotized prior to trial to help him recall details of the collision. At trial, he testifies that the other vehicle in the collision jumped the median and crashed into his car. Which of the following is true?
   a. Plaintiff lacks personal knowledge because he is suffering from brain damage
   b. Plaintiff is incompetent to testify because he suffered brain damage

(continued)

c. Plaintiff is incompetent to testify because he was hypnotized to refresh his recollection about the accident

d. Plaintiff is competent to testify because every person is competent to be a witness under Rule 601

3. Action for personal injuries. Plaintiff testifies that, at a Fourth of July party, Defendant handed Plaintiff a firecracker, ignited it, and it exploded in Plaintiff's hand. Plaintiff alleged the firecracker burned her hand and caused all her hair to fall out. After conclusion of Plaintiff's case, Defendant moves to dismiss on the ground Plaintiff offered no evidence either to prove that an exploding firecracker can cause a burn or to prove it can cause hair loss. Prior to going to law school, the judge had no experience with explosions, but she did work as a hair stylist and had personal experience that taught her that trauma can cause someone's hair to fall out. Which of the following is correct?

a. The judge may take judicial notice both that an exploding firecracker can cause a burn and can cause hair loss

b. The judge may only take judicial notice that an exploding firecracker can cause a burn, but may not take judicial notice it can cause hair loss

c. The judge may not take judicial notice that an exploding firecracker can cause a burn, but may take judicial notice it can cause hair loss

d. The judge may not take judicial notice that an exploding firecracker can cause a burn or hair loss

4. Prosecution for the commission of terrorist acts. The prosecution offers into evidence a photocopy of a written confession that the prosecution claims is signed by the defendant. A federal agent testified that he tortured Defendant and Defendant then signed the confession. The Supreme Court has definitively ruled that a coerced confession is inadmissible because it is not voluntary. At trial, defense counsel objected to the admissibility of the evidence on the ground it violates the best evidence rule and was not properly authenticated. The trial court overruled the objection and admitted the confession. Defendant was convicted. Defendant's best argument on appeal is:

a. Admitting the confession violated the best evidence rule

b. Admitting the confession was in error because it had not been properly authenticated

c. Both a and b

d. Admitting the confession was plain error

5. Prosecution for bank robbery. An eyewitness to the robbery, who is a client of the bank, is shown a video taken by an automated bank surveillance camera. The prosecutor shows the witness the video.

Which of the following should the prosecutor ask the witness in order to properly authenticate the video?

a. "Is this a fair and accurate representation of what the robbery looked like?"

b. "Is this a video of the robbery?"

c. Both a and b should be asked

d. Neither a nor b is sufficient to authenticate the video

Answers and Analysis

1. The correct answer is c. The testimony is offered to prove the contents of a writing (the newspaper) since, if the jury read that Defendant had previously been convicted of a violent assault, that might influence them to conclude Defendant would commit murder. Answer a is incorrect since this is an example of extraneous prejudicial information, which is an exception to Rule 606(b). Answer b is incorrect since the witness has personal knowledge of what was in the newspaper. Answer d is incorrect since the newspaper is not being introduced into evidence.

2. The correct answer is c. In a civil cases brought in federal district court under diversity jurisdiction, Rule 601 requires that federal courts apply state competency law. Under People v. Shirley, the California Supreme Court declared that witnesses who have been hypnotized to help refresh recollection are incompetent to testify. California Evidence Code § 795 changed this result for criminal cases, but says nothing about civil cases. This leaves *Shirley* as the prevailing standard in California for civil cases. Answer a is incorrect because, while ability to comprehend, recall, and communicate are all aspects of personal knowledge, the witness was able to give the testimony in question and, thus, appears to satisfy the minimal "sufficient to support a finding" standard of Rule 602. Answer b is incorrect because Rule 601 provides that every person is competent to be a witness and we have seen no California law (and there is none) that disqualifies witnesses because they have suffered a brain injury. Answer d is incorrect because the state law provision of Rule 601 applies.

3. The correct answer is b. A judge may take judicial notice that an exploding firecracker can cause a burn since this is a matter of general knowledge. While this judge happens to know that trauma can cause hair loss, individual (as opposed to general) knowledge is not a basis for judicial notice. Accordingly, a, c, and d are all incorrect.

4. The correct answer is d. The confession was not voluntary and, thus, was inadmissible. But the defense failed to object on that basis. Under Rule 103, to preserve for appeal an error in the form of

(continued)

admitting evidence, the objecting party must have stated the specific ground for objection at trial. Defendant failed to state any objection regarding the voluntariness of the confession. Thus, the objection is waived unless it can be said to be plain error. While Defendant objected, the specific grounds for objection were not sustainable. Answer a is incorrect because a photocopy is a duplicate and, thus, is typically admissible over a best evidence objection. Answer b is incorrect because the witness saw the Defendant sign the confession, which is a proper basis for authentication under Rule 901(b)(1). Thus, answer c also is incorrect.

5. The correct answer is a. Because the witness was at the scene, she has the personal knowledge needed to state that the video is an accurate representation of what she saw. Answer b is incorrect because the witness has no personal knowledge of the taking of the video and, thus, cannot answer the question. For that reason, answer c is also incorrect. Answer d is incorrect because a is sufficient to authenticate.

CHAPTER
2

Relevance

A.   THE DEFINITION OF RELEVANT EVIDENCE

1.   *The Basic Definition*

Most evidence rules are technical in nature. Although the rules are designed to deal with events that happen in the real world, an understanding of the rules of evidence hardly comes naturally. The relevance rules, however, are exceptions. In its most fundamental form, the concept of relevance in evidence law is exactly the same one we use to make decisions in everyday life. Set aside your legal training for a moment and think about the following problem:

On warm spring days, you like to take your valuable pet parrot, Polly, outside to the patio behind your house, where you keep a perch for it. The bird appears to enjoy this. The back yard is fenced, though there is a gate allowing access to and from an alley behind the yard. One day, about a half hour after taking the bird outside, you look through the back window and notice that Polly is missing. It is not on its perch, nor do you see it anywhere in the yard.

You now set out to determine what happened to Polly. Walking around the yard and thinking about the problem, you take note of several facts:

1. The gate leading from the back yard to the alley is open.
2. You did not hear any unusual squawking or other sounds from Polly between the time you put it on the patio and the time you noticed that it was missing.
3. You have taken the bird outside this way many times, and the bird has never before attempted to escape.
4. A few moments before you looked outside, you heard an unfamiliar voice coming from the back yard. The person said, "That's the bird!"
5. After you took Polly outside this time, you began reading a biography of Clarence Darrow. This was a change for you because you normally read fiction.
6. There is half of a leftover pizza in your refrigerator.

In deciding what happened to Polly, which of the facts noted above would matter to you? Clearly, only facts 1, 2, 3, and 4 would make any difference. Facts 5 and 6 do not. Why is that? Start with the first three facts. These facts matter to you because logic suggests they might provide a clue about what happened to the parrot. Facts 1 and 4, for example, suggest the possibility of an intruder. Fact 3 both increases the probability that an intruder stole Polly and reduces the probability that the bird escaped on its own. Fact 2 is also important because it reduces the possibility of an intruder—at least an intruder with whom the parrot is unfamiliar. Even though fact 2 tends to undercut what you might infer from facts 1 and 3, this does not make it unimportant; it only makes the problem a little more complicated.

Facts 5 and 6, on the other hand, are of no help. You are certain that the change in your reading habits would not increase or decrease the likelihood of any particular explanation for the bird's disappearance, and you also know that the presence of pizza in the refrigerator has no effect on the various possibilities. Of course, the contents of your refrigerator would be important if the question you were trying to resolve was something like, "Do I have to cook tonight or do I have enough leftovers for dinner?" But that is not a fact that will help you solve the case of the missing parrot. Absent some other facts connecting your reading habits or the pizza to the disappearance of your bird, you will ignore facts 5 and 6 as you seek to determine what happened to Polly.

This is exactly the way the definition of relevant evidence works. Rule 401 provides that evidence is relevant if it has ". . . any tendency to make a fact more or less probable than it would be without the evidence; and . . . the fact is of consequence in determining the action." Therefore, if you think you know more about a pertinent fact after you hear the evidence than you knew before you heard it, the evidence is relevant.[1]

In other words, you cannot determine whether a certain item of evidence is relevant until you know the fact it was offered to prove. And that fact must be "of consequence" in determining the outcome of the case. Once you have identified the fact the proponent offers the evidence to prove, logic determines whether the evidence actually tends to make the existence of that fact more likely or less likely.

2.   *Relevance Distinguished from Probative Value*

Evidence is relevant if it has any effect on fact-finding, even if that effect is minimal. The evidence does not have to be sufficient to prove the fact "beyond a reasonable doubt," or even to prove that the fact is true "more likely than not." In the words of Rule 401, the evidence is relevant if it has *any tendency* to increase or decrease the likelihood that a fact of consequence is true.

This points out the crucial distinction between *relevance* and a related concept, *probative value*. Relevance is an on-off proposition. Evidence is either relevant or irrelevant, regardless of the degree to which it helps to establish the existence of a fact. Probative value, on the other hand, is a matter of degree. Irrelevant evidence obviously has no probative value. But relevant evidence has high probative value if it has a significant effect on the existence of a fact, and low probative value if its effect is small. To illustrate, return to the case of the missing parrot. We have already established that facts 5 and 6 are irrelevant because they are of no assistance in determining what happened to the bird. The other facts are relevant because they tell us something about that question. But each of these facts has different probative value. Fact 3 (that the bird has never tried to escape before) has modest probative value. Perhaps nothing has happened in the past to make the bird want to escape. Fact 4, on the other hand, has high probative value. Hearing an unfamiliar voice from the back yard exclaiming, "That's the bird!" greatly increases the likelihood that the bird was stolen by an intruder. Of course, the probative value of the evidence might be undercut somewhat by the fact that you did not hear the bird squawking, but the evidence nonetheless seems very significant.

Most rules of evidence are not concerned with probative value. Rule 402 provides that if evidence is relevant, it will be admissible unless excluded by other rules or by principles of constitutional law. As we see later in this chapter, however, sometimes the court must consider the probative value of the evidence to determine its admissibility.

---

1. One of the most quoted passages in the intellectual history of evidence law encapsulates what we have explained so far:

> Relevancy, as the word itself indicates, is not an inherent characteristic of any item of evidence but exists as a relation between an item of evidence and a proposition sought to be proved. If any item of evidence tends to prove or to disprove any proposition, it is relevant to that proposition.

George F. James, *Relevancy, Probability and the Law*, 29 Cal. L. Rev. 689, 690 (1941).

3. Materiality: When Is a Fact "of Consequence"?

Note that the definition of relevant evidence has two parts: To be relevant, the evidence must (1) make more or less probable (2) a fact of consequence. As we have seen, logic and common sense tell us whether an item of evidence affects the probability that a certain fact is true. But we need knowledge about the specific substantive law governing a case to decide if that fact is "of consequence."

Whether the evidence is offered to prove "a fact that is of consequence in determining the action" is a question of what is sometimes called *materiality*. To understand the concept of materiality, we must first recognize what evidence rules are *not* designed to do: They do not establish rules of substantive law. In other words, evidence rules do not dictate what facts must be proved to establish a charge, claim, or defense. Evidence rules dictate only the allowable means by which facts of consequence may be proved.

Return again to the case of the missing parrot. Suppose Defendant is arrested and charged with burglary in connection with the missing bird. Criminal law provides that there are three essential elements of the crime of burglary: (1) an unauthorized entry, (2) of a structure or separately secured or occupied portion of the structure, that was inhabited at the time of the entry, (3) with the intent to commit a felony or theft. Thus, the criminal law determines what facts are "of consequence" or material in the case of the missing parrot. Facts are "of consequence in determining the action" if they are either necessary elements under the applicable substantive law or other facts from which a necessary element may be inferred. This means that to determine whether evidence is relevant, you have to know the substantive law applicable in the case. In a prosecution, the criminal law establishes the facts of consequence. In a civil action for breach of contract, the law of contracts controls. Thus, relevance analysis is driven by the nature of the case.

4. When Does Evidence Make a Fact More or Less Probable?

How do we know when an item of evidence has a tendency to make the existence of a fact of consequence more or less probable? In the case of the missing parrot, we say that the open gate increases the probability that an intruder stole the parrot, but how did we reach that conclusion? The answer is that we applied a *generalization* to the fact of the open gate, and used logic to infer from that generalization that there was an intruder. A generalization is an unstated assumption about reality that we believe to be true more often than not, and that is applicable to the fact in question. In the parrot case, the generalization would be something like "Gates do not open by themselves." From that generalization, we might logically infer from evidence of the open gate that an intruder entered the back yard and stole the parrot.

Consider another example: Assume that you saw a person who was standing on a fourth-floor balcony drop a large rock over the railing. You immediately closed your eyes and a moment later opened your eyes only to see another person lying under a rock on the sidewalk directly below the balcony. You probably would conclude that the person was struck by the rock that was dropped by the person on the balcony. Even though you did not see the rock fall and strike the victim, you will make the generalization that objects dropped from a height tend to fall toward the earth rather than move in other directions. From that generalization, you would infer that the injured person was hit by the rock dropped from the balcony directly above him.

To take a somewhat less obvious example, imagine that you see a cat lying dead on your lawn. Next to the cat is a bag of rat poison with a small hole in the side. If someone asks you what happened to the cat, you probably would say that the cat died when it ate poison. You would be virtually sure of this even though you did not see the cat eating the poison, you did not speak with anyone else who saw the event take place, and other explanations are possible. Why would you be so certain that the cat ate poison? The answer is that you applied a generalization to the "evidence" and arrived at the conclusion most supported by your everyday experience. Your reasoning could be described as follows:

> **EVIDENCE**: A cat was lying dead next to a bag of poison that had a small hole in its side.
>
> → **INFERENCE**: The cat ate the poison, causing its death.
>
> > **GENERALIZATION SUPPORTING INFERENCE**: An animal found dead in the presence of a poison is more likely to have died from poisoning than from other causes.

In this example, our experience of day-to-day life allows us to make the leap from the evidence to the inference. Although we might not be as certain of the conclusion as we would be if we actually saw the cat eat the poison, experience helps us to reach the conclusion with a fair degree of confidence. In any case, we can safely say that the close proximity of a deceased cat to a bag of poison with a small hole in its side provides a meaningful clue to the reason for the cat's demise.

We apply the same reasoning when we draw conclusions about the past actions of people. Suppose Victim witnesses a crime. Based on information Victim provides to the police, Zed is arrested and charged with the crime. A few days later, a hit-and-run driver strikes Victim while Victim is crossing the street. The police arrest Defendant, a member of the same criminal gang as Zed, and charge Defendant with running down Victim. He denies he was the driver of the car. Would you consider Defendant's common gang membership with Zed relevant to show that Defendant was the driver? Most likely, your answer would be yes, and your reasoning would be as follows:

> **EVIDENCE**: Defendant and Zed are members of the same criminal gang.
>
> → **INFERENCE**: Defendant had a motive to prevent Victim from testifying against Zed.
>
> > **GENERALIZATION SUPPORTING INFERENCE**: A member of the same criminal gang as another person will want to protect that person.
>
> > → **INFERENCE**: Defendant was the driver who ran down Victim.

> **GENERALIZATION SUPPORTING INFERENCE**: A person with a
> motive to act in a certain way is more likely to have acted in
> that way than is one without such a motive.

Once again, the evidence is not inherently relevant. It becomes relevant when subjected to one or more generalizations the fact-finder accepts as valid. This is the same reasoning process we use when we act in the everyday world, and it is the process the fact-finder uses in a formal trial. Indeed, the best trial lawyers are those who are able to make explicit these generalizations, creating a roadmap for the fact-finder leading from masses of conflicting evidence to the conclusion the lawyer wants the jury to reach.

Of course, concluding that the evidence in this example is relevant does not mean it proves that Defendant is guilty. It is but one piece of evidence that Defendant is the person who ran Victim down. Guilt requires proof beyond a reasonable doubt, while Rule 401 says that evidence is relevant if it has *any* *tendency* (even just a little) to affect the existence of a fact of consequence. As McCormick said, "A brick is not a wall."[2] This point is illustrated by the next case.

STATE v. JAEGER
973 P.2d 404 (Utah 1999)

HOWE, Chief Justice:

Defendant Donald L. Jaeger appeals from his second degree murder conviction, a first degree felony in violation of Utah Code Ann. § 76-5-203 (1989). He contends that (1) the trial court erroneously excluded evidence of the victim's prior suicide attempt. . . .

FACTS

On August 22, 1990, shortly after midnight, Jaeger called 911 from his home and reported that his nineteen-year-old live-in girlfriend, Mary Barndt, had shot herself. When police and paramedics arrived, they found Mary partially clothed and lying in the kitchen. A .22 caliber pistol was lying "pretty close" to her right foot, and an empty shell casing was found between her ankles. . . .

Mary was unconscious and had a weak pulse when the paramedics began to treat her injuries. The bullet entered her neck just above her clavicle and had struck the subclavian artery, causing severe internal bleeding. In an attempt to preserve evidence, one of the police officers taped brown paper bags on Mary's hands. She died shortly after arriving at the hospital.

Jaeger told one of the officers that when he arrived home from work at about 7:30 P.M., the house appeared empty. However, at 8:30 P.M., he discovered Mary's thirteen-month-old daughter alone in a back bedroom. He admitted that he was angry and upset that Mary had left the child unattended. He called Judy Clark,

---

2. McCormick on Evidence § 185, at 641 (5th ed. John W. Strong ed. 1999).

Mary's mother, in an attempt to locate Mary, but she did not know Mary's whereabouts.

Jaeger also told police that when Mary finally returned home at around 12:10 A.M., he told her that he was tired of her lying and wanted her out of the house by the next day. He said that he then called her mother again and that after a struggle, Mary reluctantly took the phone. He asserted that after Mary began talking to her mother, he threw a blanket and pillow into the hall for her and he then went to bed. He stated that he later awoke to a "bang" and that he found Mary lying unconscious on the kitchen floor. He maintained that she shot herself.

However, other evidence contradicted Jaeger's story. The police swabbed both Jaeger's and Mary's hands for gunshot residue ("GSR"). These swabs were then taken to the state crime lab and examined by two separate experts. Both experts concluded that the swabs taken from Jaeger's hands contained elements of GSR while the swabs taken from Mary's hands did not. Thus the GSR evidence suggested that Jaeger, not Mary, had fired a gun.

In addition to the GSR evidence, Dr. Edward A. Leis, the Deputy Chief Medical Examiner, performed an autopsy on Mary's body. The autopsy showed that Mary died from a gunshot wound to the neck. Moreover, on the basis of the autopsy results, Dr. Leis opined that Mary's death was a homicide, not a suicide.

The State charged Jaeger with second degree murder. . . .

The central issue at Jaeger's trial was whether Mary's death was a suicide or a homicide. During trial, Jaeger sought to admit certain medical records from Valley Mental Health's Adolescent Residential Treatment & Education Center ("ARTEC"). Mary was a resident of ARTEC from 1986 to 1987 because she was "ungovernable," ran away from home, and abused alcohol and drugs. The ARTEC records contained statements Mary allegedly made admitting that she had attempted suicide in the past but denying any suicidal ideation while a resident of the program. The State objected to the admission of the records; the court sustained the objection, ruling that they were irrelevant.

Jaeger was ultimately convicted as charged and was sentenced to serve a term of five years to life in prison. Thereafter, he moved for a new trial on the basis that the trial court erroneously excluded evidence of Mary's past suicide attempt. The court denied the motion. Jaeger now appeals.

ANALYSIS

I. EVIDENCE OF PAST SUICIDE ATTEMPT

The first issue presented is whether the trial court erred in excluding the ARTEC records which contained Mary's statements that she had attempted suicide on a previous occasion. The court excluded these records on the basis that they were irrelevant. Jaeger, however, contends that such records were relevant because the main issue at trial was whether Mary's death was a homicide or a suicide. . . . We agree that the court erred by excluding this evidence but ultimately conclude that such error was harmless.

A. *The Relevance of the ARTEC Records*

Rule 401 of the Utah Rules of Evidence defines relevant evidence as "evidence having *any* tendency to make the existence of any fact that is of consequence to the determination of the action more probable or less probable than it would be without the evidence." Utah R. Evid. 401 (emphasis added). In other words, "[e]vidence that has even the slightest probative value" is relevant under the definition in rule 401. . . .

Irrelevant evidence is inadmissible under rule 402 of the Utah Rules of Evidence. That rule provides: "All relevant evidence is admissible, except as otherwise provided by the Constitution of the United States or the Constitution of the state of Utah, statute, or by these rules. . . . *Evidence* which is *not relevant is not admissible.*" Utah R. Evid. 402 (emphasis added). Thus, where the proffered evidence has no probative value to a fact at issue, it is irrelevant and is inadmissible under rule 402. However, because the standard for determining whether evidence is relevant is so low, the issue of whether evidence is relevant is rarely an issue.

The trial court held that ninety-nine percent of the ARTEC records were *irrelevant* and that they were "very speculative, both as to content and as to the time element." Although the trial court did not cite to any particular rule, it apparently concluded that these records failed to meet rule 401's definition of relevant evidence and excluded them under rule 402. This decision was erroneous.

As stated above, the primary issue at trial was whether Mary's death was a homicide or a suicide. Jaeger sought to introduce the ARTEC records as evidence supporting his defense that Mary committed suicide. The court apparently excluded this evidence on the basis that proof that a person attempted suicide when she was a young, "ungovernable" teenager is not probative of whether this same person committed suicide when she was nineteen years old.

We noted earlier that the standard for determining whether evidence is relevant is very low. It is reasonable to believe that a person who has attempted suicide in the past may attempt suicide again. The flaw in the trial court's reasoning was its failure to recognize that while the remoteness of the evidence may reduce its probative value, rule 401 states that relevant evidence is evidence that has "*any* tendency to make the existence of any fact . . . more probable or less probable," Utah R. Evid. 401 (emphasis added), and the ARTEC records in this case met that standard.

In sum, we conclude that the trial court erred in holding that the ARTEC records were irrelevant. These records might have aided the jury in determining whether Mary's death was a homicide or a suicide. Thus this evidence was relevant under rule 401 and was not excludable under rule 402. . . .

We affirm Jaeger's conviction and sentence. Although the court erred in excluding the ARTEC records as irrelevant, we conclude that such error was harmless . . . .

The *Jaeger* court understood that evidence concerning a person's attempted suicide as a "young, 'ungovernable' teenager" is relevant to the question whether her death years later was a homicide or a suicide. Though many factors can affect the probative value of the evidence, it is a rational inference that a person who attempted suicide at an earlier point in her life is somewhat more likely to have repeated the attempt on the occasion in question.

One thing that affects the probative value of evidence is the number of inferences one must make to move from the evidence to the conclusion. The closer one looks, the more inferential steps appear in even relatively simple logical thinking. Consider the following example:

> Defendant is charged with arson for burning down the factory of Victim. Defendant denies involvement in the fire. The prosecution wishes to call a witness to testify that Defendant and Victim are business competitors who had both just learned that a third party was accepting bids on a very large contract. Is the evidence relevant?

Instinctively, we know the answer: The evidence is relevant. We hardly need to run through all the intermediate inferences leading from the evidence to the conclusion because we see the connection right away. It has to do with motive. But a more careful analysis shows that the logic actually involves a number of steps:

EVIDENCE: Defendant and Victim are business competitors who had both just learned that a third party was accepting bids on a very large contract.

→ **INFERENCE 1**: It is true that Defendant and Victim are business competitors who both had learned this information.[3]

→ **INFERENCE 2**: Defendant wanted to land the contract.

→ **INFERENCE 3**: Defendant had a motivation to eliminate competitors to land the contract.

→ **INFERENCE 4**: Defendant was willing to act on the motive by burning down Victim's factory.

→ **INFERENCE 5** (CONCLUSION): Defendant burned down Victim's factory.

In this example, what seems to be relatively simple logic actually requires a fact-finder to employ at least five inferences. If even a single link in this inferential chain is broken (i.e., if the inference cannot be drawn), the evidence is irrelevant. Here, a rational person would be able to make each inferential leap because such a person could accept the generalization that justifies each leap. Inference 1, the truth of the testimony that Defendant and Victim were competitors who both learned of a possible large deal, is reasonable because of the generalization that people typically tell the truth when they testify under oath. One then can draw the inference that Defendant wanted to land the contract (Inference 2) on the basis of a generalization that a business person tends to want to get more business. Inference 3 is supported by the generalization that a business person who has potential competition for a particular sale has a motive to eliminate the competitor. We can justify the final inference, that Defendant burned down Victim's factory, based on the generalization that people tend to

---

3. The testimony that constitutes the evidence in this hypothetical is not necessarily accurate. If the fact-finder rejects the testimony, the entire chain of inferences is broken. Thus, the first inference in the chain must be that the testimony is accurate.

act on their motives. As long as each step is supported by a defensible general-ization and an inference that can be drawn from that generalization, the evidence is relevant.

This example also demonstrates once again the essential difference between relevance and probative value. The relevance of the evidence depends only on whether it is rational to link each step in the chain to the one before it. The probative value of the evidence, on the other hand, depends on the *strength* of each inference. One way to assess probative value is to think about the mathe-matical probabilities of each link. The result of this is often striking. Assume the improbable in our hypothetical: that the prosecution has no evidence of Defen-dant's guilt other than the testimony that Defendant and Victim were business competitors who had just learned about the opportunity to bid for new business. *The probative value of that evidence then can be stated as the product of the probabilities of each link in the chain.* As we see later in this chapter, this is known as the "product rule."[4] Assume the following probabilities:

Inference 1 (Defendant and Victim were competitors who had learned of a potential opportunity)	80%
Inference 2 (Defendant wanted to land the business)	70%
Inference 3 (Defendant had a motive to eliminate the competition)	80%
Inference 4 (Defendant was willing to act on the motive)	60%
Conclusion (Defendant burned down Victim's factory)	60%

Our assumed probabilities are arbitrary, of course, in that they are not sup-ported by any data. Though the chain will remain intact even if any particular inference has a less than 50 percent chance of being true, we have deliberately chosen probabilities greater than 50 percent for each leap in the chain to sug-gest each inference is fairly strong. *If* the product rule applies to this situation, the probability (P) of Defendant's guilt should be the product of each individual probability. Here, the formula is as follows: $P = .80 \times .70 \times .80 \times .60 \times .60$. Thus, P is equal to only about 16.1 percent. Not only does the evidence, standing alone, fail to prove Defendant's guilt beyond a reasonable doubt, it even fails to satisfy the preponderance standard by a huge margin. If the numbers used above are accurate, the prosecution must lose without presenting more evidence of guilt. In fact, even if each leap is supported by a probability of *90 percent*, the resulting probability of .59 still falls short of proof beyond a reasonable doubt. In either case, the evidence is relevant, but its probative value for the proposition it is offered to prove does not satisfy the legal standard for guilt. In other words, the evidence is relevant but not sufficient to convict.

So far, we've been operating on the assumption that the generalizations applied to evidence to determine its relevance are indisputable. That is not

4. As we will see, the product rule in evidence law is usually applied to a series of facts, with the goal of determining the likelihood that all of the facts, in combination, are true. Thus, suppose an eyewitness testifies that a crime was committed by a male with blue eyes. If we assume that the witness is correct, and we know that the probability of a randomly chosen person being male is one in two, and that the probability that a person chosen at random from a particular community has blue eyes is one in four, then we can say that only one in eight people in the community could have committed the crime. Presently, we are using the product rule in a somewhat different way, apply-ing it to inferences from a single fact rather than to different facts. But the application seems reasonable, because the probability that the ultimate conclusion is correct is proportionately decreased by the less-than-certain probability of the truth of each individual inference.

true in every case, of course. At the end of this chapter, we explore whether the judge or the jury should be the final arbiter of relevance. For now, it is sufficient to point out that when there is a dispute about the validity of the generalization making certain evidence relevant, the parties should be prepared to argue the matter.

Further Reading: Ann Althouse, *Beyond King Solomon's Harlots: Women in Evidence*, 65 S. Cal. L. Rev. 1265 (1992); David Crump, *On the Uses of Irrelevant Evidence*, 34 Hous. L. Rev. 1 (1997); George F. James, *Relevancy, Probability and the Law*, 29 Cal. L. Rev. 689 (1941); Richard O. Lempert, *Modeling Relevance*, 75 Mich. L. Rev. 1021 (1977); Herman L. Trautman, *Logical or Legal Relevancy — A Conflict in Theory*, 5 Vand. L. Rev. 385 (1952).

Questions for Classroom Discussion

1. In *Jaeger*, was the evidence offered to prove a fact of consequence? If so, did it have a tendency to make that fact more or less probable?

2. How would you assess the probative value of the evidence in *Jaeger*? What factors would you take into consideration?

3. Prosecution of Defendant for assault and battery on Victim. While sitting in the stands at a football game, Victim was struck in the back by a bullet apparently fired from a handgun. Defendant denies involvement. To prove that Defendant shot Victim, the prosecution calls Witness, who was sitting near Defendant at the time, to testify that she saw Defendant pull something out of his pocket (Witness could not see what it was) and point it in Victim's direction and that, moments later, there was a loud popping noise and Victim slumped down in her seat. Defendant objects on relevance grounds. How should the court rule? What inferences connect the testimony to a fact of consequence? What generalizations justify those inferences?

4. As noted in the discussion following *Jaeger*, the first inference in the chain of inferences necessary to determine if Witness's testimony is relevant is that the testimony is accurate. In Question 3, what reasons might we have to question the accuracy of Witness's testimony?

5. Same case as in Question 3. The prosecution calls Victim to testify that a week before the shooting, Victim turned down a date with Defendant. Defendant objects on relevance grounds. How should the court rule?

6. Action against a life insurance company for refusing to pay the proceeds of a policy on the life of Deceased. Plaintiff was the beneficiary of Deceased's insurance policy. The insurance company claims Deceased committed suicide, an act that voids

(continued)

the policy. To prove Deceased took her own life, the insurance company calls Witness to testify that a few days before she died, Deceased called Witness and apologized for something that occurred many years earlier. Plaintiff objects on relevance grounds. How should the court rule? What inferences connect the testimony to a fact of consequence? What generalizations justify those inferences?

7. Same facts as in Question 6. After the court admits Witness's testimony, Plaintiff wishes to testify that she knew Deceased all her life, and that Deceased was an atheist who did not believe in an afterlife. Is this relevant to prove Deceased did not commit suicide? Is it relevant to prove she did commit suicide? What inferences connect the testimony to either conclusion? What generalizations justify those inferences?

8. Dispute between Plaintiff and Defendant over who is the birth mother of a certain baby. It is undisputed that both women gave birth to babies at about the same time, but that one of the babies died. To prove that Plaintiff is the birth mother of the living child, Plaintiff wishes to offer evidence that when an elder suggested that the child be divided in two, Plaintiff offered to give the baby to Defendant instead. Defendant objects on relevance grounds. How should the court rule?

9. Same facts as in Question 8. To prove that she is the birth mother of the living child, Defendant wishes to offer evidence that when the elder suggested that the child be divided in two, Defendant, in tears, told the elder that she would go along with the solution. Is the evidence relevant to prove Defendant is the birth mother?

10. Prosecution of Defendant for assault and battery on Victim. Defendant claims self-defense. To prove self-defense, Defendant calls Witness to testify that a week before the altercation between Defendant and Victim, Victim threatened to kill Defendant. Defendant was unaware of the threat. The prosecution objects on relevance grounds. How should the court rule? Does it matter if Defendant claims self-defense because Victim attacked Defendant first or because Defendant was justified in being the first attacker in that he was in fear of his life?

11. Prosecution of Defendant for the murder of Victim. Defendant claims she attacked Victim in self-defense because Zed told her that Victim had made a threat against her. It is conceded, however, that Zed was wrong — that in fact Victim made no such threat. The prosecution therefore objects on relevance grounds to Defendant's testimony concerning what Zed told Defendant. How should the court rule?

> 12. Prosecution of Defendant for bank robbery. To prove Defendant took part in the robbery, the prosecution calls Witness, who testifies that she was standing across the street from the bank and saw Defendant emerge with what appeared to be a bag of money. Later, Defendant offers evidence that Witness is nearsighted and was not wearing his glasses at the time the bank robbery occurred. The prosecution objects on relevance grounds. How should the court rule?
>
> 13. At a trial involving an intersection collision, Plaintiff calls Witness and begins by asking Witness to recite her name and address. Defendant objects on relevance grounds. How should the court rule?

B. BALANCING PROBATIVE VALUE AGAINST DANGERS

> ### FED. R. EVID. 403. EXCLUDING RELEVANT EVIDENCE FOR PREJUDICE, CONFUSION, WASTE OF TIME, OR OTHER REASONS

The court may exclude relevant evidence if its probative value is substantially outweighed by a danger of one or more of the following: unfair prejudice, confusing the issues, misleading the jury, undue delay, wasting time, or needlessly presenting cumulative evidence.

1. Introduction

While evidence must be relevant to be admissible, not all relevant evidence is admitted. Some relevant evidence is excluded by certain categorical exclusionary rules (such as the hearsay rule). Other evidence, although relevant, carries sufficient danger or cost to justify giving the trial court discretion to exclude. This is the function of Rule 403. Every jurisdiction maintains a rule either identical or similar to Rule 403. A close look at the rule reveals several important features:

1. The rule only applies if evidence is relevant.
2. When an attorney objects to the evidence under Rule 403, the court's responsibility is to weigh the probative value of the evidence and to compare it to a number of problems or "dangers" that might be created if the evidence is admitted ("unfair prejudice, confusing the issues, misleading the jury, undue delay, wasting time, or needlessly presenting cumulative evidence").
3. The court may exclude the evidence only if it finds that the dangers "substantially outweigh[]" probative value. This is not an even balance. Instead, the rule strongly favors admissibility. Only when the dangers posed by the evidence *substantially* outweigh its probative value may the court exclude it under Rule 403. The greater the probative value, the greater the dangers must be to justify exclusion. Evidence that carries significant probative value rarely will be excluded under this rule.

4. The rule states that the court "may" exclude evidence in appropriate circumstances. This means the court has discretion in striking the balance and deciding whether to admit or exclude the evidence.

Because Rule 403 gives trial courts discretion, appellate courts normally will defer to trial court decisions based on the rule. Appellate courts still have the authority to review such decisions, but meaningful appellate review often depends on whether the trial court placed the reasons for its ruling on the record. Counsel have the responsibility of ensuring that the trial court articulates its reasons for sustaining or overruling an objection based on Rule 403. Without such information in the record, an appellate court will have a very difficult time determining whether the trial court exercised its discretion in a reasonable fashion. Some appellate courts take the position that failure by the trial court to put such information on the record is itself an abuse of discretion under Rule 403.

2.   The "Probative Value" Side of the Equation

Rule 403 balancing begins with an examination of probative value. As we have seen, probative value is not the same as relevance. In the law of evidence, relevance is a binary concept; evidence is either relevant or irrelevant. Thus, the statement, "this evidence is highly relevant" is technically incorrect. Probative value is an assessment of *weight*— the degree to which an item of evidence affects the likelihood that a fact of consequence in the case is or is not true. Two factors influence this assessment: the logical force of the evidence and the context in which it is offered.

As we saw in the preceding section on relevance, the logical force of an item of evidence is a product of the strength and number of inferences that connect the evidence to the ultimate fact to be proven. For example, assume a robbery prosecution in which defendant denies being the robber. A witness's testimony that she saw defendant commit the robbery has more probative value than evidence defendant was in the vicinity when the crime was committed. The eyewitness testimony identifying defendant as the perpetrator requires only one inference: that the witness is testifying accurately. Her testimony has the greatest possible logical force because it is direct evidence of the ultimate fact to be proven. By contrast, evidence that defendant was in the vicinity requires at least one additional inference to establish defendant was the robber: that defendant took advantage of being in the neighborhood and committed the crime. The strength of that additional inference is relatively weak because a person can be in the vicinity of the crime scene without being the perpetrator.

Probative value is not just a function of the number and strength of inferences connecting the evidence to a fact of consequence. This is because a single item of evidence does not exist in a vacuum but is presented in the context of an entire case. Because of this, the probative value of evidence must be weighed in context. For example, in a murder case with only one eyewitness, her testimony that the perpetrator wore a red coat likely carries enormous probative value. But if ten people all had approximately the same view of the scene, the testimony of each witness that the perpetrator wore a red coat likely carries only minimal probative value once the first witness or two have testified.

3. The "Dangers" Side of the Equation

A court applying Rule 403 must assess the dangers of the evidence and compare them to its probative value. The rule specifies a number of different dangers. Some evidence, for example, would take a great deal of time to present but carries little probative value. The court may exclude the evidence because its presentation might consume more resources than it is worth, and because the time involved in presenting it might distract the jury from the primary focus of the case. Similarly, the court may exclude evidence that is cumulative, meaning it merely repeats other evidence that adequately establishes a fact. For example, in a case involving a collision of a crowded bus and a motorcycle, testimony of two or three bus passengers who each had a good view of the scene will generally suffice. If the party plans to call every bus passenger, and the opponent objects on the ground that the evidence is needlessly cumulative, the court will likely sustain the objection.

Unfair prejudice is the principal danger against which Rule 403 is designed to protect. Naturally, any item of evidence offered by a party will be prejudicial to the opponent because prejudice simply means it will influence the fact-finder. To count against admission under Rule 403, the evidence must be *unfairly* prejudicial. Unfortunately, the rule does not define the concept. The Advisory Committee Note simply states that unfair prejudice "means an undue tendency to suggest decision on an improper basis, commonly, though not necessarily, an emotional one." This is, at best, an incomplete definition. To better understand its meaning, one must consider the types of situations in which a jury might decide a case "on an improper basis." There are two main types of impropriety, each of which creates a different kind of unfair prejudice.

a. Inferential Error Prejudice

This term describes situations in which the jury misconceives the logical import of the evidence, either by deciding that the evidence is probative of a fact when it is not or deciding that it is more or less probative of a fact than it is. Consider this example: Plaintiff brings a negligence action against defendant after an auto accident. To prove her injuries, Plaintiff offers into evidence several color photos of her face taken at the hospital just minutes after the accident. The photos show blood flowing from several points on plaintiff's face. Her eyelids are swollen, apparently making it impossible for her to open her eyes, and her hair is soaked in blood. Defendant objects to the photos, claiming that if allowed to see them, the jury will be misled as to the actual extent of Plaintiff's injuries. Defendant represents that expert testimony will demonstrate that people whose injuries are relatively minor often appear horribly injured shortly after an accident, that Plaintiff recovered fully from her injuries, and that she suffers little, if any, permanent impairment. Plaintiff does not dispute this characterization of the extent of the injuries, but asserts that the photos are relevant and admissible.

The photos are certainly relevant. They have some probative value because they demonstrate that Plaintiff was in fact injured in the collision. However, because the photos are so graphic they might lead the jury to overestimate the extent of the harm she suffered and, based on that misunderstanding, render a verdict for more than Plaintiff should receive. This would be an inferential error leading to unfair prejudice, and if the court finds that the extent of the unfair prejudice greatly outweighs the legitimate probative value of the evidence, it should exclude the photos.

This example also illustrates another type of inferential error. Assume the question of negligence in the auto accident case is disputed, and that the photographs of Plaintiff reveal terrible injuries in the most shocking way possible. Because studies show that jurors often wrongly assume that the extent of injury is probative of negligence, the photographs are unfairly prejudicial. This is true not because the jury might overvalue the photographs but, rather, because the jury will think the evidence is probative of a fact (negligence) when logically it is not.

b. Nullification Prejudice

The second type of unfair prejudice is sometimes called nullification prejudice, and it occurs when the presentation of certain evidence invites the jury to lawlessness. Put another way, the evidence is of such a nature as to make the jury want to punish or reward a party regardless of guilt or legal liability, and thus ignore the law set forth in the court's instructions. Consider the following case: Defendant is charged with bank robbery, but claims he was not involved. To prove Defendant was the perpetrator, the prosecution offers evidence that Defendant is a heroin addict. The prosecution's theory is that the evidence is relevant to prove that Defendant had a motive to rob the bank because he needed money to feed his heroin addiction. It is true that the evidence is relevant to prove motive, but there is a danger that the jury might use the evidence for a different purpose: Once the jury hears that Defendant is a heroin addict it might decide to convict him because of what he is, not because of what he did. In other words, even though the judge will instruct the jury to find Defendant guilty only if the prosecution proves beyond a reasonable doubt that Defendant committed the robbery, the jury might decide that a heroin addict is the sort of person who should be locked up regardless of what he has or has not done.

This is called nullification prejudice because the evidence might move the jury to ignore or "nullify" the law. To convict on such a basis would violate the fundamental tenet of the law that a person is to be tried for conduct on the occasion in question, not on the basis of his status or some other aspect of his behavior. If the court finds that the risk of the jury deciding the case on this basis substantially outweighs the legitimate probative value of the evidence, it should exclude the evidence.

The bank robbery hypothetical also illustrates a second form of nullification prejudice: unfair prejudice that arises from the jury's inability or refusal to follow the court's instructions about the limited use of particular evidence. As we have seen, the evidence about Defendant's addiction is relevant to show a motive to commit the crime. It is also relevant to show that Defendant has the character of a law breaker because he regularly violates the law by the possession and use of illegal drugs. This character trait increases the probability that Defendant engaged in unlawful conduct like bank robbery. But we will see in Chapter 4 that the evidence is inadmissible for this purpose under Rule 404(a). If the court were to admit the evidence of Defendant's heroin addiction for the limited purpose of showing Defendant had a motive to commit the crime and instructed the jury to disregard the evidence insofar as it says anything about his character, the jury would nullify Rule 404(a) if it disregarded the court's instruction. If the court finds that the danger of such action by the jury substantially outweighs any minimal probative value the evidence might carry to prove motive, the court could exclude the evidence under Rule 403.

4. Conducting the Balance

We have yet to address an important question about the application of Rule 403. Recall the standard rule: Judges determine questions of "law," and juries decide questions of "fact." One aspect of this rule is that juries, not judges, determine the credibility of witnesses. This is because witness credibility is a fact. How, then, can the judge perform the probative value/prejudicial impact balance without evaluating the credibility of the witness who provides the evidence at issue? More specifically, is the credibility of a witness a factor in weighing the probative value of her testimony under Rule 403? That question is addressed in the following case.

FEASTER v. UNITED STATES
631 A.2d 400 (D.C. App. 1993)

ROGERS, Chief Judge:

Appellant Michael A. Feaster appeals from his convictions by a jury of sexual offenses on the grounds that his Sixth Amendment right to present a defense was violated when the trial judge excluded from the defense case a transcript of the grand jury testimony of Oscar Mitchell. . . .

I.

The complainants were seven young boys from troubled homes whom appellant took into his home and held out as his "godsons." Four of the complainants were under the age of fourteen at the time of the incidents, which occurred between the summer of 1987 and early 1989. The complainants maintained that when they began staying at appellant's home, he had treated them "nice," made sure that they went to school and did their homework, and bought clothes for them. However, this living situation ended on Saturday, February 25, 1989, when one of the boys, John, ran away from appellant's apartment to his grandmother's home. Crying and upset, he told his grandmother that appellant had sexually assaulted him. The following Monday, John was examined by a doctor. As a result of a police investigation, appellant was charged with forty-one counts of sexually assaulting the boys who lived at, or regularly visited, his home.

[At trial, the prosecution introduced the testimony of several boys, who gave similar accounts of the events in appellant's home. Three of the witnesses stated that 19-year-old Oscar Mitchell observed the sexual misconduct. When testifying before the grand jury, however, Mitchell had claimed that he was hardly ever home and he denied observing any such misconduct. Defense counsel sought to introduce at trial the transcript of Mitchell's grand jury testimony instead of calling him as a witness. Though the transcript constituted hearsay, the defendant claimed Mitchell was unavailable and that the transcript was admissible under the former testimony exception to the hearsay rule (which we study in Chapter 3). The trial court denied defendant's request, holding that because the prosecutor did not conduct a searching examination of Mitchell's "superficial" testimony, the former testimony exception did not apply.] The defense then presented its case, including two witnesses who stated that they had never seen appellant engage in sexual acts with the boys in the house and one witness who offered a possible motive for John's instigation of the allegations. The jury found appellant guilty of six counts of sodomy, sixteen counts of indecent liberties, and four counts of enticing a minor child.

II.

[The court first concluded that the hearsay objection should have been overruled because the former testimony exception to the hearsay rule applied, assuming Mitchell was unavailable to testify at trial.]

Absent a judicial finding, as well as a sufficient record to assess unavailability, the question remains whether, assuming unavailability, the exclusion of Oscar Mitchell's grand jury testimony can be upheld on some other basis. The judge based his decision to exclude the evidence on three grounds: the absence of a sufficient opportunity for the government to cross-examine Oscar Mitchell when he appeared before the grand jury, the unreliability of Oscar Mitchell's grand jury testimony, and the likelihood of juror confusion resulting from the inability of the jurors to understand Oscar Mitchell's testimony. . . . [T]hese reasons for exclusion do not withstand scrutiny.

While the trial judge has discretion . . . to exclude otherwise admissible evidence on the grounds that it is not competent, relevant, or conflicts with countervailing evidentiary policy concerns, Oscar Mitchell's grand jury testimony did not present any of these problems. The grand jury testimony was relevant to the material issue of appellant's guilt or innocence. It was also competent evidence if Oscar Mitchell was unavailable. Nevertheless, the trial judge excluded the transcript, concluding that Oscar Mitchell's testimony was unreliable and that the transcript would not provide the jury with a sufficient opportunity to understand his testimony. The judge explained, in denying appellant's motion for a new trial, that when Oscar Mitchell appeared before the grand jury, he made disparaging remarks about homosexuals, and "in every way he seemed bent on distancing himself from the defendant." The judge also found that Oscar Mitchell's denial that he and appellant had a sexual relationship stood in "stark contrast" to the testimony of other government witnesses, who did or would testify to the existence of such a relationship. Finally, the judge cited as evidence of the unreliability of Oscar Mitchell's testimony the fact that he was appellant's roommate and was "living in a house where young boys were allegedly, frequently and routinely molested, [which] would certainly have seriously undercut the proper grand jury testimony." The judge concluded:

Viewing the testimony, even in the light most favorable to the defense, it fails to persuade   me . . . that   it   contained   even   minimal   indicators   of reliability. . . . Especially given what I observed and concluded about the credibility of witnesses presented during the trial. . . .

In varying degrees [the relevant] cases look to the prior proceedings examination, that is cross examination or its equivalent, to assist in establishing a record testimony from which sufficient reliability emerges. In my view Mr. Mitchell's grand jury testimony provided no such assurances.

In [Johns v. United States, 434 A.2d 463, 473 (D.C. App. 1981)], the court cautioned against confusing the discretion that the trial court has with regard to determining whether evidence is admissible with the "'credibility and weight to be assigned to competent and admissible evidence.'" *Id.* (quoting Fowel v. Wood, 62 A.2d 636, 637 (D.C. 1948)). "It is for the jury to decide weight and credibility: 'neither the trial court nor the reviewing court can infringe upon that authority.'" *Id.* (citations omitted). . . . As in *Johns, supra,* 434 A.2d at 473, "we conclude that the trial court impermissibly invaded the province of the jury in excluding the grand jury testimony." Although a witness's credibility before the grand jury may be open to question, as appellant concedes, that question was for the petit jury and not the trial judge to decide. *See* Ballou v. Henri Studios, Inc., 656 F.2d 1147, 1154 (5th Cir. 1981) (trial judge abused discretion in excluding results of blood alcohol test on ground that results conflicted with testimony of another witness; decision "constituted a credibility choice which should properly have been reserved for the jury").

The trial judge's exclusion of the evidence because of "countervailing circumstances" focused on Oscar Mitchell's credibility. In fact, Oscar Mitchell's grand jury testimony was similar to that of Milton Cheeks, a defense witness who had lived in appellant's home and denied having a sexual relationship with him or seeing appellant engage in a sexual relationship with John. That Oscar Mitchell strongly denied that he was a homosexual and that appellant was sexually abusing John, and took some offense at efforts by the grand jury prosecutor to suggest to the contrary, and used the word "faggot," are not proper bases on which to deny appellant the right to present Oscar Mitchell's testimony as part of the defense case to the jury. Nor was it appropriate to exclude the transcript on the ground that witnesses testified appellant was a homosexual and Oscar Mitchell continued to live with him. A review of the grand jury transcript does not reveal that Oscar Mitchell's denials and explanations were inherently incredible or that he lacked an appreciation of the seriousness of the occasion.

[The court then held that the error in excluding Mitchell's testimony was not harmless.]

Accordingly, we hold that unless the defense fails to demonstrate the unavailability of Oscar Mitchell for purposes of the prior recorded testimony exception, the trial judge erred in excluding the grand jury transcript of Oscar Mitchell's testimony. Because the error could not have been harmless, . . . we remand the case to the trial court to make a finding on unavailability. . . .

Further Reading (Prejudicial Evidence): Victor J. Gold, *Limiting Judicial Discretion to Exclude Prejudicial Evidence,* 18 U.C. Davis L. Rev. 59 (1984); Victor J. Gold, *Federal Rule of Evidence 403: Observations on the Nature of Unfairly Prejudicial Evidence,* 58 Wash. L. Rev. 497 (1983); Edward J. Imwinkelried, *The Meaning of Probative Value and Prejudice in Federal Rule of Evidence 403: Can Rule 403 Be Used to Resurrect the Common Law of Evidence?,* 41 Vand. L. Rev. 879 (1988); D. Craig

Lewis, *Proof and Prejudice: A Constitutional Challenge to the Treatment of Prejudicial Evidence in Federal Criminal Cases*, 64 Wash. L. Rev. 289 (1989); J. Alexander Tanford, *A Political-Choice Approach to Limiting Prejudicial Evidence*, 64 Ind. L.J. 831 (1989); Lee E. Teitelbaum et al., *Evaluating the Prejudicial Effect of Evidence: Can Judges Identify the Impact of Improper Evidence on Juries?*, 1983 Wis. L. Rev. 1147.

Further Reading (Discretion in Evidence Rules): David P. Leonard, *Power and Responsibility in Evidence Law*, 63 S. Cal. L. Rev. 937 (1990); Thomas Mengler, *The Theory of Discretion in the Federal Rules of Evidence*, 74 Iowa L. Rev. 413 (1989); Maurice Rosenberg, *Judicial Discretion of the Trial Court, Viewed from Above*, 22 Syracuse L. Rev. 635 (1971); Eleanor Swift, *One Hundred Years of Evidence Law Reform: Thayer's Triumph*, 88 Cal. L. Rev. 2437 (2000); Jon R. Waltz, *Judicial Discretion in the Admission of Evidence Under the Federal Rules of Evidence*, 79 Nw. U. L. Rev. 1097 (1985).

Questions for Classroom Discussion

1. According to the *Feaster* court, how exactly is a trial judge to avoid making determinations of credibility when weighing probative value and prejudicial impact? How can the court determine probative value without deciding whether the evidence is credible?

2. What, exactly, was the trial judge's error in *Feaster*?

3. How should a trial court instruct a jury about its role in determining credibility?

4. Prosecution of Defendant for murder. Defendant claims self-defense. At trial, the prosecution wishes to offer several color photographs of the victim, taken during the autopsy. The photos show the victim's body from several angles, and reveal bullet entry and exit points on the torso and head. Defendant objects to the photos on Rule 403 grounds. How should the court rule? Should it matter that the photos are in color? What if the photos are tight close-ups of the wound and do not show a recognizable location on the body? What if the prosecution introduced a diagram rather than the photos?

5. Same case. The perpetrator had placed the victim's body in a bag and threw the bag in the lake. The body and bag were discovered six months later. The prosecutor offers the bag into evidence. The bag emits a pungent, disturbing odor that can be detected throughout the courtroom. Defendant objects on Rule 403 grounds. How should the court rule?

6. Negligence action by Plaintiff against Defendant following an intersection collision. Prior to trial, Defendant admits negligence and indicates that she will only contest the extent of injury suffered by Plaintiff. At trial, Plaintiff wishes to call a witness to testify that

> Defendant ran the red light, striking Plaintiff's vehicle. Defendant objects on relevance and Rule 403 grounds. How should the court rule?

C. UNDISPUTED FACTS

Suppose a party concedes the existence of a fact constituting an element of the crime or civil claim, but disputes other elements of the case. In a negligence case, for example, the defendant sometimes admits negligence but claims plaintiff suffered considerably less damage than she asserts. In such a case, the trial will focus not on the nature of defendant's conduct, but on the effect that conduct had on plaintiff. Does defendant's concession of negligence render irrelevant (and thus inadmissible) any evidence that would tend to establish such negligence? Under Rule 401, the answer is no. Rule 401 only requires that the evidence tend to prove a fact *of consequence*, not a fact *in controversy*. This differs from some definitions of relevancy under other compilations of evidence law. For example, California Evidence Code § 210 defines relevant evidence as "evidence . . . having any tendency in reason to prove or disprove any *disputed* fact that is of consequence to the determination of the action" (emphasis supplied). Under the California definition, evidence tending to show defendant's negligence would be irrelevant and thus inadmissible. Under Federal Rule 401, the evidence is considered relevant, but that does not mean it is admissible. As we have already seen, under Rule 403 the court may exclude relevant evidence for various reasons, such as unfair prejudice and waste of time.

But if a party wishes to offer evidence on an element of the case that is conceded by the opponent, does this automatically mean it is a waste of time to permit the party to offer the evidence? Suppose Defendant has been charged with the first-degree murder of her husband. Defendant admits killing him, but claims she acted impulsively on learning of her husband's infidelity, making her guilty of manslaughter or a lesser degree of murder. By stipulating to the commission of the act, may Defendant prevent the prosecution from offering any evidence concerning the killing itself? On the one hand, considerable time could be saved by limiting the prosecution's case to evidence bearing on Defendant's state of mind. In addition, limiting the issues could allow the court to minimize the potential for unfair prejudice or distraction of the jury. On the other hand, a fundamental tenet of the adversary system holds that a party should be allowed to prove its case in whatever manner it deems appropriate. In fact, party control over the way evidence is presented is one of the key differences between adversarial and inquisitorial systems. To place limits on a party's otherwise admissible evidence might unduly hamper the operation of the adversary system.

The Supreme Court explained this point in the following case.

OLD CHIEF v. UNITED STATES

519 U.S. 172 (1997)

Justice Souter delivered the opinion of the Court.

Subject to certain limitations, 18 U.S.C. § 922(g)(1) prohibits possession of a firearm by anyone with a prior felony conviction, which the Government can prove by introducing a record of judgment or similar evidence identifying the previous offense. Fearing prejudice if the jury learns the nature of the earlier crime, defendants sometimes seek to avoid such an informative disclosure by offering to concede the fact of the prior conviction. The issue here is whether a district court abuses its discretion if it spurns such an offer and admits the full record of a prior judgment, when the name or nature of the prior offense raises the risk of a verdict tainted by improper considerations, and when the purpose of the evidence is solely to prove the element of prior conviction. We hold that it does.

I

In 1993, petitioner, Old Chief, was arrested after a fracas involving at least one gunshot. The ensuing federal charges included not only assault with a dangerous weapon and using a firearm in relation to a crime of violence but violation of 18 U.S.C. § 922(g)(1). This statute makes it unlawful for anyone "who has been convicted in any court of, a crime punishable by imprisonment for a term exceeding one year" to "possess in or affecting commerce, any firearm. . . ." [Certain crimes are excluded from this definition.]

The earlier crime charged in the indictment against Old Chief was assault causing serious bodily injury. Before trial, he moved for an order requiring the Government "to refrain from mentioning — by reading the Indictment, during jury selection, in opening statement, or closing argument — and to refrain from offering into evidence or soliciting any testimony from any witness regarding the prior criminal convictions of the Defendant, *except* to state that the Defendant has been convicted of a crime punishable by imprisonment exceeding one (1) year." He said that revealing the name and nature of his prior assault conviction would unfairly tax the jury's capacity to hold the Government to its burden of proof beyond a reasonable doubt on current charges of assault, possession, and violence with a firearm, and he offered to "solve the problem here by stipulating, agreeing and requesting the Court to instruct the jury that he has been convicted of a crime punishable by imprisonment exceeding one (1) yea[r]." He argued that the offer to stipulate to the fact of the prior conviction rendered evidence of the name and nature of the offense inadmissible under Rule 403 of the Federal Rules of Evidence, the danger being that unfair prejudice from that evidence would substantially outweigh its probative value. . . .

The Assistant United States Attorney refused to join in a stipulation, insisting on his right to prove his case his own way, and the District Court agreed, ruling orally that, "If he doesn't want to stipulate, he doesn't have to." *Id.*, at 15-16. At trial, over renewed objection, the Government introduced the order of judgment and commitment for Old Chief's prior conviction. This document disclosed that on December 18, 1988, he "did knowingly and unlawfully assault

Rory Dean Fenner, said assault resulting in serious bodily injury," for which Old Chief was sentenced to five years' imprisonment. *Id.*, at 18-19. The jury found Old Chief guilty on all counts, and he appealed.

[The Ninth Circuit affirmed. The Supreme Court granted certiorari to resolve a conflict in the circuits.]

II

A

[The Court first rejected defendant's argument that the name of the prior offense was irrelevant. "[I]ts demonstration was a step on one evidentiary route to the ultimate fact, since it served to place Old Chief within a particular subclass of offenders for whom firearms possession is outlawed by § 922(g)(1). A documentary record of the conviction for that named offense was thus relevant evidence in making Old Chief's § 922(g)(1) status more probable than it would have been without the evidence."]

Nor was its evidentiary relevance under Rule 401 affected by the availability of alternative proofs of the element to which it went, such as an admission by Old Chief that he had been convicted of a crime "punishable by imprisonment for a term exceeding one year" within the meaning of the statute. The 1972 Advisory Committee Notes to Rule 401 make this point directly:

> The fact to which the evidence is directed need not be in dispute. While situations will arise which call for the exclusion of evidence offered to prove a point conceded by the opponent, the ruling should be made on the basis of such considerations as waste of time and undue prejudice (see Rule 403), rather than under any general requirement that evidence is admissible only if directed to matters in dispute. Advisory Committee's Notes on Fed. Rule Evid. 401. . . .

If, then, relevant evidence is inadmissible in the presence of other evidence related to it, its exclusion must rest not on the ground that the other evidence has rendered it "irrelevant," but on its character as unfairly prejudicial, cumulative or the like, its relevance notwithstanding.

B

The principal issue is the scope of a trial judge's discretion under Rule 403. . . . Old Chief relies on the danger of unfair prejudice.

1

The term "unfair prejudice," as to a criminal defendant, speaks to the capacity of some concededly relevant evidence to lure the fact-finder into declaring guilt on a ground different from proof specific to the offense charged. . . . So, the Committee Notes to Rule 403 explain, "'Unfair prejudice' within its context means an undue tendency to suggest decision on an improper basis, commonly, though not necessarily, an emotional one." Advisory Committee's Notes on Fed. Rule Evid. 403. . . .

Such improper grounds certainly include the one that Old Chief points to here: generalizing a defendant's earlier bad act into bad character and taking that as raising the odds that he did the later bad act now charged (or, worse, as calling for preventive conviction even if he should happen to be innocent momentarily). As then-Judge Breyer put it, "Although . . . 'propensity evidence' is relevant, the risk that a jury will convict for crimes other than those charged — or that, uncertain of guilt, it will convict anyway because a bad person deserves punishment — creates a prejudicial effect that outweighs ordinary relevance." United States v. Moccia, 681 F.2d 61, 63 (C.A.1 1982). . . . There is no question that propensity would be an "improper basis" for conviction and that evidence of a prior conviction is subject to analysis under Rule 403 for relative probative value and for prejudicial risk of misuse as propensity evidence. . . .

As for the analytical method to be used in Rule 403 balancing, two basic possibilities present themselves. An item of evidence might be viewed as an island, with estimates of its own probative value and unfairly prejudicial risk the sole reference points in deciding whether the danger substantially outweighs the value and whether the evidence ought to be excluded. Or the question of admissibility might be seen as inviting further comparisons to take account of the full evidentiary context of the case as the court understands it when the ruling must be made. This second approach would start out like the first but be ready to go further. On objection, the court would decide whether a particular item of evidence raised a danger of unfair prejudice. If it did, the judge would go on to evaluate the degrees of probative value and unfair prejudice not only for the item in question but for any actually available substitutes as well. If an alternative were found to have substantially the same or greater probative value but a lower danger of unfair prejudice, sound judicial discretion would discount the value of the item first offered and exclude it if its discounted probative value were substantially outweighed by unfairly prejudicial risk. As we will explain later on, the judge would have to make these calculations with an appreciation of the offering party's need for evidentiary richness and narrative integrity in presenting a case, and the mere fact that two pieces of evidence might go to the same point would not, of course, necessarily mean that only one of them might come in. It would only mean that a judge applying Rule 403 could reasonably apply some discount to the probative value of an item of evidence when faced with less risky alternative proof going to the same point. Even under this second approach, as we explain below, a defendant's Rule 403 objection offering to concede a point generally cannot prevail over the Government's choice to offer evidence showing guilt and all the circumstances surrounding the offense.

The first understanding of the Rule is open to a very telling objection. That reading would leave the party offering evidence with the option to structure a trial in whatever way would produce the maximum unfair prejudice consistent with relevance. He could choose the available alternative carrying the greatest threat of improper influence, despite the availability of less prejudicial but equally probative evidence. The worst he would have to fear would be a ruling sustaining a Rule 403 objection, and if that occurred, he could simply fall back to offering substitute evidence. This would be a strange rule. It would be very odd for the law of evidence to recognize the danger of unfair prejudice only to confer such a degree of autonomy on the party subject to temptation, and the Rules of Evidence are not so odd.

Rather, a reading of the companions to Rule 403, and of the commentaries that went with them to Congress, makes it clear that what counts as the Rule 403 "probative value" of an item of evidence, as distinct from its Rule 401 "relevance," may be calculated by comparing evidentiary alternatives. The Committee Notes to Rule 401 explicitly say that a party's concession is pertinent to the court's discretion to exclude evidence on the point conceded. Such a concession, according to the Notes, will sometimes "call for the exclusion of evidence offered to prove [the] point conceded by the opponent. . . ." Advisory Committee's Notes on Fed. Rule Evid. 401. . . . As already mentioned, the Notes make it clear that such rulings should be made not on the basis of Rule 401 relevance but on "such considerations as waste of time and undue prejudice (see Rule 403). . . ." The Notes to Rule 403 then take up the point by stating that when a court considers "whether to exclude on grounds of unfair prejudice," the "availability of other means of proof may . . . be an appropriate factor." Advisory Committee's Notes on Fed. Rule Evid. 403. . . . The point gets a reprise in the Notes to Rule 404(b), dealing with admissibility when a given evidentiary item has the dual nature of legitimate evidence of an element and illegitimate evidence of character: "No mechanical solution is offered. The determination must be made whether the danger of undue prejudice outweighs the probative value of the evidence in view of the availability of other means of proof and other facts appropriate for making decision[s] of this kind under 403." Advisory Committee's Notes on Fed. Rule Evid. 404. . . . Thus the notes leave no question that when Rule 403 confers discretion by providing that evidence "may" be excluded, the discretionary judgment may be informed not only by assessing an evidentiary item's twin tendencies, but by placing the result of that assessment alongside similar assessments of evidentiary alternatives. . . .

2

In dealing with the specific problem raised by § 922(g)(1) and its prior-conviction element, there can be no question that evidence of the name or nature of the prior offense generally carries a risk of unfair prejudice to the defendant. That risk will vary from case to case, for the reasons already given, but will be substantial whenever the official record offered by the Government would be arresting enough to lure a juror into a sequence of bad character reasoning. Where a prior conviction was for a gun crime or one similar to other charges in a pending case the risk of unfair prejudice would be especially obvious, and Old Chief sensibly worried that the prejudicial effect of his prior assault conviction, significant enough with respect to the current gun charges alone, would take on added weight from the related assault charge against him.

The District Court was also presented with alternative, relevant, admissible evidence of the prior conviction by Old Chief's offer to stipulate, evidence necessarily subject to the District Court's consideration on the motion to exclude the record offered by the Government. . . .

Old Chief's proffered admission would, in fact, have been not merely relevant but seemingly conclusive evidence of the element. . . . As a consequence, although the name of the prior offense may have been technically relevant, it addressed no detail in the definition of the prior-conviction element that would not have been covered by the stipulation or admission. Logic, then, seems to side with Old Chief.

3

There is, however, one more question to be considered before deciding whether Old Chief's offer was to supply evidentiary value at least equivalent to what the Government's own evidence carried. In arguing that the stipulation or admission would not have carried equivalent value, the Government invokes the familiar, standard rule that the prosecution is entitled to prove its case by evidence of its own choice, or, more exactly, that a criminal defendant may not stipulate or admit his way out of the full evidentiary force of the case as the Government chooses to present it. . . .

This is unquestionably true as a general matter. The "fair and legitimate weight" of conventional evidence showing individual thoughts and acts amounting to a crime reflects the fact that making a case with testimony and tangible things not only satisfies the formal definition of an offense, but tells a colorful story with descriptive richness. Unlike an abstract premise, whose force depends on going precisely to a particular step in a course of reasoning, a piece of evidence may address any number of separate elements, striking hard just because it shows so much at once; the account of a shooting that establishes capacity and causation may tell just as much about the triggerman's motive and intent. Evidence thus has force beyond any linear scheme of reasoning, and as its pieces come together a narrative gains momentum, with power not only to support conclusions but to sustain the willingness of jurors to draw the inferences, whatever they may be, necessary to reach an honest verdict. This persuasive power of the concrete and particular is often essential to the capacity of jurors to satisfy the obligations that the law places on them. . . .

In sum, the accepted rule that the prosecution is entitled to prove its case free from any defendant's option to stipulate the evidence away rests on good sense. A syllogism is not a story, and a naked proposition in a courtroom may be no match for the robust evidence that would be used to prove it. People who hear a story interrupted by gaps of abstraction may be puzzled at the missing chapters, and jurors asked to rest a momentous decision on the story's truth can feel put upon at being asked to take responsibility knowing that more could be said than they have heard. A convincing tale can be told with economy, but when economy becomes a break in the natural sequence of narrative evidence, an assurance that the missing link is really there is never more than second best.

4

This recognition that the prosecution with its burden of persuasion needs evidentiary depth to tell a continuous story has, however, virtually no application when the point at issue is a defendant's legal status, dependent on some judgment rendered wholly independently of the concrete events of later criminal behavior charged against him. As in this case, the choice of evidence for such an element is usually not between eventful narrative and abstract proposition, but between propositions of slightly varying abstraction, either a record saying that conviction for some crime occurred at a certain time or a statement admitting the same thing without naming the particular offense. The issue of substituting one statement for the other normally arises only when the record of conviction would not be admissible for any purpose beyond proving status, so that excluding it would not deprive the prosecution of evidence with multiple utility; if, indeed, there were a justification for receiving evidence of the nature of prior acts on some issue other than status (i.e., to prove "motive, opportunity, intent, preparation, plan, knowledge, identity, or absence of mistake or accident," Fed. Rule Evid. 404(b)), Rule 404(b) guarantees the opportunity to seek its admission. Nor can it be argued that the events behind the prior conviction are proper nourishment for the jurors' sense of obligation to vindicate the public interest. The issue is not whether concrete details of the prior crime should come to the jurors' attention but whether the name or general character of that crime is to be disclosed. Congress, however, has made it plain that distinctions among generic felonies do not count for this purpose; the fact of the qualifying conviction is alone what matters under the statute. . . . Proving status without telling exactly why that status was imposed leaves no gap in the story of a defendant's subsequent criminality, and its demonstration by stipulation or admission neither displaces a chapter from a continuous sequence of conventional evidence nor comes across as an officious substitution, to confuse or offend or provoke reproach.

Given these peculiarities of the element of felony-convict status and of admissions and the like when used to prove it, there is no cognizable difference between the evidentiary significance of an admission and of the legitimately probative component of the official record the prosecution would prefer to place in evidence. For purposes of the Rule 403 weighing of the probative against the prejudicial, the functions of the competing evidence are distinguishable only by the risk inherent in the one and wholly absent from the other. In this case, as in any other in which the prior conviction is for an offense likely to support conviction on some improper ground, the only reasonable conclusion was that the risk of unfair prejudice did substantially outweigh the discounted probative value of the record of conviction, and it was an abuse of discretion to admit the record when an admission was available.[10] What we have said shows why this will be the general rule when proof of convict status is at issue, just as the prosecutor's choice will generally survive a Rule 403 analysis when a defendant seeks to force the substitution of an admission for evidence creating a coherent narrative of his thoughts and actions in perpetrating the offense for which he is being tried.

The judgment is reversed, and the case is remanded to the Ninth Circuit for further proceedings consistent with this opinion.[11]

It is so ordered.

[Justice O'CONNOR dissented in an opinion joined by THE CHIEF JUSTICE, Justice SCALIA, and Justice THOMAS.]

---

10. There may be yet other means of proof besides a formal admission on the record that, with a proper objection, will obligate a district court to exclude evidence of the name of the offense. A redacted record of conviction is the one most frequently mentioned. Any alternative will, of course, require some jury instruction to explain it (just as it will require some discretion when the indictment is read). A redacted judgment in this case, for example, would presumably have revealed to the jury that Old Chief was previously convicted in federal court and sentenced to more than a year's imprisonment, but it would not have shown whether his previous conviction was for one of the business offenses that do not count, under § 921(a)(20). Hence, an instruction, with the defendant's consent, would be necessary to make clear that the redacted judgment was enough to satisfy the status element remaining in the case. The Government might, indeed, propose such a redacted judgment for the trial court to weigh against a defendant's offer to admit, as indeed the Government might do even if the defendant's admission had been received into evidence.

11. In remanding, we imply no opinion on the possibility of harmless error, an issue not passed upon below.

Questions for Classroom Discussion

1. As the *Old Chief* opinion points out, relevant evidence as defined in Rule 401 includes evidence offered to prove a fact that is not in dispute. In this sense, the rule differs from the definition of relevant evidence in other rules, including California Evidence Code § 210, which defines as relevant any evidence that has "any tendency in reason to prove or disprove any disputed fact that is of consequence to the determination of the action." What is the justification for the Federal Rules definition?

2. What did the Court in *Old Chief* mean by "evidentiary richness" in comparing alternate ways to prove facts?

3. Why didn't that principle apply to the facts of *Old Chief*?

4. Prosecution of Defendant for bank robbery. Defendant admits to being the person who approached a teller, pointed a shotgun at him, and threatened to kill him if he did not empty his cash drawer into a bag and hand it over. Defendant claims, however, that she had been kidnapped by the other robbers, and that they threatened to kill her if she did not help them rob the bank. At trial, the prosecution wishes to call the bank teller referred to above to describe Defendant's actions. Defendant offers to stipulate to all the facts to which the teller will testify. The prosecution refuses Defendant's offered stipulation. Defendant objects. How should the court rule?

D. PROBABILISTIC EVIDENCE

We cannot prove facts with certainty. Even in the ideal case where multiple eyewitnesses emphatically testify to the same version of an event and there is no conflicting evidence, there is still a chance that the witnesses are all mistaken or lying.[5] And the vast majority of cases are far from ideal, featuring evidence that is sparse, ambiguous, of dubious credibility, and in conflict. As a consequence, the most we can expect from evidence is that it tells us something about the probabilities of the pertinent facts. Thus, Rule 401 incorporates the concept of probability into the very definition of relevant evidence: Evidence is relevant if it makes a fact of consequence "more or less probable." Our inability to establish facts with certainty also explains why we are forced to decide lawsuits based on standards such as preponderance of the evidence or beyond a reasonable doubt. These descriptions of burden of proof are merely statements of probability—procedural acquiescence to the inescapable reality that we cannot be certain about the facts.

---

5. In fact, psychologists have shown that eyewitnesses are especially prone to make mistakes in certain situations. *See, e.g.*, Elizabeth Loftus, Eyewitness Testimony (1979).

Lay witnesses frequently testify in probabilistic terms, but are forced by the limits of perception and language to describe probabilities imprecisely. For example, an eyewitness to a crime might testify he is "pretty certain" the defendant is the person he saw commit the crime. But as the ability of modern technology to store and process data grows, it is more common to encounter evidence in the form of a seemingly more precise mathematical statement of probability. Evidence in this form can be valuable not just because it might be more precise, but also because it can assemble a large mass of data in a way that no reasonable number of eyewitnesses could ever describe. For example, laboratory tests can show that a DNA sample taken from the accused has characteristics that precisely match DNA found at a crime scene. A collection of the results of many such tests might show that only one person in a billion has such characteristics.

Probabilistic evidence often is presented in the form of an expert's opinion concerning the meaning of a large mass of data. For example, in employment discrimination cases the most important issue often is whether defendant intended to discriminate on a prohibited basis, such as race or gender. Of course, only the defendant directly perceives his or her own state of mind and typically will deny having the prohibited intention. But statistical evidence accumulating hundreds of employment decisions over the course of years can provide powerful circumstantial evidence of discriminatory intent. This happens when a certain variable, such as race, is correlated with certain employment decisions, such as hiring or promotion. Where the correlation is high, experts may testify that there is a high probability that the decisions were influenced by race.

While probabilistic evidence can be powerful, it presents dangers. The accuracy of the underlying data might be dubious and the manner in which it is assembled might be statistically invalid. Even if the evidence is reliable, it can overwhelm other compelling evidence and can even obscure the meaning of the applicable burden of proof. And because the evidence is often expressed in numerical terms, it can be manipulated in ways that might be difficult for lay juries to understand and weigh against the more familiar defects of conventional evidence.

Perhaps the simplest type of statistical evidence is based on the frequency with which two or more independent events or things can be expected to coincide. For example, if you flip a coin, there are two possible outcomes: heads or tails. And assuming the coin has not been altered and that you have not mastered a technique that allows you to control the outcome, each time you flip the coin, there is a 50 percent chance of getting heads and a 50 percent chance of getting tails. Because the outcome of one flip is independent of the outcome of another flip, we can express the probability of achieving two heads in a row as the product of the probabilities of each flip. To put it simply, the chance of flipping two heads in a row is 50% × 50%, or 25%. The chance of getting three heads in a row is 50% × 50% × 50%, or 12.5%. This is an application of what is known as the *product rule*, and it applies to any set of independent events. Thus, the probability of several things occurring together is the product of their separate probabilities.

Over the years, we have seen many students shudder when we use mathematical formulas in class. We know you didn't go to law school to do math, but the product rule is really quite simple, and you can demonstrate its validity to yourself. Think about the possible *combined* outcomes when you flip a coin twice. You should realize that there are four (H stands for heads, T for tails):

First Flip	Second Flip
T	T
T	H
H	H
H	T

Each of these four outcomes is equally probable. Thus, the chance of getting two heads in a row is one in four. Now imagine three flips. You should be able to count eight possible combined outcomes:

First Flip	Second Flip	Third Flip
H	H	H
H	H	T
H	T	H
H	T	T
T	T	T
T	T	H
T	H	T
T	H	H

From this chart, you can see that the probability of achieving three heads in a row is one in eight.

Now consider two different events. Let's say you have a coin and a six-sided die. You toss them both onto a table. What is the chance you will get heads and a six? The chance of that outcome is the product of the probability of the separate outcomes. Because the probability of getting heads is one in two, and the probability of rolling a six is one in six, there is a one in twelve chance ($1/2 \times 1/6 = 1/12$) of getting heads and a six.

The product rule works simply and easily with things like coins and dice. But what about the types of events that become the subjects of judicial trials? Does the product rule have a place in criminal cases? The following Questions for Classroom Discussion are designed to test the possible application of the product rule in that context. The questions are also designed to get you thinking about the meaning of statistical evidence and its possible effects on the jury.

Questions for Classroom Discussion

1. Prosecution for bank robbery. Eyewitnesses testify that the two perpetrators were a black man with a shaved head, beard, and mustache and a Caucasian woman with blonde hair and blue eyes. The two defendants have these characteristics. The prosecutor then calls a mathematician to testify as an expert. The prosecutor states, "Assume one in ten men has a shaved head, one in four men

have a mustache, one in ten have a beard, one in three women are blond, one in ten women have blue eyes, and one of every thousand couples are interracial. What is the probability of finding a couple that reflect all these characteristics?" The witness answers, "One in twelve million." Is the expert's math correct?

2. Same case. Is there a problem with the prosecutor's assumptions?

3. Same case. Is there any problem calculating probability in this manner? If one in three women is blond and one in ten women has blue eyes, does that mean that one in thirty women has blond hair and blue eyes?

4. Same case. Assume defense counsel finds one other couple with all the characteristics of the perpetrators. Does that mean that the probability defendants are guilty is one in two?

5. Rape prosecution. The victim testifies the perpetrator was a Hispanic male, but can offer no other description. Defendant is a Hispanic male. A blood sample taken from defendant reveals six DNA characteristics that match those present in a semen stain found on the victim's clothing. An FBI database collecting data from several hundred DNA samples of men of various races and ethnic backgrounds shows the following probabilities for the six characteristics: one in five, one in twenty, one in ten, one in two, one in fifty, and one in seven. An expert witness testifies that this means the probability of a single person having all these characteristics is one in 700,000. Assume the technology for proving a DNA match is reliable. If you are defense counsel, how might you attack the evidence?

ADAMS v. AMERITECH SERVICES, INC.

231 F.3d 414 (7th Cir. 2000)

Diane P. Wood, Circuit Judge.

Throughout the decade of the 1990s, corporate downsizing was a popular strategy for companies that believed they had become indolent, complacent, inefficient, or otherwise unsuited to the ever-increasing pace of competition in their markets. Ameritech Corporation was no exception. With the advent of more competition in the telecommunications market and the promise of much more change to come in the near future . . . its management came to the conclusion in 1992 that drastic measures were necessary if it was to succeed in its new environment. And drastic measures were taken. Both Ameritech Services, Inc. (ASI), a company jointly owned by Ameritech's five independent operating companies, and Indiana Bell Telephone Company, one of those operating companies, slashed their middle management ranks dramatically as part of a comprehensive restructuring and reduction in force.

. . . [P]laintiffs remaining on appeal claim principally that both ASI and Indiana Bell discriminated against them on the basis of age, in violation of the Age Discrimination in Employment Act (ADEA), §§ 29 U.S.C. 621 et seq., and that both companies violated their rights under sections 502 and 503 of the Employee Retirement Income Security Act (ERISA), §§ 29 U.S.C. 1132, 1133. . . .

With the exception of some incidental issues, the district court disposed of all the claims in a series of orders granting summary judgment for the defendants. It then certified those orders as final for purposes of appeal under Fed. R. Civ. P. 54(b). While we appreciate the herculean efforts the district court made to wade through the voluminous materials on summary judgment that both sides presented, we conclude that the plaintiffs presented enough evidence to withstand the defendants' motions. We therefore reverse and remand for further proceedings. . . .

Richard Notebaert became ASI's president in June of 1992, at a time when Ameritech as a whole was seeking to improve its competitiveness. Shortly before Notebaert took over his new job, Ameritech's operating committee began to discuss what it perceived as a surplus of employees, and it began to explore with ASI what to do about it. It contacted the other Bell operating companies and concluded that they too had a surplus. Both ASI and Indiana Bell (along with the other operating companies) decided that they had to undertake a significant management workforce reduction—in plain English, they had to get rid of large numbers of managers, either by persuasion or by force. . . .

The principal theories on which both sets of plaintiffs rely relate to the way in which the lay-offs were orchestrated and the interrelation between those selected for termination and their age and pension status (which the plaintiffs assert created a strong financial incentive to terminate people below the chronological age thresholds set by the Plan). . . .

A. AGE DISCRIMINATION CLAIMS

1. LEGAL STANDARDS FOR PROOF

The Supreme Court's most recent pronouncement on the legal standards a plaintiff must meet in order to prove a case of age discrimination appears in Reeves v. Sanderson Plumbing Products, Inc., 530 U.S. 133, 120 S. Ct. 2097, 147 L. Ed. 2d 105 (2000). In *Reeves*, the Court began by reiterating that in such cases, "liability depends on whether the protected trait (under the ADEA, age) actually motivated the employer's decision." *Id.* at 2105, *quoting* Hazen Paper Co. v. Biggins, 507 U.S. 604, 610, 113 S. Ct. 1701, 123 L. Ed. 2d 338 (1993). That is, it continued, "the plaintiff's age must have actually played a role in [the employer's decision-making] process and had a determinative influence on the outcome." 120 S. Ct. at 2105, *quoting Hazen Paper* at 610, 113 S. Ct. 1701 (bracketed text in *Reeves*). . . .

2. USE OF STATISTICAL EVIDENCE

At the threshold, the defendants have questioned whether statistical evidence as a whole can ever be useful in a case alleging disparate treatment or a discriminatory pattern or practice, as opposed to a disparate impact case. The short answer is yes: statistical evidence can be very useful to prove discrimination in either or both of those two kinds of cases, but it will likely not be sufficient in itself. *See generally* David C. Baldus and James W.L. Cole, Statistical Proof of Discrimination, §§ 9.02, 9.42 (1980). The Supreme Court discussed the use of statistical evidence in a pattern or practice case in Hazelwood School District v. United States, 433 U.S. 299, 97 S. Ct. 2736, 53 L. Ed. 2d 768 (1977), in which the Court approved of the use of statistics to help show that the school district was discriminating on the basis of race in its faculty hiring decisions. *See id.* at 307, 97 S. Ct. 2736. *Hazelwood* also underscored the importance of looking to the proper "community" or group when making statistical comparisons. . . .

The Court returned to the topic of statistics in Bazemore v. Friday, 478 U.S. 385, 106 S. Ct. 3000, 92 L. Ed. 2d 315 (1986). *Bazemore* involved both a pattern or practice claim brought by the United States and individual plaintiffs' discrimination claims, all arising out of alleged racial discrimination in employment and the provision of services by the North Carolina Agricultural Extension Service. The court of appeals had rejected the plaintiffs' statistical evidence because it had not taken into account every factor that might have affected the employees' salary levels. The Supreme Court disagreed, holding both that the statistical study should have been admitted and that "[n]ormally, failure to include variables will affect the analysis' probativeness, not its admissibility." *Id.* at 400, 106 S. Ct. 3000. The Court also noted that the statistical evidence had to be evaluated in the light of the remaining evidence in the record.

Studies in employment discrimination cases typically begin by defining the relevant labor market, and then ask what the results would be for the salient variable (. . . age in our case) if there were no discrimination. That is called the "null hypothesis." If the relevant market is 40% African-American, for instance, one would expect 40% of hires to be African-American under the null hypothesis. If the observed percentage of African-American hires is only 20%, then the statistician will compute the "standard deviation" from the expected norm and indicate how likely it is that race played no part in the decisionmaking. Two standard deviations is normally enough to show that it is extremely unlikely (that is, there is less than a 5% probability) that the disparity is due to chance, giving rise to a reasonable inference that the hiring was not race-neutral; the more standard deviations away, the less likely the factor in question played no role in the decisionmaking process. . . .

3.   EXCLUSION OF WERTHEIMER REPORTS

We are now in a position to consider whether . . . the statistical evidence plaintiffs have offered in the two cases before us (coupled with the other evidence they presented) was sound enough methodologically (i.e., reliable enough) and relevant, such that the district court should have taken it into account in evaluating their claim. Several points are important to bear in mind. First, the question before us is not whether the reports proffered by the plaintiffs prove the entire case; it is whether they were prepared in a reliable and statistically sound way, such that they contained relevant evidence that a trier of fact would have been entitled to consider. No one piece of evidence has to prove every element of the plaintiffs' case; it need only make the existence of "any fact that is of consequence" more or less probable. *See* Fed. R. Evid. 401. *See also, e.g.,* United States v. Porter, 881 F.2d 878, 887 (10th Cir. 1989) ("'An item of evidence, being but a single link in the chain of proof, need not prove conclusively the proposition for which it is offered. . . . It is enough if the item could reasonably show that a fact is slightly more probable than it would appear without that evidence. . . . A brick is not a wall.'"), *quoting* McCormick on Evidence, § 185 at 542-43 (E. Cleary 3d ed. 1984) (footnotes omitted). Put a little differently, the issue is whether the criticisms of the Wertheimer reports and the plaintiffs' other statistical evidence affected the admissibility of those materials, or only, as the Supreme Court put it in *Bazemore*, their "probativeness" or weight. . . .

What Wertheimer did, briefly put, was to examine the correlations that existed between the ages of employees and the companies' decisions to terminate. What he did not do (and, as far as we can tell, what the defendants' experts did not do either) was to run a multiple-regression analysis that would have isolated the relevance of age as a factor in the companies' decisions. While this omission strikes us as odd, we are not prepared to hold as a matter of law that nothing but regression analyses can produce evidence that [is admissible]. Statisticians might have good reasons to look at data in different ways. (For example, as additional variables are introduced into a regression, the less likely it is that any of them will be statistically significant, a fact that causes its own problems.) We thus evaluate here what Wertheimer did, rather than hypothetical tests that he or another expert might have done. . . .

We summarize here Wertheimer's findings at each of those levels. After making some comparisons between the age profile of ASI's workforce as a whole and that of the entire country (which we do not find particularly useful and thus disregard), he calculated the termination rates of employees by age. He did this by dividing the number of terminated workers in each age category by the number of workers in that category before the terminations. The results for the November 1992 terminations were as follows:

Age 30: 6.2%	Age 45–49: 12.6%
Age 30–34: 9.9%	Age 50–54: 12.5%
Age 35–39: 9.9%	Age 55–59: 9.5%
Age 40–44: 10.5%	Age 60–64: 26.3%

Table D-2, Wertheimer Report.

Another way he reviewed the same data was to compare the share of terminations accounted for by employees at least age 40 with the share of the under-40 group: the former accounted for 62.6% of the 1992 terminations, even though they were only 58.1% of the workforce. For the 1993 terminations, the differences were greater: employees at least 40 accounted for 79.3% of the terminations, but only 61.3% of the workforce. Last, in this report he considered the way that the selection process worked to see how the designation of the at risk employees in Stage 1 and the termination candidates at Stage 2 correlated to age. At Stage 1, the selection rate for the under-40 employees was 28.6%, and for the older employees it was 35.3%; at Stage 2 the selection rate for the younger group was 38.1%, compared with 46.7% for the older employees. These differences exceeded two standard deviations and, Wertheimer concluded, were thus statistically significant. (By that, he meant that the probability that the difference would have been observed even if the hypothesis being tested were false is less than 5%. Most likely, some other factor — perhaps age, perhaps something else correlated to age — explains at least some of the difference.) . . .

There is far more detail in the record, but this description is enough to give an idea of what Wertheimer was doing. The district court found his reports inadmissible for several reasons: . . . (2) the reports only showed that the difference in treatment between the over and under 40 aged individuals was not due to chance, but they did not affirmatively indicate what caused that difference; (3) the analysis did not take into account or control for other non-age related variables. . . . The theme of numbers two and three was that Wertheimer's analysis, standing alone, was not enough to show that age was the reason why ASI and Indiana Bell took the actions that they did. That much is true; the statistical analyses were enough to rule out chance, but the real reason for the decisions may have been age or it may have been some other factor or factors positively correlated with both advancing age and the likelihood of termination. But ruling out chance was an important step in the plaintiffs' proof, even if it was not a single leap from the starting line to the finish line. If this is all the plaintiffs had introduced, we would agree with the district court that the record would have supported summary judgment against them. It was not, however, and in our view the other items of evidence, if believed by a jury, could have done the rest of the job: that is, it could have ruled out factors other than age.

Questions for Classroom Discussion

1. Action for employment discrimination on the basis of race. Plaintiffs are African-American teachers who applied for positions with Defendant school district but were not hired. Plaintiffs tender evidence that over the preceding five years only 3 percent of Defendant's employment offers were extended to African-American applicants. Is this relevant to show intent to discriminate if Plaintiffs prove that 10 percent of the student population in the district is African American?

2. Same case. Plaintiffs tender evidence that over the preceding five years only 3 percent of Defendant's employment offers were extended to African-American applicants while 10 percent of the applicant pool for those positions was African American. An expert testifies that these data indicate there is a high probability racial discrimination was a motivating factor in Defendant's employment decisions. Assume Plaintiffs fail to offer any evidence concerning the relative qualifications of the African-American applicants. Are the data and the expert's opinion relevant to show intent to discriminate?

3. Assuming the evidence in Question 2 is relevant, would it be sufficient to sustain a judgment for Plaintiffs?

While evidence stated in probabilistic terms certainly can be relevant, the question remains whether that evidence can be stated in ways that provide the trier of fact with the means to determine the probability of issues such as guilt or innocence with a relatively high degree of precision and confidence. Some scholars and a few courts think that, through the application of a formula called Bayes' Theorem, the answer is yes.

DAVID H. KAYE, SCIENCE IN EVIDENCE
28-29 (1997)

This theorem involves three quantities—the "prior odds" in favor of some hypothesis H (which we may denote as Odds(H)), the "likelihood ratio" (LR), which states how many times more probable the new evidence E is when H is true than when H is false, and the "posterior odds" (given the new evidence) that H is true. According to Bayes' theorem, the posterior odds are simply the product of the likelihood ratio and the prior odds:

$$Odds(H/E) = LR \times Odds(H)$$

. . . For example, if there are exactly 100 individuals who might have committed a murder and each one is equally likely to be the murderer, then the prior odds on the hypothesis H that the defendant is the murderer are Odds(H) = 1 to 99. (There is one murderer and 99 innocent people in the suspect population.) If evidence E is introduced to show that the murderer left a bloodstain of a type that occurs in a population like that of the suspects only once in every 5000 people, and if defendant's blood is of this type, then it is 5000 times more likely that the murderer would have the incriminating type than an innocent suspect, so LR = 5000. Therefore, the evidence shifts the odds from the prior level of 1 to 99 to the posterior level of 5000×1 to $99 = 5000$ to 99—just over 50 to 1.

RICHARD E. MYERS II, DETECTOR DOGS AND PROBABLE CAUSE
14 Geo. Mason L. Rev. 1, 13-15 (2006)

Bayes' Theorem [is] a formula commonly used by medical doctors and scientists for taking proper account of new information, such as that provided by laboratory tests. It tells us, through a little calculation, how strong our belief should be that a particular fact or condition exists, if we are given a new piece of information to add to what we knew before. Or, in the language of statisticians, the formula allows the user to update their beliefs about certain events in light of new information.

[For example, applying] Bayes' Theorem debunks the common fallacy that an alert by a dog with a ninety percent success rate means there is a ninety percent chance that this particular vehicle contains the controlled substance. In fact, that conclusion could not be further from the truth. Yet, as the literature and the cases confirm, such a conclusion is a widely held and intuitive misconception. It should not be surprising that unless the dog is perfect, the test only increases the likelihood that there are drugs present; it does not establish it. We do not expect a ninety percent accurate test to leave us with a one hundred percent conviction that there are drugs present. But that ninety percent accurate test increases the likelihood that drugs are present far less than most people think. If the probability was low to begin with, even a really good test will still result in a relatively low number.

Imagine that a deputy sheriff has made a stop, and while he is writing the driver of the car a ticket, a colleague runs this ninety percent successful dog around the car. The handler has not talked to the other deputy at all about the stop, the reasons for it, the driver's demeanor, story, or other conditions. The dog alerts at the trunk, scratching vigorously as it has been trained to do in the presence of cocaine or marijuana. Knowing nothing else about the driver and her demeanor, what are the odds that the trunk in fact contains an illegal drug? Despite what your instincts may tell you, there is not a ninety percent chance that there will be drugs in the car. To get the true number, we need to know more.

To see how the error rate of dog alerts alters the probable cause calculation, one needs to understand some statistics. Bayes' Theorem provides a framework for this analysis. As stated above, Bayes' Theorem is concerned with updating beliefs about certain events in light of new information. That sounds technical, so consider the following example. Suppose the police, because of prior experiences, believe that one out of fifty stopped cars will contain drugs. In other words, the police officer's original assessment is that two percent of the cars stopped will possess drugs. . . . Suppose, then, that the dog alerts after the car is stopped. The legal question is whether the dog alert alone is enough to justify a search. This depends on the dog's error rate coupled with the officer's original assessment of guilt. Take first the error rate. The dog might commit two types of errors. First, the dog might fail to alert when there are drugs in the car. Second, the dog might alert when there are no drugs in the car. Assume that the dog is pretty good. He fails to alert in the presence of drugs only five percent of the time. Put another way, he has a five percent false negative rate. He alerts when drugs are not present ten percent of the time. He has a ten percent false positive rate.

For our purposes, the important number is the false positives. What we want to know is the probability the car contains drugs conditional on (or in light of) the dog alert. Given this information, Bayes' Theorem tells us the chance that the dog alert is correct and the person stopped has drugs. The formula and computation follow: First, some notation for the mathematically inclined. Let P [not equal | guilty] equal the probability the dog commits the first type of error — 5 percent. [This also means] the dog correctly alerts in the presence of drugs 95 percent of time. So, P [alert | guilty] = .95. Let P [alert | innocent] equal the probability the dog commits the second type of error — 10 percent. Hence, P [not alert | innocent] = .90.

Finally, we need the background expectations. Let P[guilty] = .02 represent the original assessment of guilt and P[innocent] = .98 represent the original assessment of innocence.

$$\frac{P[alert|guilty]P[guilty]}{P[alert|guilty]P[guilty] + P[alert|innocent]P[innocent]}$$
$$= \frac{(.95)(.02)}{(.95)(.02) + (.10)(.98)}$$
$$= .162393$$

With a pretty good dog, but a largely innocent population, a dog alert will signal drugs only about sixteen percent of the time. The reason is this: Because the officer is stopping mostly innocent people, one has to be more concerned about the false positive error (alerting when there are no drugs). Because there are more cars without drugs in them, the gross number of searches that result from the error rate will be higher than the gross number of searches that result from correct alerts. Overall, there will be many more searches of innocent people than there will be searches of guilty people.

UNITED STATES v. SHONUBI
895 F. Supp. 460 (E.D.N.Y. 1995)

WEINSTEIN, Senior District Judge.

A judge, in the position of fact-finder, enters the courtroom in much the same position as a juror. Early on, he or she may form an opinion of the likelihood that a proposition is true. This perceived likelihood then rises and falls as each item of evidence is introduced. Despite admonitions not to "decide" until all of the evidence is in, triers tend to keep a running estimate of probabilities.

As Professor David Schum has noted:

> [T]he structure of arguments we make from evidence [has] to undergo revision if we are to keep abreast of recognized changes in the world. Structural revisions . . . involve changes in our hypotheses or possible conclusions, changes in our assumptions, premises and generalizations, and, of course, changes in the amount and kind of evidence we obtain.

1 David Schum, Evidence and Inference for the Intelligence Analyst 318 (1987), *quoted in* Peter Tillers, Webs of Things in the Mind: A New Science of Evidence, 87 Mich. L. Rev. 1225, 1250 (1989).

Bayes' Theorem is useful in describing this dynamic process. Analysis begins with a "subjective probability" — the fact-finder's "opening" estimate of the likelihood of the end proposition. After each item of proof is introduced, this "subjective probability" is recalculated based on the degree to which the new evidence supports or contradicts the proposition to be proven. This recalculated probability is then treated as a "prior" assessment in processing a further item of proof, and so on. The calculation is repeated over and over, until all the items in a line of proof have been considered. The end result of all these calculations is called a "posterior probability" — a judgment accounting for each successive element of proof. . . .

These ideas have traveled from the university to the courtroom as judges have observed that, among academicians, "Bayes' Theorem . . . is practically universally accepted as valid." State v. Spann, 130 N.J. 484, 505, 617 A.2d 247 (N.J. 1993) (applying Bayesian analysis to paternity determination); *see also* State v. Klindt, 389 N.W.2d 670 (Iowa 1986) (statistical evidence properly used, in conjunction with non-statistical evidence, to prove identity of mutilated body). *But see* State v. Skipper, 228 Conn. 610, 637 A.2d 1101 (1994) (criticizing application of Bayes' Theorem in paternity hearing), discussed in Ronald J. Allen et al., Probability and Proof in State v. Skipper: An Internet Exchange, 35 Jurimetrics Journal 277 (1995).

The problem for the courts is not so much whether this type of analysis is valid, but how to make it comprehensible to the trier. . . . Research on the utility of explicit Bayesianism in jury trials remains "in an incunabular phase." D.H. Kaye & Jonathan J. Koehler, Can Jurors Understand Probabilistic Evidence?, 154 J. Royal Stat. Soc'y (A), 75, 80 (1991).

Professors Finkelstein and Fairley wisely advocate the application of Bayes' Theorem primarily to cases in which a probability assessment based on non-mathematical evidence is modified by the later introduction of explicitly quantitative proof. In fact, they have argued that Bayes' Theorem is most useful where statistical evidence is "added to the mix" after "particularistic" evidence has already been considered. In such situations, they believe, "Bayesian analysis would demonstrate that the evidentiary weight of an impressive figure like one in a thousand—which might otherwise exercise an undue influence—would depend on the other evidence in the case, and might well be relatively insignificant if the prior suspicion were sufficiently weak." Finkelstein & Fairley, *supra*, at 514. If, by contrast, the probability of guilt based on the initial, non-statistical evidence is high, jurors may be surprised at the strength of the inference of guilt flowing from the combination of their prior suspicions and the statistical evidence. But this, if the suspicions are correctly estimated, is no more than the evidence deserves.

It is possible to accept the validity of Bayes' Theorem as a guide to, and description of, decision-making, without attempting the complex calculations literal application of the Theorem would require. Bayes' Theorem is useful, even without quantification, to explain how triers think. . . . As utilized subconsciously by laypersons—or even consciously by judges—to structure their decision-making, Bayes' Theorem is often not a mathematical formula but a heuristic device.

Further Reading: Ronald J. Allen, *Rationality, Mythology, and the Acceptability of Verdicts Thesis*, 66 B.U. L. Rev. 541 (1986); L. Jonathan Cohen, *Subjective Probability and the Paradox of the Gatecrasher*, 1981 Ariz. St. L.J. 635; Michael O. Finkelstein & William B. Fairley, *A Bayesian Approach to Identification Evidence*, 83 Harv. L. Rev. 489 (1970); Charles Nesson, *Agent Orange Meets the Blue Bus: Factfinding at the Frontier of Knowledge*, 66 B.U. L. Rev. 521 (1986); Charles Nesson, *The Evidence or the Event? On Judicial Proof and the Acceptability of Verdicts*, 98 Harv. L. Rev. 1357 (1985); Laurence Tribe, *Trial by Mathematics: Precision and Ritual in the Legal Process*, 84 Harv. L. Rev. 1329 (1971); Symposium, *Probability and Inference in the Law of Evidence*, 66 B.U. L. Rev. 377 (1986).

Question for Classroom Discussion

Civil action to recover child support. Plaintiff, the mother, alleges Defendant is the father. Plaintiff admits she was sexually intimate with two other men in addition to Defendant at about the time the child was conceived. Analysis of the genetic characteristics of blood samples taken from the child and the defendant reveals that Defendant is 12 times more likely to be the father than a male randomly selected from the population. The other two men are unavailable for testing and there is

(continued)

no evidence of their genetic characteristics. Using the formula for Bayes' Theorem (Odds(H/E) = LR × Odds(H)), what are the odds that the defendant is the father? Is this sufficient to meet Plaintiff's burden of persuasion? How would you explain this to a jury?

E. A SPECIAL APPLICATION OF RELEVANCE DOCTRINE: PRELIMINARY QUESTIONS OF FACT

FED. R. EVID. 104. PRELIMINARY QUESTIONS

(a) **In General.** The court must decide any preliminary question about whether a witness is qualified, a privilege exists, or evidence is admissible. In so deciding, the court is not bound by evidence rules, except those on privilege.

(b) **Relevancy That Depends on a Fact.** When the relevancy of evidence depends on fulfilling a factual condition, the court may admit it on, or subject to, the introduction of evidence sufficient to support a finding that the condition is fulfilled.

(c) **Matters That the Jury Must Not Hear.** A hearing on a preliminary question must be conducted outside the jury's hearing if:

(1) the hearing involves the admissibility of a confession;

(2) a defendant in a criminal case is a witness and requests that the jury not be present; or

(3) justice so requires.

(d) **Testimony by a Defendant in a Criminal Case.** By testifying on a preliminary question, a defendant in a criminal case does not become subject to cross-examination on other issues in the case.

(e) **Evidence Relevant to Weight and Credibility.** This rule does not limit a party's right to introduce before the jury evidence that is relevant to the weight or credibility of other evidence.

1. Introduction: The Court's Involvement in Fact-finding

Every first-year law student learns that "questions of law" are for the court and "questions of fact" are for the jury. But students quickly discover that this is not universally true and that it can be hard to distinguish between a "question of law" and a "question of fact." For example, even in a civil action tried to a jury, the court may enter judgment for a party if the opponent "has been fully heard on an issue and there is no legally sufficient evidentiary basis for a reasonable jury to find for that party on that issue. . . ." Fed. R. Civ. Proc. 50(a). In such a situation, we might say that the court entered judgment for the moving party "as a matter of law," but in reality the court also made a decision about the facts. A court may grant such a motion only if no reasonable jury could render a verdict for the non-moving party. Similarly, in criminal cases, the court may enter judgment for the defendant even if the prosecution has offered *some* evidence to support each essential element of the charged crime. It turns out that evidence law also requires that courts make decisions about facts.

2.   *Preliminary Questions of Fact: General Doctrine*

Many rules of evidence explicitly refer to facts. These rules make evidence admissible or inadmissible only if certain facts exist. Accordingly, when a court applies one of these rules of evidence it must make a decision about the existence of those facts. Consider the following hypothetical:

> Prosecution of Defendant for the murder of Victim. Defendant denies involvement in the crime. To prove Defendant committed the crime, the prosecution wishes to present evidence that before Victim died, Victim said, "Defendant shot me." Defendant objects on hearsay grounds, and the prosecutor responds that although the statement is hearsay, it qualifies as a "dying declaration" under Federal Rule 804(b)(2). Defendant replies that Victim's statement does not qualify as a dying declaration because Victim did not believe he was about to die when he made the statement.

How should the court rule on Defendant's motion? Rule 804(b)(2) says that, for a hearsay statement to be admissible as a dying declaration, it must have been made by the speaker, "while believing [his] death to be imminent." Of course, what the speaker believed is a question of fact. Because this is a factual question that must be answered as a preliminary step in determining the admissibility of the evidence, it is called a *preliminary question of fact.*

What role should the court have in resolving questions of preliminary fact? Logically, there are only two possibilities. One possibility would be to leave the question to the jury by admitting the victim's statement and instructing the jury to ignore it unless it finds that Victim believed he was about to die. The other possibility would be for the court to decide the preliminary fact issue itself, and only allow the jury to hear the evidence if the court finds that Victim made his statement while he believed his death was imminent.[6]

The first option (leaving the preliminary factual questions to the jury) has the advantage of preserving in the broadest way the parties' constitutional right to jury trial and the jury's power to decide the facts. But this first option also has a serious and ultimately fatal disadvantage: It requires the jury to *ignore relevant evidence* if the jury does not believe that the required preliminary fact is true. In this example, the evidence (Victim's statement, "Defendant shot me") is relevant even if Victim did not think he was about to die because the evidence still makes it more probable that Defendant was the perpetrator of the crime. This means that even if the jury concludes Victim did not believe his death was imminent when he made the statement, it seems likely that the jury will still consider the evidence when reaching a verdict. That's because it is unrealistic to expect that lay jurors will simply ignore relevant evidence just to uphold technical rules of admissibility like the dying declaration exception to the hearsay rule. Human nature being what it is, the evidence probably will still influence the

---

6. In most cases such as this one, the admissibility issue should be resolved before the witness testifies to the statement, and out of the hearing of the jury.

jurors, even if just subconsciously, despite the trial court's instruction to ignore the evidence.

The other option is to give the trial court the power to decide whether the preliminary fact is true. The disadvantage of this approach is that it involves the court in fact-finding, a function normally left to the jury. The advantage, however, is that it preserves the policies and rationales behind the rules of evidence — matters jurors are not likely to comprehend or have an interest in maintaining.[7] This is the result reached by modern evidence law, as exemplified by Federal Rule 104(a).

As we explain shortly, Rule 104(a) strives to minimize the extent to which trial judges intrude on the power of the jury to decide the facts. For example, we will see that the burden of proof for preliminary facts is low and the courts normally are not confined only to admissible evidence when deciding if preliminary facts exist. These features of Rule 104(a) make it easier to establish the existence of preliminary facts, which increases the chances that evidence will be admissible. And when evidence is admissible, it means that the judge is increasing the opportunity for the jury to decide the facts.

3. *Preliminary Questions of Fact: Conditional Relevancy*

Does preservation of the rules of evidence *always* require the trial court to decide questions of preliminary fact? The answer is no. Respect for the constitutional right to trial by jury demands that the judge only engage in fact-finding when necessary to preserve other important values. Whenever those values would not be endangered by jury determination of preliminary facts, the court should allow the jury to make those findings. Consider another murder hypothetical:

> Prosecution of Defendant for the murder of Victim, whose largely decomposed body was found several months after the killing. Defendant denies any involvement in the crime. At trial, the cause of death is disputed. The prosecution claims Victim was stabbed with an antique knife with a distinctively shaped blade, and Defendant claims Victim died of some other cause. To prove Defendant was the killer, the prosecution calls Officer, one of the investigating police officers, to testify that he found an antique knife with a distinctively shaped blade in Defendant's bedroom closet.

In this example, the question of preliminary fact that must be decided before it can be determined that the testimony is admissible is whether Victim was stabbed by an antique knife with a distinctively shaped blade or died from some other cause. Officer's testimony that he found an antique knife with an unusually shaped blade in Defendant's bedroom closet is relevant only if Victim died of a stab wound with characteristics that could have been caused by such a blade. If that fact is true, evidence that the antique knife was found in Defendant's home is relevant because it increases the probability that Defendant was the killer. If Victim died from a gunshot wound, for example, testimony about the knife is irrelevant.

---

7. For example, jurors are unlikely to appreciate the complex policies supporting the exclusion of hearsay evidence, or the rationales for the rules excluding evidence of subsequent remedial measures and of efforts to compromise a disputed claim.

Is it necessary for the judge, rather than the jury, to make the factual decision whether Victim died of a stabbing or from some other cause? Consider, again, the two choices the court faces: leaving the factual question largely to the jury, or deciding the question itself. In contrast to our first hypothetical, it would be appropriate to leave this matter to the jury. The reason is that no important value would be undermined by doing so. This is because, if the court instructs the jury to consider the evidence about the knife only if it finds that Victim died from a stab wound that could have been caused by such an unusual blade, the jury will be inclined to abide by the judge's instruction. We are confident that the jury will follow the instruction because the relevance rule on which the instruction is based is not a technical rule but, instead, is based on logic and common sense. Imagine how unlikely it is that a juror would think: "I know Victim was shot rather than stabbed, but I think the presence of this antique knife in Defendant's bedroom closet shows that Defendant killed Victim." It doesn't take a law degree or an understanding of complex rules of evidence to understand why this makes no sense. Thus, the right to jury trial can be protected, and the rules of evidence will be followed, by allowing the jury to decide this question of preliminary fact.

But the judge still plays some role in deciding the question. While common sense suggests it is safe to give the jury most of the responsibility for determining if the dagger evidence is relevant, common sense also suggests that we should not waste the jury's time with that evidence unless there is at least some minimal reason to think it might be relevant. Accordingly, so long as the prosecution has made a threshold showing sufficient to *allow* (not require) a rational fact-finder to conclude that Victim died of a stab wound that could have been caused by this unusual knife, the court admits the evidence about the discovery of the knife and simply lets the jury decide the preliminary question concerning the type of weapon used in the murder. If the prosecution has not satisfied this very minimal standard, the judge does not permit the jury to hear the evidence. Thus, the judge performs a screening role even under Rule 104(b).

We call this a problem of *conditional relevancy*, or *relevancy that depends on a fact*, because the evidence is not relevant unless a particular fact is true. Rule 104(b) both describes the concept and sets forth the respective roles of judge and jury: "When the relevancy of evidence depends on fulfilling a factual condition, the court may admit it on, or subject to, the introduction of evidence sufficient to support a finding that the condition is fulfilled." Applied to our hypothetical case, Rule 104(b) provides (1) the court must consider whether the prosecution offered sufficient evidence to permit a rational juror to conclude that Victim had stab wounds that could have been caused by the blade in question, and, (2) if such evidence has been offered (or if the prosecutor promises that such evidence will be offered), the court must admit the evidence about the dagger and allow the jury to decide whether it is relevant.

Two more examples of conditional relevancy should help to solidify your understanding:

1. In an automobile accident case, a key question is whether the defendant was speeding at the time of the accident. Defendant admits being involved in the accident but denies she was driving in excess of the speed limit. If Plaintiff wishes to introduce the testimony of a witness who will claim that she saw a car speeding less than a minute before the accident, that witness's testimony

will be irrelevant if the car she saw was not in fact the Defendant's car. The court should permit the witness to testify so long as there is, or will be, evidence sufficient to support a finding that the car the witness observed was the Defendant's car.

2. In a contract case where Defendant denies entering into the contract, the letter accepting Plaintiff's offer is relevant if the letter was sent by Defendant. The court should admit the letter so long as there is, or will be, evidence sufficient to support a finding that the signature on the letter is that of Defendant. The process of showing that the letter is signed by Defendant is called authentication, an issue addressed in Chapter 1. Notice that, while there is a special rule for authentication,[8] its "sufficient to support a finding" standard is the same as the one contained in Rule 104(b).

We also saw in Chapter 1 another rule that follows logic similar to that of Rule 104(b). Rule 602 provides that a witness may testify only as to matters within her personal knowledge. Whether a witness has personal knowledge of a fact is a question left to the jury, subject only to the judge making a threshold determination that there is evidence sufficient to support a finding that the witness has personal knowledge. Again, this standard is identical to that in Rule 104(b). The reasoning behind Rule 602 is that, if the jury concludes that the witness does not have personal knowledge of the underlying facts, the jury will ignore the evidence. In other words, the rule is based on the assumption that there is little risk that the jury will consider the testimony if the witness lacks personal knowledge. Personal knowledge problems are essentially problems of conditional relevancy in that, if a witness did not perceive the facts she testifies to, her testimony does not make those facts more or less probable.

Most preliminary fact questions do not involve problems of conditional relevancy. Therefore, in most situations Rule 104(a) will apply. This means that the judge must decide whether the preliminary facts exist. Assume, for example, a witness offers to testify to the contents of a written contract for the sale of goods in a case where plaintiff sues for breach on the ground the defendant delivered the goods late. Because the testimony concerns the contents of a writing, the best evidence rule applies. As we saw in Chapter 1, the preliminary fact question under Rule 1004(a) is whether all the originals of the written contract were lost or destroyed. It will be the court's responsibility to decide that question under Rule 104(a). This is not a question of conditional relevance under Rule 104(b) because the testimony ("The contract said that the goods were to be delivered on the first of the month") would be relevant whether or not all the originals have been lost or destroyed.

In a few cases it will be difficult to determine whether the preliminary fact question arises under Rule 104(a) or is a question of conditional relevancy under Rule 104(b). But in the vast majority of cases the answer will be clear. To arrive at the correct answer, you need only apply the same two-step approach used above in the example regarding the testimony offered under Rule 1004(a). First, identify the preliminary fact on which admissibility of the evidence depends. Second, ask yourself whether the evidence would still be relevant

---

8. Rule 901(a) states: "To authenticate or identify an item of evidence in order to have it admitted, the proponent must produce evidence sufficient to support a finding that the item is what the proponent claims it is."

even if the preliminary fact was not established. If the answer is yes, the preliminary fact question should be decided under Rule 104(a). If the answer is no, the evidence would be irrelevant if the preliminary fact is not established, then the preliminary fact question arises under Rule 104(b).

4.   Comparing the Court's Role in Cases Falling into Rule 104(a) with Its Role in Cases Governed by Rule 104(b)

Why does it matter whether a preliminary question of fact falls into Rule 104(a) or Rule 104(b)? After all, we have said that the court plays some role in evaluating the admissibility of the evidence under both provisions before the evidence may be heard by the jury. There are two differences:

1.   the amount of proof of the preliminary fact needed to admit the evidence; and
2.   the nature of the evidence the court may consider in deciding whether that level of proof exists.

Both of these differences are described or at least alluded to by the text of Rule 104. Let's illustrate with a hypothetical:

> Defendant is charged with armed robbery of a convenience store, using a gun. Defendant admits robbing the store, but claims not to have used a gun or any other weapon. The prosecution calls Witness, who was at home speaking with Zed on the telephone at the time of the robbery. Zed was using a cellular phone, and was standing just outside the convenience store during the conversation. The prosecution wishes to have Witness testify that during the conversation, Zed said, "A guy with a gun just walked into the store." Defendant objects on hearsay grounds, and the prosecution responds that Zed's statement is admissible as a "present sense impression" under the exception to the hearsay rule in Rule 803(1).

Assume there is no dispute that the "guy" to whom Zed referred was Defendant. As we will see in Chapter 3, Zed's statement will be admissible under Rule 803(1) if the following preliminary fact is established: Zed made the statement at a moment in time simultaneous with perceiving Defendant and a gun, or immediately after perceiving these things. Because the statement will be relevant even if these preliminary facts are not true, this is not a case of conditional relevancy, and the court must decide whether these preliminary facts existed under Rule 104(a). While that provision does not directly describe the burden of proof, it is clearly established that the standard the court must apply is "preponderance of the evidence" or "more likely than not." It does not matter that this is a criminal case and that the jury ultimately will have to apply the standard of "beyond a reasonable doubt" to all facts essential to establishing Defendant's guilt. In deciding preliminary facts under Rule 104(a), the court is involved in the process of determining the admissibility of evidence, not the ultimate guilt or innocence of Defendant. The "preponderance" or "more likely than not" standard applies.

What evidence may the court consider in reaching this decision? The last sentence of Rule 104(a) provides the answer: "In so deciding, the court is not bound by evidence rules, except those on privilege." Thus, while it is clear that the court may consider Witness's testimony about such things as Zed's tone of voice and the circumstances surrounding the call, the court may also consider other evidence available to it, including evidence that would not be admissible. Suppose, for example, Witness and Zed had another conversation a day later during which Zed told Witness, "That person was no more than ten feet from me when I told you about the gun. I was very scared." Even if this statement would be hearsay and not admissible under any exception to the hearsay rule, the court is still permitted to take it into consideration when deciding whether the earlier statement satisfied the requirements of the present sense impression exception. According to the terms of Rule 104(a), the only type of evidence denied to the court in making its determination is evidence that falls within a privilege.[9] We will discuss privileges in Chapter 8.

Indeed, the court is permitted to take into account the very evidence at issue in deciding whether the preliminary facts necessary to its admissibility are true. Zed's original statement, "A guy with a gun *just* walked into the store," suggested that Zed was making his statement shortly after perceiving the facts described. Although it seems in some sense to be "bootstrapping" to allow the court to consider the questioned evidence itself when deciding its admissibility, this is precisely what the drafters of Rule 104 intended. The only unresolved question is whether the questioned evidence may be sufficient in and of itself to satisfy the requirements of its own admissibility. That is, if the proponent can come forward with absolutely no evidence, other than the statement itself, to support the existence of the preliminary facts, may the court nevertheless find that the preconditions for admissibility have been satisfied? At common law, the answer appears to have been no. Under the Federal Rules, the answer remains unclear, although a 1997 amendment to Rule 801(d)(2) provides that for some purposes at least, the common law rule will still be followed. It is most unlikely, however, that the questioned evidence will often be the only evidence available to support the factual preconditions for its admissibility. In virtually all cases, the proponent will have some other evidence, whether admissible or inadmissible, to support the necessary preliminary facts.

The court's role in cases of conditional relevancy (those governed by Rule 104(b)) is quite different. Recall that in discussing our examples of conditional relevancy, we did not state that the court automatically allows the jury to consider the evidence. We made it clear that the court still must play a role in controlling what the jury may consider. As Rule 104(b) states, in cases of conditional relevancy the court admits the evidence if it is presented with proof sufficient to support a finding that the preliminary fact exists. Of course, "sufficient to support a finding" is a less demanding standard than "preponderance of the evidence." It requires the judge to admit the evidence in question if a reasonable juror could conclude the preliminary fact exists. But even though Rule 104(b) sets the bar quite low, the court may not admit evidence unless it finds that this minimal standard is satisfied.

What evidence may the court consider in making this determination under Rule 104(b)? Return to the hypothetical murder case in which the prosecution wishes to have Officer testify that he found an antique knife in the closet of Defendant's bedroom. The court's role under Rule 104(b) is to determine

9. We discuss the meaning of the phrase "except those with respect to privileges" in Chapter 8.

whether a reasonable juror could conclude that Victim died of a stab wound that has characteristics that could have been caused by this knife. Logically, the only evidence the court should take into account is evidence a juror could be permitted to hear when deciding whether, in fact, Victim died this way. Because the jury is only permitted to hear admissible evidence, the judge should only consider admissible evidence when making a preliminary ruling under Rule 104(b). Therefore, if Officer's testimony includes a more detailed description of the wounds on Victim's body, the court could consider such evidence when making the preliminary determination. However, the court would not be permitted to consider a statement the coroner made to Officer if that statement would constitute inadmissible hearsay.

5. What If the Preliminary Fact Is the Same as an Ultimate Fact the Jury Must Decide?

What if the preliminary question of fact is identical to one of the factual issues the jury must decide when deliberating its verdict? Consider the following example:

> Defendant is charged with murder and conspiracy to murder Victim. The government alleges that Defendant planned the murder with Xavier and Zed. Defendant denies any involvement. To prove Defendant's complicity, the government calls Witness to testify that the day before the murder, Witness heard Xavier say to Zed, "We're going to kill Victim at Victim's office. Defendant is going to leave a getaway car for us around the corner." Defendant makes a hearsay objection, and the government argues that the evidence is admissible as a non-hearsay statement of a co-conspirator under Rule 801(d)(2)(E).

As we will see in Chapter 3, the statement will qualify as a statement of a co-conspirator under Rule 801(d)(2)(E) and will not be excluded by the hearsay rule if the following facts are true: There was a conspiracy, Xavier was a member of the conspiracy, and the statement was made during the course and in furtherance of the conspiracy. Each part of the rule raises a different question of preliminary fact. Most important for present purposes is the question of the existence of a conspiracy. If there was none, the evidence is not admissible under this rule. Because Xavier's statement would be relevant to Defendant's participation in the murder even if there was no formal conspiracy under the law, the admissibility question is not one of conditional relevancy. Thus, this is a preliminary fact question arising under Rule 104(a). Note, however, that the existence of a conspiracy is one of the ultimate questions of fact the jury must decide when deliberating a verdict. (Remember that Defendant was charged with the crime of engaging in a conspiracy.) Does this create a dilemma for division of responsibility between judge and jury?

The answer is no. Trial judges deciding the admissibility of evidence are engaged in a very different task than are juries when deliberating a verdict. The judge is simply determining what evidence may be considered by the jury; the jury's task is to add up all the admitted evidence and decide whether the legal standard at issue in the case has been met. Thus, there is nothing anomalous about permitting the court to make a preliminary determination of the same fact the jury must later decide, nor is there anything troubling about the court making that decision on a different standard of proof (preponderance of the evidence) than the jury will ultimately apply in its deliberations (beyond a reasonable doubt, in a criminal case). In its role as a filter of proffered evidence, the court must be permitted to exercise this power. The only thing the court must *not* do is inform the jury that it has found (by a preponderance of the evidence) that there was a conspiracy. Such a statement would be an improper comment on the evidence that would risk unduly prejudicing the jury against Defendant. The jury should simply hear about Xavier's statement, and not be told what findings the court had to make in order for the statement to be admitted.

Questions of preliminary fact pervade all trials, and counsel must learn to recognize preliminary fact questions as they arise. Analysis must always begin by determining whether the situation involves a problem of conditional relevancy. Once that decision is made, the rest of the analysis flows relatively easily from the rules.

6. Caveats

Before we turn to hypotheticals testing your understanding of preliminary fact-finding, it is necessary to throw a small monkey wrench into the mechanism. Here is the issue: Is all of this logical, and does it accord with the way people actually think? Begin with a simple example taken from everyday life:

> As you are driving along a street you approach a railroad crossing. You notice that there is a gate but it is in the "up" position. In addition, the light signals are not flashing and no bells are ringing. Thus, the evidence indicates that no train is approaching.

In this example, will you drive forward without looking either right or left to see if a train is coming? Hopefully not. If you are careful, you will take the evidence to mean that a train *probably* is not approaching, but you will not consider the evidence conclusive. In other words, you will still consider the possibility that the signals are not working and that a train is on its way.

We suspect that this often is the way people think (especially law students), but it is not the way the conditional relevancy rule assumes people think. That rule operates as though human decision making is a binary ("on-off") proposition — that people faced with evidence concerning some fact decide whether that fact is true and, if they decide that it is true, they then ignore the possibility that it is not. This assumption is unrealistic. Consider the following illustration:

> Personal injury action by Plaintiff against Defendant. Plaintiff claims Defendant, a driver, ran her down as Plaintiff was crossing the street in a crosswalk. Defendant admits striking Plaintiff, but claims Plaintiff was not in the crosswalk and darted out in the middle of the block from between two parked cars. To prove this fact, Defendant calls Witness to testify that, shortly before the impact, Witness saw Plaintiff trying to cross in the middle of the block. Plaintiff objects on grounds Witness lacks personal knowledge because other evidence shows Witness was, in fact, across town at the time of the accident.

Plaintiff has invoked Rule 602, which requires that a witness have personal knowledge of the facts to which she testifies. More precisely, the rule requires that there be evidence "sufficient to support a finding" that Witness has personal knowledge. This indicates that personal knowledge is a matter of conditional relevancy. The court must allow the jury to hear Witness's testimony as long as the court concludes that there is evidence sufficient to support the jury's conclusion that Witness had personal knowledge of the facts.

Suppose the judge decides that the standard in Rule 602 has been satisfied because Witness testifies she was present at the scene of the accident.[10] Rule 602 then requires that the judge permit the jury to hear Witness's testimony, even if there is conflicting evidence suggesting Witness actually was across town at the time of the accident. Of course, the conflicting evidence will then also be admissible. The assumption built into Rule 602 is that if, after the jury hears Witness's testimony and the conflicting evidence placing Witness across town, the jury "finds" that Witness did not have first-hand knowledge of the accident, the jury will entirely ignore Witness's testimony because it is irrelevant. In other words, conditional relevancy is assumed to be an on-off proposition.

But we have seen that this is not how people really think. It is more likely that the jurors will act in the same way as the driver in our railroad crossing hypothetical. They will weigh Witness's testimony in probabilistic rather than absolute terms. They might conclude that it is unlikely, maybe even very unlikely, that Witness had personal knowledge, but precisely because it remains *possible* that Witness did have first-hand knowledge, they will not completely ignore her testimony.

This suggests that the theory of conditional relevancy is flawed because it assumes a type of reasoning people do not use. It assumes that jurors will consider evidence to be either relevant or irrelevant depending on their "finding" about a preliminary fact. But it is much more likely that jurors will give some credit to the questioned evidence even if they believe it highly unlikely that the preliminary fact (in the present example, personal knowledge) is not true.[11] This is reminiscent of a point made earlier in this chapter concerning the distinction between relevance and probative value. Recall that while the concept of probative value is a matter of degree, relevance is an on-off proposition. Evidence is either relevant or irrelevant. Maybe this assumption about relevance is also flawed. Perhaps, in dealing with day-to-day decision making, we treat evidence as possibly relevant, and act according to the probabilities as we assess them. If that is true, either the concept of relevance in the law differs from the concept as used in everyday life, or the law intends the concept to mean the same thing as in everyday life but misconceives the way people think.

Our caveat has taken us into a brief examination of the validity of the received doctrine of relevance and conditional relevance. Despite its appeal, the critique holds little sway with judges and has mostly been confined to the academic world. The rules are as they are, and we must learn to use them.

---

10. Notice that Witness did not specifically state that she was looking in the direction of the accident, but only that she was there at the time.

11. The one situation in which the theory of conditional relevancy is completely valid is the (unusual) case in which the jurors have *no doubt* that the preliminary fact is true or is false. But 100 percent certainty in either direction is not common in everyday experience.

One more caveat. So far, we have not discussed the possibility that the generalizations applied to evidence to determine its relevance are subject to dispute. Consider this example: Money is missing from my wallet. I suspect that a certain person took the money. When I ask that person if she took it, she says she did not, but she does not make eye contact when she answers my question. Is it any more likely that she is lying than if she made eye contact with me? Many people would say yes. The generalization these people make is that a person who is telling the truth is more likely to look her interrogator in the eye than is a person who is lying. Not everyone, however, would agree with that generalization; some people would consider the lack of eye contact irrelevant.

Consider a more controversial example: Defendant is charged with the rape of Victim. Defendant admits having sexual intercourse with Victim, but claims that the act was consensual. To prove this, Defendant wishes to offer evidence that Victim had consensual sexual intercourse with five different men during the past two years. Is this evidence relevant? It is relevant if we accept the generalization that a person who has consented to sex with several different partners in the recent past is more likely to have consented on a particular occasion than is one who does not have this sexual history. But this is a very debatable generalization.

If there is doubt about the validity of the generalization supporting the relevance of particular evidence, how is the dispute to be resolved? One possibility would be to call expert witnesses — perhaps psychologists or criminologists in the rape example — to testify to the validity of the generalization. But that solution is cumbersome and expensive. If we were to stop the "action" every time a party challenges the validity of a generalization allegedly supporting the relevance of particular evidence, trials would be even longer and more expensive than they are already, and the fact-finder's attention would be diverted from the central issues to a series of evidentiary sideshows. One of two possible solutions makes more sense: (1) relevance arguments are addressed to the court pursuant to its authority under Rule 104(a), meaning that the judge decides whether the generalization at issue holds true; or (2) relevance arguments are addressed primarily to the jury, meaning that the court's role is constrained to the undemanding "sufficient to support a finding" standard of Rule 104(b).

Let's look more closely at the two practical options. If the judge is the final arbiter of relevance arguments, all argument concerning the validity of the generalization supporting relevance must be directed to the judge, who will apply the standard of Rule 104(a) to decide the question. This means the party offering the evidence will be appealing to the judge's experience of the world rather than the collective experiences of the jurors. The advantage of this approach is that it would keep any evidence the judge considers irrelevant from the jury. That, in turn, will avoid distracting the jury with potentially useless evidence and keep the jury focused on the important evidence offered by the parties. The disadvantage of this approach is that relevance determinations will rely on one person's life experience rather than that of a group. Remember that the relevance rule is not a technical rule of evidence; application of the rule does not require legal training, nor are there any evidentiary or substantive law policies that affect the determination whether particular evidence is relevant. Unless we believe that judges' everyday experience is broader than that of juries, leaving relevance determinations to the judge could lead to the exclusion of evidence a group of everyday citizens would consider useful.[12]

If the jury is the final arbiter of relevance, the court's role would be prescribed by Rule 104(b). According to that rule, the judge would admit the evidence upon, or subject to the introduction of, evidence sufficient to support the jury's conclusion that the questioned evidence is relevant. That rule would leave virtually all relevance issues to the jury.

To take an example, assume a case involving an alleged breach of oral contract in which Defendant claims there was no agreement. To prove the existence of the contract, Plaintiff testifies that she received a telephone call from a person identifying herself as Defendant and that during the call the person on the other end of the line said, "I accept your offer." Defendant claims she was not that person. Rule 104(b) applies here because the relevance of the telephone call is dependent on its having been placed by Defendant. Under the rule, the court need only decide whether there is evidence sufficient to support a finding that Defendant placed the call. If the court answers that question in the affirmative, it will admit the evidence, knowing that the jury will ignore the evidence if it finds that Defendant was not the person who accepted Plaintiff's offer.

Now return to the problem of relevance itself. If evidence is irrelevant, the fact-finder presumably will ignore it. That suggests that the principle, if not the letter, of Rule 104(b) applies to the determination of whether particular evidence is relevant. There does not appear to be any harm in allowing the jury to be the final arbiter of relevance.[13] But despite the apparent logic in deciding relevance questions pursuant to the standard of Rule 104(b), courts and lawyers tend to assume that relevance questions should be addressed to the court.

Further Reading: Richard D. Friedman, *Conditional Probative Value: Neoclassicism Without Myth*, 93 Mich. L. Rev. 439 (1994); Norman M. Garland & Jay A. Schmitz, *Of Judges and Juries: A Proposed Revision of Federal Rule of Evidence 104*, 23 U.C. Davis L. Rev. 77 (1989); John Kaplan, *Of Mabrus and Zorgs — An Essay in Honor of David Louisell*, 66 Cal. L. Rev. 987 (1978); John M. Maguire & Charles Epstein, *Preliminary Questions of Fact in Determining the Admissibility of Evidence*, 40 Harv. L. Rev. 392 (1927); Edmund M. Morgan, *Functions of Judge and Jury in the Determination of Preliminary Questions of Fact*, 43 Harv. L. Rev. 165 (1929); Dale A. Nance, *Conditional Relevance Reinterpreted*, 70 B.U. L. Rev. 447 (1990).

12. Assume an African-American murder defendant denies any involvement, and claims that the police, motivated by racism, planted evidence suggesting the defendant's guilt. To prove this, Defendant wishes to present evidence that one of the investigating officers had used racial slurs in the past. It is very possible that the judge will consider the evidence irrelevant but that a diverse jury drawn from the Defendant's own community might think the evidence relevant. (This hypothetical is suggested by the facts of O.J. Simpson's murder trial, in which a racially diverse criminal jury acquitted defendant of murder, and a much less diverse jury found Simpson liable in a civil case brought by the victims' families.)

13. Based on this discussion, one might begin to wonder whether there is actually a difference between relevance and conditional relevance. The entire subject of conditional relevance has given rise to spirited debate. Some authors argue that the concept is illogical. *See, e.g.*, 1 John H. Wigmore, Evidence in Trials at Common Law § 14.1 (Peter Tillers rev. 1983); Ronald J. Allen, *The Myth of Conditional Relevancy*, 25 Loy. L.A. L. Rev. 871 (1992); Vaughan C. Ball, *The Myth of Conditional Relevancy*, 14 Ga. L. Rev. 435 (1980).

Questions for Classroom Discussion

1. Breach of oral contract action between Plaintiff and Defendant, who were friends, concerning the alleged sale of a car. Plaintiff wishes to testify that Defendant phoned Plaintiff, offered to buy Plaintiff's car, and that Plaintiff accepted the offer. Defendant claims she never had this phone conversation with Plaintiff, and objects to Plaintiff's testimony concerning that conversation. What is the preliminary fact Plaintiff must prove to make the testimony admissible? Is this a 104(a) or 104(b) preliminary fact? How should the court rule on Defendant's objection?

2. Prosecution of Defendant for pick-pocketing. To prove Defendant committed the crime, the prosecution calls Witness, who was walking with the victim when the act occurred. If permitted, Witness will testify that just after Defendant reached into the victim's back pocket and removed his wallet, Witness said to the victim, "Someone just stole your wallet." Assume that the statement is hearsay but will be admissible if Witness's statement described or explained the event while she was perceiving it or immediately after she perceived it. (*See* Rule 803(1).) What is the preliminary fact that must be decided? Should it be decided according to the standard of Rule 104(a) or Rule 104(b)?

3. Negligence action by Plaintiff against Defendant following an automobile collision on a dark road at night. Plaintiff was driving one car and Defendant was driving the other car. Defendant also had a passenger in the car. Plaintiff wishes to testify that after the collision, Plaintiff walked over to Defendant's car, knocked on the window, asked what happened, and that a voice answered, "I don't know what happened. I fell asleep before the accident." Assume that if Defendant was the speaker, the evidence would not be excluded by the hearsay rule, but that if the passenger was the speaker, the evidence would be inadmissible hearsay. Defendant objects to Plaintiff's testimony. What is the preliminary fact Plaintiff must prove to make the testimony admissible? Is this a 104(a) or 104(b) preliminary fact? How should the court rule on Defendant's objection?

4. Same facts as in Question 3. Assume, however, that the voice from inside the car said, "I don't know what happened. The windshield was all fogged up." Defendant objects to Plaintiff's testimony. What is the preliminary fact Plaintiff must prove to make the testimony admissible? Is this a 104(a) or 104(b) preliminary fact? How should the court rule on Defendant's objection?

5. Prosecution of Defendant for murder. The prosecution wishes to present evidence of a written confession signed by Defendant.

Defendant admits signing the confession, but claims she only did so after the police threatened to investigate her entire family for any possible wrongdoing. Assume that Defendant is entitled to a decision as to the voluntariness of her confession. To make this decision the court will need to hear testimony from Defendant and the police. Where should the jury be during this testimony?

Assessments

1. Action for breach of contract. Defendant offers to testify that, when he said to Plaintiff, "I accept your offer," he secretly was joking and had no subjective intent to enter into a contract with Plaintiff since he had read in a newspaper earlier that same day that Plaintiff would soon be indicted for child molestation. The best objection to Defendant's testimony is:
   a. Unfair prejudice substantially outweighs probative value
   b. The testimony violates the best evidence rule
   c. The newspaper has not been properly authenticated
   d. The testimony is irrelevant

2. Prosecution for bank robbery in which the robber got away with $200,000 in cash. Defendant, who has testified he is unemployed and a drug addict, denies he was involved in the robbery. The prosecution offers evidence that, when he was arrested, Defendant was in possession of a large carton of a white powdery substance. The evidence is:
   a. Admissible if the prosecution shows by a preponderance of the evidence that the substance is cocaine
   b. Admissible if the prosecution presents evidence sufficient to support a finding that the substance is cocaine
   c. Inadmissible because the evidence is irrelevant
   d. Inadmissible because unfair prejudice outweighs probative value

3. Prosecution of John for murder. John admits killing the victim but pleads insanity as a defense. A police officer testifies for the prosecution that when he arrived at the scene the victim was still alive and said, "I am going fast . . . John shot me." A moment later the victim died. Assume that under the law that we will study in the next chapter, a hearsay objection will be overruled if it is shown that the victim believed his death to be imminent when he made his statement. The evidence is:
   a. Irrelevant because there are many people named John
   b. Irrelevant because Defendant admits shooting the victim

(continued)

c. Admissible if the prosecution shows by a preponderance of the evidence that the victim thought his death to be imminent

d. Admissible if the prosecution presents evidence sufficient to support a finding that the victim thought his death to be imminent

4. Prosecution for sexual assault. The victim testifies that the perpetrator had blond hair. The prosecution offers evidence that one in ten people has blond hair and that a DNA analysis of the perpetrator's semen revealed a rare genetic trait present in only one of every 100,000 males. Defendant has blond hair and has the genetic trait in question. The prosecution then calls a mathematics professor who offers to testify that this means the probability of finding a blond person with the genetic trait in question is one in a million. The testimony of the professor is:

a. A proper application of the product rule

b. Inadmissible because the witness lacks personal knowledge

c. Inadmissible under Rule 403 because the evidence is cumulative

d. Inadmissible without additional foundation

5. Plaintiff sued for negligence after falling down a flight of stairs in a common area of Defendant's apartment building. Plaintiff alleges there was a banana peel on the stairs that caused her fall and that Defendant was negligent in not having the stairs clean and free of debris. Defendant denies there was a banana peel on the stairs since, he testified, he has all the common areas of the building swept every day. Defendant claims Plaintiff just tripped and fell. Which of the following is most likely to be deemed relevant?

a. Plaintiff's evidence that Defendant owns other apartment buildings in which there have been instances of people falling down stairs

b. Defendant's evidence that, in the weeks prior to the accident, hundreds of other people safely used the stairs on which plaintiff fell

c. Plaintiff's evidence that the ground floor lobby of the apartment building in which she fell was littered with trash on the day she fell on the stairs

d. Defendant's evidence that Plaintiff tripped over her own feet and fell down a flight of stairs five years ago

Answers and Analysis

1. The correct answer is d. The testimony is irrelevant because it is not offered to prove a fact "of consequence." This is because the substantive law of contracts employs an objective theory of assent under which the only question is, would a reasonable person in the position of the offeror believe Defendant had accepted. The secret, unspoken intent of the defendant is not of consequence. Answer a is

incorrect since Rule 403 applies only to relevant evidence. Note that the reference to the possible indictment of Plaintiff for child molestation certainly carries with it great potential for unfair prejudice. This is a typical way multiple choice tests lure you into the wrong answer — by creating a factual scenario that obviously raises an issue you have seen before, but raises that issue in a context where some other rule controls. Answers b and c are incorrect since, logically, we never get to questions of the best evidence rule or authentication if the evidence is irrelevant.

2. The correct answer is b. Under Rule 104(b), the evidence about the carton is admissible if the prosecution makes a showing sufficient to support a finding that the substance is cocaine. This makes the evidence relevant because it shows that the unemployed defendant had the money to obtain a large amount of a very expensive drug. This increases the probability that he is the bank robber. Answer a is incorrect because the admissibility of the evidence is a matter of conditional relevancy, making the preponderance standard of Rule 104(a) inapplicable. Answer c is incorrect because, if the substance is cocaine, the evidence is relevant for the reason described above. Answer d is incorrect because the evidence has significant probative value to prove Defendant robbed the bank. The unfairly prejudicial danger of the evidence is diminished because Defendant already has testified he is a drug addict. Remember, under Rule 403, the court has the discretion to exclude only if unfair prejudice substantially outweighs probative value.

3. The correct answer is c. The admissibility of the evidence depends on proving a preliminary fact under Rule 104(a) — that victim thought his death to be imminent. This is a 104(a) fact because, even if that fact is not shown, the evidence is still relevant. Thus, answer d is incorrect. Answer a is incorrect because, even though there are others named John, the evidence increases the probability that the defendant, whose name is John, is the shooter. Answer b is incorrect because, under Rule 401, the evidence is relevant if it increases the probability of a fact of consequence, even if that fact is not in dispute.

4. The correct answer is d. Without a showing that the two characteristics (blond hair and the genetic trait) are independent variables, application of the product rule is impermissible and the evidence is irrelevant or at least misleading under Rule 403. Thus, answer a is incorrect. Answer b is incorrect since, as we saw in Chapter 1, expert witness testimony is exempt from the personal knowledge requirement of Rule 602. Answer c is incorrect since there is nothing to suggest this evidence is cumulative.

5. The correct answer is c. The relevance analysis in this question requires that we consider the extent to which each item of evidence is remote or proximate to Plaintiff's fall in terms of time, location,

(continued)

and other circumstances. The more proximate, the greater the likelihood that the evidence will be deemed to affect the probability of a fact of consequence. While the evidence in c directly relates to the lobby, not the stairway, it is in the same building. Further, it is reasonable to assume that if one common area in a building has not been cleaned and is full of trash, that increases the probability that other common areas in the same building at the same time have not been cleaned as well. Answer a relates to different buildings and there is nothing to suggest the cause or circumstances of the falls (i.e., were they related to debris on the stairs?). Answer b is incorrect because the evidence relates to use of the stairs at times other than when the accident took place. This evidence is proximate to the location of the accident, but not to the time of the accident. The evidence is that all the common areas are swept every day, but apparently not on the day in question. Thus, timing is crucial to relevancy. Answer d is incorrect since there is nothing connecting Plaintiff's prior fall to the fall in question. It is remote in both time and place and, without more circumstances connecting the two events (e.g., a showing Plaintiff was wearing the same high heeled shoes on both occasions), the evidence is irrelevant.

CHAPTER

3

The Hearsay Rule

A. INTRODUCTION: THE IDEA BEHIND THE HEARSAY RULE

No evidence rule is as vexing to law students as the hearsay rule. Before we delve into the complexities of the rule, it is best to start with the reasons that support it.

When a person tells us something we did not already know, we are likely to be at least a bit skeptical about its accuracy. Thus, if Pat, an acquaintance, approaches you and says, "I saw Lisa give Eric back his apartment key," we might not accept that this is true without at least some probing. Perhaps we would ask Pat to describe what she saw in more detail. We might want to know whether Pat was in a good position to observe the event, or whether the event took place a while ago and Pat's memory is not terribly clear. If we knew Pat had an ulterior motive (perhaps a desire to foment discord between Lisa and Eric), we would be less likely to accept her assertions as true. It's also possible that Pat's statement doesn't really convey how Pat interpreted the event. That is, a listener might interpret Pat's words as conveying a belief that Lisa and Eric were ending their relationship, but that might not be what Pat meant to convey. These problems exist because the listener is *once removed* from the event itself. In other words, we obtained our information about the event not from observing the event, but from another person who claims to have observed it. That means our perception of the event is created by the mind and the communicative behavior of another person.

We can place the possible sources of inaccuracy or inaccurate understanding just discussed into four categories:

1. Perception (the accuracy of the source's perception of the event);
2. Memory (the accuracy of the source's recollection of the event);
3. Sincerity (the source's honesty about the event); and
4. Narration (the adequacy of the source's communication of her thoughts).

If examining these possible sources of inaccuracy is important in everyday life, it is doubly important to do so in the context of a trial. This is the primary function of cross-examination. A witness has made certain assertions during her direct examination. In almost every case, those assertions support the factual theory of the party who called her to testify. Cross-examination now gives the opponent an opportunity to challenge the accuracy of the assertions by questioning the witness's perception, memory, and sincerity, and by determining whether we understand correctly what the witness was attempting to communicate.

Now imagine that instead of saying, "I saw Lisa give Eric back his apartment key," the person says to you, "Jay told me that Lisa just gave Eric back his apartment key." At this point, our information about the event, and the way we come to see it, is *twice removed* from the event. Not only do we have to be concerned with Pat's reliability (perception, memory, sincerity, and ambiguity) before we decide what happened, but we must also be concerned with Jay's reliability, as Jay was the source of Pat's information.

The rules of hearsay are not concerned with the "once-removed" problem. If the hearsay rule barred all evidence that was even once removed from the event at issue, virtually all evidence would be inadmissible. That is because most evidence consists of the testimony (in-court statements) of people about what they perceived. Their testimony is once removed from the events about which they testify. So the hearsay rule cannot apply to statements made by witnesses in the court proceeding that is currently taking place. We trust the adversary system in general, and the process of cross-examination in particular, to reveal flaws in the testimony of witnesses. To return to our hypothetical, if the question is whether Lisa gave Eric back his key and what, if any, significance that event might have had, the opponent will have an opportunity to cross-examine Pat to reveal possible problems with the testimony. Thus, a cross-examination of Pat might go as follows:

Q: Where did this event take place?
A: In front of Eric's apartment building.
Q: Why were you there?
A: I was there to pick up Lisa for work. We work in the same office.
Q: Were you in your car when you saw this happen?
A: Yes.
Q: How far was your car from Lisa and Eric when this occurred?
A: I was parked along the curb, maybe 15 feet from Lisa and Eric.
Q: Was Eric facing you?
A: Yes.
Q: So that must mean Lisa was not facing you. Is that correct?
A: I guess so. But I could see what she was doing.
Q: But you didn't actually see the key in Lisa's hand, did you?
A: Well, I saw her reach into her pocket with her right hand and take something out and then give it to Eric.
Q: You didn't actually see her remove a key, did you?
A: I can't imagine what else she might have been handing him.
Q: Could it have been a different key?
A: I suppose.
Q: Could it have been some change?
A: I guess so.
Q: You say this took place in the morning, right?

A: Yes. It was about 7:45.

Q: And the street in front of Eric's apartment runs east and west, doesn't it?

A: I think so, yes.

Q: Your car was facing east, right?

A: Yes.

Q: Was it a clear day?

A: Yes. It was very clear.

Q: And the sun was up?

A: Yes.

Q: How do you know Eric and Lisa?

A: We were all friends in college, and we stayed close after we graduated.

Q: Did you ever date Eric?

A: We went out for a while after college, but we broke up last year.

Q: The break-up was Eric's idea, wasn't it?

A: Well, he might have said something first, but things weren't going well anyway.

Q: Thinking back on the day you say you saw Lisa give Eric back his key, that was a busy day, wasn't it?

A: Do you mean at work?

Q: Yes.

A: I guess so. We had a number of important deadlines, and the boss was on us to get everything done.

Q: You say these were important deadlines. What were the clients you were working on that day?

A: I don't really remember.

Q: You don't remember which important clients you worked on that day?

A: Not really.

This hypothetical cross-examination was designed to test the witness's perception, memory, sincerity, as well as the meaning of her statement that she had seen Lisa give Eric back his key (narration). The jury's ability to assess the accuracy of Pat's account of the event has been enhanced by hearing a cross-examination shortly after Pat made her assertion about what happened. Though the credibility of Pat's statements is therefore in issue, the concerns of the hearsay rule are not implicated because the jury has observed both Pat's initial assertion and the nearly contemporaneous cross-examination.

The hearsay rule is concerned, instead, with the problem of twice-removed evidence. In our hypothetical, Pat would testify not to Pat's own observation, but to what Jay told Pat. Pat's direct examination on this point might occur in the following way:

Q: On that day, did you have a conversation with Jay concerning Lisa and Eric?

A: Yes, I did.

Q: What did Jay tell you?

A: Jay told me that he saw Lisa give Eric back his apartment key.

In this variation, Pat's testimony partly consists of Pat's first-hand knowledge (the conversation with Jay), while part merely reports what Jay said. The opponent can cross-examine Pat adequately about whether this conversation actually took place when Pat said it did, and as to the substance of the conversation (what Jay said about Lisa and Eric), but it is not possible to cross-examine Pat about the *accuracy* of Jay's statement because Jay, not Pat, is the one with personal knowledge of the event. If parties were permitted to prove facts by offering testimony about statements made out of court concerning those events, the fact-finder would be forced to decide what actually happened without the benefit of observing cross-examination of the out-of-court speaker.[1]

One prominent legal scholar summed up the issue we've just been discussing:

> The basic hearsay problem is that of forging a reliable chain of inferences, from an act or utterance of a person not subject to contemporaneous in-court cross-examination about that act or utterance, to an event that the act or utterance is supposed to reflect. Typically, the first link in the required chain of inferences is the link from the act or utterance to the belief it is thought to express or indicate. It is helpful to think of this link as involving a "trip" into the head of the person responsible for the act or utterance (the declarant) to see what he or she was really thinking when the act occurred. The second link is the one from the declarant's assumed belief to a conclusion about some external event that is supposed to have triggered the belief, or that is linked to the belief in some other way. This link involves a trip out of the head of the declarant, in order to match the declarant's assumed belief with the external reality sought to be demonstrated.
>
> The trier must obviously employ such a chain of inferences whenever a witness testifies in court. But the process has long been regarded as particularly suspect when the act or utterance is not one made in court, under oath, by a person whose demeanor at the time is witnessed by the trier, and under circumstances permitting immediate cross-examination by counsel in order to probe possible inaccuracies in the inferential chain. These inaccuracies are usually attributed to the four testimonial infirmities of ambiguity, insincerity, faulty perception, and erroneous memory. In the absence of special reasons, the perceived untrustworthiness of such an out-of-court act or utterance has led the Anglo-Saxon legal system to exclude it as hearsay despite its potentially probative value.

Laurence H. Tribe, *Triangulating Hearsay*, 87 Harv. L. Rev. 957, 958 (1974).

It should now be clear that the main problem with hearsay is *not* that it is always unreliable, though anyone who has ever played "Telephone" knows that the further a statement is removed from its source, the more likely it is that the original statement has not been repeated accurately. The problem is that the reliability of hearsay cannot be tested at the most appropriate time: just as the statement is made. Any later examination of the statement's accuracy usually will be less effective to uncover sources of inaccuracy. This is because the trier of fact does not have an opportunity to observe the declarant while she is making the statement.

Of course, there are other reasons for a rule forbidding the use of hearsay in court. Principal among these is the value of confrontation. In U.S. trials, we always have held dear the philosophy behind the Sixth Amendment's Confrontation Clause: that the fairest way to prove one's case is through the use of live

---

1. Note that an out-of-court statement is hearsay even if the person who made it is the same person who is now testifying about it. We discuss this issue further at the end of this subsection.

witnesses, testifying under oath, in court, subject to cross-examination, and in the presence of the opponent.[2] "Trial by affidavit," or simply calling witnesses to relate what others have said, does not meet our ideal of simple fairness and due process because it deprives the party of the opportunity for meaningful participation in the trial. This is particularly important in criminal cases. The hearsay rule seeks to enforce the principle of confrontation by establishing a preference for live testimony of percipient witnesses.

Even so, until recently the U.S. Supreme Court appeared to have de-emphasized the importance of face-to-face confrontation as a fundamental value, and instead focused on *accuracy* as the *raison d'être* of confrontation, just as it is for the hearsay rule itself. Under this view of the confrontation right, if a statement or conduct constituted hearsay but satisfied the requirements of one of the many exceptions to the hearsay rule, then the evidence could be offered against a criminal defendant. But in Crawford v. Washington, 541 U.S. 36 (1994), the Court re-evaluated its interpretation of the Confrontation Clause and held that a criminal defendant's right to confront witnesses does not derive principally from the accuracy interests that support the hearsay rule, but instead stems from the importance of having an opportunity to face and cross-examine a prosecution witness. The result of this change in the Court's view of the Confrontation Clause has been to place significant restrictions on the admissibility of certain classes of hearsay when offered against a criminal defendant. Though we discuss this issue in detail toward the end of this chapter, it is important to keep in mind that in criminal cases, the analysis of admissibility of hearsay against the defendant does not end with the determination that the evidence meets the requirements of a hearsay exception. One must also consider whether admitting the evidence would violate the defendant's confrontation rights.

The rationales for the hearsay rule also apply when the witness on the stand is repeating her own prior statement. Return to our earlier hypothetical involving Lisa's return of Eric's key. Suppose Jay is the witness and the following colloquy takes place during Jay's direct examination:

Q: On that day, did you happen to see Lisa and Eric together?

A: Yes.

Q: And after you saw Lisa and Eric together, did you tell Pat what you saw?

A: Yes, I did.

Q: What did you tell Pat?

A: I told Pat that I saw Lisa give Eric back his apartment key.

Why is there any problem with the testimony in this example, when the person who made the out-of-court statement is the same person now testifying about it? The difficulty is that the out-of-court statement is still twice removed from the event. Admittedly, it is possible to conduct some cross-examination about the veracity of the statement because the witness is the one who made the out-of-court statement. But *the passage of time* between the making of the statement and its repetition in court still presents a problem. For example, perhaps Jay no

---

2. The Confrontation Clause of the Sixth Amendment provides that "[i]n all criminal trials, the accused shall enjoy the right . . . to be confronted with the witnesses against him. . . ." Though this provision applies only to criminal trials, the notion behind it reverberates through both the criminal and civil justice systems.

longer remembers the event as well as he did when he observed it and made the earlier statement. Our memories of events erode with time and can even be affected by subsequent events. This is especially true when people have vested interests in a particular version of the event, as is often the case at trial. It might have been possible to judge Jay's sincerity if we had been present when he first made the statement but, by the time he repeats it in court, he has had the chance to prepare himself more effectively to hide any dishonesty. Even if the witness and the person who made the out-of-court statement are the same person, the "twice-removed" issue makes it more difficult to assess the veracity of the statement.[3]

Questions for Classroom Discussion

1. Why do we have a hearsay rule? How does it affect the fact-finding process?

2. If the witness and the declarant are the same person (i.e., if the witness is testifying about her own out-of-court statement), why should the statement ever be classified as hearsay?

3. Suppose a statement is hearsay and is not admissible under an exception. If the judge believes that the probative value of the statement is not outweighed by the danger of unfair prejudice, does the judge have the authority to admit the evidence?

B. THE RULE

FED. R. EVID. 801. DEFINITIONS THAT APPLY TO THIS ARTICLE . . .

The following definitions apply under this article:

(a) **Statement.** "Statement" means a person's oral assertion, written assertion, or nonverbal conduct, if the person intended it as an assertion.

(b) **Declarant.** "Declarant" means the person who made the statement.

(c) **Hearsay.** "Hearsay" means a statement that:

(1) the declarant does not make while testifying at the current trial or hearing; and

(2) a party offers in evidence to prove the truth of the matter asserted in the statement.

---

3. Though our point here is that a hearsay problem exists even when the witness and the declarant are the same, it remains true that the hearsay problem is more acute when a witness reports the out-of-court statement of another person. To some extent, the hearsay rule protects the interests of the declarant, who might well object to having her words reported by another person who might have misheard or misunderstood the statement. All of us have had the painful experience of learning that our words have been misrepresented or misunderstood.

> **FED. R. EVID. 802. THE RULE AGAINST HEARSAY**

Hearsay is not admissible unless any of the following provides otherwise:

- a federal statute;
- these rules; or
- other rules prescribed by the Supreme Court.

Look closely at the definition of hearsay in Rule 801(c). Hearsay means "a statement that the declarant does not make while testifying at the current trial or hearing—that a party offers in evidence to prove the truth of the matter asserted in the statement." Rule 801 adopts what has been called the *assertion-based* model of hearsay. It defines hearsay according to whether the person whose statement is at issue (the declarant) was making an "assertion" of the fact the statement is offered to prove. As we will see, this is not the only hearsay model courts have used. It is, however, the prevalent model. There are several components to the assertion-based definition. For evidence to be hearsay, several facts must be true:

1. It must be a "statement,"
2. of the "declarant,"
3. made "not . . . while testifying at the current trial or hearing,"
4. offered in evidence "to prove the truth of the matter asserted."

1. *"Statement"*

Rule 801(a) defines a *statement* as either "(1) a person's oral assertion; (2) a person's written assertion; or (3) a person's nonverbal conduct, if the person intended it as an assertion." From this definition, it can be seen that a statement need not involve the utterance—or even the writing—of words. It may also consist of conduct. But whether words or conduct, it must be an assertion. Because the rules do not define *assertion* or otherwise provide a legal-technical definition, it is worthwhile to turn to a common dictionary for a definition. Among the definitions of *assertion* in The Oxford English Dictionary (2d ed.) is "[t]he action of declaring or positively stating; declaration, affirmation, averment." WordNet, a Princeton University source, defines the term as "the act of affirming or asserting or stating something," and lists "statement" among its synonyms. Based on these definitions, it should be clear that to be an assertion, the words or conduct must be an attempt to state information. The previous sentence is an assertion, for example, as is the present sentence. The words "I saw the defendant shoot the victim" also constitute an assertion.

As the definition of *statement* in Rule 801(a)(2) makes clear, conduct is also an assertion if the actor intends by that conduct to convey information. If a person is asked which way a suspect ran, and the person points in a certain direction, the act of pointing probably asserts, "she went that way." If a professor says to a class, "raise your hands if you did last night's reading," those students who raise their hands would be making the assertion, "I did last night's reading."[4] Indeed, assuming they were listening to the professor's instructions, those who did *not* raise their hands would also be making an assertion (that they did not do last night's reading).

If words or conduct form an assertion, they constitute a statement, and satisfy the first component of the hearsay definition.

What types of words or conduct would not qualify as an assertion and, thus, as a statement? A *question* is generally not considered assertive. Thus, "What time is it?" would not be considered an assertion.[5] In addition, an *order* or *instruction* to another is not generally thought to be an assertion because it does not set forth some factual matter. Thus, there is no assertion when a parent instructs a child who is about to leave the house on a cold day "keep your jacket zipped up!" It might be *based on* a belief that would be an assertion if stated directly (in this case, that it is cold outside),[6] but it is not an assertion of that fact.

Similarly, conduct not intended to assert a fact is not a statement. So, if a person raises her umbrella after stepping outside, the act of raising the umbrella is not a statement that it is raining. Although she might have raised the umbrella because it was raining (or because she thought it was raining), it is doubtful she did it in order to *state* that it was raining. On the other hand, if someone asks that same woman, "Is it raining?", and she then raises her umbrella, this context suggests that her conduct is assertive. In other words, context is crucial to deciding whether conduct is assertive.

2.   *"Declarant"*

The *declarant* is the person who made the out-of-court statement. It is important to distinguish the declarant from the in-court witness. Hearsay doctrine revolves around the person who made the out-of-court statement, not the person who testifies about the statement in court.[7] You will not be able to determine whether a certain statement constitutes hearsay unless you have identified the declarant and the declarant's statement. Consider this example:

> During the trial of a negligence case arising from an automobile accident, plaintiff calls Wiley, who testifies that she was walking along the sidewalk just after the collision, and that another pedestrian ran up to her and screamed, "The red car just ran through the light and broadsided the blue car!"

In this example, the declarant is the pedestrian and the statement is, "the red car just ran through the light and broadsided the blue car!" Note that the part of Wiley's testimony in which she stated that the pedestrian ran up to her and screamed is *not* part of the declarant's statement. These are facts Wiley, the

4. Notice the possible sincerity problem in connection with this assertion!

5. Of course, some questions do make assertions. The question, "Joe shot the victim, didn't he?" contains the assertion that Joe shot the victim. We'll skip over the philosopher's argument that the question "What time is it?" asserts that it is *some* time.

6. Like questions, commands also can be assertions. For example, the command, "Put down the gun, Sally," asserts that Sally is holding a gun.

7. But recall that sometimes the declarant and the witness are the same person. An out-of-court statement that would be hearsay if made by a different person than the witness will still be hearsay even if the witness herself is the person who made that statement.

witness, perceived for herself. The hearsay rule will be applied only to the pedestrian's statement.

Sometimes there is more than one declarant. To return to the same hypothetical, suppose a police officer arrived at the scene a few minutes after Wiley, that the officer spoke to Wiley, and that Wiley repeated the first pedestrian's statement to the officer. Unfortunately, Wiley is not available to testify at trial, so plaintiff calls the officer to the stand and asks the officer what she learned at the scene. In response, the officer might testify, "A person named Wiley told me that she arrived at the scene a few moments after the crash, and that immediately on her arrival, another individual ran up to her and screamed, 'the red car just ran through the light and broadsided the blue car!'" In this example, there are two declarants because two different people made out-of-court statements repeated by the police officer during her testimony:

1. The pedestrian who told Wiley, "the red car just ran through the light and broadsided the blue car!"; and
2. Wiley, who told the police officer that she arrived at the scene a few moments after the crash and that immediately on her arrival, the pedestrian made the statement noted in (1) above.

In this example, the hearsay rule will be applied both to the pedestrian's statement and to Wiley's statement. If both statements are hearsay, both will be inadmissible unless each is subject to an exception. (Exceptions to the hearsay rule are contained in Rules 803, 804, and 807, discussed later in this chapter.) We call this "multiple hearsay" or "hearsay within hearsay."

Can an animal be a declarant? Though it might seem odd at first, this question has actually been debated in the case law. The definition of *statement* in Rule 801(a)(2) resolves the question as to nonverbal conduct because it makes clear that such conduct can be a statement only if it is the "person's nonverbal conduct, if the person intended it as an assertion." Rule 801(a)(1) does not resolve this question as to verbal behavior, but Rule 801(b) does. It states that the declarant is "the person who made the statement." Thus, if a witness is asked to testify about a bloodhound's tracking of a scent from the crime scene to the defendant several miles away through the woods, the act of the dog would not be treated as hearsay, even if it was intended as an assertion (which is unlikely).

Should the verbal or nonverbal conduct of an animal constitute a statement? Consider this hypothetical:

> Police arrest Doug after seizing illegal drugs at what they believe to be his apartment. Doug denies living there, and thus possessing the drugs. At trial, to prove Doug lives at the apartment, a police officer testifies that while she was in the apartment during the drug bust, an African Grey parrot sitting on a perch said over and over, "Good morning, Doug! Good morning, Doug!"

Would the parrot's utterances constitute a statement for purposes of the hearsay rule? No. The reason for this is relatively simple: If the goal of the hearsay rule is to require percipient witnesses to be called to testify and be subjected to cross-examination rather than allow their observations to be proved through hearsay witnesses, nothing would be gained by requiring the in-court testimony of an animal. To put it simply in the context of our example, you're not likely to learn much by cross-examining a bird. When the utterance of an animal is offered into evidence, the courts treat the problem as one of relevance and probative value, and hold that sufficient checks on accuracy can be made by cross-examining the witness who testifies about the animal's utterance.

Can a mechanical device be a declarant? For the same reasons just given concerning animals, mechanical devices do not make "statements" for purposes of the hearsay rule. Thus, the printout of an electrocardiogram, which records a person's heartbeat rhythm, would not be a statement, nor would the chiming of mechanized church bells at certain intervals of time. Each, when the subject of trial testimony, would be analyzed according to principles of relevance, and their probative value would be established through the examination and cross-examination of the testifying witness.

Beware, however, of situations in which what appears to be the utterance or conduct of an animal or mechanical device is actually the statement of a person. Consider the following examples:

1. To prove that a certain automobile crash occurred at 1:00 A.M., Plaintiff calls a witness who testifies that she awoke to a loud sound, turned to her husband, asked him what time it was, that he then looked at his alarm clock, and said, "It's 1:00 A.M."

    In this example, the witness is not testifying about the time shown on the alarm clock. She is testifying about what her husband said the time was. Her husband's utterance is thus a statement under the hearsay rule. To avoid the hearsay problem, Plaintiff could have called the witness's husband, whose testimony would have been that he looked at the clock and saw that it was 1:00 A.M.

2. To prove that Defendant ran the red light, Plaintiff offers in evidence an audiotape or videotape recording of a witness who saw the accident stating, "Defendant ran the red light."

    Here, the jury hears only the mechanical recording of the witness's statement, but the statement is hearsay because the machine merely preserved in a more permanent form the statement of a person. The same result would hold true if a witness testifies that she heard someone say, through an electronic megaphone, "Defendant ran the red light." The megaphone helped to amplify the declarant's voice, but the statement was still made by the declarant, and will be hearsay when offered to prove that Defendant ran the red light.

3. To prove that a bank was robbed just before 2:00 P.M., a witness testifies that she was standing outside the bank when the robber emerged, and that moments later, she heard the bells of St. Evi's Cathedral sound two times.

    In this example, it is likely that there is no statement. But suppose that the chimes of St. Evi's Cathedral are not operated by a mechanical device, but by a stooped-over man with a big lump on his back, who climbs the steeple's ladder each hour and pulls on a rope, causing the bells to chime. If this were the case, the chiming of the bells would actually be a human assertion, not the act of a machine. The accuracy of the bells would depend on the person's accuracy, and thus would constitute the person's statement.

4. To prove that a bank robbery occurred just before 2:00 P.M., a witness testifies that she was standing outside the bank when the robber emerged, that she

glanced at her quartz watch that sets itself automatically by synchronizing to a radio signal broadcast by the U.S. government, and that the time on the watch was 2:00.

Here, a court most likely would not find a statement. Certainly, that would be a valid conclusion. But what if our witness was wearing an antique watch that she must reset every three days? Even though her watch might not be so accurate, and in fact must be set by its owner quite frequently to remain even roughly accurate, courts would not treat the time revealed on the watch as a human statement. Instead, they would treat the problem as one of weight, with the opponent arguing to the jury that the inaccuracy of the watch should cause the jury to discount its reading. If, however, the witness set the watch to 2:00 just as she observed the robbery, then the situation would clearly involve the statement of a person, and would thus be hearsay if offered to prove that the robbery occurred at 2:00.

3.   *Statement Made "Other Than While Testifying at the Trial or Hearing"*

To be classified as hearsay under Rule 801(c), the statement must have been made by the declarant "not . . . while testifying at the current trial or hearing." This language is preferable to the more familiar phrase "out-of-court statement" because, as we will see, a statement made in court can qualify as hearsay.

Any statement not made at *the trial or hearing at which it is offered* qualifies under this part of the rule. Thus, a statement made to a police officer at the scene of a crime is one made "not . . . while testifying at the current trial or hearing." So, too, is a statement made in an affidavit or during a deposition. Even testimony given at trial is a statement made "not . . . while testifying at *the* current trial or hearing" if it is later offered during the trial in a different case. Indeed, a statement made during an earlier trial of the same case, if offered in evidence at a later trial following appellate reversal, would qualify. Even a statement made by a party, witness, or spectator in the courtroom where the case is being heard would qualify if it was not made "while testifying," which undoubtedly means while on the witness stand, under oath.

Questions for Classroom Discussion

1.   To prove that Defendant committed the crime, a police officer testifies that at a line-up, an eyewitness to the crime pointed to Defendant when asked whether the person who committed the crime was among those in the group. Is the eyewitness's conduct a statement?

2.   To prove that Defendant committed the crime, evidence is offered that a bloodhound trained to track a scent followed a trail from the crime scene and "pointed" to Defendant. Is this a statement?

(continued)

3. To prove that the "surf was up" at a particular beach, evidence is offered that hordes of surfers headed for that beach. Is this a statement?

4. To prove that an officer had just entered the barracks, evidence is offered that the lead enlisted person in the barracks loudly snapped to attention and yelled, "Atten-Hut!" Is this a statement?

5. To prove that Defendant committed the crime, a testifying witness points to Defendant when asked if the person who committed the crime is in the courtroom. Is this a statement for purposes of the hearsay rule? If so, is it covered by the rule?

6. During Denise's murder trial, a spectator in the gallery stands up and yells, "Denise is a murderer." Is this statement covered by the hearsay rule?

7. At a trial, a party wishes to offer in evidence a statement made by a person in a deposition. Is this statement covered by the hearsay rule?

8. Same case. A witness testifying at trial is asked, "Tell us what you said in your deposition." Is this statement covered by the hearsay rule?

9. Defendant is convicted of arson after Wally testifies Defendant hired him to "torch his plant." Defendant wins a reversal on appeal, and the case is retried. Wally has disappeared, so the prosecution calls a juror from the first trial to recount Wally's testimony. Is this statement covered by the hearsay rule?

4. Statement "a Party Offers in Evidence to Prove the Truth of the Matter Asserted"

The most difficult part of the hearsay definition is the requirement that the statement be offered "to prove the truth of the matter asserted." To determine whether a statement qualifies under this part of the rule, you must make two determinations.

First, determine the purpose for which the proponent has offered the statement.[8] Sometimes a hearsay question will tell you the purpose for which the statement is offered. When the question does not make this clear, you have to figure it out. The way to do this is to ask yourself, which party is offering the statement and how is that statement relevant to that party's case? This is what the statement is offered to prove.

Remember that all analysis of evidentiary issues must begin with relevance. This means that before you reach the hearsay question, you must have discerned

---

8. By "statement" we mean the utterance or conduct you are examining to determine whether it is hearsay.

the purpose for which the proponent offered the statement, and have decided whether the statement has a tendency to make the existence of that fact more probable or less probable than it would be without the statement. Usually, a several-step chain of inferences is involved in the relevance determination. If the statement does not pass the test of relevance, there is no reason to consider the hearsay rule. If it does, you must take the next step.

Second, determine the first inference in the chain of reasoning that leads from the statement to the conclusion. A statement is not "offer[ed] in evidence to prove the truth of the matter asserted" merely because it is relevant — merely because it *ultimately* tends to prove a "fact . . . of consequence in determining the action" (to use the language of Rule 401). Hearsay analysis requires you to consider *only the first inference* leading from the statement to the fact it is offered to prove. We call this the *first inference rule: A statement a party offers in evidence "to prove the truth of the matter asserted" only if the first inference from the statement must be true in order for the statement to prove the factual conclusion the party wishes to prove.* This sounds complicated, but it is not. The first inference rule is really just another way of saying that a statement is hearsay if the matter it asserts has to be true in order for the evidence to be relevant. If it must be true, that means the statement "offers to prove the truth of the matter asserted." Consider the following examples:

1. Prosecution of Defendant for the murder of Victim, a bank security guard, during a holdup. To prove that Defendant committed the crime, the prosecution calls Officer, a police officer, to testify that she interviewed Teller, a bank teller who knew Defendant well, and that Teller stated, "Defendant was the shooter."

    Here, Teller is the declarant, and the out-of-court statement is that Defendant was the shooter. The evidence is relevant because it tends to make it somewhat more likely than it would be without the evidence that Defendant committed the crime. In fact, to reach this conclusion from the evidence (the statement) requires only a single inferential step:

    STATEMENT: "Defendant was the shooter."

    ➔ **INFERENCE:** Defendant was the shooter.

    Because the assertion of the statement must be true for it to be relevant to prove that Defendant was the shooter, the statement is hearsay when it is offered in court.

2. Same case. To prove that Defendant committed the crime, the prosecution asks Officer about her conversation with Teller 2, another bank teller. Officer will testify that Teller 2 said that the shooter was a "tall woman with curly hair." Defendant meets this description.

    In this example, the declarant is Teller 2, and the out-of-court statement is that the shooter was a tall woman with curly hair. Once again, the prosecution's purpose for offering the statement is to prove that Defendant committed the crime. To reach that conclusion from this statement, the following simple chain of inferences is necessary:

→ **STATEMENT:** "The shooter was a tall woman with curly hair."

→ **INFERENCE:** The shooter was a tall woman with curly hair.

→ **CONCLUSION:** Defendant [who is a tall woman with curly hair] was the shooter.

Based on this reasoning, the statement is relevant. It is also hearsay. The assertion contained in the statement is that the shooter was a tall woman with curly hair. At this point, our first inference rule comes into play. Are the facts asserted in the statement the same facts as in the first inference? Yes. Note that if the first inference is not accurate, the statement will not be relevant. In other words, the relevance of the statement depends on the truth of the matter asserted. And it might not be accurate; just because Teller 2 said that the shooter was a tall woman with curly hair does not make it true. Teller 2 might have lied, misperceived, or remembered inaccurately; and Teller 2's definition of a "tall woman with curly hair" might not be the same as the fact-finder's. The absence of cross-examination contemporaneous with the making of the statement creates the kind of problem the hearsay rule is designed to address.

3. Personal injury action following a vehicle collision. Defendant claims Plaintiff suffered no injury in the accident. To prove Plaintiff was injured, Plaintiff calls Witness, who was with Plaintiff in her car at the time of the accident, to testify that a few moments after the crash, Plaintiff looked at Witness and said, "my back is killing me." Plaintiff's statement is relevant because an assertion of pain tends to make it somewhat more likely than it would be without the assertion that Plaintiff suffered an injury. The statement is also hearsay. Using the first inference rule, the reasoning is as follows:

→ **STATEMENT:** "My back is killing me."

→ **INFERENCE:** Plaintiff's back hurt.

→ **CONCLUSION:** Plaintiff suffered an injury in the collision.

Note that in this example, it does not matter that Plaintiff did not specifically assert that she was hurt in the accident. Plaintiff's assertion that her back hurt must be true in order for the evidence to be relevant to whether she suffered an injury in the accident.

As we have stated, the first inference rule is merely an alternative way of saying that the statement "offers . . . to prove the truth of the matter asserted." The statement is not relevant unless each link in the chain of inferences is true or valid; any break in the chain destroys the value of the evidence. Thus, the first inference rule is satisfied only when the first inference from the statement *must be true* in order for the chain of inferences to lead to the ultimate conclusion. If the first inference is the same as the assertion contained in the out-of-court statement, the statement is offered to prove the truth of the matter asserted.

Questions for Classroom Discussion

1. Why is a statement classified as hearsay only if a party offers it "to prove the truth of the matter asserted"?

   In each of the following hypotheticals, indicate whether the statement or conduct "offers to prove the truth of the matter asserted."

2. Prosecution of Defendant for the murder of Victim. To prove that Zed, another person, committed the crime, Defendant offers evidence that Zed confessed to the crime.

3. Same case. To prove that Zed committed the crime, Defendant offers evidence that Zed said, "I hated Victim."

4. Personal injury action arising from an automobile accident. To prove that Plaintiff was injured, evidence is offered that just after the event, Plaintiff was sitting on the street curb sobbing.

5. Same case. To prove Plaintiff was injured, evidence is offered that when someone asked him at the scene whether he was hurt, Plaintiff grabbed his own leg and began rubbing it.

6. Prosecution of Defendant for assault and battery on Victim. Defendant claims self-defense. To prove that Victim attacked Defendant first, evidence is offered that the day before the altercation, Victim said, "I want to kill Defendant."

7. Same case. Suppose that Defendant admits being the one who hit first, and claims he did so because he feared that Victim was going to kill him. Victim's statement ("I want to kill Defendant") is offered to prove that fact.

8. Personal injury action. Witness testifies that the light was green for Plaintiff. To prove that Plaintiff's light was *red*, Defendant offers evidence that at the scene of the accident, Witness said Plaintiff's light was red.

9. Same facts. Defendant offers Witness's prior statement ("Plaintiff's light was red") to impeach Witness by demonstrating that she is inconsistent and therefore unreliable.

10. To prove that a witness is insane, and thus not credible, evidence is offered that she said, "I am Elvis."

11. Same case. Suppose the witness said, "I believe I am Elvis."

12. Prosecution of Defendant for the murder of Victim. To prove that Defendant was acting in the heat of passion and did not premeditate, Defendant offers evidence that just before he killed Victim, Defendant's best friend Joy said to Defendant, "Victim attacked me."

(continued)

13. Same basic situation as in Question 12, except assume that Victim survived, and is now being prosecuted for rape of Joy. The prosecution offers Joy's statement to Defendant, "Victim attacked me."

14. Prosecution of Defendant for bank robbery. To prove that Defendant robbed the bank, evidence is offered that during a fight with his girlfriend, the girlfriend said to Defendant, "I may have B.O. but at least *I've* never robbed a bank."

15. Prosecution of Defendant for the murder of Victim. A prosecution witness offers to testify that he heard the sound of a gunshot from the next room, opened the door, saw Victim on the floor and Victim's brother choking Defendant while screaming, "Killer!"

C.   UTTERANCES AND CONDUCT THAT ARE NOT HEARSAY

There is no substitute for case-by-case analysis of hearsay problems. In theory, the discussion in the section above is about all you need to decide whether a particular utterance or conduct constitutes hearsay under the basic definition. Practically speaking, however, we can identify several recurring types of statements or conduct that do not constitute hearsay under the analysis contained in the preceding section because the evidence is relevant and offered to prove something other than the truth of the facts asserted. The following discussion surveys those categories.[9]

1.   Situations in Which the Utterance or Conduct Constitutes "Words of Independent Legal Significance" or "Verbal Acts"

Suppose Plaintiff sues Defendant for breach of contract after Defendant refuses to pay for a set of evidence notes that Plaintiff transferred to Defendant. Plaintiff claims that the transfer was part of a sale of the notes, while Defendant claims that the transfer was a gift. At trial, Plaintiff calls a witness to testify that before Plaintiff handed the notes to Defendant, Plaintiff said, "I offer to sell you my evidence notes for $20," and that Defendant had responded, "I accept your offer." Are the words spoken by Plaintiff and Defendant hearsay if offered to prove that a contract existed?

The answer is no, and the reason is that the words spoken by Plaintiff and Defendant are not *evidence* of the existence of the contract, *they are the very act of forming the contract.* Hearsay evidence consists of words or conduct *about* something; it is merely evidence of the fact asserted. But when the speaking

---

9. Some examples that follow could be classified in more than one of these categories. What is important is not that you can tell in which non-hearsay category the evidence fits. Rather, all you need to determine is whether the evidence fits at least one of these categories, and, thus, is not hearsay.

of words constitutes an act to which the substantive law attaches legal significance, such as the formation of an oral contract, the words spoken are not mere evidence of the act, they are the act itself. In our example, when Plaintiff said to defendant, "I offer to sell you my evidence notes for $20," those words were not *about* an offer, they *were* the offer, a legally significant event. The same is true for Defendant's reply, which constitutes an acceptance of the offer.

We call words spoken in situations such as these "words of independent legal significance" or "verbal acts." In such cases, it is the speaking of the words, and not the credibility of the person who speaks them, that counts. As a result, the only cross-examination that is needed is of the witness who repeats the words while testifying at the trial or hearing. It is possible to test the credibility of that witness by cross-examination to reveal flaws in perception, memory, sincerity, or narration. If the witness accurately repeats the words, the words will have legal significance. Because it is the credibility of the witness while testifying that is at issue, and not of the declarant, there is no need to treat the words spoken as hearsay.

There is another reason not to treat words of independent legal significance as hearsay: Were the courts to do otherwise, they would elevate the law of evidence above the substantive law. Put differently, the courts would be making it virtually impossible to establish the facts necessary to effectuate the elements of the substantive law. To return to our example, imagine you were Plaintiff and you knew that you would not be permitted to prove the existence of an oral contract by offering testimony about the words spoken that formed the contract. How would you go about proving that the contract existed? Perhaps you could offer testimony that the parties acted as though a contract existed. But such evidence is likely to be available only as to the Plaintiff; by the very nature of the case, it is likely that the Defendant acted as though no contract existed. The law of evidence is essentially procedural in nature. It is designed to create an orderly way to effectuate the demands of the substantive civil and criminal law. To classify as hearsay and exclude from evidence the utterance of the very words that have independent legal significance would be to undermine the substantive law — to put the cart (the law of evidence) before the horse (the substantive law).

You should not underestimate the importance of "verbal acts" in our society. The utterance or writing of words is often a significant act in itself. As one author has written:

> Giving a word to a thing is to give it life. "Let there be light," God said, "and there was light." No magic. No raised hands and thunder. The *articulation* made it possible. . . .
>
> It's the same with marriage. You say "I do" and you do. What is it, *really*, to be married? To be married is to say you are married. To say it not only in front of your spouse, but in front of your community, and in front of God. I don't believe in God, but I believe in saying things to God. I believe in prayer. Or I believe in saying aloud what you would pray for if you believed in God. Saying it brings it into an existence that it didn't have in silence.
>
> I once read an essay by a linguist about the continued creation of modern Hebrew. Until the mid-1970s, he wrote, there wasn't a word for frustrated. And so until the mid-seventies, no Hebrew speaker experienced frustration. Should his wife turn to him in the car and ask why he'd fallen so quiet, he would search his incomplete dictionary of emotions and say, "I'm upset." Or, "I'm annoyed." Or, "I'm irritated." This might have been, itself, merely frustrating, were it not for the

problem of our words being self-fulfilling prophecies: we become what we say we are. The man in the car says he's upset, annoyed, or irritated and becomes upset, annoyed, or irritated.

Exactly a year ago today, my first child was born. After much debate — the single word was the most difficult piece of writing I have ever done — we named him Sasha, after his grandmother. He is not only identified as Sasha, he *is* Sasha. My son would not exist with another name.[10]

Other examples of words of independent legal significance abound. In a slander action, defendant's utterance of the allegedly slanderous words ("You are the worst scoundrel since Stalin!") is not evidence *about* the slander, it *is* the slander. The same would be true in a libel action in which defendant printed the words in its newspaper. If the issue in a case is whether the police gave a person her Miranda warning, evidence that the police officer stated, "You have the right to remain silent" is not evidence that the warning was given, it constituted the warning itself. In a dispute as to whether a transfer of a ring was a gift or a loan, testimony that the plaintiff said to defendant "Please accept this as a token of my gratitude" as she handed defendant the ring is not evidence about the transfer. Because the words accompanied the transfer, they make the transfer a gift under the substantive law regarding the ownership of personal property. In a dispute between a tenant farmer and a landlord over payment of rent, where the tenant's rent consists of a portion of her crops, evidence that on the day the rent was due, the tenant pointed to a field and told the landlord, "the corn in that field belongs to you" is not evidence of payment; it is the act of payment. It is not hearsay.

Questions for Classroom Discussion

1. Breach of contract action. Defendant claims there was no contract. To prove a contract existed, Plaintiff offers evidence that after receiving Defendant's offer Plaintiff said, "I accept your offer." Is this hearsay?

2. Same case. Plaintiff offers, instead, his statement to Defendant, "I accepted your offer last week. Where are my widgets?" Is this hearsay?

3. Libel action by Plaintiff against the River City Times for publishing an article falsely stating that Plaintiff was a child molester. To prove the libel, Plaintiff offers in evidence a copy of the newspaper article. Is this hearsay?

4. Same case. To prove the libel, Plaintiff wishes to testify that the day after the newspaper article appeared, Zed told Plaintiff, "An article in the River City Times states that you are a child molester." Is this hearsay?

---

10. Jonathan Safran Foer, Introduction to The Diary of Petr Ginz 1941-1942, at vii (Chava Pressburger ed. 2004).

5. To prove that a corporate board of directors approved a certain resolution, evidence is offered that when the chairperson asked all in favor to say "aye," a majority of directors did so. Is this hearsay?

6. Action by Joe to quiet title to real property. Joe claims he acquired title through adverse possession. He offers evidence that, for years, he posted signs on the property reading, "Private property of Joe. Stay off!" Is this hearsay?

7. Dispute over ownership of a bracelet. To prove she owned the bracelet, Plaintiff testifies that her grandmother, the prior owner, gave her the bracelet while stating, "Here is your birthday present." Is this hearsay?

2. Situations in Which the Value of the Evidence Derives from the Fact That Words Were Spoken, Not from the Truth of the Matter Asserted

Sometimes, the fact that words were spoken is relevant in and of itself. For example, if it is necessary to know whether a person was alive at a given moment, evidence that at that time, the person said, "I'm still alive" would be non-hearsay. It is not the content of the words, but the fact that the speaker said anything at that moment, that matters.

In this example, one might object that the evidence seems to satisfy the definition of hearsay. After all, the words spoken constitute an assertion, the assertion is that the declarant is alive, the declarant spoke the words other than while testifying at the trial or hearing, and the words are being offered to prove the truth of the matter asserted (that the declarant was alive). But consider this: Suppose the person had said, "I'm dead." In that case, if offered to prove that the person was alive, the words are just as probative as if she had said, "I'm alive." Either way, the fact that she spoke indicates that she was alive. That being true, the words spoken do not derive their value from their content, but merely from the fact that they were spoken. The credibility of the speaker is not at all important. (Maybe she was being dishonest when she said, "I'm alive," because she actually believed she was dead. It would not matter.) The only person whose credibility is important is the witness who relates the speaker's words, and that person is on the stand and subject to cross-examination concerning her perception, memory, sincerity, and any ambiguity in her testimony. The very core purpose of the hearsay rule is not implicated in this situation. Thus, the statement is not hearsay.

Questions for Classroom Discussion

1. To prove that Deceased was alive at a certain moment, evidence is offered that at that moment, Deceased told a police officer, "I haven't kicked the bucket yet." Is this hearsay?

(continued)

> **2.** Same case. To prove Deceased was alive at that moment, Deceased's widow testifies that the police officer told her, at the scene, "Deceased just said he's still alive." Is this hearsay?
>
> **3.** To prove that Zelda spoke Spanish, a witness will testify he overheard Zelda say, in a restaurant, "Él es muy guapo!" Is this hearsay?

3. Situations in Which the Words Are Being Offered to Show Their Effect on the Listener Rather Than to Prove the Truth of the Matter Asserted

In some instances, a person's words or conduct are relevant because of the effect they have on a person who hears them. Take a simple example:

> Prosecution of Defendant for assault and battery on Victim. Defendant claims self-defense. To prove self-defense, Defendant wishes to testify that just before he punched Victim, Victim screamed, "I'm going to shoot you!"

In this hypothetical, Victim's statement is relevant because, according to the law of self-defense, a person is privileged to use force to protect himself against another person if he reasonably believes the other person poses an imminent threat of personal harm. Here, Victim's statement is being offered *not* to show that Victim actually was going to shoot Defendant, but that Defendant reasonably believed that she was in imminent danger of suffering personal violence at the hands of Victim.

Now consider a slightly more complicated example:

> Plaintiff sues Defendant after Defendant's car rear-ended Plaintiff's car. Plaintiff claims the accident was caused by faulty brakes, that Defendant was aware of the condition, and that Defendant's failure to have the brakes fixed before driving the car constituted negligence. To prove Defendant knew about the brake problem, Plaintiff calls a garage mechanic who worked on the car a few days before the accident. If allowed, the mechanic will testify that when Defendant arrived to pick up the car, the mechanic told Defendant that the brakes were faulty and that she should have them fixed immediately.

In this example, the mechanic's out-of-court statement is hearsay if offered to prove that the brakes were defective. That is because the statement asserts that the brakes were defective, and the statement was not made while the mechanic was testifying at the trial. The statement is therefore hearsay if offered for that purpose. (Recall, it doesn't matter that the declarant — the mechanic — is also the witness.)

There is another possible use of the mechanic's statement that does not run afoul of the hearsay rule. The statement is relevant, and non-hearsay, if offered to prove that Defendant was aware of the problem with the brakes and was therefore negligent for driving the car when it was in that condition. The reasoning would be as follows:

STATEMENT: "Your brakes are faulty and you should fix them immediately."

→ **INFERENCE:** Defendant heard the mechanic's statement.

→ **INFERENCE:** Defendant understood or should have understood what the mechanic meant.

→ **CONCLUSION:** Defendant was negligent for driving the car before fixing the brakes.

Notice that when offered according to this chain of reasoning, the truth of the statement does not matter. Naturally, Plaintiff will have to prove that the brakes were defective but, unless Plaintiff's statement fits within a hearsay exception (and none appear from the facts given above), Plaintiff will have to offer other evidence to prove the actual defect. But to prove Defendant's knowledge of the brakes' condition the statement is not hearsay *because it does not assert the fact of knowledge.* (This example would be different if the mechanic's statement had been, "You know that the brakes are defective.")

Why is it appropriate to treat statements such as this as non-hearsay when offered to show their effect on the listener rather than their truth? The answer is that the relevance of the evidence does not depend on the credibility of the declarant (here, the mechanic). Rather, the statement is relevant merely because it was made. Thus, the jury can assess the usefulness of the statement without the benefit of contemporaneous cross-examination of the mechanic. Of course, circumstances might have indicated to Plaintiff, or to a reasonable person in Plaintiff's condition, that the mechanic was wrong about the brakes, but that fact would affect the probative value of the evidence on the question of notice to Plaintiff or Plaintiff's knowledge, not its relevance. Because the declarant's credibility is not relevant, the inability to cross-examine the declarant contemporaneously with her making of the statement is of little or no consequence. To take another simple example, in Defendant's trial for bank robbery, the statement of one of the other robbers to Defendant, "We will kill you if you do not help us rob the bank," is relevant to help establish a defense of duress. The statement is not offered to prove that the other robber really would have killed Defendant if she did not take part. It is offered to show that Defendant *feared* the other robber would do so.

There are many possible situations in which this concept would apply to characterize a statement as non-hearsay. Essentially, whenever the reaction of person who heard a statement is relevant to an issue in the case, the statement is not hearsay if offered on that basis. The difficulty, of course, arises from the fact that usually the statement will also be relevant, though hearsay, to prove the truth of the matter asserted. Return to our defective brakes example. As we have stated, the mechanic's statement is relevant *both* to prove Defendant's negligence and to prove that the brakes were, in fact, defective. If offered for the latter purpose, however, the statement is hearsay. This creates a problem of *limited admissibility*, which we introduced in Chapter 1. If evidence is relevant for more than one purpose, but admissible only for one of those purposes, Rule 105 provides the usual remedy to protect the opponent: The court should issue a limiting instruction to the jury upon request. In our example, on the Defendant's request, the court must instruct the jury that the evidence is admissible only to prove Defendant's possible negligence for driving the vehicle after being notified that its brakes were defective. The court should instruct the jury that the evidence is not admissible to prove the existence of the defect. In fact, though Rule 105 makes limiting instruction mandatory if requested, the court may issue such instruction even without a request, if it chooses to do so. And although a limiting instruction is the usual remedy, the court may exercise its authority under Rule 403 and exclude the evidence if it finds that a limiting instruction will not sufficiently reduce the danger of unfair prejudice associated with the jury's misuse of the statement.

Questions for Classroom Discussion

1. Negligence action by Plaintiff against Defendant, the owner of a supermarket, after Plaintiff allegedly slipped on a ketchup spill. Defendant denies there was any ketchup spill. To prove the spill was present, Plaintiff calls Witness, another customer who was in the store at the time, to testify that 15 minutes before Plaintiff fell, Witness told Defendant's manager that there was ketchup on the floor. Is this hearsay?

2. Same case. Suppose Witness's statement is only offered to prove that Defendant was aware of the ketchup spill before the accident occurred. Is this hearsay?

3. Same case. Suppose Defendant asks the court to exclude the evidence because the risk of jury misuse is too great. How should the court rule?

4. Same case. If the evidence is only admissible to prove notice, how may Defendant prevent the jury from using it for the wrong purpose?

5. Same case. Plaintiff wishes to testify that while she was waiting for medical care, Witness told her, "I warned them about the ketchup!" Is this hearsay if offered to prove that Defendant was aware of the ketchup spill?

---

4. Situations in Which the Words or Conduct Constitute Circumstantial Evidence of the Declarant's State of Mind

Sometimes, the declarant's state of mind is itself a relevant fact. Suppose, for example, that during the trial of a negligence action involving an automobile collision, plaintiff calls a witness who testifies that she saw the collision, and that it occurred after defendant's car ran the red light. On cross-examination, defendant asks the witness if it isn't true that recently she said to a friend, "I am the Queen of England." In this example, the witness's out-of-court statement obviously is not offered to prove the truth of the matter asserted (that she is the Queen of England). Instead, it is offered to prove that the witness *believes* the fact she asserted, and is therefore a delusional person who cannot distinguish reality from fantasy. That, in turn, is relevant because it tends to impeach the witness's credibility by undermining her testimony that defendant ran the red light. The reasoning is as follows:

STATEMENT: "I am the Queen of England."

→ **INFERENCE:** Witness believes she is the Queen of England.

→ **INFERENCE:** Witness is delusional.

→ **CONCLUSION:** Witness's testimony about the accident is not worthy of belief.

Take another example. Plaintiff sues Defendant for the value of a jeweled necklace. Defendant claims Plaintiff gave the item to Defendant as a gift. Plaintiff admits giving the necklace to Defendant, but claims the transfer was part of a sale, not a gift. To prove that Plaintiff did not give the necklace to Defendant as a gift, Plaintiff calls Witness to testify that on the day before the transfer, Plaintiff told Witness, "Defendant is a lazy slob who hasn't worked a day in her life." Plaintiff's statement is relevant in two ways. First, it is relevant to Defendant's actual character. For that purpose, however, the statement is hearsay because it would be offered to prove the truth of the matter asserted (that Defendant is a lazy slob who hasn't worked a day in her life). The statement, however, also tends to prove Plaintiff's feelings about Defendant, based on the following reasoning:

STATEMENT: "Defendant is a lazy slob who hasn't worked a day in her life."

→ **INFERENCE:** Plaintiff believes Defendant is a lazy slob.

→ **INFERENCE:** Plaintiff does not like Defendant.

→ **CONCLUSION:** Plaintiff did not transfer the necklace to Defendant as a gift.

The statement is relevant if offered for this purpose because, if Plaintiff has negative feelings about Defendant, this makes it less likely Plaintiff gave Defendant a gift. If offered to show Plaintiff's feelings toward Defendant, the statement is not hearsay. Plaintiff's statement is not offered to prove the truth of the matter asserted, but is offered as circumstantial evidence of Plaintiff's feelings toward Defendant.

Note that if Plaintiff's statement had been, "I don't like Defendant," the statement would constitute hearsay when offered to prove Plaintiff's feelings toward Defendant. This is because the statement is not *circumstantial* evidence of Plaintiff's feelings about Defendant; it is a *direct* statement of her feelings. The reasoning is as follows:

STATEMENT: "I don't like Defendant."

→ **INFERENCE:** Plaintiff does not like Defendant.

→ **CONCLUSION:** Plaintiff did not transfer the necklace to Defendant as a gift.

Because the first inference in this logical chain is the same as the matter asserted, the statement is hearsay.

Why should a direct statement of a person's state of mind, which is the best evidence of that fact, be characterized as hearsay while a far more ambiguous statement, from which one must infer the declarant's state of mind, passes under the radar of the hearsay rule? The traditional answer is that the direct statement is less reliable because it poses a greater danger that the speaker was lying about the fact at issue (that Plaintiff does not like Defendant). This is based on a generalization that when a person wants to mislead a listener with a false-hood, the person usually asserts the false facts explicitly rather than asserting a different fact. This might or might not be true, but it is the view that supports calling the direct statement hearsay.[11] Though statements offered as circumstantial evidence of the declarant's state of mind are sometimes ambiguous and thus subject to misinterpretation, the opponent can point that fact out to the jury during closing argument.

Some out-of-court statements are admissible non-hearsay when offered to prove another state of mind: knowledge. For example, suppose the prosecution in a criminal case wishes to prove that Defendant was a member of a gang that had committed a crime. The prosecution wishes to present evidence that the gang's leader was arrested with a note in his pocket that contained Defendant's address and telephone number, which other evidence has shown to be correct. This evidence would be relevant to show that the leader knew defendant. From the leader's knowledge of Defendant, it is possible to infer that Defendant was also a member of the gang. (It might not be strong evidence, but it is still relevant.) In this example, the contents of the note are not being offered to prove the truth of the matters asserted (Defendant's correct address and telephone number), but only that the possessor of the note (the gang leader) had knowledge of that information.

Usually, it is easy to determine whether the declarant's knowledge is relevant to an issue in the case. Occasionally, it is more difficult. Consider the following example:

Prosecution of Defendant for kidnapping Victim, a six-year-old child. Defendant claims she was not involved. At trial, the prosecution presents evidence that the kidnapper abducted Victim from a playground and kept Victim locked in a van for several days before releasing Victim near her home. During an interview with police officers, Victim gave a detailed description of the van in which she was confined. She told the officer that the inside of the van was decorated with hand-painted drawings of zebras, elephants, and other animals. She said that the drawings looked like the real animals except for the colors, which she also

<hr/>

11. In the end, however, both statements will be admissible but for different reasons. The statement, "Defendant is a lazy slob who has never worked a day in her life" will be admissible as circumstantial evidence of Plaintiff's state of mind and, thus, non-hearsay. The statement, "I don't like Defendant" will be hearsay, but subject to an exception for statements of the declarant's then-existing state of mind, which we study later in this chapter.

described. The prosecution also presents evidence that Defendant owns a minivan matching Victim's description. The prosecution calls Victim to testify about the abduction and about the van in which she was imprisoned, but due to her tender age and general reticence, she is unable to testify. The prosecution now wishes to call the police officer who interviewed her to relate Victim's description of the van. Defendant raises a hearsay objection.

In this example, evidence of Victim's out-of-court description of the van is hearsay if offered to prove that the van in which she was kept had the appearance she described. But Victim's *knowledge* of the appearance of the van might be relevant in itself:

STATEMENT: "The van in which I was kept looked like . . ."

➔ **INFERENCE:** Victim was aware of a van that had that unique appearance.

➔ **INFERENCE:** Victim had been inside that van.

➔ **CONCLUSION:** (When combined with admissible evidence of the appearance of Defendant's van) Defendant was Victim's kidnapper.

The question, of course, is whether this is the real reason the prosecutor is offering the evidence, or whether the prosecutor is instead attempting to circumvent the hearsay rule. After all, every statement of a fact is also circumstantial evidence of the declarant's belief that the fact is true. The key is to determine whether there is any special significance to the state of mind of the declarant. In Bridges v. State, 19 N.W.2d 529 (Wis. 1945), the case on which our hypothetical is loosely based, the court held that there was. In *Bridges*, Defendant was charged with molesting a young girl in his apartment. After the event took place, the child told her mother and the police that she had been attacked in an apartment, and gave a very detailed description of the premises. Other evidence showed that the Defendant's apartment was very similar to the child's description. The court admitted the child's description to prove her knowledge of the appearance of the apartment. At least two facts seem to have been most important in *Bridges*: First, it was very unlikely that the child would have seen the apartment or learned of its appearance other than by having been there on the occasion in question. Second, the description was sufficiently detailed that it would be virtually impossible for the child to guess the details or make them up.

In our hypothetical, the same two elements very likely appear. If Victim had never met her kidnapper before the incident, Victim probably would have had no opportunity to see the van or learn of its interior's appearance. Thus, it is likely that she gained her knowledge of the van's appearance by having been there on the occasion in question. Also, Victim's description is sufficiently detailed as to be virtually impossible for her to fabricate. Thus, Victim's knowledge of the appearance of the van does appear significant in ways that are not true in run-of-the-mill assertions of facts. This does not mean the statement is admissible, however. The court might well conclude that the jury will not employ the permissible train of thought (that the statement shows Victim's knowledge of a fact that will be proven by other evidence), but instead make the more immediate, but impermissible, inference: The van in which Victim was held had the appearance Victim described. If the risk that the jury will use the forbidden reasoning is too great, the court should exclude the evidence under Rule 403.

A somewhat more common situation raises the same issue. Suppose an assault victim describes his attacker to a police sketch artist. Police then arrest Defendant, who bears a striking resemblance to the artist's picture. The victim's description would be hearsay if offered to prove the attacker actually had the appearance the victim described, but not hearsay if offered to prove the victim's knowledge of an individual who had the appearance described. If the victim's description was sufficiently detailed, and there is no suggestion that the victim had seen Defendant at another time or had been shown a photograph of Defendant, the victim's description can carry substantial probative value.

Questions for Classroom Discussion

1. Action by Plaintiff against Defendant for interference with contract. Plaintiff alleges that Defendant enticed Zed, one of Plaintiff's customers, to switch its business from Plaintiff to Defendant by falsely suggesting that Plaintiff was going to declare bankruptcy soon. To prove that Defendant did this, Plaintiff wishes to testify that Zed told Plaintiff's sales representative, "I'm switching because your future is uncertain." Is Zed's statement hearsay?

2. Same case. Suppose Zed's statement had been, "I'm afraid you will be going bankrupt soon and won't be able to fill our orders." Is Zed's statement hearsay?

3. Will contest. Testator's will left everything to Defendant, and Plaintiff claims this was because Defendant exerted undue influence on Testator. To prove Testator had fallen under Defendant's spell, Plaintiff wishes to testify that Testator told him, "Defendant really knows how to take care of an old man." Is this statement hearsay?

4. Same case. To prove that Defendant did not exert undue influence, Defendant calls Witness to testify that Testator told Witness, "I've never talked to Defendant about this, but I've changed my will and am leaving everything to him." Is any part of this statement hearsay?

5. Same case. Plaintiff claims one of the ways Defendant influenced Testator was to tell Testator lies about Plaintiff. To prove this, Plaintiff wishes to testify that around the time he changed his will, Testator said to Plaintiff, "You've robbed me blind for years!" Is this statement hearsay?

> **6.** Suit by Plaintiff, the personal representative of Deceased, against Defendant Insurance Co. for failure to pay on a policy of insurance on Deceased's life. Deceased died in an automobile crash. It is undisputed that Deceased suffered from an often fatal illness. Defendant claims the insurance policy was void because Deceased committed suicide. Plaintiff claims the automobile crash was an accident. To prove the crash was an accident, Plaintiff calls Witness, a good friend of Deceased, to testify that a few days before the crash, Deceased told Witness, who was suffering from a bout of deep depression, "Don't give up! There's always hope." Is this statement hearsay?

5.   *Situations in Which Words or Conduct Are Not Assertive or Are Assertive of Something Other Than What They Are Offered to Prove*

Suppose an issue in a case is whether Testator was mentally competent at the time she made her will. Evidence that other people who knew Testator treated Testator as though she were competent at the time she made her will would be relevant evidence of her competence. For example, assume that several of Testator's friends asked her to take care of their very young children while they went out of town on business for a few days. This evidence would be relevant on the following ground:

EVIDENCE: Testator's friends left their children in Testator's care.

→ **INFERENCE:** Testator's friends believed she was competent.

→ **CONCLUSION:** Testator was competent.

Situations of this kind have been called *non-assertive conduct* because they are relevant evidence of the fact they are offered to prove, but the actors do not intend to assert that fact. As such, this conduct constitutes a subset of the kind of behavior we studied in the last section: circumstantial evidence of state of mind. In our hypothetical, the actors who treated Testator as competent were not trying to assert (were not making the statement) that Testator was competent. Their behavior is simply relevant evidence that they believed Testator to be competent.

If we employ the "assertion-based" model of hearsay contained in the Federal Rules of Evidence, it should be clear that utterances or conduct of this kind are not hearsay because they are not assertive of the fact they are offered to prove. In fact, in our example, the conduct was not assertive of anything. But consider for a moment whether it is appropriate to treat this type of non-assertive conduct as non-hearsay. If a person behaves in a way that suggests she holds a certain belief, and the fact believed is something we need to prove, wouldn't we want to speak with the person to clarify what was in her mind and whether it was accurate? All of the testimonial infirmities are in play. Perhaps the actor misunderstood the true facts (perception). Perhaps she forgot that something had happened to

Testator that altered Testator's mental competence (memory). Perhaps we misinterpret the meaning of the actor's behavior (narration). And maybe the actor has behaved in this way to deceive us (sincerity).

At common law, non-assertive conduct offered to prove the actor's belief generally was excluded as hearsay. In fact, we based our first hypothetical (involving the mental competency of an individual) on the seminal case of Wright v. Joe dem. Tatham, 112 Eng. Rep. 488 (Exch. Ch. 1837). In that case, several persons who died before trial wrote letters to the testator that contained descriptions and requests they were unlikely to have directed toward a person they believed to be mentally incompetent. These letters, which never asserted the competence of the testator, were offered to prove his competence. Perceiving no difference between this situation and one in which the letter-writers actually asserted the competence of the testator, the House of Lords held the letters inadmissible. For more than a century, most courts took the same position.

The drafters of the Federal Rules considered, but rejected, the position that non-assertive conduct should be treated as hearsay. The Advisory Committee wrote:

> [Some] nonverbal conduct . . . may be offered as evidence that the person acted as he did because of his belief in the existence of the condition sought to be proved.
>
> . . . Admittedly evidence of this character is untested with respect to the perception, memory, and narration (or their equivalents) of the actor, but the Advisory Committee is of the view that these dangers are minimal in the absence of an intent to assert and do not justify the loss of the evidence on hearsay grounds. No class of evidence is free of the possibility of fabrication, but the likelihood is less with nonverbal than with assertive verbal conduct. The situations giving rise to the nonverbal conduct are such as virtually to eliminate question of sincerity. Motivation, the nature of the conduct, and the presence or absence of reliance will bear heavily upon the weight to be given the evidence. . . . Similar considerations govern nonassertive verbal conduct and verbal conduct which is assertive but offered as a basis for inferring something other than the matter asserted. . . .

Fed. R. Evid. 801 Advisory Committee's Note. Thus, the drafters minimized the dangers of admitting non-assertive conduct.

In most cases, the decision to treat non-assertive conduct as non-hearsay is a wise one. In some instances, for example, a person's conduct appears to be based on first-hand knowledge, there is no suggestion of a memory problem, the conduct is not ambiguous, and the conduct would be self-destructive if the actor were not sincere. Indeed, the House of Lords gave such an example in the *Wright* case itself: To prove the seaworthiness of a vessel, evidence is offered that its captain examined every part of it before boarding it with his family. If the captain did not believe the vessel was safe, his decision to sail off with his family aboard would be foolhardy. Though the House of Lords held that such evidence would be hearsay, there seems to be little reason to exclude it as unreliable. The same would be true when the issue is whether a particular employee is competent at her job and the party seeking to prove competency offers evidence that the employee's boss gave her additional responsibilities. In that case, the boss's conduct, without more, appears to be a reliable indicator of her belief in the employee's abilities. Perhaps the decision of the drafters of the Federal Rules to exclude non-assertive conduct from the definition of hearsay was, on balance, the better choice.

Still, there is something to be said for a more restrictive rule. For one thing, some conduct that appears non-assertive is actually assertive, and in fact intended to deceive. A good example appears in the 1983 film *Trading Places*. In that film, two young men manipulate the price of orange futures by trading the futures as though they had information that the crop was about to suffer a cataclysmic loss. This leads other traders to sell orange futures in a panic, which causes the price to collapse. When the futures have lost nearly all their value, the pair buy up the futures for a song and watch as their value shoots up when word breaks that the crop is in fact healthy. If you were another futures trader unaware of the young men's scheme, and you observed their behavior on the trading floor, you would have concluded they were basing their initial actions on a belief that the crop was in bad shape. In other words, you would have thought their behavior was an example of non-assertive conduct. In fact, however, it was assertive but deceptively so. Without the opportunity to cross-examine the men while they were acting, a fact-finder would reach an inaccurate conclusion about relevant facts.[12]

Another example of the ambiguity of non-assertive conduct is ripped from the headlines, so to speak. In 1971, the federal government planned to conduct a nuclear weapon test near Amchitka, Alaska. There was a good deal of public opposition, and among the opponents was Alaska Governor William Egan. James Schlesinger, who was serving as chairperson of the Atomic Energy Commission, told reporters that he was taking his wife and daughters with him to observe the test. If an issue at trial is whether the test was dangerous to those nearby, Schlesinger's statement (as well as the act of taking his wife and daughters to Amchitka) would be relevant evidence of safety. The reasoning would be that if Schlesinger, who was in a position to know the safety of the test, was willing to take his family with him to observe the blast, it must have been safe.

If all we knew was that Schlesinger announced he was taking his wife and daughters with him to observe the test, we might consider his statement and subsequent conduct as not intended to be an assertion of the safety of the test. But if we add the information that the governor and others in Alaska opposed the test on safety grounds, Schlesinger's words and behavior appear more as an effort to be communicative. In other words, his statement and follow-through were implied assertions of the safety of the test. If the opponent in the case persuades the court that Schlesinger's statement and conduct were assertive of the test's safety, the court should rule that evidence of the statement and conduct constitutes hearsay.

Some conduct or utterances are in fact assertive, but are not hearsay because the proponent does not offer the evidence to prove the truth of the matter asserted. Imagine the following scenario, based on the facts of United States v. Reynolds, 715 F.2d 99 (3d Cir. 1983):

> Two men, Zed and Abel, are arrested on suspicion of committing a crime, and both are taken to the police station for questioning. After the police interrogate Zed, Zed sees Abel waiting for his turn, and says to him, "I didn't tell them anything about you." At Abel's trial, the prosecution wishes to offer evidence of Zed's statement.

---

12. A famous old joke is another example: A man with a parrot walks into a bar and bets the bartender $50 that the parrot can recite the entire Gettysburg Address. The parrot squawks a little but is otherwise silent. When they get home the man berates the parrot for failing to perform and the parrot responds, "Idiot! Think of the odds we can get next time!"

Note that the statement is assertive: It asserts that Zed did not tell the police anything about Abel. But this is not what the prosecution is offering the statement to prove. Rather, the prosecution wishes to use the statement to prove, circumstantially, that Abel was involved in the crime. The statement is relevant evidence of this fact because it suggests that Zed knew of Abel's involvement.

As with truly non-assertive conduct, situations such as the one just given are merely a type of circumstantial evidence of the declarant's state of mind. They are, in fact, indistinguishable from the case of the person who declares, "I am the Queen of England," when the statement is offered to prove the declarant's insanity.

As we have stated, one can question the wisdom of the modern approach, which treats as non-hearsay non-assertive conduct and other conduct or utterances that evidence the declarant's state of mind. The next section explores an alternative model of hearsay that deals differently with these kinds of situations.

Further Reading: Ted Finman, *Implied Assertions as Hearsay: Some Criticisms of the Uniform Rules of Evidence*, 14 Stan. L. Rev. 682 (1962); David E. Seidelson, *Implied Assertions and Federal Rule of Evidence 801: A Quandary for Federal Courts*, 24 Duq. L. Rev. 251 (1974).

Questions for Classroom Discussion

1. Negligence action by Plaintiff against Defendant, the owner/pilot of a small airplane that crashed, injuring Plaintiff. Plaintiff claims Defendant took off even though the plane was unsafe. To prove that the plane was safe, Defendant offers testimony that before she got on board and took off, she walked around the plane looking at its wings and engine. Is this hearsay? If not, why not? Do you understand why "non-assertive conduct" can be a subset of "circumstantial evidence of the declarant's state of mind"?

2. To prove a hurricane was expected to hit the town, evidence is offered that the citizens boarded up their homes and businesses. Is this hearsay?

3. To prove a hurricane was coming, evidence is offered that the police activated the town's warning siren. Is this hearsay?

4. To prove a person had a contagious disease, evidence is offered that her doctor placed her in an isolation room. Is this hearsay?

5. Prosecution of Defendant for robbing the River City Bank. To prove Zed, a parking attendant, robbed the bank, Defendant offers evidence that shortly after the robbery, Zed purchased a $25,000 car with cash. Is this hearsay?

6. Same case. To prove Defendant committed the crime, the prosecution offers evidence that when the police tried to question Defendant shortly after the robbery, Defendant ran away. Is this hearsay?

D. AN ALTERNATIVE MODEL OF HEARSAY

As we have seen, the Federal Rules adopt the assertion-based model of hearsay. According to that model, an utterance or conduct is hearsay if it asserts a fact and is offered to prove that fact. The primary reason for excluding evidence that falls within this definition is that its reliability cannot be tested contemporaneously with its occurrence — that is, that the declarant cannot be cross-examined shortly after making the statement or engaging in the conduct. Cross-examination of the witness who repeats the declarant's statement is simply not a reasonable substitute for contemporaneous cross-examination of the declarant herself, even when the declarant and the witness are the same person. This makes hearsay different from most other evidence offered in court, the reliability of which (or of the person on whose information it was based) can be tested shortly after it is presented.

The assertion-based model captures most statements and conduct that suffer from this inability to be tested, but some statements or conduct slip below its radar. Consider the following example:

> Prosecution of Defendant for possession of cocaine with intent to distribute. The drugs were found in a house at 123 Elm Street. Defendant denies living in the house or having any connection to it. At trial, the prosecution calls Officer, a police officer, who testifies that shortly after arresting Defendant, she interviewed Zed, a close friend of Defendant. If permitted, Officer will testify that when she asked Zed where Defendant lived, Zed answered, "Defendant doesn't live at 123 Elm Street." Defendant objects on hearsay grounds.

Is Zed's statement hearsay? Obviously, the prosecution is not offering the statement to prove that Defendant does not live at 123 Elm Street. Instead, the prosecution is offering the statement as a falsehood — an effort by Zed, possibly encouraged by Defendant, to hide Defendant's guilt:

STATEMENT: "Defendant does not live at 123 Elm Street."

> ➔ **INFERENCE:** Zed knows where Defendant lives and is lying to protect Defendant.

> ➔ **INFERENCE:** Defendant lives at 123 Elm Street.

> ➔ **CONCLUSION:** Defendant possessed the drugs.

If we take the language of Rule 801(c) literally, Zed's statement will not be hearsay because it is not offered to prove the truth of the matter asserted (that Defendant does not live at 123 Elm Street).

But isn't it true that the value of Zed's statement depends on Zed's credibility? And if so, doesn't the trier of fact suffer a significant loss by not having the chance to observe a cross-examination of Zed at the time Zed made the statement? All the hearsay dangers (perception, memory, sincerity, narration) are potentially present. This fact leads to a possible alternative model of hearsay, one that encompasses the rule as understood by the House of Lords in

Wright v. Joe dem. Tatham (the testator case we discussed previously): *Hearsay is a statement made by the declarant, other than while testifying at the trial or hearing, the value of which depends on the credibility of the declarant.* We can call this the *declarant-based* model of hearsay.[13]

Virtually any utterance or conduct that would be classified as hearsay under the assertion-based definition contained in Rule 801(c) would be classified as hearsay under the declarant-based model. However, the declarant-based model would also sweep within the category of hearsay many instances of nonverbal conduct that would not be hearsay under the definition in Rule 801(c). An example would be the pilot's inspection of the aircraft before boarding and taking off. This conduct would be treated as hearsay under the declarant-based model, but not under the assertion-based definition (unless the pilot is found to have intended by her conduct to assert the safety of the aircraft). In addition, the declarant-based model would treat most assertions (both words and conduct) as hearsay even if the assertions are not being offered to prove the truth of the matter asserted. For example, the statement in *Reynolds,* "I didn't tell them anything about you," would almost certainly be classified as hearsay under the declarant-based model even if offered to prove a matter not asserted — that the person to whom the statement was made was involved in the crime.

For our purposes, it is best to assume that courts will generally stick closely to the assertion-based definition used in the Federal Rules. But this does not always happen, and when courts have departed from that definition, it is usually because they believe that the value of the utterance or conduct is highly dependent on the declarant's credibility. For this reason, it is important to be familiar with the declarant-based model, and to be prepared to argue that certain statements offered against your client should be classified as hearsay even if not technically offered "to prove the truth of the matter asserted."

Further Reading: Craig R. Callen, *Othello Could Not Optimize: Economics, Hearsay, and Less Adversary Systems,* 22 Cardozo L. Rev. 1791 (2001); Craig R. Callen, *Hearsay and Informal Reasoning,* 47 Vand. L. Rev. 43 (1994); Judson F. Falknor, *The Hearsay Rule as a "See-Do" Rule: Evidence of Conduct,* 33 Rocky Mtn. L. Rev. 133 (1961); G. Michael Fenner, *Law Professor Reveals Shocking Truth About Hearsay,* 62 UMKC L. Rev. 1 (1993); Michael H. Graham, *"Stickperson Hearsay": A Simplified Approach to Understanding the Rule Against Hearsay,* 1982 U. Ill. L. Rev. 903; Edward J. Imwinkelried, *The Importance of the Memory Factor in Analyzing the Reliability of Hearsay Testimony: A Lesson Slowly Learnt — And Quickly Forgotten,* 41 Fla. L. Rev. 215 (1989); Paul F. Kirgis, *Meaning, Intention, and the Hearsay Rule,* 43 Wm. & Mary L. Rev. 275 (2001); John M. Maguire, *The Hearsay System: Around and Through the Thicket,* 14 Vand. L. Rev. 741 (1961); Charles T. McCormick, *The Borderland of Hearsay,* 39 Yale L.J. 489 (1930); Edmund M. Morgan, *Hearsay Dangers and the Application of the Hearsay Concept,* 62 Harv. L. Rev. 177 (1948); Christopher B. Mueller, *Post-Modern Hearsay Reform: The Importance of Complexity,* 76 Minn. L. Rev. 367 (1992); Roger C. Park, *A Subject Matter Approach to Hearsay Reform,* 86 Mich. L. Rev. 51 (1987); Michael L. Siegel, *Rationalizing Hearsay: A Proposal for a Best Evidence Hearsay Rule,* 72 B.U. L. Rev. 893 (1992); Eleanor

---

13. The differences between the alternative definitions of hearsay are explored in detail in Roger C. Park, *"I didn't tell them anything about you": Implied Assertions as Hearsay Under the Federal Rules of Evidence,* 74 Minn. L. Rev. 783 (1990).

Swift, *The Hearsay Rule at Work: Has It Been Abolished De Facto by Judicial Decision?*, 76 Minn. L. Rev. 473 (1992); Eleanor Swift, *A Foundation Fact Approach to Hearsay*, 75 Cal. L. Rev. 1339 (1987); Olin Guy Wellborn III, *The Definition of Hearsay in the Federal Rules of Evidence*, 61 Tex. L. Rev. 49 (1982).

E. A CAVEAT: OTHER STATEMENTS THAT ARE NOT HEARSAY UNDER RULE 801

Even if evidence is hearsay under the definition contained in Rule 801(c), it still might not be hearsay. This is because Rule 801(d) defines as non-hearsay certain statements that would otherwise qualify as hearsay under the basic definition in Rule 801(c). These are sometimes referred to as the "exemptions" from the definition of hearsay. We turn to these rules in detail later in this chapter and in Chapter 6. At this point, we want to make one important distinction. Because the drafters of the Federal Rules chose to exempt certain categories of statements from the definition of hearsay, you must understand the difference between an *exception* to the hearsay rule and an *exemption* from the rule.

Exceptions to the hearsay rule are found in Rules 803, 804, and 807. Exceptions come into play only if the utterance or conduct qualifies as hearsay under Rule 801(c). If it does, you then must determine whether the utterance or conduct falls into one or more of the many categories covered by the exceptions. If so, it will not be excluded by Rule 802, the so-called hearsay rule. But for definitional purposes, evidence within an exception is still hearsay, albeit admissible. Of course, to say that the evidence is not excluded by the hearsay rule does not mean it is admissible. Other evidence rules might prevent its admission.

Exemptions from the definition of hearsay are found in Rule 801(d). If an utterance or conduct falls into one of the categories contained in that rule, the utterance or conduct is not hearsay even though, analytically, it satisfies the definition of hearsay found in Rule 801(c). Thus, there is no need to consult the exceptions in Rules 803, 804, and 807 to determine whether the evidence is excluded by the hearsay rule. The hearsay rule will not stand as a bar to admission because the evidence is not hearsay.

F. HEARSAY WITHIN HEARSAY

FED. R. EVID. 805. HEARSAY WITHIN HEARSAY

Hearsay within hearsay is not excluded by the rule against hearsay if each part of the combined statements conforms with an exception to the rule.

Sometimes, a witness's proposed testimony, or a document offered in evidence, will contain multiple layers of out-of-court statements. Rule 805 provides, by negative inference, that when this occurs the testimony or document will not be admissible unless an exception exists for each layer of hearsay. For present purposes, it is important only for you to teach yourself to recognize when testimony or a document presents a hearsay-within-hearsay problem.

Consider the following example:

> Prosecution of Defendant for the murder of Joe. At trial, the prosecution calls Witness, who proposes to testify that shortly after the killing took place, he was in a bar when he overheard Zed tell the bartender, "Abel told me that Defendant shot Joe."

In this example, there are two out-of-court statements:

1. Abel's statement to Zed, "Defendant shot Joe."
2. Zed's statement to the bartender, "Abel told me he saw Defendant shoot Joe."

It might help to conceptualize the statements in the following way, demonstrating that one statement is contained within the other:

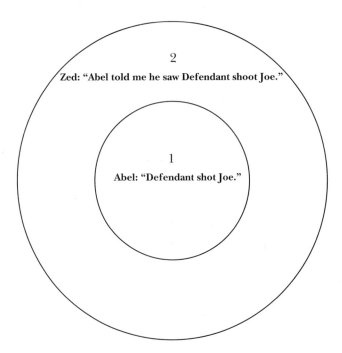

Both of these statements are hearsay. Statement (1) is hearsay because it is the assertion of Abel, made out of court, that he saw Defendant shoot Joe, and the prosecution no doubt is offering the statement to prove the truth of the assertion. Statement (2) is hearsay because it, too, is offered to prove the truth of the matter asserted. Witness's testimony concerning Zed's statement (which includes Abel's statement) will not be admissible unless there is an exception covering both Abel's and Zed's statements. Thus, if there is an exception covering Abel's statement but not Zed's, we'd treat Abel's statement as, in a sense, trapped. It is not admissible. To understand why the rule works this way, consider the implications for the case if the second statement was inaccurate: Zed's assertion is that Abel made a certain statement to him. If Abel did not make that statement to Zed, Zed's statement would be of no value in proving Defendant shot Joe. (Zed would lack personal knowledge of anything relevant to the case, in all likelihood.)

To reiterate, according to Rule 805, no part of Witness's testimony concerning what he overheard in the bar will be admissible unless there is an exception for each part. As you will be able to determine after we study the exceptions to the hearsay rule, it does not appear that there is an exception for either statement. Thus, Witness will not be permitted to testify to what he overheard.

Now consider why the following example does *not* raise a multiple hearsay problem:

> Prosecution of Defendant for bank robbery. The prosecution alleges that Defendant and Zed robbed the bank together. Defendant admits she participated in the bank robbery, but claims she acted under duress. To prove that fact, Defendant calls Witness, who will testify that a few weeks after the robbery, Defendant said to Witness, "Zed said, 'I will kill you if you do not help me rob the bank!'"

As in the previous example, there are two statements:

1. Zed's statement to Defendant, "I'll kill you if you do not help me rob the bank."
2. Defendant's statement to Witness, "Zed said, 'I will kill you if you do not help me rob the bank!'"

Here, Zed's statement to Defendant is not hearsay because it is not offered to prove the truth of the matter asserted. Zed asserted that he would kill Defendant if she did not help him rob the bank. But the statement is not offered to prove that Zed actually would have done this. Instead, it is offered to show its effect on Defendant, the listener. It is relevant for that purpose because it forms the basis for Defendant's claim that she acted under duress.

The second statement, Defendant's statement to Witness, is hearsay. It is an assertion that Zed made the threat. If Zed did not actually make the threat, the underpinning of Defendant's duress defense falls away. Thus, the statement is offered to prove the truth of the matter asserted, and is hearsay. Unless there is an exception that covers Defendant's statement to Witness (and most likely, there is not), Witness will not be permitted to testify to what Defendant told her.[14]

Situations involving hearsay within hearsay are common in trials. They arise frequently, for example, when a party offers documentary evidence such as business or public records. Thus, if a police record of an auto accident contains

---

14. Defendant could avoid the hearsay problem by taking the stand to testify that Zed made the threat. There might be strategic reasons why Defendant might choose to exercise her Fifth Amendment privilege not to testify, however.

statements of witnesses who observed the event, there is a multiple hearsay problem. And the same can be true in other contexts as well.

A related problem is presented when one out-of-court statement is contained in another but only one of those statements is hearsay while the other is not hearsay because it is within one of the exemptions established by Rule 801(d). This is literally not hearsay within hearsay as described by Rule 805 because only one of the out-of-court statements is hearsay. Nonetheless, logic of the admissibility analysis is similar to that described in Rule 805: The evidence is admissible so long as each level of out-of-court statement is either within an exemption to the hearsay definition or an exception to the hearsay rule.

G. HEARSAY VERSUS PERSONAL KNOWLEDGE OBJECTIONS

In Chapter 1 we learned that the personal knowledge requirement embodied in Rule 602 means that a witness must testify from first-hand perception. In the present chapter we have learned that the hearsay rule does something similar. Rule 802 applies when a witness testifies concerning an out-of-court statement if that statement, rather than the witness's first-hand perception related in court, is the means to prove the facts asserted in the statement.

Because Rules 602 and 802 are related, students sometimes have difficulty determining when the appropriate objection to a given item of evidence should be based on one provision or the other. For example, assume a murder prosecution against Joe. Joe calls a witness who offers to testify, "I heard Joe's brother say, 'Joe was with me in another town on the night of the murder.'" The statement clearly is offered to prove the truth of the facts asserted, which help to establish Joe's alibi. This means the evidence is hearsay. But the witness also lacks first-hand perception of the acts asserted in the statement because the brother, not the witness, was with Joe on the night in question. So is the proper objection hearsay or lack of personal knowledge? Are both objections applicable?

Hearsay is the proper objection in this example. Rule 602 is inapplicable because the witness has personal knowledge of what he heard the declarant say and the declarant has personal knowledge of what he saw.[15] The evidence is hearsay because the witness quotes an out-of-court statement for the purpose of proving the facts asserted in that statement.

But assume the witness testified, "Joe was in another town on the night of the murder." If the witness did not see Joe that night and is merely relying on what he heard Joe's brother say, the proper objection now is lack of personal knowledge. This is because the witness had no first-hand perception of the facts to which she testifies. Hearsay is not the proper objection because the witness does not purport to repeat the out-of-court statement.

---

15. Recall that the personal knowledge requirement applies not only to in-court witnesses but also to out-of-court declarants (with one exception that we learn in the next section).

This means that the proper objection is determined by the form of the testimony. If the witness quotes or paraphrases an out-of-court statement, the objection is hearsay.[16] If the witness does not quote or paraphrase, but simply relies on another person's perception as described in an out-of-court statement, the proper objection is lack of personal knowledge.

Another way to choose the correct objection is to ask whether the fact that the witness testifies to is literally the fact the witness perceived. (Does FT = FP?) If the answer is yes, then the witness has personal knowledge and the objection must be hearsay. If the answer is no, the objection is lack of personal knowledge. For example, FT = FP in the example described above when the witness testifies, "I heard Joe's brother say, 'Joe was with me in another town on the night of the murder.'" The "fact testified" to is what the witness heard the brother say. And this is exactly the fact perceived since the witness used his sense of hearing to perceive what the brother said. Thus, the correct objection is hearsay. In contrast, when the witness testified, "Joe was in another town on the night of the murder," but did not see Joe that night and is merely relying on what he heard Joe's brother say, FT ≠ FP. Thus, the correct objection is lack of personal knowledge.

Questions for Classroom Discussion

1. Civil action for injuries suffered in an automobile accident. Defendant alleges contributory negligence in that Plaintiff knowingly was driving with defective brakes, which prevented him from stopping in time to avoid the collision. To prove Plaintiff had defective brakes, Defendant calls a witness who offers to testify that on the day before the accident, she heard an auto mechanic tell Plaintiff, "I just took a look at your brakes. They are shot." Is this testimony objectionable? If so, on what basis?

2. Same case. Plaintiff admits his brakes were defective but claims he did not know this was the case. Defendant offers the same evidence only to prove Plaintiff was on notice of the defect. Is this testimony objectionable? If so, on what basis?

3. Same case. Defendant's witness testifies, "Plaintiff's brakes were shot." The witness is relying on what she heard the mechanic say. Is this testimony objectionable? If so, on what basis?

4. Same situation as in Question 3. How does Plaintiff's attorney find out and reveal to the judge that the witness lacks personal knowledge?

---

16. By paraphrase, we mean simply that the witness purports to describe the content of an out-of-court statement, but does not quote word for word. "Joe's brother said, 'Joe was in another town,'" is a word-for-word quotation. "Joe's brother said that Joe was in another town" is a paraphrase.

H.   REVIEW: HEARSAY OR NOT HEARSAY

Questions for Classroom Discussion

In each of the following questions, indicate whether the evidence is hearsay or not hearsay. Assume the definition of hearsay in Federal Rule 801(c) (and not the declarant-based model) applies unless you are instructed otherwise.

1. Prosecution of Defendant, a tall blond man, for bank robbery. Defendant denies committing the crime. To prove Defendant committed the crime, the prosecution calls Officer, a police officer, to testify that she spoke with Zed, who witnessed the robbery, and that Zed said the crime was committed by a tall blond man.

2. Same case. Assume Zed testified in an earlier trial of the same case that the robbery was committed by a tall blond man. The first trial ended in a hung jury. Before the case could be retried, Zed died. The prosecutor wishes to take the stand to testify that she was at the first trial, and heard Zed testify that the robber was a tall blond man.

3. Same case. Instead of taking the stand herself to relate the substance of Zed's testimony at the first trial, the prosecutor calls Court Reporter, the court reporter who transcribed the testimony at the first trial, to read Zed's testimony from the official transcript.

4. Same case. To prove Defendant's involvement, the prosecution calls Witness, a teller who was in the bank at the time of the robbery, to testify that just after the robbery, she told a police officer that the robber was a tall blond man.

5. Same case. The prosecution calls Investigator, the chief police investigator assigned to the case, to testify that a police forensic expert examined the stolen money for fingerprints, and that this expert told Investigator that fingerprints on the money matched those of Defendant.

6. Same case. If the court sustains a hearsay objection to the testimony in Question 5, the prosecutor will respond that the forensic expert's statement is not being offered to prove the truth of the matter asserted (that fingerprints on the money matched those of Defendant), but only to prove that the expert believed that the prints matched those of Defendant).

7. Same case. Assume the evidence of the forensic expert's statement is offered during a hearing to determine whether there was probable cause to arrest Defendant.

8. Wrongful death action by Plaintiff, administrator of the estate of Deceased, against Defendant following an automobile accident in which Deceased died. Defendant admits negligence but contests damages, claiming that Deceased died instantly in the crash. To prove that Deceased lived for a time after the crash, Plaintiff calls Witness, a bystander who observed the accident, to testify that she approached Deceased's car just after the crash, and that Deceased was moaning incomprehensibly.

9. Same case, except that Witness will testify that when she approached Deceased, Deceased said, "I'm alive."

10. Same case, except that Witness will testify that she did not speak to Deceased, but that Bystander told her that Deceased said, "I'm alive."

11. If the judge rules that the evidence in Question 10 is hearsay, how can Plaintiff's lawyer get Deceased's words before the jury?

12. Prosecution of Defendant for murder. To prove her innocence, Defendant offers a letter written by Zed, now deceased, taking responsibility for the crime.

13. To prove that the traffic signal at a particular intersection had turned green, a witness will testify that at that moment, the driver second in line at the intersection honked her horn.

14. To prove that it was raining at a particular place and time, evidence is offered that people opened their umbrellas.

15. To prove that Zed suffered pain when another person bumped into him, evidence is offered that Zed said, "Ouch!"

16. Same case. To prove Zed was in pain when brought to the hospital, an emergency room nurse testifies that when she asked Zed, "Are you in pain?" Zed looked at the nurse, put his hand on his stomach and said, "Ouch!"

17. Prosecution of Defendant for burglary. Defendant claims she never left her house on the night of the crime. To prove Defendant was home on the night of the crime, Defendant testifies that earlier that evening, before the burglary took place, she told her husband, "I have a horrible stomach ache."

18. Same case. To prove that Defendant never left her house on the night of the crime, Defendant testifies that she is a Sagittarius, that she read her horoscope in the paper on the day the crime was committed, and that the horoscope read, "Your life will take a bad turn if you don't stay home tonight."

(continued)

19. Same case. Instead of testifying that she read the horoscope in the paper, Defendant testifies that on the day the crime was committed, she got a call from Zed, a close friend, who said, "Stay home tonight. Your horoscope says that if you don't, your life will take a bad turn."

20. Same case. Instead of Defendant or Zed testifying, Abel, a mutual friend of Defendant and Zed, takes the stand to testify that on the same day, Zed told Abel that he had told Defendant to stay home because her horoscope said that her life would take a bad turn if she did not.

21. Prosecution of Defendant for the shotgun murder of Victim in Springfield. There is a dispute about the time Victim was shot. Defendant claims the shooting occurred at 6:00, when she was in River City. The prosecution claims the shooting occurred at 4:00, when it is undisputed that Defendant was in Springfield. To prove that Victim was shot at 4:00, the prosecution calls Witness to testify that on the day of the crime, she was working at her desk, heard a loud sound that could have been a gunshot or an auto backfiring, and within a minute, looked at her watch, which read 4:00.

22. Same case, except that Witness testifies that within a minute after hearing the loud sound, she asked her colleague what time it was, and that the colleague looked at her watch and said, "4:00."

23. Same case, except that instead of testifying that she looked at her watch or asked a colleague about the time, Witness testifies that within a minute after hearing the shot, she heard the automated "break whistle" on the factory floor go off four times, which she testifies indicates that it is 4:00.

24. Conversion action by Plaintiff against Defendant arising from a dispute about ownership of a certain dog. Defendant, a kennel operator, claims that Plaintiff sold the dog to Defendant for $200. Plaintiff claims she was the one who paid the $200, and that this payment was to board and care for the dog for a month while Plaintiff traveled in Europe. To prove that the arrangement was only for boarding and care, Plaintiff testifies that when she brought the dog to Defendant, she said, "I'll pay you $200 if you will care for my dog for a month."

25. Same case. Plaintiff wishes to testify that when she returned from Europe and Defendant refused to turn over the dog, Plaintiff responded, "We had a deal for board and care, not a sale!"

26. Action by Landlord against Tenant to recover rent. Both are farmers. Rent is to consist of a portion of Tenant's crops. Tenant alleges she paid the rent. To prove payment, Tenant testifies that on the day rent was due, she approached Landlord, pointed to a certain field, and said, "That corn over there is your rent."

27. Prosecution of Defendant for the murder of Victim. During the trial, while Defendant is testifying on her own behalf, a member of Victim's family, present in the courtroom, stands up and screams, "You murderer! You killed Victim, and I saw you do it." Later in the trial, a witness who heard the family member's outburst is asked to repeat what the person said.

28. Negligent entrustment action by Plaintiff against Defendant. Defendant allowed Zed to use her car, and Zed recklessly struck Plaintiff while Plaintiff was crossing the street in a crosswalk. Defendant denies she had reason to know of Zed's recklessness. To prove Defendant knew about Zed's poor driving habits, Plaintiff calls Witness to testify that a week before Defendant loaned the car to Zed, Witness told Defendant that Zed was "the most irresponsible and reckless person I've ever met."

29. Same case. Plaintiff offers into evidence an article in a local newspaper, published a week before Defendant loaned the car to Zed. The article states that Zed's driver's license had been revoked because of several arrests for reckless driving.

30. Same case. To prove Defendant was aware of Zed's recklessness, Plaintiff calls Witness to testify that several days before Defendant loaned the car to Zed, Abel told Witness that he had just told Defendant that Zed was the most reckless person he had ever met.

31. Proceeding to commit Lengold, a law professor, to an institution for the hopelessly insane. To prove Lengold is insane, evidence is offered that one day recently, Lengold grabbed a megaphone, went to the highest point on campus, and yelled, "I am the king of the Federal Rules!"

32. Employment discrimination action. Employer claims Plaintiff was fired for incompetence; Plaintiff claims racial motives. To prove Plaintiff was fired for incompetence, Employer wishes to testify that a few weeks before firing Plaintiff, she demoted Plaintiff from a supervisory job to a lower position.

33. Same case. Suppose the jurisdiction in which the case is tried uses the declarant-based model of hearsay rather than the assertion-based model. Would evidence of the demotion be hearsay?

34. Prosecution of Defendant for running a murder-for-hire operation out of his neighborhood "counseling" office. Defendant denies running such a business. To prove that Defendant ran a murder-for-hire operation, the prosecution calls a police officer who conducted an authorized wiretap of Defendant's office. If permitted, the officer will authenticate and play a tape recording of a "client" of Defendant saying to Defendant, "Please make my husband disappear."

(continued)

35. Paternity action by Plaintiff against Defendant. Plaintiff claims that Defendant is the father of Plaintiff's ten-year-old son Zed. At trial, Zed takes the stand and testifies, "Defendant is my father." If the evidence is not hearsay, is there any other objection?

36. Negligence action by Plaintiff against Defendant arising from an automobile collision. At trial, Plaintiff calls Witness, a bystander, to testify that shortly after the cars collided, another bystander asked Witness, "Did you see the Chevy run the red light?"

37. Prosecution of Defendant for arson. Defendant asserts that the crime was committed by someone else. To prove Defendant committed the crime, the prosecution wishes to offer evidence that the day after the crime was committed, the police asked Zed if Defendant committed the crime, and that Zed answered, "it wasn't a little birdy, if you know what I mean."

38. Negligence action by Plaintiff against Defendant after the car Defendant was driving ran off the road and struck Plaintiff. To prove Defendant's car was in bad condition, leading to the accident, Plaintiff offers evidence that an hour before the accident, someone said, "Your right front tire is missing two lug nuts."

39. Same case. Assume the person's statement was made in Defendant's presence, and is offered to prove that Defendant knew the car was in bad condition.

40. Prosecution of Defendant for violation of the securities laws by trading stock in Zed Corp. on inside information. To prove Defendant's guilt, the prosecution offers evidence that just before Defendant traded the stock, an insider at Zed Corp. told Defendant that the company was about to announce a huge loss for the previous quarter.

41. Prosecution of Defendant for theft of a valuable coin. The coin at issue is a one-of-a-kind double-tailed quarter. Though police found the coin buried in a field near Defendant's home, Defendant denies any involvement in the theft. At trial, the prosecution calls Officer, a police officer, who testifies that Defendant's housekeeper told Officer she saw a quarter "with two tail sides" in Defendant's home. Defendant's counsel objects on hearsay grounds. The prosecution responds that evidence of the housekeeper's statement is not being offered to prove that such a coin was in Defendant's house, but only to prove that the housekeeper had knowledge of such a coin. Defendant continues to object.

42. Negligence action by Plaintiff against Defendant arising from an automobile accident. After the accident, Plaintiff received a letter from Zed, a witness to the accident, stating that Defendant's car ran a red light and struck Plaintiff's car. Plaintiff offers Zed's letter into evidence.

43. Same case. Prior to trial, Plaintiff took Zed's deposition, and Zed repeated that Defendant's car ran the light and struck Plaintiff's car. Zed died before trial. Plaintiff wishes to use the transcript of Zed's deposition to prove that Defendant ran the light and struck Plaintiff.

44. Prosecution of Defendant, a woman, for murder. To prove Defendant committed the crime, the prosecution calls Witness, who testifies that she saw Defendant shoot the victim. To impeach Witness by showing that she tells inconsistent stories, Defendant wishes to offer evidence that just after the killing, Witness told the police the killer was a man.

45. Same case. Assume Defendant offers Witness's prior statement to prove that the killer was a man.

46. Prosecution of Defendant for murder. To prove Defendant's guilt, the prosecution offers evidence that Defendant ran away when the police tried to question her at the scene of the killing.

47. Same case. In response to the evidence offered above, Defendant calls Witness to testify that just before Defendant ran from the scene, someone told Defendant that her child had just been run over by a car on the next block.

48. Slander action by Plaintiff against Defendant. Plaintiff claims Defendant told an audience of senior citizens that Plaintiff, a stock broker, had stolen money from many of his elderly clients. To prove this, Plaintiff wishes to have Witness, who was in the audience, testify about Defendant's statement.

49. Same case. To prove that Defendant slandered her, Plaintiff calls Zed to testify that she was not in the audience, but that after the meeting, Witness told her that Defendant claimed Plaintiff had stolen money from many of his elderly clients.

I. RATIONALES FOR EXCEPTIONS TO AND EXEMPTIONS FROM THE HEARSAY RULE

If the hearsay rule protects such important values, why are there so many exceptions to and exemptions from it? The reason, in a nutshell, is that the rule is too broad. It sweeps within its principle some hearsay that is quite reliable, and also excludes some hearsay for which there is substantial need in the resolution of the issues at trial. If the hearsay rule excluded even highly reliable and much-needed evidence, it would be more difficult to determine the truth, which is the central purpose of a trial. Another way of putting it is that some hearsay is too useful and too important to do without.

The key, of course, is to figure out what types of hearsay are more reliable than other types. The common law went about this by creating *categories* of hearsay that are either more reliable as a class, or more necessary to the truth-determination process, or both, than garden variety hearsay. It's not a matter of case-by-case determination, but rather of deciding whether the hearsay at issue fits within one of these categories.

As time went on, courts identified more and more categories of reliable or necessary hearsay. The Federal Rules of Evidence now contain eight exemptions and about thirty exceptions to the hearsay rule. Virtually all of these are now also found in the law of each state.

Before we begin to study the specific categories, we should clarify the terminology. If an utterance or conduct is classified as hearsay, it may only be admitted if it fits within an *exception to* the hearsay rule. We would then say that the evidence is hearsay, but admissible. The *exceptions to* the hearsay rule are listed in Rules 803, 804, and 807.

The drafters of the Federal Rules decided to treat as *non-hearsay* some utterances or conduct that would have been hearsay at common law, but admissible under an exception. We say that such evidence fits within an *exemption from* the hearsay rule. To put it simply, if asked whether such evidence is hearsay or not hearsay, you would answer *not hearsay*. The exemptions can be found in Rule 801(d)(1) and 801(d)(2). If evidence fits within any of the exemptions created by this rule, it is not hearsay even if otherwise it would be classified as hearsay under Rule 801(c). You can think of Rule 801(d) as creating exemptions from the general definition of hearsay in Rule 801(c). This means that if the evidence is within an exemption, you do not need to consider whether the evidence would be hearsay under Rule 801(c) — it is not hearsay no matter what Rule 801(c) says. If you are having some difficulty mastering Rule 801(c), this means there is an entire category of cases where you do not have to worry about it!

Why did the drafters of the Federal Rules choose to complicate things in this way? That is a good question that has an only partly satisfactory answer. The drafters believed that evidence falling within the categories in Rule 801(d) should be admitted not because it is inherently reliable or particularly necessary, but because the adversary system will help to ensure adequate testing of its reliability. Consider the types of statements that fall within Rule 801(d)(2). These are all "admissions" of a party opponent. As such, the person who made the statement — the opposing party — will always have both an incentive and an opportunity to deny making the statement or to explain its meaning. In other words, the adversary system will provide information that helps the fact-finder assess the reliability of the evidence. The same is true for statements falling within Rule 801(d)(1), all of which are prior statements made by persons who testify at the trial. If those declarants testified as witnesses, the party who called them is able to recall them to explain or deny the prior statement.

Whether you accept this justification or not, the fact remains that we must distinguish between exceptions to the hearsay rule (statements that are hearsay but admissible because of an exception contained in Rules 803, 804, or 807) and exemptions from the definition of hearsay (statements that are not hearsay). We begin with the exemptions.

J. EXEMPTIONS FROM THE HEARSAY RULE: STATEMENTS OFFERED AGAINST A PARTY (ADMISSIONS)

> **FED. R. EVID. 801.   DEFINITIONS THAT APPLY TO THIS ARTICLE; EXCLUSIONS FROM HEARSAY**

(d) Statements which are not hearsay. A statement that meets the following conditions is not hearsay:

(2) *An Opposing Party's Statement.* The statement is offered against an opposing party and:

(A) was made by the party in an individual or representative capacity;

(B) is one the party manifested that it adopted or believed to be true;

(C) was made by a person whom the party authorized to make a statement on the subject;

(D) was made by the party's agent or employee on a matter within the scope of that relationship and while it existed; or

(E) was made by the party's co-conspirator during and in furtherance of the conspiracy.

The statement must be considered but does not by itself establish the declarant's authority under (C); the existence or scope of the relationship under (D); or the existence of the conspiracy or participation in it under (E).

1. Simple Party "Admissions"

In its basic form, the party admission rule is extremely simple: If a party has made a statement, the party's opponent is entitled to offer that statement into evidence to prove the truth of anything relevant, including the matter asserted. Because such a statement meets the requirements of Rule 801(d)(2)(A), it qualifies as non-hearsay. The rule really is as simple as it sounds. Any statement made by a party may be offered by the party's opponent. This means any party may produce a witness to testify about an opponent's statement.

Calling such a statement an *admission* is somewhat misleading and often confuses students. It does not matter whether the statement "admitted" anything, or was even against the declarant's interest at the time it was made.[17] As long as the statement is "offered against an opposing party and (A) was made by the party in an individual or representative capacity," it is defined as not hearsay by Rule 801(d)(2).

Imagine that a husband and wife are dissolving their marriage, and that they are disputing the division of assets. The husband claims that several years earlier, his wife purchased a vacation home without telling him, and that she has a great amount of equity in that home. The wife denies owning the home. To prove the wife owns the home, the husband offers evidence that after the wife allegedly purchased the home, she sought a business loan from a bank, and in the

---

17. There is, however, a hearsay exception for statements against interest: Rule 804(b)(3). Don't confuse this with party admissions.

application for that loan, she listed the home as an asset. In the dissolution proceeding, the husband may offer his wife's statement as a party admission even
though, at the time she made the statement, it was not against her interest to
make it. In fact, it was in her interest to fully disclose her financial assets, and
even to exaggerate them, to help her secure the loan. Again, all that Rule
801(d)(2) requires is that the statement be made by a party, and that it is offered
by the opponent.

Another feature of party admissions that makes them easy to admit is that
courts do not demand that the declarant have personal knowledge of the facts
contained in the statement. This is the one exception to the personal knowledge
requirement otherwise imposed on all lay witnesses and out-of-court declarants
by Rule 602. To illustrate, assume that Plaintiff, a tenant, sues Defendant, her
landlord, following Plaintiff's slip-and-fall accident on a common stairway. Plaintiff alleges that she fell because the bulb lighting the stairway burned out and
that Defendant had not replaced it. Suppose Defendant discussed the accident
with a friend, and said, "The tenant fell because the lights in the stairway were
burned out." Even if Defendant did not have personal knowledge of this fact,
but learned it from another tenant shortly after the accident, Defendant's statement to her friend qualifies under Rule 801(d)(2).[18]

Usually, it is easy to identify the "party" whose statement may be offered under
Rule 801(d)(2) as a party admission. The matter becomes somewhat more complicated when the opponent is a corporate or governmental entity, however. As we
see below, corporate and other business entities can only speak through people,
and the rules take account of that reality by creating categories of what are called
agency and authorized admissions. In criminal cases, one of the parties is the
"people" or the "state," and the issue may arise whether the statement of a police
officer, prosecutor, or other person involved in law enforcement qualifies as a
party admission. As we see when we discuss authorized and agency admissions,
courts have tended not to treat such statements as party admissions.

Offering evidence of a party admission is usually very simple: The party simply
calls a witness to testify about the opponent's statement. In the landlord-tenant
hypothetical, Plaintiff might call the Defendant's friend, and conduct the
following direct examination:

P.   Did you speak with Defendant on September 1 of last year?

W.   Yes. We met for lunch that day.

P.   Did you discuss my client's accident on the stairway?

W.   Yes. We talked about it.

P.   Did Defendant say anything about what caused my client's accident?

W.   Yes.

P.   What did he say?

W.   He said your client fell because the lights in the stairway were burned out.

---

18. Note that the landlord in this example asserted *as a fact* that the tenant fell on the stairs because
the light had burned out. She did not tell her friend that another tenant told her this fact. Had she said
to her friend, "Another tenant told me that the accident happened because a light had burned out,"
this statement would not qualify as an admission because it would be the statement of the second
tenant, not that of the defendant landlord. Unless the circumstances show that the landlord "adopted"
as true the second tenant's statement, the statement would be hearsay, and probably would not fit
within any exception. For discussion of "adoptive admissions," see the next section of this chapter.

If a party-opponent's statement is in writing, offering the statement requires authenticating the writing.

Why are the statements of a party so readily admissible when offered by an opponent? Some party admissions are indeed more reliable than other out-of-court statements. In particular, those admissions that are against the interests of the declarant when made are likely to be reliable because people normally do not say things against their interest unless they believe them to be true. But as we noted above, a party admission need not have been against the interest of the declarant when it was made. Not all admissions, therefore, are particularly reliable. (Indeed, in the marriage dissolution hypothetical discussed above, the wife had a motive to lie when she made the statement.) So, there must be another rationale for admitting these statements.

The rationale lies in the kind of consideration that caused the drafters of the Federal Rules to exempt party admissions from the definition of hearsay: Because the declarant is a party, she usually will be present at the trial and has both an opportunity and an incentive to clarify any of her own statements that have been offered against her. Thus, the adversary system will help to correct any distortions in fact-finding caused by the introduction of the statements of party-opponents. Moreover, a party who finds her own statement being offered by an opponent can hardly complain that she did not have an opportunity to cross-examine herself contemporaneously with the making of the statement. The party admission rule therefore holds parties responsible for their own statements. And because parties have an incentive to ensure that their statements are not misunderstood, we can assume that the truth-determination process is advanced rather than impeded by their admission.

As the above discussion should make clear, party admissions work only one way. A party may not offer her *own* statement as a party admission. This is generally true even when the opponent has offered a different statement of the same party. One exception is the common law "completeness" doctrine, which basically provides that if one party offers into evidence one part of an oral or written statement or exchange of statements, the opponent may offer another statement or part of the exchange if it would put the already admitted statement into context or otherwise correct a mistaken impression that might be left with the jury. Thus, suppose a person is charged with bribing an individual to remain silent about a crime. If a witness testifies about a conversation with the defendant in which the defendant said, "we could pay him off," defendant would be permitted to offer testimony that a moment later, he added, "but that would be wrong." While some courts continue to apply this doctrine, it cannot be found in the Federal Rules of Evidence. Rule 106 states a more narrow completeness principle, applicable only to writings:

> **FED. R. EVID. 106.   REST OF OR RELATED WRITINGS OR RECORDED STATEMENTS**

If a party introduces all or part of a writing or recorded statement, an adverse party may require the introduction, at that time, of any other part — or any other writing or recorded statement — that in fairness ought to be considered at the same time.

Unless the completeness doctrine applies, a party may not offer her own statement merely because the opponent has offered another of her statements. Of course, if the party can show that the statement qualifies under another exemption from or exception to the hearsay rule, it will be admissible on that basis.

Questions for Classroom Discussion

1. Negligence action by Plaintiff against Defendant following an automobile collision. Defendant claims to remember no details about the accident. At trial, to prove Defendant's liability, Plaintiff wishes to testify that a week after the collision, Defendant contacted Plaintiff and said, "I fell asleep just before the accident." Defendant objects on hearsay grounds. How should the court rule?

2. Same case. Plaintiff also wishes to testify that Defendant also said, "I crossed the center line just after I fell asleep." Defendant objects on the ground she lacked personal knowledge. How should the court rule?

3. Why do the courts refuse to impose a personal knowledge requirement on party admissions?

4. Same facts. Assume that Defendant also told Plaintiff, "Maybe somebody slipped something into my Diet Coke at dinner, because I certainly had no warning that I might fall asleep." Defendant wishes to testify to this portion of his statement. Plaintiff objects on hearsay and lack of personal knowledge grounds. How should the court rule?

5. Personal injury action by Plaintiff, the administrator of Decedent's estate, against Defendant, a paramedic, following an automobile accident and Decedent's subsequent death. Decedent was crossing the street when she was struck by Zed. (Plaintiff initially sued Zed, but they reached a settlement before trial.) At trial against Defendant, Plaintiff claims that Zed's car caused Decedent a relatively minor injury that could have been treated successfully, and that Decedent's death was caused by Defendant's negligent treatment at the scene. Defendant, however, claims that Decedent was near death when she found her. To prove Decedent was not badly injured when Defendant began to treat her, Plaintiff calls Zed to testify that when Defendant approached Decedent, Decedent said, "I'm fine. The car barely touched me." If Defendant objects on hearsay grounds, and Plaintiff claims Decedent's statement is a party admission, how should the court rule?

6. A physician brags during a party, "I am treating a superstar for insomnia." Later the superstar dies from an overdose of a prescription drug used to treat insomnia. The superstar's children sue the physician, alleging he was responsible for their father's death.

> At trial the children seek to introduce testimony about the physician's statement at the party as tending to prove he is liable for their father's death. The physician's attorney objects, arguing the proposed testimony will be inadmissible hearsay. How should counsel for the children respond?

2. *Adoptive Admissions*

Rule 801(d)(2) lists several ways that the statement of one person may be attributed to a party and, thus, be a party admission if offered against that party. One way this can happen is through what is called *adoptive admission*, which is described in Rule 801(d)(2)(B).

Sometimes one person manifests a belief in the truth of something a second person says. In such a case, the second person's statement in a sense becomes the statement of the first person. Take a simple case:

> Negligence action arising from an automobile accident. Plaintiff claims Defendant ran a red light. To prove this, Plaintiff testifies that she approached Defendant just after the accident and said, "You ran the red light," and that Defendant nodded his head up and down.

In this example, Defendant's act of nodding appears to be an acknowledgment that what Plaintiff said is true — that Defendant ran the red light. Defendant has "adopted" Plaintiff's statement, making it his own. Though Plaintiff's statement to Defendant, standing alone, is hearsay, the statement became an adoptive admission when Defendant, the adverse party, nodded his head.

Many cases are not so easy. Rule 801(d)(2)(B) directs us to consider whether the party "appeared to adopt or accept" the truth of a statement made by another person. Usually this is "manifested" by what the party says about the statement. But sometimes the party's *silence* can be an adoptive admission. Consider the following example:

> Defendant is charged with fraud for allegedly cheating on her written driver's test by having someone else take the test. Defendant denies cheating. To prove that Defendant hired Zed to take the exam, the prosecution calls Witness to testify that she was in the examination area at the same time, and that she heard an employee loudly accuse Defendant of cheating, and that Defendant did not respond. Witness will also testify that many other people were also present at the time.

Without Defendant's reaction, the employee's statement to Defendant is hearsay because it was not made while the employee was testifying at the trial, and it is offered to prove the truth of the matter asserted (that Defendant cheated). In addition, the statement does not appear to satisfy any hearsay exception. But the statement might be viewed as a party admission of Defendant if certain facts are proven to be true. In particular, *if Defendant heard and understood* what the employee said, and if *under the circumstances you would expect a person who disagreed with the employee's statement to say so,* you might view Defendant's silence as acquiescing to the employee's assertion. We would say, in such a case, that Defendant "adopted" the employee's statement by not expressing disagreement. In fact, the circumstances described in the above example might support this conclusion. Defendant must have heard the accusation because it was voiced "loudly." If the employee's accusation was clear, the only remaining question would be whether a reasonable person in Defendant's position would have denied the accusation if it was untrue. Under these circumstances, one would probably expect an innocent person to deny the truth of the accusation. Defendant's failure to do so would then be an adoptive admission under Rule 801(d)(2)(B) because Defendant's silence "appeared to adopt or accept" that the statement was true.

All jurisdictions recognize the possibility that a party's words or conduct may constitute an adoption of another's statement, and thus make that statement admissible as a party admission. A more controversial question is whether the court should decide the necessary facts by a preponderance of evidence pursuant to its authority under Rule 104(a), or whether instead the situation falls into the category of conditional relevancy, requiring that the court follow the procedure laid out in Rule 104(b).

Consider the following hypothetical, based on the facts of State v. Carlson, 808 P.2d 1002 (Or. 1991):

> Prosecution of Defendant for possession of methamphetamine. When the officer asked Defendant about what appeared to be needle marks on his arms, Defendant claimed he got them from working on a car. At that point, Defendant's wife Lisa, who was standing close by during this conversation, yelled, "You liar, you got them from shooting up in the bedroom with all your stupid friends." Defendant did not reply, but hung his head and shook it back and forth.

This would qualify as an adoptive admission if (1) Defendant heard Lisa's accusation, (2) this was a situation in which an innocent person would have denied the accusation if it was not true, and (3) Defendant's conduct was not a denial. The problem appears to be with either the second or third element. An innocent person might remain silent under these circumstances if he thinks there is nothing to be gained from denying his wife's accusation and maybe something to be lost. Further, Defendant's response, hanging his head and shaking it, is ambiguous; it might be interpreted as an adoption, but other possibilities also exist, such as that Defendant was simply showing disdain for or lack of patience with his wife.

Should this preliminary question of fact be decided by the trial court under Rule 104(a), or is this a case of conditional relevancy, governed by the standard in Rule 104(b)? In *Carlson*, the court held that Oregon's equivalent of Rule 104(a) applied:

> The objection to admissibility, based on the rule against hearsay, furthers an important legal policy of preventing the trier of fact from considering the possible truthfulness of out-of-court statements, unless the statements have sufficient guarantees of trustworthiness. The purpose of the hearsay rule is to guard against the risks of misperception, misrecollection, misstatement, and insincerity, which are associated with statements of persons made out of court. Safeguards in the trial procedure, such as the immediate cross-examination of the witness and the opportunity of the trier of fact to observe the demeanor of the witness who swears or affirms under the penalty of perjury to tell the truth, are designed to reduce those risks.

There are several difficulties with leaving the question of intent to adopt, agree or approve to the jury as a question of conditional relevancy under OEC 104(2) [equivalent to Federal Rule 104(b)]. If the OEC 104(2) conditional relevancy standard is employed, the legal policy underlying the hearsay rule would be furthered incompletely, if at all. The jury passing on the admission by conduct will have to hear not only evidence about the conduct and the surrounding circumstances, but also the out-of-court statement, as necessary predicates for understanding what the party allegedly adopted. For example, in the present case, the wife's accusatory statement, to which defendant's nonverbal conduct is a response, would have to be admitted to give meaning to defendant's conduct, and the accusation is relevant to prove the truth of the accusation even though it may not be admissible for that purpose. A juror could (a) overlook the question of intent to adopt, agree or approve, and consider the truth of the matter asserted in the out-of-court statement, (b) use the out-of-court statement before considering and resolving the preliminary question of intent to adopt, agree or approve, or (c) consider the hearsay statement regardless of what conclusion is reached on the preliminary question of adoption or belief. If the evidence is inadmissible, i.e., the jury does not find the preliminary fact (intent to adopt, agree or approve) to exist, preventing jury contamination may prove impossible. Additionally, a general verdict would not indicate the jury's resolution of whether intent to adopt existed. A record for appellate review would require a special set of preliminary jury findings.

In short, we believe that judicial intervention is required to prevent improper use of evidence. The preliminary question of intent to adopt, agree or approve, therefore, should be left to the trial judge under OEC 104(1) [equivalent to Federal Rule 104(a)].

808 P.2d at 1009.

The contrary argument (the argument that adoptive admissions present a problem of conditional relevancy) is that the defendant's conduct is irrelevant if it did not constitute an adoption of the accusation. Thus, the argument goes, if any of the foundational facts are missing, defendant's conduct or silence will not be relevant, and the jury will ignore it. But as the *Carlson* court suggests, deciding the preliminary fact questions requires consideration of the other person's accusation. For example, it is not possible to decide whether, in this context, an innocent person would deny the truth of the accusation without knowing what the accusation was. And because the accusation is relevant to the facts at issue, the jury will not ignore the accusation even if it finds that defendant did not adopt it. Nevertheless, some courts hold that the adoptive admission problem is a situation of conditional relevancy, and apply the standard in Rule 104(b). *See, e.g.,* United States v. Sears, 663 F.2d 896, 904-905 (9th Cir. 1981).

Questions for Classroom Discussion

1. Irene says to friends, in her husband's presence, "You should see the diamonds Donald picked up in his latest heist." Donald smiles and says nothing. Donald is tried for grand theft. The prosecution calls the friends to testify about Irene's statement and Donald's reaction. Donald's attorney objects, arguing the friends' testimony is hearsay and unfairly prejudicial. How should the court rule?

(continued)

2. In our hypothetical based on *Carlson*, why couldn't the court adopt the following procedure: allow the jury to decide whether defendant's head shaking was a rejection of Lisa's accusation, and if the jury decided that it was, then allow the jury to hear the accusation itself?

3. Even assuming the jury would have to hear Lisa's accusation in order to make an accurate determination of the meaning of defendant's head shaking, what harm would there have been in *Carlson* if the court had held that the preliminary facts necessary to support admission as an adoptive admission were to be decided in accordance with Oregon Evidence Code 104(2) (Oregon's equivalent of Rule 104(b))? Isn't it true that if the jury found that defendant's head shaking was a denial of the truth of his wife's statement, the jury would not use her statement against defendant?

4. What is the practical effect of the *Carlson* court's decision that the question of defendant's adoption of Lisa's accusation should be decided in accordance with Oregon Evidence Code 104(1) (Oregon's equivalent of Rule 104(a))? How exactly will this be done?

5. In *Carlson*, after deciding the issue you have read, the court held that Lisa's accusation was admissible under the "excited utterance" exception to the hearsay rule. (For the federal version, see Rule 803(2).) Make an argument that if Lisa's accusation was an excited utterance, there was no need for the court to spend so much energy deciding whether the facts supporting admission of defendant's reaction as a party admission were to be decided under the standard of Evidence Code 104(1) or that of Rule 104(2).

6. Prosecution of Defendant, a gang member, for the murder of Victim, a member of a rival gang. Defendant denies involvement. To prove Defendant killed Victim, the prosecution calls Witness, a member of Victim's gang, to testify that shortly after the killing, he approached Defendant in a bar and said, "You son of a bitch! You killed my friend!" and that Defendant just stared at him and smirked. Defendant lodges a hearsay objection to Witness's testimony. How should the court rule?

7. Same facts. Suppose that instead of making his accusation in a bar, Witness made it in front of a bunch of members of Defendant's gang, and not in the presence of any "civilians." Again, Defendant lodges a hearsay objection. How should the court rule?

8. Prosecution of Defendant for bank robbery. Shortly after Defendant's arrest, and after the police officer read him his Miranda rights, a bank teller approached Defendant and stated, "You are the one who pointed that gun at me." Defendant did not respond. The prosecution wishes to offer the teller's statement and Defendant's lack of response. Defendant makes a hearsay objection. How should the court rule?

3.   *Vicarious Party Admissions (Authorized and Agency Admissions)*

Sometimes people authorize others to speak for them. When the authorizing person is a party, the statement of the person authorized to speak is admissible under Rule 801(d)(2)(C) as an authorized admission. A simple example is a corporate spokesperson. If the corporation is a party to an action, and the spokesperson makes a statement on behalf of the company, that statement will qualify as an authorized admission if offered against the corporation. General partners are also normally authorized to speak for each other. And lawyers often speak for clients. Of course, some entities, including corporations, can *only* speak through others.[19]

The authorized admission rule applies to statements both to the outside world and within an organization. Thus, a corporate spokesperson's statements to the outside world on behalf of the company will qualify. So too will a corporation's financial records, even those that were kept internally and never intended to be shown outside the company. *See* Fed. R. Evid. 801 Advisory Committee's Note.

The authorized admission rule makes good sense, particularly because its reach is within the party's control. If the party does not wish to allow another person to speak on her behalf, she need not authorize a person for that purpose. The admissibility of authorized admissions has a long history.

That one may make an admission through an agent not authorized to speak was a more controversial concept prior to the adoption of the Federal Rules. Under Rule 801(d)(2)(D), however, a statement "made by the party's agent or employee on a matter within the scope of that relationship and while it existed" is non-hearsay regardless of whether the agent was authorized to speak concerning the matter. Consider the following example:

> A delivery truck owned by Hank's Appliances runs over and injures Plaintiff, a pedestrian. Immediately after the accident, the delivery truck driver tells Plaintiff, "I was distracted and didn't see you in time." Plaintiff brings suit against Hank's Appliances.

Prior to the advent of the agency admission rule, the driver's statement almost certainly would *not* have been admissible against her employer if (as is probably the case) the driver was authorized not to speak on the employer's behalf but only to drive on her behalf. Under Rule 801(d)(2)(D), however, the driver's statement would likely be admissible because it concerned the conduct of his job (driving the truck) and it was made while he was in the employ of the store.

Does the agency admission rule apply to statements of government agents in criminal cases? In general, the courts have held that it does not. Even though Rule 801(d)(2) provides that a statement by a party, *or its representatives and agents*, may be used against that party at trial, courts are reluctant to admit statements of government officials under this rule. Thus, if Defendant is charged with bank robbery, and wishes to offer evidence that a police officer involved in the investigation claimed another person committed the crime, the officer's statement probably would not be admissible as a party admission.

---

19. If the agent or authorized person is also a party to the lawsuit, her statement on behalf of the corporation will be admissible under Rule 801(d)(2)(A) as a statement made by a party in "a representative capacity."

The current practice of not recognizing statements by government agents as admissions in criminal cases derives from common law. Before the adoption of the Federal Rules, government officials were seen as authorized to *act* for the government, but not necessarily to *speak* for the government. *See, e.g.,* United States v. Santos, 372 F.2d 177 (2d Cir. 1967). Even though the Federal Rules no longer require that agents be "authorized" to speak for the party in order for their statements to be admissible as party admissions, courts have been slow to apply this concept to the government. *See, e.g.,* United States v. Kamiles, 609 F.2d 1233 (7th Cir. 1979) (refusing to apply new Rule 801(d)(2) to statements of government agents). To some extent, this reluctance stems from the nature of the actual party in criminal cases. When it prosecutes crimes, the government is neither an individual nor quite like a corporate entity. Instead, the government prosecutes crimes on behalf of "the people," and although courts have recognized that it seems unfair to admit the statements of criminal defendants as party admissions but not those of government employees, they have usually adhered to the common law treatment.

Some courts are now reevaluating the fairness of this approach. *See generally* Anne Bowen Poulin, *Party Admissions in Criminal Cases: Should the Government Have to Eat Its Words*, 87 Minn. L. Rev. 401 (2002). For courts inclined to treat the statements of government agents as party admissions when offered against the government, one important factor is the rank and authority of the government official who made the statement. Statements by informants or lower-level government employees are unlikely to qualify. However, statements by high-ranking government officials, or the prosecutors themselves, may be considered as admissions under some circumstances.

Laying the foundation for admission of an agent's statement is relatively straightforward. In the driver/pedestrian hypothetical, Plaintiff might take the stand and testify as follows (assume Plaintiff has already testified that she was hit by a Hank's Appliances truck as she crossed the street in a crosswalk):

Q: What happened after the truck hit you?

A: The truck knocked me over. I fell down in the middle of the street.

Q: What happened next?

A: I saw the truck pull over to the side of the road, and the driver got out.

Q: How do you know it was the driver who got out?

A: Well, I saw the person get out of the truck from the driver's-side door.

Q: What did the driver do next?

A: The driver ran over to me and asked me if I needed help. I said I did, and he helped me to get up. He helped me get off the street and onto the sidewalk.

Q: What was the driver wearing?

A: He had on a shirt that said Hank's Appliances.

Q: Did the driver say anything else?

A: Yes. He said, "I was distracted and didn't see you in time."

The Advisory Committee explained its decision to broaden the vicarious admission rule to allow statements such as the one described in our hypothetical:

The tradition has been to test the admissibility of statements by agents, as admissions, by applying the usual test of agency. Was the admission made by the agent acting in the scope of his employment? Since few principals employ agents for the purpose of making damaging statements, the usual result was exclusion of the statement. Dissatisfaction with this loss of valuable and helpful evidence has been increasing. A substantial trend favors admitting statements related to a matter within the scope of the agency or employment.

Fed. R. Evid. 801 Advisory Committee's Note. The agency admission rule can also be supported by practical considerations: Normally, the agent herself will also be a party. Consequently, the agent's own statements will be admissible against her at trial. If the agent's statements were not also admissible against the principal, the principal would be entitled to a limiting instruction pursuant to Rule 105. That instruction would tell the jury that it could only consider the agent's statements against the agent, and not against the principal. But a jury is unlikely to be able to follow such instruction, and even if able, the jury might not be willing to do so. The agency admission rule eliminates the need for such an instruction by making the agent's statements admissible against the principal as long as the foundational facts are shown to exist.

Not all states have adopted this reasoning. In California, for example, there is no general agency admission rule, and there is a general rule (treated as a hearsay exception rather than an exemption) for authorized party admissions. *See* Cal. Evid. Code § 1222.

The final sentence of Rule 801(d)(2) makes clear that the court may consider the purported authorized or agency admission itself in deciding whether the declarant had authority to speak (authorized admissions) or the existence and scope of the agency (agency admissions). However, the rule also provides that the statements themselves are not alone sufficient to establish any of these facts. This will rarely be a problem, however; in almost all cases, the proponent will present other evidence tending to establish the preliminary facts.

Questions for Classroom Discussion

1. Should the preliminary facts necessary to the application of the authorized admission rule (Rule 801(d)(2)(C)) be decided in accordance with the standard of Rule 104(a) or that of Rule 104(b)? Should agency admissions (Rule 801(d)(2)(D)) be treated the same way?

2. California Evidence Code § 1222 provides that a "statement made by a person authorized by the party to make a statement or statements concerning the subject matter of the statement" is admissible if it is "offered either after admission of evidence sufficient to sustain a finding of such authority, or, in the court's discretion as to the order of proof, subject to the admission of such evidence." Does this rule establish the same standard for admissibility of authorized admissions as the federal version of the authorized admission rule?

(continued)

3.   Suppose that the only evidence of the authority of the declarant is the declarant's own statement ("I am authorized to tell you . . ."). In the absence of any other evidence of authority, may the court find that the declarant was authorized to speak for the party?

4.   Negligence action by Plaintiff against Ron's, a supermarket, to recover for personal injuries Plaintiff suffered when he fell in the produce aisle. Plaintiff claims the fall was caused by a puddle of water on the floor. Defendant denies there was a puddle on the floor. At trial, to prove the puddle existed, Plaintiff wishes to testify that shortly after the fall, Zed, the store's produce department manager, apologized to Plaintiff for "not cleaning up the puddle." Defendant objects on hearsay grounds. How should the court rule?

5.   Same facts. Suppose Defendant argues that it never authorized Zed to make any statements on its behalf concerning accidents. Should this affect the court's ruling?

6.   Same facts. Suppose that prior to trial, but after Zed made the statement, Defendant fired Zed. Is Zed's statement still admissible?

7.   Same facts. On cross-examination of Plaintiff, Defendant wishes to ask whether Zed also told Plaintiff that Plaintiff was trying to carry too much produce and should have been watching where he was going. Plaintiff objects on hearsay grounds. How should the court rule?

8.   Negligence action by Plaintiff against Defendant, the owner of a business, after Plaintiff's car and a delivery truck operated by one of Defendant's employees collided in an intersection. Defendant denies the driver was negligent. To prove negligence, Plaintiff wishes to testify that just after the accident, the driver approached Plaintiff and said, "I didn't notice that the light had changed. My company will pay your damages." Defendant objects on hearsay grounds. How should the court rule?

9.   Breach of contract action by Plaintiff, a movie studio, against Defendant, a famous actor, for reneging on a commitment to star in the studio's musical version of *Citizen Kane*. Defendant claims he was unable to perform because he broke both of his legs in a snow sled accident two weeks prior to the date on which filming was to commence. To prove that Defendant was physically fit to meet his commitment, Plaintiff calls Witness, a reporter, to testify that shortly after the alleged snow sled accident, Defendant's publicist told her that Defendant was feeling fine and looked forward to his planned mountain climbing expedition scheduled for the following week. Defendant objects on hearsay grounds. How should the court rule?

4. *Co-conspirator Statements*

Rule 801(d)(2)(E) creates an exemption from the definition of hearsay in Rule 801(c) for a statement "made by the party's coconspirator during and in furtherance of the conspiracy." It is not clear why such statements should be exempted, but several explanations are possible. One is that a criminal conspiracy is like a business (except that it exists for illicit purposes rather than legitimate ones). When people in a business speak for each other, they usually have an incentive to speak carefully and accurately because doing so will be to the benefit of the business. The reasoning then suggests that if people in a legitimate business are allowed to speak for each other, the same should be true for people involved in an illegitimate one. This rationale is questionable because criminal conspiracies are not like regular businesses. There is not likely to be the same premium placed on truthfulness and accuracy among criminal conspirators. In fact, given the illegal nature of their "business," criminal conspirators are often likely to speak inaccurately if doing so will help them avoid detection. Criminals tend to apply the old saying, "every man for himself," when the heat is on.

A second rationale is more persuasive. Criminal conspiracy is difficult to prove. It requires an inquiry into the minds of people who have every reason not to tell what they are thinking, and a constitutional right not to incriminate themselves. Because tangible evidence of a conspiracy is often difficult to find, the words of the conspirators themselves are often the best evidence of its existence.

Whatever the strength of the rationales supporting it, the co-conspirator rule is widely recognized and frequently used. Rule 801(d)(2)(E) contains several preliminary fact requirements:

1. There must have been a conspiracy;
2. The declarant must have been a member of the conspiracy;
3. The statement must have been made while the conspiracy was in existence (during its "course"); and
4. The statement must have been made "in furtherance of" the conspiracy.

These preliminary facts should be decided by the court pursuant to the standard set forth in Rule 104(a). That is because the statement at issue almost always will be relevant whether or not the facts are all true. Consider this example:

> Defendant is charged with bank robbery and conspiracy to commit bank robbery. Defendant denies involvement. To prove Defendant was involved, the prosecution calls Witness, an alleged co-conspirator who pleaded guilty in exchange for leniency. If permitted, Witness will testify that a few days before the robbery, she tried to recruit Zed into the plan, telling Zed, "Defendant is the best safe-cracker in the business, and we've got her for this job."

In this example, Witness's statement is hearsay under Rule 801(c) unless it qualifies as non-hearsay under the co-conspirator rule. But the statement will be relevant even if one or more of the preliminary facts are not true. For example, suppose that at the time Witness made the statement to Zed, Witness was no longer a member of the conspiracy, having been "fired" for incompetence. Witness's assertion of Defendant's involvement would still be relevant (even if perhaps a little less credible than if Witness was still involved in the conspiracy). The same logic would apply if the facts reveal that Witness was not really trying to recruit Zed, but was just boasting about the bank robbery plot. In such a case, the statement probably would not have been "in furtherance" of the conspiracy, but it would still be relevant.

Because the preliminary facts supporting admission of a co-conspirator statement must be decided by the court, a strange phenomenon appears: In deciding on the admissibility of evidence, the court will have to make the same factual finding (the existence of a conspiracy) that the jury will be asked to make at the end of the case. This might seem incongruous at first, but it need not be troublesome. Remember that Rule 801(d)(2)(E) is a rule about the admission of evidence. It is not a substantive rule about ultimate liability or guilt. Thus, the preliminary facts necessary for admissibility are only that — facts necessary for the evidence to be admitted. The judge need not, and in fact must not, inform the jury that she has already decided that a conspiracy existed as part of her job to determine the admissibility of evidence. It should also be noted that the court's finding will not be based on the same standard the jury will ultimately apply. To admit the evidence, the court need only determine by the "more likely than not" standard that all of the preliminary facts are true. To convict Defendant of conspiracy, the jury will have to employ the "beyond a reasonable doubt" standard to the elements of the crime, including the existence of a conspiracy.

Note that the apparent incongruousness of both judge and jury determining that a conspiracy existed will only come up if conspiracy is one of the crimes charged in the case. This is not a requirement of the co-conspirator rule, however. Co-conspirator statements are admissible whether or not conspiracy is actually charged. If no conspiracy is charged, the jury will not be required to determine whether a conspiracy existed.

Note also that the co-conspirator rule applies even if the declarant is not a party. There is also no requirement that the declarant be produced at trial and be made subject to cross-examination. It is in fact quite common for the statements of an absent, unindicted co-conspirator to be offered against a criminal defendant.

Needless to say, the co-conspirator rule is controversial. As Judge Richard Posner of the Seventh Circuit observed, "This translation of commercial principles of agency into the laws of evidence is one of the less impressive examples of what Coke called the 'artificial reason' of the law. . . . Whatever the justification for the rule — and there may be none — its dependence on agency principles makes the scope of the conspiracy critical." United States v. DiDomenico, 78 F.3d 294, 303 (7th Cir. 1996).

Though situations exist in which the defendant rather than the government will offer such statements in evidence, it is the prosecution that benefits from the admission of co-conspirator statements in virtually every instance.

As with authorized and agency admissions under Rule 801(d)(2)(C) and (D), the co-conspirator statement may not form the entire basis for finding the preliminary facts necessary to its admission. The final sentence of Rule 801(d)(2) states that "[t]he statement must be considered but does not by itself establish . . . the existence of the conspiracy or participation in it." This will rarely be a problem, however, because in almost all cases, there will be *some* evidence outside of the statement itself that tends to prove the existence of the conspiracy and the participation of the declarant and the defendant in it. Such evidence might not be particularly strong, but all the rule requires is that there be some evidence in addition to the statement itself.

Further Reading: Edmund M. Morgan, *Admissions as an Exception to the Hearsay Rule*, 30 Yale L.J. 355 (1921); Christopher B. Mueller, *The Federal Coconspirator Exception: Action, Assertion, and Hearsay*, 12 Hofstra L. Rev. 323 (1984); Roger C. Park, *The Rationale of Personal Admissions*, 21 Ind. L. Rev. 509 (1988); John S. Strahorn, *A Reconsideration of the Hearsay Rule and Admissions*, 85 U. Pa. L. Rev. 484 (1937).

Questions for Classroom Discussion

1. Prosecution of Defendant for murder and conspiracy to commit murder. Defendant denies any involvement. To prove Defendant supplied the poison used to kill the victim, the prosecution calls Witness, a bartender, to testify that a few months before the killing took place, Defendant and Zed were sitting at the bar and that Zed said to Defendant, "If you can get the anthrax, I'll take care of the delivery." Defendant objects on hearsay grounds. How should the court rule?

2. Same facts. Assume all the physical evidence suggests that the crime was committed by a single individual, and the only evidence of the involvement of more than one person was Zed's statement to Defendant. Is the statement admissible under the co-conspirator rule?

3. Same facts. Assume Defendant is only charged with murder, not conspiracy to commit murder. How would this affect the admissibility of Zed's statement?

4. Same basic facts. Assume, however, that instead of calling Witness (the bartender) to testify, the prosecution calls Witness's spouse. If permitted, the spouse will state that Witness told her that he heard Zed say to Defendant, "If you can get the anthrax, I'll take care of the delivery." Defendant objects on hearsay grounds. How should the court rule?

5. Same case. Assume that after the killing, the police captured Zed and Defendant together, and that on the way to the police station, Zed said to Defendant, "We should have picked something less detectable in the body." If a police officer overheard the statement, may the prosecution call her to testify about it?

(continued)

6. Prosecution of Defendant for bank robbery. The prosecution alleges that Defendant was the "lookout" whose job was to alert the other robbers if the police were in the vicinity. Defendant denies any involvement. To prove he was not involved, Defendant calls Witness to testify that, just before the robbery, he was in a coffee shop when he overheard Zed tell Abel, "If you take care of the inside, I'll keep an eye out for the cops." The prosecution objects on hearsay grounds. Defendant claims Zed's statement is admissible as a co-conspirator statement. How should the court rule?

7. Same facts. Assume the statement is not admissible as a co-conspirator statement, and that no hearsay exception applies. Can you make an argument that the court must admit it anyway?

K. EXEMPTIONS FROM THE HEARSAY RULE: PRIOR STATEMENTS OF WITNESSES

FED. R. EVID. 801 . . .

(d) **Statements That Are Not Hearsay.** A statement that meets the following conditions is not hearsay:

(1) *A Declarant-Witness's Prior Statement.* The declarant testifies and is subject to cross-examination about a prior statement, and the statement:

(A) is inconsistent with the declarant's testimony and was given under penalty of perjury at a trial, hearing, or other proceeding or in a deposition;

(B) is consistent with the declarant's testimony and is offered:

(i) to rebut an express or implied charge that the declarant recently fabricated it or acted from a recent improper influence or motive in so testifying; or

(ii) to rehabilitate the declarant's credibility as a witness when attacked on another ground; or

(C) identifies a person as someone the declarant perceived earlier.

1. Introduction

Suppose that at some point before testifying at the trial, a trial witness made a statement relevant to the case. If offered to prove the truth of the matters asserted, the prior statement normally would be hearsay. While it might seem strange that prior statements of a person who is in court and subject to cross-examination would constitute hearsay, the hearsay rule sweeps within its orbit even statements made by witnesses. We discussed early in this chapter why that is so.

Some prior statements of witnesses are admissible to prove the truth of what they assert, however. Rule 801(d)(1) creates three narrow categories of such statements:

1.   Statements inconsistent with the witness's trial testimony;
2.   Statements consistent with the witness's trial testimony; and
3.   Statements identifying a person and made after perceiving that person.

Not all prior inconsistent, prior consistent, and prior identification statements qualify as non-hearsay under Rule 801(d)(1). We will see that each type of statement must meet certain qualifications, and that in addition, each has its own separate set of requirements.

There are two common requirements, however. As stated in Rule 801(d)(1):

1.   The declarant must testify at the trial or hearing; and
2.   The declarant must be subject to cross-examination concerning the prior statement.

The first requirement is simple: The person must be a witness at the trial or hearing. The second requirement is more complicated. In Chapter 6 we discuss that requirement in detail. For now, it is sufficient to know that wisely or not, the Supreme Court has held that a witness normally will be considered "subject to cross-examination" for purposes of Rule 801(d)(1) if the witness is "placed on the stand, under oath, and responds willingly to questions." United States v. Owens, 484 U.S. 554 (1988).

Because prior inconsistent statements and prior consistent statements are so often associated with impeachment and rehabilitation of witnesses, we discuss those types of statements in depth in Chapter 6. We provide a brief overview here; following that, we treat in greater detail the use of statements of prior identification.

2.   *Prior Inconsistent and Prior Consistent Statements: A Primer*

Suppose a blue car driven by Plaintiff and a green car driven by Defendant collided in an intersection. Plaintiff sues Defendant for personal injuries sustained in the accident, and calls Witness, who testifies, "The green car ran the red light." Just after the accident, however, Witness said, "The blue car ran the red light." No doubt Defendant will want to apprise the jury of Witness's prior statement, and there might be two purposes for doing so. *First*, Defendant might want to use Witness's prior statement to show that the blue car ran the red light. *Second*, Defendant might want to use Witness's prior statement to impeach her credibility—to show that she speaks inconsistently and thus should not be viewed as a believable source of information about the accident.

We will call the first use of Witness's prior statement its *substantive use* because Defendant will seek to use it to prove the facts of the case—here, that Plaintiff's blue car ran the light. For that purpose, the statement is hearsay under the definition in Rule 801(c). It was made by the declarant (who happens to be the witness) other than while testifying at the trial, and it will be offered to prove the truth of the matter asserted (that the blue car ran the red light). Assuming the statement does not qualify for any hearsay exception, the statement will not be admissible for this purpose unless it satisfies all of the requirements of Rule 801(d)(1)(A). Aside from requiring that the declarant testify at the trial or hearing and be subject to cross-examination concerning the statement, that rule states that the statement is not hearsay and will be admissible substantively only if both of the following conditions are met:

1. The statement is inconsistent with the witness's testimony at the trial; and
2. The statement "was given under oath subject to the penalty of perjury at a trial, hearing, or other proceeding, or in a deposition. . . ."

By hypothesis, the first requirement is met here because the statement "the blue car ran the red light" is clearly inconsistent with the statement "the green car ran the red light." But the facts do not show that Witness made the prior statement under oath, subject to the penalty of perjury at another formal proceeding. Usually, of course, that will not be true. Most prior statements are made informally to other bystanders, friends, and law enforcement authorities. Even a sworn affidavit given to the police will not qualify, because an affidavit is not given "at a trial, hearing, or other proceeding, or in a deposition." Essentially, the rule requires that for the prior inconsistent statement to be admissible substantively (to prove the truth of the matter asserted), it must have been made by a witness in a formal proceeding. Formal proceedings include not only trials and depositions, but also grand jury proceedings. In fact, a witness's prior grand jury testimony is a common source of prior inconsistent statements.

As we stated above, the second possible use of a prior inconsistent statement is simply to impeach the witness's credibility. For this purpose, it is sufficient to know that the witness has spoken inconsistently. That fact alone tends to impeach her because it suggests that the person is unclear about the facts, is forgetful, or is otherwise unreliable. Because mere inconsistency is sufficient for impeachment purposes, the truth of the prior statement is not important. In our example, the statement is not offered to prove that the blue car ran the light, but merely to show that this witness, who testified at trial that the green car ran the light, is unreliable. Accordingly, the statement is not hearsay when offered for this limited purpose. When a prior inconsistent statement is offered only to impeach, the requirements of Rule 801(d)(1)(A) do not apply. This is because that rule assumes that prior statements are being offered to prove the truth of the matter asserted (which would otherwise make them hearsay). As we see in Chapter 6, there are some restrictions on the impeachment use of prior inconsistent statements, but there is no requirement, for example, that the prior statements have been made under oath.[20]

Just as a person may speak inconsistently, a person may speak consistently. To return to our example, suppose that instead of stating just after the accident that the blue car ran the red light, Witness stated that the green car ran the light. This statement would be consistent with Witness's trial testimony. This time, it would

20. Some states' rules are much more permissive about the substantive use of prior inconsistent statements. For example, Cal. Evid. Code § 1235 is a hearsay exception, making prior inconsistent statements admissible whether or not they were given under oath. In a jurisdiction that adopts such an approach it is not necessary for the court to issue a limiting instruction when a prior inconsistent statement is offered because the statement may be used both substantively and to impeach the witness's credibility.

be Plaintiff rather than Defendant who might wish to offer the prior statement and, in theory, there could be two purposes for the evidence. *First,* Plaintiff might wish to use the statement substantively—to prove that the prior statement is true. In other words, Plaintiff might wish to use the statement as further substantive proof that Defendant's green car ran the red light. *Second,* Plaintiff might wish to use the statement simply to support Witness's credibility. The theory would be that the jury should give greater credit to a witness who speaks consistently.

As we explain in Chapter 6, although both purposes are theoretically valid, the law restricts prior consistent statements as though they were always being offered substantively. For that purpose, such statements normally would be hearsay because they would be offered to prove the truth of the matter asserted. Only if all the requirements of Rule 801(d)(1)(B) are satisfied will prior consistent statements be admissible as non-hearsay. Aside from the general requirements that the declarant testify at the trial or hearing and be subject to cross-examination concerning the statement, a prior consistent statement is only admissible if:

1.   the statement is consistent with the witness's testimony at trial; and
2.   the statement is being offered "to rebut an express or implied charge of recent fabrication or improper influence or motive, or to rehabilitate the declarant's credibility as a witness when attacked on another ground."

In Tome v. United States, 513 U.S. 150 (1995) (discussed in Chapter 6), the Supreme Court held that in addition, the statement must have been made *before the alleged fabrication, or before the alleged improper influence or motive arose.*

As with prior inconsistent statements, these requirements are quite strict, but for different reasons. Prior consistent statements need not have been made under oath to be admissible. But most consistent statements do not satisfy the requirement that they be offered to rebut a charge that the witness fabricated or had been subject to improper influence or motive. Even if a statement satisfies this second requirement, the statement often will not have been made prior to the time the witness is alleged to have fabricated the account or prior to the time the improper influence or motive was brought to bear.

In our hypothetical, suppose Defendant learns that at some point before trial, Plaintiff offered Witness a bribe to testify in Plaintiff's favor. If Defendant introduces, or intends to introduce, evidence to that effect at the trial, Rule 801(d)(1)(B) would permit Plaintiff to offer evidence that Witness made the consistent statement, *as long as that statement was made at a point in time before the alleged bribe was offered.* Similarly, if Defendant claims Witness fabricated the story about Defendant's green car running the light, Witness's consistent statement to the same effect, made *before* she is alleged to have fabricated the story, would be admissible. A statement consistent with the witness's trial testimony but made *after* the alleged bribe or *after* the alleged fabrication would not be admissible.

For further discussion of prior inconsistent and consistent statements, along with hypotheticals testing your understanding of the rules, *see* Chapter 6.

3.   Statements of Prior Identification

When, shortly after an event, a witness to the event sees and specifically identifies one or more of the people involved, the identification is usually much more

reliable than a subsequent in-court identification. After all, the in-court identification takes place much later, often months or even years after the event, by
which time the witness's memory might have faded. In addition, when (as is
usually the case) the person identified is a criminal defendant, how difficult is it
for the witness to point to the person sitting at counsel table next to his attorney?
Sometimes the defendant will be dressed in prison orange. Even when he is not,
it is usually abundantly clear who the prosecutor wants the witness to identify.[21]
As the drafters of the Federal Rules wrote, "The basis [of the prior identification
rule] is the generally inconclusive nature of courtroom identifications as compared with those made at an earlier time under less suggestive conditions." Fed.
R. Evid. 801 Advisory Committee's Note.

There is a related but somewhat more subtle reason why the earlier identification should carry more weight than the in-court procedure: When the witness
points out the individual in court, there is a very real possibility that her memory
of the individual's appearance is based more on the prior identification than on
the actual event that is the subject of the trial. This is especially true when the
prior identification took the form of a line-up or similar procedure that gave the
witness ample time to look closely at the people or photographs presented to her
and to select the person she saw at the time of the event at issue. The mental
image of the individual that the witness carries with her to the trial is much more
likely to derive from the prior identification than from the crime or other event
at issue. It is only fair that the fact-finder be made aware that this is the case. What
if the witness picked the wrong person out of the line-up? What if the actual
perpetrator was not among those exhibited to the witness? The jury should know
that the in-court identification might consist of a compounded error.

The prior identification, however, is analytically hearsay. It is a statement
(whether verbal or non-verbal) amounting, essentially, to the assertion, "He
is the one who did it." The statement will have been made other than while
testifying at the trial or hearing at which it is being offered. And the proponent is
offering it to prove the truth of the matter asserted — that the person identified
is the one who "did it." Unless such statements are exempted from the definition of hearsay, or an exception is created that admits them, the hearsay rule
would bar the fact-finder from learning of the identification.

The drafters of the Federal Rules chose the exemption route. Rule
801(d)(1)(C) sets forth the prerequisites for the introduction of evidence of
a prior identification. Those requirements are as follows (the first two are the
same as for the other types of statements falling within Rule 801(d)(1)):

1. The declarant (the person who made the identification) must testify at the
   trial or hearing;
2. The declarant must be "subject to cross-examination about the prior statement"; and
3. The statement must be one that "identifies a person as someone the declarant perceived earlier."

---

21. Undoubtedly, many students have seen television programs or films in which defense
counsel arranges to substitute another person for the defendant prior to the testimony of an
eyewitness. This has been done in real trials. Defense counsel senses that the witness will automatically point to the person sitting in the defendant's position, and uses this trick to highlight the
weakness of the in-court identification. As you might expect, not all judges appreciate these tactics,
and counsel planning such a tactic are best advised to obtain advance permission from the court.

The first requirement is simple: The declarant must testify at the trial at which the prior identification is offered into evidence. Note that the rule does not require that the witness testify *about the identification*. It merely requires that the person testify at the trial. Thus, another person who observed the identification (commonly a police officer) might be the witness who actually informs the fact-finder about the identification procedure.

The second requirement raises the same issues as with prior consistent and inconsistent statements. We cover this in greater depth in Chapter 6. For now, you should know that it will usually be sufficient if the declarant takes the witness stand and willingly answers questions. Even if she has little or no memory of the prior identification, it is likely that she will be characterized as "subject to cross-examination concerning the statement."

The third requirement is that the statement be one of "identification of a person made after perceiving the person." Only identifications of a person fall within the rule, and the identification must be of a specific person. Descriptions of a person's appearance ("the robber was about six feet six inches tall and had short brown hair") are not made admissible by this rule.

The drafters of this rule primarily had in mind situations such as formal line-ups, but other prior identifications are also within the scope of the rule. Thus, other formal procedures are within the rule, including "show-ups" (in which only the suspect is paraded before the witness, and the witness is asked if he is the person who committed the crime), and completely informal and unstaged identifications (such as a situation in which the witness spots the perpetrator in a crowd not long after the crime occurred, and points out the individual to a police officer or other person present at the moment). Indeed, there is nothing in the rule that requires the identification to have been made in person. One common way in which witnesses to crimes identify perpetrators is to be shown an array of photographs. The person's identification of one of the photos as that of the perpetrator would qualify as an identification of a person "the declarant perceived earlier." Basically, the rule might apply to allow the statement to be admitted as non-hearsay any time an individual with personal knowledge identifies a person after perceiving either the person or a photo of the person.

If each of the three requirements is satisfied, a statement of prior identification will be admissible as non-hearsay unless there are other reasons for its exclusion. For example, if police created a procedure that unfairly suggested the guilt of a particular person, the declarant's identification of that person will probably be excluded for constitutional reasons. So, if the declarant previously described the perpetrator as a "Caucasian male," and defendant was the only Caucasian male in the line-up, the court would probably exclude evidence that the declarant selected Defendant as the perpetrator.

To illustrate the prior identification rule, consider a case in which Defendant is charged with bank robbery. A few days after the robbery, one of the bank tellers who was working at the time of the robbery picked Defendant out of a line-up at the police station. At trial, the teller testifies about the robbery, but has difficulty remembering who she identified at the line-up. It is therefore necessary for the prosecution to call a police officer who conducted the line-up to provide that information. The relevant parts of the direct examinations of the teller (T) and the officer (Jones) might proceed as follows (assume any issues concerning the constitutionality of the line-up have already been resolved):

Pros: Did you visit the police station two days after the robbery?

T: Yes. I got a call from Officer Jones asking me to come down to the station to look at some people and tell them whether one of them was the robber.

Pros: Did you go to the station that day?

T: Yes. I went down after lunch.

Pros: What happened first?

T: Officer Jones told me that he would take me into a room and that a group of people would line up on the stage in front of me. He told me that I should look at the people, take as much time as I needed, and to let him know whether the person who robbed the bank was one of them.

Pros: What happened next?

T: I went into the room and took a seat. Five or six men walked onto the stage. Officer Jones asked each one of them to turn left, right, and so forth.

Pros: How long did this take?

T: I don't remember. It seemed like a long time. I was still very scared from the robbery, and being around these people made me more nervous.

Pros: Did you identify one of the men as the person who robbed the bank?

T: I think so, but that whole thing was so frightening that I don't remember anymore.

At this point, defense counsel will be given an opportunity to cross-examine the witness. The prosecution next calls Officer Jones. Jones testifies about the basic line-up procedure, and then the following colloquy takes place:

Pros: Did the teller identify anyone as the bank robber?

Jones: Yes.

Pros: How did she do so?

Jones: She pointed to one of the men and said, "He's the one I saw in the bank. He's the robber."

Pros: Is the person the teller identified present in the courtroom today?

Jones: Yes.

Pros: Would you please point out that person?

Jones: It's the defendant, the man sitting right there.

Pros: Your Honor, may the record show that the witness has pointed to Defendant?

By the Court: The record will reflect that the witness indicated the defendant.

Pros: After the teller identified the defendant, what happened next?

Jones: I asked her if she was certain that the man she selected was the robber.

Pros: Did she reply?

Jones: Yes. She said she was very sure.

At this point, defense counsel will be given an opportunity to cross-examine Officer Jones.

Questions for Classroom Discussion

1. Prosecution of Defendant for robbery of a convenience store. Two days after the robbery, the police arranged a formal line-up, and Witness, the clerk who was on duty when the robbery occurred, identified Defendant as the perpetrator. At trial, after presenting evidence about the line-up procedure, the prosecutor asks Witness who she identified. Defendant objects on hearsay grounds. How should the court rule?

2. Prosecution of Defendant for murder. Witness observed the killing, described the perpetrator to the police, and picked Defendant out of a line-up the next day. Witness died before trial. Does Witness's statement qualify as a statement of prior identification?

3. Same case. Suppose Witness did not die before trial, and appears as a prosecution witness. On direct examination, Witness only testifies about the facts of the killing itself; the prosecutor does not ask her about the line-up. The prosecutor calls Officer, the police officer who arranged the line-up, to testify about the line-up and about Witness's identification of Defendant. Defendant objects on hearsay grounds. How should the court rule?

4. Same case. Assume the court overrules Defendant's hearsay objection. Defendant now objects to Officer's testimony on the ground Officer lacks personal knowledge of the perpetrator because she was not present when the killing took place. How should the court rule?

5. Same case. Suppose that instead of arranging a line-up, the police showed Witness 20 photographs of persons with characteristics matching Witness's description of the perpetrator. Does this procedure satisfy the prior identification rule?

6. Same case. Suppose that instead of identifying Defendant in a line-up or photo array, Witness was at the police station giving a statement when she noticed Defendant being interrogated, and told the police officer that Defendant was the one who committed the crime. Does this statement qualify as a statement of prior identification?

7. Negligence action. Plaintiff claims Defendant ran a red light and struck Plaintiff as she crossed the street. Defendant claims she was in another state when the accident occurred. To prove Defendant was the one who struck Plaintiff, Plaintiff calls Witness to testify that she saw the accident, and described the driver to the police shortly afterward. (Defendant fits the description.) Defendant makes a hearsay objection to Witness's testimony concerning the description she gave to the police. How should the court rule?

L. EXCEPTIONS TO THE HEARSAY RULE: FORM AND STRUCTURE

Both at common law and under the Federal Rules, the exceptions to the hearsay rule are divided into two basic groups. Those exceptions falling into the first group (found in Rule 804) apply only if the declarant is "unavailable." Exceptions in the second, and much larger, group (Rules 803 and 807) apply without regard to whether the witness is available or unavailable.

Why should the availability of the declarant matter in determining whether a hearsay exception will apply? To begin to answer that question, it is necessary to recall the rationales for creating exceptions to the hearsay rule. Some out-of-court statements are made in circumstances that suggest reasonably high reliability—maybe even greater than testimony offered in court. Though the assumptions supporting the reliability of some types of statements admitted under the hearsay exceptions are of questionable validity, the assumed reliability of these statements helps to explain why hearsay exceptions in Rule 803 apply even if the declarant is available. Put simply, the statements are thought to be probative enough because of the context in which they were made that, on balance, the truth-finding process would be advanced by admitting them.

As noted above, evidence admitted pursuant to some exceptions might not be as reliable as tradition assumes. An interesting feature of the modern law of evidence is that the traditional exceptions have been maintained even as the assumptions supporting the purported reliability of certain categories of hearsay have been found to be faulty. For example, one of the oldest exceptions is the one admitting "excited utterances." That exception continues to be recognized today even as the assumptions about the reliability of statements made under stress have been severely undercut. In hearsay law, there is a lot to be said for sheer momentum.

Other types of out-of-court statements are not necessarily as reliable as the in-court testimony of the declarant would be, but the declarant's unavailability presents a choice between two imperfect options: excluding the evidence, thereby denying the fact-finder the opportunity to weigh it; or admitting the evidence and hoping that the fact-finder can evaluate its weight appropriately. For some classes of statement, the second choice has been made, based on the belief that the need for such statements as an aid to the truth-finding process outweighs their dangers. What we mean by "need" is that there are certain classes of hearsay that tend to contain information that is unlikely to be available through other sources or other types of evidence. A clear example is the exception for "former testimony." When a person has testified at a prior trial or hearing, and is no longer available, that person's testimony is unlikely to be replicable. The rules therefore permit the former testimony to be read into the record in the present case if certain conditions are met. Though need for the evidence is sometimes an important factor in the exceptions that do not require the declarant's unavailability, it has been a particularly strong factor in the recognition of Rule 804 exceptions, which apply only if the declarant is unavailable.

Today, state and federal courts recognize 30 or more exceptions. The categories of hearsay for which exceptions exist do not all have the same level of reliability or need. Some exceptions are strongly supported, others less so. But the approach of the hearsay rule in every jurisdiction has traditionally been a categorical one: The proponent must demonstrate that the statement at issue satisfies all the requirements of a specific exception, or the statement will be excluded.[22] Traditionally, hearsay law was not like the game of darts or horse-shoes; in hearsay law, a near-miss was as much of a miss as a shot that missed by a country mile. Hearsay either fit an exception or it did not. With the adoption of the Federal Rules and its "residual" or "catch-all" exception in Rule 807, this categorical feature of hearsay law began to break down. Today, in federal court and in jurisdictions that have followed the federal lead by adopting a residual exception, hearsay that does not satisfy the requirements of any specific exception might nevertheless be admitted if it meets certain criteria regarding reliability and need. The residual exception adds one more layer of complexity to an already rich and complicated body of law. Depending on how it is interpreted in the coming years, the residual exception might herald a new approach to hearsay that results in admission whenever the court deems its probative value to be sufficiently high or the need for it to be great.

Finally, keep in mind that the fact that hearsay fits within an exception does not guarantee its admission. In some circumstances, admission of the evidence would violate a specific rule of evidence. In some cases, the constitutional rights of a party might be violated by admission of the evidence. And as usual, Rule 403 is available to exclude evidence when its probative value is substantially outweighed by the dangers and concerns enumerated in that rule.

M. EXCEPTIONS TO THE HEARSAY RULE: AVAILABILITY OF DECLARANT IMMATERIAL

1. Time-Sensitive Statements (Rules 803(1) and (2))

FED. R. EVID. 803. EXCEPTIONS TO THE RULE AGAINST HEARSAY— REGARDLESS OF WHETHER THE DECLARANT IS AVAILABLE AS A WITNESS

The following are not excluded by the rule against hearsay, regardless of whether the declarant is available as a witness:

(1) *Present Sense Impression.* A statement describing or explaining an event or condition, made while or immediately after the declarant perceived it.

(2) *Excited Utterance.* A statement relating to a startling event or condition, made while the declarant was under the stress or excitement that it caused.

---

22. To be admissible, a given piece of hearsay need only satisfy the requirements of one exception. Generally speaking, the fact that the hearsay does not satisfy the requirements of other exceptions does not make it inadmissible as long as it fits into one exception. We discuss a limited qualification to this generalization later in this chapter.

a. Excited Utterances (Rule 803(2))

One of the oldest hearsay exceptions to be recognized by the courts admits statements made by a person who was suffering under the stress of a startling event. As Wigmore explained, the exception is

> based on the experience that, under certain external circumstances of physical shock, a stress of nervous excitement may be produced which stills the reflective faculties and removes their control, so that the utterance which then occurs is a spontaneous and sincere response to the actual sensations and perceptions already produced by the external shock. Since this utterance is made under the immediate and uncontrolled domination of the senses, and during the brief period when considerations of self-interest could not have been brought fully to bear by reasoned reflection, the utterance may be taken as particularly trustworthy (or, at least, as lacking the usual grounds of untrustworthiness), and thus as expressing the real tenor of the speaker's belief as to the facts just observed by him; and may therefore be received as testimony to those facts.

3 Wigmore, Evidence §1747 (1904). Note the assumption contained within Wigmore's explanation: that statements made while "under the stress of nervous excitement" caused by a shocking experience are likely to be *sincere* because the person's "reflective faculties" will not have an opportunity to work. Thus, the assumption is that it is difficult for a person to lie in these circumstances.

This is not the only assumption supporting the reliability of excited utterances. Such statements are also thought to be *accurate*. The theory is that an exciting event elevates a person's senses, leading to clear perceptions.

The excited utterance exception is therefore based on the assumption that the testimonial infirmities of insincerity and faulty perception are not likely to be present (or at least, are likely to be reduced) under the circumstances described. Together, these assumptions almost suggest that the utterance is caused by the event rather than any active cognition on the part of the observer — that the utterance is part of the event itself. This notion gave rise to the unfortunate term *res gestae* (literally translated as "things done"), which was applied to excited utterances and other similar statements so as to exempt them from the reach of the hearsay rule. The theory was that the utterance was part of the event rather than a person's statement about the event. Obviously, the notion that a person's statement could be part of the event it describes is nonsense. Even when a person reacts verbally to an event, the verbalization and the event are two different things. The term *res gestae* is out of favor today, and is not found in the Federal Rules.

Another problem with the excited utterance exception is that the human mind most likely does not work the way the courts assumed it does. Experimental research beginning in the first part of the twentieth century in fact suggests that both assumptions about excited utterances are false: Under stress, people are not accurate observers, and even when they are under stress, people can make up lies, sometimes extremely quickly. Our daily experience tells us that this is so. Many of us are familiar with the classroom experiment in which the teacher stages an unexpected event and then asks the students to give a detailed description of the event or the people involved. We know that the reactions of different students are often startlingly different. Empirical research also validates another thing we know from experience: Some people are excellent and lightning-fast liars, even when caught off-guard.[23]

Despite the likely invalidity of the assumptions supporting the reliability of excited utterances, courts continued to recognize this hearsay exception, and codifiers, including the drafters of the Federal Rules, have ensured its place in the modern law of evidence. Under Federal Rule 803(2), "A statement relating to a startling event or condition, made while the declarant was under the stress or excitement that it caused" qualifies as an excited utterance. Note that there are several prerequisites contained within this brief rule:

1. There must be a "startling event or condition";
2. The statement must "relat[e]" to that event or condition; and
3. The declarant must have been "under the stress or excitement that it caused" when she made the statement.

The existence or non-existence of each of these preliminary facts must be determined by the court pursuant to Rule 104(a) because the statement will be relevant even if one or more of the preliminary facts are not true. For example, a bystander's statement, following an automobile crash, "That car just ran right through the light!" is relevant even if the event was not startling. (Indeed, the installation of automated "red light cameras" at many intersections in this country attests to the frequency with which drivers run red lights.) Thus, this is not a case in which the evidence is relevant only if a certain condition of fact exists.

There is no clear or precise limit to the amount of time that may pass before a statement will no longer be considered to have been made "under the stress of excitement" caused by the event. In some situations, the stress of the event will dissipate very quickly, perhaps within a few seconds. In others, at least in theory, the stress can last for minutes or perhaps hours. The rule of thumb is this: If sufficient time has passed to give a person time to reflect on the event, the statement will not qualify. Courts tend to lengthen the time during which they may conclude a declarant will be unable to reflect when the declarant is directly involved in the exciting event (as compared to a bystander). Courts also tend to allow for the passage of additional time if the event is severe or unusual.

Sometimes, the statement or the circumstances will provide hints about this matter. For example, if the statement appears to have been a reasoned response to a question ("Did you see what happened?"), there is likely to have been reflection on the part of the respondent, and, if so, the statement will not qualify as an excited utterance.

b. Present Sense Impressions (Rule 803(1))

Early in the twentieth century, courts began to recognize a new hearsay exception related to the excited utterance. If excited utterances are reliable because

---

23. The empirical attack on perceptual accuracy under stress is probably more devastating than the attack on sincerity of statements made under stress. If so, it is possible that the continued acceptance of the excited utterance exception can be explained partly by the courts' greater concern with the inability to test the declarant's sincerity than with inability to test inaccurate perception. In other words, perhaps courts are more confident in the ability of the fact-finder to detect problems of the declarant's perception than those of insincerity.

insufficient time passes for a still-excited declarant to lie, the courts reasoned, the same could be true for people observing any event. As long as there has been no time for reflection (and thus insincerity), comments about any event or condition would be reliable. In addition, the courts noted, such statements almost always are made to another person who is able to verify their accuracy. Thus was born the present sense impression rule.

One of the earliest cases was Houston Oxygen Co. v. Davis, 161 S.W.2d 474 (Tex. App. 1942), an auto accident case. The trial court refused to allow defendant to introduce testimony that just after plaintiff's car passed another car four or five miles from the scene of the impending accident, an occupant in the other car commented that the people in plaintiff's car must have been drunk, and that they would have a wreck if they kept up that rate of speed. On appeal, the court held that exclusion of this evidence was error.[24] A few years later, McCormick laid out the reasons why statements of present sense impression are thought to be reliable:

> If a person observes some situation or happening which is not at all startling or shocking in its nature, nor actually producing excitement in the observer, the observer may yet have occasion to comment on what he sees (or learns from other senses) *at the very time that he is receiving the impression.* Such a comment, as to a situation then before the declarant, does not have the safeguard of impulse, emotion, or excitement, but as Morgan points out, there are other safeguards. In the first place, the report at the moment of the things then seen, heard, etc., is safe from any error from defect of *memory* of the declarant. Secondly, there is little or no *time* for calculated misstatement, and thirdly, the statement will usually be made to another . . . who would have equal opportunities to observe and hence to check a misstatement.

Charles T. McCormick, Evidence § 273, at 584 (1954) (emphasis in original).

Not all of the "safeguards" referred to by McCormick have been preserved by Rule 803(1), which creates a hearsay exception for "[a] statement describing or explaining an event or condition made while the declarant was perceiving the event or condition, or immediately thereafter." Rule 803(1) contains the following requirements:

1. There must have been an "event" or "condition";
2. The statement must describe or explain that "event" or "condition"; and
3. The declarant must have made the statement "while or immediately after [he] perceived it."

While McCormick would have required the statement to have been made "at the very time that he is receiving the impression," Rule 803(1) allows a statement to qualify under this exception if it was made "while or immediately after the declarant perceived it." In addition, there is no requirement that the statement have been made to an observer who had an equally good opportunity to observe the event or condition and who can therefore validate the declarant's statement. (Even McCormick might not have required this; he merely stated that "usually" such statements are made to a person with equally good opportunities to

---

24. A possible objection to the testimony that the appellate court did not address is that it contained an opinion that might not have been permissible for a lay witness. For discussion of the limits of lay opinion testimony, see Chapter 7.

perceive.) Even if the witness is the declarant, and the witness testifies that she said aloud but to herself, "that car is going awfully fast for this narrow, winding street," the statement potentially qualifies as a present sense impression. A more common situation in which there is no equally percipient witness would be a phone conversation between the declarant and another person, during which the declarant makes a statement about something occurring at that same time.

Note that although the excited utterance exception requires that a statement "relate to" a startling event or condition, statements admitted under the present sense impression exception must "describe" an event or condition. The difference can be important. A statement may qualify as an excited utterance even if it does not describe the event or condition; it qualifies as long as it "relates" to it. Thus, a child's exclamation "My mom's going to have a cow!" uttered after noticing that he'd tracked mud into the house might qualify as an excited utterance, but because it does not "describe" the act of tracking mud nor the condition of the carpet, it might not qualify as a present sense impression.

Note also that the event or condition described in a present sense impression need not be "startling" and the declarant need not be excited. Thus, the child's dispassionate statement, "looks like I tracked mud on the carpet—whatever," qualifies as a present sense impression but not an excited utterance. So the essential difference between Rules 803(1) and 803(2) is that the former focuses upon the timing of the statement while the latter focuses upon the psychological state of the declarant.

What does "immediately thereafter" mean in Rule 803(1)? As you might expect, this is purely a matter of context. But these statements are more time-restricted than excited utterances. An excited utterance can be made fairly long after an event, as long as the declarant is found still to be suffering from the stress of excitement caused by the event. A present sense impression, on the other hand, must be made very quickly. Though there is no per se rule providing for the amount of time that can pass before the statement becomes inadmissible, a reasonable rule of thumb would be as follows: If the court determines that sufficient time has passed to have allowed the declarant an opportunity to reflect on the events about which she has spoken, the statement will be inadmissible.

Despite the differences between excited utterances and present sense impressions, some statements satisfy the requirements for both. Suppose, for example, that two bicyclists collide on a bike path. Moments before the collision, one of the riders had yelled to the other, "You're veering into my path!" That statement probably qualifies as an excited utterance because there appears to be a startling event (the other bicycle veering into the declarant's path), the statement describes that event, and it seems to have been made while the declarant was under the stress of excitement caused by the event. The statement is also a present sense impression because it described an event and was made while the declarant was perceiving it.

Further Reading: Douglas E. Beloof & Joel Shapiro, *Let the Truth Be Told: Proposed Hearsay Exceptions to Admit Domestic Violence Victims' Out of Court Statements as Substantive Evidence*, 11 Colum. J. Gender & L. 1 (2002); Robert M. Hutchins & Donald Slesinger, *Some Observations on the Law of Evidence: Spontaneous Exclamations*, 28 Colum. L. Rev. 432 (1928); Jon R. Waltz, *The Present Sense Impression Exception to the Rule Against Hearsay: Origins and Attributes*, 66 Iowa L. Rev. 869 (1981).

Questions for Classroom Discussion

1. Prosecution of Defendant for murder. To prove that the killing took place outside a bank at 1:00 P.M., the prosecution calls Witness who testifies that she was in front of the bank at 1:00 P.M. that day when she heard Bystander scream, "Did you hear that gunshot?" Defendant makes a hearsay objection to Witness's testimony concerning Bystander's statement. How should the court rule?

2. Same case. Suppose Witness will testify that Bystander did not scream, "Did you hear that gunshot?" until Witness noticed Bystander looking frantically around her and asked Bystander what happened. Defendant objects on hearsay grounds. How should the court rule?

3. Same case and same circumstances as described in Question 2. Suppose that after listening to the proposed testimony of Witness and the arguments presented by counsel for both sides, the court is in equipoise as to whether Bystander's utterance was a spontaneous reaction to the event or a deliberative reaction to Witness's question. ("Equipoise" means evenly balanced; here, that means the court is not persuaded either way.) How should the court rule on Defendant's objection?

4. Prosecution of Defendant for assault and battery on Victim, his spouse. The incident occurred on a busy street corner when Defendant allegedly pushed Victim to the ground. A police officer arrived at the scene about five minutes after the incident. The prosecution wishes to have the officer testify that when she approached Victim, Victim was sitting on the sidewalk sobbing, and that when Victim saw the officer, Victim immediately said, through her sobs, "My husband hit me!" Defendant lodges a hearsay objection to the testimony about Victim's statement. The prosecution argues that the evidence is relevant and admissible as an excited utterance. How should the court rule?

5. Same facts as in Question 4. Assume the prosecution argues that Victim's utterance is also admissible as a present sense impression. How should the court rule?

6. Prosecution of Defendant for the attempted murder of Victim, her boyfriend. Defendant denies being the person who pushed Victim off a cliff. Victim did not die, but was knocked out by the fall and remained comatose for several weeks before waking up in the hospital. The prosecution calls Witness, a nurse, to testify that as Victim was emerging from his coma, he opened his eyes and screamed, "You did it, Defendant!" Defendant objects on hearsay grounds. The prosecution responds that the statement is admissible as an excited utterance. How should the court rule?

7. Prosecution of Defendant for the murder of Victim. Defendant claims he was in another town on the day of the murder. The prosecution calls Witness to testify that he was talking to Victim on the telephone

on the day of the murder when Victim said, "Defendant just walked into the room. It looks like he wants to show me his new chainsaw. I will call you right back." He never did. Defendant objects on hearsay grounds. How should the court rule?

8. Prosecution of Defendant for vehicular manslaughter. The driver ran down the victim in a crosswalk and fled. The car left a tire track clearly showing the tread pattern. Police took a photo of this track, and also took a photo of the tread pattern of the tires on Defendant's car. At trial, the prosecution calls a police officer, who testifies that he showed the two photos to a police tire track expert, and that the expert looked at them and said, "The tread patterns match." Defendant raises a hearsay objection to the testimony concerning the expert's statement. How should the court rule?

9. Negligence action arising from a bicycle collision. Plaintiff alleges that the cyclists had been heading in opposite directions when Defendant suddenly veered into Plaintiff's path, causing the collision. To prove Defendant veered into Plaintiff's path, Plaintiff calls Witness, who testifies she heard Plaintiff yell, "You're in my path!" Witness did not observe the crash itself, and only looked toward the bike path after the two cyclists were already sprawled on the ground, their twisted bikes wrapped around them. Plaintiff and Defendant were knocked out by the crash, so neither remembers what happened just before and during the accident. There were no eyewitnesses, and there is no physical evidence to show whether Defendant veered into Plaintiff's path. Defendant makes a hearsay objection. May Plaintiff's statement qualify as either an excited utterance or a present sense impression?

2.   Statements Concerning State of Mind and Physical Condition

> **FED. R. EVID.   803. EXCEPTIONS TO THE RULE AGAINST HEARSAY — REGARDLESS OF WHETHER THE DECLARANT IS AVAILABLE AS A WITNESS**

The following are not excluded by the rule against hearsay, regardless of whether the declarant is available as a witness:

(3) *Then-Existing Mental, Emotional, or Physical Condition.* A statement of the declarant's then-existing state of mind (such as motive, intent, or plan) or emotional, sensory, or physical condition (such as mental feeling, pain, or bodily health), but not including a statement of memory or belief to prove the fact remembered or believed unless it relates to the validity or terms of the declarant's will.

(4) *Statement Made for Medical Diagnosis or Treatment.* A statement that:

(A) is made for — and is reasonably pertinent to — medical diagnosis or treatment; and

(B) describes medical history; past or present symptoms or sensations; their inception; or their general cause.

a.   Statements of Declarant's Then-Existing State of Mind or Physical Condition (Rule 803(3))

Rule 803(3), sometimes referred to as the *state of mind exception*, is actually much broader than that phrase suggests. With one caveat, it allows the court to admit statements of the declarant's "then existing state of mind (such as motive, intent, or plan) or emotional, sensory, or physical condition (such as mental feeling, pain, or bodily health). . . ." Earlier in this chapter, we looked at one type of "state of mind" utterance: one that constitutes circumstantial evidence of the declarant's state of mind. In that situation, the statement is not hearsay because it is not offered to prove the truth of the matter asserted. Here, we discuss statements that directly assert the declarant's state of mind, and thus must be classified as hearsay, but may be admissible under an exception.

To understand the difference, imagine a conversion action by Plaintiff against Defendant. The suit concerns Defendant's possession of a valuable ring. Plaintiff alleges that Defendant stole it. Defendant admits possessing the ring, but claims Plaintiff gave it to him as a gift. To prove Plaintiff did not transfer the ring to Defendant voluntarily, Plaintiff calls Witness to testify that a few days before the transfer, Plaintiff said, "Defendant is the kind of person who would steal milk from a starving baby." The relevance of that statement is based on the following logic:

> **STATEMENT:** "Defendant is the kind of person who would steal milk from a starving baby."
>
> **INFERENCE:** Plaintiff did not like Defendant.
>
> **CONCLUSION:** Plaintiff did not give the ring to Defendant voluntarily.

The first inference is supported by the generalization that one who says a terrible thing about another person more likely dislikes that person than one who does not make such a statement. The conclusion that Plaintiff did not voluntarily transfer the ring to Defendant is based on the generalization that a person who does not like another person is not as likely to give that person a valuable gift as is one who does like the other person. The statement is therefore relevant. In this example, Plaintiff's statement is not hearsay because it is not offered to prove the truth of the matter asserted. We know this because the *first inference* from the statement (that Plaintiff did not like Defendant) is not the same thing it asserts (that Defendant is the kind of person who would steal milk from a starving baby). If Plaintiff were offering the statement to prove that Defendant would steal milk from a starving baby, the statement would be hearsay. But this is not the purpose for which Plaintiff is offering the statement. The statement is being offered to show, circumstantially, that Plaintiff did not like Defendant. Therefore, it is not hearsay.

Imagine, however, that Plaintiff had said something different to Witness: "I don't like Defendant one bit." Now the chain of inferences is as follows:

STATEMENT: "I don't like Defendant one bit."

INFERENCE: Plaintiff did not like Defendant.

CONCLUSION: Plaintiff did not give the ring to Defendant voluntarily.

Notice what has changed: The first inference from the statement is the same thing the statement asserts. Plaintiff said she didn't like Defendant, and the statement is being offered to show the same thing. The statement is hearsay.

At this point, we imagine that some students might wonder if the law of evidence makes any sense at all. One would think that the admissibility of statements offered to prove a person's state of mind would not depend on small details in the words the person chose. Fortunately, the law reaches the same *ultimate* conclusion with respect to both types of statements: Both are generally admissible. Statements that constitute circumstantial evidence of the declarant's state of mind are admissible non-hearsay, and statements that directly assert the declarant's state of mind are hearsay but fit within the exception in Rule 803(3).

Still, it is a useful test of your understanding of the hearsay rule to distinguish between the two types of statements. Generally, this is relatively easy. In our example above, the first statement clearly does not constitute an *assertion* that the declarant (Plaintiff) does not like Defendant. Certainly, the inferential leap from the statement to Plaintiff's feelings about Defendant is not very long, but a leap is still required. At the other end of the spectrum, no similar inferential leap is required for the statement, "I don't like Defendant one bit." One must still decide whether Plaintiff is being sincere, and whether there is any ambiguity in the statement that might cause us to misunderstand Plaintiff's meaning, but the statement is a direct assertion of Plaintiff's state of mind.

Some statements are much more difficult to classify. For example, if the statement "I'm meeting Keesha for dinner" is offered to prove the declarant's intention to do something in the future, is that statement hearsay or non-hearsay? If the declarant had said, "I'm planning to meet Keesha for dinner," this would fairly clearly constitute hearsay because the declarant is speaking in terms of her state of mind ("I am planning . . ."). But when she merely stated as a fact what she was going to do, is this non-hearsay? Some courts would treat the statement as circumstantial evidence of the declarant's then-existing state of mind (the intention to do something in the future), and thus non-hearsay. (See the discussion of this in section C.4 of this chapter.) Others would treat the statement as direct evidence of the declarant's state of mind, and thus hearsay, but admissible under the "state of mind" exception embodied in Rule 803(3).[25]

---

25. The distinction between circumstantial evidence of state of mind (non-hearsay) and a direct statement of the declarant's state of mind (hearsay but admissible under the "state of mind" exception) is sometimes difficult to discern.

Let's return to the scope of Rule 803(3). An important limitation is that any statement must be of the declarant's *then-existing* state of mind.[26] This means that backward-looking statements ("Yesterday I was pretty depressed") are not admissible under the rule. On the other hand, note that one's present state of mind about the future does qualify. So, the statement "I'm thinking about driving to New York tomorrow" is within the scope of Rule 803(3) because the declarant is referring to the plans she now has in her mind.

The "state of mind" exception is not limited to statements of emotion. It also encompasses such things as physical sensations (pain, hunger, thirst, and so forth) as well as intentions (plans, desires, needs). The rationale for the exception can be traced both to *necessity* and *reliability*. None of these matters can be proven directly; we cannot read a person's mind (at least not yet). Thus, when a person's thoughts are relevant, we must look to outward manifestations, and the best of these is what the person says about the matter. And, as described above, statements of one's state of mind are also considered relatively reliable because people are reasonably good at perceiving their own thoughts[27] and there is no problem of memory because the rule is limited to the declarant's *then-existing* state of mind.

Note that there is some overlap between the state of mind exception and both the excited utterance and the present sense impression exceptions. Some statements may qualify under two or three of these exceptions. For example, if a person exclaims as he grabs his stomach, "Oh! That cramp really hurts!" that statement would probably qualify as an excited utterance, a present sense impression, and a statement of the declarant's then-existing physical sensation. If the declarant had not reacted in an excited way, the statement would not qualify as an excited utterance, but probably would satisfy the other two exceptions.

i. Statements That Look Forward

One of the most interesting questions about the scope of the state of mind rule concerns the admissibility of a person's statement of her intention to do something in the future. The courts have tended to admit forward-looking statements. Even the U.S. Supreme Court weighed in on this question, in the famous case that follows.

---

26. Interestingly, Cal. Evid. Code § 1251 creates an exception for "evidence of a statement of the declarant's state of mind . . . at a time prior to the statement" if the declarant is unavailable as a witness and if "[t]he evidence is offered to prove such prior state of mind . . . when it is itself an issue in the action and the evidence is not offered to prove any fact other than such state of mind. . . ."

27. Even when we cannot say for certain how we feel about someone or something, this generalization is still true—we correctly perceive our thoughts, but those thoughts are ambivalent.

MUTUAL LIFE INS. CO. OF NEW YORK v. HILLMON

145 U.S. 285 (1892)

Statement by Mr. Justice Gray.

On July 13, 1880, Sallie E. Hillmon, a citizen of Kansas, brought an action against the Mutual Life Insurance Company, a corporation of New York, on a policy of insurance, dated December 10, 1878, on the life of her husband, John W. Hillmon, in the sum of $10,000, payable to her within 60 days after notice and proof of his death. On the same day the plaintiff brought two other actions, — the one against the New York Life Insurance Company, a corporation of New York, on two similar policies of life insurance, dated, respectively, November 30, 1878, and December 10, 1878, for the sum of $5,000 each; and the other against the Connecticut Mutual Life Insurance Company, a corporation of Connecticut, on a similar policy, dated March 4, 1879, for the sum of $5,000.

In each case the declaration alleged that Hillmon died on March 17, 1879, during the continuance of the policy, but that the defendant, though duly notified of the fact, had refused to pay the amount of the policy, or any part thereof; and the answer denied the death of Hillmon, and alleged that he, together with John H. Brown and diverse other persons, on or before November 30, 1878, conspiring to defraud the defendant, procured the issue of all the policies, and afterwards, in March and April, 1879, falsely pretended and represented that Hillmon was dead, and that a dead body which they had procured was his, whereas in reality he was alive and in hiding. . . .

At the trial plaintiff introduced evidence tending to show that on or about March 5, 1879, Hillmon and Brown left Wichita, in the state of Kansas, and traveled together through southern Kansas in search of a site for a cattle ranch; that on the night of March 18th, while they were in camp at a place called "Crooked creek," Hillmon was killed by the accidental discharge of a gun; that Brown at once notified persons living in the neighborhood, and that the body was thereupon taken to a neighboring town, where, after an inquest, it was buried. The defendants introduced evidence tending to show that the body found in the camp at Crooked creek on the night of March 18th was not the body of Hillmon, but was the body of one Frederick Adolph Walters. Upon the question whose body this was there was much conflicting evidence, including photographs and descriptions of the corpse, and of the marks and scars upon it, and testimony to its likeness to Hillmon and to Walters.

The defendants introduced testimony that Walters left his home at Ft. Madison, in the state of Iowa, in March, 1878, and was afterwards in Kansas in 1878, and in January and February, 1879; that during that time his family frequently received letters from him, the last of which was written from Wichita; and that he had not been heard from since March, 1879. The defendants also offered the following evidence:

Elizabeth Rieffenach testified that she was a sister of Frederick Adolph Walters, and lived at Ft. Madison; and thereupon, as shown by the bill of exceptions, the following proceedings took place:

> Witness further testified that she had received a letter written from Wichita, Kansas, about the 4th or 5th day of March, 1879, by her brother Frederick Adolph; that the letter was dated at Wichita, and was in the handwriting of her brother; that she

had searched for the letter, but could not find the same, it being lost; that she remembered and could state the contents of the letter.

Thereupon the defendants' counsel asked the question, "State the contents of that letter;" to which the plaintiff objected, on the ground that the same is incompetent, irrelevant, and hearsay. The objection was sustained, and the defendants duly excepted. The following is the letter as stated by witness:

Wichita, Kansas, March 4th or 5th or 3d or 4th, — I don't know, — 1879. Dear Sister and All: I now in my usual style drop you a few lines to let you know that I expect to leave Wichita on or about March the 5th with a certain Mr. Hillmon, a sheep trader, for Colorado, or parts unknown to me. I expect to see the country now. News are of no interest to you, as you are not acquainted here. I will close with compliments to all inquiring friends. Love to all. I am truly your brother, FRED. ADOLPH WALTERS.

[Defendants presented testimony concerning a second letter sent by Walters, the content of which was much the same.] . . .

The jury, being instructed by the court to return a separate verdict in each case, returned verdicts for the plaintiff against the three defendants respectively for the amounts of their policies and interest, upon which separate judgments were rendered. The defendants sued out four writs of error, one jointly in the three cases as consolidated, and one in each case separately.

Mr. Justice GRAY, after stating the case as above, delivered the opinion of the court. . . .

There is . . . one question of evidence so important, so fully argued at the bar, and so likely to arise upon another trial, that it is proper to express an opinion upon it.

This question is of the admissibility of the letters written by Walters on the first days of March, 1879, which were offered in evidence by the defendants, and excluded by the court. In order to determine the competency of these letters it is important to consider the state of the case when they were offered to be read.

The matter chiefly contested at the trial was the death of John W. Hillmon, the insured; and that depended upon the question whether the body found at Crooked creek on the night of March 18, 1879, was his body or the body of one Walters.

Much conflicting evidence had been introduced as to the identity of the body. The plaintiff had also introduced evidence that Hillmon and one Brown left Wichita, in Kansas, on or about March 5, 1879, and traveled together through southern Kansas in search of a site for a cattle ranch; and that on the night of March 18th, while they were in camp at Crooked creek, Hillmon was accidentally killed, and that his body was taken thence and buried. The defendants had introduced evidence, without objection, that Walters left his home and his betrothed in Iowa in March, 1878, and was afterwards in Kansas until March, 1879; that during that time he corresponded regularly with his family and his betrothed; that the last letters received from him were one received by his betrothed on March 3d, and postmarked at "Wichita, March 2," and one received by his sister about March 4th or 5th, and dated at Wichita a day or two before; and that he had not been heard from since.

The evidence that Walters was at Wichita on or before March 5th, and had not been heard from since, together with the evidence to identify as his the body found at Crooked creek on March 18th, tended to show that he went from Wichita to Crooked creek between those dates. Evidence that just before

March 5th he had the intention of leaving Wichita with Hillmon would tend to corroborate the evidence already admitted, and to show that he went from Wichita to Crooked creek with Hillmon. Letters from him to his family and his betrothed were the natural, if not the only attainable, evidence of his intention.

The position taken at the bar that the letters were competent evidence, within the rule stated in Nicholls v. Webb, 8 Wheat. 326, 337, as memoranda made in the ordinary course of business, cannot be maintained, for they were clearly not such.

But upon another ground suggested they should have been admitted. A man's state of mind or feeling can only be manifested to others by countenance, attitude, or gesture, or by sounds or words, spoken or written. The nature of the fact to be proved is the same, and evidence of its proper tokens is equally competent to prove it, whether expressed by aspect or conduct, by voice or pen. When the intention to be proved is important only as qualifying an act, its connection with that act must be shown, in order to warrant the admission of declarations of the intention. But whenever the intention is of itself a distinct and material fact in a chain of circumstances, it may be proved by contemporaneous oral or written declarations of the party.

The existence of a particular intention in a certain person at a certain time being a material fact to be proved, evidence that he expressed that intention at that time is as direct evidence of the fact as his own testimony that he then had that intention would be. After his death there can hardly be any other way of proving it, and while he is still alive his own memory of his state of mind at a former time is no more likely to be clear and true than a bystander's recollection of what he then said, and is less trustworthy than letters written by him at the very time and under circumstances precluding a suspicion of misrepresentation.

The letters in question were competent not as narratives of facts communicated to the writer by others, nor yet as proof that he actually went away from Wichita, but as evidence that, shortly before the time when other evidence tended to show that he went away, he had the intention of going, and of going with Hillmon, which made it more probable both that he did go and that he went with Hillmon than if there had been no proof of such intention. In view of the mass of conflicting testimony introduced upon the question whether it was the body of Walters that was found in Hillmon's camp, this evidence might properly influence the jury in determining that question.

The rule applicable to this case has been thus stated by this court: "Wherever the bodily or mental feelings of an individual are material to be proved, the usual expressions of such feelings are original and competent evidence. Those expressions are the natural reflexes of what it might be impossible to show by other testimony. If there be such other testimony, this may be necessary to set the facts thus developed in their true light, and to give them their proper effect. As independent, explanatory, or corroborative evidence it is often indispensable to the due administration of justice. Such declarations are regarded as verbal acts, and are as competent as any other testimony, when relevant to the issue. Their truth or falsity is an inquiry for the jury." Insurance Co. v. Mosley, 8 Wall. 397, 404, 405. . . .

Upon an indictment of one Hunter for the murder of one Armstrong at Camden, the court of errors and appeals of New Jersey unanimously held that Armstrong's oral declarations to his son at Philadelphia, on the afternoon before the night of the murder, as well as a letter written by him at the same time and place to his wife, each stating that he was going with Hunter to Camden on business, were rightly admitted in evidence. Chief Justice Beasley said: "In the ordinary course of things, it was the usual information that a man about leaving home would communicate, for the convenience of his family, the information of his friends, or the regulation of his business. At the time it was given, such declarations could, in the nature of things, mean harm to no one. He who uttered them was bent on no expedition of mischief or wrong, and the attitude of affairs at the time entirely explodes the idea that such utterances were intended to serve any purpose but that for which they were obviously designed. If it be said that such notice of an intention of leaving home could have been given without introducing in it the name of Mr. Hunter, the obvious answer to the suggestion, I think, is that a reference to the companion who is to accompany the person leaving is as natural a part of the transaction as is any other incident or quality of it. If it is legitimate to show by a man's own declarations that he left his home to be gone a week, or for a certain destination, which seems incontestable, why may it not be proved in the same way that a designated person was to bear him company? At the time the words were uttered or written they imported no wrongdoing to any one, and the reference to the companion who was to go with him was nothing more, as matters then stood, than an indication of an additional circumstance of his going. If it was in the ordinary train of events for this man to leave word or to state where he was going, it seems to me it was equally so for him to say with whom he was going." Hunter v. State, 40 N.J. Law, 495, 534, 536-538.

Upon principle and authority, therefore, we are of opinion that the two letters were competent evidence of the intention of Walters at the time of writing them, which was a material fact bearing upon the question in controversy; and that for the exclusion of these letters, as well as for the undue restriction of the defendants' challenges, the verdicts must be set aside, and a new trial had.

As the verdicts and judgments were several, the writ of error sued out by the defendants jointly was superfluous, and may be dismissed without costs; and upon each of the writs of error sued out by the defendants severally the order will be:

Judgment reversed, and case remanded to the circuit court, with directions to set aside the verdict and to order a new trial.

The *Hillmon* rule is still followed in U.S. courts. It is now clear that a person's statement of her intention to do something in the future is admissible both to prove that the speaker had such an intention and that the person acted upon that intention.[28] What is not so clear is the breadth of the rule. Consider the following hypothetical:

28. As we noted when we introduced the issue of the admissibility of statements of intention earlier in this chapter, it is not always clear whether such statements are hearsay but subject to the exception for state of mind, or non-hearsay circumstantial evidence of the declarant's state of mind. Of course, there is little practical difference between the statement, "I'm going to the movies tonight" and the statement, "I intend to go to the movies tonight." Both are statements of an intention to do something in the future. If one is admissible, the other should also be admissible.

> Prosecution of Defendant for the murder of Victim. Defendant denies any involvement and denies seeing Victim on the day she was killed. At trial, the prosecution wishes to present evidence that several hours before she was killed, Victim told a friend, "I'm going to a movie tonight with Defendant."

Is Victim's statement admissible under the *Hillmon* doctrine? If Victim had simply said, "I'm going to a movie tonight," there would be no problem. The statement would qualify as a statement of Victim's intention to do something in the future, and under the *Hillmon* doctrine would be admissible to prove both that Victim intended to go to the movies and, in fact, that Victim did go to the movies. But, of course, this is not the primary reason the prosecution is offering the evidence. Primarily, the prosecution's interest is in putting Victim together with Defendant on the night Victim was killed. Is Victim's statement admissible not only to show that Victim acted in accordance with her intention to go to a movie with Defendant, but also to show that Defendant went to the movies?

Some courts would hold the evidence admissible to show both Victim's and Defendant's conduct. In People v. Alcalde, 148 P.2d 627 (Cal. 1944), for example, the California Supreme Court held that a murder victim's statement that she was going out to dinner that night with "Frank" was admissible against the defendant, who used the name Frank. The majority held that "[f]rom the declared intent to do a particular thing an inference that the thing was done may fairly be drawn. Such declarations have been deemed admissible where they possessed a high degree of trustworthiness. Where they are relevant to an issue in the case and the declarant is dead or otherwise unavailable the necessity for their admission has been recognized." *Id.* at 631. *See also* United States v. Pheaster, 544 F.2d 353, 376-377 (9th Cir. 1976) (declarant told friends he was going to meet Angelo in the parking lot of a certain restaurant; the court held the statement admissible to prove declarant and Angelo were together on the night in question). Some courts have admitted such statements, but only in the presence of evidence corroborating the involvement of the person to whom the statement referred. *See, e.g.,* United States v. Cicale, 691 F.2d 95, 103-104 (2d Cir. 1982) (declarant told an undercover agent that he was going to meet his source to arrange a heroin deal; the court held the evidence admissible because other evidence corroborated defendant's involvement in the conspiracy).

Other courts have held that statements of an intention to do something in the future that involve a third person should not be admitted to show the third party's conduct. Justice Traynor issued a strong dissent in *Alcalde*. He wrote:

> A declaration of intention is admissible to show that the *declarant* did the intended act, if there are corroborating circumstances and if the declarant is dead or unavailable and hence cannot be put on the witness stand. . . . A declaration as to what one person intended to do, however, cannot safely be accepted as evidence of what another probably did. . . . The declaration of the deceased in this case that she was going out with Frank is also a declaration that he was going out with her, and it could not be admitted for the limited purpose of showing that she went out with him at the time in question without necessarily showing that he went with her. . . . Such a declaration could not be admitted without the risk that the jury would conclude that it tended to prove the acts of the defendant as well as of the declarant, and it is clear that the prosecution used the declaration to that end. There is no dispute as to the identity of the deceased or as to where she was at the time of her death. Since the evidence is overwhelming as to who the deceased was and

where she was when she met her death, no legitimate purpose could be served by admitting her declarations of what she intended to do on the evening of November 22d. The only purpose that could be served by admitting such declarations would be to induce the belief that the defendant went out with the deceased, took her to the scene of the crime and there murdered her. Her declarations cannot be admitted for that purpose without setting aside the rule against hearsay.

Arguably, the reason for allowing the admission of state of mind statements does not justify admitting statements of one person's state of mind to prove the conduct of another person. Recall that as long as we do not have the technology to read people's minds directly, the best available evidence of a person's state of mind is her own statement about it. We can reasonably assume that when a person says what is on her mind, she accurately perceives her own mental state. But this is hardly true when one person purports to speak of the state of mind of a different person. I might think I know what my friend intends to do tonight, but I might well be mistaken. Thus, the accuracy of state of mind statements does not extend beyond the speaker. Some courts accept this argument and would rule, in our hypothetical, that the evidence is not admissible. The effect of such a ruling would be either to exclude Victim's statement entirely, or, more likely, to redact the statement as reported to the jury, so that only Victim's intention to go to the movies that night is mentioned. This, of course, likely gives the prosecution little or none of what it wants, but the result (exclusion of the evidence) is supported by the unreliability of the statement when it concerns the intentions of another person.

Further Reading: Diane Kiesel, Comment, *One Person's Thoughts, Another Person's Acts: How the Federal Circuit Courts Interpret the* Hillmon *Doctrine*, 33 Cath. U. L. Rev. 699 (1984); John M. Maguire, *The* Hillmon *Case — Thirty-Three Years After*, 38 Harv. L. Rev. 709 (1925); David E. Seidelson, *The State of Mind Exception to the Hearsay Rule*, 13 Duq. L. Rev. 251 (1974).

ii. Statements That Look Backward

If forward-looking statements are admissible, at least to prove the intentions of the declarant, what about statements that look backward? Consider this hypothetical:

> Defendant is charged with the murder of Victim, who died from ingesting cyanide-laced lemonade. Defendant claims there was no murder — that Victim's death was a suicide. To prove that Victim did not take her own life, the prosecution calls Witness, Victim's friend, to testify that after drinking the lemonade, Victim said to Witness, "Somebody tried to poison me."

Because Victim's statement asserts that someone was trying to poison her, and the statement was not made while testifying at the trial or hearing, the statement is hearsay if offered to prove that someone actually tried to poison her:

STATEMENT: "Someone tried to poison me."

CONCLUSION: Someone tried to poison Victim.

However, Victim might seek to offer the statement for another purpose that does not depend on its truth:

STATEMENT: "Someone tried to poison me."

➔ **INFERENCE:** Victim believed the drink was poisoned by someone else.

➔ **INFERENCE:** Victim did not put the poison in the drink.

➔ **CONCLUSION:** Victim did not commit suicide.

On this line of reasoning, the statement is not hearsay because the first inference from the statement does not have to be true in order for the statement to be relevant. The first inference from the statement is not the truth of its assertion (that someone was trying to poison Victim), but rather that Victim *believed* that to be the case. The statement is relevant to prove Victim's belief because it is somewhat more likely that a person who asserts a fact actually believes it is true than if the person does not assert the fact. Victim's belief, in turn, is relevant because it suggests that Victim did not poison the drink, and thus did not take her own life.

Thus, it is possible that some statements about past events might be relevant non-hearsay because they constitute circumstantial evidence of the declarant's belief. This does not mean the statements are admissible, however. As we have already seen, an important limitation on the use of the state of mind theory to explain events in the past is the possibility of unfair prejudice. This is the issue the U.S. Supreme Court faced in the following case.

SHEPARD v. UNITED STATES
290 U.S. 96 (1933)

Mr. Justice CARDOZO delivered the opinion of the Court.

The petitioner, Charles A. Shepard, a major in the medical corps of the United States Army, has been convicted of the murder of his wife, Zenana Shepard, at Fort Riley, Kan., a United States military reservation. The jury having qualified their verdict by adding thereto the words "without capital punishment" . . . , the defendant was sentenced to imprisonment for life. The judgment of the United States District Court has been affirmed by the Circuit Court of Appeals for the Tenth Circuit, one of the judges of that court dissenting. . . . A writ of certiorari brings the case here.

The crime is charged to have been committed by poisoning the victim with bichloride of mercury. The defendant was in love with another woman, and wished to make her his wife. There is circumstantial evidence to sustain a finding by the jury that to win himself his freedom he turned to poison and murder. Even so, guilt was contested, and conflicting inferences are possible. The defendant asks us to hold that by the acceptance of incompetent evidence the scales were weighted to his prejudice and in the end to his undoing.

The evidence complained of was offered by the government in rebuttal when the trial was nearly over. On May 22, 1929, there was a conversation in the absence of the defendant between Mrs. Shepard, then ill in bed, and Clara Brown, her nurse. The patient asked the nurse to go to the closet in the defendant's room and bring a bottle of whisky that would be found upon a shelf. When the bottle was produced, she said that this was the liquor she had taken just before collapsing. She asked whether enough was left to make a test for the presence of poison, insisting that the smell and taste were strange. And then she added the words, "Dr. Shepard has poisoned me."

The conversation was proved twice. After the first proof of it, the government asked to strike it out, being doubtful of its competence, and this request was granted. A little later, however, the offer was renewed; the nurse having then testified to statements by Mrs. Shepard as to the prospect of recovery. "She said she was not going to get well; she was going to die." With the aid of this new evidence, the conversation already summarized was proved a second time. There was a timely challenge of the ruling.

She said, "Dr. Shepard has poisoned me." The admission of this declaration, if erroneous, was more than unsubstantial error. As to that the parties are agreed. The voice of the dead wife was heard in accusation of her husband, and the accusation was accepted as evidence of guilt. If the evidence was incompetent, the verdict may not stand.

1. Upon the hearing in this court the government finds its main prop in the position that what was said by Mrs. Shepard was admissible as a dying declaration. This is manifestly the theory upon which it was offered and received. The prop, however, is a broken reed. To make out a dying declaration, the declarant must have spoken without hope of recovery and in the shadow of impending death. The record furnishes no proof of that indispensable condition. . . .
2. We pass to the question whether the statements to the nurse, though incompetent as dying declarations, were admissible on other grounds.

The Circuit Court of Appeals determined that they were. Witnesses for the defendant had testified to declarations by Mrs. Shepard which suggested a mind bent upon suicide, or at any rate were thought by the defendant to carry that suggestion. More than once before her illness she had stated in the hearing of these witnesses that she had no wish to live, and had nothing to live for, and on one occasion she added that she expected some day to make an end to her life. This testimony opened the door, so it is argued, to declarations in rebuttal that she had been poisoned by her husband. They were admissible, in that view, not as evidence of the truth of what was said, but as betokening a state of mind inconsistent with the presence of suicidal intent. . . .

(b) [T]he accusatory declaration must have been rejected as evidence of a state of mind [even if] the purpose thus to limit it had been brought to light upon the trial. The defendant had tried to show by Mrs. Shepard's declarations to her friends that she had exhibited a weariness of life and a readiness to end it, the testimony giving plausibility to the hypothesis of suicide. . . . By the proof of these declarations evincing an unhappy state of mind, the defendant opened the door to the offer by the government of declarations evincing a different state of mind, declarations consistent with the persistence of a will to live. The defendant would have no grievance if the testimony in rebuttal had been narrowed to that point. What the government put in evidence, however, was something very different. It did not use the declarations by Mrs. Shepard to prove her present thoughts and feelings, or even her thoughts and feelings in times past. It used the declarations as proof of an act committed by some one else, as evidence that she was dying of poison given by her husband. This fact, if fact it was, the government was free to prove, but not by hearsay declarations. It will not do to say that the jury might accept the declarations for any light that they cast upon the existence of a vital urge, and reject them to the extent that they charged the death to some one else. Discrimination so subtle is a feat beyond the compass of ordinary minds. The reverberating clang of those accusatory words would drown all weaker sounds. It is for ordinary minds, and not for psychoanalysts, that our rules of evidence are framed. They have their source very often in considerations of administrative convenience, of practical expediency, and not in rules of logic. When the risk of confusion is so great as to upset the balance of advantage, the evidence goes out. . . .

These precepts of caution are a guide to judgment here. There are times when a state of mind, if relevant, may be proved by contemporaneous declarations of feeling or intent. Mutual Life Ins. Co. v. Hillmon, 145 U.S. 285, 295, 12 S. Ct. 909, 36 L. Ed. 706; . . . Thus, in proceedings for the probate of a will, where the issue is undue influence, the declarations of a testator are competent to prove his feelings for his relatives, but are incompetent as evidence of his conduct or of theirs. . . . In suits for the alienation of affections, letters passing between the spouses are admissible in aid of a like purpose. . . . In damage suits for personal injuries, declarations by the patient to bystanders or physicians are evidence of sufferings or symptoms . . . , but are not received to prove the acts, the external circumstances, through which the injuries came about. . . . Even statements of past sufferings or symptoms are generally excluded . . . though an exception is at times allowed when they are made to a physician. . . . So also in suits upon insurance policies, declarations by an insured that he intends to go upon a journey with another may be evidence of a state of mind lending probability to the conclusion that the purpose was fulfilled. Mutual Life Ins. Co. v. Hillmon, *supra*. The ruling in that case marks the high-water line beyond which courts have been unwilling to go. It has developed a substantial body of criticism and commentary. Declarations of intention, casting light upon the future, have been sharply distinguished from declarations of memory, pointing backwards to the past. There would be an end, or nearly that, to the rule against hearsay if the distinction were ignored.

The testimony now questioned faced backward and not forward. This at least it did in its most obvious implications. What is even more important, it spoke to a past act, and, more than that, to an act by some one not the speaker. Other tendency, if it had any, was a filament too fine to be disentangled by a jury.

The judgment should be reversed and the cause remanded to the District Court for further proceedings in accordance with this opinion.

Reversed.

The *Shepard* opinion states an important limitation on the *Hillmon* reasoning — that it does not allow the court to admit statements concerning a fact remembered or believed if offered to prove the fact remembered or believed. Thus, if Mrs. Shepard says, "I think Dr. Shepard has poisoned me" (instead of "Dr. Shepard has poisoned me"), this statement would be hearsay if offered to prove what Mrs. Shepard thought, but it would be admissible if offered to prove simply that Mrs. Shepard had such a state of mind. But the hearsay would not be admissible if offered to further prove the fact remembered or believed; that Dr. Shepard had poisoned Mrs. Shepard. If it were admissible for that purpose, the state-of-mind exception would swallow the hearsay rule because every statement about something that took place in the past is, at least implicitly, a statement of the declarant's memory of that event. The language of Rule 803(3) incorporates the limitation stated in *Shepard*: "but not including a statement of memory or belief to prove the fact remembered or believed. . . ."

Another way to understand this distinction is to think about the rationale for this exception. Rule 803(3) makes admissible statements of a declarant's then-existing physical condition or state of mind because, when a person is speaking only about what is happening internally to his or her own person, it is reasonable to think that the person is not misperceiving that internal reality. We know how we feel and we know what is in our heads. In contrast, we can easily misperceive events that occur in the external world for a myriad of reasons, such as bad eyesight, distraction, and the like. The problem is that sometimes people make statements about external events using language of internal states of mind. For example, "I remember Dr. Shepard poisoned me" or "I believe Dr. Shepard poisoned me." But the mere fact that the statement makes reference to an internal state of mind does not make the statement any more reliable. If that statement is being used to prove the external event remembered or believed, the declarant could be misperceiving that event. Thus, Rule 803(3) makes such statements inadmissible.

There is one exception to this limitation. Rule 803(3) states that a statement or memory or belief may be admitted if "it relates to the validity or terms of the declarant's will." This somewhat obscure provision rests "on practical grounds of necessity and expedience rather than logic," in the words of the Advisory Committee. Its purpose can be understood more clearly by reviewing the language of the California counterpart, which creates an exception for "[e]vidence of a statement made by a declarant unavailable as a witness that he has or has not made a will, or has or has not revoked his will, or that identifies his will. . . ." Cal. Evid. Code § 1260. When there is a dispute about whether a deceased person made or revoked a will, or whether a particular document is that person's last will, the absence of the decedent to answer this question creates a gap in available evidence that can be filled by the decedent's statements.

Questions for Classroom Discussion

1. In *Shepard*, why was Mrs. Shepard's statement hearsay if offered to prove Dr. Shepard's guilt?

2. What non-hearsay argument did the government make to justify admission of Mrs. Shepard's statement? Why did the Supreme Court reject the argument? Was the Court correct?

3. Did the Court need to discuss the limits of the *Hillmon* doctrine to resolve the issues in *Shepard*?

b.   Statements for Purposes of Medical Diagnosis or Treatment (Rule 803(4))

Rule 803(4) creates an exception for a statement that "(A) is made for — and is reasonably pertinent to — medical diagnosis or treatment; and (B) describes medical history; past or present symptoms or sensations; their inception; or their general cause." The rationale for the rule is simple: If a person is seeking medical diagnosis or treatment, she is unlikely to lie because the resulting diagnosis or treatment could be ineffectual or harmful. Thus, sincerity is not a great problem. Additionally, a person normally has relatively accurate perception concerning her medical condition. Laypersons are not necessarily good diagnosticians, but we are able to describe our symptoms with reasonable accuracy.

There are some problems in assessing the reliability of statements for purposes of medical diagnosis or treatment. Though the opponent's inability to conduct contemporaneous cross-examination of the declarant regarding her sincerity and perception is not a major disadvantage, the testimonial infirmities of memory and narration can present a problem. Memory can be a problem because the rule covers statements of medical history or past symptoms as well as present ones. And narration can be a problem because laypersons' descriptions of medical conditions are often difficult to understand. One would prefer to be able to clarify these descriptions at the time they are made.

The medical diagnosis or treatment exception is supported by considerations of *necessity*. Though the need is not as great as for statements admitted under the state of mind exception, a person's utterances concerning his physical condition or medical history are often the best available evidence of those facts. Though some facts, such as past symptoms and treatment, are often documented in writing, others, such as symptoms not previously reported, are not documented.

In one important way, the exception sweeps more broadly than the version that developed at common law. While the common law exception was usually limited to statements made for purposes of medical *treatment*, the modern exception also covers statements made for purposes of *diagnosis*. This is significant because the exception would admit a patient's statement to a physician from whom she had no intention of seeking treatment. Yet this is a common situation: People who have brought or are contemplating bringing personal injury actions often consult physicians to aid a lawyer in assessing the damages that might be sought in the case. When this occurs, the patient does not lose all reason to be sincere, but does have some incentive to maximize or exaggerate the nature of her condition. It was this concern for lack of reliability of statements made for purpose of diagnosis rather than treatment that caused the courts at common law to limit the exception to statements made for purposes of medical treatment.

Some states have taken a middle ground. In Maryland, for example, a statement is admissible if made "for purposes of medical treatment or medical diagnosis in contemplation of treatment." Md. R. Evid. 803(b)(4). When a person seeks a medical diagnosis for purposes of receiving treatment, she is more likely to be honest about her condition than when she is seeking a diagnosis only for purposes of litigation.

Note that the medical diagnosis or treatment exception is not limited to statements made to medical professionals. If a skateboarder suffers a fall on a public sidewalk, for example, her statement to a passerby, "Please get me help. I can't feel my legs," is covered by the exception. Nor is the exception limited to statements concerning the declarant's own medical condition. If a parent takes a child to the doctor and tells the doctor, "my son has been running a high fever all day," that statement, too, is covered by the exception.

The exception only covers statements that are "reasonably pertinent to medical diagnosis or treatment." This limitation is based on concern for reliability because only statements or parts of statements that are relevant to diagnosis or treatment are likely to be sufficiently trustworthy to admit. This does not mean the rule is very limited, however. Anything reasonably pertinent to diagnosis or treatment is within the rule's reach. This can include such things as descriptions of events. Suppose an injured person tells an emergency room physician, "I was riding my bike when a car hit me." If a diagnosing or treating physician would consider it significant that the patient was riding a bicycle at the time of the accident, or that she was hit by a vehicle, the exception would cover that detail as well as the patient's specific descriptions of her injuries. One might imagine, for example, that the information in our example would help the physician determine the proper tests to perform or the likelihood of internal injuries that might dictate the need for immediate care. If so, the exception will apply. Of course, there are some fairly clear limits to this concept. If the patient mentioned the license number of the vehicle, or its color, those details will not be pertinent to diagnosis or treatment, and are therefore not likely to be sufficiently reliable to fit within the exception.

Most courts hold that the exception applies only to statements made for the purposes of *obtaining* medical diagnosis or treatment, not to statements *giving* medical diagnosis or treatment. Thus, a physician's statement to the patient, "you have cancer," would not be admissible under Rule 803(4). This makes good sense. Remember that when the court admits hearsay, the effect is to allow the proponent to present a person's statement without making that person subject to cross-examination at the time the statement is made (and if the declarant never testifies, the declarant is never subjected to cross-examination in front of the jury). When a physician makes a diagnosis, it is only fair that such an important statement be made under circumstances that allow its testing through cross-examination. In our example, the proponent should not be able to avoid such testing by offering the physician's diagnosis through hearsay.

Finally, remember that evidence is not necessarily admissible just because it falls within the scope of an exception to the hearsay rule such as Rule 803(4). Objections other than hearsay might still be applicable. Specifically, statements covered by Rule 803(4) will frequently raise admissibility questions under the physician-patient privilege, discussed in Chapter 8.

Further Reading: Robert P. Mosteller, *Child Sexual Abuse and Statements for the Purpose of Medical Diagnosis or Treatment,* 67 N.C. L. Rev. 257 (1989).

Questions for Classroom Discussion

1. Why is it important to admit statements of a person's state of mind, or statements that stand as circumstantial evidence of one's state of mind?

2. Personal injury action by Plaintiff against Defendant following an auto collision. To prove Plaintiff suffered injuries in the collision, Plaintiff calls Witness to testify that at the scene, when Witness asked Plaintiff if she was hurt, Plaintiff said, "My leg is killing me." Is the statement admissible under either Rule 803(3) or 803(4)?

3. Same case. Suppose that in response to Witness's question, Plaintiff added, "I was feeling fine just before the accident." Is the statement admissible under either Rule 803(3) or 803(4)?

4. Same case. To prove that Plaintiff was not injured, Defendant wishes to offer evidence that a paramedic who responded to the accident told Plaintiff at the scene, "luckily, your leg is not broken." Is the statement admissible under either Rule 803(3) or 803(4)?

5. Negligence action by Plaintiff, a young child, against Defendant, the driver of a car who allegedly ran into the child on the street in front of Plaintiff's school. Defendant claims her car did not strike Plaintiff and that Plaintiff did not suffer any injury. To prove that the car struck Plaintiff, causing a hip injury, Plaintiff calls the emergency room doctor who treated her to testify that when the paramedic brought Plaintiff into the emergency room, the paramedic said, "Plaintiff says her hip hurts." Is the statement admissible under either Rule 803(3) or 803(4)?

6. Same case. Suppose that after saying, "my hip hurts," Plaintiff added, "I fell hard after that car hit me." Is the statement admissible under either Rule 803(3) or 803(4)?

7. Personal injury action by Plaintiff against Defendant. To prove that she was injured in the accident, Plaintiff calls Dr. Witness to testify that she examined Plaintiff at the request of Plaintiff's attorney, and that Plaintiff said, "My head has been hurting ever since the accident." Is the statement admissible under either Rule 803(3) or 803(4)?

8. Prosecution of Defendant for assault and battery on Victim. Defendant claims he had nothing to do with the crime. To prove Defendant was the perpetrator, the prosecution calls Officer, a police officer, to testify that the day after the crime, she interviewed Victim while Victim was recovering in the hospital, and that Victim said, "I distinctly remember that the guy had long, straight hair and was well over six feet tall." Is the statement admissible under either Rule 803(3) or 803(4)?

(continued)

9. Action for involuntary commitment of a law professor to a mental institution. To prove that the professor is in serious need of inpatient psychiatric treatment, a psychiatrist testifies that the professor, a man, said, "I am Queen Caroline, and I hereby invoke the rule in my case." Is the statement admissible under either Rule 803(3) or 803(4)? Is the statement hearsay?

10. Same case. Suppose the professor's statement was, "I believe I am Queen Caroline." Is the statement admissible under either Rule 803(3) or 803(4)?

11. Prosecution of Defendant for the murder of Victim. To prove Defendant was the killer, the prosecution wishes to offer evidence that a few days before he was killed, Victim said, "I am afraid of Defendant." Is the statement admissible under either Rule 803(3) or 803(4)?

12. Same case. Suppose Victim's statement had been, "I'm scared because Defendant threatened to hurt me." Is the statement admissible under either Rule 803(3) or 803(4)?

13. In *Hillmon*, who was the declarant, what was the statement, and why did the Supreme Court classify it as non-hearsay?

14. Why was Walters' statement in *Hillmon* relevant?

15. What if Walters had written, "A certain Mr. Hillmon plans to leave Wichita . . ."? Would the statement be relevant? Would it be hearsay? If it is hearsay, would it be admissible under the state of mind exception?

16. Was Walters' statement strictly about his own intentions? If not, why didn't Hillmon's representatives object to the statement, insofar as it mentioned Hillmon as well as Walters?

17. Prosecution of Zed and Abel for the kidnapping and murder of Victim. In the guilt phase of the trial, both Zed and Abel were found guilty of participating in the crime. During the sentencing phase, to achieve a harsher sentence for Zed, the prosecution wishes to show that Zed was the one who killed Victim. To prove this, the prosecution wishes to offer evidence that the day before the crime took place, Abel wrote a letter to her husband in which she said, "Tomorrow, Zed and I are going ahead with a risky plan. All I can say is that I will stand guard, but I don't want to have anything to do with any violence." Is the statement admissible under Rule 803(3)?

18. Prosecution of Defendant for the murder of Victim. To prove Defendant committed the crime, the prosecution offers evidence that earlier in the day she was killed, Victim told a friend, "Defendant is planning to come over for dinner tonight." Is the statement admissible under Rule 803(3)?

19.   Prosecution of Roger for murder. The prosecution case against Roger is entirely circumstantial—no eyewitness can place Roger in the company of Victim on the day the murder occurred. The prosecution offers testimony of Willa, a friend of the Victim, that on the day she last saw Victim he said, "I am going to meet Roger at The Diner for lunch today (the last day Victim was seen alive)." Is this testimony hearsay? Is it admissible under Rule 803(3)?

20.   Same case. The prosecution offers the testimony of Ella, another friend of Victim, that he told her, "Roger is going to be at The Diner today." Is this testimony hearsay? Is it admissible under Rule 803(3)?

3.   *Recorded Recollection (Rule 803(5))*

FED. R. EVID. 803.   EXCEPTIONS TO THE RULE AGAINST HEARSAY— REGARDLESS OF WHETHER THE DECLARANT IS AVAILABLE AS A WITNESS

The following are not excluded by the rule against hearsay, regardless of whether the declarant is available as a witness:

(5) *Recorded Recollection.* A record that:

(A) is on a matter the witness once knew about but now cannot recall well enough to testify fully and accurately;

(B) was made or adopted by the witness when the matter was fresh in the witness's memory; and

(C) accurately reflects the witness's knowledge.

If admitted, the record may be read into evidence but may be received as an exhibit only if offered by an adverse party.

a.   The Rule

Human memory is fallible. Over time, our recollection of events becomes more vague, and some things pass from memory altogether. Yet it is an unfortunate fact that a great deal of time often passes between the events at issue in a case and the trial. In criminal cases, it is usually months before the trial occurs, and in civil cases, years can pass before a case comes to trial. As a result, the reliability of witness testimony, particularly as to details, is often doubtful. Clearly, if we could examine witnesses when the relevant events were fresh in their minds, we would be considerably more confident in the accuracy of their testimony.

Sometimes, we get lucky because a person with knowledge of facts decides to make a written record of what she knows at a time when the facts are fresh in her mind. In such a case, it would be irrational for the evidence rules to demand an inferior source of evidence (the witness's diminished memory at the time of trial) over the superior source of evidence (the witness's recorded recollections). The recognition that recorded recollection is more reliable than impaired memory, and the need for the evidence, gives rise to the recorded recollection exception to the hearsay rule. The exception, sometimes called *past recollection recorded*, is embodied in Rule 803(5). The rule provides that if all of the following conditions are met, the recording may be read to the jury:

1. The witness must once have had personal knowledge about the matter;
2. The witness must now not be able to "recall well enough to testify fully and accurately";
3. The memorandum or record of the witness's knowledge must have been "made or adopted by the witness when the matter was fresh in the witness's memory"; and
4. The memorandum or record must reflect the witness's prior knowledge accurately.

The first requirement listed above is self-explanatory. The witness must testify that she once had personal knowledge about the event or condition. The second requirement clarifies that the prior knowledge must have been better than the witness's current knowledge. In that situation, it is not possible for the witness now to testify "fully and accurately." The witness must also testify that when she made or adopted the memorandum or record, the matter was fresh in her mind. To have "adopted" the memorandum or record simply means that if the witness did not actually make the memorandum or record, she read it when the matter was fresh in her mind and concluded it was correct. Finally, the witness must testify that the record accurately reflects what she knew (a strange requirement, as it requires a person who no longer knows a fact to testify that a written record of that fact is accurate).

Note that the rule allows the memorandum or record to be read into the record but states that it may not be offered as an exhibit except by the adverse party. This important limitation on the recorded recollection doctrine helps us to understand its nature: The memorandum or record is merely a substitute for oral testimony. If the witness's recollection is good enough to permit "full[] and accurate[]" testimony, the exception will not apply and the jury must settle for the witness's oral testimony. Because the transcript of oral testimony may not be offered as an exhibit (and taken into the jury deliberation room), evidence admitted pursuant to the recorded recollection doctrine should receive no greater emphasis.

On the other hand, if the opponent wishes to offer the memorandum or record into evidence, the rule allows her to do so. Usually, the opponent will not have any reason to do this, but in some situations the memorandum contains statements that are useful to the opponent's case. In this sense, the risk is on the party who made use of the recorded recollection exception, and that party should consider the opponent's right to offer the item into evidence before deciding to lay the foundation for the exception.

Though the rule does not explicitly require it, the person whose prior knowledge is preserved in the memorandum or record must testify in order for the exception to apply. In this sense, the exception is somewhat unusual because the availability of the declarant is generally immaterial to the application of the Rule 803 exceptions. With recorded recollection, however, the proponent of the evidence must persuade the court that each of the prerequisites is satisfied, and this can only be done through the declarant—the person who made or adopted the memorandum or record.

The court has the responsibility, under Rule 104(a), to decide whether the factual prerequisites for the application of the recorded recollection exception have been satisfied. This is because these facts do not present a case of conditional relevance; the record will be relevant even if some of the requirements are not satisfied.

b.   Distinguishing Recorded Recollection from Refreshing a Witness's Recollection

You must be careful not to confuse the recorded recollection exception with a party's right to refresh a witness's recollection. That is something judges and lawyers sometimes do. The concept of refreshing a witness's memory has nothing to do with the hearsay rule, and thus is not a hearsay exception. In fact, it is not even a formal rule of evidence. But because refreshing recollection sometimes goes by the name *present recollection refreshed* or *present recollection revived*, and those titles are similar to *past recollection recorded*, confusion often results.

You might think of refreshing recollection this way: Witnesses often forget details, but some forgetfulness is momentary. Whether caused by the stress of testifying or by some other factor, it is common for a witness to forget details important to her testimony. When this occurs, the lawyer's first option should be to try to help the witness remember the facts—to try to refresh her recollection. The law places no limits on the manner in which the witness's recollection may be refreshed. The lawyer may show the witness a document that contains the facts at issue. The lawyer may ask the witness the leading question, even on direct examination.[29] The lawyer may attempt to refresh recollection by asking the witness to look at a certain person, or may even play a tune for the witness; as one court noted, rather whimsically, ". . . the memory aid itself need not even be a writing. . . . It may be a line from Kipling or the dolorous refrain of 'The Tennessee Waltz'; a whiff of hickory smoke; the running of the fingers across a swatch of corduroy; the sweet carbonation of a chocolate soda; the sight of a faded snapshot in a long-neglected album." Baker v. State, 35 Md. App. 593, 602-603 (1977). Counsel may remind the witness of their conversation earlier in the day when they were discussing the witness's proposed testimony.

None of these methods of jarring the witness's memory are themselves "evidence." If the effort is unsuccessful, and the witness still does not remember, nothing presented to the witness, said to her, or otherwise taking place becomes evidence of the missing fact. If the lawyer wishes to prove the forgotten fact, she must present admissible evidence. This then leads to use of the recorded recollection exception.

When a party uses a writing in an effort to refresh a witness's recollection, Rule 612 applies. That rule provides as follows:

---

29. We will see in Chapter 6 that Rule 611(c) typically bars the use of leading questions on direct examination, but recognizes an exception "as necessary to develop the witness' testimony."

FED. R. EVID. 612.   WRITING USED TO REFRESH A WITNESS'S MEMORY

(a) Scope. This rule gives an adverse party certain options when a witness uses a writing to refresh memory:

    (1) while testifying; or

    (2) before testifying, if the court decides that justice requires a party to have those options.

(b) Adverse Party's Options; Deleting Unrelated Matter. Unless 18 U.S.C. § 3500 provides otherwise in a criminal case, an adverse party is entitled to have the writing produced at the hearing, to inspect it, to cross-examine the witness about it, and to introduce in evidence any portion that relates to the witness's testimony. If the producing party claims that the writing includes unrelated matter, the court must examine the writing in camera, delete any unrelated portion, and order that the rest be delivered to the adverse party. Any portion deleted over objection must be preserved for the record.

(c) Failure to Produce or Deliver the Writing. If a writing is not produced or is not delivered as ordered, the court may issue any appropriate order. But if the prosecution does not comply in a criminal case, the court must strike the witness's testimony or — if justice so requires — declare a mistrial.

This rule allows the opponent to examine any writing used to refresh the recollection of a witness if the document was used during her testimony, and also to examine any such document if it was used to refresh the witness's recollection before she testified, "if the court in its discretion determines it is necessary in the interests of justice." The rule also allows the adverse party to cross-examine the witness concerning the writing, and to introduce into evidence those parts of the writing that relate to the witness's testimony. The rule's purpose is to assist the adverse party in determining whether the witness's recollection actually has been refreshed, or whether she is simply repeating what the writing says. To put it more simply, the rule gives the adverse party an opportunity to show that it is the writing, and not the witness's memory, that is the true source of the testimony. If the judge concludes that this is the case, she may strike the testimony on the ground it is inadmissible hearsay.

Suppose the witness whose recollection is incomplete wrote a memorandum at a time when the facts were fresh in her mind, and the memorandum satisfies all the requirements for the recorded recollection doctrine. The usual procedure is as follows: First, the lawyer will attempt to refresh the witness's memory, even using the memorandum itself. If that succeeds, the recorded recollection doctrine will not apply because the witness does, in fact, remember the events sufficiently. If the effort to refresh the witness's memory fails, however, the lawyer may then seek to lay the recorded recollection foundation, thus permitting the memorandum to be read into evidence. Throughout this process, the opponent may take the witness on "voir dire" to inquire into the actual state of her recollection.

All of this sounds rather complicated, but it is actually fairly simple, and the procedure is quite familiar to all trial lawyers. An example will demonstrate more clearly how the recorded recollection rule and the doctrine of refreshing recollection interact:

Prosecution of Defendant for burglary and robbery of Victim's home. The indictment alleges that Defendant broke into the home while Victim was at work and stole three items: a television, a set of sterling silver flatware, and a diamond necklace. During its case-in-chief, the prosecution calls Victim to testify about the items that were missing from her home. Unfortunately, Victim remembers only that the necklace and sterling silver were missing, and does not recall that her television was also missing.

Shortly after the burglary/robbery, and at the suggestion of the police, Victim wrote down a list of the three items that were missing from her home.

The direct examination below begins when the prosecutor asks Victim to list the missing items. ("Pros" stands for Prosecutor and "Def" for defense counsel.)

Pros: Did you notice whether anything was missing when you returned home from work?

V: Yes.

Pros: Please tell the court what was missing.

V: When I looked around the house, I noticed that my diamond necklace and my sterling silver flatware were gone.

Pros: Was anything else missing?

V: I think there might have been something else, but I can't remember.

Pros: Was it something you used for enjoyment?

V: I think so, but I just can't remember now.

Pros: Your Honor, may I approach the witness?

By the Court: Go ahead, counsel.

Pros: I would like to show you a sheet of paper and ask that you look at it for a moment. Your Honor, I have shown this paper to defense counsel, and also provided a photocopy.

Pros: Have you had a chance to look over the paper?

V: Yes, I have.

Pros: Would you please hand it back to me?

[The witness hands back the paper.]

Pros: Thank you. After looking over the paper, do you now recall if anything else was missing from your home?

V: Yes, I do.

Pros: Would you please tell the court what else was missing?

Def: Your Honor, may I take the witness on voir dire?

By the Court: Go ahead, but keep it short.

Def: Thank you, Your Honor. [Defense counsel then asks a series of questions — most of them leading questions — seeking to establish that the witness does not actually remember that the television was missing.]

Def: Your Honor, we object to the question on grounds of lack of personal knowledge.

By the Court: Objection overruled.

Pros: Would the reporter please read back my last question?

[The court reporter reads the prosecutor's last question.]

V: I also noticed that my television was missing.

In our example, the prosecutor's attempt to refresh the witness's recollection succeeded. Suppose now that it did not.

Pros: After looking over the paper, do you now recall if anything else was missing from your home?

V: I'm sorry, but I still don't remember.

Pros: You testified earlier that you met with the police on the day of the break-in. Is that correct?

V: Yes.

Pros: After that meeting, did you do anything to preserve your memory of the event?

V: Yes. I made a list of the things that were missing from my home.

Pros: Your Honor, may I approach the witness?

By the Court: You may.

Pros: I would now like to show you the paper I showed you before. Do you recognize it?

V: Yes, I do.

Pros: What is it?

V: It's the list I made of the things that were missing from my home.

Pros: How do you know it is the list?

V: It has my signature at the bottom, and it's dated the day after the burglary. I also remember making the list, and I'm certain this is it.

Pros: When you wrote this list, did you have a good memory of the things that were missing from your home when you returned from work the day before?

V: Yes. I was very upset, and thought about these things all day at work.

Pros: And at the present time, do you remember the third item that was missing?

V: I know it sounds a little crazy, but I really don't remember.

Pros: That's okay. You need to be honest. Now, when you made the list, did you make it accurately? Did you write down only the things that were missing after the burglary, and nothing else?

V: Yes. I'm sure I did.

Pros: Would you please read to the court the last item on the list, the one you have not already testified about?

Def: Your Honor, may I take the witness on voir dire?

By the Court: Go ahead.

Def: Thank you. [Defense counsel then asks a series of questions—most of them leading questions—seeking to establish that one or more of the elements of the recorded recollection doctrine have not been established.]

Def: Your Honor, I object to the witness reading the last item from the list.

The prosecution has not established . . . [Defense counsel names the preliminary facts that arguably have not been proven. The prosecutor responds.]

By the Court: Objection overruled.

Pros: Would the reporter please read back my last question?

[The court reporter reads the prosecutor's last question.]

V: It says, "my television set."

Pros: Thank you.

Questions for Classroom Discussion

1. Prosecution of Defendant, a Caucasian man, for assault and battery on Victim following a barroom brawl. Defendant denies being involved. To prove that he was not involved, Defendant calls Witness, the bartender, and asks the bartender to describe the person who started the fight. Witness testifies that she cannot remember what the person looked like. Defendant then wishes to show Witness a copy of a note Witness wrote after the event, which contains a description of the attacker as an Asian male. The prosecution objects. Defendant responds that he is merely trying to refresh Witness's recollection. How should the court rule?

2. Same case. Assume that the court allows Defendant to show the note to Witness, but that after looking at it, Witness states that she still has no independent memory of the attacker's appearance. Defendant then asks Witness if, shortly after the brawl, she wrote an account of the incident that included a description of the person who started the fight, whether the person's appearance was fresh in her memory when she wrote the document, and whether the document contained an accurate description. After each question, Witness answers, "Yes." Defendant then shows Witness the same document referred to in Question 1, and Witness identifies it as the account she wrote. Defendant asks Witness to read the part of the account that describes the person who started the fight. (The document states that the perpetrator was an "Asian male.") The prosecution objects on hearsay grounds. How should the court rule?

3. Same case. Assume that instead of objecting, the prosecutor makes a motion to interrupt the direct examination to conduct a "voir dire" of Witness concerning the document. Should the court grant that motion?

4. Same case. During the voir dire examination, Witness admits that she can't remember exactly when she wrote the description, and

(continued)

that it might have been several weeks after the brawl took place. The prosecutor renews her objection. How should the court rule?

5. Same case. Assume the court overrules the prosecutor's objection and allows Witness to read into the record her description of the perpetrator. The prosecutor, having seen a copy of the document, knows that Witness had apparently written "white" before "male," but had crossed it off and written the word "Asian." The prosecutor moves for admission of the document into evidence as an exhibit. Defendant objects. How should the court rule?

6. Same case. Assume Witness did not write the document. It is a note from a bar patron scribbled as the brawl was occurring. The police found the note on the floor of the bar while they were investigating the incident. The police were not able to identify the person who wrote the note. Defendant wishes to show the note to Witness in an effort to refresh Witness's recollection. The prosecution objects this is improper because Witness did not write the note and the identity of the author is unknown. How should the court rule?

7. Same case. Assume that Witness did not write the document. Instead, it was written by Officer, a police officer to whom Witness spoke shortly after the brawl. After Witness testifies that she no longer remembers what the perpetrator looked like, Defendant calls Officer, elicits testimony about the document, and asks Officer to read the description into the record. The prosecutor objects. How should the court rule?

8. Same case. Suppose that instead of calling Officer, Defendant asks Witness whether she gave a description to Officer when the perpetrator's appearance was fresh in her mind. Witness answers that she did. Defendant then asks whether her description was accurate. Witness says yes. Defendant then asks if she saw what Officer wrote down. Witness says yes. Defendant then asks whether Officer accurately wrote down what Witness told Officer. Again, Witness answers yes. Defendant asks Witness to read the description into the record. The prosecutor objects. How should the court rule?

9. Same case. Defendant asks the court for permission to play an excerpt of a recording of a football game. The prosecution objects on the ground of relevancy. Defendant responds that the game was on the bar's television sets when the brawl occurred, and that seeing the excerpt might refresh Witness's recollection. How should the court rule?

4. *Business and Public Records*

**FED. R. EVID. 803. EXCEPTIONS TO THE RULE AGAINST HEARSAY—
REGARDLESS OF WHETHER THE DECLARANT IS AVAILABLE AS A WITNESS**

The following are not excluded by the rule against hearsay, regardless of whether the declarant is available as a witness:

(6) *Records of a Regularly Conducted Activity.* A record of an act, event, condition, opinion, or diagnosis if:

(A) the record was made at or near the time by—or from information transmitted by—someone with knowledge;

(B) the record was kept in the course of a regularly conducted activity of a business, organization, occupation, or calling, whether or not for profit;

(C) making the record was a regular practice of that activity; and

(D) all these conditions are shown by the testimony of the custodian or another qualified witness, or by a certification that complies with Rule 902(b)(11) or (12) or with a statute permitting certification; and

(E) neither the source of information nor the method or circumstances of preparation indicate a lack of trustworthiness.

(7) *Absence of a Record of a Regularly Conducted Activity.* Evidence that a matter is not included in a record described in paragraph (6) if:

(A) the evidence is admitted to prove that the matter did not occur or exist; and

(B) a record was regularly kept for a matter of that kind; and

(C) neither the possible source of the information nor other circumstances indicate a lack of trustworthiness.

(8) *Public Records.* A record or statement of a public office if:

(A) it sets out:

(i) the office's activities;

(ii) a matter observed while under a legal duty to report, but not including, in a criminal case, a matter observed by law-enforcement personnel; or

(iii) in a civil case or against the government in a criminal case, factual findings from a legally authorized investigation; and

(B) neither the source of information nor other circumstances indicate a lack of trustworthiness.

(10) *Absence of a Public Record.* Testimony—or a certification under Rule 902—that a diligent search failed to disclose a public record or statement if:

(A) the testimony or certification is admitted to prove that:

(i) the record or statement does not exist; or

(ii) a matter did not occur or exist, if a public office regularly kept a record or statement for a matter of that kind.

(B) in a criminal case, a prosecutor who intends to offer a certification provides written notice of that intent at least 14 days before trial, and the defendant does not object in writing within 7 days of receiving the notice—unless the court sets a different time for the notice or the objection.

a.   Records of Regularly Conducted Activity (Rule 803(6))

Commonly called the business records exception, Rule 803(6) assumes that records of regularly conducted activity are sufficiently reliable to admit even if hearsay. The reasoning runs something like this: An enterprise cannot stay in business for long without accurate records. For this reason, businesses develop procedures for ensuring accurate recordkeeping. In addition, the employees who maintain those records understand that their very jobs may depend on the successful implementation of those procedures. As a consequence, if the record was kept in the regular course of business and if it was the regular practice of the business to make such a record, it is sufficiently reliable to admit over a hearsay objection. Of course, the assumption that business records are reliable might be challenged in light of revelations concerning the magnitude of corporate fraud. But there is some vindication for Rule 803(6) even in the sordid stories of Enron and WorldCom: After the first revelations of wrongdoing, the perpetrators often began shredding business records, which, they feared, reliably recorded incriminating facts.

Necessity is another rationale for Rule 803(6). In the complex world of modern business, many employees may contribute information to be compiled into a single business record. If the record is not admissible, it might be impractical to call each individual to testify to the few bits of information for which she was responsible. Even if practical and possible to call all these witnesses, it might be fruitless. Employees often have no detailed recollection of information they compile in the regular, but often mundane, course of business. Imagine, for example, how a large Internet-based company would prove that it had received a particular order for goods, processed the order, and shipped the goods if the company's own records could not be used to establish the details of the transaction. It is not likely that any of the company's employees who might have handled different aspects of the order would remember what they did. Without a business records exception, the company would not likely be able to prove the essential facts.

Rule 803(6) is the longest of all the hearsay exceptions, necessitating a careful breakdown of its various elements.

"A record . . ."   Although the rule does not define "record," it should be clear that included within the term are all modern forms of digital data collection as well as more conventional written documents.

"[O]f an act, event, condition, opinion, or diagnosis . . ."   Rule 803(6) also broadly defines the permissible content of business records. The key here is that the exception is not limited to records of a clerical nature, such as the accounts that log the details of each sale and purchase. Also included are records that contain more subjective matters such as opinions or diagnoses. Thus, included within the scope of Rule 803(6) are notes of an attending physician or employee performance evaluations penned by the job supervisor. Of course, records containing opinions must not only overcome a hearsay objection, but also must satisfy the requirements of Article VII of the Federal Rules of Evidence, discussed in Chapter 7.

"[M]ade at or near the time . . ."   Business records tend to be reliable when they are compiled close in time to the events described. As time passes, however, the recollection of the person compiling the record may begin to fail. What

constitutes "near the time" is a function of circumstances. Mundane and complex details should be recorded quickly because it is likely that recollections concerning such matters will soon deteriorate. More general information is likely to remain in memory for longer.

"[B]y — or from information transmitted by — someone with knowledge . . ." Rule 803(6) requires that the person who makes the business record either has personal knowledge of the matters described in it or receives input from another person who has that knowledge. For example, the regional sales manager of a large company might compile sales data from employees in the field and produce a report summarizing facts about which the sales manager has no personal knowledge. The report is admissible under the business records exception as long as the employees transmitting the information had personal knowledge. Similarly, the vice-president for sales of that company might receive reports from various regional sales managers and compile the data into yet another document summarizing sales nationally. This national sales report is admissible under Rule 803(6) because each employee in the field had personal knowledge of her few bits of data, each regional sales manager had personal knowledge of what each employee in the field said, and the vice-president had personal knowledge of what each regional sales manager said. It does not matter that the vice-president did not have personal knowledge of the *facts* reported by the regional sales managers. What matters is that the people who supplied the information — the sales managers — had a business duty to collect the information carefully and report it accurately. The vice-president, in turn, had a duty to listen carefully to the information provided and to record it accurately.

This also means that this single exception can cover multiple layers of hearsay, as long as each person contributing a layer of hearsay was acting in the course of business and her statements otherwise conformed to the requirements of Rule 803(6). But when a declarant is not acting under a business duty, Rule 803(6) will not apply to her statements (although they might be admissible under some other exception). Thus, in the pre-rules wrongful death case of Johnson v. Lutz, 170 N.E. 517 (N.Y. 1930), the plaintiff offered into evidence an accident report compiled by the investigating police officer. The report was based on statements that the officer took from eyewitnesses. The New York high court ruled that the business records exception could not apply because, while the police officer was acting under a business duty to record the eyewitness statements accurately,[30] those eyewitnesses had no similar duty to be accurate. The Advisory Committee Note to Rule 803(6) explicitly endorsed the decision of Johnson v. Lutz and observed, "If, however, the supplier of the information does not act in the regular course, an essential link is broken; the assurance of accuracy does not extend to the information itself and the fact that it may be recorded with scrupulous accuracy is of no avail."[31]

Suppose, however, that a police officer arrives at an accident scene moments after the crash and approaches a sobbing witness who looks up and exclaims,

---

30. While we might not usually think of a police officer as being engaged in a "business," Rule 803(6) defines the term very broadly, as we discuss below.

31. The fact that a record contains information supplied by persons not under a business duty to observe and report accurately does not necessarily disqualify the entire report. If the part of the report reporting or based on such statements can be removed from the record, the remaining parts may qualify under Rule 803(6).

"That red car ran through the stop sign and smashed that blue car!" The police officer records the witness's statement in her report, and the report is later offered at trial to prove that the driver of the red car was responsible for the accident. As noted above, records that contain information supplied by persons who are not under a business duty to observe and record events accurately normally do not qualify under Rule 803(6). But in our example, there is another indication of trustworthiness: The witness's statement appears to qualify as an excited utterance under Rule 803(2). If it does, the record might be admissible under the business records exception.

"[K]ept in the course of a regularly conducted activity of a business . . ." The reliability of a firm's business records depends in large part on whether the record concerns the firm's regular activities. For example, imagine a firm in the business of manufacturing and selling widgets. Records directly relating to that activity would include documents concerning the sales of widgets to the firm's customers. Because the firm is engaged in the regular activity of selling widgets, it is reasonable to expect that the firm has established practices to ensure that the records of those transactions are accurate. Now imagine that the same firm rents its factory to a studio to be the location for a movie scene. Because this is not the type of transaction in which the firm regularly engages, the firm may have no internal policies or practices that ensure that records concerning this rental transaction are accurate. Those records are not kept in the course of a regularly conducted business activity and, thus, are not admissible under Rule 803(6).

This principle has important implications for the admissibility of records prepared for purposes of litigation. For example, in Palmer v. Hoffman, 318 U.S. 109 (1943), a railroad investigating a grade crossing collision asked the train's engineer to prepare an accident report, which was offered into evidence at the ensuing trial. The Supreme Court ruled that the report was not admissible under the business record exception because the business of the railroad was running trains, not litigating. But subsequent cases suggest that reports prepared for litigation are not invariably outside the scope of Rule 803(6). This makes sense because the compiling of records such as accident reports often has a business purpose in addition to the use of those records in litigation. Assuming a record prepared for purposes of litigation is made in the regular course of business, admissibility under Rule 803(6) still may be questioned on the ground the circumstances surrounding the creation of that report indicate lack of trustworthiness, which is an element of the rule described more fully below. For example, trustworthiness may depend on whether the person who provides the information for an accident report is a potential party with an interest in stretching the truth or, instead, is a neutral eyewitness.

"[M]aking the record was a regular practice of that activity . . ." Even if a record is kept in the course of a regularly conducted business activity, Rule 803(6) also requires that it is the regular practice of the business to make the type of report in question. The *motive* to be accurate is supplied by the first element, since the record relates to activities at the heart of the business. The *ability* to be accurate is secured by the second aspect of regularity, which establishes that the business has had the opportunity to develop procedures to compile reliable records of the type in question. Returning to the example of our widget manufacturer, a record of widget sales would qualify as being kept in the course of a regularly

conducted business activity. But if the sales manager had been in the habit of keeping sales information in his head rather than making such records, the record in question would not be admissible under Rule 803(6) because it was not the regular practice of the business to make such a record.

"[A]ll these conditions are shown by the testimony of the custodian or another qualified witness, or by a certification that complies with Rule 902(b)(11) or (12) or with a statute permitting certification." This element identifies who may testify to the facts necessary to establish that a document qualifies as a business record. The rule does not demand that the author of the record or the person with knowledge of the matters described in the record testify to the requisite foundational facts. Instead, the provision permits anyone to give testimony as long as that person is familiar with the business, its mode of operation, and its recordkeeping practices. This includes but is not limited to the so-called custodian of records for the business. This is simply the person whose responsibility is to maintain the files of the business.

In 2000, Rule 803(6) was amended to the form presented above, which indicates that in certain situations, it is unnecessary to call a witness to lay the foundation for the record. Pursuant to Rules 902(11) and 902(12), which were added by amendment to Rule 902 at the same time, the proponent may present a declaration of a qualified person certifying that the record:

1. was made at or near the time of the occurrence of the matters set forth by, or from information transmitted by, a person with knowledge of those matters;
2. was kept in the course of the regularly conducted activity; and
3. was made by the regularly conducted activity as a regular practice.

In addition, the proponent must provide prior written notice of its intention to introduce the record in this manner, must make the record and declaration available for inspection, and must provide the opponent with a fair opportunity to challenge the record. The Advisory Committee explained that the reason for allowing declarations in lieu of live witnesses is to avoid the "expense and inconvenience of producing time-consuming foundation witnesses." Fed. R. Evid. 803(6) Advisory Committee Note to 2000 Amendment.

"Neither the source of information nor other circumstances of preparation indicate a lack of trustworthiness." Even if all the other requirements of Rule 803(6) are met, the court still may refuse to admit the business record if it appears untrustworthy. The source of information for a business record might be deemed untrustworthy if, for example, a person prepared the record for use in litigation and that person had a personal stake in the outcome of that action. The method or circumstances of preparation might indicate lack of trustworthiness when a business simply fails to keep its records in a "businesslike" manner.

Rule 803(6)(B) employs a broad concept of what constitutes a "business." That concept encompasses professions (such as physicians, dentists, and attorneys), and any occupation or calling (think of your corner auto mechanic and the neighborhood gardener). It is clear that nonprofit activities are included within the concept as well. Thus, the records of a nonprofit organization or charity could be considered business records.

Similarly, the records of public agencies could be considered business records, including even police records. But some courts have held that, notwithstanding this broad definition of "business," the admissibility of certain kinds of public records must be determined under Rule 803(8), the so-called public records exception. Other courts have held that public records could be admissible under Rule 803(6) even if not admissible under Rule 803(8). We discuss this issue shortly.

To illustrate how the foundation for Rule 803(6) is usually established, assume a suit for breach of contract brought by Widgets, Inc., against Ben Buyer for failure to pay for a shipment of 1,000 widgets. Defendant alleges the goods were never delivered. Plaintiff calls the supervisor of its shipping department to testify. ("P" stands for Plaintiff's counsel, "D" for Defendant's counsel, and "W" for the witness.)

P. Please state your name.

W. My name is Saul Supervisor.

P. What do you do for a living?

W. I am the supervisor of the delivery department for Widgets, Inc.

P. How long have you held that position?

W. Seven years. Before that I was a delivery driver for twelve years.

P. What is Widget, Inc.'s business?

W. We manufacture and sell widgets.

P. Do your responsibilities as supervisor of the delivery department include anything having to do with the delivery records for Widgets, Inc.?

W. Yes. It's my job to make sure that my delivery staff properly completes all delivery forms. I then collect those forms and am responsible for keeping them in a file cabinet in my office.

P. Describe what you do to make sure that your staff properly fills out the delivery forms.

W. At the end of every shift each driver of a delivery truck gives me his or her delivery records. The drivers have to fill out a record for every delivery on that shift. I check the records to make sure each states what goods were delivered, the address where the goods were delivered, the date and time of delivery, and the name of the person who accepted delivery. I check to make sure each driver has signed each record.

P. Do drivers have to fill out all this information on a delivery form for every delivery?

W. For deliveries over ten widgets, yes. We require this to make sure delivery was properly made. We also send a copy of this form to our billing department, which needs all that information to send the customer a proper statement. For the small deliveries, it is not worth our driver's time to fill out the form.

P. So for the deliveries over ten widgets, when do the drivers fill out those forms?

W. They have to fill them out at the time delivery is made. I guess they might sometimes fill out a form later. But the form is always completed before the end of the shift because that's when I check it.

P. I show you now a document that has been marked as Plaintiff's Exhibit 1. Do you know what that is?

    W: Yes. It's one of our delivery records. In fact, it's one I took from my file cabinet and gave to you this morning.

    P: Do you remember seeing Exhibit 1 before today?

    W: No. I get dozens of these every day. Over the years, thousands. I just don't remember this one.

    P: Do you recognize the signature on Exhibit 1?

    W: Yes, it's the signature of Sally, one of my delivery drivers. She has been working for me for over a year. I have seen her signature a couple of hundred times.

    P: Would you please read Exhibit 1 to the jury?

    D: Objection, hearsay.

    P: Your Honor, the evidence is admissible as a business record under Rule 803(6).

By the Court: Objection overruled. The witness may read Exhibit 1.

    W: It says delivery was made of 1,000 widgets to Ben Buyer at 1441 Main Street on May 14, 2003, at 1 P.M.

Questions for Classroom Discussion

1. What part or parts of Saul Supervisor's testimony established each foundational requirement of Rule 803(6)? Was the court correct in overruling defendant's hearsay objection?

2. Civil action to recover for personal injuries suffered in an automobile accident. After the accident, Plaintiff was taken to the emergency room at General Hospital. To prove the extent of his injuries, Plaintiff offers into evidence a record of the emergency room, written by the attending physician, which states "Preliminary diagnosis: Permanent impairment of anterior keester." Is this hearsay? If so, what must Plaintiff show to have the record admitted as a business record?

3. Same case. Under Rule 803(6), does it matter that General Hospital is a nonprofit hospital? That the record contains a diagnosis rather than merely reciting observations?

4. Same case. Assume the record states, "Admitting nurse informs me that patient was unconscious when he arrived. My preliminary diagnosis is permanent impairment of anterior keester." Defendant objects to admissibility on the ground this is double hearsay. How should the court rule? Suppose the doctor's statement was not contained in the record, but was an oral statement reported in the testimony of a witness who heard the doctor make the statement. Would it be admissible?

5. Same case. Assume the record states, "Admitting nurse informs me that patient stated he had abdominal pain. My preliminary diagnosis is permanent impairment of anterior keester." Defendant objects to admissibility on the ground this is triple hearsay. How should the court rule?

(continued)

6. Same case. Assume the record states, "Admitting nurse informs me that patient stated the other driver ran the red light. My preliminary diagnosis is permanent impairment of anterior keester." Defendant objects to admissibility on the ground this is triple hearsay. How should the court rule?

7. Action by Hospital against Patient to recover an unpaid bill. Hospital offers evidence that its accounting records reveal Patient owed $100,000 for services and has paid nothing. Patient offers his checking account register, which shows he paid in full. Are these both admissible under Rule 803(6)? Can you argue that the provision's preference for the records of a business over the personal records of an individual is unwarranted?

b. Public Records and Reports (Rule 803(8))

At first glance, the public records exception appears superfluous. This is because Rule 803(6) will apply to many public records since it broadly defines "business" to include "callings of every kind, whether or not conducted for profit." But remember that the business records exception only applies to records "kept in the course of a regularly conducted business activity" and when "it was the regular practice of that business activity to make the memorandum, report, record or data compilation." Public records that fail to meet these requirements will not be admissible under Rule 803(6). On the other hand, those records might be admissible under Rule 803(8), which does not demand regularity of activity or record making.

One justification for the public records exception is that public officials are trustworthy or are at least careful because they have a legal duty to be accurate. Many might challenge these assumptions, claiming that the expression "good enough for civil service" better describes the work ethic of certain public officials. While the reliability of public records is debatable, a more convincing rationale for Rule 803(8) is that, without this exception, it may be very difficult if not impossible to prove the activities of public offices or the facts uncovered by investigations conducted by those offices. This is because public officials called to testify often are unable to recall much of what is recorded in the mountains of records maintained in their offices.

Rule 803(8) sets forth different standards for the admission of three different types of public records. Rule 803(8)(A)(i) allows for the admission, without limitation, of public records "setting out the office's activities." This refers to documents concerning the internal workings of an agency, such as payroll records, personnel files, purchase receipts, and the like. In contrast, subdivisions (ii) and (iii) of Rule 803(8)(A) significantly limit the admissibility of public records setting forth observations of and investigations by public officials.

Subdivision (ii) of Rule 803(8)(A) applies to records concerning matters observed by public officials when there was a duty both to make the observation and to report on the matters observed. Included within the scope of the provision are government reports on all manner of observable data, such as weather records, maps, and a court reporter's transcript. In a criminal case, the provision excludes from its coverage matters observed by law enforcement personnel. Rule 803(8)(A)(iii) similarly does not extend to records offered by the prosecution in a criminal case. The reason for these features of Rule 803(8) is that, in a criminal prosecution, observations by or findings of police officers might be unreliable due to the adversarial nature of the relationship between the police and a defendant. While subdivision (ii) seems to preclude the admission of police records in a criminal case no matter which party offers the document, the reason for the ban has led some courts to conclude that it applies only when the prosecution offers the police record. Public records clearly may be offered by either party under subdivision (ii) in a civil case and in a criminal case when the record is created by a public agency that is not engaged in law enforcement.

Because Rule 803(8) limits the admissibility in a criminal case of public records created by law enforcement, some courts refuse to undermine that limitation by permitting such records to be admitted against the defendant in a criminal case under Rule 803(6), the business records exception, even when the terms of that provision seem to be satisfied. These courts argue that Rules 803(8)(A)(ii) and (iii) effectuate Congress's desire to prevent "trial by affidavit" in criminal cases and that other hearsay exceptions, particularly the business records exception, should not be used to circumvent that policy. *See, e.g.,* United States v. Oates, 560 F.2d 45 (2d Cir. 1977) (in drug prosecution, chemist's report concluding that substance was heroin, which was inadmissible under Rule 803(8), could not be offered under Rule 803(6) even though it appeared to meet the requirements of that rule).

Rule 803(8)(A)(iii) makes admissible in a civil case and, when offered against the government in a criminal case, "factual findings from a legally authorized investigation." Included in the scope of this provision are reports of an evaluative nature that produce factual findings after an investigation, such as an administrative finding about employment discrimination or the safety of a plane that crashed. In contrast, subdivision (ii) applies to records that simply describe observed data without analysis leading to factual findings. The Supreme Court, in Beech Aircraft Corp. v. Rainey, 499 U.S. 153 (1988), held that the coverage of subdivision (iii)[32] includes reports containing opinions, as long as those opinions are based on investigations and factual findings. A public record may be admitted under subdivision (iii) even when the factual finding in that record is based on statements from persons who are not public officials. For example, a report of the Federal Aviation Administration that reaches a finding concerning the cause of an airplane crash could be admitted under Rule 803(8)(A)(iii) even if that finding was based in part on interviews with eyewitnesses to the crash. The eyewitness statements, however, would not be admissible unless within another hearsay exception.

Admission under subdivision (iii) is denied when the sources of information or other circumstances indicate lack of trustworthiness. Factors bearing on trustworthiness include the timeliness of the investigation, the skill or experience of the investigator, the extent of the investigation, and bias or prejudice of the investigator. While the Advisory Committee's Note suggests that this

---

32. At the time *Beech Aircraft Corp.* was decided, that provision was designated as Rule 803(8)(C).

trustworthiness issue applies only to subdivision (iii), some cases extend the provision to subdivisions (i) and (ii) as well.

It is not necessary in all cases to call a foundational witness to qualify a public record. Public records are admissible without a sponsoring witness as long as they have been authenticated, and public records can be self-authenticating under Rules 902(1), (2), or (4). As we have seen, a 2000 amendment to the business records exception, Rule 803(6), also permits business records to be admitted under certain circumstances without a foundational witness.

Questions for Classroom Discussion

1. Murder prosecution. The state offers into evidence the report of the police forensic specialist who retrieved and then tested two blood samples she found at the murder scene and a blood sample she took from Defendant after his arrest. The report describes the genetic characteristics of each sample and concludes that one crime scene sample is a match for Defendant's blood sample. Defendant objects to the report on the ground of hearsay. How should the court rule?

2. Same case. Assuming the prosecution could establish all the requisite foundational facts, should the court admit the report as a business record under Rule 803(6)?

3. Same case. The defense offers into evidence a portion of the same report that states the other crime scene sample does not match Defendant's blood. The prosecution objects on the ground of hearsay. How should the court rule?

4. Same case. If the defense successfully admits the portion of the report described in Question 3, what argument can the prosecution make about the admissibility of the portion of the report described in Question 1?

5. Same case. The prosecution offers into evidence just that portion of the report in which the forensic specialist stated that she found the crime scene blood samples under the victim's fingernails. The defense objects on the ground of hearsay. How should the court rule?

6. Same case. The police forensic specialist testifies that Defendant's blood matches a blood sample found at the crime scene. On cross-examination, the defense challenges the witness's expert qualifications. The prosecution then offers into evidence records from the witness's personnel file at the police department that shows he passed all regular proficiency tests with flying colors. The defense objects on the ground of hearsay. How should the court rule?

c. Absence of Entry in Business or Public Record (Rules 803(7) and 803(10))

Rules 803(6) and 803(8) permit business and public records to be admitted for the purpose of proving facts described in those records. But sometimes business and public records are relevant because of what is *not* contained in those records. Rule 803(7) makes evidence that a matter is not included in a business record admissible for the purpose of showing the non-occurrence or non-existence of that matter. For example, Rule 803(7) could make the records of a credit card company pertaining to a specific individual's account admissible to prove that those records have no entry showing payment for charges to that account. Rule 803(10) performs the same function for public records. This provision is used in cases in which the absence of a public record or an entry in such a record shows that a required public filing did not take place, as in a prosecution for possession of an unregistered firearm.

To illustrate, imagine a personal injury action in which Plaintiff seeks recovery for hospital expenses incurred in the days following the accident. Defendant claims Plaintiff's injuries were very minor and that she was not hospitalized. To prove this, Defendant calls the custodian of records of the hospital to which Plaintiff claims to have been admitted:

> *D:* Please describe your job at the hospital.
>
> *Cust:* I am in charge of all patient records. I am in charge of the office that contains those records.
>
> *D:* Among the records you maintain, is there a record of all patient admissions and discharges?
>
> *Cust:* Yes. We prepare a running log of all admissions and discharges.
>
> *D:* How is the log prepared?
>
> *Cust:* The hospital has a staff of patient representatives. Their job is to log all information about a patient into a patient computer database. Whenever a person is admitted to the hospital, one of the patient representatives enters all information pertaining to that person in the main patient database. When the patient is discharged, one of the representatives makes a notation in the database showing that the patient was discharged.
>
> *D:* You indicated that all the information is entered into a single database. How do you prepare the admission/discharge log?
>
> *Cust:* Every 24 hours, one of the representatives accesses the database and runs a query for the names of all patients currently admitted to the hospital. The computer prepares a report, which the representative prints and posts in a specified place in the patient records office.
>
> *D:* Other than the name, what information is contained in this report?
>
> *Cust:* The report also lists the date of admission, the patient's room number, and the phone number of the patient's next-of-kin.
>
> *D:* What happens to each report at the end of the 24-hour period?

Cust: When a new report is posted, the representative leaves the old report on my desk. I then place the report in a special patient archive file.

D: Your Honor, may I approach the witness?

By the Court: You may.

D: I'd now like to show you a document that has been marked for identification as Defendant's Exhibit 3. Do you recognize it?

Cust: Yes, I do.

D: Please tell the court what the document is.

Cust: This is the list of patients covering the 24-hour period from noon on September 1 of last year to 11:59 A.M. on September 2.

[At this point, Defendant's attorney shows the witness several other documents, which the witness identifies as the records for the next several days. The days are the ones on which Plaintiff claims to have been in the hospital.]

D: Your Honor, I move the admission into evidence of Defendant's Exhibits 3 through 8.

By the Court: Hearing no objection, Defendant's Exhibits 3 through 8 will be admitted.

D: Please look over Defendant's Exhibit 3 and tell the court whether it contains Plaintiff's name.

Cust: It does not.

D: Please review Defendant's Exhibit 4 and tell the court whether it contains Plaintiff's name.

Cust: It does not.

[Defendant's attorney goes through the remainder of the exhibits and the custodian gives the same answers.]

In this hypothetical, the hospital's business records were offered in evidence under Rule 803(7) to prove, by virtue of the absence of information concerning Plaintiff, that Plaintiff was not a patient at the hospital during the dates at issue.

Question for Classroom Discussion

State court prosecution for possession of an unregistered firearm. The prosecution calls the custodian of records of the State Department of Public Safety, who offers to testify that a diligent search of the records of that public agency reveals the absence of any registration for the firearm found in Defendant's possession. Defendant objects on the ground of hearsay. The state evidence rules do not have a provision comparable to Rule 803(10) but follow a definition of hearsay identical to that in Rule 801(c). Make an argument that the testimony does not contain hearsay.

N. EXCEPTIONS TO THE HEARSAY RULE: UNAVAILABILITY OF DECLARANT REQUIRED

1. *Unavailability*

FED. R. EVID. 804. EXCEPTIONS TO THE RULE AGAINST HEARSAY — WHEN THE DECLARANT IS UNAVAILABLE AS A WITNESS

(a) Criteria for Being Unavailable. A declarant is considered to be unavailable as a witness if the declarant:

    (1) is exempted from testifying about the subject matter of the declarant's statement because the court rules that a privilege applies;

    (2) refuses to testify about the subject matter despite a court order to do so;

    (3) testifies to not remembering the subject matter;

    (4) cannot be present or testify at the trial or hearing because of death or a then-existing infirmity, physical illness, or mental illness; or

    (5) is absent from the trial or hearing and the statement's proponent has not been able, by process or other reasonable means, to procure:

        (A) the declarant's attendance, in the case of a hearsay exception under Rule 804(b)(1) or (5); or

        (B) the declarant's attendance or testimony, in the case of a hearsay exception under Rule 804(b)(2), (3), or (4).

But this subdivision (a) does not apply if the statement's proponent procured or wrongfully caused the declarant's unavailability as a witness in order to prevent the declarant from attending or testifying.

As we have stated previously, the exceptions to the hearsay rule are divided into 23 that apply under Rule 803 and one that applies under Rule 807 regardless of the availability of the declarant and only five that apply under Rule 804 when the declarant is unavailable.

Because a statement within the hearsay exceptions will be relevant regardless of the availability of the declarant, unavailability is a preliminary fact that must be decided by the court under Rule 104(a).

The meaning of the term *unavailable* is much broader in evidence law than in the language of everyday life. Rule 804(a) sets forth five circumstances in which a declarant will be deemed unavailable. The most obvious is listed fourth. Rule 804(a)(4) provides that a declarant is unavailable when she "is unable to be present or to testify at the hearing because of death or then existing physical or mental illness or infirmity." Similarly, Rule 804(a)(5) states that a declarant is unavailable if she "is absent from the trial or hearing and the statement's proponent has not been able, by process or other reasonable means, to procure the declarant's attendance." Proof of unavailability under the latter rule requires the proponent to demonstrate that reasonable means were used to locate the declarant. Though what is reasonable will vary from case to case, perfunctory measures such as a letter or telephone call to a recent address usually will not suffice. Depending on the circumstances, the proponent should also look for forwarding orders with the post office, inquire at the declarant's last known workplace, ask the declarant's family members and acquaintances for information about her whereabouts, and take other steps appropriate to the situation.

A declarant also may be deemed unavailable if she is in court, on the witness stand. Rule 804(a)(1) provides that a declarant is unavailable if she has a privilege that exempts her from testifying. For example, if a party's spouse is called as a witness, she has a privilege under certain circumstances to refuse to testify about confidential communications that took place between the spouses while they were married. (We discuss this and another marital privilege in Chapter 8.) If, therefore, the opponent calls the spouse to testify, she may refuse to answer questions relating to such confidential communications, and as to the subjects of those communications, the spouse is deemed unavailable. Similarly, a person has a constitutional privilege against compulsory self-incrimination. If a question calls for testimony that might subject the declarant to criminal sanctions, she may refuse to answer the question, and she will be deemed unavailable as to the subject of that question.

Even a groundless claim of privilege or the claim of a legally unrecognized excuse may render a declarant unavailable. Rule 804(a)(2) states that a declarant is unavailable if she "refuses to testify about the subject matter despite a court order to do so."

A declarant also is unavailable under Rule 804(a)(3) if she "testifies to not remembering the subject matter." Earlier in this chapter we discussed this issue in passing in connection with the meaning of the phrase, "subject to cross-examination" as used in Rule 801(d)(1). A witness who does not remember the subject matter of her prior statement is "unavailable as a witness" for purposes of the exceptions in Rule 804 even though she is considered "subject to cross-examination" for purposes of prior statements offered pursuant to Rule 801(d)(1). Although the language of Rule 804(a)(3) seems to apply only when the declarant has no memory of the subject matter of her prior statement, it would be reasonable for a court to declare the witness unavailable if she remembers the subject matter of the statement, but does not remember sufficient detail to make her testimony very useful. Finally, this ground of unavailability will not apply unless the declarant herself testifies to lack of memory. Fed. R. Evid. 804 Advisory Committee's Note.

Rule 804(a) concludes by providing that a declarant is not to be deemed unavailable "if the statement's proponent procured or wrongfully caused the declarant's unavailability as a witness in order to prevent the declarant from attending or testifying." The primary purpose of this rule is to prevent a person from procuring the unavailability of a witness in order to make that person's prior statements admissible. For example, suppose Defendant is on trial for the murder of Victim and the attempted murder of Zed. The prosecution plans to call Zed to identify Defendant as the perpetrator. Defendant is aware that shortly after the crime occurred, Zed, believing she was about to die, named another person as the attacker. Zed's statement would be admissible under Rule 804(b)(2) as a "statement under the belief of imminent death" (commonly called a "dying declaration" and discussed later in this chapter) only if Zed is unavailable. If Defendant kills Zed or threatens her to prevent her from attending the trial, the last sentence of Rule 804(a) declares that Zed is not unavailable. The effect will be to prevent Defendant from offering evidence of Zed's prior statement. This rule makes sense, of course. A person should not be allowed to manipulate the trial process in this way.[33]

Questions for Classroom Discussion

1. Civil action for battery. Defendant denies involvement in the fight. Shortly after Plaintiff was attacked, she named Defendant as her attacker. She then lapsed into a coma and has not recovered. Plaintiff wishes to offer her statement into evidence under the dying declaration exception to the hearsay rule. Defendant objects on grounds Plaintiff is not unavailable. How should the court rule?

2. Same case. Suppose Plaintiff is not comatose but is still hospitalized because she is not well enough to go home. Defendant makes the same objection. How should the court rule?

3. Same case, and same situation as in Question 2. Suppose Defendant argues that if Plaintiff cannot come to court, the court can go to Plaintiff by having court officers, attorneys, and jury go to the hospital, where Plaintiff can testify from her room. Is Plaintiff available now?

4. Same case. Zed was an eyewitness to the attack on Plaintiff. Assume Zed testified for Plaintiff at an earlier trial of the same action that resulted in a mistrial. At the earlier trial, Zed testified that she saw Defendant attack Plaintiff. Before the second trial, Plaintiff lost track of Zed. Plaintiff's investigator learned that she no longer lived at the address she had given previously, and she did not leave any forwarding information. In addition, Zed's employer reported that she had quit abruptly, saying only that she "needed to get away." No further effort was made to find Zed. At trial, Plaintiff wishes to offer the transcript of Zed's preliminary hearing testimony under the former testimony exception. Defendant objects on the ground Plaintiff has failed to demonstrate Zed's unavailability. How should the court rule?

5. Same case. Plaintiff's investigator testifies he had remained in "constant contact" with Zed before she disappeared, and Zed had never indicated she was going to leave the area. The investigator further testifies that as soon as he realized Zed was gone he made multiple efforts to locate her. The investigator contacted each of Zed's known relatives—and each claimed they had no knowledge of Zed's whereabouts. The investigator searched the

(continued)

---

33. As we discuss below, Rule 804(b)(6) operates in a similar fashion by allowing a party to offer the statement of a declarant whose unavailability was procured or acquiesced in by the party's opponent.

public records of all 50 states, and conducted Google and other Internet searches with no success. Defendant objects on the ground Plaintiff has failed to demonstrate Zed's unavailability. How should the court rule?

6. Prosecution of Defendant for corporate securities fraud. At Defendant's preliminary hearing, the prosecution called Witness, an alleged co-conspirator of Defendant. Witness testified that Defendant was involved. Witness refuses to testify at trial, however, asserting her privilege against compulsory self-incrimination. The prosecutor then confers "use immunity" on Witness, meaning that the government may not use any of Witness's testimony against her. Despite having use immunity, and despite the court's demands that Witness testify, she persists in her refusal. The prosecution now offers the transcript of Witness's preliminary hearing testimony under the former testimony exception. Defendant objects on the ground Witness is not unavailable. How should the court rule?

7. Retrial of a negligence action by Plaintiff against Defendant arising from a skateboard collision. At the first trial, Plaintiff called Witness, who testified that Defendant skated directly into Plaintiff's path. Plaintiff calls Witness at the second trial, and although Witness remembers the incident vaguely, she does not remember the events immediately before the actual collision. Plaintiff asks to have the transcript of Witness's testimony from the first trial read into the record. Defendant objects on the ground Witness is not unavailable. How should the court rule?

8. Same case. Suppose that shortly after the accident, a police officer approached Witness and asked her to point to the person who caused the collision. Witness then pointed to the person. At trial, however, Witness does not remember who she pointed out in response to the officer's request. Plaintiff then calls the officer to testify that Witness pointed to Defendant. Defendant objects on hearsay grounds. Plaintiff responds that Witness's act qualifies as prior identification under Rule 801(d)(1)(C). Defendant argues that because Witness is unavailable, she is not "subject to cross-examination about the [prior identification]." How should the court rule?

9. Same case. Suppose Plaintiff sent a letter to Witness asking her to appear at the second trial. Witness responded in writing that she would appear. However, Witness does not show up on the specified date. Plaintiff offers into evidence the transcript of Witness's testimony at the first trial. Defendant objects on the ground Witness is not unavailable. How should the court rule?

> **10.**   Prosecution of a professional athlete charging he committed per-
> jury when he testified he never "knowingly" took steroids. During
> the trial of the athlete's trainer for administering steroids the
> trainer testified, "I always told my athletes when I gave them ster-
> oids." At trial in the perjury prosecution, the judge sends the
> trainer to jail for contempt of court after he refuses to testify.
> The prosecution offers the transcript of the trainer's testimony
> from his criminal trial. Defendant objects on the ground the
> trainer is not unavailable. How should the court rule?

---

2.   The Former Testimony Exception (Rule 804(b)(1))

> **FED. R. EVID. 804.   EXCEPTIONS TO THE RULE AGAINST
> HEARSAY — WHEN THE DECLARANT IS UNAVAILABLE AS A WITNESS**

(b) The Exceptions. The following are not excluded by the rule against hearsay if the declarant is unavailable as a witness:
  (1) *Former Testimony.* Testimony that:
    (A) was given as a witness at a trial, hearing, or lawful deposition,
  whether given during the current proceeding or a different one; and
    (B) is now offered against a party who had — or, in a civil case, whose
  predecessor in interest had — an opportunity and similar motive to develop
  it by direct, cross-, or redirect examination.

Consider the following hypothetical:

A wrongful death case comes to trial. Plaintiff calls Witness, who testifies that
Defendant ran a stop sign and plowed into the deceased's car. After the court
enters judgment (it does not matter for which party), an appeal is taken and
the appellate court orders a new trial. Unfortunately, Witness, who testified for
Plaintiff at the first trial, dies before the second trial begins. Plaintiff would like to
introduce Witness's testimony from the first trial. Is this permissible?

The problem is that when offered at the second trial, Witness's testimony from
the first trial is hearsay. That is, the testimony is "a prior statement, — one the
declarant does not make while testifying at the *current* trial or hearing — that a
party offers in evidence to prove the truth of the matter asserted by the declarant." Fed. R. Evid. 801(c) (emphasis added). Even though Witness's testimony
was given at an earlier trial of the same case, not the "*current* trial," it is now being
offered at this second trial.

Even so, would it be sensible to exclude the evidence of Witness's earlier
testimony? One argument would support doing so: Because Witness's testimony
would not be presented "live," the jury in the present trial would not have the
opportunity to assess the credibility of the declarant. This violates our strongly

held belief in the importance of face-to-face confrontation of witnesses, even in civil cases.

But if Witness has become unavailable, protecting the value of face-to-face confrontation comes at a rather high price. The party who called Witness is not responsible for her unavailability. (If the party were responsible for it, the final sentence of Rule 804(a) would declare Witness not to be unavailable.) Witness's testimony at the first trial was offered for the same purpose for which it is being offered at the current trial. And the party against whom the testimony is offered (Defendant) had both an opportunity to cross-examine Witness at the first trial and a motive to do so that was identical to the motives it has in the second trial. The testimony, after all, accused Defendant of running a stop sign and plowing into Plaintiff's car. Now consider the most serious problem with hearsay in general: the absence of cross-examination of the statement contemporaneously with its making. That problem is minimized with formal testimony because, by hypothesis, the statement was subject to contemporaneous cross-examination. It is only the present jury that is unable to observe such cross-examination. As Rule 804's drafters noted, "[t]he only missing one of the ideal conditions for the giving of testimony is the presence of trier and opponent ('demeanor evidence'). This is lacking with all hearsay exceptions. Hence it may be argued that former testimony is the strongest hearsay. . . ." Fed. R. Evid. 804 Advisory Committee's Note.

These considerations strongly suggest that former testimony should be admitted, and that is the purpose of Rule 804(b)(1). That rule establishes several foundational requirements in addition to the declarant's unavailability:

1. The testimony must have been "given as a witness at a trial, hearing, or lawful deposition, whether given during the current proceeding or a different one."
2. If the current case is a criminal prosecution, the party against whom the evidence is now offered:
    a. must have "had an opportunity . . . to develop it by direct, cross, or redirect examination"; and
    b. must have had a "similar motive" to develop the testimony by such examination.
3. If the current case is a civil action, the party against whom the evidence is now offered, *or a predecessor in interest of that party,* must have had an opportunity and similar motive to develop the witness's testimony.

The first requirement is simple. The declarant must have been a "witness" at another trial or hearing, or must have been a deponent. To be a witness or deponent requires the observance of certain formalities, including an oath or affirmation. (*See* Rule 603, which we discuss in Chapter 1.) But it is important to note that the former testimony need not have been given at a trial. A deposition qualifies. Even a preliminary hearing in a criminal case might qualify, though the defendant might be able to argue that there is little motive to cross-examine the prosecution's witnesses in that forum.

The more problematic requirements deal with the opportunity and motive to develop the declarant's testimony at the earlier trial, hearing, or deposition.[34]

---

34. For the sake of simplicity, we refer to the earlier "trial" instead of trial, hearing, or deposition.

Because students often find the language of the rule confusing, we have broken it down according to the *type of case in which the former testimony is being offered.* If the case is a criminal prosecution, the party against whom the testimony is now offered must have had an opportunity and similar motive to develop the declarant's testimony at the earlier trial. In practical terms, what that means is that the person must have been a party to the earlier trial.

If the current case is a civil action, the rule relaxes the "opportunity and similar motive" requirement. The rule will apply if the party against whom the evidence is now offered *either* was a party to the earlier action *or* a "predecessor in interest" was a party to the earlier action. The courts have varied in the extent to which they give the term *predecessor in interest* the same meaning it carries in property or contract law. Thus, for some courts it is not limited solely to a person in privity with the party against whom the evidence is now offered, such as the prior owner of real property now held by that party. For those courts, that person must have been one whose interests and motivations track those of the party against whom the evidence is now offered. In fact, some federal courts have tended to read the term *predecessor in interest* as surplusage, requiring no foundation beyond the opportunity and similar motive requirement. In those jurisdictions, the evidence qualifies under Rule 804(b)(1) as long as *anyone* had an opportunity to examine the witness in the earlier trial and had a motive to do so sufficiently similar to the motive that the party against whom the evidence is now offered has.

Even where the predecessor in interest language does not impose any burdens on the party offering the evidence beyond those imposed by the opportunity and similar motive requirement, it is particularly important to remember that it only applies if the current case is civil rather than criminal. As originally proposed, the rule would have allowed the court to admit the evidence against any party as long as a party with similar interest and motive had an opportunity to examine the witness at the prior trial. The House Judiciary Committee was uncomfortable applying this language to criminal cases:

> The committee considered that it is generally unfair to impose upon the party against whom the hearsay evidence is being offered responsibility for the manner in which the witness was previously handled by another party. The sole exception to this . . . is when a party's predecessor in interest in a civil action or proceeding had an opportunity and similar motive to examine the witness. The Committee amended the Rule to reflect these policy determinations.

House Comm. on Judiciary, Fed. Rules of Evidence, H.R. Rep. No. 650, 93d Cong., 1st Sess., p. 15 (1973). Although this statement does not clarify the meaning of "predecessor in interest," it is reasonable to infer from this statement that Congress was concerned about protecting the Sixth Amendment rights of a criminal defendant who did not have the opportunity to confront a witness whose testimony is now being offered against him. Recent Supreme Court decisions interpreting the Confrontation Clause, which we discuss later in this chapter, lend considerable support to this position.

The prior party must have had an "opportunity" to develop the witness's testimony. This simply means that the party was afforded the chance to cross-examine the witness, if the witness was called by the opponent. If the party against whom the evidence is now offered was the one who initially called the witness, and the witness provided evidence on cross-examination that was detrimental to the interests of the party who called the witness, redirect examination would suffice to meet the opportunity requirement. To take an example, suppose that in our automobile accident case Plaintiff's witness testified on direct examination that Defendant's car ran the stop sign. On cross-examination, however, the witness admitted that it might have been the deceased's car that ran the stop sign. As long as Plaintiff has an opportunity to conduct redirect examination to further "develop" the witness's testimony, the opportunity requirement of the former testimony exception would be satisfied. Naturally, this requirement does not guarantee a *successful* cross- or redirect examination. The rule only demands an *opportunity* to test the witness further.

In civil cases in which the party against whom the evidence is now offered was not a party to the earlier trial, the opportunity requirement just discussed applies to the predecessor in interest.

The key requirement of the former testimony exception concerns the party's (or predecessor's) similar motive to develop the witness's testimony at the earlier trial. What does it mean to have a "similar motive"? When the earlier trial and the current trial are of the same case, and when the parties have not changed the purpose for which the witness's testimony will be used, the requirement is satisfied. To return to our auto accident case, if on retrial Plaintiff does not change in any significant way the purpose of the witness's testimony, the similar motive requirement will be satisfied. Defendant's motive at the first trial would have been to challenge the credibility of the witness or her testimony that Defendant ran the stop sign, and if the witness were available to testify at the second trial, Defendant would have had the same goals. Similar motive in this case actually means identical motive.

Suppose, however, that the first trial in our auto accident hypothetical had been a criminal prosecution for vehicular manslaughter, and that the witness had been called by the prosecution. Would Defendant's motive to examine the witness in that trial be similar to the motive Defendant would have to examine the witness if she were available to testify at the present civil trial? The answer is yes. It is true that the stakes are different in criminal trials and civil trials. In the first trial, Defendant's strong motive to cross-examine the witness would have been supplied largely by Defendant's desire to avoid a substantial fine or prison sentence. In the current trial, on the other hand, compensation of the deceased's estate would be the consequence of an adverse judgment. Even though the results in the civil and criminal cases are not identical, they are similar in that both adverse judgments would be of great consequence. The rule only requires that the party's *factual purpose* in developing the witness's testimony be similar; the ultimate goal of the trial would not be important.

The rule is not categorical, however. There is room to argue that in some situations, the adverse party had no significant motive to develop the witness's testimony at the first trial, but would have such a motive in the second trial. Suppose, for example, that at the first trial Plaintiff called several eyewitnesses, each of whom had roughly the same view of the scene as the witness in question, and all of whom testified that Defendant's car ran the stop sign. Under those circumstances, Defendant might have had a motive to cross-examine the first several witnesses vigorously, but to limit cross-examination of the remaining witnesses, including the witness whose testimony is now being offered, so as not to bore the jury and lengthen the trial. By the time the witness whose testimony is now offered was called at the first trial, Defendant chose to spend little time on cross-examination. At the retrial, however, suppose Plaintiff calls only one or two eyewitnesses and then offers the testimony of the unavailable witness through the former testimony exception. Defendant now has a much more urgent need to conduct cross-examination, and the absence of the witness would prevent that. It is conceivable that under these circumstances, the court will hold that Defendant's motive was not sufficiently similar in the two trials to permit Plaintiff to use the former testimony of the unavailable witness.

What if Defendant changed lawyers for the second trial? Would Defendant be forced to accept the decisions made and tactics used by her first lawyer (or her predecessor in interest's lawyer) in conducting cross-examination of the witness? The answer is yes. The rule requires only that the factual issues raised by the witness's testimony be similar. A change in tactics would not affect the application of the former testimony exception as long as Defendant's factual purpose in conducting cross-examination is sufficiently similar to the former lawyer's purpose.

It is possible, however, for the purpose to change. Suppose in our hypothetical auto accident case that Plaintiff has brought suit not only against the driver, but also against the car's owner and that, at the time of the accident, the driver was an employee of the owner making a delivery for the owner. At the vehicular manslaughter trial, the driver cross-examined the witness, seeking to discredit her direct examination testimony that the driver ran the stop sign. In the current civil action for wrongful death, Plaintiff seeks to hold both the driver and the owner liable, the latter on respondeat superior grounds. Legally, the owner might have two defenses. First, she might argue, along with the driver, that the driver did not run the stop sign and cause the accident. For this purpose, the driver's cross-examination of the witness at the earlier criminal trial would suffice and the evidence would be admissible pursuant to the former testimony exception.

But suppose that the owner adopts a different defense: the driver was, in fact, at fault, but the owner should not be held liable because the driver was not acting in the scope of her employment. Perhaps the driver had deviated very substantially from the proper route at the time of the accident. Or perhaps the driver acted with the sort of malice for which an employer would not be held vicariously liable. Would it be appropriate to bind the owner with the driver's criminal trial cross-examination of the witness? Arguably not. In fact, if the witness were available to testify at the current trial, the owner's motive might be to support, rather than impeach, the witness's testimony that the driver ran the stop sign. If this is true, the court should hold that the witness's former testimony should be admissible only against the driver, and not the owner. If the danger that the jury will not abide by a limiting instruction to this effect is too great, the court might find it necessary to hold two separate trials, one for each defendant. If that is done, the jury in the employer's trial would not be exposed to the former testimony.

Assuming the former testimony is admissible, the next question is the manner in which that testimony is shown. Note that nothing in the former testimony exception requires that the former testimony be proved in any particular manner. Obviously, the most accurate way to prove the witness's prior testimony is by offering the court reporter's transcript. The court reporter's job is to record accurately the words spoken, and in some situations, the witness has an opportunity to correct what she perceives to be errors in the transcript. The document is therefore extremely reliable evidence of the witness's testimony. Although the use of the transcript introduces another layer of hearsay (because the transcript is the court reporter's assertion that these words were spoken by the witness), the transcript will qualify as the reporter's business record, and might also qualify as the reporter's recorded recollection or even as a public record.

Another way to prove the substance of the witness's prior testimony is to call a witness with first-hand knowledge of that testimony. That individual could testify to what she remembers of the witness's testimony. She need not have personal knowledge of the *truth* of the earlier testimony; she need only have personal knowledge of the testimony itself. Though the testimony of a witness who observed another person testifying at the earlier trial is not likely to be as complete or accurate as the court reporter's transcript, there is no requirement that the "best evidence" be used. Remember that the best evidence rule only applies when a party seeks to prove the contents of a writing. (See Chapter 1.) In our situation, therefore, the best evidence rule would only be applicable if the witness proposes to testify to what the transcript says.

Finally, do not confuse the admissibility of former testimony under an exception to the hearsay rule with the question of whether a prior adjudication can be used to preclude relitigation of an issue under the concepts of res judicata or collateral estoppel. Questions of issue preclusion are not matters of evidence law. Our concern is with the admissibility of the former testimony, assuming the issue may be tried in the present case. Thus, when determining the applicability of the former testimony exception, it is not necessary for the court to apply the standards of issue preclusion. As McCormick's handbook states, "insistence upon precise identity of issues, which might have some appropriateness if the question were one of res judicata or estoppel by judgment, is out of place with respect to former testimony, where the question is not of binding anyone but merely of salvaging the testimony of an unavailable witness." 2 McCormick on Evidence § 304, at 296 (5th ed. John W. Strong ed. 1999).

Questions for Classroom Discussion

1. Prosecution of Defendant for bank robbery. At an earlier trial, which resulted in a hung jury, Witness testified for the prosecution that she saw Defendant and Zed point weapons at the bank tellers and demand all the money. At the new trial, the prosecution calls Witness to give the same testimony, but Witness refuses to testify, claiming a non-existent privilege, and continues to refuse even after the court orders Witness to testify. The prosecution wishes to offer into evidence the transcript of Witness's testimony from the first trial. Defendant objects on hearsay grounds. How should the court rule?

2. Same case. Assume Zed, the other person with whom Defendant allegedly robbed the bank, disappeared after the robbery and was not found until a few weeks before the second trial. The prosecutor

at the second trial offers the transcript of Witness's testimony against both Defendant and Zed. Is it admissible against Zed?

3.   Same case. Assume once again that Witness's former testimony is only being offered against Defendant. Instead of offering the transcript of Witness's testimony, the prosecution calls a newspaper reporter who was in court during Witness's testimony at the first trial, covering the case. The prosecutor asks the newspaper reporter to relate the substance of Witness's testimony. Defendant objects on hearsay and best evidence rule grounds. How should the court rule?

4.   Second trial of a negligence action by Plaintiff against Defendant arising from a skateboarding accident. Plaintiff claims Defendant suddenly swerved into Plaintiff's path and struck Plaintiff. At the first trial, to prove Defendant swerved into Plaintiff's path, Plaintiff called Witness, expecting Witness to testify to that effect. But Witness's direct examination testimony was at best ambiguous, and on cross-examination, Witness testified that it was Plaintiff who swerved into Defendant's path. Plaintiff's redirect examination failed to discredit Witness's testimony. Defendant prevailed. On appeal, the court reversed and remanded the case for a new trial. Unfortunately, Witness died between the two trials. Defendant wishes to introduce the transcript of Witness's testimony from the first trial. Plaintiff raises a hearsay objection. How should the court rule?

5.   Same facts. Suppose Plaintiff did not attempt to undermine the testimony Witness gave on cross-examination, preferring to leave well enough alone and not risk making the situation even worse. May Defendant introduce the transcript of Witness's testimony at the retrial?

6.   Prosecution of Defendant for racketeering. The indictment resulted from a grand jury investigation during which Witness, an alleged member of Defendant's "family," testified that Defendant ran a huge illegal drug importation operation. At trial, the prosecutor calls Witness, but Witness refuses to testify despite a court order, citing fear of reprisal. The prosecutor then offers into evidence the transcript of Witness's grand jury testimony accusing Defendant. Defendant objects on hearsay grounds. How should the court rule?

7.   Same case. Suppose that when he testified before the grand jury, Witness insisted that Defendant did *not* have anything to do with illegal drug importation. Other witnesses, however, provide sufficient evidence to lead the grand jury to indict Defendant. Witness dies in a plane crash before trial, due to no fault of the prosecution or Defendant. At trial, Defendant offers into evidence

(continued)

the transcript of Witness's grand jury testimony. The prosecution objects. How should the court rule?

8. Same facts. Suppose Witness had not died in the plane crash and Defendant calls Witness to testify at the trial. Witness refuses, however, claiming a fear of prosecution based on his testimony. What steps may Defendant take to obtain Witness's testimony?

9. Same facts. Suppose Witness's grand jury testimony had been favorable to the government's case. At Defendant's trial, if Witness is reluctant to repeat his testimony, what steps might the government take to require Witness to testify?

10. Is it fair that the government has a far greater chance of being able to make use of inculpatory grand jury testimony than a criminal defendant has of making use of exculpatory grand jury testimony?

11. Civil action for battery by Plaintiff against Zed and Corporation. Plaintiff alleges that Zed, who worked as a security guard at Corporation headquarters, committed battery when she forced Plaintiff to submit to an invasive full body search in the lobby of the building before allowing Plaintiff to take an elevator to a Corporation office. The state also filed criminal assault and battery charges against Zed. At that trial, the prosecution called Witness, who testified that she observed Zed's search of Plaintiff. Zed cross-examined Witness, seeking without success to get Witness to admit that Zed did not conduct the invasive search alleged by the government. Zed was acquitted. Witness died before the civil action came to trial. Plaintiff now offers against both defendants the transcript of Witness's testimony at the criminal trial. Assume Plaintiff claims Corporation is liable on a theory of respondeat superior. Both Zed and Corporation raise hearsay objections to admission of the transcript. How should the court rule?

3. The Dying Declaration Exception (Rule 804(b)(2))

> **FED. R. EVID. 804.   EXCEPTIONS TO THE RULE AGAINST HEARSAY — WHEN THE DECLARANT IS UNAVAILABLE AS A WITNESS**

(b) The Exceptions. The following are not excluded by the rule against hearsay if the declarant is unavailable as a witness: . . .

   (2) *Statement Under the Belief of Imminent Death.* In a prosecution for homicide or in a civil case, a statement that the declarant, while believing the declarant's death to be imminent, made about its cause or circumstances.

As we have already seen in the case of excited utterances and present sense impressions, evidence law bases its conclusions about the reliability of certain classes of hearsay on outmoded assumptions about human psychology and behavior. The "dying declaration" exception, probably the oldest widely recognized hearsay exception, presents another example. Simply put, the rationale for the exception is that a person who believes she is about to die is not likely to lie. As the U.S. Supreme Court wrote in Mattox v. United States, 156 U.S. 237, 244 (1895), "the sense of impending death is presumed to remove all temptation to falsehood and to enforce as strict an adherence to the truth as would the obligation of an oath." A British court used similarly colorful language to express the same idea: "[N]o person, who is immediately going into the presence of his Maker, will do so with a lie upon his lips." Queen v. Osman, 15 Cos. Crim. Cas. 1, 3 (Eng. N. Wales Cir. 1881).

The assumption underlying the dying declaration rule may apply to some people, especially those who hold certain religious views about an afterlife. But the assumption is hardly true universally and might not reflect attitudes about life and death prevailing in modern western culture. As the authors of one article have written, the dying declaration exception

> arises from the cultural experience of "facing one's Maker" as a moment of truth. But in a culture that only grows more cynical about the authenticity of religious experience, the exception loses its rhetorical force. Dying declarations no longer evoke the image of a person making a solemn statement on the death bed, before a confessor, surrounded by family members. Instead, we more commonly envision a drugged, whispering patient in an impersonal hospital, alone except for a detective holding a little black book and straining to hear a name gasped against the flow of pure oxygen. The contemporary image lacks the comforting effect of the traditional one.

Charles R. Nesson & Yochai Benkler, *Constitutional Hearsay: Requiring Foundational Testing and Corroboration Under the Confrontation Clause*, 81 Va. L. Rev. 149, 156 (1995). Emphasizing the cultural assumptions underlying the dying declaration exception, a nineteenth-century British treatise writer quoted a native of Madras, India, who stated that "'[s]uch evidence . . . ought never to be admitted in any case. What motive for telling the truth can any man possibly have when he is at the point of death?'" 1 Sir James Fitzjames Stephen, A History of the Criminal Law of England 449 (1883). The author reports that when the English law of evidence, including the dying declaration exception, was introduced in India, it became common in the Punjab region for a mortally wounded person to "make[] a statement bringing all his hereditary enemies on to the scene at the time of his receiving his wound, thus using his last opportunity to do them an injury." *Id.* at 448. Obviously, the culture of India at that time hardly guaranteed that dying declarations were reliable.

The drafters of the Federal Rules recognized that "the original religious justification for the exception may have lost its conviction for some persons over the years," but asserted that "it can scarcely be doubted that powerful psychological pressures are present." Fed. R. Evid. 804 Advisory Committee's Note. Based on that claim, the drafters codified the exception in Rule 804(b)(2), and a version of it exists in all states. Under the Federal Rule, there are several prerequisites to the rule's applicability, in addition to the unavailability of the declarant:

1.   The case in which the evidence is offered must be a civil action or a homicide prosecution;
2.   The statement must have been made by the declarant while believing that his or her death was imminent; and
3.   The statement must concern the cause or circumstances of what the declarant believed to be impending death.

It is important to note that the rule does not require that the declarant died. Thus, so long as the declarant is unavailable for other reasons and the three elements listed above are present, the statement is admissible as a dying declaration even though the declarant is still very much alive.

Perhaps the strongest arguments supporting the admissibility of dying declarations are strong considerations of necessity. This is obviously the case in homicide prosecutions, when the victim might well have known who was responsible for her impending death, and her statements about that fact often would not be admissible absent an exception. Because this evidence is especially crucial in homicide prosecutions, the common law tended to apply the exception only to such cases. The drafters of the Federal Rules, however, believed that considerations of necessity justified extending the exception to civil cases, though they did not extend the exception to criminal prosecutions for crimes other than homicide.

In practice, the most difficult element of the rule to establish is the requirement that the declarant has made the statement "while believing . . . death to be imminent." Proving state of mind is always difficult, and having to do so without being able to question the unavailable declarant makes this especially problematic. Nevertheless, because the declarant's belief that death is imminent is the factor that supposedly lends reliability to the statement, that state of mind must be proven by a preponderance of the evidence for the statement to be admissible. We have already seen that in deciding preliminary facts pursuant to Rule 104(a), the court is not bound by the rules of evidence except those with respect to privileges. In the context of dying declarations, this means the court may consider the statement itself in deciding whether it was made in anticipation of imminent death. Thus, the statement, "I don't think I have long to live. It was George who shot me" contains indications of the declarant's state of mind that the court may consider in determining whether the requirement has been satisfied. In deciding if the declarant believed her death was imminent, the court may also consider any other pertinent circumstances as well as other statements made by the declarant at or near the time of the purported dying declaration. For example, the declarant's expression of hope for recovery would undermine (though not necessarily defeat) the claim that the statement at issue was made under a sense of impending death. In addition, statements that the declarant plans to take action in the future (such as exacting revenge or engaging in conduct typical of a healthy person) suggest that the declarant did not believe death was imminent.

The final requirement—that the statement concerns the "cause or circumstances"—occasionally creates difficulty for admission. It will usually be clear whether the statements concerns the cause or circumstances surrounding the declarant's supposed impending death; when it is not clear, the court should look at the statement and the surrounding circumstances to determine its context and meaning.

Questions for Classroom Discussion

1. Prosecution of Defendant for the attempted murder of Victim. Defendant denies involvement. The attack on Victim left her critically injured, and she lapsed into a coma from which she has not recovered at the time of trial. The prosecution wishes to offer evidence that before becoming comatose, Victim told an attending nurse, "I don't expect to make it. I hope Defendant pays for this." Defendant objects on hearsay grounds. How should the court rule?

2. Same facts, except assume that Victim died and the charge is murder. Defendant lodges a hearsay objection to the evidence of Victim's statement. How should the court rule?

3. Same facts. Assume Victim did not die until several weeks after making the statement. How does this affect its admissibility as a dying declaration?

4. Civil action for battery by Plaintiff against Defendant. The action stems from a barroom brawl during which Plaintiff, who claims he was an innocent bystander, was seriously injured. Defendant also claims he was a bystander. To prove that Defendant was involved in the fight, Plaintiff wishes to offer evidence that while Zed, who was injured trying to stop the brawl, was recovering in the hospital, she suddenly sat upright in bed and said to a nurse, "I must follow the white light. Defendant put me here, but I will be at peace soon." At the time of the trial, Zed has recovered but is on a long trip out of the country and beyond the reach of the court's subpoena power. Defendant makes a hearsay objection to testimony concerning Zed's statement. How should the court rule?

5. Same case. Suppose that during her argument to the court about the admissibility of the purported dying declaration, Defendant represents that a few minutes before making the statement to the nurse, Zed told a visiting family member, "I plan to sue Defendant when I get out of here." Based on this statement, Defendant asks the court to exclude Zed's statement to the nurse. How should the court rule?

6. Same case. Suppose the court overrules Defendant's objection to evidence of Zed's statement to the nurse. Defendant now offers the statement Zed made to the family member. Plaintiff objects on both relevance and hearsay grounds. How should the court rule?

7. Prosecution of Defendant for the murder of Victim. Defendant denies involvement. Just before Victim died, Victim told her

(continued)

husband, "The end is very near. Defendant did this to me." The prosecution offers Victim's statement as a dying declaration. Defendant objects, and presents uncontested evidence that Victim was a lifelong atheist who did not believe in any kind of afterlife. How should the court rule?

8. **Will contest.** The testator died from injuries sustained in an automobile accident. Plaintiff offers evidence that, shortly before she died, the testator said, "I'm going fast. My will was the product of undue influence!" Defendant objects on hearsay grounds. How should the court rule?

Further Reading: Charles W. Quick, *Some Reflections on Dying Declarations*, 6 How. L.J. 109 (1960).

4. *The Declaration Against Interest Exception (Rule 804(b)(3))*

FED. R. EVID. 804.   EXCEPTIONS TO THE RULE AGAINST HEARSAY — WHEN THE DECLARANT IS UNAVAILABLE AS A WITNESS

(b) **The Exceptions.** The following are not excluded by the rule against hearsay if the declarant is unavailable as a witness:

(3) *Statement Against Interest.* A statement that:

(A) a reasonable person in the declarant's position would have made only if the person believed it to be true because, when made, it was so contrary to the declarant's proprietary or pecuniary interest or had so great a tendency to invalidate the declarant's claim against someone else or to expose the declarant to civil or criminal liability; and

(B) is supported by corroborating circumstances that clearly indicate its trustworthiness, if it is offered in a criminal case as one that tends to expose the declarant to criminal liability.

a. Rationale for the Exception

The declaration against interest exception to the hearsay rule is based on a common sense idea: People are reluctant to make statements that are against their interest, and if they do make such statements, the statements are likely to be trustworthy. Nevertheless, the scope of the exception was very limited at common law and, though the drafters of the Federal Rules expanded its scope, many statements against a person's interest still are not admissible. For example, if the declarant is available, the exception does not apply. This is because one is always a bit suspicious about situations in which one makes a statement against her interest and, if the declarant is available to testify, we would prefer to take the opportunity to cross-examine the declarant regarding the statement.[35]

b.   Nature of "Interests" Covered by the Exception

Prior to the adoption of the Federal Rules, the exception for declarations against interest was usually limited to statements against the declarant's "pecuniary or proprietary" interests. The rationale was that statements placing the declarant's finances or property in jeopardy are especially trustworthy. Though courts often found ways to characterize statements as fitting within this limited language, they were nevertheless relatively steadfast about excluding certain types of statements, especially those that tended to subject the declarant to criminal prosecution. This limitation primarily arose from the fear that if the exception extended to statements against penal interest, criminal defendants would take advantage of the rule by having a witness testify that another person, no longer available, had confessed to the crime. As the Advisory Committee explained, "one senses in the decisions a distrust of evidence of confessions by third persons offered to exculpate the accused arising from suspicions of fabrication either of the fact of the making of the confession or in its contents, enhanced in either instance by the required unavailability of the declarant." Fed. R. Evid. 804 Advisory Committee's Note.

The common law exclusion of statements against penal interest bothered many leading authorities, including Justice Holmes, whose dissent in Donnelly v. United States, 228 U.S. 243, 277-278 (1913), argued:

> The confession of Joe Dick, since deceased, that he committed the murder for which the plaintiff in error was tried, coupled with circumstances pointing to its truth, would have a very strong tendency to make anyone outside of a court of justice believe that Donnelly did not commit the crime. I say this, of course, on the supposition that it should be proved that the confession really was made, and that there was no ground for connecting Donnelly with Dick. The rules of evidence in the main are based on experience, logic, and common sense, less hampered by history than some parts of the substantive law. . . . [T]he exception to the hearsay rule in the case of declarations against interest is well known; no other statement is so much against interest as a confession of murder; it is far more calculated to convince than dying declarations, which would be let in to hang a man . . . ; and when we surround the accused with so many safeguards, some of which seem to me excessive; I think we ought to give him the benefit of a fact that, if proved, commonly would have such weight.

In addition, as Holmes implies, some doubts about the veracity of an exculpatory statement against penal interest can be resolved through cross-examination of the witness reporting the statement.

---

35. This logic is somewhat strained. If the trustworthiness of a statement is doubtful, one would think that instead of requiring the unavailability of the declarant, the law would require that the declarant be *available* to be cross-examined concerning the statement. But the only hearsay exception that appears to require the declarant to testify (and thus be available) is the exception for recorded recollection embodied in Rule 803(5). (In addition, as we have seen, the types of statements *exempted* from the definition of hearsay in Rule 801(d)(1) do require that the declarant be "subject to cross-examination about the prior statement.") A more likely explanation for the requirement of unavailability here is that of need. If the declarant is unavailable, there is not likely to be any other way to reveal that she made a statement against her interest that is relevant to the facts at issue in the case.

Views such as those expressed by Justice Holmes proved persuasive to the drafters of the Federal Rules, who broadened the scope of the exception to include declarations against penal interest. But as Justice Holmes implied, some declarations against penal interest can be highly suspect. The drafters took this into consideration when they added the requirement that when a criminal defendant offered a statement that subjected the declarant to criminal liability, the statement would not be admissible unless there were "corroborating circumstances that clearly indicate its trustworthiness."

The Federal Rules have therefore discarded only the categorical exclusion of statements against penal interest. Consider the following scenario:

> Zed is questioned in connection with a crime. During the interrogation, Zed admits committing the crime, and states that she acted alone. Before seeking charges against Zed, the police decide to conduct further investigation. During that time, Zed disappears. Eventually, Defendant is charged with the crime.

If Defendant wishes to offer Zed's statement into evidence to prove that Defendant did not commit the crime, the rule requires that there be "corroborating circumstances that clearly indicate" Zed's statement is trustworthy. Defendant has the burden of producing such evidence, of course, and the prosecution has little incentive to do so. If Defendant is unable to present sufficient corroboration of the statements' trustworthiness, it will not be admissible.

Suppose, however, that Zed's statement inculpated both Zed and Defendant. If Zed disappears before Defendant's trial, at one time the prosecution might have been permitted to introduce Zed's statement against Defendant without presenting evidence demonstrating the trustworthiness of the statement, particularly the part that inculpates Defendant. There was no logical reason to impose a one-sided corroboration requirement, and the Judicial Conference amended the rule in 2010 to remove the imbalance. Now the prosecution is also required to present sufficient corroboration of the statement's trustworthiness.

With the exception of this limitation, the drafters of the Federal Rules intended that the exception would be "expand[ed] to the full logical limit. One result is to remove doubt as to the admissibility of declarations tending to establish a tort liability against the declarant or to extinguish one which might be asserted by him. . . ." Fed. R. Evid. 804 Advisory Committee's Note. On its face, the rule does in fact appear to be very broad, covering any statement that was "contrary to the declarant's proprietary or pecuniary interest or had . . . a tendency to invalidate the declarant's claim against someone else or to expose the declarant to civil or criminal liability. . . ." Most likely, however, the rule does not cover less tangible potential harms such as social opprobrium or embarrassment. In contrast, the California rule explicitly allows admission of statements that "create[] . . . a risk of making [the declarant] an object of hatred, ridicule, or social disgrace in the community. . . ." Cal. Evid. Code § 1230.

c. The Standard of the Rule

The rule is couched in objective terms. On its face, what matters is not what the declarant thought, but what a reasonable person in the declarant's position would have thought. Thus, the proponent must demonstrate that the statement was "so contrary" to certain interests, or had "so great a tendency" to subject the declarant to certain risks, "that a reasonable person in the declarant's position would have made only if the person believed it to be true." The court, exercising its authority under Rule 104(a), must make this determination on a case-by-case basis, taking into account all the circumstances surrounding the making of the statement. The words themselves obviously will be important, as will such factors as the identities of the people present to hear what the declarant says.

Consider the following statement: "I'm the one who shot that guy on the street corner yesterday." If the declarant made this statement to police after having been informed of his Miranda rights, the statement is probably very reliable because it is unlikely that a person would tell the police such a thing if it were not true. Suppose, however, that declarant is a member of a criminal gang, the victim was a member of a rival gang, and declarant made the statement to a number of his gang colleagues. Under these circumstances, the statement's reliability is more doubtful because a person in declarant's position might well speak boastfully, and inaccurately, in order to gain status within the group. Thus, whether a statement is truly against the interest of the declarant is a question that often can be answered only by looking at the circumstances in which the statement was made. The reliability of the same statement made to a mixed group of strangers and acquaintances would likely fall between that of the first two situations. In each case, the statement will not be admissible unless the court concludes that it is so far against the declarant's interests that a reasonable person in his position would not have made the statement unless he believed it was true.

Questions for Classroom Discussion

1. Negligence action arising from an automobile collision. Plaintiff claims Defendant's car crossed the center line and struck Plaintiff's car. To prove that it was Plaintiff's car that crossed the center line, Defendant calls Zed, a passenger in Plaintiff's car, and asks Zed if it isn't true that, after the accident, Zed admitted to a police officer that she grabbed Plaintiff's steering wheel as a joke and that the car veered left, crossing the center line. Plaintiff objects on hearsay grounds. How should the court rule?

2. Same case. Suppose Zed refuses to answer the question even though the court orders her to do so. Defendant now calls the police officer to whom Zed made the statement, and asks that person to relate what Zed said. Plaintiff objects on hearsay grounds. How should the court rule?

3. Battery action by Plaintiff against Defendant. Plaintiff claims Defendant knew she had a sexually transmitted disease and had sex with Plaintiff without informing him of that fact. Defendant denies she has an STD. To prove that Zed, another person with whom Plaintiff had a sexual relationship, was the one who transmitted

(continued)

the disease to Plaintiff, Defendant offers evidence that before Zed learned she had an STD, she told a friend about her relationship with Plaintiff. Zed disappeared before trial and cannot be located. Plaintiff raises a hearsay objection to the evidence of Zed's statement to her friend. How should the court rule?

4. Same facts. Assume that Zed made the statement after she learned that she had the STD. Plaintiff objects on hearsay grounds to evidence of the statement. How should the court rule?

5. Prosecution of Defendant for distribution of cocaine. Defendant denies involvement, and claims that Zed was the guilty party. To prove that Zed, and not Defendant, committed the crime, Defendant offers evidence that Zed, a member of an underworld "family," told his "don" that he had set up a "terrific cocaine distribution network," just as the "don" had told him to do. Zed died before trial. The prosecution raises a hearsay objection to the evidence of Zed's statement. How should the court rule?

6. Same case. Assume, however, that Zed made the statement to an undercover police officer posing as a would-be buyer of a large quantity of drugs. Again, the prosecution objects on hearsay grounds. How should the court rule?

7. Same case. Assume that Zed made the statement to a police detective while being interrogated in connection with the cocaine distribution ring. Assume, also, that Defendant presents evidence that when the police searched Zed's apartment, they found a large quantity of cocaine and a computerized list of prospective buyers. Again, the prosecution raises a hearsay objection. How should the court rule?

d. Applicability of the Exception to Neutral or Self-Serving Statements

One of the most controversial issues concerning the scope of the declaration against interest exception is whether, when only part of a statement is against the declarant's interest, the exception applies just to that part or also makes admissible those parts of the statement that are either neutral or self-serving. For example, suppose a person questioned in connection with a bank robbery tells the police after his arrest, "I was involved but all I did was keep watch outside the bank. The plan called for Zed to drive the getaway car and dump it on Route 1 after the robbery, and Abel was the one whose job was to get the money from the bank teller." The declarant enters into a plea bargain in exchange for leniency and a promise to testify at the trial of Zed and Abel. The declarant, however, refuses to testify when called to the stand, even after the court orders him to do so. What parts of this statement, if any, are admissible against Zed and Abel under the declaration against interest exception? Obviously, the part of the statement ("I was involved. . . .") in which the declarant took responsibility for involvement in the robbery is against his interest. Even if the declarant was trying to curry favor with the police to avoid being charged or to show cooperation and thus get the charge against him reduced, this part of the statement still takes responsibility for participation in a serious crime.

But what about the other parts of the statement? The part in which the declarant claims only to have kept watch outside the bank can be viewed as in his favor, not against his interest, because it shows he played a relatively unimportant role in the robbery. The same can be said for the part that accuses Zed and Abel of more active roles; if Zed and Abel played the roles the declarant described, the declarant's own involvement was likely not as great. On the other hand, declarant's statements about the roles of Zed and Abel and of the fate of the getaway car are as against his interest in that they demonstrate his knowledge of details of the crime, which might tend to show his more active involvement, perhaps in planning. From this discussion, it should be clear that context is extremely important in determining whether any given statement is actually against the interest of the declarant at the time it is made. (The statement "I owe Joe $500" might be against interest in some contexts, but not if it is made in response to a claim that the declarant owes Joe $5,000.)

From the time the Federal Rules went into effect until the Supreme Court decided Williamson v. United States, 512 U.S. 594 (1994), lower federal courts took a number of different positions about the scope of the rule. Some admitted any statement that contained material against the declarant's interest. Others admitted only those parts of a statement that were clearly against the declarant's interest. Still others took positions in between. The Supreme Court attempted to resolve the issue in *Williamson.*

WILLIAMSON v. UNITED STATES
512 U.S. 594 (1994)

Justice O'CONNOR delivered the opinion of the Court, except as to Part II-C.

In this case we clarify the scope of the hearsay exception for statements against penal interest. Fed. Rule Evid. 804(b)(3).

I

A deputy sheriff stopped the rental car driven by Reginald Harris for weaving on the highway. Harris consented to a search of the car, which revealed 19 kilograms of cocaine in two suitcases in the trunk. Harris was promptly arrested.

Shortly after Harris' arrest, Special Agent Donald Walton of the Drug Enforcement Administration (DEA) interviewed him by telephone. During that conversation, Harris said that he got the cocaine from an unidentified Cuban in Fort Lauderdale; that the cocaine belonged to petitioner Williamson; and that it was to be delivered that night to a particular dumpster. Williamson was also connected to Harris by physical evidence: The luggage bore the initials of Williamson's sister, Williamson was listed as an additional driver on the car rental agreement, and an envelope addressed to Williamson and a receipt with Williamson's girlfriend's address were found in the glove compartment.

Several hours later, Agent Walton spoke to Harris in person. During that interview, Harris said he had rented the car a few days earlier and had driven it to Fort Lauderdale to meet Williamson. According to Harris, he had gotten the cocaine from a Cuban who was Williamson's acquaintance, and the Cuban had put the cocaine in the car with a note telling Harris how to deliver the drugs. Harris repeated that he had been instructed to leave the drugs in a certain dumpster, to return to his car, and to leave without waiting for anyone to pick up the drugs.

Agent Walton then took steps to arrange a controlled delivery of the cocaine. But as Walton was preparing to leave the interview room, Harris "got out of [his] chair . . . and . . . took a half step toward [Walton] . . . and . . . said, . . . 'I can't let you do that,' threw his hands up and said 'that's not true, I can't let you go up there for no reason.'" Harris told Walton he had lied about the Cuban, the note, and the dumpster. The real story, Harris said, was that he was transporting the cocaine to Atlanta for Williamson, and that Williamson was traveling in front of him in another rental car. Harris added that after his car was stopped, Williamson turned around and drove past the location of the stop, where he could see Harris' car with its trunk open. Because Williamson had apparently seen the police searching the car, Harris explained that it would be impossible to make a controlled delivery.

Harris told Walton that he had lied about the source of the drugs because he was afraid of Williamson. Though Harris freely implicated himself, he did not want his story to be recorded, and he refused to sign a written version of the statement. Walton testified that he had promised to report any cooperation by Harris to the Assistant United States Attorney. Walton said Harris was not promised any reward or other benefit for cooperating.

Williamson was eventually convicted of possessing cocaine with intent to distribute, conspiring to possess cocaine with intent to distribute, and traveling interstate to promote the distribution of cocaine. When called to testify at Williamson's trial, Harris refused, even though the prosecution gave him use immunity and the court ordered him to testify and eventually held him in contempt. The District Court then ruled that, under Rule 804(b)(3), Agent Walton could relate what Harris had said to him:

> The ruling of the Court is that the statements . . . are admissible under [Rule 804(b)(3)], which deals with statements against interest.
>
> First, defendant Harris' statements clearly implicated himself, and therefore, are against his penal interest.
>
> Second, defendant Harris, the declarant, is unavailable.
>
> And third, as I found yesterday, there are sufficient corroborating circumstances in this case to ensure the trustworthiness of his testimony. Therefore, under [United States v. Harrell], these statements by defendant Harris implicating [Williamson] are admissible. . . .

II

A

To decide whether Harris' confession is made admissible by Rule 804(b)(3), we must first determine what the Rule means by "statement," which Federal Rule of Evidence 801(a)(1) defines as "an oral or written assertion." One possible meaning, "a report or narrative," Webster's Third New International Dictionary, connotes an extended declaration. Under this reading, Harris' entire confession — even if it contains both self-inculpatory and non-self-inculpatory parts — would be admissible so long as in the aggregate the confession sufficiently inculpates him. Another meaning of "statement," "a single declaration or remark," would make Rule 804(b)(3) cover only those declarations or remarks within the confession that are individually self-inculpatory. . . .

Although the text of the Rule does not directly resolve the matter, the principle behind the Rule, so far as it is discernible from the text, points clearly to the narrower reading. Rule 804(b)(3) is founded on the commonsense notion that reasonable people, even reasonable people who are not especially honest, tend not to make self-inculpatory statements unless they believe them to be true. This notion simply does not extend to the broader definition of "statement." The fact that a person is making a broadly self-inculpatory confession does not make more credible the confession's non-self-inculpatory parts. One of the most effective ways to lie is to mix falsehood with truth, especially truth that seems particularly persuasive because of its self-inculpatory nature.

In this respect, it is telling that the non-self-inculpatory things Harris said in his first statement actually proved to be false, as Harris himself admitted during the second interrogation. And when part of the confession is actually self-exculpatory, the generalization on which Rule 804(b)(3) is founded becomes even less applicable. Self-exculpatory statements are exactly the ones which people are most likely to make even when they are false; and mere proximity to other, self-inculpatory, statements does not increase the plausibility of the self-exculpatory statements.

We therefore cannot agree with Justice Kennedy's suggestion that the Rule can be read as expressing a policy that collateral statements — even ones that are not in any way against the declarant's interest — are admissible. Nothing in the text of Rule 804(b)(3) or the general theory of the hearsay Rules suggests that admissibility should turn on whether a statement is collateral to a self-inculpatory statement. The fact that a statement is self-inculpatory does make it more reliable; but the fact that a statement is collateral to a self-inculpatory statement says nothing at all about the collateral statement's reliability. We see no reason why collateral statements, even ones that are neutral as to interest, should be treated any differently from other hearsay statements that are generally excluded.

. . . In our view, the most faithful reading of Rule 804(b)(3) is that it does not allow admission of non-self-inculpatory statements, even if they are made within a broader narrative that is generally self-inculpatory. The district court may not just assume for purposes of Rule 804(b)(3) that a statement is self-inculpatory because it is part of a fuller confession, and this is especially true when the statement implicates someone else. "[T]he arrest statements of a codefendant have traditionally been viewed with special suspicion. Due to his strong motivation to implicate the defendant and to exonerate himself, a codefendant's statements about what the defendant said or did are less credible than ordinary hearsay evidence." Lee v. Illinois, 476 U.S. 530, 541, 106 S. Ct. 2056, 2062, 90 L. Ed. 2d 514 (1986) (internal quotation marks omitted). . . .

B

We also do not share Justice Kennedy's fears that our reading of the Rule "eviscerate[s] the against penal interest exception," or makes it lack "meaningful effect." There are many circumstances in which Rule 804(b)(3) does allow the admission of statements that inculpate a criminal defendant. Even the confessions of arrested accomplices may be admissible if they are truly self-inculpatory, rather than merely attempts to shift blame or curry favor.

For instance, a declarant's squarely self-inculpatory confession — "yes, I killed X" — will likely be admissible under Rule 804(b)(3) against accomplices of his who are being tried under a co-conspirator liability theory. Likewise, by showing that the declarant knew something, a self-inculpatory statement can in some situations help the jury infer that his confederates knew it as well. And when seen with other evidence, an accomplice's self-inculpatory statement can inculpate the defendant directly: "I was robbing the bank on Friday morning," coupled with someone's testimony that the declarant and the defendant drove off together Friday morning, is evidence that the defendant also participated in the robbery.

Moreover, whether a statement is self-inculpatory or not can only be determined by viewing it in context. Even statements that are on their face neutral may actually be against the declarant's interest. "I hid the gun in Joe's apartment" may not be a confession of a crime; but if it is likely to help the police find the murder weapon, then it is certainly self-inculpatory. "Sam and I went to Joe's house" might be against the declarant's interest if a reasonable person in the declarant's shoes would realize that being linked to Joe and Sam would implicate the declarant in Joe and Sam's conspiracy. And other statements that give the police significant details about the crime may also, depending on the situation, be against the declarant's interest. The question under Rule 804(b)(3) is always whether the statement was sufficiently against the declarant's penal interest "that a reasonable person in the declarant's position would not have made the statement unless believing it to be true," and this question can only be answered in light of all the surrounding circumstances.

C

In this case, however, we cannot conclude that all that Harris said was properly admitted. Some of Harris' confession would clearly have been admissible under Rule 804(b)(3); for instance, when he said he knew there was cocaine in the suitcase, he essentially forfeited his only possible defense to a charge of cocaine possession, lack of knowledge. But other parts of his confession, especially the parts that implicated Williamson, did little to subject Harris himself to criminal liability. A reasonable person in Harris' position might even think that implicating someone else would decrease his practical exposure to criminal liability, at least so far as sentencing goes. Small fish in a big conspiracy often get shorter sentences than people who are running the whole show, especially if the small fish are willing to help the authorities catch the big ones.

Nothing in the record shows that the District Court or the Court of Appeals inquired whether each of the statements in Harris' confession was truly self-inculpatory. As we explained above, this can be a fact-intensive inquiry, which would require careful examination of all the circumstances surrounding the criminal activity involved; we therefore remand to the Court of Appeals to conduct this inquiry in the first instance.

. . . The judgment of the Court of Appeals is vacated, and the case is remanded for further proceedings.

So ordered.

Justice SCALIA, concurring. . . .

Employing the narrower definition of "statement," so that Rule 804(b)(3) allows admission of only those remarks that are individually self-inculpatory, does not, as Justice Kennedy states, "eviscerate the against penal interest exception." A statement obviously can be self-inculpatory (in the sense of having so much of a tendency to subject one to criminal liability that a reasonable person would not make it without believing it to be true) without consisting of the confession "I committed Z element of crime Y." Consider, for example, a declarant who stated: "On Friday morning, I went into a gunshop and (lawfully) bought a particular type of handgun and particular type of ammunition. I then drove in my 1958 blue Edsel and parked in front of the First City Bank with the keys in the ignition and the driver's door ajar. I then went inside, robbed the bank, and shot the security guard." Although the declarant has not confessed to any element of a crime in the first two sentences, those statements in context are obviously against his penal interest, and I have no doubt that a trial judge could properly admit them.

Moreover, a declarant's statement is not magically transformed from a statement against penal interest into one that is inadmissible merely because the declarant names another person or implicates a possible codefendant. For example, if a lieutenant in an organized crime operation described the inner workings of an extortion and protection racket, naming some of the other actors and thereby inculpating himself on racketeering and/or conspiracy charges, I have no doubt that some of those remarks could be admitted as statements against penal interest. Of course, naming another person, if done, for example, in a context where the declarant is minimizing culpability or criminal exposure, can bear on whether the statement meets the Rule 804(b)(3) standard. The relevant inquiry, however — and one that is not furthered by clouding the waters with manufactured categories such as "collateral neutral" and "collateral self-serving," — must always be whether the particular remark at issue (and *not* the extended narrative) meets the standard set forth in the Rule.

Justice GINSBURG, with whom Justice BLACKMUN, Justice STEVENS, and Justice SOUTER join, concurring in part and concurring in the judgment.

I join Parts I, II-A, and II-B of the Court's opinion. I agree with the Court that Federal Rule of Evidence 804(b)(3) excepts from the general rule that hearsay statements are inadmissible only "those declarations or remarks within [a narrative] that are individually self-inculpatory." As the Court explains, the exception for statements against penal interest "does not allow admission of non-self-inculpatory statements, even if they are made within a broader narrative that is generally self-inculpatory"; the exception applies only to statements that are "sufficiently against the declarant's penal interest 'that a reasonable person in the declarant's position would not have made the statement unless believing it to be true.'"

Further, the Court recognizes the untrustworthiness of statements implicating another person. . . .

Unlike Justice O'Connor, however, I conclude that Reginald Harris' statements, as recounted by Drug Enforcement Administration (DEA) Special Agent Donald E. Walton, do not fit, even in part, within the exception described in Rule 804(b)(3), for Harris' arguably inculpatory statements are too closely intertwined with his self-serving declarations to be ranked as trustworthy. Harris was caught redhanded with 19 kilos of cocaine — enough to subject even a first-time offender to a minimum of 12 1/2 years' imprisonment. He could have denied knowing the drugs were in the car's trunk, but that strategy would have brought little prospect of thwarting a criminal prosecution. He therefore admitted involvement, but did so in a way that minimized his own role and shifted blame to petitioner Fredel Williamson (and a Cuban man named Shawn).

Most of Harris' statements to DEA Agent Walton focused on Williamson's, rather than Harris', conduct. . . .

To the extent some of these statements tended to incriminate Harris, they provided only marginal or cumulative evidence of his guilt. They project an image of a person acting not against his penal interest, but striving mightily to shift principal responsibility to someone else. . . .

[The concurring opinion of Justice KENNEDY, joined by Chief Justice REHNQUIST and Justice THOMAS, is omitted.]

Later in this chapter, we discuss the effect of the Sixth Amendment's Confrontation Clause on the use of hearsay against criminal defendants. Recent developments in the Supreme Court's view of the Confrontation Clause will make so-called testimonial statements by an unavailable declarant inadmissible against the defendant unless the defendant had an opportunity at an earlier time to cross-examine the declarant concerning the statement. Based on that rule, the government's use of the declaration against interest exception is now more restricted than at the time the Court decided *Williamson*. Under the very facts of *Williamson*, for example, Harris's statement to the DEA agent probably would be inadmissible because it was "testimonial" in nature, the defendants never had an opportunity to cross-examine Harris, and he refused to testify at the trial, rendering him unavailable for purposes of Rule 804(a).

Questions for Classroom Discussion

1. In Williamson v. United States, why did the Supreme Court hold that "neutral" statements made during the course of an otherwise self-incriminating statement were not within the scope of the declaration against interest exception?

2. Prosecution of Defendant for kidnapping. Defendant denies involvement. During their investigation, the police questioned Zed. At first, Zed denied having any knowledge of the crime. After being warned that his lack of cooperation might lead to his

being charged as a principal in the crime, Zed admitted involvement, but claimed his only role was to develop information about the victim's daily routine and to pass it along to Defendant, who Zed claimed actually captured and held the victim. Zed also told the police how and where Defendant captured the victim. Zed was killed in an auto accident before trial. The prosecution offers Zed's statements into evidence. Defendant objects on hearsay grounds. How should the court rule?

e. Comparison to Statements Offered Against a Party ("Admissions")

It is important not to confuse declarations against interest with statements offered against a party (Rule 801(d)(2) ("party admissions")). The latter rule applies only to statements of parties (or those speaking or acting on their behalf), and applies to any statement of a party, whether against the party's interest or in her favor. Even the personal knowledge requirement is not imposed on statements offered against a party. And Rule 801(d)(2) does not require unavailability of the declarant; indeed, by definition, the party will almost always be available.[36] The only limitation is that the statement of a party is admissible only when offered *against* the party.

Declarations against interest, on the other hand, must be against the interest of the declarant when made, need not be made by a party, and the declarant must be unavailable at the time her statement is introduced into evidence. Moreover, the statement is objectionable under Rule 602 if the declarant lacks personal knowledge of the facts contained in her statement. The declaration against interest exception to the hearsay rule is designed to permit the use of out-of-court statements only if they were against the interest of the declarant when they were made.

5. The Forfeiture by Wrongdoing Exception (Rule 804(b)(6))

> **FED. R. EVID. 804.   EXCEPTIONS TO THE RULE AGAINST HEARSAY — WHEN THE DECLARANT IS UNAVAILABLE AS A WITNESS . . .**

(b) The Exceptions. The following are not excluded by the rule against hearsay if the declarant is unavailable as a witness: . . .

(6) *Statement Offered Against a Party That Wrongfully Caused the Declarant's Unavailability.* A statement offered against a party that wrongfully caused — or

---

36. It is possible for a party to be "unavailable" for purposes of Rule 804(a). A criminal defendant who asserts her privilege not to be called as a witness by the prosecution would be "unavailable" for purposes of that rule. But a party's opponent would never have to resort to Rule 804 to present evidence of a party's out-of-court statement because such statements always qualify as party admissions.

acquiesced in wrongfully causing — the declarant's unavailability as a witness, and did so intending that result.

For more than 20 years after the Federal Rules went into effect, no new hearsay exceptions were added. Rule 804(b)(6) was added in 1997. The rationale for the "forfeiture by wrongdoing" exception is that parties should not be able to manipulate the trial process by wrongfully preventing an individual from testifying by making him unavailable or by acquiescing in such an arrangement undertaken by another person. Thus, this is more of a prophylactic rule than one recognizing the reliability of a particular class of hearsay.

The most obvious application of the exception is in the case where a criminal defendant arranges to murder a prosecution witness or to intimidate that person into refusing to testify. A party who would engage in such behavior is not entitled to the protection of the hearsay rule. This is a rule of forfeiture, not of waiver. The party does not agree to forgo the exercise of a right; the rule withdraws that right because of the party's conduct.

The principle that a party could forfeit the protection of the hearsay rule by procuring the unavailability of an adverse witness was recognized at common law in many jurisdictions, including all federal circuits that had addressed the issue prior to the enactment of Rule 804(b)(6). And the rule makes good sense. As one court stated, arranging the unavailability of a witness who will testify against you "strikes at the heart of the system of justice itself." United States v. Mastrangelo, 693 F.2d 269, 273 (2d Cir. 1982).

At the same time, courts need to apply the rule cautiously, as its effect might be to deprive a party of the constitutional right to confront the witnesses against her. This is particularly true with respect to situations in which the party did not directly procure the absence of the witness, but was only involved indirectly or tangentially. What, exactly, does the rule mean when it states that an absent declarant's statement may be offered against a party who "acquiesced" in wrongdoing that procured the declarant's absence? Is mere knowledge that someone else plans to procure the declarant's unavailability sufficient? Is it enough that the party and the person who made the declarant unavailable were both participants in a criminal conspiracy about which the declarant would have testified? The rule is too new to have been definitively interpreted. One court's struggle with this problem appears in the following case.

UNITED STATES v. CHERRY
217 F.3d 811 (10th Cir. 2000)

LUCERO, Circuit Judge.

This interlocutory appeal from the district court's grant of a motion to suppress out-of-court statements made by a murdered witness requires us to address the difficult question of how the doctrine of waiver by misconduct and Fed. R. Evid. 804(b)(6) apply to defendants who did not themselves directly procure the unavailability of a witness, but allegedly participated in a conspiracy, one of the members of which murdered the witness. . . . [W]e conclude that co-conspirators can be deemed to have waived confrontation and hearsay objections as a result of certain actions that are in furtherance, within the scope, and reasonably foreseeable as a necessary or natural consequence of an ongoing conspiracy. We therefore remand to the district court for findings under our newly-enunciated standard.

I

The government charged five defendants with involvement in a drug conspiracy: Joshua Price ("Joshua"), Michelle Cherry, LaDonna Gibbs, Teresa Price ("Price"), and Sonya Parker. Much of the evidence in their case came from a cooperating witness, Ebon Sekou Lurks. Prior to trial, however, Lurks was murdered. The government moved to admit out-of-court statements by Lurks, pursuant to Fed. R. Evid. 804(b)(6), on the grounds that the defendants wrongfully procured Lurks's unavailability.

In support of their motion, the government offered the following evidence. Lurks's ex-wife told Joshua of Lurks's cooperation with the government in retaliation for his obtaining custody of the Lurks's children. After this, Lurks reported being followed by Joshua and by Price. Approximately one week later, Price arranged to borrow a car from a friend, Beatrice Deffebaugh, explaining that she wanted to go on a date with another man without attracting her steady boyfriend's notice by using her usual car. So that Deffebaugh could pick up her children after work, Price loaned her another car, one that Deffebaugh described to an investigating agent as belonging to Gibbs. Joshua picked up Deffebaugh's car, which a witness noticed near Lurks's home at around 10 P.M. on January 28, 1998. One of Joshua's girlfriends, Kenesha Colbert, testified to receiving a call from him around 10:40 P.M. and hearing Price's voice singing in the background.

Around 11 P.M., several shots were fired in the vicinity of Lurks's home. Two witnesses saw a tall, thin black man (a description consistent with Joshua Price's appearance) chasing a short, stout black man (a description consistent with Lurks's appearance). Another witness stated she saw a car in the vicinity of Lurks's home, resembling the one borrowed by Joshua and Price, immediately after hearing shots fired. Additionally, one witness reported a license plate for the vehicle identical to that of the vehicle borrowed from Deffebaugh, save for the inversion of two digits. Police found Lurks's body not long after midnight. Price returned the borrowed car to her friend between midnight and 12:30 A.M. on January 29, 1998. Further investigation discovered physical evidence linking Joshua to the murder: "debris" on Joshua's tennis shoes matching Lurks's DNA.

The district court held that Joshua procured the absence of Lurks and hence Lurks's statements were admissible against him. It held, however, that there was insufficient evidence that Price procured Lurks's absence and "absolutely no evidence [that Cherry, Gibbs, and Parker] had actual knowledge of, agreed to or participated in the murder of . . . Lurks." . . . The district court therefore refused to find that those defendants had waived their Confrontation Clause and hearsay objections to the admission of Lurks's statements.

II

"We review a trial court's evidentiary decisions for abuse of discretion. However, we subject to de novo review a trial court's legal conclusions about the Federal Rules of Evidence and the Confrontation Clause." . . .

A. RULE 804(b)(6) AND THE WAIVER BY MISCONDUCT DOCTRINE

The Confrontation Clause of the Sixth Amendment protects a criminal defendant's "fundamental right" to confront the witnesses against him or her, including the right to cross-examine such witnesses. . . . "There is a presumption against the waiver of constitutional rights, and for a waiver to be effective it must be clearly established that there was an intentional relinquishment or abandonment of a known right or privilege." Brookhart v. Janis, 384 U.S. 1, 4, 86 S. Ct. 1245, 16 L. Ed. 2d 314 (1966) (internal quotations and citations omitted).

The Supreme Court has held repeatedly that a defendant's intentional misconduct can constitute waiver of Confrontation Clause rights. . . . We have applied this principle to conclude that a defendant can waive confrontation rights by threatening a witness's life. . . .

At issue in the instant case is whether Rule 804(b)(6) and the Confrontation Clause permit a finding of waiver based not on direct procurement but rather on involvement in a conspiracy, one of the members of which wrongfully procured a witness's unavailability. The government argues that under the principle of conspiratorial liability articulated in Pinkerton v. United States, 328 U.S. 640, 66 S. Ct. 1180, 90 L. Ed. 1489 (1946), defendants-appellees are responsible for the murder of Lurks as a foreseeable result of the drug conspiracy in which they were allegedly involved, and they thereby waive their Confrontation Clause and hearsay objections to his out-of-court statements. . . .

Turning to the language of Rule 804(b)(6), the use of the words "engaged or acquiesced in wrongdoing" lends support to the government's assertion that, at least for purposes of the hearsay rules, waiver can be imputed under an agency theory of responsibility to a defendant who "acquiesced" in the wrongful procurement of a witness's unavailability but did not actually "engage[]" in wrongdoing apart from the conspiracy itself. Fed. R. Evid. 804(b)(6). The proper scope of such imputed waiver as applied to a criminal defendant is best defined in the context of the Confrontation Clause doctrine of waiver by misconduct. While the Confrontation Clause and the hearsay rules are not coextensive, . . . it is beyond doubt that evidentiary rules cannot abrogate constitutional rights. We therefore read the plain language of Rule 804(b)(6) to permit the admission of those hearsay statements that would be admissible under the constitutional doctrine of waiver by misconduct, and hold that, in the context of criminal proceedings, the Rule permits the admission of hearsay statements by unavailable witnesses against defendants if those statements are otherwise admissible under the doctrine of waiver by misconduct. Our analysis of whether and under what circumstances waiver can be imputed under that doctrine and the acquiescence prong of the Rule is guided by two important but sometimes conflicting principles: the right to confrontation is "a fundamental right essential to a fair trial in a criminal prosecution," *Pointer*, 380 U.S. at 404, 85 S. Ct. 1065; and "courts will not suffer a party to profit by his own wrongdoing". . . .

B. *PINKERTON* CONSPIRATORIAL LIABILITY

. . . The *Pinkerton* Court held that evidence of direct participation in a substantive offense is not necessary for criminal liability under the principles holding conspirators liable for the substantive crimes of the conspiracy . . . .

This Circuit has . . . described *Pinkerton* liability as follows:

> During the existence of a conspiracy, each member of the conspiracy is legally responsible for the crimes of fellow conspirators. Of course, a conspirator is only responsible for the crimes of the conspirators that are committed in furtherance of the conspiracy. As stated by the Supreme Court, conspirators are responsible for crimes committed "within the scope of the unlawful project" and thus "reasonably foreseen as a necessary or natural consequence of the unlawful agreement."

United States v. Russell, 963 F.2d 1320, 1322 (10th Cir. 1992) (quoting *Pinkerton*, 328 U.S. at 646-648, 66 S. Ct. 1180). . . . To extend substantive *Pinkerton* liability in the manner urged by the government would apparently render every minor drug distribution co-conspirator, regardless of knowledge, the extent of the conspiracy, its history of violence, and like factors, liable for first-degree murder. Such a result appears incompatible with the due process limitations inherent in *Pinkerton*.

. . . We . . . agree . . . that *Pinkerton*'s formulation of conspiratorial liability is an appropriate mechanism for assessing whether the actions of another can be imputed to a defendant for purposes of determining whether that defendant has waived confrontation and hearsay objections. It would make little sense to limit forfeiture of a defendant's trial rights to a narrower set of facts than would be sufficient to sustain a conviction and corresponding loss of liberty. Therefore, we conclude that the acquiescence prong of Fed. R. Evid. 804(b)(6), consistent with the Confrontation Clause, permits consideration of a *Pinkerton* theory of conspiratorial responsibility in determining wrongful procurement of witness unavailability, and we turn to waiver-by-misconduct case law to define the precise contours of such responsibility.

C. CONSPIRATORIAL RESPONSIBILITY AND "ACQUIESCENCE" UNDER RULE 804(B)(6)

The court held that "[b]y analogy to *Pinkerton*, mere participation in a conspiracy does not suffice — yet participation may suffice when combined with findings that the wrongful act at issue was in furtherance and within the scope of an ongoing conspiracy and reasonably foreseeable as a natural or necessary consequence thereof. . . ." It then stated the following interpretation of the "acquiescence" aspect of Rule 804(b)(6): "A defendant may be deemed to have waived his or her Confrontation Clause rights (and, a fortiori, hearsay objections) if a preponderance of the evidence establishes one of the following circumstances: (1) he or she participated directly in planning or procuring the declarant's unavailability through wrongdoing . . . ; or (2) the wrongful procurement was in furtherance, within the scope, and reasonably foreseeable as a necessary or natural consequence of an ongoing conspiracy. . . ."

D. APPLICATION OF RULE 804(B)(6)

We therefore examine the district court's order in light of our newly-elucidated standard. We conclude the district court did not abuse its discretion in holding that the government failed to show by a preponderance of the evidence that any of the defendants directly participated in the execution of the murder, but remand for application of the planning and *Pinkerton* tests. We take this opportunity to note that, even if the district court finds the standard for waiver by acquiescence to be met for some or all appellees, and thereby their Confrontation Clause and hearsay objections to be forfeited, the district court is still free to consider concerns of weighing prejudice against probative value under Fed. R. Evid. 403.

1. Scope of Conspiracy, Furtherance, and Reasonable Foreseeability as a Necessary and Natural Consequence

Relying on *White*, 838 F. Supp. at 618, the district court concluded that "the mere fact [that defendants] may have participated in the drug conspiracy did not constitute a waiver of [their] constitutional confrontation rights." . . . This statement is correct, as far as it goes. However, today we hold that participation in an ongoing drug conspiracy *may* constitute a waiver of constitutional confrontation rights if the following additional circumstances are present: the wrongdoing leading to the unavailability of the witness was in furtherance of and within the scope of the drug conspiracy, and such wrongdoing was reasonably foreseeable as a "necessary or natural" consequence of the conspiracy. We therefore remand to the district court for findings on the *Pinkerton* factors as to Lurks's murder: whether it was in furtherance and within the scope of the conspiracy, and whether it was reasonably foreseeable as a necessary or natural consequence of that conspiracy. We note that the scope of the conspiracy is not necessarily limited to a primary goal — such as bank robbery — but can also include secondary goals relevant to the evasion of apprehension and prosecution for that goal — such as escape, or, by analogy, obstruction of justice. . . . We further reiterate that, under *Pinkerton*, a defendant is not responsible for the acts of co-conspirators if that defendant meets the burden of proving he or she took affirmative steps to withdraw from the conspiracy before those acts were committed. . . .

We note that the district court found "there is absolutely no evidence" that defendants Cherry, Gibbs, and Parker (although not Teresa Price) "had actual knowledge of, agreed to or participated in the murder of Ebon Sekou Lurks." . . . After complete review of the record, we conclude that this finding of fact is not clearly erroneous. It does not, however, foreclose the possibility of waiver under a *Pinkerton* theory. Actual knowledge is not required for conspiratorial waiver by misconduct if the elements of *Pinkerton* — scope, furtherance, and reasonable foreseeability as a necessary or natural consequence — are satisfied. . . . A defendant's actual knowledge of a co-conspirator's intent to murder a witness in order to prevent discovery or prosecution of the conspiracy may prove relevant to those elements.

2. Planning

Although the district court found the evidence was "insufficient to show that by a preponderance of the evidence the Defendant Teresa Price procured the absence of Ebon Sekou Lurks," it did not discuss whether the evidence that she obtained the car used in Lurks's murder under false pretenses, combined with her apparent proximity to Joshua around the time of the murder, would be sufficient circumstantial evidence to support a finding that she participated in the planning of the murder. . . . We therefore remand for specific findings on whether the government can meet its burden of showing that Price participated in the planning of Lurks's murder so as to permit a finding of waiver by misconduct.

III

To summarize, we remand to the district court for findings on the following issues: (1) did Teresa Price participate in the planning or carrying out of Lurks's murder by Joshua Price; (2) was Joshua Price's murder of Lurks within the scope, in furtherance, and reasonably foreseeable as a necessary or natural consequence, of an ongoing drug distribution conspiracy involving the defendants? The district court's order is REVERSED and REMANDED for proceedings consistent with this opinion.

Further Reading: Leonard Birdsong, *The Exclusion of Hearsay Through Forfeiture by Wrongdoing — Old Wine in a New Bottle — Solving the Mystery of the Codification of the Concept into Federal Rule 804(b)(6)*, 80 Neb. L. Rev. 891-919 (2001).

Questions for Classroom Discussion

1. Negligence action by Plaintiff against Defendant arising from an automobile collision. Witness observed the collision, and Plaintiff plans to call Witness to testify at trial. Prior to trial, Defendant pays Witness to "disappear" for a while, making Witness unavailable to testify at the trial. Plaintiff wishes to offer into evidence Witness's statement to a police officer the day after the accident, in which Witness said that Defendant ran a red light and struck Plaintiff. Defendant objects on hearsay grounds. How should the court rule?

2. Prosecution of Defendant for the murder of Victim. The prosecution alleges that Defendant killed Victim to prevent her from testifying at Defendant's racketeering trial. Defendant denies having anything to do with Victim's death. Before she was killed, Victim accused Defendant of being a "big time mobster who is involved in all kinds of illegal activities." The prosecution wishes to offer Victim's statement into evidence at the murder trial. Defendant objects. How should the court rule?

3. Prosecution of Defendant for the murder of Victim. An intruder killed Victim as he slept in his home. Defendant denies being the intruder. A few days before Victim was killed, he told a friend, "Defendant is going to kill me." The prosecution offers Victim's statement, and Defendant objects on hearsay grounds. How should the court rule?

4. Prosecution of Defendant for bank robbery. A few days before the trial was to begin, Zed, one of Defendant's co-defendants, killed

(continued)

Witness, a bank customer who was present during the robbery. Zed did this to prevent Witness from testifying against the defendants. Defendant knew nothing of Zed's plan to kill Witness before Zed carried it out, though Defendant did not inform the police of Zed's act after Defendant learned of what Zed had done. The prosecution wishes to offer in evidence Witness's statement to the police in which she gave a description of the robbers. Defendant objects on hearsay grounds. How should the court rule?

5. Same case. Suppose that Defendant knew of Zed's intention before Zed acted, and that Defendant attempted without success to talk Zed out of killing Witness. When it was clear that Zed would not change his mind, Defendant told him, "Do what you want. I can't stop you." Defendant objects on hearsay grounds to admission of Witness's statement to the police. How should the court rule?

6. Prosecution of Defendant for involvement in an ongoing drug distribution scheme. Before the authorities arrested Defendant and others, Witness, a rival drug dealer, threatened to go to the police and tell them about the operation in which Defendant allegedly participated. To prevent Witness from doing this, Zed, one of Defendant's alleged co-conspirators, without the knowledge of the others, threatened to kill Witness if he went to the police or cooperated in any way with a possible prosecution of Defendant's group. At trial, Witness refuses to testify despite a court order to do so. The prosecution wishes to offer into evidence a statement by Witness to a friend in which Witness claimed Defendant was a drug distributor. Defendant objects on hearsay grounds. How should the court rule?

O.   THE RESIDUAL EXCEPTION (RULE 807)

FED. R. EVID. 807.   RESIDUAL EXCEPTION

(a) In General. Under the following circumstances, a hearsay statement is not excluded by the rule against hearsay even if the statement is not specifically covered by a hearsay exception in Rule 803 or 804:

(1) the statement has equivalent circumstantial guarantees of trustworthiness;

(2) it is offered as evidence of a material fact;

(3) it is more probative on the point for which it is offered than any other evidence that the proponent can obtain through reasonable efforts; and

(4) admitting it will best serve the purposes of these rules and the interests of justice.

(b) Notice. The statement is admissible only if, before the trial or hearing, the proponent gives an adverse party reasonable notice of the intent to offer the statement and its particulars, including the declarant's name and address, so that the party has a fair opportunity to meet it.

1.   Background

As this chapter has shown, the approach taken by courts and codifiers to the hearsay rule has traditionally been one of the slow accumulation of exceptions (and in the case of the Federal Rules, of exemptions as well as exceptions). Courts and codifiers created specific exceptions when certain categories of hearsay were found to be particularly reliable, necessary, or both. We can call this the "categorical approach" to hearsay: A statement that qualifies as hearsay is inadmissible unless it meets all the requirements of an exception that describes a specific category of hearsay.

   This is not the only way the hearsay rule could have developed. For example, the rule could have been crafted as one of discretionary exclusion, providing that hearsay is inadmissible unless the court finds that it is particularly reliable, necessary to the case, or both. A case-by-case decision about admissibility has its disadvantages, the most important of which are the lack of predictability and consistency. On the other hand, a flexible rule has the advantage of allowing the court to admit evidence when it would help lead to accurate fact-finding. But this is not the way the hearsay rule developed, and courts got by for quite a long time applying a categorical approach.

   The drafters of the Federal Rules originally proposed a discretionary approach to hearsay, which listed traditional exceptions as simply examples of trustworthy statements and gave the trial court the authority to admit other hearsay that the court determined to be sufficiently reliable. In doing so, the drafters were undoubtedly influenced by Judge Wisdom's opinion in Dallas County v. Commercial Union Assurance Co., 286 F.2d 388 (5th Cir. 1961), in which the court held that an old newspaper account of a courthouse fire was admissible even though it did not fit within an existing common law exception to the hearsay rule. Judge Wisdom wrote of the "two requisites" for the creation of hearsay exceptions: necessity and trustworthiness:

> If they are worth their salt, evidentiary rules are to aid the search for truth. [Federal Rule of Civil Procedure] 43(a) . . . carries out that purpose by enabling federal courts to apply a liberal, flexible rule for the admissibility of evidence, unencumbered by common law archaisms. . . .
>
>   The first of the two requisites is necessity. As to necessity, Wigmore points out this requisite means that unless the hearsay statement is admitted, the facts it brings out may otherwise be lost, either because the person whose assertion is offered may be dead or unavailable, or because the assertion is of such a nature that one could not expect to obtain evidence of the same value from the same person or from other sources. Wigmore, § 1421 (3rd ed.). "In effect, Wigmore says that, as the word necessity is here used, it is not to be interpreted as uniformly demanding a showing of total inaccessibility of firsthand evidence as a condition precedent to the acceptance of a particular piece of hearsay, but that necessity exists where otherwise great practical inconvenience would be experienced in making the desired proof. (Wigmore, 3rd ed., Vol. V, sec. 1421; Vol. VI, sec. 1702). . . . If it were otherwise, the result would be that the exception created to

the hearsay rule would thereby be mostly, if not completely, destroyed." United States v. Aluminum Co. of America, D.C. 1940, 35 F. Supp. 820, 823.

The fire referred to in the newspaper account occurred fifty-eight years before the trial of this case. Any witness who saw that fire with sufficient understanding to observe it and describe it accurately, would have been older than a young child at the time of the fire. We may reasonably assume that at the time of the trial he was either dead or his faculties were dimmed by the passage of fifty-eight years. It would have been burdensome, but not impossible, for the defendant to have discovered the name of the author of the article (although it had no by-line) and, perhaps, to have found an eye-witness to the fire. But it is improbable — so it seems to us — that any witness could have been found whose recollection would have been accurate at the time of the trial of this case. And it seems impossible that the testimony of any witness would have been as accurate and as reliable as the statement of facts in the contemporary newspaper article.

The rationale behind the "ancient documents" exception is applicable here: after a long lapse of time, ordinary evidence regarding signatures or handwriting is virtually unavailable, and it is therefore permissible to resort to circumstantial evidence. Thus, in Trustees of German Township, Montgomery County v. Farmers & Citizens Savings Bank Co., Ohio Com. Pl. 1953, 113 N.E.2d 409, 412, *affirmed* Ohio App., 115 N.E.2d 690, the court admitted as ancient documents newspapers eighty years old containing notices of advertisements for bids relating to the town hall: "Such exhibits, by reason of age, alone, and unquestioned authenticity, qualify as ancient documents." The ancient documents rule applies to documents a generation or more in age. Here, the Selma Times-Journal article is almost two generations old. The principle of necessity, not requiring absolute impossibility or total inaccessibility of first-hand knowledge, is satisfied by the practicalities of the situation before us.

The second requisite for admission of hearsay evidence is trustworthiness. According to Wigmore, there are three sets of circumstances when hearsay is trustworthy enough to serve as a practicable substitute for the ordinary test of cross-examination: "Where the circumstances are such that a sincere and accurate statement would naturally be uttered, and no plan of falsification be formed; where, even though a desire to falsify might present itself, other considerations, such as the danger of easy detection or the fear of punishment, would probably counteract its force; where the statement was made under such conditions of publicity that an error, if it had occurred, would probably have been detected and corrected." 5 Wigmore, Evidence, § 1422 (3rd ed.). These circumstances fit the instant case.

There is no procedural canon against the exercise of common sense in deciding the admissibility of hearsay evidence. In 1901 Selma, Alabama, was a small town. Taking a common sense view of this case, it is inconceivable to us that a newspaper reporter in a small town would report there was a fire in the dome of the new courthouse — if there had been no fire. He is without motive to falsify, and a false report would have subjected the newspaper and him to embarrassment in the community. The usual dangers inherent in hearsay evidence, such as lack of memory, faulty narration, intent to influence the court proceedings, and plain lack of truthfulness are not present here. To our minds, the article published in the Selma Morning-Times on the day of the fire is more reliable, more trustworthy, more competent evidence than the testimony of a witness called to the stand fifty-eight years later.

We hold, that in matters of local interest, when the fact in question is of such a public nature it would be generally known throughout the community, and when the questioned fact occurred so long ago that the testimony of an eye-witness would probably be less trustworthy than a contemporary newspaper account, a federal court, under Rule 43(a), may relax the exclusionary rules to the extent of admitting the newspaper article in evidence. We do not characterize this newspaper as a "business record," nor as an "ancient document," nor as any other readily identifiable and happily tagged species of hearsay exception. It is admissible because it is necessary and trustworthy, relevant and material, and its admission is within the trial judge's exercise of discretion in holding the hearing within reasonable bounds.

Later drafts of the Federal Rules retreated from the discretionary position, and took what the drafters thought was a modest step away from the categorical approach by adopting new, flexible, "residual" exceptions.[37] The Advisory Committee explained its rationale:

> The preceding 23 exceptions of Rule 803 and the first [four] exceptions of Rule 804(b) . . . are designed to take full advantage of the accumulated wisdom and experience of the past in dealing with hearsay. It would, however, be presumptuous to assume that all possible desirable exceptions to the hearsay rule have been catalogued and to pass the hearsay rule to oncoming generations as a closed system. [The residual exceptions] are accordingly included.

Fed. R. Evid. 803 Advisory Committee's Note. The Advisory Committee did not intend for the residual exceptions to open the hearsay floodgates. The Committee wrote that the exceptions "do not contemplate an unfettered exercise of judicial discretion, but they do provide for treating new and presently unanticipated situations which demonstrate a trustworthiness within the spirit of the specifically stated exceptions." *Id.*

Congress was clearly troubled by the proposed residual exceptions. The House Judiciary Committee at first deleted the residual exceptions, fearing they would "inject[] too much uncertainty into the law of evidence and impair[] the ability of practitioners to prepare for trial. . . . The Committee believed that if additional hearsay exceptions are to be created, they should be by amendments to the Rules, not on a case-by-case basis." House Comm. on Judiciary, Fed. Rules of Evidence, H.R. Rep. No. 650, 93d Cong., 1st Sess., p. 5 (1973). The Senate Judiciary Committee did not favor eliminating the residual exceptions entirely, but narrowed the Supreme Court's proposed draft so as to limit the exceptions to "certain exceptional circumstances where evidence is found by a court to have guarantees of trustworthiness equivalent to or exceeding the guarantees reflected by the presently listed exceptions, and to have a high degree of probativeness and necessity. . . ." Senate Comm. on Judiciary, Fed. Rules of Evidence, S. Rep. No. 1277, 93d Cong., 2d Sess., p. 118 (1974). Emphasizing the limited nature of the residual exceptions, the Senate Judiciary Committee wrote:

> It is intended that the residual hearsay exceptions will be used very rarely, and only in exceptional circumstances. The committee does not intend to establish a broad license for trial judges to admit hearsay statements that do not fit within one of the other exceptions contained in Rules 803 and 804(b). The residual exceptions are not meant to authorize major judicial revisions of the hearsay rule, including its present exceptions. Such major revisions are best accomplished by legislative action.

---

37. Originally, the Federal Rules contained two identical exceptions, one numbered Rule 803(24) and the other numbered Rule 804(b)(5). In 1997, these rules were eliminated and a single rule with the same language was substituted as Rule 807.

Id. Congress ultimately adopted the Senate view. No substantive changes have been made to the language of the rules. As written, the residual exception allows courts to admit a hearsay statement not covered by the other exceptions if admitting that statement will serve "the interests of justice." When considering whether to admit evidence under the residual exception, a court's decision should be guided by the necessity for and trustworthiness of the evidence. The residual exception, however, is only meant to be applied in exceptional situations.

2. *Requirements for Application of the Residual Exception*

The residual exception will not apply unless the court makes four specific preliminary findings and unless the party planning to offer hearsay under the exception has provided proper notice to the opponent.

Reliability.   First, the evidence is admissible if the "statement [is] not specifically covered by a hearsay exception in Rule 803 or 804 and "it [has] equivalent circumstantial guarantees of trustworthiness." This is a difficult element to understand and apply. Though there is room for disagreement as to the specifics, all agree that the nearly 30 specific categories of statements contained in Rules 803 and 804 have vastly different levels of trustworthiness. We have already seen, for example, that the trustworthiness of excited utterances and dying declarations is highly suspect. Some declarations against interest, on the other hand, are particularly trustworthy, as are some types of business and public records as well as statements made for purposes of medical treatment (though perhaps not diagnosis). Other categories of hearsay admit evidence that falls anywhere on the spectrum from marginally trustworthy to extremely trustworthy.

What benchmark, then, is the court to use when determining whether a particular item of evidence offered under the residual exception has "equivalent circumstantial guarantees of trustworthiness"? Requiring that the evidence be as trustworthy as the most trustworthy evidence covered by a Rule 803 or Rule 804 exception seems unduly restrictive, particularly since evidence that is far less trustworthy is routinely admitted under other exceptions. On the other hand, admitting evidence that is only as reliable as evidence meeting the requirements of the least reliable category might make too much evidence admissible.

In the end, any effort to define the test in the abstract is probably pointless. There is enormous room for disagreement about the relative trustworthiness of evidence admitted under the various exceptions. At most, the requirement serves as a reminder to the court to inquire into the trustworthiness of the evidence at issue, and to refuse to admit evidence that appears, under the circumstances, to be lacking in trustworthiness.

Materiality.   The second requirement is that the statement must be "offered as evidence of a material fact." It is doubtful that this prerequisite adds anything to the requirement that any evidence offered at trial be logically relevant and that it be offered to prove a fact that is properly provable in the case. If Congress intended anything more in adding this requirement to the Supreme Court's draft of the rule, perhaps it is that the evidence must be offered to prove a fact that is of particular importance to the case. If so, the requirement is hardly necessary, as it is doubtful that a party will often attempt to jump through the hoops otherwise set up by the residual exception unless the evidence bears on an important issue.

Probative value. The third requirement is that the evidence must be "more probative on the point for which it is offered than any other evidence that the proponent can obtain through reasonable efforts." This prerequisite for admission establishes a meaningful barrier to admission because it imposes on the proponent the obligation to use reasonable efforts to find other admissible evidence to prove the fact and then to demonstrate why the hearsay in question is more probative than the other evidence. Though what is reasonable will depend on the circumstances of each case, the drafters clearly intended that the proponent's burden not be taken lightly.

Interests of justice. The fourth requirement is that the proponent must persuade the court that "admitting it will best serve the purposes of these rules and the interests of justice." This is an amorphous requirement, but not entirely without standards. Rule 102, for example, states that the court must construe the rules "to administer every proceeding fairly, eliminate unjustifiable expense and delay, and promote the development of evidence law, to the end of ascertaining the truth and securing a just determination." Rule 403 requires the court to consider the dangers of unfair prejudice and jury confusion, and Rule 611(a) instructs the court to "protect witnesses from harassment or undue embarrassment."[38] These rules are not mere aspirational verbiage. They require the court to administer the trial with the goals of fairness, efficiency, truth-determination, and justice in mind, and to consider the effects its evidence rulings might have on witnesses and on the continued development of the law. These considerations are especially important when construing rules as vaguely written as the residual exception.

Notice. Finally, the residual exception contains a specific notice requirement. Evidence may only be admitted under the rule if "the proponent gives an adverse party reasonable notice of the intent to offer the statement and its particulars, including the declarant's name and address, so that the party has a fair opportunity to meet it." Pretrial notice serves the goal of fairness by giving the opponent an opportunity to investigate the statement and the declarant, and perhaps to develop evidence to rebut the statement. In practice, however, courts have not always followed the strict requirements of the rule. It is not uncommon, for example, for courts to admit the statement if the proponent gives notice sufficiently in advance of offering the evidence to permit the opponent to prepare to meet the evidence, even if the notice was given after the trial began. This violates the rule's plain language, of course. Perhaps it is justified in some situations, such as when the proponent reasonably did not learn of the evidence until the trial had begun. Still, courts must exercise caution

38. Rules 403 and 611 also repeat some of the concerns encompassed within the language of Rule 102. Rule 403 mentions avoidance of "undue delay, wasting time, or needlessly presenting cumulative evidence," and Rule 611(a) instructs the court to control the mode and order of witness interrogation and presentation of evidence to "make those procedures effective for determining the truth" and "avoid wasting time."

before they violate the plain language of the rule. If situations exist in which pretrial notice should not be required, perhaps the best solution would be to amend the rule to describe those situations.

3. *The "Near Miss" Problem*

One of the most controversial issues surrounding the application of the residual exception concerns the following question: What if the evidence at issue fits very generally into a category covered by one of the Rule 803 or Rule 804 exceptions, but fails to satisfy one or more of the prerequisites for admission under that exception? May the court admit the evidence under the residual exception, or is the evidence simply inadmissible? To some extent, the resolution of this question hangs on the meaning of the phrase "[a] statement . . . not specifically covered by a hearsay exception in Rule 803 or 804" in the residual exception. This phrase is subject to at least two reasonable interpretations. One interpretation holds that the residual exception may be used to admit a statement that is the *type* covered by one of the exceptions in Rules 803 and 804, but that fails to meet all the requirements of that rule. The other interpretation holds that the residual exception may only be used for evidence that is not of a type covered by one of the exceptions in Rules 803 and 804. Unfortunately, neither Rule 807 nor the official commentary provides clues to the drafters' intentions.

Consider the following example:

> Negligence action arising from the collision of Plaintiff's sports car and Defendant's SUV at a remote intersection controlled only by stop signs. Each party contends that the other ran the stop sign, and the physical evidence is ambiguous. To prove that Defendant ran the stop sign, Plaintiff calls Witness, the only other person on the scene at the time, and who observed the collision. Two or three minutes after the collision, Witness called a friend and told her that she had just seen a "huge SUV" run a stop sign and strike a "small sports car." At trial, Witness does not remember which car ran the light, and Plaintiff is unable to refresh her recollection. Plaintiff now wishes to call the friend to testify about Witness's statement. Defendant objects on hearsay grounds.

Witness's statement to the friend is hearsay because it asserts that the SUV ran the stop sign and hit the sports car, and it is offered to prove those very facts. The statement does not qualify as an excited utterance under Rule 803(2) because the facts do not demonstrate that Witness made the statement under the stress of excitement caused by this undoubtedly startling event. The statement is also not admissible as a present sense impression under Rule 803(1) because Witness did not make the statement while observing the event, and the passage of even two or three minutes is probably sufficient to permit some reflection, thus reducing the supposed source of trustworthiness. Had Witness made a written record of her observation while the matter was fresh in her mind, that writing probably would be admissible as Witness's recorded recollection under Rule 803(5), but she did not do so. Does the court have the authority to admit the statement under the residual exception?

Note that the statement is probably reliable. Given the great difference between the two vehicles, it is not very likely that Witness would become confused about which one ran the stop sign (assuming Witness was in a good position to view both vehicles as they approached the intersection). In the two or three minutes that passed between the accident and Witness's statement, Witness is very unlikely to have forgotten which vehicle ran the stop sign. Witness's statement describing the vehicle that ran the stop sign was unambiguous in context because the two vehicles were so different. The witness had no connection with either party that might cause her to slant her testimony. And finally, the witness is available to be cross-examined concerning her memory of other aspects of the accident.

There is probably great need for the statement as well. Given the ambiguity of the physical evidence (the condition of the vehicles, skid marks, and so forth), the only other evidence pointing to which vehicle ran the light is each party's statement, and both are of questionable value because of the parties' self-interest. Witness's statement is probably the best evidence available on this crucial — and likely dispositive — question.

It is also easy to argue that the interests of justice require admission of the statement. If it is trustworthy, the jury's ability to render an accurate verdict might well hinge on its hearing Witness's statement, and even though Witness no longer remembers which vehicle ran the stop sign, she is available to answer other questions about the accident.

The circumstances appear strongly to suggest the evidence ought to be admitted. But a court may only reach this conclusion if the residual exception authorizes it to do so. If a court lacks the authority to admit evidence that falls within a type of statement generally covered by an exception in Rule 803 or Rule 804, but which fails to meet one or more requirements of either rule, the evidence should be excluded. If the court has authority to admit near misses under the residual exception, the court should admit the evidence. The resolution of this problem depends on which interpretation of the residual exception is more appropriate.

In a nutshell, the argument that the rule should be interpreted to apply only to statements of a general type not covered by the Rules 803 and 804 exceptions is as follows: The exceptions in Rules 803 and 804 are based on experience in the admission and exclusion of hearsay evidence. Each requirement for application of the rule is an important part of the basis on which the statement is deemed reliable, necessary, or both. If a statement satisfies all prerequisites for one of those exceptions, experience therefore tells us it should be admitted. If a statement fails to satisfy one or more of the prerequisites, it should be excluded because part of the basis for concluding that it is reliable or necessary is missing. To put it simply, the hearsay exceptions do not work like a game of darts. Whereas in darts one may still receive points for a shot that misses the bull's-eye (as long as the shot lands somewhere on the target), a statement that fails to hit the bull's-eye (meet all requirements) of a hearsay exception is inadmissible. A near miss is a miss.

The argument that a near miss can still qualify for admission under the residual exception is as follows: The main purpose of Rule 807 is to admit reliable and necessary hearsay that would be excluded otherwise. The mere fact that hearsay in a particular instance is of a type covered by one of the exceptions in Rules 803 and 804, but does not qualify, is not sufficient to conclude that in all instances, the evidence is so unreliable or so unnecessary that it must be excluded. Rather than exclude the evidence, the interests of justice and the achievement of accurate verdicts can be served better by allowing the court to determine admissibility on a case-by-case basis. In other words, there should be an analogy between the operation of the hearsay exceptions and a game of darts.

It is possible to find court decisions supporting both positions on the near miss problem. Some courts exclude near miss evidence, while others make the decision on a case-by-case basis. To return to our auto accident hypothetical, some courts would hold that because Rules 803(1) and 803(2) govern the admissibility of contemporaneous statements, and because the statement in the hypothetical is a type of contemporaneous statement, it must be analyzed according to the requirements of those exceptions. In this situation, the evidence fails to satisfy the requirements of either exception. Thus, the court must exclude it.

Courts taking the opposite position might reason that the statement in our hypothetical does not lose all of its trustworthiness merely because it was made two or three minutes after the accident rather than while the accident was taking place or within a few seconds after it occurred. As discussed above, the statement is probably trustworthy, much needed to prove the crucial facts of the case, and the interests of justice would counsel admission. A court applying the looser interpretation of Rule 807 might well decide to admit the statement.

Nowhere have the two positions on the near miss problem come into sharper focus than in connection with the admission in a criminal trial of a person's prior grand jury testimony. Grand jury witnesses rarely can be cross-examined, and those under investigation by the grand jury have neither a right to be present for the testimony of witnesses nor a right to be represented by counsel at the proceedings. Because the defendant in a criminal trial had no opportunity to cross-examine witnesses who testified before the grand jury, their testimony may not be admitted under the former testimony exception found in Rule 804(b)(1).

Courts taking the view that a near miss is simply a miss hold that because grand jury testimony is former testimony, its admissibility is governed by the former testimony exception. And because it fails to satisfy the requirements of that exception, it is inadmissible. Courts taking the view that a near miss can sometimes be counted as a "hit" hold that grand jury testimony is admissible if it satisfies the requirements of Rule 807 (the residual exception), even if it does not satisfy the requirements of the former testimony exception.

However one views the near miss problem in general, the Supreme Court's recent decisions interpreting the Sixth Amendment's Confrontation Clause, which we discuss later in this chapter, make clear that the grand jury testimony of a witness whom the defendant did not have a prior opportunity to cross-examine is inadmissible unless the grand jury witness testifies at the trial.

4. Is the Residual Exception Party-Neutral?

With few exceptions, the evidence rules are written in a party-neutral way. They are not written so as to allow one party, but not the other, to offer a particular kind of evidence. Hearsay exceptions, for example, do not apply only to prosecutors, or to civil plaintiffs. Thus, an excited utterance may be offered by any party, and the same is true of evidence satisfying the other hearsay exceptions. The rules operate symmetrically.

This, at least, is the theory. In practice, the situation is quite different. Consider party admissions in criminal cases. It is simple for the prosecution to offer evidence of the defendant's statements. But how often will statements by the "government" be relevant and admissible as party admissions? Though an attorney for the prosecuting authority sometimes may stand in for the government for purposes of party admissions under Rules 801(d)(2)(C) and (D), a prosecuting attorney's statements will not often be relevant to an issue in a criminal case (and usually will not be based on personal knowledge). Therefore, it is not surprising that although the party admissions rule is written in neutral language, it is far more often of use to prosecutors than to criminal defendants.

What about evidence offered under the residual exception? This rule, as well, is written in party-neutral language, and none of its foundational requirements appear to favor one party over the other in either civil or criminal cases. In practice, though, the government in criminal cases has been far more successful than criminal defendants in making use of the residual exception. That may change because of the Supreme Court's recent Confrontation Clause jurisprudence, but it is difficult to resist the conclusion that the prosecution will often have the advantage when it comes to making use of the residual exception as well as the other hearsay exceptions.

Further Reading: Edward J. Imwinkelried, *The Scope of the Residual Hearsay Exceptions in the Federal Rules of Evidence*, 15 S.D. L. Rev. 239 (1978); Randolph N. Jonakait, *The Subversion of the Hearsay Rule: The Residual Hearsay Exceptions, Circumstantial Guarantees of Trustworthiness, and Grand Jury Testimony*, 36 Case W. Res. L. Rev. 431 (1986); Myrna S. Raeder, *The Effect of the Catchalls on Criminal Defendants: Little Red Riding Hood Meets the Hearsay Wolf and Is Devoured*, 25 Loy. L.A. L. Rev. 925 (1992); Joseph W. Rand, Note, *The Residual Exceptions to the Hearsay Rule: The Futile and Misguided Attempt to Restrain Judicial Discretion*, 80 Geo. L.J. 873 (1992); David E. Sonenshein, *The Residual Exceptions to the Federal Hearsay Rule: Two Exceptions in Search of a Rule*, 57 N.Y.U. L. Rev. 867 (1982).

Questions for Classroom Discussion

1. Product liability action by Plaintiff against Defendant, an automobile manufacturer. Plaintiff claims that Husband, her husband, was driving a new car manufactured by Defendant when the car's defectively designed steering mechanism failed, causing him to lose control and crash. Husband died from injuries he sustained in the crash, but lived long enough to tape-record a description of what happened. Plaintiff offers the tape recording into evidence. Assume that Zed was also in the car with Husband when the accident occurred, and that the car, though badly damaged, has been preserved. Defendant makes a hearsay objection to the admission of the tape recording. How should the court rule?

2. Same facts. Assume, however, that Husband was alone in the car and that the car was damaged so badly in the accident that it is not

(continued)

possible for experts to determine what happened. Plaintiff asks the court to admit Husband's tape under Rule 807, the residual exception. Defendant objects on hearsay grounds. How should the court rule?

3. Prosecution of Defendant for possession of cocaine with intent to distribute. The grand jury indicted Defendant after hearing the testimony of Zed, who had been granted transactional immunity before giving her grand jury testimony. In that testimony, Zed admitted that she conspired with Defendant to obtain and sell a large quantity of cocaine, and also testified about important details of the planning and execution of the crime. Before the trial, Zed died in an automobile accident. At trial, the prosecution offers Zed's grand jury testimony. Defendant objects on hearsay grounds. How should the court rule?

4. Same facts, except suppose that in her grand jury testimony, Zed declared that she knew a great deal about Defendant's activities, and that she was certain Defendant had nothing to do with the crime. Zed died before trial. Defendant wishes to offer Zed's grand jury testimony. The prosecution objects on hearsay grounds. How should the court rule?

P. MISCELLANEOUS EXCEPTIONS

We have already discussed the most commonly used hearsay exceptions. Most of the remaining exceptions are relatively minor and technical; we give them brief treatment.

1. *Public Records of Vital Statistics (Rule 803(9)), Records of Religious Organizations Concerning Personal or Family History (Rule 803(11)), and Certificates of Marriage, Baptism, and Similar Ceremonies (Rule 803(12))*

FED. R. EVID. 803. EXCEPTIONS TO THE RULE AGAINST HEARSAY—REGARDLESS OF WHETHER THE DECLARANT IS AVAILABLE AS A WITNESS

The following are not excluded by the rule against hearsay, regardless of whether the declarant is available as a witness:

(9) *Public Records of Vital Statistics.* A record of a birth, death, or marriage, if reported to a public office in accordance with a legal duty.

(11) *Records of Religious Organizations Concerning Personal or Family History.* A statement of birth, legitimacy, ancestry, marriage, divorce, death, relationship by blood or marriage, or similar facts of personal or family history, contained in a regularly kept record of a religious organization.

(12) *Certificates of Marriage, Baptism, and Similar Ceremonies.* A statement of fact contained in a certificate:

    (A) made by a person who is authorized by a religious organization or by law to perform the act certified;

    (B) attesting that the person performed a marriage or similar ceremony or administered a sacrament; and

    (C) purporting to have been issued at the time of the act or within a reasonable time after it.

All three of these exceptions cover documents related to personal history, including records of births, deaths, and marriages.

The first exception covers records of birth, death, and marriage made to a public office pursuant to a legal duty to report. The exception rests primarily on a foundation of trustworthiness. This is especially true since most such records are filed by doctors, hospitals, religious authorities, and others who have no motive to lie. The exception also exists for reasons of efficiency, as it makes the proof of an important fact simple. Some such records can even be self-authenticating under Rule 902(4), (8), or (11). Finally, the exception has a basis in necessity because in some instances, the best (or only) available evidence of a person's birth, death, or marriage is in a document filed with a public authority.

Rule 803(11) (records of religious organizations concerning personal or family history) covers similar subject matter and has a similar basis. It applies to "[a] statement of birth, legitimacy, ancestry, marriage, divorce, death, relationship by blood or marriage, or similar facts of personal or family history" if part of a "regularly kept record of a religious organization." Like businesses, such organizations have a motive to keep accurate records. Indeed, the beliefs of some religions require the keeping of such records.

Rule 803(12) (certificates of marriage, baptism, and similar ceremonies) allows the court to admit certificates made by clergy, public officials, and other authorized persons that purport to record the occurrence of a marriage or other ceremony or sacrament. The rule requires that the certificate purports to have been "issued at the time of the act or within a reasonable time after it." Again, trustworthiness is the primary basis for the exception.

2. Family Records (Rule 803(13)) and Statements of Personal or Family History (Rule 804(b)(4))

> **FED. R. EVID. 803.** **EXCEPTIONS TO THE RULE AGAINST HEARSAY—REGARDLESS OF WHETHER THE DECLARANT IS AVAILABLE AS A WITNESS**

The following are not excluded by the rule against hearsay, regardless of whether the declarant is available as a witness:

    (13) *Family Records.* A statement of fact about personal or family history contained in a family record, such as a Bible, genealogy, chart, engraving on a ring, inscription on a portrait, or engraving on an urn or burial marker.

FED. R. EVID. 804.   EXCEPTIONS TO THE RULE AGAINST HEARSAY — WHEN THE DECLARANT IS UNAVAILABLE AS A WITNESS

(b) The Exceptions. The following are not excluded by the rule against hearsay if the declarant is unavailable as a witness:

(4) *Statement of Personal or Family History.* A statement about:

(A) the declarant's own birth, adoption, legitimacy, ancestry, marriage, divorce, relationship by blood or marriage, or similar facts of personal or family history, even though the declarant had no way of acquiring personal knowledge about that fact; or

(B) another person concerning any of these facts, as well as death, if the declarant was related to the person by blood, adoption, or marriage or was so intimately associated with the person's family that the declarant's information is likely to be accurate.

Rule 803(13) creates an exception for statements of fact about personal or family history when those facts are recorded in "a Bible, genealogy, chart, engraving on a ring, inscription on a family portrait, or engraving on an urn or burial marker." The exception takes note of a tradition in many families to keep records of family history, often in bibles and other keepsakes. Family members generally do this to preserve a history of their ancestors. The motivation to record these matters accurately therefore is strong. In addition, the need for such records is often great, especially when the relationships among persons are at issue and where no witness with personal knowledge of the historical origins of those relationships is available to testify.

Rule 804(b)(4) allows the court to admit statements of an unavailable declarant concerning her birth, adoption, marriage, relationship to others, and similar matters, even though the declarant could not have had personal knowledge of the matter stated. Thus, if the parentage of an unavailable person is relevant to a case, the person's statement that she was the daughter of Zed and Abel would be admissible even though the declarant could not have possessed first-hand knowledge of that fact. The exception also covers the same types of statements about another person if the declarant was related to that person by blood, adoption, or marriage, or was so closely associated with the person that she is likely to have possessed accurate information about the matter asserted. As to both types of statements covered, the exception is clearly justified more by necessity than by trustworthiness. This explains why it applies only if the declarant is unavailable.

3. Records of Documents That Affect an Interest in Property (Rule 803(14)) and Statements in Such Documents (Rule 803(15))

FED. R. EVID. 803.   EXCEPTIONS TO THE RULE AGAINST HEARSAY — REGARDLESS OF WHETHER THE DECLARANT IS AVAILABLE AS A WITNESS

The following are not excluded by the rule against hearsay, regardless of whether the declarant is available as a witness:

(14) *Records of Documents That Affect an Interest in Property.* The record of a document that purports to establish or affect an interest in property if:

 (A) the record is admitted to prove the content of the original recorded document, along with its signing and its delivery by each person who purports to have signed it;

 (B) the record is kept in a public office; and

 (C) a statute authorizes recording documents of that kind in that office.

(15) *Statements in Documents That Affect an Interest in Property.* A statement contained in a document that purports to establish or affect an interest in property if the matter stated was relevant to the document's purpose — unless later dealings with the property are inconsistent with the truth of the statement or the purport of the document.

Rule 803(14) covers records that purport to affect an interest in property if those records are kept by a public office authorized by law to record such documents. The exception allows such records in evidence "to prove the content of the original recorded document, along with its signing and its delivery by each person who purports to have signed it." A simple example would be a deed conveying title to land that has been recorded in a county recorder's office. The deed itself would not be hearsay (it has independent legal significance), but a writing containing a public official's statement that it is a true and correct copy of the original kept in the recorder's office is hearsay when offered to prove that it is a true and correct copy of the original. The exception permits the court to admit the record. In its Note explaining this exception, the Advisory Committee recognized that if the records were not receivable as evidence of the contents of the recorded document, "the recording process would be reduced to a nullity."

Rule 803(15) allows a record of the same type to be admitted to prove any facts recited in it as long as those facts are relevant to the purpose of the document. The Advisory Committee Note explains that "[t]he circumstances under which dispositive documents are executed and the requirement that the recital be germane to the purpose of the document are believed to be adequate guarantees of trustworthiness. . . ." The rule states, however, that it does not apply if "dealings with the property are inconsistent with the truth of the statement or the purport of the document."

4. *Statements in Ancient Documents (Rule 803(16))*

**FED. R. EVID. 803. EXCEPTIONS TO THE RULE AGAINST HEARSAY —
REGARDLESS OF WHETHER THE DECLARANT IS AVAILABLE AS A WITNESS**

The following are not excluded by the rule against hearsay, regardless of whether the declarant is available as a witness: . . .

(16) *Statements in Ancient Documents.* A statement in a document that is at least 20 years old and whose authenticity is established.

If individuals have treated a particular document as authentic for a long period of time, it is reasonable to assume that statements made in the document are accurate. This is the basis for the "ancient documents" exception. In fact, a document need not be very old to qualify. If the document has been in existence for at least 20 years, and if it has been authenticated, the exception will apply.

One method of authenticating ancient documents is set forth in Rule 901(b)(8), which states that a document that has been in existence 20 years or more at the time it is offered into evidence may be authenticated if it "(A) is in a condition that creates no suspicion about its authenticity; [and] (B) was in a place where it, if authentic, would likely be . . .". If the proponent persuades the trial court by a preponderance of the evidence that each of these conditions is satisfied, the court should admit the document under the exception to the hearsay rule contained in Rule 803(16).

5. *Market Reports and Similar Commercial Publications (Rule 803(17))*

**FED. R. EVID. 803.   EXCEPTIONS TO THE RULE AGAINST HEARSAY —
REGARDLESS OF WHETHER THE DECLARANT IS AVAILABLE AS A WITNESS**

The following are not excluded by the rule against hearsay, regardless of whether the declarant is available as a witness:

   (17) *Market Reports and Similar Commercial Publications.* Market quotations, lists, directories, or other compilations that are generally relied on by the public or by persons in particular occupations.

Rule 803(17) makes admissible "[m]arket quotations, lists, directories, or other compilations that are generally relied on by the public or by persons in particular occupations." The primary justification for the exception is trustworthiness; because the people who make them usually do so for commercial gain, they have a significant motive to report accurately.

6. *Learned Treatises (Rule 803(18))*

**FED. R. EVID. 803.   EXCEPTIONS TO THE RULE AGAINST HEARSAY —
REGARDLESS OF WHETHER THE DECLARANT IS AVAILABLE AS A WITNESS**

The following are not excluded by the rule against hearsay, regardless of whether the declarant is available as a witness: . . .

   (18) *Statements in Learned Treatises, Periodicals, or Pamphlets.* A statement contained in a treatise, periodical, or pamphlet if:

      (A) the statement is called to the attention of an expert witness on cross-examination or relied on by the expert on direct examination; and

      (B) the publication is established as a reliable authority by the expert's admission or testimony, by another expert's testimony, or by judicial notice.

If admitted, the statement may be read into evidence but not received as an exhibit.

———————————

It is common for experts to rely on learned treatises in preparing their testimony. It is also common for the party cross-examining an expert to call the expert's attention to a statement in a treatise that tends to cast doubt on the expert's direct examination testimony. Experts, in fact, will rely on treatises whether a hearsay exception applies or not. And as we learn in Chapter 7, the jury is entitled to learn the basis of an expert's opinion as a means to help it assess the credibility of the expert's opinion. This exception allows the jury to consider the statement in the treatise as proof of the matter asserted rather than simply as evidence of the basis for the expert's opinion.

The difference between permitting the jury to hear that the expert relied on a treatise and allowing the jury to consider the statement in the treatise as substantive evidence — as proof of the fact asserted — is, of course, virtually impossible for a juror to understand. Jurors are also not likely to appreciate the difference between the cross-examiner's reference to a statement in a treatise merely to contradict (and thus impeach) the witness and its use to prove the truth of the matter asserted. In this sense, the exception takes account of the practical effect of testimony concerning the assertions of a treatise writer. Nevertheless, prior to the adoption of the Federal Rules, most courts did not recognize an exception for learned treatises.

The rule applies to a broad range of treatises as long as the treatise has been "established as reliable authority by the expert's admission or testimony, by another expert's testimony, or by judicial notice." This helps to ensure that only reliable treatises may be used as substantive evidence.

For the statement in the treatise to be admissible under the exception, the proponent must show that the treatise is authoritative. This is usually accomplished through the testimony of the proponent's expert witness. The treatise must also be shown to an expert on the witness stand, whether it is the proponent's own witness or the opponent's expert. And the treatise itself is not admissible as an exhibit (it would not be wise to allow the jury to peruse the book during deliberations). Instead, relevant parts of the treatise may be read into evidence.

7. Reputation (Rules 803(19), 803(20), and 803(21))

> **FED. R. EVID. 803.   EXCEPTIONS TO THE RULE AGAINST HEARSAY —
> REGARDLESS OF WHETHER THE DECLARANT IS AVAILABLE AS A WITNESS**

The following are not excluded by the rule against hearsay, regardless of whether the declarant is available as a witness:

   (19) *Reputation Concerning Personal or Family History.* A reputation among a person's family by blood, adoption, or marriage — or among a person's associates or in the community—concerning the person's birth, adoption, legitimacy, ancestry, marriage, divorce, death, relationship by blood, adoption, or marriage, or similar facts of personal or family history.

(20) *Reputation Concerning Boundaries or General History.* A reputation in a community—arising before the controversy—concerning boundaries of land in the community or customs that affect the land, or concerning general historical events important to that community, state, or nation.

(21) *Reputation Concerning Character.* A reputation among a person's associates or in the community concerning the person's character.

Reputation consists of the combined out-of-court statements of many people concerning a person or thing. The reputation evidence is hearsay if offered to prove that the person or thing actually has the reputed characteristic. Thus, when an attorney asks a witness to recite the reputation of a person for honesty, the response "Zed's reputation is that she is honest" is hearsay if offered to prove that Zed is honest because it constitutes an out-of-court, mass statement that Zed is honest.

Like all hearsay, reputation evidence is inadmissible in the absence of an applicable exception. Because both the common law and the Federal Rules sometimes allow evidence of reputation to prove a person's character (*see* Rules 405(a) and 608(b)), a hearsay exception is necessary to allow the evidence to be admitted. This is the purpose of Rule 803(21). Note that this exception only covers evidence of a *person's* reputation concerning character. It does not cover the reputation of organizations or other entities. And the reputation must concern character; it may not concern other matters.

The Federal Rules contain two additional exceptions covering reputation evidence. Rule 803(19) allows the court to admit evidence of reputation among members of a person's family, associates, or community concerning the person's birth, adoption, marriage, divorce, death, family relationships, or similar facts. Rule 803(20) creates an exception for community reputation concerning "boundaries of land in the community or customs that affect the land, or concerning general historical events important to that community, state, or nation" in which the land is located.

8. *Judgment of Previous Conviction (Rule 803(22)) and Involving Personal, Family, or General History, or a Boundary (Rule 803(23))*

> **FED. R. EVID. 803. EXCEPTIONS TO THE RULE AGAINST HEARSAY—REGARDLESS OF WHETHER THE DECLARANT IS AVAILABLE AS A WITNESS**

The following are not excluded by the rule against hearsay, regardless of whether the declarant is available as a witness:

(22) *Judgment of a Previous Conviction.* Evidence of a final judgment of conviction if:

(**A**) the judgment was entered after a trial or guilty plea, but not a nolo contendere plea;

(**B**) the judgment was for a crime punishable by death or by imprisonment for more than a year;

(**C**) the evidence is admitted to prove any fact essential to the judgment; and

(**D**) when offered by the prosecutor in a criminal case for a purpose other than impeachment, the judgment was against the defendant.

The pendency of an appeal may be shown but does not affect admissibility.

(**23**) *Judgments Involving Personal, Family, or General History or a Boundary.* A judgment that is admitted to prove a matter of personal, family, or general history, or boundaries, if the matter:

(**A**) was essential to the judgment; and

(**B**) could be proved by evidence of reputation.

In some cases, it is necessary to prove or useful to prove that a person has been convicted of a crime. Rule 803(22) allows the court to admit a judgment of conviction when offered to prove "any fact essential to the judgment." The most reliable evidence of a conviction is the court's record of the judgment of conviction, though the rule does not limit proof to such records. A judgment of conviction may be proven, for example, by the testimony of a witness who heard the judge pronounce the defendant guilty of the crime.

In one sense, a judgment of conviction is particularly trustworthy because it may only be made upon a guilty plea or after a trial at which the fact-finder was convinced of the individual's guilt beyond a reasonable doubt of all factual elements of the offense. But not all judgments are equally reliable and, thus, the exception is limited to situations in which the judgment is particularly reliable. Accordingly, it only applies when the conviction was of a crime punishable by death or imprisonment in excess of a year — the traditional definition of a felony. The reason for this limitation is that many people plead guilty to minor crimes simply to avoid the time and expense of a trial, and not because they are in fact guilty of the crime. This is particularly true of traffic offenses. Judgments of conviction based on pleas of *nolo contendere* are also not admissible pursuant to this rule; the very purpose of the *nolo* plea is to permit the defendant to accept the punishment for the charged crime without having to deal with adverse collateral consequences at a later time.

The exception also does not allow the government to offer evidence of the conviction of a person other than the defendant, unless the conviction is offered to impeach the person's credibility. (In Chapter 6, we learn when a prior conviction is admissible to impeach under Rule 609.)

Rule 803(23) allows the court to admit judgments concerning matters of personal, family, or general history, and also covers judgments concerning boundaries of land. The exception will operate if the same "could be proved by evidence of reputation," which is covered by Rules 803(19) and 803(20) (discussed above).

Q.   THE HEARSAY RULE AND THE CONSTITUTION

1.   Introduction

The Sixth Amendment to the United States Constitution provides:

> In all criminal prosecutions, the accused shall enjoy the right . . . to be confronted with the witnesses against him. . . .

This very brief phrase emerged from a centuries-long process that saw the development of the accusatorial system of justice, the values upon which it is based, and the adversarial system that effectuates it in day-to-day practice. The right to confront witnesses is only one of a series of rights guaranteed to an accused by the Fifth and Sixth Amendments, including the right against compulsory self-incrimination and the right to a public trial. As Wright and Graham explain:

> If the Confrontation Clause did not prevent the state from deposing the accusers in private and using their depositions rather than their testimony, the public nature of the trial would be diminished. By forcing "the witnesses against" the defendant into the open, the two Sixth Amendment Clauses [public trial and confrontation] make an acquittal more meaningful to the accused and a conviction more justifiable to the community, thereby increasing the acceptability of jury verdicts and increasing the independence of the jurors. By requiring that the confrontation between the accused and the accuser be public, the two clauses combine to increase the formality of the event, to impress the accuser with the significance of the accusation, and to place psychological pressure on all the participants to behave responsibly.

30 Charles A. Wright & Kenneth W. Graham, Jr., Federal Practice and Procedure: Evidence § 6341, at 191 (1997) (footnotes omitted).

The confrontation right is also closely bound up with the right to trial by jury. "By requiring that the accusers be produced before the jury, the Confrontation Clause requires the evidence in a form that is most accessible to the special talents the jurors are supposed to bring to their task; the ability to assess demeanor, knowledge of the community and thus the context from which the crime and the accusation arose, and understanding of the common discourse of ordinary people." *Id.* at 191-192.

Thus, the right of the accused to confront witnesses is fundamental to our system of criminal jurisprudence. Though the Confrontation Clause raises many important issues, we must limit our focus to the interplay between this constitutionally guaranteed right and the admission of hearsay against a criminal defendant. To put the matter bluntly, if the Constitution requires that the accused be "confronted with the witnesses against him," and if the constitutional right to trial by jury ensures that the jury will have the opportunity to test the credibility of the witnesses against the accused, how can *any* hearsay be offered against the accused at trial?

There are many possible answers to this question. First consider the extreme positions. At one extreme, it is possible to argue that all the Confrontation Clause guarantees is that the defendant have the right to confront the *witnesses* called by the prosecution to testify against her at trial. This would forbid the taking of testimony in the absence of the accused. It might also require that the accused have the literal opportunity to look the witnesses in the eye as they testify, and to cross-examine them. But under this approach the Constitution would not forbid the use of hearsay, as long as the defendant has the opportunity to "confront" the witness who reports the hearsay at trial. This interpretation would not affect the constitutionality of the hearsay rule as applied against a criminal defendant.

A position at the other extreme would forbid the use of almost all hearsay against a criminal defendant. That position would view anyone who supplies information against an accused as a "witness" against her. Presumably, the only exception would be when the declarant testifies at trial, thus allowing the accused to confront her.

Though the Supreme Court did not issue an interpretation of the Confrontation Clause until about a century after the Constitution's adoption, the Court has never taken either extreme position. At the same time, it was not until about 1980 that the Court adopted a relatively clear interpretation. And that interpretation only survived until 2004, when the Court replaced it with a fundamentally different position about the nature and scope of the confrontation right.

2.   History and Purposes of the Right of Confrontation

It is not possible to offer here a lengthy history of the right to confront witnesses.[39] Passages in the New Testament suggest that Roman law recognized a type of confrontation right.[40] English history, however, is replete with examples of procedures that denied even the most rudimentary forms of confrontation, some of which affected the American colonists themselves. The Framers' fear of "trial by affidavit," therefore, was not misplaced. The Star Chamber, created in England during the middle of the fifteenth century, was the most infamous example of the type of system the Framers wanted to avoid. In Star Chamber proceedings, the prosecutor would use written depositions of witnesses, sometimes obtained by torture. The accused was then placed under oath and interrogated, without having seen the depositions and without the benefit of counsel. The trial itself was conducted by the Lord Chancellor without a jury, and consisted entirely of a reading of the witness depositions. The Framers found this kind of procedure odious, and the Confrontation Clause clearly was intended to prevent its use in the courts of the United States.

But it was not only the Framers of the U.S. Constitution who viewed confrontation as fundamental. Even in sixteenth-century England, criminal defendants and other parties argued for the right to confront the witnesses against them. A series of controversial treason trials during that century led Parliament to enact laws giving rudimentary protections to the accused, but not including

39. For an exhaustive and fascinating discussion of the development of the right to confront witnesses, *see* 30-30A Charles A. Wright & Kenneth W. Graham, Federal Practice and Procedure: Evidence (1997 & 2000).

40. During the trial of Paul in a Roman court, Paul argued: "[I]t is not the manner of the Romans to deliver any man to die, before that he which is accused have the accusers face to face, and have license to answer for himself concerning the crime laid against him." King James Bible, Acts 25:16. The trials of Jesus also supply evidence that accused parties considered confrontation to be important. *See, e.g.,* John 18:20-34 (recounting a colloquy between Jesus and the High Priest concerning the statements of absent accusers). Though we cannot be certain that this states the clear practice under Roman law, it reveals that confrontation, as a value, is very old.

face-to-face confrontation during trial. And the courts continued to build an elaborate system of trial by the sworn depositions of witnesses, which were simply read at trial.

The most celebrated English trial in which confrontation was denied was that of Sir Walter Raleigh, who in 1603 was charged with participating in a plot to overthrow King James I and install Lady Arabella Stuart in his place. The prosecution of Raleigh was based on the confessions of Cobham, an alleged co-conspirator who in fact had retracted the confessions. Raleigh complained that the confessions were unsigned, and he pleaded with the court to produce Cobham at the trial:

> I claim to have my accuser brought here face to face to speak. . . . If you proceed to condemn me by bare inferences, without an oath, without subscription, upon a paper accusation, you try me by the Spanish inquisition. If my accuser were dead or abroad, it were something; but he liveth, and is in this very house. Consider, my Lords, it is not rare case for a man to be falsely accused; aye, and falsely condemned too.

Raleigh made other arguments for confrontation, and concluded, "if [Cobham] will maintain his accusation to my face, I will confess myself guilty." The court was unmoved, and proceeded to admit still more hearsay, Chief Justice Popham explaining that "[t]here must not such a gap be opened for the destruction of the King as would be if we should grant [the right to confront the accusers]." All of Raleigh's efforts failed, and he was convicted of treason.[41] By the end of the seventeenth century, the right of confrontation had become established for trials in England. As Wright and Graham explain:

> Somehow, in the period between 1640 and 1660, a time when the English fought a long civil war, tried and executed a king, and converted their nation from an aristocratic monarchy to a republican commonwealth, confrontation switched from a claim made by dissidents to a right available to all. Although no law was enacted requiring this, during the Commonwealth defendants were confronted with all the available witnesses against them. The government created some new mechanisms of repression, but generally trials became more accusatorial. Though many of the other accusatorial features adopted by the Puritans were rolled back with the Restoration of the monarchy, confrontation of witnesses continued under the later Stuarts. Following the Glorious Revolution, Parliament enacted statutes that fixed the main features of the accusatorial system, reenacting some of the Puritan legal reforms.

30 Wright & Graham § 6343. Why this happened is not clear, but it did coincide with the rise of the jury and with the Puritan movement, which redefined "truth" as something human rather than divine and which could be discovered through a combination of reason and intuition. Of particular importance was the concept that truth could emerge through the use of the five senses, something rather difficult to do if one did not have an opportunity to observe the accuser and the accused, face to face.

---

41. Some years later, after a strange series of events, Raleigh was executed on the original charges.

To the Puritans, there was no need for an "intermediary" between oneself and the law. This led to the vilification of lawyers but also to the notion that, because a witness is a sort of intermediary in the process of determining the truth, the jury needed to be able to see and hear the witness with its own eyes and ears so that it might judge the truth of his testimony. Wright and Graham summarize the importance of this aspect of Puritan thinking to the development of the right of confrontation:

> All witnesses are intermediaries between the trier of fact and the knowledge it needs to decide the case. Often, however, they are necessary. . . . Hence . . . it is necessary for the jury to directly encounter the intermediary because the truth of the message is not to be determined from the words alone but from how they resonate with the experience and practical knowledge of the jury.

30 Wright & Graham § 6343, at 295 (footnotes omitted).

The development of the right of confrontation and the hearsay rule proceeded separately; one was not the outgrowth of the other. Nor did the confrontation right arise from the same concern — lack of contemporaneous cross-examination — that motivated the development of the hearsay rule. Indeed, historical records suggest that hearsay evidence was commonly admitted in English courts well into the eighteenth century, by which time the right of confrontation had already become reasonably well established.

In the American Colonies, the right of confrontation also underwent a long development; American practice did not mimic the English and a right to confront witnesses had developed well before it was written into the Sixth Amendment. There was a long history of distrust of judges and of executive power in the Colonies. The "Great Awakening" proceeded on principles similar to those espoused by the English Puritans. For example, colonial thinkers picked up the idea that there is no need for an intermediary between the individual and God. This undercut the authority of the clergy, and also helped to foment distrust of civil authority.

Over time, the Colonies' legal systems began to resemble more and more the English system. Colonists had strong reactions to high profile political trials conducted in ways similar to those used in Tudor and Stuart England. Arguments for procedural reform became more common. Still, the confrontation right was not recognized in the Colonies until some time after it had been secured in England. In part, this might have been caused by the relative lack of lawyers in the Colonies, as well as by public dislike of the legal profession.

One factor in the growth of the confrontation right in both England and the United States was the English Enlightenment. As Wright and Graham explain:

> [S]cientists adopted a humility, a lowering of expectations, a sense of the limits of scientific knowledge; since certainty . . . was not possible, the most we could hope for was probability. [Also], scientists believed that the probability of finding truth would be enhanced if science was seen as a collective rather than an individual endeavor. These views resonated with legal notions of burden of proof and the advantages of the adversary over the inquisitorial system.
>
> Scientists also sought standards for evaluating evidence. It was generally agreed that one's own senses provided the best evidence and that the "testimony" of others was distinctly inferior. Nonetheless, scientists could not rely on their own perceptions for everything so they had to devise methods for determining when

statements from others were reliable; not surprisingly, the factors they suggested were similar if not identical to those now common in legal analysis; e.g., the bias and interest of the "witness," the number of similar witnesses, and the disregard of "mere hearsay."

30 Wright & Graham § 6345, at 452-453 (footnotes omitted). Colonial authorities considered both trial by jury and confrontation as essential to the legal fact-finding process. They were also an important check on governmental power.

The Colonies' legal and political struggles with Britain also advanced the drive toward a right of confrontation. In the decade or two before the Revolution, colonial anger at British rule increased rapidly. Particularly galling were the courts set up to try colonists for violation of various laws the colonists despised, especially those imposing taxes. The colonists reserved much hatred for the vice-admiralty courts, partly for their inquisitorial style. In these courts, the defendant had no right to jury trial, witnesses were often informants who stood to benefit financially from any fines imposed or property confiscated, and there was no opportunity for face-to-face confrontation. In essence, the colonists saw that the court was employing the inquisitorial style that the British had fought so hard to eliminate. As was the case in Britain so many years earlier, several widely publicized trials, including that of John Hancock, served to focus public anger at the system.

Included among the grievances listed in the Declaration of Independence was depriving the colonists of "the benefits of trial by jury" and "transporting us beyond seas to be tried for pretended offenses." The Declaration's adoption of egalitarian principles and its reliance on "self-evident" truths, central to Puritan thinking, made confrontation particularly important. "The notion of truths that transcend logic lies at the root of the notion that a lay jury by observing the confrontation of accuser and accused will be better able to determine truth than a trained judge poring over depositions into the night." 30 Wright & Graham § 6345, at 559.

Confrontation, then, is about more than simply the right of cross-examination. It derives from values deeply rooted in English and American history, religion, and political philosophy.

3. Current Supreme Court Jurisprudence About the Relationship Between Hearsay and the Confrontation Clause

Whether or not the Confrontation Clause was meant to serve the same purposes as the hearsay rule, that is how the Supreme Court viewed it for some time. In a series of cases beginning in 1980, the Supreme Court crafted a test under which virtually any otherwise admissible hearsay will also satisfy the demands of the Confrontation Clause. Keep in mind that Confrontation Clause analysis is only necessary if the evidence satisfies a hearsay exception recognized in that jurisdiction. If it does not, the evidence is simply inadmissible; no resort to confrontation analysis is needed. By the same token, in those cases in which evidence satisfies a hearsay exception but its admission would violate the defendant's confrontation right, the evidence is inadmissible.

We begin with Ohio v. Roberts, 448 U.S. 56 (1980). Roberts was charged with forgery of a check in the name of Bernard Isaacs, and with possession of stolen credit cards in Isaacs' name. At the preliminary hearing, the defense called Anita, the Isaacs' daughter, and tried unsuccessfully to elicit her admission that she had given Roberts the checks and credit cards without telling him she did not have permission to use them. Anita did not respond to subpoenas to appear at trial, and her whereabouts at that time were unknown. The prosecution therefore sought to use Anita's preliminary hearing testimony against Roberts under Ohio's hearsay exception covering the preliminary hearing testimony of an unavailable witness (a version of the former testimony exception). Roberts objected on Confrontation Clause grounds.

Writing for a majority of six, Justice Blackmun began his analysis by holding that the Framers evinced a preference for face-to-face accusation. Employing language from which the Court would later find it necessary to retreat, the Court held that "the Sixth Amendment establishes a rule of necessity. In the usual case (including cases where prior cross-examination has occurred), the prosecution must either produce, or demonstrate the unavailability of, the declarant whose statement it wishes to use against the defendant." Second, even if the declarant is unavailable, the trial court may only admit hearsay "marked with such trustworthiness that 'there is no material departure from the reason of the general rule.'" The key, the Court held, was to find "indicia of reliability":

> The Court has applied this "indicia of reliability" requirement principally by concluding that certain hearsay exceptions rest upon such solid foundations that admission of virtually any evidence within them comports with the "substance of the constitutional protection." This reflects the truism that "hearsay rules and the Confrontation Clause are generally designed to protect similar values" . . . and "stem from the same roots." It also responds to the need for certainty in the workaday world of conducting criminal trials.
>
> In sum, when a hearsay declarant is not present for cross-examination at trial, the Confrontation Clause normally requires a showing that he is unavailable. Even then, his statement is admissible only if it bears adequate "indicia of reliability." *Reliability can be inferred without more in a case where the evidence falls within a firmly rooted hearsay exception. In other cases, the evidence must be excluded, at least absent a showing of particularized guarantees of trustworthiness.*

(Emphasis added.)

The Court then held that there was no important difference between Anita's examination by Robert's counsel at the preliminary hearing, which was conducted much like a cross-examination, and the typical cross-examination of a prosecution witness at trial. As a result, the transcript "bore sufficient 'indicia of reliability'" and was admissible.

The Court continued to develop its confrontation analysis in United States v. Inadi, 475 U.S. 387 (1986), a federal drug prosecution. The statements at issue were on audiotapes of legally intercepted telephone calls among alleged co-conspirators, including one Lozaro. The statements qualified as co-conspirator statements under Rule 801(d)(2)(E). Inadi objected to admission of the tapes on confrontation grounds, asserting, quite understandably, that *Roberts* required the prosecution either to produce the declarant or demonstrate his unavailability, and that the prosecution had done neither.

Speaking through Justice Powell, a majority of seven rejected Inadi's argument, and held that the Court in *Roberts* did not intend "such a wholesale revision of the law of evidence, nor does [*Roberts*] support such a broad interpretation of the Confrontation Clause." Co-conspirator statements may be admitted against a criminal defendant even if the prosecution has not produced the declarant or demonstrated the declarant's unavailability. The Court explained that such statements are more probative than former testimony, largely because they are made while the conspiracy is in progress. In contrast, former testimony is "only a weaker substitute for live testimony" that "seldom has independent evidentiary significance of its own." The Court also held that an unavailability requirement would produce little or no benefit: "First, if the declarant either is unavailable, or is available and produced by the prosecution, the statements can be introduced anyway." Second, such a requirement would be unlikely to produce much testimony that would not be produced otherwise because either the prosecution or the defense is likely to subpoena some available declarants, and only those who are believed unhelpful will not be subpoenaed.

Inadi thus holds that a co-conspirator statement may satisfy the demands of the Confrontation Clause even if the prosecution neither produces the declarant nor demonstrates that the declarant is unavailable. The following year, in Bourjaily v. United States, 483 U.S. 171 (1987), the Supreme Court held that the co-conspirator rule (Rule 801(d)(2)(E)) is "firmly rooted." This means, under *Roberts*, that no further inquiry into reliability was required. Statements that satisfy the requirements of the co-conspirator rule generally would be admissible against criminal defendants.

Other cases continued to explore and refine the *Roberts* test. In Idaho v. Wright, 497 U.S. 805 (1990), the Supreme Court limited the evidence a trial court may consider when deciding whether evidence offered under an exception that is not "firmly rooted" had "particularized guarantees of trustworthiness." The Court held that trustworthiness "must be shown from the totality of the circumstances, but [that] the relevant circumstances include only those that surround the making of the statement and that render the declarant particularly worthy of belief." This means the court may *not* look to corroborating evidence to verify the accuracy of the statement. In other decisions, the Court also explored the meaning of "firmly rooted," apparently relying primarily on the age and degree of acceptance the hearsay exception at issue had achieved as well as on whether the hearsay admitted under the exception is reliable. *See* White v. Illinois, 502 U.S. 346 (1992); Lilly v. Virginia, 527 U.S. 116 (1999).

After these cases, it appeared that the Confrontation Clause still retained some life as a tool to prevent the admission of hearsay evidence against the criminal defendant. Though most hearsay exceptions would satisfy the Court's "firmly rooted" standard (meaning that the government need not demonstrate that the evidence is otherwise reliable), there was room to argue that some hearsay exceptions are not firmly rooted and that other exceptions contain sub-classes that are not firmly rooted even though other sub-classes do satisfy the firmly rooted criteria. And when evidence offered against a criminal defendant did not fit within a firmly rooted exception or part of such an exception, there was room to argue that the government failed to demonstrate the required "particularized guarantees of trustworthiness" demanded by the Confrontation Clause.

In 2004, the Supreme Court took a sharp turn with its decision in Crawford v. Washington, 541 U.S. 36 (2004). Defendant Michael Crawford was charged with assault and attempted murder of Kenneth Lee, a man he believed had attempted to rape his wife Sylvia. The police interrogated Michael and Sylvia, and took tape-recorded statements from each. Michael Crawford's statement set forth facts supporting a self-defense claim. Sylvia's statement corroborated her husband's in a number of respects, but provided much weaker support for the self-defense claim. Sylvia did not testify at trial because of Washington's adverse spousal testimony privilege, which bars a spouse from testifying without the other spouse's consent. (For discussion of the spousal privileges, see Chapter 8.) Washington's privilege does not prevent the adverse party from offering into evidence a statement that satisfies a hearsay exception, however. Sylvia's statement was hearsay but qualified as a declaration against interest because she admitted leading her husband to Lee's apartment, which facilitated the assault. Over Michael's confrontation objection, the trial court allowed the prosecution to play the tape of Sylvia's statement to the jury, and Michael was convicted.

The United States Supreme Court held that admission of Sylvia's statement violated Michael's confrontation rights. Writing for a majority of seven, Justice Scalia reviewed the history of the confrontation right from Roman times to the present. Placing primary emphasis on what he saw as the state of the common law at the time of the Sixth Amendment's framing, Scalia wrote:

> First, the principal evil at which the Confrontation Clause was directed was the civil-law mode of criminal procedure, and particularly its use of *ex parte* examinations as evidence against the accused. . . .
>
> Accordingly, we once again reject the view that the Confrontation Clause applies of its own force only to in-court testimony, and that its application to out-of-court statements introduced at trial depends upon "the law of Evidence for the time being." . . . Leaving the regulation of out-of-court statements to the law of evidence would render the Confrontation Clause powerless to prevent even the most flagrant inquisitorial practices. Raleigh was, after all, perfectly free to confront those who read Cobham's confession in court. . . .
>
> The text of the Confrontation Clause reflects this focus. It applies to "witnesses" against the accused — in other words, those who "bear testimony." . . . "Testimony," in turn, is typically "[a] solemn declaration or affirmation made for the purpose of establishing or proving some fact." . . . An accuser who makes a formal statement to government officers bears testimony in a sense that a person who makes a casual remark to an acquaintance does not. The constitutional text, like the history underlying the common-law right of confrontation, thus reflects an especially acute concern with a specific type of out-of-court statement.

Id. at 50-52. Though the Court declined to provide a precise definition of "testimonial," it held that the category included, "at a minimum . . . prior testimony at a preliminary hearing, before a grand jury or at a former trial; and to police interrogations." *Id.* at 68.

The Court held that "[t]he historical record . . . supports [the] proposition that the Framers would not have allowed admission of testimonial statements of a witness who did not appear at trial unless he was unavailable to testify, and the defendant had a prior opportunity for cross-examination." *Id.* at 53-54. Thus, the Court established a bright-line rule for "testimonial" hearsay offered against a criminal defendant: Such hearsay is only admissible if (1) the declarant testifies at trial; or (2) the declarant is unavailable *and* the defendant had a prior opportunity to cross-examine the declarant.[42] By so holding, the Court abolished the *Roberts* test in cases of "testimonial" hearsay. Under *Roberts*, trustworthy hearsay could be admitted where the declarant was unavailable, even if the hearsay was testimonial. After *Crawford*, even a high degree of trustworthiness does not satisfy the Confrontation Clause. The Court wrote that "[d]ispensing with confrontation because testimony is obviously reliable is akin to dispensing with jury trial because a defendant is obviously guilty." *Id.* at 62.

Crawford was a turning point in the Court's Confrontation Clause jurisprudence. Now, even if hearsay fits within exceptions that admit "testimonial" statements, it will not be admissible against a criminal defendant unless the declarant testifies at the trial, or, if the declarant does not testify, she is unavailable to testify and the defendant had a prior opportunity for cross-examination. This will certainly mean that grand jury testimony of a person who does not testify at trial will no longer be admissible against a criminal defendant because such statements are not subject to cross-examination. For the same reason, statements of individuals other than the criminal defendant, made during police interrogation, will not be admissible against the defendant. *Crawford* also casts doubt on the validity of state child hearsay exceptions, at least to the extent the child's statement is "testimonial" because it was made formally during police questioning. At the same time, the results of many pre-*Crawford* cases will not change. To take the facts of *Roberts* itself, defendant had an opportunity to cross-examine the declarant at the preliminary hearing and the declarant was unavailable at the time of trial. Thus, the requirements of *Crawford* would have been satisfied.

When hearsay is not "testimonial," *Crawford* strongly suggests that the Confrontation Clause does not apply at all, and that the only barrier to admission is the hearsay rule. However, the facts before the Court in *Crawford* did not involve "nontestimonial" hearsay, so the case did not settle the matter clearly.

After the Supreme Court decided *Crawford*, the lower federal courts, as well as state courts, struggled to come to terms with the issues left open or only partially resolved by the Court. Among the many issues are the meaning of "testimonial"; the timing of the prior opportunity for cross-examination; the possibility that some hearsay exceptions (most notably the dying declaration exception) are *sui generis*, and thus not subject to confrontation analysis; and the relationship between forfeiture doctrine and the Confrontation Clause.

In 2006, the Court revisited the confrontation issue in Davis v. Washington, 547 U.S. 813 (2006). *Davis* considered the facts of two cases, one from Washington and the other from Indiana. In the Washington case, Michelle McCottry, Davis's former girlfriend, made a 911 call during which she claimed that Davis was present and "jumpin' on" her, using his fists. The 911 operator, whom the Court treated as an agent of law enforcement, ascertained certain other facts during the call, including McCottry's assertion that Davis had just left the scene,

42. Dying declarations may be exempt from Confrontation Clause analysis. Justice Scalia acknowledged that "[a]lthough many dying declarations may not be testimonial, there is authority for admitting even those that clearly are." 541 U.S. at 56, n.6. The majority opinion declined to decide whether the Sixth Amendment incorporates that exception. Some state courts have held, after *Crawford*, that dying declarations are exempt from Confrontation Clause exclusion: e.g., *People v. Monterroso*, 101 P.3d 956, 971-972 (Cal. 2004); *State v. Lewis*, 235 S.W.3d 136, 147-148 (Tenn. 2007).

why Davis said he had come to McCottry's house, and Davis's full name and birth date. The police arrived within four minutes of the 911 call, saw that McCottry was shaken and had fresh bruises on her forearm and face, and noticed that McCottry was frantically trying to gather her belongings and children so she could leave. Davis was charged with violating a domestic no-contact order. At trial, the only witnesses against him were the two police officers who responded to the 911 call; McCottry did not testify. The police witnesses testified about what they observed, but of course were unable to identify who caused McCottry's injuries. Over Davis's objection, key portions of the tape recording of the 911 call were admitted.

In the second case decided in *Davis*, police responded to a report of a domestic disturbance at the home of Hershel and Amy Hammon. When they arrived, the police saw Amy alone on the front porch. She appeared frightened but said nothing was wrong. She gave the officers permission to search the house, where the officers observed a gas heating unit with flames coming out of the front. Broken glass was on the floor in front of the unit. Hershel was in the kitchen, and told police that he and Amy had had an argument, that the argument had not gotten physical, and that everything was fine. One of the officers then took Amy aside and asked her what had happened. The other officer restrained Hershel from joining that conversation. After listening to Amy's story, the officer asked her to fill out and sign a "battery affidavit." She handwrote the document, stating that Hershel had broken the furnace, shoved her down on the floor into the broken glass, hit her in the chest, thrown her down, and broken other items. She also asserted that Hershel "tore up my van where I couldn't leave the house" and attacked her daughter. Hershel was charged with domestic battery and probation violation and tried at a bench trial. Amy was subpoenaed to appear at trial, but failed to do so. The state called the officer who had questioned Amy and asked him to recount what she told him and to authenticate the affidavit. Over Hershel's objection, the court then admitted the affidavit as a "present sense impression" and Amy's oral statements as "excited utterances." The judge convicted Hershel.

With Justice Scalia writing for an eight-to-one majority, the Supreme Court held that the tape of the 911 call in the Washington case was not testimonial and thus was properly admitted in Davis's trial. It held, however, that the Indiana court erred in admitting the affidavit against Hammon. Because the statements in both cases were made in the context of interrogation by police officers or their agents,[43] the Court began its analysis with an effort to determine what statements made to law enforcement are "testimonial" in nature:

> Without attempting to produce an exhaustive classification of all conceivable statements — or even all conceivable statements in response to police interrogation — as either testimonial or nontestimonial, it suffices to decide the present cases to hold as follows: Statements are nontestimonial when made in the course of police interrogation under circumstances objectively indicating that the primary purpose of the interrogation is to enable police assistance to meet an ongoing emergency. They are testimonial when the circumstances objectively indicate that there is no

---

43. The Court considered the 911 operator in *Davis* to be an agent of law enforcement even if not a police officer herself.

such ongoing emergency, and that the primary purpose of the interrogation is to establish or prove past events potentially relevant to later criminal prosecution.[44]

The key feature of this holding is the objective nature of the test. Statements are nontestimonial when the "circumstances objectively indicat[e] that the primary purpose of the interrogation is to enable the police to meet an ongoing emergency." They are testimonial when "the primary purpose of the interrogation is to establish or prove past events potentially relevant to later criminal prosecution."

The Court then explicitly held what it had strongly hinted in *Crawford*: that the Confrontation Clause applies only to "testimonial" hearsay. Citing early state confrontation cases, the Court noted that each involved testimony of one kind or another. Indeed, the Court stated, "[w]ell into the 20th century, our own Confrontation Clause jurisprudence was carefully applied only in the testimonial context." Though some more recent cases had muddied the waters, the right to confrontation attaches only to such statements:

> When we said in *Crawford* . . . that "interrogations by law enforcement officers fall squarely within [the] class" of testimonial hearsay, we had immediately in mind (for that was the case before us) interrogations solely directed at establishing the facts of a past crime, in order to identify (or provide evidence to convict) the perpetrator. The product of such interrogation, whether reduced to a writing signed by the declarant or embedded in the memory (and perhaps notes) of the interrogating officer, is testimonial."

A 911 call, the Court held, does not meet this definition because the "call . . . and at least the initial interrogation conducted in connection with a 911 call, is ordinarily not designed primarily to 'establis[h] or prov[e]' some past fact, but to describe current circumstances requiring police assistance." Thus, it differs from the interrogation in *Crawford* because it concerned "events *as they were actually happening*," and that any reasonable listener would recognize that the caller was describing an ongoing emergency rather than past events. In addition, "the nature of what was asked and answered in *Davis*, again viewed objectively, was such that the elicited statements were necessary to be able to *resolve* the present emergency, rather than simply to learn (as in *Crawford*), what had happened in the past." Finally, the Court noted "the difference in the level of formality" between the interviews in *Crawford* and *Davis*. Apparently, the more formal the interview, the more likely the hearsay is "testimonial." Concluding, the Court wrote that McCottry "simply was not acting as a *witness*; she was not *testifying*. What she said was not 'a weaker substitute for live testimony' at trial," as was the testimony in *Inadi* (discussed in the text).[45]

The Court then turned to *Hammon*, which it considered an easier case because the statements were similar to those in *Crawford*: "It is entirely clear from the

44. In a footnote, the Court stressed that although the statements at issue in these cases were both made during police interrogation, "[t]his is not to imply . . . that statements made in the absence of any interrogation are necessarily nontestimonial."
45. The Court recognized that a 911 call that begins in a nontestimonial context can become testimonial once the need for emergency assistance has ended. In *Davis*, for example, after the 911 operator learned what she needed to address the emergency and Davis had left the premises, the answers McCottry gave to the operator's questions were most likely testimonial, "not unlike the 'structured police questioning' that occurred in *Crawford*." Trial courts should redact any testimonial hearsay through *in limine* procedures.

circumstances that the interrogation was part of an investigation into possibly criminal past conduct. . . . There was no emergency in progress. . . . Objectively viewed, the primary, if not indeed the sole, purpose of the interrogation was to investigate a possible crime." Even though the *Crawford* interrogation was more formal, the interview in *Hammon* was sufficiently similar to be considered testimonial:

> Both declarants were actively separated from the defendant. . . . Both statements deliberately recounted, in response to police questioning, how potentially criminal past events began and progressed. And both took place some time after the events described were over. Such statements under official interrogation are an obvious substitute for live testimony, because they do precisely *what a witness does* on direct examination; they are inherently testimonial.

The Court was careful to note that its holding does not mean that questioning on the scene of alleged crime will never yield nontestimonial answers. Officers called to investigate domestic disputes need to learn who they are dealing with so they can assess the situation, including any possible threats to their own safety or to that of the victim. Thus, "[s]uch exigencies may *often* mean that 'initial inquiries' produce nontestimonial statements." But this was not the case in *Hammon*, "where Amy's statements were neither a cry for help nor the provision of information enabling officers immediately to end a threatening situation."

Davis helped to clarify the broad scope of the Court's new confrontation jurisprudence. For example, the Court made clear what it implied in *Crawford*: that the Confrontation Clause does not apply to "nontestimonial" hearsay. This holding cleared the way for admission of any "nontestimonial" hearsay that satisfies a hearsay exception. The Court also forged a rough test for determining when hearsay fits within one category or the other: The key is whether the declarant was acting in a manner similar to a trial witness. If the statement was made to police, the trial court should consider whether it was given to help police deal with an ongoing emergency (nontestimonial) or whether it was part of an investigation into past events (testimonial). The more formal the questioning, the more likely the declarant's statements are testimonial. And trial courts should be aware that the character of statements can change, requiring careful redaction of inadmissible parts.

Finally, the *Davis* opinion took note of the availability of forfeiture doctrine to deal with situations in which a domestic violence victim is intimidated or coerced into refusing to testify. When this occurs, the Confrontation Clause might appear to grant a "windfall" to the guilty, but the Sixth Amendment does not require courts to acquiesce. While defendants have no duty to assist the State in proving their guilt, they *do* have the duty to refrain from acting in ways that destroy the integrity of the criminal trial system. Justice Scalia wrote: "We reiterate what we said in *Crawford*: that 'the rule of forfeiture by wrongdoing . . . extinguishes confrontation claims on essentially equitable grounds.' . . . That is, one who obtains the absence of a witness by wrongdoing forfeits the constitutional right to confrontation."

In 2008, the Court discussed the application of the forfeiture doctrine to Confrontation Clause issues in Giles v. California, 554 U.S. 353 (2008). Dwayne Giles was prosecuted for the murder of his ex-girlfriend Brenda Avie. At trial Giles testified he shot Avie in self-defense. To counteract Giles's claim of self-defense and impeach his testimony, the prosecution offered statements Avie made to a police officer three weeks before the shooting alleging Giles had punched and choked her, then threatened her with a knife. The trial court admitted these statements. It relied on a California Evidence Code provision that permitted admission of hearsay statements describing the infliction or threat of physical injury on a declarant when the declarant was unavailable and the statements were deemed trustworthy. The California Supreme Court concluded admitting Avie's statement did not violate the Confrontation Clause, reasoning that because Giles's intentional criminal act made Avie unavailable, he had forfeited his constitutional right to confront her.

Justice Scalia, writing for five members of the Court, concluded the forfeiture doctrine applies only where there is a showing that the defendant engaged in conduct designed to prevent the declarant from testifying. To hold otherwise, Justice Scalia reasoned, would allow judges to strip a defendant of the right of confrontation, "a right that the Constitution deems essential to a fair trial," on the basis of a judicial assessment that the defendant is "guilty as charged." Three dissenting Justices argued the forfeiture doctrine should not require a showing the defendant specifically intended to prevent the declarant from testifying because the law generally holds an individual responsible for the likely consequences of an action as if that person intended to achieve them.

In 2011, the Supreme Court revisited the definition of "testimonial statements" in the context of police questioning. In Michigan v. Bryant, 131 S. Ct. 1143 (2011), police officers responding to a 911 call found Anthony Covington, mortally wounded, in a gas station parking lot. In response to police questioning Covington told the officers he had been shot about 25 minutes before they arrived at the home of defendant Bryant. Covington then provided a description of Bryant.[46] Covington told the officers he drove his car to the gas station after he was shot. Covington died within hours after he was transported to a hospital.

The trial court admitted police testimony recounting Covington's statements describing the shooting and identifying Bryant as his assailant. After Bryant was convicted of murder he appealed, arguing that admission of Covington's statements to the police violated the Confrontation Clause. The Michigan Supreme Court, invoking the broad language of the *Davis* opinion, concluded that Covington's statements to the police were testimonial because no emergency existed when the questioning occurred.

A majority of the U.S. Supreme Court disagreed. Writing for five members of the Court,[47] Justice Sotomayor explained how a court should analyze a claim that statements made to the police are testimonial:

46. The police questioning is described in Justice Scalia's dissenting opinion:

... in less than 10 minutes five different Detroit police officers questioned Covington about the shooting. Each asked him a similar battery of questions: "what happened" and when, ... "who shot" the victim, ... and "where" did the shooting take place. ... After Covington would answer, they would ask follow-up questions, such as "how tall is" the shooter, ... "[h]ow much does he weigh," ... what is the exact address or physical description of the house where the shooting took place, and what chain of events led to the shooting. The battery relented when the paramedics arrived and began tending to Covington's wounds.

47. Justice Thomas concluded the statements were not testimonial because the questioning by the police officers "lacked sufficient formality and solemnity for [Covington's] statements to be considered 'testimonial.'"

> ... [W]hen a court must determine whether the Confrontation Clause bars the admission of a statement at trial, it should determine the "primary purpose of the interrogation" by objectively evaluating the statements and actions of the parties to the encounter, in light of the circumstances in which the interrogation occurs. The existence of an emergency or the parties' perception that an emergency is ongoing is among the most important circumstances that courts must take into account in determining whether an interrogation is testimonial because statements made to assist police in addressing an ongoing emergency presumably lack the testimonial purpose that would subject them to the requirement of confrontation. ... The existence and duration of an emergency depend upon the type and scope of danger posed to the victim, the police, and the public.

The majority held that a judicial assessment of whether an emergency existed cannot focus solely on whether the threat to the victim had been neutralized, and that the duration of the emergency may depend upon the type of weapon involved. The majority stressed that the existence of an emergency is only one factor in determining the primary purpose of an interrogation. Also important is the formality or informality of the encounter between the declarant and the police, the primary purpose of the interrogation, and the medical condition of the declarant at the time the disputed statement was made.

A gun was involved in the incident, and Covington was seriously wounded. The majority concluded this suggested an emergency still existed. The questioning of Covington took place in the parking lot of a gas station before medical assistance arrived, which led the majority to conclude it was "informal," as opposed to the station house interrogation that occurred in *Crawford*. And the circumstances, for both the police and the victim, objectively indicated to the majority that neither party had the primary purpose of establishing past events potentially relevant to a later criminal prosecution. Based on this accumulation of factors, the majority concluded Covington's statements to the police were not testimonial, and therefore admitting them did not violate the Confrontation Clause.[48]

In Ohio v. Clark, 135 S. Ct. 2173 (2015), the Supreme Court further refined its *Crawford* analysis. In *Clark*, the defendant was accused of assault, domestic abuse, and child endangerment. A three-year-old boy made statements to his preschool teachers, who questioned him after they noticed he had bloodshot eyes and red marks and bruises on his body. When the child told the teachers the defendant caused his injuries, they called a child abuse hotline, and the prosecution ensued.

The trial court concluded the child was incompetent to testify. An Ohio statute allowed the introduction of reliable hearsay statements of alleged victims of child abuse. Defendant moved to exclude the statements made by the alleged victim, arguing that admission would violate the Confrontation Clause. The trial court admitted the statements; ultimately the Ohio Supreme Court reversed, agreeing with the defendant.

The U.S. Supreme Court unanimously reversed. The Justices declined to hold categorically that statements made to persons other than law enforcement officers cannot be "testimonial." However, they agreed that statements made to someone "not principally charged with uncovering and prosecuting criminal behavior," such as the teachers in *Clark*, are significantly less likely to be testimonial. The Justices further agreed that statements made by very young

---

48. In his dissent, Justice Scalia wrote that the majority opinion "distorts our Confrontation Clause jurisprudence and leaves it in a shambles."

children will rarely, "if ever," be testimonial. The Justices reached this conclusion by observing that it is "extremely unlikely" a young child would intend his or her statements to be a substitute for trial testimony.

The majority opinion also suggested a rationale for concluding that statements admitted under the dying declaration exception are exempt from Confrontation Clause exclusion: "Neither *Crawford* nor any of the cases that it has produced has mounted evidence that the . . . Confrontation Clause was understood to require the exclusion of evidence that was regularly admitted in criminal cases at the time of the founding."[49]

Much remains to be clarified about the application of the Confrontation Clause to evidentiary questions. It is reasonable to speculate that the Supreme Court will revisit these issues in the future. However, much of that clarification will be provided by the state and lower federal courts.[50]

Confrontation issues can arise in somewhat different settings as well. In Bruton v. United States, 391 U.S. 123 (1968), the Court held that when two people are charged criminally, and the confession of one defendant would not be admissible against the other defendant, it is normally necessary to sever the two cases and hold separate trials. In cases subsequent to *Bruton*, the courts explored situations in which separate trials are not necessary, but in Gray v. Maryland, 523 U.S. 185 (1998), the Court reaffirmed the requirement of severance in most situations in which two persons are charged with a crime and the confession of one implicates the second but is not admissible against that second defendant. The prosecution in *Gray* tried to avoid severance by removing any references to the non-confessing defendant from the co-defendant's confession and replacing them with the word *deleted* or *deletion*. The Court held that this did not adequately protect the rights of the non-confessing defendant because a jury could readily guess that the original version of the statement implicated the non-confessing defendant.

Further Reading: Margaret A. Berger, *The Deconstitutionalization of the Confrontation Clause: The Fallacy That Hearsay Rules and the Confrontation Clause Protect Similar Values*, 76 Minn. L. Rev. 557 (1992); Richard D. Friedman, *Confrontation: The Search for Basic Principles*, 86 Geo. L. Rev. 1011 (1998); Richard D. Friedman & Bridget McCormack, *Dial-In Testimony*, 150 U. Pa. L. Rev. 1171 (2002); Kenneth W. Graham, Jr., *The Right of Confrontation and the Hearsay Rule: Sir Walter Raleigh Loses Another One*, 8 Crim. L. Bull. 99 (1972); Randolph N. Jonakait, *Restoring the Confrontation Clause to the Sixth Amendment*, 46 UCLA L. Rev. 557 (1988); Laird C. Kirkpatrick, *Confrontation and Hearsay: Exemptions from the Constitutional Unavailability Requirement*, 70 Minn. L. Rev. 665 (1986); Roger W. Kirst, *The Procedural Dimension of the Confrontation Clause*, 66 Neb. L. Rev. 485 (1987); Penny J. White, *Rescuing the Confrontation Clause*, 54 S.C. L. Rev. 537 (2003).

---

49. In a concurring opinion, Justice Scalia agreed with this conclusion, but pointedly argued that the burden should be on the prosecution to prove ". . . a long established practice of introducing *specific* kinds of evidence, such as dying declarations. . . ." (Emphasis in original.)

50. Richard D. Friedman, a law professor whose theories were cited by the Supreme Court in *Crawford*, and who was appointed counsel to Hammon in the Supreme Court, maintains a blog devoted to the Confrontation Clause at http://confrontationright.blogspot.com/.

Questions for Classroom Discussion

1. Prosecution of Bob for bank robbery. Alice, an alleged accomplice, told police while under interrogation that she was the mastermind of the crime but that Bob was also involved. Alice died while in custody. Would admission of Alice's statement against Bob violate the Confrontation Clause?

2. Same case. While in jail, Alice made the same statement to Sally, her cellmate. Unknown to Alice, Sally was a police officer who was posing as a prisoner. Would admission of Alice's statement violate the Confrontation Clause?

3. Prosecution of Dennis for the shooting murder of Victim on a street corner. Dennis claims he was just in the wrong place at the wrong time, and that the killing was committed by another person. At trial, the prosecution calls Wilma to testify that she arrived at the street corner moments after the shooting and saw Walker kneeling next to Victim, sobbing. If permitted, Wilma will next testify that Walker suddenly pointed to Dennis and screamed, "You did it!" Walker died before the trial. Would admission of Walker's statement violate the Confrontation Clause?

4. Prosecution of Charlie in state court for possession of cocaine. Police Officer Anne testifies that when she stopped Charlie for speeding, she saw a vial containing a "white powdery substance" on the console of his car. The prosecution next offers in evidence affidavits from two police lab analysts stating they each tested the contents of the vial and independently concluded it was powder cocaine. Charlie's attorney objects, arguing admission of the affidavits would violate the Confrontation Clause. How should the court rule, and why?

5. Prosecution of Anh, a teacher, for statutory rape — she allegedly had sexual relations with an underage student. The student told the police about his relationship with the teacher during questioning. At trial the student refuses to testify, telling the court "I saw her again last week. I cannot hurt the woman I love." The state has a law that makes such statements admissible over a hearsay objection if there is evidence the defendant "convinced or coerced the declarant not to testify." Would admission of the student's statement to the police violate the Confrontation Clause?

4. Constitutional Limits on the Exclusion of Hearsay

Before we conclude our study of hearsay, we need to explore one more aspect of its relationship to the Constitution. The issue we must consider is whether a criminal defendant's constitutional rights ever *require* the trial court to permit the defendant to present otherwise inadmissible hearsay. The brief answer is yes. The difficulty is in isolating the precise factors that might lead to such a conclusion. The following case is generally considered the starting point for modern analysis of the issue.

CHAMBERS v. MISSISSIPPI

410 U.S. 284 (1973)

Mr. Justice POWELL delivered the opinion of the Court.

Petitioner, Leon Chambers, was tried by a jury in a Mississippi trial court and convicted of murdering a policeman. The jury assessed punishment at life imprisonment, and the Mississippi Supreme Court affirmed, one justice dissenting. . . . Subsequently, the petition for certiorari was granted . . . to consider whether petitioner's trial was conducted in accord with principles of due process under the Fourteenth Amendment. We conclude that it was not.

I

The events that led to petitioner's prosecution for murder occurred in the small town of Woodville in southern Mississippi. On Saturday evening, June 14, 1969, two Woodville policemen, James Forman and Aaron "Sonny" Liberty, entered a local bar and pool hall to execute a warrant for the arrest of a youth named C. C. Jackson. Jackson resisted and a hostile crowd of some 50 or 60 persons gathered. The officers' first attempt to handcuff Jackson was frustrated when 20 or 25 men in the crowd intervened and wrestled him free. Forman then radioed for assistance and Liberty removed his riot gun, a 12-gauge sawed-off shotgun, from the car. Three deputy sheriffs arrived shortly thereafter and the officers again attempted to make their arrest. Once more, the officers were attacked by the onlookers and during the commotion five or six pistol shots were fired. Forman was looking in a different direction when the shooting began, but immediately saw that Liberty had been shot several times in the back. Before Liberty died, he turned around and fired both barrels of his riot gun into an alley in the area from which the shots appeared to have come. The first shot was wild and high and scattered the crowd standing at the face of the alley. Liberty appeared, however, to take more deliberate aim before the second shot and hit one of the men in the crowd in the back of the head and neck as he ran down the alley. That man was Leon Chambers.

Officer Forman could not see from his vantage point who shot Liberty or whether Liberty's shots hit anyone. One of the deputy sheriffs testified at trial that he was standing several feet from Liberty and that he saw Chambers shoot him. Another deputy sheriff stated that, although he could not see whether Chambers had a gun in his hand, he did see Chambers "break his arm down" shortly before the shots were fired. The officers who saw Chambers fall testified that they thought he was dead but they made no effort at that time either to examine him or to search for the murder weapon. Instead, they attended to Liberty, who was placed in the police car and taken to a hospital where he was declared dead on arrival. A subsequent autopsy showed that he had been hit with four bullets from a .22-caliber revolver.

Shortly after the shooting, three of Chambers' friends discovered that he was not yet dead. James Williams, Berkley Turner, and Gable McDonald loaded him into a car and transported him to the same hospital. Later that night, when the county sheriff discovered that Chambers was still alive, a guard was placed outside his room. Chambers was subsequently charged with Liberty's murder. He pleaded not guilty and has asserted his innocence throughout.

The story of Leon Chambers is intertwined with the story of another man, Gable McDonald. McDonald, a lifelong resident of Woodville, was in the crowd on the evening of Liberty's death. Sometime shortly after that day, he left his wife in Woodville and moved to Louisiana and found a job at a sugar mill. In November of that same year, he returned to Woodville when his wife informed him that an acquaintance of his, known as Reverend Stokes, wanted to see him. Stokes owned a gas station in Natchez, Mississippi, several miles north of Woodville, and upon his return McDonald went to see him. After talking to Stokes, McDonald agreed to make a statement to Chambers' attorneys, who maintained offices in Natchez. Two days later, he appeared at the attorneys' offices and gave a sworn confession that he shot Officer Liberty. He also stated that he had already told a friend of his, James Williams, that he shot Liberty. He said that he used his own pistol, a nine-shot .22-caliber revolver, which he had discarded shortly after the shooting. In response to questions from Chambers' attorneys, McDonald affirmed that his confession was voluntary and that no one had compelled him to come to them. Once the confession had been transcribed, signed, and witnessed, McDonald was turned over to the local police authorities and was placed in jail.

One month later, at a preliminary hearing, McDonald repudiated his prior sworn confession. He testified that Stokes had persuaded him to confess that he shot Liberty. He claimed that Stokes had promised that he would not go to jail and that he would share in the proceeds of a lawsuit that Chambers would bring against the town of Woodville. On examination by his own attorney and on cross-examination by the State, McDonald swore that he had not been at the scene when Liberty was shot but had been down the street drinking beer in a cafe with a friend, Berkley Turner. When he and Turner heard the shooting, he testified, they walked up the street and found Chambers lying in the alley. He, Turner, and Williams took Chambers to the hospital. McDonald further testified at the preliminary hearing that he did not know what had happened, that there was no discussion about the shooting either going to or coming back from the hospital, and that it was not until the next day that he learned that Chambers had been felled by a blast from Liberty's riot gun. In addition, McDonald stated that while he once owned a .22-caliber pistol he had lost it many months before the shooting and did not own or possess a weapon at that time. The local justice of the peace accepted McDonald's repudiation and released him from custody. The local authorities undertook no further investigation of his possible involvement.

Chambers' case came on for trial in October of the next year. At trial, he endeavored to develop two grounds of defense. He first attempted to show that he did not shoot Liberty. Only one officer testified that he actually saw Chambers fire the shots. Although three officers saw Liberty shoot Chambers and testified that they assumed he was shooting his attacker, none of them examined Chambers to see whether he was still alive or whether he possessed a gun. Indeed, no weapon was ever recovered from the scene and there was no proof that Chambers had ever owned a .22-caliber pistol. One witness testified that he was standing in the street near where Liberty was shot, that he was looking at Chambers when the shooting began, and that he was sure that Chambers did not fire the shots.

Petitioner's second defense was that Gable McDonald had shot Officer Liberty. He was only partially successful, however, in his efforts to bring before the jury the testimony supporting this defense. Sam Hardin, a lifelong friend of McDonald's, testified that he saw McDonald shoot Liberty. A second witness, one of Liberty's cousins, testified that he saw McDonald immediately after the shooting with a pistol in his hand. In addition to the testimony of these two witnesses, Chambers endeavored to show the jury that McDonald had repeatedly confessed to the crime. Chambers attempted to prove that McDonald had admitted responsibility for the murder on four separate occasions, once when he gave the sworn statement to Chambers' counsel and three other times prior to that occasion in private conversations with friends.

In large measure, he was thwarted in his attempt to present this portion of his defense by the strict application of certain Mississippi rules of evidence. Chambers asserts in this Court, as he did unsuccessfully in his motion for new trial and on appeal to the State Supreme Court, that the application of these evidentiary rules rendered his trial fundamentally unfair and deprived him of due process of law. It is necessary, therefore, to examine carefully the rulings made during the trial.

II

Chambers filed a pretrial motion requesting the court to order McDonald to appear. Chambers also sought a ruling at that time that, if the State itself chose not to call McDonald, he be allowed to call him as an adverse witness. Attached to the motion were copies of McDonald's sworn confession and of the transcript of his preliminary hearing at which he repudiated that confession. The trial court granted the motion requiring McDonald to appear but reserved ruling on the adverse-witness motion. At trial, after the State failed to put McDonald on the stand, Chambers called McDonald, laid a predicate for the introduction of his sworn out-of-court confession, had it admitted into evidence, and read it to the jury. The State, upon cross-examination, elicited from McDonald the fact that he had repudiated his prior confession. McDonald further testified, as he had at the preliminary hearing, that he did not shoot Liberty, and that he confessed to the crime only on the promise of Reverend Stokes that he would not go to jail and would share in a sizable tort recovery from the town. He also retold his own story of his actions on the evening of the shooting, including his visit to the cafe down the street, his absence from the scene during the critical period, and his subsequent trip to the hospital with Chambers.

At the conclusion of the State's cross-examination, Chambers renewed his motion to examine McDonald as an adverse witness. The trial court denied the motion, stating: "He may be hostile, but he is not adverse in the sense of the word, so your request will be overruled." On appeal, the State Supreme Court upheld the trial court's ruling, finding that "McDonald's testimony was not adverse to appellant" because "(n)owhere did he point the finger at Chambers." . . .

Defeated in his attempt to challenge directly McDonald's renunciation of his prior confession, Chambers sought to introduce the testimony of the three witnesses to whom McDonald had admitted that he shot the officer. The first of these, Sam Hardin, would have testified that, on the night of the shooting, he spent the late evening hours with McDonald at a friend's house after their return from the hospital and that, while driving McDonald home later that night, McDonald stated that he shot Liberty. The State objected to the admission of this testimony on the ground that it was hearsay. The trial court sustained the objection.

Berkley Turner, the friend with whom McDonald said he was drinking beer when the shooting occurred, was then called to testify. In the jury's presence, and without objection, he testified that he had not been in the cafe that Saturday and had not had any beers with McDonald. The jury was then excused. In the absence of the jury, Turner recounted his conversations with McDonald while they were riding with James Williams to take Chambers to the hospital. When asked whether McDonald said anything regarding the shooting of Liberty, Turner testified that McDonald told him that he "shot him." Turner further stated that one week later, when he met McDonald at a friend's house, McDonald reminded him of their prior conversation and urged Turner not to "mess him up." Petitioner argued to the court that, especially where there was other proof in the case that was corroborative of these out-of-court statements, Turner's testimony as to McDonald's self-incriminating remarks should have been admitted as an exception to the hearsay rule. Again, the trial court sustained the State's objection.

The third witness, Albert Carter, was McDonald's neighbor. They had been friends for about 25 years. Although Carter had not been in Woodville on the evening of the shooting, he stated that he learned about it the next morning from McDonald. That same day, he and McDonald walked out to a well near McDonald's house and there McDonald told him that he was the one who shot Officer Liberty. Carter testified that McDonald also told him that he had disposed of the .22-caliber revolver later that night. He further testified that several weeks after the shooting, he accompanied McDonald to Natchez where McDonald purchased another .22 pistol to replace the one he had discarded. The jury was not allowed to hear Carter's testimony. Chambers urged that these statements were admissible, the State objected, and the court sustained the objection. On appeal, the State Supreme Court approved the lower court's exclusion of these witnesses' testimony on hearsay grounds. . . .

In sum, then, this was Chambers' predicament. As a consequence of the combination of Mississippi's "party witness" or "voucher" rule and its hearsay rule, he was unable either to cross-examine McDonald or to present witnesses in his own behalf who would have discredited McDonald's repudiation and demonstrated his complicity. Chambers had, however, chipped away at the fringes of McDonald's story by introducing admissible testimony from other sources indicating that he had not been seen in the cafe where he said he was when the shooting started, that he had not been having beer with Turner, and that he possessed a .22 pistol at the time of the crime. But all that remained from McDonald's own testimony was a single written confession countered by an arguably acceptable renunciation. Chambers' defense was far less persuasive than it might have been had he been given an opportunity to subject McDonald's statements to cross-examination or had the other confessions been admitted.

III

The right of an accused in a criminal trial to due process is, in essence, the right to a fair opportunity to defend against the State's accusations. The rights to confront and cross-examine witnesses and to call witnesses in one's own behalf have long been recognized as essential to due process. . . .

. . . Both of these elements of a fair trial are implicated in the present case.

A

Chambers was denied an opportunity to subject McDonald's damning repudiation and alibi to cross-examination. He was not allowed to test the witness' recollection, to probe into the details of his alibi, or to "sift" his conscience so that the jury might judge for itself whether McDonald's testimony was worthy of belief. . . . The right of cross-examination is more than a desirable rule of trial procedure. It is implicit in the constitutional right of confrontation, and helps assure the "accuracy of the truth-determining process." . . . It is, indeed, "an essential and fundamental requirement for the kind of fair trial which is this country's constitutional goal." . . . Of course, the right to confront and to cross-examine is not absolute and may, in appropriate cases, bow to accommodate other legitimate interests in the criminal trial process. . . . But its denial or significant diminution calls into question the ultimate "integrity of the fact-finding process" and requires that the competing interest be closely examined. . . .

In this case, petitioner's request to cross-examine McDonald was denied on the basis of a Mississippi common-law rule that a party may not impeach his own witness. The rule rests on the presumption—without regard to the circumstances of the particular case—that a party who calls a witness "vouches for his credibility." . . . Although the historical origins of the "voucher" rule are uncertain, it appears to be a remnant of primitive English trial practice in which "oath-takers" or "compurgators" were called to stand behind a particular party's position in any controversy. Their assertions were strictly partisan and, quite unlike witnesses in criminal trials today, their role bore little relation to the impartial ascertainment of the facts.

Whatever validity the "voucher" rule may have once enjoyed, and apart from whatever usefulness it retains today in the civil trial process, it bears little present relationship to the realities of the criminal process. It might have been logical for the early common law to require a party to vouch for the credibility of witnesses he brought before the jury to affirm his veracity. Having selected them especially for that purpose, the party might reasonably be expected to stand firmly behind their testimony. But in modern criminal trials, defendants are rarely able to select their witnesses: they must take them where they find them. Moreover, as applied in this case, the "voucher" rule's impact was doubly harmful to Chambers' efforts to develop his defense. Not only was he precluded from cross-examining McDonald, but, as the State conceded at oral argument, he was also restricted in the scope of his direct examination by the rule's corollary requirement that the party calling the witness is bound by anything he might say. He was, therefore, effectively prevented from exploring the circumstances of McDonald's three prior oral confessions and from challenging the renunciation of the written confession.

In this Court, Mississippi has not sought to defend the rule or explain its underlying rationale. Nor has it contended that its rule should override the accused's right of confrontation. Instead, it argues that there is no incompatibility between the rule and Chambers' rights because no right of confrontation exists unless the testifying witness is "adverse" to the accused. The State's brief asserts that the "right of confrontation applies to witnesses 'against' an accused." Relying on the trial court's determination that McDonald was not "adverse," and on the State Supreme Court's holding that McDonald did not "point the finger at Chambers," the State contends that Chambers' constitutional right was not involved.

The argument that McDonald's testimony was not "adverse" to, or "against," Chambers is not convincing. The State's proof at trial excluded the theory that more than one person participated in the shooting of Liberty. To the extent that McDonald's sworn confession tended to incriminate him, it tended also to exculpate Chambers. And, in the circumstances of this case, McDonald's retraction inculpated Chambers to the same extent that it exculpated McDonald. It can hardly be disputed that McDonald's testimony was in fact seriously adverse to Chambers. The availability of the right to confront and to cross-examine those who give damaging testimony against the accused has never been held to depend on whether the witness was initially put on the stand by the accused or by the State. We reject the notion that a right of such substance in the criminal process may be governed by that technicality or by any narrow and unrealistic definition of the word "against." The "voucher" rule, as applied in this case, plainly interfered with Chambers' right to defend against the State's charges.

B

We need not decide, however, whether this error alone would occasion reversal since Chambers' claimed denial of due process rests on the ultimate impact of that error when viewed in conjunction with the trial court's refusal to permit him to call other witnesses. The trial court refused to allow him to introduce the testimony of Hardin, Turner, and Carter. Each would have testified to the statements purportedly made by McDonald, on three separate occasions shortly after the crime, naming himself as the murderer. The State Supreme Court approved the exclusion of this evidence on the ground that it was hearsay.

The hearsay rule, which has long been recognized and respected by virtually every State, is based on experience and grounded in the notion that untrustworthy evidence should not be presented to the triers of fact. Out-of-court statements are traditionally excluded because they lack the conventional indicia of reliability: they are usually not made under oath or other circumstances that impress the speaker with the solemnity of his statements; the declarant's word is not subject to cross-examination; and he is not available in order that his demeanor and credibility may be assessed by the jury. . . . A number of exceptions have developed over the years to allow admission of hearsay statements made under circumstances that tend to assure reliability and thereby compensate for the absence of the oath and opportunity for cross-examination. Among the most prevalent of these exceptions is the one applicable to declarations against interest — an exception founded on the assumption that a person is unlikely to fabricate a statement against his own interest at the time it is made. Mississippi recognizes this exception but applies it only to declarations against pecuniary interest. It recognizes no such exception for declarations, like McDonald's in this case, that are against the penal interest of the declarant. . . .

This materialistic limitation on the declaration-against-interest hearsay exception appears to be accepted by most States in their criminal trial processes, although a number of States have discarded it. Declarations against penal interest have also been excluded in federal courts . . . although exclusion would not be required under the newly proposed Federal Rules of Evidence. Exclusion, where the limitation prevails, is usually premised on the view that admission would lead to the frequent presentation of perjured testimony to the jury. It is believed that confessions of criminal activity are often motivated by extraneous considerations and, therefore, are not as inherently reliable as statements against pecuniary or proprietary interest.

While that rationale has been the subject of considerable scholarly criticism, we need not decide in this case whether, under other circumstances, it might serve some valid state purpose by excluding untrustworthy testimony.

The hearsay statements involved in this case were originally made and subsequently offered at trial under circumstances that provided considerable assurance of their reliability. First, each of McDonald's confessions was made spontaneously to a close acquaintance shortly after the murder had occurred. Second, each one was corroborated by some other evidence in the case—McDonald's sworn confession, the testimony of an eyewitness to the shooting, the testimony that McDonald was seen with a gun immediately after the shooting, and proof of his prior ownership of a .22-caliber revolver and subsequent purchase of a new weapon. The sheer number of independent confessions provided additional corroboration for each. Third, whatever may be the parameters of the penal-interest rationale, each confession here was in a very real sense self-incriminatory and unquestionably against interest. . . . McDonald stood to benefit nothing by disclosing his role in the shooting to any of his three friends and he must have been aware of the possibility that disclosure would lead to criminal prosecution. Indeed, after telling Turner of his involvement, he subsequently urged Turner not to "mess him up." Finally, if there was any question about the truthfulness of the extrajudicial statements, McDonald was present in the courtroom and was under oath. He could have been cross-examined by the State, and his demeanor and responses weighed by the jury. . . . The availability of McDonald significantly distinguishes this case from the prior Mississippi precedent, . . . and from the *Donnelly*-type situation, since in both cases the declarant was unavailable at the time of trial.

Few rights are more fundamental than that of an accused to present witnesses in his own defense. . . . In the exercise of this right, the accused, as is required of the State, must comply with established rules of procedure and evidence designed to assure both fairness and reliability in the ascertainment of guilt and innocence. Although perhaps no rule of evidence has been more respected or more frequently applied in jury trials than that applicable to the exclusion of hearsay, exceptions tailored to allow the introduction of evidence which in fact is likely to be trustworthy have long existed. The testimony rejected by the trial court here bore persuasive assurances of trustworthiness and thus was well within the basic rationale of the exception for declarations against interest. That testimony also was critical to Chambers' defense. In these circumstances, where constitutional rights directly affecting the ascertainment of guilt are implicated, the hearsay rule may not be applied mechanistically to defeat the ends of justice.

We conclude that the exclusion of this critical evidence, coupled with the State's refusal to permit Chambers to cross-examine McDonald, denied him a trial in accord with traditional and fundamental standards of due process. In reaching this judgment, we establish no new principles of constitutional law. Nor does our holding signal any diminution in the respect traditionally accorded to the States in the establishment and implementation of their own criminal trial rules and procedures. Rather, we hold quite simply that under the facts and circumstances of this case the rulings of the trial court deprived Chambers of a fair trial.

The judgment is reversed and the case is remanded to the Supreme Court of Mississippi for further proceedings not inconsistent with this opinion.

Chambers is not the only case in which the Supreme Court has held that the hearsay rule and other rules of evidence sometimes must yield to a criminal defendant's constitutional rights. The Court applied the same analysis in Green v. Georgia, 442 U.S. 95 (1979), a rape and murder prosecution. The Court reversed the death sentence of Green, who was prevented from offering the statement of his co-defendant asserting that he, and not defendant, had killed the victim. The prosecution had used that same evidence to obtain a death sentence for the co-defendant, but objected to its use by Green because Georgia's hearsay rule did not include an exception for statements against penal interest. The Court rested its decision on the defendant's right to due process.

Whether couched in terms of due process or one of the many rights embedded in the Sixth Amendment, the decisions of various state and federal courts demonstrate that a criminal defendant sometimes has the right to present evidence that otherwise would be excluded by the hearsay rule or other rules of evidence. The right is not broad; in most instances, a criminal defendant is just as bound by the rules of evidence as is the government. But to quote the Supreme Court in *Chambers*, "the hearsay rule may not be applied mechanistically to defeat the ends of justice," and the same principle applies to other evidence rules as well.[51]

Further Reading: Robert Clinton, *The Right to Present a Defense: An Emergent Constitutional Guarantee in Criminal Trials*, 9 Ind. L. Rev. 711 (1976); David Robinson, Jr., *From Fat Tony and Matty the Horse to the Sad Case of A.A.: Defensive and Offensive Use of Hearsay Evidence in Criminal Cases*, 32 Hous. L. Rev. 895 (1995); Peter Westen, *Confrontation and Compulsory Process: A Unified Theory of Evidence for Criminal Cases*, 91 Harv. L. Rev. 567 (1978); Peter Westen, *The Compulsory Process Clause*, 73 Mich. L. Rev. 71 (1974); Welsh S. White, *Evidentiary Privileges and the Defendant's Constitutional Right to Introduce Evidence*, 80 J. Crim. L. & Criminology 377 (1989).

51. For an analysis of the variety of situations in which a criminal defendant's constitutional rights — particularly the right to present a defense — demand that the evidence rules give way, see Edward J. Imwinkelried & Norman M. Garland, Exculpatory Evidence (2d ed. 1996).

Questions for Classroom Discussion

1. In *Chambers*, what factors appear to have motivated the Supreme Court to hold that the Mississippi evidence rules could not be used to prevent Chambers from presenting evidence of McDonald's confession and other statements?

2. Prosecution of Defendant for murder. The crime was witnessed by several people, each of whom independently identified Defendant in non-suggestive line-ups. At trial, Defendant calls Witness and wishes to have her testify that Zed, a casual acquaintance of Defendant, confessed that he had committed the murder. Zed is unavailable. Defendant is unable to present any evidence corroborating the trustworthiness of Zed's statement to Witness. The prosecution objects on hearsay grounds. Defendant responds that exclusion of the evidence would violate his constitutional rights. How should the court rule?

Assessments

The first four questions are hearsay/not hearsay questions. You should determine whether the "statement" is, analytically, hearsay considering the purpose for which it is offered. <u>Do not consider any exceptions to the hearsay rule, or any of the provisions of the Federal Rules of Evidence that create exemptions from the hearsay rule.</u>

1. When asked to identify her assailant in a constitutionally acceptable line-up at the police station, Marsha pointed to David Defendant. At David's trial, Marsha testifies she pointed to David at the station.

2. Romeo and Juliet rob a bank. After the robbery, Romeo tells Juliet, "I will head for Tijuana. When I run for it the cops will suspect only me. After the heat dies down you will join me in Cabo San Lucas where we will live happily ever after." During his trial for bank robbery, the prosecution offers testimony that Romeo was caught trying to cross the border, as tending to prove his guilt.

<u>Questions 3 and 4 are based upon this scenario:</u> A bridge over a river is damaged during a storm. A city engineer instructs a work crew to erect a sign reading "Danger — Bridge unsafe." The next day a driver attempts to cross the bridge, and crashes into the river when the bridge collapses. The driver sues the city for his injuries. During the trial, a properly authenticated photograph of the sign, taken one day after the accident, is marked for identification:

3. The photograph is offered by the city as tending to show the driver was contributorily negligent.

4. The photograph is offered by the defendant as tending to show the bridge was damaged.

<u>The following multiple choice questions will test your knowledge of the hearsay rule, and the application of the exemptions and exceptions under the Federal Rules of Evidence.</u>

5. Williams' children file an action seeking to have him committed to a mental institution. On the issue of Williams' insanity, his students will testify Williams stated in class, "I am Stephen Curry!" This testimony is:
   a. Hearsay because the inference that Williams is insane depends on the truth of the matter asserted
   b. Not hearsay because the statement is not offered to prove the truth of the matter asserted
   c. Hearsay but admissible under the state of mind exception to the hearsay rule
   d. Not hearsay because the statement has independent legal significance

6. Phil is being tried for the murder of Lana. Immediately before Lana died Phil's chauffeur heard her say, "I see a bright white light. I know that I am leaving this world for a better life. The little troll shot me because I would not sleep with him." The chauffeur is called by the prosecution to testify to the above.
   a. This is hearsay, but may be admissible as a dying declaration exception
   b. This is inadmissible hearsay
   c. This is hearsay, but may be admissible under the state of mind exception
   d. This is hearsay, and the prosecution must present non-hearsay evidence that Lana was under a sense of impending death before the court may admit the testimony

7. Jerry is attacked. The evening after the attack, Jerry calls the police when he sees Geraldo at a celebrity party and identifies Geraldo as the man who attacked him. During the trial of Geraldo on assault charges, Jerry testifies he remembers identifying his attacker for the police, but no longer remembers whom he identified. The prosecution then calls Detective Crane who was present when Geraldo was arrested. Crane will testify that Jerry identified Geraldo as his attacker. Crane's proposed testimony is:
   a. Inadmissible because Jerry cannot recall who he identified
   b. Not hearsay

(continued)

    c. Hearsay, but admissible under the prior identification exception
    d. Hearsay, but admissible under the state of mind exception

8. Taylor is prosecuted for assault with a deadly weapon. As tending to prove Taylor had a weapon, the prosecution calls Walter, who testifies that he calmly told his wife, as Taylor was walking by their home, "Dear, look at the .457 Magnum in that man's jacket." Walter's testimony is:
    a. Inadmissible hearsay
    b. Hearsay, but admissible as an excited utterance
    c. Not hearsay because Walter is on the stand and subject to cross-examination
    d. Hearsay, but admissible as a present sense impression

Answers and Analysis

1. The correct answer is "hearsay." Marsha's conduct is assertive; by pointing to David she intended to assert that he was her assailant. Therefore analytically this is hearsay—Marsha's out of court statement is being offered to prove the truth of the matter asserted. If the Federal Rules applied the correct answer would become "not hearsay because this is a statement of identification. FRE 801(d)(1)(c).

2. The correct answer is "hearsay." Fleeing after committing a crime is, typically, non-assertive conduct. However Romeo says his conduct is intended to divert suspicion from Juliet. His conduct is, therefore assertive. It is being offered to prove the truth of the matter asserted, that Romeo robbed the bank. Analytically that makes this testimony hearsay. If the Federal Rules applied the correct answer would become "not hearsay" because this "statement" of Romeo is being offered against him. FRE 801(d)(2)(A).

3. The correct answer is "not hearsay.' In this instance the city wants to show the driver knew, or should have known, the bridge was unsafe. The existence of the sign is being offered to show its impact upon the driver—it is not being offered to prove the bridge was damaged.

4. The correct answer is "hearsay." The engineer intended to communicate to drivers that the bridge was unsafe when she ordered the sign erected. The sign is the assertion that the bridge was unsafe—and here the defendant is offering that statement to prove the truth of the matter asserted.

5. The correct answer is "b." Williams' children are not trying to prove the truth of the matter asserted in his statement—that he is the most valuable player in professional basketball. The children are using Williams' statement as indirect evidence of his state of mind—it tends to show that he is not quite sane. Because the statement is not being offered to prove the truth of the matter asserted, it is not hearsay.

6. The correct answer is "a." This is a fairly straightforward example of a dying declaration. The statement concerns the cause and circumstances of Lana's death. Her statement tends to show she was under a sense of impending death when she spoke. The court may use her statement as evidence of that foundational requirement because Rule 104(a) provides that a court is not bound by the evidence Rules when determining preliminary questions of fact.

7. The correct answer is "b." This is an example of one of the exemptions in the Federal Rules at work. Jerry's statement to the police is an assertion that Geraldo attacked him. Officer Crane's testimony is offered to prove the truth of that assertion. Because Jerry's statement was one of identification, it is defined as "not hearsay." Rule 801(d)(1)(c).

8. The correct answer is "d." This testimony is hearsay because Walter is testifying about his out-of-court statement to his wife. The inference to be drawn, that Taylor had a gun, depends upon the truthfulness of Walter's out of court statement. It qualifies as a present sense impression because Walter made the statement to his wife as he was observing Taylor walk by their home. FRE 803(1).

CHAPTER

4

Evidence of Character, Uncharged Misconduct, and Similar Events

A. INTRODUCTION

The primary purpose of this chapter is to explore the complex problems created by a party's presentation of evidence shedding light on a person's character. As we will see, U.S. law strongly disfavors what has been called *trial by character*. Trials should be about what people have done, not about the kinds of people they are. As a result of this policy, parties are usually forbidden from offering character evidence and, instead, must present evidence that focuses the fact-finder's attention on the parties' conduct and state of mind. For several reasons, however, any rule that categorically forbade the use of evidence from which the fact-finder might infer an actor's character would be overbroad. First, deeply held considerations of fairness and policy support the use of some character evidence by criminal defendants seeking to show their innocence. Second, the substantive law sometimes makes character an issue in a case, making its admission necessary. Third, some evidence of a person's character is also useful to prove facts other than character. If evidence law categorically prohibited all such evidence, the fact-finder would be shielded from much useful — and even occasionally required — information.

The materials in this chapter describe the ways in which the law of evidence attempts to walk the thin line between avoiding trial by character and allowing the parties to present sufficient legitimate evidence to support their claims. As you will see, the admissibility of character evidence is highly dependent on the type of case in which it is offered, the purpose for which it is offered, and the factual context of the case.

In this chapter, we also explore two other related types of evidence, each of which is subject to its own set of rules. First is evidence of "habit." We will see that habit, a rather narrow category of evidence, is far more likely to be admissible than is evidence of character. The second type of evidence concerns similar events. As with habit, if the evidence qualifies, it is more readily admissible than character evidence.

The subjects of this chapter are not easy to learn. It is essential to keep your eye on the ball. We suggest that you analyze any problem that potentially involves character evidence by asking yourself the following questions:

1. What is the evidence?
2. What is it offered to prove?
3. Is it relevant when offered for that purpose? (If it is not, the analysis is over and the evidence is inadmissible.)
4. If the evidence is relevant, is it character evidence?
5. If the evidence *is* character evidence,
    a. Do the rules permit the use of character evidence for this purpose in this type of case?
    b. If character evidence can be used for this purpose, does it prove character through a proper method?
    c. Has the party offering the evidence complied with any procedural rules regarding its admission (timing, for example)?
6. If the evidence *is not* character evidence,
    a. Is it evidence of "*other crimes, wrongs, or acts*" offered to prove a fact other than character? If so, has the party offering the evidence complied with the rules and standards governing its use for that purpose?
    b. Is it evidence of *habit?* If so, has the party offering the evidence complied with the rules and standards governing its use for that purpose?
    c. Is it evidence of *similar events?* If so, has the party offering the evidence complied with the rules and standards governing its use for that purpose?

Students who fail to follow this general roadmap are bound to ask such questions as "Is character evidence admissible in a civil case?" This is a useless question because it is far too general. One must ask, instead, whether evidence of character is admissible for *this* specific purpose under *these* circumstances in *this* type of case. The questions above are designed to help you analyze those more specific issues.

B.   CHARACTER EVIDENCE

> ### FED. R. EVID. 404.   CHARACTER EVIDENCE; CRIMES, WRONGS, OR OTHER ACTS

(a) Character Evidence.

(1) **Prohibited Uses.** Evidence of a person's character or character trait is not admissible to prove that on a particular occasion the person acted in accordance with the character or trait.

(2) **Exceptions for a Defendant or Victim in a Criminal Case.** The following exceptions apply in a criminal case:

(A) a defendant may offer evidence of the defendant's pertinent trait, and if the evidence is admitted, the prosecutor may offer evidence to rebut it;

(B) subject to the limitations in Rule 412, a defendant may offer evidence of an alleged crime victim's pertinent trait, and if the evidence is admitted, the prosecutor may:

      (i) offer evidence to rebut it; and

      (ii) offer evidence of the defendant's same trait; and

      (C) in a homicide case, the prosecutor may offer evidence of the alleged victim's trait of peacefulness to rebut evidence that the victim was the first aggressor.

Exceptions for a Witness. Evidence of a witness's character may be admitted under Rules 607, 608, and 609.

  (b) Crimes, Wrongs, or Other Acts.

    (1) *Prohibited Uses.* Evidence of a crime or other act is not admissible to prove a person's character in order to show that on a particular occasion the person acted in accordance with the character.

    (2) *Permitted Uses; Notice.* This evidence may be admissible for another purpose, such as proving motive, opportunity, intent, preparation, plan, knowledge, identity, absence of mistake, or lack of accident. On request by a defendant in a criminal case, the prosecutor must:

      (A) provide reasonable notice of the general nature of any such evidence that the prosecutor intends to offer at trial; and

      (B) do so before trial — or during trial if the court, for good cause, excuses lack of pretrial notice.

FED. R. EVID. 405. METHODS OF PROVING CHARACTER

  (a) By Reputation or Opinion. When evidence of a person's character or character trait is admissible, it may be proved by testimony about the person's reputation or by testimony in the form of an opinion. On cross-examination of the character witness, the court may allow an inquiry into relevant specific instances of the person's conduct.

  (b) By Specific Instances of Conduct. When a person's character or character trait is an essential element of a charge, claim, or defense, the character or trait may also be proved by relevant specific instances of the person's conduct.

Discussion

1. Introduction

With very limited exceptions, trials in the United States are about conduct, not character. This is a fundamental principle, and it runs very deep. The government can prosecute a person for possessing drugs, or for being under the influence of certain substances, but it is unconstitutional to prosecute a person for *being* a drug addict. A defendant can be a bad person and still be innocent. She can be a good person but still guilty. Rather than focusing generally on what kind of a person a party may be, our system focuses on whether she engaged in specific conduct with a specific state of mind on a specific occasion or series of occasions. A person may have a bad character, or may have participated in criminal or other wrongful conduct at times other than those that formed the basis of the charge or claim, but neither character nor uncharged misconduct may be made the ultimate issue in this action.

But while this limitation on the subject matter of U.S. trials is clear, it leaves open a number of interesting and sometimes troubling questions. What kind of evidence may be used to prove the specific events at issue, the identity of the individuals who committed the acts in question, or the actors' states of mind? To say, for example, that one may not be prosecuted for being addicted to drugs does not resolve all questions concerning the admissibility of evidence concerning drug addiction. The question remains, can such evidence be used to prove conduct such as drug possession? The fact of a defendant's addiction is certainly relevant to the question whether defendant possessed drugs; it might even be highly probative evidence of possession. Consider the following hypothetical:

Defendant is charged with the murder of Victim, who was shot by a person hiding in the bushes in front of Victim's home, apparently waiting for Victim to return from work. Defendant denies any involvement. To prove Defendant's guilt, the prosecution wishes to offer evidence that a week before Victim was murdered, Defendant had robbed a bank, that Victim was a teller at the bank, and that Victim was about to identify Defendant as the perpetrator.

This evidence clearly is relevant. One possible chain of reasoning would be as follows:

> **EVIDENCE:** Victim could identify Defendant as the perpetrator of a bank robbery.
>
> > **➜INFERENCE:** Defendant had a motive to prevent Victim from making the identification.
> >
> > > **➜CONCLUSION:** Defendant murdered Victim to prevent this disclosure.

This reasoning is logical, sensible, and, in some cases, compelling. Defendant is not on trial for robbing the bank, but evidence of the robbery, and of Victim's ability to identify Defendant as the robber, creates a motive that makes it somewhat more likely than it would be without the evidence that Defendant murdered Victim.

Of course, the reasoning outlined above is not the only possible set of inferences that might arise from the facts of the case. The following reasoning is also possible:

> **EVIDENCE**: Victim could identify Defendant as the perpetrator of a bank robbery.
>
> > **➜INFERENCE**: Defendant is a bad person who commits serious crimes.
> >
> > > **➜CONCLUSION**: Defendant was the person who murdered Victim.

This reasoning is also logical. Our experience leads us to believe that people who have committed serious crimes are more likely to commit other serious crimes than are people who have not been involved in such conduct. The problem with this reasoning is that it seems to violate the basic principle with which we began: that people must be tried based on their conduct on the charged occasion, not on their past conduct or on how highly they rate in the pantheon of human character.

For the past two centuries, Anglo-American courts have sought to place appropriate limits on the admissibility of character and misconduct evidence. This is a delicate task, and it has often led to inconsistency and controversy. On the one hand, courts must hew to the basic principle we've been discussing. But on the other hand, courts must not place such strict limits on the admissibility of relevant evidence that it becomes virtually impossible to prove the elements of a charge or claim.

As you study the subjects covered in this chapter, it is vital to keep in mind the basic mode of analysis that we have set forth from the beginning of this book. Remember that the rules of evidence are based on classification. We classify types of evidence and we classify specific purposes for which the evidence might be offered. To resolve any question regarding the admissibility of character or misconduct evidence, one must always begin by classifying that evidence: What is the questioned evidence? What is it offered to prove? What type of evidence is it? What limitations does the law place on that type of evidence, offered for that purpose, in this situation?

2. *Character Evidence Offered for Non-credibility Purposes*

a. **Character Defined**

What is *character*? Unfortunately, we do not have a good definition. Almost everyone would agree that when we speak of the character of a person, we are thinking about something both *internal* and *general* about that person. We think of character as internal because we see it as a fundamental and integral part of the person — as much or more a part of her being as any physical characteristic. We think of character as general because we see it as informing many of a person's actions, rather than merely describing a reaction the person has to a particular situation. Thus, when we heard in elementary school that Abraham Lincoln was known as "Honest Abe," we believed we had learned something internal about Lincoln that would affect his conduct in a variety of situations. Having heard that Lincoln was honest, we were more likely to believe that as a young store clerk, he once walked for miles to catch up with a customer to whom he owed a penny in change. Similarly, if we hear that a person participated in a barroom brawl, we believe we have learned about something internal to that person (a character for violent behavior) that would make her act in similar ways under certain circumstances.

Because we think of character as an internal motivator of a person's conduct, evidence of character can thus be seen as a form of *propensity* evidence. By "propensity evidence," we mean evidence that shows a person's tendency to act in a certain way. But character is not the only kind of propensity evidence. We know that people have tendencies to act in many different ways, and that we would not see all of them as motivated by character. For example, if you hear that your Evidence professor has a tendency to look more toward the left side of the classroom than the right when she is teaching, and you are the type of student who prefers not to be called on in class, you would consider that information when deciding where to sit in the classroom. In other words, you would take the information as a predictor of how the professor would behave in class. But it is unlikely that you would consider the professor's behavior to be evidence of her character. Similarly, if you heard that a person was blind, left-handed, or a cancer survivor, you would believe that you had learned something internal about the person that might affect her behavior, but you are unlikely to consider that behavior to be character-driven. Another type of propensity is habitual behavior. If we learn that a person always turns on the television when she gets home from work, or that a dry cleaner always gives a customer a receipt when the customer drops off a load of clothes, we have learned something about the person's propensity to act in a certain way, but we probably do not consider that propensity to be character-driven. These pieces of information suggest what a person's propensities might be, but do not arise from what we would call character.

Thus, character evidence is a form of general propensity evidence, but it is merely a subset of propensity evidence. As one scholar has written, "[a]ll character evidence offered to show action in conformity with character is propensity evidence, but not all propensity evidence is character evidence."[1] We therefore must add something to our definition of character to distinguish it from other forms of propensity. Perhaps the distinguishing factor is that character must have a *moral or ethical component*. Wigmore defined character as "the actual moral or psychical disposition or sum of traits."[2] In a frequently quoted passage, McCormick defined it as "a generalized description of one's disposition, or of one's disposition in respect to a general trait, such as honesty, temperance, or peacefulness,"[3] which suggests that he, also, thought character had something to do with a person's moral or ethical bearing. The Advisory Committee suggested that "character is defined as the kind of person one is,"[4] and distinguished it from habit, which, as some of our examples show, is also a form of propensity evidence.

Based on the foregoing, we take the following as our working understanding of *character evidence*. It is evidence concerning the propensity of a person to act in a certain manner that makes a general statement about that person and conveys a moral or ethical judgment. As the materials in the sections that follow show, the limits on the admissibility of character evidence, so defined, make sense for a number of reasons. Most important, character evidence, though probative of conduct, carries significant danger of unfair prejudice because it tends to focus the jury's attention on the moral or ethical worthiness of the person in question. Other forms of propensity do not create so great a risk.[5]

1. Richard B. Kuhns, *The Propensity to Misunderstand the Character of Specific Acts Evidence*, 66 Iowa L. Rev. 777, 794 (1981).

2. 1A John H. Wigmore, Evidence in Trials at Common Law §52, at 1148 (Peter Tillers rev. 1983).

3. Charles T. McCormick, Handbook on the Law of Evidence §162, at 340 (1954).

4. Fed. R. Evid. 405 Advisory Committee's Note.

5. Although our materials adopt this view of character, we should point out that some courts and commentators use a broader definition. In their view, a person's character includes, but is not limited to, attributes that indicate something about a person's morals or ethics. We understand this broader view of character, but do not believe it adequately explains or reflects the goals of the rules restricting the use of character evidence at trial.

A word about character theory.   The law accepts a largely outmoded theory of character usually known as *trait theory*. That theory holds that people possess fairly consistent traits of character, and that those traits manifest themselves, more or less, in the varying circumstances of everyday life. Thus, a person may possess a trait for peacefulness. A peaceful person, it is thought, will tend to be peaceful in circumstances that might cause a more violence-prone person to erupt. The circumstances may be different, but the person will exhibit the same tendency toward peacefulness whenever confronted with a situation that calls on the use of that trait or its opposite.

By the middle of the twentieth century, trait theory was largely abandoned by experimental psychologists. Clinical studies showed that people exhibit very little cross-situational consistency. For example, a child who declines to cheat on one kind of school test administered in one type of setting might cheat on another kind of test in a different setting, or even the same type of test in a different setting. Once the assumed consistency of character traits was undermined, our confidence in the predictive value of character traits was also significantly lessened.

In place of trait theory, psychologists substituted what is sometimes called *situationism.* As its name suggests, this theory is based on the assumption that to predict how a person might behave in a given situation, it is necessary to know how that person behaved in very similar situations in the past. Only extremely similar situations would provide meaningful predictability. Thus, to predict whether a particular third-grader will cheat on a math test administered in class with 25 other students, it would be crucial to know how she behaved in that exact situation before. Any differences between the two situations would significantly undermine the predictive value of the earlier one. Situationism is therefore a very strict theory.

Some psychologists have recently suggested that the greatest accuracy of predictions may be achieved through a combination of trait theory and situationism. This new theory is called *interactionism.* As its nature suggests, predictability requires a rather large amount of information about a person. But if one can accurately assess an individual's general tendencies (traits), and research about the person's past behavior reveals that she has been faced with situations very similar to the one at issue, it is theoretically possible to make a reasonable prediction about how she will behave. The prediction will not carry enormous confidence, of course, but it should prove more accurate than one based solely on traits or solely on behavior in similar situations.

Unfortunately, as we will see, the law of evidence is still mired in trait theory. Faced with determining how a person might have acted in a particular situation (the occasion of the charged crime, for example), the law largely forbids evidence of how that person acted in very similar situations. Instead, the law usually allows only the broadest generalities about the person's character traits, revealed by her community reputation or by the opinion of a person who knows her well. It remains to be seen whether the law will ever catch up with human behavioral experts.

b. Potential Uses of Character Evidence

The key to determining the admissibility of character evidence is ascertaining the purpose for which that evidence is offered. There are three main purposes for which a party may wish to offer evidence of character:

1. to prove character when character itself is an essential element of a charge, claim, or defense (when character is "in issue");
2. to prove character as circumstantial evidence of how a person behaved other than as a witness while testifying (circumstantial evidence of out-of-court conduct); and
3. to prove character as circumstantial evidence of the truthfulness of a witness.

In this chapter, we focus on the first two purposes. The third purpose, which concerns impeachment or rehabilitation of a witness through evidence of the witness's character for truthfulness, is covered in Chapter 6. To say that character evidence may be offered in each of these situations is not to say that it is *always* admissible for those purposes. As we will see, though the law is necessarily lenient with respect to evidence of character when character is "in issue," it is extremely restrictive when character is offered as circumstantial evidence of a person's out-of-court conduct.

c.   Methods of Proving Character: Rule 405

Just as it is vital to identify the purpose for which character evidence is offered, it is also important to consider the method the party is using to prove character. A person's character may not be proven directly. This is because character is not something tangible that can be perceived by a witness, such as blond hair or brown eyes. Instead, one must look for traces in a person's life to find circumstantial evidence of her character. As illustrated by Rule 405, quoted at the beginning of this chapter, the law envisions three methods of proving character: *evidence of reputation, opinion, and specific instances of conduct.*

Reputation is not character. It is what people in the community say about a person's character and, as we all know, it is not always accurate. (Wigmore called reputation "the secondhand, irresponsible product of multiplied guesses and gossip. . . .") Indeed, testimony about reputation is hearsay, though Rule 803(21) contains an exception for "reputation among a person's associates or in the community concerning the person's character." If a party wishes to have a witness testify to a person's reputation for having a particular character trait, the party must demonstrate that the witness has sufficient knowledge of the person's community reputation; reputation among a small circle of people is usually not sufficient. The witness may not testify to a person's reputation unless the witness has been part of the community in question long enough to have gained sufficient exposure to what people in the community think about the person. In the following example, assume that Defendant has been charged with murder, and has called Witness to testify to Defendant's reputation for peacefulness.

D: How long have you lived in Springfield?

W: All my life. Thirty-five years.

D: And have you ever heard people in the community speak about Defendant's character?

W: Yes, I have.

D: Are you aware of Defendant's reputation for peacefulness within the community at large?

W: Yes.

D: What is Defendant's community reputation for peacefulness?

W: Defendant has a reputation as an extremely peaceful person.

In this example, Witness has testified to her knowledge of defendant's general community reputation for peacefulness, and has stated what that reputation is. The examination consumes little time and involves no detail; even the possible factual basis for Defendant's reputation is not included (and might not be permitted).

The second method of proving character is with opinion evidence. Opinion evidence generally consists of the testimony of someone who knows the person's character well enough to assert an opinion about it. Rule 701 governs the admissibility of lay opinion, which is the type of opinion testimony most commonly offered to prove character. Among other things, Rule 701 requires that lay opinion must be rationally based on perception. Thus, one who knows a person well and for a long period of time is likely to have a sufficient basis for testifying about the person's honesty, peacefulness, and other traits that would have manifested themselves in daily life. A person who works closely with another is likely to have a sufficient basis for testifying about her character for care in her work, her character for promptness, and perhaps other things. Absent unusual circumstances at work, however, such a witness is unlikely to have gained sufficient insight into the person's character for peacefulness to be permitted to testify about that character trait. See Chapter 7 for a detailed discussion of lay opinion evidence under Rule 701.

To return to our murder hypothetical, Defendant might call as a character witness someone who has known Defendant for a sufficient period of time and has observed Defendant in a sufficient variety of circumstances:

D: Do you know Defendant personally?

W: Yes.

D: What is the nature of your relationship?

W: Friends.

D: How long have you been friends?

W: I guess you could say a long time. We've been friends since grade school.

D: Have you and Defendant been together in different types of social and business situations?

W: Yes. Over the years, we've spent a lot of time together.

D: Based on your knowledge of and observation of Defendant, do you have an opinion as to Defendant's character for peacefulness?

W: Yes, I do.

D: What is your opinion about Defendant's character for peacefulness?

W: In my opinion, Defendant is an extremely peaceful person.

As with evidence of reputation, the process of eliciting opinion evidence of character is swift and its substance is general. Usually, the witness may not explain the basis for an opinion by referring to specific instances of the person's conduct.

So far, we have been speaking of the opinion of a lay witness. But it is also possible that one might offer an expert's opinion of a person's character. A psychiatrist, for example, might be called to testify to a person's character. The expert witness may have formed that opinion from a number of sources, including face-to-face interviews, examination of answers to a questionnaire, the results of a battery of psychological tests, review of a social worker's report, or other sources. The expert may also be presented with the data while testifying, such as through a lengthy hypothetical question based on evidence supported by the record. As set forth in Rule 703, the expert's opinion must be based on data that "experts in the particular field would reasonably rely on . . . in forming an opinion on the subject." Further, Rule 702 provides that the expert's opinion must be reliable in the sense that it is grounded in valid science. See Chapter 7 for our discussion of expert testimony.

The final form character evidence may take is evidence of specific instances of a person's conduct. When this type of evidence is permitted, the witness will be asked to relate specific instances of conduct that demonstrate a particular character trait. To take a new hypothetical, suppose Plaintiff sues Defendant for libel, alleging that Defendant's newspaper published an untruthful article referring to Plaintiff, a produce dealer, as a "crooked businesswoman." Because the article will not be libelous unless the allegation is untrue, one way for Defendant to prevail is by proving that Plaintiff is, in fact, a crooked businesswoman. In other words, Defendant must prove that Plaintiff's character actually is as portrayed in the article. Examination of a character witness might proceed as follows:

D: Are you employed?

W: Yes.

D: What is the nature of your business?

W: I am the produce purchasing manager for a large supermarket chain.

D: Do you know Plaintiff?

W: Yes.

D: What is the nature of your relationship?

W: We did business with each other for a number of years. For quite a while, I bought produce from her.

D: Did you stop ordering produce from Plaintiff?

W: Yes.

D: Why did you stop?

W: I concluded that plaintiff was totally crooked in her business dealings.

D: Can you give the court an example of a situation in which Plaintiff acted dishonestly in her transactions with you?

W: I could give you a lot of examples, but one in particular sticks out in my mind. About three years ago, I made an order for Pippin apples, which were in short supply at the time because of a drought. Plaintiff charged me double the price I had paid the previous year, and then, instead of shipping Pippins, she sent my stores a bunch of cheap substitutes that looked a little like Pippins but were practically useless because they tasted horrible.

In this example, the witness has both stated her opinion of Plaintiff's honesty and provided the basis of the opinion through reference to a specific instance of conduct. The drafters of the Federal Rules recognized that this form of character evidence is the "most convincing." However, it takes longer to prove, and, particularly when the evidence is of a bad character trait, it can carry with it a high risk of unfair prejudice. For these and other reasons, the rules are far more restrictive about admitting evidence of specific instances of conduct than they are about evidence of reputation or opinion. In our hypothetical, the specific conduct evidence presented by the witness's last answer would be admissible because it is offered to prove character where character is itself "in issue." But as we will see, in other situations, this evidence would not be admissible on the direct examination of the witness.

Rule 405 tells us when character evidence may be proven with reputation, opinion, or specific instances evidence. It is important to understand that Rule 405 does not govern when character evidence is admissible. It only specifies the type of character evidence a party may offer *if* character is admissible. Subdivision (a) of Rule 405 provides that, when character evidence is otherwise admissible, reputation and opinion are permissible methods of proving character. The final sentence of subdivision (a) states the general rule that specific instances evidence may be used only during cross-examination. Subdivision (b), however, adds that when character is an "essential element of a charge, claim, or defense," specific instances evidence may be used to prove character evidence on direct examination (in addition to reputation and opinion). It is commonly said that character is "in issue" in such a case.

d. Proving Character When Character Is "In Issue"

Character is rarely "in issue" in a case. It is not in issue unless the law *requires* a party to prove character in order to establish an element of a charge, claim, or defense. Consider the following hypotheticals:

1. Prosecution of Defendant for assault and battery on Victim. Defendant admits striking Victim but claims she acted in self-defense when Victim attacked Defendant. To prove that Defendant was the first aggressor, the prosecution offers evidence that Defendant is a violent person.

   In this hypothetical, Defendant's character is not in issue because the substantive law does not require the prosecution to prove Defendant's violent character as an element of the offense of assault and battery. The issue in the case is not whether Defendant is a violent person; she could not be prosecuted for that character flaw. Obviously, Defendant generally could be a non-violent person and still commit a violent crime. Rather, the issue is whether Defendant in fact committed an assault and battery on Victim, or whether she acted in self-defense. Evidence of Defendant's character for violence is relevant *circumstantial evidence* that Defendant was the first aggressor based on the generalization that violent people are more likely to be the first aggressors in fights than non-violent people. But that does not make Defendant's character an essential element of the charge. Indeed, as we will see, the evidence is generally not admissible even as circumstantial evidence of Defendant's actions.

2. Same case. To prove that Victim was the first aggressor, Defendant offers evidence of Victim's violent character.

Once again, the character of the person is not in issue because it is not necessary to prove character to prevail. Victim's character for violence might help to show that Victim was the first aggressor, but proving character is not essential to establish the defense. Thus, Victim's character is not an essential element of Defendant's defense.

3. Same case, except that Defendant admits being the first aggressor but claims she attacked Victim only because she had heard that Victim was a violent person who planned to kill Defendant the next time he saw Defendant.

    Same result again. Here, Defendant's self-defense claim does not rest on proof of Victim's actions, but on proof that Defendant reasonably believed Victim planned to kill her. What counts is not the kind of person Victim actually is, but the kind of person Defendant believed him to be. Thus, once again, Victim's character is not in issue.

4. Defamation action by Plaintiff, owner of a car dealership, against Defendant, publisher of a newspaper, after Defendant published an article calling Plaintiff a liar. Defendant asserts the "truth" defense. To prove that Plaintiff is a liar, Defendant wishes to call several witnesses to testify that they purchased cars from Plaintiff, and that the cars lacked much of the "standard" equipment Plaintiff stated would be included.

    In this case, Plaintiff's character is an "essential element of a . . . defense." To establish the defense of truth, Defendant must prove that Plaintiff is what Defendant claimed: a liar. Thus, Plaintiff's character is in issue. (Incidentally, this is why the cause of action is sometimes called *defamation of character*.)

5. Same case. Assume, however, that Defendant concedes the article was inaccurate (that Plaintiff is not a liar), but that Defendant made reasonable efforts to verify the content of the article before publishing it. (As long as Plaintiff is not a public figure, this would be a valid defense.) To prove reasonable belief that Plaintiff was a liar, Defendant wishes to call a witness to testify that Plaintiff has a community reputation as a liar.

    When Defendant asserts the reasonable belief defense, Plaintiff's character is *not* an essential element. To prevail, Defendant need not prove Plaintiff's actual character. Unlike the situation in Hypothetical 4, the defense is not based on the kind of person Plaintiff actually is, but on what Defendant reasonably believed Plaintiff is. Thus, Defendant is not offering evidence of Plaintiff's reputation as a liar to prove that Plaintiff is a liar, but only to establish the information that caused Defendant to conclude that Plaintiff is a liar.[6] Thus, our conclusion that character is not in issue in this hypothetical does not mean the evidence will be inadmissible. It is admissible not to prove Plaintiff's character but, instead, to prove Defendant's state of mind.

6. Negligent entrustment action by Plaintiff against Defendant. Defendant loaned her power boat to Zed, who ran into Plaintiff while Plaintiff was water skiing. Plaintiff's theory is that Zed is a reckless operator, that

---

6. It is important to understand that reputation evidence is actually two things. First, it is a form of character evidence. That is, reputation is one way of proving a person's character. (What people say about a person helps to establish what that person's character actually is.) Second, reputation is sometimes an end in itself. That is the case here, where Defendant does not ask the jury to draw any inference of Plaintiff's actual character from Plaintiff's reputation. Plaintiff's reputation itself tends to support Defendant's defense.

Defendant should have been aware of that fact, and that Defendant was negligent in allowing Zed to borrow the boat. To prove Zed's recklessness, Plaintiff wishes to offer evidence of Zed's reckless character.

Zed's reckless character *is* in issue in this case. To prevail in the negligent entrustment action, it is necessary for Plaintiff to prove Zed's character for recklessness. That character trait is the foundation for Defendant's liability.

As we stated previously, Rule 405(b) makes clear that when a person's character is an "essential element of a charge, claim, or defense," all forms of character evidence are admissible. The rule makes good sense. When the substantive law *requires* that a fact be proven, the law of evidence should be very reluctant to restrict the permissible means of proving the fact, especially when the restrictions leave available only the weaker forms of evidence as to that fact. A rule restricting character evidence in this context to reputation and opinion would do just that. Thus, in Hypotheticals 4 and 6, where character is an essential element, all three forms of character evidence are allowed.

e. Proving Character as Circumstantial Evidence of Out-of-Court Conduct

i. *The Basic Rule*

Recall Hypothetical 1 in subsection d, above. Defendant is charged with assault and battery on Victim. To support her self-defense claim based on Victim's allegedly having attacked first, Defendant wishes to offer evidence of Victim's violent character. In that case, we showed that Victim's character is not in issue. Rather, Defendant wishes to use Victim's character to prove, circumstantially, how Victim behaved in the fight. Assume Defendant wishes to call a witness to testify to Victim's community reputation as a violent person. The reasoning is as follows:

EVIDENCE: Victim has a community reputation for being a violent person.

→**INFERENCE:** Victim is a violent person.

→**CONCLUSION:** Victim acted in conformity with his character by being the first aggressor in the fight.

This reasoning uses character evidence as circumstantial evidence of a person's out-of-court behavior. As such, it is subject to the basic prohibition found in the first sentence of Rule 404(a): "Evidence of a person's character or character trait is not admissible to prove that on a particular occasion the person acted in accordance with the character or trait."

Why maintain this rule? Clearly, it is not because the evidence is irrelevant; the reasoning set forth above is supported by the entirely rational generalization that character traits *are* predictive — that people do tend, in some degree, to behave according to their characters. (The evidence might not be highly probative, but it satisfies the lenient definition of relevance.) The real reason for the rule appears to be that allowing evidence of a person's character to prove action in conformity would create substantial risk of unfair prejudice. As we discussed in Chapter 2, unfair prejudice takes two basic forms. Both of those are applicable to character evidence.

Inferential error prejudice. Permitting conduct to be proved by character evidence creates the risk that the jury will over-value the character evidence as an indicator of the person's conduct. We have already noted that character evidence has only very limited value in predicting behavior. But there is a gulf between what clinical research shows and what people believe. The popular view is that character is more predictive than it actually is. If character evidence were generally admissible to prove behavior, the jury would be likely to overvalue it. This would cause the accuracy of results reached at trial to suffer, undermining the most important goal of the trial: to find the truth.

Nullification prejudice. This type of prejudice occurs when jurors convict a person not for what she has done on the charged occasion, but for being a bad person. In other words, nullification prejudice occurs when jurors discard the question of whether the individual committed the charged acts and convict either for the person's other wrongdoing or simply to remove a dangerous person from free society. This is not entirely irrational or even unjustified; we would consider our lives safer if we were able to imprison those whose characters might lead them to commit crimes. But as we stated at the beginning of this chapter, our system holds to a deeply held principle that people must be tried not for the kind of persons they are, but for what they have done on the charged occasion. If we admit evidence of a person's character, jurors might tend to ignore this principle in exchange for the more immediate impulse to prevent the person from committing any further crimes. Because that reaction would nullify the law requiring proof of the charged behavior, use of the "bad person" reasoning is unfairly prejudicial. (The same is true for "good person" reasoning. It is no more appropriate for the jury to acquit a person charged with a crime because the jury views the person as generally good than it is to convict because the jury views the person unfavorably.)

These types of potential prejudice have led to the general rule, expressed in Rule 404(a), that prohibits the use of character evidence to prove a person's conduct in conformity with her character.

Questions for Classroom Discussion

1. Negligence action by Plaintiff against Defendant arising from an automobile accident. Plaintiff claims Defendant ran a red light and struck Plaintiff's car, causing the injury. To prove Defendant ran the light, Plaintiff calls Witness, who is familiar with Defendant's community reputation, to testify that Defendant is known as a careless driver. Defendant objects. How should the court rule?

> **2.** Same case. Is the evidence Plaintiff wishes to present relevant? Why or why not?
>
> **3.** If the evidence is relevant, why does the rule require its exclusion? Why not allow the court to admit it unless its probative value is substantially outweighed by the danger of unfair prejudice or other concerns contained in Rule 403?

As Rule 404(a) makes clear, there are exceptions to the prohibition of character evidence to prove out-of-court conduct. The Supreme Court examined the common law form of this rule in the well-known case of Michelson v. United States.

ii. *Evidence of a Criminal Defendant's Character*

In general

MICHELSON v. UNITED STATES
335 U.S. 469 (1948)

Mr. Justice JACKSON delivered the opinion of the Court.

In 1947 petitioner Michelson was convicted of bribing a federal revenue agent. The Government proved a large payment by accused to the agent for the purpose of influencing his official action. The defendant, as a witness on his own behalf, admitted passing the money but claimed it was done in response to the agent's demands, threats, solicitations, and inducements that amounted to entrapment. It is enough for our purposes to say that determination of the issue turned on whether the jury should believe the agent or the accused.

On direct examination of defendant, his own counsel brought out that, in 1927, he had been convicted of a misdemeanor having to do with trading in counterfeit watch dials. On cross-examination it appeared that in 1930, in executing an application for a license to deal in second-hand jewelry, he answered "No" to the question whether he had theretofore been arrested or summoned for any offense.

Defendant called five witnesses to prove that he enjoyed a good reputation. Two of them testified that their acquaintance with him extended over a period of about thirty years and the others said they had known him at least half that long. . . .

On cross-examination, four of the witnesses were asked, in substance, this question: "Did you ever hear that Mr. Michelson on March 4, 1927, was convicted of a violation of the trademark law in New York City in regard to watches?" This referred to the twenty-year-old conviction about which defendant himself had testified on direct examination. Two of them had heard of it and two had not.

To four of these witnesses the prosecution also addressed the question the allowance of which, over defendant's objection, is claimed to be reversible error:

"Did you ever hear that on October 11th, 1920, the defendant, Solomon Michelson, was arrested for receiving stolen goods?"

None of the witnesses appears to have heard of this.

The trial court asked counsel for the prosecution, out of presence of the jury, "Is it a fact according to the best information in your possession that Michelson was arrested for receiving stolen goods?" Counsel replied that it was, and to support his good faith exhibited a paper record which defendant's counsel did not challenge.

The judge also on three occasions warned the jury, in terms that are not criticized, of the limited purpose for which this evidence was received.[3]

Defendant-petitioner challenges the right of the prosecution to cross-examine his character witnesses. The Court of Appeals held that it was permissible. The opinion, however, points out that the practice has been severely criticized and invites us, in one respect, to change the rule.[4] Serious and responsible criticism has been aimed, however, not alone at the detail now questioned by

3. In ruling on the objection when the question was first asked, the Court said: ". . . I instruct the jury that what is happening now is this: the defendant has called character witnesses, and the basis for the evidence given by those character witnesses is the reputation of the defendant in the community, and since the defendant tenders the issue of his reputation the prosecution may ask the witness if she has heard of various incidents in his career. I say to you that regardless of her answer you are not to assume that the incidents asked about actually took place. All that is happening is that this witness' standard of opinion of the reputation of the defendant is being tested. Is that clear?" In overruling the second objection to the question the Court said: "Again I say to the jury there is no proof that Mr. Michelson was arrested for receiving stolen goods in 1920, there isn't any such proof. All this witness has been asked is whether he had heard of that. There is nothing before you on that issue. Now would you base your decision on the case fairly in spite of the fact that that question has been asked? You would? All right." The charge included the following: "In connection with the character evidence in the case I permitted a question whether or not the witness knew that in 1920 this defendant had been arrested for receiving stolen goods. I tried to give you the instruction then that that question was permitted only to test the standards of character evidence that these character witnesses seemed to have. There isn't any proof in the case that could be produced before you legally within the rules of evidence that this defendant was arrested in 1920 for receiving stolen goods, and that fact you are not to hold against him; nor are you to assume what the consequences of that arrest were. You just drive it from your mind so far as he is concerned, and take it into consideration only in weighing the evidence of the character witnesses."

4. Footnote 8 to that court's opinion reads as follows (165 F.2d 735): "Wigmore, Evidence (3d ed. 1940) 988, after noting that 'such inquiries are almost universally admitted,' not as 'impeachment by extrinsic testimony of particular acts of misconduct,' but as means of testing the character 'witness' grounds of knowledge, continues with these comments: 'But the serious objection to them is that practically the above distinction — between rumors of such conduct, as affecting reputation, and the fact of it as violating the rule against particular facts — cannot be maintained in the mind of the jury. The rumor of the misconduct, when admitted, goes far, in spite of all theory and of the judge's charge, towards fixing the misconduct as a fact upon the other person, and thus does three improper things, — (1) it violates the fundamental rule of fairness that prohibits the use of such facts, (2) it gets at them by hearsay only, and not by trustworthy testimony, and (3) it leaves the other person no means of defending himself by denial or explanation, such as he would otherwise have had if the rule had allowed that conduct to be made the subject of an issue. Moreover, these are not occurrences of possibility, but of daily practice. This method of inquiry or cross-examination is frequently resorted to by counsel for the very purpose of injuring by indirection a character which they are forbidden directly to attack in that way; they rely upon the mere putting of the question (not caring that it is answered negatively) to convey their convert insinuation. The value of the inquiry for testing purposes is often so small and the opportunities of its abuse by underhand ways are so great that the practice may amount to little more than a mere subterfuge, and should be strictly supervised by forbidding it to counsel who do not use it in good faith.' Because, as Wigmore says, the jury almost surely cannot comprehend the judge's limiting instruction, the writer of this opinion wishes that the United States Supreme Court would tell us to follow what appears to be the Illinois rule, i.e., that such questions are improper unless they relate to offenses similar to those for which the defendant is on trial. *See* Aiken v. People, 183 Ill. 215, 55 N.E. 695; *cf.* People v. Hannon, 381 Ill. 206, 44 N.E.2d 923."

the Court of Appeals but at common-law doctrine on the whole subject of proof of reputation or character. It would not be possible to appraise the usefulness and propriety of this cross-examination without consideration of the unique practice concerning character testimony, of which such cross-examination is a minor part.

Courts that follow the common-law tradition almost unanimously have come to disallow resort by the prosecution to any kind of evidence of a defendant's evil character to establish a probability of his guilt. Not that the law invests the defendant with a presumption of good character, Greer v. United States, 245 U.S. 559, 38 S. Ct. 209, 62 L. Ed. 469, but it simply closes the whole matter of character, disposition and reputation on the prosecution's case-in-chief. The State may not show defendant's prior trouble with the law, specific criminal acts, or ill name among his neighbors, even though such facts might logically be persuasive that he is by propensity a probable perpetrator of the crime. The inquiry is not rejected because character is irrelevant; on the contrary, it is said to weigh too much with the jury and to so overpersuade them as to prejudge one with a bad general record and deny him a fair opportunity to defend against a particular charge. The overriding policy of excluding such evidence, despite its admitted probative value, is the practical experience that its disallowance tends to prevent confusion of issues, unfair surprise and undue prejudice.

But this line of inquiry firmly denied to the State is opened to the defendant because character is relevant in resolving probabilities of guilt. He may introduce affirmative testimony that the general estimate of his character is so favorable that the jury may infer that he would not be likely to commit the offense charged. This privilege is sometimes valuable to a defendant for this Court has held that such testimony alone, in some circumstances, may be enough to raise a reasonable doubt of guilt and that in the federal courts a jury in a proper case should be so instructed. Edgington v. United States, 164 U.S. 361, 17 S. Ct. 72, 41 L. Ed. 467.

When the defendant elects to initiate a character inquiry, another anomalous rule comes into play. Not only is he permitted to call witnesses to testify from hearsay, but indeed such a witness is not allowed to base his testimony on anything but hearsay. What commonly is called "character evidence" is only such when "character" is employed as a synonym for "reputation." The witness may not testify about defendant's specific acts or courses of conduct or his possession of a particular disposition or of benign mental and moral traits; nor can he testify that his own acquaintance, observation, and knowledge of defendant leads to his own independent opinion that defendant possesses a good general or specific character, inconsistent with commission of acts charged. The witness is, however, allowed to summarize what he has heard in the community, although much of it may have been said by persons less qualified to judge than himself. The evidence which the law permits is not as to the personality of defendant but only as to the shadow his daily life has cast in his neighborhood. This has been well described in a different connection as "the slow growth of months and years, the resultant picture of forgotten incidents, passing events, habitual and daily conduct, presumably honest because disinterested, and safer to be trusted because prone to suspect. . . . It is for that reason that such general repute is permitted to be proven. It sums up a multitude of trivial details. It compacts into the brief phrase of a verdict the teaching of many incidents and the conduct of years. It is the average intelligence drawing its conclusion." Finch J., in Badger v. Badger, 88 N.Y. 546, 552, 42 Am. Rep. 263.

While courts have recognized logical grounds for criticism of this type of opinion-based-on-hearsay testimony, it is said to be justified by "overwhelming considerations of practical convenience" in avoiding innumerable collateral issues which, if it were attempted to prove character by direct testimony, would complicate and confuse the trial, distract the minds of jurymen and befog the chief issues in the litigation. People v. Van Gaasbeck, 189 N.Y. 408, 418, 82 N.E. 718, 22 L.R.A., N.S., 650, 12 Ann. Cas. 745.

Another paradox in this branch of the law of evidence is that the delicate and responsible task of compacting reputation hearsay into the "brief phrase of a verdict" is one of the few instances in which conclusions are accepted from a witness on a subject in which he is not an expert. However, the witness must qualify to give an opinion by showing such acquaintance with the defendant, the community in which he has lived and the circles in which he has moved, as to speak with authority of the terms in which generally he is regarded. To require affirmative knowledge of the reputation may seem inconsistent with the latitude given to the witness to testify when all he can say of the reputation is that he has "heard nothing against defendant." This is permitted upon assumption that, if no ill is reported of one, his reputation must be good.[13] But this answer is accepted only from a witness whose knowledge of defendant's habitat and surroundings is intimate enough so that his failure to hear of any relevant ill repute is an assurance that no ugly rumors were about.

Thus the law extends helpful but illogical options to a defendant. Experience taught a necessity that they be counterweighted with equally illogical conditions to keep the advantage from becoming an unfair and unreasonable one. The price a defendant must pay for attempting to prove his good name is to throw open the entire subject which the law has kept closed for his benefit and to make himself vulnerable where the law otherwise shields him. The prosecution may pursue the inquiry with contradictory witnesses to show that damaging rumors, whether or not well-grounded, were afloat—for it is not the man that he is, but the name that he has which is put in issue. Another hazard is that his own witness is subject to cross-examination as to the contents and extent of the hearsay on which he bases his conclusions, and he may be required to disclose rumors and reports that are current even if they do not affect his own conclusion.[16] It may test the sufficiency of his knowledge by asking what stories were circulating concerning events, such as one's arrest, about which people normally comment and speculate. Thus, while the law gives defendant the option to show as a fact that his reputation reflects a life and habit incompatible with commission of the

13. People v. Van Gaasbeck, 189 N.Y. 408, 420, 82 N.E. 718, 22 L.R.A., N.S., 650, 12 Ann. Cas. 745. The law apparently ignores the existence of such human ciphers as Kipling's Tomlinson, of whom no ill is reported but no good can be recalled. They win seats with the righteous for character evidence purposes, however hard their lot in literature.

16. A classic example in the books is a character witness in a trial for murder. She testified she grew up with defendant, knew his reputation for peace and quiet, and that it was good. On cross-examination she was asked if she had heard that the defendant had shot anybody and, if so, how many. She answered, "Three or four," and gave the names of two but could not recall the names of the others. She still insisted, however, that he was of "good character." The jury seems to have valued her information more highly than her judgment, and on appeal from conviction the cross-examination was held proper. People v. Laudiero, 192 N.Y. 304, 309, 85 N.E. 132. *See also* People v. Elliott, 163 N.Y. 11, 57 N.E. 103.

offense charged, it subjects his proof to tests of credibility designed to prevent him from profiting by a mere parade of partisans.

To thus digress from evidence as to the offense to hear a contest as to the standing of the accused, at its best opens a tricky line of inquiry as to a shapeless and elusive subject matter. At its worst it opens a veritable Pandora's box of irresponsible gossip, innuendo and smear. In the frontier phase of our law's development, calling friends to vouch for defendant's good character, and its counterpart — calling the rivals and enemies of a witness to impeach him by testifying that his reputation for veracity was so bad that he was unworthy of belief on his oath — were favorite and frequent ways of converting an individual litigation into a community contest and a trial into a spectacle. Growth of urban conditions, where one may never know or hear the name of his next-door neighbor, have tended to limit the use of these techniques and to deprive them of weight with juries. The popularity of both procedures has subsided, but courts of last resort have sought to overcome danger that the true issues will be obscured and confused by investing the trial court with discretion to limit the number of such witnesses and to control cross-examination. Both propriety and abuse of hearsay reputation testimony, on both sides, depend on numerous and subtle considerations, difficult to detect or appraise from a cold record, and therefore rarely and only on clear showing of prejudicial abuse of discretion will Courts of Appeals disturb rulings of trial courts on this subject.

Wide discretion is accompanied by heavy responsibility on trial courts to protect the practice from any misuse. The trial judge was scrupulous to so guard it in the case before us. He took pains to ascertain, out of presence of the jury, that the target of the question was an actual event, which would probably result in some comment among acquaintances if not injury to defendant's reputation. He satisfied himself that counsel was not merely taking a random shot at a reputation imprudently exposed or asking a groundless question to waft an unwarranted innuendo into the jury box.[18]

The question permitted by the trial court, however, involves several features that may be worthy of comment. Its form invited hearsay; it asked about an arrest, not a conviction, and for an offense not closely similar to the one on trial; and it concerned an occurrence many years past.

Since the whole inquiry, as we have pointed out, is calculated to ascertain the general talk of people about defendant, rather than the witness' own knowledge of him, the form of inquiry, "Have you heard?" has general approval, and "Do you know?" is not allowed.

---

18. This procedure was recommended by Wigmore. But analysis of his innovation emphasizes the way in which law on this subject has evolved from pragmatic considerations rather than from theoretical consistency. The relevant information that it is permissible to lay before the jury is talk or conversation about the defendant's being arrested. That is admissible whether or not an actual arrest had taken place; it might even be more significant of repute if his neighbors were ready to arrest him in rumor when the authorities were not in fact. But before this relevant and proper inquiry can be made, counsel must demonstrate privately to the court an irrelevant and possibly unprovable fact — the reality of arrest. From this permissible inquiry about reports of arrest, the jury is pretty certain to infer that defendant had in fact been arrested and to draw its own conclusions as to character from that fact. The Wigmore suggestion thus limits legally relevant inquiries to those based on legally irrelevant facts in order that the legally irrelevant conclusion which the jury probably will draw from the relevant questions will not be based on unsupported or untrue innuendo. It illustrates Judge Hand's suggestion that the system may work best when explained least. Yet, despite its theoretical paradoxes and deficiencies, we approve the procedure as calculated in practice to hold the inquiry within decent bounds.

A character witness may be cross-examined as to an arrest whether or not it culminated in a conviction, according to the overwhelming weight of authority. . . .

Arrest without more may . . . impair or cloud one's reputation. False arrest may do that. Even to be acquitted may damage one's good name if the community receives the verdict with a wink and chooses to remember defendant as one who ought to have been convicted. . . .

The inquiry as to an arrest is permissible also because the prosecution has a right to test the qualifications of the witness to bespeak the community opinion. If one never heard the speculations and rumors in which even one's friends indulge upon his arrest, the jury may doubt whether he is capable of giving any very reliable conclusions as to his reputation.

In this case the crime inquired about was receiving stolen goods; the trial was for bribery. The Court of Appeals thought this dissimilarity of offenses too great to sustain the inquiry in logic, though conceding that it is authorized by preponderance of authority. It asks us to substitute the Illinois rule which allows inquiry about arrest, but only for very closely similar if not identical charges, in place of the rule more generally adhered to in this country and in England. We think the facts of this case show the proposal to be inexpedient.

The good character which the defendant had sought to establish was broader than the crime charged and included the traits of "honesty and truthfulness" and "being a law-abiding citizen." Possession of these characteristics would seem as incompatible with offering a bribe to a revenue agent as with receiving stolen goods. The crimes may be unlike, but both alike proceed from the same defects of character which the witnesses said this defendant was reputed not to exhibit. It is not only by comparison with the crime on trial but by comparison with the reputation asserted that a court may judge whether the prior arrest should be made subject of inquiry. By this test the inquiry was permissible. It was proper cross-examination because reports of his arrest for receiving stolen goods, if admitted, would tend to weaken the assertion that he was known as an honest and law-abiding citizen. The cross-examination may take in as much ground as the testimony it is designed to verify. To hold otherwise would give defendant the benefit of testimony that he was honest and law-abiding in reputation when such might not be the fact; the refutation was founded on convictions equally persuasive though not for crimes exactly repeated in the present charge.

The inquiry here concerned an arrest twenty-seven years before the trial. Events a generation old are likely to be lived down and dropped from the present thought and talk of the community and to be absent from the knowledge of younger or more recent acquaintances. The court in its discretion may well exclude inquiry about rumors of an event so remote, unless recent misconduct revived them. But two of these witnesses dated their acquaintance with defendant as commencing thirty years before the trial. Defendant, on direct examination, voluntarily called attention to his conviction twenty years before. While the jury might conclude that a matter so old and indecisive as a 1920 arrest would shed little light on the present reputation and hence propensities of the defendant, we cannot say that, in the context of this evidence and in the absence of objection on this specific ground, its admission was an abuse of discretion.

We do not overlook or minimize the consideration that "the jury almost surely cannot comprehend the Judge's limiting instructions," which disturbed the Court of Appeals. The refinements of the evidentiary rules on this subject are such that even lawyers and judges, after study and reflection, often are confused, and surely jurors in the hurried and unfamiliar movement of a trial must find them almost unintelligible. However, limiting instructions on this subject are no more difficult to comprehend or apply than those upon various other subjects; for example, instructions that admissions of a co-defendant are to be limited to the question of his guilt and are not to be considered as evidence against other defendants, and instructions as to other problems in the trial of conspiracy charges. A defendant in such a case is powerless to prevent his cause from being irretrievably obscured and confused; but, in cases such as the one before us, the law foreclosed this whole confounding line of inquiry, unless defendant thought the net advantage from opening it up would be with him. Given this option, we think defendants in general and this defendant in particular have no valid complaint at the latitude which existing law allows to the prosecution to meet by cross-examination an issue voluntarily tendered by the defense. *See* Greer v. United States, 245 U.S. 559, 38 S. Ct. 209, 62 L. Ed. 469.

We end, as we began, with the observation that the law regulating the offering and testing of character testimony may merit many criticisms. England, and some states have overhauled the practice by statute. But the task of modernizing the longstanding rules on the subject is one of magnitude and difficulty which even those dedicated to law reform do not lightly undertake. . . .

We concur in the general opinion of courts, textwriters and the profession that much of this law is archaic, paradoxical and full of compromises and compensations by which an irrational advantage to one side is offset by a poorly reasoned counter-privilege to the other. But somehow it has proved a workable even if clumsy system when moderated by discretionary controls in the hands of a wise and strong trial court. To pull one misshapen stone out of the grotesque structure is more likely simply to upset its present balance between adverse interests than to establish a rational edifice.

The present suggestion is that we adopt for all federal courts a new rule as to cross-examination about prior arrest, adhered to by the courts of only one state and rejected elsewhere. The confusion and error it would engender would seem too heavy a price to pay for an almost imperceptible logical improvement, if any, in a system which is justified, if at all, by accumulated judicial experience rather than abstract logic.

The judgment is
Affirmed.

The concurring opinion of Justice FRANKFURTER, and the dissenting opinion of Justice RUTLEDGE (joined by Justice MURPHY), are omitted.

———————————

Though it was decided in 1947, *Michelson* fairly accurately states the law as it exists today in virtually all U.S. jurisdictions. Rule 404(a)(1) is the applicable federal provision. Under that rule, the prosecution may not offer evidence of defendant's character to prove defendant acted in conformity with her character, but the defendant may offer evidence of her character to prove her innocence. Once defendant has done so, the prosecution may respond by cross-examining defendant's character witnesses and by offering its own character witnesses to contradict the testimony defendant offered. Thus, the inconsistencies and logical flaws in the common law, so elegantly described in *Michelson*, remain in the law today.

There are only three important differences between *Michelson* and current law. First, under Rule 405(a), character evidence in the form of personal opinion is admissible whenever evidence of reputation is admissible.

The second difference comes into play when a criminal defendant offers evidence of the alleged victim's character to prove innocence. As we will see in subsection iii below, Rule 404(a)(2) allows a criminal defendant to offer "evidence of an alleged crime victim's pertinent trait." Before Rule 404(a)(1) was amended in 2000, the prosecution's rebuttal of such evidence was limited to cross-examining the witnesses who testified about the alleged victim's character or calling its own witnesses to show that the alleged victim's character was, in fact, good. Pursuant to the 2000 amendment, the prosecution now has a new weapon: When the defendant offers evidence of a pertinent trait of the *victim*'s character, the prosecution may respond by offering evidence concerning the same trait of the *defendant*'s character. Thus, if the defendant is charged with assault and battery, claims self-defense, and seeks to prove the alleged victim's character for violence, the prosecution may now offer evidence concerning the defendant's character for violence.

There is a third difference between the common law approach to character evidence concerning the criminal defendant and the approach used today in the federal courts. It concerns evidence of a person's prior instances of sexual assault or child molestation when the person is alleged to have committed those acts in the present case. We take up that subject next.

An aside: In 2006, an amendment to Rule 404(a) made clear that the exceptions created in the rule apply only in criminal cases. The Advisory Committee Note to the amendment states that "[t]he Rule has been amended to clarify that in a civil case evidence of a person's character is never admissible to prove that the person acted in conformity with the character trait." But, as the saying goes, never say "never." The Advisory Committee forgot about Rule 415.

Questions for Classroom Discussion

1. Why does the law allow a criminal defendant to prove her innocence by offering evidence of her good character, but, except in very limited circumstances, does not allow the prosecution to present character evidence during its case-in-chief to prove the defendant's guilt?

2. What restrictions do *Michelson*, and Rules 404 and 405, place on the defendant's right to prove innocence with character evidence?

3. Once the defendant offers character evidence to prove her innocence, how may the prosecution respond?

4. Does the court still retain the authority to forbid the prosecution from asking about specific instances of conduct on cross-examination? If so, why?

5. If the prosecution chooses to call its own witness to "rebut" the defendant's character evidence, may defendant raise specific instances of conduct on cross-examination of that witness?

6. Prosecution of Defendant for the murder of Victim. The prosecution alleges that Defendant planned and carried out the murder of Victim, Defendant's business rival. To prove Defendant committed the crime, the prosecution calls Witness during its case-in-chief to testify that she has known Defendant for many years, and that in her opinion, Defendant is a violent person. Defendant objects. How should the court rule?

7. Same case. During his case-in-chief, Defendant calls Witness to testify that she has lived in the same community as Defendant for many years, that she knows Defendant's reputation for peacefulness, and that Defendant's reputation is that he is a peaceful person. The prosecution objects that Defendant has offered inadmissible character evidence. How should the court rule?

8. Same case. If the prosecution also objects to the evidence in Question 7 on hearsay grounds, how should the court rule?

9. Same case. On direct examination, Defendant also asks Witness, "Have you heard about an occasion two years ago when Defendant refused an opportunity to fight with a person who had attacked Defendant's child?" The prosecution objects. How should the court rule?

10. Same case. During its cross-examination of Witness, the prosecution asks, "Did you hear that last year, Defendant was involved in a violent altercation while attending a high school football game?" Defendant objects. How should the court rule?

11. Same case. During the argument on Defendant's objection to the prosecution's question, Defendant's attorney points out that although Defendant attended the football game where the fight occurred, Defendant was not involved in that fight. The prosecution responds that the key question is not whether Defendant in fact was involved, but whether rumors circulated throughout the community that Defendant was involved, and that the prosecution has good reason to believe that such rumors existed. How should the court rule?

12. Same case. Assume the court allows the prosecution to question Witness about rumors of Defendant's involvement in the fight at the high school football game. On redirect examination, Defendant asks Witness, "Did you ever hear that Defendant once refused an opportunity to fight with the person who attacked Defendant's girlfriend?" The prosecution objects. How should the court rule?

(continued)

13. Prosecution of Defendant for burglary of a store late at night after the store had closed. Defendant allegedly hid in the store at closing time and stole merchandise after everyone else had left. In her defense, Defendant calls Witness to testify that she has known Defendant for many years, and that in her opinion, Defendant is a law-abiding, peaceful person. The prosecution objects. How should the court rule?

14. Prosecution of Defendant for the murder of Victim. Defendant calls Witness to testify that she has lived in the same community as Defendant for many years, and that Defendant has a community reputation as a peaceful person. The prosecution then asks Witness, "Did you know that Defendant was arrested last year for the attempted murder of a bartender?" Defendant objects on the ground that this is an impermissible form of cross-examination. How should the court rule?

15. Civil action for battery by Plaintiff against Defendant following a brawl in a bar. Defendant denies striking Plaintiff. To prove that Defendant did not strike Plaintiff, Defendant calls Witness to testify that she knows Defendant well, and that in her opinion, Defendant is a non-violent person. Plaintiff objects. How should the court rule?

16. Civil action where the plaintiff alleges a police officer violated her deceased husband's civil rights by shooting and killing deceased. The trial court admits evidence of deceased's history of violent encounters with police officers as tending to show deceased attacked the officer first. The judge reasons the evidence is admissible because the claim against the officer is criminal in nature. Plaintiff appeals on the ground this was inadmissible character evidence. How should the appellate court rule?

Additional exceptions to the exclusion of character evidence to prove conduct; special rule for homicide prosecutions.   Rule 404(a)(2) contains a special provision that applies only in homicide prosecutions in which the defendant claims that the alleged victim was the "first aggressor." In those cases, the prosecution may offer evidence of the victim's character for peacefulness to rebut *any* evidence offered by the defendant to prove that the victim was the first aggressor. In other words, in such cases there are two keys that can open the door to prosecution evidence of the victim's character: defense evidence of the victim's character and defense evidence that the victim attacked first.

There are, of course, numerous ways in which the defendant might seek to prove that the victim was the first aggressor. The most simple and common way to do this is for the defendant to testify that the victim was the first aggressor or to call another witness who was present at the time of the altercation to testify to the same effect. In either event, once such testimony is offered the prosecution may rebut the defendant's claim with evidence of the victim's peaceful character.

Note that this is the only instance in Rules 404(a)(1) and (2) in which the prosecution may be the first party to offer evidence of a person's character when the purpose is to prove that person's conduct. In every other situation, the prosecution is forbidden to offer character evidence about a person unless and until the defendant has "opened the door" by offering evidence on her own behalf about that person's character. True, the prosecution sometimes may be the first to offer evidence of the *defendant*'s character under the recent amendment to Rule 404(a)(1), but even that step may not be taken until the defendant has chosen to offer evidence of the same trait of the *alleged victim's* character. Except for the very narrow provision in Rule 404(a)(2) concerning homicide victims, the defendant may preclude any character evidence to prove a person's conduct simply by not offering any such evidence herself. And even in cases falling into this narrow exception, it is the defendant who has opened the door to the prosecution's use of character by raising the first aggressor claim. (As we have already discussed, Rules 413-415 create other exceptions to this general rule.)

It is somewhat difficult to understand why this special rule applies only to homicide prosecutions, and not, for example, to assault and battery prosecutions in which the defendant asserts that the alleged victim was the first aggressor. Perhaps the rule is justified by considerations of fairness because the homicide victim is not able to speak for herself at trial. In any event, the exception is narrow.

Sexual assault and child molestation cases.   Rules 404 and 405 are not the only rules governing the use of character evidence to prove the behavior of a person on a specific occasion. In 1994, as part of major crime control legislation, Congress added Rules 413-415 to the Federal Rules of Evidence. These rules provide as follows:

> ### FED. R. EVID. 413.   SIMILAR CRIMES IN SEXUAL ASSAULT CASES

(a) Permitted Uses. In a criminal case in which a defendant is accused of a sexual assault, the court may admit evidence that the defendant committed any other sexual assault. The evidence may be considered on any matter to which it is relevant.

(b) Disclosure. If the prosecutor intends to offer this evidence, the prosecutor must disclose it to the defendant, including witnesses' statements or a summary of the expected testimony. The prosecutor must do so at least 15 days before trial or at a later time that the court allows for good cause.

(c) Effect on Other Rules. This rule does not limit the admission or consideration of evidence under any other rule.

(d) [Defines "offense of sexual assault."]

> ### FED. R. EVID. 414.   SIMILAR CRIMES IN CHILD MOLESTATION CASES

[Rule is identical to Rule 413 except substituting definitions of *child* and *offense of child molestation* in appropriate places. For the text of the rule, see Appendix A.]

> FED. R. EVID. 415.   SIMILAR ACTS IN CIVIL CASES INVOLVING
> SEXUAL ASSAULT OR CHILD MOLESTATION

(a) Permitted Uses. In a civil case involving a claim for relief based on a party's alleged sexual assault or child molestation, the court may admit evidence that the party committed any other sexual assault or act of child molestation. The evidence may be considered as provided in Rules 413 and 414.

(b) Disclosure. If a party intends to offer this evidence, the party must disclose it to the party against whom it will be offered, including witnesses' statements or a summary of the expected testimony. The party must do so at least 15 days before trial or at a later time that the court allows for good cause.

(c) Effect on Other Rules. This rule does not limit the admission or consideration of evidence under any other rule.

Rules 413-415 became a part of federal law as a result of major crime legislation passed by Congress in 1994. Though they are controversial, the rules have influenced many states. (California, for example, has enacted a similar, though somewhat more limited rule. *See* Cal. Evid. Code § 1108.) As their language suggests, the rules do away with the character prohibition in sexual assault and child molestation prosecutions as well as in civil cases based on those types of misconduct. Other similar conduct of the charged person may now be introduced on the precise reasoning formerly forbidden: that a person who has engaged in such conduct on one occasion is likely to engage in that same type of conduct on the charged occasion. This is character evidence. Thus, Rules 413, 414, and 415 carve out exceptions to Rule 404(a)'s general ban on character evidence to prove conduct.

Before the enactment of these and similar rules, all jurisdictions allowed evidence of such misconduct under some circumstances. For example, if a rape defendant had used the same unusual and distinctive method of attracting and then sexually attacking women as was used by the perpetrator in the present case, the other instances of defendant's conduct might be admissible to prove his identity as the perpetrator by means of "modus operandi" reasoning (see section C of this chapter). And in child molestation cases, many courts would admit evidence of the defendant's other assaults on the same child to prove his opportunity, plan, or perhaps motive to commit the assault on the charged occasion. A few states even approved of the so-called depraved sexual instinct theory by which a defendant's other sexual assaults could be offered to show that the defendant had a tendency to commit such crimes. The flawed theory was that such a tendency was not character-based, but akin to a disease. What distinguishes these and all other theories admitting other misconduct from what is allowed under Rules 413-415 is that the new rules unabashedly permit the evidence to be offered on a character-propensity basis. In federal courts and in jurisdictions adopting these or similar rules, it will no longer be necessary to justify admission of other sexual assaults or acts of child molestation on a non-character ground.

The new rules arose in part from the difficulty of prosecuting sexual assault and child molestation cases in which often the only witnesses are the perpetrator and the victim. Both child and adult victims are often reluctant to testify, and when they do take the stand, their testimony is often weak and their characters vilified by innuendo. When the victim is a child, the difficulty of obtaining useful and persuasive testimony is particularly great. Congress no doubt was motivated by these considerations when it adopted the rules, as well as by the social outcry about what was perceived to be an epidemic of sexual assault and child molestation. The rules were also justified by the belief that character evidence in these types of cases has greater probative value than in other types of cases, even serious crimes such as murder. Though this rationale is difficult to support by crime studies and statistics, it has also proven difficult to refute.

It is useful to contrast the new rules admitting evidence concerning a defendant's prior sexual wrongdoing with the rules governing the admissibility of evidence concerning an alleged rape victim's sexual history. As we will see in subsection 3.b of this chapter, the latter is generally inadmissible. This creates an imbalance that can best be illustrated by an example. Suppose Defendant is charged with sexual assault on Victim. Defendant does not deny that he had sexual intercourse with Victim, but claims Victim consented after they met at a bar and conversed for a time. If Defendant wishes to offer evidence that Victim had consented to sexual intercourse with other men after meeting them at bars, Rule 412 almost certainly would exclude the evidence. On the other hand, if the prosecution wishes to present evidence that Defendant had committed other acts of sexual assault in the past, that evidence is almost certainly admissible under Rule 413. Thus, in the same case, the prosecution will be permitted to prove certain instances of Defendant's past sexual conduct, but Defendant will not be permitted to respond with evidence of Victim's conduct.

This imbalance can be justified, of course. As we will see, serious considerations of unfair prejudice to rape victims as well as public policy motivated legislatures to enact rules restricting evidence of a rape victim's sexual history. In addition, the type of evidence made admissible by Rules 413-415 is in most cases quite different from the type of evidence defendants might want to present concerning the alleged victim.

Even under Rules 413-415, the trial court retains the authority to exclude the evidence when its probative value is substantially outweighed by the danger of unfair prejudice or by other considerations embodied in Rule 403. Thus, for example, if the court is convinced that the jury is likely to be misled by the evidence, or distracted from its task of determining what happened on the charged occasion, the court should exclude the evidence. The rules also contain notice protections.

Questions for Classroom Discussion

1. Prosecution of Defendant for rape of Victim, who was attacked while walking to her car after seeing a movie. Defendant denies being the perpetrator. To prove that Defendant committed the crime, the prosecution calls Witness to testify that Defendant has committed several rapes in the past few years. Defendant objects. How should the court rule?

(continued)

2. Same case as in Question 1. The prosecution also wishes to offer evidence that Defendant has a community reputation as a dangerous sexual criminal. Defendant objects. How should the court rule?

3. Same case as in Question 1. The prosecution wishes to offer evidence that Defendant has committed two acts of child molestation. Defendant objects. How should the court rule?

4. Defendant is sued for sexual assault. Plaintiff offers evidence Defendant was charged with sexual assault in two instances. Defendant objects, arguing the charge was dropped in one case, and that he was acquitted in the second. How should the court rule?

iii. Evidence of an Alleged Crime Victim's Character

We have seen that in criminal cases, the law affords the defendant an opportunity to prove innocence by showing she has a character inconsistent with the kind of criminality for which she is on trial. There is another situation in which a criminal defendant may also offer evidence of character to prove innocence: Under Rule 404(a)(2), defendant may offer evidence of a pertinent trait of the *alleged victim*'s character. The simplest example would be a prosecution for assault and battery in which defendant claims self-defense. To prove that she acted in response to the alleged victim's attack, or to prove that she reasonably feared that the alleged victim was about to attack her, defendant may offer evidence that the alleged victim is a violent person. In either case, the alleged victim's character for violence would support defendant's self-defense claim.

Note that this is simply another example of character evidence offered as circumstantial evidence of a person's behavior — in this case, the alleged crime victim. Therefore, the same rules we have already studied that limit the permissible forms of character evidence apply. In our example, on direct examination of a defense character witness, defendant may offer only reputation or opinion evidence concerning the alleged victim's character for violence.

If the defendant chooses to "open the door" in this way, the rule also permits the prosecution to rebut the defendant's evidence. Once again, the rules we have already studied apply. The prosecution may rebut the defendant's character evidence by cross-examining the witnesses who testified about the alleged victim's character. The cross-examination of a reputation witness, for example, may further inquire into reputation, opinion, or may raise relevant specific instances of conduct that cast doubt on the witness's testimony. The prosecution may also call its own witnesses to establish the alleged victim's character, presumably by showing a character for peacefulness rather than violence in our example. And, of course, the defense is entitled to cross-examine any character witnesses the prosecution calls. On direct examination of a prosecution witness, only reputation and opinion evidence are permitted. On cross-examination, the defense may also inquire about the witness's knowledge of specific instances of conduct.

It will be easier to remember the details of Rule 404(a) if you visualize the following: At the start of the trial there are two doors at the front of the courtroom. One is the door through which evidence of defendant's character may pass. The other door is for evidence of the victim's character. When the prosecution begins its case, both doors are closed. Only the defendant has the keys to these doors. The defendant opens one door by offering evidence of his own character. Now that this first door is open, the prosecution may rebut with its own evidence of defendant's character. The defendant unlocks the second door by offering evidence of the victim's character. Now the prosecution can walk through that door and present rebuttal evidence about the victim's character. It is important to remember that these doors normally open separately. If defendant opens one door, the other door usually is still closed.

There is one exception. As we mentioned earlier, when the defendant offers evidence of the alleged victim's character he opens the door to *victim's* character. But Federal Rule 404(a)(1) says that he also opens, at least a crack, the door to *defendant's* character. The prosecution may respond to defendant's evidence concerning the victim's character by presenting evidence that defendant has the *same character trait.* For example, if defendant presents evidence that the alleged assault and battery victim had a violent character, the prosecution is permitted to present evidence that defendant also possessed that character trait. The rules concerning the type of evidence permitted on direct and cross-examination, however, do not change. Thus, Rule 405(a) permits direct examination about reputation and opinion. On cross-examination, reputation and opinion remain admissible, as well as "relevant specific instances of the person's conduct."

While Rules 404(a) and 405 lay out the usual standards for the admissibility of evidence of defendant's and victim's character to prove conduct, don't forget that Rules 413, 414, and 415 override those provisions where evidence is offered to prove defendant's character in a case of sexual assault or child molestation. In the next section we learn that Rule 412 also overrides Rules 404(a) and 405 where evidence is offered to prove the victim's character in a sexual assault case.

iv. Evidence of Character of an Alleged Victim of Sexual Assault

Limitations regarding evidence of character of rape victims. Historically, the courts and the law have not treated victims of rape with kindness. Until very recently, a common strategy of defendants in such cases was to encourage the jury to blame the victim, particularly in acquaintance rape cases in which the outcome turns on consent or lack of consent. The easiest way to blame the victim is to parade evidence of her sexual history before the jury to suggest she consented, or to present evidence that she is an untruthful person who is lying to avoid social scorn. The tendency of the courts to admit such evidence was well known, and contributed to the underreporting of rape crimes and the refusal of known victims to testify and thereby subject themselves to further attack and humiliation in court.

To combat these disturbing realities, legislatures began in the 1960s to enact what have come to be known as "rape-shield" statutes, the effect of which is to prevent the unwarranted admission of evidence concerning the character of the alleged rape victim. The legislation differs from state to state, but Rule 412 is a typical example:

**FED. R. EVID. 412.   SEX OFFENSE CASES:
THE VICTIM'S SEXUAL BEHAVIOR OR PREDISPOSITION**

(a) Prohibited Uses. The following evidence is not admissible in a civil or criminal proceeding involving alleged sexual misconduct:

(1) evidence offered to prove that a victim engaged in other sexual behavior; or

(2) evidence offered to prove a victim's sexual predisposition.

(b) Exceptions.

(1) *Criminal Cases.* The court may admit the following evidence in a criminal case:

(A) evidence of specific instances of a victim's sexual behavior, if offered to prove that someone other than the defendant was the source of semen, injury, or other physical evidence;

(B) evidence of specific instances of a victim's sexual behavior toward the defendant, if offered by the prosecutor or if offered by the defendant to prove consent; and

(C) evidence whose exclusion would violate the defendant's constitutional rights.

(2) *Civil Cases.* In a civil case, the court may admit evidence offered to prove a victim's sexual behavior or sexual predisposition if its probative value substantially outweighs the danger of harm to any victim and of unfair prejudice to any party. The court may admit evidence of a victim's reputation only if the victim has placed it in controversy.

(c) Procedure to Determine Admissibility.

(1) *Motion.* If a party intends to offer evidence under Rule 412(b), the party must:

(A) file a motion that specifically describes the evidence and states the purpose for which it is to be offered;

(B) do so at least 14 days before trial unless the court, for good cause, sets a different time;

(C) serve the motion on all parties; and

(D) notify the victim or, when appropriate, the victim's guardian or representative.

(2) *Hearing.* Before admitting evidence under this rule, the court must conduct an in-camera hearing and give the victim and parties a right to attend and be heard. Unless the court orders otherwise, the motion, related materials, and the record of the hearing must be and remain sealed.

(d) Definition of "Victim." In this rule, "victim" includes an alleged victim.

Rule 412 begins with a general provision: In a criminal or civil proceeding involving sexual misconduct, evidence that the alleged victim engaged in other sexual behavior is generally inadmissible. Also inadmissible is other evidence of the alleged victim's sexual predisposition, which is a way of referring to the character trait defense counsel would like to attack. This broad prohibition is followed by narrow exceptions. In criminal cases, (1) evidence of specific instances of the victim's sexual behavior is admissible "to prove that someone other than the defendant was the source of semen, injury, or other physical evidence"; (2) evidence of the victim's sexual behavior *with the accused* is admissible at the behest of the defendant if offered to prove consent, or at the behest of the prosecution to prove other things; and (3) otherwise prohibited evidence is admissible if its exclusion would violate the defendant's constitutional rights. In civil cases, evidence of the victim's sexual behavior or predisposition is admissible if not excluded by any other rules and if "its probative value substantially outweighs the danger of harm to any victim and of unfair prejudice to any party." Note that this is the reverse of the Rule 403 probative value-prejudicial effect balancing test, which gives the court discretion to exclude if unfair prejudice and related costs of evidence substantially outweigh its probative value. This reversal of the balance places a heavy burden on the proponent to demonstrate that the court should admit the evidence. Further, in civil cases, evidence of the victim's reputation is only admissible if the victim placed her reputation "in controversy."

The rule also provides a procedure for all cases in which a party wishes to offer evidence pursuant to any of its exceptions. The purpose of the procedure is to give the opponent an opportunity to contest admissibility as well as to protect the privacy of the alleged victim and prevent unfair prejudice.

The exceptions set forth in Rule 412 for criminal cases are designed to admit this type of evidence only in those situations in which it may have significant probative value or where defendant's right to present a defense overcomes concern for protecting the alleged victim from unwarranted character attack. When, for example, blood or semen found on the victim or on her clothing is from a person other than the defendant, such evidence carries high probative value. Additionally, when the defendant claims the victim consented, evidence that the two had engaged in consensual sexual relations at other times may be probative of consent on the occasion in question. The third exception, providing for admission when the constitutional rights of the accused so require, is more amorphous. The Supreme Court addressed that exception in the following case.

OLDEN v. KENTUCKY

488 U.S. 227 (1988)

PER CURIAM.

[Olden and his friend Harris, both African Americans, were charged with kidnapping, rape, and forcible sodomy. The alleged victim, Matthews, was white. She testified that she and a friend went to Princeton, Kentucky, to exchange gifts with Russell, Olden's half-brother. They then went to a bar, where Matthews had several beers and became somewhat intoxicated. Olden was also present at the bar. When Olden told Matthews that her friend had been in a car accident, she left with Olden and Harris in Harris's car to another location where Olden threatened her with a knife and sexually assaulted her, with Harris holding Matthews' arms. Later, she was taken to another location where Olden again raped her before dropping her off near Russell's house. On cross-examination, Olden's counsel pointed out a number of inconsistencies in the various accounts Matthews had given about the events. Russell testified for the prosecution that he saw Matthews get out of Harris's car, and that Matthews immediately told him that Olden and Harris had raped her. Olden and Harris claimed Matthews consented to the sexual acts, and that they dropped Matthews off in the vicinity of Russell's home at Matthews' request. Other witnesses corroborated their version of the events. One witness testified that he saw Matthews, Harris, and Olden at a store when a police officer was present, and that Matthews made no attempt to signal for help.]

Although Matthews and Russell were both married to and living with other people at the time of the incident, they were apparently involved in an extramarital relationship. By the time of trial the two were living together, having separated from their respective spouses. Petitioner's theory of the case was that Matthews concocted the rape story to protect her relationship with Russell, who would have grown suspicious upon seeing her disembark from Harris's car. In order to demonstrate Matthews' motive to lie, it was crucial, petitioner contended, that he be allowed to introduce evidence of Matthew's and Russell's current cohabitation. Over petitioner's vehement objections, the trial court nonetheless granted the prosecutor's motion in limine to keep all evidence of Matthews' and Russell's living arrangement from the jury. Moreover, when the defense attempted to cross-examine Matthews about her living arrangements, after she had claimed during direct examination that she was living with her mother, the trial court sustained the prosecutor's objection.

Based on the evidence admitted at trial, the jury acquitted Harris of being either a principal or an accomplice to any of the charged offenses. Petitioner was likewise acquitted of kidnaping and rape. However, in a somewhat puzzling turn of events, the jury convicted petitioner alone of forcible sodomy. He was sentenced to 10 years' imprisonment.

Petitioner appealed, asserting, inter alia, that the trial court's refusal to allow him to impeach Matthews' testimony by introducing evidence supporting a motive to lie deprived him of his Sixth Amendment right to confront witnesses against him. The Kentucky Court of Appeals upheld the conviction. The court specifically held that evidence that Matthews and Russell were living together at the time of trial was not barred by the State's rape shield law. Moreover, it acknowledged that the evidence in question was relevant to petitioner's theory of the case. But it held, nonetheless, that the evidence was properly excluded as "its probative value [was] outweighed by its possibility for prejudice." By way of explanation, the court stated: "[T]here were the undisputed facts of race; Matthews was white and Russell was black. For the trial court to have admitted into evidence testimony that Matthews and Russell were living together at the time of the trial may have created extreme prejudice against Matthews." Judge Clayton, who dissented but did not address the evidentiary issue, would have reversed petitioner's conviction both because he believed the jury's verdicts were "manifestly inconsistent," and because he found Matthews' testimony too incredible to provide evidence sufficient to uphold the verdict.

The Kentucky Court of Appeals failed to accord proper weight to petitioner's Sixth Amendment right "to be confronted with the witnesses against him." That right, incorporated in the Fourteenth Amendment and therefore available in state proceedings, Pointer v. Texas, 380 U.S. 400, 85 S. Ct. 1065, 13 L. Ed. 2d 923 (1965), includes the right to conduct reasonable cross-examination. Davis v. Alaska, 415 U.S. 308, 315-316, 94 S. Ct. 1105, 1109-1110, 39 L. Ed. 2d 347 (1974).

In Davis v. Alaska, we observed that, subject to "the broad discretion of a trial judge to preclude repetitive and unduly harassing interrogation . . . , the cross-examiner has traditionally been allowed to impeach, i.e., discredit, the witness." We emphasized that "the exposure of a witness' motivation in testifying is a proper and important function of the constitutionally protected right of cross-examination." Recently, in Delaware v. Van Arsdall, 475 U.S. 673, 106 S. Ct. 1431, 89 L. Ed. 2d 674 (1986), we reaffirmed *Davis,* and held that "a criminal defendant states a violation of the Confrontation Clause by showing that he was prohibited from engaging in otherwise appropriate cross-examination designed to show a prototypical form of bias on the part of the witness, and thereby 'to expose to the jury the facts from which jurors . . . could appropriately draw inferences relating to the reliability of the witness.'"

In the instant case, petitioner has consistently asserted that he and Matthews engaged in consensual sexual acts and that Matthews — out of fear of jeopardizing her relationship with Russell — lied when she told Russell she had been raped and has continued to lie since. It is plain to us that "[a] reasonable jury might have received a significantly different impression of [the witness'] credibility had [defense counsel] been permitted to pursue his proposed line of cross-examination."

. . . While a trial court may, of course, impose reasonable limits on defense counsel's inquiry into the potential bias of a prosecution witness, to take account of such factors as "harassment, prejudice, confusion of the issues, the witness' safety, or interrogation that [would be] repetitive or only marginally relevant," the limitation here was beyond reason. Speculation as to the effect of jurors' racial biases cannot justify exclusion of cross-examination with such strong potential to demonstrate the falsity of Matthews' testimony.

In Delaware v. Van Arsdall, we held that "the constitutionally improper denial of a defendant's opportunity to impeach a witness for bias, like other Confrontation Clause errors, is subject to *Chapman* harmless-error analysis." Thus we stated:

> The correct inquiry is whether, assuming that the damaging potential of the cross-examination were fully realized, a reviewing court might nonetheless say that the error was harmless beyond a reasonable doubt. Whether such an error is harmless in a particular case depends upon a host of factors, all readily accessible to reviewing courts. These factors include the importance of the witness' testimony in the prosecution's case, whether the testimony was cumulative, the presence or absence of evidence corroborating or contradicting the testimony of the witness on material points, the extent of cross-examination otherwise permitted, and, of course, the overall strength of the prosecution's case.

Here, Matthews' testimony was central, indeed crucial, to the prosecution's case. Her story, which was directly contradicted by that of petitioner and Harris, was corroborated only by the largely derivative testimony of Russell, whose impartiality would also have been somewhat impugned by revelation of his relationship with Matthews. Finally, as demonstrated graphically by the jury's verdicts, which cannot be squared with the State's theory of the alleged crime, and by Judge Clayton's dissenting opinion below, the State's case against petitioner was far from overwhelming. In sum, considering the relevant *Van Arsdall* factors within the context of this case, we find it impossible to conclude "beyond a reasonable doubt" that the restriction on petitioner's right to confrontation was harmless.

The . . . case is remanded for further proceedings not inconsistent with this opinion.

It is so ordered.

Further Reading: Ann Althouse, *Thelma and Louise and the Law: Do Rape Shield Rules Matter?*, 25 Loy. L.A. L. Rev. 757 (1992); Vivian Berger, *Man's Trial, Woman's Tribulation: Rape Cases in the Courtroom*, 77 Colum. L. Rev. 1 (1977); Harriett R. Galvin, *Shielding Rape Victims in the State and Federal Courts: A Proposal for the Second Decade*, 70 Minn. L. Rev. 763 (1986); Elizabeth Kessler, *Pattern of Sexual Conduct Evidence and Present Consent: Limiting the Admissibility of Sexual History Evidence in Rape Prosecutions*, 14 Women's Rts. L. Rep. 79 (1992).

Questions for Classroom Discussion

1. What exactly was the questioned evidence in *Olden*?

2. Why was this evidence relevant?

3. Does this evidence carry significant probative value?

4. Why did the trial court exclude the evidence? Was the court's reason rational?

5. After *Olden*, would any sexual-assault defendant be encouraged to investigate the alleged victim's sex life to determine if she is engaged, or has ever engaged, in an illicit relationship? If so, would that situation undermine the purposes of the rape-shield laws?

6. Prosecution of Defendant for sexual assault on Victim. Defendant admits having sex with Victim but claims Victim consented. To prove consent, Defendant wishes to testify that prior to the alleged sexual assault, Defendant and Victim had engaged in consensual sexual intercourse on two occasions. The prosecution objects. How should the court rule?

7. Defendant is prosecuted for sexual assault. The prosecution's theory is that Victim went to defendant's hotel room willingly, but said "No" after he bit her. As tending to prove consent the defense calls a witness who will testify he dated Victim, and their physical relationship was "kinky."

---

v.   *Illustrating the Basic Rules*

The following transcript illustrates how parties might use some of the basic rules governing the use of character evidence to prove a person's out-of-court conduct. Doug is prosecuted for assault and battery on Vic. Assume that during the prosecution's case-in-chief, Vic testified that he and Doug were coaches of opposing kids' soccer teams, and that they got into an argument during a game about a referee's call. Vic testifies that Doug suddenly became violent and struck Vic on the head with the edge of a clipboard, inflicting a severe cut.

As part of Doug's defense, defense counsel calls Wilma, a parent whose child was on Vic's soccer team. "Pros" indicates the prosecutor; "Def" indicates defense counsel.

Def:	Do you know Vic?
Wilma:	Yes.
Def:	How long have you known him?
Wilma:	About two years.
Def:	And how do you know him?
Wilma:	For the last couple of years, my son has played on soccer teams, and Vic has been his coach both years.
Def:	In the course of those two soccer seasons, did you have occasion to observe Vic's behavior?
Wilma:	Sure. I always go to the games.
Def:	And do you have an opinion about whether Vic is a peaceful or violent person?
Wilma:	Yes. I think Vic gets mad very easily and sometimes tends to be pretty violent.
Def:	Thank you. No further questions.
By The Court:	Cross-examination?
Pros:	Thank you, Your Honor. Wilma, have you ever heard of an organization called "Talk First"?
Wilma:	Yes.
Pros:	And what is the purpose of that organization?
Wilma:	I think it promotes non-violent solutions to disputes.
Pros:	Did you know that Vic received that organization's "Talker of the Year" award last year?
Def:	Objection. This is not proper rebuttal.
Pros:	Your Honor, this is similar to evidence of specific instances of conduct, which are allowed under Rule 405(a).
By The Court:	I'll allow it. It's not exactly the typical sort of specific instance of conduct, but I think it reflects peaceful conduct. Objection overruled. The witness will answer the question.
Wilma:	No, I hadn't heard that.
Pros:	Do you know Doug?
Wilma:	Not personally, but we live in the neighborhood and our kids have been involved in sports together for a few years.
Pros:	Do you ever hear people speak about Doug's character for peacefulness?
Wilma:	I suppose I hear some things.
Pros:	Did you ever hear that Doug threatened to punch a referee during a soccer game last year?

> *Wilma:*   No, I never heard such a thing.
>
> *Pros:*   Thank you. Your Honor, I have no further questions.

Defense counsel then calls Walker to the witness stand.

> *Def:*   Are you familiar with Doug, the defendant in this case?
>
> *Walker:*   Yes.
>
> *Def:*   How do you know Doug?
>
> *Walker:*   We work together at the auto parts plant in town.
>
> *Def:*   How long have you worked together?
>
> *Walker:*   About three years.
>
> *Def:*   Do you work in the same part of the plant?
>
> *Walker:*   Yes. I first met Doug when I started to work on the engine line. He was already on that line, and he's been there with me ever since.
>
> *Def:*   Have you had occasion to observe Doug's behavior with his co-workers?
>
> *Walker:*   Yes.
>
> *Def:*   And do you have an opinion about Doug's character for peacefulness?
>
> *Walker:*   Yes. I think he's a real peacemaker around the plant. He often breaks up fights and I've never seen him get involved in one.
>
> *Pros:*   Your Honor. I move to strike the last part of the witness's answer as a violation of Rule 405(a).
>
> *By the Court:*   Motion granted. The jury will ignore everything the witness said after describing Doug as a peacemaker.
>
> *Def:*   No further questions, Your Honor.
>
> *By the Court:*   Cross-examination?
>
> *Pros:*   Did you know that several months ago, Doug was reprimanded for roughing up a workmate following a dispute?
>
> *Def:*   Your Honor, I object. May we approach?
>
> *By the Court:*   Counsel will approach.
>
> *Def:*   This is the first I've heard of such an incident. The prosecutor has to have some proof that it occurred.
>
> *Pros:*   Your Honor, I have interviewed the victim of this attack and am prepared to bring him in if you would like to hear from him.
>
> *Def:*   Your Honor, I've looked at Doug's personnel file, and there's nothing about this incident.
>
> *Pros:*   That's because the employer agreed to make this an informal reprimand. It won't go in the defendant's personnel file.
>
> *By the Court:*   Objection overruled. I'll allow the question.
>
> *Pros:*   Will the court reporter please read back the question?
>
> [The court reporter reads back the question.]
>
> *Walker:*   No. I didn't know of such an incident.
>
> *Pros:*   No further questions.
>
> *Def:*   Just one question, Your Honor.
>
> *By the Court:*   Go ahead, counsel.
>
> *Def:*   If your son was assigned to play soccer on Doug's team, would you have

	any problem with that?
Pros:	I object, Your Honor. This goes beyond allowable limits under the character evidence rules.
Def:	It does not, Your Honor. I am only seeking to demonstrate the witness's opinion more fully. I am not asking the witness to relate any specific instances of conduct.
By the Court:	Objection overruled. You may answer the question, Walker.
Walker:	I'd have no problem if my kid were assigned to Doug's team.
Def:	Thank you. I have no further questions.

In this example, the prosecution did not offer any evidence of Doug's character during its case-in-chief, nor would the rules have allowed the prosecution to do so under these circumstances. Doug's first witness, Wilma, was a character witness. Rule 404(a)(2) allows the defendant in a criminal case to be the first to present evidence of a pertinent trait of the victim's character. Peacefulness is a pertinent character trait, and Wilma probably knows Vic well enough to have an opinion about Vic's character for peacefulness. Rule 405(a) limits character evidence on direct examination to reputation and opinion. This was opinion. On cross-examination, the prosecutor sought to rebut the inference of Vic's violent character. This was permissible because Doug has opened the door. The prosecutor sought to rebut by asking Wilma about Vic's receipt of an award for promoting non-violence. Rule 405(a) allows the use of specific instances of conduct on cross-examination of a character witness. Although receipt of an award is not exactly a specific instance of conduct, the court's ruling on Doug's objection was probably correct. Receipt of an award of this kind can be seen as circumstantial evidence of a specific instance or instances of conduct. It can also be seen as circumstantial evidence of the organization's opinion that Vic is a peaceful person.

The prosecutor then continued the cross-examination of Wilma by eliciting evidence of Doug's violent character. Rule 404(a)(1) allows the prosecutor to respond to the defendant's presentation of character evidence concerning the victim with evidence concerning the same trait of character in the defendant. The prosecutor's questions sought testimony about Doug's reputation, which is permitted under Rule 405, and the witness appears to have been qualified to offer such testimony.

Doug's next witness was Walker, who was a typical character witness. Walker appears to have been sufficiently familiar with Doug to present an opinion about Doug's character for peacefulness. (Observation of Doug in a work setting over a period of three years is probably sufficient, though the judge certainly has discretion to rule that it is not.) Defense counsel sought Walker's opinion, but after offering it, Walker backed up the opinion with evidence of specific instances of conduct (stating that Doug often breaks up fights and doesn't get involved in fights himself). The prosecutor's motion to strike the last part of the answer was proper because the answer went beyond the allowable form of character testimony during direct examination. Thus, the court's ruling striking the last part of Walker's answer was correct. The prosecutor's cross-examination of Walker was also proper, as long as the prosecutor had a good faith belief that the event inquired about actually occurred. That was the purpose of the colloquy at sidebar. The court's ruling appears correct; the prosecutor has shown a good faith basis for believing that the event actually took place.

Doug's brief redirect examination was probably also proper. Asking the witness whether he would allow his kid to play soccer on a team coached by Doug appears to be a further explanation of the basis of her opinion that Doug is a peaceful person.

Further Reading: David P. Bryden & Roger C. Park, *"Other Crimes" Evidence in Sex Offense Cases*, 78 Minn. L. Rev. 529 (1994); Russell L. Jones, *"If It Ain't Broke, Don't Fix It!" An Unnecessary Tampering with a Well Established Rule: Louisiana Code of Evidence Article 412.2 Admits Criminal Propensity Evidence*, 48 Loy. L. Rev. 17-51 (2002); David P. Leonard, *In Defense of the Character Evidence Prohibition: Foundations of the Rule Against Trial by Character*, 73 Ind. L.J. 1161 (1998); David P. Leonard, *The Use of Character to Prove Conduct: Rationality and Catharsis in the Law of Evidence*, 58 U. Colo. L. Rev. 1 (1986-1987); Miguel A. Mendez, *California's New Law on Character Evidence: Evidence Code Section 352 and the Impact of Recent Psychological Studies*, 31 UCLA L. Rev. 1003 (1984); Chris William Sanchirico, *Character Evidence and the Object of Trial*, 101 Colum. L. Rev. 1227 (2001); Andrew E. Taslitz, *Myself Alone: Individualizing Justice Through Psychological Character Evidence*, 52 Md. L. Rev. 1 (1993); H. Richard Uviller, *Evidence of Character to Prove Conduct: Illusion, Illogic, and Injustice in the Courtroom*, 130 U. Pa. L. Rev. 845 (1982); Glen Weissenberger, *Character Evidence Under the Federal Rules: A Puzzle with Missing Pieces*, 48 U. Cin. L. Rev. 1 (1979); Richard C. Wydick, *Character Evidence: A Guided Tour of the Grotesque Structure*, 21 U.C. Davis L. Rev. 123 (1987).

Questions for Classroom Discussion

1. Prosecution of Defendant for arson. The prosecution claims that Defendant set fire to the office building of Victim, a business rival, after Victim beat Defendant in bidding on a large contract. Defendant claims Victim burned the building for the insurance money. To prove that Victim was responsible for the fire, Defendant calls Witness to testify that she has known Victim for many years, and that in her opinion, Victim is a dishonest person. The prosecution objects. How should the court rule?

2. Same case. During its rebuttal case, the prosecution calls Witness 2 to testify that Defendant is known in the community as a dishonest person. Defendant objects. How should the court rule?

3. Same case. The prosecutor asks Witness 2 to relate an instance of Defendant's dishonesty. Defendant objects. How should the court rule?

4. Same case. During its rebuttal case, the prosecution calls Witness 3 to testify that Defendant is known in the community as a mobster. Defendant objects. How should the court rule?

5. Prosecution of Defendant for the murder of Victim. To prove that Victim was the first aggressor, Defendant calls Witness, who testifies that she knew Victim for many years, and that in her opinion, Victim was a violent person. During its rebuttal case, the prosecution calls Witness 2 to testify that she knew Victim for many years, and that in her opinion, Victim was a non-violent person. Defendant objects. How should the court rule?

6. Same case. Assume that instead of testifying as in Question 5, Witness states that she was present at the time of the incident, that Victim attacked Defendant with a knife without notice or provocation, and that Defendant responded by shooting Victim. During its rebuttal case, the prosecution wishes to call Witness 2 to testify to Victim's character for peacefulness. Defendant objects. How should the court rule?

C. OTHER CRIMES, WRONGS, OR ACTS

> FED. R. EVID. 404(B).   CRIMES OR OTHER ACTS

(1) *Prohibited Uses.* Evidence of a crime or other act is not admissible to prove a person's character in order to show that on a particular occasion the person acted in accordance with the character.

(2) *Permitted Uses; Notice.* This evidence may be admissible for another purpose, such as proving motive, opportunity, intent, preparation, plan, knowledge, identity, absence of mistake, or lack of accident. On request by a defendant in a criminal case, the prosecutor must:

(A) provide reasonable notice of the general nature of any such evidence that the prosecutor intends to offer at trial; and

(B) do so before trial — or during trial if the court, for good cause, excuses lack of pretrial notice.

Discussion

1. Introduction

No single rule of evidence has been litigated as often, and with as much inconsistency of outcome, as the "crimes and other acts" rule. On its face the principle of the rule is relatively straightforward. The first sentence is redundant, essentially repeating the provision of Rule 404(a) that says character evidence is not admissible to prove that the individual acted in accordance with her character. The only difference is that the first sentence of Rule 404(b) refers to a particular type of evidence: other crimes, wrongs, or acts. This is a type of specific instance of conduct. Such conduct may not be offered to prove that the actor possesses a character trait, and that she acted in accordance with that character trait. For simplicity, we will sometimes refer to "crimes and other acts" evidence as *uncharged misconduct* evidence. By that term, we mean simply that the evidence concerns conduct that is not the subject of the charge or claim in the case at hand. In many cases, the conduct will have been the subject of another prosecution or claim, but it is still "uncharged misconduct" in the present case.

Under the second sentence of Rule 404(b), evidence of crimes or other acts is inadmissible only if its relevance *requires* an inference of character at any point in the chain of inferences leading from the evidence to the conclusion sought to be proved. If the evidence is relevant through any chain of inferences that does not include the actor's character, it is potentially admissible. The rule then provides a non-exclusive list of non-character purposes for which crimes or other acts may be offered: motive, opportunity, intent, preparation, plan, knowledge, identity, and absence of mistake or accident.[7] The rule is not restricted to criminal cases, but when the prosecution in a criminal case plans to offer such evidence against the defendant, the prosecution must provide notice, preferably before trial, of its intention to introduce the evidence and of the general nature of the evidence.

The discussion to follow highlights the logic behind the rule as well as its basic operation.

2. *The Basic Principle*

The rule's basic principle can be illustrated with a simple hypothetical:

> Bank robbery prosecution. The perpetrator used explosives to break open the safe. Defendant claims she was not involved and testifies that, in any event, she had been drinking heavily just before the robbery occurred and so would not have had the ability to commit such a crime. The prosecution wishes to present evidence that just before the bank robbery took place and during the time Defendant claims to have been drunk, Defendant robbed another bank nearby.

Consider how evidence of Defendant's participation in another bank robbery might be relevant. First, the evidence could demonstrate Defendant's criminal character:

EVIDENCE: At the time Defendant claims to have been drunk, Defendant committed another bank robbery.

→**INFERENCE:** Defendant is a person who commits serious crimes.

→**CONCLUSION:** Defendant committed the bank robbery for which she is charged.

---

7. Generations of law students have memorized the list of non-character facts in Rule 404(b) using the word "MIMIC" (*M* stands for Motive; *I* stands for Intent; *M* stands for Mistake or absence of Mistake; *I* stands for Identity; *C* stands for Common plan). These are often referred to as the "MIMIC facts." Unfortunately, MIMIC does not encompass all the possible facts that uncharged misconduct evidence might be admissible to prove under Rule 404(b). The most notable omission is "opportunity."

Used in this way, the evidence violates the character rule because its purpose is to expose Defendant's character, and from that, to suggest that she committed the crime. Though relevant, the evidence is inadmissible for this purpose.

Suppose, however, the prosecution argues that the evidence is not being offered to show Defendant's criminal character, but merely to show that she had the *ability* or *opportunity* to commit the crime:

> **EVIDENCE:** At the time Defendant claims to have been drunk, Defendant committed another bank robbery.
>
> → **INFERENCE:** Defendant was sober enough to rob another bank.
>
> → **INFERENCE:** Defendant was sober enough to rob the bank at issue just a few minutes later.
>
> → **CONCLUSION:** Defendant committed the bank robbery for which she is charged.

This series of inferences does not include any reference to Defendant's character, and the relevance of the evidence does not depend on any inference that Defendant has a bad character. Thus, it does not violate the character evidence rule if used in this way, and it is potentially admissible.

Take a second example:

> Defendant is charged with the murder of Victim. Defendant admits backing her car over Victim, but claims it was an accident. To prove Defendant's intent to kill Victim, the prosecution wishes to present evidence that the day before the incident, Defendant and Victim had robbed a bank together, netting a large sum of money.

As in the previous example, this evidence would not be admissible to prove that Defendant is the kind of person who would commit a serious crime, such as murder. It might be admissible, however, to prove that Defendant had a *motive* to kill Victim:

> **EVIDENCE:** The day before the incident, Defendant and Victim robbed a bank, getting a large sum of money.
>
> → **INFERENCE:** Defendant had a motive to obtain sole possession of the entire loot.
>
> → **CONCLUSION:** Defendant intentionally killed Victim so as not to have to share the loot.

In these examples, we say that the evidence is *potentially* admissible because, like most evidence rules, the rule permitting evidence of crimes or other acts is not a rule of automatic admission. The court must also decide, for example, whether a limiting instruction sufficiently protects Defendant from unfair prejudice. As we will see, this is a central issue in the application of Rule 404(b), especially in criminal trials.

Recall that character-based propensity is only one type of propensity inference, and that Rule 404(a) only prohibits that type of propensity inference. The same is true for Rule 404(b). In most cases, evidence admissible under Rule 404(b) requires the use of a propensity inference. As long as the propensity inference is not character-based, the rule does not forbid it. Consider the following example:

> Bank robbery prosecution. Defendant denies involvement. To prove Defendant's involvement, the prosecution wishes to present evidence that the day before the robbery, Defendant stole the car that was used as the getaway vehicle.

In this example, the evidence of Defendant's theft of the getaway car would not be admissible to prove Defendant's character for criminality, and thus his propensity to commit the bank robbery. The evidence would, however, be relevant, and probably admissible, to prove Defendant's *plan* to commit the robbery, and from that, Defendant's involvement. The reasoning is as follows:

> **EVIDENCE:** The day before the bank robbery, Defendant stole the getaway car.
>
> ➔**INFERENCE:** Defendant had a plan to commit the robbery.
>
> ➔**CONCLUSION:** Defendant committed the bank robbery.

This series of logical steps does not require an inference of character-based propensity, but it does not avoid all propensity inferences. To move from the inference that Defendant had a plan to commit bank robbery to Defendant's commission of the robbery, one must employ the generalization that a person who has a plan to act in a certain way is somewhat more likely than one without such a plan to carry out the act. Certainly, this involves a propensity inference, but arguably it is not one based on a trait of Defendant's individual character. Rather, it is simply general human nature — a characteristic we all share that helps to explain why and how we tend to act. When we plan to act in a certain way, we are more likely to act in that way than if we do not have such a plan. This is especially true once we take a step in the direction of implementing our plan, as would be the case whenever there is uncharged misconduct evidence of the plan such as the theft of the getaway vehicle. You can think of this as propensity in the sense that, once we formulate and set a plan in motion, the sheer momentum of that conduct has a tendency to carry us forward. Character, our propensity to be good or bad, has nothing to do with this momentum. In fact, it does not even matter whether the plan is to commit legal or illegal conduct since the momentum of the plan exerts its force in either case. Seen in that way, the evidence does not violate the character rule. Propensity it is, but character-based propensity it is not.

If all applications of Rule 404(b) were this straightforward, the rule would not be particularly difficult to apply or controversial in nature. Unfortunately, many uses of the rule are considerably more problematic. Consider the following hypothetical:

> Prosecution of Defendant for stealing cocaine from a clinical laboratory. The lab had been using the cocaine in government-sanctioned research. Defendant denies

involvement. To prove Defendant's involvement, the prosecution wishes to present evidence that Defendant is addicted to cocaine.[13]

In this example, the evidence would not be admissible to prove that Defendant, as a cocaine addict, has a criminal character that would lead him to commit crimes such as theft. The government will argue, however, that the evidence of Defendant's addiction shows that Defendant had a *motive* to commit the crime, and thus that Defendant might have been the perpetrator. The reasoning is as follows:

EVIDENCE: Defendant is addicted to cocaine.

→**INFERENCE:** Defendant had a motive to obtain cocaine.

→**CONCLUSION:** Defendant robbed the laboratory to obtain cocaine.

Most courts would admit this evidence under Rule 404(b) on the ground that as used above, it is not character evidence.

But the line between motive and character in this example, if it exists at all, is extremely thin. If we view addiction as arising from a character flaw, then there would be essentially no difference between using the evidence to prove "motive" and using it to prove "character" and the court should exclude the evidence as a violation of the character prohibition. If we view addiction as a disease, then there is no reason to treat it any differently, in theory at least, from a disease such as Parkinson's. Clearly, such a disease affects a person's behavior, but we do not think of a person so afflicted as having a particular character trait. This analysis would lead to a strange result, however: If the court categorizes the evidence as character evidence, the court would be required to exclude it. That would mean the jury would not learn of Defendant's addiction and, therefore, would be less likely to convict. But if the court accepts the position that drug addiction is not evidence of a character trait, the court would have the authority to admit it. A decision to admit, however, would create a risk of unfair prejudice. Specifically, there is a risk that the jury would adhere to the more common belief that addiction to illegal drugs is indicative of a bad character and convict on that basis. Theoretically, of course, the court could hold that the evidence is not character evidence but exclude it because the risk of unfair prejudice is too great. But it is hard to escape the irony of convicting a morally innocent person and acquitting an immoral one.

Unfortunately, the type of problem sometimes raised by motive evidence is not unique to that theory of admissibility. A number of theories for admissibility under Rule 404(b) suffer from similar problems.

In each example we have discussed to this point, the analysis begins with the assumption that the actor committed the uncharged misconduct. From that fact, a series of inferences will flow, leading to the ultimate issue for which the evidence is offered. Not all uses of uncharged misconduct operate this way. Take the famous English case of Rex v. Smith, 11 Cr. App. R. 229, 84

13. This hypothetical is loosely based on the facts of United States v. Cunningham, 103 F.3d 553 (7th Cir. 1996) (evidence of nurse's prior addiction to Demerol admissible to prove motive to steal Demerol from locked hospital medicine cabinet to which she had access; existence of motive tended to prove identity).

L.J.K.B. 2153 (1915). Smith was charged with the murder of Bessie Mundy, a woman with whom Smith had gone through a marriage ceremony even though he was married to another woman at the time. Mundy was found drowned in the bathtub. Smith claimed that no crime occurred — that Mundy drowned accidentally while bathing. To prove that a crime occurred and that Smith was responsible, the prosecution offered evidence that after Mundy's death, Smith went through marriage ceremonies with two other women, that both women also drowned in the bath, that all three women had obtained life insurance at defendant's suggestion, and that shortly before the death of each woman, defendant took her to the doctor, explaining that she was in ill health.

In Rex v. Smith, the relevance of the evidence regarding the deaths of defendant's subsequent wives does not depend, first, on an inference that defendant actually murdered them. Instead, it flows from an intuitive idea that has been called the *doctrine of chances*. As one author explains:

> Common sense suggests that the typical, innocent person will rarely suffer the type of loss involved in *Smith* — the death of a spouse by drowning in his or her own bathtub. When the number of losses suffered by the accused exceeds the ordinary incidence of such events, the extraordinary coincidence is some evidence of criminal agency. Either Smith was one the unluckiest persons on the face of the planet, or one or some of the deaths in question were caused by an actus reus. Thus, under the doctrine of chances, an accused's similar uncharged misconduct can be relevant in this context to prove one element of the charged offense, that is, the actus reus.[9]

To put it simply, the doctrine of chances proceeds from the intuitive reaction, "that can't be a coincidence! What are the odds?!" In *Smith*, we would naturally think that the odds that three "wives" of the same man would all drown in the bath accidentally are very small, while the probability that the man was responsible for the three deaths is rather high.

Doctrine of chances reasoning therefore does not move from a given act to the charged act, but rather considers a series of acts or events as a group. If, taken together, the likelihood of innocent coincidence appears small, the evidence of the uncharged acts is relevant and likely admissible. Consider the following case:

ROBBINS v. STATE

88 S.W.3d 256 (Tex. Crim. App. 2002)

In this capital murder case the prosecution did not seek the death penalty against appellant, who was convicted and sentenced to life for killing the seventeen-month-old daughter of his live-in girlfriend. The issue in this case is whether during the guilt/innocence phase of appellant's trial, the trial court abused its discretion to admit evidence of previous injuries the victim suffered while she was in appellant's care. We will refer to this evidence as "relationship evidence."

9. Edward J. Imwinkelried, *A Small Contribution to the Debate over the Proposed Legislation Abolishing the Character Evidence Prohibition in Sex Offense Prosecutions*, 44 Syracuse L. Rev. 1125, 1131-1132 (1993) (footnotes omitted).

The prosecution presented evidence that the victim received the injuries that caused her death while she was alone with, and in the care of, the appellant in their home. Appellant and the victim lived with appellant's mother and the victim's mother. The victim's mother left the victim alone with appellant at home. When the victim's mother returned, appellant told her that the victim was taking a nap; appellant left soon thereafter. About an hour later, when the victim's mother attempted to wake the victim up from her nap, she noticed that the victim was cold and not breathing. The prosecution presented medical evidence that the victim was dead at this time.

Appellant suggested through vigorous cross-examination of prosecution witnesses that the victim's death was not the result of an intentional act by appellant. Through his cross-examination of one prosecution witness, appellant presented the defensive theory that the victim could have died from Sudden Infant Death Syndrome (SIDS) and not from an intentional act by appellant. Through his cross-examination of his parole officer who saw appellant and the victim on the day of the victim's death, appellant presented the defensive theory that he was treating the victim "kindly" with the obvious inference being that appellant would not have intentionally harmed the victim. And through his cross-examination of another prosecution witness, appellant presented the defensive theory that bruises on the victim's body could have been caused by incorrectly performed CPR efforts to save her life rather than from an intentional act by appellant. . . .

The victim's mother and other witnesses later testified over appellant's objection about the relationship evidence. They testified that on three separate occasions the victim received injuries while she was in appellant's care. For example, the victim's mother testified that on one occasion while in appellant's care, the victim received a black eye. On another occasion while in appellant's care, the victim's "leg was so badly injured she couldn't stand up." And, on another occasion while in appellant's care, the victim "appeared with bruises in her ear and on the side of her face."

Appellant testified that he loved the victim and would not have harmed her. Appellant presented seemingly innocent explanations for how the victim suffered the injuries described in the relationship evidence. Appellant also presented medical expert testimony that the victim's cause of death was "undeterminable" and that the victim's death-causing injuries could have occurred at a time when appellant did not have access to her.

During closing jury arguments, appellant argued that if "anything, he is guilty of the offense of loving a child." He also pointed to the testimony of the two medical examiners who came to "two diametrically-opposed conclusions" about the victim's death: one that "this is a death of undeterminant cause" and the other that it is "a homicide." Appellant put forth the SIDS scenario, and he also emphasized that the bruises on the victim's body could have been caused by incorrectly performed CPR efforts to save the victim's life. Finally, appellant argued:

[Appellant] loved the [victim]. The [victim's] own mother said she never saw him yell at the [victim], discipline the [victim]. And everybody else, save for [two witnesses], said they had a loving relationship, got along well; and told how much he loved [the victim] and spent time caring for her. And I don't think there is any doubt about the relationship they had up to [the day of the victim's death]; and there is nothing, nothing that would explain [appellant] doing this terrible thing.

Our reading of the record indicates that the trial court admitted the relationship evidence under Article 38.36(a), V.A.C.C.P., and also overruled appellant's objections that this evidence was inadmissible under Rules 404(b) and 403 of the Texas Rules of Evidence. The Court of Appeals decided that this evidence was "probative of intent and lack of accident" under Rule 404(b) and that it was not "unfairly prejudicial" under Rule 403 because "the prejudicial effect lies in its probative value rather than an unrelated matter." . . .

RULE 404(B)

Relevant evidence of a person's bad character is generally not admissible for the purpose of showing that he acted in conformity therewith. This evidence, however, may be admissible when it is relevant to a noncharacter conformity issue of consequence in the case such as establishing intent or rebutting a defensive theory.

Because trial courts are in the best position to decide these admissibility questions, an appellate court must review a trial court's admissibility decision under an abuse of discretion standard. This standard requires an appellate court to uphold a trial court's admissibility decision when that decision is within the zone of reasonable disagreement. An appellate court would misapply the appellate abuse of discretion standard of review to reverse a trial court's admissibility decision solely because the appellate court disagreed with it. . . .

Notwithstanding the foregoing, the trial court would not have abused its discretion to have decided that the relationship evidence was relevant for the noncharacter conformity purpose of rebutting appellant's various defensive theories including the defensive theory that the victim's death resulted from an accident due to improperly performed CPR efforts to save her life. . . . It too is subject to reasonable debate whether the relationship evidence made these defensive theories less probable.

RULE 403

An appellate court also reviews a trial court's Rule 403 decision under the above-mentioned abuse of discretion standard. The Rule 403 appellate issue is usually whether the trial court abused its discretion to decide that the probative value of the evidence "is substantially outweighed by the danger of unfair prejudice."

In making this determination, it is important to remember that each word in Rule 403 is significant. For example, it appears that appellant misquoted Rule 403 in the Court of Appeals by arguing "the probative value of the [relationship] evidence was outweighed by its prejudicial effect." This is a misstatement of Rule 403 which, in relevant part, actually reads "evidence may be excluded if its probative value is *substantially* outweighed by the danger of *unfair* prejudice." (Emphasis supplied.)

The Rule 403 analysis advances the "overriding policy" of excluding what most agree is relevant and probative character evidence when it is offered solely for the purpose of showing that a defendant acted in conformity therewith. *See generally* Michelson v. United States, 335 U.S. 469, 69 S. Ct. 213, 218-19, 93 L. Ed. 168 (1948).

> Courts that follow the common-law tradition almost unanimously have come to disallow resort by the prosecution to any kind of evidence of a defendant's evil character to establish a probability of his guilt. (Footnote Omitted.) Not that the law invests the defendant with a presumption of good character, (citation omitted), but it simply closes the whole matter of character, disposition and reputation on the prosecution's case-in-chief. The State may not show defendant's prior trouble with the law, specific criminal acts, or ill name among his neighbors, even though such facts might logically be persuasive that he is by propensity a probable perpetrator of the crime. (Footnote Omitted.) The inquiry is not rejected because character is irrelevant; (footnote omitted) it is said to weigh too much with the jury and to so overpersuade them as to prejudge one with a bad general record and deny him a fair opportunity to defend against a particular charge. The overriding policy of excluding such evidence, despite its admitted probative value, is the practical experience that its disallowance tends to prevent confusion of issues, unfair surprise and undue prejudice. (Footnote Omitted.)

Id.

This "overriding policy" of preventing "undue prejudice" is meant primarily to prevent a jury, with a reasonable doubt of a defendant's guilt of the charged offense, from nevertheless convicting the defendant of the charged offense based solely on the defendant's "wicked or criminal disposition" or solely because the defendant is a bad person generally. . . .

With these considerations in mind, we cannot say that the Court of Appeals wrongly decided that the trial court was within its discretion to decide that the probative value of the relationship evidence was not *substantially* outweighed by the danger of *unfair* prejudice especially in light of the defensive theories that appellant presented. Though "prejudicial," the evidence was not "unfairly prejudicial." And, any "unfair prejudice" did not "substantially" outweigh the probative value of the evidence even if it could be said that it "outweighed" its probative value. On this record, there was no reason to believe that the jury had a reasonable doubt for appellant's guilt of the charged offense but convicted appellant based on the relationship evidence.

The judgment of the Court of Appeals is affirmed.

COCHRAN, J., filed a concurring opinion joined by WOMACK, and JOHNSON, JJ.

I concur in the majority's conclusion that the trial court did not abuse its discretion in admitting evidence of previous injuries that seventeen-month-old Tristen suffered while she was in appellant's sole care. I would hold that evidence showing that Tristen repeatedly suffered various physical injuries when left in appellant's care was admissible to prove the *corpus delicti* of murder. . . .

The situation here is . . . similar to that in the renowned English case, Rex v. Smith. . . . The logical proposition was that one drowned bride is an accident, two are suspicious, and three make murder. Smith was convicted upon what Wigmore called "the doctrine of chances" because the likelihood of three such coincidental events occurring naturally was logically improbable. The evidence was not offered to prove that Mr. Smith had a "drowning" or "murderous" character trait, but to show that it was more likely that Ms. Mundy died from a criminal act because two of Mr. Smith's other brides had died under very similar circumstances. The repetition of similar unusual events over time, involving Smith and different brides, made it possible for the jury to conclude that Mundy's drowning was caused by Smith's intentional act rather than by an inadvertent accident or a health problem.

In the present case, the fact that, as the State notes, "things started to happen to Tristen physically" when she was in appellant's sole care, increases the probability, however minimally, that "something" happened to Tristen while appellant took care of her on the day of her death. None of these incidents, taken alone, conclusively demonstrates that appellant intentionally harmed Tristen on those prior occasions or on the charged occasion. None of them prove any character trait possessed by appellant. But evidence that Tristen repeatedly suffered physical injuries while she was in appellant's care increases the probability that Tristen's injury on the day of her death was the result of some act, careless or otherwise, committed by appellant. . . .

Here, as in Rex v. Smith, one physical injury may be purely the result of accident. But because Tristen suffered four such injuries within a single six month period, each of them while under appellant's care, the probability that sheer accident caused each injury decreases significantly.

Therefore, because the evidence of Tristen's prior injuries was admissible for a non-character purpose to prove the *corpus delicti* of the crime, I concur in the judgment.

The probative value of the uncharged misconduct evidence in doctrine of chances cases will vary, of course. In *Smith*, for example, if the evidence were merely that one other "wife" had died under somewhat ambiguous, tough, different circumstances, the doctrine of chances probably would not apply, and the evidence would not be admissible unless some other ground could be found. The evidence in *Robbins* falls between the actual facts of *Smith* and this hypothetical variation. Though the numerous other injuries suffered by the victim while in defendant's care strongly suggests defendant was responsible for her death, the lack of similarity among the instances makes a somewhat less compelling case for application of the doctrine of chances.

Because the variety of circumstances in which the "crimes or other acts" principle might apply is virtually infinite, we cannot hope to discuss all possible patterns. Instead, we uncover some common uses of the rule, and set forth the basic principles common to all situations in which it is used. First, prepare the following questions, which test your understanding of the material we have covered up to this point.

Questions for Classroom Discussion

1. Veep, the vice-president of a bank, loses money betting with a bookie. To cover his losses, he embezzles money from the bank. He learns that bank examiners will examine the bank's books the next day. Fearing they will discover that cash is missing, he sets the bank on fire. Veep is charged with arson, and the prosecutor offers

evidence of Veep's gambling and embezzlement. Veep objects. How should the court rule?

2. Murder prosecution. Victim Roadrunner was shot. Defendant Coyote admits shooting Roadrunner but claims it was accidental. The prosecution offers evidence that, in the week before the shooting, Coyote tried to drop an anvil on Roadrunner, gave Roadrunner a birthday cake with sticks of dynamite for candles, and put a black widow spider in Roadrunner's athletic supporter. Coyote objects. How should the court rule?

3. Prosecution of Defendant for bank robbery. The perpetrator entered the bank wearing a Smokey the Bear costume, approached a teller, told the teller that money was needed to "feed the hungry bears," held out a large burlap sack for the teller to fill, and left after the teller did as she was told. Defendant claims to have been in another city when the crime was committed. The prosecution calls a witness to testify that on two occasions in the past month, he served as lookout for Defendant when Defendant committed bank robberies in the same city using the method just described. Defendant does not deny committing the other robberies, but objects to admission of the evidence on the ground it violates the character evidence rule. How should the prosecutor respond? How should the court rule?

4. Same case. Defendant argues that because the charged and uncharged crimes are so similar, there is a great danger that the jury will convict Defendant for being a bank robbing type, without finding whether Defendant committed the charged robbery. As a result, Defendant argues, the court should exclude the evidence as too prejudicial. How should the court rule?

5. Prosecution of Defendant for possession of a stolen laptop computer. Defendant admits possessing the computer, but claims she had just found it at a bus stop and planned to turn it in to the bus company. To prove Defendant planned to keep the laptop, the prosecutor wishes to present evidence that police found three other laptops in Defendant's home. None of these machines belonged to Defendant. Defendant objects to the prosecution's evidence on the ground it constitutes inadmissible character evidence. How should the court rule?

6. Prosecution of Defendant for failing to stop her car on police orders after she ran a red light. The police followed Defendant for many miles before finally shooting out Defendant's tires, forcing her to stop. Defendant claims she did not know the police were chasing her. To prove Defendant's knowledge, the prosecution wishes to offer evidence that a few days before the incident, Defendant robbed a bank. Defendant objects on grounds the evidence is irrelevant except on the basis that it shows her bad character, and that it is not admissible for that purpose. How should the court rule?

3. *What Is a "Crime or Other Act"?*

Except for its notice provision applicable to criminal cases where the prosecution is offering the evidence, Rule 404(b) is unnecessary. As noted above, the first sentence simply repeats the basic rule contained in Rule 404(a) that character evidence is usually not admissible to prove a person acted in conformity with her character on a specific occasion. The rest of Rule 404(b) merely states what is implicit in the first sentence: that evidence of crimes or other acts is not automatically excluded if offered for a different purpose.

The rule applies to crimes or other acts of a person. Most likely, it does not deal with arrests or convictions, which is conduct of the police or the courts, but with the underlying conduct that gave rise to the arrest or conviction.[10] That the rule refers to a person's "acts" almost certainly does not mean that it applies to *any* conduct of the person. This is because the main concern of the rule, in the context of a criminal prosecution, is to ensure that courts carefully scrutinize evidence of *misconduct*. Only acts of this type give rise to the concerns about unfair prejudice that the rule addresses. Thus, it is reasonable to assume that in most instances the term *acts* in the rule refers to misconduct rather than neutral or good conduct.

The rule only covers other crimes, wrongs, or acts that are not part of the event or transaction at issue in the case. Obviously, courts have no desire to prevent the parties from proving the very conduct that caused the case to be brought in the first place. Thus, any conduct that forms part of the matter at issue is not covered by Rule 404(b). Unfortunately, some courts have used that fact to hold that the rule does not apply to other misconduct close in time to the charged actions. Some courts, for example, would admit evidence that a burglary defendant stole the tool that was used at a later time to gain access to the building that was burglarized. Calling such conduct "inextricably intertwined" with the charged acts, or stating that it helps to "complete the story" of the charged acts, leads courts away from the central task of preventing unfair prejudice while admitting relevant evidence of meaningful probative value. Unless the other crimes, wrongs, or acts are actually a part of the charged conduct, they should be scrutinized under Rule 404(b) to determine their admissibility. In the burglary example, defendant's theft of the tool might be admissible if it can be shown that she stole it in preparation for the charged burglary. But if she did not commit the theft in anticipation of the charged burglary, the evidence is hardly inextricably intertwined with the charged act. Thus, though evidence of other, related acts is sometimes admissible, it is important for the courts to analyze that evidence according to the rule's requirements rather than to sweep in all arguably related conduct by calling it "inextricably intertwined" or by saying that it helps to "complete the story."

An interesting question is whether a person's status can constitute an "act" that will be governed by the rule. For example, is a person's addiction to drugs or membership in a gang a "crime or other act"? Most likely, the answer is yes. Remember that the purpose of the rule is to call attention to the need for caution in admitting evidence that is relevant to prove a person's character

---

10. We do not mean to suggest by this that arrests and convictions are admissible and unregulated by Rule 404. On the contrary, arrests and convictions are generally considered inadmissible character evidence under Rule 404(a).

but inadmissible for that purpose. Though the rule specifically only governs conduct, the conduct necessarily associated with the status of being a drug addict or gang member is put at issue by evidence of such status. This issue is likely to arise in a number of contexts. One example would be a hate crime case in which the defendant is a member of a hate-related organization and the victim is a member of a group targeted by that organization.

Questions for Classroom Discussion

1. Prosecution of Defendant for theft of valuable jewelry from a neighbor's home. Defendant denies involvement. To prove Defendant committed the crime, the prosecution wishes to present evidence that Defendant had a key to the neighbor's home. Defendant objects on the ground the evidence constitutes inadmissible character evidence. How should the court rule?

2. Prosecution of Defendant for bank robbery. Defendant denies involvement. The prosecution claims Defendant needed the money to pay her bills. To prove Defendant needed the money and therefore had a motive to rob the bank, the prosecution wishes to present evidence that Defendant was involuntarily forced into bankruptcy a few days before the bank robbery occurred. Defendant objects on inadmissible character evidence grounds. How should the court rule?

3. Plaintiff athlete sues Defendant agent for embezzlement of money Plaintiff entrusted to Defendant. Defendant claims one of his employees took the money. To show Defendant needed the money, Plaintiff wishes to introduce evidence Defendant's automobile was repossessed two weeks before Plaintiff's money disappeared. Defendant objects on relevancy and inadmissible character evidence grounds. How should the court rule?

---

4. Timing of Uncharged Misconduct

Nothing in Rule 404(b) requires that the uncharged misconduct evidence consist of acts committed *before* the act at issue in the case. The only limitation, of course, is relevance. In the following example, the evidence is relevant even though it concerns conduct that occurred, in part, subsequent to the charged act:

> Prosecution of Defendant for arson, arising from the burning of Victim's home. Defendant denies committing the crime. To prove that Defendant committed the crime, the prosecution offers evidence that Defendant set fire to two other properties owned by Victim. One of the fires was set before the fire at issue in the case, and the other was set after it.

In this example, the timing of the two uncharged fires is not important. Presumably, the prosecution's theory is that Defendant had a plan, perhaps motivated by hatred, to destroy Victim's property, and that the act at issue was one of several committed in pursuance of the plan. That the uncharged acts occurred both before and after the charged act does not matter.

In other cases, the timing of the uncharged misconduct is important. Consider the following example:

> Prosecution of Defendant for passing a counterfeit 100 dollar bill. Defendant admits using the bill to pay for a store purchase, but claims she did not know it was counterfeit. To prove Defendant's knowledge, the prosecution wishes to present evidence that a few days later, Defendant tried to spend another counterfeit 100 dollar bill, but that the clerk refused to take it, claiming it was fake.

In this example, timing does matter. The prosecution's evidence does not tend to prove that Defendant had knowledge at the time of the charged crime, but only later, when she tried to pass a similar bill. If the uncharged act had occurred prior to the charged crime, evidence of that act almost certainly would have been admissible to prove knowledge.

Questions for Classroom Discussion

1. Prosecution of Defendant for bank robbery. The perpetrators gained entry to the safe using a very rare type of explosive. Defendant denies involvement. To prove that Defendant committed the crime, the prosecution wishes to present evidence that two weeks after the charged robbery, Defendant robbed another bank using the same type of explosive. Defendant argues that the evidence is inadmissible. How should the court rule?

2. Same case. Suppose that instead of committing the uncharged robbery two weeks after the charged crime, Defendant committed it three years earlier. Defendant objects to the evidence. How should the court rule?

3. Prosecution of Defendant for unlawful possession of a prohibited type of firearm. Defendant admits she possessed the gun, but claims she did not know it was of an illegal type. To prove knowledge, the prosecution wishes to present evidence that on a later occasion, Defendant illegally purchased another gun of the same type on the black market after the seller told Defendant the gun was illegal. Defendant objects. How should the court rule?

---

5. Degree of Required Similarity Between Charged and Uncharged Conduct

In many cases, evidence of uncharged misconduct is relevant and admissible to prove a non-character fact under Rule 404(b) because of some similarity between that misconduct and the conduct directly at issue in the case.

As with the timing of the uncharged misconduct in relation to the acts at issue in the case, the necessary degree of similarity between the charged and uncharged conduct varies according to the circumstances and the theory under which the evidence is offered. In some situations, the acts must be virtually identical for the evidence to be admissible under Rule 404(b). In other situations, almost no similarity is needed. In still other cases, some similarity is needed, but not a great deal. The following hypotheticals illustrate the various possibilities.

1. Prosecution of Defendant for robbing a convenience store. Defendant denies committing the crime. The robbery was committed by a person dressed in an Elvis costume. The person first gathered up all the donuts in the store, then approached the clerk, said he was hungry, and told the clerk to "clean out the register before I step on you with my blue suede shoes." The prosecution wishes to present evidence that on two occasions fairly close in time to the charged robbery, Defendant robbed convenience stores wearing an Elvis costume and acting in exactly the same way.

2. Prosecution of Defendant for the murder of Victim. Victim was stabbed in the heart. Defendant denies involvement. To prove Defendant's involvement, the prosecution offers evidence that Defendant previously stabbed another person in the heart.

3. Prosecution of Defendant for the murder of Victim by poison. Victim was Defendant's sister. Defendant denies involvement in Victim's killing. Defendant and Victim were the only surviving children of a wealthy woman who was in bad health. To prove Defendant's involvement, the prosecution offers evidence that Defendant killed her other two siblings recently, one with a firearm and the other with a kitchen knife.

4. Prosecution of Defendant for armed robbery of a supermarket. The robber approached the store manager, demanded that the manager open the safe, and then took all the money from inside. Defendant denies involvement. To prove Defendant was involved, the prosecution offers evidence that in the two weeks before the supermarket robbery, Defendant robbed two other supermarkets very near to the one charged in the case, using the same method that was used in the charged robbery.

5. Prosecution of Defendant for sale of cocaine. Defendant claims that the police arrested the wrong person — that he did not engage in any sale of drugs. To prove Defendant sold the cocaine, the prosecution offers evidence that in the several months surrounding the charged sale, Defendant sold heroin in the same city.

In Hypothetical 1, the prosecution will argue admissibility under the *modus operandi* theory. The idea behind the theory is that, because of the unusual way all three robberies were committed, it is likely that the same person committed each. Thus, the evidence may be admitted under Rule 404(b) to prove the identity of the perpetrator. If Defendant committed the two uncharged robberies, it is therefore more likely that Defendant committed the charged robbery. To avoid the claim that the real value of the evidence is to show Defendant's character-based propensity to rob convenience stores, the prosecution must argue that the circumstances of the charged and uncharged acts are so similar as to represent a sort of fingerprint or signature of the perpetrator. To appreciate the probative value of the evidence, imagine that Defendant had worn conventional clothing in the prior robberies. The prior robbery evidence does not "identify" Defendant as the perpetrator of the convenience store robbery except insofar as it demonstrates Defendant's character as a robber — reasoning forbidden by Rule 404(a).

In Hypothetical 2, the prior act is similar to the charged conduct. But is similarity sufficient here to prove a 404(b) fact? There is not enough similarity in this example to demonstrate identity through the mechanism of *modus operandi*. This is because many murderers stab their victims in the heart. This is a preferred methodology for murderers because it is an effective way to dispatch a victim. To permit a *modus operandi* inference, the similarities between the charged and uncharged conduct must relate to something unique, such as the use of a distinctive knife.

In Hypothetical 3, similarity is completely unnecessary except insofar as the victims were all siblings of Defendant. The prosecution's theory is that Defendant had a monetary motive to kill her siblings, and that the uncharged acts show the existence of a plan to become the only surviving child. It makes no difference if there are similarities in how Defendant killed the other two siblings; the fact of the killings, alone, shows that Defendant is more likely to have committed the charged crime.

The admissibility of the evidence in Hypothetical 4 depends on some similarity between the charged and uncharged conduct, but not so much as needed to fit the *modus operandi* theory. The prosecution's theory here is that Defendant had a specific plan to rob supermarkets in a certain area over a short period of time, and that the charged robbery was committed in furtherance of that plan. Absent more similarities, the theory would be weak, and admissibility of the uncharged misconduct evidence would invite the forbidden character inference that Defendant is the type of person who robs supermarkets, rather than the permitted inference that Defendant had a plan to rob certain supermarkets within a short period of time.

In Hypothetical 5, there is some similarity among the charged and uncharged acts: all are drug crimes, all involve sale of drugs, and all occurred in the same city. But what is the prosecution's theory for admission of the evidence? If it is *modus operandi*, that theory certainly should fail because there is nothing unique about the circumstances of the charged and uncharged sales. If it is that Defendant had a plan to sell drugs in that city and the court accepted the theory, any similar crimes committed in a widely described geographical area could be offered to prove guilt. On that reasoning, one might also be permitted to present evidence of an uncharged murder to prove a charged murder, or even an uncharged assault and battery to prove a charged murder, and the ban on character to prove conduct would become nearly meaningless.

These examples demonstrate that there is no single formula for the degree of similarity required between the charged and uncharged conduct. Instead, one must consider carefully both the theory for admissibility and the particular circumstances of the case.

Questions for Classroom Discussion

1. Prosecution of Defendant for the murder of Victim. The murderer waited outside Victim's home, accosted him when he got out of his car, forced him into the house, took all the money and jewelry from the house, and shot him. Defendant denies committing the crime. To prove Defendant was the killer, the prosecution wishes to present evidence that several weeks earlier, Defendant had committed a murder in a nearby town using the same method. Defendant objects on the ground the two acts are not sufficiently similar. How should the court rule?

2. Prosecution of Defendant, a restaurant parking valet, for car theft. The day before the car was stolen, its owner had driven it to the restaurant, and Defendant parked it. Defendant denies committing the crime. To prove Defendant committed the crime, the prosecution wishes to present evidence that when Defendant parked the car the day before it was stolen, he made a clay impression of the key. Defendant objects on the ground that the uncharged and charged acts are not sufficiently similar. How should the court rule?

3. Prosecution of Defendant for possession of heroin. Defendant admits the heroin was found in her apartment, but claims she thought it was something else. To prove Defendant knew the substance was heroin, the prosecution wishes to present evidence that Defendant was a regular marijuana smoker. Defendant objects on the ground the charged and uncharged conduct are not similar enough. How should the court rule?

---

6.   *Purposes for Which Evidence May Be Offered*

Remember that the list of "other purposes" in Rule 404(b) is not exclusive. Instead, the rule states that evidence of "crimes or other acts" is admissible for any relevant purpose except to prove a person's character and action in conformity with that character. The key is relevance and, in most situations, evidence offered under Rule 404(b) tends to prove a fact that forms only one link along a chain of inferences leading to an ultimate fact. For example, "motive" is not an ultimate fact in a crime, claim, or defense. Instead, it can form one link in a chain leading to an ultimate fact such as the identity of an actor, the actor's intent at the time of the act, or the actual occurrence of the act in question. "Preparation" is another example. That fact, in itself, is not a required element of a crime. Instead, it tends to lead to an ultimate fact such as intent or identity.[11] The proponent of Rule 404(b) evidence must be

---

11. The exceptions in the list are "intent," "identity," and "absence of mistake or lack of accident." These are often ultimate facts in civil and criminal cases.

prepared to meet a relevance objection by demonstrating that the evidence is relevant to an ultimate fact in the case. Take the following two examples:

1. Prosecution of Defendant for the first degree murder of Victim, her boy-friend. The crime was committed by a person dressed in camouflage clothing. Defendant denies involvement. To prove Defendant committed the crime, the prosecution presents evidence that Defendant stole the camouflage clothing on the day before the murder.
2. Same case. Assume Defendant admits killing Victim, but claims she did so in the heat of passion after learning, just moments earlier, that Victim had been seeing another woman. The prosecution presents the same evidence about Defendant stealing camouflage clothing.

In both of these examples, Defendant's theft of the camouflage clothing is uncharged misconduct that tends to prove the existence of a plan to commit the crime. In the first example, however, the theft ultimately tends to prove that Defendant was the perpetrator:

EVIDENCE: Defendant stole the camouflage clothing.

→**INFERENCE:** Defendant harbored a plan to kill Victim.

→**CONCLUSION:** Defendant was the person who killed Victim.

In the second example, the evidence also tends to prove the existence of a plan. Because Defendant has admitted being the killer in this example, the prosecution most likely offers the evidence to prove malice aforethought, a required element of first degree murder:

EVIDENCE: Defendant stole the camouflage clothing.

→**INFERENCE:** Defendant harbored a plan to kill Victim.

→**CONCLUSION:** Defendant acted with malice aforethought in killing Victim.

The lesson here should be clear: Whenever a party offers uncharged misconduct evidence, the proponent must specify not only the general theory, but the ultimate purpose for which the evidence is offered. Only after the party has revealed both matters may the court properly determine the admissibility of the evidence.

7. Procedure for Determining Admissibility

In Huddleston v. United States, 485 U.S. 681 (1988), the Supreme Court held that the trial court must engage in a four-step inquiry when determining the admissibility of uncharged misconduct evidence. *First*, the evidence must be offered for a "proper purpose." This means the court must decide whether admission of the evidence would violate the ban on character to prove conduct — whether, in other words, the relevance of the evidence depends on an inference as to the actor's character. As long as it does not, the evidence is potentially admissible. As we have already noted, the party seeking admission of the evidence under Rule 404(b) bears the burden of expressing the precise purpose for which it is offered, and, if necessary, demonstrating why the evidence does not violate the character rule. In most cases, simply stating that the evidence "goes to identity" or "shows intent" is not enough. The party should set forth the reasoning that supports admissibility, and, if necessary, explain why its admission does not require an inference as to the actor's character.

Second, the evidence must be relevant to prove the Rule 404(b) fact in question. Because a fact need not be "in dispute" to be relevant under the Federal Rules (see Chapter 2), this will not be a difficult requirement to satisfy. The evidence would not be admissible, however, if the fact sought to be proved with the uncharged misconduct evidence is not one "of consequence to the determination of the action." For example, because an action based on the doctrine of respondeat superior does not require any wrongdoing by the master, evidence of the master's improper motive is not "of consequence" to that claim. (If the plaintiff asserts a separate claim for the master's own wrongdoing, the motive evidence would be of consequence to that claim.)

Third, the probative value of the evidence must not be substantially outweighed by the danger of unfair prejudice or other concerns under Rule 403. Because uncharged misconduct evidence can always lead to a character inference, evidence offered to prove a 404(b) fact will almost always pose a significant potential for unfair prejudice. There are several ways this potential can be realized. The jury might not use the evidence for its legitimate purpose, opting instead to use the evidence for its forbidden character purpose. Another possibility is that the jury will give the evidence more weight than it carries legitimately. Another is that the jury will nullify the law by rendering a verdict adverse to the party not because of responsibility in the case at hand, but for the party's other misdeeds. Sometimes the evidence will have little value because the matter on which it is offered is not in dispute, making its introduction a waste of time or creating a risk of distracting the jury from its proper function. In each of these cases, the court must determine whether the probative value of the evidence *for its legitimate purpose* is sufficiently great so as not to be outweighed substantially by any of these dangers.

Consider the following example:

> Prosecution of Defendant for bank robbery. Defendant denies involvement. To prove Defendant was involved, the prosecution offers evidence that Defendant needed money to support a heroin habit and was unemployed because he had just gotten out of prison after a child molestation conviction.

The court probably should not admit this evidence. Even though Defendant's other bad conduct is relevant to prove a 404(b) fact, Defendant's motive to rob the bank, the court should exercise its discretion to exclude this evidence since its probative value for that purpose seems to be substantially outweighed by the unfairly prejudicial tendency of this obviously inflammatory evidence to induce the jury to draw improper character inferences.

Fourth, pursuant to Rule 105, the court must issue a limiting instruction if a party requests it to do so, and may issue an instruction even in the absence of a

388 4. Evidence of Character, Uncharged Misconduct, and Similar Events

request. The instruction must inform the jury of the proper use of the evidence, and the court should set forth its instruction in clear, understandable language. Indeed, one ground for excluding the evidence altogether, under Rule 403, is the court's conclusion that a limiting instruction will not be understood or followed by the jury.

It is not uncommon to find courts stating additional, more specific tests for admissibility. For example, some courts state that the uncharged misconduct must be "sufficiently similar" to the conduct at issue in the case. As we have seen, such statements are overbroad because different theories require different levels of similarity and some theories require no similarity at all. The most accurate general statement of the requirements for admissibility of uncharged misconduct evidence is that set forth in *Huddleston*, which takes into account the many variations of fact and theory that might be brought within the rule's orbit. We discuss *Huddleston* immediately after the following set of questions.

8. *Putting It All Together*

The following questions test your understanding of all aspects of Rule 404(b) analysis covered so far.

Questions for Classroom Discussion

1. Prosecution of Defendant for possession of cocaine. Defendant admits that the cocaine was found in his apartment, but claims he thought it was flour. To prove Defendant knew the substance was cocaine, the prosecution wishes to prove that several months earlier, Defendant was convicted of cocaine possession. Defendant objects. How should the court rule?

2. Same case. Assume Defendant argues that the prosecution should not be permitted to offer the evidence because Defendant was acquitted in the prior trial. How should the court rule?

3. Prosecution of Defendant for bank robbery. After obtaining the money, the robbers fled in a minivan. Defendant denies involvement. To prove Defendant's involvement, the prosecution offers evidence that Defendant stole the minivan the day before the bank robbery. Defendant objects. How should the court rule?

4. Prosecution of Defendant for the murder of Victim. Defendant admits running Victim over with a car, but claims it was an accident. The prosecution alleges that Defendant, Victim, Zed, and Abel had all participated in a successful bank robbery. The prosecution wishes to present evidence that just after killing Victim, Defendant shot Zed to death and cut the brake cable on Abel's car, causing Abel to be involved in a fatal accident. Defendant objects to evidence of the killings of Zed and Abel, alleging lack of similarity

---

between those acts and the charged crime. How should the court rule?

5. Prosecution of Defendant, a nurse, for theft of Demerol, an addictive drug, from a locked medicine cabinet in the hospital in which Defendant worked. Defendant was one of only five people who had a key to the cabinet. Defendant denies being the thief. To prove Defendant stole the Demerol, the prosecution wishes to present evidence that in the past, Defendant was addicted to Demerol, and that she had stolen some Demerol from the hospital at which she then worked. Defendant objects to admission of the evidence. How should the court rule?

6. Prosecution of Defendant for sale of cocaine. Defendant was present in an apartment when a police informant wearing a "wire" purchased cocaine from another person. Defendant did not live in the apartment. Defendant admits being present when the sale was conducted, but denies knowing that any drugs were present. To prove Defendant's involvement, the prosecution wishes to offer evidence that on three separate occasions in the past year, Defendant has been present in other apartments when cocaine was sold by the same people Defendant was with on the charged occasion. Defendant objects. How should the court rule?

7. Plaintiff sues Defendant for battery following an altercation in a bar. Defendant claims she was not involved, or even present, at the time of the fight. To prove that another person, Zed, was the responsible party, Defendant wishes to offer evidence that Plaintiff had previously attacked Zed at a football game. Plaintiff objects. How should the court rule?

8. Prosecution of Defendant for sexually molesting Victim, Defendant's ten-year-old child. Defendant admits entering Victim's bedroom on the night in question, but claims he only "tucked Victim into bed," and committed no act of molestation. To prove that an act of molestation occurred, the prosecution wishes to offer evidence that on two prior occasions, Defendant sexually molested the same child. Defendant objects. How should the court rule? How should the court rule in the absence of Rule 414?

9. Same case. Assume, however, that the victim of the uncharged molestation was not Victim, but Victim's sibling, also a young child. Would the evidence be admissible absent Rule 414?

10. Same case. Assume, however, that the uncharged acts of molestation were committed on a child or children not related to Defendant. Would the evidence be admissible absent Rule 414?

9. Judge/Jury Functions: Required Quantum of Proof of Uncharged Misconduct

To this point, we have generally assumed that there is no dispute whether the person at issue committed or was otherwise involved in the uncharged misconduct. That will not be true in all cases. Sometimes the subject of the uncharged misconduct evidence (usually a criminal defendant) denies that the misconduct took place as alleged. The question is how much evidence of that conduct is necessary to justify its admission under Rule 404(b). Remember that, in addressing this issue, we are not dealing with the substantive issue of guilt or innocence of the current charge or liability for the current claim. These issues are for the fact-finder to determine based on the applicable burden of persuasion — usually preponderance of the evidence in a civil case and beyond a reasonable doubt in a criminal prosecution. Rather, here we are dealing only with threshold requirements the court must apply to determine the admissibility of evidence. As we saw in our discussion of preliminary facts in Chapter 2, facts that form part of the foundation for the admission of evidence do not need to be proven by the same standard that will eventually govern the outcome of the case. The question we address in this section is the following: What is the standard of proof for those facts necessary to the admission of uncharged misconduct evidence?

In some cases, the uncharged misconduct will have been the subject of a prior criminal prosecution. If the actor was convicted of the crime, even the most stringent standard for its admission in the current case will be satisfied. Conviction requires a finding of guilt "beyond a reasonable doubt," certainly the highest standard of persuasion in modern law. And among the ways the conviction may be proven is by an official record, which would be admissible under Rule 803(22) (judgment of a previous conviction). But suppose the person was acquitted in the earlier trial. Might the evidence of defendant's uncharged misconduct yet be admissible in the current trial? Somewhat surprisingly, the answer given by most courts is yes. An acquittal does not necessarily mean innocence; its only clear meaning is that the prosecution has not persuaded the jury of the defendant's guilt beyond a reasonable doubt. In a subsequent case the issue is only the admissibility of the misconduct evidence in support of another charge. What standard applies? And what if the person was never charged in connection with the conduct? Does that matter?

In 1988, the Supreme Court considered how such cases should be handled under the Federal Rules.

HUDDLESTON v. UNITED STATES
485 U.S. 681 (1988)

Chief Justice REHNQUIST delivered the opinion of the Court.

This case presents the question whether the district court must itself make a preliminary finding that the Government has proved the "other act" by a preponderance of the evidence before it submits the evidence to the jury. We hold that it need not do so.

[Huddleston was charged with selling stolen goods and possessing stolen property, both in connection with a shipment of Memorex videotapes. To prevail, the prosecution had to prove that Huddleston knew the tapes were stolen. The prosecution presented evidence that a trailer containing 32,000 videotapes with a manufacturing cost of $4.53 per tape was stolen from an Overnight Express yard. Several days later, Huddleston offered to sell a large number of tapes in lots of at least 500 for between $2.75 and $3.00 per tape. The only issue was Huddleston's knowledge that the tapes were stolen. To prove this fact, the court allowed the government to present evidence that shortly before these events, Huddleston offered to sell a number of new black and white televisions for $28 apiece, and that not long after the charged events, Huddleston tried to sell a large number of stolen appliances. Huddleston testified that he obtained the tapes, televisions, and appliances from one Wesby, who told him the goods were obtained legally.] . . .

We granted certiorari to resolve a conflict among the Courts of Appeals as to whether the trial court must make a preliminary finding before "similar act" and other Rule 404(b) evidence is submitted to the jury.[2] We conclude that such evidence should be admitted if there is sufficient evidence to support a finding by the jury that the defendant committed the similar act.

Federal Rule of Evidence 404(b) — which applies in both civil and criminal cases — generally prohibits the introduction of evidence of extrinsic acts that might adversely reflect on the actor's character, unless that evidence bears upon a relevant issue in the case such as motive, opportunity, or knowledge. Extrinsic acts evidence may be critical to the establishment of the truth as to a disputed issue, especially when that issue involves the actor's state of mind and the only means of ascertaining that mental state is by drawing inferences from conduct. The actor in the instant case was a criminal defendant, and the act in question was "similar" to the one with which he was charged. Our use of these terms is not meant to suggest that our analysis is limited to such circumstances.

. . . The threshold inquiry a court must make before admitting similar acts evidence under Rule 404(b) is whether that evidence is probative of a material issue other than character. The Government's theory of relevance was that the televisions were stolen, and proof that petitioner had engaged in a series of sales of stolen merchandise from the same suspicious source would be strong evidence that he was aware that each of these items, including the Memorex tapes, was stolen. As such, the sale of the televisions was a "similar act" only if the televisions were stolen. Petitioner acknowledges that this evidence was admitted for the proper purpose of showing his knowledge that the Memorex tapes were stolen. He asserts, however, that the evidence should not have been admitted

---

2. The First, Fourth, Fifth, and Eleventh Circuits allow the admission of similar act evidence if the evidence is sufficient to allow the jury to find that the defendant committed the act. United States v. Ingraham, 832 F.2d 229, 235 (CA1 1987); United States v. Martin, 773 F.2d 579, 582 (CA4 1985); United States v. Beechum, 582 F.2d 898, 914 (CA5 1978) (en banc), *cert. denied*, 440 U.S. 920, 99 S. Ct. 1244, 59 L. Ed. 2d 472 (1979); United States v. Dothard, 666 F.2d 498, 502 (CA11 1982). Consistent with the Sixth Circuit, the Second Circuit prohibits the introduction of similar act evidence unless the trial court finds by a preponderance of the evidence that the defendant committed the act. United States v. Leonard, 524 F.2d 1076, 1090-1091 (CA2 1975). The Seventh, Eighth, Ninth, and District of Columbia Circuits require the Government to prove to the court by clear and convincing evidence that the defendant committed the similar act. United States v. Leight, 818 F.2d 1297, 1302 (CA7), *cert. denied*, 484 U.S. 958, 108 S. Ct. 356, 98 L. Ed. 2d 381 (1987); United States v. Weber, 818 F.2d 14 (CA8 1987); United States v. Vaccaro, 816 F.2d 443, 452 (CA9), *cert. denied sub nom.* Alvis v. United States, 484 U.S. 914, 108 S. Ct. 262, 98 L. Ed. 2d 220 (1987); United States v. Lavelle, 243 U.S. App. D.C. 47, 57, 751 F.2d 1266, 1276, *cert. denied*, 474 U.S. 817, 106 S. Ct. 62, 88 L. Ed. 2d 51 (1985).

because the Government failed to prove to the District Court that the televisions were in fact stolen.

Petitioner argues from the premise that evidence of similar acts has a grave potential for causing improper prejudice. For instance, the jury may choose to punish the defendant for the similar rather than the charged act, or the jury may infer that the defendant is an evil person inclined to violate the law. Because of this danger, petitioner maintains, the jury ought not to be exposed to similar act evidence until the trial court has heard the evidence and made a determination under Federal Rule of Evidence 104(a) that the defendant committed the similar act. Rule 104(a) provides that "[p]reliminary questions concerning the qualification of a person to be a witness, the existence of a privilege, or the admissibility of evidence shall be determined by the court, subject to the provisions of subdivision (b)." According to petitioner, the trial court must make this preliminary finding by at least a preponderance of the evidence.

We reject petitioner's position, for it is inconsistent with the structure of the Rules of Evidence and with the plain language of Rule 404(b). Article IV of the Rules of Evidence deals with the relevancy of evidence. Rules 401 and 402 establish the broad principle that relevant evidence — evidence that makes the existence of any fact at issue more or less probable — is admissible unless the Rules provide otherwise. Rule 403 allows the trial judge to exclude relevant evidence if, among other things, "its probative value is substantially outweighed by the danger of unfair prejudice." Rules 404 through 412 address specific types of evidence that have generated problems. Generally, these latter Rules do not flatly prohibit the introduction of such evidence but instead limit the purpose for which it may be introduced. Rule 404(b), for example, protects against the introduction of extrinsic act evidence when that evidence is offered solely to prove character. The text contains no intimation, however, that any preliminary showing is necessary before such evidence may be introduced for a proper purpose. If offered for such a proper purpose, the evidence is subject only to general strictures limiting admissibility such as Rules 402 and 403.

Petitioner's reading of Rule 404(b) as mandating a preliminary finding by the trial court that the act in question occurred not only superimposes a level of judicial oversight that is nowhere apparent from the language of that provision, but it is simply inconsistent with the legislative history behind Rule 404(b). The Advisory Committee specifically declined to offer any "mechanical solution" to the admission of evidence under 404(b). Rather, the Committee indicated that the trial court should assess such evidence under the usual rules for admissibility: "The determination must be made whether the danger of undue prejudice outweighs the probative value of the evidence in view of the availability of other means of proof and other factors appropriate for making decisions of this kind under Rule 403."

Petitioner's suggestion that a preliminary finding is necessary to protect the defendant from the potential for unfair prejudice is also belied by the Reports of the House of Representatives and the Senate. The House made clear that the version of Rule 404(b) which became law was intended to "plac[e] greater emphasis on admissibility than did the final Court version." The Senate echoed this theme: "[T]he use of the discretionary word 'may' with respect to the admissibility of evidence of crimes, wrongs, or other acts is not intended to confer any arbitrary discretion on the trial judge." Thus, Congress was not nearly so concerned with the potential prejudicial effect of Rule 404(b) evidence as it was with ensuring that restrictions would not be placed on the admission of such evidence.

We conclude that a preliminary finding by the court that the Government has proved the act by a preponderance of the evidence is not called for under Rule 104(a). This is not to say, however, that the Government may parade past the jury a litany of potentially prejudicial similar acts that have been established or connected to the defendant only by unsubstantiated innuendo. Evidence is admissible under Rule 404(b) only if it is relevant. "Relevancy is not an inherent characteristic of any item of evidence but exists only as a relation between an item of evidence and a matter properly provable in the case." In the Rule 404(b) context, similar act evidence is relevant only if the jury can reasonably conclude that the act occurred and that the defendant was the actor. In the instant case, the evidence that petitioner was selling the televisions was relevant under the Government's theory only if the jury could reasonably find that the televisions were stolen.

Such questions of relevance conditioned on a fact are dealt with under Federal Rule of Evidence 104(b). . . .

In determining whether the Government has introduced sufficient evidence to meet Rule 104(b), the trial court neither weighs credibility nor makes a finding that the Government has proved the conditional fact by a preponderance of the evidence. The court simply examines all the evidence in the case and decides whether the jury could reasonably find the conditional fact — here, that the televisions were stolen — by a preponderance of the evidence. The trial court has traditionally exercised the broadest sort of discretion in controlling the order of proof at trial, and we see nothing in the Rules of Evidence that would change this practice. Often the trial court may decide to allow the proponent to introduce evidence concerning a similar act, and at a later point in the trial assess whether sufficient evidence has been offered to permit the jury to make the requisite finding. If the proponent has failed to meet this minimal standard of proof, the trial court must instruct the jury to disregard the evidence.

We emphasize that in assessing the sufficiency of the evidence under Rule 104(b), the trial court must consider all evidence presented to the jury. . . . In assessing whether the evidence was sufficient to support a finding that the televisions were stolen, the court here was required to consider not only the direct evidence on that point — the low price of the televisions, the large quantity offered for sale, and petitioner's inability to produce a bill of sale — but also the evidence concerning petitioner's involvement in the sales of other stolen merchandise obtained from Wesby, such as the Memorex tapes and the Amana appliances. Given this evidence, the jury reasonably could have concluded that the televisions were stolen, and the trial court therefore properly allowed the evidence to go to the jury.

We share petitioner's concern that unduly prejudicial evidence might be introduced under Rule 404(b). We think, however, that the protection against such unfair prejudice emanates not from a requirement of a preliminary finding by the trial court, but rather from four other sources: first, from the requirement of Rule 404(b) that the evidence be offered for a proper purpose; second, from the relevancy requirement of Rule 402 — as enforced through Rule 104(b); third, from the assessment the trial court must make under Rule 403 to determine whether the probative value of the similar acts evidence is substantially outweighed by its potential for unfair prejudice; and fourth, from Federal Rule of Evidence 105, which provides that the trial court shall, upon request, instruct the jury that the similar acts evidence is to be considered only for the proper purpose for which it was admitted.

Affirmed.

As the Court makes clear in *Huddleston*, the law prior to the case was quite unsettled. Many courts—indeed, the majority of federal circuit courts—took the position that the trial court must decide whether the individual in fact engaged in the uncharged misconduct. Some courts even held that the trial court must apply to this question a standard higher than preponderance of the evidence, such as "clear and convincing evidence." That conclusion is difficult to justify according to the logic of Rule 104, as the Court demonstrates in *Huddleston.* After all, one would think that a jury would disregard any uncharged misconduct evidence if it finds that the individual did not commit the misconduct in question. Thus, the Court seems to have been correct in holding that the matter should be decided according to the "sufficient to support a finding" standard of Rule 104(b).

However, the Court's ruling that Rule 104(b) governs perhaps does not adequately account for the significant prejudice that uncharged misconduct evidence sometimes threatens. It seems likely that, in the real world, jurors often will be undecided as to the existence of the preliminary facts and that sometimes they will be willing to err on the side of protecting society from a defendant who is only potentially dangerous. Thus, jurors might be willing to take uncharged misconduct evidence into account even if they have doubts that the defendant engaged in that conduct. Trial courts should consider this possibility when conducting the Rule 403 balance in situations involving the admissibility of other crimes, wrongs, or acts.

Further Reading: Edward J. Imwinkelried, *The Use of Evidence of an Accused's Uncharged Misconduct to Prove Mens Rea: The Doctrines Which Threaten to Engulf the Character Evidence Prohibition*, 51 Ohio St. L.J. 575 (1990); Edward J. Imwinkelried, *The Need to Amend Federal Rule of Evidence 404(b): The Threat to the Future of the Federal Rules of Evidence*, 30 Vill. L. Rev. 1465 (1985); David Kaloyanides, Comment, *The Depraved Sexual Instinct Theory: An Example of Propensity for Aberrant Application of Federal Rule of Evidence 404(b)*, 25 Loy. L. Rev. 1297 (1992); Richard B. Kuhns, *The Propensity to Misunderstand the Character of Specific Facts Evidence*, 66 Iowa L. Rev. 777 (1981); David P. Leonard, *The Use of Uncharged Misconduct Evidence to Prove Knowledge*, 81 Neb. L. Rev. 115 (2002); David P. Leonard, *Character and Motive in Evidence Law*, 34 Loy. L.A. L. Rev. 439 (2001); Judith M.G. Patterson, *Evidence of Prior Bad Acts: Admissibility Under the Federal Rules*, 38 Baylor L. Rev. 331 (1986); William Roth, *Understanding Admissibility of Prior Bad Acts: A Diagrammatic Approach*, 9 Pepp. L. Rev. 297 (1982); M.C. Slough & J. William Knightly, *Other Vices, Other Crimes*, 41 Iowa L. Rev. 325 (1956); Calvin W. Sharpe, *Two-Step Balancing and the Admissibility of Other Crimes Evidence: A Sliding Scale of Proof*, 55 Notre Dame L. Rev. 556 (1984); Glen Weissenberger, *Making Sense of Extrinsic Act Evidence: Federal Rule of Evidence 404(b)*, 70 Iowa L. Rev. 579 (1985).

Questions for Classroom Discussion

1. Explain the reasoning behind the Supreme Court's holding in *Huddleston* that Rule 104(b) applies to the question whether a person actually committed the uncharged misconduct. Use the following hypothetical to illustrate your explanation: prosecution of Defendant for the murder of Victim, the lover of Defendant's spouse. Defendant denies committing the crime. To prove guilt, the prosecution offers evidence that a week before Victim was killed, Defendant attempted to run Victim over while Victim was crossing the street. Defendant denies being the person whose car nearly ran Victim over.

2. Can you make an argument that even if this reasoning is valid on its face, the court should apply the standard of Rule 104(a) anyway? Use the same hypothetical given in Question 1 to illustrate.

3. An earlier hypothetical stated as follows: "Prosecution of Defendant for bank robbery. The perpetrator entered the bank wearing a Smokey the Bear costume, approached a teller, told the teller that money was needed to 'feed the hungry bears,' held out a large burlap sack for the teller to fill, and left after the teller did as she was told. Defendant claims to have been in another city when the crime was committed. The prosecution calls a witness to testify that on two occasions in the past month, he served as lookout for Defendant when Defendant committed bank robberies in the same city using the method just described." Suppose Defendant denies committing the two previous robberies and objects to admission of the evidence. How should the court rule?

4. Return to the facts of *Huddleston*. Huddleston was charged with possessing and selling stolen goods (a trailer of blank Memorex videocassette tapes). The government was required to prove, among other things, that Huddleston knew the items were stolen, which he denied. To prove his knowledge, the government offered evidence that in the past, Huddleston had obtained other stolen goods, including some televisions, from the same source. What type of theory supports the admission of this evidence? Is it a legitimate non-character theory?

Before we leave the subject, it is important to remember that Rule 404(b) also applies to civil litigation, and that its language is not limited to evidence of misconduct. The rule allows introduction of other acts evidence, if relevant, to prove an aspect of a civil case. And in many instances that other act or acts may not involve "misconduct." Consider the following example:

An athlete sues her manager, contending he siphoned some of the athlete's funds for personal use. The manager denies the allegation, claiming the loss of the funds was caused by investment losses for which the manager, per contract, is not liable. At trial the athlete seeks to introduce evidence that just prior to the financial loss the manager made a late payment on his home, and subsequently declared bankruptcy.

The manager's conduct is relevant to prove a 404(b) fact—that he had a motive to siphon the athlete's money. Notice, though, that the manager's actions are not necessarily "misconduct." Homeowners make late mortgage payments from time to time for a variety of often innocent reasons. And declaring bankruptcy is a legally sanctioned way to restructure debt. In exercising its discretion, a court is unlikely to exclude this evidence because its probative value is high, and the danger of unfair prejudice seems very low.

D. HABIT EVIDENCE

> **FED. R. EVID. 406.   HABIT; ROUTINE PRACTICE**

Evidence of a person's habit or an organization's routine practice may be admitted to prove that on a particular occasion the person or organization acted in accordance with the habit or routine practice. The court may admit this evidence regardless of whether it is corroborated or whether there was an eyewitness.

Discussion

We have previously defined character evidence as evidence concerning the propensity of a person to act in a certain manner that makes a general statement about that person and conveys a moral or ethical judgment. "Habit evidence" and "character evidence" are related but distinct concepts that are treated very differently under evidence law. Both are forms of propensity evidence. Both involve internalized patterns of behavior characteristic of particular individuals. But habit is thought to be much more specific than character. McCormick explained:

> Character and habit are close akin. Character is a generalized description of one's disposition, or of one's disposition in respect to a general trait, such as honesty, temperance, or peacefulness. "Habit," in modern usage, both lay and psychological, is more specific. It describes one's regular response to a repeated specific situation. If we speak of character for care, we think of the person's tendency to act prudently in all the varying situations of life, in business, family life, in handling automobiles and in walking across the street. A habit, on the other hand, is the person's regular practice of meeting a particular kind of situation with a specific type of conduct, such as the habit of going down a particular stairway two stairs at a time, or of giving the hand-signal for a left turn, or of alighting from railway cars

while they are moving. The doing of the habitual acts may become semi-automatic.[12]

Thus, habit evidence may be defined as evidence concerning the propensity of a person repeatedly to act in a certain manner in a specific situation. And because habit evidence only describes conduct in a specific situation rather than describing general propensity, it does not convey a moral or ethical judgment about the person. While character evidence says something general about a person and conveys a moral or ethical judgment, habit evidence describes specific behavior of a person and is neutral from a moral and ethical standpoint. The Advisory Committee adopted this theory of habit evidence and embodied it in Rule 406.

The admissibility of propensity evidence frequently depends on whether it may be classified as habit or character evidence. In contrast to the rules governing character evidence, Rule 406 treats habit as generally admissible. This is because if evidence satisfies the definition of habit, it carries considerably greater probative value as a predictor of conduct than does character. In addition, because habit evidence does not convey a moral judgment about the person, there is less concern about unfair prejudice. There also are no limits on the types of evidence that may be offered to prove habit, though one would expect that in most cases, the evidence consists of first-hand testimony that the person "always" or "almost always" engages in certain specific conduct in a specific situation. Evidence that a person did so on only a modest number of occasions generally would not be sufficient to prove the existence of a habit. The party offering habit evidence need not jump through any specific procedural hoops before being permitted to present it, though the court retains its authority under Rule 403 to exclude the evidence when necessary to avoid unfair prejudice, waste of time, or other dangers.

To qualify as a habit under Rule 406, behavior does not need to be automatic — behavior engaged in without conscious thought. Some behavior that requires conscious deliberation is also included. For example, one might "habitually" check all the gas burners on the stove before going to bed every night. Doing so requires some thought, but in a case involving a gas fire and in which defendant claims plaintiff contributed to her injury by leaving a gas burner on, evidence that plaintiff "always" checks the burners before going to bed would be admissible as habit to prove that she did so on the night of the fire. The key to admissibility is not the absence of consciousness (though the more unconscious the behavior, the more likely the person did it on a particular occasion). Instead, the key is the existence of evidence supporting a conclusion of the virtually invariable conduct of the person — a repeated, specific response to a specific stimulus. Often, this requirement will be satisfied by testimony concerning a sufficient number of instances of the same specific behavior to persuade a court that it rises to the level of habit.

Note that Rule 406 allows for the admission of more than just the habitual behavior of a person. It also encompasses the "organization's routine practice." Thus, for example, a store's routine practice of issuing a specific type of receipt to each customer most likely would be admissible to prove that the store issued a receipt on a particular occasion.

---

12. Charles T. McCormick, Handbook on the Law of Evidence § 162, at 340 (1954).

Questions for Classroom Discussion

1. Negligence action arising from an intersection collision. Plaintiff claims that Defendant ran the stop sign. To prove that Defendant did so, Plaintiff calls Witness to testify that for the past year, she has ridden with Defendant almost every day to school, that they always cross the intersection in question, and that Defendant almost always fails to stop at the stop sign. Defendant objects on grounds Witness's testimony is inadmissible character evidence. How should the court rule?

2. Same case. Suppose Witness's testimony will be that she has ridden with Defendant three times, and that Defendant failed to stop at the stop sign all three times. Again, Defendant objects on grounds Witness's testimony is inadmissible character evidence. How should the court rule?

3. Same case. Defendant calls Witness 2 to testify that she has known Defendant for many years, has ridden with Defendant on hundreds of occasions, and that in her opinion, Defendant is a careful driver. Plaintiff objects on grounds Witness 2's testimony is inadmissible character evidence. How should the court rule?

4. Personal injury action following a freeway collision. Plaintiff claims that Defendant was going at least 80 miles per hour when she lost control and struck Plaintiff's car. Defendant denies speeding. At trial, Plaintiff calls Witness to testify that she has ridden with Defendant on scores of occasions, and that Defendant almost always drives "very fast." Defendant objects. How should the court rule?

5. Plaintiff is injured while driving a taxi. He sues the taxi company, claiming the brakes on his taxi were defective. The taxi company claims Plaintiff was driving carelessly. To prove Plaintiff was at fault, the taxi company calls a company safety engineer to testify each time a taxi is brought into the garage its brakes are checked, and any taxi with "the slightest problem" is immediately taken out of service and not put back on the road until the brakes are repaired. Plaintiff objects that the engineer's testimony is irrelevant because she did not see anyone inspect Plaintiff's taxi on the day of the accident. How should the court rule?

E. EVIDENCE OF SIMILAR EVENTS

In some cases, a party will seek to prove that an event occurred in a particular way using evidence that one or more similar events have occurred under similar circumstances. Consider the following hypothetical:

Negligence action by Plaintiff against Defendant, a supermarket owner, for
injuries suffered when Plaintiff exited the store carrying several packages and
accidentally walked into a pole near the exit door. Defendant installed the four-
foot-tall solid metal pole near the door to prevent vehicles from driving into the
store. Plaintiff alleges that the pole's location makes it unreasonably dangerous
for patrons exiting the store carrying packages because they would not be able to
see the pole. Defendant claims the pole is not unreasonably dangerous. To
prove the existence of the danger, Plaintiff wishes to present evidence that
since Defendant installed the pole a year earlier, five patrons carrying packages
suffered accidents similar to Plaintiff's.

In this hypothetical, evidence of the similar accidents is relevant because it
tends to suggest that Plaintiff's collision was not a fluke. Evidence that other
patrons had walked into the pole under similar conditions makes it somewhat
more likely than it would be without the evidence that the condition is unreasonably dangerous.

Note the differences between similar happenings evidence, on the one hand,
and evidence of character or habit, on the other hand. Similar happenings
evidence is not evidence of propensity—the tendency of a person to act in a
certain way. In fact, similar happenings evidence need not even be about the
conduct of a person. Further, character evidence conveys a moral or ethical
judgment. Similar happenings evidence is morally and ethically neutral.
Habit evidence refers to repeated conduct, whereas a single event can be a
similar happening.

Drawing a distinction between character, habit, and similar happenings
evidence is important. While Rules 404 and 405 regulate character and Rule
406 regulates habit, there is no rule specific to similar happenings evidence. The
admissibility of such evidence is determined by analyzing relevance and probative value. The probative value of similar happenings evidence, and even its
relevance, will depend on proof that the events took place under the same or
closely similar circumstances. In our hypothetical, for example, the allegedly
dangerous condition was static—it was the same when Plaintiff walked into the
pole as it was when the five other patrons suffered their accidents. Had the
circumstances been different, the evidence would lack sufficient probative
value to warrant admission. Suppose, for example, that at the time the other
patrons walked into the pole, it was only two feet tall, and that Defendant had
replaced it with the four-foot pole before Plaintiff's accident. This is probably a
significant change because a four-foot pole is most likely more visible than a two-
foot pole. In that case, courts are likely to exclude the evidence of the earlier
accidents.

Even if the pole with which the other patrons collided was shorter, however,
wouldn't the evidence still be relevant? That is, wouldn't it be reasonable to
conclude that a package-laden customer leaving the store might fail to see any
pole shorter than, say, six or eight feet? If that is true, the evidence probably
satisfies the lenient definition of relevance contained in Rule 401. The problem,
however, is that the evidence also carries significant potential for unfair
prejudice. A jury hearing of other accidents at the supermarket might well overestimate the probative value of the evidence, or even decide to hold Defendant
liable because too many accidents have occurred, regardless of Defendant's
fault. Alternatively, a jury might use the other accidents to create a sort of
bad character inference about the store management's behavior, and opt to

punish the store regardless of its actual fault in the case at hand. Consider, as well, that offering evidence of the other accidents takes time and might distract the jury from its principal task of determining what happened on this occasion, not at other times.

The problem is, therefore, somewhat analogous to that raised by evidence of other crimes, wrongs, or acts under Rule 404(b). The court must consider the probative value of the evidence, and compare that factor with the dangers the evidence presents. When dealing with similar events evidence, courts tend to look for close similarity between the event at issue and the other events about which the party seeks to inform the jury.

We should note that, just as the occurrence of other events under similar conditions is relevant and admissible to prove unreasonable danger, the *absence* of similar accidents under similar conditions has a tendency to prove *lack* of unreasonable danger. Thus, in our hypothetical, a court would likely allow Defendant to introduce evidence that, since it installed the four-foot pole, no other patron has reported walking into it. This is quite potent evidence that the pole does not present unreasonable danger. The same would be true if Defendant wished to introduce evidence that thousands of people had exited the store through that door, and that only a tiny fraction had suffered an accident.

Students should not confuse the issues under consideration here with the problems raised by evidence of subsequent remedial measures, which we discuss in Chapter 5.

Questions for Classroom Discussion

1. Negligence action by Plaintiff against Defendant, a railroad company, following a collision between Plaintiff's vehicle and Defendant's train. Plaintiff was driving her vehicle when she approached a railroad crossing. Plaintiff claims that the gate was not down and the light was not flashing, so she started to cross the tracks. Defendant denies that the gate and signal were not working. To prove that the gate and signal were not working, Plaintiff wishes to present evidence that on two occasions in the year before her accident, drivers narrowly avoided collisions at the same crossing because the gate and signal were not operating. Defendant objects. How should the court rule?

2. Negligence action by Plaintiff against Defendant, a supermarket owner, for injuries suffered when Plaintiff slipped and fell on the floor of the produce section. It was raining outside when the accident occurred. Plaintiff claims the floor was wet and slippery, causing her fall. Defendant denies that the floor was unreasonably slippery when wet. To prove that the floor surface was unreasonably dangerous, Plaintiff wishes to present evidence that in the past two years, several customers have suffered slip-and-fall accidents

in the produce section. Defendant objects. How should the court rule?

3. Negligence action by Plaintiff against Defendant, a store owner, following an incident in which Plaintiff tripped on the sidewalk in front of Defendant's store. Plaintiff alleges that the cracked sidewalk created unreasonable danger to customers and others passing by the store. Assume Defendant is responsible for maintaining a reasonably safe sidewalk. Defendant admits the presence of the crack but denies that the sidewalk is unreasonably dangerous. To prove the existence of unreasonable danger, Plaintiff wishes to present evidence that in the period from six months before Plaintiff's fall until six months after Plaintiff's fall, five other people had tripped on the same crack, all of them under similar weather conditions. Defendant objects. How should the court rule?

4. Same facts. Assume that in support of its motion to exclude Plaintiff's evidence of the other falls, Defendant wishes to present evidence that during the same time period, thousands of pedestrians walked over the same spot in the sidewalk, and that Defendant had received no other reports of falls or injuries. How should the court rule?

5. Employment discrimination action by Plaintiff, an unsuccessful job applicant, against Defendant, the company with which she had sought employment. Plaintiff claims Defendant did not hire her because of gender. Defendant admits not hiring Plaintiff, but claims its reasons had nothing to do with Plaintiff's gender. To prove Defendant based its decision on gender, Plaintiff wishes to present evidence that the person in charge of hiring filled the last 50 engineering jobs with men despite having applications from qualified women each time. Defendant objects. How should the court rule?

6. Plaintiff fell in the perfume department of Defendant department store. Plaintiff alleges that perfumes and lotions spilled from the counter, and Defendant did nothing to correct the condition. Plaintiff's fall occurred at 1:30 P.M. on January 7. Plaintiff's attorney makes an offer of proof that Shakira will testify she fell in the same floor area of the Defendant's store at approximately 1:45 P.M. on January 7. Defendant objects. How should the court rule?

Assessments

1. James sues Nick, alleging that Nick threw him into a glass case during a fight. Nick's defense is that James started the fight. At trial Nick calls Sasha, who will testify she has known Nick for 10 years, knows his friends and acquaintances, and that in her opinion Nick is a peaceful person. Which of the following statements is most accurate?
   a. The testimony is admissible because it tends to prove Nick did not start the fight
   b. The testimony is inadmissible hearsay
   c. The testimony is inadmissible character evidence
   d. The testimony is irrelevant

2. Joe is on trial for assault with a deadly weapon. Joe calls Tina, the alleged Victim's former girlfriend, who will testify that in her opinion Victim is a violent person, and that is why she broke up with him. In rebuttal the prosecution calls Ellen, who will testify she has lived next door to Joe for 15 years, and that Joe has a reputation as a violent person. Joe's lawyer objects, arguing the evidence is inadmissible hearsay, and inadmissible character evidence. The judge should:
   a. Overrule the objection because Joe's character is an essential element of the charge.
   b. Sustain the objection because the testimony is inadmissible hearsay
   c. Overrule the objection
   d. Sustain the objection because the prosecution may not place a defendant's character in issue

3. Phil is charged with murder. The prosecution theory is that Phil shot the victim because she refused his sexual advances. Phil's attorney announces during opening statement that she will prove the shooting was accidental. During its case in chief the prosecution calls a woman who will testify that Phil pointed a gun to her head after she refused to stay overnight at his mansion. Phil's counsel objects that this testimony is inadmissible character evidence. The judge should rule:
   a. The testimony is admissible because it tends to prove the shooting was not an accident
   b. The testimony is inadmissible because the prosecution may not offer evidence of Phil's character during its case in chief
   c. The testimony is admissible because it tends to prove Phil's pattern of threatening women with guns
   d. The testimony is inadmissible because it is specific act evidence

4. Gabe is accused of rape. His defense is consent. Gabe's attorney notifies the prosecution he intends to call a witness who will testify the accuser had an "intimate relationship" with her boyfriend who is

"insanely jealous." The witness will further testify the accuser was worried her boyfriend might find out she met with Gabe voluntarily. The prosecution makes a motion *in limine* seeking to exclude this testimony on the grounds that it is inadmissible sexual history evidence, and unfairly prejudicial. The trial judge should:

  a. Grant the motion because sexual history evidence is inadmissible to prove consent
  b. Grant the motion because the proposed testimony is irrelevant to the question of consent
  c. Deny the motion because the evidence may tend to impeach the alleged victim
  d. Grant the motion because the probative value of the proposed testimony is substantially outweighed by the danger of undue prejudice

5. Plaintiff sues his employer, claiming he suffered a back injury when the brakes failed as he was working on a freight car. The employer calls its safety engineer to testify that the brakes of every freight car are inspected at 4:00 A.M. every day. The proposed testimony is:

  a. Inadmissible circumstantial character evidence
  b. Inadmissible because it is irrelevant
  c. Admissible only if the safety engineer witnessed the inspection of the freight car involved, on the day Plaintiff's accident occurred
  d. Admissible

6. Clifford sues Jordan Marsh (JM) after he slipped and fell in the perfume department of a JM store. Clifford alleges JM negligently permitted a slippery floor to develop after perfumes spilled from the counter. Clifford's fall occurred at 1:30 P.M. on December 7. Clifford's attorney calls Shakira, who will testify she slipped and fell in the same area of the same JM store at approximately 1:20 P.M. on January 7. The court should:

  a. Admit the testimony because it tends to show a dangerous condition existed
  b. Admit the testimony because it tends to show JM knew about the dangerous condition
  c. a & b
  d. Refuse to admit the testimony. It is irrelevant because Shakira fell before Clifford fell

Answers and Analysis

1. The correct answer is "c." Circumstantial character evidence may not be used in most civil trials. This is made clear by the statement in FRE 404 (a) that "Evidence of a person's character or character trait is not admissible to prove that on a particular occasion the person acted in accordance with the character or trait." The exception stated in FRE 404 (a)(2) applies to a defendant in a criminal case.

(continued)

  Evidence of Character, Uncharged Misconduct, and Similar Events

2. The correct answer is "c." By placing the alleged victim's character for violence in issue, Joe has opened up the issue of his character for the same trait. FRE 404(b)(2)(ii). While the testimony about Joe's reputation is hearsay, it is admissible for this purpose. FRE 405(a); 804(21).

3. The correct answer is "a." Phil's attorney contended in her opening statement that the evidence will show the shooting was accidental. Thus the prosecution may introduce this testimony as part of its case in chief to show "lack of accident." FRE 404(b)(2).

4. The correct answer is "c." The defense is attempting to show the accuser had a motive to falsely accuse Gabe of rape. As was the case in Olden v. Kentucky, the sexual history evidence is not being offered as tending to prove consent, and it is highly probative. Therefore the motion should be denied.

5. The correct answer is "d." It does not matter whether the engineer witnessed the particular inspection; her testimony establishes the regular practice of the employer. The existence of that practice tends to prove the brakes were not defective. FRE 406.

6. The correct answer is "c." This is evidence of a similar event. The proximity in time of the two accidents is probably a sufficient basis for a court to conclude the evidence is relevant. Because Shakira fell before Clifford, the evidence is relevant as tending to show knowledge, and the existence, of the dangerous condition. If Shakira fell after Clifford, the evidence would be relevant regarding the existence of the condition, but would have no bearing on the issue of knowledge.

CHAPTER
5

Exclusion of Other Relevant Evidence for Reasons of Policy

A. INTRODUCTION

As we have seen throughout our study of evidence law, not all relevant evidence is admissible. Though modern evidence rules favor admission of relevant evidence, considerations of policy, as well as other factors, sometimes override that general principle. We have already noted that Rule 403 confers wide-ranging authority on the trial court to exclude relevant evidence when the dangers associated with it, in context, substantially outweigh its legitimate probative value. We also have seen instances in which broader considerations require adherence to a general prohibition of certain types of evidence unless certain narrowly defined exceptions apply. Character evidence is one obvious example.

In this chapter, we study several rules limiting the admission of certain categories of relevant evidence. One common thread among these rules of exclusion is that admission of the evidence in question threatens a policy important to the law. The policies usually are not the same policies supporting most of the evidence rules discussed so far: promoting accurate fact-finding and judicial efficiency. Another common thread is that the admissibility of the evidence in question usually depends on what it is offered to prove. As we have seen in other contexts, if the evidence is relevant for more than one purpose, it can be admissible for one and inadmissible for another.

As you read the materials in this chapter, keep the following questions in mind: Will the rules generally exclude the evidence, or do the purposes for which the evidence is admissible overwhelm the exclusionary provisions? Do the rules actually help to effectuate the policies that supposedly support them, or are the rules based on faulty or unproven assumptions about human behavior? Finally, what is the court's role in determining whether the evidence fits into one of the excluded categories or is offered for a permissible purpose?

B.   SUBSEQUENT REMEDIAL MEASURES

> ### FED. R. EVID. 407.   SUBSEQUENT REMEDIAL MEASURES

When measures are taken that would have made an earlier injury or harm less likely to occur, evidence of the subsequent measures is not admissible to prove:

- negligence;
- culpable conduct;
- a defect in a product or its design; or
- a need for a warning or instruction.

But the court may admit this evidence for another purpose, such as impeachment or — if disputed — proving ownership, control, or the feasibility of precautionary measures.

Discussion

1.   *Rationale for the Rule*

One of the primary goals of tort law is to encourage people to take steps to avoid accidents. One way to achieve this goal is to create rules that do not penalize such conduct. Evidence that the defendant improved a condition after an accident to make future accidents less likely would be relevant in an ensuing lawsuit because it tends to show the defendant believed the condition was dangerous at the time of the accident. But a rule of evidence that permitted an injured party to prove that the defendant improved the condition after the accident might discourage the defendant from making the improvement and, thus, increase the risk of future accidents. The main purpose of Rule 407, the subsequent remedial measures rule, is to avoid discouraging repairs and similar conduct. The rule promotes this purpose by excluding such evidence when it is offered to prove fault.

Other policy considerations also support the rule. One such consideration is to prevent people from being punished for doing the right thing, like taking safety measures. Allowing evidence of those measures to be used against the actor is tantamount to punishing the actor for engaging in laudable conduct. The rule also is justified on the ground that remedial measures evidence has dubious probative value as an indication of unreasonable danger at the time of the prior accident. Maybe the condition was already reasonably safe, but the actor wished to make it even safer. Maybe the remedial measure was taken for purposes unrelated to safety. Maybe the actor's own judgment about the danger, reflected in her decision to repair, was not correct. A subsequent remedial measure is, at best, ambiguous evidence of danger.

2.   *Efficacy and Necessity of Exclusionary Rule*

Little or no empirical evidence exists to support (or, for that matter, challenge) the assumption that, in the absence of Rule 407, people would be discouraged from undertaking remedial measures. Though it is perilous to generalize, one might reasonably suggest that the rule would be most effective, and thus most justified, in cases involving individuals or small organizations and one-time events rather than large organizations that regularly face accident claims. Thus, the owner of a small grocery store being sued by a customer who slipped and fell on a piece of fruit might well hesitate to start cleaning the floor right after an accident if he thought that evidence of his conduct could be offered to prove his fault in the plaintiff's case. Rule 407 might actually change the conduct of such a person, if she only knew the rule existed. Of course, the less sophisticated the party, the less likely the party is to *know* about the exclusionary rule. This means the rule is unlikely to have the intended impact with those whose conduct the rule might actually influence.

The situation is probably different for larger, more sophisticated parties that potentially could be subjected to extensive liability if they do not undertake remedial measures. Suppose, for example, that an automobile manufacturer learns that a design element of its automobile has led to one or more accidents. It is reasonable to predict that, to prevent even more accidents, the manufacturer will change the design even if it knows evidence of the change could be used in lawsuits concerning accidents that have already occurred. Simple cost-benefit analysis could persuade the manufacturer of the wisdom of such conduct. Reasoning such as this has been partly responsible for the decision of a minority of states, including California, to decline to extend the remedial measures rule to product liability cases. Unlike the Federal Rule, those jurisdictions would permit the admission of remedial measures evidence in product liability cases.

Despite the different effects that the rule might have in different types of cases, the majority of states hold that the exclusionary rule applies across the board whenever a party undertakes a subsequent remedial measure and the evidence is offered for the forbidden purpose. The same result holds in the federal courts; Rule 407 was amended to make clear that it applies in product liability cases.

3. Limited Exclusionary Principle

The subsequent remedial measures rule is not a categorical rule of exclusion — *it applies only when the evidence is offered to show fault or product defect, and then, only when its relevance depends on an inference that the remedial measure stands as the actor's implied recognition of fault or that the product is defective.* Thus, Rule 407 provides that remedial measures evidence "is not admissible to prove negligence, culpable conduct, a defect in a product or its design, or a need for a warning or instruction." The rule does not forbid any other use of the evidence, stating "[t]he court may admit this evidence for another purpose, such as impeachment or — if disputed — proving ownership, control, or the feasibility of precautionary measures." The rule's basic operation can be illustrated by the following hypothetical:

> Plaintiff sues Defendant for negligence after Plaintiff slipped and fell on a piece of fruit on the sidewalk in front of a supermarket owned by Defendant. Defendant denies negligence. Plaintiff wishes to present evidence that following the accident, Defendant began requiring store employees to clean the sidewalk in front of the

store every 15 minutes instead of once an hour. Had the policy been changed before Plaintiff's accident, Plaintiff probably would not have fallen.

In this example, the rule would exclude the evidence if it is offered based on the following reasoning:

EVIDENCE: After Plaintiff's accident, Defendant changed her policy, requiring sidewalk cleaning every 15 minutes instead of once an hour.

→**INFERENCE:** Defendant believed her prior policy did not offer customers sufficient protection from slip-and-fall accidents.

→**CONCLUSION:** Defendant's previous policy posed an unreasonable danger to store customers.

The generalization supporting the move from the evidence to the first inference is that store owners who believe their procedures do not adequately protect the safety of customers are more likely to change those procedures than are store owners who do not hold such a belief. The generalization supporting the move from the first inference to the conclusion is that a store owner is in a better position to judge the adequacy of safety measures than is a person without the owner's knowledge and experience. Because the generalizations are valid, the evidence is relevant. But the subsequent remedial measures rule requires the court to exclude the evidence upon Defendant's objection.

Suppose, however, that Defendant defends the case on the ground that it is not responsible for maintaining the sidewalk in front of the store. In that situation, the evidence would still be relevant and the subsequent remedial measures rule would not exclude it. The relevance of the evidence can be shown as follows:

EVIDENCE: After Plaintiff's accident, Defendant changed her policy, requiring sidewalk cleaning every 15 minutes instead of once an hour.

→**INFERENCE:** Defendant believed she was responsible for maintaining the sidewalk in front of the store.

→**CONCLUSION:** Defendant was responsible for maintaining the sidewalk in front of the store.

In this situation, the relevance of the evidence still depends on a judgment about Defendant's belief and, ultimately, Defendant's responsibility for the accident. Because the evidence is not directly offered to prove Defendant's negligence by means of an implied recognition of fault, however, the rule does not forbid the court from admitting it.

In the variation just discussed, the evidence, of course, remains relevant for its forbidden purpose. Thus, the situation is one of limited admissibility and the court must issue a limiting instruction if asked (and may do so even if not asked). In addition, if the court believes that the danger that the jury will use the evidence for a forbidden purpose substantially outweighs its probative value for the legitimate purpose (showing Defendant's control), the court may exclude the evidence altogether.

As the illustrative and non-exclusive list of permissible uses contained in Rule 407 demonstrates, there are many purposes for which evidence of subsequent remedial measures may be admitted. That possibility might make us pause if we are very serious about the policy behind the rule. If we wanted to avoid any risk that admissibility would discourage repair, the rule would be a categorical one, excluding the evidence regardless of the purpose for which it is offered. Reasonable people may well hesitate to take subsequent remedial measures if they know that evidence of their conduct could be offered for *any* reason. But the rule is not written so broadly, and the reason is probably that, while subsequent remedial measures evidence is of dubious value as an indication of fault, it is often of considerable value for other purposes. To return once again to our hypothetical, evidence of the change in the cleaning schedule might not be particularly probative on the issue of fault, but the fact that Defendant has been cleaning the sidewalk since before the accident is highly probative on the issue of Defendant's control of, and responsibility for, the sidewalk.

4. Meaning of "Negligence [or] Culpable Conduct"

As originally enacted, Rule 407 applied only when a party offered evidence of subsequent remedial measures to prove "negligence or culpable conduct." That phrase clearly applies to cases based on negligence and, presumably, intentional torts. But what about strict liability litigation, including certain product liability cases? As noted in the discussion above concerning the efficacy and necessity of the exclusionary rule, some jurisdictions held, and a few still hold, that the evidence is not excludable in such cases. But most courts hold that the policy of the rule applies regardless of the theory supporting liability, and the federal rule was amended to make clear that product liability cases are within the exclusionary reach of the rule. Whether the rule will apply in other types of strict liability litigation is not as clear, though there are good arguments that it should apply.

5. What Is a "Subsequent Remedial Measure"?

Rule 407 refers to measures that, if taken before the accident, would have made the accident less likely to occur. While one normally thinks of measures such as fixing the stairs after a person trips, or replacing burned-out bulbs in a common corridor, the rule actually encompasses many other types of measures. In the hypothetical discussed above, for example, a post-accident change in policy qualified as a subsequent remedial measure. Presumably, a post-accident internal investigation (sometimes called self-critical analysis) designed to uncover possible systemic problems also could qualify. Firing or reassigning an employee whose conduct contributed to the accident could constitute a subsequent remedial measure. In products cases, recall letters or changes in operating instructions could qualify, as could design changes. Whatever the conduct at issue, the common element is that, had the party taken that measure before the accident at issue, the accident would have been less likely to occur.

6. Timing of Subsequent Remedial Measure

The language of the rule makes clear that the remedial measure must have been taken *after* the event that gave rise to the action. This was not always clear. An earlier version of the rule was ambiguous, and some courts held that this sequence of events was not always required. The issue arose primarily in product liability cases based on alleged design defects. Suppose plaintiff suffers an injury when her 2006 vehicle's steering mechanism breaks, causing plaintiff to lose control of the car and strike a tree. Suppose further that the accident occurs in 2008, after plaintiff has owned the car for two years. However, for model years 2007 and later, the manufacturer redesigned that model's steering system in a way that would likely have prevented plaintiff's accident. If the main purpose of the rule is to encourage the taking of safety measures, the rule arguably should apply to a pre-accident but post-sale remedial measure because the manufacturer is less likely to make the repair if it knows its conduct will be admissible in litigation involving older model cars such as plaintiff's. In fact, it is likely that the design change was motivated in part by the occurrence of other accidents prior to plaintiff's.

Despite the possibility that parties' conduct might be affected by potential admissibility in pre-accident, post-sale cases such as our hypothetical, Rule 407 was amended to make clear that it only excludes remedial conduct undertaken *after* the accident at issue in the case. Though perhaps unwise in some respects, the amendment can be justified on the ground that it limits the exclusionary reach of the rule, thus admitting more relevant evidence for the fact-finder's consideration. This accords with the general direction of the rules in favor of the admissibility of relevant evidence.

7. Admissibility to Prove "Feasibility of Precautionary Measures"

While Rule 407 precludes the admission of subsequent remedial measures to prove negligence or culpable conduct, it allows a party to introduce such evidence to prove "feasibility of precautionary measures" if the issue is in controversy. Thus, it is important to understand the distinction. Consider this example, based on Flaminio v. Honda Motor Co., 733 F.2d 463 (7th Cir. 1984). Suppose plaintiff is injured when she loses control of her motorcycle, which was manufactured by defendant. Plaintiff claims that the accident was caused by excessive "wobble" at freeway speeds, and that the wobble, in turn, resulted from a weakness in the motorcycle's struts. Defendant responds that wobble at high speed is unavoidable in motorcycles. That defense amounts to a claim that it is not feasible to change the design of the motorcycle to avoid wobble. After all, if something is not possible, it is not feasible. Notice that this is a bolder defense than a claim that, while the motorcycle could have been engineered to avoid excessive wobble, defendant was not negligent because the design that was employed was safe or reasonable. Where defendant makes the bold claim that it was not feasible or possible to avoid the problem, the rule permits plaintiff to present evidence that after the accident, defendant thickened the motorcycle's struts in a way that eliminated the wobble.

Suppose, however, that defendant does not claim it is impossible to eliminate the wobble, but asserts that doing so would involve the substitution of materials so costly as to put the motorcycle out of reach to all but the very rich. If one views the term *feasible* as including elements of cost and benefit, defendant's claim would certainly challenge the feasibility of the alternate design, and the rule would permit plaintiff to offer evidence of the subsequent change. This is a broad definition of feasibility that, if adopted, would result in the admission of more subsequent remedial measures evidence.

Now suppose defendant claims it could have changed the motorcycle's struts so as to eliminate wobble, but that doing so would increase the risk of "weave," another potential danger. Such a defense also involves features of cost and benefit, but of a different kind. If the court views this type of claim as challenging feasibility, it will permit plaintiff to prove the subsequent design change. Once again, this would limit the scope of the exclusionary rule.

The courts have not settled on a single approach to the meaning of feasibility. The following case reviews two basic approaches and chooses a more narrow definition that makes it more likely that the evidence will be excluded.

TUER v. McDONALD

701 A.2d 1101 (Md. 1997)

WILNER, Judge.

This is a medical malpractice action filed by Mary Tuer, the surviving spouse and personal representative of her late husband, Eugene, arising from Eugene's death at St. Joseph's Hospital on November 3, 1992. Although the hospital and several doctors were initially joined as defendants, we are concerned here only with the action against Mr. Tuer's two cardiac surgeons, Drs. McDonald and Brawley, and their professional association. [Defendants prevailed in the lower courts.] We granted *certiorari* to consider whether the trial court erred in excluding evidence that, after Mr. Tuer's death, the defendants changed the protocol regarding the administration of the drug Heparin to patients awaiting coronary artery bypass surgery. . . . We shall hold that the court did not err and therefore shall affirm the judgment of the Court of Special Appeals.

FACTUAL BACKGROUND

The relevant underlying facts are not in substantial dispute. Mr. Tuer, 63, had suffered from angina pectoris for about 16 years. In September, 1992, his cardiologist, Dr. Louis Grenzer, recommended that he undergo coronary artery bypass graft (CABG) surgery and referred him to the defendants for that purpose. The surgery was initially scheduled for November 9, 1992. On October 30, however, Mr. Tuer was admitted to St. Joseph's Hospital after suffering chest pains the night before, and the operation was rescheduled for the morning of November 2.

After a second episode of chest pain following Mr. Tuer's admission, Dr. Grenzer prescribed Atenolol, a beta blocker that reduces pressure on the heart, and Heparin, an anti-coagulant, to help stabilize the angina. The Heparin was administered intravenously throughout the weekend, and, with the other medication Mr. Tuer was receiving, it achieved its purpose; there were no further incidents of chest pains or shortness of breath. The defendants assumed responsibility for Mr. Tuer on November 1. Dr. McDonald was to perform the operation, with Dr. Brawley assisting.

The operation was scheduled to begin between 8:00 and 9:00 A.M. on November 2. In accordance with the protocol then followed by the defendants and by St. Joseph's Hospital, an anesthesiologist caused the administration of Heparin to be discontinued at 5:30 that morning. That was done to allow the drug to metabolize so that Mr. Tuer would not have an anticoagulant in his blood when the surgery commenced.

Both Mr. Tuer and Dr. McDonald prepared for the 9:00 A.M. surgery. Shortly before the surgery was due to begin, however, Dr. McDonald was called to deal with an emergency involving another patient, whose condition was more critical than that of Mr. Tuer, and that required a three- to four-hour postponement of Mr. Tuer's operation. Mr. Tuer was taken to the coronary surgery unit (CSU) in the meanwhile, where he could be closely monitored. Dr. McDonald considered restarting the Heparin but decided not to do so.

Dr. McDonald next saw Mr. Tuer just after 1:00 P.M., when he was summoned to the CSU and found his patient short of breath and with arrhythmia and low blood pressure. Quickly thereafter, Mr. Tuer went into cardiac arrest. Appropriate resuscitation efforts, including some seven hours of surgery, were undertaken, and, although Mr. Tuer survived the operation, he died the next day. Following Mr. Tuer's death — apparently because of it — the defendants and St. Joseph's Hospital changed the protocol with respect to discontinuing Heparin for patients with unstable angina. Under the new protocol, Heparin is continued until the patient is taken into the operating room; had that protocol been in effect on November 2, 1992, the Heparin would not have been discontinued at 5:30 A.M., and no issue would have arisen as to restarting it. . . .

The Heparin issue first arose at trial when the plaintiff called Dr. McDonald as an adverse witness. In direct examination, Dr. McDonald stated that he approved discontinuation of the Heparin at 5:30 so that it would metabolize before the scheduled surgery. That decision, he said, was taken to minimize the risk attendant to an inadvertent puncture of the carotid artery by the anesthesiologist.

Dr. McDonald explained that, in the initial stage of CABG surgery, the anesthesiologist inserts a catheter into the internal jugular vein in the neck and that the procedure for doing so involves, first, puncturing the vein with a needle and then, after inserting a guide wire, making an incision and inserting the catheter. He pointed out that the jugular vein lies in close proximity to the carotid artery, which is a high pressure vessel that brings blood from the heart to the brain, and that, in his experience, there was a 5% to 10% incidence of the anesthesiologist inadvertently puncturing the carotid artery when attempting to insert the needle into the jugular vein. A puncture of the carotid artery, he said, could produce a serious bleeding problem, and it was for that reason that the protocol called for patients not to have an anticoagulant in their blood when the surgery commenced. He first said that he was unaware of whether any fatalities had resulted at St. Joseph's Hospital or in his particular practice from such an inadvertent puncture, but he did recall that they had had "some serious consequences from inadvertent carotid artery puncture in our hospital." In later testimony, he recounted that he was "very familiar with fatalities in the literature from inadvertent carotid puncture in patients who are having cardiac surgery." In response to a specific question, he confirmed that "the procedure in place on November the 2nd, 1992, at St. Joseph's Hospital, for coronary artery bypass patients on Heparin therapy was to discontinue the Heparin three to four hours prior to the time of the surgery ..." and that that practice and procedure "was required by the standard of care applicable at that time." He explained: "[t]hat is what we did at our hospital."

Following that answer, the plaintiff attempted to set up a basis for inquiring as to the subsequent change. He elicited from Dr. McDonald that there were no circumstances prior to November 2, 1992 in Dr. McDonald's practice at St. Joseph's Hospital in which a patient with Mr. Tuer's clinical profile — unstable angina stabilized in the hospital with Heparin therapy pending coronary bypass surgery — would not have had their Heparin discontinued three to four hours prior to their surgery. Dr. McDonald confirmed that "that was our policy at the time. It would have been a departure, and sitting here this morning I just can't think of a reason offhand why that could be." He added that he had considered restarting the Heparin once the surgery was postponed and elected not to do so because he did not want the drug in Mr. Tuer's blood when the surgery commenced. Counsel asked whether it was "feasible to restart Heparin for Mr. Tuer after your decision to postpone the surgery," but the court sustained an objection to that question. Counsel then inquired whether it was Dr. McDonald's contention "that it would have been *unsafe* to restart Mr. Tuer's Heparin after your decision to postpone his surgery," (emphasis added) to which the witness responded in the affirmative, for the reason already given.

With that answer, plaintiff urged that she was entitled to ask about the change in protocol for impeachment purposes — presumably to show that it is *not* unsafe to bring a patient into surgery with Heparin in his or her system. The court again rejected that argument, distinguishing between the situation presented, of the doctor changing his mind about the relative safety of the protocol, apparently as a result of the unfortunate death of Mr. Tuer, and the case of the doctor not really believing at the time that it would have been unsafe to restart the Heparin. The latter, the court concluded, would constitute grounds for impeachment, but not the former: "In order to impeach his opinion that it was unsafe on November the 1st, 1992, there need be evidence that he didn't think it was unsafe on November the 1st, 1992, not what he thought in January or February of 1993."

On cross-examination, Dr. McDonald noted that, had Mr. Tuer redeveloped chest pains, indicative of an episode of unstable angina, he would have restarted the Heparin, but that no such episode occurred until about 1:00, at which point Mr. Tuer was given a large dose of nitroglycerine. He also pointed out that Heparin is, in fact, used routinely *during* CABG surgery, to prevent clotting as the blood passes through a heart-lung machine. The doctor explained that the Heparin is introduced *after* the initial incision is made, just before the patient is hooked up to the heart-lung machine. That occurs, he said, from 15 to 30 minutes after the initial puncturing of the internal jugular vein by the anesthesiologist. . . .

[There was conflicting expert testimony about the medical wisdom of not restarting Heparin.]

DISCUSSION . . .

The plaintiff offers two grounds for the admissibility of the change in procedure adopted after her husband's death, both hinging on Dr. McDonald's testimony and that of his expert witnesses regarding the risk associated with taking patients into CABG surgery with Heparin in their blood. That testimony, she urges, effectively controverted the feasibility of protecting patients with Heparin until taken into the operating room, which she was then entitled to establish through evidence of the revised protocol. That evidence was also admissible, she claims, to impeach Dr. McDonald's statement that restarting the drug would have been "unsafe." Although these arguments overlap, we shall deal with them separately.

FEASIBILITY

Rule 5-407(b) exempts subsequent remedial measure evidence from the exclusionary provision of § (a) when it is offered to prove feasibility, if feasibility has been controverted. That raises two questions: what is meant by "feasibility" and was feasibility, in fact, controverted? These two questions also tend to overlap and are often dealt with together; whether a defendant has controverted feasibility may well depend on how one defines the term.

The exception allowing subsequent conduct evidence to show feasibility has been a troublesome one, especially in negligence cases, for, as Judge Weinstein points out, "negligence and feasibility [are] often indistinct issues. The feasibility of a precaution may bear on whether the defendant was negligent not to have taken the precaution sooner." 2 *Weinstein's Federal Evidence, supra,* § 407.04[3]. The Court of Special Appeals noted that two seemingly divergent approaches have been taken in construing the feasibility exception. . . . Some courts have construed the word narrowly, disallowing evidence of subsequent remedial measures under the feasibility exception unless the defendant has essentially contended that the measures were not physically, technologically, or economically possible under the circumstances then pertaining. Other courts have swept into the concept of feasibility a somewhat broader spectrum of motives and explanations for not having adopted the remedial measure earlier, the effect of which is to circumscribe the exclusionary provision.

Courts in the first camp have concluded that feasibility is not controverted — and thus subsequent remedial evidence is not admissible under the Rule — when a defendant contends that the design or practice complained of was chosen because of its perceived comparative advantage over the alternative design or practice . . . or when the defendant merely asserts that the instructions or warnings given with a product were acceptable or adequate and does not suggest that additional or different instructions or warnings could not have been given . . . or when the defendant urges that the alternative would not have been effective to prevent the kind of accident that occurred. . . .

Courts announcing a more expansive view have concluded that "feasible" means more than that which is merely possible, but includes that which is capable of being utilized successfully. In Anderson v. Malloy, 700 F.2d 1208 (8th Cir. 1983), for example, a motel guest who was raped in her room and who sued the motel for failure to provide safe lodging, offered evidence that, after the event, the motel installed peepholes in the doors to the rooms. The appellate court held that the evidence was admissible in light of the defendant's testimony that it had considered installing peepholes earlier but decided not to do so because (1) there were already windows next to the solid door allowing a guest to look out, and (2) based on the advice of the local police chief, peepholes would give a false sense of security. Although the motel, for obvious reasons, never suggested that the installation of peepholes was not possible, the court, over a strident dissent, concluded that, by inferring that the installation of peepholes would create a lesser level of security, the defendant had "controverted the feasibility of the installation of these devices." *Id.* at 1214. . . .

The apparent divergence indicated by these cases may, at least to some extent, be less of a doctrinal division than a recognition that the concept of practicability is implicit in the notion of feasibility and allows some leeway in the application of the rule. Part of the problem is that dictionaries, which are often resorted to by the courts, contain several definitions of the word "feasible." Webster's New Universal Unabridged Dictionary (2d ed. 1983), for example, contains three definitions: (1) "that may be done, performed, executed, or effected; practicable; possible"; (2) "likely; reasonable; probable; as, a *feasible* story"; (3) "that may be used or dealt with successfully; as, land *feasible* for cultivation." Each of those definitions embody, to some extent, the concept of practicability. Some courts have tended to follow the first definition and have thus articulated the notion of feasibility in terms of that which physically, technologically, or economically is capable of being done; others, like the Eighth Circuit in Anderson v. Malloy, have latched on to the third definition, which brings more into play the concepts of value, effectiveness, and overall utility.

To some extent, the problem may be driven by special considerations arising from application of the rule to product liability cases, especially those grounded on strict liability. When the plaintiff is obliged to establish that there were feasible alternatives to the design, manufacturing method, or warnings used by the defendant, he or she necessarily injects the question of feasibility into the case, to which the defendant ordinarily responds by showing why those alternatives were not used. As Saltzburg, Martin, and Capra point out, if a remedial measure has, in fact, been taken that could have been taken earlier, the defendant is not likely to claim that the measure was not possible or practicable, and, indeed, defendants often are willing to stipulate to feasibility in order to avoid having the subsequent remedial evidence admitted. The issue arises when the defendant offers some other explanation for not putting the measure into effect sooner — often a judgment call as to comparative value or a trade-off between cost and benefit or between competing benefits — and the plaintiff characterizes that explanation as putting feasibility into issue. . . . To the extent there can be said to be a doctrinal split among the courts, it seems to center on whether that kind of judgment call, which is modified later, suffices to allow the challenged evidence to be admitted.

That is essentially what occurred in this case. At no time did Dr. McDonald or any of his expert witnesses suggest that the Heparin could not have been restarted following the postponement of Mr. Tuer's surgery. Indeed, they indicated quite the opposite; Dr. McDonald, in fact, made clear that, had Mr. Tuer exhibited signs of renewed unstable angina, he would have restarted the Heparin. The only fair reading of his testimony and that of his supporting experts is that the protocol then in effect was the product of a professional judgment call that the risk to Mr. Tuer of having CABG surgery commence while there was a significant amount of Heparin in his blood outweighed the prospect of harm accruing from allowing him to remain Heparin-free for several hours.

Dr. McDonald's brief response to one question that, *at the time,* he regarded it as "unsafe" to restart the Heparin cannot be viewed in isolation but has to be read in the context of his whole testimony. Under any reasonable view of the meaning of feasibility, a flat assertion by a physician that the remedial measure was inappropriate because it was medically "unsafe" would ordinarily be tantamount to asserting that the measure was not feasible and would thus suffice to controvert the feasibility of the measure. In a medical context at least, feasibility has to include more than mere physical possibility; as we have so sadly learned from history, virtually anything can physically be done to the human body. The practice of medicine is quintessentially therapeutic in nature. Its purpose is to comfort and to heal, and a determination of whether a practice or procedure is feasible has to be viewed in that light. The assertion that a given course would be unsafe, in the sense that it would likely cause paramount harm to the patient, necessarily constitutes an assertion that the course would not be feasible. Dr. McDonald was not asserting, however, in any absolute sense, that restarting the Heparin would have been unsafe but only that, given the complications that could have arisen, and that, in other cases had arisen, from an inadvertent puncture of the carotid artery, weighed against Mr. Tuer's apparently stable condition at the time and the intensive monitoring he would receive during the waiting period, there was a relative safety risk that, at the time, he and the hospital believed was not worth taking. That does not, in our view, constitute an assertion that a restarting of the Heparin was not feasible. It was feasible but, in their view, not advisable.

[The court then discussed whether the evidence was admissible to impeach the testimony of Dr. McDonald. We take up that question next.]

[Affirmed.]

8. *Admissibility to Impeach*

Rule 407 permits a party to offer evidence of subsequent remedial measures to impeach the credibility of a witness. Return to our motorcycle hypothetical. Defendant calls its chief design engineer, who testifies that it is not possible to change the strut design in a way that would eliminate wobble. Plaintiff is aware that defendant did in fact change the struts to eliminate wobble. As we learn in Chapter 6, one way to impeach the credibility of a witness is to *contradict* her—to show that she is wrong about a fact to which she testified. In our example, evidence of the subsequent design change directly contradicts the engineer's testimony and, thus, impeaches her. The evidence is therefore relevant and possibly admissible to impeach even if it is inadmissible for the purpose of proving negligence or culpable conduct. Unless the court is persuaded that the jury will misuse the evidence to infer negligence and that such a result substantially outweighs its legitimate probative value for impeachment, the court will admit the evidence along with a limiting instruction informing the jury of the proper use of the evidence.

Examples such as the one just given are relatively straightforward because the subsequent remedial measure directly contradicts the witness's testimony. Suppose, however, that the contradiction is more subtle. If the engineer had testified on direct examination that the strut design of plaintiff's motorcycle was "safe," or "effective," or "a good balance of cost and benefit," would the subsequent design change be admissible to impeach her testimony? This has been a matter of significant controversy, with some courts holding that the evidence is admissible to impeach and others taking the position that, unless the contradiction is quite direct, the court should exclude the evidence. After discussing admissibility to show feasibility, the *Tuer* court took up the question of admissibility to impeach. As with the use of the evidence to prove feasibility, the court took a cautious approach:

TUER v. McDONALD
701 A.2d 1101 (Md. 1997)

WILNER, Judge. . . .

IMPEACHMENT

The exception in the Rule for impeachment has created some of the same practical and interpretive problems presented by the exception for establishing feasibility. As Saltzburg, Martin, and Capra point out, "almost any testimony given by defense witnesses could be contradicted at least in some minimal way by a subsequent remedial measure. If the defendant's expert testifies that the product was safe, a subsequent remedial measure could be seen as contradicting that testimony. If the defendant is asked on cross-examination whether he thinks that he had taken all reasonable safety precautions, and answers in the affirmative, then a subsequent remedial measure can be seen as contradicting that testimony."

The prevailing, and pragmatically necessary, view is that the impeachment exception cannot be read in so expansive a manner. . . . As Wright and Graham note, even at common law it would likely have been impermissible for the plaintiff to "have called the defendant to the stand, asked him if he thought he had been negligent, and impeached him with evidence of subsequent repairs if he answered 'no.'" Thus, as Saltzburg, Martin, and Capra point out, most courts have held that subsequent remedial measure evidence is not ordinarily admissible for impeachment "if it is offered for simple contradiction of a defense witness' testimony."

To some extent, that begs the question; whether the evidence is allowed for impeachment seems to depend more on the nature of the contradiction than on the fact of it. In Muzyka v. Remington Arms Co., 774 F.2d 1309, 1313 (5th Cir. 1985), for example, where a defense witness asserted that the challenged product constituted "perhaps the best combination of safety and operation yet devised," a design change made after the accident but before the giving of that testimony was allowed as impeachment evidence, presumably to show either that the witness did not really believe that to be the case or that his opinion should not be accepted as credible. . . . In Dollar v. Long Mfg., N.C., Inc., 561 F.2d 613 (5th Cir. 1977), the court allowed evidence of a post-accident letter by the manufacturer to its dealers warning of "death dealing propensities" of the product when used in a particular fashion to impeach testimony by the defendant's design engineer, who wrote the letter, that the product was safe to operate in that manner. *See also* Patrick v. South Central Bell Tel. Co., 641 F.2d 1192 (6th Cir. 1980) (evidence that defendant subsequently raised height of telephone lines admissible to impeach testimony that lines met minimum statutory height at time of accident). In these circumstances, the subsequent remedial measure falls neatly within the scope of classic impeachment evidence and directly serves the purpose of such evidence — to cast doubt on the credibility of the witness's testimony; it is not a mere pretext for using the evidence to establish culpability. *Compare,* however, Davenport v. Ephraim McDowell Mem. Hosp., 769 S.W.2d 56 (Ky. App. 1988) (evidence that, after the decedent's death, the defendant reactivated alarms on heart monitoring machines held admissible to impeach defense testimony that the alarms had been made inoperative at the time of the event because they went off unnecessarily on false readings and were distracting to the nursing staff).

Consistent with the approach taken on the issue of feasibility, however, subsequent remedial measure evidence had been held inadmissible to impeach testimony that, at the time of the event, the measure was not believed to be as practical as the one employed . . . , or that the defendant was using due care at the time of the accident. . . .

Largely for the reasons cited with respect to the feasibility issue, we do not believe that the change in protocol was admissible to impeach Dr. McDonald's brief statement that restarting the Heparin would have been unsafe. As we observed, that statement must be read in context, and, when so read, would not be impeached by the subsequent change in protocol. It is clear that Dr. McDonald made a judgment call based on his knowledge and collective experience at the time. He had read about and, in 5% to 10% of the cases had experienced, problems arising from an inadvertent puncture of the carotid artery; he had not experienced a patient in Mr. Tuer's circumstances dying from the lack of Heparin during a four-hour wait for surgery. He was aware that the same protocol, of allowing the Heparin to metabolize, was used at Johns Hopkins Hospital. The fact that the protocol was changed following Mr. Tuer's death in no way suggests that Dr. McDonald did not honestly believe that his judgment call was appropriate at the time. The only reasonable inference from his testimony, coupled with counsel's proffer as to why the protocol was changed, was that Dr. McDonald and his colleagues reevaluated the relative risks in light of what happened to Mr. Tuer and decided that the safer course was to continue the Heparin. That kind of reevaluation is precisely what the exclusionary provision of the Rule was designed to encourage.

9. *Other Permissible Uses of Subsequent Remedial Measures Evidence; Viability of the Exclusionary Rule*

The only forbidden use of subsequent remedial measures evidence is to prove negligence, culpable conduct, or product defect through an inference that the action represents the actor's implied recognition of responsibility. In this discussion, we have seen how subsequent remedial measures evidence can be admissible to prove anything else, such as feasibility of precautionary measures or control over the instrumentality of the accident. We have also seen how the evidence might be used to impeach the credibility of a witness. The rule does not forbid any use of the evidence other than as an implied recognition of responsibility; the list of permissible purposes in the rule is not exclusive. Of course, admission of the evidence is not automatic just because a party offers it for a permissible purpose. The court retains the authority to exclude the evidence when its probative value for the permissible purpose is substantially outweighed by the danger that the jury will use the evidence for a prohibited purpose, thereby unfairly prejudicing the opponent.

Some courts and commentators have expressed concern that the evidence is potentially admissible on so many grounds that the exclusionary rule can become overwhelmed. It does seem worth inquiring whether the existence of so many routes to admissibility threatens to undermine the rule's primary rationale: to avoid discouraging remedial conduct. That concern explains in part why some courts have taken a cautious approach to the feasibility and impeachment uses of subsequent remedial measures evidence.

Further Reading: Charles R. Gamble & Gwen L. Windle, *Subsequent Remedial Measures Doctrine in Alabama: From Exclusion to Admissibility and the Death of Policy,* 37 Ala. L. Rev. 547 (1986); Roger C. Henderson, *Product Liability and Admissibility of Subsequent Remedial Measures: Resolving the Conflict by Recognizing the Difference Between Negligence and Strict Tort Liability,* 64 Neb. L. Rev. 1 (1985); Malcolm E. McLorg, Note, *Exceptions to the Subsequent Remedial Conduct Rule,* 18 Hast. L.J. 677 (1967); John R. Schmertz, Jr., *Relevancy and Its Policy Counterweights: A Brief Excursion Through Article IV of the Proposed Federal Rules of Evidence,* 33 Fed. B.J. 1 (1974); M.C. Slough, *Relevancy Unraveled,* 5 U. Kan. L. Rev. 675 (1957); Victor E. Schwartz, *The Exclusionary Rule on Subsequent Repairs — A Rule in Need of Repair,* 7 Forum 1 (1971).

Questions for Classroom Discussion

1. Plaintiff sues Defendant, the owner of a convenience store, for negligence after Plaintiff tripped and fell over a can of fruit that had fallen off a shelf on a display near the store's front door. Defendant admits that Plaintiff tripped in this way, but denies its negligence led to Plaintiff's fall. To prove Defendant was negligent in allowing the can to fall from the shelf, Plaintiff wishes to present evidence that after the accident, Defendant began placing the cans in staggered (brick-like) stacks rather than one directly on top of the other. Defendant objects. How should the court rule?

2. Same case. Defendant claims the can on which Plaintiff tripped was no longer the store's property, but had fallen out of a customer's bag after the customer had paid for his purchases. How should the court rule on Defendant's objection to the subsequent remedial measures evidence?

3. Same case. Defendant admits that the can fell from the display, but testifies that this was the "best possible way" to stack cans. How should the court rule on Defendant's objection?

(continued)

4. Same case. Defendant admits that the can fell from the display. Instead of testifying that this was the "best possible way" to stack cans, Defendant testifies that this method was "safe." How should the court rule on Defendant's objection?

5. Same case. On cross-examination of Defendant, Plaintiff's counsel establishes that when the can fell, the cans in the display were stacked one atop the other. Counsel then asks, "Is this the way you always stack them?" Defendant answers yes. Plaintiff now wishes to offer evidence of the subsequent remedial measure to impeach Defendant. Defendant objects. How should the court rule?

C.   COMPROMISE AND PAYMENT OF MEDICAL AND SIMILAR EXPENSES

FED. R. EVID. 408.   COMPROMISE OFFERS AND NEGOTIATIONS

(a) Prohibited Uses. Evidence of the following is not admissible — on behalf of any party — either to prove or disprove the validity or amount of a disputed claim or to impeach by a prior inconsistent statement or a contradiction:

(1) furnishing, promising, or offering — or accepting, promising to accept, or offering to accept — a valuable consideration in compromising or attempting to compromise the claim; and

(2) conduct or a statement made during compromise negotiations about the claim — except when offered in a criminal case and when the negotiations related to a claim by a public office in the exercise of its regulatory, investigative, or enforcement authority.

(b) Exceptions. The court may admit this evidence for another purpose, such as proving a witness's bias or prejudice, negating a contention of undue delay, or proving an effort to obstruct a criminal investigation or prosecution.

FED. R. EVID. 409.   OFFERS TO PAY MEDICAL AND SIMILAR EXPENSES

Evidence of furnishing, promising to pay, or offering to pay medical, hospital, or similar expenses resulting from an injury is not admissible to prove liability for the injury.

Discussion: Compromise

1.   Introduction

Compromise of claims is essential to the survival of our system of civil justice. If even a quarter of civil actions proceeded to trial, the backlog would be so serious that, in some jurisdictions, litigants might have to wait decades to have their day in court. Our nation simply has not committed the huge infrastructure and personnel resources that would be necessary to support a system in which a sizeable percentage of cases went to trial. As a result, settlement is more than a convenience. It is a necessity.

Compromise and settlement are also good for the soul. In a perfect society, disputes would be resolved in a cooperative rather than belligerent way. People would air their differences, state frankly their perceptions of the facts, and work out a solution that recognizes the dignity of each person.

Unfortunately, our tradition of adversarial justice tends to make lawyers fight and posture for somewhat longer than we might think appropriate. Lawyers are also wary of the possibility that, to use the familiar phrase, everything they (or their clients) say may be used against them in a court of law. Achieving compromise, however, requires frankness and straight talk.

The law has attempted to reconcile the conflicting incentives brought about by the adversary system on the one hand, and the need for settlement on the other, by creating a rule forbidding a party to present evidence of efforts to compromise the claim. The idea behind the rule is similar to that behind the subsequent remedial measures rule: If people are aware that what they say may not be used against them, they are more likely to speak freely. The favored outcome, a compromise, is more likely to result.

Federal Rule 408 has a number of important features:

- The rule applies to the efforts of both the party claiming a right to relief and the party against whom the claim is made.
- One or both parties must be engaged in a bona fide effort to compromise a claim that is disputed as to either validity or amount.
- The rule applies both to completed compromises and to unsuccessful efforts to compromise.
- The rule excludes both settlement demands/offers and "conduct or a statement made during compromise negotiations." This includes statements of fact, even if such statements otherwise would be admissible as party admissions. A party need not state a fact "arguendo" or "without prejudice" for it to be excluded under the rule. Pursuant to an amendment adopted in 2006, however, if the evidence is being offered in a criminal case, and if "the negotiations related to a claim by a public office in the exercise of its regulatory, investigative, or enforcement authority," statements made in the course of those negotiations are admissible. This somewhat controversial amendment may chill discussions seeking to compromise claims made by public agencies such as the SEC, the FTC, and other bodies. It remains to be seen whether states will follow suit by amending their compromise rules in the same fashion.
- The rule only applies when the evidence is offered to "prove or disprove the validity or amount of a disputed claim." If offered for any other purpose, including but not limited to "proving a witness's bias or prejudice, negating a contention of undue delay, or proving an effort to obstruct a criminal investigation or prosecution," it is potentially admissible. The 2006 amendment to Rule 408(a) made clear that compromise evidence may not be used to impeach a witness through contradiction or prior inconsistent statement.
- If rules permit discovery of certain evidence, a party may not shield that evidence from admission at trial simply by presenting it to the opponent in the course of compromise discussions.

- Application of the rule is not limited to the parties currently at trial. Evidence that a person previously settled a claim is excluded if offered to prove, in a case involving a different person, liability for that claim, its invalidity, or the proper amount.

2. Rationales for the Rule

As the preceding discussion indicates, the primary purpose of the rule excluding evidence of compromise is to avoid discouraging compromise. This is because compromise is socially beneficial behavior. In that sense, the rule is similar to the subsequent remedial measures rule. And as with that rule, other considerations also support the exclusion of compromise evidence. One such consideration is low probative value. Evidence of compromise efforts satisfies the very lenient definition of relevance because one rational inference from such behavior is that the person engaging in those efforts believes there are weaknesses in her claim or defense. Thus, as with the taking of subsequent remedial measures, efforts to compromise can be seen as an implied recognition of a relevant fact. The problem, however, is that numerous other rational inferences can flow from the same conduct. For example, a compromise offer might stem from the actor's desire to avoid the time and expense of litigation and trial, regardless of the merits. The actor might also wish to avoid the negative publicity likely to attend certain claims.

Naturally, the strength of the various inferences that may be derived from compromise evidence will depend on the facts of the case and the nature of the parties. A defendant's offer of $100 to settle a $500 claim might have a reasonable amount of probative value on the defendant's belief in the strength of the plaintiff's case, while the probative value of the same offer to settle a multimillion dollar claim is negligible. The fact of the matter is that so many conflicting inferences can flow from compromise behavior that the value of the evidence as an implied recognition of responsibility is often extremely low.

Another reason for the rule is fairness. People should not be punished for doing the right thing. As is the case with the subsequent remedial measures rule, admitting evidence of a person's laudable behavior both punishes and discourages that behavior.

Finally, the rule can be supported by concern about unfair prejudice. One fear is that the jury will over-value compromise behavior as evidence of the person's belief in the strength or weakness of her claim or defense. Perhaps this concern is misplaced since, in many instances, a jury is likely to understand the various reasons for seeking settlement. But such concern might be justified in other cases. For example, jurors might have difficulty understanding that a large corporation's offer of millions of dollars to settle a billion dollar claim might be motivated almost entirely by the desire to avoid the cost of litigation and that the corporation can make such an offer while still believing that the claim against it has no merit.

3. Special Situation: The Biased Witness

Rule 408 provides that the court may admit compromise evidence to prove "a witness's bias or prejudice." Because the meaning of this provision is not obvious, this situation deserves special attention. Consider the following facts:

Plaintiff charters a small plane from Charter Co. for a business trip. Plaintiff hires Pilot, an experienced pilot, to fly the plane. During the flight, the plane suddenly goes into a dive. Pilot manages to regain partial control, but the plane lands in a field, injuring Plaintiff. Plaintiff sues Pilot, alleging negligent operation, and Charter Co., alleging negligent maintenance. Before the case comes to trial, Pilot settles with Plaintiff for about 10 percent of Plaintiff's claim. As part of the settlement agreement, Pilot promises to testify for Plaintiff at the trial against Charter Co. Plaintiff, in turn, has promised to reimburse Pilot if Plaintiff obtains a judgment against Charter Co. in excess of a certain amount of money. At trial, Pilot testifies that an engine problem caused the plane to dive. Charter Co. seeks to present evidence of Pilot's settlement agreement with Plaintiff.

In this case, Pilot's settlement agreement has many of the elements of a "Mary Carter" agreement. Named for Booth v. Mary Carter Paint Co., 202 So. 2d 8 (Fla. App. 1967), such an agreement exists, broadly speaking, when one defendant agrees with the plaintiff to settle the case for a certain amount but remains a party to the suit and retains a financial stake in the outcome of the plaintiff's action against the remaining defendants. In those cases, the settling defendant has a significant incentive to testify against the interests of the non-settling defendants because the greater the plaintiff's recovery against them, the less the settling defendant ultimately will have to pay.

If the terms of this kind of agreement are not disclosed to the jury, the jury will not possess the tools needed to evaluate the credibility of the settling defendant's testimony. Some states, in fact, simply outlaw Mary Carter agreements. A majority of states, while not outlawing the agreements, hold that the agreements are admissible to prove bias or prejudice of a witness and, thus, are not excluded by the compromise rule.

In our hypothetical, even if the court does not void the agreement, it should allow the jury to learn of its contents. Though Pilot is no longer a party, Pilot's incentive to testify against the interests of Charter Co. is substantial because Pilot has a financial interest in the outcome of the case. If the jury does not know of the agreement, the jury might give Pilot's testimony far more credit than it deserves.

This is not the only situation in which compromise evidence is relevant to show the bias or prejudice of a witness. While the compromise rule permits the court to admit compromise evidence when offered for that purpose, the court retains the authority to exclude the evidence pursuant to Rule 403.

Questions for Classroom Discussion

1.   Plaintiff sues Defendant for negligence following an intersection collision between their cars after one of them ran a red light. Plaintiff's car was damaged, though Plaintiff suffered no physical injury. Plaintiff wishes to testify that immediately after the collision, before Plaintiff said anything, Defendant got out of his car, approached Plaintiff, and said, "It's my fault. Please let me pay your damages." Defendant objects on hearsay grounds. How should the court rule?

(continued)

2. Same case. Defendant objects on grounds of the compromise rule. How should the court rule?

3. Same case, except that Defendant's statement to Plaintiff was "It's my fault, but I don't want to go through our insurance companies. If you'll agree to bypass the insurance companies, I'll pay you now for your damages." Defendant objects. How should the court rule?

4. Same case. Assume that at the scene, both parties claimed the other ran the red light. Plaintiff wishes to testify that a month later, after Plaintiff notified Defendant in writing that it cost $2,500 to fix the car, Defendant called Plaintiff and said, "I admit that I ran the light, but there's no way your car had that much damage. I think we can work things out more reasonably." Defendant objects. How should the court rule?

5. Same as Question 4, except that Defendant's statement to Plaintiff was "I was in the wrong, but I can only scrape together $1,000. Will you accept that?" Defendant objects. How should the court rule?

6. Same as Question 5. Assume, however, that Defendant denies ever calling Plaintiff at all. How should the court rule on Defendant's objection?

7. Same case. At trial, Plaintiff wishes to testify that a few weeks after the accident, Plaintiff called Defendant, seeking payment of $2,500 to fix the car, and threatening to sue if Defendant does not pay. Defendant responds, "You're the one who ran the light, but I'll pay you $100 to drop this thing." Defendant objects. How should the court rule?

8. Plaintiff, a pedestrian, sues Defendant, a driver, for negligence for striking Plaintiff as Plaintiff crossed the street in a crosswalk. Defendant denies striking Plaintiff, and claims she was elsewhere when the event took place. The police began a criminal investigation, and, based on Plaintiff's identification of Defendant as the driver, charged Defendant with reckless driving. At trial, Defendant wishes to testify that shortly after Defendant was charged, Plaintiff phoned Defendant and said that if Defendant agreed to a private settlement of the civil case, Plaintiff would tell the police she was mistaken in her identification of Defendant as the driver. Plaintiff objects. How should the court rule?

9. Plaintiff sues Defendant, a store owner, after Plaintiff slipped and fell in the store. Plaintiff claims she suffered an injury in the fall. A few days after the accident, Defendant said to Plaintiff, "That floor was slippery, but I'm not sure you were really injured." Defendant then offered to pay some of Plaintiff's medical expenses in exchange for a signed release. The case did not settle. At trial, Defendant testifies that the floor was not slippery. Plaintiff wishes

to testify about Defendant's prior statement admitting that the floor was slippery. Defendant objects. How should the court rule?

10. Action by Plaintiff against Defendant to recover a debt Defendant allegedly owes. Defendant claims that the debt was discharged. To prove discharge, Defendant wishes to testify that the parties negotiated a settlement of the matter, and that the parties performed their obligations pursuant to the agreement. Plaintiff objects. How should the court rule?

11. After a three-car collision involving Plaintiff, Defendant, and Zed, Plaintiff brought suit against both Defendant and Zed. After some negotiation, Plaintiff agreed to settle with Zed for a small percentage of the total damages. Zed, in turn, agreed to remain a party to the action but testify favorably to Plaintiff at trial. In addition, Plaintiff agrees that if she obtains a judgment against Defendant in excess of a certain amount, Zed will receive a share of the excess. At trial, Zed testifies that Defendant started the chain of events by speeding and running a red light. Defendant wishes to ask Zed on cross-examination about the settlement agreement with Plaintiff. Plaintiff objects, citing the compromise rule. How should the court rule?

Discussion: Humanitarian Measures

Generally speaking, U.S. law does not require people to assist others in need. At the same time, the law does not wish to discourage such efforts nor does it wish to punish the Good Samaritan. Rule 409 follows these principles, though in a limited way. The rule protects those who "offer[] to pay medical, hospital, or similar expenses resulting from an injury" by making evidence of those measures inadmissible to prove liability for the injury. Like Rules 407 and 408, the rule tries to treat fairly those who have done the "right thing."

It is easy to imagine a typical situation for the application of Rule 409: After an automobile accident leading to an injury, one of the drivers offers to pay the other driver's hospital bill. In that case, evidence of the offer is relevant to the offeror's liability because that evidence makes it somewhat more likely than it would be without the evidence that the offer was motivated by a sense of responsibility for the accident. Certainly other inferences are possible, such as the offeror's desire to help another person in need without regard to fault. But because we would accept the generalization that a person who believes herself responsible for an accident is more likely to offer medical aid than one who does not hold such a belief, the evidence satisfies the minimal test of relevance.

Note that the rule does not require that the person making the offer or payment was involved in the accident or is even a party to the suit. Any person's offer will be excluded by the rule if it is offered to prove liability for the accident. In addition, the humanitarian conduct need not occur immediately after an accident; payment of another's hospital bill weeks after the accident would also be excluded if offered to prove liability.

As we have noted above, the scope of the rule is limited. It only applies to "medical, hospital, or similar expenses." Thus, an offer to pay or actual payment of another's towing charges after an accident would not be excluded by the rule, nor would payment of wages lost due to the injury. Some expenses closely related to medical or hospital charges, such as payment for rehabilitation services, medications, or medical equipment, should be covered, however.

The behavior covered by Rule 409 overlaps to a degree with compromise behavior covered by Rule 408. For example, suppose that following an accident, one driver says to the other, "We can't agree who's responsible for the accident, but I'll pay your hospital bill and we'll forget the whole thing." This statement is both an offer to compromise a disputed claim and the type of humanitarian assistance covered by Rule 409. The overlap is not complete, however. Rule 409, for example, excludes offers or payments even in the absence of a disputed claim. By the same token, an offer to compromise by payment of the other person's non-medical expense, such as a towing charge, would not be excluded by Rule 409. It would, however, be excluded by Rule 408 if the underlying claim was disputed.

Another important difference between the compromise rule and the medical expenses rule concerns how those provisions deal with the admissibility of statements of fact made in connection with the underlying excluded conduct. As we have seen, the compromise rule excludes not only the actual compromise offer, payment, or acceptance of payment, but also any statements of fact made in connection with that conduct. This is not true with the medical expenses rule. The drafters of Rule 409 believed that statements of fact are not as central to humanitarian conduct as they are to compromise efforts. To put it another way, the drafters believed that frank factual discussion is essential to negotiating a successful compromise but is not necessary to the rendering of humanitarian assistance. Thus, in the latter case, the need for relevant evidence to resolve factual disputes outweighs the value to be gained in encouraging humanitarian conduct by excluding statements of fact made in connection with that conduct.

Note that, unlike the compromise rule, the rule excluding offers or payments of medical, hospital, and similar expenses does not contain a list of permissible uses of such evidence. Even so, the rule states a limiting principle: The evidence is to be excluded only when offered to prove "liability." The implication is that, if the evidence is offered for any other purpose, the rule does not exclude the evidence.

If the law excludes evidence of the payment of medical expenses, should it also exclude evidence of conduct that heals psychic, not physical, injury? In recent years, the concept of "therapeutic jurisprudence" has emerged in the legal literature. According to its proponents, certain acts and statements, including apologies, have a beneficial effect on both the aggrieved party and the party against whom a claim is made or might be made in the future. Specifically, humanitarian gestures such as apologies are thought to defuse incendiary situations and make the peaceful settlement of disputes more likely. Studies of medical malpractice, for example, have suggested that when a physician expresses remorse or apologies after a bad outcome, the patient is less likely to bring suit. Several states have enacted rules that exclude evidence of apologies or other benevolent gestures in civil cases. The Massachusetts rule, for example, provides that "[s]tatements, writings, or benevolent gestures expressing sympathy or a general sense of benevolence relating to the pain, suffering, or death of a person involved in an accident and made to such person or to the family of such person shall be inadmissible as evidence of an admission of liability in a civil action. Mass. Ann. Laws ch. 233, § 23D. California Evidence Code § 1160 sets out a similar rule. These rules, however, are not intended to exclude actual admissions of fault. The Federal Rules have no comparable provision.

Further Reading: George M. Bell, *Admissions Arising Out of Compromise—Are They Irrelevant?*, 31 Tex. L. Rev. 239 (1953); Newell H. Blakely, *Article IV: Relevancy and Its Limits*, 20 Hous. L. Rev. 151 (1983); June F. Entman, *Mary Carter Agreements: An Assessment of Attempted Solutions*, 38 U. Fla. L. Rev. 521 (1986); Judson F. Falknor, *Extrinsic Policies Affecting Admissibility*, 10 Rutgers L. Rev. 574 (1956); Aviva Orenstein, *Apology Excepted: Incorporating a Feminist Analysis into Evidence Policy Where You Would Least Expect It*, 28 Sw. U. L. Rev. 221 (1999); Symposium, *Therapeutic Jurisprudence: Issues, Analysis, and Applications*, 24 Seattle U. L. Rev. 215 (2000).

Questions for Classroom Discussion

1. Plaintiff sues Defendant for negligence following Plaintiff's fall in Defendant's restaurant. Plaintiff claims Defendant's employees failed to mop up a coffee spill near one of the tables, and that Plaintiff slipped on the coffee, causing her injury. Defendant denies that there was spilled coffee on the floor. To prove Defendant's responsibility, Plaintiff wishes to testify that after her fall, Defendant offered to send her to a doctor "at our expense." Defendant objects. How should the court rule?

2. Same case. Assume the statement had been made by a waiter rather than by Defendant. Defendant objects. How should the court rule?

3. Same case. Assume, as in Question 1, that the statement was made by Defendant, and that the entire statement was, "looks like the floor was pretty slippery. Why don't you see your doctor at our expense?" Defendant objects. How should the court rule?

4. Same as Question 3, except that Defendant says, "looks like the floor was pretty slippery. If you will sign a release, you can see your doctor at our expense." Defendant objects. How should the court rule?

5. Same case, and same statement as in Question 3. Suppose Defendant made the statement to Plaintiff during a telephone call after being contacted by a waiter about Plaintiff's fall. Defendant argues that the statement about the spill is inadmissible for lack of personal knowledge. How should the court rule?

6. Personal injury action by Plaintiff against Defendant arising from an auto accident. To prove liability, Plaintiff wishes to testify that after

(continued)

the collision Defendant said, "Let me give you a lift to the hospital." Defendant objects. How should the court rule?

7. Same case as in Question 6. To prove liability, Plaintiff wishes to testify that after the collision, Defendant said, "Just let me know how I can help, and I'll do it." Defendant objects. How should the court rule?

D. PLEA EVIDENCE

FED. R. EVID. 410.   PLEAS, PLEA DISCUSSIONS,
AND RELATED STATEMENTS

(a) Prohibited Uses. In a civil or criminal case, evidence of the following is not admissible against the defendant who made the plea or participated in the plea discussions:

(1) a guilty plea that was later withdrawn;

(2) a nolo contendere plea;

(3) a statement made during a proceeding on either of those pleas under Federal Rule of Criminal Procedure 11 or a comparable state procedure; or

(4) a statement made during plea discussions with an attorney for the prosecuting authority if the discussions did not result in a guilty plea or they resulted in a later-withdrawn guilty plea.

(b) Exceptions. The court may admit a statement described in Rule 410(a)(3) or (4):

(1) in any proceeding in which another statement made during the same plea or plea discussions has been introduced, if in fairness the statements ought to be considered together; or

(2) in a criminal proceeding for perjury or false statement, if the defendant made the statement under oath, on the record, and with counsel present.

Discussion

1.   Unwithdrawn Guilty Pleas

A plea of guilty poses several evidentiary issues. It is a statement made by the declarant other than while testifying at the present trial or hearing. If it is offered to prove the truth of the matter asserted (the declarant's guilt of the crime), the person who entered the plea is a party in the present case, and if it is offered into evidence against that party, it constitutes a party admission pursuant to Rule

801(d)(2)(A). Otherwise, the plea may be inadmissible hearsay. Even if the plea is not inadmissible hearsay, it might be excluded under Rule 410.

Guilty pleas are highly probative of the truth. This is because guilty pleas can carry significant consequences for the person, including, of course, imprisonment. Thus, assuming fair trial procedures, it is unlikely that a person will choose to plead guilty unless there is a clear factual basis for the plea. In fact, a court is not permitted to accept a plea of guilty absent such a basis. Fed. R. Crim. P. 11(f). Before accepting a plea, the court must also ensure that the defendant understands such important matters as the nature of the charge, possible penalties, the right to counsel, the right to plead not guilty or nolo contendere, the right to jury trial, the right to examine and cross-examine trial witnesses, the right against compelled self-incrimination, and, if the plea agreement so provides, waiver of the right to appeal or to mount a collateral attack on the conviction. Fed. R. Crim. P. 11(c). The court must also ensure that the plea was entered voluntarily. Fed. R. Crim. P. 11(d).

Because of all these protections, it is safe to assume that a criminal defendant will not enter a plea of guilty unless he knows there is a significant chance he will be convicted at trial. If a defendant then enters such a plea and does not later withdraw it, his conduct is highly probative of guilt. Thus, it would be foolish for courts in subsequent proceedings to exclude evidence of that plea if offered to prove guilt. This is true even though there is as much of a social interest in the settlement of criminal cases as in the settlement of civil cases. In either situation, the resources of our justice system could not support the trial of every case. But there are many incentives for guilty parties to plead guilty, especially when presented with the opportunity to plead to a lesser charge. Thus, the settlement rate might not be reduced severely by allowing evidence of a guilty plea to be used against the pleader in a later proceeding. For these reasons, a guilty plea that was never withdrawn may be admitted against the pleader in a later action. Rule 410 excludes guilty pleas only if they were withdrawn before judgment was entered on that plea.

Does the reasoning limiting the scope of Rule 410 apply to all types of crimes? There is little question that a guilty plea that was never withdrawn is highly probative of guilt if the offense in question is a serious crime such as a felony and even some misdemeanors. But what about offenses like traffic violations? Doesn't common experience suggest that many people plead guilty to such violations (often simply by paying a fine) even if they believe themselves innocent? Often the time, effort, and expense of pleading not guilty and going to trial vastly outweigh a person's interest in avoiding false convictions. Though the issue will not arise frequently in the federal courts, many states accept this argument and refuse to allow the later use of evidence that a person charged with a traffic infraction chose to pay the fine rather than contest the violation. Even so, a categorical rule either way probably is not justified. A person who pays a traffic fine without contest following an injury-causing accident may well understand that the injured party is likely to bring a civil action for damages. In that situation, payment of a fine is highly probative of guilt. Regardless of the strength of the rationale behind the rule as applied to certain types of guilty pleas, Rule 410 treats all alike: All are admissible against the person who entered the plea, as long as the person did not withdraw the plea.

2.   Withdrawn Guilty Pleas[1]

For many reasons, criminal defendants who initially enter guilty pleas sometimes change their minds and wish to withdraw the pleas and go to trial. Aware of the constitutional implications of denying a trial to a person who no longer wishes to plead guilty, the courts generally grant motions to withdraw guilty pleas. The question then arises: Is the government entitled to prove that the defendant first pleaded guilty to the charge? The answer, supplied by Rule 410, is no. This is a sensible answer. If a court permitted the government to offer such damning evidence, it would severely disadvantage a defendant who wishes to put the government to its proof. Rather than so severely burdening a defendant, the rule ensures that the defendant is given a fresh start.

3.   Pleas of Nolo Contendere

The federal courts and a majority of jurisdictions also permit a criminal defendant to plead "nolo contendere," which literally means "I will not contest it." Like the guilty plea, the nolo plea amounts to an admission of all essential elements of the charge, and is thus a party admission when offered to prove those elements. Moreover, the consequences of entering a nolo plea are similar to those attending a guilty plea: A conviction based on a nolo plea subjects the person to the same penalties as a guilty plea. Most of the protections afforded a defendant pleading guilty also apply to the entry of a nolo plea. There is, however, one important difference between the two: In return for the nolo plea, the government gives up the right to use the plea against the defendant in any subsequent proceeding. And it is this difference that makes the nolo plea attractive to the criminal defendant.

Because the nolo plea does not create evidence that may be used in a subsequent proceeding, Rule 410 prohibits its use against the defendant. For evidentiary purposes, this is the primary difference between nolo pleas and pleas of guilty.

4.   Statements Made at Hearing to Enter Plea

Rule 410 also excludes "a statement about either of those pleas made during a proceeding under Federal Rule of Criminal Procedure 11 or a comparable state procedure. . . ." This part of the rule also is intended to protect defendants from adverse consequences should they be permitted to plead nolo contendere or to withdraw a guilty plea. Recall that before it may accept a guilty plea, the court must determine that there is a factual basis for the plea. Normally, the court satisfies this requirement by asking the defendant about the facts. Since the defendant has decided to plead guilty he cannot avoid making self-incriminating statements. But if the court later permits the defendant to withdraw the guilty plea, giving the defendant a fresh start requires also denying the government the opportunity to use against the defendant the statements he made at a

---

1. The present discussion applies as well to withdrawn pleas of nolo contendere. Because even an unwithdrawn nolo plea is inadmissible against the person who entered the plea, it is not necessary to discuss such situations separately.

formal plea hearing. The rule therefore forbids the government to use these statements.

The same result holds true for statements made during a hearing to enter a nolo contendere plea. Holding otherwise would effectively deny the defendant the advantages otherwise offered by the nolo plea. To ensure that the consequences of the nolo plea stop at the case in which the plea is entered, it is necessary also to prevent statements made during the hearing from being used against the defendant in any later case. This rule applies, of course, whether the nolo plea was withdrawn at a later time or not.

5. Statements Made in the Course of Plea Bargaining

Rule 410(a)(4) provides for exclusion of "a statement made during plea discussions with an attorney for the prosecuting authority if the discussions did not result in a guilty plea or they resulted in a later-withdrawn guilty plea." The purpose of this rule is to promote plea bargaining. That process requires negotiation, and criminal defendants are more likely to enter into serious negotiations if they know that statements they make in connection with those negotiations will not be admissible against them at a later time.

The rule, however, is not absolute. Note, first, that the statement must have been made during discussion with "an attorney for the prosecuting authority." This limitation can be important. Statements made to the police, for example, are not protected. Thus, a suspect who tries to plea bargain with police by offering information in exchange for leniency will find that her statements are not protected from later use against her. (This assumes, of course, that the police have advised the suspect of her Miranda rights if those rights have attached.) At the same time, the mere fact that a police officer is present during the suspect's discussions with a prosecutor will not remove the rule's protection. In addition, there may be situations in which a police officer or other official conducts plea discussions as an agent of the prosecutor. In those cases, the rule should also protect the discussions. But the basic message of this part of the rule is clear: Criminal defense attorneys should advise their clients to refrain from discussions with the police or other authorities concerning the case. Indeed, it makes sense to advise clients to avoid discussing the case with anybody except when defense counsel is present.

6. Exceptions to Rule Excluding Statements Made in Formal Plea Hearings or During Plea Bargaining

There are a number of situations in which statements made during a plea hearing or in the course of plea bargaining will be admissible against the defendant. The rule provides that such statements are admissible "(b)(1) in any proceeding in which another statement made during the same plea or plea discussions has been introduced, if in fairness both statements ought to be considered together; or (b)(2) in a criminal proceeding for perjury or false statement, if the defendant made the statement under oath, on the record, and in the presence of counsel."

The first exception is a specialized application of the "completeness" principle exemplified by Rule 106.[2] The goal is to avoid misleading the fact-finder. If, for example, the defendant offers one statement made during plea bargaining, and the court finds that another statement is necessary to clarify the meaning of the first statement, the court will permit the government to introduce the other statement.

The second exception applies to situations in which the defendant is later prosecuted for perjury or false statement. A typical scenario would be as follows:

Following negotiations with the prosecutor, a murder defendant agrees to plead guilty and provide information about Zed, another person involved in the crime, all in exchange for leniency. During the hearing for entry of his plea, the defendant testifies under oath, on the record, and in the presence of his counsel. In his testimony, defendant minimizes his role in the murder and claims that Zed played the major role in the crime. Later, the government comes to believe that defendant testified falsely at the plea hearing, and charges defendant with perjury.

Under the rule, the statements made at the plea hearing would be admissible against him. This result makes good sense. For one thing, defendant most likely did not act in good faith to carry out his obligations under the plea deal. It seems fair under such circumstances to permit the government to use defendant's statements at the perjury trial. If the rule did not contain this exception, a plea bargaining defendant would have no incentive to be truthful in negotiating or carrying out his end of the bargain. In addition, were the rule to deny the government that right, it would be virtually impossible to bring a perjury action against the defendant because the very basis of the perjury — the perjurious testimony itself — would not be admissible. The statement, moreover, is not hearsay because it constitutes words of independent legal significance. That is, the statement is not being offered to prove the truth of the matters asserted, but rather as the act of committing perjury itself. Thus, it is not *evidence* of anything, but is instead the thing at issue (the act of committing perjury).

7. Impeachment Use of Plea Evidence

Unlike Rules 407, 408, and 409, Rule 410 does not focus on the purpose for which the evidence is offered. It is, instead, *party-oriented*, forbidding the use of the evidence against a specified party (the criminal defendant) regardless of the purpose for which that evidence might be offered. As a result, the government may not argue that plea bargaining evidence is admissible when offered for a limited purpose, such as impeachment. Indeed, this was precisely the intent of Congress, which decided after much debate that plea evidence should not be admissible even for impeachment purposes. A typical situation would be one in which a suspect enters into plea negotiations, during the course of which she admits to involvement in the crime. The negotiations fail, the case goes to trial,

---

2. Rule 106 provides: "If a party introduces all or part of a writing or recorded statement, an adverse party may require the introduction, at that time, of any other part — or any other writing or recorded statement — that in fairness ought to be considered at the same time."

and defendant testifies inconsistently with her statements made during plea bargaining. In that situation, Rule 410 forbids the government from using what defendant said during plea bargaining as prior inconsistent statements to impeach her credibility. Not all states follow this approach; some state versions of Rule 410 explicitly permit impeachment use of plea bargaining statements.

8. Waiver of the Rule's Protections

Suppose the prosecutor offers a criminal defendant a deal that calls for defendant to plead guilty to a lesser charge. One of the prosecutor's terms is that, should the deal break down and the case go to trial, any statements the defendant made during the course of plea bargaining will be admissible to impeach her if she testifies at trial inconsistently with those statements. Suppose, further, that the prosecutor states that the inclusion of the waiver term is a "make-or-break" thing; there will be no deal if defendant does not accept that term. If defendant agrees, is the waiver term enforceable? The Supreme Court resolved that question in the following case.

UNITED STATES v. MEZZANATTO
513 U.S. 196 (1995)

Justice THOMAS delivered the opinion of the Court.

Federal Rule of Evidence 410 and Federal Rule of Criminal Procedure 11(e)(6) provide that statements made in the course of plea discussions between a criminal defendant and a prosecutor are inadmissible against the defendant. The court below held that these exclusionary provisions may not be waived by the defendant. We granted certiorari to resolve a conflict among the Courts of Appeals, and we now reverse.

I

[Shuster was arrested by police for having a methamphetamine laboratory at his home. He agreed to cooperate with the police, and set up a meeting with respondent Mezzanatto purportedly to sell him drugs.] On October 17, 1991, respondent and his attorney asked to meet with the prosecutor to discuss the possibility of cooperating with the Government. The prosecutor agreed to meet later that day. At the beginning of the meeting, the prosecutor informed respondent that he had no obligation to talk, but that if he wanted to cooperate he would have to be completely truthful. As a condition to proceeding with the discussion, the prosecutor indicated that respondent would have to agree that any statements he made during the meeting could be used to impeach any contradictory testimony he might give at trial if the case proceeded that far. Respondent conferred with his counsel and agreed to proceed under the prosecutor's terms.

Respondent then admitted knowing that the package he had attempted to sell to the undercover police officer contained methamphetamine, but insisted that he had dealt only in "ounce" quantities of methamphetamine prior to his arrest. Initially, respondent also claimed that he was acting merely as a broker for Shuster and did not know that Shuster was manufacturing methamphetamine at his residence, but he later conceded that he knew about Shuster's laboratory. Respondent attempted to minimize his role in Shuster's operation by claiming that he had not visited Shuster's residence for at least a week before his arrest. At this point, the Government confronted respondent with surveillance evidence showing that his car was on Shuster's property the day before the arrest, and terminated the meeting on the basis of respondent's failure to provide completely truthful information.

Respondent eventually was tried on the methamphetamine charge and took the stand in his own defense. He maintained that he was not involved in methamphetamine trafficking and that he had thought Shuster used his home laboratory to manufacture plastic explosives for the CIA. He also denied knowing that the package he delivered to the undercover officer contained methamphetamine. Over defense counsel's objection, the prosecutor cross-examined respondent about the inconsistent statements he had made during the October 17 meeting. Respondent denied having made certain statements, and the prosecutor called one of the agents who had attended the meeting to recount the prior statements. The jury found respondent guilty, and the District Court sentenced him to 170 months in prison. . . .

II

Federal Rule of Evidence 410 and Federal Rule of Criminal Procedure 11(e)(6) (Rules or plea-statement Rules) are substantively identical. . . .

The Ninth Circuit noted that these Rules are subject to only two express exceptions, neither of which says anything about waiver, and thus concluded that Congress must have meant to preclude waiver agreements such as respondent's. . . .

The Ninth Circuit's analysis is directly contrary to the approach we have taken in the context of a broad array of constitutional and statutory provisions. Rather than deeming waiver presumptively unavailable absent some sort of express enabling clause, we instead have adhered to the opposite presumption. A criminal defendant may knowingly and voluntarily waive many of the most fundamental protections afforded by the Constitution. Likewise, absent some affirmative indication of Congress' intent to preclude waiver, we have presumed that statutory provisions are subject to waiver by voluntary agreement of the parties.

Our cases interpreting the Federal Rules of Criminal Procedure are consistent with this approach. The provisions of those Rules are presumptively waivable, though an express waiver clause may suggest that Congress intended to occupy the field and to preclude waiver under other, unstated circumstances.

The presumption of waivability has found specific application in the context of evidentiary rules. Absent some "overriding procedural consideration that prevents enforcement of the contract," courts have held that agreements to waive evidentiary rules are generally enforceable even over a party's subsequent objections. Courts have "liberally enforced" agreements to waive various exclusionary rules of evidence. Thus, at the time of the adoption of the Federal Rules of Evidence, agreements as to the admissibility of documentary evidence were routinely enforced and held to preclude subsequent objections as to authenticity. And although hearsay is inadmissible except under certain specific exceptions, we have held that agreements to waive hearsay objections are enforceable.

Indeed, evidentiary stipulations are a valuable and integral part of everyday trial practice. Prior to trial, parties often agree in writing to the admission of otherwise objectionable evidence, either in exchange for stipulations from opposing counsel or for other strategic purposes. Both the Federal Rules of Civil Procedure and the Federal Rules of Criminal Procedure appear to contemplate that the parties will enter into evidentiary agreements during a pretrial conference. During the course of trial, parties frequently decide to waive evidentiary objections, and such tactics are routinely honored by trial judges.

III

Because the plea-statement Rules were enacted against a background presumption that legal rights generally, and evidentiary provisions specifically, are subject to waiver by voluntary agreement of the parties, we will not interpret Congress' silence as an implicit rejection of waivability. Respondent bears the responsibility of identifying some affirmative basis for concluding that the plea-statement Rules depart from the presumption of waivability.

Respondent offers three potential bases for concluding that the Rules should be placed beyond the control of the parties. We find none of them persuasive.

A

Respondent first suggests that the plea-statement Rules establish a "guarantee [to] fair procedure" that cannot be waived. We agree with respondent's basic premise: There may be some evidentiary provisions that are so fundamental to the reliability of the factfinding process that they may never be waived without irreparably "discredit[ing] the federal courts." But enforcement of agreements like respondent's plainly will not have that effect. The admission of plea statements for impeachment purposes *enhances* the truth-seeking function of trials and will result in more accurate verdicts. Under any view of the evidence, the defendant has made a false statement, either to the prosecutor during the plea discussion or to the jury at trial; making the jury aware of the inconsistency will tend to increase the reliability of the verdict without risking institutional harm to the federal courts.

Respondent nevertheless urges that the plea-statement Rules are analogous to Federal Rule of Criminal Procedure 24(c), which provides that "[a]n alternate juror who does not replace a regular juror shall be discharged after the jury retires to consider its verdict." Justice Kennedy's concurrence in United States v. Olano, 507 U.S. 725, 741, 113 S. Ct. 1770, 1781, 123 L. Ed. 2d 508 (1993), suggested that the guarantees of Rule 24(c) may never be waived by an agreement to permit alternate jurors to sit in on jury deliberations, and respondent asks us to extend that logic to the plea-statement Rules. But even if we assume that the requirements of Rule 24(c) are "the product of a judgment that our jury system should be given a stable and constant structure, one that cannot be varied by a court with or without the consent of the parties," the plea-statement Rules plainly do not satisfy this standard. Rules 410 and 11(e)(6) "creat[e], in effect, a privilege of the defendant," and, like other evidentiary privileges, this one may be waived or varied at the defendant's request. The Rules provide that statements made in the course of plea discussions are inadmissible "against" the defendant, and thus leave open the possibility that a defendant may offer such statements into evidence for his own tactical advantage. Indeed, the Rules contemplate this result in permitting admission of statements made "in any proceeding wherein another statement made in the course of the same . . . plea discussions *has been introduced* and the statement ought in fairness be considered contemporaneously with it." Thus, the plea-statement Rules expressly contemplate a degree of party control that is consonant with the background presumption of waivability.

B

Respondent also contends that waiver is fundamentally inconsistent with the Rules' goal of encouraging voluntary settlement. The Ninth Circuit expressed similar concerns, noting that Rules 410 and 11(e)(6) "aid in obtaining th[e] cooperation" that is often necessary to identify and prosecute the leaders of a criminal conspiracy and that waiver of the protections of the Rules "could easily have a chilling effect on the entire plea bargaining process." According to the Ninth Circuit, the plea-statement Rules "permit the plea bargainer to maximize what he has 'to sell'" by preserving "the ability to withdraw from the bargain proposed by the prosecutor without being harmed by any of his statements made in the course of an aborted plea bargaining session."

We need not decide whether and under what circumstances substantial "public policy" interests may permit the inference that Congress intended to override the presumption of waivability, for in this case is no basis for concluding that waiver will interfere with the Rules' goal of encouraging plea bargaining. The court below focused entirely on the *defendant's* incentives and completely ignored the other essential party to the transaction: the prosecutor. Thus, although the availability of waiver may discourage some defendants from negotiating, it is also true that prosecutors may be unwilling to proceed without it.

Prosecutors may be especially reluctant to negotiate without a waiver agreement during the early stages of a criminal investigation, when prosecutors are searching for leads and suspects may be willing to offer information in exchange for some form of immunity or leniency in sentencing. In this "cooperation" context, prosecutors face "painfully delicate" choices as to "whether to proceed and prosecute those suspects against whom the already produced evidence makes a case or whether to extend leniency or full immunity to some suspects in order to procure testimony against other, more dangerous suspects against whom existing evidence is flimsy or nonexistent." Because prosecutors have limited resources and must be able to answer "sensitive questions about the credibility of the testimony" they receive before entering into any sort of cooperation agreement, prosecutors may condition cooperation discussions on an agreement that the testimony provided may be used for impeachment purposes. If prosecutors were precluded from securing such agreements, they might well decline to enter into cooperation discussions in the first place and might never take this potential first step toward a plea bargain.

Indeed, as a logical matter, it simply makes no sense to conclude that mutual settlement will be encouraged by precluding negotiation over an issue that may be particularly important to one of the parties to the transaction. A sounder way to encourage settlement is to permit the interested parties to enter into knowing and voluntary negotiations without any arbitrary limits on their bargaining chips. To use the Ninth Circuit's metaphor, if the prosecutor is interested in "buying" the reliability assurance that accompanies a waiver agreement, then precluding waiver can only stifle the market for plea bargains. A defendant can "maximize" what he has to "sell" only if he is permitted to offer what the prosecutor is most interested in buying. And while it is certainly true that prosecutors often need help from the small fish in a conspiracy in order to catch the big ones, that is no reason to preclude waiver altogether. If prosecutors decide that certain crucial information will be gained only by preserving the inadmissibility of plea statements, they will agree to leave intact the exclusionary provisions of the plea-statement Rules.

In sum, there is no reason to believe that allowing negotiation as to waiver of the plea-statement Rules will bring plea bargaining to a grinding halt; it may well have the opposite effect. Respondent's unfounded policy argument thus provides no basis for concluding that Congress intended to prevent criminal defendants from offering to waive the plea-statement Rules during plea negotiation.

c

Finally, respondent contends that waiver agreements should be forbidden because they invite prosecutorial overreaching and abuse. Respondent asserts that there is a "gross disparity" in the relative bargaining power of the parties to a plea agreement and suggests that a waiver agreement is "inherently unfair and coercive." Because the prosecutor retains the discretion to "reward defendants for their substantial assistance" under the Sentencing Guidelines, respondent argues that defendants face an "'incredible dilemma'" when they are asked to accept waiver as the price of entering plea discussions.

The dilemma flagged by respondent is indistinguishable from any of a number of difficult choices that criminal defendants face every day. The plea bargaining process necessarily exerts pressure on defendants to plead guilty and to abandon a series of fundamental rights, but we have repeatedly held that the government "may encourage a guilty plea by offering substantial benefits in return for the plea." "While confronting a defendant with the risk of more severe punishment clearly may have a 'discouraging effect on the defendant's assertion of his trial rights, the imposition of these difficult choices [is] an inevitable' — and permissible — 'attribute of any legitimate system which tolerates and encourages the negotiation of pleas.'"

The mere potential for abuse of prosecutorial bargaining power is an insufficient basis for foreclosing negotiation altogether. "Rather, tradition and experience justify our belief that the great majority of prosecutors will be faithful to their duty." Thus, although some waiver agreements "may not be the product of an informed and voluntary decision," this possibility "does not justify invalidating *all* such agreements." Instead, the appropriate response to respondent's predictions of abuse is to permit case-by-case inquiries into whether waiver agreements are the product of fraud or coercion. We hold that absent some affirmative indication that the agreement was entered into unknowingly or involuntarily, an agreement to waive the exclusionary provisions of the plea-statement Rules is valid and enforceable.

IV

Respondent conferred with his lawyer after the prosecutor proposed waiver as a condition of proceeding with the plea discussion, and he has never complained that he entered into the waiver agreement at issue unknowingly or involuntarily. The Ninth Circuit's decision was based on its *per se* rejection of waiver of the plea-statement Rules. Accordingly, the judgment of the Court of Appeals is reversed.

It is so ordered.

[The concurring opinion of Justice Ginsburg, joined by Justices O'Connor and Breyer, and the dissenting opinion of Justice Souter, joined by Justice Stevens, are omitted.]

———————————

As might have been expected, the practice of obtaining waivers of Rule 410's protections has increased dramatically since the Court decided *Mezzanatto*. Today, it is standard practice in many jurisdictions to condition plea agreements on such waivers.

Further Reading: Brian M. Barkey, Comment, *Relevancy and Its Limits in the Proposed Federal Rules of Evidence*, 16 Wayne L. Rev. 167 (1969); Michael S. Gershowitz, *Waiver of the Plea-Statement Rules*, 86 J. Crim. L. & Criminology 1439 (1996); Eric Rasmusen, Mezzanatto *and the Economics of Self-Incrimination*, 19 Cardozo L. Rev. 1541 (1998); Daniel C. Richman, *Bargaining about Future Jeopardy*, 48 Vand. L. Rev. 1181 (1996).

Questions for Classroom Discussion

1. Prosecution of Defendant for possession of narcotics with intent to distribute. At trial, the prosecution wishes to present evidence that after being read her Miranda rights, and while she was being transported to the police station after her arrest, Defendant said to one of the officers, "Can't we work something out? I was only going to sell enough of the stuff to make sure I could pay the rent." Defendant objects. How should the court rule?

2. Prosecution of Defendant and Zed for murder. At trial, the prosecution wishes to present evidence that while in custody, during a meeting with the prosecutor, Defendant admitted being involved and said she would testify that Zed was the "trigger man" if the prosecutor would drop the charges against her. Defendant and Zed both object to the testimony. How should the court rule?

3. Same case as in Question 2. Assume, however, that Defendant's statement was made to police rather than to a prosecutor. Both Defendant and Zed object. How should the court rule?

4. Prosecution of Defendant for bank robbery. The perpetrator approached a teller with a realistic-looking gun fashioned from a large bar of soap, told the teller that he was the "Mr. Clean Bandit," and ordered the teller to place all the small bills from her cash drawer into the laundry sack he was carrying. After the teller did this, the perpetrator sprayed her with Mr. Clean and fled. Defendant denies involvement. To prove Defendant's guilt, the prosecution offers evidence that a year earlier, Defendant had pled guilty to a bank robbery committed in exactly the same way. That plea was never withdrawn. Defendant objects. How should the court rule?

5. Same case as in Question 4. Assume, however, that in the earlier case, Defendant pleaded nolo contendere instead of guilty. The prosecution wishes to offer evidence of the nolo plea to prove Defendant's guilt in the present case. Defendant objects. How should the court rule?

6. Prosecution of Defendant for bank robbery. At a hearing before the judge, the court accepts Defendant's guilty plea after being satisfied that there is a factual basis for the plea and that Defendant understands all the rights she is giving up by pleading guilty. Before the sentencing hearing, Defendant changes her mind and moves to withdraw the guilty plea and substitute a plea of not guilty. The court agrees, and the case goes to trial. At trial, the prosecutor wishes to offer evidence that Defendant first pled guilty at a hearing at which all her rights were explained and the court satisfied itself that there was sufficient factual support for the plea. Defendant objects. How should the court rule?

7. After Defendant's arrest for the crime of murder, Defendant worked out a plea bargain, the terms of which required him to give a full statement of facts at his plea hearing. At the hearing, the court accepted Defendant's guilty plea to a lesser charge after hearing Defendant's statement, which named Zed as also involved in the crime. Later, upon investigating Zed, the prosecution learned that Zed was not involved in the crime. Defendant had lied at the plea hearing about Zed's involvement. Defendant is now being prosecuted for perjury, and the prosecution wishes to put in evidence the statement Defendant gave at the plea hearing. Defendant objects. How should the court rule?

8. Prosecution of Defendant for murder. Earlier, Defendant pled guilty in exchange for leniency in sentencing. As a condition of entering into the agreement, the prosecutor stated that Defendant would have to waive the right not to have statements made during plea bargaining admitted against her if she later withdrew her plea and testified at trial inconsistently with those statements. Defendant agreed to the term. Later, Defendant asks the court to allow her to withdraw the plea and enter a plea of not guilty. The court grants

(continued)

Defendant's motion. At trial, Defendant testifies inconsistently with a statement made during plea negotiations, and the government offers her prior statement to impeach Defendant. Defendant objects. How should the court rule?

9. Do you agree with the Supreme Court's analysis in *Mezzanatto*? Will the government's ability to demand waiver of protection for plea bargaining statements in the event the deal falls through or defendant later violates the terms of the agreement have a significant chilling effect on plea negotiations? To what extent may a criminal defendant waive other protections of Rule 410? For example, would the government be permitted to condition its acceptance of a guilty plea to a lesser charge on the defendant's agreement that the plea would be admissible at trial if it was later withdrawn? Could the government condition acceptance of a plea on the defendant's agreement that he would never seek to withdraw the plea?

E.   EVIDENCE OF LIABILITY INSURANCE

FED. R. EVID. 411.   LIABILITY INSURANCE

Evidence that a person was or was not insured against liability is not admissible to prove whether the person acted negligently or otherwise wrongfully. But the court may admit this evidence for another purpose, such as proving a witness's bias or prejudice or proving agency, ownership, or control.

Discussion

1.   *Rationale for the Rule*

Generally speaking, people do not act less carefully simply because they are covered by liability insurance. It is unlikely that a driver who speeds past us while engaged in personal grooming and dialing a cell phone is thinking, "I'm insured." That person will probably drive recklessly whether insured or not. This being the case, the fact that at some point in the past, a person has obtained a policy of liability insurance is most likely irrelevant on the issue whether the person acted with care on the occasion in question. Rule 411 therefore can be justified, in part, on the basis that the evidence is irrelevant.[3]

---

3. One might even argue that the act of obtaining liability insurance demonstrates a person's care and concern for others, something less likely to be exhibited by a careless driver. Thus, a person who obtains liability insurance might well be more careful than one who does not.

In addition, unlike the conduct governed by the other rules discussed in this chapter, the act of obtaining liability insurance occurs *before* (sometimes long before) the events at issue in the case. For example, the making of a compromise offer occurs after the events at issue and logically can be motivated by a person's feelings of responsibility. The same is true of a party's plea bargaining efforts or the undertaking of subsequent remedial measures. When the conduct occurs before the accident or event that is the subject of litigation, as is the case when the defendant-to-be obtains liability insurance, it is difficult to see a link to one's feeling of responsibility for the future accident except in the most abstract sense.[4]

The liability insurance rule also can be justified by considerations of social policy and fairness. Encouraging people to obtain policies of liability insurance is one way to help ensure compensation of accident victims. Were liability insurance evidence admissible to prove fault, it is possible that fewer people would obtain the insurance, making compensation of accident victims less likely.[5] Connected with this rationale is the notion that obtaining liability insurance is the right thing to do, and that allowing that act to be used against a person at a later trial is simply unfair. Of course, in many jurisdictions it is illegal to drive without liability insurance. Admitting evidence of liability insurance in such a jurisdiction would have the effect of punishing someone for obeying the law.

Finally, and perhaps most important, the liability insurance rule can be supported by concerns of unfair prejudice. The danger presented by admitting such evidence is not that juries are likely to view liability insurance as an implied recognition of fault. Rather, the concern is that juries might use the existence of insurance as an excuse to compensate an injured victim without regard to the legal merits of her liability claim. While juries may look upon an injured victim of an accident with compassion, they tend not to view insurance companies in a positive light. In addition, insurance companies are often perceived (accurately or not) as having virtually unlimited resources. It is not unreasonable to expect that, if we allowed the fact-finder to know about the defendant's liability insurance policy, the fact-finder would decide the case on a basis other than that of legal responsibility.

Particularly because of the risk of unfair prejudice, counsel should be extremely cautious about offering any evidence of the existence of liability insurance, and about making any statement or argument that even suggests the existence of liability insurance. Though there are some situations in which such evidence is admissible, counsel should be aware that courts tend to apply the rule quite strictly and that a violation can bring not only an admonition to counsel, but even a mistrial. Having to explain that one's own error has resulted in a mistrial, and that the trial will have to be restarted from square one (most likely at a later date) is not a way to engender the client's trust and confidence. If counsel believes that liability insurance evidence might be admissible for a particular purpose, the safest course is to make a motion *in limine* seeking a ruling to that effect.

Of course, none of this makes much sense, and it is foolish to speculate about the motives of a particular person in obtaining liability insurance, particularly given that most states require drivers and others to have such policies.

4. No doubt there are some people who know they are careless drivers and who obtain insurance against liability in the inevitable event of an accident. But even in these cases, general carelessness is not proof of carelessness on the occasion in question, and indeed, such evidence is generally excluded by the character evidence rule, as discussed in Chapter 4.

5. This rationale would carry less weight in the large number of states that require drivers to carry liability insurance.

2. Limited Exclusionary Principle

For the reasons discussed above, Rule 411 and comparable rules in virtually every state forbid a party from presenting evidence of liability insurance to prove negligence or other wrongful conduct. The rule does not, however, require exclusion when the evidence is offered for another purpose. Several permissible uses of insurance evidence are common.

First, when a party contests ownership of or legal responsibility for the instrumentality of the accident or event at issue, evidence that the person had obtained a policy of liability insurance covering that instrumentality is highly probative of ownership or responsibility. Thus, in the case of a pedestrian injured by an automobile driven by Driver and allegedly owned by Owner, evidence that Owner obtained a policy of liability insurance covering the vehicle would contravene her claim that she did not own, or was not responsible for, the vehicle. In fact, under general principles of insurance law, a person may not obtain insurance covering a thing or event unless she has an "insurable interest" in it. If Owner did not own or have legal responsibility for the vehicle, she would not be permitted to take out a liability insurance policy covering it. Similarly, when the car was driven by a person other than the defendant, evidence that defendant carried liability insurance covering the actions of a driver who injured plaintiff would tend to contravene the defendant's claim that the driver was an independent contractor rather than an employee.

A second common use of liability insurance evidence is to prove a witness's bias. Suppose that in an automobile accident case, there is a dispute about the degree of damage sustained to plaintiff's expensive sports car. During its case-in-chief, defendant calls an expert witness to testify that the damage to plaintiff's expensive car was far less significant than plaintiff claims. If defendant's witness is a claims adjuster for defendant's liability insurance company, the witness is likely to be biased and informing the jury of that fact would assist the jury in evaluating credibility. At the same time, this would reveal to the jury that the defendant has liability insurance. Despite the potential for unfair prejudice to the defendant from such revelation, courts tend to hold that the probative value of the evidence on the issue of credibility is sufficiently great to require admission. (Defendant could have avoided this problem by calling an expert not connected with the insurance company, though such an expert might not give testimony as favorable as defendant would like.)

A third permissible use of liability insurance evidence occurs in the context of jury selection. One of the primary functions of that process is to reveal potential bias of jurors, and one source of bias is employment by, or other relatively close connection to, a party. Though most states do not allow direct action against the defendant's liability insurer, the insurer is likely to play a key role in conducting the defense (most likely supplying defendant's representation), and it is entirely possible that the prospective juror will learn during the course of the trial that her employer is involved in the case. That person should not serve as a juror in the case because she might not be able to judge the facts fairly. To a lesser degree, one who holds stock in the defendant's insurance company, or who is herself insured by that company, might harbor a bias in favor of the company. It is even possible that a prospective juror, for some reason, will have a bias against insurance companies in general or this insurance company in particular. In all of these cases, to ensure a fair trial it might be necessary to ask prospective jurors questions that directly or indirectly reveal that defendant carries liability insurance. Courts sometimes allow such questions, but they try to limit the scope and specificity of the questions to minimize potential prejudice. For example, to ensure that no one employed by the defendant's liability insurance company serves on the jury, prospective jurors can be asked to state the name of their employers. This provides the court and parties with the necessary information, but avoids disclosing the existence of liability insurance. It is somewhat more difficult to fashion questions concerning prospective jurors' own liability insurance without revealing that defendant has such insurance, and courts are more reluctant to attempt to do so unless the circumstances clearly warrant it.

The presence of liability insurance often can be revealed in various ways either incidentally or indirectly during the trial. For example, a witness might mention that she gave a statement to defendant's insurance company after the accident, or a witness might reveal that she works for the auto repair shop that fixed the car after receiving a check from the insurance company. Such incidental disclosure is not entirely avoidable, and despite earlier authority that the court was obliged to declare a mistrial when this happens, most courts today hold that a simple jury instruction notifying jurors that they are not to draw any inferences from the mention of insurance will suffice.

One final word about the scope of evidence excluded by Rule 411: Both the language of that provision and our discussion of its rationale make it clear that the rule excludes only *liability* insurance evidence. The rule has no impact on the admissibility of evidence concerning other types of insurance. For example, evidence that the defendant purchased a fire insurance policy shortly before his building burnt down under suspicious circumstances would be relevant to prove motive and Rule 411 would be inapplicable.

Further Reading: Dale W. Broeder, *The University of Chicago Jury Project*, 38 Neb. L. Rev. 744 (1959); Alan Calnan, *The Insurance Exclusionary Rule Revisited: Are Reports of Its Demise Exaggerated?*, 52 Ohio St. L.J. 1177 (1991); Leon Green, *Blindfolding the Jury*, 33 Tex. L. Rev. 157 (1954); Samuel R. Gross, *Make-Believe: The Rules Excluding Evidence of Character and Liability Insurance*, 49 Hast. L.J. 843 (1998); Elizabeth Loftus, *Insurance Advertising and Jury Awards*, 65 A.B.A. J. 68 (1979); J.E. Lyerly, Comment, *Evidence: Revealing the Existence of Defendant's Liability Insurance to the Jury*, 6 Cumb. L. Rev. 123 (1975); Richard A. Pettigrew, Note, *Another Look at That Forbidden Word—Insurance*, 10 U. Fla. L. Rev. 68 (1957); Bernard R. Rapoport, Note, *Evidence: Proper Disclosure During Trial That Defendant Is Insured*, 26 Cornell L.Q. 137 (1940).

Questions for Classroom Discussion

1. Negligence action by Plaintiff against Defendant, the owner of a grocery store, for injuries suffered when Plaintiff fell on the floor of the store's produce section. To prove that Defendant negligently permitted the floor to become slippery, Plaintiff wishes to offer evidence that Defendant was covered by a policy of liability

(continued)

insurance. Defendant objects on *relevance* grounds. How should the court rule?

2. Same case. Assume the court overrules Defendant's relevance objection. Defendant also objects on the ground that the evidence is excluded by Rule 411, the liability insurance rule. How should the court rule?

3. Same case. Defendant claims that the produce section of the store is stocked and maintained by a separate company, and that the company operates as an independent contractor. Plaintiff offers evidence that Defendant maintains a liability insurance policy covering accidents in the produce section caused by such things as slippery floors. Defendant objects on grounds the evidence is excluded by Rule 411. How should the court rule?

4. Same case. Prior to trial, Plaintiff asks the court to permit inquiry of prospective jurors concerning their employment status to learn whether any of these individuals are employed by Defendant's insurance company or by any insurance company. Defendant objects. How should the court rule?

5. Same case. During jury selection, Plaintiff wishes to inquire whether any prospective jurors own stock in Defendant's insurance company or any insurance company. Defendant objects. How should the court rule?

6. Same case. To prove that Plaintiff did not suffer significant injury in the fall, Defendant calls Witness, a physician, who testifies that she examined Plaintiff and found little actual injury. On cross-examination of Witness, Plaintiff wishes to reveal that Witness was hired by Defendant's liability insurer to examine Plaintiff, and that much of Witness's business derives from such referrals. Defendant objects. How should the court rule?

Assessments

1. Harry sues Dice Pizza for injuries he suffered when he was hit by a driver trying to make good on Dice Pizza's 30-minute delivery guarantee. During his case-in-chief, Harry offers evidence that after his accident Dice Pizza changed its delivery guarantee to 45 minutes. The attorney for Dice Pizza objects that this evidence is inadmissible.
   a. The evidence is inadmissible because the change in the guarantee is irrelevant to the issue of whether the driver was negligent

b. The evidence is admissible because it tends to show the 30-minute guarantee was a cause of the accident

c. The evidence is admissible because changing the guarantee is non-assertive conduct that tends to show Dice Pizza's liability

d. The evidence is inadmissible because the change in the guarantee is being offered as tending to prove the Dice Pizza driver was negligent

2. Madonna and Guy are getting a divorce. After several acrimonious meetings between their lawyers, Madonna and Guy agree to meet alone to discuss their differences. During this meeting, Madonna comments, "Guy, you raised my career to the next level." This discussion breaks down. At trial, Guy wants to testify to Madonna's statement as tending to increase the amount of spousal support he should receive (assume Guy's contribution to Madonna's career is relevant for this purpose). Guy's proposed testimony is:
   a. Admissible because Madonna did not say, "Assume, for purposes of our negotiation, that you took my career to the next level"
   b. Hearsay, but admissible under the admissions exception
   c. Inadmissible because the statement was made during settlement discussions
   d. Admissible because it is not hearsay

3. Ralph is involved in an automobile accident. Ralph visits Minnie Driver at the hospital, and offers to pay her medical expenses. As Minnie seemingly dozes off, Ralph muses, "I really should not have been texting." Minnie sues Ralph for negligence. At trial, she seeks to testify about Ralph's offer of payment of her expenses, and about his statement about texting, as tending to prove Ralph was at fault in the accident. Minnie's proposed testimony is:
   a. Inadmissible hearsay
   b. Admissible because Ralph's offer to pay is non-assertive conduct
   c. Ralph's offer to pay Minnie's expenses is inadmissible. However, his statement about texting is admissible non-hearsay evidence
   d. Ralph's statement is admissible under the admissions exception to the hearsay rule

4. Lift Ride Services Company is sued by drivers claiming the company pays less than the minimum wage. Lift's defense is that the minimum wage law does not apply because Lift has no control over its drivers, who are independent contractors. During trial, the drivers offer evidence that Lift requires them to purchase automobile liability insurance. The drivers argue this shows they are Lift employees. The judge should rule that the evidence is:
   a. Admissible as tending to show Lift exercised some control over the drivers
   b. Inadmissible because it is evidence of liability insurance
   c. Inadmissible because it is unfairly prejudicial
   d. Inadmissible because it is irrelevant

(continued)

Answers and Analysis

1. The correct answer is d. Harry is offering evidence of the change in the delivery guarantee as part of his case-in-chief. That makes it clear Harry is offering the change as tending to prove liability, which makes it inadmissible subsequent remedial measure evidence. FRE 407.

2. The correct answer is c. The discussion between Guy and Madonna was part of a negotiation. Madonna made the statement about Guy's assistance during that negotiation, making it inadmissible to prove the "amount of a disputed claim" — in this case how much spousal support Madonna should pay. FRE 408.

3. The correct answer is c. Ralph's offer to pay Minnie's medical expenses is inadmissible to prove negligence. However, his statement that he was texting is admissible because statements made in connection with an offer to pay medical expenses are not excluded. Minnie's testimony is not hearsay because Ralph's statement is being offered against him. FRE 409; 801(d)(2)(A).

4. The correct answer is a. The fact that Lift requires the drivers to carry liability insurance has some tendency to prove that Lift exercises some control over those drivers — an element of an employer-employee relationship. Because the evidence of liability insurance is not being offered as tending to show that Lift or any of its drivers acted negligently, it is admissible. FRE 411.

CHAPTER
6

Examining Witnesses: Attacking and Supporting the Credibility of Witnesses

A. MODE OF WITNESS EXAMINATION

> **FED. R. EVID. 611.   MODE AND ORDER OF EXAMINING WITNESSES AND PRESENTING EVIDENCE**

(a) Control by the Court; Purposes. The court should exercise reasonable control over the mode and order of questioning witnesses and presenting evidence so as to:

  (1) make those procedures effective for determining the truth;

  (2) avoid wasting time; and

  (3) protect witnesses from harassment or undue embarrassment.

(b) Scope of Cross-Examination. Cross-examination should not go beyond the subject matter of the direct examination and matters affecting a witness's credibility. The court may allow inquiry into additional matters as if on direct examination.

(c) Leading Questions. Leading questions should not be used on direct examination except as necessary to develop the witness's testimony. Ordinarily, the court should allow leading questions:

  (1) on cross-examination; and

  (2) when a party calls a hostile witness, an adverse party, or a witness identified with an adverse party.

Discussion

1. Control over Mode and Order of Interrogating Witnesses and Presenting Evidence

Most of the evidence rules we have studied thus far regulate *what* the jury can hear or see. Rule 611(a) gives courts power to regulate *how* the evidence may be presented. During the course of a trial the judge will exercise her powers under

Rule 611(a) more often than she will invoke any other evidence rule. In fact, that rule commands that courts "shall" exercise these powers. The rule makes this command because the trial court's active involvement in regulating the presentation of evidence is essential to achieving the stated goals of the rule — revealing the truth, saving time, and protecting witnesses from abuse. The court's involvement is essential because counsel in an adversary system often are focused on winning, not on the system's goal of getting at the truth.

Rule 611(a) is most commonly employed to regulate the form of counsel's questions. Objections that a question is ambiguous, confusing, or misleading refer to defects that threaten truth in slightly different ways. A question is *ambiguous* or *unintelligible* when it is unclear what facts it seeks to reveal. This defect is often the result of a poorly worded question. As a consequence, the appropriate judicial response usually will be to sustain an objection to the question but give the examiner an opportunity to rephrase her inquiry. A question is *confusing* when it may cause the jury to misconstrue its significance to the case. This may occur, for example, when the subject of the question is only remotely connected to the issues in the case and the question and answer may divert the jury's attention away from those issues. The appropriate judicial response usually will be to sustain the objection to the question and not permit that question to be rephrased because the problem stems from the subject of the inquiry and not just the form of the question. Finally, a question is *misleading* if it mischaracterizes earlier received evidence or in some other manner tricks the witness and the jury into assuming a fact that has not been proven. A common solution is to compel the examining party to restate the question in a form that eliminates its misleading aspects, if that is possible. If it is not possible to restate the question in a non-misleading form, the court may preclude further questions on the subject and strike from the record any answer the witness already may have given.

The objection that a question is *argumentative* is closely related to the objections just mentioned. At the outset, it is important to distinguish between an argumentative question and cross-examination that has a sharp edge. An argumentative question is a question only in form. It is, in substance, an argument because it asserts facts with such a forceful tone it suggests that those facts are established and the answer of the witness is of no consequence. For example: "Isn't it correct that your testimony on direct makes absolutely no sense?" In contrast, even a vigorous cross-examination has as its central object the extraction of answers from the witness. Like a question that assumes facts not in evidence, the danger of an argumentative question is that it is suggestive without evidentiary support and, thus, may be misleading. Further, because argumentative questions are often stated in a manner that ridicules the witness and any testimony contrary to the question's assertion, those questions often unduly harass and embarrass the witness. The appropriate judicial response to an argumentative question is to sustain an objection and permit counsel to rephrase the question to remove its argumentative aspects.

A *compound question* simultaneously poses more than one inquiry and calls for more than one answer. Such a question presents two problems. First, the question might be ambiguous because of its complexity. Second, any answer might be confusing because of uncertainty as to which part of the compound question the witness intended to answer. When a compound question has been posed but not yet answered, the court may respond to an objection by requiring that its component questions be posed separately. When a witness answers a compound question before an objection is raised, the court may require that the witness makes clear which part of the compound question the witness intended to answer. Even where the question leaves room for confusion, the court has discretion under Rule 611(a) to overrule objections on the ground the objecting party has the opportunity to clarify matters on cross-examination.

A question that *assumes facts not in evidence* goes beyond merely mischaracterizing prior evidence; it invents facts not supported by any admitted evidence. When this is done on direct examination with a friendly witness, the danger is that the questions are suggestive to that witness. Thus, the question may also be objectionable under Rule 611(c) (discussed below) on the grounds it is leading. When a question on cross-examination assumes facts not in evidence, there is no objection on the grounds that the question is suggestive to the witness. Rule 611(c) permits cross-examination to be conducted with leading questions, which by definition are suggestive. Rather, the danger on cross-examination is that the question suggests the assumed facts to the jury even if the witness denies them. This is not objectionable as long as the cross-examiner believes in good faith that the assumed fact may be true. On the other hand, once the witness has answered the question by denying the assumed fact, the direct examiner may be entitled to an instruction that the jury should disregard the suggestions contained within the question.

Rule 611(a) also has been used as a basis for precluding questions because they waste time. Thus, the courts have discretion to preclude questions that seek evidence that is said to be *cumulative* in that it goes to facts well established by evidence already admitted. Difficulty results from the fact that witness examination is usually repetitive or cumulative only in a relative sense; while much of the effort may be duplicative, it is rare that a line of questioning has absolutely no prospect of uncovering something new. Thus, the issue courts must decide is whether that point has been reached in witness examination when the probable benefits of further questioning do not justify the time that further questioning will consume.

Similarly, the objection that a question has been *asked and answered* asserts that the examiner is simply repeating a question to which there has already been an adequate response. Usually, the objection is stated when the examiner is repeating a question she herself has asked. Courts are reluctant to sustain this objection when a question posed by one party previously was asked and answered during examination by an opposing party. This is because one of the most effective ways for the cross-examiner to undermine testimony given on direct examination is to ask the same questions that were posed on direct for the purpose of showing inconsistencies, a failure of memory, or as a foundation to delve into additional details that undermine the impact of the direct. Similarly, restatement during redirect examination of a question first posed on cross-examination may give the witness an opportunity to provide explanation and elaboration not permitted the witness by the cross-examiner. While courts have the discretion to preclude questions that have been asked and answered, it is also clear they may permit such questions if there is a reasonable chance that new evidence will be revealed.

Finally, a question is objectionable if it *calls for a narrative answer*. Such a question poses an open-ended inquiry that invites the witness to give a lengthy narrative response. For example: "Tell the jury what you know about the accident." The main problem with such questions is that they give the witness room to say virtually anything, including matters that are irrelevant, unfairly prejudicial, or otherwise inadmissible, without giving the court or the opponent any warning that such a response is forthcoming. For example, "Tell the jury what you know about the accident" might elicit the response, "Well, I know the driver of the Chevy is a convicted child molester." While a court undoubtedly would be willing to strike such an answer, the damage might not be repairable once the jury has heard the prejudicial matter. Conversely, questions that are specific and seek particular bits of information give a warning when objectionable matters are about to be mentioned. For example, "Does the Chevy driver have a criminal record?" gives the opponent a chance to object before the witness ever answers. Note that a question is not objectionable as calling for a narrative just because it asks the witness to give a full description of an event or condition. As long as the question limits the witness in a reasonable way, it will be permissible. Thus the question, "What did the drivers do after they exited their vehicles?" is probably permissible.

2. Scope of Cross-Examination

Rule 611(b) provides that cross-examination should be limited to the subject matter of the direct examination and matters affecting the credibility of witnesses. But this provision grants the judge discretion to "allow inquiry into additional matters as if on direct-examination."

The policy justification for the subject-matter limitation is that it permits the direct examiner to determine the topics on which each of her witnesses will testify, thereby presenting the evidence in an orderly and comprehensible manner. In other words, by limiting cross-examination to the subject matter of the direct, subdivision (b) precludes the cross-examiner from creating diversions and digressions into different topics that might confuse or otherwise unfairly prejudice the jury. In theory, the subject-matter limitation is only a minimal inconvenience to the cross-examiner, who may recall the witness during her case for purposes of exploring new subjects.

Application of the subject-matter limitation is made difficult by the fact that the term *subject matter* is ambiguous. The subject matter of direct examination might be just the specific facts to which the witness testified or could include all the inferences to be derived from those facts, right up to the ultimate issues in the case. Given the ambiguity of the subject-matter standard, courts have significant discretion in deciding how far the cross-examiner may stray from the specifics of the direct examination. Ultimately, the issue under Rule 611(b) is where to draw the lines within the spectrum of relevant subjects so as to promote an orderly and comprehensible presentation of evidence. An appellate court will rarely second-guess a trial court's judgment on this matter.

If the court determines that the cross-examination goes beyond the scope of the direct, the second sentence of Rule 611(b) gives the court discretion to permit the questioning to proceed "as if on direct examination." This means that the cross-examination cannot be conducted with leading questions, in accordance with the rules established by Rule 611(c).

Questions for Classroom Discussion

1. Prosecution of Defendant for bank robbery. At trial, Defendant takes the stand and denies any involvement in the robbery. On cross-examination, the prosecutor asks Defendant to admit that she owed thousands of dollars in gambling debts at the time of the robbery. Defendant objects on the ground that the question goes beyond the scope of the direct examination. How should the court rule?

2. Plaintiff sues Defendant for negligence after the two skateboarders collided on a sidewalk. Plaintiff claims she was skating along when Defendant struck her head-on. Defendant denies this and claims Plaintiff lost control of her skateboard and ran into Defendant. At trial, Plaintiff testifies that Defendant skated into her path. On cross-examination, Defendant asks Plaintiff to admit that this was the first time she had gone skateboarding. Plaintiff objects on the ground the question goes beyond the scope of the direct examination. How should the court rule?

3. Same case as in Question 2. Plaintiff calls Witness, who testifies that she saw Defendant looking backward just before the two skaters collided. On cross-examination, Defendant asks Witness to admit that Plaintiff paid Witness to testify as she did. Plaintiff objects on the ground that the question goes beyond the scope of the direct examination. How should the court rule?

---

3. Leading Questions

Rule 611(c) states that leading questions are usually permissible on cross-examination and impermissible on direct examination. A leading question is a question that suggests the answer. For example, "You ran the red light, didn't you?" and "Isn't it true that you shot the victim?" are leading questions.

The law restricts the use of leading questions because they are suggestive. Suggestive questions can be dangerous when the question might induce a false memory of facts the witness did not perceive. Susceptibility to suggestion may be especially high if counsel posing the leading question prepared the witness for his testimony and the witness is biased in favor of the party represented by that attorney. Accordingly, Rule 611(c) discourages the use of leading questions on direct examination, when it is common for one or both of these circumstances to exist. On the other hand, the risks of suggestion are thought to be slight when the witness seems to have an interest in promoting a version of the facts contrary to that suggested. As a consequence, Rule 611(c) generally permits leading questions on cross-examination, when the witness usually is interested in defending against attack the version of facts described in his direct examination testimony.

For the same reason, Rule 611(c) permits leading questions on direct examination when the witness is adverse or hostile to the direct examiner. Even when the risk of suggestion is real, sometimes it might be outweighed by the fact that, without the aid of suggestion, the witness might be unable, or unwilling, to give important testimony. Thus, Rule 611(c) grants the court discretion to permit leading questions where the witness has a memory failure, is a child, or is an adult with communication or comprehension problems.

Further Reading: Ronald L. Carlson, *Scope of Cross-Examination and the Proposed Federal Rules,* 32 Fed. B.J. 244 (1973); John M. Conley et al., *The Power of Language: Presentation Style in the Courtroom,* 1978 Duke L.J. 1375; Ronan E. Degnan, *Non-Rules Evidence Law: Cross-Examination,* 6 Utah L. Rev. 323 (1959); J. Alexander Tanford, *Keeping Cross-Examination Under Control,* 18 Am. J. Trial Advoc. 245 (1994).

Questions for Classroom Discussion

Following is a portion of a transcript in a divorce case in which Wife, the plaintiff, seeks a divorce based on the alleged adultery and acts of mental cruelty of Husband, the defendant. She seeks substantial alimony and child support. Does the judge correctly rule on the objections? What other objections could have been made?

By the Court: Plaintiff may call its first witness.

      P: Thank you, Your Honor. Plaintiff calls Husband. [Husband is duly sworn and takes the stand.]

      P: Where do you live?

      H: I live at 123 Main Street.

      P: Isn't it true that you live there with a certain Ms. Fifi LaRue?

      D: Objection, leading.

By the Court: Overruled. The witness will answer the question.

      H: Yes, we both reside at that address.

      P: In fact, you and Ms. LaRue are having an affair, correct?

      H: No. We sleep in separate bedrooms.

      P: You expect the jury to believe that?

      H: It's the truth.

      P: You started your affair with Ms. LaRue the day after you had a fight with your wife during which you called her a fat pig and struck her in the face, correct?

      H: I never struck my wife. We got into an argument and shoved each other.

      P: No further questions.

By the Court:	Cross-examination?
D:	Yes, thank you, Your Honor. Mr. Husband, the day after you had the argument with your wife, did you send her a bouquet of roses?
P:	Objection, leading, assumes facts not in evidence.
By the Court:	Overruled. The witness may answer.
H:	Yes, and a very nice box of chocolates.
D:	And she then called you and said the argument was all her fault, right?
P:	That's leading and hearsay.
By the Court:	It is leading but not hearsay. Rephrase the question.
D:	What did she tell you?
H:	She said she was sorry for starting the argument.
D:	Are you having an affair with Ms. LaRue?
P:	Objection, asked and answered.
By the Court:	Overruled. You may answer.
H:	Absolutely not.
D:	One further question. How much is your monthly income?
H:	Zero. I just lost my job.
D:	Nothing further, Your Honor.
By the Court:	Any redirect?
P:	Just one question. Did you call your wife a fat pig before or after you struck her?
D:	Objection, that's misleading, Your Honor.
By the Court:	Sustained.
P:	Nothing further, Your Honor.

B. IMPEACHMENT: INTRODUCTION

When all the witnesses to the event at issue tell the same story, the case usually will be disposed of through agreement of the parties or by pretrial motion. Cases go to trial when the witnesses tell conflicting stories. This means that the winner is often the party whose witnesses are the most convincing. Thus, the fact-finder's evaluation of witness credibility is crucial.

Part of counsel's role in examining witnesses is to help the fact-finder perform this evaluation. One way to do this involves presenting evidence concerning a witness's credibility. Other ways jurors evaluate credibility are not the subject of formal testimony, but are based only on their common-sense judgment of what they see and hear in the courtroom.

Consider the following list of ways in which a witness's credibility can be attacked or supported. While this is a section from the California Evidence Code, it reflects practice in the federal courts and the vast majority of states.

> ### CAL. EVID. CODE § 780. TESTIMONY; PROOF OF TRUTHFULNESS; CONSIDERATIONS

Except as otherwise provided by statute, the court or jury may consider in determining the credibility of a witness any matter that has any tendency in reason to prove or disprove the truthfulness of his testimony at the hearing, including but not limited to any of the following:

(a) His demeanor while testifying and the manner in which he testifies.

(b) The character of his testimony.

(c) The extent of his capacity to perceive, to recollect, or to communicate any matter about which he testifies.

(d) The extent of his opportunity to perceive any matter about which he testifies.

(e) His character for honesty or veracity or their opposites.

(f) The existence or nonexistence of a bias, interest, or other motive.

(g) A statement previously made by him that is consistent with his testimony at the hearing.

(h) A statement made by him that is inconsistent with any part of his testimony at the hearing.

(i) The existence or nonexistence of any fact testified to by him.

(j) His attitude toward the action in which he testifies or toward the giving of testimony.

(k) His admission of untruthfulness.

Some of the credibility factors mentioned in this statute require the presentation of evidence. For example, to contradict a witness (as implied by item (i)), it is almost always necessary to introduce evidence to prove the contradictory fact. Similarly, a witness's bias, interest, or other motive (item (f)) normally must be revealed through cross-examination of the witness or the presentation of another witness's testimony.

Other credibility factors are brought to the jury's attention without the formal presentation of evidence. For example, the jury's observation of witness demeanor (item (a)) helps the jury evaluate credibility, and the way in which a witness presents herself in the courtroom can reveal a good deal about her attitude toward the case (item (j)), which in turn suggests what weight should be given to her testimony. Further, simply evaluating the inherent *plausibility* of testimony in light of what fact-finders know from experience is a good way to judge the value of testimony.

The effort to cast doubt on the credibility of witnesses is called "impeachment." Black's Law Dictionary defines witness impeachment as "call[ing] in question the veracity of a witness, by means of evidence adduced for such purpose, or the adducing of proof that a witness is unworthy of belief." Evidence also may be offered to support the credibility of a witness whose testimony has been attacked. We use the terms *supporting* and *rehabilitating* interchangeably to refer to this process.

Students often find the law regulating impeaching and supporting the credibility of a witness to be quite complicated and confusing. It need not be so. As we have seen throughout this book, all evidence issues can be analyzed by following these steps: Identify the evidence, ask what it is offered to prove, determine its relevance for that purpose, and then apply the rules governing admission for that purpose. This approach works for credibility evidence just as it works for other evidence issues. Here is a specialized set of questions that adapts this approach to evidence of witness credibility:

1.   What is the evidence?
2.   Is it offered to support the credibility of a witness? If so, has credibility been attacked?
3.   Is it offered to impeach the credibility of a witness? If so, determine the method of impeachment and ask, is the evidence relevant and admissible under the law governing this method? To determine its relevance, apply the principle of Rule 401. To determine its admissibility, ask:
    a.   Does the law for the method in question require that proof of the impeaching facts be elicited during cross-examination of the witness being impeached, or does that law permit proof from other sources (so-called extrinsic evidence)?
    b.   Are all other foundational requirements for this method of impeachment satisfied?
4.   Would admission of the evidence violate any other rules, such as Rule 403?

This part of the chapter begins with the general question of who may impeach a witness, then moves to a brief examination of methods of witness impeachment or support that are not governed by specific rules. The remaining sections of the chapter examine the specific rule-based methods for impeaching or supporting witness credibility.

Before we begin, two more points: First, Article VI, the section of the Federal Rules of Evidence dealing with witness credibility, is short and incomplete. A number of common law rules governing specific methods of impeachment and support are not mentioned at all. This gap in the Federal Rules leaves open a key question: Did the drafters intend to wipe out all common law rules not specifically mentioned, did they intend to retain them, or did they intend to leave the question open for future development of the law "in the light of reason and experience"? The answer is, in the absence of explicit mention of particular common law rules, the drafters probably intended the courts to reach consensus by application of the same common law process that led to the development of the common law rules in the first place. As we will see, in many cases in which the Federal Rules are silent, the courts have opted to retain the preexisting common law.

Second, a number of impeachment methods, including impeachment by contradiction, impeachment by acts evidencing untruthfulness, and impeachment by prior inconsistent statement, limit the admissibility of something called "extrinsic evidence." As we will see, impeachment evidence is "extrinsic" if it comes from any source other than the mouth of the witness who is the target of impeachment while that witness is testifying in the proceeding in which the impeachment is attempted. Thus, anything the witness says during her direct, cross, or redirect examination would not be considered extrinsic evidence. But a statement of that witness at any other time, such as in a deposition, would be extrinsic evidence. The testimony of another witness also would be extrinsic evidence, and the same would usually be true for any documentary evidence offered to impeach.

Further Reading: Mark R. Kebbell & Shane D. Johnson, *Lawyers' Questioning: The Effect of Confusing Questions on Witness Confidence and Accuracy,* 24 Law & Hum. Behav. 629 (2000); Mason Ladd, *Some Observations on Credibility: Impeachment of Witnesses,* 52 Cornell L.Q. 238 (1967); Lt. Col. James Moody & Lt. Col. LeEllen Coacher, *A Primer on Methods of Impeachment,* 45 A.F. L. Rev. 161 (1998).

C.   WHO MAY IMPEACH

> **FED. R. EVID. 607.   WHO MAY IMPEACH A WITNESS**

Any party, including the party that called the witness, may attack the witness's credibility.

Discussion

Rule 607 abolishes the common law "voucher" principle, which precluded a party from attacking the credibility of a witness that party called to testify. One justification for the voucher principle was the idea that a party who calls a witness represents her as worthy of belief, or "vouches" for that witness. The Advisory Committee's Note to Rule 607 rejects this reasoning because, except for a few types of witnesses such as character witnesses or experts, a party rarely has a free choice in selecting witnesses. But even if the voucher principle reflected reality, precluding a party from impeaching its own witness might deprive the trier of fact of evidence essential to weighing witness reliability. Thus, the goal of accurate fact-finding compels admission of impeaching evidence even from a party who "vouches" for the witness.

The U.S. Supreme Court in Chambers v. Mississippi, 410 U.S. 484 (1973),[1] suggested that the old voucher principle may be unconstitutional in some situations. Chambers had been charged with a murder to which another individual, McDonald, had confessed out of court. McDonald then repudiated his confession. When the state refused to call McDonald to testify, the defendant called him and proceeded to read his confession to the jury. On cross-examination, the state showed that McDonald had repudiated the confession. When Chambers tried to challenge this repudiation on redirect, the court ruled that he could not impeach his own witness under the Mississippi voucher rule. The trial court also concluded that the hearsay rule precluded defendant from presenting evidence regarding statements McDonald made that would support the reliability of his confession. In reversing defendant's conviction, the Supreme Court held that excluding this evidence, coupled with the refusal to permit impeachment of

---

1. *Chambers* is discussed at length in Chapter 3.

McDonald, would deny the defendant due process. The Supreme Court made it clear, however, that it was not concluding that the voucher rule is unconstitutional as a general matter.

A more complex question relating to Rule 607 is raised by the possible abuse of the right to impeach one's own witness. For example, a party might call a witness with the expectation that she will testify in a way inconsistent with a prior statement. Under Rule 607, this could provide the party calling the witness with an opportunity to offer that prior statement to impeach. But the party's real purpose in doing this might not be to attack the credibility of the witness, since there would be little point in calling a witness just to impeach her. Rather, the purpose could be to permit the jury to hear the prior inconsistent statement in the hope that the jury will consider the statement for the truth of the matter asserted, even when the statement would be inadmissible hearsay if openly offered for that purpose. This amounts to using impeachment as a pretense to conceal an effort to avoid the hearsay rule.

Commentators have proposed various approaches to dealing with the threat that Rule 607 might be exploited in this fashion. The first approach would interpret Rule 607 as precluding a party from impeaching its own witness unless her testimony damaged that party's case and was a surprise. The presence of damage and surprise suggests that there is legitimate impeachment value in the prior inconsistent statement and that Rule 607 is not being used merely as a pretense for exposing the jury to hearsay. Another solution would reach the same result by reading damage and surprise requirements into Rule 403. A third approach would simply apply Rule 403 as written, permitting the courts to balance probative value against unfair prejudice.

While no federal court has directly held that Rule 607 imposes the requirements of damage and surprise, all the federal courts that have considered the issue acknowledge that impeachment by prior inconsistent statement may not be permitted when employed as a mere subterfuge to get before the jury evidence that is not otherwise admissible. In deciding whether a subterfuge has been attempted, a few federal courts have focused on the presence and degree of damage and surprise. This means that impeachment would be permitted only when the party offering the prior inconsistent statement could show that the witness's trial testimony damaged the case of the party calling the witness and was unexpected. The most obvious problem with this approach is that the language of Rule 607 is unequivocal in its rejection of the voucher principle and is not explicitly conditioned by anything, much less requirements of damage and surprise. Accordingly, other federal courts have refused to read into Rule 607 a damage and surprise requirement. Thus, it remains unclear exactly how the courts will react to a party's attempt to abuse the power to impeach its own witness.

UNITED STATES v. HOGAN
763 F.2d 697 (5th Cir. 1985)

[Prosecution of the Hogan brothers for smuggling drugs from Mexico to Texas. Carpenter, the pilot of an airplane owned by one of the brothers, was arrested in Mexico and confessed while in the custody of the Mexican authorities. In his confession, Carpenter also implicated the Hogan brothers in drug smuggling. After he returned to the United States, Carpenter recanted his confession and claimed it was obtained through torture. At trial the prosecution called Carpenter to testify, expecting that he would deny the smuggling and also deny any involvement by the Hogans. Carpenter testified as expected. The prosecution then offered into evidence Carpenter's statement to the Mexican authorities, which, of course, was inconsistent with his trial testimony. The avowed purpose of offering this statement was to impeach Carpenter's credibility. The trial court admitted the evidence and the Hogans were convicted. They appealed on the ground admission of Carpenter's prior statement was error.]

CLARK, Chief Judge:

The Hogans contend that the government called Carpenter solely to present otherwise inadmissible hearsay testimony to the jury under the guise of impeachment. Defendants claim this "straw-man" ploy violated the Federal Rules of Evidence (FRE), and deprived them of a fair trial. . . .

The prosecution contends that it has a right pursuant to FRE 607 to impeach its own witnesses. Rule 607 provides, "the credibility of a witness may be attacked by any party, including the party calling him." In addition, they assert that a prior inconsistent statement of the witness may be admitted to attack his credibility even if the statement tends to directly inculpate the defendant. These contentions are correct.

The rule in this Circuit, however, is that "the prosecutor may not use such a statement under the guise of impeachment for the primary purpose of placing before the jury substantive evidence which is not otherwise admissible."

Despite this consistent precedent, the government contends it has the right to place on the stand a witness whom it suspects will fabricate his story, despite indications by the witness that his story has changed. They assert that in the formal courtroom setting, where the witness must swear an oath before the judge and is subject to the penalties of perjury, the witness is under maximum compulsion to tell the truth. Under these conditions, the fact-finder should be allowed to observe the witness's demeanor when confronted with the conflicting statements and decide which version is true. In addition, they point out that if the prosecution could not introduce the testimony of any witness who had once made incriminating statements but later announced that he would recant that story at trial, declarants could effectively negate all incriminating statements made during questioning.

The apparent conflict in theories is not real. The government may call a witness it knows may be hostile, and it may impeach that witness's credibility. Surprise is not a necessary prerequisite to impeaching one's own witness under FRE 607. The prosecution, however, may not call a witness it knows to be hostile for the primary purpose of eliciting otherwise inadmissible impeachment testimony, for such a scheme merely serves as a subterfuge to avoid the hearsay rule.

The danger in this procedure is obvious. The jury will hear the impeachment evidence, which is not otherwise admissible and is not substantive proof of guilt, but is likely to be received as such proof. The defendant thus risks being convicted on the basis of hearsay evidence that should bear only on a witness's credibility. See also FRE 403, 404. Limiting instructions can ameliorate a jury's confusion. Because none were requested or given in this trial, we review whether the introduction of Carpenter's testimony and the subsequent impeachment evidence constituted plain error. We find that it did.

The prosecution announced to the jury that Carpenter would be hostile and that it would impeach him. This is not a case where the government needed to determine whether a witness would adhere to his story under oath and subject to perjury. In the cases recognizing the right to put the witness to a trial test, the witness had not testified under oath and subject to perjury. In contrast, Carpenter had already testified twice under oath, and both times he adhered to his account of fabrication. He testified at the grand jury proceedings in a related case and a perjury indictment and conviction resulted. He again testified on voir dire in this proceeding. The government was not entitled to another test of Carpenter's sworn testimony. It well knew what he would say under oath.

The government also contends that the primary purpose of calling Carpenter was to link the Hogans to the smuggling operation, and to help solidify in the jury's mind the drug operation, especially because Carpenter was the only conspirator apprehended at the scene of the crime. Again, while these are legitimate purposes for calling a witness, they cannot be considered the primary purpose for calling Carpenter in this case. The testimony they knew he would give provided no link between the drug transaction in Mexico and the Hogans other than the undisputed fact that the plane belonged to Barry Hogan and that Carpenter was employed by Hogan. The primary if not sole purpose in calling him to testify again was focused on getting Carpenter's prior statements before the jury. . . .

The admission of this evidence constituted plain, not harmless, error. Errors in the admission of evidence affecting the substantial rights of a party may be corrected on appeal, even if they were not brought to the attention of the trial court. FRE 103; Fed. R. Crim. P. 52(b). The danger that the uninstructed jury relied on the impeaching statements as substantive proof is great. In addition, in its closing arguments the government relied on Carpenter's hearsay statements to corroborate [another witness's] testimony. This request for affirmative use of impeachment testimony as substantive evidence unfairly prejudiced the Hogans. The remaining evidence does not so overwhelmingly establish guilt that we could say the error is harmless under Fed. R. Crim. P. 52(a). The convictions of the Hogans must be reversed.

Further Reading: Lee Lofton Sheppard, Commentary, *Subterfuge: Improper Impeachment of a Party's Own Witness in Alabama,* 53 Ala. L. Rev. 1003 (2002); Don Johnsen, Note, *Impeachment with an Unsworn Prior Inconsistent Statement as Subterfuge,* 28 Wm. & Mary L. Rev. 295 (1987).

Questions for Classroom Discussion

1. The prosecution called Carpenter to testify even though the prosecution knew he would deny the smuggling and defendants' involvement. Why did the prosecution do this?

(continued)

2. Was the prosecution prohibited from attacking Carpenter's credibility merely because the prosecution was trying to impeach its own witness? Read Rule 607.

3. If Carpenter's prior statement implicating defendants was offered to prove defendants were involved in the smuggling, what's the objection? If the prior statement is offered to prove that the witness made an inconsistent statement and is unreliable, does the same objection apply? A different objection? How should the court rule on that different objection?

4. Same facts as in *Hogan* except assume Carpenter made his prior inconsistent statement while testifying under oath before a grand jury. Should this produce a different result?

5. Same facts as in *Hogan* except assume the prosecutor was surprised by Carpenter's testimony because the prosecutor assumed Carpenter would testify consistently with his earlier statement in which he incriminated defendants. Should the prosecution then be permitted to introduce evidence of the prior statement to impeach the witness?

6. Assume you are defense counsel and you suspect the prosecution is going to call a witness just for impeachment as in *Hogan*. If that happens, you can always move to strike the witness's testimony. Is there anything you should do before the witness even testifies?

D. IMPEACHMENT BY METHODS NOT COVERED BY SPECIFIC COMMON LAW OR STATUTORY RULES

Discussion

1. Introduction

When we studied the subject of hearsay we noted that the reliability of an out-of-court statement is affected chiefly by four factors: *perception, memory, sincerity,* and *narration.* These same "testimonial infirmities" apply to the in-court utterances of witnesses. Ultimately, all tools for assessing the credibility of a witness's testimony are concerned with one or more of these four factors. Some tools are subject to meaningful control by rules of evidence, others less so. Still other factors enhancing or reducing credibility are beyond the control of evidence rules. Recall the factors affecting witness credibility listed in §780 of the California Evidence Code. Some items in that list are governed by specific law and are discussed in ensuing sections. For example, there are laws governing impeachment by prior inconsistent statement (and its converse, support by prior consistent statement); impeachment by character for honesty or veracity; bias, interest, or motive; and the existence or nonexistence of a fact to which the witness has testified (impeachment by contradiction and its opposite). All of these tools for evaluating witness credibility, as well as others, will require extended, individual discussion.

As noted, however, some factors that enhance or weaken credibility cannot be subjected to such close control. This section addresses those factors.

2. Factors Affecting the Witness's Opportunity to Perceive

The accuracy of a witness's testimony can be affected by the quality of the opportunity she had to perceive the event. Suppose a witness testifies that an automobile ran a red light and struck another vehicle that entered the intersection on the green. Evidence that the witness's view of the intersection was obstructed by a tree casts doubt on the accuracy of her testimony. Evidence that the witness was facing a bright sun while looking in the direction of the accident would have a similar effect, as would evidence that another event distracted the witness's attention just as the accident was occurring. Demonstrating impaired opportunity to observe is a common way to impeach a witness, just as proving the witness's superior position to observe is a common way to show that the witness's testimony is accurate. No rules limit the way in which opportunity to perceive may be proved or disproved.

3. Factors Affecting the Witness's Capacity to Perceive

Some witnesses lack the normal capacity to perceive an event accurately. A person with poor vision and who was not wearing corrective lenses is less likely to have observed an automobile accident accurately than is a person whose vision at the time was normal. A person with a hearing impairment is less likely to hear accurately the words spoken by another person, or to hear whether a train issued a warning as it approached an intersection, than is one whose hearing is normal. It is fair to point out to the jury anything that casts doubt on the capacity of a witness to use her five senses, or that shows the witness's acute sensory abilities. There are no specific rules limiting the use of this technique.

A witness's capacity to perceive accurately also can be affected by mental or emotional factors. For example, the accuracy of the witness's testimony about an event might be suspect if the witness suffers from a mental disorder that affects her ability to distinguish reality from fantasy. Similarly, the jury is probably entitled to learn that an adult witness possesses the mind of a young child, or that a witness suffers from schizophrenia. On the other hand, the mere fact that a witness has somewhat lower than average intelligence, or suffers from depression, would not normally be a proper subject of proof. These factors have little, if any, effect on the witness's capacity to perceive and admitting proof of them would only serve to embarrass the witness and prolong the trial unnecessarily. The trial court has the power under Rule 611(a) to prevent such abuses.

Of course, when it is permissible to prove a witness's impaired mental capacity to perceive, it will sometimes be necessary to call an expert witness to establish the impairment and explain its likely effect. We discuss the admissibility of expert testimony in Chapter 7.

Finally, it is proper to reveal to the fact-finder that a witness was intoxicated or under the influence of mind-altering drugs at the time she observed the events to which she has testified. Clearly, such conditions can affect the accuracy of a person's perceptions and courts allow evidence to establish these conditions if there is a reasonable basis for concluding that they existed at the relevant time. Evidence that the person is an alcoholic or regular drug abuser, on the other hand, usually is excluded on the ground it is intoxication or drug use at the time of the events observed that is relevant to credibility, not the witness's status as an alcohol or drug abuser. On the other hand, we will see later in the chapter that certain aspects of a witness's character sometimes are admissible under Rules 608 and 609.

4.   *Factors Affecting the Witness's Capacity to Recollect*

Some of the same factors that affect a witness's capacity to perceive accurately also can affect a person's memory. For example, a person's consumption of alcohol or drugs either at the time of the events in issue or later might affect not only her capacity to perceive, but also her memory of the events perceived. The same can be true of certain psychiatric conditions.

In addition, some people have worse than average memories. Whether caused by physiological factors or just "absent-mindedness," poor memory in general casts doubt on the accuracy of testimony. This is common sense. But what is not so clear is whether, and how, one may prove that a witness possesses a poor memory. If having a poor memory is a character trait (which we doubt), admissibility would be governed by Rule 608(a), a rule we study later in this chapter. If poor memory is not a character trait, no specific rule of evidence applies. The simplest way to prove poor memory, and the means most likely to be permitted, is to elicit the witness's admission. Cross-examination as to the fact will consume little time, and will seldom prove unduly distracting to the jury. On the other hand, the effectiveness of this technique depends on the willingness of the witness to admit to memory problems.

Assuming the witness refuses to admit to memory problems, is extrinsic evidence admissible to prove such problems? Evidence of the witness's reputation for having a poor memory would be excluded as hearsay. (The hearsay exception for community reputation applies only to reputation for character. *See* Rule 803(21).) Would it be permissible to call another witness who knows the first witness to testify that, in her opinion, the first witness has a poor memory? There is no rule specifically forbidding the practice, although Rule 701 places some limits on lay opinion evidence. Under that provision, the opinion would be admissible as long as the witness's testimony is rationally based on the perception of the witness and the court finds that the evidence would help the trier of fact to assess the issues in the case. Opinion of an expert also might be admissible to prove a witness has a poor memory. In such a case, admissibility would be determined under the standard of Rule 702. As we will see, the demands of that provision require substantial analysis. For present purposes, it is sufficient to note that Rule 702 requires that expert testimony be helpful to the trier of fact and that it be based on valid science. We discuss the admissibility of lay and expert opinion testimony in Chapter 7.

Note that opinion evidence concerning a witness's poor memory, whether in the form of lay or expert testimony, consumes considerably more time than eliciting an admission during cross-examination. As a consequence, courts might apply Rule 403 to exclude opinion evidence on the grounds it is a waste of time.

5. *Factors Affecting the Witness's Capacity to Narrate*

Some people have poor communication skills. Juries can perceive this, and should be expected to take the fact into consideration when judging the credibility of a witness. It would be a rare circumstance in which it will be necessary or helpful to call another witness to testify about the principal witness's poor communication skills. Whether arising from physiological or other factors, a witness's inability to relate events she has witnessed will affect the trier of fact's assessment of the credibility of her testimony.

6. *Appearance and Status Factors*

Imagine that in the course of a criminal trial, the prosecution calls a witness. The witness is not dressed in street clothes. In fact, the witness is wearing an orange jumpsuit emblazoned with the words "County Jail." The witness is also handcuffed and shackled, and is escorted into the courtroom by two uniformed law officers. Before this witness utters even a single word, the jury already will have formed an impression of her credibility. It is only human to do so. There is no way to prevent the jury from drawing inferences from the appearance and status of a witness.

This same principle applies to a criminal defendant, whether the defendant testifies or just sits at the defense table. When Bobby Seale, charged with crimes in connection with the disruption of the 1968 Democratic National Convention, appeared in the courtroom bound, gagged, and tied to his chair, the jury was certain to form an impression of his credibility and guilt. In contrast, O.J. Simpson's lawyers made sure that during his criminal trial he appeared in court impeccably attired in an expensive business suit. However dressed, a defendant's mere status as the accused will have some effect on the jury's evaluation of guilt. An instruction from the court about the "presumption of innocence," or a reminder that defendant is "innocent until proven guilty" helps to protect a defendant from some prejudice, but it is unrealistic to think that such an instruction removes all taint.

Appearance or status also can enhance a witness's credibility. A priest who appears in formal attire normally will be accorded considerable credibility even before he utters a word of testimony. A well-dressed business person with a briefcase, a neat haircut, and a confident gait will receive much more consideration than an unshaven man in a tee shirt and jeans.

The witness's appearance is not "evidence" in the usual sense and is not the subject of testimony or other formal presentation. While rule-based control of appearance or behavior is not practical, the court may still exercise some control over such matters. For example, the court may order that a criminal defendant and any jailed witnesses be permitted to wear street clothes in the courtroom. The court may admonish the jury to avoid prejudging parties or witnesses, using language and examples that bring home the point. Complete control, however, is impossible.

7. Demeanor

In our daily lives we judge a person's credibility, in part, by his demeanor. The same is true of our assessment of witnesses. Demeanor of a witness manifests itself in an infinite number of ways. One witness avoids eye contact while relating a story. Another constantly shifts in the chair while testifying. Another seems hostile to questions, appears evasive, or answers questions sarcastically. Of course, there are also witnesses who exhibit none of these negative qualities. They appear honest, forthright, and cooperative. They look counsel, the parties, and the jury in the eye while testifying. They present themselves in all ways as sincere. Jurors bring into the courtroom their own interpretations of demeanor. Some interpretations are based on valid assumptions about behavior, and some are not.

A witness's demeanor is not "evidence" in the usual sense, and thus it is not subject to control by rules. The jury may consider any aspect of a witness's demeanor in determining the credibility of that witness.

8. Plausibility of the Witness's Testimony

Perhaps the most convincing indicator of a witness's credibility is whether the witness tells a plausible story. Do the parts of her story fit together into a coherent whole? Does the story fit in with the testimony of other witnesses the jury finds credible? Or does the testimony seem implausible, incoherent, and inconsistent with other evidence? In the presentation of testimony, and in closing argument, it is counsel's job to construct a complete story that makes sense to the jury. And just as a chain is only as strong as its weakest links, a story is only as plausible as its least plausible part. This is not the realm of rules, but of common sense and daily experience.

9. Illustration

To illustrate some of the ways to judge witness credibility discussed above, imagine a personal injury action in which Plaintiff claims Defendant ran a red light and struck Plaintiff's car as it passed through the busy intersection of First and Main. Plaintiff was traveling on First, and Defendant was driving along Main. To prove Defendant ran the light, Plaintiff calls Witness, who testifies that she was driving on First when she saw Defendant run the light and strike Plaintiff's car. The following cross-examination attempts to impeach the credibility of Witness's testimony on direct. (You should assume that defense counsel's characterizations of Witness's direct examination testimony are accurate.)

Def: You testified on direct that the light was red for cars traveling on Main Street. Is that correct?

W: Yes.

Def. And you also testified that you were about half a block from the intersection of First and Main when you saw the cars collide?

W. Yes.

Def. And the cars collided in the middle of the intersection?

W. Yes.

Def. That must mean Defendant entered the intersection at least a few moments before you saw the cars collide, isn't that correct?

W. I suppose. But it couldn't have been long.

Def. But you don't know how fast Defendant was traveling before the collision, do you?

W. No.

Def. So that means you can't say how long it was before the collision that Defendant entered the intersection, right?

W. I guess so.

Def. You testified on direct that after you saw the crash, you noticed the light for cars on Main was red, correct?

W. Yes. It was red.

Def. And you testified that you know this because you saw that you had a green light at that time.

W. Correct.

Def. So you didn't actually see the color of the light on Main before the crash, did you?

W. Well, I think I saw the cross-street light, the light on Main.

Def. This was from about half a block away, and maybe more?

W. Yes. I pay attention when I drive. And also, I know the light on Main was red before the accident because I had a green light. It was green for a while.

Def. But you don't remember how long your light was green before you saw the crash, do you?

W. No. Not exactly. But I'm pretty sure it was for a while.

Def. You were not alone in your car, were you?

W. No. My kids were in the back seat.

Def. One of these kids was your second-grader, right?

W. Yes. He was 7 at the time.

Def. And the other was your fourth-grader, correct?

W. Yes. Age 9.

Def. And they weren't sitting quietly, were they?

W. What do you mean?

Def. They were arguing and pushing each other, weren't they?

W. Maybe a little horseplay. They're kids.

Def. But you weren't ignoring them, were you?

W. No, I was trying to get them to stop.

Def. And this was happening while you were driving on First, approaching the corner of Main.

W. Yes.

Def: You were driving in a westerly direction, weren't you?

W: I think so. First runs east-west, and I was going west.

Def: And this was at about 4:00 in the afternoon on March 30, correct?

W: Yes.

Def: Was it a sunny day?

W: There was some sun, yes. And some clouds as well.

Def: And you would have been facing the sun as you drove on First, isn't that correct?

W: Yes.

Def: You were not wearing sunglasses, were you?

W: I don't remember for sure, but I don't think so.

Def: The streets were quite crowded at that time, weren't they?

W: Yes. It was rush hour.

Def: And both First and Main are commercial streets, aren't they?

W: There are stores, gas stations, and so forth, if that's what you mean.

Def: So it's fair to say that some of the vehicles on the street on that day and at that time were commercial ones?

W: Maybe.

Def: Trucks, vans, and so forth?

W: I think some of the vehicles were trucks, yes.

Def: And you were driving a regular sedan, weren't you?

W: Yes. I drive a Honda Accord.

Def: At the time you saw this accident, you had just picked up your kids from school, correct?

W: They stayed late for some club meetings, yes. I picked them up a little before 4:00.

Def: And just before you picked up your kids, you finished a late lunch with three friends, correct?

W: Yes.

Def: You had a couple of glasses of wine at lunch, didn't you?

W: Maybe, but I certainly was not drunk. I would never drive drunk, never mind with kids in the car.

Def: I didn't ask if you were intoxicated. I just asked if you had had a couple of glasses of wine. Is it correct that you drank two glasses of wine with lunch?

W: Yes.

Def: And you had the second glass with dessert, not long before you left the restaurant?

W: I think so, yes.

Def: I have no further questions.

Look closely at Defendant's cross-examination of Witness. Some questions were designed to show that Witness's *opportunity to observe* was limited. For example, she did not see the color of Defendant's light before the accident, she was driving into the sun, there were other, larger vehicles on the street that might have impeded her view, and her children were fighting in the back seat.

Her *capacity to observe* might have been affected by the wine she consumed at a late lunch that ended not long before the accident took place. Her *memory* of how long her own light had been green before the accident was hazy. Defendant's questions also undermined the *plausibility* of her testimony, especially her statement that she saw that the light was red on Main when she was about a half-block away, on First. Aspects of Witness's *demeanor* during her direct and cross-examination would also affect the jurors' perceptions of her credibility; though it is difficult to tell from a transcript, it does appear that she was somewhat defensive.

None of the ways in which Defendant attempted to impeach Witness in this example are subject to specific rules. Had the cross-examiner's tone been angry or argumentative, Plaintiff might well have objected, and the court would have instructed Defendant's counsel to tone it down. But Plaintiff would have no specific rule-based objection to any of the types of impeachment Defendant used in this situation.

Questions for Classroom Discussion

All of the following hypotheticals are based on the following facts: Prosecution of Defendant for a murder committed in the course of a bank robbery. The prosecution calls Witness 1, who testifies that she was in the bank and saw Defendant shoot the victim. On cross-examination, Witness 1 claims to have had "an unobstructed view" of the shooter. In each case, assume that the prosecution objects, claiming the impeachment is improper. How should the court rule in each case?

1. Defendant calls Witness 2, a friend of Witness 1, who testifies that she was with Witness 1 in the bank, that the two of them were about 50 feet from the robber at the time of the shooting, and that there were many people between them and the shooter.

2. Witness 2 testifies that Witness 1 is nearsighted and normally wears eyeglasses, but that she was not wearing them in the bank on the day in question.

3. On direct examination, Witness 1 testifies that she had just made a withdrawal at a teller window when the shooting occurred. Witness 2 testifies for Defendant that Witness 1 had made a deposit, not a withdrawal.

4. Witness 2 testifies for Defendant that recently Witness 1 told Witness 2, "When I hit 40, my memory started slipping away."

5. Witness 2 testifies for Defendant that she is familiar with Witness 1's community reputation, and that Witness 1 is notorious for having a bad memory.

(continued)

6. Witness 2 testifies for Defendant that she has known Witness 1 for many years, and that in her opinion, Witness 1 has a terrible memory.

7. Defendant calls Witness 3, a psychiatrist who sat in the courtroom during Witness 1's testimony. After qualifying Witness 3 as an expert in psychiatry, Witness 3 testifies for Defendant that, based on her observation of Witness 1 while testifying, she believes that Witness 1 suffers from a mental disorder that renders her unable to distinguish reality from fantasy.

8. Defendant also wishes to have Witness 3, the psychiatrist, testify that, based on her observations of Witness 1 while testifying, she believes Witness 1 was lying.

9. During her closing argument, Defendant's attorney makes the following statement: "Did you notice that during her testimony, Witness 1 never once looked directly at you or at the defendant? Did you notice that when Witness 1 answered my questions about her identification of my client, Witness 1 looked toward the floor? What is Witness 1 hiding? Could it be that she isn't as certain of her testimony as she, and the prosecutor, would like you to believe?" Is this proper argument?

E. WITNESS'S CHARACTER

1. *Introduction*

This section addresses the admissibility of evidence concerning a witness's character for truthfulness or untruthfulness. This evidence can take three forms: (1) opinion and reputation for truthfulness, (2) specific instances of conduct involving lying or telling the truth, and (3) criminal convictions that suggest a character for untruthfulness. We will see that there is a different rule for each. There is also a special rule prohibiting character impeachment on the basis of a witness's religious beliefs or lack thereof.

Here is a definition of witness character evidence that will help you differentiate it from other evidence bearing on witness credibility: Evidence of witness character relates to the general credibility of the witness, rather than just the believability of specific testimony, and suggests something about the ethics or morals of that witness.

For example, assume that in a murder case the prosecution calls a witness who testifies that she saw the defendant commit the crime. The defense then offers evidence that the witness once lied on a job application that was unrelated to the murder. This evidence says nothing specific about the credibility of her testimony concerning the murder. But the evidence permits the inference that she is generally untruthful, a conclusion that carries with it an ethical or moral judgment about the witness. This is character evidence. In contrast, consider evidence that the witness suffers from a vision disability that calls into question the accuracy of what she claims to have seen. This is not character evidence because it does not convey an ethical or moral judgment about the witness. Similarly, imagine that other evidence shows the witness and the defendant are lifelong enemies. Bias evidence usually is not character evidence because it does not make a general statement about truthfulness but, instead, merely shows the witness has an interest in the outcome of the specific case. For the same reason, evidence of a witness's prior inconsistent statement usually is not character evidence. An inconsistent statement normally suggests only that the witness lied or was mistaken with respect to the specific facts described in the statement. The evidence conveys no encompassing generalization about the witness's truthfulness.

But while there is a clear theoretical distinction between character impeachment and other methods of attacking credibility, drawing that distinction in a given case is not always easy. Sometimes the same evidence undermines the credibility of a witness based on both a character and a non-character inference. The admissibility of the evidence to prove these two inferences may be governed by two different rules. Accordingly, the evidence might be admissible to prove one inference and inadmissible for the other. For example, assume a criminal prosecution in which the defense calls an alibi witness. The prosecution then seeks to impeach the alibi witness with evidence that the witness and the accused are members of the same criminal gang. The evidence shows that the alibi witness is biased but also shows something about the witness's character that has a bearing on credibility — he is not law abiding. The admissibility issues raised by such a case are discussed later in this chapter, in connection with United States v. Abel, 469 U.S. 45 (1984).

Because evidence of a witness's character only says something general about the witness's truthfulness, it may have less probative value than evidence directly bearing on credibility in the specific case. For example, evidence that a prosecution witness lied on a job application unrelated to the case usually says less about credibility than does evidence that she hates defendant and, thus, is biased.

While its probative value is generally low, character evidence about a witness can threaten to inflict a high level of unfair prejudice. This is primarily because evidence of witness character can distract the jury from the issues in the case and induce a decision on an improper basis. For example, when the jury hears evidence that a witness has a reputation for being a liar, the jury may be more inclined to punish the party who called to the stand a witness of such low moral fiber. When the witness is herself a party, the ramifications of this inclination can be especially serious — the jury may ignore the issues in the case and decide against the party it perceives to be a bad person. Because the probative value of evidence concerning a witness's character for truthfulness may be low while its potential for unfair prejudice is high, we will see that the rules often place significant limits on admissibility.

Because we are once again concerned with character evidence, it is important to understand when the rules described in this section apply and when the character evidence rules discussed in Chapter 4 apply. The answer depends on what the character evidence is offered to prove. The rules described in this chapter apply only when character evidence is offered for the purpose of attacking or supporting witness credibility. For example, assume a prosecution for bank robbery in which defendant testifies and denies committing the crime. Evidence that defendant has a prior conviction for auto theft permits the inference that defendant is not law abiding. This permits the further inference that defendant may have been willing to commit perjury when he testified. If the evidence is offered to impeach defendant as a witness, Rule 609, which is described below, applies. But the rules described in this chapter do not apply when character evidence is offered for some other purpose, such as proving character for purposes of showing the defendant's conduct. Rule 404 applies if evidence concerning the conviction for auto theft is offered to prove that the defendant has the character of a thief and, thus, is more likely to have committed the bank robbery. Because different rules apply depending on the purpose for which the character evidence is offered, that evidence might be admissible for one purpose and not the other. As we will see, this means the trial court might admit the evidence for limited purposes (giving the jury a limiting instruction pursuant to Rule 105) or might exclude the evidence entirely under Rule 403.

2.   *Reputation or Opinion Concerning Truthfulness*

> FED. R. EVID. 608(a)

Reputation or Opinion Evidence. A witness's credibility may be attacked or supported by testimony about the witness's reputation for having a character for truthfulness or untruthfulness, or by testimony in the form of an opinion about that character. But evidence of truthful character is admissible only after the witness's character for truthfulness has been attacked.

Discussion

a.   Reputation and Opinion

Rule 608(a) regulates the admissibility of opinion and reputation evidence concerning a witness's character for truthfulness or untruthfulness. The rule places few limits on the admissibility of such evidence. This contrasts with Rule 608(b), which addresses the admissibility of evidence of specific instances of a witness's conduct to prove her character for truthfulness. Subdivision (b) of Rule 608, unlike its partner in subdivision (a), makes extrinsic evidence inadmissible. Under subdivision (a), once a witness has testified, a second witness may be called to give an opinion concerning the first witness's character for truthfulness or may describe the first witness's reputation for truthfulness. This second witness is often referred to as a "character witness." But while the character witness usually may give an opinion or testify as to reputation, she generally is prohibited from testifying as to specific instances of the first witness's conduct. While Rule 608(a) fails to establish any bar to the admissibility of reputation and opinion testimony, it states only that such evidence "may" be admitted. This signifies that the evidence is still subject to other rules regulating admissibility and that the court retains the discretion under Rule 403 to exclude the evidence where that is appropriate.

Opinion evidence consists of a personal assessment of a person's character by one who has sufficient knowledge of that individual's character to give an opinion worth considering. The Federal Rules of Evidence recognize two types of opinion evidence, lay and expert. Rule 608 draws no distinction between these two types of opinion evidence, suggesting that both can be acceptable under that rule. Thus, admissibility of opinion as to truthfulness requires compliance not only with Rule 608(a) but also with Rule 701 for lay opinion or Rule 702 for expert opinion.

Reputation evidence under Rule 608 has both an out-of-court component and an in-court component. The out-of-court component consists of what persons in a community have said or done that reflects their opinion of the witness whose credibility is at issue. The in-court component consists of the reputation of witness's testimony as to whether those persons regard the witness in question as truthful or untruthful. Wigmore noted the inherent unreliability of such evidence, calling it "the secondhand, irresponsible product of multiplied guesses and gossip."

To ensure that reputation evidence is reliable, the courts require proof of certain foundational facts. Thus, it must be shown that the persons whose opinions make up the out-of-court component must have had sufficient exposure to the witness being impeached to form reliable opinions about her character. This means that if the witness is a relative newcomer to the community, the members of that community might have insufficient familiarity with her to reliably evaluate her truthfulness. In addition, the character witness's in-court testimony must be supported by a showing that she had sufficient contact with the community in question to form accurate conclusions about the reputations prevailing there. So if the character witness had minimal contact with the community, the court might reject the reputation testimony.

b. Character for Truthfulness or Untruthfulness

Credibility under subdivision (a) "may be attacked or supported by testimony about the witness's reputation for having a character for truthfulness or untruthfulness, or by testimony in the form of opinion about that character." Thus, opinion or reputation testimony pertaining to any other character trait, such as recklessness or inclination toward violence, is inadmissible to prove witness credibility. This also means that testimony concerning the general moral character of the witness will not be admissible under Rule 608(a).

c. Evidence of Truthfulness Admissible Only After Attack on Character for Truthfulness

Rule 608(a) also states that "evidence of truthful character is admissible only after the witness's character for truthfulness has been attacked." This limitation is a product of balancing two policies underlying Rule 608: the promotion of accurate fact-finding and the elimination of unjustifiable expense and delay. In the absence of an attack on character for truthfulness, Rule 608(a) assumes that evidence of truthful character is of insufficient probative value to warrant the time necessary to consider it.

Not every attack on credibility provides a basis for the admission of evidence of truthful character. Evidence of character for truthfulness is admissible only when the impeaching evidence undermines credibility by suggesting character for untruthfulness. Thus, evidence of truthful character would not be admissible when, for example, credibility was attacked by a showing that the witness misperceived events, suffered a memory lapse, or was otherwise honestly mistaken. This is because evidence of truthful character does not logically refute such attacks on credibility. Without this logical connection, the probative value of evidence of truthful character is insufficient to warrant its consideration.

Questions for Classroom Discussion

1. Civil action for personal injuries suffered in an auto accident. The defense is contributory negligence. Plaintiff testifies that Defendant ran the red light. Plaintiff then calls his minister who offers to testify that he has known Plaintiff for years and that he believes Plaintiff to be a truthful person. Is the minister's testimony admissible under Rule 608(a)?

2. Same case. Defendant calls a witness who offers to testify that he has worked in the same small office with Plaintiff for years and that, in his opinion, Plaintiff is careless. Is the witness's testimony admissible under Rule 608(a)? Is it admissible if offered to prove that Plaintiff was negligent?

3. Same case. Defendant calls a witness who offers to testify that he has lived in the same large apartment building with Plaintiff for years and that, in his opinion, Plaintiff is a liar. Is the witness's testimony admissible under Rule 608(a)?

4. Same case. Defendant calls a witness who testifies that he has lived next door to Plaintiff for years and that, in his opinion, Plaintiff is a liar. On cross-examination Plaintiff asks, "Isn't it true that everyone else in the neighborhood says Plaintiff is truthful?" The witness answers, "Yes." Is this cross-examination testimony admissible under Rule 608(a)? Should it be excluded as hearsay?

---

3. *Conduct Probative of Truthfulness*

FED. R. EVID. 608(b)

(b) Specific Instances of Conduct. Except for a criminal conviction under Rule 609, extrinsic evidence is not admissible to prove specific instances of a witness's conduct in order to attack or support the witness's character for truthfulness. But the court may, on cross-examination, allow them to be inquired into if they are probative of the character for truthfulness or untruthfulness of:

    (1) the witness; or

    (2) another witness whose character the witness being cross-examined has testified about.

Discussion

a. Rationale for Admitting Evidence of Witness Conduct Probative of Truthfulness

Evidence of instances in a witness's life in which she lied or told the truth can reveal her character for truthfulness or untruthfulness. The story about a young George Washington admitting he chopped down a cherry tree, though probably apocryphal, became an enduring symbol of his integrity. Such snapshots of personal history can provide a valuable perspective on the credibility of a witness. This is because witnesses are often carefully groomed and coached by counsel to project in the courtroom an image of truthfulness. Evidence of a witness's conduct in unguarded moments outside the courtroom can be used to poke holes in this facade.

But while evidence of specific instances of witness conduct has some probative value, the extent of that value should not be overestimated. After all, over the course of a lifetime every person engages in countless instances of truthtelling or lying. Any given specific instance might be atypical and not a true reflection of that person's character. Thus, even a few specific instances of conduct will have relatively low probative value. And while the probative value of such evidence is low, the dangers and costs of admitting that evidence can be high because evidence of witness conduct bearing on truthfulness can cause unfair prejudice or lead the jury to draw improper inferences. For example, assume a tax fraud prosecution in which defendant testifies he did not commit the crime. Impeachment evidence that defendant lied on his law school application might induce the jury to decide that defendant has character traits that make it more likely he committed tax fraud. As we saw in Chapter 4, this is a use of character evidence that usually is barred by Rule 404(a). The jury also might infer from this evidence that defendant is simply a bad person. Jurors then might vote to convict because they dislike defendant, not because they think defendant committed tax fraud. As we saw in Chapter 2, this would be unfairly prejudicial. The only permissible inference from the evidence about defendant lying on his law school application is that defendant also might have lied when he testified at his tax fraud trial. If the court concludes that the probative value of the evidence when considered for this purpose is substantially outweighed by the danger that the jury will use the evidence for one or more of the impermissible purposes, the court may exclude the evidence under Rule 403.

Evidence offered under Rule 608(b) also raises questions that can be time consuming and expensive to address. Notice that the provision regulates the admissibility of specific instances of the conduct of a witness to attack or support credibility, "except for a criminal conviction under Rule 609." This means that Rule 608(b), unlike Rule 609, deals with evidence of conduct that has not been proven in court beyond a reasonable doubt. Thus, the nature or even occurrence of that conduct may be disputed. Resolving these disputes could distract and confuse the jury with lengthy diversions from the central issues. Accordingly, Rule 608(b) imposes significant limits on the admissibility of such evidence.

b. Extrinsic Evidence Inadmissible

The first sentence of Rule 608(b) makes the admissibility of conduct evidence depend on the source for that evidence. Extrinsic evidence is inadmissible, subject to one exception recognized by the second sentence of the rule that we discuss below. Earlier in this chapter, we discussed briefly the meaning of *extrinsic evidence.* That term is not defined in Rule 608(b), but its meaning can be inferred from the second sentence of the rule. While Rule 608(b) states that "extrinsic evidence is not admissible to prove specific instances of witness conduct," the provision goes on to give courts discretion to admit specific-instances evidence on cross-examination of the witness whose character is the subject of that evidence. This suggests that the testimony of such a witness while being cross-examined in the proceeding in question *is not* extrinsic evidence. This further suggests that evidence from any other source *is* extrinsic evidence. For example, assume an action for breach of contract in which the defendant testifies he never accepted plaintiff's offer. Testimony from another witness that the defendant once lied about his military service is extrinsic evidence. Documentary evidence, like a letter revealing defendant's lie, also is extrinsic evidence. Even defendant's own testimony about his conduct is extrinsic evidence when given in a deposition or some proceeding other than the one in which that evidence is now offered. But if defendant admits to the lie while being cross-examined at this trial, that testimony is not extrinsic and is permitted. Of course, a savvy defendant simply might deny having committed the lie, knowing that extrinsic evidence to prove the lie is inadmissible and, thus, the prosecution has no recourse other than a later prosecution for perjury.

In sum, the first sentence of Rule 608(b) means that counsel can ask a witness about that witness's conduct, but if the witness denies the conduct it cannot be proved through other evidence. This accounts for the saying that, under Rule 608(b), counsel must usually "take the answer of the witness."

c. Discretion to Admit Specific Instances Probative of Truthfulness or Untruthfulness

Notice that Rule 608(b) states that specific instances of conduct "may" be admissible. This suggests that admissibility is not mandatory but a matter of judicial discretion. The first point to make about discretion under the second sentence of Rule 608(b) is that it is limited. Courts have discretion to admit specific instances evidence only if all other aspects of the rule are satisfied. Thus, the court has discretion to admit evidence only if it is probative of truthfulness or untruthfulness and fits into one of the two situations described in the second sentence of Rule 608(b). If the evidence is probative of truthful character, the limitation we saw in Rule 608(a) also applies here — discretion to admit exists only if character for truthfulness has been attacked.

The second sentence of Rule 608(b) recognizes two situations in which courts have discretion to admit evidence of specific instances of conduct probative of truthfulness or untruthfulness. Under Rule 608(b)(1), one source of that evidence can be the witness whose character for truthfulness or untruthfulness is at issue. This person is sometimes referred to as the "principal witness." As just indicated, testimony given by the principal witness in this proceeding *is not* extrinsic evidence. Under Rule 608(b)(2), another source for specific-instances evidence can be a witness who testified as to the principal witness's character for truthfulness or untruthfulness. This witness is sometimes referred to as a "character witness." While testimony from a character witness *is* extrinsic evidence under the definition offered above, Rule 608(b)(2) states that it may be admitted.

For example, suppose defendant is prosecuted for murder. On direct examination by the government, Alice testifies that she saw defendant commit the crime. On cross-examination, defense counsel asks, "Isn't it true that you lied on your tax return?" Alice answers, "Yes." This is permitted by Rule 608(b)(1). The evidence is being elicited from Alice during her cross-examination, and the question concerns an act (lying on a tax return) that is probative of Alice's character for untruthfulness. Then assume that the prosecution calls a second witness, Bob, who offers the opinion that Alice is a truthful person. Recall that this is permitted by Rule 608(a). On cross-examination of Bob, defense counsel then asks, "Did you know that Alice lied on a job application?" Bob answers, "Yes." This is permitted by Rule 608(b)(2) because Bob is a character witness who has testified as to the character for truthfulness of Alice, the principal witness.

Note that Rule 608(b) allows the court to admit evidence concerning specific instances of a witness's conduct only if that conduct is "probative of truthfulness or untruthfulness." Conduct is probative of truthfulness or untruthfulness when it implicates the general character of the witness for veracity rather than some other character trait, such as carelessness or propensity for violence. For example, evidence of specific instances is probative of truthfulness or untruthfulness when the conduct consists of acts such as fraud, lying, using a false name, making a false claim, engaging in deceptive business practices, and the like.

Even where the requirements of Rule 608(b) are otherwise satisfied, recall that the provision does not require the admission of specific instances evidence but only recognizes the discretion to admit. The Advisory Committee's Note makes clear that Rules 403 and 611 supply the principles that govern the exercise of this discretion:

> [T]he overriding protection of Rule 403 requires that probative value not be outweighed by danger of unfair prejudice, confusion of issues or misleading the jury, and that of Rule 611 bars harassment and undue embarrassment.

For example, assume defendant is charged with perjury. He testifies in his own defense and admits he made a false statement but denies he knew it was false when he made it. The prosecution then asks defendant on cross-examination if he had sex with someone after first lying to that person by saying that he was not HIV positive. Defendant's conduct is an act of lying and, thus, bears on his character for truthfulness. Moreover, defendant's response to the question would not be extrinsic evidence. However, the court still might exercise its discretion under Rule 403 to exclude the evidence because it could unfairly prejudice the jury in two ways. First, since defendant is charged with a crime of lying, the jury might use the evidence to draw an inference about his conduct in this case, which would be prohibited under Rule 404. Second, because the evidence reveals that defendant is HIV positive and was willing to lie about it to entice a person to have sex with him, the jury might ignore the issues in this perjury case and convict simply because it dislikes defendant.

Further Reading: Fred Warren Bennett, *Is the Witness Believable: A New Look at Truth and Veracity Character Evidence and Bad Acts Relevant to Truthfulness in a Criminal Case*, 9 St. Thomas L. Rev. 569 (1997); Diane H. Mazur, *Sex and Lies: Rules of Ethics, Rules of Evidence, and Our Conflicted Views on the Significance of Honesty*, 14 Notre Dame J.L. Ethics & Pub. Pol'y 679 (2000); Kevin C. McMunigal & Calvin William Sharpe, *Reforming Extrinsic Impeachment*, 33 Conn. L. Rev. 363 (2001); H. Richard Uviller, *Credence, Character, and the Rules of Evidence: Seeing Through the Liar's Tale*, 42 Duke L.J. 776 (1993).

Questions for Classroom Discussion

1.   Prosecution for drug dealing. Defendant testifies and denies committing the crime. On cross-examination, the prosecutor asks Defendant if he lied on a job application about a misdemeanor conviction for marijuana possession. Is evidence of the marijuana conviction admissible to prove Defendant was dealing drugs in this case?

2.   Same case. Is evidence of the marijuana conviction admissible under Rule 608(b) to impeach Defendant?

3.   Same case. If the marijuana conviction is not admissible to impeach under Rule 608(b), does the prosecutor's cross-examination in Question 1 refer to any other specific instance of conduct that is probative of truthfulness or untruthfulness?

4.   Same case. If your answer to Question 3 is "yes," on what basis might the court still exclude the evidence under Rule 608(b)?

5.   Same case. Assume that on cross-examination Defendant denied lying on his job application. Could the prosecution prove the lie with the application itself? With testimony from the personnel officer who received the application?

> **6.** Same case. Assume the prosecution calls a witness who testifies Defendant has a reputation for lying. Is this permitted under Rule 608? If so, can the defense cross-examine and ask, "Have you heard that Defendant truthfully admitted to chopping down the cherry tree?"

4. Conviction of Crime

> **FED. R. EVID. 609.   IMPEACHMENT BY EVIDENCE OF A CRIMINAL CONVICTION**

(a) In General. The following rules apply to attacking a witness's character for truthfulness by evidence of a criminal conviction:

(1) for a crime that, in the convicting jurisdiction, was punishable by death or by imprisonment for more than one year, the evidence:

(A) must be admitted, subject to Rule 403, in a civil case or in a criminal case in which the witness is not a defendant; and

(B) must be admitted in a criminal case in which the witness is a defendant, if the probative value of the evidence outweighs its prejudicial effect to that defendant; and

(2) for any crime regardless of the punishment, the evidence must be admitted if the court can readily determine that establishing the elements of the crime required proving—or the witness's admitting—a dishonest act or false statement.

(b) Limit on Using the Evidence After 10 Years. This subdivision (b) applies if more than 10 years have passed since the witness's conviction or release from confinement for it, whichever is later. Evidence of the conviction is admissible only if:

(1) its probative value, supported by specific facts and circumstances, substantially outweighs its prejudicial effect; and

(2) the proponent gives an adverse party reasonable written notice of the intent to use it so that the party has a fair opportunity to contest its use.

(c) Effect of a Pardon, Annulment, or Certificate of Rehabilitation. Evidence of a conviction is not admissible if:

(1) the conviction has been the subject of a pardon, annulment, certificate of rehabilitation, or other equivalent procedure based on a finding that the person has been rehabilitated, and the person has not been convicted of a later crime punishable by death or by imprisonment for more than one year; or

(2) the conviction has been the subject of a pardon, annulment, or other equivalent procedure based on a finding of innocence.

(d) Juvenile Adjudications. Evidence of a juvenile adjudication is admissible under this rule only if:

(1) it is offered in a criminal case;

(2) the adjudication was of a witness other than the defendant;

(3) an adult's conviction for that offense would be admissible to attack the adult's credibility; and

(4) admitting the evidence is necessary to fairly determine guilt or innocence.

(e) **Pendency of an Appeal.** A conviction that satisfies this rule is admissible even if an appeal is pending. Evidence of the pendency is also admissible.

Discussion

a.   Rationale for Admitting Conviction Evidence to Impeach

Admitting evidence of a witness's criminal conviction has been justified on the ground it helps the trier of fact determine the credibility of a person who might otherwise appear to have led a blameless life. Rule 609 assumes that convictions for crimes involving lying increase the probability that the witness is an untruthful person and, thus, may lie when testifying. The provision further assumes that convictions for other serious crimes reveal a more general character trait — that the witness is not a law-abiding person. This trait suggests the witness may be willing to break the law again by committing perjury while testifying. Many legal commentators have questioned the conclusions about a witness's character that Rule 609 assumes can be drawn from a conviction.[2]

While evidence of a conviction might tell us something about a witness's credibility, it also poses some dangers. These dangers are particularly serious when the witness being impeached is also the defendant in a criminal prosecution. For example, assume the defendant in a prosecution for perjury testifies and the prosecution then offers impeachment evidence in the form of the defendant's prior conviction for child molestation. In such a case, the jury might ignore the issues in the perjury prosecution because evidence of defendant's conviction suggests the defendant is a bad person who, if not guilty of the specific crime charged, still may be deserving of punishment. Next, assume that the conviction was for perjury in a matter unconnected with the present perjury prosecution. Because defendant previously was convicted of the same type of crime for which the defendant now is charged, the jury might use this conviction evidence to infer that defendant has the character of a perjurer and, thus, committed the perjury charged in this case. In Chapter 4 we learned that Rule 404 generally prohibits this use of bad-acts evidence.

Because a jury might misuse conviction evidence to the defendant's detriment, the mere threat that such evidence might be admitted to impeach can discourage defendants from taking the stand. This could deprive the jury of a valuable source of evidence. Because an accused has a right to testify, questions of a constitutional dimension may be raised when the exercise of that right is

2. The philosopher and jurist Jeremy Bentham ridiculed the notion that convictions for any serious crime should be admissible to impeach: "Take homicide in the way of duelling. Two men quarrel; one of them calls the other a liar. So highly does he prize the reputation of veracity, that, rather than suffer a stain to remain upon it, he determines to risk his life, challenges his adversary to fight, and kills him [and is guilty of a felony]. . . . The man prefers death to the imputation of a lie, — and the inference of the law is, that he cannot open his mouth but lies will issue from it." Bentham, Rationale of Judicial Evidence 406 (Brownings ed. 1827).

discouraged. Luce v. United States, 469 U.S. 38 (1984), which appears later in this chapter, addresses these issues.

The statutory history of Rule 609 reveals that, while Congress was aware of the possible benefits of conviction evidence, it also was concerned with the dangers. The complex structure of Rule 609 is understandable in light of the tension between the benefits and costs of conviction evidence.

b.   Scope of Rule 609

Rule 609 does not apply to all character evidence offered for the purpose of attacking witness credibility. It only applies to criminal convictions of the witness. As we have seen, Rule 608(a) applies to reputation and opinion evidence concerning a witness's character for truthfulness or untruthfulness and Rule 608(b) controls when evidence of misconduct that did not result in a conviction is offered to impeach a witness. Knowing which of these rules to apply is essential to determining whether character evidence is admissible to impeach. For example, recall that Rule 608(b) imposes strict limits on the admissibility of extrinsic evidence. Rule 609 contains *no* limit on extrinsic evidence of convictions.

Rule 609 only applies when the conviction is offered to prove the "character for truthfulness" of the witness. It does not apply to conviction evidence offered for non-character purposes. Thus, the provision does not control the admissibility of a conviction if the fact of conviction is an element of an offense. For example, assume defendant is prosecuted for being a felon in possession of a firearm. He testifies, denying he had a gun. Rule 609 does not apply if defendant's previous conviction for perjury is offered to prove merely that he is a felon — an element of the crime with which he is now charged. On the other hand, Rule 609 does apply if the conviction is offered to prove that defendant lied when he denied having a gun.

Finally, Rule 609 is inapplicable when a conviction is offered to prove motive, opportunity, intent, or other facts under Rule 404(b). And, of course, Rule 609 says nothing about the admissibility of evidence to impeach through any method other than conviction of crime.

c.   Rule 609(a) — General Rule

The two subdivisions of Rule 609(a) apply to convictions for different types of crimes. Subdivision (1) applies only to convictions for crimes "punishable by death or by imprisonment for more than one year." This is the definition of a felony. Thus, misdemeanors will not be admissible under subdivision (1). Subdivision (2) controls when "the court can readily determine that establishing the elements of the crime required proving — or the witness's admitting — a dishonest act or false statement," regardless of the punishment. The crime can be but need not have been a felony under subdivision (2); if it is a crime involving "a dishonest or false statement," even a misdemeanor is admissible. If a conviction is admissible under subdivision (2), there is no need to consider its admissibility under the more complex provisions of subdivision (1).

It has never been entirely clear what crimes qualify under the "dishonest act or false statement" standard of subdivision (2). Prior to 2006, the rule simply referred to crimes "involving dishonesty or false statement." Some courts interpreted this to mean only crimes in which lying is an essential element, such as perjury or fraud. Other courts would admit evidence of a conviction if the crime was actually committed *using* dishonesty or false statement, regardless of whether lying is an essential element of the crime. In 2006, the wording of subdivision (2) was changed to cover conviction for a crime, "if it readily can be determined that establishing the elements of the crime required proof or admission of an act of dishonesty or false statement by the witness." Unfortunately, this amendment did not resolve the matter definitively. The U.S. Justice Department had sought an amendment that would adopt a broader interpretation, admitting evidence of a conviction if the method used to commit the crime involved lying. Initially, the Evidence Rules Advisory Committee and Judicial Conference agreed, but public comment helped to persuade the Judicial Conference to adopt somewhat narrower language that refers to the "elements of the crime." This appears to mean that the only convictions that may be admitted under subdivision (2) are for crimes the elements of which require "a dishonest act or false statement." Judicial interpretation will be needed to clarify this standard further. The restyling of the Federal Rules that became effective in 2011 modified the provision in question to read: ". . . if the court can readily determine that establishing the elements of the crime required proving—or the witness's admitting—a dishonest act or false statement." There are other important differences between subdivisions (1) and (2). Notice that subdivision (2) states that conviction for a crime involving a dishonest act or false statement "must be admitted." This command makes it clear that a trial judge has no discretion to exclude such evidence even if she thinks it is unfairly prejudicial. In contrast, the terms of subdivision (1) compel the trial judge to weigh unfair prejudice against probative value.

How the trial judge strikes this balance under subdivision (1) depends on whether the witness being impeached is a defendant in a criminal prosecution or is some other type of witness. When the witness is not the accused, the evidence is admitted unless the party opposing the impeachment shows that probative value of the conviction for impeachment purposes is substantially outweighed by unfair prejudice. This is the usual burden imposed by Rule 403 on the party objecting to evidence. But when the witness is the accused, Rule 609(a)(1) shifts the burden of proving how the balance is struck to the party offering the evidence. The evidence can be admitted to impeach the accused only if the prosecution shows that the "probative value . . . outweighs its prejudicial effect."

For example, assume a prosecution for murder in which an alibi witness testifies that the accused was with him when the crime was committed across town. The prosecution offers evidence that the witness has a conviction for felony assault. The evidence is admitted under Rule 609(a)(1) unless the defense shows that prejudicial effect substantially outweighs probative value. Now assume that the accused testifies he did not commit the crime and the prosecution then offers evidence that the accused also has a conviction for felony assault. The evidence may be admitted under Rule 609(a)(1) only if the prosecutor shows that probative value outweighs prejudice.

This shifting of the burden makes sense when the witness is the accused because the evidence of the accused's assault conviction presents a high risk of unfair prejudice while providing what is likely to be minimal probative value. The risk is that the evidence might induce the jury to decide the case on an improper basis by concluding the accused is a bad person deserving of punishment regardless of whether he committed the murder with which he is charged. The jury might think this way because, before the jury can draw the permitted inference concerning lack of truthfulness, it logically must first conclude that the accused is a law breaker. But this is the same general inference that might lead the jury to conclude that the accused is a bad person who deserves to be punished even if innocent of the murder. Recall that in Chapter 4 we learned that Rule 404(a) generally bars this use of evidence. At the same time this evidence inflicts unfair prejudice, it adds little to the jurors' understanding of the accused's credibility as a witness. This is because the jurors already know that the accused is an interested witness who, if guilty of the murder, probably would not hesitate to commit the crime of perjury to avoid execution or a long jail sentence. Thus, the conviction evidence tells the jury nothing that it does not already know. One commentator illustrates the logic of this conclusion with this example of how *contrary* reasoning would obviously be illogical: "At first I thought it was very unlikely, if Defoe committed robbery, he would be willing to lie about it. But now that I know he committed forgery a year before, that possibility seems substantially more likely."[3]

Rule 609(a)(2) in part can be understood using a similar analysis. Recall that evidence under this provision is not subject to exclusion even when unfair prejudice outweighs probative value. This approach makes sense because usually the probative value of evidence offered under this provision is relatively high while its prejudicial effect is relatively low. Convictions that qualify for admission under Rule 609(a)(2) involve "a dishonest or false statement" and, thus, are necessarily more probative of untruthful character than are convictions for other crimes that might suggest other character traits, like violence or sexual immorality. At the same time, convictions for crimes involving a dishonest or false statement usually present less risk of inducing unfair prejudice because the jury need not infer from the fact of the conviction that the witness has a *general* propensity for breaking the law. Rather, the jury need only infer that the witness has the *specific* propensity for lying.

Because Rule 609(a) is so complicated, we provide the following chart to summarize some of the details in that provision:[4]

Crime	Impeaching accused	Impeaching other witness
Crime of dishonesty or false statement [609(a)(2)]	Admissible. No discretion to exclude for unfair prejudice	Admissible. No discretion to exclude for unfair prejudice

(continued)

---

3. Richard D. Friedman, *Character Impeachment Evidence: Psycho-Bayesian [!?] Analysis and a Proposed Overhaul*, 38 UCLA L. Rev. 637 (1991).

4. Note that the chart only summarizes the features of Rule 609(a). Other parts of Rule 609, if applicable, might alter the admissibility analysis.

Crime	Impeaching accused	Impeaching other witness
Other crimes punishable by death or imprisonment in excess of a year (felonies) [609(a)(1)]	Admissible only if prosecution shows probative value outweighs danger of unfair prejudice	Admissible unless party opposing impeachment shows, under Rule 403, that unfair prejudice, etc., substantially out-weighs probative value
Other crimes not punishable by death or imprisonment in excess of a year (misdemeanors) [609(a)]	Not admissible	Not admissible

d. Rule 609(b) — Old Convictions

Rule 609(b) excludes evidence otherwise admissible under subdivision (a) if more than ten years have passed since the witness's conviction or release from confinement for that conviction, whichever is later. However, the rule still permits such evidence to be admitted if the court concludes that, in light of the specific facts and circumstances surrounding the conviction, probative value substantially outweighs prejudice. This standard for admissibility sup-plants, for old convictions, the standards that otherwise would apply under Rule 609(a). This provision embodies the important policy judgment that it is often unfair and misleading to brand someone as a criminal, or a liar, based on something that happened many years in the past.

Note that the balancing standard of Rule 609(b) is *not* the same as that in Rule 403. Rule 403 is heavily slanted in favor of admission; only if prejudicial effect or other dangers substantially outweigh probative value may the court exclude the evidence. Rule 609(b), on the other hand, creates a standard heavily slanted in favor of exclusion; only if the probative value substantially outweighs prejudicial effect or other dangers may the court admit the evidence. The rule also contains a requirement that the party intending to present the evidence provide written notice of its intention.

e. Rule 609(c) — Effect of Pardon, Annulment, or Certificate of Rehabilitation

Subdivision (c) recognizes two situations in which conviction evidence should be excluded when it otherwise would be admissible under subdivisions (a) and (b). First, the evidence is inadmissible if a pardon or its equivalent was granted upon a finding of rehabilitation, so long as the witness was not subsequently convicted of a felony. Excluding the evidence when the witness has been reha-bilitated makes sense because rehabilitation is inconsistent with the assumption that conviction evidence proves the witness has a propensity toward lawlessness and, thus, may commit perjury. But because a subsequent conviction gives new life to this inference, it also makes sense then to disregard the finding of rehabilitation and admit the evidence. Second, subdivision (c) makes conviction evidence inadmissible when a pardon or its equivalent was based on a finding of innocence. This is also appropriate because such a finding demonstrates that there is no basis for inferring the witness is anything other than law abiding.

f. Rule 609(d) — Juvenile Adjudications

Subdivision (d) regulates the admissibility of "juvenile adjudications." The provision gives courts discretion to admit the evidence in a criminal case against a witness other than the accused. The court may exercise that discretion and admit the evidence if the evidence would otherwise be admissible under Rule 609 and it "is necessary to fairly determine guilt or innocence." The admissibility of juvenile adjudications is restricted because the actions of a person when a juvenile might not be indicative of his character as an adult. Just as subdivision (b) assumes that time permits rehabilitation, subdivision (d) assumes that maturity can have the same effect. The policy reasons for making the latter assumption are strong. The primary purpose of the juvenile justice system is to rehabilitate, not punish. Excluding juvenile adjudications serves this purpose by helping to ensure that the stigma of conviction does not follow the juvenile and interfere with his efforts to reform.

g. Rule 609(e) — Pendency of Appeal

Subdivision (e) establishes that the pendency of an appeal does not make evidence of a conviction inadmissible. The Advisory Committee's Note states that this provision is based on the "presumption of correctness that ought to attend judicial proceedings." The same rationale suggests that the pendency of post-trial motions attacking the validity of the judgment should also be no bar to the admissibility of conviction evidence to impeach.

h. Preserving the Right to Appeal Under Rule 609

LUCE v. UNITED STATES
469 U.S. 38 (1984)

[In a prosecution for drug-related crimes, defendant made a pretrial motion asking the court to rule that evidence of his prior drug conviction was inadmissible under Rule 609. The trial court denied the motion, concluding the evidence would be admissible to impeach defendant if he testified. The defendant declined to testify at trial, which, of course, precluded the prosecution from offering the prior conviction to impeach his credibility. He was convicted, and appealed, claiming that the trial court erred in its pretrial ruling.]

Chief Justice BURGER delivered the opinion of the Court.

It is clear, of course, that had petitioner testified and been impeached by evidence of a prior conviction, the District Court's decision to admit the impeachment evidence would have been reviewable on appeal along with any other claims of error. The Court of Appeals would then have had a complete record detailing the nature of petitioner's testimony, the scope of the cross-examination, and the possible impact of the impeachment on the jury's verdict.

A reviewing court is handicapped in any effort to rule on subtle evidentiary questions outside a factual context. This is particularly true under Rule 609(a)(1), which directs the court to weigh the probative value of a prior conviction against the prejudicial effect to the defendant. To perform this balancing, the court must know the precise nature of the defendant's testimony, which is unknowable when, as here, the defendant does not testify.

Any possible harm flowing from a district court's *in limine* ruling permitting impeachment by a prior conviction is wholly speculative. The ruling is subject to change when the case unfolds, particularly if the actual testimony differs from what was contained in the defendant's proffer. Indeed even if nothing unexpected happens at trial, the district judge is free, in the exercise of sound judicial discretion, to alter a previous *in limine* ruling. On a record such as here, it would be a matter of conjecture whether the District Court would have allowed the Government to attack petitioner's credibility at trial by means of the prior conviction.

When the defendant does not testify, the reviewing court also has no way of knowing whether the Government would have sought to impeach with the prior conviction. If, for example, the Government's case is strong, and the defendant is subject to impeachment by other means, a prosecutor might elect not to use an arguably inadmissible prior conviction.

Because an accused's decision whether to testify "seldom turns on the resolution of one factor," . . . a reviewing court cannot assume that the adverse ruling motivated a defendant's decision not to testify. In support of his motion a defendant might make a commitment to testify if his motion is granted; but such a commitment is virtually risk free because of the difficulty of enforcing it.

Even if these difficulties could be surmounted, the reviewing court would still face the question of harmless error. . . . Were *in limine* rulings under Rule 609(a) reviewable on appeal, almost any error would result in the windfall of automatic reversal; the appellate court could not logically term "harmless" an error that presumptively kept the defendant from testifying. Requiring that a defendant testify in order to preserve Rule 609(a) claims will enable the reviewing court to determine the impact any erroneous impeachment may have had in light of the record as a whole; it will also tend to discourage making such motions solely to "plant" reversible error in the event of conviction. . . .

We hold that to raise and preserve for review the claim of improper impeachment with a prior conviction, a defendant must testify. Accordingly, the judgment of the Court of Appeals is

Affirmed.

Further Reading: Robert D. Dodson, *What Went Wrong with Federal Rule of Evidence 609: A Look at How Jurors Really Misuse Prior Conviction Evidence*, 48 Drake L. Rev. 1 (1999); Victor Gold, *Impeachment by Conviction Evidence and the Politics of Rule 609*, 15 Cardozo L. Rev. 2295 (1994); Alan D. Hornstein, *Between a Rock and a Hard Place: The Right to Testify and Impeachment by Prior Conviction*, 42 Vill. L. Rev. 1 (1997); Robert Okun, *Character and Credibility: A Proposal to Realign Federal Rules of Evidence 608 and 609*, 37 Vill. L. Rev. 533 (1992); David A. Sonenshein, *Circuit Roulette: The Use of Prior Convictions to Impeach Credibility in Civil Cases Under the Federal Rules of Evidence*, 57 Geo. Wash. L. Rev. 279 (1988);

David Williams, Jr., Comment, *Witness Impeachment by Evidence of Prior Felony Convictions: The Time Has Come for the Federal Rules of Evidence to Put on the New Man and Forgive the Felon*, 65 Temp. L. Rev. 893 (1992).

Questions for Classroom Discussion

1. What assumptions does Rule 609 make about the connection between a witness's prior conviction and that witness's character for truthfulness? Do you agree with the assumptions? If an accused testifies and denies committing the crime charged, does evidence that the accused has a prior conviction for an unrelated offense tell us much about the reliability of his testimony that we do not already know?

2. Recall that Rule 608(b) limits the admissibility of misconduct evidence bearing on truthfulness because, in part, resolving doubts concerning whether the misconduct occurred might require time-consuming presentation of extrinsic evidence. Why doesn't Rule 609 place greater limits on the admission of conviction evidence on the ground that there may be doubts about whether the witness committed the crime?

3. Prosecution for perjury. Defendant testifies that, while he made false statements, he did not know they were false at the time. On cross-examination of Defendant, the prosecutor asks, "Isn't it true that last year you were convicted of a misdemeanor for lying on your driver's license application? Defendant answers "Yes." Admissible? Is there discretion under Rule 403 to exclude for unfair prejudice? What if the conviction is more than ten years old?

4. Same case. Defendant denies the conviction occurred. Is a certified copy of the judgment of conviction admissible?

5. Same case. Defendant denies the conviction occurred. A police officer is prepared to testify that he arrested Defendant for lying on his driver's license application. Is the officer's testimony admissible?

6. Same case. The prosecutor offers evidence that Defendant was convicted of petty theft, a misdemeanor. Admissible?

7. Prosecution for bank robbery. Defendant testifies and denies committing the crime. The prosecutor offers evidence Defendant has a prior conviction for bank robbery, a felony. Admissible?

8. Same case. An alibi witness testifies for the defense that he and Defendant were at the movies at the time the crime was committed across town. The prosecutor offers evidence that the witness had an eight-year-old prior conviction for bank robbery, a felony. There is no other evidence concerning the witness's credibility. Admissible?

(continued)

9. Same case. The alibi witness was convicted of felony bank robbery but was sentenced to probation and was never imprisoned. Admissible?

10. Same case. The alibi witness was convicted of perjury and was released from prison in 1988. Admissible?

11. In *Luce*, the defendant declined at trial to testify in his own defense. Why? Does the decision in *Luce* have costs?

12. Murder prosecution. The trial court denies Defendant's pretrial motion to exclude, in the event he testified, a misdemeanor conviction for assault. If Defendant fails to testify, has he waived the issue for appeal? Is *Luce* distinguishable?

5. *Religious Beliefs or Opinions*

FED. R. EVID. 610.   RELIGIOUS BELIEFS OR OPINIONS

Evidence of a witness's religious beliefs or opinions is not admissible to attack or support the witness's credibility.

Discussion

Rule 610 makes inadmissible evidence of a witness's beliefs or opinions on matters of religion when offered for certain purposes pertaining to witness credibility. Defining *religion* for purposes of Rule 610 can be difficult. But it should be clear that, in addition to mainstream religions, the rule extends to evidence of unconventional beliefs. In fact, disclosure of unconventional beliefs has the greatest potential to incite the sort of prejudice Rule 610 exists to prevent. Further, imposition by a judge of a narrow personal notion of religion may, in and of itself, violate the values of religious liberty inherent in both Rule 610 and the Free Exercise Clause of the U.S. Constitution. However, it also should be clear that Rule 610 is not intended to make inadmissible evidence that a witness subscribes to an ideology that is political or philosophical, rather than religious. The difficulty comes in distinguishing between religious beliefs on the one hand and political or philosophical beliefs on the other hand.

The policy assumptions underlying Rule 610 provide some help in classifying beliefs or opinions as religious. Evidence is excluded under that provision because it threatens unfair prejudice. This prejudice can occur in two ways. First, the evidence is unfairly prejudicial if it impairs the jury's estimation of witness credibility by revealing that the witness subscribes to ideas offensive to conventional religious beliefs. Second, the evidence is unfairly prejudicial if it enhances the jury's estimation of witness credibility by revealing that the witness adheres to conventional beliefs. This suggests that when a jury of conventional believers would not consider their religious beliefs to be implicated by the witness's opinions, there is no need to treat those opinions as religious under Rule 610. This does not mean, however, that evidence of such opinions is necessarily admissible. That evidence might still be irrelevant to credibility or otherwise objectionable.

Rule 610 does not exclude all evidence of religious belief offered for impeachment. The evidence is inadmissible only if offered for a purpose that threatens the sort of prejudice just described. Thus, the Advisory Committee's Note states that religious-belief evidence is inadmissible only when offered to show that a witness's character for truthfulness or untruthfulness is influenced by the nature of that belief. This means that Rule 610 is inapplicable when such evidence is offered for any other purpose, even when it affects credibility in some other way. For example, the courts have held that Rule 610 is inapplicable when evidence of religious belief is offered to show the bias of a witness, the basis for an assertion of clerical privilege, damages, *modus operandi*, motive, conduct, and the basis for a claim or defense. On the other hand, even when evidence of religious belief is offered for some purpose other than to prove credibility, Rule 403 gives the court discretion to exclude if probative value is substantially outweighed by the danger of unfair prejudice. When the court chooses to admit the evidence, an instruction should be given limiting its use to matters other than the witness's character for truthfulness.

Questions for Classroom Discussion

1. Prosecution of Defendant for tax fraud. Defendant's accountant testifies that Defendant scrupulously observed the requirements of the Internal Revenue Code. The prosecutor offers evidence that the accountant is a member of a religious organization that believes in animal sacrifice and worships a golden calf. Admissible?

2. Same case. The prosecutor offers evidence that the accountant is a member of a religious organization that believes Defendant is the messiah. Admissible?

F.   BIAS, MOTIVE, AND INTEREST

There is no specific Federal Rule of Evidence regulating impeachment for bias, motive, and interest.

Discussion

1. Effects of Bias

Bias is a state of mind that may cause a witness to favor or disfavor a party. Motive and interest are related states of mind that may influence the testimony of a witness regardless of the witness's connection to a party. For example, a witness may be biased in favor of a party if the party and the witness are friends. A witness has a motive to alter her testimony if she has been threatened with physical harm in the event she testifies to certain facts. Finally, a witness also may alter her testimony if she has an interest in the outcome of the case, as would be the case if she was promised a part of any monetary recovery. The lines between bias, motive, and interest may be difficult to draw in a given case. Fortunately, the law makes no significant distinctions between impeachment on these grounds. Accordingly, in the remainder of this section we refer to these states of mind collectively as "bias."

Evidence of bias provides a powerful ground for impeachment because it can undermine all the attributes on which the credibility of a witness depends. Bias can impair perception because people tend to interpret what they see and hear in ways consistent with their prejudices and interests. Similarly, bias can put in doubt the reliability of recollection by moving people to engage in selective recall and even confabulation. Evidence of bias raises questions concerning a witness's sincerity because people may lie to gain some advantage. Even the accuracy of witness narration is threatened by bias, which can influence the very words we choose. Some of these effects may occur unconsciously. This makes it difficult for witnesses to control their biases even when they want to testify truthfully.

2.   *Proving Bias*

Bias often can be proven only circumstantially. One reason is that witnesses resist admitting their biases. Another reason is that only a given witness can testify directly about her state of mind. Because the forces that motivate an individual can be highly idiosyncratic, circumstantial evidence of bias may take a wide variety of forms. However, a limited number of scenarios are common. Thus, the credibility of a witness frequently has been attacked for bias when there is evidence that the witness is favorably disposed toward a party because of family or financial relationship, romantic entanglement, friendship, employment, shared beliefs or background, or payment of money. Bias also exists when there is enmity between a witness and a party. This enmity can be due to a fight, insult, prior lawsuit, differences in background, fear, and numerous other factors.

Bias also exists when the witness has a personal interest in the outcome of the litigation or the matters about which she testifies. Cases in this category include those in which the witness is a party, has a claim against a party that is related to the proceeding in which she testifies, has settled such a claim, is the insurer of a party, is a shareholder of a corporate party, or may be subject to criticism for the content of her testimony. Self-interest is a particularly important basis for impeachment in criminal cases in which the witness testifies for the state and has received immunity, has been promised or given leniency in exchange for testimony, has been indicted, is awaiting sentencing, is a paid informant, is being held in protective custody, is on parole or probation, or has obtained some other benefit for testifying.

3. Admissibility of Bias Evidence

The Federal Rules of Evidence do not explicitly regulate proof of bias. However, in United States v. Abel, 469 U.S. 45 (1984), an excerpt of which appears below, the Supreme Court held that the relevance rules and other provisions within the Federal Rules of Evidence imply that evidence of witness bias should be admissible. The opinion in *Abel* is a landmark in the jurisprudence of the Federal Rules of Evidence because it helps define the relationship between those rules and the common law that preceded adoption of the rules.

The law regards bias as a favored and powerful basis for attacking credibility. An accused may have a constitutional right to impeach prosecution witnesses for bias.[5] Similarly, the courts generally do not impose admissibility limits on extrinsic evidence of bias. Thus, even if a witness does not admit to the facts suggesting her bias, those facts may be proved through other evidence, such as the testimony of another witness. This is because bias is never collateral to the issues in a case; it probably will affect testimony about important matters because it is on those matters that the force of bias is most likely to be felt. By contrast, we have seen that the admissibility of extrinsic evidence is sometimes limited when credibility is attacked on other grounds, such as using specific instances of conduct to prove a witness's character for untruthfulness.

But this does not mean that bias evidence is always admissible. Occasionally, the admission of such evidence will violate a constitutional right or a rule of evidence. Courts also may exclude bias evidence under the discretionary powers granted to them by Rules 403 and 611(a). This is because evidence of bias sometimes has the potential to confuse and prejudice the jury or unduly embarrass and harass the witness. Thus, courts have exercised their discretion to exclude when bias is revealed by evidence of wrongful acts, insurance, a settlement, or inflammatory matters. It should be noted that, when the witness is also a party, the potential for bias evidence to produce unfair prejudice may be increased significantly, as when bias is shown by the party's commission of wrongful acts. In such a case, the jury might improperly consider the evidence as revealing character traits suggestive of the party's conduct. We have seen in Chapter 4 that Rule 404 generally makes evidence inadmissible for such purposes.

4. Admitting Extrinsic Evidence of a Witness's Prior Statements Revealing Bias

A final question concerning bias evidence is whether the impeaching party must give the witness an opportunity to admit or deny the facts demonstrating bias *before* extrinsic evidence of those facts is admissible. For example, assume a prosecution witness testifies that she does not know the defendant, but defense

---

5. *See* Davis v. Alaska, 415 U.S. 308 (1974) (the Sixth Amendment Confrontation Clause gives criminal defendants the right to have an opportunity to prove that a prosecution witness is biased). See also Chapter 4 for discussion of Olden v. Kentucky, 488 U.S. 227 (1988), a case in which the Supreme Court held that a defendant accused of rape had a constitutional right to impeach the alleged victim by showing her extramarital relationship with another man. Because of that relationship, the alleged victim had a motive to testify that she did not consent to the sexual conduct with defendant.

counsel has extrinsic evidence that the witness made a prior statement in which she said she had a fight with defendant. Citing to Rule 613(b), several courts and commentators conclude that an impeaching party normally must give a witness an opportunity to admit or deny bias as a condition to admitting extrinsic evidence of a prior statement of the witness proving that bias. Some authorities further require that the impeaching party call the attention of the witness to the time, place, and persons involved in the making of the statement that reveals bias.

If the courts impose such requirements, the next issue is whether extrinsic evidence of a prior statement is admissible if the witness admits to making the statement revealing bias. As a general matter, if the witness denies the facts indicating bias, extrinsic evidence of those facts is freely admissible. However, if a witness unequivocally admits to making the statement, extrinsic evidence might be cumulative and a time-waster. On the other hand, sometimes a witness's bias is not adequately revealed simply by admitting to making a statement. Words are ambiguous. The witness's admission may not disclose the tone of the statement or the circumstances under which it was made. After all, if a witness is biased, her testimony about her statements will itself be affected by bias. Extrinsic evidence that reveals additional facts concerning the statement may be crucial to revealing the bias and its full impact. In such a case, the principles underlying Rules 403 and 611 suggest that the extrinsic evidence should be admitted. Because the Federal Rules do not specifically address the question, trial courts must determine admissibility on a case-by-case basis, applying the standards of Rules 403 and 611.

For similar reasons, if the witness is given a chance to admit to and explain her statement, sometimes it might make sense to provide this opportunity *after* the extrinsic evidence has been admitted. The prior disclosure of such evidence may go a long way to inspiring the witness to control the effects of bias when she is called to the stand. In the case of impeachment with prior inconsistent statement, Rule 613 dispenses with the requirement of a preliminary foundation so long as the impeached witness eventually gets a chance to explain the inconsistent statement. Similarly, it seems unnecessary always to insist on a preliminary foundation in the case of prior statements evidencing bias. However, when extrinsic evidence of the statement might add little to the witness's admission, it makes sense to require the foundation first so that the court can consider the need to spend more time on the matter. The court has authority under Rule 611 to require a party to take that step.

UNITED STATES v. ABEL
469 U.S. 45 (1984)

[Abel was charged with bank robbery. An alleged accomplice, Ehle, testified for the prosecution. Abel then called Mills to impeach Ehle by testifying that Ehle said he would falsely implicate Abel to gain favor with the prosecutors. The prosecution then recalled Ehle to impeach Mills. Ehle testified that he, Abel, and Mills were all members of a secret prison gang that required its members to lie, cheat, and steal to protect each other. The implication of Ehle's testimony was that Mills had lied to protect Abel. Abel was convicted but the conviction was reversed by the Court of Appeals on the ground the trial court erred in admitting Ehle's testimony to impeach Mills. (You might need a scorecard to keep track of the players.)]

Justice REHNQUIST delivered the opinion of the Court.

We hold that the evidence showing Mills' and respondent's membership in the prison gang was sufficiently probative of Mills' possible bias towards respondent to warrant its admission into evidence. Thus it was within the District Court's discretion to admit Ehle's testimony, and the Court of Appeals was wrong in concluding otherwise.

Both parties correctly assume, as did the District Court and the Court of Appeals, that the question is governed by the Federal Rules of Evidence. But the Rules do not by their terms deal with impeachment for "bias," although they do expressly treat impeachment by character evidence and conduct, Rule 608, by evidence of conviction of a crime, Rule 609, and by showing of religious beliefs or opinion, Rule 610. Neither party has suggested what significance we should attribute to this fact. Although we are nominally the promulgators of the Rules, and should in theory need only to consult our collective memories to analyze the situation properly, we are in truth merely a conduit when we deal with an undertaking as substantial as the preparation of the Federal Rules of Evidence. In the case of these Rules, too, it must be remembered that Congress extensively reviewed our submission, and considerably revised it.

Before the present Rules were promulgated, the admissibility of evidence in the federal courts was governed in part by statutes or Rules, and in part by case law. This Court had held . . . that a trial court must allow some cross-examination of a witness to show bias. This holding was in accord with the overwhelming weight of authority in the state courts as reflected in Wigmore's classic treatise on the law of evidence. . . . Our decision in Davis v. Alaska, 415 U.S. 308, 94 S. Ct. 1105, 39 L. Ed. 2d 347 (1974), holds that the Confrontation Clause of the Sixth Amendment requires a defendant to have some opportunity to show bias on the part of a prosecution witness.

With this state of unanimity confronting the drafters of the Federal Rules of Evidence, we think it unlikely that they intended to scuttle entirely the evidentiary availability of cross-examination for bias. One commentator, recognizing the omission of any express treatment of impeachment for bias, prejudice, or corruption, observes that the Rules "clearly contemplate the use of the above-mentioned grounds of impeachment." E. Cleary, McCormick on Evidence § 40, p. 85 (3d ed. 1984).

We think this conclusion is obviously correct. Rule 401 defines as "relevant evidence" evidence having any tendency to make the existence of any fact that is of consequence to the determination of the action more probable or less probable than it would be without the evidence. Rule 402 provides that all relevant evidence is admissible, except as otherwise provided by the United States Constitution, by Act of Congress, or by applicable rule. A successful showing of bias on the part of a witness would have a tendency to make the facts to which he testified less probable in the eyes of the jury than it would be without such testimony.

The correctness of the conclusion that the Rules contemplate impeachment by showing of bias is confirmed by the references to bias in the Advisory Committee Notes to Rules 608 and 610, and by the provisions allowing any party to attack credibility in Rule 607, and allowing cross-examination on "matters affecting the credibility of the witness" in Rule 611(b). The Courts of Appeals have upheld use of extrinsic evidence to show bias both before and after the adoption of the Federal Rules of Evidence. . . .

We think the lesson to be drawn from all of this is that it is permissible to impeach a witness by showing his bias under the Federal Rules of Evidence just as it was permissible to do so before their adoption. In this connection, the comment of the Reporter for the Advisory Committee which drafted the Rules is apropos:

> "In principle, under the Federal Rules no common law of evidence remains. 'All relevant evidence is admissible, except as otherwise provided. . . .' In reality, of course, the body of common law knowledge continues to exist, though in the somewhat altered form of a source of guidance in the exercise of delegated powers." Cleary, Preliminary Notes on Reading the Rules of Evidence, 57 Neb. L. Rev. 908, 915 (1978) (footnote omitted).

Ehle's testimony about the prison gang certainly made the existence of Mills' bias towards respondent more probable. Thus it was relevant to support that inference. Bias is a term used in the "common law of evidence" to describe the relationship between a party and a witness which might lead the witness to slant, unconsciously or otherwise, his testimony in favor of or against a party. Bias may be induced by a witness' like, dislike, or fear of a party, or by the witness' self-interest. Proof of bias is almost always relevant because the jury, as finder of fact and weigher of credibility, has historically been entitled to assess all evidence which might bear on the accuracy and truth of a witness' testimony. The "common law of evidence" allowed the showing of bias by extrinsic evidence, while requiring the cross-examiner to "take the answer of the witness" with respect to less favored forms of impeachment. . . .

Mills' and respondent's membership in the Aryan Brotherhood supported the inference that Mills' testimony was slanted or perhaps fabricated in respondent's favor. A witness' and a party's common membership in an organization, even without proof that the witness or party has personally adopted its tenets, is certainly probative of bias. . . . Mills' and respondent's membership in the Aryan Brotherhood was not offered to convict either of a crime, but to impeach Mills' testimony. Mills was subject to no sanction other than that he might be disbelieved. . . . For purposes of the law of evidence the jury may be permitted to draw an inference of subscription to the tenets of the organization from membership alone, even though such an inference would not be sufficient to convict beyond a reasonable doubt in a criminal prosecution under the Smith Act.

Respondent argues that even if the evidence of membership in the prison gang were relevant to show bias, the District Court erred in permitting a full description of the gang and its odious tenets. Respondent contends that the District Court abused its discretion under Federal Rule of Evidence 403, because the prejudicial effect of the contested evidence outweighed its probative value. In other words, testimony about the gang inflamed the jury against respondent, and the chance that he would be convicted by his mere association with the organization outweighed any probative value the testimony may have had on Mills' bias.

Respondent specifically contends that the District Court should not have permitted Ehle's precise description of the gang as a lying and murderous group. Respondent suggests that the District Court should have cut off the testimony after the prosecutor had elicited that Mills knew respondent and both may have belonged to an organization together. This argument ignores the fact that the type of organization in which a witness and a party share membership may be relevant to show bias. If the organization is a loosely knit group having nothing to do with the subject matter of the litigation, the inference of bias arising from common membership may be small or nonexistent. If the prosecutor had elicited that both respondent and Mills belonged to the Book of the Month Club, the jury probably would not have inferred bias even if the District Court had admitted the testimony. The attributes of the Aryan Brotherhood — a secret prison sect sworn to perjury and self-protection — bore directly not only on the fact of bias but also on the source and strength of Mills' bias. The tenets of this group showed that Mills had a powerful motive to slant his testimony towards respondent, or even commit perjury outright.

A district court is accorded a wide discretion in determining the admissibility of evidence under the Federal Rules. Assessing the probative value of common membership in any particular group, and weighing any factors counseling against admissibility is a matter first for the district court's sound judgment under Rules 401 and 403 and ultimately, if the evidence is admitted, for the trier of fact.

Before admitting Ehle's rebuttal testimony, the District Court gave heed to the extensive arguments of counsel, both in chambers and at the bench. In an attempt to avoid undue prejudice to respondent the court ordered that the name "Aryan Brotherhood" not be used. The court also offered to give a limiting instruction concerning the testimony, and it sustained defense objections to the prosecutor's questions concerning the punishment meted out to unfaithful members. These precautions did not prevent all prejudice to respondent from Ehle's testimony, but they did, in our opinion, ensure that the admission of this highly probative evidence did not unduly prejudice respondent. We hold there was no abuse of discretion under Rule 403 in admitting Ehle's testimony as to membership and tenets.

Respondent makes an additional argument based on Rule 608(b). That Rule allows a cross-examiner to impeach a witness by asking him about specific instances of past conduct, other than crimes covered by Rule 609, which are probative of his veracity or "character for truthfulness or untruthfulness." The Rule limits the inquiry to cross-examination of the witness, however, and prohibits the cross-examiner from introducing extrinsic evidence of the witness' past conduct.

Respondent claims that the prosecutor cross-examined Mills about the gang not to show bias but to offer Mills' membership in the gang as past conduct bearing on his veracity. This was error under Rule 608(b), respondent contends, because the mere fact of Mills' membership, without more, was not sufficiently probative of Mills' character for truthfulness. Respondent cites a second error under the same Rule, contending that Ehle's rebuttal testimony concerning the gang was extrinsic evidence offered to impugn Mills' veracity, and extrinsic evidence is barred by Rule 608(b)....

It seems clear to us that the proffered testimony with respect to Mills' membership in the Aryan Brotherhood sufficed to show potential bias in favor of respondent; because of the tenets of the organization described, it might also impeach his veracity directly. But there is no rule of evidence which provides that testimony admissible for one purpose and inadmissible for another purpose is thereby rendered inadmissible; quite the contrary is the case. It would be a strange rule of law which held that relevant, competent evidence which tended to show bias on the part of a witness was nonetheless inadmissible because it also tended to show that the witness was a liar.

We intimate no view as to whether the evidence of Mills' membership in an organization having the tenets ascribed to the Aryan Brotherhood would be a specific instance of Mills' conduct which could not be proved against him by extrinsic evidence except as otherwise provided in Rule 608(b). It was enough that such evidence could properly be found admissible to show bias.

The judgment of the Court of Appeals is
Reversed.

Questions for Classroom Discussion

1. The prosecution in United States v. Abel offered evidence that defendant and a defense witness were members of the same secret society that required its members to lie, cheat, and steal to protect each other. Identify three relevant facts that might be inferred from this evidence. Was it *admissible* to prove each of those facts?

2. What does *Abel* say about the relationship between the Federal Rules of Evidence and the common law of evidence that was in existence at the time the Federal Rules were enacted? What does *Abel* say about the power of the courts to make evidence law after enactment of the Federal Rules?

3. The Court in *Abel* adopted the traditional common law approach that extrinsic evidence is admissible to prove bias. Recall that there are limits on the admissibility of extrinsic evidence when offered to impeach under other methods of impeachment, such as contradiction or specific instances of conduct under Rule 608(b). Why is the law more willing to admit extrinsic evidence of bias?

4. Murder prosecution. Defendant calls Joe, who testifies, "Defendant was with me at the movies on the night of the crime." On cross-examination, the prosecutor asks, "Defendant paid you $1,000 for the alibi, didn't he?" The witness answers, "No." The prosecutor then calls a second witness who offers to testify, "Joe told me that Defendant paid him $1,000 to provide an alibi." Does Rule 613(b) apply?

5. Prosecution for cruelty to animals. Defendant is charged with sacrificing a goat in a religious ritual. A defense witness testifies Defendant did not commit the act charged. The prosecution offers evidence that both the defense witness and Defendant are members of a religious sect that believes in animal sacrifice. Is this evidence admissible to impeach the witness?

6. Civil action to recover for personal injuries sustained in an automobile accident. A witness testifies for the defense that Plaintiff drove through a red light and then struck Defendant's car. On cross-examination, Plaintiff's counsel asks the witness, "Isn't it true that you are the president of Defendant's automobile insurance company? Doesn't Defendant have $100,000 of liability insurance?" What objection should Defendant raise? How should the court rule?

7. Civil trial. Plaintiff claims Defendant broke his jaw during a bar fight. A witness testifies she was at the bar that evening, and that Defendant started the brawl. On cross-examination, Defendant's lawyer asks, "You began dating the defendant shortly after you met him in his lawyer's office, didn't you?" Defendant objects. Should the court permit the witness to answer, on the theory that it may tend to impeach the witness?

8. Murder trial. A witness testifies that while she was Defendant's cellmate Defendant said she committed the homicide. Should defense counsel be allowed to introduce a document showing the witness is a paid informant? Should counsel be required to ask the witness whether she is a paid informant before he is allowed to introduce the document?

9. In a civil rights trial, an expert witness testifies on behalf of Plaintiffs. On cross-examination, defense counsel asks, "You are not charging the plaintiffs for your testimony, are you?" Plaintiffs' counsel objects, arguing the question is irrelevant, or in the alternative, that it is unfairly prejudicial. How should the court rule?

G. IMPEACHMENT BY CONTRADICTION

There is no specific Federal Rule of Evidence regulating impeachment by contradiction.

Discussion

1. Introduction

A person who is wrong about one thing might be wrong about other things. For example, a witness who testifies inaccurately that the weather was clear on the day she observed an automobile accident might also have testified inaccurately about who ran the red light. This is a commonly accepted and intuitively accurate observation about people. Of course, the mere fact that a person is wrong about one fact does not necessarily make that person generally unreliable. Also, a witness's inaccuracy about a minor detail might not say much about whether she has accurately described important details of an event. After all, everyone is wrong sometimes. Nonetheless, demonstrating that a witness has testified inaccurately can be a very effective means of impeaching her credibility. This is impeachment by contradiction.

Note that impeachment by contradiction is common. One witness testifies that the day of the bank robbery was cloudy, while another testifies that it was sunny. One witness testifies that the bank robber was a tall woman, while another states that the robber was a short man. Again, the testimony of each witness tends to undercut that of the other by contradicting it, and if we know that the first witness was wrong and the second right about one fact, we will accord less credibility to the former concerning other details of her testimony and more to the latter. Ultimately, it is up to the trier of fact to sort out the differences and decide which witnesses to believe. The lawyer's role is to reveal and highlight the differences in the stories told by the witnesses.

As should be expected, the law generously allows impeachment by contradiction when the matter about which there is disagreement is important to the case. It is only when a witness is demonstrably wrong about something entirely unimportant that the common law restricted (but did not disallow completely) the use of impeachment by contradiction. The discussion that follows explains and illustrates the restrictions.

2.   *Common Law Rule Restricting Impeachment by Contradiction*

Contradiction of one witness by the testimony of a second witness can serve two purposes. First, the testimony of the second witness can be used to establish the facts to which that witness testifies. Second, it can be used to show that the first witness lacks credibility. In most cases, the evidence serves both purposes. Suppose, for example, that in a bank robbery trial, the prosecutor calls a witness who testifies that as she was driving past the bank on the day in question, she saw a male running out of the bank carrying a rifle. Defendant is a male. If the defendant then offers the testimony of another witness that the bank robber was a woman, that evidence serves two purposes: It has the tendency to prove defendant's innocence because the robber was a woman and it casts doubt on the credibility of the prosecution witness as to all matters about which she testified. Of course, the jury might decide that it was the defense witness who incorrectly described the perpetrator. In that case, the contradiction works the other way.

While contradiction evidence is not regulated by a specific rule, it still is subject to the general rules governing the form of questions; the dangers of unfair prejudice, distraction, or waste of time; and by other limits on witness examination.

The one common law rule specifically governing and limiting impeachment by contradiction is as follows: *Extrinsic evidence is not admissible to contradict a witness on a collateral matter.* We will examine the rule in the context of the following hypothetical:

> Prosecution of Defendant for the murder of Victim. The charge stems from a barroom brawl that left Victim dead. The prosecution claims Defendant instigated the fight and killed Victim without provocation. Defendant claims he acted in self-defense. At trial, the prosecution calls Witness 1, who testifies that Defendant started the fight and stabbed Victim without reason. In response, Defendant

calls Witness 2, who testifies that just before Defendant stabbed Victim, Victim threatened to kill Defendant.

Let's take apart the impeachment by contradiction rule piece by piece. *First*, it is a rule applied only to the form of impeachment known as impeachment by contradiction. If another method of impeachment is being used, such as proof of bias or conviction of a crime, you must consider the specific rules that govern those forms of impeachment. The present discussion does not address those rules.

Second, the contradiction rule applies only when the contradiction concerns "collateral matters." What is a collateral matter? It is a factual matter that has no importance to the case except in its tendency to undercut the credibility of a witness *by contradiction* rather than in some other manner. In our example, Witness 2's testimony does not concern a collateral matter. Evidence that Victim threatened Defendant has significant substantive value. Not only does it tend to impeach Witness 1's credibility by contradicting Witness 1, it also tends to supply Defendant with a substantive defense to the murder charge. Evidence that is relevant to a substantive issue in the case is not collateral.

Even if contradiction evidence is not relevant to a substantive issue, it still is non-collateral if it says something about the credibility of the witness beyond contradicting her. For example, suppose Witness 1 testified on direct examination that when the fight between Defendant and Victim broke out, she was sitting alone at a table watching the other people in the bar. Defendant offers evidence that Witness 1 was actually intently watching a football game on the bar television during that time. This evidence contradicts Witness 1 and does not directly challenge any of Witness 1's testimony about who started the fight. But, the evidence *also* casts doubt on whether Witness 1 really observed the events preceding the stabbing. If Witness 1 was watching a football game on television, it is less likely that she saw the events leading up to the stabbing than if she was sitting quietly at a table watching the other bar patrons. The evidence is not collateral and is admissible. In fact, it tends to impeach her by showing an impaired opportunity to observe caused by distraction.

Suppose, further that Witness 1 testified that she observed the fight while she was sipping a diet cola. Defendant then offers evidence that Witness 1 was sipping a regular cola, not a diet cola. That testimony certainly contradicts Witness 1, and if Witness 1 is wrong about the type of drink she was having, she might be wrong about other details. However, the question of what type of soft drink Witness 1 was sipping is certainly collateral. The only purpose of the evidence would be to impeach Witness 1 by contradiction; it would have no value on the substantive issues of the case. But consider how the analysis changes if Defendant offers evidence that Witness 1 was enjoying her fifth gin and tonic when the fight broke out. Now the contradiction evidence proves a fact that is not collateral because it tells us something about the credibility of Witness 1 beyond just the contradiction; namely, she may have been drunk when perceiving the events in question.

Third, the rule limiting admissibility applies only to the use of extrinsic evidence to prove the collateral matter. As we have seen already, the word *extrinsic* is not easy to define, but the idea behind that term is relatively simple. "Extrinsic" means from without, or outside. Thus, extrinsic evidence is evidence that comes from outside the witness who is being impeached. Here is a more complete definition of the term, as applied to the rule we are now considering: Extrinsic evidence is any evidence offered to contradict a witness that comes from a source other than that witness while she is testifying in this trial. The most obvious example of extrinsic evidence offered to impeach a witness is the testimony of *another* witness. Similarly, documents are extrinsic evidence. Even a statement by the very witness being impeached is extrinsic evidence if that statement was made at any time other than while the witness was testifying here in the proceeding where the impeachment evidence is offered. The most obvious example of *intrinsic* (non-extrinsic) evidence is testimony elicited on cross-examination of the witness herself.

To return to our hypothetical, Defendant's cross-examination of Witness 1 in an effort to bring forth contradictory information is not extrinsic. It seeks to contradict Witness 1 out of her own mouth. So Defendant is permitted to ask Witness 1 on cross-examination, "Isn't it true that you were drinking a regular cola and not, as you claimed on direct, a diet cola?" While Witness 1's affirmative answer goes to a collateral matter, it is admissible because it is not extrinsic evidence. But if Witness 1 still insists she was drinking a diet cola, Defendant may not prove otherwise through the testimony of Witness 2 since this would be an attempt to use extrinsic evidence to contradict on a collateral matter.

This is yet another example of something we have seen before in connection with certain other impeachment techniques that limit the admissibility of extrinsic evidence: If the witness being impeached denies the basis for impeachment when cross-examined, the cross-examiner must "take the answer" of the witness. In our hypothetical case, even if Defendant *knows* that Witness 1 is wrong when she denies drinking a regular cola, Defendant may not use extrinsic evidence to prove that fact.

3. Modern Treatment of the Rule

As noted at the beginning of this section, there is no provision of the Federal Rules of Evidence specifically governing impeachment by contradiction. This method of impeachment simply is not mentioned in the rules. This does not mean, of course, that the rules do not permit impeachment by contradiction. As we have seen in connection with the discussion of bias impeachment, the absence of a specific rule does not signal an intent to discard a principle of admissibility followed by the common law. In most circumstances, the courts can use their authority under Rule 403 to forbid extrinsic evidence that impeaches by contradiction on a collateral matter because it is a waste of time and distracts the jury.

4. Overlap with Other Impeachment Methods

The same evidence that impeaches by contradiction can also impeach by other means. We already saw this in the discussion of the hypothetical case involving a murder in a bar when the evidence concerned the witness watching television just before the stabbing. We saw that if the contradiction evidence is also relevant to impeach by other means, such as by showing that the witness's attention was not on the stabbing, the common law rule excluding extrinsic evidence is inapplicable because the evidence is not collateral. Consider the following additional illustration:

Negligence action by Plaintiff against Defendant arising from an automobile-pedestrian collision at the corner of First and Main Streets. Plaintiff was crossing First Street when he was struck by Defendant, who was driving on Main. Plaintiff claims he was crossing on a green light; Defendant claims she had the green light and that Plaintiff darted across the street on the red. To prove he was crossing on green, Plaintiff calls Witness 1, who testifies that she was leaving a dry cleaner on the northeast corner of First and Main when she saw Defendant run a red light and strike Plaintiff. Defendant wishes to call Witness 2 to testify that she was with Witness 1 at the scene, and that the business at the corner of First and Main, from which they were exiting, was a coffee house, not a dry cleaner. Plaintiff objects to Witness 2's testimony.

Witness 2's testimony contradicts that of Witness 1, and therefore tends to impeach Witness 1's credibility. The matter is collateral, however. All else being equal, it makes no difference whether Witness 1 and Witness 2 were coming out of a dry cleaner or a coffee house when the accident happened. Therefore, at common law Defendant would not be permitted to offer extrinsic evidence to contradict Witness 1. If Witness 1 refuses to acknowledge that the business was a coffee house and not a dry cleaner, Defendant is "stuck" with Witness 1's answer.

Suppose, however, that Witness 2's testimony is that she and Witness 1 were coming out of a coffee house immediately next door to the dry cleaner and 50 feet further away from the intersection where the accident occurred. Now the evidence also tends to cast doubt on Witness 1's testimony for at least one other reason: It might affect Witness 1's opportunity to perceive the accident. Was the view of the collision as good from the sidewalk in front of the coffee house as from the sidewalk in front of the dry cleaner? If it was not, the evidence would be admissible to impeach Witness 1's opportunity to observe, a method of impeachment not governed by the same rules as impeachment by contradiction or indeed by any specific rules. The evidence would not be collateral, so the common law limitation on impeachment by contradiction using extrinsic evidence would not apply. Witness 2's testimony would be admissible. The same result would occur under the Federal Rules. Because the evidence tends to impeach Witness 1's opportunity to observe, its probative value for impeachment purposes would be sufficiently great so as to defeat an argument that the court should exclude it under Rule 403.

The lesson here is relatively simple: The same evidence that tends to impeach by contradiction might also impeach by another means. If it does, the evidence is not collateral.

Questions for Classroom Discussion

1. Negligence action by Plaintiff against Defendant following a collision between their two cars. Plaintiff calls Witness 1, who testifies that she was a passenger in Plaintiff's car, that she looked down for a moment to change the radio from a rock station to a country music

(continued)

station, and that when she looked up, she saw Defendant cross the center line, veer into Plaintiff's path, and strike Plaintiff's car head-on. On cross-examination, Defendant asks Witness 1, "Isn't it true that Plaintiff is the one who crossed the center line?" Plaintiff objects that this is improper impeachment. How should the court rule?

2. Same case. Assume Witness 1 refuses to acknowledge that it was Plaintiff who crossed the center line. May Defendant now call Witness 2 to testify to that effect?

3. Same case. Defendant calls Witness 3, a back-seat passenger in Plaintiff's car, to testify that just before the accident, Witness 1 was not looking down to tune the radio, but had her head turned toward the back seat, was engaged in a conversation with Witness 3, and never turned her head forward before the crash. Plaintiff objects that this is improper impeachment. How should the court rule?

4. Same case. Assume that instead of testifying as in Question 3, Witness 3 will testify that Witness 1 was not changing the station from rock to country, but from country to rock, just before the accident. Plaintiff objects that this is improper impeachment. How should the court rule?

H. PRIOR STATEMENTS OF WITNESSES

1. Prior Inconsistent Statements

FED. R. EVID. 801(d)(1)(A)

A statement that meets the following conditions is not hearsay. . . . The declarant testifies and is subject to cross-examination about a prior statement, and the statement . . . is inconsistent with the declarant's testimony and was given under penalty of perjury at a trial, hearing, or other proceeding or in a deposition . . . .

FED. R. EVID. 613

(a) **Showing or Disclosing the Statement During Examination.** When examining a witness about the witness's prior statement, a party need not show it or disclose its contents to the witness. But the party must, on request, show it or disclose its contents to an adverse party's attorney.

(b) **Extrinsic Evidence of a Prior Inconsistent Statement.** Extrinsic evidence of a witness's prior inconsistent statement is admissible only if the witness is given an opportunity to explain or deny the statement and an adverse party is given an opportunity to question the witness about it, or if justice so requires. This subdivision (b) does not apply to an opposing party's statement under Rule 801(d)(2).

a.   Introduction

People often make statements that are inconsistent. For example, a witness to an automobile accident might state at the scene that the Chevy had the green light, and might say at a later time that the Ford had the green. It is not necessarily a question of dishonesty (though it might be), or of obfuscation (though that is true in some cases). In many situations, there are innocent explanations for why a witness at different times offers differing accounts of the same event or condition. But whatever the reason for the inconsistency, it reduces the credibility of the witness. Thus, evidence of a witness's prior inconsistent statement is an important tool for the cross-examiner. In our automobile accident hypothetical, if the plaintiff who was driving the Ford calls the witness to testify that the Ford had the green light, defendant's attorney almost certainly will want to reveal that at the scene of the accident the same person said that it was the Chevy (defendant's car) that had the green light.

There are two reasons why a party might offer into evidence a witness's prior inconsistent statement. *First*, the party might want the fact-finder to accept the truth of the prior statement in place of the testimony offered at trial. We call this the *substantive* use of a prior inconsistent statement. *Second*, the party might want the jury to be aware that the witness who has testified to a particular fact has made a statement inconsistent with the testimony and, thus, should not be viewed as a credible witness. We call this the *impeachment* use of a prior inconsistent statement. It is conceivable that a party might want the jury to use a prior inconsistent statement for both purposes, but sometimes that tactic backfires because it asks the jury at once to both believe and disbelieve the same witness.

Using the example of our automobile collision hypothetical, defendant's counsel might wish to prove either that defendant actually had the green light, a substantive use of the prior inconsistent statement, or that the witness who has given two conflicting accounts of the accident should not be believed, an impeachment use of the prior inconsistent statement.

b.   Substantive Use of Prior Inconsistent Statements

As discussed in Chapter 3, Rule 801(c) defines hearsay as a statement made by a person other than while testifying at the trial or hearing, offered in evidence to prove the truth of the matter asserted.[6] This definition of hearsay does not distinguish the prior, out-of-court statements of people who testify at trial from out-of-court statements of any other person; all are hearsay if offered to prove the truth of the matter asserted. Moreover, this is true regardless of the context in which the witness made the prior statement. As far as Rule 801(c) goes, it does not matter if the statement was made at the scene of the accident or in a prior judicial proceeding. As long as the statement was not made in *this* trial or hearing, and now is offered to prove the truth of the matter asserted, it is

---

6. Put aside for present purposes party admissions under Rule 801(d)(2).

hearsay. Thus, returning once again to the automobile accident case, when defendant offers the witness's prior statement that the Chevy had the green light, the evidence is hearsay if offered to prove that the Chevy had the green light.

There is no special reason why most prior inconsistent statements should be made admissible. As a class, prior inconsistent statements are not more trustworthy than other out-of-court statements, and there is usually no substantial need for prior statements that would render their probative value especially great or make their exclusion unfair. Sometimes, however, prior inconsistent statements are made under circumstances enhancing their trustworthiness, or at least allowing their trustworthiness to be tested. In these limited circumstances, admission can be justified. This is the theory behind Federal Rule 801(d)(1)(A), which classifies prior inconsistent statements as non-hearsay, and thus makes them substantively admissible, if three conditions can be met:

1. The declarant testifies at the trial or hearing;
2. The declarant is subject to cross-examination concerning the statement; and
3. The inconsistent statement was made under oath subject to the penalty for perjury "at a trial, hearing, or other proceeding or in a deposition."

The rule assumes that these conditions enhance the trustworthiness of the statement for two reasons. First, because the prior statement must have been given under oath, the possibility of prosecution for perjury decreases the likelihood that the witness lied. Second, the accuracy of the prior statement can be tested at trial since the rule requires that the declarant testify at trial and be subject to cross-examination.[7]

Consider this example:

> Plaintiff sues Defendant for negligence after Plaintiff's slip-and-fall in the produce section of Defendant's supermarket. At trial, Plaintiff calls Witness who testifies that he saw a "large puddle of liquid" on the floor moments before Plaintiff fell. On cross-examination of Witness, Defendant wishes to introduce evidence that at a deposition prior to trial Witness stated that the floor where Plaintiff fell was dry.

Here, all three requirements of Rule 801(d)(1)(A) are satisfied: Witness's prior statement (the deposition testimony) is inconsistent with his trial testimony, it was given under oath subject to the penalty for perjury (a witness at a deposition is placed under oath), and Witness is available at trial for cross-examination concerning the statement. The prior inconsistent statement is therefore admissible substantively to prove that the floor was dry because Rule 801(d)(1)(A) classifies it as not hearsay.

The result in this hypothetical would be different if Witness had made the prior statement while not under oath. If, for example, Witness had simply told a friend that the floor appeared to be dry, one essential element of Rule 801(d)(1)(A) would not be met, and the statement would be inadmissible to prove the matter asserted (that the floor was dry). The statement would only be admissible as not hearsay under Rule 801(c) to impeach Witness's credibility.

---

7. Some jurisdictions deem this second element to be sufficient, making admissible all prior inconsistent statements of a person now testifying in court even if those statements were not given under oath. *See, e.g.,* Cal. Evid. Code § 1235.

The evidence would not be hearsay for this limited purpose because it would be offered only to prove that Witness made the inconsistent statement, not that the facts Witness asserted in the statement are true.

The same would be the result if the prior inconsistent statement was given under oath but not "at a trial, hearing, or other proceeding, or in a deposition." Thus, a prior inconsistent statement in an affidavit, even though under oath, would still be hearsay if offered to prove the truth of the matters asserted in it, but would not be hearsay under Rule 801(c) if offered only to impeach.

Suppose Witness's prior inconsistent statement *was* given under oath "at a trial, hearing, or other proceeding, or in a deposition," but Witness now testifies at trial he does not recall the incident in the supermarket, or does not recall the substance of his prior statement. Is Witness "subject to cross-examination concerning the statement"? The U.S. Supreme Court took up that question in connection with Federal Rule 801(d)(1)(C), concerning statements of prior identification which, like Rule 801(d)(1)(A), contains the "subject to cross-examination" requirement.

UNITED STATES v. OWENS
484 U.S. 554 (1988)

[Owens, a prison inmate, was charged with assault with intent to commit murder. The victim, Foster, was a correctional counselor. Because the attacker struck Foster on the head, Foster's memory of the attack was severely impaired. In an interview conducted by an FBI agent while Foster was still in the hospital, Foster named Owens as his attacker and identified his photograph. At trial, Foster testified on direct examination that he remembered identifying Owens. On cross-examination, however, Foster admitted that he could not remember seeing the person who attacked him, could not remember any of the visits he received while in the hospital save that of the FBI agent, and could not recall if any of his visitors had suggested that Owens had been the attacker. Defendant's efforts to refresh Foster's memory were unsuccessful. Owens was convicted. The Ninth Circuit reversed. The Supreme Court reinstated the conviction.]

Justice SCALIA delivered the opinion of the Court.

This case requires us to determine whether either the Confrontation Clause of the Sixth Amendment or Rule 802 of the Federal Rules of Evidence bars testimony concerning a prior, out-of-court identification when the identifying witness is unable, because of memory loss, to explain the basis for the identification. . . .

It seems to us that the more natural reading of "subject to cross-examination concerning the statement" includes what was available here. Ordinarily a witness is regarded as "subject to cross-examination" when he is placed on the stand, under oath, and responds willingly to questions. Just as with the constitutional prohibition, limitations on the scope of examination by the trial court or assertions of privilege by the witness may undermine the process to such a degree that meaningful cross-examination within the intent of the Rule no longer exists. But that effect is not produced by the witness' assertion of memory loss — which, as discussed earlier, is often the very result sought to be produced by cross-examination, and can be effective in destroying the force of the prior statement. Rule 801(d)(1)(C), which specifies that the cross-examination need only "concer[n] the statement," does not on its face require more.

This reading seems even more compelling when the Rule is compared with Rule 804(a)(3), which defines "[u]navailability as a witness" to include situations in which a declarant "testifies to a lack of memory of the subject matter of the declarant's statement." Congress plainly was aware of the recurrent evidentiary problem at issue here — witness forgetfulness of an underlying event — but chose not to make it an exception to Rule 801(d)(1)(C).

The reasons for that choice are apparent from the Advisory Committee's Notes on Rule 801 and its legislative history. The premise for Rule 801(d)(1)(C) was that, given adequate safeguards against suggestiveness, out-of-court identifications were generally preferable to courtroom identifications. Thus, despite the traditional view that such statements were hearsay, the Advisory Committee believed that their use was to be fostered rather than discouraged. Similarly, the House Report on the Rule noted that since, "[a]s time goes by, a witness' memory will fade and his identification will become less reliable," minimizing the barriers to admission of more contemporaneous identification is fairer to defendants and prevents "cases falling through because the witness can no longer recall the identity of the person he saw commit the crime." To judge from the House and Senate Reports, Rule 801(d)(1)(C) was in part directed to the very problem here at issue: a memory loss that makes it impossible for the witness to provide an in-court identification or testify about details of the events underlying an earlier identification.

Respondent argues that this reading is impermissible because it creates an internal inconsistency in the Rules, since the forgetful witness who is deemed "subject to cross-examination" under 801(d)(1)(C) is simultaneously deemed "unavailable" under 804(a)(3). This is the position espoused by a prominent commentary on the Rules, *see* 4 J. Weinstein & M. Berger, Weinstein's Evidence 801-120 to 801-121, 801-178 (1987). It seems to us, however, that this is not a substantive inconsistency, but only a semantic oddity resulting from the fact that Rule 804(a) has for convenience of reference in Rule 804(b) chosen to describe the circumstances necessary in order to admit certain categories of hearsay testimony under the rubric "Unavailability as a witness." These circumstances include not only absence from the hearing, but also claims of privilege, refusals to obey a court's order to testify, and inability to testify based on physical or mental illness or memory loss. Had the rubric instead been "unavailability as a witness, memory loss, and other special circumstances" there would be no apparent inconsistency with Rule 801, which is a definition section excluding certain statements entirely from the category of "hearsay." The semantic inconsistency exists not only with respect to Rule 801(d)(1)(C), but also with respect to the other subparagraphs of Rule 801(d)(1). It would seem strange, for example, to assert that a witness can avoid introduction of testimony from a prior proceeding that is inconsistent with his trial testimony, *see* Rule 801(d)(1)(A), by simply asserting lack of memory of the facts to which the prior testimony related. But that situation, like this one, presents the verbal curiosity that the witness is "subject to cross-examination" under Rule 801 while at the same time "unavailable" under Rule 804(a)(3). Quite obviously, the two characterizations are made for two entirely different purposes and there is no requirement or expectation that they should coincide.

Although the Supreme Court's decision in *Owens* adopted a broad interpretation of "subject to cross-examination about the prior statement," this does not mean *any* witness appearing at trial automatically will be deemed subject to cross-examination. As the Court recognized, "limitations on the scope of examination by the trial court or assertions of privilege by the witness may undermine the process to such a degree that meaningful cross-examination within the intent of the Rule no longer exists." Thus, if a court's rulings too greatly impede the cross-examiner's effort to question the witness, or if the witness's assertion of a privilege undermines efforts to cross-examine, there is a chance the witness will not be deemed "subject to cross-examination," and the prior inconsistent statement will fail to satisfy the requirements of Rule 801(d)(1)(A).

c. Impeachment Use of Prior Inconsistent Statements

The second possible use for a prior inconsistent statement is to impeach the credibility of a witness. It is important to understand how a prior inconsistent statement tends to impeach. The key to prior inconsistent statement impeachment is not dishonesty, but simply inconsistency. We accord more credibility to people who speak consistently than to those whom we know to make inconsistent statements. To return to our automobile accident hypothetical, recall that both Plaintiff and Defendant claim they had the green light. Suppose that to prove Defendant ran the red light, Plaintiff calls Witness, who testifies on direct examination that she saw Defendant's car run through the red light and broadside Plaintiff's car. Further suppose that Defendant's attorney is aware that a few days after the accident, Witness told an acquaintance the opposite story — that she had seen Plaintiff's car run the red light and strike Defendant's car. Defendant knows that because Witness's prior inconsistent statement was not made under oath subject to penalty of perjury, that statement could not be admitted under Rule 801(d)(1)(A) to prove that Plaintiff ran the red light. If Defendant wishes to have the jury hear Witness's prior inconsistent statement, it may be used only to impeach Witness's credibility. The jury will be asked to take note of the inconsistency in Witness's accounts of the incident, and then to apply its everyday experience about the credibility of people who speak inconsistently.

It is easy to see that a prior inconsistent statement is not hearsay when it is offered merely to impeach: Although it is a statement the declarant does not make while testifying at the current trial or hearing, it is not being offered to prove the truth of the matter asserted. Rather, the statement is offered merely to show that it was made. Thus, the hearsay rule is not a barrier to admission of the statement. At the same time, the common law did not allow unimpeded admission of prior inconsistent statements to impeach. Instead, a series of rules regulated their use. First, an opponent was not permitted to offer evidence of a prior inconsistent statement until the witness who made the statement was first given an opportunity to admit or deny making the statement. This generally meant that the opponent would be required to show the statement to the witness if it was in writing or otherwise disclose its contents before attempting to impeach the witness with the statement. In addition, if the witness denied making the statement, the impeaching party was not allowed to introduce extrinsic evidence of the statement unless the party first provided the declarant-witness with specific information about the prior statement: the date it was made, where it was made, and who was present at the time. Only then could the impeaching party offer extrinsic evidence of the statement, generally consisting of the testimony of another witness with first-hand knowledge of the statement. Recall that we have defined extrinsic evidence as any evidence offered to impeach a witness that comes from a source other than that witness while she is testifying in this proceeding.

Although these common law rules appear somewhat quaint when viewed through a modern lens, the reasons for the rules are still valid. As we have noted, there can be many explanations why a witness might testify inconsistently with a prior statement; intent to deceive is only one. It is entirely possible, for example, that the witness's memory at the time of trial is not as good as it was when the prior statement was made and that, when confronted with the specifics of the prior statement, the witness's memory of the events will be refreshed and the inconsistency clarified. ("Hearing what I said before, I have a better memory of what happened. I was right when I said before that Plaintiff's car ran the red light.") The truth-determination function of the trial is better served by a procedure ensuring that the declarant-witness is given a meaningful opportunity to explain a prior statement than by one that allows the opponent free rein in creating impressions of dishonesty or improper motive in testifying. Our general desire to conduct trials in a fair manner also helps to explain a rule without which honest and well-meaning witnesses can be made to look unintelligent at best and dishonest at worst.

Nevertheless, a blanket rule imposing burdensome prerequisites to the introduction of extrinsic evidence of a witness's prior inconsistent statement is not justifiable, nor is it in line with the modern trend away from rigidly formulaic evidence rules. Sometimes it can be unduly burdensome, or even impossible, to learn all the necessary details of the making of the prior statement. At other times, the opponent knows that providing the witness with the necessary information before offering extrinsic evidence will be futile because the witness, a convincing liar, will persist in denying having made the prior statement or exploit the information in devising a convincing but false explanation for the inconsistency.

These and other drawbacks have led courts to relax the common law rule and replace it with one intended to promote truth-determination and fairness while not impeding the presentation of potentially persuasive impeachment evidence. Federal Rule 613(a) provides, first, that it is not necessary to show the declarant-witness the prior statement or to disclose its contents *before* using the statement to impeach the witness. This would allow the cross-examiner in our hypothetical simply to ask Witness, "isn't it true that you once told someone that Plaintiff is the one who ran the red light?" Rule 613 allows this question, doing away with the requirement that Witness first be given detailed information about the prior statement.

Rule 613(b) also liberalizes the portion of the common law rule that concerns extrinsic evidence. The provision makes extrinsic evidence of a prior statement admissible so long as the witness is afforded, *at some time during the trial,* an opportunity to explain or deny the statement and the opponent has a chance to examine the witness. The rule does away with the common law requirement that the cross-examiner provide this opportunity *before* offering extrinsic evidence to prove the inconsistent statement was made. This means it is usually permissible to first offer extrinsic evidence of the inconsistent statement and then give the witness who has been impeached an opportunity to explain the inconsistency or deny altogether that the statement was made.

The reasons for these changes to the common law rules is plain: By eliminating the need first to show the inconsistent statement to the witness, then explain the circumstances under which it was made, and finally provide an opportunity to explain or deny, all *before* offering extrinsic evidence of that statement, Rule 613 preserves the element of surprise often so vital to effective impeachment.

Another common law rule applied to extrinsic proof of prior inconsistent statements has largely survived the recent liberalizing trend. Earlier, we learned that, at common law, extrinsic evidence was inadmissible to impeach a witness by contradiction on a collateral matter and that, even though the Federal Rules did not explicitly adopt this rule, courts often use Rule 403 as a basis for its continued application. The same standard is often applied to impeachment by prior inconsistent statement since it is a form of contradiction impeachment; it is self-contradiction. For example, suppose that in our auto accident hypothetical Witness testified that she was emerging from a video store after renting a movie when she saw Defendant's car run the light and strike Plaintiff's car. On an earlier occasion Witness told her friend much the same thing but with one difference: Instead of saying that she had rented a movie at the video store, Witness told the friend that she had just *returned* a movie. The two statements are in fact inconsistent and, thus, in some minor way the evidence impairs Witness's credibility. Witness's purpose in going to the video store has no bearing on the outcome of the case. Although the court would probably permit the opponent to cross-examine Witness about this inconsistency, it would be a waste of time to permit the opponent to offer extrinsic evidence of this unimportant self-contradiction. In addition, revealing the inconsistency may be unnecessarily embarrassing to Witness who, in preparing to testify, undoubtedly focused on what was important about her observations, not on details unconnected with the event at issue. This limitation can also be justified under Rule 611(a), which instructs the trial judge to "exercise reasonable control over the mode and order of questioning witnesses and presenting evidence so as to . . . protect witnesses from harassment or undue embarrassment."

Finally, note that the prior statements of *non-testifying declarants* sometimes may be offered as bearing on their credibility. This is permitted by Rule 806:

FED. R. EVID. 806. ATTACKING AND SUPPORTING THE DECLARANT'S CREDIBILITY

When a hearsay statement—or a statement described in Rule 801(d)(2)(C), (D), or (E)—has been admitted in evidence, the declarant's credibility may be attacked, and then supported, by any evidence that would be admissible for those purposes if the declarant had testified as a witness. The court may admit evidence of the declarant's inconsistent statement or conduct, regardless of when it occurred or whether the declarant had an opportunity to explain or deny it. If the party against whom the statement was admitted calls the declarant as a witness, the party may examine the declarant on the statement as if on cross-examination.

The credibility of the declarant becomes an issue where an out-of-court statement is offered to prove the truth of the matter asserted. If the declarant does not testify it is impossible to cross-examine her about facts bearing on credibility. Thus, extrinsic evidence becomes the only means to prove those facts. But, as we have seen, the law places various limits on the admissibility of extrinsic evidence to impeach. In the case of impeachment through inconsistent statement, Rule 613 would require the exclusion of extrinsic evidence unless the declarant is given an opportunity to explain or deny the statement. Rule 806 deals with the fact that it is impossible to provide this opportunity to a declarant who does not testify in court. The solution adopted by this provision is simply to exempt the statements of non-testifying declarants from this requirement.

For example, suppose that in a murder case, the prosecution offers into evidence a dying declaration of the victim accusing defendant of committing the crime. In that situation, the defendant would be permitted to offer into evidence a prior statement of the victim accusing a different person. Even if the prior statement does not qualify as a dying declaration it would be admissible to impeach the victim/declarant since it would not be hearsay if offered for this limited purpose. Moreover, Rule 806 establishes that extrinsic evidence of the prior statement is admissible to impeach even though there is no means of providing the victim/declarant with an opportunity to explain or deny the statement.

d.   A Note About Limited Admissibility

In several contexts, we have noted that evidence that is admissible for one purpose or against one party might not be admissible for another purpose or against other parties. Federal Rule 105, which we introduced in Chapter 1, embodies this principle. It requires the trial court, on request, to "restrict the evidence to its proper scope and instruct the jury accordingly." Because many prior inconsistent statements are admissible only to impeach, and not to prove the truth of the matter asserted, it is particularly important to consider the limited admissibility problem in connection with this type of evidence.

When a prior inconsistent statement is only admissible to impeach, most often the appropriate action is for the trial court to instruct the jury about the limited purpose for which the evidence may be considered. Such a "limiting instruction," however, will not always be effective. Particularly when the prior statement is directed to a crucial, disputed issue in the case, the jury is very unlikely to ignore the statement for its substantive value and consider it only for its less intuitively relevant impeachment purpose. In such cases, as well as in others in which the danger of jury misuse is great, the objecting party should consider asking the court to exclude the evidence altogether pursuant to Rule 403. The argument would be that the prejudice to the objecting party from the jury's likely use of the evidence for its improper purpose substantially outweighs the probative value of the evidence for its impeachment purpose. This is not inconsistent with Rule 105, which contemplates the use of limiting instructions. In some cases, that remedy does not provide sufficient protection to the opposing party. Although the standard of Rule 403 is heavily weighted in favor of admissibility, the trial court should carefully consider exclusion in situations in which the danger of misuse is especially great.

Further Reading (Prior Inconsistent Statements): Michael H. Graham, *Employing Inconsistent Statements for Impeachment and as Substantive Evidence: A Critical Review and Proposed Amendments of Federal Rules of Evidence 801(d)(1)(A), 613, and 607,* 75 Mich. L. Rev. 1565 (1977); Steven Lubet, *Understanding Impeachment,* 15 Am. J. Trial. Advoc. 483 (1992).

Further Reading (Impeaching a Non-Testifying Declarant): Fred Warren Bennett, *How to Administer the "Big Hurt" in a Criminal Case: The Life and Times of Federal Rule of Evidence 806,* 44 Cath. U. L. Rev. 1135 (1995); Margaret Meriwether Cordray, *Evidence Rule 806 and the Problem of Impeaching the Nontestifying Declarant,* 56 Ohio St. L.J. 495 (1995); David A. Seidelson, *Extrinsic Evidence on a Collateral Matter May Not Be Used to Impeach Credibility: What Constitutes "Collateral Matter"?,* 9 Rev. Litig. 203 (1990); David Sonenshein, *Impeaching the Hearsay Declarant,* 74 Temp. L. Rev. 163 (2001).

Questions for Classroom Discussion

1. Prosecution of Defendant for robbery of Victim's jewelry store. The prosecutor calls Witness, who testifies that she saw a woman running from the store just after the alarm started to sound. On cross-examination, Defendant asks Witness, "Isn't it true that just after the robbery, you told the police that the robbery was committed by a man?" Is this evidence admissible? If so, for what purpose?

2. Same case. To prove that Witness made the prior statement, Defendant calls the police officer with whom Witness spoke, and asks the officer to relate Witness's statement that the robbery was committed by a man. Is this evidence admissible? If so, for what purpose? Is there any additional foundational requirement imposed on the officer's testimony?

3. Same case. Assume that Witness's prior statement was made in a deposition rather than orally to the police officer. The prosecutor objects. Is this evidence admissible? If so, for what purpose? What if the prior statement was contained in a sworn affidavit?

4. Same case. The prosecutor calls Victim, who testifies about the robbery but states that she cannot remember what the robber was wearing. On cross-examination, Defendant asks Victim if it isn't true that hours after the robbery, Victim told the police that the robber was wearing blue jeans. If the prosecutor objects, how should the court rule?

(continued)

5. Same case. Suppose Victim's prior statement that the robber was wearing blue jeans was made just before Victim took the stand. May Defendant now offer the statement as a prior inconsistent statement?

6. Civil fraud action by Plaintiff against Defendant arising from a failed land development deal. At trial, Defendant testifies that he warned Plaintiff that land development deals are risky and that Plaintiff should consult an attorney before investing. On cross-examination Plaintiff asks Defendant to admit that Defendant never made such a statement, and in fact told Plaintiff that the deal was "good as gold." Defendant denies making that representation and sticks to his story that he warned Plaintiff about the risks of investing. May Plaintiff call a witness to testify that she overheard the conversation, that Defendant never mentioned the risks, and that Defendant made the "good as gold" statement? For what purposes, if any, is the evidence admissible?

7. Prosecution of Defendant for the murder of Victim, allegedly committed during a brawl at a football game. Defendant denies involvement. The prosecutor calls Witness 1, Victim's spouse, who testifies that a week after the incident, just before Victim died, Victim said, "I'm done for. See to it that Defendant pays for this." Defendant objects on hearsay grounds. How should the court rule?

8. Same facts as in Question 7. After Witness 1 testifies Defendant calls Witness 2, the doctor who treated Victim at the hospital following the incident. Witness 2 testifies that some time before Victim made the statement apparently accusing Defendant, Victim said, "Zed is the one who did this, and when I get out of here, I'll see that she suffers for it." Is Witness 2's testimony about Victim's earlier statement admissible? If so, for what purpose? Is the evidence objectionable on the ground Victim was never given an opportunity to explain or deny the statement to Witness 2?

9. Prosecution of Defendant in a California state court for robbery of a convenience store. Witness testifies for the prosecution that she saw Defendant commit the crime. On cross-examination of Witness, Defendant establishes that on the day of the crime, Witness identified another person as the robber. Cal. Evid. Code § 1235, a hearsay exception, provides: "Evidence of a statement made by a witness is not made inadmissible by the hearsay rule if the statement is inconsistent with his testimony at the hearing and is offered in compliance with Section 770." (Section 770 is similar to Fed. R. Evid. 613(b).) For what purpose, if any, is Witness's prior statement admissible? How does this differ from the result under the Federal Rules?

10. Prosecution of Defendant for bank robbery. The prosecution alleges that Defendant, a man, approached a teller, showed the teller a firearm hidden under his raincoat, demanded that the teller fill a bag with cash, and then struck the teller over the head before escaping with the cash. At trial Defendant calls the teller who testifies that the robbery was committed by a woman. On cross-examination the prosecutor asks the teller to admit that she testified before the grand jury that the robber was a male. The teller responds that she has suffered from memory problems since being struck on the head and has no recollection of testifying before the grand jury. The prosecutor then offers into evidence a certified transcript of the teller's grand jury testimony in which she stated, "The robber was a man." Defendant objects on the ground the transcript is inadmissible hearsay and teller's memory problem means the teller is not "subject to cross-examination" as required by Rule 801(d)(1)(A). How should the court rule?

2. Prior Consistent Statements

Fed. R. Evid. 801(d)(1)(B)

A statement that meets the following conditions is not hearsay . . . The declarant testifies and is subject to cross-examination about the prior statement, and the statement . . . is consistent with the declarant's testimony and is offered to rebut an express or implied charge that the declarant recently fabricated it or acted from a recent improper influence or motive in so testifying.

a. Introduction

People who give consistent accounts of the same event or condition are more credible than people who are inconsistent. Thus, evidence that a witness previously made a statement consistent with her current testimony suggests that the witness is entitled to somewhat greater credence than would be the case if the witness gave an inconsistent statement. Despite this logic, the law of evidence is stingy about the admission of prior consistent statements made by a witness who testifies at trial. Rule 801(d)(1)(B) allows such statements to be admissible over a hearsay objection only if offered under very narrow circumstances.

Before we discuss what those circumstances might be, it is worth considering why the law does not just allow all prior consistent statements to be admitted to support credibility. We previously have seen that prior inconsistent statements can be relevant to prove two different propositions: (1) the witness is not credible because she has uttered a statement inconsistent with her testimony, and (2) the facts asserted in the prior statement are true. We have also seen that, if offered to prove the first proposition only, a prior inconsistent statement is not hearsay and can be admitted for this limited purpose. But can we say something comparable about prior consistent statements? Are they relevant to prove (1) the witness is a credible person because she has uttered a statement consistent with her testimony, and (2) the facts asserted in the prior statement are true? If so, does it make sense to say we can overcome hearsay problems by admitting it for the first proposition only?

Suppose Plaintiff sues Defendant for negligence after Plaintiff allegedly tripped over a skateboard in Defendant's house. At trial, Defendant calls Witness who testifies that Plaintiff did not trip over a skateboard but fell while trying to ride her bicycle with no hands. Defendant wants Witness to testify that Witness told the same story to a friend the next day. The argument that this evidence is relevant to show that Witness is credible goes something like this:

> → **EVIDENCE:** The day after the accident, Witness told a friend the same story (that Plaintiff fell while trying to ride her bicycle with no hands, not by tripping over a skateboard).
>
> > → **INFERENCE:** Witness gives consistent accounts of events.
> >
> > > → **CONCLUSION:** Witness should be believed when she testifies that Plaintiff fell while trying to ride her bicycle with no hands.

There is nothing inherently wrong with this logic. *The trouble is that virtually all witnesses who testify to a fact will have said much the same thing on a prior occasion and maybe on many prior occasions.* This creates at least two problems with allowing unlimited admission of prior consistent statements. *First*, if we allowed all prior consistent statements into evidence, already long trials could take considerably longer. And to what end? The evidence proves only what we would already expect to be the case: that the witness has told the same story before testifying. At best, evidence of the prior consistent statement enhances the witness's credibility only marginally. *Second*, jurors are very unlikely to be able or willing to distinguish between the substantive use of the prior consistent statement (to prove the truth of the matter asserted) and its use simply to show that the witness is credible. It is hard even for a lawyer to explain why "the witness is credible" is different from "what the witness said is true."

Because a jury will find this line difficult to draw, allowing unlimited use of prior consistent statements to enhance credibility would seriously undermine the hearsay rule. This is something U.S. law has been unwilling to let happen, much to the dismay of law students. In the end, the limits on the admissibility of prior consistent statements inherent in Rule 801(d)(1)(B) are justified by the same considerations that motivate Rule 403: Broad admissibility would add little in probative value while increasing to an unacceptable degree the dangers of unfair prejudice, confusion, waste of time, and needless presentation of cumulative evidence.

Thus, prior consistent statements are only admissible — for whatever purpose — under very limited circumstances. We now turn to an examination of those circumstances.

b. Foundation for Admission of Prior Consistent Statements

We have already seen in connection with the discussion of Rule 608(a) that evidence supporting credibility usually is admissible only if credibility has been attacked. This principle is based on the conclusion that, in the absence of such an attack, evidence supporting credibility is of insufficient probative value to warrant the time necessary to consider it. This conclusion is itself based on the assumption that, unless impeached, every witness has normal perceptual recall, and narrative abilities as well as normal inclinations toward truthfulness. Where these presumed abilities and inclinations are unchallenged, the courts conclude that further efforts to support credibility are a waste of time and, thus, objectionable under Rule 403. Accordingly, prior consistent statements are not admissible to support credibility unless the credibility of the witness has been attacked. Typically, the attack comes in the form of evidence of a prior inconsistent statement or evidence that the witness developed a motive to lie, as would be the case where she was offered a bribe to testify to certain facts or was threatened with harm if she did not testify to those facts.

Even if credibility has been attacked, evidence supporting credibility is worth considering only if it logically refutes the specific focus of the attack. This suggests that prior consistent statements should not always be admissible after credibility has been attacked, even if the attack has been by prior inconsistent statement. As described above, the theory of impeachment by prior inconsistent statement usually is that, when a witness changes her story, she is revealed to be either a liar or mistaken in her testimony. This permits the further inference that the witness is generally an unreliable source of information. Evidence of a prior consistent statement does not always refute these inferences since it is possible that the consistent statement also could be the product of the same lie or mistake underlying the testimony. The logic of this argument dictates that consistent statements should be admissible to rehabilitate credibility only when made under circumstances that refute the implication that the statement is itself the product of that same lie or mistake.

This helps us to understand the meaning of Rule 801(d)(1)(B)'s declaration that a consistent statement is admissible where it rebuts a charge that the witness "recently fabricated . . . or acted from a recent improper influence or motive." If the impeacher charges that the witness's testimony is the product of a fabrication or a motive to lie that emerged before the witness took the stand, a consistent statement logically rebuts that charge if it was made at some moment in time *before* that fabrication or motive arose. The timing of such a consistent statement compels the conclusion that the fabrication or motive to lie could not have affected the consistent statement. The consistency between the statement and the testimony then permits the further inference that the testimony itself was not affected by that fabrication or motive to lie.

Returning to the hypothetical slip-and-fall case, suppose that at trial, Plaintiff claims that Defendant paid Witness to testify that Plaintiff fell while trying to ride her bicycle with no hands rather than by tripping over a skateboard. If it turns out that Witness told her friend the same story *before* Defendant allegedly paid Witness, Witness's statement to the friend takes on added significance. In effect, it tends strongly to rebut Plaintiff's claim that Witness was improperly influenced to testify against Plaintiff. If, after all, Witness offered the same account before the alleged bribe, this suggests either there was no bribe or that it had no influence on Witness's testimony. Either way, the evidence makes it more likely that Witness testified truthfully at trial.

Consider another example. Suppose Defendant is charged with murder. Defendant denies any involvement. At trial, Defendant calls Witness, who testifies that she was with Defendant in another state when the murder was committed. The prosecution claims that Witness's testimony was coerced — that Defendant told Witness that Defendant would kill Witness if Witness did not provide the alibi. If believed, this evidence severely undercuts the credibility of Witness's testimony. But Witness's testimony is more credible if there is evidence that, *before* Defendant allegedly made the threat, Witness told the same story about being with Defendant in another state. Such evidence tends to refute the making of the threat and/or its effect on Witness's testimony.

Notice the importance of timing in these examples. If Witness had made the consistent statement *after* the alleged bribe or threat, that statement would have little or no value in terms of rebutting the effect of the bribe or threat. Indeed, one would expect that a person with a motive to lie would willingly make the same statement many times after the motive arose. The repetition of the statement would not make the statement more credible because each telling could have been corrupted by the same motive. But when a statement consistent with later trial testimony was made *before* the motive arose, that statement is untainted and permits us to infer that the consistent trial testimony also was not improperly influenced.

The common law recognized the peculiar reliability and high probative value of prior consistent statements made under the types of circumstances mentioned above, and generally recognized an exception to the hearsay rule for such situations. Statements satisfying these requirements were admissible not only to support the credibility of the witness but also to prove the truth of the matter asserted.

The drafters of the Federal Rules generally agreed with this approach. Rule 801(d)(1)(B) exempts from the hearsay rule prior consistent statements of a witness if offered to rebut an express or implied charge of recent fabrication or improper influence or motive. But the drafters did not explicitly include in Rule 801(d)(1)(B) the timing element found in the common law rule. The question thus arose whether, under Rule 801(d)(1)(B), a prior statement must have been made *before* the alleged improper influence was brought to bear or the motive existed. The Supreme Court addressed that question in 1995.

TOME v. UNITED STATES

513 U.S. 150 (1995)

Justice KENNEDY delivered the opinion of the Court, except as to Part IIB.

I

Petitioner Tome was charged in a one-count indictment with the felony of sexual abuse of a child, his own daughter, aged four at the time of the alleged crime. [At trial, A.T., then six and a half years old, testified, but she proved to be a reluctant witness, having difficulty concentrating and often taking close to a minute to begin to answer questions. The trial judge stated, "We have a very difficult situation here." The government then produced six witnesses, who testified about seven prior statements A.T. made describing the alleged assaults.]

A.T.'s out-of-court statements, recounted by the six witnesses, were offered by the Government under Rule 801(d)(1)(B). The trial court admitted all of the statements over defense counsel's objection, accepting the Government's argument that they rebutted the implicit charge that A.T.'s testimony was motivated by a desire to live with her mother. . . . Following trial, Tome was convicted and sentenced to 12 years' imprisonment.

On appeal, the Court of Appeals for the Tenth Circuit affirmed, adopting the Government's argument that all of A.T.'s out-of-court statements were admissible under Rule 801(d)(1)(B) even though they had been made after A.T.'s alleged motive to fabricate arose. . . .

II

The prevailing common-law rule for more than a century before adoption of the Federal Rules of Evidence was that a prior consistent statement introduced to rebut a charge of recent fabrication or improper influence or motive was admissible if the statement had been made before the alleged fabrication, influence, or motive came into being, but it was inadmissible if made afterwards. As Justice Story explained: "[W]here the testimony is assailed as a fabrication of a recent date, . . . in order to repel such imputation, proof of the antecedent declaration of the party may be admitted." Ellicott v. Pearl, 35 U.S. (10 Pet.) 412, 439, 9 L. Ed. 475 (1836) (emphasis added). . . .

A

Rule 801 defines prior consistent statements as nonhearsay only if they are offered to rebut a charge of "recent fabrication or improper influence or motive." Fed. Rule Evid. 801(d)(1)(B). Noting the "troublesome" logic of treating a witness' prior consistent statements as hearsay at all (because the declarant is present in court and subject to cross-examination), the Advisory Committee decided to treat those consistent statements, once the preconditions of the Rule were satisfied, as nonhearsay and admissible as substantive evidence, not just to rebut an attack on the witness' credibility. *See* Advisory Committee's Notes on Fed. Rule Evid. 801(d)(1), 28 U.S.C. App., p. 773. A consistent statement meeting the requirements of the Rule is thus placed in the same category as a declarant's inconsistent statement made under oath in another proceeding, or prior identification testimony, or admissions by a party opponent. *See* Fed. Rule Evid. 801.

The Rules do not accord this weighty, nonhearsay status to all prior consistent statements. To the contrary, admissibility under the Rules is confined to those statements offered to rebut a charge of "recent fabrication or improper influence or motive," the same phrase used by the Advisory Committee in its description of the "traditiona[l]" common law of evidence, which was the background against which the Rules were drafted. *See* Advisory Committee's Notes, *supra*, at 773. Prior consistent statements may not be admitted to counter all forms of impeachment or to bolster the witness merely because she has been discredited. In the present context, the question is whether A.T.'s out-of-court statements rebutted the alleged link between her desire to be with her mother and her testimony, not whether they suggested that A.T.'s in-court testimony was true. The Rule speaks of a party rebutting an alleged motive, not bolstering the veracity of the story told.

This limitation is instructive, not only to establish the preconditions of admissibility but also to reinforce the significance of the requirement that the consistent statements must have been made before the alleged influence, or motive to fabricate, arose. That is to say, the forms of impeachment within the Rule's coverage are the ones in which the temporal requirement makes the most sense. Impeachment by charging that the testimony is a recent fabrication or results from an improper influence or motive is, as a general matter, capable of direct and forceful refutation through introduction of out-of-court consistent statements that predate the alleged fabrication, influence, or motive. A consistent statement that predates the motive is a square rebuttal of the charge that the testimony was contrived as a consequence of that motive. By contrast, prior consistent statements carry little rebuttal force when most other types of impeachment are involved.

There may arise instances when out-of-court statements that postdate the alleged fabrication have some probative force in rebutting a charge of fabrication or improper influence or motive, but those statements refute the charged fabrication in a less direct and forceful way. Evidence that a witness made consistent statements after the alleged motive to fabricate arose may suggest in some degree that the in-court testimony is truthful, and thus suggest in some degree that that testimony did not result from some improper influence; but if the drafters of Rule 801(d)(1)(B) intended to countenance rebuttal along that indirect inferential chain, the purpose of confining the types of impeachment that open the door to rebuttal by introducing consistent statements becomes unclear. If consistent statements are admissible without reference to the timeframe we find imbedded in the Rule, there appears no sound reason not to admit consistent statements to rebut other forms of impeachment as well. Whatever objections can be leveled against limiting the Rule to this designated form of impeachment and confining the rebuttal to those statements made before the fabrication or improper influence or motive arose, it is clear to us that the drafters of Rule 801(d)(1)(B) were relying upon the common-law temporal requirement.

The underlying theory of the Government's position is that an out-of-court consistent statement, whenever it was made, tends to bolster the testimony of a witness and so tends also to rebut an express or implied charge that the testimony has been the product of an improper influence. Congress could have adopted that rule with ease, providing, for instance, that "a witness' prior consistent statements are admissible whenever relevant to assess the witness' truthfulness or accuracy." The theory would be that, in a broad sense, any prior statement by a witness concerning the disputed issues at trial would have some relevance in assessing the accuracy or truthfulness of the witness' in-court testimony on the same subject. The narrow Rule enacted by Congress, however, cannot be understood to incorporate the Government's theory.

B

Our conclusion that Rule 801(d)(1)(B) embodies the common-law premotive requirement is confirmed by an examination of the Advisory Committee's Notes to the Federal Rules of Evidence. . . .

D

The case before us illustrates some of the important considerations supporting the Rule as we interpret it, especially in criminal cases. If the Rule were to permit the introduction of prior statements as substantive evidence to rebut every implicit charge that a witness' in-court testimony results from recent fabrication or improper influence or motive, the whole emphasis of the trial could shift to the out-of-court statements, not the in-court ones. The present case illustrates the point. In response to a rather weak charge that A.T.'s testimony was a fabrication created so the child could remain with her mother, the Government was permitted to present a parade of sympathetic and credible witnesses who did no more than recount A.T.'s detailed out-of-court statements to them. Although those statements might have been probative on the question whether the alleged conduct had occurred, they shed but minimal light on whether A.T. had the charged motive to fabricate. At closing argument before the jury, the Government placed great reliance on the prior statements for substantive purposes but did not once seek to use them to rebut the impact of the alleged motive.

The judgment of the Court of Appeals for the Tenth Circuit is reversed, and the case is remanded for further proceedings consistent with this opinion.

The Court suggests in *Tome* that the Federal Rules admit prior consistent statements only if they meet the requirements of Rule 801(d)(1)(B) or satisfy a hearsay exception. The Court reads Rule 801(d)(1)(B) as suggesting that a prior consistent statement is admissible only if made *before* the claim of fabrication was made or *before* the alleged motive or improper influence arose. Most prior consistent statements will not satisfy these stringent requirements.

We can now summarize the foundation for admission of prior consistent statements:

1. The declarant testifies at the trial or hearing;
2. The declarant is subject to cross-examination concerning the statement;
3. The prior consistent statement is offered to rebut an express or implied charge or recent fabrication or improper influence or motive; and
4. The prior consistent statement was made before the alleged improper influence or motive arose.

c. Purposes for Which Prior Consistent Statements May Be Offered; Comparing Prior Consistent and Prior Inconsistent Statements

For what purpose is a prior consistent statement admissible? A statement that meets the requirements of Rule 801(d)(1)(B) is defined as non-hearsay. This means that such a statement is admissible substantively, that is, to prove the truth of the matter asserted. Thus, to return to our skateboard hypothetical, if Witness testifies that Plaintiff fell while riding her bicycle with no hands on the handlebars, and not from tripping over a skateboard, and Witness had previously said the same thing before allegedly accepting a bribe to testify for Defendant, Witness's prior statement would be admissible to prove that this is, indeed, how the accident happened.

Witness's testimony also is admissible to support her credibility. This is because any rational juror will consider the statement both as proof that Plaintiff was the cause of his own injury and to show that Witness should be believed when she testifies to that effect. The two propositions are logically inseparable. This illustrates a qualitative difference between prior consistent and prior inconsistent statements. While it is difficult to distinguish the credibility-enhancing effect of a prior consistent statement from its use to prove the truth of the matter asserted, it is not so difficult to compartmentalize the two potential uses of prior inconsistent statements. Jurors are considerably more likely to understand the difference between a prior inconsistent statement offered to impeach a witness and one offered to prove the truth of the matter asserted. For example, if your professor makes inconsistent statements in class, you might think to yourself, "While I don't know which of these statements is true, I certainly know the professor is unreliable." But if what your professor says is always consistent with what she said in previous classes, you are likely to think, "I know my professor is reliable and, thus, what she says must be true."

Because of this, a prior consistent statement is not admissible to support credibility unless it is also admissible to prove the truth of the matters asserted in that statement. In other words, a prior consistent statement is either admissible for all purposes or it is not admissible for any purpose. This is different from how the law treats prior inconsistent statements, which may be admitted for the limited purpose of impeachment even if not admissible for substantive purposes.

Note another key difference between the treatment of prior consistent and prior inconsistent statements. To be admissible substantively, a prior inconsistent statement must have been "made under oath, subject to the penalty for perjury." That is not the case for prior consistent statements. The latter have their own stringent requirements, but making the statement under oath is not one of them.

We have already seen that Rule 613 imposes certain procedural requirements when evidence of a prior inconsistent statement is offered. Do the requirements of Rule 613 apply to consistent statements? Both the language and the policy goals of the rule suggest that the answer is no.

First, Rule 613 is designed to liberalize a common law practice that restricted the proof of prior inconsistent statements, not other prior statements of witnesses. Second, the very language of the rule is directed to prior inconsistent, rather than consistent, statements. Rule 613(b), which regulates proof by extrinsic evidence, explicitly applies only to prior inconsistent statements. And Rule 613(a), which concerns examination of the witness herself concerning the prior statement, is intended primarily to overturn the categorical practice of the common law to require informing the witness of certain details concerning the prior inconsistent statement, a practice that did not apply to prior consistent statements. Finally, the provisions of Rule 613 are designed to protect the witness whose credibility is being attacked from unfair surprise or embarrassment and to avoid the unwarranted appearance that the witness has deliberately lied. Giving a witness an opportunity to explain the meaning of or deny the making of a prior inconsistent statement serves both purposes. By contrast, there is simply no issue of embarrassment or surprise when the prior statement at issue is consistent with the witness's trial testimony. Nor is the fact-finder likely to be misled by proving the statement through extrinsic evidence rather than through the witness-declarant herself. If the opponent is concerned that the testimony creates a false impression of truthfulness and consistency, the opponent is free to cross-examine the witness or present other evidence to refute the facts asserted or impeach the witness's credibility.

3. Illustrating the Use of Prior Consistent and Inconsistent Statements

Defendant is charged with the murder of Vic during a botched attempt to rob the Springfield branch of First State Bank. Defendant claims she was not involved, and intends to call an alibi witness.

At trial, the prosecution calls Will. After establishing that Will works as a teller at the bank, the following colloquy takes place. "Def" indicates the defense attorney; "Pros" indicates the prosecutor.

Pros: Where were you during the early afternoon of May 2 of last year?

Will: I was at work at the bank.

Pros: Do you remember what happened at approximately 2:30?

Will: Yes. Someone entered the bank and attempted to rob the teller who was stationed next to me.

Pros: Did you have an opportunity to see the robber clearly?

Will: Yes.

Pros: How close were you to the robber during this time?

Will: Maybe 6 or 8 feet.

Pros: Was the robber male or female?

Will: Female.

Pros: Please describe the robber's appearance.

Will: She was average height and had very short dark brown hair and brown eyes. She appeared to be Caucasian.

Pros: What clothes was the robber wearing?

Will: She was wearing a light-colored raincoat and long pants.

Pros: [The prosecutor questions the witness further concerning the robbery, and then concludes.] I have no further questions for this witness, Your Honor.

By the Court: Cross-examination?

Def: Thank you, Your Honor. Will, do you recall a conversation with Ward, the bank manager, on the day after the robbery?

Will: Yes.

Def: During that conversation, didn't you say that the robber was wearing dark sunglasses?

Pros: Objection. Calls for hearsay.

Def: No, Your Honor. I am trying to establish the witness's inconsistency. I do not intend to offer the witness's prior statement to prove its truth.

Pros: The statement, even if made, would not be inconsistent with the witness's direct examination testimony. She said nothing about sunglasses, one way or the other.

Def: The witness testified that the robber had brown eyes. If the robber was wearing dark sunglasses, the witness could not have determined the robber's eye color.

By the Court: Objection overruled. The witness will answer the question.

Will: I don't remember saying that.

Def: And didn't you describe the robber as tall?

Will: I did not.

Def: Nothing further, Your Honor.

By the Court: Any redirect?

Pros: Just a couple of questions. Will, do you recall a conversation with a police detective at the bank just a few minutes after the robbery?

Will: Yes. We were all told to stay there until the detective had a chance to interview us.

Pros: And during that interview, did you describe the color of the robber's eyes?

Will: Yes. I said the robber had brown eyes.

Def: Move to strike. This is hearsay.

Pros: Not hearsay, Your Honor. This is a prior consistent statement.

By the Court: Motion to strike granted. The jury will disregard the question and answer.

Pros: Nothing further, Your Honor.

After the prosecution rests, defense counsel calls Ward, the bank manager.

Def: What do you do for a living?

Ward: I am the manager of the Springfield branch of First State Bank.

Def: Do you recall a conversation with Will on May 3, the day after the robbery?

Ward: Yes. I remember the conversation.

Def: During that conversation, did Will describe what the robber was wearing?

Ward: Yes.

Def: Did Will say whether the robber was wearing sunglasses?

Pros: I renew my earlier hearsay objection, Your Honor.

Def: I'm only impeaching, Your Honor. This is not hearsay.

By the Court: Objection overruled.

Ward: Yes. Will told me the robber was wearing dark sunglasses.

Def: Did Will say anything about the robber's eye color?

Ward: No.

Def: And did Will say anything about the robber's height?

Ward: Yes. He said the robber was tall.

Pros:	Would the court please instruct the jury about the limited admissibility of this testimony?
By the Court:	Members of the jury, you are not to consider this witness's testimony about what Will said as any evidence concerning the appearance of the robber, including whether the robber was wearing sunglasses and the robber's height. You may consider this testimony only insofar as it tends to affect the witness's credibility.
Def:	Nothing further, Your Honor.
By the Court:	Cross-examination?
Pros:	No questions, Your Honor.

In this example, the prosecutor has elicited Will's testimony that the robber had brown eyes. On cross-examination, defense counsel asks Will whether he made a statement to the bank manager the next day that the robber was wearing dark sunglasses. Though not inconsistent on its face, such a statement is inconsistent in the sense that it is doubtful the witness could have determined the robber's eye color if the robber was wearing dark glasses. The prosecutor's objection that the question calls for hearsay should be overruled. This is because defense counsel is not trying to prove the robber was wearing dark glasses. Rather, she is trying to prove only that the witness said so, that the statement is inconsistent with the witness's direct examination testimony and, thus, that the witness should not be believed. Of course, the witness denies making the statement, which means that at this point, there is no evidence of the prior inconsistent statement. (The lawyer's question is not testimony.)

Later during the cross-examination, defense counsel also seeks to elicit Will's admission that, during the same conversation the day after the robbery, he told the bank manager that the robber was tall. Again, Will denies making the statement.

On redirect examination, the prosecutor hopes to rehabilitate Will's credibility by demonstrating that, very shortly after the robbery, Will told a police officer that the robber had brown eyes. This is a prior *consistent* statement because it is consistent with Will's direct examination testimony. Prior consistent statements are governed by Rule 801(d)(1)(B). To be admissible, (1) the declarant must testify at the trial or hearing, (2) declarant must be subject to cross-examination about the prior statement, (3) the statement must be offered to "rebut an express or implied charge that the declarant recently fabricated it or acted from a recent improper influence or motive," and (4) the consistent statement must have been made before the alleged fabrication took place or the alleged improper influence or motive arose. The third requirement is not met. Defendant is not claiming that Will fabricated his trial testimony or otherwise had a motive to testify that the robber had brown eyes. Thus, the statement is not admissible. The trial judge correctly sustained defense counsel's objection.

Defense counsel then calls Ward for the purpose of proving the prior inconsistent statements that Will denied making. This constitutes extrinsic evidence of the statement because the proof is coming through another witness, not through Will during his cross-examination. Thus, Rule 613 is implicated. That rule requires that extrinsic evidence of a prior inconsistent statement may not be offered unless the declarant has an opportunity to explain the statement or deny making it. Because defense counsel already confronted

Will with the statement during his cross-examination, that requirement has been satisfied. Thus, it is proper to call Ward to establish the making of the statement. For the same reasons, defense counsel may also establish that Will told Ward the robber was tall.

Further Reading: Frank W. Bullock, Jr. & Steve Gardner, *Prior Consistent Statements and the Premotive Rule*, 24 Fla. St. U. L. Rev. 509 (1997); Leslie E. Daigle, Note, *Tell Me No Timing Rule and I'll Tell You No Lies: Why a Child's Prior Consistent Statements Should Be Admissible Without a Pre-Motive Requirement — A Critique of Tome v. United States*, 17 Rev. Litig. 91 (1998); Richard D. Friedman, *Prior Statements of Witnesses: A Nettlesome Corner of the Hearsay Thicket*, 1995 Sup. Ct. Rev. 277; E. Desmond Hogan, Casenote, *A Consistent Interpretation for 801(d)(1)(B) Prior Consistent Statement*, 39 How. L.J. 819 (1996).

Questions for Classroom Discussion

1. Negligence action by Plaintiff against Defendant arising from an intersection collision. Plaintiff claims Defendant ran the red light; Defendant claims Plaintiff ran the red. Plaintiff calls Witness, who testifies that she saw Defendant run the red light. Plaintiff then seeks to elicit from Witness testimony that she said the same thing when Defendant took her deposition prior to trial. Defendant objects to admission of the deposition testimony on hearsay grounds. How should the court rule?

2. Same case. In response to Defendant's objection, Plaintiff argues that the prior statement is only being offered to support Witness's credibility, not to prove that Defendant ran the red light. How should the court rule?

3. Same case. Assume Plaintiff did not try to elicit Witness's prior statement during direct examination. On cross-examination, Defendant asks Witness to admit that Plaintiff offered Witness money in exchange for Witness's favorable testimony. Witness denies this (or admits receiving the offer but claims that her testimony would have been favorable in any event). On redirect examination, Plaintiff wishes to elicit testimony that Witness's deposition was taken before the date on which Defendant claims Plaintiff offered the bribe. If Defendant objects to admission of the deposition testimony, how should the court rule?

4. Prosecution of Defendant for murder. Defendant denies any involvement. The prosecutor calls Witness, who was arrested for the crime along with Defendant and who previously pleaded guilty in exchange for leniency. Witness testifies that she and Defendant planned and executed the murder together. On cross-examination, Witness admits that she was arrested for and has been charged with

the same crime. On redirect, the prosecutor proposes to ask Witness whether she made the same statement to the police (that she and Defendant planned and executed the murder together) shortly after she was arrested. If Defendant objects to admission of the prior statement, how should the court rule?

5. Prosecution of Defendant for the murder of Victim. The prosecution calls Witness, the doctor who treated Victim in the weeks before Victim died. After ruling on a hearsay objection, the court permits Witness to testify that just before Victim died, Victim accused Defendant of attacking her. Defendant then calls Police Officer as an adverse witness, and elicits Police Officer's admission that a day before Victim's statement to the doctor, Police Officer told Victim that Defendant was a violent person who posed a risk to society, and that if Victim named Defendant as the shooter, Defendant could be "put away for good." During its rebuttal case, the prosecutor recalls Witness, the doctor, and seeks to elicit Witness's testimony that several times before Victim's conversation with Police Officer, Victim named Defendant as the shooter. If Defendant objects to Witness's testimony about Victim's earlier statements to Witness, how should the court rule?

6. Prosecution of Defendant for murder. Defendant calls Witness, who testifies that she was with Defendant in another city when the murder took place. On cross-examination, to show Witness's motive to lie, the prosecution elicits Witness's admission that she and Defendant have been close friends for many years. On redirect examination, Witness wishes to testify that she had told the police the same story (that she and Defendant were in another state when the murder occurred) after the police told her that they had a witness who could challenge Witness's story, and that if Witness didn't tell them the truth, they would prosecute her for obstruction of justice and move to revoke her parole from a lengthy prison term. If the prosecutor objects to Witness's proposed testimony, how should the court rule?

I. TRANSCRIPT EXERCISE: EMPHASIS ON WITNESS IMPEACHMENT

General Facts

Prosecution of Delta for assault and battery on Vic following a barroom brawl that left Vic seriously injured. The bar was located a block from a baseball stadium at which a baseball game between the Red Sox and the Yankees had just taken place. Delta is a fan of the Yankees, who lost. The prosecution alleges that Delta was in the bar having a beer when she saw Vic wearing a Red Sox baseball cap. Delta allegedly noticed Vic's cap and attacked Vic with a beer bottle without provocation. Delta claims she acted in self-defense. She alleges that Vic walked up to Delta and began to taunt Delta about the game, calling the Yankees "slime," and that when Delta asked Vic to stop and "move away," Vic pulled a knife and threatened to kill Delta. At that point, Delta claims, she struck Vic with the beer bottle in self-defense.

The prosecution first calls Vic, who testifies about the incident consistently with the prosecution's theory. Delta's counsel cross-examines Vic. The next witness for the prosecution is White. Throughout the transcript, "Pros" stands for Prosecutor, "DC" for defense counsel.

As you read this transcript ask yourself (1) does the court properly rule on the lawyers' motions and objections, and (2) should the lawyers have stated other motions and objections?

Pros:	Mr. White, where were you on the evening of July 19 of this year, at about 11:00?
White:	I was in the Red Sox bar. I had just come from the Red Sox–Yankees game.
Pros:	Where were you sitting?
White:	At the bar.
Pros:	From the position in which you were seated, could you see much of the room?
White:	Pretty much.
Pros:	Have you ever seen the defendant, Delta, before today?
White:	Yes. I saw her in the bar on the night of July 19, the night we're talking about.
Pros:	Where was Delta when you saw her?
White:	Delta was sitting at a table about 10 feet from the bar.
Pros:	Which way was Delta facing?
White:	Delta was facing the door to the bar.
Pros:	Do you know Vic?
White:	Yes. In fact, I was waiting for Vic. We were planning to meet at the bar after the game.
Pros:	Did Vic enter the bar?
White:	Yes.
Pros:	What time was that?
White:	It was about 11:15.
Pros:	What did Vic do when he came into the bar?
White:	Well, I waved at him to let him know where I was. He looked in my direction and started to walk toward me.
Pros:	Was Vic wearing anything on his head?
White:	Sure. He was wearing a Red Sox cap. He's a big fan.
Pros:	What happened after Vic sat down?
White:	Well, that lady, Delta, sitting at the table there, she just ran up to Vic and hit him over the head with a beer bottle.

Pros:	Were any words exchanged between Delta and Vic before the attack, as far as you could tell?
White:	I don't know. It was hard to hear with all the noise.
Pros:	Before Delta hit Vic with the beer bottle, did Vic make any move toward Delta?
White:	No.
Pros:	Did Vic appear to have any weapon such as a knife?
White:	No.
Pros:	From the positions of both Vic and Delta, does it seem likely to you that Vic could see Delta before the attack?
White:	I doubt it. But Vic wouldn't attack a stranger. That's not the kind of sh —, um, stuff, Vic would do. He's just not like that. Vic was just walking toward me, you know, maybe smiling a little. The Red Sox had just killed the Yankees, you know.
DC:	Move to strike, Your Honor. Inadmissible character evidence.
By the Court:	Motion denied. This involves the character of the victim.
Pros:	What happened after Delta hit Vic with the bottle?
White:	Well, Vic just kind of slumped to the floor. People ran up to him to see if he was okay. Delta, meanwhile, she just stood there like nothing happened.
Pros:	Thank you. Your Honor, I have no further questions at this time.
By the Court:	Cross-examination?
DC:	Yes, Your Honor. Mr. White, you testified that you do not know Delta, is that correct?
White:	Yes.
DC:	And you also testified that you saw Delta sitting at a table in the bar?
White:	That's right.
DC:	And this was before the incident involving the beer bottle?
White:	Yeah. Just a little before.
DC:	Mr. White, were there many people in the bar at about 11:00 that night?
White:	I guess so, yes. It was pretty crowded because the game had just ended, and lots of people like to walk over there, especially after the Red Sox win.
DC:	Was there anything about Delta that drew her to your attention before the incident?
White:	Not really. I wasn't checking her out, if that's what you mean.
DC:	So it's your testimony that even though you are not familiar with Delta, you noticed Delta in a crowded bar before there was any special reason to focus on her?
White:	Yeah, I guess so. So what?
DC:	How well do you know Vic, Mr. White?
White:	We're friends.
DC:	Isn't there something else? Don't you also work for Vic?
White:	Not really. Sometimes I do stuff for Vic, but I also work for a lot of other people.

DC: Let's focus on what you saw. Is it your testimony that when Delta saw Vic enter the bar, Delta just walked up to Vic and broke a bottle over his head, just like that?

White: Just like that.

DC: And no words were exchanged between Delta and Vic before this happened?

White: Right. No fight, no words.

DC: Mr. White, do you remember talking to the police shortly after the incident in the bar?

White: Sure, I remember.

DC: And do you recall making a statement at that time about the incident?

White: Yes. I did.

DC: Did you sign that statement?

White: Yes. I talked into a tape recorder, the officer had it typed up, and then I signed it.

DC: And when you signed it, did you swear to tell the truth?

White: I didn't say anything, if that's what you mean.

DC: But above your signature, did you notice that there was language advising you that you swore under penalty of perjury that what you said in the statement was correct?

White: Yes, I saw it.

DC: And did you understand what it meant?

White: Sure. It meant I had to tell the truth, and I did.

DC: In that statement, you didn't say anything about seeing Delta before the incident, did you?

White: No, I didn't say anything about that.

DC: In fact, didn't you state, and I quote, I noticed Vic enter the bar and start to walk toward me when this woman just came out of nowhere, just walked up to Vic and hit him over the head with a bottle. Unquote. Did you make that statement?

Pros: Objection, Your Honor. Calls for hearsay.

By the Court: Objection overruled.

White: Yes, I said that.

DC: Let's turn to what happened after Vic fell to the floor. You testified that after Vic fell to the floor, people went over to Vic to see if they could help. Correct?

White: Yes.

DC: And you also testified that Delta just stood there, quote, like nothing happened, unquote.

White: Right.

DC: I have nothing further, Your Honor.

[At this time, the prosecutor indicated that she had no further witnesses to call. After a recess, the Defense calls Ward. On direct examination, Ward testifies that he was in the bar having a drink when he saw Vic walk up to Delta and taunt her about the game, calling the Yankees "slime," and that when Delta asked Vic to stop and get away, Vic pulled a knife and threatened to kill Delta. Ward testifies that at that point, Delta struck Vic with the beer bottle.

Ward also testifies that less than five minutes after hitting Vic with the bottle, Delta, excitedly and in tears, told Ward, "I've never been so frightened of anyone in my life!" The court admitted this testimony as an excited utterance, over the prosecutor's objection.

Following is a transcript of the prosecutor's cross-examination of Ward.]

Pros: Mr. Ward, you testified that Delta only struck Vic after Vic pulled a knife on her, is that correct?

Ward: That's right.

Pros: Isn't it true that you arrived at the bar at approximately 9:00 that evening?

Ward: I don't remember exactly. Maybe about that time. Could have been later.

Pros: And isn't it true that by 11:00 or so, you had consumed quite a few beers?

Ward: I had a few. I wouldn't say quite a few. Two or three, maybe.

Pros: It was more like five, wasn't it, Mr. Ward?

Ward: No.

Pros: And if I had a witness who could testify that you had five beers, that witness would be lying?

DC: Objection, Your Honor. Asked and answered.

By the Court: Overruled.

Ward: I wouldn't say lying. Mistaken.

Pros: Mr. Ward, do you know Delta, the defendant?

Ward: Yeah, I guess so.

Pros: Are you friends?

Ward: Yes.

Pros: More than that?

Ward: Friends.

Pros: Mr. Ward, to your knowledge, has Delta ever been convicted of the crime of assault and battery?

DC: Objection, Your Honor, and I move for a mistrial. This evidence is obviously inadmissible and highly inflammatory. Even with a cautionary instruction, the jury will not put this highly prejudicial question out of its mind.

Pros: Offered to impeach, Your Honor.

DC: Your Honor, impeach who? My client has not testified.

By the Court: Objection sustained. The jury is instructed to ignore this question. You are not to assume that the defendant has been convicted of a previous crime. That has nothing to do with this case. Motion for mistrial denied. Move on to something else, counsel.

Pros: I have nothing further.

[The defense next called Will, who testifies as follows:]

DC: Please state your profession.

Will: I'm a bartender.

DC: Where did you work last year?

Will: I worked at a place called Betty's.

DC: In March of last year, did you see White at Betty's?

Will: Yes, I did.

DC: How do you remember?

Will: I remember because he caused some trouble when I carded him.

DC: What do you mean by carded?

Will: Asked for his identification, for proof of his age. He looked like he might not be 21, so I asked for I.D.

DC: And what happened?

Will: He showed me a driver's license. I could tell he'd changed the date of birth. So I told him to leave.

DC: Did he leave?

Will: Not at first. He started yelling, calling me names. Racial things. Bad stuff.

Pros: Move to strike, Your Honor. Irrelevant and inflammatory.

By the Court: Overruled.

DC: What happened next?

Will: I told him again to leave, and he did. That was it.

DC: Nothing further, Your Honor.

By the Court: Cross-examination?

Pros: Will, have you ever been convicted of a felony?

Will: Absolutely not.

Pros: You don't recall being convicted of felony burglary six years ago?

Will: I do not.

Pros: Your Honor, I offer into evidence a document titled, "Judgment of Conviction," which bears the seal of the Clerk of the Superior Court of this county. It is dated six years ago, signed by Judge Jefferson, and records a conviction of this witness for the crime of felony burglary.

DC: I object, Your Honor. Hearsay and not authenticated.

By the Court: Overruled.

DC: In addition, Your Honor, it is irrelevant.

Pros: Your Honor, it is offered to impeach this witness.

By the Court: Objection sustained. The exhibit will not be received.

Pros: I have no more questions for this witness, Your Honor.

[The defense next called Gil.]

DC: Gil, do you know White?

Gil: Yes. We've been friends for a long time.

DC: And did you ever speak with White about the incident in the Red Sox Bar on the night of July 19 of this year?

Gil: Yes. I think we talked about it once.

DC: And during that conversation, did White tell you anything about people going to help Vic after he was hit with the beer bottle?

Gil: I think he might have said something about that.

DC: What did he say?

Pros: Objection. Calls for hearsay.

DC: Offered to impeach, Your Honor.

By the Court: Objection overruled. You may answer the question.

Gil: I think he told me that a bunch of people went over to help Vic.

DC: Did White say anything about Delta being one of those people?

Gil: I think so. Yes, he said Delta was one of them.

DC: No more questions, Your Honor.

By the Court: Cross-examination?

Pros: No, Your Honor.

Assessments

For Questions 1 and 2, answer "true" or "false."

1. James testifies he saw the red car run the stop sign. You may ask James on cross-examination whether he was drinking during the hour before he claims to have seen the incident.

2. Same facts as in Question 1. James testifies that he was "sober" when he witnessed the incident. After James is excused as a witness, you may not call a bartender who will testify James drank four martinis one hour before the accident.

3. The prosecution alleges Tony rigged the bidding on large construction contracts in exchange for kick-backs. Jimmy signed a sworn affidavit stating that Tony was engaged in bid rigging. Jimmy repeated this accusation during his grand jury testimony. At trial, the government calls Jimmy to testify. Jimmy testifies that Tony was not engaged in bid rigging. The prosecutor begins to cross-examine Jimmy using his affidavit. Tony's attorney objects, arguing this is improper impeachment. The trial court should:
   a. Sustain the objection because the government called Jimmy as its witness
   b. Overrule the objection. The prosecutor may attack Jimmy's credibility because his testimony is contrary to his earlier statements
   c. Sustain the objection. The prosecutor may not impeach Jimmy using the affidavit because she did not disclose the circumstances under which he signed the affidavit
   d. The court should allow Tony's attorney to question Jimmy out of the presence of the jury. If Jimmy continues to deny Tony's guilt, the court should sustain the objection because the cross-examination is improper impeachment

4. Walter testifies the blue car ran the stop sign. On cross-examination, the lawyer for the defendant gets Walter to admit he told friends a few days after the accident that the red car may have run the stop sign. The judge should:

(continued)

a. Admit the testimony as tending to prove the red car ran the stop sign
b. Admit the testimony as tending to impeach Walter's testimony on direct
c. Upon request, instruct the jury it may only consider the testimony to the extent it might impeach Walter's testimony on direct
d. Both b and c

5. The prosecution introduces testimony about a statement made by a decedent that the defendant helped her embezzle money. The judge ruled the testimony was admissible as a declaration against interest. In response, defense counsel offers testimony that, before decedent made the disputed statement, she stated that she alone embezzled the money. The prosecution objects that this testimony is hearsay, and improper impeachment. How should the judge rule?
a. The testimony is inadmissible because the declarant will not have an opportunity to deny or explain her inconsistent statement
b. The testimony is admissible as tending to impeach the declarant introduced by the prosecution
c. The testimony is admissible as tending to prove the defendant did not help the decedent embezzle money
d. The testimony is inadmissible hearsay

Answers and Analysis

1. True. You may always attempt to impeach a witness by challenging her/his ability to perceive and recollect accurately. If James was drinking before the incident, his perception and memory may have been adversely affected.

2. False. You may attempt to impeach James by introducing testimony that contradicts his denial. While the bartender's testimony is "extrinsic," it will be allowed because James's ability to perceive and recollect is central to the jury's assessment of his credibility.

3. The correct answer is "b." The prosecutor should be allowed to impeach Jimmy even though she called him as a witness. Jimmy twice stated the defendant was engaged in bid rigging before he testified. The prosecution may attempt to impeach his testimony using his prior inconsistent statement. There is no requirement that the prosecutor show Jimmy the affidavit, or disclose its contents before questioning him about it; that common law requirement was eliminated by the FRE. FRE 607, 613.

4. The correct answer is "c." Walter's prior inconsistent statement may be used to impeach his testimony. It may not be used to prove the truth of the matter asserted because the inconsistent statement was not made penalty of perjury at a trial, hearing, or other proceeding.

Therefore the court should, upon request, instruct the jury it may only consider the testimony for its impeachment value.

5. The correct answer is "b." This prior inconsistent statement tends to impeach the hearsay declarant. Because she is unavailable, there is no requirement that the declarant be given an opportunity to explain or deny the prior inconsistent statement. FRE 806, Advisory Committee Note.

CHAPTER
7

Lay and Expert Opinion Evidence

A. INTRODUCTION

The rules governing opinion evidence are designed to limit admission to opinions that are reliable and necessary. To achieve these goals, the rules focus on four issues. You can resolve most problems in this chapter by considering these questions:

1. Who is competent to give opinion testimony?
2. What may opinion testimony be based on?
3. Is the opinion helpful?
4. What sort of methodology or reasoning process must form the foundation for the opinion evidence?

The rules we are about to study do not define *opinion*. Courts in the nineteenth century attempted to give content to the concept by distinguishing opinion from fact. These courts discouraged testimony based on the former in favor of testimony based on the latter. However, the distinction became impossible to apply because it is ephemeral. All testimony consists of opinions in the form of inferences drawn from perception.

For example, assume a witness is called by the prosecution and testifies, "I saw the defendant pick up a gun and shoot the victim." On the surface, the witness appears to describe her perception of facts entirely free of opinion. But in truth the witness has based her testimony on a series of inferences or opinions produced by relating perception to her prior knowledge of guns and their effect on people. In other words, the witness opined that the metallic object that the witness saw was a gun. The witness also came to the opinion that, when the witness saw a puff of white smoke come out of the metallic object simultaneously with hearing a loud sound, and then saw red liquid spurt out of the victim, this meant that the defendant shot the victim. These may be very safe opinions to draw, but they are *still* opinions. Thus, the failure of the rules to define opinion is not the result of oversight; the drafters of the Federal Rules of Evidence were mindful of the difficulties of distinguishing between opinion and fact.

There are two types of opinion testimony: lay and expert. The admissibility issues posed by these two types of opinion testimony are different. Accordingly, they are regulated by different provisions in the Federal Rules of Evidence.

B. LAY OPINION

> **FED. R. EVID. 701.   OPINION TESTIMONY BY LAY WITNESSES**

If a witness is not testifying as an expert, testimony in the form of an opinion is limited to one that is:

(a) rationally based on the witness's perception;

(b) helpful to clearly understanding the witness's testimony or to determining a fact in issue; and

(c) not based on scientific, technical, or other specialized knowledge within the scope of Rule 702.

1. *Function of Rule 701: Requiring the Witness to Be More Specific*

By leaving the concept of opinion undefined, the drafters bestowed upon the courts considerable discretion to determine the scope of Rule 701. But this discretion has less to do with *admissibility* of a witness's testimony than it has to do with controlling the *form* of that testimony. The reason admissibility usually is not affected is that similar tests for admissibility apply whether or not the testimony is said to consist of opinion. For example, if a court concludes that the testimony of a lay witness contains opinion, Rule 701 commands that the opinion be "rationally based on the witness's perception" and "helpful." But if a court concludes that the testimony does not contain opinion, we already have seen that the testimony still must be based on perception under Rule 602 and must be helpful or face exclusion under Rule 403 as a waste of time.

This means that the real aim of Rule 701 is not to create another limit on admissibility but to afford the courts a vehicle for forcing a witness to give testimony that is more specific. For example, assume an action for injuries sustained in an automobile accident. A witness testifies, "The driver of the blue car was reckless." The testimony gives the jurors the witness's opinion as to who should win the case, but does not give them the information they need to make that decision for themselves. By requiring that a lay opinion be helpful, Rule 701 empowers the court to exclude such an opinion, forcing the witness to be more specific: "The driver of the blue car was going the wrong way on a one-way street."

2. *Who May Give Lay Opinions?*

The scope of Rule 701 also is limited in that it relates only to opinion testimony from a witness who "is not testifying as an expert." Such a person is commonly called a *lay witness.* Rule 702, discussed in the next section, regulates expert opinion testimony.

How do you tell the difference between lay and expert testimony? Rule 701 supplies the answer, stating that lay opinion is "not based on scientific, technical, or other specialized knowledge within the scope of Rule 702." This means that Rule 702 applies rather than Rule 701 if the witness arrives at her opinion through the application of special skill or erudition beyond the realm of common knowledge. The Advisory Committee's Note to this part of Rule 701 gives a good example of the distinction: "[A] lay witness with experience could testify that a substance appeared to be blood, but . . . a witness would have to qualify as an expert before he could testify that bruising around the eyes is indicative of skull trauma."

The rationale for creating separate rules regulating lay and expert opinion is that juries have a more difficult time weighing expert opinion because of the very nature of that type of opinion — it is based on matters beyond the ken of most laypeople. As a consequence, we will see that the expert witness rules are more complex and demanding than Rule 701.

3. What Is a Proper Basis for Lay Opinion Testimony?

Rule 701 tells us that lay opinion must be "rationally based on the witness's perception." By restricting lay opinions to those based on the perception of the witness, one implication of Rule 701 is that lay opinion may not be based on hearsay. This is because a witness who bases an opinion on hearsay may have perceived the out-of-court statement with her sense of hearing, but the "matter asserted" by that statement usually relates to facts perceived by the hearsay declarant and not the witness. This means that if a witness bases a lay opinion on the statement of someone else, the application of Rule 701 depends on whether the opinion relies on the mere fact that the statement was made or on the truth of the facts asserted within that statement. The former is proper but the latter is not.

For example, assume that a lay witness offers to testify that he heard a person say out of court, "I am the Queen of England." Based on hearing this statement the witness offers her opinion that the speaker is insane. Because this opinion is based only on the fact that the statement was made, and the witness perceived the statement with her sense of hearing, the opinion is not based on hearsay and is proper under Rule 701. But the opinion is improper if the witness uses the statement as the basis for an opinion that the speaker is the rightful heir to the English throne. In that case, the opinion of the witness relies on a fact the speaker asserts. While the speaker may have personal knowledge of that fact, the witness does not. This means that the opinion is based on hearsay and not "on the witness's perception," as required by Rule 701.

Rule 701 requires not only that the opinion be based on perception but also that there be a rational connection between that perception and the opinion. Two issues can be raised under this requirement that the opinion be "rationally based." First, there must be some logical connection between the subject of the opinion and the matters perceived. Second, the quality and quantity of the perception must be sufficient to logically permit the witness to base an opinion on it.

The logical connection between perception and lay opinion depends on the validity of the proposition linking the perception to the opinion. For example, when a witness offers the opinion that the substance he smelled on defendant's breath was alcohol, the opinion is "rationally based" only if the factual assumption the witness made concerning the smell of alcohol on a person's breath is valid. This usually means that the witness must have some experience smelling alcohol on a person's breath. But when the factual assumption underlying the lay opinion is invalid (e.g., alcohol in a person's breath smells like fried onions), that opinion is not rationally based even when the witness bases that opinion on first-hand observation.

The second aspect of the requirement that lay opinion be rationally based on perception is that the perception must be sufficient in quality and quantity to permit the opinion. For example, assume a lay witness offers an opinion as to the sanity of another person. Because behavior and demeanor can be indicators of mental condition, the courts conclude that a lay opinion as to sanity is rationally based on perception when the witness observed the behavior and demeanor of the person in question. But most authorities permit the opinion only if the witness had a *significant* opportunity to observe that person. A solitary, fleeting observation is not considered to be a rational basis for such an opinion because experience tells us that sane people frequently engage in isolated behavior that may seem crazy and that insane people can have occasional moments of lucidity. Thus, without an opportunity to view the context of an individual's actions and a large enough sample of those actions, an opinion as to sanity will have little value and might even be misleading.

This means that lay opinion founded on limited perception is not rationally based when our knowledge and experience of the opinion's subject suggest significant perception is needed to arrive at an accurate opinion. On the other hand, the duration and extent of perception is not an issue with respect to opinions on many subjects. For example, the courts have held that opinions founded on minimal perception can be rationally based if the opinion relates to a specific fact or event, such as the identification of a person or the speed of a moving vehicle. In such cases, questions concerning the sufficiency of perception usually go only to the weight of the opinions, not their admissibility.

4. When Is Lay Opinion "Helpful"?

Rule 701 requires that lay opinion must be "helpful to clearly understanding the witness's testimony or to determining a fact in issue." Deciding whether an opinion is helpful often requires balancing the benefits of the opinion against its costs. Thus, this aspect of Rule 701 necessarily gives trial courts a significant degree of flexibility in determining whether lay opinion is admissible. Lay opinion produces benefits when it saves time or provides information that would not be conveyed by testimony limited to specific facts. There are at least five situations where lay opinion produces such benefits.

In the first situation, lay opinion conveys information that the witness cannot otherwise clearly relate to the jury because of limitations on the descriptive abilities of that witness. An example is lay opinion identifying a voice heard on a recording or over the telephone. Though an expert witness might be able to articulate the specific distinguishing characteristics of a person's voice, such as tone quality or speech patterns, a lay witness might be unable to give such a description. This is because the lay witness may not be consciously aware of the aspects of her perception that she used to arrive at her opinion. The opinion of the witness is helpful in such a case because, while we believe a witness can accurately identify the voice of a person with whom she is familiar, we also know that the witness may be unable to describe to the jury the specific characteristics of the voice that allow her to make that identification.

In the second situation where lay opinion produces benefits, the witness can describe some, but not all, of the perceptual details that produce the opinion. For example, when a lay witness gives an opinion as to the emotional state of another person, the witness might be able to describe some of the perceptual details that produced that opinion. Thus, assume a witness offers the opinion that a certain person appeared angry. The witness might be able to explain her opinion by pointing out that the person furrowed his brow, was frowning, and had a flushed complexion. However, the witness might be unable to describe the additional but more subtle details that led the witness to conclude that the person was not experiencing some other emotion or sensation that could induce the same facial expressions. In such a case the lay opinion is helpful because it fills gaps that would be left by an incomplete description of her perceptions.

In the third situation where lay opinion is helpful, the witness can describe all the components of his perception but the opinion still conveys additional information — an example of the notion that the whole is sometimes more than the sum of its parts. For example, when a lay witness gives an opinion as to the speed of a vehicle, the witness may be able to state that the roar of the engine was loud, there was a cloud of dust, and the vehicle was a blur as it passed. But even after a complete description of these details the jury may be uncertain as to whether the vehicle had been traveling closer to 50 or 80 miles per hour, which could be a crucial distinction. In such a case, lay opinion as to the speed of the vehicle ("He was going about 80") is helpful because only the witness is in a position to assemble all the details into a clear picture.

In the fourth situation where lay opinion produces benefits, the witness can interpret evidence the full meaning of which would not otherwise be apparent to the jury. For example, if the jury cannot determine whether the defendant is the bank robber depicted in surveillance photos because of the robber's disguise or the poor quality of the photos, a lay witness familiar with the defendant still might be able to make the identification. On the other hand, if the appearance of the robber in the photos is clear or the witness is unfamiliar with the defendant's appearance, lay opinion may be of no help.

Finally, lay opinion also produces a benefit when it saves time, even though the opinion may convey no more information than would testimony limited to the details of perception. An opinion usually saves time because it summarizes into a single statement the meaning of many specific details. For example, it takes only a moment to state that a person "looked drunk." It takes much longer for the witness to explain that the person had slurred speech, bloodshot eyes, an uneven gait, and reeked of beer. Lay opinion also may save time because witnesses are unaccustomed to limiting their speech to particulars, commonly mixing the general with the specific. Thus, a witness may find it natural to state that a person "staggered like he was drunk." It takes time to resolve objections aimed at precluding a witness from using this natural manner of speech. Further, if those objections are sustained, the witness may find it difficult to reformulate her testimony. In such a case, permitting the witness to state opinions may be "helpful to clearly understanding the witness's testimony."

Of course, on cross-examination, the opponent might choose to require the witness to state why she reached her conclusion, a strategy designed to undercut the witness by showing that she cannot articulate the basis of her opinion. (This strategy can backfire, however, if the witness is able to state a clear basis for her opinion.)

On the other hand, there are at least three ways in which lay opinion might not be helpful because it imposes costs on the fact-finding process. First, when lay opinion is offered in lieu of the individual components of perception, the jury may be deprived of information it needs to determine the facts. For example, when a witness in an automobile accident case testifies that the defendant drove recklessly, but omits the specific details supporting that opinion, the jury is unable to draw its own conclusions or even determine what weight to give the opinion. Second, even where the opinion is accompanied by testimony as to particular facts, it is a waste of time if it adds no information beyond that conveyed by those facts. Finally, lay opinion can mislead the jury if the witness lacks a sufficient basis for that opinion. Thus, even when the witness combines opinion testimony with testimony concerning the factual basis for his opinion, the jury may be lulled by a convincing witness into accepting a flawed or unfounded opinion. Such opinions not only fail to be helpful, they may also violate the "rationally based" requirement.

Thus, lay opinion testimony can both bestow benefits and impose costs. The likely benefits of such testimony must outweigh its costs before the evidence can be considered helpful. In striking that balance, the courts commonly focus on two factors.

First, the costs of lay opinion increase and the benefits diminish the closer the opinion approaches the crucial issues in the case. For example, assume defendant is on trial for the crime of public inebriation. Lay opinion that defendant was "drunk" on the evening in question is of limited benefit because it provides the jury with no independent basis to resolve the central issue in the case. When the opinion is offered without supporting factual details, it represents little more than choosing sides and it would be appropriate for the court to exclude it. Whatever time would be saved might not justify receiving the opinion in lieu of supporting details because the opinion goes to the heart of the case, making worthwhile a full airing of the facts pertinent to that issue. But even though a court will be more likely to exclude an opinion that goes to the heart of the case, there is plenty of room to allow the opinion when the court concludes that, on balance, the value of the opinion exceeds any dangers it might create.

On the other hand, the balance shifts in the direction of admitting lay opinion as the distance increases between the opinion and the ultimate issues. For example, if the issue is the fitness of a parent to retain custody of a child, the admission of lay opinion that the parent was "drunk" on a given occasion presents little danger that jurors will fail to exercise independent judgment as to the much broader question of overall fitness. Similarly, receiving the opinion in lieu of a recitation of all the details that led the witness to his opinion may be justifiable on the ground of saving time. This savings is beneficial because, now that the issue is the broader question of fitness, the sobriety of the parent on a single evening may be of insufficient consequence to warrant extensive proof.

The second factor important to balancing the costs and benefits of lay opinion is the extent to which those costs can be minimized by cross-examination and argument. In most cases, cross-examination and argument by the party opposing the opinion can effectively reveal defects in the judgment of the witness or the adequacy of his perception. Further, such problems usually can be revealed without undue expenditure of time. When cross-examination and argument can be effective, the costs of lay opinion diminish and the balance may tip in favor of admitting lay opinion. On the other hand, when those adversarial mechanisms do not work, the courts may be inclined to exclude lay opinion.

Because application of the helpfulness requirement necessitates a careful balance of the benefits and costs of lay opinion, each case must be decided under its particular facts and circumstances. The determination of whether lay opinion is helpful under Rule 701 is a question for the trial court under Rule 104(a). In striking the balance between benefits and costs, trial courts have significant room to exercise discretion. However, certain categories of cases can be recognized in which the courts have tended toward striking the balance in favor of admissibility.

For example, lay opinion traditionally has been received as to the mental, emotional, or physical condition of a person observed by the witness. Thus, the courts have admitted lay opinion as to sanity, insanity, feelings, knowledge, intent, character, appearance, age, suffering, intoxication, and the like. Similarly, lay opinion has also been received on a myriad of subjects having to do with the nature or condition of objects. Thus, lay witnesses have been permitted to give opinions as to appearance of objects, condition of an accident site, value of property or profits, quality or acceptability, adequacy of safety precautions or devices, the nature of a substance, smell, and related matters. Further, courts have been open to lay opinion concerning the nature of certain conduct and other events. Thus, the courts have admitted opinions as to speed of a vehicle, meaning of a statement, cause of an accident, *modus operandi*, and the like. The courts have also been open to lay opinion concerning identity or origin. Thus, evidence has been admitted under Rule 701 concerning voice identification, genuineness of handwriting, and identity of a person depicted in a photograph or videotape. Of course, the types of lay opinions mentioned here have not been admitted in every case. Courts exercise their judgment in each situation to determine the admissibility of the opinion.

Illustrating the lay opinion rule. Plaintiff sues Defendant for negligence after Defendant's black SUV struck Plaintiff as Plaintiff was crossing Evergreen Street between First and Second Avenues. This was in a residential neighborhood. Plaintiff claims Defendant was driving at excessive speed through the neighborhood, sped around a corner, and was not able to stop in time to avoid striking Plaintiff. At trial, Plaintiff calls Wyn, and the following colloquy takes place. "Pl" indicates Plaintiff's counsel; "Def" indicates Defendant's counsel.

> *Pl:* Ms. Wyn, where were you at 12:15 P.M. on June 4 of last year?
>
> *Wyn:* I was on my daily run. I was on Evergreen, headed east.
>
> *Pl:* Were you on the street?
>
> *Wyn:* Yes. I was running along the left side of the street, close to the curb.

Pl:	Were you approaching a cross street at that time?
Wyn:	Yes. I was about halfway between First and Second Streets, heading toward Second.
Pl:	Was the road ahead of you straight?
Wyn:	No. The road made a fairly sharp turn from the left ahead of me, about a half block past the Second Street intersection.
Pl:	Did you notice a black SUV at that time?
Wyn:	Yes.
Pl:	In what direction was it heading?
Wyn:	The SUV was heading west, so it was coming toward me.
Pl:	What drew your attention to the SUV?
Wyn:	Well, I was looking straight ahead, so cars coming toward me along Evergreen were in my range of vision.
Pl:	Okay. Did other cars come into your range of vision at about that time?
Wyn:	There might have been a few. I don't really remember.
Pl:	So what caused you to pay attention to the black SUV?
Wyn:	Well, first I noticed it because I heard screeching brakes, so I focused on the road ahead and saw this black SUV.
Pl:	Was the screeching sound you mentioned caused by that vehicle?
Def:	Objection, Your Honor. Lack of foundation for the opinion.
Pl:	Your Honor, with the court's permission, I will lay the foundation.
By the Court:	Go ahead.
Pl:	Were you able to tell what caused this screeching sound?
Wyn:	It was clearly a car. I know the sound of screeching brakes when I hear it.
Pl:	Were you able to determine which vehicle made the sound?
Wyn:	Yes.
Pl:	Which vehicle made the sound?
Def:	Your Honor, I renew my objection. Though I am sure the witness can testify that a sound was caused by a vehicle's screeching brakes, as the record stands counsel has not shown how the witness could have determined which vehicle made the noise.
Pl:	This witness is perfectly capable of stating that, Your Honor.
By the Court:	I do not believe you have shown how the proposed testimony will be rationally based on the witness's perception. Objection sustained.
Pl:	May I continue with this line of questions, Your Honor? I would like another opportunity to make the showing.
By the Court:	I'll allow a few more questions.
Pl:	Thank you, Your Honor. Ms. Wyn, were you looking at any vehicles when you heard the sound?
Wyn:	I don't remember. I just remember hearing a screeching sound and then focusing on this SUV rounding the bend.
Pl:	Let's move ahead. Did the SUV pass you?
Wyn:	Yes.
Pl:	Can you estimate the SUV's speed when it passed you?

Def:	Objection. Lacks foundation for an opinion.
Pl:	Your Honor, the witness is capable of estimating the speed of a moving vehicle. This is a matter of common experience, and the witness had a sufficient opportunity to make the necessary observation.
By the Court:	I'll allow it. Objection overruled.
Def:	May I be heard, Your Honor?
By the Court:	Go ahead.
Def:	If the witness intends to state an actual speed in miles per hour, I think that is not rationally based on her perception. First, she was not in another moving vehicle and so could not use her own speedometer as a reference point. Second, she was running in the opposite direction of the vehicle. It is very difficult to estimate speed under those circumstances.
Pl:	Your Honor, as I said, this is a matter of common experience.
By the Court:	I'll allow the witness to estimate within ranges, but not a specific speed.
Pl:	Ms. Wyn, is it your opinion that the SUV was moving faster or slower than 25 miles per hour?
Wyn:	Definitely faster.
Pl:	Was it faster than 40 miles per hour?
Wyn:	Yes.
Pl:	Faster than 60?
Wyn:	I don't think so.
Pl:	I have no further questions for this witness, Your Honor.

In this example, Plaintiff's counsel seeks to elicit several opinions from the witness. Because Wyn is a lay witness, Rule 701 applies. As we have seen, that rule limits lay opinions to those that are (1) rationally based on the perceptions of the witness; (2) helpful to a clear understanding of the witness's testimony or in determining a fact in issue; and (3) not based on specialized knowledge of the sort that would call for application of the rule regulating expert testimony. The witness gave three opinions.

First, the witness properly was permitted to testify that the screeching sound came from a person applying the brakes on a vehicle. Note that defense counsel did not object to this opinion. This opinion is permissible because a lay witness has experience with the sound of screeching tires caused by the hard application of a vehicle's brakes. The opinion is helpful to the jury because testimony limited just to describing the noise ("a loud, high-pitched, screeching sound") that the witness heard would not give the fact-finder a sufficiently complete picture of what the witness actually perceived.

Second, Plaintiff's counsel wanted to elicit Wyn's opinion that the sound came from the SUV, which other evidence shows was Defendant's vehicle. The problem here is that it does not appear that Wyn actually saw the vehicle as it was making the sound. If the SUV was the only vehicle in the area from which the sound came, perhaps the opinion would be rationally based on the witness's perception. But Plaintiff's counsel did not develop that information either at first or after defense counsel objected. This example also can be viewed as one that implicates the personal knowledge rule (Rule 602). Arguably, the problem here was that Wyn lacked the kind of sensory perception necessary to provide her with personal knowledge of the source of the sound. Whether based on the opinion rule or the personal knowledge rule, the court acted properly in sustaining Defendant's objection.

Third, Plaintiff's counsel wanted to have Wyn testify how fast the SUV was traveling. This is a close case. Certainly, there are situations in which a lay witness may testify about the speed of a vehicle. If, for example, the witness was traveling in another vehicle alongside the one at issue, and if the witness knew the speed of her own vehicle, a court probably would allow her to offer an opinion as to the speed of the other car (even if the two were traveling at somewhat different speeds). Here, however, Wyn was running in one direction and the SUV was traveling toward her. It is much more difficult to say that Wyn's estimate of the vehicle's speed in such a situation is rationally based on her perception. Certainly, a court would be acting well within its discretion if it disallows the opinion. Note, however, that Plaintiff's counsel did not give up. The court allowed counsel to elicit the speed of the vehicle within a rough range. This is much more likely to be rationally based on Wyn's perception, and though the result might not have been as useful to Plaintiff's case as a specific opinion as to speed, the testimony still gives Plaintiff's counsel something from which to argue at the close of the case.

Questions for Classroom Discussion

1. Divorce action. The issue is which parent should have custody of the children, who currently reside with their mother. The father calls a neighbor to testify that, in her opinion, the mother is not fit to retain custody. Is the opinion admissible? Why or why not?

2. Same case. The neighbor offers to testify that, in her opinion, the mother frequently had many male guests stay overnight. The opinion is based on the fact that the neighbor saw cars other than those owned by the mother parked in the mother's driveway at night when the neighbor went to bed and would see the same cars in the driveway in the morning. Is the opinion admissible? Why or why not?

3. Same case. The neighbor offers to testify that, in her opinion, the mother is an alcoholic because the neighbor once smelled alcohol on the mother's breath. Is the opinion admissible? Why or why not?

4. Same case. The neighbor offers to testify that, in her opinion, the mother uses drugs because she has a tattoo and a nose ring. Is the opinion admissible? Why or why not?

5. Same case. The father calls a psychologist who offers to testify, based on the testimony of other witnesses, that the mother is not fit to retain custody. Is the opinion admissible under Rule 701? Why or why not?

C. EXPERT OPINION

FED. R. EVID. 702. TESTIMONY BY EXPERT WITNESSES

A witness who is qualified as an expert by knowledge, skill, experience, train-ing, or education may testify in the form of an opinion or otherwise if:

(a) the expert's scientific, technical, or other specialized knowledge will help the trier of fact to understand the evidence or to determine a fact in issue;

(b) the testimony is based on sufficient facts or data;

(c) the testimony is the product of reliable principles and methods; and

(d) the expert has reliably applied the principles and methods to the facts of the case.

1. Introduction

The Advisory Committee's Note to Rule 702 describes the importance of expert testimony: "An intelligent evaluation of facts is often difficult or impossible without the application of some scientific, technical, or other specialized knowl-edge." These words are doubtless even more accurate today than when they were written. In the decades since the drafters made this observation, science and technology have intruded into nearly every aspect of life and litigation. Today there are many cases that a jury could not begin to understand without the help of experts, and there are few cases in which experts cannot at least assist understanding.

On the other hand, expert testimony also can undermine the fact-finder's search for the truth. Because experts often deal with esoteric matters of great complexity, the jury might be incapable of critically evaluating an expert's testimony. In addition, experts present themselves as people with special qua-lifications. As a consequence, there is a significant danger that a jury may view an expert as surrounded by what some psychologists call an "aura of infalli-bility." Thus, even when the trier of fact has some basis for questioning an expert's reliability, it may be disinclined to do so. In an era when the opinions of professional witnesses are available for purchase in virtually every field of science and technology, a jury's unquestioning deference to expert opinion may seriously jeopardize accurate fact-finding. Rule 702 mitigates the effect of these dangers by imposing several limits on the admissibility of expert testimony.

2. Expert Testimony Must "Help the Trier of Fact"

Rule 702 requires that expert testimony relate to specialized knowledge that will "help the trier of fact." Many factors have a bearing on whether expert testimony meets this requirement. The first factor is whether the expert testimony is relevant. Thus, expert testimony does not "help" if it is unrelated to facts at issue or is based on factual assumptions that are not supported by the evidence. For example, in a wrongful death case, testimony of an economist as to lost future income is irrelevant and does not assist if it is based on assumptions concerning the deceased's past earnings that have no basis in fact. Similarly, an opinion that defendant's product causes a certain disease is irrelevant and does not assist when offered to prove that the same product might have caused plaintiff's different and unrelated disease. Expert testimony also is irrelevant and fails to assist if the reasoning behind that testimony is so illogical that it cannot affect the probabilities of the existence of facts at issue.

Assuming expert testimony is relevant, the most important factor in determining whether expert testimony will help is the jury's need for expert testimony to determine the facts accurately. Thus, expert testimony helps when it relates to esoteric matters beyond the experience of most laypeople and this knowledge is needed to determine the facts at issue. For example, expert testimony normally will help the jury in a medical malpractice action because the issues in such cases usually relate to facts that cannot be evaluated properly without a medical background. Similarly, experts are needed when the case concerns complex matters that challenge the comprehension of laypeople, such as intricate financial transactions. Expert testimony also can be helpful when other evidence is confusing but can be explained by an expert. Finally, expert testimony helps even when the laypeople on the jury can understand the evidence, but their understanding without expert assistance will be incomplete or inaccurate in some respect. In all these cases, expert testimony can explain the evidence so that the jury can then draw its own conclusions. On the other hand, expert testimony does not assist if the jury has no need for an opinion because it easily can be derived from common sense, common experience, the jury's own perceptions, or simple logic. Thus, expert testimony might not be admissible in a medical malpractice case to explain the enormity of a physician's blunder in amputating the wrong leg of a patient.

Another factor in applying the "help" requirement is whether expert testimony will undermine the judge's power to decide the law or the trier of fact's powers to decide the meaning of evidence and the credibility of witnesses. Accordingly, courts generally exclude expert opinion as to whether a witness is or is not telling the truth. This in part also explains the hostility of many courts toward polygraph (so-called lie-detector) evidence. Similarly, courts often exclude expert opinions that involve legal conclusions if those opinions tell the jury nothing about the facts. For example, courts will often refuse to receive expert testimony stating the conclusion that the defendant's conduct was negligent. Such opinions merely function like jury instructions and, thus, infringe upon the trial judge's role to decide the applicable law. Furthermore, because such summary conclusions often are given in lieu of testimony describing the details of the allegedly negligent conduct, the testimony denies the jury the very data it needs to reach its own conclusions.

Courts generally assume that expert testimony can assist the trier of fact even when the expert's opinion is equivocal. In these situations, the courts reason that the expert's lack of certainty is a matter the jury can consider in weighing the testimony. In fact, an expression of certainty in matters of complexity is often a mask for bias or incompetence. Thus, an expert usually is permitted to give an opinion that there is a causal link between defendant's product and plaintiff's illness even where the expert is unable to state the opinion with a high degree of medical certainty. But courts will reject expert testimony based on rank speculation.

Questions for Classroom Discussion

1. Murder prosecution. The defense calls an astrologer to testify that, based on Defendant's birthday and the alignment of the planets on the night of the murder, Defendant could not be the perpetrator. Does the testimony "help the trier of fact"?

2. Same case. A prosecution witness with a PhD in criminology testifies that, based on the fact that bloody shoeprints led from the murder scene to Defendant's apartment, Defendant must be guilty. Does the testimony "help the trier of fact"?

3. Same case. A prosecution witness who has extensive experience analyzing shoeprints testifies that the shoeprints leading to Defendant's apartment were made by a size 12EEE shoe, which other evidence demonstrates to be Defendant's shoe size. Does the testimony "help the trier of fact"?

4. Prosecution for sexual assault. The alleged victim testifies that Defendant attacked her. The defense calls a psychiatrist to testify that, based on his observation of the alleged victim, she is suffering from psychosis and is not telling the truth. Does the testimony "help the trier of fact"?

5. Same case. A psychiatrist testifies that, based on his observation of the alleged victim, she is suffering from psychosis and that people who have this condition often cannot distinguish between fantasy and reality. Does the testimony "help the trier of fact"?

---

3. Expert Witnesses Must Be Qualified

Rule 702 permits a witness to testify as to scientific, technical, or other specialized knowledge as long as that witness is qualified as an expert. The rule recognizes five bases for qualifying an expert: "knowledge, skill, experience, training, or education." It is clear that a background in just one of these five may be sufficient. For example, a witness with an academic background in a given area but no practical experience may still qualify as an expert. The same is true for a witness with experience but no formal education.

The degree of "knowledge, skill, experience, training, or education" sufficient to qualify an expert witness is only that necessary to ensure that the witness's testimony will "help" the trier of fact. Thus, the courts have found witnesses to be qualified as experts based on only a relatively modest degree of specialized knowledge. As a consequence, it is not necessary that the witness be recognized as a leading authority in the field in question. Gaps in an expert witness's qualifications or knowledge generally go to the weight of the witness's testimony, not its admissibility. On the other hand, there are cases in which a witness lacks sufficient background to qualify as an expert. For example, a witness can fail to qualify as an expert even if that witness has some special education or experience if that background is so limited that there is no reasonable expectation the witness can help the trier of fact.

Special knowledge or experience in one area is not sufficient to qualify a witness to testify as an expert in another area. The area of the witness's competence must match the subject matter of the witness's testimony. For example, a scientist with an expertise in dealing with diseases of animals might not be qualified to give an opinion as to what caused a human disease. The question is whether the expert's area of expertise is relevant to the issue at hand.

Several procedural issues are related to expert-witness qualification. Of course, the party proffering a witness as an expert has the burden of laying a foundation that establishes that the witness is qualified. The question of expert witness qualification is a matter to be resolved by the court under Rule 104(a). Rule 702 does not require that courts employ any specific procedure for receiving evidence concerning expert qualifications. Normally, a trial court will hear qualification evidence before permitting the witness to give opinion testimony. This may take place either in the presence or absence of the jury, at the discretion of the court. Before the court rules on whether a witness is qualified to testify as an expert, the opposing party should be afforded an opportunity to conduct a voir dire examination of the witness concerning the witness's qualifications.

Questions for Classroom Discussion

1. Murder prosecution. The victim was killed when a washing machine exploded. The defense claims it was an accident. The prosecution calls a plumber, who quit school after the sixth grade, to testify that, based on 20 years of professional experience fixing washing machines, it is impossible for one to explode accidentally. Is this testimony admissible, even though witness lacks any academic qualifications?

2. Medical malpractice action against a cosmetic surgeon. Plaintiff seeks damages for injuries following from an alleged botched nose job. Plaintiff's expert is shown to be an experienced cosmetic surgeon. If permitted, she will testify that the procedures followed by Defendant doctor were improper and that Plaintiff suffered $1,000,000 lost income as a result of her injuries. Is the witness's testimony admissible?

3. Same case. Defendant calls a physician with a general family practice who offers to testify that procedures used by Defendant to perform surgery conformed to the professional standard of care. Is the witness's testimony admissible?

> **4.** Prosecution for burglary. The sole witness to the crime speaks only
> Bulgarian. A police officer translates the witness's testimony. The
> officer took one year of college Bulgarian several years ago. Does the
> officer have to be an expert to translate the witness's testimony? Is
> she qualified as an expert?

4. Expert Testimony Must Be Reliable: The Daubert Decision

As we have seen repeatedly throughout this book, the Federal Rules of Evidence generally take a liberal approach to admissibility, eliminating many old doctrines that led to the exclusion of evidence. This approach reflects faith in the ability of the jury to properly discount unreliable evidence. But this faith might not be warranted when the jury is confronted with expert testimony that relates to complex scientific or technical matters. This is because laypeople on an ordinary jury might be unable to evaluate such testimony critically.

Several developments in the last few decades intensified concern over this issue. First, the pace of scientific research and development dramatically accelerated, thereby expanding the volume and diversity of issues on the frontiers of science. Some of these same developments led to the creation of innovative but occasionally dangerous products that spawned an enormous amount of products liability and mass tort litigation. At the same time, lawyers expanded their use of scientific expert testimony wherever scientific developments had possible forensic application. As a consequence, courts have been confronted with a huge amount of expert testimony, some based on cutting-edge breakthroughs, some based on theories over which even the experts are divided, and some based on what has been called "junk science."

A decision in 1923 by the District of Columbia Circuit Court of Appeals, Frye v. United States, 293 F. 1013 (D.C. Cir. 1923), established what would become for decades the standard for deciding the admissibility of scientific evidence, including expert opinion on scientific matters. Under *Frye*, scientific evidence was admissible only if based on principles generally accepted as valid by the relevant scientific community. This approach had the virtue of relieving courts of the need to evaluate independently the reliability of scientific evidence, a task that might be beyond the ability of judges schooled in law rather than science. Rather, the matter was left to the judgment of the scientific community. On the other hand, the inflexibility of this "general acceptance" test presented serious disadvantages. That test excluded cutting-edge scientific evidence that might be both relevant and reliable under traditional legal standards but was not yet widely accepted by scientists. Furthermore, deciding admissibility under *Frye* frequently was not easy because the meaning of "general acceptance" is often unclear. Accordingly, the *Frye* test was widely criticized. In addition, the enactment of the Federal Rules of Evidence in 1975 posed a new problem for *Frye*. The rules did not explicitly codify that test, nor was it even mentioned in the Advisory Committee Notes. Moreover, the rules relaxed other limits on opinion evidence and generally adopted a liberal approach toward admitting relevant evidence. For these reasons, many commentators argued that *Frye* had not survived adoption of the Evidence Rules. The federal circuit courts were in conflict on the issue.

The Supreme Court resolved the question for the federal courts in Daubert v. Merrell Dow Pharmaceuticals, 509 U.S. 579 (1993), concluding that the *Frye* test had been superseded by adoption of the Evidence Rules.

DAUBERT v. MERRELL DOW PHARMACEUTICALS, INC.

509 U.S. 579 (1993)

BLACKMUN, J., delivered the opinion of the Court.

Petitioners Jason Daubert and Eric Schuller are minor children born with serious birth defects. They and their parents sued respondent in California state court, alleging that the birth defects had been caused by the mothers' ingestion of Bendectin, a prescription antinausea drug marketed by respondent. Respondent removed the suits to federal court on diversity grounds.

After extensive discovery, respondent moved for summary judgment, contending that Bendectin does not cause birth defects in humans and that petitioners would be unable to come forward with any admissible evidence that it does. In support of its motion, respondent submitted an affidavit of Steven H. Lamm, physician and epidemiologist, who is a well-credentialed expert on the risks from exposure to various chemical substances. Doctor Lamm stated that he had reviewed all the literature on Bendectin and human birth defects — more than 30 published studies involving over 130,000 patients. No study had found Bendectin to be a human teratogen (i.e., a substance capable of causing malformations in fetuses). On the basis of this review, Doctor Lamm concluded that maternal use of Bendectin during the first trimester of pregnancy has not been shown to be a risk factor for human birth defects.

Petitioners did not (and do not) contest this characterization of the published record regarding Bendectin. Instead, they responded to respondent's motion with the testimony of eight experts of their own, each of whom also possessed impressive credentials. These experts had concluded that Bendectin can cause birth defects. Their conclusions were based upon "in vitro" (test tube) and "in vivo" (live) animal studies that found a link between Bendectin and malformations; pharmacological studies of the chemical structure of Bendectin that purported to show similarities between the structure of the drug and that of other substances known to cause birth defects; and the "reanalysis" of previously published epidemiological (human statistical) studies.

[The District Court concluded that plaintiffs' evidence of causation did not meet the applicable "general acceptance" standard for the admission of expert testimony. The Court of Appeals agreed and affirmed, citing Frye v. United States. The Supreme Court reversed.] . . .

Nothing in the text of [Rule 702] establishes "general acceptance" as an absolute prerequisite to admissibility. Nor does respondent present any clear indication that Rule 702 or the Rules as a whole were intended to incorporate a "general acceptance" standard. The drafting history makes no mention of *Frye*, and a rigid "general acceptance" requirement would be at odds with the "liberal thrust" of the Federal Rules and their "general approach of relaxing the traditional barriers to 'opinion' testimony." . . . Given the Rules' permissive backdrop and their inclusion of a specific rule on expert testimony that does not mention "general acceptance," the assertion that the Rules somehow assimilated *Frye* is unconvincing. *Frye* made "general acceptance" the exclusive test for admitting expert scientific testimony. That austere standard, absent from and incompatible with the Federal Rules of Evidence, should not be applied in federal trials.

That the *Frye* test was displaced by the Rules of Evidence does not mean, however, that the Rules themselves place no limits on the admissibility of purportedly scientific evidence. Nor is the trial judge disabled from screening such evidence. To the contrary, under the Rules the trial judge must ensure that any and all scientific testimony or evidence admitted is not only relevant, but reliable.

Faced with a proffer of expert scientific testimony, then, the trial judge must determine at the outset, pursuant to Rule 104(a), whether the expert is proposing to testify to (1) scientific knowledge that (2) will assist the trier of fact to understand or determine a fact in issue. This entails a preliminary assessment of whether the reasoning or methodology underlying the testimony is scientifically valid and of whether that reasoning or methodology properly can be applied to the facts in issue. We are confident that federal judges possess the capacity to undertake this review. Many factors will bear on the inquiry, and we do not presume to set out a definitive checklist or test. But some general observations are appropriate.

Ordinarily, a key question to be answered in determining whether a theory or technique is scientific knowledge that will assist the trier of fact will be whether it can be (and has been) tested. "Scientific methodology today is based on generating hypotheses and testing them to see if they can be falsified; indeed, this methodology is what distinguishes science from other fields of human inquiry." . . . Another pertinent consideration is whether the theory or technique has been subjected to peer review and publication. . . . [S]ubmission to the scrutiny of the scientific community is a component of "good science," in part because it increases the likelihood that substantive flaws in methodology will be detected. . . . Additionally, in the case of a particular scientific technique, the court ordinarily should consider the known or potential rate of error . . . and the existence and maintenance of standards controlling the technique's operation. . . . Finally, "general acceptance" can yet have a bearing on the inquiry. . . . Widespread acceptance can be an important factor in ruling particular evidence admissible, and "a known technique which has been able to attract only minimal support within the community," . . . may properly be viewed with skepticism.

The inquiry envisioned by Rule 702 is, we emphasize, a flexible one. Its overarching subject is the scientific validity and thus the evidentiary relevance and reliability — of the principles that underlie a proposed submission. The focus, of course, must be solely on principles and methodology, not on the conclusions that they generate.

The inquiries of the District Court and the Court of Appeals focused almost exclusively on "general acceptance," as gauged by publication and the decisions of other courts. Accordingly, the judgment of the Court of Appeals is vacated, and the case is remanded for further proceedings consistent with this opinion.

It is so ordered.

5. *Expert Testimony Must Be Reliable: The* Kumho Tire *Decision*

While a few jurisdictions still apply the general acceptance test, *Daubert* has emerged as the prevailing standard. But many issues concerning the admissibility of expert testimony were left unresolved by *Daubert*. Not the least of these was whether *Daubert* is limited to scientific evidence or applies in some way to all expert testimony. The Supreme Court answered this question in Kumho Tire Co. v. Carmichael, 526 U.S. 137 (1999). In *Kumho Tire*, plaintiffs brought a products liability action against a tire manufacturer and distributor for injuries sustained when a tire failed. The plaintiffs rested their case in significant part on deposition testimony provided by an expert in tire-failure analysis. In his deposition, the expert testified that the tire failed due to a defect in design or manufacture. The trial court granted defendant's motion to exclude the expert's testimony on the ground it failed to meet the *Daubert* requirement that expert testimony be reliable. The trial court then granted defendant's motion for summary judgment. The court of appeals reversed, holding that *Daubert* applied only to scientific evidence.

The Supreme Court reversed, concluding that the admissibility of all expert testimony must be determined by application of the *Daubert* requirements of relevance and reliability. The Court further concluded that the *Daubert* reliability factors (testing, error rate, standards and controls, peer review and publication, reasonable level of acceptance) may be, but are not necessarily, pertinent to expert testimony on non-scientific subjects and that other factors might also have a bearing on reliability, depending on the case. Whether the *Daubert* factors or other factors are pertinent to reliability depends, said the Court, on the nature of the issue, the expert's particular expertise, and the subject of his testimony. Accordingly, the Court held that trial judges have broad latitude to determine the pertinent reliability factors in a given case. This is not to say, however, that the Court regarded this discretion as unlimited. *Kumho Tire* recognized that a trial judge may abuse her discretion if she applies factors to determine reliability that are inappropriate to the circumstances of a given case.

Kumho Tire also makes clear that, in addition to gauging reliability in light of factors specific to the area of expertise involved, the trial court also may consider whether the expert's testimony holds together based on logic and common sense. As applied to the facts of *Kumho Tire*, the Supreme Court noted that the expert testimony was suspect because the expert could not adequately explain some aspects of his analysis, there were inconsistencies in his testimony, the expert did not adequately examine the allegedly defective tire, the expert failed to consider all the pertinent facts, the expert could not convincingly explain how the facts led to his opinion, and the expert was unable to answer questions that should have been within his command if his other testimony was reliable.

Kumho Tire does not suggest that expert testimony should be excluded whenever there is any doubt as to reliability. Few, if any, expert witnesses will offer opinions that are impervious to attack. The issue is whether, under Rule 104(a), the party offering the expert testimony can persuade the court by a preponderance of the evidence that it is reliable. Courts should be reluctant to exclude expert testimony when the reliability problems can be understood by the laypeople on the jury, who then can properly weigh that testimony in light of these problems. This is consistent with the notion that, by limiting the circumstances under which a witness may give an opinion, Rules 701 and 702 seek to preserve the jury's power to decide what evidence means. As one lower court has stated, trial judges have the responsibility to exclude unreliable expert evidence, but they should be viewed as gatekeepers, not armed guards.

While there are limits on the power of a trial judge to exclude expert testimony under *Daubert/Kumho Tire*, an appellate court will rarely reverse for error in applying that standard. In General Electric Co. v. Joiner, 522 U.S. 136 (1997), the Supreme Court concluded that an appellate court should apply an abuse of discretion standard in reviewing a trial court's decision to admit or exclude expert testimony. This means that appellate courts usually will defer to the discretion of the trial judge and will reverse only in cases of egregious error.

6. Expert Testimony Must Be Reliable and Sufficient: Requirements of Rule 702

Rule 702 was amended in 2000 in response to *Daubert* and *Kumho Tire*. The rule now states that an expert may testify if "(b) the testimony is based on sufficient facts or data, (c) the testimony is the product of reliable principles and methods, and (d) the expert has reliably applied the principles and methods to the facts of the case." The amendment did not codify the specific *Daubert* factors, leaving room for trial courts to determine the factors pertinent to reliability in each case. However, it is clear that the amendment endorses *Daubert* and *Kumho Tire*. As we describe below, the *Daubert* factors (testing, error rate, peer review and publication, general acceptance) still are pertinent to resolving the issues raised by Rule 702 when the expert offers an opinion in an area of science.

Rule 702(b) requires that expert testimony be "based on sufficient facts or data." The Advisory Committee's Note to Rule 702(b) states that this calls for a quantitative rather than qualitative analysis. The question is whether the expert considered *enough* information to make the proffered opinion reliable. This is different from the question posed by a provision we discuss shortly (Rule 703), which asks whether the opinion was based on evidence of a *type* that is reliable. Included in the analysis under Rule 702(b) is whether the expert considered all the pertinent physical and eyewitness evidence. For example, assume that in an auto accident case plaintiff calls an accident reconstruction expert who testifies defendant must have been traveling over the speed limit. The expert bases her opinion entirely on the extent of damage to the vehicles and admits she did not measure the skid marks, consider the extent of the personal injuries, or examine any other physical evidence pertinent to estimating the speed at which the vehicles must have been travelling at the time of impact. This opinion may be challenged under Rule 702(b) on the ground it is not based on sufficient facts or data. In the same case, assume that defendant's expert testifies that, based on an inspection of plaintiff's car, the cause of the accident was brake failure due to defective design. But this expert admits she failed to question eyewitnesses who might testify as to whether plaintiff could have avoided the accident had her brakes functioned properly. This opinion also can be challenged under Rule 702(b) on the basis that an expert failed to consider and eliminate alternative theories.

Rule 702(c) requires that expert testimony be "the product of reliable principles and methods." A "principle" is a theory that can be used to explain the meaning of observations. For example, expert testimony concerning the meaning of polygraph ("lie detector") evidence is based on the theory that certain metabolic processes, such as heart rate and respiration, are affected by the stress of lying and that changes in these processes can reveal whether a person is answering questions truthfully. Doubts about the validity of this theory have led many courts to reject polygraph evidence. Even non-scientific experts employ principles to explain their observations. For example, assume a police officer testifies that the participants in an alleged drug transaction who seemingly were making innocuous statements were, in fact, using code words that revealed criminality. In such a case, the officer's opinion relies on the principle or theory that drug dealers commonly use code words to conceal their activities.

Expert testimony is the product of a reliable principle if the theory employed by the expert to explain the meaning of her observations is shown to be valid. With respect to scientific evidence, the validity of an expert's principle may be evaluated under the *Daubert* factors. For example, polygraph evidence might be admitted if the theory connecting metabolic processes to the stress of lying was validated by a reasonable level of acceptance in the scientific community as well as research that was published and peer reviewed. With respect to non-scientific expert testimony, *Kumho Tire* indicates that validity of an expert's explanatory theory depends on consideration of other factors that are specific to the non-scientific area of expertise in question, in addition to logic and common sense.

While "principle" refers to the theories an expert employs to explain observed facts, "method" refers to *how* the expert derives those theories. Expert testimony regarding scientific matters is reliable if the expert's theories were derived through the so-called scientific method. This includes the use of testing, appropriate standards and controls, and acceptable error rates. These *Daubert* factors focus on the reliability of the expert's methods rather than the validity of the expert's conclusions. In the non-scientific context, the reliability of an expert's methodology will be determined by common sense, logic, and practices common to or accepted in the area of expertise in question. For example, when a police officer employs the theory that code words are commonly used in a drug transaction, the officer arguably uses a reliable method to derive the theory if she calls on extensive experience in dealing with criminal activity of that specific nature.

Rule 702(d) states that expert testimony is admissible only if the witness applies her principles and methods reliably to the facts of the case. Thus, even if the expert employs reliable general principles developed by reliable methods, evidence may be excluded under Rule 702(d) if the specific application of those principles to the facts of the case is suspect. For example, when an expert testifies that defendant's fingerprints match those found on the murder weapon, she employs the simple and long-accepted principle that human fingerprints are sufficiently unique to permit inferences as to identity. How the expert applies that principle, however, may be more complex and open to question. The conclusion that two fingerprints are a match might depend on the validity of many questions concerning the application of the general principle, such as whether the subject fingerprints were properly recovered and secured, what characteristics of the subject fingerprints should be compared, how many characteristics should be compared, how a partial or smudged print should be interpreted, and how similar the characteristics must be to declare a match. Even if there is no question concerning the validity of the general principle, each specific question of application can raise reliability issues.

Questions for Classroom Discussion

1. Murder prosecution. Defendant is an aging, bald, overweight law professor. A prosecution expert witness offers to testify that, based on application of a radical new technology for DNA testing, the perpetrator's blood found at the crime scene reveals the perpetrator had all these characteristics. While the validity of the test is not yet generally accepted among scientists, the test has been *published* in scientific journals, has a *low error rate*, the results are *subject to retesting*, and the test at least has *a reasonable level of acceptance* in the scientific community. Is the expert's opinion admissible?

2. Same case. A prosecution expert witness testifies that conventional DNA tests of blood stains on Defendant's clothing show a match with the victim's blood. The validity of this DNA technology is well established. However, the expert admits that the lab technician who performed the tests utterly failed to follow procedures aimed at avoiding contamination and degradation of blood samples. Under what subpart of Rule 702 should Defendant object?

3. Same case. Assume that the lab technician deviated from established procedures only in that, while on a lunch break, she failed to refrigerate one of the blood samples. While this might lead to degradation of the sample, the test results show that degradation did not occur. Should the court exclude expert testimony based on the test results?

4. Action against a seatbelt manufacturer for personal injuries suffered in an auto accident. Defendant alleges Plaintiff was injured because he did not secure his seatbelt properly. Plaintiff calls an accident reconstruction expert, who proposes to testify that Plaintiff was injured because the seatbelt popped open upon impact even though it was secured prior to the crash. The expert admits she failed to consider eyewitness testimony that Plaintiff did not buckle his seatbelt properly. Under what subpart of Rule 702 should Defendant object?

5. Same case. The expert admits she failed to test the seatbelt to determine if the force of impact could have caused the seatbelt to open. Under what subpart of Rule 702 should Defendant object?

6. Action for wrongful death against a pharmaceutical company, manufacturer of the product that allegedly caused decedent's fatal disease. Plaintiff's expert testifies that Defendant's product can cause this disease. She bases her opinion on laboratory studies with mice that show these animals developed this disease after exposure to Defendant's product. Under what subpart of Rule 702 should Defendant object?

7. *Expert Testimony Must Be Reliable: Problems Applying* Daubert/Kumho Tire

Recall that the Supreme Court's decisions in *Daubert* and *Kumho Tire* were, at least in part, reactions to the complaints (usually by large corporations) that the nation's courtrooms were being inundated with "junk science." It is not surprising, then, that the Court would conclude that trial judges need to be gatekeepers and exclude expert evidence if it is unreliable. But giving judges this job raises many problems, some of which the Court might not have expected. For example, trial judges rarely have the technical or scientific background needed to assess reliability. Furthermore, since *Daubert* was decided, the trial courts have found it necessary to spend significant time and effort on hearings to determine the reliability of expert testimony. Finally, the *Daubert* and *Kumho Tire* decisions have called into question the admissibility of much expert testimony previously thought irreproachable. In the following opinion, the trial judge struggles with the application of the *Daubert/Kumho Tire* standards to fingerprint evidence, long a mainstay of criminal prosecutions.

UNITED STATES v. LLERA PLAZA
188 F. Supp. 2d 549 (E.D. Pa. 2002)

POLLACK, District Judge.

In the government's list of witnesses expected to be called at the upcoming trial, on drug and murder charges, of defendants Carlos Ivan Llera Plaza, Wilfredo Martinez Acosta and Victor Rodriguez, there are four Federal Bureau of Investigation (FBI) fingerprint examiners and one FBI fingerprint specialist. To bar the testimony of these anticipated witnesses, the defendants filed a Motion to Preclude the United States from Introducing Latent Fingerprint Identification Evidence. . . . The principal question posed by the defendants' motion . . . was whether, as the government contended, fingerprint identification evidence is sufficiently reliable to meet the standards for expert testimony set by Rule 702 of the Federal Rules of Evidence as explicated by the Supreme Court in Daubert v. Merrell Dow Pharmaceuticals, Inc. . . . and reaffirmed in Kumho Tire Co., Ltd. v. Carmichael. . . . By stipulation of the parties, the evidence with respect to these questions consisted of a copy of the transcript of a five-day hearing addressed to the same question presided over by my colleague Judge Joyner, in 1999, in United States v. Mitchell. While no new evidence was presented before me, the parties in the case at bar supplemented the *Mitchell* materials with extensive briefs.

On January 7, 2002, I filed an opinion and order addressed to the defendants' motion and the government's counter-motion.

First, I concluded that, as the government had contended, it was beyond reasonable dispute that the fingerprints of each person (a) are unique to that person and (b) are (barring some serious and deeply penetrating wound to the hand that substantially alters or defaces the surface of one or more of the fingers or of the palm) permanent from birth to death. I therefore ruled that, pursuant to Rule 201, I would, for the purposes of the up-coming trial, take judicial notice of the uniqueness and permanence of fingerprints. In agreeing to take judicial notice of the uniqueness and permanence of fingerprints, I was in effect, accepting the theoretical basis of fingerprint identification — namely, that a showing that a latent print replicates (is a "match" of) a rolled print constitutes a showing that the latent and rolled prints are fingerprints of the same person.

Second, I considered whether the ACE-V fingerprint identification system employed by the FBI sufficiently conforms to the *Daubert* standards of reliability laid down by the Court as guidelines in determining the admissibility of expert testimony under Rule 702. . . . Based on the *Mitchell* record, I came to the following conclusions with respect to ACE-V's conformity to the *Daubert* factors:

> The one *Daubert* factor that ACE-V satisfies in significant fashion is the fourth factor: ACE-V has attained general acceptance within the American fingerprint examiner community . . . .
>
> . . . [T]he court finds that ACE-V does not adequately satisfy the "scientific" criterion of testing (the first *Daubert* factor) or the "scientific" criterion of "peer review" (the second *Daubert* factor). Further, the court finds that the information of record is unpersuasive, one way or another, as to ACE-V's "scientific" rate of error (the first aspect of *Daubert*'s third factor), and that, at the critical evaluation stage, ACE-V does not operate under uniformly accepted "scientific" standards (the second aspect of *Daubert*'s third factor).
>
> The *Daubert* difficulty with the ACE-V process is by no means total. The difficulty comes into play at the stage at which . . . the ACE-V process becomes "subjective" — namely, the evaluation stage. By contrast, the antecedent analysis and comparison stages are, according to the testimony, "objective": analysis of the rolled and latent prints and comparison of what the examiner has observed in the two prints. Up to the evaluation stage, the ACE-V fingerprint examiner's testimony is descriptive, not judgmental. Accordingly, this court will permit the government to present testimony by fingerprint examiners who, suitably qualified as "expert" examiners by virtue of training and experience, may (1) describe how the rolled and latent fingerprints at issue in this case were obtained, (2) identify and place before the jury the fingerprints and such magnifications thereof as may be required to show minute details, and (3) point out observed similarities (and differences) between any latent print and any rolled print the government contends are attributable to the same person. What such expert witnesses will not be permitted to do is to present "evaluation" testimony as to their "opinion" (Rule 702) that a particular latent print is in fact the print of a particular person.

I

The government moved for reconsideration of the ruling. The government felt that its prosecutorial effectiveness, both in the case at bar and in other cases in which fingerprint identification could be expected to play a significant role, would be seriously compromised by the preclusion of opinion testimony at the "evaluation" stage "that a particular latent print is in fact the print of a particular person." Arguing that the analysis underlying the ruling was both factually and legally flawed, the government contended that the ruling was "at odds with Rule 702 of the Federal Rules of Evidence, and should be reconsidered and reversed." . . .

[T]he defendants were on sound ground in contending that neither of the circumstances conventionally justifying reconsideration — new, or hitherto unavailable, facts or new controlling law — was present here. It seemed to me, nonetheless, that there was a factor peculiar to this case which militated in favor of agreeing to reconsider the January 7 ruling. That factor was that the record underlying the January 7 opinion did not consist of testimony by witnesses I had actually seen and heard; my field of vision was a transcript of testimony presented in another courtroom more than two years ago. Therefore, it seemed prudent to hear such live witnesses as the government wished to present, together with any rebuttal witnesses the defense would elect to present.

Accordingly, I agreed to reconsider the January 7 ruling. The parties required a period of time to prepare for the evidentiary hearing requested by the government. The hearing was held on February 25, 26 and 27.

II

[In this section of the opinion, the court described the conflicting testimony of the various experts presented by the prosecution and defense at the evidentiary hearing.]

III

(1) IS ACE-V A "SCIENTIFIC" TECHNIQUE?

The opinion of January 7, which was based on the *Mitchell* record, undertook to respond to the parties' competing arguments as to whether ACE-V meets *Daubert*'s requirements. . . . In the January 7 opinion I accepted the battleground as the parties had defined it, and on that basis I concluded that: (1) and (2), ACE-V was not supported by "testing" or by "peer review" in the "scientific" sense contemplated by *Daubert*; (3) the rate of error was "in limbo" and consensus on controlling standards was lacking; and (4) while there was "general acceptance" of ACE-V in the fingerprint identification community, that community was not a "'scientific community'" in *Daubert*'s use of the term. . . .

(2) CE-V AS A "TECHNICAL" DISCIPLINE: *DAUBERT* THROUGH THE PRISM OF *KUMHO TIRE* . . .

The *Kumho Tire* Court's injunction that the gatekeeping requirement is designed to insure "that an expert . . . employs in the courtroom the same level of intellectual rigor that characterizes the practice of an expert in the relevant field" serves as a reminder that fingerprint identification is not a discipline that is confined to courtroom use. It is a discipline relied on in other settings—e.g., in identifying the dead in mass disasters. Properly to determine whether an FBI fingerprint examiner operates at a proper level of intellectual rigor when she comes to court as an expert witness, it becomes necessary, on this motion for reconsideration of my January 7 ruling, to reexamine the grounds on which I found that ACE-V did not satisfy three of the *Daubert* factors and only marginally met the fourth ("general acceptance" by the fingerprint community, which I deemed not a "scientific community"). In this reexamination there are two points to be addressed. One is the extent to which the several *Daubert* factors "are reasonable measures of the reliability of expert testimony." The other is whether the recent enlargement of the record—the three days of hearings on the motion for reconsideration—alters in some significant way the pertinent facts drawn from the *Mitchell* record.

(a) "Peer Review" and "General Acceptance"

First I consider the "peer review" and "general acceptance" factors. The fact that fingerprint specialists are not "scientists," and hence that the forensic journals in which their writings on fingerprint identification appear are not "scientific" journals in *Daubert*'s peer review sense, does not seem to me to militate against the utility of the identification procedures employed by fingerprint specialists, whether on the witness stand or at the disaster site. By the same token, I conclude that the fingerprint community's "general acceptance" of ACE-V should not be discounted because fingerprint specialists — like accountants, vocational experts, accident-reconstruction experts, appraisers of land or of art, experts in tire failure analysis, or others — have "technical, or other specialized knowledge," (Rule 702), rather than "scientific . . . knowledge," and hence are not members of what *Daubert* termed a "scientific community."

(b) "Testing"

Next I consider the "testing" factor. The key to the admissibility of expert testimony under *Daubert* and *Kumho Tire* is reliability, and this, of course, derives directly from the text of Rule 702, which contemplates that "(1) the testimony is based upon sufficient facts or data, (2) the testimony is the product of reliable principles and methods, and (3) the witness has applied the principles and methods reliably to the facts of the case." Bearing this in mind, one would welcome "testing" in the *Daubert* sense as a criterion of reliability. Disagreeing with contentions that the "verification" phase of ACE-V constitutes *Daubert* "testing," or, in the alternative, that a century of litigation has been a form of "adversarial" testing that meets *Daubert*'s criteria, I concluded in the January 7 opinion that *Daubert*'s testing factor was not met, and I have found no reason to depart from that conclusion.

(c) "Rate of Error" and "Standards Controlling the Technique's Operation"

The last *Daubert* question to be addressed is whether *Daubert*'s third factor — "the known or potential rate of error . . . and the existence and maintenance of standards controlling the technique's operation" — offers support for fingerprint identification testimony. In the January 7 opinion, on the basis of the *Mitchell* record, I answered this question in the negative: I found no persuasive information with respect to rate of error. And with respect to "the existence and maintenance of [controlling] standards" I found (1) "whether a minimum number of Galton points must be identified before a match can be declared, varies from jurisdiction to jurisdiction. Sergeant Ashbaugh testified that the United Kingdom employs a sixteen-point minimum, Australia mandates that twelve points be found in common, and Canada uses no minimum point standard. . . . In the United States, state jurisdictions set their own minimum point standards, while the FBI has no minimum number that must be identified to declare an 'absolutely him' match"; (2) there appeared to be no uniformly accepted qualifying standards for fingerprint examiners; and (3) the identification judgments made by fingerprint examiners at ACE-V's "evaluation" stage — i.e., in determining whether there is a "match" — are "subjective."

What new light — if any — is shed upon rate of error, or upon controlling standards, by the recent three days of hearings?

(i) "rate of error"

The factual case presented by the government was chiefly devoted to demonstrating, through the testimony of Mr. Meagher, that certified FBI fingerprint examiners have scored spectacularly well on the in-house annual proficiency tests. . . . The evident theory of the government's demonstration was that, in the absence of actual data on rate of error, proficiency test scores of those who would be expert witnesses should be taken as a surrogate form of proof: if certified examiners rarely make a mistake on ACE-V proficiency tests, it stands to reason (so the theory would have it) that they rarely make a mistake when presenting ACE-V testimony in court. To rebut the government's proof, the defense witnesses undertook to demonstrate that the proficiency tests were inadequate. . . .

. . . [O]n the present record I conclude that the proficiency tests are less demanding than they should be. To the extent that this is the case, it would appear that the tests can be of little assistance in providing the test makers with a discriminating measure of the relative competence of the test takers. But the defense witnesses offered not a syllable to suggest that certified FBI fingerprint examiners as a group, or any individual examiners among them, have not achieved at least an acceptable level of competence. I conclude, therefore, on the basis of the limited information in the record as expanded, that there is no evidence that the error rate of certified FBI fingerprint examiners is unacceptably high.

(ii) "standards controlling the technique's operation"

. . . On reviewing these issues on the basis of the expanded record I reach the following conclusions:

(a) Whatever may be the case for other law enforcement agencies, the standards prescribed for qualification as an FBI fingerprint examiner are clear. . . . The uniformity and rigor of these FBI requirements provide substantial assurance that, with respect to certified FBI fingerprint examiners, properly controlling qualification standards are in place and are in force.

(b) As previously noted, the *Mitchell* record pointed to wide disagreements, from jurisdiction to jurisdiction, with respect to the minimum number of Galton points required to permit an examiner to find a "match." . . . However, it appears that the July 7, 1999 *Mitchell* testimony with respect to the United Kingdom did not accurately reflect the then state of United Kingdom law and is now entirely out of date. . . .

. . . [T]he fact that England has, after many years of close study, moved to the position which prevails in Canada and which the FBI has long subscribed to, leads me to conclude that there is sufficient uniformity within the principal common law jurisdictions to satisfy *Daubert*.

(iii)

In the January 7 opinion, the aspect of the *Daubert* inquiry into "the existence and maintenance of standards controlling the technique's operation," that was of greatest concern was the acknowledged subjectivity of the fingerprint examiner's stated opinion that a latent print and a known exemplar are both attributable to the same person. . . . I concluded that "[w]ith such a high degree of subjectivity, it is difficult to see how fingerprint identification — the matching of a latent print to a known print — is controlled by any clearly describable set of standards to which most examiners prescribe." On further reflection, I disagree with myself. I think my assessment stopped with the word "subjective" when I should have gone on to focus on the process the word describes. There are, to be sure, situations in which the subjectiveness of an opinion properly gives rise to reservations about the opinion's reliability. But there are many situations in which an expert's manifestly subjective opinion . . . is regarded as admissible evidence in an American courtroom. . . . [T]he subjective ingredients of opinion testimony presented by a competent fingerprint examiner appear to be of substantially more restricted compass. . . . In sum, contrary to the view expressed in my January 7 opinion, I am now persuaded that the standards which control the opining of a competent fingerprint examiner are sufficiently widely agreed upon to satisfy *Daubert*'s requirements.

(3) COMPLETING THE *DAUBERT/KUMHO TIRE* ASSESSMENT

Having re-reviewed the applicability of the *Daubert* factors through the prism of *Kumho Tire*, I conclude that the one *Daubert* factor which is both pertinent and unsatisfied is the first factor — "testing." *Kumho Tire*, as I have noted above, instructs district courts to "consider the specific factors identified in *Daubert* where they are reasonable measures of the reliability of expert testimony." Scientific tests of ACE-V — i.e., tests in the *Daubert* sense — would clearly aid in measuring ACE-V's reliability. But, as of today, no such tests are in hand. The question, then, is whether, in the absence of such tests, a court should conclude that the ACE-V fingerprint identification system, as practiced by certified FBI fingerprint examiners, has too great a likelihood of producing erroneous results to be admissible as evidence in a courtroom setting. There are respected authorities who, it appears, would render such a verdict. In a recent OpEd piece in The New York Times, Peter Neufeld and Barry Scheck, who direct Cardozo Law School's Innocence Project, have this to say:

> No one doubts that fingerprints can, and do, serve as a highly discriminating identifier, and digital photographic enhancement and computer databases now promise to make fingerprint identification more useful than ever before. But to what degree incomplete and imperfect fingerprints can be reliably used to identify individuals requires more scientific examination. . . . Forensic science has rarely been subjected to the kind of scrutiny and independent verification applied to other fields of applied and medical science. Instead, analysts testifying in courts about fingerprint analysis, bite marks, handwriting comparisons and the like have often argued that in their field the courtroom itself provided the test. . . . As the National Institutes of Health finance basic scientific research, the National Institute of Justice should put money into verification and validation before a technique of identification is admitted into court.

As explained in Part II of this opinion, I have found, on the record before me, that there is no evidence that certified FBI fingerprint examiners present erroneous identification testimony, and, as a corollary, that there is no evidence that the rate of error of certified FBI fingerprint examiners is unacceptably high. With those findings in mind, I am not persuaded that courts should defer admission of testimony with respect to fingerprinting — which Professors Neufeld and Scheck term "[t]he bedrock forensic identifier of the 20th century" — until academic investigators financed by the National Institute of Justice have made substantial headway on a "verification and validation" research agenda. . . .

The ACE-V regime . . . is, I conclude, a regime whose reliability should, subject to a similar measure of trial court oversight, be regarded by the federal courts of the United States as satisfying the requirements of Rule 702 as the Supreme Court has explicated that rule in *Daubert* and *Kumho Tire*.

CONCLUSION

Motions for reconsideration are not favorites of the law. It is an important feature of a judge's job to arrive at a decision and then move on to the next issue to be decided, whether in the pending case or the case next to be addressed on the judge's docket. This judicial convention has special force for trial judges, for if a trial judge's ruling is mistaken it can, and if need arises will, be corrected on appeal. But there are occasions when a motion for reconsideration has its uses. This is such an occasion. . . .

In short, I have changed my mind. "Wisdom too often never comes, and so" — as Justice Frankfurter admonished himself and every judge — "one ought not to reject it merely because it comes late."

Accordingly, in an order filed today accompanying this opinion, this court GRANTS the government's motion for reconsideration of the January 7 order; VACATES the January 7 order; DENIES the defendants' Motion to Preclude the United States from Introducing Latent Fingerprint Evidence; and GRANTS the government's Motion in Limine to Admit Latent Prints.

Questions for Classroom Discussion

1. Applying the *Daubert/Kumho Tire* test, the judge in *Llera Plaza* initially ruled that prosecution experts cannot testify that crime scene fingerprints match fingerprints of defendants. In the opinion printed above, however, the judge granted a motion for reconsideration, even though the judge admitted that this is unusual. What might have motivated the judge to take this step?

2. What was the cost in judicial resources of conducting the *Daubert/Kumho Tire* hearing in *Llera Plaza*? How is this effort unlike the manner in which the law resolves the vast majority of other evidentiary issues?

3. What demands does *Daubert/Kumho Tire* place on counsel?

4. Do all four *Daubert* factors bearing on reliability have to be satisfied before scientific evidence is admissible? What does *Llera Plaza* suggest?

One of the most difficult problems in applying *Daubert/Kumho Tire* is judging the reliability of expert testimony in areas where the factors identified in *Daubert* might be inapplicable as measures of reliability. Recall that those factors are (1) testing, (2) error rate, (3) the existence of standards and controls, (4) peer review and publication, and (5) level of acceptance in the relevant scientific community. It makes little sense to apply criteria like these in judging the reliability of expert testimony on many subjects to which *Daubert/Kumho Tire* has been applied. Consider, for example, expert testimony from a police detective concerning the modus operandi of drug dealers[1] or the nature of the relationship between a pimp and his prostitutes.[2] It seems unlikely that police detectives with experience in such matters engage in testing, publishing, or other academic exercises. As a consequence, it is clear that the courts cannot rely on the *Daubert* factors in all situations, but must be flexible and develop reliability criteria properly tailored to fit the situation.

This can be true even in cases involving expert medical testimony such as that offered in *Daubert* itself. Recall that in *Daubert* the issue was whether plaintiffs' expert could give an opinion that defendant's product caused plaintiffs' birth defects. Causation typically is the primary issue in toxic tort or product liability cases, where the defendant usually concedes plaintiff is ill or has been injured, but disputes that defendant caused the problem. One way causation of disease can be shown is through data produced by *epidemiological* studies. Epidemiology is the study of the incidence, distribution, and etiology (a fancy word for "cause") of disease. For example, a famous series of epidemiological studies published in the 1950s showed that people who smoked 10 to 20 cigarettes a day had a lung cancer mortality rate about 10 times higher than the non-smoking population. An expert opinion based on a published epidemiological study clearly can satisfy all the *Daubert* factors.

But sometimes an illness is so unusual that there is insufficient data to produce a proper study. In addition, few practicing physicians have time to conduct and publish epidemiological studies. In fact, practicing physicians generally are willing to give opinions based on first-hand observations of a single patient, viewed through the filter of their medical knowledge and experience. While those opinions might not satisfy all the *Daubert* factors, most patients are willing to bet their lives on them. Does it make sense for the courts to reject those opinions, or can a court adapt the *Daubert* factors to such a situation?

PIPITONE v. BIOMATRIX, INC.

288 F.3d 239 (5th Cir. 2002)

W. EUGENE DAVIS, Circuit Judge:

Thomas Pipitone and his wife, Bonnie, brought suit against Biomatrix, Inc. ("Biomatrix"), alleging that a product that Biomatrix manufactures, known as Synvisc, caused Mr. Pipitone to develop a salmonella infection in his knee after a physician injected his knee with Synvisc. The district court excluded the testimony of the plaintiffs' experts, Doctors Millet and Coco, under the standard set forth in Daubert v. Merrell Dow Pharmaceuticals, Inc. The district court concluded that without the testimony of their two witnesses, the plaintiffs could not establish their case and granted summary judgment in favor of Biomatrix. Because we conclude that the district court abused its discretion in excluding

1. *See, e.g.,* United States v. Romero, 189 F.3d 576 (7th Cir. 1999).
2. *See, e.g.,* United States v. Taylor, 239 F.3d 994 (9th Cir. 2001).

the testimony of Dr. Coco, we reverse the district court's grant of summary judgment in favor of Biomatrix and remand the case to the district court.

[Pipitone sought medical treatment for severe osteoarthritic pain in his knees. He consulted a physican, Dr. Millet, who specialized in joints. Because of an unrelated condition, Pipitone was not a candidate for surgery. Dr. Millet suggested treatment with Synvisc.]

Synvisc is a replacement synovial fluid manufactured by Biomatrix. Synvisc is made from rendered rooster combs, which are bathed in formaldehyde for a full day and then subjected to other chemical and detergent treatments. The product is put through a sterile filtration system and into syringes. Biomatrix packages Synvisc in boxes of three, factory-sealed syringes to be administered by injection directly into the knee once a week for three weeks. When injecting Synvisc, the doctor supplies only the needle. . . .

Pipitone decided to go forward with the Synvisc treatment. He filled the prescription for Synvisc at a Walgreen's pharmacy and returned to Dr. Millet's office on the morning of January 25, 2000, to receive the injection. Dr. Millet's nurse, who was not scrubbed down, opened the Synvisc package and one of the shrink-wrapped syringes inside. She also opened the packaging for the needle and aspiration syringe, both of which Dr. Millet's office supplied. The nurse then attached the needle, still in its sterile sheath, to the empty aspiration syringe, and placed all of these items on an injection tray next to unsterile gauze.

Wearing unsterile gloves, Dr. Millet prepared Pipitone's knee with an antibiotic cleanser and then with alcohol. Following Biomatrix's instructions, Dr. Millet inserted the needle attached to the empty aspiration syringe into Pipitone's knee and withdrew a small amount of synovial fluid. He noted that the fluid was clear and normal in appearance and indicated no sign of infection. Dr. Millet then detached the fluid-filled aspiration syringe from the needle, which remained in place in Pipitone's knee, removed the rubber tip from the Synvisc syringe, and attached the Synvisc syringe to the needle. Dr. Millet then injected the Synvisc and removed the needle. He placed a bandage over the entry site, and Pipitone went home.

Later that evening, Pipitone began having severe pain in his knee. His wife took his temperature, which was 101 degrees, but they did not report these symptoms to a doctor at that time because they believed that they were attributable to the injection. As Pipitone's knee pain worsened, the Pipitones made several attempts to contact Dr. Millet's office and succeeded in meeting him on the morning of January 27, two days after the injection. Dr. Millet aspirated some of the synovial fluid from Pipitone's knee and found that it was cloudy and turbid, indicating infection. Dr. Millet immediately hospitalized Pipitone and drained Pipitone's infected knee completely. The hospital laboratory tested the fluid from Pipitone's knee and discovered that the infection was salmonella, which is extremely rare in joints.

Because the culture showed such a rare infection, Dr. Millet asked Dr. Jeffrey Coco, a physician who limits his practice to infectious diseases, to examine Pipitone. When Dr. Coco evaluated Pipitone in the hospital, he found that Pipitone had no fever, chilled sweats, diarrhea, nausea, or vomiting. . . . Dr. Coco ordered a second check of the synovial fluid from Pipitone's knee, but the laboratory had already rechecked the fluid due to the rarity of the result. The second test showed again that the infection was salmonella.

When Biomatrix was informed of Pipitone's infection, it tested the other two syringes in the Synvisc package that Pipitone purchased and found no evidence of salmonella. It also tested the twenty syringes held back from the production lot that had included the Synvisc sold to Pipitone and found no salmonella.

[Dr. Coco was willing to testify that, in his opinion, Synvisc caused Pipitone's infection. The District Court granted summary judgment for Biomatrix after ruling that the doctor's testimony was inadmissible under *Daubert*.]

Many factors bear on the inquiry into the reliability of scientific and other expert testimony. In *Daubert*, the Supreme Court offered an illustrative, but not an exhaustive, list of factors that district courts may use in evaluating the reliability of expert testimony. These factors include whether the expert's theory or technique: (1) can be or has been tested; (2) has been subjected to peer review and publication; (3) has a known or potential rate of error or standards controlling its operation; and (4) is generally accepted in the relevant scientific community. In the later case of Kumho Tire Co. v. Carmichael, the Supreme Court emphasized that the *Daubert* analysis is a "flexible" one, and that "the factors identified in *Daubert* may or may not be pertinent in assessing reliability, depending on the nature of the issue, the expert's particular expertise, and the subject of his testimony." The district court's responsibility is "to make certain that an expert, whether basing testimony upon professional studies or personal experience, employs in the courtroom the same level of intellectual rigor that characterizes the practice of an expert in the relevant field." . . .

The district court based its decision to exclude Dr. Coco's testimony on several factors. First, after discussing Dr. Coco's great expertise in the area of epidemiology and infectious diseases, the district court noted that Dr. Coco performed no epidemiological study in the instant case. The district court also found that Dr. Coco's literature search, which yielded no report of any salmonella infection arising from a contaminated injectable knee product of any kind, undermined Dr. Coco's hypothesis that Synvisc caused the salmonella infection in this case. Finally, the district court stated that Dr. Coco had failed to eliminate "many viable alternative sources" for the salmonella infection.

The four factors identified in *Daubert* form the starting point of the inquiry into the admissibility of expert testimony. However, as the Supreme Court noted in *Kumho Tire*, "the factors identified in *Daubert* may or may not be pertinent in assessing reliability, depending on the nature of the issue, the expert's particular expertise, and the subject of his testimony." It is a fact-specific inquiry.

First, Dr. Coco did not test his hypothesis that a Synvisc syringe that contains salmonella would cause a salmonella infection in a knee injected with the Synvisc. Neither side disputes, however, that if the Synvisc was in fact contaminated, Pipitone's knee would probably have been infected. Dr. Coco did not conduct an epidemiological study of Pipitone's infection. He explained, however, that such a study is not necessary or appropriate in a case such as this in which only one person is infected.

Dr. Coco did conduct a literature search and found no evidence of a salmonella infection arising from any injectable knee product, such as Cortisone, which has been injected into joints for years. Dr. Coco excluded Synvisc from his search. The district court found that excluding the defendant's product from the search discredited Dr. Coco's conclusion that the Synvisc was the source of the salmonella.

Dr. Coco decided to exclude Synvisc from his search of the relevant scientific literature primarily because Synvisc is the only knee injectable product made from chicken parts, a known source of salmonella. By excluding Synvisc, he sought to isolate the question he was researching—whether a salmonella infection had ever arisen from the injection process. Dr. Coco reasoned that if Pipitone's salmonella infection in this case was caused by unsterile injection technique or some other cause unrelated to Synvisc, one would reasonably expect to find other occurrences of salmonella infections arising from injections of any product into the knee. The lack of literature on injection-related salmonella infections of the joint does not undermine Dr. Coco's hypothesis. As the Supreme Court explained in *Kumho Tire*, "[i]t might not be surprising in a particular case, for example, that a claim made by a scientific witness has never been the subject of peer review, for the particular application at issue may never previously have interested any scientist." Where, as here, there is no evidence that anyone has ever contracted a salmonella infection from an injection of any kind into the knee, it is difficult to see why a scientist would study this phenomenon. We conclude, therefore, that the lack of reports in the literature that any knee injectable other than Synvisc has caused a salmonella infection, supports, rather than contradicts, Dr. Coco's conclusion that the infection did not arise due to unsterile technique or other source not related to Synvisc.

There is no known or potential rate of error or controlling standards associated with Dr. Coco's hypothesis. Again, however, this factor is not particularly relevant, where as here, the expert derives his testimony mainly from firsthand observations and professional experience in translating these observations into medical diagnoses.

The final consideration under *Daubert* is whether Dr. Coco's hypothesis is generally accepted in the relevant scientific community. Dr. Coco based his opinion on how Pipitone contracted salmonella in large part on accepted medical knowledge of the ways in which salmonella functions as an organism and how it infects humans. Dr. Coco's elimination of various alternative causes, as discussed more thoroughly below, such as infection through the gastrointestinal ("GI") tract or the bloodstream, were based on generally accepted diagnostic principles related to these conditions. Dr. Coco personally examined Pipitone in the hospital and found him to be lacking the symptoms that a physician would expect to find if salmonella had been introduced into the body through one of these alternative routes.

In a case such as this one, however, it is appropriate for the trial court to consider factors other than those listed in *Daubert* to evaluate the reliability of the expert's testimony. In this case, the expert's testimony is based mainly on his personal observations, professional experience, education and training. The trial court, therefore, must probe into the reliability of these bases when determining whether the testimony should be admitted. . . .

Dr. Coco specializes in infectious diseases. He is employed by three local hospitals in the area of hospital epidemiology and concentrates in this area as it relates to infectious diseases and the prevention thereof. He has been on the Specialty Board of Infectious Diseases and has written on the subject. For the last twelve years, Dr. Coco has been a Clinical Assistant Professor at Louisiana State University School of Medicine in the Department of Infectious Disease. Dr. Coco drew on this experience when he personally examined Pipitone in January 2000. Based on his experience as an infectious disease specialist and his personal observation of Pipitone and his symptoms, Dr. Coco concluded that the most likely cause of Pipitone's infection was the Synvisc that had been injected into his knee two days before. Specifically, Dr. Coco based this opinion on the timeliness of the infection (symptoms of which began to appear hours after the Synvisc injection), the source of the Synvisc, the type of organism (salmonella) that infected Pipitone, and the elimination of all other likely alternatives. . . .

It bears reminding that "the trial court's role as gatekeeper [under *Daubert*] is not intended to serve as a replacement for the adversary system." Rather, as *Daubert* makes clear, "[v]igorous cross-examination, presentation of contrary evidence, and careful instruction on the burden of proof are the traditional and appropriate means of attacking shaky but admissible evidence." Thus, while exercising its role as a gatekeeper, a trial court must take care not to transform a *Daubert* hearing into a trial on the merits. In this case, we conclude that the standard of reliability that the district court applied to Dr. Coco's testimony was overly stringent. The fact-finder is entitled to hear Dr. Coco's testimony and decide whether it should accept or reject that testimony after considering all factors that weigh on credibility, including whether the predicate facts on which Dr. Coco relied are accurate.

REVERSED AND REMANDED.

Questions for Classroom Discussion

1. In *Pipitone*, Dr. Coco opined that Synvisc caused Pipitone's infection. Which *Daubert* factors did Dr. Coco's opinion satisfy? Which were not satisfied? What was the justification for not strictly applying the *Daubert* factors? What other reliability factors justified the admission of Dr. Coco's opinion?

2. Assume Dr. Coco conducted an epidemiological study of the incidence of salmonella infections within the population of patients injected with Synvisc. After reviewing thousands of case studies, he concluded that 3 percent of the patients developed salmonella. He still opines that Synvisc caused Pipitone's infection. Does Coco's study support or undermine his conclusion? In answering that question, what additional information might you want to have?

Further Reading: 29 Charles Alan Wright & Victor J. Gold, Federal Practice and Procedure 2d §§ 6261-6270 (West, 2016); Michael R. Barnett, Casenote, *The Admissibility Determination of Expert Testimony on Eyewitness Identification: United States v. Smithers*, 212 F.3d 306 (6th Cir. 2000), 70 U. Cin. L. Rev. 751 (2002); Robert Epstein, *Fingerprints Meet* Daubert: *The Myth of Fingerprint "Science" Is Revealed*, 75 S. Cal. L. Rev. 605 (2002); David L. Faigman, *Making the Law Safe for the Science: A Proposed Rule for the Admission of Expert Testimony*, 35 Washburn L. Rev. 401 (1996); David L. Faigman, *To Have and Have Not: Assessing the Value of Social Science to the Law as Science and Policy*, 38 Emory L.J. 1005 (1989); Peter Huber, *Junk Science in the Courtroom*, 26 Val. U. L. Rev. 723 (1992); Toni M.

Massaro, *Experts, Psychology, Credibility, and Rape: The Rape Trauma Syndrome Issue and Its Implications for Expert Psychological Testimony*, 69 Minn. L. Rev. 395 (1985); David McCord, *Syndromes, Profiles and Other Mental Exotica: A New Approach to the Admissibility of Nontraditional Psychological Evidence in Criminal Cases*, 66 Or. L. Rev. 19 (1987); Jennifer L. Mnookin, *Scripting Expertise: The History of Handwriting Identification Evidence and the Judicial Construction of Reliability*, 87 Va. L. Rev. 1723 (2001); Jennifer L. Mnookin, *Fingerprint Evidence in an Age of DNA Profiling*, 67 Brook. L. Rev. 13 (2001); Steven D. Penrod & Brian L. Cutler, *Eyewitness Expert Testimony and Jury Decisionmaking*, 52 Law & Contemp. Probs. 43 (1989); D. Michael Risinger et al., *The* Daubert/Kumho *Implications of Observer Effects in Forensic Science: Hidden Problems of Expectation and Suggestion*, 90 Cal. L. Rev. 1 (2002); D. Michael Risinger & Michael J. Saks, *Science and Nonscience in the Courts:* Daubert *Meets Handwriting Identification Expertise*, 82 Iowa L. Rev. 21 (1996); Symposium, *Special Theme: The Other-Race Effect and Contemporary Criminal Justice: Eyewitness Identification and Jury Decision Making*, 7 Psych. Pub. Pol'y & L. 3 (2001); Neil Vidmar & Shari Seidman Diamond, *Juries and Expert Evidence*, 66 Brook. L. Rev. 1121 (2001).

8. *Expert Testimony Must Have a Proper Basis*

> **FED. R. EVID. 703. BASES OF AN EXPERT'S OPINION TESTIMONY**

An expert may base an opinion on facts or data in the case that the expert has been made aware of or personally observed. If experts in the particular field would reasonably rely on those kinds of facts or data in forming an opinion on the subject, they need not be admissible for the opinion to be admitted. But if the facts or data would otherwise be inadmissible, the proponent of the opinion may disclose them to the jury only if their probative value in helping the jury evaluate the opinion substantially outweighs their prejudicial effect.

Rule 703 permits expert opinion to be based on three possible sources of information: first-hand knowledge, admitted evidence, and facts or data not admitted into evidence if "experts in the particular field would reasonably rely on those kinds of facts or data in forming an opinion on the subject." Expert testimony that is not based on one or more of these three sources should be excluded.

In pre-rules practice, many courts permitted expert opinion to be based only on either the expert's first-hand knowledge or on other admissible evidence. Because relatively few experts have personal knowledge of all the facts or data pertinent to their courtroom opinions, this meant that most experts needed to rely on evidence admitted through other witnesses. This created two serious problems. First, when experts relied on data produced by other experts, substantial trial time was needed to produce the other experts as witnesses and secure their testimony. Second, during the examination of an expert it was necessary to create a record of the facts or data on which the expert relied in order to demonstrate that all those matters already had been admitted into evidence. A lawyer typically would create this record by posing to the expert what is referred to as a "hypothetical question" that identified the facts or data on which the expert intended to base her opinion. The use of these hypothetical questions often ignited disputes over whether the question accurately reflected evidence in the record or, instead, mischaracterized that evidence. To meet such objections, the examining attorney was commonly required to augment, qualify, and complicate the question to such a degree that the relationship between the ensuing expert testimony and the issues in the case often became unclear.

While still permitting hypothetical questions, Rule 703 clearly is intended to streamline trials by reducing the need for that mechanism as a basis for expert testimony. Since Rule 703 permits experts to rely on evidence that has not been admitted, there is no longer any need to pose a hypothetical question for the purpose of showing that the opinion is based on admitted evidence. In fact, Rule 705 (described later in this chapter) provides that experts may give their opinions without first giving any testimony as to the bases for that opinion. In the name of efficiency, Rules 703 and 705 shift the burden to the cross-examiner to reveal the bases of an expert's opinion and the deficiencies therein.

What is the rationale for permitting an expert to base an opinion on inadmissible evidence if experts in the particular field would reasonably rely on those kinds of facts or data? Experts, more so than judges, can be presumed to know what sort of evidence is sufficiently trustworthy for them to use as a basis for their opinions. Thus, if experts in the relevant field use a particular type of evidence in forming their out-of-court opinions, that evidence should be a sufficiently trustworthy basis for in-court opinions, regardless of the admissibility of that evidence. The Advisory Committee's Note to Rule 703 provides a good example:

> [A] physician in his own practice bases his diagnosis on information from numerous sources and of considerable variety, including statements by patients and relatives, reports and opinions from nurses, technicians and other doctors, hospital records, and X rays. Most of them are admissible in evidence, but only with the expenditure of substantial time in producing and examining various authenticating witnesses. The physician makes life-and-death decisions in reliance upon them. His validation, expertly performed and subject to cross-examination, ought to suffice for judicial purposes.

The most difficult issue raised by Rule 703 is determining the extent of the trial court's power to exclude expert opinion under the "reasonably rely on" clause. Some courts interpret this part of Rule 703 as providing the trial judge only limited gatekeeping power. Under this limited gatekeeper approach, if the party offering the expert testimony shows that experts in the field rely on the type of facts or data in question, the trial court usually makes no further inquiry into reliability. Courts following the limited gatekeeper approach generally conclude that, if the expert witness in question testifies that experts in her field typically base opinions on the sorts of matters relied on by the witness, that testimony is conclusive. However, most courts conclude Rule 703 gives the trial judge more power as a gatekeeper. Under this active gatekeeper approach, the admissibility of expert opinion depends on a showing of two separate preliminary facts under Rule 104(a). First, the party offering the expert testimony must show that the expert relied on facts and data of a type relied on by experts in the field. Second, that party must show such reliance is reasonable. Thus, under the active gatekeeper approach the trial court exercises a measure of independent judgment as to reliability. This means the court may conclude that an expert cannot reasonably rely on certain facts or data even if, as the witness claims, experts in the field typically rely on the same type of facts or data. While *Daubert* and *Kumho Tire* were decided under Rule 702, not Rule 703, those decisions assume that trial judges have substantial discretion to evaluate the reliability of expert testimony. The active gatekeeper approach under Rule 703 is consistent with that assumption and those decisions.

Assuming Rule 703 permits an expert to give an opinion based on inadmissible evidence, the next question is whether the expert also can testify about that evidence to show that the opinion has a sound basis. This raises a problem in some cases. The problem is that the jury might consider the evidence not just for what it says concerning the expert's opinion, but also for a purpose for which the evidence otherwise would be inadmissible. For example, assume an engineer testifies on direct examination that a product was defective and that, in forming this opinion, he relied on the fact that the manufacturer redesigned the product after plaintiff was injured. In such a case, the jury might use this testimony to determine whether the expert's opinion had a sound basis, but might also use this testimony to draw an inference that Rule 407 forbids — that the product was defective. In fact, it is almost inevitable that the jury will draw the prohibited inference that the product was defective because the offered opinion goes to that very question.

Similarly, assume that a physician offers expert testimony in a personal injury action that plaintiff's injuries are permanent. She bases her opinion on a review of plaintiff's medical records, which contain the statement of an unidentified doctor, "Patient is permanently paralyzed." If the medical records are admitted to show the witness's opinion was sound, it is likely that the jury also will consider the statement of the other doctor for the hearsay purpose of concluding that the facts asserted in it (that plaintiff is permanently paralyzed) are true. This is improper because, if the medical records do not qualify under an exception to the hearsay rule, they constitute inadmissible hearsay and may not be considered for the truth of the matters asserted.

The last sentence of Rule 703 addresses the problem: "But if the facts or data would otherwise be inadmissible, the proponent of the opinion may disclose them to the jury only if their probative value in helping the jury evaluate the opinion substantially outweighs their prejudicial effect." The Advisory Committee's Note describes the approach as follows:

> When information is reasonably relied upon by an expert and yet is admissible only for the purpose of assisting the jury in evaluating an expert's opinion, a trial court applying this Rule must consider the information's probative value in assisting the jury to weigh the expert's opinion on the one hand, and the risk of prejudice resulting from the jury's potential misuse of the information for substantive purposes on the other. The information may be disclosed to the jury, upon objection, only if the trial court finds that the probative value of the information in assisting the jury to evaluate the expert's opinion substantially outweighs its prejudicial effect.

Illustrating the permissible bases of expert opinions. Following a fire that destroyed her commercial building, Plaintiff made a claim on her fire insurance policy. The insurer refused to pay, however, claiming that the fire was set deliberately and that Plaintiff was responsible. Plaintiff has sued the insurer to require it to make payment on the policy. At trial, the insurer's counsel calls Inspector Fox, a county fire inspector who investigated the fire. After establishing Fox's expert credentials and eliciting Fox's opinion that the fire was set deliberately, the following colloquy takes place. "Def" indicates counsel for the Defendant insurance company; "Pl" indicates Plaintiff's counsel.

Def:	Inspector Fox, why did you conclude that the fire was set intentionally?
Fox:	I followed guidelines set by the National Fire Protection Association.
Def:	What is this organization?
Fox:	The NFPA is dedicated to reducing the effects of fires on quality of life. It does so by providing and advocating scientifically based consensus codes and standards, research, training, and education.
Def:	Does NFPA have inspection standards for determining the origins of fires?
Fox:	Yes. Those standards are always evolving, of course, but there is a set of standards currently in place.
Def:	Where can those standards be found?
Fox:	They are published in NFPA 21, which is called the Guide for Fire and Explosion Investigations. It came out in 1998.
Def:	May I approach, Your Honor?
By the Court:	Yes.
Def:	Can you identify the document I am now showing you?
Fox:	Yes. This is a copy of NFPA 21.
Def:	Your Honor, prior to trial, I supplied a copy of this document to Plaintiff's counsel.
By the Court:	Proceed with your examination, counsel.
Def:	Did you follow those standards in your inspection of this fire?
Fox:	Yes.
Def:	How did you conduct the investigation then?
Fox:	My first step was to examine the scene. We always try to arrive as quickly as possible after the fire has been extinguished, before the scene has been altered in any way.
Def:	When did you begin your inspection in this case?
Fox:	I arrived just after the fire was out.
Def:	Had anyone else been through the building before you, other than the firefighters who were involved in extinguishing the fire?
Fox:	Not to my knowledge.
Def:	What did your inspection show?
Fox:	I always look for traces of accelerant, and I found some in this case.
Def:	What is an accelerant?
Fox:	It is a substance used to cause the fire to spread quickly.
Def:	What accelerant did you find in this case?

Fox: I found traces of kerosene, which is a common accelerant used by arsonists.

Def: Where did you find the traces of kerosene?

Fox: In the northeast corner of the first floor.

[Counsel then takes the witness through a detailed description of his examination of the remains of the building.]

Def: Other than your personal inspection of the building's remains, did you rely on anything else in reaching your conclusion that this fire was deliberately set?

Fox: I interviewed several neighbors who were present just as the fire broke out.

Def: And what did these people tell you?

PL: Objection, Your Honor. Calls for hearsay and improper basis for an expert's opinion.

Def: If the Court will permit, I will demonstrate that experts in this field rely on the statements of witnesses when conducting investigations of this kind. And we will not be using those statements to prove the truth of the matters stated by the witnesses, but only to demonstrate the basis of Inspector Fox's opinion.

By the Court: Objection overruled.

Def: Inspector Fox, is it proper procedure for fire inspectors to interview percipient witnesses when seeking to determine the cause of a fire?

Fox: Yes. We consider direct observations about the places where smoke was first seen, the color of flames, the speed with which the fire spread, and other similar matters to be important indicators of a fire's cause. These are the kinds of things about which neighbors and other percipient witnesses might have knowledge.

Def: And what did you learn from those interviews in this case?

Fox: Information supplied by these witnesses concerning the place where smoke first appeared, the color of the flames, and the speed of the fire's spread supported my view that the fire was of incendiary origin and that it began in the northeast corner of the first floor, where I found kerosene residue.

Def: No further questions, Your Honor.

In this example, Defendant's counsel has successfully demonstrated the bases of the expert's opinion, primarily personal inspection and interviews of witnesses. In addition, counsel has shown that these sources are of a type reasonably relied upon by fire investigation experts.

Further Reading: 29 Charles Alan Wright & Victor J. Gold, Federal Practice and Procedure 2d §§ 6271-6275 (West, 2016); Ronald L. Carlson, *Policing the Bases of Modern Expert Testimony*, 39 Vand. L. Rev. 577 (1986); Ronald L. Carlson, *Collision Course in Expert Testimony: Limitations on Affirmative Introduction of Underlying Data*, 36 Fla. L. Rev. 234 (1984); Edward J. Imwinkelried, *The "Bases" of Expert Testimony: The Syllogistic Structure of Scientific Testimony*, 67 N.C. L. Rev. 1 (1988); Paul R. Rice, *Inadmissible Evidence as a Basis for Expert Testimony: A Response to Professor Carlson*, 40 Vand. L. Rev. 583 (1987).

Questions for Classroom Discussion

1. Murder prosecution. The murder victim died when a toilet exploded. The defense calls Dr. Bidet, the famous French expert on exploding toilets. Dr. Bidet has no personal knowledge of the facts. His opinion is that the explosion was caused by an accidental buildup of water pressure. May he base this opinion on already received testimony of the investigating officer? On his personal inspection of the debris?

2. Same case. The investigating officer testifies that water was shooting 200 feet up into the air from a crater in the bathroom floor, there was no trace of explosives, and the victim was clutching a note in his lifeless hand that read, "You are a dead man!" The defense calls an expert, Professor Plunge, and asks, "Assume, professor, that the investigating officer testified water was shooting 200 feet up into the air from a crater in the bathroom floor and there was no trace of explosives. What is your opinion as to cause of death?" Is this question permissible?

3. Same case. The prosecution calls a pathologist whose knowledge of the case is entirely based on a lab report that already has been ruled inadmissible hearsay. Testifying that she customarily relies on such lab reports when rendering professional opinions at the hospital, the pathologist then offers an opinion that the cause of death was homicide. Is the pathologist's opinion admissible?

---

9. Expert Testimony: Limits on Opinions Going to Ultimate Issues

FED. R. EVID. 704. OPINION ON AN ULTIMATE ISSUE

(a) **In General — Not Automatically Objectionable.** An opinion is not objectionable just because it embraces an ultimate issue.

(b) **Exception.** In a criminal case, an expert witness must not state an opinion about whether the defendant did or did not have a mental state or condition that constitutes an element of the crime charged or of a defense. Those matters are for the trier of fact alone.

Rule 704(a) states that opinion testimony, lay or expert, is not objectionable on the ground that it "embraces an ultimate issue" in the case. Based on this provision, courts permit expert witnesses to offer answers to the very questions the jury will be asked to resolve. Courts most commonly cite the provision as a basis for permitting opinions stated in the same terms employed by the law that the jury will be instructed to apply. For example, an expert may be permitted to give the opinion that the design defect in a product "caused" plaintiff's injury even though causation may be the very legal issue on which the case turns.

Rule 704(a) does not declare any evidence admissible. Instead, it simply says that the evidence is "not objectionable just because it embraces an ultimate issue." Accordingly, the court still may exclude opinion testimony on ultimate issues if the court concludes that it is objectionable under any other provision in the Evidence Rules. Thus, opinions that merely tell the trier of fact what result to reach or state a legal conclusion in a way that says nothing about the facts are still objectionable. This is because such opinions are not "helpful" as required by Rule 701 and do not "help" as required by Rule 702.

The Advisory Committee's Note to Rule 704 provides an illustration of this principle:

> [Rules 403, 701, and 702] stand ready to exclude opinions phrased in terms of inadequately explored legal criteria. Thus the question, "Did T have capacity to make a will?" would be excluded, while the question, "Did T have sufficient mental capacity to know the nature and extent of his property and the natural objects of his bounty and to formulate a rational scheme of distribution?" would be allowed.

While both questions in this example employ the same legal term, *capacity*, the difference between them is a matter of the jury's ability to understand the witness's answers to these questions. In the first example, the question asks the witness to apply the legal test for enforceability of wills referred to as capacity. Capacity has a particular meaning in the law of wills that is not intuitively obvious to a layperson and may differ from a layperson's understanding of that word. The first question fails to explain how the legal test relates to the facts in the case. Without such an explanation, an answer to the first question cannot help the jury decide those facts. The jury may not understand the answer and even may attribute to "capacity" a meaning that the witness did not intend. This is what the Advisory Committee referred to, in the passage quoted above, as "inadequately explored legal criteria."

In contrast, the second question also refers to capacity but adds a description that explains how the legal test for capacity relates to the facts. As a consequence, a jury presumably is better able to understand an answer to the second question and employ that answer in resolving the factual issues in the case. For this reason, the drafters considered the first question improper and the second permissible.

Even when a witness uses language that has a legal meaning and that meaning is not explained, the courts still might admit the witness's opinion. This is proper when the language also has a meaning understandable to laypeople and the lay meaning is the same as the legal meaning or, if the legal and lay meanings differ, the witness clearly intended to employ the lay meaning. For example, in a conspiracy prosecution a police officer might be permitted to state the opinion that the defendants "were in a conspiracy" because that term has a common-sense meaning understandable to lay jurors.

Rule 704(b) recognizes an exception to the principle established in subdivision (a). The provision was added to Rule 704 in the wake of the attempted assassination of President Reagan in 1981 and the subsequent acquittal of his assailant on the ground of insanity. The scope of Rule 704(b) is limited in several respects:

1. The provision applies only to expert opinion testimony and only when that testimony concerns the defendant in a criminal case.
2. The provision applies only when the subject of the expert's testimony is "a mental state or condition" of the defendant.
3. The provision bars admission only when the content of the expert's opinion relates to "whether the defendant did or did not have a mental state or condition that constitutes an element of the crime charged or of a defense."

The imprecision of the language imposing these subject and content restrictions on subdivision (b) has raised many difficult issues concerning the application of that provision.

The legislative history of Rule 704(b) suggests that Congress mainly was concerned with limiting the admissibility of psychiatric testimony when an accused relies on the defense of insanity. Thus, the rule clearly excludes expert opinions as to whether an accused was legally sane when the accused claims insanity as a defense. The language of subdivision (b) makes it clear that the provision also excludes testimony on mental state or condition that is pertinent to "an element of the crime charged or of a defense." Accordingly, courts have held that subdivision (b) applies to exclude expert testimony as to whether the accused acted with the intent or knowledge required to commit the crimes charged. Furthermore, the courts agree that subdivision (b) regulates expert testimony concerning a defense other than insanity that is based on the accused's mental state. Thus, Rule 704(b) has been applied to expert opinion concerning entrapment, duress, and diminished capacity defenses. The legislative history of subdivision (b) confirms that Congress intended the provision to apply to such evidence.

It is also clear that testimony concerning any subject other than the accused's mental state or condition is not regulated by Rule 704(b). But drawing this line may be difficult. This is because an expert opinion concerning an accused's conduct or physical condition can speak indirectly to his mental state or condition. For example, prosecutors frequently offer expert testimony by a law enforcement agent that the accused's conduct is typical of the *modus operandi* employed in a certain type of criminal activity. The evidence usually is offered to permit the jury to infer that the accused intended to engage in that criminal activity. This connection to intent permits the argument that Rule 704(b) applies to exclude such opinions because the expert is testifying with respect to "a mental state or condition" of the accused. But most courts presented with such testimony conclude that the provision does not make the evidence in question inadmissible.

A similar problem with the scope of Rule 704(b) is presented whenever a psychiatrist testifies with respect to "a mental state or condition [of a defendant]." Rule 704(b) forbids admission only of opinions "about whether the defendant did or did not have a mental state or condition that constitutes an element of the crime charged or of a defense." If the scope of this language is extended as far as logic permits, virtually no psychiatric testimony about an accused would be admissible in a criminal trial. This is because almost all such testimony is offered to prove whether the accused acted with the mental state required to commit the crime.

The courts are unwilling to read the scope of Rule 704(b) so broadly, preferring a liberal approach to admissibility of expert testimony on issues such as sanity and intent. Subdivision (b) usually is interpreted to bar expert opinion only when it goes to the last step in the inferential process concerning a defendant's mental state or condition. Thus, when the issue is defendant's sanity, the courts permit an expert to testify as to the diagnosis of the accused's disease, the characteristics of that disease, and the effect that disease *could* have on a person's ability to appreciate the wrongfulness of conduct. Most courts only bar experts from testifying in terms of the ultimate question posed by the applicable legal definition of insanity. Accordingly, experts are precluded from testifying that the accused was or was not legally sane. Similarly, experts cannot testify that the accused did or did not appreciate the wrongfulness of his conduct or the nature or quality of his acts. However, the decisions in this area are not uniform and sometimes appear result oriented, drawing lines on seemingly minor distinctions. Courts frequently employ language in these cases that betrays their uncertainty about the legal standard.

The courts take a similar approach when the issue is not sanity but whether the accused acted with the intent or knowledge required to commit the crime. Rule 704(b) usually bars only a direct statement that the accused did or did not have the required mental state. Opinions that stop just short of this last step in the inferential process are generally admitted. The courts draw a distinction between testimony that the accused "could" have a certain intent and testimony that he "did" have that intent. Thus, the courts usually will reject opinion testimony that, based on his disease, the accused *did or did not* have a particular mental state. But the courts will admit opinions as to whether the accused suffered from a disease and, if so, whether his disease *could* have had a particular effect on the accused's mental state. For example, various courts are willing to admit evidence that the accused suffered from battered-woman syndrome and that the syndrome could have affected her state of mind at the time of the crime. But Rule 704(b) should bar testimony that, as a consequence of suffering from that syndrome, the accused believed she was in imminent danger of death or great bodily injury at the time of the crime, which is the specific mental state necessary to establish self-defense.

Again, however, the courts sometimes have difficulty drawing clear lines. This is most obvious in cases where law enforcement officers offer expert testimony as to the meaning of the accused's conduct. Most courts attempt to draw a distinction between testimony about the accused's conduct that suggests or permits an inference concerning the accused's intent and testimony about the accused's conduct that directly asserts the accused's intent. For example, most courts will permit a witness to testify that "the large quantity of drugs found in defendant's possession is consistent with intent to sell." On the other hand, the courts usually will preclude a witness from testifying, "the large quantity of drugs in defendant's possession means he had the intent to sell." Whether juries appreciate these fine semantic distinctions is open to question.

Further Reading: 29 Charles Alan Wright & Victor J. Gold, Federal Practice and Procedure 2d §§ 6281-6286 (West, 2016); Deon J. Nossel, Note, *The Admissibility of Ultimate Issue Expert Testimony by Law Enforcement Officers in Criminal Trials*, 93 Colum. L. Rev. 231 (1993).

Questions for Classroom Discussion

1. Prosecution for possession of drugs with intent to sell. A police officer, qualified as an expert, testifies that, based on the fact Defendant was arrested with a kilo of cocaine in his possession, he must have had the intent to sell. Is this opinion permitted under Rule 704(a)? 702? 704(b)?

2. Same case. What could the officer say without violating Rule 704(b)?

3. Prosecution for attempted assassination of the President. A psychiatrist is called to testify for the defense. Which is more likely to be admissible under 704(b)? (a) "Given defendant's mental condition, it is my opinion that he *did not* have the mental state required to commit the crime." (b) "Given defendant's mental condition, it is my opinion that he *could not* have the mental state required to commit the crime."

---

10. Expert Testimony: Disclosing Facts Underlying Opinion

> **FED. R. EVID. 705. DISCLOSING THE FACTS OR DATA UNDERLYING AN EXPERT'S OPINION**

Unless the court orders otherwise, an expert may state an opinion — and give the reasons for it — without first testifying to the underlying facts or data. But the expert may be required to disclose those facts or data on cross-examination.

In our discussion of Rule 703 we learned that many pre-rules cases permitted expert opinion to be based only on first-hand knowledge or on other admissible evidence. Because relatively few experts have personal knowledge of all the facts or data pertinent to their courtroom opinions, this meant that most experts needed to rely on evidence admitted through other witnesses and restated in the form of a hypothetical question. As we have seen, Rule 703 expands the permissible bases for expert opinion to also include inadmissible evidence, if of the kind reasonably relied on by experts in the pertinent field. Rule 703 ends with this sentence: "But if the facts or data [on which expert opinion is based] would otherwise be inadmissible, the proponent of the opinion may disclose them to the jury only if their probative value in helping the jury evaluate the opinion substantially outweighs their prejudicial effect."

By sometimes permitting expert opinion to be based on inadmissible matters, Rule 703 makes Rule 705 necessary. Obviously, if an opinion can be admitted even if the data on which it is based cannot be heard by the jury, it makes little sense to require testimony about that data prior to admission of the opinion. Rule 705 simply confirms this conclusion.

But Rule 705 even goes beyond what is logically required by Rule 703. Even if the expert's underlying facts and data are admissible, Rule 705 gives the party offering expert opinion testimony the power to present that opinion without prior disclosure of that material. However, this power is subject to one proviso — "unless the court orders otherwise." This phrase suggests that the trial court has considerable discretion in determining the order in which the expert's opinion and its underlying bases will be presented. The court may require prior disclosure when, for example, Rules 703, 702, or 403 pose serious questions concerning the admissibility of an expert's opinion and those questions are raised by the basis for that opinion. In such a case, prior disclosure of the basis may help resolve the admissibility issue.

For example, assume that a physician offers to testify for plaintiff that defendant's product caused plaintiff's disease. The doctor's opinion is based entirely on a speech the doctor heard at a scientific conference concerning animal studies linking defendant's product to a completely different disease. This opinion might not assist the trier of fact under Rule 702 because it relies on studies that could be irrelevant to plaintiff's condition. For the same reason, the opinion also might be objectionable under Rule 703 if based on inadmissible hearsay that is not the type of evidence on which experts in the pertinent field reasonably rely. In such a case, the trial court might conclude that the underlying facts and data must be disclosed *before* the opinion is offered because the court could not otherwise determine if the opinion is admissible. This disclosure could take place before the jury or, if that might lead to unfair prejudice, in the absence of the jury.

On the other hand, this departure from the usual procedure under Rule 705 should be limited. Many potential attacks on the basis of an expert's opinion raise questions only as to the weight of that opinion, not its admissibility. When this is the case, the party offering expert opinion retains the discretion to present that opinion without prior disclosure of the expert's basis. Rule 705 primarily relies on cross-examination by the opponent to enable the trier of fact to weigh the opinion properly.

The final question is the extent of a cross-examiner's power under the second sentence of Rule 705. That provision gives the cross-examiner the right to inquire into the facts and data underlying the expert's opinion. Because Rule 705 is not a rule of admissibility, it does not make admissible evidence that is otherwise inadmissible under some other rule. On the other hand, Rule 703 frequently permits the receipt of otherwise inadmissible evidence merely to show the basis of an expert's opinion. Accordingly, cross-examination concerning the basis of an expert's opinion generally is permitted for the limited purpose of showing that the basis was unreliable or otherwise insufficient.

Question for Classroom Discussion

Murder prosecution. An expert testifies for the prosecution that a new DNA test shows an irrefutable match between Defendant's DNA and blood found at the crime scene. Because of limitations on pretrial discovery in criminal cases, Defendant did not know the prosecution would present this highly technical evidence. Make an argument that the judge should exercise her discretion under Rule 705 to require the prosecution to present the basis of the expert's opinion before the opinion is received.

11. Expert Testimony: Court-Appointed Experts

FED. R. EVID. 706. COURT-APPOINTED EXPERT WITNESSES

(a) **Appointment Process.** On a party's motion or on its own, the court may order the parties to show cause why expert witnesses should not be appointed and may ask the parties to submit nominations. The court may appoint any expert witness that the parties agree on and any of its own choosing. But the court may only appoint someone who consents to act.

(b) **Expert's Role.** The court must inform the expert of the expert's duties. The court may do so in writing and have a copy filed with the clerk or may do so orally at a conference in which the parties have an opportunity to participate. The expert:

(1) must advise the parties of any findings the expert makes;

(2) may be deposed by any party;

(3) may be called to testify by the court or any party; and

(4) may be cross-examined by any party, including the party that called the expert.

(c) **Compensation.** The expert is entitled to a reasonable compensation, as set by the court. The compensation is payable as follows:

(1) in a criminal case or in a civil case involving just compensation under the Fifth Amendment, from any funds that are provided by law; and

(2) in any other civil case, by the parties in the proportion and at the time that the court directs—and the compensation is then charged like other costs.

(d) **Disclosing the Appointment to the Jury.** The court may authorize disclosure to the jury that the court appointed the expert.

(e) **Parties' Choice of Their Own Experts.** This rule does not limit a party in calling its own experts.

One justification for our adversary system is that adversarial conflict usually is an effective means of getting at the truth. When the parties are in control of presenting the evidence, their conflicting interests make it likely that the trier of fact will be exposed to a wide spectrum of relevant data. Evidence presented by one side typically contradicts evidence presented by the other side. The conclusion that this system promotes accurate fact-finding is based on the assumption that the trier of fact can reliably sift through this evidence, accord each item its proper weight, and determine if the truth resides with one side or somewhere in the middle.

But this assumption is particularly tenuous when the case turns on expert testimony. Expert testimony frequently concerns complex matters with which the trier of fact is unfamiliar. When the adversaries present conflicting expert testimony on such matters, the trier of fact may be incapable of determining which expert is correct or even locating a sensible middle-ground position. This problem is exacerbated by the fact that, due to the financial rewards of testifying, expert witnesses can be found to champion many unworthy propositions and theories. As a result, the reliability of the fact-finding process may be undermined if the trier of fact hears only from experts called (and paid for) by the parties.

Rule 706 gives courts discretion to appoint their own expert witnesses in order to mitigate these weaknesses of the adversary process. A court-appointed expert in theory provides the trier of fact with a neutral and more reliable perspective on the issues. The availability of court-appointed experts also provides the parties with reason to moderate their views and move toward settlement. Finally, the involvement of a court-appointed expert may induce the parties' experts to be more careful in their own testimony.

While Rule 706 fails to provide a standard by which the exercise of the court's discretion should be judged, the policy of promoting accurate fact-finding supplies sufficient guidance. Thus, Rule 706 powers are properly invoked when the issues are complex and the parties' experts have presented conflicting testimony that is difficult to reconcile or have otherwise failed to provide a sufficient basis for deciding the issues. Invocation of Rule 706 powers is especially appropriate to protect the rights of an accused, a child, or the public interest. In such cases, many courts rightly assume there is a heightened judicial duty to see that the abuses and inadequacies of the adversaries should not be permitted to obscure the truth. However, even in such cases the exercise of Rule 706 powers remains a matter of discretion with the trial court.

But while accurate fact-finding sometimes may be promoted by judicial appointment of expert witnesses, it also can undermine that value. The opinion of a court's expert may become decisive because the expert wears the mantle of judicial authority and impartiality. This can mislead the jury because, in fact, no expert is entirely impartial. Although a court's expert may be free of financial ties to a party, that expert still enters the courtroom with all the vested professional interests and biases developed over the course of a career. In addition, that expert may reflect the biases of the judge. A court-appointed expert also can be wrong for reasons unconnected to bias. But because of the expert's link to the court, a jury may fail to scrutinize his testimony to the same extent it would the testimony of party experts. Thus, the testimony of a court-appointed expert can undermine rather than promote accurate fact-finding.

Accordingly, Rule 706 tries to balance the need for judicial involvement in the presentation of expert testimony against the dangers associated with that involvement. While recognizing the judicial power to appoint expert witnesses, the provision gives the adversaries various opportunities to forestall inappropriate appointments and expose defective testimony. For example, subdivision (a) provides that a court may appoint an expert only on motion for an order to show cause why such an expert should not be appointed. This ensures that the parties are afforded an opportunity to be heard on the matter. That provision also gives the parties the right to participate at the conference at which the expert is informed of his duties, to receive notice of the expert's findings, and to take the expert's deposition. These safeguards ensure that the parties are not surprised by the expert's opinions and can prepare to the extent necessary to reveal the expert's biases or errors. Subdivision (a) also permits the parties to call the expert to testify, and to cross-examine the expert. This provides the parties with the opportunity to promote or attack the expert's testimony as they see fit. Subdivision (d) gives the court discretion to decide whether to disclose to the jury the fact that the court appointed the expert. By making this a matter of discretion, Rule 706 provides the parties with the means to raise the appropriateness of disclosure as an issue. Finally, subdivision (e) preserves the parties' right to call experts of their own selection, thereby again permitting the parties to attack, support, or supplement the testimony of the court's expert.

Question for Classroom Discussion

Much of the law concerning expert witness testimony seems to address reliability concerns caused by a combination of two factors: (1) most expert witnesses are not impartial because they are hired by the parties, and (2) jurors and judges are not well equipped to evaluate the reliability of testimony offered by expert witnesses because that testimony usually addresses complex or esoteric subjects. *Daubert/Kumho Tire* provides only one possible, albeit imperfect, approach to the problem. Other suggestions have been made. They include sending highly technical cases to a special court where the judges have a scientific background, or impaneling a jury of experts, rather than the traditional "jury of one's peers." What do you think of these suggestions?

Assessments

1. Prosecution for possession of marijuana. A witness testifies that as she walked past Defendant she could smell that he was smoking something and, in her opinion, it was not tobacco but was marijuana. Witness says she is familiar with the smell of tobacco smoke but admits that she has never previously smelled marijuana smoke. Defendant objects to the admissibility of her testimony. Which of the following is correct?
   a. The witness's opinion that Defendant was not smoking tobacco is inadmissible because it is not helpful
   b. The witness's opinion that Defendant was smoking marijuana is inadmissible because it is not helpful
   c. The witness's opinion that Defendant was smoking marijuana is inadmissible because it is not rationally based on her perception
   d. The witness's opinions that Defendant was not smoking tobacco but was smoking marijuana are both admissible

(continued)

2. Personal injury action in which Plaintiff seeks to recover for both physical and psychological injuries. Plaintiff calls his family doctor who testifies that, based on her physical examination of Plaintiff, which revealed the extent of his physical injuries, she has concluded that Plaintiff also must have suffered permanent psychological damage. Defendant's best objection is:
   a. The opinion is based on privileged matters
   b. The opinion is based on hearsay
   c. The opinion is not rationally based on the perception of the witness
   d. The witness is not qualified as an expert

3. Prosecution for possession of drugs with intent to distribute. A retired police officer with extensive experience in drug investigations testifies for the defense that the quantity of drugs found in Defendant's pocket when arrested was consistent with the intent to possess for personal use rather than drug dealing. On cross-examination, the officer admits that he has no relevant academic credentials. He also admits that his assumption concerning the amount of drugs indicative of drug dealing is based only on his experience and is not based on peer reviewed publications or testing. The officer also admits that, in arriving at his conclusions, he did not consider the fact that when Defendant was arrested he also had ten thousand dollars cash in his pocket. The prosecution's best objection to the testimony of the witness is:
   a. The opinion of the witness does not satisfy the *Daubert* factors
   b. The opinion is unreliable because the witness did not consider all the pertinent evidence
   c. The opinion of the witness is inadmissible because it describes whether Defendant had the mental state or condition that is an element of the crime charged
   d. The witness has not been qualified as an expert

4. Action for products liability arising out of an automobile accident in which Plaintiff was injured when the brakes on his car allegedly failed. An automotive engineer testifies for Plaintiff that, in his opinion, the brakes had a defective design. He further testifies that one of the bases for his opinion is that, immediately after the accident in which Plaintiff was injured, Defendant redesigned the brakes on that model car. Defendant objects to the expert's testimony. Which of the following is correct?
   a. Testimony that the brakes had a defective design is inadmissible because it goes to an ultimate issue in the case
   b. Testimony that the defendant redesigned the brakes after the accident is inadmissible because it is a subsequent remedial measure
   c. All the expert's testimony is admissible
   d. Testimony that the brakes had a defective design is admissible but testimony that the expert based his opinion on redesign of

the brakes is admissible only if probative value substantially outweighs prejudicial effect

5. Action for wrongful death arising out of a crash of a race car into the crowd during the Indianapolis 500. Plaintiff alleges that Defendant was negligent in driving at an unsafe speed while taking a turn on the racecourse. Plaintiff calls a witness to testify that, as Defendant was entering the turn just before the crash, Defendant's car was travelling at least 240 miles per hour. Which of the following is correct?
   a. The testimony is admissible so long as the witness had personal knowledge of the car in motion at the time of the accident
   b. The testimony is admissible so long as the witness's opinion was rationally based on perception
   c. The testimony is admissible so long as the witness is qualified as an expert regarding the subject of his opinion
   d. The testimony is inadmissible

Answers and Analysis

1. The correct answer is c. Witness's opinion that it was marijuana smoke is not rationally based on her perception because she has no prior experience with marijuana smoke. Thus, she has no basis for her assumptions concerning what marijuana smoke smells like. Answer a is incorrect because the witness might have difficulty describing what tobacco smoke smells like (or doesn't smell like) and, thus, it would be helpful to permit the witness to give the opinion that Defendant was not smoking tobacco. Answer b is incorrect for the same reason. Answer d is incorrect because the witness's opinion that Defendant was smoking marijuana is not rationally based on her perception.

2. The correct answer is d. While Plaintiff's family doctor is qualified to testify as an expert as to medical matters, it seems unlikely that she has the background to qualify as an expert regarding psychological injuries. One would normally expect a psychiatrist or psychologist to offer such an opinion. On the other hand, it is possible that a family doctor with significant relevant experience could qualify as an expert regarding emotional or psychological injury, but the facts of the question do not make this apparent. Importantly, the other alternatives are clearly incorrect. Thus, this is an example of a multiple choice question that requires eliminating the other alternatives before it is clear that d is the best answer. Answer a is incorrect because, even though the witness's opinion is based on matters that might be privileged in some jurisdiction, Plaintiff (the patient) is the holder of the privilege. Thus, Defendant has no standing to assert privilege here. Answer b is incorrect because the results of the witness's physical examination of Plaintiff are not hearsay and, even so, experts can base opinions on inadmissible evidence so long as it is the type of evidence experts in the field reasonably rely upon.

(continued)

Doctors reasonably rely upon physical exams of patients in arriving at a diagnosis. Answer c is incorrect because it states an admissibility standard for lay, not expert, opinion. Even if a similar type of requirement might be inferred from the terms of Rule 702, the witness's perceptions of Plaintiff's physical injuries could be a rational basis from which to infer psychological damage.

3.   The correct answer is b. Under *Kumho Tire*, courts may reject expert opinion that appears to be unreliable because it fails to consider all the pertinent evidence. The fact that Defendant had ten thousand dollars cash in his pocket is pertinent because it suggests Defendant may already have sold a large quantity of drugs before he was arrested. Thus, an opinion may be unreliable if it is based only on the amount of drugs in Defendant's pocket at the time of arrest, while ignoring the other pertinent contents of his pocket. Answer a is incorrect because the *Daubert* factors, such as publication, peer review, and testing, are not necessarily applicable to expert opinion in non-scientific areas like this. Answer c is incorrect because the opinion does not explicitly state that Defendant had (or did not have) a specific intent. Rather, the opinion merely states that the amount of drugs in question is consistent with intent to use, not distribute. This is a distinction adhered to by the cases arising under Rule 703. Answer d is also incorrect because a witness may be qualified as an expert based on experience. Academic background is not essential.

4.   The correct answer is d. While opinion testimony that the brakes had a defective design goes directly to the ultimate issue in a products liability case, Rule 704(a) makes it clear that such testimony is not objectionable on that basis. The evidence concerning redesign of the brakes would normally be inadmissible under Rule 407, which we saw in a previous chapter applies in products liability cases. But Rule 703 makes such evidence admissible if its probative value in helping the jury evaluate the opinion evidence substantially outweighs the prejudicial effect of such evidence. Answer a is incorrect because of Rule 704(a). Answer b is incorrect if, as just stated, under Rule 703 the probative value of the evidence substantially outweighs its prejudicial effect. Answer c might be correct, but only if the redesign evidence is admissible after this balancing. Thus, d is the best answer.

5.   The correct answer is c. While lay witnesses usually may give an opinion as to the speed of a conventional automobile, estimating the speed of a Indy type race car requires specialized knowledge of the sort that only experts have. Rule 701 makes it clear that lay witnesses may not offer opinions as to such matters. Thus, answer a is incorrect because personal knowledge of the car in motion is not enough to warrant admissibility of the witness's opinion. Similarly, answer b is incorrect since it states the standard for admissibility of lay opinion. Answer d is incorrect because, if the witness is properly qualified as an expert, the opinion could be admitted.

CHAPTER

8

Privileges

A. INTRODUCTION

If truth-determination was the only goal of the trial, there could be no rule categorically excluding evidence that reveals the truth. In such a system of adjudication, the judge might be given discretion to exclude relevant evidence under a provision like Rule 403, but only when the admission of evidence might impede, rather than advance, the truth. But we do not have such a system. We have seen that there are many rules that exclude evidence for reasons other than the potential of that evidence to impede the truth. This is because, as we also have seen, these rules serve goals in addition to promoting the truth. In Chapter 1, we stated that one such goal is "vindicating the rights and expectations of parties." Although this goal is mainly served by the substantive civil and criminal law, it is also advanced by evidence rules that protect the privacy of certain relationships. This is the objective of privileges. But there is a cost to privilege law. By promoting these relationships, evidentiary privileges undermine the goal of truth-determination.

How do privileges impede truth-determination? Suppose Defendant is charged with robbing a convenience store. There were few customers in the store at the time of the robbery, none of whom got a good look at the perpetrator. The physical evidence left behind is not compelling, but much of it points to Defendant. Defendant claims he was not involved. He has reason to believe, however, that another person who has since fled the country confessed to his attorney that he committed the crime. At trial, Defendant wishes to call the attorney to testify about the other person's confession.[1] If the attorney asserts her client's attorney-client privilege — as she must unless the client waived the privilege — the court may not compel the attorney to testify to her client's confession. The result might be that Defendant is convicted.[2] If Defendant is innocent, the attorney-client privilege would have prevented exposure of the truth.

---

1. The confession would be hearsay but might qualify as a statement against interest under Rule 804(b)(3).

2. Of course, if Defendant suspected a particular person might have committed the crime, the existence of the attorney-client privilege between that person and his attorney would not prevent Defendant from trying to develop other information proving the person's guilt.

This means that the privilege must serve other values. The existence of the privilege encourages a client to speak openly and frankly with her attorney, who should inform her of the privilege. If no privilege protects their conversation, it is the attorney's duty to tell the client that she might be required to repeat their conversation in court, and such a revelation certainly could discourage the client from revealing sensitive information. By withholding that information, the client would make it difficult for the attorney to represent her effectively. Some courts and commentators have noted that this dynamic means that, in the absence of privilege, there will be no communication in the first place and, thus, no evidence for the opponent to discover. This means the opponent might be in no worse position with the privilege than without.

The utilitarian or instrumental rationale for privilege — promotion of full and frank communication — is the value most often cited for the existence of privileges. In fact, Wigmore, the most influential of twentieth-century evidence scholars, believed that the *only* reason to recognize privileges was to promote communication and that a privilege should be recognized only when it is necessary to promote communication between particular classes of people. As a result, Wigmore supported privileges only for the attorney-client, priest-penitent, and husband-wife relationships. He did not support adoption of a privilege for other relationships, such as physician-patient. Wigmore argued that a doctor-patient privilege was not necessary to promote communication because, even in the absence of such a privilege, patients would disclose their medical conditions fully to ensure that they receive proper treatment.

Although highly influential and useful in understanding the scope of privileges, this utilitarian rationale does not take account of at least one other key value served by privileges: the dignitary interest of privacy in certain close relationships. When spouses communicate with each other in confidence, they are entitled to privacy. When a client confides in her attorney, or a patient confides in her physician, she might or might not be aware of the formal evidentiary privilege, but the law still should respect the privacy of their communications. Some have argued that basic human dignity and a sense of fundamental fairness demand no less. This argument is perhaps most convincingly made in connection with confidential communications between a person seeking spiritual guidance and a member of the clergy, where the non-utilitarian values at stake include those enshrined in the Free Exercise Clause of the First Amendment. Most jurisdictions have concluded that, at least in these relationships the values to be promoted by protecting confidential communications can overcome the value of truth-determination at trial. The same can be argued about the value of privacy in other relationships, such as parent-child and accountant-client, but fewer jurisdictions have seen fit to recognize privileges protecting these relationships.

As we shall see, the value of privacy has not had a great influence on the development of privileges in modern U.S. law. Though some new privileges have emerged in recent years, others, such as the physician-patient privilege, have been hedged with numerous exceptions in some jurisdictions, and simply abandoned in others. Wigmore's utilitarian rationale still holds sway with courts and legislatures.

In this chapter, we explore some basic principles applicable to all testimonial privileges, and then we discuss certain specific privileges. Keep in mind that we are only studying privileges established by evidence law. We are not discussing constitutional privileges (such as the Fifth Amendment right not to incriminate oneself), nor are we discussing government privileges (such as executive privilege or the protection of state secrets).

The history of the development of privilege law is rich. Even before courts in Britain began to recognize evidentiary privileges, there were rules that simply made certain persons *incompetent* to testify at trial. Among them were convicted criminals and interested persons, including parties to the present action. The history of the recognition of testimonial privileges is intertwined with the slow erosion of the many rules of witness incompetency. For a detailed review of the history of privilege law, consult Edward J. Imwinkelried, The New Wigmore: Privileges (2002).

B. THE FEDERAL RULE

FED. R. EVID. 501. PRIVILEGE IN GENERAL

The common law—as interpreted by United States courts in the light of reason and experience — governs a claim of privilege unless any of the following provides otherwise:

- the United States Constitution;
- a federal statute; or
- other rules prescribed by the Supreme Court.

But in a civil case, state law governs privilege regarding a claim or defense for which state law supplies the rule of decision.

Rule 501 is the main provision in the Federal Rules of Evidence applicable to privileges.[3] The rule simply provides that the federal courts should continue to develop the common law of privileges "in the light of reason and experience." This approach, however, does not apply in civil actions when "state law supplies the rule of decision." This means that state privilege law controls if the claim or defense in a civil case is governed by state substantive law, as usually will be true in diversity cases. This provision was added to recognize the *Erie* doctrine, which limits the application of federal common law. In other civil cases and in criminal cases, Rule 501 calls for the application of the federal law of privileges.

In adopting Rule 501, Congress rejected a series of rules proposed by the Supreme Court that would have codified nine specific privileges (attorney-client, psychotherapist-patient, spousal, clergy-penitent, political vote, trade secrets, official information and state secrets, identity of informer, and required reports). Congress also rejected a proposed rule that would have precluded

---

3. Congress later added Rule 502 in 2008. We will discuss that rule in connection with the attorney-client privilege.

federal courts from recognizing any other privileges unless created by Congress. These rejected rules are set forth in Appendix B of this volume. With the adoption of Rule 501, the federal courts will continue to develop the law of privileges as they did prior to the adoption of the Federal Rules of Evidence. Indeed, as we shall see, the federal courts have actively engaged in the development of the law, most recently adopting a broad psychotherapist-patient privilege.

We will occasionally refer to the proposed federal rules regarding privileges. Though never enacted, these proposed rules are useful because, for the most part, they would have codified commonly followed principles concerning privileges or principles that the Supreme Court thought should be followed. As such, many courts have referred to the proposed rules in exercising their responsibility under Rule 501 to develop the common law of privilege.

Question for Classroom Discussion

Diversity action in federal district court by Plaintiff against Defendant, a trucking company. Plaintiff seeks damages for personal injury following a collision between her car and Defendant's 18-wheeler. At trial, Defendant calls Witness, who secretly "bugged" Plaintiff's attorney's office and listened in during a private conversation between Plaintiff and her attorney. In that conversation, Plaintiff allegedly admitted being responsible for causing the accident. Plaintiff objects on grounds of attorney-client privilege. The federal courts in the state whose substantive law governs the case hold that otherwise privileged conversations overheard by an eavesdropper are privileged if the parties took reasonable steps to ensure confidentiality. The state's own courts, however, hold that otherwise confidential communications lose their privileged status if they are overheard. How should the court rule on Plaintiff's objection?

C. GENERAL PRINCIPLES

Before studying specific privileges, it is necessary to understand several principles applicable to all privileges. This section sets forth these basic principles. The privilege rules of all jurisdictions are founded on these basic concepts.

1. The Nature of Privileges

The privileges we will study for the most part prevent disclosure in a judicial context of confidential communications between people in certain relationships. As such, these privileges operate much like other evidence rules, excluding at trial particular categories of evidence or preventing compelled disclosure in other formal proceedings such as a deposition. Privileges are not addressed to other situations in which disclosure might be compelled, such as in the performance of duties imposed by common law or statute. For example, in Tarasoff v. The Regents of the University of California, 131 Cal. Rptr. 14 (Cal. 1976), the California Supreme Court held that psychotherapists have a duty to warn prospective victims of a client's threat to cause them bodily harm. Disclosure to the prospective victim, or to law enforcement on the victim's behalf, does not in itself destroy the patient's privilege to prevent the psychotherapist from disclosing confidential communications in a judicial proceeding such as a trial.[4]

In one way, privileges apply more broadly than other rules of evidence. Whereas other rules typically do not apply during discovery, the privilege rules apply at all stages of a judicial proceeding. Indeed, if a party wishes to maintain a privilege, she *must* assert it even during discovery because a voluntary disclosure during discovery of material otherwise protected by privilege generally will constitute a waiver of the privilege at trial.

2. Covered Relationships

Though some privileges differ,[5] all the confidential communication privileges we will study in detail protect persons involved in specific relationships. As we review each privilege, consider its breadth as well as its particular limitations. Not only are communications within some relationships more fully protected than those that occur within others, but some relationships in which confidentiality is important are not covered at all. Why, for example, is the attorney-client privilege so broad while the physician-patient privilege is so narrow and, indeed, not recognized at all in a number of jurisdictions? Why do only a handful of states recognize a privilege for confidential communications between parent and child, between accountant and client, or between teacher and student?

In part, these differences can be explained by the relative political influence possessed by persons involved in different types of relationships. Lawyers enjoy enormous influence over the political process. Judges, the makers of common law rules, are lawyers, and the legal profession is by far the profession most represented in legislatures. In contrast, few doctors or teachers serve in lawmaking capacities, and the interests of parents and children are not represented by many organized lobbyists. For some time, the relative influence of different branches of the counseling profession was even more strikingly apparent in California privilege law. Before the California Evidence Code was amended fairly recently, communications between psychiatrists and patients, as well as those between Ph.D. psychologists and their clients, enjoyed broad protection, while communications between clients and other types of counselors, including social workers, received little protection. Under this regime, those with the means to pay the high cost of psychiatric counseling or assistance by licensed clinical psychologists could be assured of strict confidentiality, while those in

---

4. Other rules might provide an exception to the privilege, however. In California, for example, the so-called dangerous patient exception to the psychotherapist-patient privilege is contained in Cal. Evid. Code § 1024. It provides: "There is no privilege under this article if the psychotherapist has reasonable cause to believe that the patient is in such mental or emotional condition as to be dangerous to himself or to the person or property of another and that disclosure of the communication is necessary to prevent the threatened danger." These issues are discussed below, in connection with the medical privileges.

5. Privileges protecting political votes, trade secrets, and state secrets do not involve the types of relationships found in the privileges on which we will focus most of our attention.

lower economic classes could expect far less protection. Though that inequity no longer exists in California law, it is important to scrutinize carefully your jurisdiction's privilege law to determine the extent to which it protects confidential communications within particular relationships.

3.   "Confidential Communications"

Most of the privileges we study in this chapter protect "confidential communications" between the parties in a particular relationship. Only communications that qualify as confidential communications are protected from disclosure, and even if the communication is protected, the information communicated is not. Consider this example:

> Plaintiff brings a negligence action against Defendant after Defendant's car ran into Plaintiff as she crossed the street. Defendant consults an attorney for purposes of obtaining representation. In the course of their confidential discussion, Defendant admits that Plaintiff was in a crosswalk when Defendant's car struck her, and that Defendant did not see Plaintiff before the collision because Defendant was distracted.

If the privilege applies in this situation, it will prevent disclosure only of the confidential discussion, not of the facts related by Defendant. The effect will be that Plaintiff may not force Defendant's attorney to disclose what Defendant told her,[6] nor may Plaintiff force Defendant to relate what he said to his attorney. But the existence of the privilege does not prevent Plaintiff from asking Defendant about the *facts*—whether, for example, Plaintiff was in a crosswalk, or whether Defendant was paying attention just before the collision. To put it simply, Defendant may not prevent disclosure of the facts by including them in a confidential communication with his attorney.

In addition, the privilege does not protect non-communicative behavior, including physical evidence. For example, if a person charged with murder gives her attorney the gun used to shoot the victim, most states require the attorney to turn over the gun to the prosecution (though some permit the attorney to obtain use or source immunity for her client before doing so). Similarly, in an accident case, the privilege would not prevent an attorney from being asked whether her client, who now claims permanent physical impairment, in fact walked without a limp when he met with the attorney to discuss the case. Also not subject to the privilege in most situations is the fact that an attorney has been hired to represent a particular individual. And even if the substance of an attorney's confidential communication with a client is subject to the privilege, the mere fact that the attorney and client spoke, if relevant, normally is not privileged.

The definition of *communication* is broader than one might expect. Normally, of course, a communication is an oral or written transmission of information. But for privilege purposes a communication can be in the form of a non-assertive transmission of information. The physician-patient privilege, for example, covers

---

6. In effect, this means the attorney is not a proper witness in the case. Because she did not see the accident, and only "knows" the facts because they were related by defendant, she lacks personal knowledge.

any information the doctor obtains during a private examination or testing of the patient. In addition, suppose a personal injury plaintiff alleges that she suffered permanent loss of motion in her arm as a result of the accident. In the course of a private meeting with her lawyer, plaintiff demonstrates the limited range of motion in her arm. The information conveyed by this demonstration is subject to protection by the attorney-client privilege, meaning that the lawyer may not be compelled to reveal her knowledge of the plaintiff's condition.

When does a communication qualify as "confidential"? Proposed Federal Rule 503, concerning the attorney-client privilege, defines a communication as confidential if it is "not intended to be disclosed to third persons other than those to whom disclosure is in furtherance of the rendition of professional legal services to the client or those reasonably necessary for the transmission of the communication." California Evidence Code § 952 sets forth a somewhat more complex definition:

> "[C]onfidential communication between client and lawyer" means information transmitted between a client and his or her lawyer in the course of that relationship and in confidence by a means which, so far as the client is aware, discloses the information to no third persons other than those who are present to further the interest of the client in the consultation or those to whom disclosure is reasonably necessary for the transmission of the information or the accomplishment of the purpose for which the lawyer is consulted, and includes a legal opinion formed and the advice given by the lawyer in the course of that relationship. A communication between a client and his or her lawyer is not deemed lacking in confidentiality solely because the communication is transmitted by facsimile, cellular telephone, or electronic means between the client and his or her lawyer.

In addition, California law establishes a "presumption" that communications taking place within certain protected relationships (including lawyer and client) are "made in confidence and the opponent of the claim of privilege has the burden of proof to establish that the communication was not confidential." Cal. Evid. Code § 917.

While the privilege depends on a showing that the client intended the communication be confidential, the proposed federal rule and the California law determine the client's intent under an objective standard: Looking at the communication and the surrounding circumstances apparent to the client when the communication was made, would a reasonable person in that position believe that the communication was confidential? For example, if the client consulted her lawyer in a private conference room with the doors closed and used a soft tone of voice not likely to be heard outside the room, the court is likely to treat the communication as confidential even if a hidden eavesdropper overhears the conversation. But if the client chose to communicate with her lawyer in a public place, and used a loud tone of voice that could be overheard by people in plain view, the court is unlikely to hold that the communication was confidential, no matter how vociferously the client asserts that she subjectively intended her conversation to be confidential. In some cases, the communication can only take place in circumstances where others might hear, as where a client who is a prisoner is permitted to communicate with her attorney only in the presence of a guard. Where this is the case, it would seem fair to conclude under the objective standard that the client still intended the communication to be confidential.

4. Who Can Participate in the Communication?

To establish and preserve a confidential communication privilege, the parties must take reasonable steps to prevent disclosure to persons who are not necessary to the protected relationship. This requires not just choosing an appropriate location and method of conducting the conversation to avoid accidental disclosure, but also taking steps to intentionally include in the conversation only those people whose presence is essential to that relationship. Thus, while the presence of a legal secretary or law clerk might be necessary to the provision of legal services, a lawyer from another firm or a friend of the client probably is not. In the context of spousal communications, the presence of almost any third party, even a child of the spouses, can destroy the privilege.

Thus, privilege may extend to a communication between many different people, so long as all of them are participating in that communication for the purpose of facilitating the protected relationship. For example, a communication between a client's employee and the attorney's secretary can be protected, even though neither the client nor the attorney participated in the conversation. Similarly, the attorney-client privilege will extend to a communication from the client in the presence of her employee, the attorney, the attorney's paralegal, an investigator, and a doctor hired by the attorney to help prepare the case for trial. This is because, even though the room is rather crowded, everyone present is there to help facilitate the rendition of professional legal services to the client. In the following diagram, A stands for attorney, C for Client, AR for attorney's representative, and CR for client's representative. Communications along any and all of the dotted lines can be protected if intended to facilitate legal services.

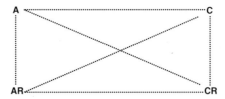

The same principle applies to the physician-patient privilege.

In some situations, the application of multiple privileges can lead to protection of a communication even if a person not necessary to one of the protected relationships is present. Suppose, for example, that a woman accompanies her spouse on a visit to his physician, and is present during her spouse's consultation with the doctor. Even if the woman's presence is not necessary to the provision of medical services to her spouse, the existence of a privilege between spouses will probably lead a court to conclude that the physician-patient privilege, if otherwise applicable, has not been lost merely because the woman was present during the consultation.[7]

Sometimes effective communication is not possible without the assistance of a third person who is not otherwise a part of the protected relationship. For example, if a doctor and her patient do not speak the same language, it

---

7. This result is suggested by proposed Federal Rule 512, which would have provided that a privilege is not waived if the disclosure of a confidential communication "is itself a privileged communication."

might be necessary to employ the services of a translator. The translator's presence during the communication will not, of course, destroy the privilege between physician and patient because the translator is present to facilitate the rendition of professional services. Similarly, if an attorney asks her personal injury client to visit a particular physician for purposes of evaluating the client's medical condition in anticipation of trial, the physician's confidential report to the attorney following the examination will not likely be subject to the physician-patient privilege,[8] but probably will be protected by attorney-client privilege. This is because the doctor has been hired to facilitate the rendition of legal services to the client, not medical services. In a sense, the physician serves as a "translator" of the client's medical condition; without the physician's services, effective communication between client and attorney would not be possible. Even some communications the client never intended to be transmitted directly to the attorney also will be subject to the privilege. For example, a client might provide the attorney's secretary, law clerk, or paralegal with information relevant to the case. Such a communication will also be protected under the attorney-client privilege.

5.   *"Holder" of the Privilege*

The holder of a privilege is the person who has the authority to determine whether the privilege will be asserted or waived. For example, the client is the holder of the attorney-client privilege. The other participant in the confidential communication, the attorney in this example, may have the authority to *assert* the privilege on behalf of the holder, but only the holder may *waive* the privilege. While the holder may give the other party authority to waive the privilege by disclosing the communication, the decision to waive the privilege belongs to the holder alone.

The law determines who holds a privilege. The decision is made on a privilege-by-privilege basis, not on a case-by-case basis. In all jurisdictions, the client is the holder of the attorney-client privilege, and the patient is the holder of the physician-patient and psychotherapist-patient privileges. This is quite sensible, as it resides the privilege in the person who has sought professional services. Some privileges are held by both parties. In California, for example, both spouses are holders of the privilege for confidential communications between spouses. *See* Cal. Evid. Code § 980, Law Revision Commission Comment.

One interesting exception to these general principles can be found in the California privileges protecting clergy and penitents. Rather than designate a holder of a single privilege, the law provides privileges for *both* participants in the communication. *See* Cal. Evid. Code § 1033 (penitent privilege); § 1034 (clergy privilege). In these rules, the law recognizes the practical necessity of establishing a separate privilege for clergy, many of whom by the tenets of their religious practice could not reveal confidential communications even if a court ordered them to do so and threatened to hold them in contempt for failure to comply. Though the same result could have been achieved by making both parties the holders of a single privilege, establishing a separate clergy privilege

---

8. As we discuss later in this chapter, there is no physician-patient privilege when a party places her medical condition in issue.

acknowledges the constitutional value of avoiding state intrusion into religious practice. Proposed Federal Rule 503 would have made the person confiding in the member of the clergy the only holder of the privilege, though the rule also provided that the member of the clergy "may claim the privilege on behalf of the person [and the] authority to do so is presumed in the absence of evidence to the contrary."

6. *"Waiver" of the Privilege*

As we have said, the holder of a privilege is the only one who may decide to waive it. What constitutes waiver? Proposed Federal Rule 511 would have provided for waiver if the holder "voluntarily discloses or consents to disclosure of any significant part of the matter or communication." California Evidence Code § 912(a) provides that a privilege

> is waived with respect to a communication protected by such privilege if any holder of the privilege, without coercion, has disclosed a significant part of the communication or has consented to such disclosure made by anyone. Consent to disclosure is manifested by any statement or other conduct of the holder of the privilege indicating consent to the disclosure, including failure to claim the privilege in any proceeding in which the holder has the legal standing and opportunity to claim the privilege.

Thus, behavior that explicitly or implicitly indicates a willingness to have a communication revealed outside of the privileged relationship will constitute a waiver. In addition, a holder's conduct inconsistent with a desire to maintain a privilege will lead to a waiver. For example, if a patient, having a clear opportunity to do so, fails to object to her physician's sharing confidential information with medical students for educational purposes, she likely will be held to have waived the physician-patient privilege. Similarly, a client who authorizes her attorney to disclose a confidential communication during a contract negotiation has waived the attorney-client privilege.

It is also clear from the above definition that waiver requires voluntary disclosure. This means that a disclosure coerced by an improper threat does not constitute a waiver. Reasonably mistaken disclosure probably should not be treated as voluntary. As with the eavesdropper scenario, if the parties take reasonable steps to preserve the confidentiality of their communications, inadvertent disclosure to a third person should not waive the privilege.

Finally, what if the holder has disclosed only a part of a confidential communication? The rule suggests that voluntary disclosure of a substantial part of a confidential communication will waive the privilege at least as to the remainder of that communication. Some courts go further, and hold that disclosure of a substantial part of a confidential communication constitutes a waiver of all confidential communications regarding the subject matter of the communication voluntarily revealed. As we will see in the section that follows, there is a specific provision in the Federal Rules of Evidence dealing with waiver of the attorney-client privilege.

Further Reading: Edward J. Imwinkelried, The New Wigmore: A Treatise on Evidence: Privileges (2002) (2 vols.); Kenneth S. Broun, *Giving Codification a Second Chance — Testimonial Privileges and the Federal Rules of Evidence*, 53 Hastings L.J. 769-815 (2002); Sanford Levinson, *Testimonial Privileges and the Preferences of Friendship*, 1984 Duke L.J. 631 (1984); David W. Louisell, *Confidentiality, Conformity and Confusion: Privileges in Federal Court Today*, 32 Tul. L. Rev. 101 (1956).

Questions for Classroom Discussion

1. Plaintiff, who has brought a personal injury action, meets with her attorney in a busy pub to discuss Plaintiff's case. Though they speak in hushed tones, their conversation is overheard by Witness, a friend of Defendant, who is sitting at the next table. At trial, Defendant calls Witness to testify about the conversation she overheard. Plaintiff objects on grounds the conversation was privileged. How should the court rule?

2. Defendant, out on bail awaiting trial on a criminal charge, speaks with her attorney about the case using a cellular phone. Unknown to Defendant, a glitch in the signals causes the conversation to be transmitted to Witness, who is located nearby speaking on her own cellular phone. Witness reports the conversation to the police, and the prosecution calls her to testify at trial about what she heard. Defendant objects on grounds of privilege. How should the court rule?

3. Defendant has been charged with murder and is housed in the county jail awaiting trial. In preparation for trial, Defendant meets with her attorney in a conference room provided for that purpose. Unknown to Defendant and her attorney, part of their conversation is overheard by a jail guard who was sitting in the room next to the conference room. At trial, the prosecution calls the employee to testify about the conversation. Plaintiff objects on grounds of privilege. How should the court rule? What if the guard is in plain view but the jail refuses for security purposes to allow prisoners to meet privately with visitors, including lawyers?

4. Breach of contract action. Plaintiff takes Defendant's deposition, and asks Defendant about conversations she had with her attorney. Defendant objects on the basis of the attorney-client privilege. Plaintiff responds that the privilege does not apply because the deposition is part of the discovery process, not the trial, and the rules of evidence do not apply during discovery. If Defendant persists in asserting the objection, should a court grant Plaintiff's motion to compel an answer?

5. Same case. At trial, Defendant calls Secretary, who works for Plaintiff's attorney, and asks Secretary to relate the substance of a meeting between Plaintiff and Plaintiff's attorney during which Secretary

(continued)

took notes. Plaintiff is not in the courtroom when the question is asked. What should Plaintiff's attorney do?

6. Murder prosecution. Prior to trial, Defendant's attorney held a press conference during which she stated, "My client wants everyone to know that he was halfway around the world when this horrible killing took place. He had nothing to do with it." At trial, Defendant admits killing the victim, but defends on the basis of self-defense. The prosecutor calls a reporter who attended the press conference to testify about Defendant's attorney's statement. Defendant makes privilege and hearsay objections. How should the court rule?

D. THE ATTORNEY-CLIENT PRIVILEGE

1. In General

The attorney-client privilege is the "oldest of the privileges for confidential communications," beginning to take shape as early as the sixteenth-century reign of Elizabeth I. 8 Wigmore, Evidence § 2290, at 542 (John T. McNaughton rev. 1961). Understanding how to maintain this privilege is among the most important lessons any law student can learn since, even if the student does not plan to be a courtroom lawyer, attorneys in all aspects of law practice need to protect the confidentiality of their clients' communications.

There are many ways to express the basic elements of the attorney-client privilege. A simple statement of the privilege is found in California Evidence Code § 954:

> [T]he client, whether or not a party, has a privilege to refuse to disclose, and to prevent another from disclosing, a confidential communication between client and lawyer. . . .

Proposed Federal Rule 503(b) states:

> A client has a privilege to refuse to disclose and to prevent any other person from disclosing confidential communications made for the purpose of facilitating the rendition of professional legal services to the client, (1) between himself or his representative and his lawyer or his lawyer's representative, or (2) between his lawyer and the lawyer's representative, or (3) by him or his lawyer to a lawyer representing another in a matter of common interest, or (4) between representatives of the client or between the client and a representative of the client, or (5) between lawyers representing the client.

From these descriptions of the rule, it should be clear that the client is the holder of the attorney-client privilege. As a result, only the client may waive the privilege, and the attorney is obligated to assert the privilege on the client's behalf unless the client has manifested the intent to waive the privilege or has otherwise acted in a manner inconsistent with maintaining the privilege.

Note also that the privilege is limited, in the words of Proposed Federal Rule 503(b), to communications "made for the purpose of facilitating the rendition of professional legal services to the client." This can become an issue when the client consults the attorney in the capacity both of a legal expert and in some other capacity, such as a business advisor. For example, suppose a client engages an attorney in connection with a real estate transaction. Communications between the individuals concerning the legal requirements and effects of the transaction will be within the protection of the privilege. But discussions concerning the financial wisdom of the transaction might well be outside the scope of the privilege even if the participants intended the discussions to be confidential. Another area in which this issue can arise is in connection with tax advice. Some tax advice is clearly legal in nature, while other advice might be characterized by an opponent as calling on the lawyer's business judgment. Often, legal and non-legal advice will be intertwined within the same communications. If it is not possible to separate the two aspects of the communication, courts should err on the side of protection as long as a significant part of the communication called on the lawyer's legal expertise.

2. Definition of Client and Attorney

To be a "client," it is not necessary for the person to have paid the attorney or even reached the point of actually engaging the attorney's services. The rules require simply that the attorney be consulted for the purpose of obtaining legal advice. To hold otherwise would leave unprivileged preliminary discussions about a case between a lawyer and a potential client that often are essential to the client deciding what lawyer to hire and the lawyer deciding what cases to take. This, in turn, would chill the sort of frank discussion necessary to help the attorney assess the prospective client's legal position and give advice. Thus, the law extends the privilege to these preliminary discussions.

The meaning of "client" is not complicated in the case of a natural person who seeks legal services. But when the entity seeking legal advice is a fictional "person" such as a corporation, the definition of *client* becomes problematic. Who speaks for the client corporation for purposes of determining whether a communication is from a client and, therefore, privileged? In the period leading up to the Supreme Court's decision in the case to follow, lower federal courts took a number of approaches. Observers had hoped that the Court would resolve the issue clearly. As you will see from the decision, the Court failed to do so.

UPJOHN CO. v. UNITED STATES
449 U.S. 393 (1981)

Justice REHNQUIST delivered the opinion of the Court.

We granted certiorari in this case to address important questions concerning the scope of the attorney-client privilege in the corporate context and the applicability of the work-product doctrine in proceedings to enforce tax summonses. . . . With respect to the privilege question the parties and various *amici* have described our task as one of choosing between two "tests" which have gained adherents in the courts of appeals. We are acutely aware, however, that we sit to decide concrete cases and not abstract propositions of law. We decline to lay down a broad rule or series of rules to govern all conceivable future questions in this area, even were we able to do so. We can and do, however, conclude that the attorney-client privilege protects the communications involved in this case from compelled disclosure and that the work-product doctrine does apply in tax summons enforcement proceedings.

I

Petitioner Upjohn Co. manufactures and sells pharmaceuticals here and abroad. In January 1976 independent accountants conducting an audit of one of Upjohn's foreign subsidiaries discovered that the subsidiary made payments to or for the benefit of foreign government officials in order to secure government business. The accountants so informed petitioner, Mr. Gerard Thomas, Upjohn's Vice President, Secretary, and General Counsel. Thomas is a member of the Michigan and New York Bars, and has been Upjohn's General Counsel for 20 years. He consulted with outside counsel and R. T. Parfet, Jr., Upjohn's Chairman of the Board. It was decided that the company would conduct an internal investigation of what were termed "questionable payments." As part of this investigation the attorneys prepared a letter containing a questionnaire which was sent to "All Foreign General and Area Managers" over the Chairman's signature. The letter began by noting recent disclosures that several American companies made "possibly illegal" payments to foreign government officials and emphasized that the management needed full information concerning any such payments made by Upjohn. The letter indicated that the Chairman had asked Thomas, identified as "the company's General Counsel," "to conduct an investigation for the purpose of determining the nature and magnitude of any payments made by the Upjohn Company or any of its subsidiaries to any employee or official of a foreign government." The questionnaire sought detailed information concerning such payments. Managers were instructed to treat the investigation as "highly confidential" and not to discuss it with anyone other than Upjohn employees who might be helpful in providing the requested information. Responses were to be sent directly to Thomas. Thomas and outside counsel also interviewed the recipients of the questionnaire and some 33 other Upjohn officers or employees as part of the investigation.

On March 26, 1976, the company voluntarily submitted a preliminary report to the Securities and Exchange Commission on Form 8-K disclosing certain questionable payments. A copy of the report was simultaneously submitted to the Internal Revenue Service, which immediately began an investigation to determine the tax consequences of the payments. Special agents conducting the investigation were given lists by Upjohn of all those interviewed and all who had responded to the questionnaire. On November 23, 1976, the Service issued a summons pursuant to 26 U.S.C. § 7602 demanding production of:

> All files relative to the investigation conducted under the supervision of Gerard
> Thomas to identify payments to employees of foreign governments and any

political contributions made by the Upjohn Company or any of its affiliates since January 1, 1971 and to determine whether any funds of the Upjohn Company had been improperly accounted for on the corporate books during the same period.

   The records should include but not be limited to written questionnaires sent to managers of the Upjohn Company's foreign affiliates, and memorandums or notes of the interviews conducted in the United States and abroad with officers and employees of the Upjohn Company and its subsidiaries.

The company declined to produce the documents specified in the second paragraph on the grounds that they were protected from disclosure by the attorney-client privilege and constituted the work product of attorneys prepared in anticipation of litigation. On August 31, 1977, the United States filed a petition seeking enforcement of the summons under 26 U.S.C. §§ 7402(b) and 7604(a) in the United States District Court for the Western District of Michigan. That court adopted the recommendation of a Magistrate who concluded that the summons should be enforced. Petitioners appealed to the Court of Appeals for the Sixth Circuit which rejected the Magistrate's finding of a waiver of the attorney-client privilege, . . . but agreed that the privilege did not apply "[t]o the extent that the communications were made by officers and agents not responsible for directing Upjohn's actions in response to legal advice . . . for the simple reason that the communications were not the 'client's.'" . . . The court reasoned that accepting petitioners' claim for a broader application of the privilege would encourage upper-echelon management to ignore unpleasant facts and create too broad a "zone of silence." Noting that Upjohn's counsel had interviewed officials such as the Chairman and President, the Court of Appeals remanded to the District Court so that a determination of who was within the "control group" could be made. In a concluding footnote the court stated that the work-product doctrine "is not applicable to administrative summonses issued under 26 U.S.C. § 7602." . . .

II

Federal Rule of Evidence 501 provides that "the privilege of a witness . . . shall be governed by the principles of the common law as they may be interpreted by the courts of the United States in light of reason and experience." The attorney-client privilege is the oldest of the privileges for confidential communications known to the common law. 8 J. Wigmore, Evidence § 2290 (McNaughton rev. 1961). Its purpose is to encourage full and frank communication between attorneys and their clients and thereby promote broader public interests in the observance of law and administration of justice. The privilege recognizes that sound legal advice or advocacy serves public ends and that such advice or advocacy depends upon the lawyer's being fully informed by the client. As we stated last Term in Trammel v. United States, 445 U.S. 40, 51, 100 S. Ct. 906, 913, 63 L. Ed. 2d 186 (1980): "The lawyer-client privilege rests on the need for the advocate and counselor to know all that relates to the client's reasons for seeking representation if the professional mission is to be carried out." . . .

   The Court of Appeals, however, considered the application of the privilege in the corporate context to present a "different problem," since the client was an inanimate entity and "only the senior management, guiding and integrating the several operations, . . . can be said to possess an identity analogous to the corporation as a whole." . . . The first case to articulate the so-called "control group test" adopted by the court below, Philadelphia v. Westinghouse Electric Corp., 210 F. Supp. 483, 485 (ED Pa.), *petition for mandamus and prohibition denied sub nom.* General Electric Co. v. Kirkpatrick, 312 F.2d 742 (CA3 1962), *cert. denied,* 372 U.S. 943, 83 S. Ct. 937, 9 L. Ed. 2d 969 (1963), reflected a similar conceptual approach:

> "Keeping in mind that the question is, Is it the corporation which is seeking the lawyer's advice when the asserted privileged communication is made?, the most satisfactory solution, I think, is that if the employee making the communication, of whatever rank he may be, is in a position to control or even to take a substantial part in a decision about any action which the corporation may take upon the advice of the attorney, . . . then, in effect, *he is (or personifies) the corporation* when he makes his disclosure to the lawyer and the privilege would apply." (Emphasis supplied.)

Such a view, we think, overlooks the fact that the privilege exists to protect not only the giving of professional advice to those who can act on it but also the giving of information to the lawyer to enable him to give sound and informed advice. . . . The first step in the resolution of any legal problem is ascertaining the factual background and sifting through the facts with an eye to the legally relevant. . . .

> In the case of the individual client the provider of information and the person who acts on the lawyer's advice are one and the same. In the corporate context, however, it will frequently be employees beyond the control group as defined by the court below — "officers and agents . . . responsible for directing [the company's] actions in response to legal advice" — who will possess the information needed by the corporation's lawyers. Middle-level — and indeed lower-level — employees can, by actions within the scope of their employment, embroil the corporation in serious legal difficulties, and it is only natural that these employees would have the relevant information needed by corporate counsel if he is adequately to advise the client with respect to such actual or potential difficulties. . . .

The control group test adopted by the court below thus frustrates the very purpose of the privilege by discouraging the communication of relevant information by employees of the client to attorneys seeking to render legal advice to the client corporation. The attorney's advice will also frequently be more significant to noncontrol group members than to those who officially sanction the advice, and the control group test makes it more difficult to convey full and frank legal advice to the employees who will put into effect the client corporation's policy. . . .

The communications at issue were made by Upjohn employees to counsel for Upjohn acting as such, at the direction of corporate superiors in order to secure legal advice from counsel. As the Magistrate found, "Mr. Thomas consulted with the Chairman of the Board and outside counsel and thereafter conducted a factual investigation to determine the nature and extent of the questionable payments *and to be in a position to give legal advice to the company with respect to the payments.*" (Emphasis supplied.) Information, not available from upper-echelon management, was needed to supply a basis for legal advice concerning compliance with securities and tax laws, foreign laws, currency regulations, duties to shareholders, and potential litigation in each of these areas. The communications concerned matters within the scope of the employees' corporate duties, and the employees themselves were sufficiently aware that they were being questioned in order that the corporation could obtain legal advice . . . .

The Court of Appeals declined to extend the attorney-client privilege beyond the limits of the control group test for fear that doing so would entail severe burdens on discovery and create a broad "zone of silence" over corporate affairs. Application of the attorney-client privilege to communications such as those involved here, however, puts the adversary in no worse position than if the communications had never taken place. The privilege only protects disclosure of communications; it does not protect disclosure of the underlying facts by those who communicated with the attorney:

> "[T]he protection of the privilege extends only to *communications* and not to facts. A fact is one thing and a communication concerning that fact is an entirely different thing. The client cannot be compelled to answer the question, 'What did you say or write to the attorney?' but may not refuse to disclose any relevant fact within his knowledge merely because he incorporated a statement of such fact into his communication to his attorney." . . . Philadelphia v. Westinghouse Electric Corp., 205 F. Supp. 830, 831.

. . . Here the Government was free to question the employees who communicated with Thomas and outside counsel. Upjohn has provided the IRS with a list of such employees, and the IRS has already interviewed some 25 of them. While it would probably be more convenient for the Government to secure the results of petitioner's internal investigation by simply subpoenaing the questionnaires and notes taken by petitioner's attorneys, such considerations of convenience do not overcome the policies served by the attorney-client privilege. As Justice Jackson noted in his concurring opinion in Hickman v. Taylor, 329 U.S., at 516, 67 S. Ct., at 396: "Discovery was hardly intended to enable a learned profession to perform its functions . . . on wits borrowed from the adversary."

Needless to say, we decide only the case before us, and do not undertake to draft a set of rules which should govern challenges to investigatory subpoenas. Any such approach would violate the spirit of Federal Rule of Evidence 501. . . . While such a "case-by-case" basis may to some slight extent undermine desirable certainty in the boundaries of the attorney-client privilege, it obeys the spirit of the Rules. At the same time we conclude that the narrow "control group test" sanctioned by the Court of Appeals, in this case cannot, consistent with "the principles of the common law as . . . interpreted . . . in the light of reason and experience," Fed. Rule Evid. 501, govern the development of the law in this area.

III . . .

Accordingly, the judgment of the Court of Appeals is reversed, and the case remanded for further proceedings.

It is so ordered.

Chief Justice BURGER, concurring in part and concurring in the judgment.

I join in Parts I and III of the opinion of the Court and in the judgment. As to Part II, I agree fully with the Court's rejection of the so-called "control group" test, its reasons for doing so, and its ultimate holding that the communications at issue are privileged. As the Court states, however, "if the purpose of the attorney-client privilege is to be served, the attorney and client must be able to predict with some degree of certainty whether particular discussions will be protected." For this very reason, I believe that we should articulate a standard that will govern similar cases and afford guidance to corporations, counsel advising them, and federal courts.

The Court properly relies on a variety of factors in concluding that the communications now before us are privileged. Because of the great importance of the issue, in my view the Court should make clear now that, as a general rule, a communication is privileged at least when, as here, an employee or former employee speaks at the direction of the management with an attorney regarding conduct or proposed conduct within the scope of employment. The attorney must be one authorized by the management to inquire into the subject and must be seeking information to assist counsel in performing any of the following functions: (a) evaluating whether the employee's conduct has bound or would bind the corporation; (b) assessing the legal consequences, if any, of that conduct; or (c) formulating appropriate legal responses to actions that have been or may be taken by others with regard to that conduct. . . . Other communications between employees and corporate counsel may indeed be privileged—as the petitioners and several *amici* have suggested in their proposed formulations—but the need for certainty does not compel us now to prescribe all the details of the privilege in this case.

Upjohn shows how difficult it can be to determine who qualifies as the "client" for purposes of applying the attorney-client privilege. Surprisingly, even the definition of *attorney* is not always what we might expect. Some rules do not even require that the person consulted actually be licensed to practice law to be classified as an attorney for purposes of the privilege. For example, proposed Federal Rule 503(a)(2) defines a *lawyer* as "a person authorized, or reasonably believed to be authorized, to practice law in any state or nation." The California definition is almost identical. (*See* Cal. Evid. Code § 950.) In a jurisdiction employing such a definition, a good liar with no legal training is a lawyer for privilege purposes if the client reasonably believed the individual was licensed to practice law.

The reason for this broad definition of attorney is to protect a would-be client from loss of the privilege when reliance on the "attorney's" representations is reasonable. It would not be fair to penalize a person for such reliance.

Questions for Classroom Discussion

1. Following an automobile accident, Plaintiff consulted Attorney 1, an attorney licensed to practice in another state, about representing her. They spoke in Attorney 1's office. After hearing the facts of

the case, Attorney 1 declined to represent Plaintiff. Plaintiff found another lawyer, Attorney 2, to take her case. Prior to trial, Defendant takes Attorney 1's deposition and asks about the conversation with Plaintiff. Attorney 2 claims Plaintiff's attorney-client privilege and Attorney 1 refuses to answer. How should the court rule on Defendant's motion to compel Attorney 1's answers?

2. Same case. At trial, Plaintiff calls Defendant and asks Defendant whether her attorney suggested that Defendant try to settle the case. Defendant objects on grounds of attorney-client privilege. Plaintiff responds that because she is not seeking disclosure of Defendant's communications with the attorney, but only the attorney's communications with Defendant, the privilege does not apply. How should the court rule?

3. Same case. A few weeks before trial, Plaintiff meets Attorney 2 at Attorney 2's office to go over Plaintiff's expected testimony. During the meeting, Zed, Attorney 2's secretary, is in the office taking notes. In the course of the conversation, Plaintiff says to Attorney 2, "I might have taken my eyes off the road for a moment, but I was distracted by a sudden noise from the car next to me." Zed, dissatisfied with his salary, goes to Defendant's attorney and tells the attorney about the conversation between Attorney 2 and Plaintiff. Defendant wishes to have Zed testify at trial about the conversation. Plaintiff objects. How should the court rule?

4. Same case. At trial, Defendant calls Plaintiff and asks whether Plaintiff ever took her eyes off the road in the moments before the accident. Plaintiff objects on grounds of attorney-client privilege. How should the court rule?

5. Same case. At trial, Defendant calls Attorney 2 and asks whether Plaintiff ever took her eyes off the road in the moments before the accident. Plaintiff objects on grounds of attorney-client privilege. How should the court rule? What other objection might Plaintiff make?

6. Same case. Suppose that Attorney 2's office door was open during the conversation mentioned in Question 3. When Plaintiff made the admission about being distracted, a courier from Defendant's lawyer happened to be in the corridor dropping off a settlement offer, and overheard Plaintiff's statement. At trial, Defendant wishes to have the courier testify about Plaintiff's statement. Plaintiff objects on privilege and hearsay grounds. How should the court rule?

7. Same case. Suppose that a summer associate in Attorney 2's office was in the room during the meeting. The summer associate is not working on Plaintiff's case, nor was she expecting to be involved. Attorney 2 asked her to be there to observe how one prepares a

(continued)

witness for her trial testimony. Defendant learns of the summer associate's presence and seeks to compel her testimony at trial. Plaintiff objects. How should the court rule?

8. Prosecution of Defendant for murder. Defendant brought her husband along for a meeting with her attorney, and the husband heard the entire conversation. At trial, the prosecution calls the husband to testify about the conversation between Defendant and her attorney. Defendant objects on privilege grounds. How should the court rule?

9. Why shouldn't all confidential communications between a corporate employee and the corporation's attorney be subject to attorney-client privilege, assuming the conversation concerns the corporation's legal matters?

10. Why did the Court in *Upjohn* reject the "control group" test for attorney-client privilege in the corporate context?

11. Negligence action by Plaintiff against Defendant, a corporation in the package delivery business. Plaintiff alleges that one of Defendant's trucks ran over Plaintiff while Plaintiff was in a crosswalk. At trial, Plaintiff calls Driver, the driver of the delivery truck that struck Plaintiff, and asks Driver to relate what she said to Defendant's attorney during a confidential interview following the accident. Defendant objects on hearsay and privilege grounds. How should the court rule?

3. Survival of Attorney-Client Privilege After Death of Client

Does the privilege survive the death of the client? If the primary purpose of the attorney-client privilege is to encourage frank communication, it probably makes sense to hold that the privilege does not expire when the client dies. This is because some people will be reluctant to speak frankly with their attorneys if they know that at *any* point in the future, even after they die, the attorney can be forced to reveal the communication. Similarly, if one accepts the view that the purpose of the attorney-client privilege is to protect the privacy of individuals who enter into such relationships, the privilege's protection should not end when the client dies. On the other hand, privileges often thwart the truth-determination process. Though the policy of encouraging frank communication might well outweigh the need for accurate fact-finding while the individual client is alive or the organizational client still exists, it might not outweigh that important concern once the client is no longer in existence.

Little empirical data exists to validate or challenge the assumption that the threat of disclosure will chill frank attorney-client communications. Given this, it is not possible to determine the degree to which the potential for disclosure after death will chill frank communication from client to attorney.

One approach is to hold that the privilege survives until all legal matters involving the deceased client have been resolved. This would have been the effect of the proposed federal rule,[9] and it is the law in California.[10] Most courts, however, appear to hold that the privilege survives even after all legal matters involving the former client have been resolved. The Supreme Court addressed the question in 1998 in a case arising out of the investigation of President Bill Clinton by Kenneth Starr, who was appointed Independent Counsel to investigate the suicide of deputy White House counsel, Vince Foster. The investigation later was expanded to include, among other things, the affair between the President and Monica Lewinsky, which featured prominently in the efforts to impeach Clinton.

SWIDLER & BERLIN v. UNITED STATES
524 U.S. 399 (1998)

Chief Justice REHNQUIST delivered the opinion of the Court.

Petitioner, James Hamilton, an attorney, made notes of an initial interview with a client shortly before the client's death. The Government, represented by the Office of Independent Counsel, now seeks his notes for use in a criminal investigation. We hold that the notes are protected by the attorney-client privilege.

This dispute arises out of an investigation conducted by the Office of the Independent Counsel into whether various individuals made false statements, obstructed justice, or committed other crimes during investigations of the 1993 dismissal of employees from the White House Travel Office. Vincent W. Foster, Jr., was Deputy White House Counsel when the firings occurred. In July 1993, Foster met with petitioner Hamilton, an attorney at petitioner Swidler & Berlin, to seek legal representation concerning possible congressional or other investigations of the firings. During a 2-hour meeting, Hamilton took three pages of handwritten notes. One of the first entries in the notes is the word "Privileged." Nine days later, Foster committed suicide.

In December 1995, a federal grand jury, at the request of the Independent Counsel, issued subpoenas to petitioners Hamilton and Swidler & Berlin for, *inter alia*, Hamilton's handwritten notes of his meeting with Foster. Petitioners filed a motion to quash, arguing that the notes were protected by the attorney-client privilege and by the work-product privilege. The District Court, after examining the notes *in camera*, concluded they were protected from disclosure by both doctrines and denied enforcement of the subpoenas.

The Court of Appeals for the District of Columbia Circuit reversed. . . . While recognizing that most courts assume the privilege survives death, the Court of Appeals noted that holdings actually manifesting the posthumous force of the privilege are rare. . . .

. . . [W]e now reverse. . . .

The Independent Counsel argues that the attorney-client privilege should not prevent disclosure of confidential communications where the client has died

---

9. Proposed Federal Rule 503(c) would have allowed the privilege to be claimed "by the client, his guardian or conservator, the personal representative of a deceased client, or the successor, trustee, or similar representative of a corporation, association, or other organization, whether or not in existence." By implication, when none of these successors exists, the privilege ceases to exist as well.

10. Cal. Evid. Code § 953 is similar to the proposed federal rule.

and the information is relevant to a criminal proceeding. There is some authority for this position. One state appellate court, Cohen v. Jenkintown Cab Co., 238 Pa. Super. 456, 357 A.2d 689 (1976), and the Court of Appeals below have held the privilege may be subject to posthumous exceptions in certain circumstances. In *Cohen*, a civil case, the court recognized that the privilege generally survives death, but concluded that it could make an exception where the interest of justice was compelling and the interest of the client in preserving the confidence was insignificant. *Id.*, at 462-464, 357 A.2d, at 692-693.

But other than these two decisions, cases addressing the existence of the privilege after death — most involving the testamentary exception — uniformly presume the privilege survives, even if they do not so hold. . . .

Such testamentary exception cases consistently presume the privilege survives. . . . They view testamentary disclosure of communications as an exception to the privilege: "[T]he general rule with respect to confidential communications . . . is that such communications are privileged during the testator's lifetime and, also, after the testator's death unless sought to be disclosed in litigation between the testator's heirs." . . . The rationale for such disclosure is that it furthers the client's intent.[2] . . .

The great body of this case law supports, either by holding or considered dicta, the position that the privilege does survive in a case such as the present one. Given the language of Rule 501, at the very least the burden is on the Independent Counsel to show that "reason and experience" require a departure from this rule.

The Independent Counsel contends that the testamentary exception supports the posthumous termination of the privilege because in practice most cases have refused to apply the privilege posthumously. He further argues that the exception reflects a policy judgment that the interest in settling estates outweighs any posthumous interest in confidentiality. He then reasons by analogy that in criminal proceedings, the interest in determining whether a crime has been committed should trump client confidentiality, particularly since the financial interests of the estate are not at stake.

But the Independent Counsel's interpretation simply does not square with the case law's implicit acceptance of the privilege's survival and with the treatment of testamentary disclosure as an "exception" or an implied "waiver." And the premise of his analogy is incorrect, since cases consistently recognize that the rationale for the testamentary exception is that it furthers the client's intent. . . . There is no reason to suppose as a general matter that grand jury testimony about confidential communications furthers the client's intent. . . .

---

2. About half the States have codified the testamentary exception by providing that a personal representative of the deceased can waive the privilege when heirs or devisees claim through the deceased client (as opposed to parties claiming against the estate, for whom the privilege is not waived). *See, e.g.,* Ala. Rule Evid. 502 (1996); Ark. Code Ann. § 16-41-101, Rule 502 (Supp. 1997); Neb. Rev. Stat. § 27-503, Rule 503 (1995). These statutes do not address expressly the continuation of the privilege outside the context of testamentary disputes, although many allow the attorney to assert the privilege on behalf of the client apparently without temporal limit. *See, e.g.,* Ark. Code Ann. § 16-41-101, Rule 502(c) (Supp. 1997). They thus do not refute or affirm the general presumption in the case law that the privilege survives. California's statute is exceptional in that it apparently allows the attorney to assert the privilege only so long as a holder of the privilege (the estate's personal representative) exists, suggesting the privilege terminates when the estate is wound up. *See* Cal. Code Evid. Ann. §§ 954, 957 (West 1995). But no other State has followed California's lead in this regard.

[W]e think there are weighty reasons that counsel in favor of posthumous application. Knowing that communications will remain confidential even after death encourages the client to communicate fully and frankly with counsel. While the fear of disclosure, and the consequent withholding of information from counsel, may be reduced if disclosure is limited to posthumous disclosure in a criminal context, it seems unreasonable to assume that it vanishes altogether. Clients may be concerned about reputation, civil liability, or possible harm to friends or family. Posthumous disclosure of such communications may be as feared as disclosure during the client's lifetime.

The Independent Counsel suggests, however, that his proposed exception would have little to no effect on the client's willingness to confide in his attorney. He reasons that only clients intending to perjure themselves will be chilled by a rule of disclosure after death, as opposed to truthful clients or those asserting their Fifth Amendment privilege. This is because for the latter group, communications disclosed by the attorney after the client's death purportedly will reveal only information that the client himself would have revealed if alive.

The Independent Counsel assumes, incorrectly we believe, that the privilege is analogous to the Fifth Amendment's protection against self-incrimination. But as suggested above, the privilege serves much broader purposes. Clients consult attorneys for a wide variety of reasons, only one of which involves possible criminal liability. Many attorneys act as counselors on personal and family matters, where, in the course of obtaining the desired advice, confidences about family members or financial problems must be revealed in order to assure sound legal advice. The same is true of owners of small businesses who may regularly consult their attorneys about a variety of problems arising in the course of the business. These confidences may not come close to any sort of admission of criminal wrongdoing, but nonetheless be matters which the client would not wish divulged.

The contention that the attorney is being required to disclose only what the client could have been required to disclose is at odds with the basis for the privilege even during the client's lifetime. In related cases, we have said that the loss of evidence admittedly caused by the privilege is justified in part by the fact that without the privilege, the client may not have made such communications in the first place. . . . This is true of disclosure before and after the client's death. Without assurance of the privilege's posthumous application, the client may very well not have made disclosures to his attorney at all, so the loss of evidence is more apparent than real. In the case at hand, it seems quite plausible that Foster, perhaps already contemplating suicide, may not have sought legal advice from Hamilton if he had not been assured the conversation was privileged. . . .

Finally, the Independent Counsel, relying on cases such as United States v. Nixon, 418 U.S. 683, 710, 94 S. Ct. 3090, 3108, 41 L. Ed. 2d 1039 (1974), and Branzburg v. Hayes, 408 U.S. 665, 92 S. Ct. 2646, 33 L. Ed. 2d 626 (1972), urges that privileges be strictly construed because they are inconsistent with the paramount judicial goal of truth seeking. But both *Nixon* and *Branzburg* dealt with the creation of privileges not recognized by the common law, whereas here we deal with one of the oldest recognized privileges in the law. And we are asked, not simply to "construe" the privilege, but to narrow it, contrary to the weight of the existing body of case law.

It has been generally, if not universally, accepted, for well over a century, that the attorney-client privilege survives the death of the client in a case such as this. While the arguments against the survival of the privilege are by no means frivolous, they are based in large part on speculation — thoughtful speculation, but speculation nonetheless — as to whether posthumous termination of the privilege would diminish a client's willingness to confide in an attorney. In an area where empirical information would be useful, it is scant and inconclusive.

Rule 501's direction to look to "the principles of the common law as they may be interpreted by the courts of the United States in the light of reason and experience" does not mandate that a rule, once established, should endure for all time. . . . But here the Independent Counsel has simply not made a sufficient showing to overturn the common-law rule embodied in the prevailing case law. Interpreted in the light of reason and experience, that body of law requires that the attorney-client privilege prevent disclosure of the notes at issue in this case. The judgment of the Court of Appeals is
Reversed.

Justice O'CONNOR, with whom Justice SCALIA and Justice THOMAS join, dissenting.

Although the attorney-client privilege ordinarily will survive the death of the client, I do not agree with the Court that it inevitably precludes disclosure of a deceased client's communications in criminal proceedings. In my view, a criminal defendant's right to exculpatory evidence or a compelling law enforcement need for information may, where the testimony is not available from other sources, override a client's posthumous interest in confidentiality. . . .

Question for Classroom Discussion

1. In *Swidler & Berlin*, why did the Supreme Court hold that the attorney-client privilege survives the client's death?

2. What would be the effect on the attorney-client privilege if the Court had adopted the position taken by Justice O'Connor in her dissenting opinion in *Swidler & Berlin*? What would attorneys representing criminal defendants be required to tell their clients?

---

4. Exceptions to the Attorney-Client Privilege

Proposed Federal Rule 503(d) sets forth the following exceptions to the attorney-client privilege:

(d) Exceptions. There is no privilege under this rule:
(1) *Furtherance of crime or fraud.* If the services of the lawyer were sought or obtained to enable or aid anyone to commit or plan to commit what the client knew or reasonably should have known to be a crime or fraud; or
(2) *Claimants through same deceased client.* As to a communication relevant to an issue between parties who claim through the same deceased client, regardless of whether the claims are by testate or intestate succession or by *inter vivos* transaction; or

(3) *Breach of duty by lawyer or client.* As to a communication relevant to an issue of breach of duty by the lawyer to his client or by the client to his lawyer; or

(4) *Documents attested by lawyer.* As to a communication relevant to an issue concerning an attested document to which the lawyer is an attesting witness; or

(5) *Joint clients.* As to a communication relevant to a matter of common interest between two or more clients if the communication was made by any of them to a lawyer retained or consulted in common, when offered in an action between any of the clients.

As the Advisory Committee Note to Rule 503 states, these are all "well established" exceptions. Exception (3), for example, would allow disclosure in malpractice suits by the client against the attorney, as well as in actions brought by the attorney against the client, such as a suit to recover unpaid fees. Exception (4) would apply, for example, when the lawyer is an attesting witness to the client's will; in such circumstances, "the approval of the client to [the lawyer's testimony] may be safely assumed, and waiver of the privilege as to any relevant lawyer-client communications is a proper result." *Id.*

The exception that has received the most attention is the crime-fraud exception. It is clear that a client does not deserve the protection of privilege where she employs an attorney to assist in the commission of a crime or fraud. Society has nothing to gain, and much to lose, from the employment of attorneys for such purposes, and there should be no expectation of privacy with regard to communications that have such an objective.

But it is often difficult to determine the purpose of a client's communications. Because protected attorney-client communications usually take place in private, even general information about their purpose will be hard to come by. And even if such general information exists, it may be ambiguous and insufficient to allow a court to conclude with any reasonable degree of certainty whether the client had a legitimate or illegitimate purpose.

Sometimes circumstantial evidence will support a reasonable inference about the client's purpose. But the significance of that circumstantial evidence also can be ambiguous. For example, suppose a client being sought by law enforcement concerning a serious crime is seen in her attorney's office. The client then disappears, never returning to her home or place of work. Those circumstances might lead an observer to believe that the client sought the attorney's help in taking flight. On the other hand, it might also be reasonable to conclude that the client found the attorney's legitimate legal advice troubling and fled on her own. Similarly, if a client under suspicion of committing a shotgun murder is seen entering his attorney's office with a long, narrow package, and the package is never again seen, it might be reasonable to suspect that the client sought the attorney's assistance in disposing of evidence, which is a crime. But even under these circumstances, there may be a benign explanation for the package.

Sometimes, however, an opponent will be in possession of detailed information about the attorney-client communication or even a rendition of the communication itself in tangible form, such as a recording or transcript. In such a case it is easy to determine the client's purpose in consulting the attorney by simply reading the transcript or listening to the recording. But there is a legal obstacle to pursuing this practical solution to the problem. Recall the final sentence of Rule 104(a): "In so deciding [admissibility], the court is not bound by evidence rules, except those on privilege." What is the meaning of that sentence? From our discussion of the so-called bootstrapping problem in Chapter 3, we already know that in other situations, the court *may* consider the evidence at issue in determining its own admissibility. For example, where the declarant/victim said, "I am a goner . . . Joe murdered me," the court may conclude that the evidence is admissible under Rule 804(b)(2), the dying declaration exception, relying just on the statement itself to conclude that the declarant believed her death was imminent.

Does the final sentence of Rule 104(a) mean that this is improper when the admissibility issue involves a privilege? In 1989, the Supreme Court addressed that question in a case involving the Church of Scientology.

UNITED STATES v. ZOLIN
491 U.S. 554 (1989)

Justice BLACKMUN delivered the opinion of the Court.

This case arises out of the efforts of the Criminal Investigation Division of the Internal Revenue Service (IRS) to investigate the tax returns of L. Ron Hubbard, founder of the Church of Scientology (the Church), for the calendar years 1979 through 1983. . . .

. . . The specific question presented is whether the applicability of the crime-fraud exception must be established by "independent evidence" (i.e., without reference to the content of the contested communications themselves), or, alternatively, whether the applicability of that exception can be resolved by an *in camera* inspection of the allegedly privileged material. We reject the "independent evidence" approach and hold that the district court, under circumstances we explore below, and at the behest of the party opposing the claim of privilege, may conduct an *in camera* review of the materials in question. Because the Court of Appeals considered only "independent evidence," we vacate its judgment on this issue and remand the case for further proceedings.

In the course of its investigation, the IRS sought access to 51 documents that had been filed with the Clerk of the Los Angeles County Superior Court in connection with a case entitled Church of Scientology of California v. Armstrong, No. C420 153. The *Armstrong* litigation involved, among other things, a charge by the Church that one of its former members, Gerald Armstrong, had obtained by unlawful means documentary materials relating to Church activities, including two tapes. Some of the documents sought by the IRS had been filed under seal.

The IRS, by its Special Agent Steven Petersell, served a summons upon the Clerk on October 24, 1984, pursuant to 26 U.S.C. § 7603, demanding that he produce the 51 documents. The tapes were among those listed. . . . On November 21, IRS agents were permitted to inspect and copy some of the summoned materials, including the tapes. . . .

Respondents asserted the privilege as a bar to disclosure of the tapes. The IRS argued, among other things, however, that the tapes fell within the crime-fraud exception to the attorney-client privilege, and urged the District Court to listen to the tapes in the course of making its privilege determination. In addition, the IRS submitted to the court two declarations by Agent Petersell. In the first, Petersell stated his grounds for believing that the tapes were relevant to the investigation. In the second, Petersell offered a description of the tapes' contents, based on information he received during several interviews. Appended to this declaration—over respondents' objection—were partial transcripts of the tapes, which the IRS lawfully had obtained from a confidential source. *See* March 15, 1985, declaration (filed under seal).[5] In subsequent briefing, the IRS reiterated its request that the District Court listen to the tapes *in camera* before making its privilege ruling. . . .

Turning to the tapes, the District Court ruled that respondents had demonstrated that they contain confidential attorney-client communications, that the privilege had not been waived, and that "[t]he 'fraud-crime' exception to the attorney-client privilege does not apply. . . ."

Respondents appealed to the Court of Appeals for the Ninth Circuit, and the IRS cross-appealed. . . .

The panel of the Court of Appeals agreed with respondents that, under *Shewfelt,* "the Government's evidence of crime or fraud must come from sources independent of the attorney-client communications recorded on the tapes." . . . On the basis of its review of the "independent evidence," the Court of Appeals affirmed the District Court's determination that the IRS had failed to establish the applicability of the crime-fraud exception. . . .

III . . .

[T]he remaining obstacle to respondents' successful assertion of the privilege is the Government's contention that the recorded attorney-client communications were made in furtherance of a future crime or fraud.

[T]he initial question in this case is whether a district court, at the request of the party opposing the privilege, may review the allegedly privileged communications *in camera* to determine whether the crime-fraud exception applies. If such *in camera* review is permitted, the second question we must consider is whether some threshold evidentiary showing is needed before the district court may undertake the requested review. Finally, if a threshold showing is required, we must consider the type of evidence the opposing party may use to meet it: i.e., in this case, whether the partial transcripts the IRS possessed may be used for that purpose.

A

We consider first the question whether a district court may *ever* honor the request of the party opposing the privilege to conduct an *in camera* review of allegedly privileged communications to determine whether those communications fall within the crime-fraud exception. We conclude that no express provision of the Federal Rules of Evidence bars such use of *in camera* review, and that it would be unwise to prohibit it in all instances as a matter of federal common law.

(1)

At first blush, two provisions of the Federal Rules of Evidence would appear to be relevant. Rule 104(a) provides: "Preliminary questions concerning the

5. The IRS denied that the transcripts were made using tapes obtained from the Superior Court or from any other illicit source. . . . As the District Court made no finding of illegality, we assume for present purposes that the transcripts were legally obtained.

qualification of a person to be a witness, *the existence of a privilege*, or the admissibility of evidence shall be determined by the court. . . . In making its determination it is not bound by the rules of evidence *except those with respect to privileges*." (Emphasis added.) Rule 1101(c) provides: "The rule with respect to privileges applies at all stages of all actions, cases, and proceedings." Taken together, these Rules might be read to establish that in a summons-enforcement proceeding, attorney-client communications cannot be considered by the district court in making its crime-fraud ruling: to do otherwise, under this view, would be to make the crime-fraud determination without due regard to the existence of the privilege.

Even those scholars who support this reading of Rule 104(a) acknowledge that it leads to an absurd result. . . .

We find this Draconian interpretation of Rule 104(a) inconsistent with the Rule's plain language. The Rule does not provide by its terms that all materials as to which a "clai[m] of privilege" is made must be excluded from consideration. In that critical respect, the language of Rule 104(a) is markedly different from the comparable California evidence rule, which provides that "the presiding officer may not require disclosure of information *claimed to be privileged* under this division in order to rule on the claim of privilege." Cal. Evid. Code Ann. § 915(a) (West Supp. 1989) (emphasis added). There is no reason to read Rule 104(a) as if its text were identical to that of the California rule.

Nor does it make sense to us to assume, as respondents have throughout this litigation, that once the attorney-client nature of the contested communications is established, those communications must be treated as *presumptively* privileged for evidentiary purposes until the privilege is "defeated" or "stripped away" by proof that the communications took place in the course of planning future crime or fraud. . . .

We see no basis for holding that the tapes in this case must be deemed privileged under Rule 104(a) while the question of crime or fraud remains open. Indeed, respondents concede that "if the *proponent* of the privilege is able to sustain its burden only by submitting the communications to the court" for *in camera* review, the court is not required to avert its eyes (or close its ears) once it concludes that the communication would be privileged, if the court found the crime-fraud exception inapplicable. Rather, respondents acknowledge that the court may "then consider the same communications to determine if the opponent of the privilege has established that the crime-fraud exception applies." Were the tapes truly deemed privileged under Rule 104(a) at the moment the trial court concludes they contain potentially privileged attorney-client communications, district courts would be required to draw precisely the counterintuitive distinction that respondents wisely reject. We thus shall not adopt a reading of Rule 104(a) that would treat the contested communications as "privileged" for purposes of the Rule, and we shall not interpret Rule 104(a) as categorically prohibiting the party opposing the privilege on crime-fraud grounds from relying on the results of an *in camera* review of the communications.

(2)

Having determined that Rule 104(a) does not prohibit the *in camera* review sought by the IRS, we must address the question as a matter of the federal common law of privileges. *See* Rule 501. We conclude that a complete prohibition against opponents' use of *in camera* review to establish the applicability of the crime-fraud exception is inconsistent with the policies underlying the privilege.

We begin our analysis by recognizing that disclosure of allegedly privileged materials to the district court for purposes of determining the merits of a claim of privilege does not have the legal effect of terminating the privilege. Indeed, this Court has approved the practice of requiring parties who seek to avoid disclosure of documents to make the documents available for *in camera* inspection. . . . Respondents do not dispute this point: they acknowledge that they would have been free to request *in camera* review to establish the fact that the tapes involved attorney-client communications, had they been unable to muster independent evidence to serve that purpose.

Once it is clear that *in camera* review does not destroy the privileged nature of the contested communications, the question of the propriety of that review turns on whether the policies underlying the privilege and its exceptions are better fostered by permitting such review or by prohibiting it. In our view, the costs of imposing an absolute bar to consideration of the communications *in camera* for purpose of establishing the crime-fraud exception are intolerably high.

"No matter how light the burden of proof which confronts the party claiming the exception, there are many blatant abuses of privilege which cannot be substantiated by extrinsic evidence. This is particularly true . . . of . . . situations in which an alleged illegal proposal is made in the context of a relationship which has an apparent legitimate end." Note, *The Future Crime or Tort Exception to Communications Privileges*, 77 Harv. L. Rev. 730, 737 (1964). A *per se* rule that the communications in question may never be considered creates, we feel, too great an impediment to the proper functioning of the adversary process. This view is consistent with current trends in the law. . . .

B

We turn to the question whether *in camera* review at the behest of the party asserting the crime-fraud exception is *always* permissible, or, in contrast, whether the party seeking *in camera* review must make some threshold showing that such review is appropriate. In addressing this question, we attend to the detrimental effect, if any, of *in camera* review on the policies underlying the privilege and on the orderly administration of justice in our courts. We conclude that some such showing must be made.

Our endorsement of the practice of testing proponents' privilege claims through *in camera* review of the allegedly privileged documents has not been without reservation. This Court noted in United States v. Reynolds, 345 U.S. 1, 73 S. Ct. 528, 97 L. Ed. 727 (1953), a case which presented a delicate question concerning the disclosure of military secrets, that "examination of the evidence, even by the judge alone, in chambers" might in some cases "jeopardize the security which the privilege is meant to protect." *Id.*, at 10, 73 S. Ct., at 533. Analogizing to claims of Fifth Amendment privilege, it observed more generally: "Too much judicial inquiry into the claim of privilege would force disclosure of the thing the privilege was meant to protect, while a complete abandonment of judicial control would lead to intolerable abuses." *Id.*, at 8, 73 S. Ct., at 532.

The Court in *Reynolds* recognized that some compromise must be reached. *See* also United States v. Weisman, 111 F.2d 260, 261-262 (CA2 1940). In *Reynolds*, it declined to "go so far as to say that the court *may automatically require* a complete disclosure to the judge before the claim of privilege will be accepted *in any case*."

345 U.S., at 10, 73 S. Ct., at 533 (emphasis added). We think that much the same result is in order here.

A blanket rule allowing *in camera* review as a tool for determining the applicability of the crime-fraud exception, as *Reynolds* suggests, would place the policy of protecting open and legitimate disclosure between attorneys and clients at undue risk. There is also reason to be concerned about the possible due process implications of routine use of *in camera* proceedings. . . . Finally, we cannot ignore the burdens *in camera* review places upon the district courts, which may well be required to evaluate large evidentiary records without open adversarial guidance by the parties.

There is no reason to permit opponents of the privilege to engage in groundless fishing expeditions, with the district courts as their unwitting (and perhaps unwilling) agents. . . . Indeed, the Government conceded at oral argument (albeit reluctantly) that a district court would be mistaken if it reviewed documents *in camera* solely because "the government beg[ged it]" to do so, "with no reason to suspect crime or fraud." We agree.

In fashioning a standard for determining when *in camera* review is appropriate, we begin with the observation that "*in camera* inspection . . . is a smaller intrusion upon the confidentiality of the attorney-client relationship than is public disclosure." Fried, *Too High a Price for Truth: The Exception to the Attorney-Client Privilege for Contemplated Crimes and Frauds*, 64 N.C. L. Rev. 443, 467 (1986). We therefore conclude that a lesser evidentiary showing is needed to trigger *in camera* review than is required ultimately to overcome the privilege. *Ibid.* The threshold we set, in other words, need not be a stringent one.

We think that the following standard strikes the correct balance. Before engaging in *in camera* review to determine the applicability of the crime-fraud exception, "the judge should require a showing of a factual basis adequate to support a good faith belief by a reasonable person," Caldwell v. District Court, 644 P.2d 26, 33 (Colo. 1982), that *in camera* review of the materials may reveal evidence to establish the claim that the crime-fraud exception applies.

Once that showing is made, the decision whether to engage in *in camera* review rests in the sound discretion of the district court. The court should make that decision in light of the facts and circumstances of the particular case, including, among other things, the volume of materials the district court has been asked to review, the relative importance to the case of the alleged privileged information, and the likelihood that the evidence produced through *in camera* review, together with other available evidence then before the court, will establish that the crime-fraud exception does apply. The district court is also free to defer its *in camera* review if it concludes that additional evidence in support of the crime-fraud exception may be available that is *not* allegedly privileged, and that production of the additional evidence will not unduly disrupt or delay the proceedings.

c

The question remains as to what kind of evidence a district court may consider in determining whether it has the discretion to undertake an *in camera* review of an allegedly privileged communication at the behest of the party opposing the privilege. Here, the issue is whether the partial transcripts may be used by the IRS in support of its request for *in camera* review of the tapes.

The answer to that question, in the first instance, must be found in Rule 104(a), which establishes that materials that have been determined to be privileged may not be considered in making the preliminary determination of the existence of a privilege. Neither the District Court nor the Court of Appeals made factual findings as to the privileged nature of the partial transcripts, so we cannot determine on this record whether Rule 104(a) would bar their consideration.

Assuming for the moment, however, that no rule of privilege bars the IRS' use of the partial transcripts, we fail to see what purpose would be served by excluding the transcripts from the District Court's consideration. There can be little doubt that partial transcripts, or other evidence directly but incompletely reflecting the content of the contested communications, generally will be strong evidence of the subject matter of the communications themselves. Permitting district courts to consider this type of evidence would aid them substantially in rapidly and reliably determining whether *in camera* review is appropriate.

. . . We conclude that the party opposing the privilege may use any nonprivileged evidence in support of its request for *in camera* review, even if its evidence is not "independent" of the contested communications as the Court of Appeals uses that term.[12]

D

In sum, we conclude that a rigid independent evidence requirement does not comport with "reason and experience," Fed. Rule Evid. 501, and we decline to adopt it as part of the developing federal common law of evidentiary privileges. We hold that *in camera* review may be used to determine whether allegedly privileged attorney-client communications fall within the crime-fraud exception. We further hold, however, that before a district court may engage in *in camera* review at the request of the party opposing the privilege, that party must present evidence sufficient to support a reasonable belief that *in camera* review may yield evidence that establishes the exception's applicability. Finally, we hold that the threshold showing to obtain *in camera* review may be met by using any relevant evidence, lawfully obtained, that has not been adjudicated to be privileged.

Because the Court of Appeals employed a rigid independent-evidence requirement which categorically excluded the partial transcripts and the tapes themselves from consideration, we vacate its judgment on this issue and remand the case for further proceedings consistent with this opinion. On remand, the Court of Appeals should consider whether the District Court's refusal to listen to the tapes *in toto* was justified by the manner in which the IRS presented and preserved its request for *in camera* review.[13] In the event the Court of Appeals holds that the IRS' demand for review was properly preserved,

12. In addition, we conclude that evidence that is not "independent" of the contents of allegedly privileged communications — like the partial transcripts in this case — may be used not only in the pursuit of *in camera* review, but also may provide the evidentiary basis for the ultimate showing that the crime-fraud exception applies. We see little to distinguish these two uses: in both circumstances, if the evidence has not itself been determined to be privileged, its exclusion does not serve the policies which underlie the attorney-client privilege. *See generally* Note, *The Future Crime or Tort Exception to Communications Privileges*, 77 Harv. L. Rev. 730, 737 (1964).

13. The Court of Appeals also will have the opportunity to review the partial transcripts, and to determine whether, even without *in camera* review of the tapes, the IRS presented sufficient evidence to establish that the tapes are within the crime-fraud exception.

the Court of Appeals should then determine, or remand the case to the District Court to determine in the first instance, whether the IRS has presented a sufficient evidentiary basis for *in camera* review, and whether, if so, it is appropriate for the District Court, in its discretion, to grant such review.

It is so ordered.

Justice BRENNAN took no part in the consideration or decision of this case.

Questions for Classroom Discussion

1. Bank robbery prosecution. During Defendant's initial meeting with Attorney, Defendant admitted that he robbed the bank and asked for Attorney's help in preparing a defense. Defendant later hired a different attorney to represent him. The prosecution calls Attorney and asks Attorney about Defendant's statement. Defendant objects on grounds of attorney-client privilege, and the prosecutor responds that the crime-fraud exception applies. Assuming the facts about Defendant's initial meeting with Attorney are true, does the crime-fraud exception apply?

2. Same case. Suppose the prosecutor simply wants to call Attorney to testify whether Defendant ever consulted her. Defendant objects on relevance and privilege grounds. How should the court rule?

3. Same case. Assume the robber's hands were cut during the robbery. Assume further that during the initial meeting with Attorney, Defendant asked Attorney if she knew of a plastic surgeon "who can fix up my hands so nobody can tell they were ever cut." The prosecution learns about the statement and calls Attorney to testify at trial about it. Attorney refuses on grounds of the attorney-client privilege. The prosecution responds that the crime-fraud exception applies. Does it? Even if the exception is inapplicable, can you think of an argument that the client's statement is simply not privileged?

4. Civil fraud action. Plaintiff alleges that over the course of several years, Defendant, a financial planner, engaged in a scheme to steal money from her clients. Prior to trial, one of Defendant's former employees approaches Plaintiff and states that Defendant's attorney, Attorney, was "helping Defendant cover up the scam for three weeks just before the scam fell apart." She states that during several of the meetings between Defendant and Attorney, she heard the sound of a shredder working for long periods of time. Plaintiff notifies Attorney that she intends to take Attorney's deposition, and demands that Attorney produce all notes "taken during meetings held with Defendant" during the three-week period. Defendant refuses to produce the notes, asserting attorney-client privilege. Plaintiff responds that the crime-fraud exception applies, and asks

the court to take possession of Attorney's notes and conduct an *in camera* inspection to determine whether the crime-fraud exception applies. How should the court proceed?

5.   Several years ago, when Plaintiff and Defendant decided to start a business together, they hired Attorney to prepare their partnership agreement. After meeting several times with Attorney and going over two or three drafts, Plaintiff and Defendant approved and executed a final draft. Recently, Plaintiff and Defendant had a falling out, and are involved in litigation against each other to dissolve the partnership and allocate its assets. Each party has retained her own attorney. At trial, Plaintiff calls Attorney to testify about certain aspects of the discussions surrounding the formation of the partnership agreement. Defendant objects on grounds of privilege. How should the court rule?

6.   Malpractice action by Client against Attorney after Client's breach of contract action against a third party was dismissed for failure to file before the expiration of the applicable statute of limitation. At trial, Client wishes to testify that she discussed her contract dispute with Attorney almost a year before the statute expired, and that Attorney told her she had a valid action and that she would file the complaint within a month. Attorney objects on attorney-client privilege grounds. How should the court rule?

7.   Same case. Attorney wishes to testify that in several private conversations between the one described above and the expiration of the limitations period, she told Client that she could not file the complaint unless Client provided her with certain documents, that Client promised to provide the documents, but that Client did not do so until after the limitations period expired. Client objects on hearsay and privilege grounds. How should the court rule?

8.   Will contest. To prove the testator was incompetent when he made the will, the party contesting the will calls Attorney as a witness. Attorney both prepared the will and served as one of the attesting witnesses. The party asks Attorney to relate the conversations she had with the testator during the meeting at which the will was signed and witnessed. The party representing the estate objects on privilege grounds. How should the court rule?

5.   *A Note About the Attorney's Ethical Obligation of Confidentiality*

It is important to distinguish between the attorney-client privilege and the attorney's ethical obligation to maintain the client's secrets. The latter obligation is imposed by ethical standards, applies to all situations, not only to disclosure in formal judicial proceedings, and is generally broader than the attorney-client privilege. American Bar Association Model Rule of Professional Conduct 1.6, titled "Confidentiality of Information," provides as follows:

(a) A lawyer shall not reveal information relating to the representation of a client unless the client gives informed consent, the disclosure is impliedly authorized in order to carry out the representation or the disclosure is permitted by paragraph (b).

(b) A lawyer may reveal information relating to the representation of a client to the extent the lawyer reasonably believes necessary:

(1) to prevent reasonably certain death or substantial bodily harm;

(2) to prevent the client from committing a crime or fraud that is reasonably certain to result in substantial injury to the financial interests or property of another and in furtherance of which the client has used or is using the lawyer's services;

(3) to prevent, mitigate or rectify substantial injury to the financial interests or property of another that is reasonably certain to result or has resulted from the client's commission of a crime or fraud in furtherance of which the client has used the lawyer's services;

(4) to secure legal advice about the lawyer's compliance with these Rules;

(5) to establish a claim or defense on behalf of the lawyer in a controversy between the lawyer and the client, to establish a defense to a criminal charge or civil claim against the lawyer based upon conduct in which the client was involved, or to respond to allegations in any proceeding concerning the lawyer's representation of the client;

(6) to comply with other law or a court order; or

(7) to detect and resolve conflicts of interest arising from the lawyer's change of employment or from changes in the composition or ownership of a firm, but only if the revealed information would not compromise the attorney-client privilege or otherwise prejudice the client.

(c) A lawyer shall make reasonable efforts to prevent the inadvertent or unauthorized disclosure of, or unauthorized access to, information relating to the representation of a client.

The limits of the lawyer's obligation to maintain confidentiality are properly the subject of a course in professional responsibility, and are not discussed further in this text. Always keep the above rule in mind, however, because it imposes obligations beyond those required by the attorney-client privilege.

6. *A Note About the Attorney Work Product Doctrine*

The attorney-client privilege should not be confused with the work product doctrine. In the federal courts, that doctrine was first established in Hickman v. Taylor, 329 U.S. 495 (1947), and its current form can be found in Federal Rule of Civil Procedure 26(b)(3):

[A] party may not discover documents and tangible things that are prepared in anticipation of litigation or for trial by or for another party or its representative (including the other party's attorney, consultant, surety, indemnitor, insurer, or agent). But . . . those materials may be discovered if . . . the party shows that it has substantial need for the materials to prepare its case and cannot, without undue hardship, obtain their substantial equivalent by other means. . . . If the court orders discovery of those materials, it must protect against disclosure of the mental impressions, conclusions, opinions, or legal theories of a party's attorney or other representative concerning the litigation.

As the rule implies, the work product doctrine is designed to protect the efforts (hence the title, "work product") of the attorney, not specifically the attorney's communications with the client. The policy behind the doctrine is to prevent an indolent litigation opponent from waiting until the other attorney does her legwork, and then demanding the fruits of her labor. This is quite different from the policies behind the attorney-client privilege which, as we have seen, mostly focus on the interests of the client in privacy and effective representation.

Although some materials are covered by both the attorney-client privilege and the work product doctrine, the rules have several important differences. *First*, the types of communications and materials covered are different. The attorney-client privilege protects confidential communications between attorney and client while the work product doctrine protects from disclosure the trial preparation work product of the attorney, whether communicated to the client or not, and whether based on confidential disclosures or not. For example, suppose that following the collision of automobiles driven by plaintiff and defendant, plaintiff's lawyer interviews several witnesses and records their statements in preparation for trial. Because those statements are not confidential communications between attorney and client, they are not protected by the attorney-client privilege. But they are covered by the work product doctrine. If the attorney interviews plaintiff and takes notes of what plaintiff says, both the privilege and work product doctrine would apply.

Second, the work product doctrine covers only materials prepared in anticipation of litigation. No such restriction applies to the attorney-client privilege. Thus, confidential communications between attorney and client related to transactional matters for which the attorney has been engaged, rather than communications in preparation for trial, are covered by the attorney-client privilege but not the work product doctrine.

Third, the attorney-client privilege is absolute unless the client has waived it or a specific exception applies. It will not give way to a showing of need. The work product doctrine, on the other hand, is absolute only insofar as it protects the attorney's "impressions, conclusions, opinions, or legal research or theories." Anything else may be discovered if the opponent demonstrates "substantial need for the materials to prepare its case and cannot, without undue hardship, obtain their substantial equivalent by other means."

Question for Classroom Discussion

1. Negligence action by Plaintiff against Defendant Corporation. Plaintiff alleges that one of Defendant's trucks ran over Plaintiff while Plaintiff was in a crosswalk. Before trial Attorney, representing Plaintiff, sends her investigator to interview the only two eyewitnesses to the accident. The investigator takes notes of what the witnesses said. The investigator then gives his notes to Attorney, who prepares a memorandum describing how each witness might be used at trial. Defendant in pretrial discovery requests a copy of the interview notes

(continued)

and the memorandum. Attorney objects on the grounds of the attorney-client privilege and work product doctrine. Defendant makes a motion to compel production. How should the court rule? What if the witnesses are now both dead?

2. Same case. After the accident, Defendant's president began a routine internal investigation to determine whether company rules and procedures were followed by the driver, and whether any changes should be made to enhance safety. The process resulted in a report to the company's president and the company's inside counsel. Plaintiff learns of the investigation and requests a copy of the report. Defendant objects on the grounds of attorney-client privilege and work product doctrine. Plaintiff makes a motion to compel production. How should the court rule?

7. *Waiver of the Attorney-Client Privilege and the Work Product Doctrine*

> ### FED. R. EVID. 502.   ATTORNEY CLIENT PRIVILEGE AND WORK PRODUCT; LIMITATIONS ON WAIVER

The following provisions apply, in the circumstances set out, to disclosure of a communication or information covered by the attorney-client privilege or work-product protection.

(a) **Disclosure Made in a Federal Proceeding or to a Federal Office or Agency; Scope of a Waiver.** When the disclosure is made in a federal proceeding or to a federal office or agency and waives the attorney-client privilege or work-product protection, the waiver extends to an undisclosed communication or information in a federal or state proceeding only if:

(1) the waiver is intentional;

(2) the disclosed and undisclosed communications or information concern the same subject matter; and

(3) they ought in fairness to be considered together.

(b) **Inadvertent Disclosure.** When made in a federal proceeding or to a federal office or agency, the disclosure does not operate as a waiver in a federal or state proceeding if:

(1) the disclosure is inadvertent;

(2) the holder of the privilege or protection took reasonable steps to prevent disclosure; and

(3) the holder promptly took reasonable steps to rectify the error, including (if applicable) following Federal Rule of Civil Procedure 26 (b)(5)(B).

(c) **Disclosure Made in a State Proceeding.** When the disclosure is made in a state proceeding and is not the subject of a state-court order concerning waiver, the disclosure does not operate as a waiver in a federal proceeding if the disclosure:

(1) would not be a waiver under this rule if it had been made in a federal proceeding; or

(2) is not a waiver under the law of the state where the disclosure occurred.

(d) Controlling Effect of a Court Order. A federal court may order that the privilege or protection is not waived by disclosure connected with the litigation pending before the court—in which event the disclosure is also not a waiver in any other federal or state proceeding.

(e) Controlling Effect of a Party Agreement. An agreement on the effect of disclosure in a federal proceeding is binding only on the parties to the agreement, unless it is incorporated into a court order.

(f) Controlling Effect of this Rule. Notwithstanding Rules 101 and 1101, this rule applies to state proceedings and to federal court-annexed and federal court-mandated arbitration proceedings, in the circumstances set out in the rule. And notwithstanding Rule 501, this rule applies even if state law provides the rule of decision.

(g) Definitions. In this rule:

(1) "attorney-client privilege" means the protection that applicable law provides for confidential attorney-client communications; and

(2) "work-product protection" means the protection that applicable law provides for tangible material (or its intangible equivalent) prepared in anticipation of litigation or for trial.

The general principles governing waiver of privileges were discussed in the first section of this chapter. Congress added Rule 502 some 33 years after the Federal Rules of Evidence were initially enacted to clarify the application of some of those principles to the attorney-client privilege and the work product doctrine. Clarification became necessary because of two aspects of modern litigation.

First, many cases involve complex matters involving thousands if not millions of documents, copies of which often are produced electronically. It can be hugely expensive to meticulously review each document to ensure that no material protected by the attorney-client privilege or work product doctrine is produced. But if such an effort is not expended and a document with protected matter is produced, there is a risk of waiver. Rule 502 tries to mitigate this risk by establishing that waiver will not occur if disclosure was inadvertent and the party producing the material took reasonable steps to avoid disclosing protected matter.

Second, protected matter can be disclosed in a suit subject to the terms of a confidentiality order of the court. Those orders can limit the extent to which disclosure results in waiver. Rule 502 is aimed at ensuring the effectiveness of those orders in other federal and state proceedings.

The other aspects of this complex rule are described in the explanatory note of the Judicial Conference Advisory Committee on Evidence Rules, which you can find in Appendix A.

Further Reading: Martha J. Aaron, Comment, *Resolving the Conflict Between Federal Rule of Evidence 612 and the Work Product Doctrine: A Proposed Solution,* 38

U. Kan. L. Rev. 1039 (1990); Ronald J. Allen et al., *A Positive Theory of the Attorney-Client Privilege and the Work Product Doctrine*, 19 J. Leg. Stud. 359 (1990); Wesley M. Ayres, Comment, *Attorney-Client Privilege: The Necessity of Intent to Waive the Privilege in Inadvertent Disclosure Cases*, 18 Pac. L.J. 59 (1986); Geoffrey C. Hazard, Jr., *An Historical Perspective on the Attorney-Client Privilege*, 66 Cal. L. Rev. 1061 (1978); Robert P. Mosteller, *Child Abuse Reporting Laws and Attorney-Client Confidences: The Reality and the Specter of Lawyer as Informant*, 42 Duke L.J. 203 (1992); Stephen A. Saltzburg, *Communications Falling within the Attorney-Client Privilege*, 66 Iowa L. Rev. 811 (1981); John E. Sexton, *A Post-Upjohn Consideration of the Corporate Attorney-Client Privilege*, 57 N.Y.U. L. Rev. 443 (1982).

E. MEDICAL PRIVILEGES

1. Physician-Patient Privilege

A general privilege for physician and patient has lost favor in American courts. As mentioned earlier, Wigmore argued that there is no need for such a privilege because he believed that confidentiality is not essential to the maintenance of an effective physician-patient relationship. The proposed Federal Rules of Evidence did not contain a general physician-patient privilege largely because, even though the common law recognized such a privilege, the number and scope of the exceptions to that common law privilege were so large as to leave "little if any basis for the privilege." Proposed Federal Rule of Evidence 504 Advisory Committee Note. While Rule 501 gives the federal courts the power to recognize a physician-patient privilege, the federal courts have not done so. Most states still have a version of the privilege, usually subject to broad exceptions. Keep in mind, however, that in a civil action brought in federal court under diversity jurisdiction, Rule 501 provides that state privilege law normally applies. Thus, federal courts sitting in states that retain the physician-patient privilege may be required to apply that law in an appropriate case.

Where the general physician-patient privilege does exist, it operates much like the attorney-client privilege. The holder is the patient, meaning that the patient is the only one who may waive the privilege by authorizing disclosure of protected information. The privilege covers only confidential communications, though the definition of "communication" in the physician-patient context is a little broader than one might at first think. Specifically, if a patient submits to a physical examination and tests conducted in confidence, any information gathered is privileged. You might think of the situation as one in which the patient's body, not just her voice, "communicates" to the physician.[11]

As suggested by the Advisory Committee's Note to proposed Rule 504, there are numerous exceptions to the physician-patient privilege. The most common exception, and the one that precludes application of the privilege in most cases

---

11. Cal. Evid. Code § 992 defines confidential communication in this context as "information, including information obtained by an examination of the patient, transmitted between a patient and his physician in the course of the relationship and in confidence. . . ."

in which it otherwise might be asserted, is the "patient-litigant" exception. California Evidence Code § 996 expresses the exception as follows:

> There is no privilege . . . as to a communication relevant to an issue concerning the condition of the patient if such issue has been tendered by:
> (a) The patient;
> (b) Any party claiming through or under the patient;
> (c) Any party claiming as a beneficiary of the patient through a contract to which the patient is or was a party; or
> (d) The plaintiff in an action brought . . . for damages for the injury or death of the patient.

This exception creates a gaping hole in the privilege. Almost any time the medical condition of a patient is relevant to an issue in the case, the court will hold that the patient's condition has been tendered. If the court finds that either explicitly or by implication the patient has made her medical condition an issue in the case, the privilege will not apply to communications concerning that condition.

Prink v. Rockefeller Center Inc., 422 N.Y.S.2d 911 (1979), presents a good example of the breadth of the patient-litigant exception.[12] An associate in a New York law firm tumbled to his death from his office window on the 36th floor of Rockefeller Center. His wife brought a wrongful death action against the owners and architects of the building, claiming that her husband fell when he was trying to open a stuck window. Her complaint did not mention the decedent's mental state or any possibility that he might have jumped from the window. Defendants claimed, however, that decedent's death was a suicide, and moved to compel plaintiff to testify about conversations she had had with her husband's psychiatrist after his death. The court denied plaintiff's claim that the psychiatrist's disclosures to her were protected by her husband's psychotherapist-patient privilege,[13] on the ground that the patient-litigant exception applied:

> Whatever the ultimate determination of the triers of fact may be in the present case and notwithstanding the presumption against suicide which they will have to consider in reaching their determination, we conclude that it is a matter of common knowledge which we can judicially notice . . . that many apparently accidental deaths are in fact suicides and that a wrongful death complaint predicated upon an alleged accidental fall from a 36th story window is sufficiently equivocal in that respect to put in issue, by plaintiff's affirmative act in bringing the action, decedent's mental condition. . . . An additional reason, not however, essential to our conclusion, for holding the privileges waived by the bringing of the action is that determination of the pecuniary injury sustained by Mr. Prink's death necessarily involved his mental condition.[14]

In *Prink*, therefore, the patient-litigant exception applied even though plaintiff brought the case on a theory completely independent of her husband's mental

12. Though *Prink* involved the psychotherapist-patient privilege, the patient-litigant exception limits that privilege in the same way it limits the physician-patient privilege.
13. Note that the psychiatrist's disclosure to the plaintiff, his patient's wife, did not waive the privilege. As the court recognized, the privilege was not the psychiatrist's to waive. In addition, the court held that his disclosure was made in his professional capacity under New York law. *Id.* at 914-915.
14. *Id.* at 916.

condition. Although the court noted that his mental condition would be relevant to the issue of damages, the court held that the patient-litigant exception would apply even if this was not an issue in the case.

There are a number of other common exceptions to the physician-patient privilege. These include exceptions for the patient's efforts to obtain the physician's assistance in committing a "crime or tort"; cases involving malpractice claims against the physician or claims for fees by the physician; a deceased patient's communications related to her intentions in preparing a deed, will, or other document affecting an interest in property; proceedings to commit the patient or otherwise place the patient or her property under the control of another person because of the patient's alleged physical or mental problems; and proceedings to establish the patient's competence. Some states also provide that there is no physician-patient privilege in criminal cases. Given the number and breadth of these exceptions, it is difficult to find a case in which the physician-patient privilege actually applies.

2. *Psychotherapist-Patient Privilege*

The opposite is true for the psychotherapist-patient privilege. The proposed Federal Rules contained such a privilege (proposed Rule 504), and every state today recognizes the privilege in some form. The Advisory Committee was persuaded of the need for such a privilege by a 1960 report of the Group for the Advancement of Psychiatry, which stated:

> Among physicians, the psychiatrist has a special need to maintain confidentiality. His capacity to help his patients is completely dependent upon their willingness and ability to talk freely. This makes it difficult if not impossible for him to function without being able to assure his patients of confidentiality and, indeed, privileged communication. . . . The relationship may well be likened to that of the priest-penitent or the lawyer-client. Psychiatrists not only explore the very depths of their patients' conscious, but their unconscious feelings and attitudes as well. Therapeutic effectiveness necessitates going beyond a patient's awareness and, in order to do this, it must be possible to communicate freely.

Report No. 45, Group for the Advancement of Psychiatry 92 (1960).

The psychotherapist-patient privilege operates in much the same way as the attorney-client privilege. The patient is the holder, and is therefore the only one who may waive the privilege by authorizing disclosure of covered communications. One key question is who qualifies as a psychotherapist. This is important because not all people who seek psychological counseling obtain the services of a psychiatrist or licensed clinical psychologist. In fact, psychiatrists and licensed psychologists largely tend to be available only to those with the means to pay their fees, those with health insurance that covers their services, and those for whom such services are specifically ordered by a court. Many people obtain psychological counseling from social workers; marriage, family, and child counselors; and others who do not possess medical or doctorate degrees. To avoid making the availability of the psychotherapist-patient privilege dependent on one's economic class, some states define "psychotherapist" very broadly. The California statute, for example, includes M.D. psychiatrists, licensed psychologists, licensed clinical social workers, credentialed school psychologists, psychological assistants, associate clinical social workers, psychological interns and certain other trainees, registered nurses who possess master's degrees in psychiatric mental health nursing, and others. Cal. Evid. Code § 1010.

Other definitions of psychotherapist are considerably narrower. Proposed Federal Rule 504, for example, would have limited the definition to medical doctors engaged in diagnosis or treatment of mental or emotional conditions, including drug addiction, and licensed psychologists engaged in similar practice. In 1996, the Supreme Court adopted a broader position, recognizing a federal psychotherapist-patient privilege, and holding that it applies to a clinical social worker.

JAFFE v. REDMOND

518 U.S. 1 (1998)

Justice STEVENS delivered the opinion of the Court.

After a traumatic incident in which she shot and killed a man, a police officer received extensive counseling from a licensed clinical social worker. The question we address is whether statements the officer made to her therapist during the counseling sessions are protected from compelled disclosure in a federal civil action brought by the family of the deceased. Stated otherwise, the question is whether it is appropriate for federal courts to recognize a "psychotherapist privilege" under Rule 501 of the Federal Rules of Evidence.

I . . .

Petitioner filed suit in Federal District Court alleging that Redmond had violated Allen's constitutional rights by using excessive force during the encounter at the apartment complex. The complaint sought damages under Rev. Stat. § 1979, 42 U.S.C. § 1983, and the Illinois wrongful-death statute, Ill. Comp. Stat., ch. 740, § 180/1 *et seq.* (1994). At trial, petitioner presented testimony from members of Allen's family that conflicted with Redmond's version of the incident in several important respects. They testified, for example, that Redmond drew her gun before exiting her squad car and that Allen was unarmed when he emerged from the apartment building.

During pretrial discovery petitioner learned that after the shooting Redmond had participated in about 50 counseling sessions with Karen Beyer, a clinical social worker licensed by the State of Illinois and employed at that time by the Village of Hoffman Estates. Petitioner sought access to Beyer's notes concerning the sessions for use in cross-examining Redmond. Respondents vigorously resisted the discovery. They asserted that the contents of the conversations between Beyer and Redmond were protected against involuntary disclosure by a psychotherapist-patient privilege. The district judge rejected this argument. Neither Beyer nor Redmond, however, complied with his order to disclose the contents of Beyer's notes. At depositions and on the witness stand both either refused to answer certain questions or professed an inability to recall details of their conversations.

In his instructions at the end of the trial, the judge advised the jury that the refusal to turn over Beyer's notes had no "legal justification" and that the jury could therefore presume that the contents of the notes would have been unfavorable to respondents. The jury awarded petitioner $45,000 on the federal claim and $500,000 on her state-law claim.

The Court of Appeals for the Seventh Circuit reversed and remanded for a new trial. . . .

The United States Courts of Appeals do not uniformly agree that the federal courts should recognize a psychotherapist privilege under Rule 501. . . . Because of the conflict among the Courts of Appeals and the importance of the question, we granted certiorari. . . . We affirm.

II

Rule 501 of the Federal Rules of Evidence authorizes federal courts to define new privileges by interpreting "common law principles . . . in the light of reason and experience." . . .

The common-law principles underlying the recognition of testimonial privileges can be stated simply. "'For more than three centuries it has now been recognized as a fundamental maxim that the public . . . has a right to every man's evidence. When we come to examine the various claims of exemption, we start with the primary assumption that there is a general duty to give what testimony one is capable of giving, and that any exemptions which may exist are distinctly exceptional, being so many derogations from a positive general rule.'" United States v. Bryan, 339 U.S. 323, 331, 70 S. Ct. 724, 730, 94 L. Ed. 884 (1950) (*quoting* 8 J. Wigmore, Evidence § 2192, p.64 (3d ed. 1940)). . . .

Guided by these principles, the question we address today is whether a privilege protecting confidential communications between a psychotherapist and her patient "promotes sufficiently important interests to outweigh the need for probative evidence. . . ." 445 U.S., at 51, 100 S. Ct., at 912. Both "reason and experience" persuade us that it does.

III

Like the spousal and attorney-client privileges, the psychotherapist-patient privilege is "rooted in the imperative need for confidence and trust." . . . Treatment by a physician for physical ailments can often proceed successfully on the basis of a physical examination, objective information supplied by the patient, and the results of diagnostic tests. Effective psychotherapy, by contrast, depends upon an atmosphere of confidence and trust in which the patient is willing to make a frank and complete disclosure of facts, emotions, memories, and fears. Because of the sensitive nature of the problems for which individuals consult psychotherapists, disclosure of confidential communications made during counseling sessions may cause embarrassment or disgrace. For this reason, the mere possibility of disclosure may impede development of the confidential relationship necessary for successful treatment. [The Court then quoted the report of the Group for Advancement of Psychiatry, discussed above.] By protecting confidential communications between a psychotherapist and her patient from involuntary disclosure, the proposed privilege thus serves important private interests.

Our cases make clear that an asserted privilege must also "serv[e] public ends." Upjohn Co. v. United States, 449 U.S. 383, 389, 101 S. Ct. 677, 682, 66 L. Ed. 2d 584 (1981). . . . The psychotherapist privilege serves the public interest by facilitating the provision of appropriate treatment for individuals suffering the effects of a mental or emotional problem. The mental health of our citizenry, no less than its physical health, is a public good of transcendent importance.[10]

In contrast to the significant public and private interests supporting recognition of the privilege, the likely evidentiary benefit that would result from the denial of the privilege is modest. If the privilege were rejected, confidential conversations between psychotherapists and their patients would surely be chilled, particularly when it is obvious that the circumstances that give rise to the need for treatment will probably result in litigation. Without a privilege, much of the desirable evidence to which litigants such as petitioner seek access — for example, admissions against interest by a party — is unlikely to come into being. This unspoken "evidence" will therefore serve no greater truth-seeking function than if it had been spoken and privileged.

That it is appropriate for the federal courts to recognize a psychotherapist privilege under Rule 501 is confirmed by the fact that all 50 States and the District of Columbia have enacted into law some form of psychotherapist privilege. We have previously observed that the policy decisions of the States bear on the question whether federal courts should recognize a new privilege or amend the coverage of an existing one. . . . Because state legislatures are fully aware of the need to protect the integrity of the factfinding functions of their courts, the existence of a consensus among the States indicates that "reason and experience" support recognition of the privilege. In addition, given the importance of the patient's understanding that her communications with her therapist will not be publicly disclosed, any State's promise of confidentiality would have little value if the patient were aware that the privilege would not be honored in a federal court.[12] Denial of the federal privilege therefore would frustrate the purposes of the state legislation that was enacted to foster these confidential communications.

The uniform judgment of the States is reinforced by the fact that a psychotherapist privilege was among the nine specific privileges recommended by the Advisory Committee in its proposed privilege rules. . . .

Because we agree with the judgment of the state legislatures and the Advisory Committee that a psychotherapist-patient privilege will serve a "public good

---

10. This case amply demonstrates the importance of allowing individuals to receive confidential counseling. Police officers engaged in the dangerous and difficult tasks associated with protecting the safety of our communities not only confront the risk of physical harm but also face stressful circumstances that may give rise to anxiety, depression, fear, or anger. The entire community may suffer if police officers are not able to receive effective counseling and treatment after traumatic incidents, either because trained officers leave the profession prematurely or because those in need of treatment remain on the job.

12. At the outset of their relationship, the ethical therapist must disclose to the patient "the relevant limits on confidentiality." *See* American Psychological Association, Ethical Principles of Psychologists and Code of Conduct, Standard 5.01 (Dec. 1992). *See also* National Federation of Societies for Clinical Social Work, Code of Ethics V(a) (May 1988); American Counseling Association, Code of Ethics and Standards of Practice A.3.a (effective July 1995).

626   8. Privileges

transcending the normally predominant principle of utilizing all rational means for ascertaining truth," . . . we hold that confidential communications between a licensed psychotherapist and her patients in the course of diagnosis or treatment are protected from compelled disclosure under Rule 501 of the Federal Rules of Evidence.

IV

All agree that a psychotherapist privilege covers confidential communications made to licensed psychiatrists and psychologists. We have no hesitation in concluding in this case that the federal privilege should also extend to confidential communications made to licensed social workers in the course of psychotherapy. The reasons for recognizing a privilege for treatment by psychiatrists and psychologists apply with equal force to treatment by a clinical social worker such as Karen Beyer. Today, social workers provide a significant amount of mental health treatment. . . . Their clients often include the poor and those of modest means who could not afford the assistance of a psychiatrist or psychologist, . . . but whose counseling sessions serve the same public goals. Perhaps in recognition of these circumstances, the vast majority of States explicitly extend a testimonial privilege to licensed social workers. We therefore agree with the Court of Appeals that "[d]rawing a distinction between the counseling provided by costly psychotherapists and the counseling provided by more readily accessible social workers serves no discernible public purpose." . . .

We part company with the Court of Appeals on a separate point. We reject the balancing component of the privilege implemented by that court and a small number of States. Making the promise of confidentiality contingent upon a trial judge's later evaluation of the relative importance of the patient's interest in privacy and the evidentiary need for disclosure would eviscerate the effectiveness of the privilege. As we explained in *Upjohn*, if the purpose of the privilege is to be served, the participants in the confidential conversation "must be able to predict with some degree of certainty whether particular discussions will be protected. An uncertain privilege, or one which purports to be certain but results in widely varying applications by the courts, is little better than no privilege at all." . . .

V

The conversations between Officer Redmond and Karen Beyer and the notes taken during their counseling sessions are protected from compelled disclosure under Rule 501 of the Federal Rules of Evidence. The judgment of the Court of Appeals is affirmed.

It is so ordered.

Justice SCALIA, with whom THE CHIEF JUSTICE joins as to Part III, dissenting.

The Court has discussed at some length the benefit that will be purchased by creation of the evidentiary privilege in this case: the encouragement of psychoanalytic counseling. It has not mentioned the purchase price: occasional injustice. That is the cost of every rule which excludes reliable and probative evidence — or at least every one categorical enough to achieve its announced policy objective. In the case of some of these rules, such as the one excluding confessions that have not been properly "Mirandized," *see* Miranda v. Arizona, 384 U.S. 436, 86 S. Ct. 1602, 16 L. Ed. 2d 694 (1966), the victim of the injustice is always the impersonal State or the faceless "public at large." For the rule proposed here, the victim is more likely to be some individual who is prevented from proving a valid claim — or (worse still) prevented from establishing a valid defense. The latter is particularly unpalatable for those who love justice, because it causes the courts of law not merely to let stand a wrong, but to become themselves the instruments of wrong. . . .

The exceptions to the psychotherapist-patient privilege are similar to those applicable to the physician-patient privilege but usually are not quite as broad. But there is one additional exception applicable only to the psychotherapist-patient privilege. Many jurisdictions maintain a so-called dangerous patient exception. Cal. Evid. Code § 1024 is typical:

> There is no privilege . . . if the psychotherapist has reasonable cause to believe that the patient is in such mental or emotional condition as to be dangerous to himself or to the person or property of another and that disclosure of the communication is necessary to prevent the threatened danger.

It is important to distinguish the "dangerous patient" exception from a substantive tort law duty recognized by some states. This duty, which gained acceptance after the California Supreme Court's decision in Tarasoff v. Regents of the University of California, 131 Cal. Rptr. 14 (Cal. 1976), generally requires a psychotherapist to exercise reasonable care to determine if a patient poses a threat of harm to other persons, and to take reasonable steps to warn that such a threat exists. Where recognized, that duty is one for which a psychotherapist may be held liable in tort, generally through the payment of damages. This is to be distinguished from the psychotherapist's duty under the law of testimonial privilege to maintain the confidentiality of communications with the patient.[15] The next case helps to highlight the ways in which the privilege, the tort duty, and the psychotherapist's ethical duty interact.

STATE v. AGACKI
595 N.W.2d 31 (Wis. Ct. App. 1999)

SCHUDSON, J.

Curtis M. Agacki appeals from the judgment of conviction entered after he pled guilty to carrying a concealed weapon. Contending that the trial court erred in denying his motion to suppress evidence, Agacki argues that the police

---

15. It should also be distinguished from the psychotherapist's duty, imposed by her profession's ethical code, to maintain her patients' secrecy and privacy. As with the attorney's ethical duty of secrecy, that duty can be broader than the duty imposed by rules of testimonial privilege.

officer's basis for stopping him and seizing the gun came from a privileged communication with his psychotherapist and, therefore, that his disclosure to his psychotherapist was not admissible to support a finding of probable cause. We conclude, however, that Agacki's disclosure that he was carrying a gun was not a privileged communication, and, therefore, that the trial court correctly considered evidence of the communication. Accordingly, we affirm.

I. BACKGROUND

The facts essential to the resolution of this appeal are undisputed. Evidence at the suppression motion hearing established that Agacki was a patient of David Baldridge, a licensed psychotherapist with a master's degree in social work. Baldridge testified that on Friday, May 17, 1996, in a telephone conversation, Agacki told him that he had been in a fight at a restaurant and had missed several days of work. Concerned, Baldridge called Agacki the next day to check on him. Agacki then told him that he had "torched" a motorcycle after a bar fight, that he believed people were watching him, but that he was not afraid because, Agacki declared: "[I]f they try anything[,] I will pull my piece out and blow their fucking heads off. I will kill them. I don't care what happens to me. . . . I am not afraid of . . . dying." Alarmed, Baldridge encouraged Agacki to see him and, fearing that Agacki was impaired by alcohol or medication, Baldridge suggested that they meet within walking distance of Agacki's residence. They agreed to get together later that afternoon at a tavern near Agacki's home.

Before leaving for the tavern, Baldridge telephoned the Milwaukee Police Department and requested assistance with what he believed might develop into the need for Agacki's mental health hospitalization. Baldridge then went to the tavern, waited for the police but, before police arrived, entered the tavern, where Agacki was waiting. They then sat at a table and talked. When Agacki, with words and gestures, indicated that he was armed, Baldridge excused himself, exited the tavern and alerted a police officer who was then waiting outside.

The evidence established that Baldridge informed Milwaukee Police Officer Charles Henn that Agacki was emotionally unstable, in need of hospitalization, and armed with a gun. Moments later, Agacki exited the tavern. Officer Henn stopped Agacki, frisked him, recovered an unloaded .41 caliber Smith and Wesson six-inch revolver from Agacki's left jacket pocket, and arrested him.

Agacki moved to suppress the statements and the gun, contending that his disclosure to his therapist was part of their confidential communication, protected by the psychotherapist-patient privilege. Rejecting Agacki's argument, the trial court concluded that the privilege applied but, under Schuster v. Altenberg, 144 Wis. 2d 223, 424 N.W.2d 159 (1988), his disclosure about the gun fell within the exception for a psychotherapist's "duty to warn third parties or to institute proceedings for the detention or commitment of a dangerous individual for the protection of the patient or the public." *Id.* at 239-40, 424 N.W.2d at 166. . . .

Accordingly, the trial court concluded that Agacki's disclosure to Baldridge was admissible and could establish the basis for Officer Henn's seizure of the gun.

II. Analysis

. . . To resolve the issue in this case, . . . we must interpret the psychotherapist-patient privilege. . . . The interpretation of a statute presents a question of law, which we review *de novo*. . . .

Mental health professionals have not only a duty of confidentiality to their patients, but also a duty *to others* to exercise reasonable care in the treatment of their patients. Under certain circumstances, the duty to exercise reasonable care includes a duty to warn potential victims and/or contact the police. As the Supreme Court declared:

> The concern regarding the preservation of patient trust in the confidentiality of communications is legitimate, yet one which must yield in those limited circumstances where the public interest in safety from violent assault is threatened. The reason why the interest of public safety commands some limited intrusion upon confidentiality was well-explained in *Tarasoff*:
>
>> Our current crowded and computerized society compels the interdependence of its members. In this risk-infested society we can hardly tolerate the further exposure to danger that would result from a concealed knowledge of the therapist that his patient was lethal.

Schuster [v. Altenberg, 144 Wis. 2d 223, 249, 424 N.W.2d 159, 170 (1988)] (citation omitted). . . .

We further note that, in Wisconsin, the principle that confidentiality of communications must give way to certain instances is reflected in the evidence code. In particular, [the privilege] accords to a patient a privilege to refuse to disclose and to prevent another person from disclosing confidential patient-therapist communications. However, an exception to this privilege is recognized. "There is no privilege under this rule as to communications and information relevant to an issue in proceedings to hospitalize the patient for mental illness, *if the physician . . . or psychologist in the course of diagnosis or treatment has determined that the patient is in need of hospitalization.*" (Emphasis added.) At the very least, the statutory exception to the evidentiary privilege suggests a balance struck by the legislature between patient confidentiality and public safety. *More generally, the exception to the general rule of privilege demonstrates that "the privilege is not sacrosanct and can properly be waived in the interest of public policy under appropriate circumstances." Schuster,* 144 Wis. 2d at 250-51, 424 N.W.2d at 170-71 (footnote and citation omitted; second emphasis added) . . . .

In applying *Schuster* to the instant case, we gain guidance from *Tarasoff*, on which *Schuster* heavily relied, and its progeny. . . . The California Supreme Court . . . held that psychotherapists have an affirmative duty to warn their patients' potential victims. . . . Our supreme court noted that "the duty which was recognized in *Tarasoff* was not limited to a duty to warn but extended to 'whatever other steps are reasonably necessary under the circumstances.'" Indeed, the court acknowledged that *Tarasoff* "mandates a duty to protect," and flatly rejected any "distinction between a psychotherapist's duty to warn on the basis of whether the patient particularizes potential victims of his or her violent tendencies or makes generalized statements of dangerous intent."

More recently, the California Supreme Court, articulating the standards for measuring the *Tarasoff* duty, clarified:

[A] psychotherapist's *Tarasoff* warning to the patient's intended victim is not covered by the privilege even if it relates an otherwise protected communication, provided that the conditions of the exception are satisfied, viz, there is *reasonable cause for the psychotherapist to believe that (1) the patient is dangerous and (2) disclosure of the communication is necessary to prevent any harm.*

Menendez v. Superior Court, 3 Cal. 4th 435, 11 Cal. Rptr. 2d 92, 834 P.2d 786, 794 (1992) (citing People v. Wharton, 53 Cal. 3d 522, 280 Cal. Rptr. 631, 809 P.2d 290 (1991)) (emphasis added). These standards are sound. Thus, if "there is reasonable cause for the psychotherapist to believe that (1) the patient is dangerous and (2) disclosure of the communication is necessary to prevent any harm," a psychotherapist has a duty to warn and, of course, police have a duty to take appropriate action. It would be absurd, then, to impose a testimonial privilege to prevent courts from considering the very communication leading to the responsible and lawful conduct of the psychotherapist and the police officer.

Here, Baldridge had "reasonable cause . . . to believe" that his patient was dangerous and that contacting police would not only prevent harm to the public, but would also assist Agacki by facilitating his hospitalization. Accordingly, we conclude that Agacki's statements to his psychotherapist were not privileged; they fell within the dangerous patient exception. Thus, the trial court correctly considered the evidence of Officer Henn's basis for searching Agacki, and correctly denied Agacki's motion to suppress.

Judgment affirmed.

Further Reading: Zechariah Chafee, *Privileged Communications: Is Justice Served or Obstructed by Closing the Doctor's Mouth on the Witness Stand?*, 52 Yale L.J. 607 (1943); Catharina J.H. Dubbelday, Comment, *The Psychotherapist-Client Testimonial Privilege: Defining the Professional Involved*, 34 Emory L.J. 777 (1985); B. Abbott Goldberg, *The Physician-Patient Privilege—An Impediment to Public Health*, 16 Pac. L.J. 787 (1985); George C. Harris, *The Dangerous Patient Exception to the Psychotherapist-Patient Privilege: The* Tarasoff *Duty and the* Jaffe *Footnote*, 74 Wash. L. Rev. 33 (1999); Daniel W. Shuman, *The Origins of the Physician-Patient Privilege and Professional Secret*, 39 Sw. L.J. 661 (1985); Daniel W. Shuman & Myron F. Weiner, *The Privilege Study: An Empirical Examination of the Psychotherapist-Patient Privilege*, 60 N.C. L. Rev. 893 (1982); Ralph Slovenko, *Psychiatry and a Second Look at the Medical Privilege*, 6 Wayne L. Rev. 175 (1960).

Questions for Classroom Discussion

1. Plaintiff sues Defendant for negligence following a collision between their two vehicles. After the accident, Plaintiff sought treatment for her injuries from Doctor, an orthopedic physician. Prior to trial, Defendant takes the deposition of Doctor, and asks Doctor to produce all records relating to the treatment of Plaintiff for injuries allegedly sustained in the accident. Doctor refuses to produce the papers, and refuses to answer any questions relating to injuries sustained in the accident.

Defendant asks the court to order Doctor to produce the papers and to answer Defendant's questions. How should the court rule?

2. Same case. Plaintiff's attorney asks Plaintiff to visit Ortho, a different orthopedic specialist, to help the attorney prepare for trial. Plaintiff does so, and Ortho sends the attorney a report concerning Plaintiff's condition. Plaintiff's attorney does not plan to call Ortho as a witness at trial. Defendant seeks to take Ortho's deposition, and demands that Ortho produce a copy of the report she sent Plaintiff's attorney. Must Ortho comply?

3. Vehicular homicide prosecution. At trial, the prosecutor calls Witness, who was crossing the street with Victim. Witness was the only eyewitness to the accident other than Defendant. Witness testifies that Defendant drove through a red light and struck and killed Victim and that Defendant's car narrowly missed Witness. Defendant testifies that she was driving properly and that Victim and Witness darted out in front of her car. Defendant wishes to establish that Witness suffers from a mental condition that causes her not to be able to distinguish reality from fantasy and that this condition led Witness to give an incorrect version of the facts. To

 establish this, Defendant calls Witness's psychiatrist and asks her about her treatment of Witness. The prosecutor objects on grounds of the psychotherapist-patient privilege. How should the court rule?

4. Proceeding to determine the competence of Defendant to stand trial for a crime. Prior to the hearing, the court appointed Psych, a psychiatrist, to conduct a mental evaluation of Defendant. At the hearing Defendant raises a privilege objection to Psych's testimony about the sessions Defendant and Psych had together. How should the court rule?

5. Proceeding to probate the will of Deceased. One party challenges the will on the ground Deceased was not competent to make a will at the time she signed it. To prove lack of competence, the party calls Psych, who had been Deceased's psychiatrist in the months prior to her death, to testify about Deceased's mental condition. The other party objects on grounds of the psychotherapist-patient privilege. How should the court rule?

6. Prosecution of Defendant for attempted murder of Victim. At trial, the prosecution calls Psych, a psychiatrist who had been treating Defendant in the months prior to the alleged attempted murder. The prosecutor asks Psych if, during one of their sessions, Defendant said, "I should kill Victim if I ever have a chance." Defendant objects on grounds of privilege. How should the court rule?

F. CLERGY PRIVILEGE

1. *In General*

Some people discuss spiritual or emotional issues with a psychotherapist or spouse. Others turn instead to members of the clergy. In each case, confidentiality is usually essential to encourage discussion. But this is not the only reason for a clergy confidential communication privilege. Imagine what would happen if no privilege existed, and the prosecution in a criminal case subpoenaed a Catholic priest to testify against the defendant who had confessed her crimes to the priest. Because his religious vows prohibit disclosure of the secrets of the confessional, the priest will not testify. And no court order or action, including jailing the priest for contempt, is likely to change the priest's mind. Thus, another reason for the clergy confidential communication privilege is that it protects the First Amendment right to the free exercise of religion. Requiring disclosure of such communications in court would bring the practice of religion and the judicial process into direct conflict.

The clergy privilege was first recognized in the context of the Catholic confessional. Once such a privilege was provided to Roman Catholic priests, it was inevitable that it would be extended to others. Today, protection is afforded to clergy of all religions, whether or not they practice formal modes of "confession."

But who is the holder of the clergy privilege — the clergy or the layperson communicating in confidence with clergy (sometimes called "the penitent")? The state versions of this privilege do not take a uniform stance on the question. A few states recognize two privileges, one for clergy and one for the penitent. *See* Cal. Evid. Code § 1034; Ill. Comp. Stat. ch. 735, 5/8-803. In other states, only the penitent is the holder. This is the case, for example, in New York. *See* De'udy v. De'udy, 495 N.Y.S.2d 616 (N.Y. Sup. 1985). Proposed Federal Rule 506 would have made only the penitent the holder, but recognizes that the clergy member may claim the privilege on behalf of the penitent.

Some definitions are in order. First is the meaning of the term *clergy*. Though it is clear that a priest, rabbi, minister, or other similar functionary would qualify, not all persons who serve in some religious capacity are "clergy." In State v. Gooding, 989 P.2d 304 (Mont. 1999), for example, the court held that the wife of a church deacon was not a member of the clergy for purposes of that state's clergy-penitent privilege. Similarly, in State v. Buss, 887 P.2d 920 (Wash. Ct. App. 1995), the court held that incriminating statements made to a non-ordained Catholic church counselor during a counseling session were not privileged under the Washington statute. Not all courts scrutinize the meaning of clergy so closely, but care must be exercised before concluding that the privilege applies.

Second, not all communications to clergy are covered by the privilege. To be protected, most states require that the communication was intended to be confidential and was "penitential," meaning that it was made in search of spiritual guidance.[16] New York, for example, requires that the information have been

---

16. Note that these two elements are distinct. As the following story illustrates, not all penitential communications are intended to be confidential: A man goes into the confessional and tells the priest, "Father, I am eighty-two years old and last night I made love to two twenty-year-old girls at the same time." The priest responds, "When was the last time you went to confession?" The man says, "Never, I'm Jewish." Taken aback, the priest says, "Then why are you telling this to me?" The old man answers, "I'm telling everybody!"

imparted by the penitent "in confidence and for the purpose of obtaining spiritual guidance." People v. Carmona, 606 N.Y.S.2d 879, 882 (1993). And though it does not explicitly so provide, the California rule implies as much:

> As used in this article, "penitential communication" means a communication made in confidence, in the presence of no third person so far as the penitent is aware, to a clergyman who, in the course of the discipline or practice of his church, denomination, or organization, is authorized or accustomed to hear such communications and, under the discipline or tenets of his church, denomination, or organization, has a duty to keep such communications secret.

Cal. Evid. Code § 1032.

A court facing uncertainty about whether a communication qualifies as "penitential" might find itself uncomfortably embroiled in a matter of religious practice. That was the situation in the case that follows.

PEOPLE v. EDWARDS

248 Cal. Rptr. 53 (Ct. App. 1988)

RACANELLI, Presiding Justice.

Defendant was convicted by the court, sitting without a jury, on four counts of grand theft following denial of her claim of a clergy-penitent privilege. . . . On appeal from the order granting probation, we affirmed the determination of the trial court. We granted rehearing to reconsider defendant's claim that inculpatory statements made by her to Father Rankin, an Episcopalian priest, were in the nature of a sacramental confession or "penitential communication" privileged from disclosure. We refile our original opinion as modified.

FACTS

We recite the factual background against which the claim of statutory privilege is presented. (The facts underlying the embezzlement counts are essentially undisputed.)

Around 8:30 P.M. on Sunday, August 5, 1984, defendant Sheridan Edwards telephoned Father William Rankin, the rector of St. Stephen's Episcopal Church in Belvedere, and said she urgently needed to talk to him about "a problem" Father Rankin, who was scheduled to leave early the next morning to attend a week-long meeting in Oklahoma, asked defendant, a church member, if her problem could wait until he returned. After defendant related she had already talked to Father Gompertz, another priest affiliated with St. Stephen's, who told her it was imperative to see Father Rankin immediately, they arranged to meet that evening at Father Rankin's office. At the meeting, defendant first declared she had done something almost "as bad as murder" She then requested that their conversation be confidential; Father Rankin agreed.

Defendant proceeded to tell Father Rankin that she needed his help in stopping payment on certain checks drawn against the account of St. Stephen's Guild, of which she served as treasurer. (In fact, the Guild account was practically depleted due to her embezzlement of nearly $30,000 over a period of many months.) Defendant told him she had arranged to borrow money to cover her misappropriation but needed his help because the loan proceeds would not be available in time to prevent the checks authorized for issuance to various charities from being dishonored.

Because he was leaving the following day, Father Rankin believed he would be unable to provide a solution and eventually suggested two alternatives to defendant: he could keep her revelation in confidence as agreed, or he could talk to the church wardens on her behalf seeking their help in solving the problem.[3] Defendant consented to the latter option. Father Rankin repeated the question whether that was the course of action defendant wanted to pursue, and she assured him it was. However, defendant testified that she felt she had no choice but to agree.

Later that evening, Father Rankin called Daniel King, the senior warden, and informed him of defendant's visit and the two alternatives he presented. King agreed to handle the problem in Father Rankin's absence. Father Rankin also called Sandra Ogden, the junior warden, and asked her to attempt retrieval of the (worthless) checks before they were presented for payment; her efforts ultimately proved successful.

During the week of his absence, Father Rankin and the two wardens remained in frequent contact with defendant, but no resolution was reached. King testified that defendant told him she had taken some $27,000, which could not be discovered in an audit. (According to Ogden, defendant told her she had burned the incriminating checks.[5])

King thereafter scheduled a meeting of the 15-member vestry for Saturday, August 11. Before the meeting, defendant showed Father Rankin a telegram from a loan agency indicating her loan had been approved. Upon the request of the vestry, defendant delivered to them pertinent records and documents with the explanation that she had destroyed some of the checks. Acting upon the advice of the controller of the diocese, the vestry decided the missing funds had to be reported to the police because their fidelity bond was otherwise at risk. Soon thereafter, King and other church members reported the incident to the local police resulting in the issuance of a search warrant. Various bank records, ledgers and cancelled checks seized during the authorized search of defendant's house were admitted in evidence at trial.

At the conclusion of the evidentiary stage of trial, the court determined that the clergy-penitent privilege did not apply and, in any event, was limited to testimonial as opposed to extrajudicial statements. The court then found defendant guilty as charged, including an enhancement pursuant to Penal Code section 12022.6, subdivision (a). Thereafter, sentence was suspended and defendant placed on formal probation subject to certain conditions including four months in jail.

---

3. As the lay leaders of the church, the wardens were responsible for its financial affairs.

5. Defendant testified that her purpose in seeking Father Rankin's help was to prevent the imminent public disclosure of insufficient funds in the Guild's bank account. She stated her intention was to cover up her misdeeds once she had replenished the depleted account with funds from the materialized loan.

DISCUSSION

Defendant argues that the trial court erred in allowing into evidence the content of her confidential statements to Father Rankin and other incriminating evidence obtained as a direct result thereof. We cannot agree.

Under the relevant statutory scheme, "a penitent . . . has a privilege to refuse to disclose, and to prevent another from disclosing, a penitential communication. . . ." A penitent is defined as one who has made a "penitential communication to a clergyman" which in turn is defined as a confidential communication to a clergyman "who, in the course of the discipline or practice of his church, denomination, or organization, is authorized or accustomed to hear such communications and, under the discipline or tenets of his church, denomination, or organization, has a duty to keep such communications secret." The focus of our inquiry is whether defendant's confidential statements to Father Rankin constituted a penitential communication within the meaning of the statutory privilege. . . .

Clearly, not every communication to a member of the clergy is privileged in the eyes of the law. (*See, e.g.*, People v. Johnson (1969) 270 Cal. App. 2d 204, 207, 75 Cal. Rptr. 605 [fleeing robber ran into nearby church requesting help from minister dressed in street clothes].)

In order for a statement to be privileged, it must satisfy all of the conceptual requirements of a penitential communication: 1) it must be intended to be in confidence; 2) it must be made to a member of the clergy who in the course of his or her religious discipline or practice is authorized or accustomed to hear such communications; and 3) such member of the clergy has a duty under the discipline or tenets of the church, religious denomination or organization to keep such communications secret. . . . And while there is a presumption of confidentiality whenever the statutory penitent's privilege is claimed, the right to claim such privilege may be waived where the claimant freely discloses, or consents to disclosure of, "a significant part of the communication."

At trial, defendant claimed her original conversation with Father Rankin was intended as a penitential communication. She testified that she sought out Father Rankin at the direction of Father Gompertz to whom she had initially confessed and asked forgiveness. Father Gompertz confirmed he had so directed defendant to whom he gave absolution, but he invoked the clergyman's privilege and declined to testify as to the substance of their conversation. Father Rankin testified that he believed defendant's statements to him were in the nature of a secular request seeking counselling and not absolution; that when he offered to assist in her predicament requiring that the substance of their confidential discussion be divulged, defendant willingly agreed.

Ultimately, the trial court determined that Father Rankin's characterization of the conversation was more credible and that defendant's statements made in confidence did not "fall within the area of the church law or the statute as far as the privilege is concerned."

Such judicial determination constituted an implicit finding that the conversation was not a penitential communication within the reach of the statutory privilege. As with all factual determinations based upon conflicting evidence, the findings of the trial judge will be upheld on appeal if supported by substantial evidence; the judgment is presumed correct, and the evidence cannot be reweighed. . . .

Extensive testimony was given by church officials as to the discipline and tenets of the Episcopal Church. Floyd Frisch, attorney and chancellor of a neighboring diocese, testified for the defense that an Episcopalian priest is under an *absolute* duty to maintain the secrecy of the confession. He stated that the Episcopal Book of Common Prayer provides for this principle with the force of law; further, that in difficult cases, the benefit of the doubt should be given to the penitent . . . .

The expert witnesses agreed that the Episcopal Church recognizes the inviolability of an act of confession by a penitent seeking God's forgiveness and absolution through a priest. And both church experts and Father Rankin concurred that the aid of priests is frequently sought for the disparate purposes of religious confession and pastoral counselling. Father Rankin had no recollection of defendant's request to make a true "confession" seeking forgiveness or absolution, the very essence of the spiritual relationship privileged under the statute. . . .

However, Father Rankin had a clear recollection that defendant stated she needed his help in order that the bad checks would not bounce and thereby disclose her wrongdoing and inflict hurt in the process. He emphasized that the conversation did not even "remotely resemble" a religious confession; rather, that the mutual encounter involved a "problem-solving" entreaty under a promise of confidence from which defendant ultimately released him. Bishop Swing and other church officials he consulted confirmed his belief that the situation involved no more than pastoral counselling which was not subject to the seal of a confession.

Since the trial court fully considered and evaluated all of the conflicting evidence in reaching its factual determination that the questioned statement was not a penitential communication within legal contemplation, no privilege attached preventing Father Rankin from otherwise consensually disclosing the content of the nonpenitential, though private, communication to the church officials and, ultimately, to the authorities. Where such determination is supported by substantial, credible evidence, as shown, we are duty bound to uphold it. . . .

The order appealed from is affirmed.

2. Exceptions

Unlike the other privileges we have studied, the clergy-penitent privilege has few if any exceptions. Proposed Federal Rule 506, for example, contains no exceptions. The absence of exceptions can best be explained by reference to the realities of the situation. If a member of the clergy is bound by the tenets of her religion to maintain the sanctity of penitential communications, she is unlikely to recognize secular exceptions to the privilege. And the same is true of the penitent, who undoubtedly relies on the practices of her religion when she engages in the kind of penitential communications protected by the privilege. Put simply, exceptions are unlikely to have much practical effect.

Questions for Classroom Discussion

1. Prosecution of Defendant for the murder of Victim. Shortly after the killing, Defendant, a practicing Roman Catholic, visited the confessional and admitted to committing the crime. At trial, the prosecution calls Priest, the priest who heard Defendant's confession, and asks Priest what Defendant said. Defendant objects on grounds of privilege. How should the court rule?

2. Same case. Assume the case is being tried in a jurisdiction that maintains privileges for both clergy and penitent. Assume further that Defendant objects, but that Priest believes that, in this situation, it is appropriate to waive his privilege and testify. How should the court rule?

3. Prosecution of Defendant for the murder of Victim, which took place in a brothel. Defendant claims self-defense. Assume the jurisdiction grants a privilege to both clergy and penitent. At trial, Defendant calls Witness, a bystander who witnessed the altercation between Defendant and Victim. Witness testifies that Defendant shot Victim after Victim attacked Defendant with a knife. On cross-examination, the prosecution asks Witness if it isn't true that shortly before trial Defendant offered Witness a high-paying job with Defendant's company. Witness admits receiving the offer, but sticks to his story about the fight. Defendant calls Priest, a Roman Catholic priest who heard Witness's confession shortly after Witness saw the altercation. Defendant wishes to elicit Priest's testimony that during his confession, Witness told Priest that he had been in a brothel when he saw Victim attack Defendant with a knife and Defendant shoot Victim in self-defense. The prosecution makes a hearsay objection, and Priest refuses to testify, asserting his clergy privilege. How should the court rule?

4. Prosecution of Defendant for bank robbery. At trial, the prosecution calls Lay, a lay minister at Defendant's church, and seeks to elicit testimony that shortly after the bank robbery, Defendant met with Lay in a church office and told Lay that she had robbed a bank. Defendant objects on grounds of privilege. How should the court rule?

5. Bank robbery prosecution. Defendant denies involvement. To prove Defendant's involvement, the prosecution calls Minister, the leader of Defendant's church, and seeks to elicit testimony that shortly after the bank robbery, Defendant took part in one of the church's weekly "group unburdening" sessions, and admitted to robbing a bank. Members of this church are encouraged to attend these meetings to confess their sins in front of other members and Minister. Defendant objects on grounds of privilege. How should the court rule?

6. Prosecution of Defendant for assault and battery on Victim. Defendant claims self-defense. At trial, the prosecution calls Bartender, the bartender at the Church of the Holy Mug, and seeks

(continued)

> to elicit testimony that shortly after the altercation between
> Defendant and Victim, Defendant met with Bartender at the church
> and told Bartender, in confidence over a few beers, that she had just
> "beat up some guy who looked at me the wrong way." Defendant
> objects on grounds of privilege. How should the court rule?

G. SPOUSAL PRIVILEGES

1. In General

Two privileges can apply to spouses. The first is a privilege for confidential
communications between spouses. This privilege operates much like the privileges we have studied to this point. The second privilege is a privilege not to
testify against a spouse. This privilege is different from the ones we have studied
up to now, because it is not limited to testimony concerning confidential communications, but extends to any testimony adverse to a spouse. In the sections to
follow, we examine each of these privileges separately.

2. The Privilege for Confidential Communications Between Spouses

The first privilege is one protecting confidential communications between
spouses. This privilege is exemplified by California Evidence Code § 980:

> [A] spouse (or his guardian or conservator . . .), whether or not a party, has a
> privilege during the marital relationship and afterwards to refuse to disclose, and
> to prevent another from disclosing, a communication if he claims the privilege and
> the communication was made in confidence between him and the other spouse
> while they were husband and wife.

Today, nearly all jurisdictions recognize the privilege for confidential spousal
communications in both civil and criminal cases.[17] As the California rule suggests, the privilege operates much like the other privileges we have discussed.
One notable difference, however, is that under the California rule both parties
to the communication are holders of the privilege. This is sensible, as the relationship in this situation is on an even footing, while the attorney and client, as
well as physician and patient, occupy different status. To put it differently, both
spouses have the same interest in preventing both their own communications
and those of the other spouse from being disclosed without permission. When
both spouses are holders of the privilege, one may prevent disclosure of protected communications even when the other wishes to disclose. But the majority
of states take a different approach, making only the communicating spouse the
holder.[18] This means that if the spouse who made the confidential

---

17. *See* Edward J. Imwinkelried, The New Wigmore: A Treatise on Evidence: Privileges § 6.2.1, at
447 (2002). Oddly, the proposed federal rules on privileges did not include a privilege for confidential communications between spouses.
    18. *Id.* at § 6.5.1(b), at 554-555.

communication does not claim the privilege, the other spouse may be compelled to testify about that communication.

Note that the privilege applies only to communications that occurred during a marriage. Thus, communications before marriage are not privileged even if the participants in that communication are married at the time of trial. It also means that the privilege applies to communications made during the marriage even if, at the time of trial, the marriage is over.

In most jurisdictions the privilege applies only to legally married couples. This means that unmarried cohabitants may not claim the privilege. This is one reason why the question of whether gay and lesbian couples can legally marry is of such consequence.

The primary justification for the spousal confidential communication privilege is that it encourages full and frank communication, which is thought to be essential to the maintenance of a successful marriage. Even Wigmore, who disfavored privileges, approved of a privilege for confidential communications between spouses. The policy behind the privilege accounts for the fact that it is recognized even after the marriage is ended. If it was not, the argument goes, spouses experiencing marital difficulties would be less likely to communicate openly and, thus, less likely to engage in the kind of behavior that will help to preserve the union. The spouses' dignitary interest in maintaining the privacy of their communications also supports the existence of the privilege and its continuation beyond the end of the marital relationship. Similar reasoning accounts for the notion that the privilege does not extend to communications between couples before they are married even though, by the time of the trial, they are wed: If the marriage did not exist at the time of the communication there necessarily was no need at that time to encourage behavior that would preserve a marriage.

3. The Adverse Testimony Privilege

The second spousal privilege is very different. It is not based on confidentiality, but on the principle that partners in marriage should not be pitted against each other in litigation. It is, simply, a witness's privilege not to testify against his or her spouse as to anything.[19] This "testimonial privilege" is recognized in many U.S. jurisdictions, though some apply it only to criminal proceedings, while others apply the privilege in any case in which a spouse is a party. Proposed Federal Rule 505, for example, limits the privilege to criminal cases, while California Evidence Code § 970 applies the privilege in "any proceeding."

Note that the privilege not to testify against one's spouse is not limited to confidential communications. It applies to any testimony that would be adverse to the spouse. For example, assume that one evening, Husband arrives home carrying a duffel bag. When Wife opens it a few minutes later, she sees that the bag is filled with $20 bills. If Husband is later charged with bank robbery, Wife has a privilege not to testify against him, which in this situation

---

19. Some jurisdictions maintain a related privilege not to be *called as a witness* against a spouse. *See, e.g.*, Cal. Evid. Code § 971. This privilege allows the spouse to avoid having to take the witness stand and claim a privilege not to testify against her spouse; even being called as a witness is not permissible.

means a privilege not to testify that Husband arrived home that evening carrying a bag full of money. It would not matter if Husband made no effort to keep his possession of the bag confidential. The bag, the cash, and the Husband's possession of these items are not even communications. Yet the testimonial privilege will allow Wife to refuse to testify against him as to the existence of the bag and anything else.

The policy behind the testimonial privilege is similar to that supporting the privilege for confidential communications between spouses in that it is also designed to preserve marriages. It operates quite differently, however. Whereas the confidential communication privilege preserves marriages by promoting full and frank communication, the testimonial privilege preserves marriages by refusing to compel one spouse to prejudice the other spouse in court. It is hard to argue with the notion that a marriage will be compromised if the testimony of one spouse is the basis for sending the other to prison, even if that testimony is compelled rather than volunteered. This difference in how the privileges protect marriages has an important effect on the duration of the privilege. Unlike the spousal communication privilege, the testimonial privilege ends when the marriage ends. The reason is rather simple: Once the marriage is over, there is no longer a need to avoid pitting the spouses against each other in court. While public policy sometimes favors having former spouses maintain a relationship with each other (such as when there are children), after the marriage has ended the interest in achieving accurate verdicts overrides the policy behind the testimonial privilege.

Thus, the key question in applying the testimonial privilege is whether defendant and witness are married at the time of trial. If not, there is no testimonial privilege even though the events about which the witness will be questioned occurred when the witness and defendant were married. If they are married at the time of trial, the witness may assert the testimonial privilege even though the events about which she would have been questioned took place before the marriage began.[20]

Who is the holder of the testimonial privilege? Some states give the privilege to both parties, some to the testifying spouse, and some to the spouse against whom the testimony would be offered. Proposed Federal Rule 505 would have given the privilege to the party-spouse. The California rule, by providing that "a married person has a privilege not to testify against his spouse . . . ," gives the privilege to the testifying spouse. In 1980, the Supreme Court answered this question for purposes of federal law, overturning prior authority.

TRAMMEL v. UNITED STATES
445 U.S. 40 (1980)

Mr. Chief Justice BURGER delivered the opinion of the Court.

We granted certiorari to consider whether an accused may invoke the privilege against adverse spousal testimony so as to exclude the voluntary testimony

---

20. This means it might be a good strategy for defendants to marry the key eyewitness. It also suggests the possibility of a new way to meet prospective marriage partners: hang around crime scenes.

of his wife. . . . This calls for a re-examination of Hawkins v. United States, 358 U.S. 74, 79 S. Ct. 136, 3 L. Ed. 2d 125 (1958).

I

On March 10, 1976, petitioner Otis Trammel was indicted with two others, Edwin Lee Roberts and Joseph Freeman, for importing heroin into the United States from Thailand and the Philippine Islands and for conspiracy to import heroin in violation of 21 U.S.C. §§ 952(a), 962(a), and 963. The indictment also named six unindicted co-conspirators, including petitioner's wife Elizabeth Ann Trammel.

According to the indictment, petitioner and his wife flew from the Philippines to California in August 1975, carrying with them a quantity of heroin. Freeman and Roberts assisted them in its distribution. Elizabeth Trammel then traveled to Thailand where she purchased another supply of the drug. On November 3, 1975, with four ounces of heroin on her person, she boarded a plane for the United States. During a routine customs search in Hawaii, she was searched, the heroin was discovered, and she was arrested. After discussions with Drug Enforcement Administration agents, she agreed to cooperate with the Government.

Prior to trial on this indictment, petitioner moved to sever his case from that of Roberts and Freeman. He advised the court that the Government intended to call his wife as an adverse witness and asserted his claim to a privilege to prevent her from testifying against him. At a hearing on the motion, Mrs. Trammel was called as a Government witness under a grant of use immunity. She testified that she and petitioner were married in May 1975 and that they remained married.[1] She explained that her cooperation with the Government was based on assurances that she would be given lenient treatment.[2] She then described, in considerable detail, her role and that of her husband in the heroin distribution conspiracy.

After hearing this testimony, the District Court ruled that Mrs. Trammel could testify in support of the Government's case to any act she observed during the marriage and to any communication "made in the presence of a third person"; however, confidential communications between petitioner and his wife were held to be privileged and inadmissible. The motion to sever was denied.

At trial, Elizabeth Trammel testified within the limits of the court's pretrial ruling; her testimony, as the Government concedes, constituted virtually its entire case against petitioner. He was found guilty on both the substantive and conspiracy charges. . . .

II

The privilege claimed by petitioner has ancient roots. Writing in 1628, Lord Coke observed that "it hath beene resolved by the Justices that a wife cannot be produced either against or for her husband." 1 E. Coke, A Commentarie upon

---

1. In response to the question whether divorce was contemplated, Mrs. Trammel testified that her husband had said that "I would go my way and he would go his."

2. The Government represents to the Court that Elizabeth Trammel has not been prosecuted for her role in the conspiracy.

Littleton 6b (1628). *See, generally,* 8 J. Wigmore, Evidence § 2227 (McNaughton rev. 1961). This spousal disqualification sprang from two canons of medieval jurisprudence: first, the rule that an accused was not permitted to testify in his own behalf because of his interest in the proceeding; second, the concept that husband and wife were one, and that since the woman had no recognized separate legal existence, the husband was that one. From those two now long-abandoned doctrines, it followed that what was inadmissible from the lips of the defendant-husband was also inadmissible from his wife.

Despite its medieval origins, this rule of spousal disqualification remained intact in most common-law jurisdictions well into the 19th century. . . . Indeed, it was not until 1933, in Funk v. United States, 290 U.S. 371, 54 S. Ct. 212, 78 L. Ed. 369, that this Court abolished the testimonial disqualification in the federal courts, so as to permit the spouse of a defendant to testify in the defendant's behalf. *Funk,* however, left undisturbed the rule that either spouse could prevent the other from giving adverse testimony. . . . The rule thus evolved into one of privilege rather than one of absolute disqualification. . . .

The modern justification for this privilege against adverse spousal testimony is its perceived role in fostering the harmony and sanctity of the marriage relationship. Notwithstanding this benign purpose, the rule was sharply criticized. . . .

In Hawkins v. United States, 358 U.S. 74, 79 S. Ct. 136, 3 L. Ed. 2d 125 (1958), this Court considered the continued vitality of the privilege against adverse spousal testimony in the federal courts. There the District Court had permitted petitioner's wife, over his objection, to testify against him. With one questioning concurring opinion, the Court held the wife's testimony inadmissible; it took note of the critical comments that the common-law rule had engendered, . . . but chose not to abandon it. Also rejected was the Government's suggestion that the Court modify the privilege by vesting it in the witness-spouse, with freedom to testify or not independent of the defendant's control. The Court viewed this proposed modification as antithetical to the widespread belief, evidenced in the rules then in effect in a majority of the States and in England, "that the law should not force or encourage testimony which might alienate husband and wife, or further inflame existing domestic differences." . . .

Hawkins, then, left the federal privilege for adverse spousal testimony where it found it, continuing "a rule which bars the testimony of one spouse against the other unless both consent." . . . However, in so doing, the Court made clear that its decision was not meant to "foreclose whatever changes in the rule may eventually be dictated by 'reason and experience.'" . . .

III

A . . .

Although Rule 501 confirms the authority of the federal courts to reconsider the continued validity of the *Hawkins* rule, the long history of the privilege suggests that it ought not to be casually cast aside. That the privilege is one affecting marriage, home, and family relationships — already subject to much erosion in our day — also counsels caution. At the same time, we cannot escape the reality that the law on occasion adheres to doctrinal concepts long after the reasons which gave them birth have disappeared and after experience suggest the need for change. . . .

B

Since 1958, when *Hawkins* was decided, support for the privilege against adverse spousal testimony has been eroded further. Thirty-one jurisdictions, including Alaska and Hawaii, then allowed an accused a privilege to prevent adverse spousal testimony. 358 U.S., at 81, n.3, 79 S. Ct., at 140 (Stewart, J., concurring). The number has now declined to 24. . . .

C

Testimonial exclusionary rules and privileges contravene the fundamental principle that "'the public . . . has a right to every man's evidence.'" United States v. Bryan, 339 U.S. 323, 331, 70 S. Ct. 724, 730, 94 L. Ed. 884 (1950). As such, they must be strictly construed and accepted "only to the very limited extent that permitting a refusal to testify or excluding relevant evidence has a public good transcending the normally predominant principle of utilizing all rational means for ascertaining truth." Elkins v. United States, 364 U.S. 206, 234, 80 S. Ct. 1437, 1454, 4 L. Ed. 2d 1669 (1960) (Frankfurter, J., dissenting). Accord, United States v. Nixon, 418 U.S. 683, 709-710, 94 S. Ct. 3090, 3108-3109, 41 L. Ed. 2d 1039 (1974). Here we must decide whether the privilege against adverse spousal testimony promotes sufficiently important interests to outweigh the need for probative evidence in the administration of criminal justice.

It is essential to remember that the *Hawkins* privilege is not needed to protect information privately disclosed between husband and wife in the confidence of the marital relationship — once described by this Court as "the best solace of human existence." Stein v. Bowman, 13 Pet., at 223. Those confidences are privileged under the independent rule protecting confidential marital communications. . . . The *Hawkins* privilege is invoked, not to exclude private marital communications, but rather to exclude evidence of criminal acts and of communications made in the presence of third persons.

No other testimonial privilege sweeps so broadly. The privileges between priest and penitent, attorney and client, and physician and patient limit protection to private communications. . . .

The *Hawkins* rule stands in marked contrast to these three privileges. Its protection is not limited to confidential communications; rather it permits an accused to exclude all adverse spousal testimony. As Jeremy Bentham observed more than a century and a half ago, such a privilege goes far beyond making "every man's house his castle," and permits a person to convert his house into "a den of thieves." 5 Rationale of Judicial Evidence 340 (1827). It "secures, to every man, one safe and unquestionable and every ready accomplice for every imaginable crime." . . .

The ancient foundations for so sweeping a privilege have long since disappeared. Nowhere in the common-law world — indeed in any modern society — is a woman regarded as chattel or demeaned by denial of a separate legal identity and the dignity associated with recognition as a whole human being. Chip by chip, over the years those archaic notions have been cast aside so that "[n]o longer is the female destined solely for the home and the rearing of the family, and only the male for the marketplace and the world of ideas." Stanton v. Stanton, 421 U.S. 7, 14-15, 95 S. Ct. 1373, 1377-1378, 43 L. Ed. 2d 688 (1975).

The contemporary justification for affording an accused such a privilege is also unpersuasive. When one spouse is willing to testify against the other in a criminal proceeding — whatever the motivation — their relationship is almost certainly in disrepair; there is probably little in the way of marital harmony for the privilege to preserve. In these circumstances, a rule of evidence that permits an accused to prevent adverse spousal testimony seems far more likely to frustrate justice than to foster family peace.[12] Indeed, there is reason to believe that vesting the privilege in the accused could actually undermine the marital relationship. For example, in a case such as this the Government is unlikely to offer a wife immunity and lenient treatment if it knows that her husband can prevent her from giving adverse testimony. If the Government is dissuaded from making such an offer, the privilege can have the untoward effect of permitting one spouse to escape justice at the expense of the other. It hardly seems conducive to the preservation of the marital relation to place a wife in jeopardy solely by virtue of her husband's control over her testimony.

<h1 style="text-align:center">IV</h1>

Our consideration of the foundations for the privilege and its history satisfy us that "reason and experience" no longer justify so sweeping a rule as that found acceptable by the Court in *Hawkins*. Accordingly, we conclude that the existing rule should be modified so that the witness-spouse alone has a privilege to refuse to testify adversely; the witness may be neither compelled to testify nor foreclosed from testifying. This modification — vesting the privilege in the witness-spouse — furthers the important public interest in marital harmony without unduly burdening legitimate law enforcement needs.

Here, petitioner's spouse chose to testify against him. That she did so after a grant of immunity and assurances of lenient treatment does not render her testimony involuntary. . . . Accordingly, the District Court and the Court of Appeals were correct in rejecting petitioner's claim of privilege, and the judgment of the Court of Appeals is

Affirmed.

4. *Exceptions to the Spousal Privileges*

The spousal privileges have a number of common exceptions. Neither privilege applies in (1) proceedings to commit either spouse because of the spouse's mental or physical condition; (2) proceedings to determine the competency of a spouse; (3) proceedings between spouses; and (4) criminal prosecutions of one spouse for crimes committed against the other spouse or their child. In addition, the confidential communication privilege has an exception for communications made to enable one or both spouses to commit or plan to commit a crime or fraud.

---

12. It is argued that abolishing the privilege will permit the Government to come between husband and wife, pitting one against the other. That, too, misses the mark. Neither *Hawkins*, nor any other privilege, prevents the Government from enlisting one spouse to give information concerning the other or to aid in the other's apprehension. It is only the spouse's testimony in the courtroom that is prohibited.

None of these exceptions should prove surprising. All involve situations in which the policy behind the privileges either does not apply or does not outweigh the probative value of the evidence a privilege might otherwise conceal.

Further Reading: Richard O. Lempert, *A Right to Every Woman's Evidence*, 66 Iowa L. Rev. 725 (1981); Comment, *The Spousal Testimonial Privilege After Trammel v. United States*, 58 Denv. L.J. 357 (1981).

Questions for Classroom Discussion

1. Does the Supreme Court's decision in *Trammel* take better account of the modern realities of marriage than would a decision to make both spouses holders of the spousal testimonial privilege?

2. Why should the privilege for confidential communications between spouses continue to exist after a marriage has ended? Is there something left to "save" at that point? Why should the testimonial privilege apply if the witness and the accused are married at the time of trial but not at the time of the events in question? Do you see any potential for abuse of this aspect of the law?

3. Murder prosecution. Defendant is married to Witness, but the two have not lived together, or even seen each other, for more than a decade. Each, in fact, is now living with another person. The murder took place when the two were together, however, and the prosecution calls Witness to testify to confidential communications Defendant made that are relevant to the murder. Witness is willing to testify, but Defendant objects. How should the court rule?

4. Bank robbery prosecution. Defendant and Witness are married, but the robbery was committed before they got married. At Defendant's trial, the prosecution wishes to compel Witness to testify that just after she married Defendant, Defendant confided to her that he had robbed the bank. Defendant objects. How should the court rule?

5. Prosecution of Defendant for the murder of Victim. The prosecution alleges that Defendant hid in some bushes next to Victim's home one evening, and attacked Victim when she returned home after work. At trial, the prosecution calls Husband, Defendant's husband, and seeks to elicit testimony that when Husband saw Defendant later that evening, Defendant had mud on her shoes and leaf residue in her hair. Defendant objects on grounds of privilege. How should the court rule?

6. Prosecution of Husband for spousal abuse. At trial, the prosecution calls Wife to testify concerning the abuse. Wife refuses to testify on grounds of privilege. How should the court rule?

H. MISCELLANEOUS PRIVILEGES

At the beginning of this chapter, we noted that the utilitarian rationale for privileges has predominated in the debate over which privileges to recognize. That rationale, for example, explains in large part why the privilege for confidential communications between physician and patient is on the wane, while the privilege for confidential communications between psychotherapist and patient is on the rise. That rationale has rich explanatory value, but it can do little to enlighten us as to why states rarely recognize certain other privileges.

Accountant-client privilege.   Only a few states recognize a privilege for the accountant-client relationship. With respect to many functions accountants serve, including provision of tax services and auditing of financial statements, can it really be said that confidentiality is not essential? Practically speaking, it seems doubtful that a client will be equally as frank with her accountant if she knows the accountant can be compelled to testify about their communications than if she knows confidentiality will be maintained. The absence of widespread recognition of an accountant-client privilege perhaps can better be understood as a result of accountants' relative lack of political influence on lawmaking bodies than as a function of lack of need for confidentiality.

Parent-child privilege.   A similar analysis might explain the rarity of a parent-child privilege, which is recognized in only a few states.[21] Any parent of a teenager can attest to the difficulty of establishing a line of communication about even the most mundane of subjects, and will acknowledge that communication is only possible when the teenager trusts that the discussion will remain confidential. In addition, one would think that parents and children are entitled to privacy in their communications with each other at least as much as attorney and client. As with the accountant-client relationship, the absence of a privilege can be understood as a reflection of the lack of political influence, but it might also stem from a judgment that the loss of relevant information in the resolution of legal disputes is greater than the benefits to be achieved from the existence of a privilege. Nevertheless, the cost of refusing to recognize a privilege can also be great. Consider the following.

---

21. Those few states that do recognize a privilege often limit the privilege to confidential communications from the child to the parent, and hedge the privilege with a number of exceptions. *See, e.g.,* Minn. Stat. § 595.02(1)(j) (limiting privilege to confidential communications from minor child to parent, but creating exception for communications involving crimes against family members); Idaho R. Evid. 514 (privilege applies only in actions or proceedings in which the child is a party, and does not apply to civil actions by child or parent against the other or to criminal prosecution of child or parent for crimes committed against the person or property of the other).

MONICA S. LEWINSKY, *TELL MAMA ALL ABOUT IT? NOT WITHOUT A LAWYER: PARENTS AND CHILDREN SHOULDN'T BE REQUIRED TO TESTIFY AGAINST EACH OTHER*

Los Angeles Times, May 11, 2003, at M5

On Feb. 12, 1998, my mother appeared before a grand jury at the federal courthouse in Washington, D.C. She was not subpoenaed to testify about a robbery she witnessed, or to describe some aspect of a securities fraud, but to be questioned about me—her only daughter.

I was horrified and sickened. Not unlike many young women, I had confided in my mom—to a certain extent—and expected our conversations to remain between us. In a million years I could never have fathomed a situation where we would find our bond—a deep, important and inviolate one—tested to the extent and in the manner that it was.

Few people are aware that, in our country, parents can be forced to testify against their children and vice versa. . . .

All of these existing privileges place value on certain relationships in order to foster and then protect them. Their inviolability is deemed more important than the truth-finding function of the courts.

Isn't the parent-child relationship every bit as important, if not more so?

It is paradoxical that in a country where we often say that our children are our future, and every parent has said, at least once, "you can always come to me," that our system actually undermines the very values it extols.

Today, on Mother's Day, it seems appropriate to express hope that this privilege will soon be nationally afforded.

Just because a parent wants to protect her child's confidence doesn't mean that objectionable behavior is being condoned. But such protection does help ensure a haven as children negotiate the labyrinth of life.

It is completely unreasonable that discussions between parents and children are not protected—be it a teenager who has been caught at school with drugs or a parent who has been wrongly accused and needs to explain herself to her son. The Department of Justice Manual's guidelines discourage a prosecutor from compelling testimony from a defendant's parents or children. But without a formal parent-child privilege, a dodgy prosecutor is free to disregard the department's guidance—which is exactly what happened in my case. Trust me, the mere hint of a parent being subpoenaed—and it's often done just as a tactic to increase pressure on the defendant—is terrifying for a child. (It is a lesser-known fact that there was a threat to subpoena my father too.)

While researching a paper for a Columbia University law and psychology class, I learned the term for the nightmare in which my mother found herself. It's called the "cruel trilemma," in which a person has a three-pronged choice: to commit perjury; testify truthfully and risk harming the relationship; or refuse to testify and go to jail for contempt of court without benefit of trial. No one in a society that calls itself civilized should have such a devastating Hobson's choice. . . .

Further Reading: Larry M. Bauer, *Recognition of a Parent-Child Testimonial Privilege*, 23 St. Louis U. L.J. 676 (1979).

Journalist privilege.   Some jurisdictions recognize a privilege for confidential communications between journalists and their sources. Such a privilege allows journalists to develop information of interest to the public by assuring sources of confidentiality. The privilege also serves to avoid the inevitable conflict that arises when a journalist refuses to comply with a court order to reveal a source and the court must determine whether it is necessary to jail the journalist for contempt of court. Like members of the clergy, journalists often consider the ability to maintain confidentiality essential to their calling, and adherence to their beliefs has led to some celebrated cases of journalists being jailed for long periods of time for refusal to reveal such information. Judges rarely win those confrontations, either by successfully obtaining the journalist's testimony or in the court of public opinion. Still, a journalist's privilege has not achieved universal recognition.

Privilege for political vote.   Because "[s]ecrecy in voting is an essential aspect of effective democratic government, insuring free exercise of the franchise and fairness in elections,"[22] there is a general privilege not to reveal the tenor of one's political vote.

State secrets and official information.   Finally, courts have long recognized certain governmental privileges for state secrets and other official information the disclosure of which might bring harm to the United States. Proposed Federal Rule 509 would have codified a privilege for "secrets of state" "relating to the national defense or the international relations of the United States" and certain types of "official information," defined as follows:

> (2) *Official Information.* "Official information" is information within the custody or control of a department or agency of the government the disclosure of which is shown to be contrary to the public interest and which consists of: (A) intragovernmental opinions or recommendations submitted for consideration in the performance of decisional or policymaking functions, or (B) subject to the provisions of 18 U.S.C. § 3500, investigatory files compiled for law enforcement purposes and not otherwise available, or (C) information within the custody or control of a government department or agency whether initiated within the department or agency or acquired by it in the exercise of its official responsibilities and not otherwise available to the public pursuant to 5 U.S.C. § 552.

Governmental privileges of this type sometimes must yield, as when a criminal defendant can demonstrate that the information is essential to an issue in the trial and that there is a specific need for the information.

---

22. Proposed Fed. R. Evid. 507 Advisory Committee's Note.

Assessments

In answering the following questions, assume that the Federal Rules of Evidence apply, including those rules regarding privileges that were proposed but not enacted.

1. Defendant is being prosecuted for murdering his parents. Defendant met with his attorney in the presence of Defendant's spouse, who he married after the parents were murdered. During the meeting, Defendant said to the attorney, "Sure, I shot them. But your job is to keep me out of jail. Should I plead insanity or self-defense?" Which of the following is correct?

    a. Defendant's statement is not protected by the attorney-client privilege because it was made to further a crime or fraud

    b. Defendant's statement is not protected by the spousal confidential communications privilege because it does not relate to matters that took place during the marriage

    c. Defendant waived the attorney-client privilege by making the communication in the presence of his spouse

    d. Defendant's statement is protected by both the attorney-client privilege and the spousal confidential communications privilege

2. Civil action in federal court under diversity jurisdiction. The federal court sits in a state that has both a spousal confidential communications privilege and a spousal testimonial privilege that applies in both civil and criminal cases. Plaintiff was injured in an automobile accident and claims Defendant drove negligently. Plaintiff calls a witness who at the time of trial is Defendant's husband. The accident occurred before they were married. Plaintiff asks the witness, "On the night of the accident, did Defendant tell you that she got into an accident because she drove through a red light?" Which of the following is correct?

    a. The testimonial privilege applies but the communications privilege does not

    b. The communications privilege applies but the testimonial privilege does not

    c. Both privileges apply

    d. Neither privilege applies

3. Prosecution for attempted murder of Victim. Defendant calls as a witness a priest who serves as a prison chaplain and was present at the execution of Zed for an unrelated murder of a different person. Just before Zed was administered a lethal injection, he was given a final opportunity to speak to the priest, but only in the presence of prison guards. Zed whispered to the priest, "Father, I confess that I tried to kill Victim too." At trial, the priest refuses to testify regarding Zed's confession. Which of the following is correct?

    a. Zed's statement is hearsay, but admissible under the dying declaration exception

(continued)

b. The priest has a privilege to refuse to disclose the confession

c. The priest may assert Zed's privilege and refuse to disclose the confession

d. The confession is not privileged because it was not intended to be confidential and Zed is dead

4. Negligence action arising out of a hit-and-run traffic accident in which Plaintiff, a pedestrian, was injured. Defendant denies he was the driver of the vehicle involved. Plaintiff calls Zed to testify. Zed, an eyewitness to the accident, identifies Defendant as the driver. Zed has a history of psychological and vision problems. To impeach Zed, Defendant offers into evidence the testimony of two doctors. Dr. Abel, a psychiatrist, was retained by Plaintiff's lawyer to evaluate Zed and testify for Plaintiff at trial as an expert witness. Plaintiff never called Dr. Abel to testify. If permitted to testify, Dr. Abel will state that Zed admitted to him that a voice in his head told him Defendant was the hit-and-run driver. Dr. Baker, an ophthalmologist, was retained by Plaintiff's lawyer to test Zed's eyesight and report back to the lawyer on the results. The purpose of this was to help Plaintiff's lawyer prepare Zed to testify. If permitted to testify, Dr. Baker will state that his report indicated Zed suffers from poor eyesight. Which of the following is correct?

a. A privilege objection will be sustained regarding the testimony of both doctors

b. A privilege objection will be sustained regarding the testimony of Dr. Baker but not regarding the testimony of Dr. Abel

c. A privilege objection will be sustained regarding the testimony of Dr. Abel but not regarding the testimony of Dr. Baker

d. The privilege objections will be overruled regarding the testimony of both doctors

5. Plaintiff Zed Corporation, a mobile phone manufacturer, brought an action in federal court for patent infringement against its main competitor, PhoneTech Corporation. To prepare for trial, the attorney for PhoneTech interviewed employees of the company that work in its research and development department. All employees were told before the interviews that conversations with the company's attorney were to be kept confidential. Zed Corporation takes the deposition of one of those employees, Alice, whose job title is assistant technician, third class. The attorney for Zed Corporation asks Alice to relate any communications she had with PhoneTech's attorneys regarding the case. Which of the following is correct?

a. If Alice is not within the control group of PhoneTech, her communications to the company lawyer are not privileged

b. Confidential communications between corporate employees at any rank or level and the company lawyers are privileged

c. Alice's communications to the company lawyer are not privileged because she is not the lawyer's client

d. Alice's communications to the company lawyer are privileged if they were made to facilitate legal services, upper-level management did not possess all the information needed to facilitate those services, and the communications concerned matters within the scope of Alice's job

Answers and Analysis

1. The correct answer is d. Defendant made a confidential communication to his attorney to facilitate professional legal services and made that communication in the presence of someone who was his wife at the time he made the communication. Thus, the basic requirements of both privileges (attorney-client and spousal communications) are satisfied. Answer a is incorrect because the crime-fraud exception does not apply to a communication defendant has with his attorney about defense strategy. This is not in furtherance of the crime. Instead, it is in furtherance of the rendering of professional legal services, which is the point of the privilege. Answer b is incorrect because the spousal confidential communications privilege protects communications made during the marriage, even if they relate to matters that took place prior to the marriage. Answer c is incorrect because, even if the spouse is not present to facilitate professional legal services, there is no waiver of one confidential communication privilege if all those present are within the scope of another confidential communication privilege.

2. The correct answer is a. The communications privilege does not apply because the communication took place before Defendant and the witness were married. Normally, the testimonial privilege would not apply in federal court because the federal version of that privilege applies only in criminal cases. However, Rule 501 states that in cases where state substantive law applies (as in a civil case under diversity jurisdiction), state privilege law applies. Since the state spousal testimonial privilege applies in all cases, that privilege would apply in this civil case. Answer b is incorrect because both propositions there are wrong. Answer c is incorrect because the communications privilege does not apply. Answer d is incorrect because the testimonial privilege applies.

3. The correct answer is c. Proposed Rule 506 recognizes that a person who engages in a confidential communication with a member of the clergy has a privilege to refuse to disclose that communication. Subdivision (c) of that rule provides that the member of the clergy may claim the privilege on behalf of the person. Answer a is incorrect because, while the evidence is hearsay, the federal dying declaration exception only applies in homicide cases and requires that the statement related to the cause or circumstances of the declarant's impending death. Neither of these elements are satisfied here.

(continued)

Answer b is incorrect because proposed Rule 506 does not give the clergy a separate privilege; it only permits the priest to assert Zed's privilege on his behalf. Answer d is incorrect because, since Zed was not given the opportunity to speak to the priest in private, we can conclude that a reasonable person in that position would still intend his confession to be confidential (even though others were present). The fact that he whispered the confession supports this conclusion. While Zed is dead, this does not prevent application of the privilege since proposed Rule 506 specifically states that the privilege can be asserted if the person who communicated with a member of the clergy is deceased.

4.   The correct answer is b. While there is no doctor-patient privilege under federal law, Dr. Baker's testimony is within the scope of the attorney-client privilege. This is because Dr. Baker was retained by the plaintiff's attorney to evaluate Zed's eyesight and report back to the attorney to help prepare the case. As such, the report from Dr. Baker is a confidential communication between an attorney's representative and an attorney. (It might also be protected under the work product doctrine.) Dr. Abel's testimony is not privileged because communications to someone retained by an attorney to testify as an expert witness are not intended to be confidential. Answer a is incorrect because, as just noted, Dr. Baker's testimony regarding the report to Plaintiff's attorney is privileged. Answer c is incorrect because, as stated above, the testimony of Dr. Abel is not privileged but the testimony of Dr. Baker is privileged. Answer d is incorrect because Dr. Baker's testimony is privileged.

5.   The correct answer is d. While *Upjohn* did not establish a clear test for when communications between a corporate employee and the corporation's lawyer are privileged, this answer lists several factors the court identified as justifying the application of the privilege. Answer a is incorrect because *Upjohn* declined to adopt the control group test. Answer b is incorrect because the Court clearly did not intend such a broad coverage of the attorney-client privilege in the corporate context. Answer c is wrong because it suggests that only communications directly between the lawyer and the client can be privileged. Since a corporation is a legal entity and can only speak through its representatives, this is incorrect.

CHAPTER
9

Burdens of Proof and Presumptions

A. BURDENS OF PROOF

There are no Federal Rules of Evidence governing burdens of proof.

1. Introduction

The term *burden of proof* encompasses two concepts: burden of persuasion and burden of production. Burden of persuasion is established by the substantive law, and concerns the final decision in a case. Burden of production is more a creature of evidence law, and guides the court's rulings on motions to dismiss or other motions designed to dispose of the case without submitting it to the jury. The terms thus serve quite different purposes, and must be distinguished.

2. Burden of Persuasion

There are two parts to the burden of persuasion, both established by the substantive law. *First*, the law determines the quantum of evidence that must exist for a party to prevail in a charge, claim, or defense. *Second*, the law determines which party bears the burden of establishing that the required quantum of proof exists.

a. Specifying the Quantum of Evidence

There are three familiar standards defining the quantum of evidence required to prevail on a criminal charge, a civil claim, or a defense. First is the level of proof variously referred to as "more likely than not," "greater weight of the evidence," or "preponderance of the evidence." This is the lowest ultimate burden of persuasion and applies in most civil cases. The party bearing this burden needs only persuade the jury that it is more likely than not that the essential facts exist. Because the party with this burden must tip the scales just past the 50 percent point to prevail, the question of who bears that burden only matters in one instance: when the jury simply cannot decide whether the essential facts of a claim or defense are true. In sports, this would be called a "tie." In the courtroom, we say that the jury is in "equipoise" after considering all the evidence. In such a case, the party bearing the burden of persuasion must lose. That is why the burden of persuasion is sometimes called the *risk of non-persuasion*.

A second level of proof is on the other extreme and applies in criminal cases. In every U.S. jurisdiction, a person may be convicted of a crime only if the fact-finder is persuaded of her guilt "beyond a reasonable doubt." The standard sets a high bar, but it is difficult to describe this standard more precisely. The meaning of *beyond a reasonable doubt* has been the subject of much litigation over the centuries, and, in the end, little clarity has emerged from this debate. Some state courts issue pattern jury instructions that attempt to define the standard. California, for example, uses a jury instruction that defines "reasonable doubt" as follows: "Proof beyond a reasonable doubt is proof that leaves you with an abiding conviction that the charge is true. The evidence need not eliminate all possible doubt because everything in life is open to some possible or imaginary doubt." Cal. Jury Instr. — Crim. 220.

A third standard rests between "more likely than not" and "beyond a reasonable doubt," and generally is described by the phrases "clear and convincing evidence" or "plain, clear, and convincing evidence." Many states apply this standard in civil fraud cases or to those situations in which a party seeks punitive damages. As with "beyond a reasonable doubt," the precise meaning of this standard is elusive. The most that can be said is that a higher degree of proof is needed than applies under the usual civil standard, but that the bar is not as high as with the criminal standard.

b. Identifying Which Party Bears the Burden

Just as the substantive law determines the required quantum of evidence to establish a charge, claim, or defense, it also determines which party bears the burden of establishing that the required quantum of evidence exists. In the criminal law, the answer is always the same with respect to the elements of the crime: The burden is on the prosecution and that burden may never shift to the defendant. The government must prove each fact essential to the crime beyond a reasonable doubt and the court must instruct the jury to that effect. An accused may be required to bear some burden as to affirmative defenses, but never as to the prima facie case.

In civil cases the matter is somewhat more complicated. Usually, the law places the burden on the party that wishes to change the status quo, though other reasons, such as access to evidence, sometimes lead to a different conclusion. Thus, in most tort litigation, it is the plaintiff who seeks to change the status quo by forcing a shift in resources from defendant to plaintiff in order to compensate for loss or to punish for particularly egregious behavior. Thus, the plaintiff bears the burden of persuasion as to the essential elements of the affirmative claim for relief. The same is generally true in other civil litigation as well. As to affirmative defenses, the defendant generally bears the burden of persuasion.

3. Burden of Production

At every moment in a trial, only one party has the responsibility to offer evidence in support of its position. The party bearing that responsibility at any given time is said to have the *burden of production* (sometimes called the *burden of producing evidence* or the *burden of going forward*). The identity of the party who has the burden of production is important when the court is asked to end the case early by dismissal, summary judgment, directed verdict, or similar means. When such a motion is made, the court must determine whether the party who has the burden of production has offered enough evidence to allow the case to continue. If the party has done so, the court will deny the motion. If the party has not done so, the court will grant the motion and end the case or that part of the case to which the motion was addressed.

Usually, the burden of *production* begins with the party who has the burden of *persuasion* as to a particular charge, claim, or defense. Thus, in a criminal case, the prosecution has the burden of persuasion and must offer affirmative evidence to support the elements of the charge. If it fails to do so, the court will dismiss because the prosecution has not met its burden of production. In a civil action, the plaintiff generally bears the burden of persuasion as to the elements of the claim and, thus, must proceed with evidence to support its claim. Failure to do so will result in dismissal because, again, plaintiff has not met its burden of production. The same is true for affirmative defenses where defendant has the burden of persuasion; if the defendant fails to offer evidence to support the defense, the court will not submit that defense to the jury because defendant did not meet its burden of production.

Usually, meeting a burden of production is not difficult. It is sometimes said that meeting a burden of production requires "more than a scintilla" of evidence, but that term has never been defined and is not helpful. It is more useful to think of the problem this way: The party with the burden of production must only offer enough evidence to *support* a verdict in its favor, but need not offer evidence to *require* such a verdict. In ruling on a motion to decide the case early without letting it go to the jury, the court must decide whether there is sufficient evidence to justify a jury verdict in favor of the non-moving party. If so, it must deny the motion. The court might believe that the moving party has the better case, but that does not justify the court's substituting its judgment for that of the jury. The party opposing the motion has met its burden of production so long as the court would not feel the need to overturn a jury verdict in favor of that party.

Most courts hold that, while the burden of production sets a low bar, it must be met with *affirmative* evidence. In Dyer v. MacDougall, 201 F.2d 265 (2d Cir. 1952), for example, plaintiff sued defendant for libel and slander, but plaintiff was unable to produce even a single witness who would verify that the allegedly defamatory statements were actually made. Defendant moved for summary judgment, and plaintiff argued that he should be permitted to go to trial, call the defendant and other witnesses, and have the jury observe their demeanor when they denied that defendant had made the statements. Plaintiff asserted that the jury would be entitled to find that the witnesses were lying, and that, even in the absence of affirmative evidence, plaintiff had proven his case. The court rejected this argument, affirming summary judgment in favor of defendant. In recent years, the Supreme Court has supported this general position in several cases.

The terminology we have employed thus far may seem daunting, but some examples will make the concepts considerably clearer:

1. Prosecution of Defendant for robbery of a convenience store. At trial, the prosecutor's only evidence is the testimony of Witness, the clerk who was on duty when the robbery allegedly occurred. Witness testifies that she was standing behind the register when a person wearing a ski mask walked in, pointed a gun at her, and told her to empty the register. Witness testifies that she did so, giving the robber several hundred dollars, that the robber then told Witness not to call the police and ran out of the store, but that Witness called the police as soon as the robber disappeared. The prosecutor then rests. Defendant moves for a directed verdict on the ground that the evidence is insufficient to support a verdict against him.

   The court should grant the motion. The prosecution has both the burden of persuasion (beyond a reasonable doubt) and the burden of production as to all essential elements of the charge. One such element is the identity of the perpetrator. In this case, the prosecution has offered no evidence connecting Defendant to the crime. As a result, a jury verdict in favor of the prosecution would not be justified, and the court must grant the motion.

2. Same case. After calling Witness, the prosecutor calls Officer, who testifies that she arrested Defendant two blocks from the convenience store ten minutes after the robbery, and that Defendant had about $100 in his wallet when arrested. Again, Defendant moves for a directed verdict.

   Once again, the court should grant Defendant's motion. In this example, the prosecution has offered some circumstantial evidence connecting Defendant to the crime, but the evidence is so weak that no rational jury could find beyond a reasonable doubt that defendant is the person who robbed the store. Evidence that merely places Defendant near the scene and in possession of a modest sum of money would not be sufficient to justify a conviction.

3. Same case. Assume that Witness, the clerk, also testifies that she remembers that two of the $20 bills she gave the perpetrator had been defaced in ink, though she does not recall what markings were made on the bills. The prosecutor produces two $20 bills and establishes a chain of custody leading back to Defendant's wallet, where Officer testified he found them when he arrested Defendant. Someone had written religious messages in ink on the back of each bill. Again, Defendant moves for a directed verdict.

   This is a closer case. The court probably would be justified in either granting or denying the motion. Denying the motion would amount to stating that the jury could find, on the evidence presented and beyond a reasonable doubt, that defendant was the perpetrator. Granting the motion would signify the judge's belief that no rational jury could convict by that high standard on the meager evidence presented.

4. Same case. Assume that in addition to all other testimony, Witness testifies that the robber was male, about six feet tall, wore a green jacket, and walked with a limp. Officer testifies that when she arrested Defendant, Defendant was wearing a green jacket, and that he walked with a limp. The jury can also see that Defendant is about six feet tall. Again, Defendant moves for a directed verdict.

On the state of the evidence in this situation, the court should deny the motion. Certainly, the prosecution has now offered sufficient evidence to meet its burden of production. As already explained, this does not mean that the prosecution has proven its case as a matter of law. (The Constitution, in fact, does not allow the court to direct a verdict for the prosecution in a criminal case.) It merely means that the court must not throw out the case at this point in the trial.

In some situations, a party bearing a burden of production will do more than simply meet that burden. Its evidence might be so compelling that, in the absence of any contrary evidence, a jury could only be justified in finding in favor of the party. What happens in that situation? Suppose that in a lawsuit, Plaintiff must prove that Defendant owned a building where an accident occurred. At trial, Plaintiff offers in evidence a grant deed showing Defendant as the grantee. In addition, Plaintiff calls the county custodian of records, who testifies that she searched the county records for any change of ownership between the date of the grant deed and the date of Plaintiff's accident, and that she could find no record of any other transactions. Plaintiff also calls as a witness the owner of a landscaping company. This witness authenticates a recent contract between her company and Defendant under which the landscaper assumes responsibility for cutting the grass and maintaining flower beds on the property. The court admits both documents into evidence. Plaintiff rests, and Defendant does not offer any evidence contesting ownership or negligence. Plaintiff asks the court to direct a verdict in her favor.

In this case, Plaintiff's proof of ownership almost certainly did more than meet the burden of production. The evidence is so strong that the court would be justified in granting Plaintiff's motion for a directed verdict on the ground that no reasonable jury could reach any conclusion other than that Defendant owned the building in question. In such a case, we say that Plaintiff's evidence has *shifted* the burden of production to Defendant, at least on the issue of Defendant's ownership or control of the property. Once that burden of production has shifted, Defendant must produce some evidence or risk a directed verdict in Plaintiff's favor. Because Defendant did not offer any evidence on this issue, the court will direct a verdict for Plaintiff.

Unlike the burden of persuasion, the burden of production can shift many times during a trial. In our example, Defendant would probably meet the burden of production if it was able to produce some meaningful evidence of non-ownership. In some situations, the evidence might be so compelling to shift the burden of production back to the opponent. Such shifts back and forth are common. The main point is that the identity of the party who has the burden of production at any given point in the trial will determine how the court will view a motion to dispose of the case, or part of the case, summarily.

Questions for Classroom Discussion

1. What rule normally (though not always) determines the party who will have a burden of persuasion in a civil action? Why should the rule operate in that way?

(continued)

2. Can you think of a situation in which this general rule should not apply?

3. Why should a party who bears the burden of persuasion and production as to an issue be denied the opportunity to take a case to trial if the party has no affirmative evidence to support the claim? Why not allow the party to proceed to trial and show, through cross-examination and impeachment of adverse witnesses, that they should not be believed?

4. Negligence action by Plaintiff against Defendant after Plaintiff fell on some stairs in an apartment building allegedly owned by Defendant. Plaintiff claims the stairs were unreasonably dangerous because the handrails were loose, causing her to lose her balance and fall. At trial, Plaintiff testifies about the loose handrails, and calls a doctor to opine about her injuries. Plaintiff then rests, and Defendant moves for a directed verdict. How should the court rule?

5. Same case. In addition to the evidence described above, Plaintiff offers evidence that a sign in front of the building listed Defendant as owner. Plaintiff then rests, and Defendant moves for a directed verdict. How should the court rule?

6. Same case. Assume that the court denies Defendant's motion. Defendant rests without offering any evidence in her defense. Plaintiff moves for a directed verdict. How should the court rule?

7. Same case. In addition to the evidence described above, Plaintiff offers in evidence a self-authenticating, certified copy of a deed dated five years before the accident. The deed purports to grant title to the building to Defendant. Plaintiff then rests, and Defendant moves for a directed verdict. How should the court rule?

8. Same case. Suppose that Defendant offers no evidence to challenge the prima facie case, nor does Defendant offer any evidence to support an affirmative defense such as comparative negligence. Plaintiff moves for a directed verdict on the issue of ownership. How should the court rule?

B. PRESUMPTIONS

FED. R. EVID. 301.   PRESUMPTIONS IN A CIVIL CASE GENERALLY

In a civil case, unless a federal statute or these rules provide otherwise, the party against whom a presumption is directed has the burden of producing evidence to rebut the presumption. But this rule does not shift the burden of persuasion, which remains on the party who had it originally.

FED. R. EVID. 302.   EFFECT OF STATE LAW ON
PRESUMPTIONS IN A CIVIL CASE

In a civil case, state law governs the effect of a presumption regarding a claim or defense for which state law supplies the rule of decision.

1. Inferences and Presumptions

Suppose you are standing on a street corner waiting for the traffic light to change so you can cross the street. The light changes and you start to cross. After you have taken several steps, you hear a loud screeching sound. Looking to your right, you see a vehicle skidding in the intersection with its front end edging downward, its smoking tires locked. Before that vehicle comes to a stop, another vehicle, traveling on the cross street and now having the green light, enters the intersection, where the two vehicles collide. If the drivers subsequently are engaged in litigation, and you are called to testify about what happened, you will likely want to state that the light changed, the driver of the first vehicle tried to brake too late, and the vehicles collided.

The truth, of course, is that you did not see the driver of the first vehicle enter the intersection after the traffic light changed, and you did not see the driver apply the brakes. You are quite certain of these conclusions, however. This is because you feel quite comfortable *inferring* these facts from facts of which you do have knowledge directly from your senses. You saw the light change, you know that a very small amount of time passed after which you saw the vehicle skidding in the intersection with its nose pointing downward and its tires locked and smoking. From these direct observations, you inferred that the vehicle entered the intersection on the red light, that the driver applied the brakes, but that the driver was unable to stop the vehicle in time to avoid the collision.

The process just described is one of *inferential reasoning*. We infer facts from other facts of which we have knowledge. It is a common-sense process that all human beings use every day. But the process is not foolproof; the inferences we make might be wrong. In this example, it is possible that the first vehicle was struck from behind by another car and pushed into the intersection while the light was still green and that its driver applied the brakes to try to control the car's movement. But without any perception of another car, it is logical to infer that this is not what happened.

The fact-finder uses the process of inferential reasoning throughout the trial. Most evidence is circumstantial, and requires the application of a human mind to reach conclusions about the critical facts. Often it is not clear what inferences we should draw from the evidence. In a trial, as in life, we rarely can be absolutely certain.

A *presumption*, in contrast, is a conclusion of fact that the law *requires* the fact-finder to draw from another fact or group of facts. Thus, unlike an inference, which is permissive, where a presumption applies it is mandatory. If certain facts exist, the presumption will *require* that another fact or set of facts be found to exist. But to say that a presumption is mandatory and requires a particular finding of fact is only partly correct. True presumptions are *rebuttable*, meaning that their effect can be overcome under some circumstances, which we will study shortly.

2. A Word About "Conclusive" or "Irrebuttable" Presumptions

Occasionally, we run across a situation in which a court will declare (often in accordance with a statute) that a certain fact is "conclusively" or "irrebuttably" presumed to be true on proof of another fact or series of facts. For example, Article 13 § 30 of the California Constitution provides that "[e]very tax shall be conclusively presumed to have been paid after 30 years from the time it became a lien unless the property subject to the lien has been sold in the manner provided by the Legislature for the payment of the tax." Similarly, California Business and Professions Code § 2660.1 provides: "A patient, client, or customer of a licentiate under this chapter is conclusively presumed to be incapable of giving free, full, and informed consent to any sexual activity which is a violation of Section 726." These are not examples of the kind of presumptions with which we are mainly concerned in this chapter. "Conclusive presumptions" are not actually presumptions because they are not devices for proving certain facts through proof of other facts. Rather, they are rules of law that change the legally significant fact from one to another. To take the example from the California Constitution, payment of tax on certain property normally would be the legally significant fact. But if 30 years has passed from the time a certain tax lien has attached to the property, it no longer matters whether the tax was actually paid since the law will act as if it was paid. The tax is presumed to have been paid and no contrary evidence will be heard. Similarly, the second conclusive presumption essentially provides that a person falling under the provisions of that chapter of the code is incapable as a matter of law of giving consent to sexual activity. This will be true even if, *in fact*, the person is competent. The law *deems* the person incompetent, and no contrary evidence will be heard. We will not pause longer on conclusive or irrebuttable presumptions. Our concern is with rebuttable presumptions.

3. Why We Use Presumptions

Whether a presumption exists is not governed by the law of evidence. A court does not declare in the middle of a case that a new presumption has come into being. Rather, legislatures and courts have created presumptions over the years, many of which are now contained in various places in state and federal codes. Why do legislatures and courts create presumptions? There are at least two reasons. First, some presumptions exist for adjudicative reasons—to ease the proof of facts that are almost certainly true but that might be difficult to prove. For example, it is common for jurisdictions to adhere to a presumption that a letter was received if it was properly stamped, addressed, and mailed. Receipt almost invariably occurs, but it is difficult for the sender to prove. Employing this presumption helps a party to prove the fact and thus avoid the possibility of an inaccurate factual finding. In addition, because the party to whom the letter was sent is in a better position to know and have evidence regarding whether it was received, the presumption helps to ease the imbalance of access to evidence, and thus serves the goal of fairness.

Second, some presumptions serve a public policy of one sort or another. For example, a presumption that a child born to a married woman is the biological child of her husband serves the social function of protecting children from unseemly litigation over their legitimacy.

Some presumptions serve both adjudicative and substantive purposes. For example, a presumption that a person is dead when that person has not been seen or heard from for a specified period of years, both eases proof of a fact almost certainly true but difficult to prove and serves the goal of helping the person's family to wrap up her affairs and put a difficult matter to rest.

4. How Presumptions Operate: Some Terminology

To understand how presumptions operate, you must learn some terminology. We call the facts proven, and from which another fact is to be presumed, the *basic* or *foundational* facts. We call the fact to be presumed the *presumed* fact. When we speak of *rebutting* the presumption, we mean that the party against whom the presumption would operate has offered evidence contradicting either the foundational facts or the presumed fact.

5. Causing a Presumption to Take Effect

A presumption will come into existence once the party wishing to make use of it has offered sufficient evidence of the foundational facts to support a finding that those facts exist. The amount of evidence needed is an amount that would meet a burden of production as to those facts. (See the discussion of burdens of production earlier in this chapter.) Once the party has done this, the presumption comes into play, knocking the ball into the opponent's court.

To take an example, suppose Plaintiff and Defendant are involved in a dispute over the ownership of a valuable antique ring. Suppose further that Plaintiff wishes to make use of the following presumption:[1]

A deed or will or other writing purporting to create, terminate, or affect an interest in real or personal property is presumed to be authentic if it

  (a) is at least 30 years old;
  (b) is in such condition as to create no suspicion concerning its authenticity;
  (c) was kept, or was found, in a place where such writing, if authentic, would be likely to be kept or found; and
  (d) has been generally acted upon as authentic by persons having an interest in the matter.

During the presentation of her case-in-chief, Plaintiff produces a letter signed by her grandmother and dated a few weeks before her death 40 years ago. The letter describes the ring in detail and purports to give it to Plaintiff. Plaintiff testifies that from the time she received the letter 40 years ago, she has kept it in her safe deposit box at a local bank, that nobody ever challenged the letter's

---

1. The presumption is found in Cal. Evid. Code § 643.

authenticity, and that until she let Defendant borrow the ring, she always wore it. Defendant's position is that the letter is a forgery, that Defendant owns the ring, that it was Plaintiff who borrowed the ring, and that when Plaintiff handed the ring to Defendant, Plaintiff was returning a borrowed item.

In this situation, the enumerated facts in subsections (a) through (d) of the statutory presumption are the foundational facts. If Plaintiff offers evidence sufficient to support a finding that each of those facts is true, the presumption that the letter is authentic will go into effect. It appears that the letter and Plaintiff's testimony are sufficient to permit those findings. The letter contains a date more than 30 years ago, nobody had ever challenged its authenticity, the letter was kept in a secure place where one would normally keep important documents, and Plaintiff has worn the ring, apparently without challenge, for the entire period. If the fact-finder determines that each of these foundational facts is true, the presumption will come into effect.

This does not necessarily mean that the case is over, however. Recall that presumptions are rebuttable. We must now discuss how presumptions are rebutted.

6. Rebutting Presumptions

In our example of the antique ring, Plaintiff has offered evidence sufficient to support a finding that the letter conveying the ring to Plaintiff is authentic. That knocks the ball into Defendant's court, and Defendant has four choices:

1. Do nothing;
2. Offer evidence challenging one or more of the foundational facts;
3. Offer evidence challenging the presumed fact (authenticity); or
4. Offer evidence challenging both the foundational and the presumed facts.

We must consider each of these possibilities separately. First, however, let's look at an actual case demonstrating that presumptions can have a very real effect in everyday litigation.

DE FEO v. MERCHANT
115 Misc. 2d 286, 454 N.Y.S.2d 576 (1982)

Sam EISENBERG, City Judge.

This is a summary proceeding instituted under Section 52 of the Tenant Protection Regulations for failure of the tenant to renew his lease under Section 45 of those regulations. The pertinent provisions of Section 45 of the Tenant Protection Regulations are as follows:

> Notice for renewal of lease. On a form prescribed by the Division, every landlord shall notify the tenant in occupancy not more than 90 days and not less than 60 days prior to the end of the tenant's lease term, by certified mail, of such termination of the lease term and offer to renew the lease at the legal regulated rent permitted for such renewal lease and otherwise on the same conditions as the

expiring lease and shall give such tenant a period of 30 days from the date of mailing of such notice to renew such lease and accept the offer. . . .

Section 52 of the Tenant Protection Regulations provides in relevant part as follows:

> Proceedings for eviction — wrongful acts of tenant. An Action or proceeding to recover possession of any housing accommodation shall be maintainable after service and filing of the notice required by Section 53 only upon one or more of the following grounds wherein wrongful acts of the tenants are established. . . .
>   (f) The tenant has refused following notice pursuant to Section 45 to execute a renewal lease at the legal regulated rent authorized under these Regulations and the Act.

The tenants defend against this eviction proceeding by asserting that they never received the notice for renewal of the lease either by certified mail or otherwise and that their experience with respect to delivery of mail within the building by the U.S. Post Office would justify a finding that the notice had not been delivered. Admittedly, the notice for such renewal was mailed by the landlord by certified mail. The issue is therefore sharply drawn. The landlord asserts that all that he need prove is the fact that he mailed the requisite notice by certified mail and his rights flow therefrom without regard to whether the notice was or was not received. Stated otherwise, it is an absolute presumption of receipt from the fact of mailing. In taking this position, the landlord relies upon case law to that effect and an opinion by the Hon. Robert E. Herman, Assistant Commissioner of the State Division of Housing and Community Renewal and the State Rent Administrator. [The Commissioner took the position that the Tenant Protection Regulations do not require receipt of the notice. The court rejected this conclusion.] . . .

It is a general rule that the law presumes that a letter properly addressed, stamped and mailed has been duly delivered to the addressee. In essence there is a presumption of receipt which flows from the fact of mailing. . . . The presumption of receipt from mailing does not bar the acceptance of competent evidence to establish that there was not, in fact, proper mailing. Indeed, the presumption of receipt from mailing does not arise until adequate proof of mailing has been adduced.

A party who seeks to invoke the presumption makes out a prima facie case of receipt by establishing that the mailing was properly made. But, how far may an intended addressee go in rebutting that prima facie case? In the cited case of Trust and Guarantee Company v. Barnhardt, [270 N.Y. 350, 1 N.E.2d 459 (1936),] the Court adopted what appears to be a most rigid position. It determined that a prima facie case of receipt established by competent evidence of proper mailing may not be rebutted by the mere assertion by the addressee that he did not receive the mailed document. It even rejected testimony of failure of delivery by the Post Office "arising from delinquencies or accidents in the post office department." Yet, courts have received testimony of non-receipt despite proof of proper mailing. Thus, in Aetna Ins. Co. v. Millard, 25 A.D.2d 341, 269 N.Y.S.2d 588 [1966], while the Court found that receipt had been proved, it accepted testimony that another letter allegedly mailed the same day had not been received. Similarly, in Michael Caprino v. Nationwide, *supra* and Boyce v.

National Commercial Bank & Trust Co., 41 Misc. 2d 1071, 247 N.Y.S.2d 521, *affd.* 22 A.D.2d 848, 254 N.Y.S.2d 127 [1964], testimony was taken as to the action within the Post Office. In the words of the Court in Teichberg v. Blair, [63 Misc. 2d 1073, 314 N.Y.S.2d 284 [1970], there are three parties involved in the mailing of notices: the sender, the Post Office and the addressee. It would appear therefore that testimony of the Post Office failure should ordinarily be heard on the question of receipt of the mailing.

There is no inconsistency between the determination in Trusts v. Barnhardt, *supra* and the acceptance of rebuttal testimony despite proof of initial mailing. The case of Trusts v. Barnhardt, *supra,* involved a matter of notice of dishonor and protest of a promissory note under a Canadian statute which by its express language provided that,

> Such notice so addressed shall be sufficient, although the place of residence of such party is other than either of the places aforesaid, and shall be deemed to have been duly served and given for all purposes if it is deposited in any post office, with the postage paid thereon, at any time during the day on which presentment has been made. . . .

Both as a matter of public policy related to the commercial requirements of notice of protest and dishonor and by reason of the statutory provision, the Court rejected testimony of non-receipt, so long as mailing by the sending party was established.

We may conclude, therefore, that where a statute makes the mailing sufficient to establish receipt, or where public policy so dictates, so long as proper mailing has been established, no rebuttal testimony of non-receipt will be accepted. On the other hand, absent such a statute or a countervailing public policy, testimony is admissible of non-receipt and of inadequate mailing. That testimony may include proof of improper mailing by the sender or of Post Office failure or any other pertinent evidence which would tend to establish non-delivery of the requisite notice.

Applying these rules to this case, the Court finds the following: The petitioner did mail the notice by certified mail. There is no statute or regulation which makes such mailing absolute proof of receipt. There has been a denial of receipt and that denial is supported by evidence of frequent failures by the Post Office to properly deposit the mail within the mail boxes in the building. The likelihood of non-delivery and non-receipt is further supported by the prompt reaction of the tenants in seeking to renew their lease upon learning of the proposed action to terminate their tenancy.

For these reasons the Court finds for the tenants. No legal fees are awarded to the respondents, since the proceeding was necessary to resolve and determine the rights of the parties. Costs are awarded to the respondents.

De Feo was a bench trial. Even so, note the importance of the presumption in that case. If the tenant defendants had not been able to rebut the presumption that they received the notice terminating their tenancy, the court would have deemed their tenancy legally terminated, and they would have been forced to vacate their homes.

We now turn to the various ways in which parties may respond to a presumption that would operate against them.

a. What If the Opponent Does Nothing?

Return to our hypothetical involving the antique ring. If Defendant fails to offer any evidence challenging either the foundational facts or the presumed fact that the letter is authentic, *and* the fact-finder determines that each foundational fact is true, the presumption will require that the letter be deemed authentic. The way this works is that, at the conclusion of the case, the court will issue to the jury an instruction providing essentially as follows:

> The law presumes that a writing is authentic if it is at least 30 years old, if its condition does not create any suspicion about its authenticity, if it was kept in a place where such a writing, if authentic, would likely be kept, and if the writing has generally been acted upon as authentic by persons having an interest in the matter. In the present case, Plaintiff has offered evidence as to each of these facts. If you find from all the testimony in this case that Plaintiff has proven each of these facts to you, by a preponderance of the evidence, then you must find that the letter conveying ownership of the ring to Plaintiff is authentic.

The jury will then determine whether each foundational fact is true. If the jury finds by a preponderance of the evidence that each such fact is true, the jury will be required to decide that the letter from Plaintiff's grandmother giving the ring to Plaintiff is authentic.

Note how the presumption differs from an inference. If the presumption did not exist, the jury might well decide, based on the letter and Plaintiff's testimony, that the letter is authentic. That decision would be logical in these circumstances. But the jury would not be *required* to make that decision because an inference is always permissive. Once a presumption is created, the presence of the foundational facts *requires* a decision that the ring was conveyed to Plaintiff.

b. What If the Opponent Only Challenges One or More of the Foundational Facts?

Suppose in our hypothetical that Defendant calls an expert document examiner who testifies that the paper stock on which the letter was written was not produced until ten years ago and that, therefore, the letter could not be more than ten years old. That testimony would challenge the first foundational fact (that the writing is at least 30 years old). Assume Defendant offers no other evidence concerning any of the foundational facts and does not otherwise offer evidence establishing that she, not Plaintiff, owned the ring. What happens to the presumption?

The answer is that nothing happens to the presumption. Plaintiff's testimony about each foundational fact did not *establish* those facts; it only created a question for the jury to decide. By the same token, the testimony of Defendant's expert did not establish that one of the foundational facts is untrue; it only challenged Plaintiff's testimony. Thus, the court should do the same thing it would do if Defendant did *not* produce any evidence challenging the foundational or presumed facts: Let the jury decide if the foundational facts are true and instruct that jury that, if it so finds, it must find that the letter is authentic.

c. What If the Opponent Only Challenges the Presumed Fact?

Suppose Defendant offers no testimony concerning the foundational facts, but calls a witness who claims she had personal knowledge that the grandmother's signature on the letter was forged when the letter was written 40 years ago. That testimony would challenge the presumed fact that the letter is authentic. In addition, the evidence is certainly strong enough to meet a burden of production as to the non-existence of the presumed fact (that is, strong enough to support a finding that the fact is not true). What happens to the presumption now?

This is where things get a little complicated. There are at least two basic approaches about the effect of evidence challenging the existence of the presumed fact. Each approach is associated with two American evidence scholars. The first, usually known as the "Thayer-Wigmore" or "bursting bubble" approach, claims that the only effect of a presumption is to shift the *burden of production* to the party against whom it operates (in our hypothetical, Defendant). The theory is that although presumptions might have some substantive grounding, their primary purpose is adjudicative — to ease proof of facts that are almost certainly true but might be difficult to prove. On that view, once light has been shed on the presumed fact (by the presentation of evidence challenging its existence), the presumption disappears. The metaphor is that presumptions are "like bats of the law flitting in the twilight, but disappearing in the sunshine of actual facts."[2]

According to the bursting bubble theory, what is left after evidence sufficient to support a finding that the presumed fact exists is not the presumption, but simply a permissible inference. The court has no reason to mention the presumption to the jury, and indeed should not do so because the instruction would likely have too much influence. Rather, the court should submit the case to the jury on all the evidence, as though a presumption never existed.

The second approach about the effect of evidence challenging the existence of the presumed fact is usually associated with Professors Morgan and McCormick. These scholars argued that presumptions exist primarily for reasons of substantive policy and that, if they were to disappear whenever evidence was presented challenging the presumed fact, they would have too little effect. The Morgan-McCormick view therefore provides that when a presumption comes into effect, it shifts to the opponent the *burden of persuasion* as to the presumed fact.[3] This means the opponent must now *prove* that the presumed fact is untrue, or the jury must find that it is true. On this view, the presentation of evidence challenging the existence of the presumed fact does not defeat the presumption and cause it to disappear like some bursting bubble; it merely presents the jury with contrary evidence.

---

2. Mackowik v. Kansas City, St. Josephs & Council Bluffs R. Co., 94 S.W. 256, 262 (Mo. 1906).
3. The burden of persuasion is discussed earlier in this chapter.

Because the Morgan-McCormick view of presumptions is that they shift the burden of persuasion as to the presumed fact, a court following that approach would have to instruct the jury about the presumption even if the party against whom it would operate presents evidence challenging the presumed fact. In our hypothetical, the instruction might provide as follows:

> The law presumes that a writing is authentic if it is at least 30 years old, if its condition does not create any suspicion about its authenticity, if it was kept in a place where such a writing, if authentic, would likely be kept, and if the writing has generally been acted upon as authentic by persons having an interest in the matter. In the present case, Plaintiff has offered evidence as to each of these facts. Defendant, in turn, has presented evidence that the signature on the letter was forged. If you find from all the testimony in this case that Plaintiff has proven each of the facts set forth in this instruction, by a preponderance of the evidence, then the burden of persuasion will be on Defendant to prove that the letter is not authentic. That is, unless Defendant has proven to you, by a preponderance of the evidence, that the letter is a forgery, you must find that the letter is authentic.

There is at least one more possible approach to the effect of evidence challenging the existence of the presumed facts. When one considers the many types of presumptions contained in law, it becomes apparent that some are entirely or largely based on adjudicative considerations such as facilitating proof, while others are mainly based on considerations of substantive policy. Assuming it is possible to determine the strongest basis for each presumption, one could divide presumptions along these lines and treat those that are based primarily on adjudicative considerations as bursting bubble presumptions (shifting only the burden of producing evidence), and treat those based primarily on substantive policy considerations as Morgan-McCormick presumptions (shifting the burden of persuasion). This is the approach of the California Evidence Code, which groups rebuttable presumptions in two classes, one of which shifts the burden of production only, while the other shifts the burden of proof, meaning the burden of persuasion. Of course, the list of presumptions in the Evidence Code is hardly exhaustive; many other presumptions exist in California law and it is not always easy to determine the primary reason for each presumption. But the California approach is eminently reasonable, albeit complicated, and largely avoids the unnecessary conflict between the bursting bubble and Morgan-McCormick theories of presumptions. (The California Evidence Code includes the presumption in our hypothetical among those that shift only the burden of production. That means it is subject to the bursting bubble theory.)

d. What If the Opponent Challenges Both the Foundational and the Presumed Facts?

Under the bursting bubble theory of presumptions, nothing changes. Assuming Defendant's evidence is sufficient to meet a burden of production as to the non-existence of the presumed fact, the presumption, if it would ever have taken effect, will disappear, leaving only a permissive inference of Plaintiff's ownership.

Under the Morgan-McCormick view, things are more complicated. The court's task will be to examine the evidence both sides have offered concerning both the foundational and presumed facts, and act accordingly. A proposed Federal Rule of Evidence that would have provided a procedure for such cases was all but incomprehensible and was never enacted. It will not be mentioned further here.

e. A Caveat

Regardless of the theory of presumptions being used by the court, it is possible that either party's evidence might be so strong as to take the case from the jury altogether. In that situation, the court should simply instruct the jury that the presumption exists. In our case of the antique ring, suppose that Plaintiff's evidence tending to establish the foundational facts concerning the letter from her grandmother is so compelling that no rational jury could decide that the facts are untrue, and that Defendant challenges neither the foundational facts nor the presumed facts. The court should simply instruct the jury that the letter is authentic.

By the same token, suppose Defendant presents a copy of a judgment convicting another person of forging the letter. In that situation, Defendant's evidence suggesting the non-existence of the foundational facts does far more than meet a burden of production; it almost certainly creates an inference so strong that no rational jury would reject it. The court therefore should instruct the jury that the letter was not authentic.

7. *Conflicting Presumptions in the Same Case*

What if the foundational facts for two presumptions can be found to exist in the same case, but the presumed facts for the two presumptions are in conflict with each other? Imagine the following case:

> Plaintiff, a tenant, sues Defendant, the landlord, following Plaintiff's May 15 fall on a common stairway in the building. Plaintiff claims the handrails were loose and that she fell when she tried to use one to help her descend the stairway. Plaintiff claims she notified Defendant of the defect at least a week before the accident. To prove notice, Plaintiff testifies that on May 5, she wrote a letter to Defendant describing the condition, that she addressed the letter properly to Defendant at Defendant's address in the same city, that she placed a stamp on the letter, and that she mailed it at a post office the same day. Plaintiff also produces a photocopy of the letter, made just before she sent it. Defendant denies receiving the letter and points out that, in any event, the photocopy produced by Plaintiff shows that the letter was dated June 5, three weeks *after* the accident.

Two common presumptions are as follows:

1. A letter correctly addressed and properly mailed is presumed to have been received in the ordinary course of mail.[4]
2. A writing is presumed to have been truly dated.[5]

---

4. *See* Cal. Evid. Code § 640.
5. *See* Cal. Evid. Code § 641.

The parties appear to have offered sufficient evidence to support a finding of the foundational facts for each of these presumptions, but application of both presumptions would lead to a direct conflict concerning the fact. Plaintiff's testimony was sufficient to meet a burden of production on the foundational facts of proper addressing and mailing of the letter on May 5. Because Defendant's address was in the same city from which Plaintiff mailed the letter, a presumption would come into being that Defendant received the letter no more than two or three days after Plaintiff mailed it, well before the accident. The date on the letter, however, establishes the foundational fact for the presumption on which Defendant relies: that the letter was not written until June 5. What should the court do?

Some courts hold that in such a case, the court must apply the presumption that has a stronger basis in logic and policy. If, for example, one presumption is based on a strong social policy, and its application would appear to lead to the outcome most in step with logic and everyday experience, that presumption might trump a presumption that exists only to facilitate proof and perhaps has a weaker logical basis in this situation. But here, neither presumption appears to be based strongly on policy; both probably exist almost entirely to facilitate proof. In addition, most letters properly addressed and mailed are received in the ordinary course of the mail, and most writings bearing a date are correctly dated. When neither presumption trumps the other on grounds of policy or logic, the best course for the court is probably to ignore both presumptions and simply let the case go to the jury on the facts. In our hypothetical, the jury would hear all the evidence and simply determine when Defendant received the notice. This is an entirely rational and reasonable approach.[6]

8. Presumptions in Criminal Cases

An accused should not be convicted except upon "proof beyond a reasonable doubt of every fact necessary to constitute the crime with which he is charged." In re Winship, 397 U.S. 358 (1970). Moreover, the Fifth and Fourteenth Amendments to the Constitution give criminal defendants the right to trial by jury. Taken together, these principles make the application of presumptions against an accused quite problematic. In a series of cases, the U.S. Supreme Court has made clear that there is little or no room for the application of such devices (which it calls mandatory presumptions) in criminal cases.[7] If a presumption, either as written or as the court describes it to the jury, *requires* the jury to reach a certain finding of fact based on the existence of other facts, the presumption, at

6. This is the approach taken by the Maine Supreme Court in Atkinson v. Hall, 556 A.2d 651 (Me. 1989), a paternity action. Plaintiff, who was married to another man when the child was born, wished to make use of a presumption that blood tests showing a "paternity index" of 98.27 created a presumption of paternity that could only be rebutted by clear and convincing evidence of non-paternity. Defendant wished to use a presumption that a child born during a lawful marriage is presumed to be the child of the husband unless the party claiming otherwise proves the husband's non-paternity beyond a reasonable doubt. The court held that the blood test presumption was founded on stronger considerations of logic, but that the marital presumption was based on stronger considerations of policy. Accordingly, the court held that both presumptions should be ignored, and that the plaintiff simply had the burden of proving defendant's paternity by a preponderance of the evidence.

7. Francis v. Franklin, 471 U.S. 307 (1985); Ulster County v. Allen, 442 U.S. 140 (1979); Sandstrom v. Montana, 442 U.S. 510 (1979).

least as applied by the court, is likely unconstitutional. The Court has held that a presumption can be saved if the court applies it in a non-mandatory way (making it what the court calls a *permissive presumption*), but that in virtually all situations, a true "mandatory" presumption may not be employed against an accused.

9. *Presumptions Under the Federal Rules of Evidence*

Federal Rules 301 and 302, quoted earlier, govern the use of presumptions in civil actions. Rule 301 most likely adopts the "bursting bubble" theory of presumptions because it provides that the "party against whom a presumption is directed has the burden of going forward with evidence to rebut the presumption. But this rule does not shift the burden of proof in the sense of the risk of nonpersuasion. . . ." Rule 302, however, follows the *Erie* doctrine by leaving to state law the application of presumptions that "regard [] a claim or defense for which state law supplies the rule of decision." Thus, in diversity actions, presumptions that would supply facts that constitute elements of claims or defenses are governed by state law. If, for example, state law applied the Morgan-McCormick view of presumptions, that view would be applied in such a situation.

The Federal Rules do not address the use of presumptions in criminal cases. As we indicated previously, the Supreme Court has addressed that issue as a matter of constitutional law.

Further Reading: Ronald J. Allen, *Presumptions in Civil Actions Reconsidered*, 66 Iowa L. Rev. 843 (1981); Ronald J. Allen, *Structuring Jury Decisionmaking in Criminal Cases: A Unified Constitutional Approach to Evidentiary Devices*, 94 Harv. L. Rev. 321 (1980); James Joseph Duane, *What Message Are We Sending to Criminal Jurors When We Ask Them to "Send a Message" with Their Verdict?*, 22 Am. J. Crim. L. 565 (1995); Michael H. Graham, *Presumptions — More Than You Ever Wanted to Know and Yet Were Too Disinterested to Ask*, 17 Crim. L. Bull. 431 (1981); Charles V. Laughlin, *In Support of the Thayer Theory of Presumptions*, 52 Mich. L. Rev. 195 (1953); Charles T. McCormick, *What Shall the Trial Judge Tell the Jury about Presumptions?*, 13 Wash. L. Rev. 185 (1938); Charles Nesson, *Rationality, Presumptions, and Judicial Comment: A Response to Professor Allen*, 94 Harv. L. Rev. 1574 (1981); Stephen A. Saltzburg, *Standards of Proof and Preliminary Questions of Fact*, 27 Stan. L. Rev. 271 (1975); Leo H. Whinery, *Presumptions and Their Effect*, 54 Okla. L. Rev. 553 (2001).

Questions for Classroom Discussion

1. How does a presumption differ from an inference?

2. In *De Feo*, what was the effect of the landlord's evidence that notice was mailed to the tenants?

3. What evidence did the tenants offer concerning the question of receipt of the notice?

---

4. What was the effect of the tenants' evidence of non-receipt?

5. What would have happened if the tenants simply testified that they did not receive the notice, but offered no further evidence concerning that issue?

6. A state maintains a presumption that an automobile driven by a relative of the owner is driven with the permission of the owner and for the owner's purposes. Plaintiff is injured when struck by a car driven by Zed, Defendant's cousin. Plaintiff sues Defendant on the theory that Defendant was negligent for letting Zed use the car. Assume Zed is a reckless driver, and that a reasonable person would have recognized that to be true. If Plaintiff wishes to make use of this presumption, and Defendant argues that under the circumstances, even a rational inference would not be possible or would be extremely weak, what should the court do?

7. If a particular presumption is based on the very high likelihood that certain facts are true, but there might be an imbalance of access to the evidence or the fact is otherwise difficult to prove, why would it be unconstitutional to apply the presumption against a criminal defendant? Wouldn't our refusal to apply the presumption more likely lead to an inaccurate outcome?

All of the remaining questions are based on the following basic facts:

Negligence action by Plaintiff, a business tenant in Defendant's office building, arising from Plaintiff's slip-and-fall on a common walkway leading to the building. Plaintiff alleges that the walkway is dangerously slippery when wet, that she notified Defendant of the condition two weeks before the accident, but that Defendant did nothing to make it safer. To prove that she notified Defendant of the condition, Plaintiff testifies that, two weeks before the accident, she wrote a letter to Defendant, addressed it to Defendant's office, which was in the same building, stamped the letter, and deposited the letter in a regular postal service mailbox. The jurisdiction maintains a presumption that "a letter correctly addressed and properly mailed is received in the ordinary course of the mail." Assume that the ordinary course of the mail in this instance is two days.

8. Defendant does not cross-examine Plaintiff concerning the letter, offers no evidence to contradict Plaintiff's testimony, and does not testify concerning receipt or non-receipt of the letter. Plaintiff asks the court to instruct the jury that if it finds that Plaintiff properly addressed and mailed the letter, Defendant received it in approximately two days. Should the court issue the instruction?

9. To prove Plaintiff did not mail the letter, Defendant calls Witness, who testifies that on the day Plaintiff claims to have mailed the

letter to Defendant, Plaintiff was out of the state on business. Defendant offers no other evidence concerning the mailing or receipt of the letter. Plaintiff asks for the same instruction as in Question 8. Should the court issue it?

10. Defendant testifies that she personally picked up her mail each day from the date on which Plaintiff claims to have mailed the letter until at least two weeks later, that she examined each piece of mail, and that she saw no letter from Plaintiff. Plaintiff asks for the same jury instruction as in Question 8. Should the court issue it?

Assessments

1. Action for breach of contract in connection with the sale of widgets by Plaintiff to Defendant. Assume that Plaintiff has the burden of persuasion as to each of the elements of a claim for breach including that Plaintiff and Defendant entered into this contract, Defendant breached its promise under the contract, Plaintiff fulfilled its promise under the contract or was excused from doing so, and Plaintiff suffered damage as a consequence of Defendant's breach. Assume Plaintiff calls a witness who testifies that she overheard Defendant say to Plaintiff, "I accept your offer for widgets." Assuming Defendant offers no evidence as to whether the contract was created, which of the following is correct?
   a. The court should allow the jury to decide whether, by a preponderance of the evidence, Plaintiff has shown that they entered into the contract
   b. The court should instruct the jury that Plaintiff and Defendant entered into the contract
   c. The court should instruct the jury that Defendant now has the burden of persuasion on the question of whether they entered into a contract and should allow the jury to decide whether, by a preponderance of the evidence, Defendant has shown that they did not enter into a contract
   d. The court should direct a verdict for Plaintiff and award judgment

2. Same case. Assume that Plaintiff offers evidence to prove Plaintiff and Defendant entered into the contract, Defendant breached the contract, and Plaintiff fulfilled its promise under the contract. However, Plaintiff failed to offer any evidence to show it suffered damage as a result of Defendant's breach. If Defendant moves for a directed verdict at the close of Plaintiff's case, which of the following should the court do?

    a. Deny the motion because a reasonable jury could decide the case for Plaintiff

    b. Deny the motion and order Defendant to present its case

    c. Defer ruling on the motion until the close of Defendant's case

    d. Grant the motion

3. Plaintiff and Defendant both claim ownership of a strip of land between their properties. The jurisdiction recognizes a rebuttable presumption that a deed affecting an interest in real property is presumed to be authentic if it is at least 30 years old, is kept in a place where a deed would be expected to be found if authentic, does not on its face present any irregularities that suggest it is not authentic, and has been acted upon as authentic by persons who have an interest in the property. The jurisdiction also follows the "bursting bubble" theory of presumptions. The deed purports be signed by the prior owner of the disputed land, Zed, and conveys the land to Plaintiff. At trial, Plaintiff offers evidence as to each of the foundational facts that give rise to the presumption of authenticity. Defendant then calls to testify a handwriting expert and a lay witness who is familiar with Zed's signature. Both witnesses offer the opinion that the signature on the document is not Zed's. Plaintiff then asks the judge to instruct the jury that, if it finds all the foundational facts giving rise to the presumption exist, it must find that the deed conveying the land to Plaintiff is authentic. Which of the following is correct?

    a. Assuming the court finds that Plaintiff produced sufficient evidence to meet her burden of production on the foundational facts, it should give the requested instruction to the jury

    b. Assuming the court finds that Plaintiff produced sufficient evidence to meet her burden of production on the foundational facts, it should instruct the jury that the deed is authentic

    c. Even if the court finds that Plaintiff produced sufficient evidence to meet her burden of production on the foundational facts, it should not give the requested instruction

    d. Assuming the court believes the expert and lay witness testimony disputing the authenticity of the signature, the court should instruct the jury that the deed is not authentic

4. Plaintiff, the mother of a baby, brings a paternity action against Defendant. Defendant denies that he is the father. Plaintiff and Defendant are not married. The jurisdiction recognizes that, if a man and a woman who are not married to each other were living together and the woman subsequently gives birth to a child, there is a rebuttable presumption that the child was fathered by that man if the child was born within 300 days of the last date on which the man and woman were living together. At trial, Plaintiff testifies that she and Defendant were not married to each other and lived together for years. She further testifies that they only stopped living together three months before the child was born. Defendant then testifies that he moved out a year before the birth of the child. No other

(continued)

evidence regarding paternity is introduced. Plaintiff asks the court to instruct the jury that, if it finds that Plaintiff and Defendant were living together within 300 days of the birth of the child, it must find that Defendant is the father of the child. Which of the following is correct?

a. The court should find that Plaintiff produced sufficient evidence to meet her burden of production on the foundational fact of cohabitation and give the requested instruction

b. If the court believes Plaintiff, it should instruct the jury that it must conclude that Defendant is the father

c. The court should conclude that Defendant has produced sufficient evidence to meet his burden of production on the foundational fact of cohabitation and, thus, should refuse to give Plaintiff's instruction

d. If the court believes Defendant, it should instruct the jury that it must conclude that Defendant is not the father

5. Plaintiff, the mother of a baby, brings a paternity action against Defendant. Defendant denies that he is the father. Plaintiff and Defendant were married at the time the child was born. The jurisdiction has a statute that provides: "The child of a wife born while the wife is cohabiting with her husband is conclusively presumed to be the child of the husband." Plaintiff testifies that the child was born while she was married to and cohabiting with Defendant. Defendant offers into evidence the testimony of an expert witness that a blood test established that Defendant is not the father of the child. Which of the following is correct?

a. The testimony of the expert witness should be admitted and the court should instruct the jury that it may weigh that evidence against the presumption

b. The testimony of the expert witness should be admitted and the court should instruct the jury that Defendant has the burden of persuading the jury that he is not the father

c. The testimony of the expert witness should not be admitted and the court should instruct the jury that Defendant is the father

d. The testimony of the expert witness should not be admitted and the court should instruct the jury that, if it finds Plaintiff and Defendant were married and cohabiting at the time of birth, it must find that Defendant is the father of the child

Answers and Analysis

1. The correct answer is a. Since Plaintiff has the burden of persuasion on the question of whether Plaintiff and Defendant entered into the contract, it typically will also have the burden of producing evidence of that fact. Plaintiff has met its burden of production by presenting witness testimony that Defendant said, "I accept your offer for widgets." But the mere fact that Plaintiff has met its burden of production

does not mean it has met its burden of persuasion. It only means that the jury will be permitted to consider whether Plaintiff has met its burden of persuasion (as opposed to having the court grant a motion to dismiss in Defendant's favor). And the fact that Plaintiff met its burden of production does not shift the burden of persuasion to Defendant. Thus, answer a is correct since the jury must decide whether Plaintiff met its burden of persuasion (preponderance of the evidence in this civil case). Answer b is incorrect since, even if Defendant fails to offer any evidence, the jury still must decide if Plaintiff met its burden of persuasion. Answer c is wrong because it incorrectly assumes that if Plaintiff meets its burden of production, that shifts the burden of persuasion to Defendant. Answer d is wrong because the court will not direct a verdict on the strength of evidence going only to one element in Plaintiff's prima facie case.

2. The correct answer is d. Plaintiff has the burden of persuasion as to each element of the prima facie case for breach of contract and also has the burden of producing evidence on each of those elements. Failure to present any evidence as to damages means Plaintiff has not met these burdens. The court should direct a verdict for Defendant even though Plaintiff met its burden of persuasion regarding the other elements of its prima facie case. Answer a is incorrect because, since Plaintiff did not meet its burden as to damages, no reasonable jury could find for Plaintiff. Answer b is incorrect because, if Plaintiff does not meet the burden of producing evidence as to damages, Defendant is under no obligation to present any evidence on that issue. Answer c is incorrect for the same reason. Thus, there is no need to wait until Defendant has put on its case to rule on the motion.

3. The correct answer is c. In this problem, Defendant contests the existence of the presumed fact (i.e., that the deed bears the authentic signature of Zed) but does not contest the foundational facts. Under the "bursting bubble" theory of presumptions, a presumption only shifts the burden of production regarding the presumed fact to the opponent. This means that when the opponent offers evidence of the non-existence of the presumed fact that is sufficient to meet the burden of production, the presumption disappears from the case. The jury is then free to consider all the conflicting evidence and draw whatever logical inferences it wants. In this case, Plaintiff produced evidence sufficient to meet her burden of production as to each foundational fact giving rise to the presumption that the deed is authentic. This shifted the burden of production regarding the presumed fact to Defendant. Defendant's evidence was sufficient to meet that burden. This means the presumption of authenticity has no further impact, leaving the jury to draw whatever inferences it wants from all the pertinent evidence. Answer a is incorrect because Defendant met its burden of production, which

(continued)

negated the presumption. Answer b is wrong for the same reason. Answer d is incorrect because, while the presumption has no further effect when Defendant met its burden of production, Defendant's evidence was not so overwhelming as to require what is essentially a directed verdict for Defendant. When the "bubble bursts" the jury can still draw logical inferences from the evidence proving the foundational facts that gave rise to the presumption. Thus, it could still infer from that evidence that the deed is authentic.

4. The correct answer is a. In this problem, Defendant contests the existence of the foundational fact (that the couple were living together within 300 days from the date of the child's birth). This means it is up to the jury to weigh the conflicting testimony and decide if the foundational fact exists. But if the jury so finds, the presumption applies and the jury must find the presumed fact (paternity). This is precisely what Plaintiff asks the court to instruct the jury. Since Plaintiff met her burden of producing evidence by testifying that they lived together until just three months before birth, a is correct. Answers b and d are incorrect because it is not up to the judge to decide which party's testimony to believe. That is the job of the jury. Answer c is incorrect because, while it is true that Defendant has met his burden of production, this does not justify an instruction that amounts to a directed verdict for Defendant. Instead, it simply means that the factual question of when cohabitation terminated goes to the jury for decision.

5. The correct answer is d. A so-called conclusive presumption is really a substantive rule of law that provides that, if the foundational facts are true, the truth of the presumed fact will be established and cannot be refuted by contrary evidence. A conclusive presumption is created to promote a certain public policy. Here, the presumption is designed to protect the legitimacy of children born to married, cohabiting couples. Evidence concerning the blood test is simply irrelevant because this rule of substantive law establishes that the facts of consequence are marriage and cohabitation — not actual biological parentage. But the jury still needs to determine if the foundation facts of marriage and cohabitation existed. Thus, the court should instruct the jury that if it finds those facts to be true, it must conclude Defendant is the father. Answer a is incorrect because this is a conclusive, not a rebuttable, presumption. As such, evidence offered to rebut that presumption should not be received. Answer b is incorrect for the same reason. Answer c is wrong because, even in the case of a conclusive presumption, the jury still needs to determine the existence of the foundational facts that give rise to that presumption.

APPENDIX A

The Federal Rules of Evidence

ARTICLE I. GENERAL PROVISIONS

Rule 101. Scope; Definitions

(a) Scope. These rules apply to proceedings in United States courts. The specific courts and proceedings to which the rules apply, along with exceptions, are set out in Rule 1101.

(b) Definitions. In these rules:

(1) "civil case" means a civil action or proceeding;

(2) "criminal case" includes a criminal proceeding;

(3) "public office" includes a public agency;

(4) "record" includes a memorandum, report, or data compilation;

(5) a "rule prescribed by the Supreme Court" means a rule adopted by the Supreme Court under statutory authority; and

(6) a reference to any kind of written material or any other medium includes electronically stored information.

(Pub. L. 93-595, § 1, Jan. 2, 1975, 88 Stat. 1929; Mar. 2, 1987, eff. Oct. 1, 1987; Apr. 25, 1988, eff. Nov. 1, 1988; Apr. 22, 1993, eff. Dec. 1, 1993; Apr. 26, 2011, eff. Dec. 1, 2011.)

RESTYLED RULE 101 — ADVISORY COMMITTEE'S NOTE

The language of Rule 101 has been amended, and definitions have been added, as part of the general restyling of the Evidence Rules to make them more easily understood and to make style and terminology consistent throughout the rules. These changes are intended to be stylistic only. There is no intent to change any result in any ruling on evidence admissibility.

The reference to electronically stored information is intended to track the language of Fed. R. Civ. P. 34.

The Style Project

The Evidence Rules are the fourth set of national procedural rules to be restyled. The restyled Rules of Appellate Procedure took effect in 1998. The restyled Rules of Criminal Procedure took effect in 2002. The restyled Rules of Civil Procedure took effect in 2007.

The restyled Rules of Evidence apply the same general drafting guidelines and principles used in restyling the Appellate, Criminal, and Civil Rules.

1. General Guidelines

Guidance in drafting, usage, and style was provided by Bryan Garner, *Guidelines for Drafting and Editing Court Rules,* Administrative Office of the United States Courts (1969) and Bryan Garner, *A Dictionary of Modern Legal Usage* (2d ed. 1995). *See also* Joseph Kimble, *Guiding Principles for Restyling the Civil Rules,* in *Preliminary Draft of Proposed Style Revision of the Federal Rules of Civil Procedure,* at page x (Feb. 2005) (*available at* http://www.uscourts .gov/rules/Prelim_draft_proposed_pt1.pdf); Joseph Kimble, *Lessons in Drafting from the New Federal Rules of Civil Procedure,* 12 Scribes J. Legal Writing 25 (2008-2009). For specific commentary on the Evidence restyling project, *see* Joseph Kimble, *Drafting Examples from the Proposed New Federal Rules of Evidence,* 88 Mich. B.J. 52 (Aug. 2009); 88 Mich. B.J. 46 (Sept. 2009); 88 Mich. B.J. 54 (Oct. 2009); 88 Mich. B.J. 50 (Nov. 2009).

2. Formatting Changes

Many of the changes in the restyled Evidence Rules result from using format to achieve clearer presentations. The rules are broken down into constituent parts, using progressively indented subparagraphs with headings and substituting vertical for horizontal lists. "Hanging indents" are used throughout. These formatting changes make the structure of the rules graphic and make the restyled rules easier to read and understand even when the words are not changed. Rules 103, 404(b), 606(b), and 612 illustrate the benefits of formatting changes.

3. Changes to Reduce Inconsistent, Ambiguous, Redundant, Repetitive, or Archaic Words

The restyled rules reduce the use of inconsistent terms that say the same thing in different ways. Because different words are presumed to have different meanings, such inconsistencies can result in confusion. The restyled rules reduce inconsistencies by using the same words to express the same meaning. For example, consistent expression is achieved by not switching between "accused" and "defendant" or between "party opponent" and "opposing party" or between the various formulations of civil and criminal action/case/proceeding.

The restyled rules minimize the use of inherently ambiguous words. For example, the word "shall" can mean "must," "may," or something else, depending on context. The potential for confusion is exacerbated by the fact the word "shall" is no longer generally used in spoken or clearly written English. The restyled rules replace "shall" with "must," "may," or "should," depending on which one the context and established interpretation make correct in each rule.

The restyled rules minimize the use of redundant "intensifiers." These are expressions that attempt to add emphasis, but instead state the obvious and create negative implications for other rules. The absence of intensifiers in the restyled rules does not change their substantive meaning. *See, e.g.,* Rule 104(c) (omitting "in all cases"); Rule 602 (omitting "but need not"); Rule 611(b) (omitting "in the exercise of discretion").

The restyled rules also remove words and concepts that are outdated or redundant.

4. Rule Numbers

The restyled rules keep the same numbers to minimize the effect on research. Subdivisions have been rearranged within some rules to achieve greater clarity and simplicity.

5. No Substantive Change

The Committee made special efforts to reject any purported style improvement that might result in a substantive change in the application of a rule. The Committee considered a change to be "substantive" if any of the following conditions were met:

a. Under the existing practice in any circuit, the change could lead to a different result on a question of admissibility (e.g., a change that requires a court to provide either a less or more stringent standard in evaluating the admissibility of particular evidence);

b. Under the existing practice in any circuit, it could lead to a change in the procedure by which an admissibility decision is made (e.g., a change in the time in which an objection must be made, or a change in whether a court must hold a hearing on an admissibility question);

c. The change would restructure a rule in a way that would alter the approach that courts and litigants have used to think about, and argue about, questions of admissibility (e.g., merging Rules 104(a) and 104(b) into a single subdivision); or

d. It changes a "sacred phrase" — one that has become so familiar in practice that to alter it would be unduly disruptive to practice and expectations. Examples in the Evidence Rules include "unfair prejudice" and "truth of the matter asserted."

ADVISORY COMMITTEE'S NOTE
56 F.R.D. 183, 194 (1973)

Rule 1101 specifies in detail the courts, proceedings, questions, and stages of proceedings to which the rules apply in whole or in part.

ADVISORY COMMITTEE'S NOTE — 1987 AMENDMENT

United States bankruptcy judges are added to conform this rule with Rule 1101(b) and Bankruptcy Rule 9017.

ADVISORY COMMITTEE'S NOTE — 1988 AMENDMENT

The amendment is technical. No substantive change is intended.

ADVISORY COMMITTEE'S NOTE — 1993 AMENDMENT

This revision is made to conform the rule to changes made by the Judicial Improvements Act of 1990.

Rule 102.   Purpose

These rules should be construed so as to administer every proceeding fairly, eliminate unjustifiable expense and delay, and promote the development of evidence law, to the end of ascertaining the truth and securing a just determination.

(Pub. L. 93-595, § 1, Jan. 2, 1975, 88 Stat. 1929; Apr. 26, 2011, eff. Dec. 1, 2011.)

RESTYLED RULE 102 — ADVISORY COMMITTEE'S NOTE

The language of Rule 102 has been amended as part of the restyling of the Evidence Rules to make them more easily understood and to make style and terminology consistent throughout the rules. These changes are intended to be stylistic only. There is no intent to change any result in any ruling on evidence admissibility.

ADVISORY COMMITTEE'S NOTE
56 F.R.D. 183, 194 (1973)

For similar provisions *see* Rule 2 of the Federal Rules of Criminal Procedure, Rule 1 of the Federal Rules of Civil Procedure, California Evidence Code § 2, and New Jersey Evidence Rule 5.

Rule 103.   Rulings on Evidence

(a) **Preserving a Claim of Error.** A party may claim error in a ruling to admit or exclude evidence only if the error affects a substantial right of the party and:

(1) if the ruling admits evidence, a party, on the record:

(A) timely objects or moves to strike; and

(B) states the specific ground, unless it was apparent from the context; or

(2) if the ruling excludes evidence, a party informs the court of its substance by an offer of proof, unless the substance was apparent from the context.

(b) **Not Needing to Renew an Objection or Offer of Proof.** Once the court rules definitively on the record — either before or at trial — a party need not renew an objection or offer of proof to preserve a claim of error for appeal.

(c) **Court's Statement About the Ruling; Directing an Offer of Proof.** The court may make any statement about the character or form of the evidence, the objection made, and the ruling. The court may direct that an offer of proof be made in question-and-answer form.

(d) **Preventing the Jury from Hearing Inadmissible Evidence.** To the extent practicable, the court must conduct a jury trial so that inadmissible evidence is not suggested to the jury by any means.

(e) **Taking Notice of Plain Error.** A court may take notice of a plain error affecting a substantial right, even if the claim of error was not properly preserved.

(Pub. L. 93-595, § 1, Jan. 2, 1975, 88 Stat. 1930; Apr. 17, 2000, eff. Dec. 1, 2000; Apr. 26, 2011, eff. Dec. 1, 2011.)

RESTYLED RULE 103 — ADVISORY COMMITTEE'S NOTE

The language of Rule 103 has been amended as part of the restyling of the Evidence Rules to make them more easily understood and to make style and terminology consistent throughout the rules. These changes are intended to be stylistic only. There is no intent to change any result in any ruling on evidence admissibility.

ADVISORY COMMITTEE'S NOTE
56 F.R.D. 183, 195 (1973)

Subdivision (a) states the law as generally accepted today. Rulings on evidence cannot be assigned as error unless (1) a substantial right is affected, and (2) the nature of the error was called to the attention of the judge, so as to alert him to the proper course of action and enable opposing counsel to take proper corrective measures. The objection and the offer of proof are the techniques for accomplishing these objectives. For similar provisions *see* Uniform Rules 4 and 5; California Evidence Code §§ 353 and 354; Kansas Code of Civil Procedure §§ 60-404 and 60-405. The rule does not purport to change the law with respect to harmless error. *See* 28 U.S.C. § 2111, F. R. Civ. P. 61, F. R. Crim. P. 52, and decisions construing them. The status of constitutional error as harmless or not is treated in Chapman v. California, 386 U.S. 18, 87 S. Ct. 824, 17 L. Ed. 2d 705 (1967), *reh. denied, id.* 987, 87 S. Ct. 1283, 18 L. Ed. 2d 241.

Subdivision (b). The first sentence is the third sentence of Rule 43(c) of the Federal Rules of Civil Procedure virtually verbatim. Its purpose is to reproduce for an appellate court, insofar as possible, a true reflection of what occurred in the trial court. The second sentence is in part derived from the final sentence of Rule 43(c). It is designed to resolve doubts as to what testimony the witness would have in fact given, and, in nonjury cases, to provide the appellate court with material for a possible final disposition of the case in the event of reversal of a ruling which excluded evidence. *See* 5 Moore's Federal Practice § 43.11 (2d ed. 1968). Application is made discretionary in view of the practical impossibility of formulating a satisfactory rule in mandatory terms.

Subdivision (c). This subdivision proceeds on the supposition that a ruling which excludes evidence in a jury case is likely to be a pointless procedure if the excluded evidence nevertheless comes to the attention of the jury. Bruton v. United States, 389 U.S. 818, 88 S. Ct. 126, L. Ed. 2d 70 (1968). Rule 43(c) of the Federal Rules of Civil Procedure provides: "The court may require the offer to be made out of the hearing of the jury." In re McConnell, 370 U.S. 230, 82 S. Ct. 1288, 8 L. Ed. 2d 434 (1962), left some doubt whether questions on which an offer is based must first be asked in the presence of the jury. The subdivision answers in the negative. The judge can foreclose a particular line of testimony and counsel can protect his record without a series of questions before the jury, designed at best to waste time and at worst "to waft into the jury box" the very matter sought to be excluded.

Subdivision (d). This wording of the plain error principle is from Rule 52(b) of the Federal Rules of Criminal Procedure. While judicial unwillingness to be constructed by mechanical breakdowns of the adversary system has been more pronounced in criminal cases, there is no scarcity of decisions to the same effect in civil cases. In general, *see* Campbell, Extent to Which Courts of Review Will Consider Questions Not Properly Raised and Preserved, 7 Wis. L. Rev. 91, 160 (1932); Vestal, Sua Sponte Consideration in Appellate Review, 27 Fordham L. Rev. 477 (1958-59); 64 Harv. L. Rev. 652 (1951). In the nature of things the application of the plain error rule will be more likely with respect to the admission of evidence than to exclusion, since failure to comply with normal requirements of offers of proof is likely to produce a record which simply does not disclose the error.

ADVISORY COMMITTEE'S NOTE — 2000 AMENDMENT

The amendment applies to all rulings on evidence whether they occur at or before trial, including so-called "*in limine*" rulings. One of the most difficult questions arising from *in limine* and other evidentiary rulings is whether a losing party must renew an objection or offer of proof when the evidence is or would be offered at trial, in order to preserve a claim of error on appeal. Courts have taken differing approaches to this question. Some courts have held that a renewal at the time the evidence is to be offered at trial is always required. *See, e.g.*, Collins v. Wayne Corp., 621 F.2d 777 (5th Cir. 1980). Some courts have taken a more flexible approach, holding that renewal is not required if the issue decided is one that (1) was fairly presented to the trial court for an initial ruling, (2) may be decided as a final matter before the evidence is actually offered, and (3) was ruled on definitively by the trial judge. *See, e.g.*, Rosenfeld v. Basquiat, 78 F.3d 84 (2d Cir. 1996) (admissibility of former testimony under the Dead Man's Statute; renewal not required). Other courts have distinguished between objections to evidence, which must be renewed when evidence is offered, and offers of proof, which need not be renewed after a definitive determination is made that the evidence is inadmissible. *See, e.g.*, Fusco v. General Motors Corp., 11 F.3d 259 (1st Cir. 1993). Another court, aware of this Committee's proposed amendment, has adopted its approach. Wilson v. Williams, 182 F.3d 562 (7th Cir. 1999) (en banc). Differing views on this question create uncertainty for litigants and unnecessary work for the appellate courts.

The amendment provides that a claim of error with respect to a definitive ruling is preserved for review when the party has otherwise satisfied the objection or offer of proof requirements of Rule 103(a). When the ruling is definitive, a renewed objection or offer of proof at the time the evidence is to be offered is more a formalism than a necessity. *See* Fed. R. Civ. P. 46 (formal exceptions unnecessary); Fed. R. Cr. P.51 (same); United States v. Mejia-Alarcon, 995 F.2d 982, 986 (10th Cir. 1993) ("Requiring a party to review an objection when the district court has issued a definitive ruling on a matter that can be fairly decided before trial would be in the nature of a formal exception and therefore unnecessary."). On the other hand, when the trial court appears to have reserved its ruling or to have indicated that the ruling is provisional, it makes sense to require the party to bring the issue to the court's attention subsequently. *See, e.g.*, United States v. Vest, 116 F.3d 1179, 1188 (7th Cir. 1997) (where the trial court ruled *in limine* that testimony from defense witnesses could not be admitted, but allowed the defendant to seek leave at trial to call the witnesses should their testimony turn out to be relevant, the defendant's failure to seek such leave at trial meant that it was "too late to reopen the issue now on appeal"); United States v. Valenti, 60 F.3d 941 (2d Cir. 1995) (failure to proffer evidence at trial waives any claim of error where the trial judge had stated that he would reserve judgment on the *in limine* motion until he had heard the trial evidence).

The amendment imposes the obligation on counsel to clarify whether an *in limine* or other evidentiary ruling is definitive when there is doubt on that point. *See, e.g.*, Walden v. Georgia-Pacific Corp., 126 F.3d 506, 520 (3d Cir. 1997) (although "the district court told plaintiffs' counsel not to reargue every ruling, it did not countermand its clear opening statement that all of its rulings were tentative, and counsel never requested clarification, as he might have done").

Even where the court's ruling is definitive, nothing in the amendment prohibits the court from revisiting its decision when the evidence is to be offered. If the court changes its initial ruling, or if the opposing party violates the terms of the initial ruling, objection must be made when the evidence is offered to preserve the claim of error for appeal. The error, if any, in such a situation occurs only when the evidence is offered and admitted. United States Aviation Underwriters, Inc. v. Olympia Wings, Inc., 896 F.2d 949, 956 (5th Cir. 1990) ("objection is required to preserve error when an opponent, or the court itself, violates a motion *in limine* that was granted"); United States v. Roenigk, 810 F.2d

809 (8th Cir. 1987) (claim of error was not preserved where the defendant failed to object at trial to secure the benefit of a favorable advance ruling).

A definitive advance ruling is reviewed in light of the facts and circumstances before the trial court at the time of the ruling. If the relevant facts and circumstances change materially after the advance ruling has been made, those facts and circumstances cannot be relied upon on appeal unless they have been brought to the attention of the trial court by way of a renewed, and timely, objection, offer of proof, or motion to strike. *See* Old Chief v. United States, 519 U.S. 172, 182, n.6 (1997) ("It is important that a reviewing court evaluate the trial court's decision from its perspective when it had to rule and not indulge in review by hindsight."). Similarly, if the court decides in an advance ruling that proffered evidence is admissible subject to the eventual introduction by the proponent of a foundation for the evidence, and that foundation is never provided, the opponent cannot claim error based on the failure to establish the foundation unless the opponent calls that failure to the court's attention by a timely motion to strike or other suitable motion. *See* Huddleston v. United States, 485 U.S. 681, 690, n.7 (1988) ("It is, of course, not the responsibility of the judge *sua sponte* to ensure that the foundation evidence is offered; the objector must move to strike the evidence if at the close of the trial the offeror has failed to satisfy the condition.").

Nothing in the amendment is intended to affect the provisions of Fed. R. Civ. P. 72(a) or 28 U.S.C. § 636(b)(1) pertaining to nondispositive pretrial rulings by magistrate judges in proceedings that are not before a magistrate judge by consent of the parties. Fed. R. Civ. P. 72(a) provides that a party who fails to file a written objection to a magistrate judge's nondispositive order within ten days of receiving a copy "may not thereafter assign as error a defect" in the order. 28 U.S.C. § 636(b)(1) provides that any party "may serve and file written objections to such proposed findings and recommendations as provided by rules of court" within ten days of receiving a copy of the order. Several courts have held that a party must comply with this statutory provision in order to preserve a claim of error. *See, e.g.*, Wells v. Shriners Hospital, 109 F.3d 198, 200 (4th Cir. 1997) ("[i]n this circuit, as in others, a party 'may' file objections within ten days or he may not, as he chooses, but he 'shall' do so if he wishes further consideration"). When Fed. R. Civ. P. 72(a) or 28 U.S.C. § 636(b)(1) is operative, its requirement must be satisfied in order for a party to preserve a claim of error on appeal, even where Evidence Rule 103(a) would not require a subsequent objection or offer of proof.

Nothing in the amendment is intended to affect the rule set forth in Luce v. United States, 469 U.S. 38 (1984), and its progeny. The amendment provides that an objection or offer of proof need not be renewed to preserve a claim of error with respect to a definitive pretrial ruling. *Luce* answers affirmatively a separate question: whether a criminal defendant must testify at trial in order to preserve a claim of error predicated upon a trial court's decision to admit the defendant's prior convictions for impeachment. The *Luce* principle has been extended by many lower courts to other situations. *See* United States v. DiMatteo, 759 F.2d 831 (11th Cir. 1985) (applying *Luce* where the defendant's witness would be impeached with evidence offered under Rule 608). *See also* United States v. Goldman, 41 F.3d 785, 788 (1st Cir. 1994) ("Although *Luce* involved impeachment by conviction under Rule 609, the reasons given by the Supreme Court for requiring the defendant to testify apply with full force to the kind of Rule 403 and 404 objections that are advanced by Goldman in this case."); Palmieri v. DeFaria, 88 F.3d 136 (2d Cir. 1996) (where the plaintiff decided to take an adverse judgment rather than challenge an advance ruling by putting on evidence at trial, the *in limine* ruling would not be reviewed on appeal); United States v. Ortiz, 857 F.2d 900 (2d Cir. 1988) (where uncharged misconduct is ruled admissible if the defendant pursues a certain defense, the defendant must actually pursue that defense at trial in order to preserve a claim of error on appeal); United States v. Bond, 87 F.3d 695 (5th Cir. 1996) (where the trial court rules *in limine* that the defendant would waive his fifth amendment privilege were he to testify, the defendant must take the stand and testify in order to challenge that ruling on appeal).

The amendment does not purport to answer whether a party who objects to evidence that the court finds admissible in a definitive ruling, and who then offers the evidence to "remove the sting" of its anticipated prejudicial effect, thereby waives the right to appeal the trial court's ruling. *See, e.g.,* United States v. Fisher, 106 F.3d 622 (5th Cir. 1997) (where the trial judge ruled *in limine* that the government could use a prior conviction to impeach the defendant if he testified, the defendant did not waive his right to appeal by introducing the conviction on direct examination); Judd v. Rodman, 105 F.3d 1339 (11th Cir. 1997) (an objection made *in limine* is sufficient to preserve a claim of error when the movant, as a matter of trial strategy, presents the objectionable evidence herself on direct examination to minimize its prejudicial effect); Gill v. Thomas, 83 F.3d 537, 540 (1st Cir. 1996) ("by offering the misdemeanor evidence himself, Gill waived his opportunity to object and thus did not preserve the issue for appeal"); United States v. Williams, 939 F.2d 721 (9th Cir. 1991) (objection to impeachment evidence was waived where the defendant was impeached on direct examination).

Rule 104.   Preliminary Questions

(a) **In General.** The court must decide any preliminary question about whether a witness is qualified, a privilege exists, or evidence is admissible. In so deciding, the court is not bound by evidence rules, except those on privilege.

(b) **Relevance That Depends on a Fact.** When the relevance of evidence depends on whether a fact exists, proof must be introduced sufficient to support a finding that the fact does exist. The court may admit the proposed evidence on the condition that the proof be introduced later.

(c) **Conducting a Hearing So That the Jury Cannot Hear It.** The court must conduct any hearing on a preliminary question so that the jury cannot hear it if:

    (1) the hearing involves the admissibility of a confession;

    (2) a defendant in a criminal case is a witness and so requests; or

    (3) justice so requires.

(d) **Cross-Examining a Defendant in a Criminal Case.** By testifying on a preliminary question, a defendant in a criminal case does not become subject to cross-examination on other issues in the case.

(e) **Evidence Relevant to Weight and Credibility.** This rule does not limit a party's right to introduce before the jury evidence that is relevant to the weight or credibility of other evidence.

(Pub. L. 93-595, §1, Jan. 2, 1975, 88 Stat. 1930; Mar. 2, 1987, eff. Oct. 1, 1987; Apr. 26, 2011, eff. Dec. 1, 2011.)

RESTYLED RULE 104 — ADVISORY COMMITTEE'S NOTE

The language of Rule 104 has been amended as part of the restyling of the Evidence Rules to make them more easily understood and to make style and terminology consistent throughout the rules. These changes are intended to be stylistic only. There is no intent to change any result in any ruling on evidence admissibility.

ADVISORY COMMITTEE'S NOTE
56 F.R.D. 183, 196 (1973)

Subdivision (a). The applicability of a particular rule of evidence often depends upon the existence of a condition. Is the alleged expert a qualified physician? Is a witness whose former testimony is offered unavailable? Was a stranger present during a conversation between attorney and client? In each instance the admissibility of evidence will turn upon the answer to the question of the existence of the condition. Accepted practice, incorporated in the rule, places on the judge the responsibility for these determinations. McCormick § 53; Morgan, Basic Problems of Evidence 45-50 (1962).

To the extent that these inquiries are factual, the judge acts as a trier of fact. Often, however, rulings on evidence call for an evaluation in terms of a legally set standard. Thus when a hearsay statement is offered as a declaration against interest, a decision must be made whether it possesses the required against-interest characteristics. These decisions, too, are made by the judge.

In view of these considerations, this subdivision refers to preliminary requirements generally by the broad term "questions," without attempt at specification.

This subdivision is of general application. It must, however, be read as subject to the special provisions for "conditional relevancy" in subdivision (b) and those for confessions in subdivision (d).

If the question is factual in nature, the judge will of necessity receive evidence pro and con on the issue. The rule provides that the rules of evidence in general do not apply to this process. McCormick § 53, p. 123, n.8, points out that the authorities are "scattered and inconclusive," and observes:

> Should the exclusionary law of evidence, "the child of the jury system" in Thayer's phrase, be applied to this hearing before the judge? Sound sense backs the view that it should not, and that the judge should be empowered to hear any relevant evidence, such as affidavits or other reliable hearsay.

This view is reinforced by practical necessity in certain situations. An item, offered and objected to, may itself be considered in ruling on admissibility, though not yet admitted in evidence. Thus the content of an asserted declaration against interest must be considered in ruling whether it is against interest. Again, common practice calls for considering the testimony of a witness, particularly a child, in determining competency. Another example is the requirement of Rule 602 dealing with personal knowledge. In the case of hearsay, it is enough, if the declarant "so far as appears [has] had an opportunity to observe the fact declared." McCormick, § 10, p. 19.

If concern is felt over the use of affidavits by the judge in preliminary hearings on admissibility, attention is directed to the many important judicial determinations made on the basis of affidavits. Rule 47 of the Federal Rules of Criminal Procedure provides:

> An application to the court for an order shall be by motion. . . . It may be supported by affidavit.

The Rules of Civil Procedure are more detailed. Rule 43(e), dealing with motions generally, provides:

> When a motion is based on facts not appearing of record the court may hear the matter on affidavits presented by the respective parties, but the court may direct that the matter be heard wholly or partly on oral testimony or depositions.

Rule 4(g) provides for proof of service by affidavit. Rule 56 provides in detail for the entry of summary judgment based on affidavits. Affidavits may supply the foundation for temporary restraining orders under Rule 65(b).

The study made for the California Law Revision Commission recommended an amendment to Uniform Rule 2 as follows:

> "In the determination of the issue aforesaid [preliminary determination], exclusionary rules shall not apply, subject, however, to Rule 45 and any valid claim of privilege." Tentative Recommendation and a Study Relating to the Uniform Rules of Evidence (Article VIII, Hearsay), Cal. Law Revision Comm'n, Rep., Rec. & Studies, 470 (1962).

The proposal was not adopted in the California Evidence Code. The Uniform Rules are likewise silent on the subject. However, New Jersey Evidence Rule 8(1), dealing with preliminary inquiry by the judge, provides:

> In his determination the rules of evidence shall not apply except for Rule 4 [exclusion on grounds of confusion, etc.] or a valid claim of privilege.

Subdivision (b). In some situations, the relevancy of an item of evidence, in the large sense, depends upon the existence of a particular preliminary fact. Thus when a spoken statement is relied upon to prove notice to X, it is without probative value unless X heard it. Or if a letter purporting to be from Y is relied upon to establish an admission by him, it has no probative value unless Y wrote or authorized it. Relevance in this sense has been labelled "conditional relevancy." Morgan, Basic Problems of Evidence 45-46 (1962). Problems arising in connection with it are to be distinguished from problems of logical relevancy, e.g., evidence in a murder case that accused on the day before purchased a weapon of the kind used in the killing, treated in Rule 401.

If preliminary questions of conditional relevancy were determined solely by the judge, as provided in subdivision (a), the functioning of the jury as a trier of fact would be greatly restricted and in some cases virtually destroyed. These are appropriate questions for juries. Accepted treatment, as provided in the rule, is consistent with that given fact questions generally. The judge makes a preliminary determination whether the foundation evidence is sufficient to support a finding of fulfillment of the condition. If so, the item is admitted. If after all the evidence on the issue is in, pro and con, the jury could reasonably conclude that fulfillment of the condition is not established, the issue is for them. If the evidence is not such as to allow a finding, the judge withdraws the matter from their consideration. Morgan, *supra*; California Evidence Code § 403; New Jersey Rule 8(2). *See also* Uniform Rules 19 and 67.

The order of proof here, as generally, is subject to the control of the judge.

Subdivision (c). Preliminary hearings on the admissibility of confessions must be conducted outside the hearing of the jury. *See* Jackson v. Denno, 378 U.S. 368, 84 S. Ct. 1774, 12 L. Ed. 2d 908 (1964). Otherwise, detailed treatment of when preliminary matters should be heard outside the hearing of the jury is not feasible. The procedure is time consuming. Not infrequently the same evidence which is relevant to the issue of establishment of fulfillment of a condition precedent to admissibility is also relevant to weight or credibility, and time is saved by taking foundation proof in the presence of the jury. Much evidence on preliminary questions, though not relevant to jury issues, may be heard by the jury with no adverse effect. A great deal must be left to the discretion of the judge who will act as the interests of justice require.

Subdivision (d). The limitation upon cross-examination is designed to encourage participation by the accused in the determination of preliminary matters. He may testify concerning them without exposing himself to cross-examination generally. The provision is necessary because of the breadth of cross-examination under Rule 611(b). The rule does not address itself to questions of the subsequent use of testimony given by an accused at a hearing on a preliminary matter. *See* Walder v. United States, 347 U.S. 62 (1954); Simmons v. United States, 390 U.S. 377 (1968); Harris v. New York, 401 U.S. 222 (1971).

Subdivision (e). For similar provisions *see* Uniform Rule 8; California Evidence Code § 406; Kansas Code of Civil Procedure § 60-408; New Jersey Evidence Rule 8(1).

ADVISORY COMMITTEE'S NOTE — 1987 AMENDMENT

The amendments are technical. No substantive change is intended.

Rule 105.   Limiting Evidence That Is Not Admissible Against Other Parties or for Other Purposes

If the court admits evidence that is admissible against a party or for a purpose — but not against another party or for another purpose — the court, on timely request, must restrict the evidence to its proper scope and instruct the jury accordingly.

(Pub. L. 93-595, § 1, Jan. 2, 1975, 88 Stat. 1930; Apr. 26, 2011, eff. Dec. 1, 2011.)

RESTYLED RULE 105 — ADVISORY COMMITTEE'S NOTE

The language of Rule 105 has been amended as part of the restyling of the Evidence Rules to make them more easily understood and to make style and terminology consistent throughout the rules. These changes are intended to be stylistic only. There is no intent to change any result in any ruling on evidence admissibility.

ADVISORY COMMITTEE'S NOTE
56 F.R.D. 183, 200 (1973)

A close relationship exists between this rule and Rule 403 which requires exclusion when "probative value is substantially outweighed by the danger of unfair prejudice, confusion of the issues, or misleading the jury." The present rule recognizes the practice of admitting evidence for a limited purpose and instructing the jury accordingly. The availability and effectiveness of this practice must be taken into consideration in reaching a decision whether to exclude for unfair prejudice under Rule 403. In Bruton v. United States, 389 U.S. 818, 88 S. Ct. 126, 19 L. Ed. 2d 70 (1968), the Court ruled that a limiting instruction did not effectively protect the accused against the prejudicial effect of admitting in evidence the confession of a codefendant which implicated him. The decision does not, however, bar the use of limited admissibility with an instruction where the risk of prejudice is less serious.

Similar provisions are found in Uniform Rule 6; California Evidence Code § 355; Kansas Code of Civil Procedure § 60-406; New Jersey Evidence Rule 6. The wording of the present rule differs, however, in repelling any implication that limiting or curative instructions are sufficient in all situations.

Rule 106.   Remainder of or Related Writings or Recorded Statements

If a party introduces all or part of a writing or recorded statement, an adverse party may require the introduction, at that time, of any other part—or any other writing or recorded statement—that in fairness ought to be considered at the same time.

(Pub. L. 93-595, § 1, Jan. 2, 1975, 88 Stat. 1930; Mar. 2, 1987, eff. Oct. 1, 1987; Apr. 26, 2011, eff. Dec. 1, 2011.)

RESTYLED RULE 106—ADVISORY COMMITTEE'S NOTE

The language of Rule 106 has been amended as part of the restyling of the Evidence Rules to make them more easily understood and to make style and terminology consistent throughout the rules. These changes are intended to be stylistic only. There is no intent to change any result in any ruling on evidence admissibility.

ADVISORY COMMITTEE'S NOTE
56 F.R.D. 183, 201 (1973)

The rule is an expression of the rule of completeness. McCormick § 56. It is manifested as to depositions in Rule 32(a)(4) of the Federal Rules of Civil Procedure, of which the proposed rule is substantially a restatement.

The rule is based on two considerations. The first is the misleading impression created by taking matters out of context. The second is the inadequacy of repair work when delayed to a point later in the trial. *See* McCormick § 56; California Evidence Code § 356. The rule does not in any way circumscribe the right of the adversary to develop the matter on cross-examination or as part of his own case.

For practical reasons, the rule is limited to writings and recorded statements and does not apply to conversations.

ADVISORY COMMITTEE'S NOTE—1987 AMENDMENT

The amendments are technical. No substantive change is intended.

ARTICLE II.   JUDICIAL NOTICE

Rule 201.   Judicial Notice of Adjudicative Facts

(a) **Scope.** This rule governs judicial notice of an adjudicative fact only, not a legislative fact.

(b) **Kinds of Facts That May Be Judicially Noticed.** The court may judicially notice a fact that is not subject to reasonable dispute because it:

(1) is generally known within the trial court's territorial jurisdiction; or

(2) can be accurately and readily determined from sources whose accuracy cannot reasonably be questioned.

(c) **Taking Notice.** The court:

(1) may take judicial notice on its own; or

(2) must take judicial notice if a party requests it and the court is supplied with the necessary information.

(d) **Timing.** The court may take judicial notice at any stage of the proceeding.

(e) **Opportunity to Be Heard.** On timely request, a party is entitled to be heard on the propriety of taking judicial notice and the nature of the fact to be noticed. If the court takes judicial notice before notifying a party, the party, on request, is still entitled to be heard.

(f) **Instructing the Jury.** In a civil case, the court must instruct the jury to accept the noticed fact as conclusive. In a criminal case, the court must instruct the jury that it may or may not accept the noticed fact as conclusive.

(Pub. L. 93-595, § 1, Jan. 2, 1975, 88 Stat. 1930; Apr. 26, 2011, eff. Dec. 1, 2011.)

RESTYLED RULE 201 — ADVISORY COMMITTEE'S NOTE

The language of Rule 201 has been amended as part of the restyling of the Evidence Rules to make them more easily understood and to make style and terminology consistent throughout the rules. These changes are intended to be stylistic only. There is no intent to change any result in any ruling on evidence admissibility.

ADVISORY COMMITTEE'S NOTE
56 F.R.D. 183, 201 (1973)

Subdivision (a). This is the only evidence rule on the subject of judicial notice. It deals only with judicial notice of "adjudicative" facts. No rule deals with judicial notice of "legislative" facts. Judicial notice of matters of foreign law is treated in Rule 44.1 of the Federal Rules of Civil Procedure and Rule 26.1 of the Federal Rules of Criminal Procedure.

The omission of any treatment of legislative facts results from fundamental differences between adjudicative facts and legislative facts. Adjudicative facts are simply the facts of the particular case. Legislative facts, on the other hand, are those which have relevance to legal reasoning and the lawmaking process, whether in the formulation of a legal principle or ruling by a judge or court or in the enactment of a legislative body. The terminology was coined by Professor Kenneth Davis in his article An Approach to Problems of Evidence in the Administrative Process, 55 Harv. L. Rev. 364, 404-407 (1942). The following discussion draws extensively upon his writings. In addition, *see* the same author's Judicial Notice, 55 Colum. L. Rev. 945 (1955); Administrative Law Treatise, ch. 15 (1958); A System of Judicial Notice Based on Fairness and Convenience, in Perspectives of Law 69 (1964).

The usual method of establishing adjudicative facts is through the introduction of evidence, ordinarily consisting of the testimony of witnesses. If particular facts are outside of reasonable controversy, this process is dispensed with as unnecessary. A high degree of indisputability is the essential prerequisite.

Legislative facts are quite different. As Professor Davis says:

> "My opinion is that judge-made law would stop growing if judges, in thinking about questions of law and policy, were forbidden to take into account the facts they believe, as distinguished from facts which are 'clearly . . . within the domain of the indisputable.' Facts most needed in thinking about difficult problems of law and policy have a way of being outside the domain of the clearly indisputable."
> A System of Judicial Notice Based on Fairness and Convenience, *supra*, at 82.

An illustration is Hawkins v. United States, 358 U.S. 74, 79 S. Ct. 136, 3 L. Ed. 2d 125 (1958), in which the Court refused to discard the common law rule that one spouse could not testify against the other, saying, "Adverse testimony given in criminal proceedings would, we think, be likely to destroy almost any marriage." This conclusion has a large intermixture of fact, but the factual aspect is scarcely "indisputable." *See* Hutchins and Slesinger, Some Observations on the Law of Evidence — Family Relations, 13 Minn. L. Rev. 675 (1929). If the destructive effect of the giving of adverse testimony by a spouse is not indisputable, should the Court have refrained from considering it in the absence of supporting evidence?

> "If the Model Code or the Uniform Rules had been applicable, the Court would have been barred from thinking about the essential factual ingredient of the problems before it, and such a result would be obviously intolerable. What the law needs as its growing points is more, not less, judicial thinking about the factual ingredients of problems of what the law ought to be, and the needed facts are seldom 'clearly' indisputable." Davis, *supra*, at 83.

Professor Morgan gave the following description of the methodology of determining domestic law:

> "In determining the content or applicability of a rule of domestic law, the judge is unrestricted in his investigation and conclusion. He may reject the propositions of either party or of both parties. He may consult the sources of pertinent data to which they refer, or he may refuse to do so. He may make an independent search for persuasive data or rest content with what he has or what the parties present. . . . [T]he parties do no more than to assist; they control no part of the process." Morgan, Judicial Notice, 57 Harv. L. Rev. 269, 270-271 (1944).

This is the view which should govern judicial access to legislative facts. It renders inappropriate any limitation in the form of indisputability, any formal requirements of notice other than those already inherent in affording opportunity to hear and be heard and exchanging briefs, and any requirement of formal findings at any level. It should, however, leave open the possibility of introducing evidence through regular channels in appropriate situations. *See* Borden's Farm Products Co. v. Baldwin, 293 U.S. 194, 55 S. Ct. 187, 79 L. Ed. 281 (1934), where the cause was remanded for the taking of evidence as to the economic conditions and trade practices underlying the New York Milk Control Law.

Similar considerations govern the judicial use of nonadjudicative facts in ways other than formulating laws and rules. Thayer described them as a part of the judicial reasoning process.

> "In conducting a process of judicial reasoning, as of other reasoning, not a step can be taken without assuming something which has not been proved; and the capacity to do this with competent judgement and efficiency, is imputed to judges and juries as part of their necessary mental outfit." Thayer, Preliminary Treatise on Evidence 279-280 (1898).

As Professor Davis points out, A System of Judicial Notice Based on Fairness and Convenience, in Perspectives of Law 69, 73 (1964), every case involves the use of hundreds or thousands of non-evidence facts. When a witness in an automobile accident case says "car," everyone, judge and jury included, furnishes, from non-evidence sources within himself, the supplementing information that the "car" is an automobile, not a railroad car, that it is self-propelled, probably by an internal combustion engine, that it may be assumed to have four wheels with pneumatic rubber tires, and so on. The judicial process cannot construct every case from scratch, like Descartes creating a world based on the postulate *Cogito, ergo sum.* These items could not possibly be introduced into evidence, and no one suggests that they be. Nor are they appropriate subjects for any formalized treatment of judicial notice of facts. *See* Levin and Levy, Persuading the Jury with Facts Not in Evidence: The Fiction-Science Spectrum, 105 U. Pa. L. Rev. 139 (1956).

Another aspect of what Thayer had in mind is the use of non-evidence facts to appraise or assess the adjudicative facts of the case. Pairs of cases from two jurisdictions illustrate this use and also the difference between non-evidence facts thus used and adjudicative facts. In People v. Strook, 347 Ill. 460, 179 N.E. 821 (1932), venue in Cook County had been held not established by testimony that the crime was committed at 7956 South Chicago Avenue, since judicial notice would not be taken that the address was in Chicago. However, the same court subsequently ruled that venue in Cook County was established by testimony that a crime occurred at 8900 South Anthony Avenue, since notice would be taken of the common practice of omitting the name of the city when speaking of local addresses, and the witness was testifying in Chicago. People v. Pride, 16 Ill. 2d 82, 156 N.E.2d 551 (1951). And in Hughes v. Vestal, 264 N.C. 500, 142 S.E.2d 361 (1965), the Supreme Court of North Carolina disapproved the trial judge's admission in evidence of a state-published table of automobile stopping distances on the basis of judicial notice, though the court itself had referred to the same table in an earlier case in a "rhetorical and illustrative" way in determining that the defendant could not have stopped her car in time to avoid striking a child who suddenly appeared in the highway and that a non-suit was properly granted. Ennis v. Dupree, 262 N.C. 224, 136 S.E.2d 702 (1964). *See also* Brown v. Hale, 263 N.C. 176, 139 S.E.2d 210 (1964); Clayton v. Rimmer, 262 N.C. 302, 136 S.E.2d 562 (1964). It is apparent that this use of non-evidence facts in evaluating the adjudicative facts of the case is not an appropriate subject for a formalized judicial notice treatment.

In view of these considerations, the regulation of judicial notice of facts by the present rule extends only to adjudicative facts.

What, then, are "adjudicative" facts? Davis refers to them as those "which relate to the parties," or more fully:

"When a court or an agency finds facts concerning the immediate parties — who did what, where, when, how, and with what motive or intent — the court or agency is performing an adjudicative function, and the facts are conveniently called adjudicative facts. . . .

"Stated in other terms, the adjudicative facts are those to which the law is applied in the process of adjudication. They are the facts that normally go to the jury in a jury case. They relate to the parties, their activities, their properties, their businesses." 2 Administrative Law Treatise 353.

Subdivision (b). With respect to judicial notice of adjudicative facts, the tradition has been one of caution in requiring that the matter be beyond reasonable controversy. This tradition of circumspection appears to be soundly based, and no reason to depart from it is apparent. As Professor Davis says:

"The reason we use trial-type procedure, I think, is that we make the practical judgment, on the basis of experience, that taking evidence, subject to cross-examination and rebuttal, is the best way to resolve controversies involving disputes of adjudicative facts, that is, facts pertaining to the parties. The reason we require a determination on the record is that we think fair procedure in resolving disputes of adjudicative facts calls for giving each party a chance to meet in the appropriate fashion the facts that come to the tribunal's attention, and the appropriate fashion for meeting disputed adjudicative facts includes rebuttal evidence, cross-examination, usually confrontation, and argument (either written or oral or both). The key to a fair trial is opportunity to use the appropriate weapons (rebuttal evidence, cross-examination, and argument) to meet adverse materials that come to the tribunal's attention." A System of Judicial Notice Based on Fairness and Convenience, in Perspectives of Law 69, 93 (1964).

The rule proceeds upon the theory that these considerations call for dispensing with traditional methods of proof only in clear cases. Compare Professor Davis' conclusion that judicial notice should be a matter of convenience, subject to requirements of procedural fairness. *Id.*, 94.

This rule is consistent with Uniform Rule 9(1) and (2) which limit judicial notice of facts to those "so universally known that they cannot reasonably be the subject of dispute," those "so generally known or of such common notoriety within the territorial jurisdiction of the court that they cannot reasonably be the subject of dispute," and those "capable of immediate and accurate determination by resort to easily accessible sources of indisputable accuracy." The traditional textbook treatment has included these general categories (matters of common knowledge, facts capable of verification), McCormick § 324, 325, and then has passed on into detailed treatment of such specific topics as facts relating to the personnel and records of the court, *Id.* § 327, and other governmental facts, *Id.* § 328. The California draftsmen, with a background of detailed statutory regulation of judicial notice, followed a somewhat similar pattern. California Evidence Code § 451, 452. The Uniform Rules, however, were drafted on the theory that these particular matters are included within the general categories and need no specific mention. This approach is followed in the present rule.

The phrase "propositions of generalized knowledge," found in Uniform Rule 9(1) and (2) is not included in the present rule. It was, it is believed, originally included in Model Code Rules 801 and 802 primarily in order to afford some minimum recognition to the right of the judge in his "legislative" capacity (not acting as the trier of fact) to take judicial notice of very limited categories of generalized knowledge. The limitations thus imposed have been discarded herein as undesirable, unworkable, and contrary to existing practice. What is left, then, to be considered, is the status of a "proposition of generalized knowledge" as an "adjudicative" fact to be noticed judicially and communicated by the judge to the jury. Thus viewed, it is considered to be lacking practical significance. While judges use judicial notice of "propositions of generalized knowledge" in a variety of situations: determining the validity and meaning of statutes, formulating common law rules, deciding whether evidence should be admitted, assessing the sufficiency and effect of evidence, all are essentially nonadjudicative in nature. When judicial notice is seen as a significant vehicle for progress in the law, these are the areas involved, particularly in developing fields of scientific knowledge. *See* McCormick 712. It is not believed that judges now instruct juries as to "propositions of generalized knowledge" derived from encyclopedias or other sources, or that they are likely to do so, or, indeed, that it is desirable that they do so. There is a vast difference between ruling on the basis of judicial notice that radar evidence of speed is admissible and explaining to the jury its principles and degree of accuracy, or between using a table of stopping distances of automobiles at various speeds in a judicial evaluation of testimony and telling the jury its precise application in the case. For cases raising doubt as to the propriety of the use of medical texts by lay triers of fact in passing on disability claims in administrative proceedings, *see* Sayers v. Gardner, 380 F.2d 940 (6th Cir. 1967); Ross v. Gardner, 365 F.2d 554 (6th Cir. 1966); Sosna v. Celebrezze, 234 F. Supp. 289 (E.D. Pa. 1964); Glendenning v. Ribicoff, 213 F. Supp. 301 (W.D. Mo. 1962).

Subdivisions (c) and (d). Under subdivision (c) the judge has a discretionary authority to take judicial notice, regardless of whether he is so requested by a party. The taking of judicial notice is mandatory, under subdivision (d), only when a party requests it and the necessary information is supplied. This scheme is believed to reflect existing practice. It is simple and workable. It avoids troublesome distinctions in the many situations in which the process of taking judicial notice is not recognized as such.

Compare Uniform Rule 9 making judicial notice of facts universally known mandatory without request, and making judicial notice of facts generally known in the jurisdiction or capable of determination by resort to accurate sources discretionary in the absence of request but mandatory if request is made and the information furnished. *But see* Uniform Rule 10(3), which directs the judge to decline to take judicial notice if available information fails to convince him that the matter falls clearly within Uniform Rule 9 or is insufficient to enable him to notice it judicially. Substantially the same approach is found in California Evidence Code § 451-453 and in New Jersey Evidence Rule 9. In contrast, the present rule treats alike all adjudicative facts which are subject to judicial notice.

Subdivision (e). Basic considerations of procedural fairness demand an opportunity to be heard on the propriety of taking judicial notice and the tenor of the matter noticed. The rule requires the granting of that opportunity upon request. No formal scheme of giving notice is provided. An adversely affected party may learn in advance that judicial notice is in contemplation, either by virtue of being served with a copy of a request by another party under subdivision (d) that judicial notice be taken, or through an advance indication by the judge. Or he may have no advance notice at all. The likelihood of the latter is enhanced by the frequent failure to recognize judicial notice as such. And in the absence of advance notice, a request made after the fact could not in fairness be considered untimely. *See* the provision for hearing on timely request in the Administrative Procedure Act, 5 U.S.C. § 556(e). *See also* Revised Model State Administrative Procedure Act (1961), 9C U.L.A. § 10(4) (Supp. 1967).

Subdivision (f). In accord with the usual view, judicial notice may be taken at any stage of the proceedings, whether in the trial court or on appeal. Uniform Rule 12; California Evidence Code § 459; Kansas Rules of Evidence § 60-412; New Jersey Evidence Rule 12; McCormick § 330, p.712.

Subdivision (g). Much of the controversy about judicial notice has centered upon the question whether evidence should be admitted in disproof of facts of which judicial notice is taken.

The writers have been divided. Favoring admissibility are Thayer, Preliminary Treatise on Evidence 308 (1898); 9 Wigmore § 2567; Davis, A System of Judicial Notice Based on Fairness and Convenience, in Perspectives of Law, 69, 76-77 (1964). Opposing admissibility are Keeffe, Landis and Shaad, Sense and Nonsense about Judicial Notice, 2 Stan. L. Rev. 664, 668 (1950); McNaughton, Judicial Notice — Excerpts Relating to the Morgan-Whitmore Controversy, 14 Vand. L. Rev. 779 (1961); Morgan, Judicial Notice, 57 Harv. L. Rev. 269, 279 (1944); McCormick 710-711. The Model Code and the Uniform Rules are predicated upon indisputability of judicially noticed facts.

The proponents of admitting evidence in disproof have concentrated largely upon legislative facts. Since the present rule deals only with judicial notice of adjudicative facts, arguments directed to legislative facts lose their relevancy.

Within its relatively narrow area of adjudicative facts, the rule contemplates there is to be no evidence before the jury in disproof. The judge instructs the jury to take judicially noticed facts as established. This position is justified by the undesirable effects of the opposite rule in limiting the rebutting party, though not his opponent, to admissible evidence, in defeating the reasons for judicial notice, and in affecting the substantive law to an extent and in ways largely unforeseeable. Ample protection and flexibility are afforded by the broad provision for opportunity to be heard on request, set forth in subdivision (e).

Authority upon the propriety of taking judicial notice against an accused in a criminal case with respect to matters other than venue is relatively meager. Proceeding upon the theory that the right of jury trial does not extend to matters which are beyond reasonable dispute, the rule does not distinguish between criminal and civil cases. People v. Mayes, 113 Cal. 618, 45 P. 860 (1896); Ross v. United States, 374 F.2d 97 (8th Cir. 1967). Cf. State v. Main, 94 R.I. 338, 180 A.2d 814 (1962); State v. Lawrence, 120 Utah 323, 234 P.2d 600 (1951).

ADVISORY COMMITTEE'S NOTE — JUDICIAL NOTICE OF LAW
56 F.R.D. 183, 207 (1973)

By rules effective July 1, 1966, the method of invoking the law of a foreign country is covered elsewhere. Rule 44.1 of the Federal Rules of Civil Procedure; Rule 26.1 of the Federal Rules of Criminal Procedure. These two new admirably designed rules are founded upon the assumption that the manner in which law is fed into the judicial process is never a proper concern of the rules of evidence but rather of the rules of procedure. The Advisory Committee on Evidence, believing that this assumption is entirely correct, proposes no evidence rule with respect to judicial notice of law, and suggests that those matters of law which, in addition to foreign-country law, have traditionally been treated as requiring pleading and proof and more recently as the subject of judicial notice be left to the Rules of Civil and Criminal Procedure.

ARTICLE III.   PRESUMPTIONS IN CIVIL CASES

Rule 301.   Presumptions in Civil Cases Generally

In a civil case, unless a federal statute or these rules provide otherwise, the party against whom a presumption is directed has the burden of producing evidence to rebut the presumption. But this rule does not shift the burden of persuasion; which remains on the party who had it originally.

(Pub. L. 93-595, § 1, Jan. 2, 1975, 88 Stat. 1931; Apr. 26, 2011, eff. Dec. 1, 2011.)

RESTYLED RULE 301 — ADVISORY COMMITTEE'S NOTE

The language of Rule 301 has been amended as part of the restyling of the Evidence Rules to make them more easily understood and to make style and terminology consistent throughout the rules. These changes are intended to be stylistic only. There is no intent to change any result in any ruling on evidence admissibility.

ADVISORY COMMITTEE'S NOTE
56 F.R.D. 158, 208 (1973)

This rule governs presumptions generally. *See* Rule 302 for presumptions controlled by state law and Rule 303 [deleted] for those against an accused in a criminal case.

Presumptions governed by this rule are given the effect of placing upon the opposing party the burden of establishing the nonexistence of the presumed fact, once the party invoking the presumption establishes the basic facts giving rise to it. The same considerations of fairness, policy, and probability which dictate the allocation of the burden of the various elements of a case as between the prima facie case of a plaintiff and affirmative defenses also underlie the creation of presumptions. These considerations are not satisfied by giving a lesser effect to presumptions. Morgan and Maguire, Looking Backward and Forward at Evidence, 50 Harv. L. Rev. 909, 913 (1937); Morgan, Instructing the Jury upon Presumptions and Burden of Proof, 47 Harv. L. Rev. 59, 82 (1933); Cleary, Presuming and Pleading: An Essay on Juristic Immaturity, 12 Stan. L. Rev. 5 (1959).

The so-called "bursting bubble" theory, under which a presumption vanishes upon the introduction of evidence which would support a finding of the nonexistence of the presumed fact, even though not believed, is rejected as according presumptions too "slight and evanescent" an effect. Morgan and Maguire, *supra*, at p.913.

In the opinion of the Advisory Committee, no constitutional infirmity attends this view of presumptions. In Mobile, J. & K.C.R. Co. v. Turnipseed, 219 U.S. 35, 31 S. Ct. 136, 55 L. Ed. 78 (1910), the Court upheld a Mississippi statute which provided that in actions against railroads proof of injury inflicted by the running of trains should be prima facie evidence of negligence by the railroad. The injury in the case had resulted from a derailment. The opinion made the points (1) that the only effect of the statute was to impose on the railroad the duty of producing some evidence to the contrary, (2) that an inference may be supplied by law if there is a rational connection between the fact proved and the fact presumed, as long as the opposite party is not precluded from presenting his evidence to the contrary, and (3) that considerations of public policy arising from the character of the business justified the application in question. Nineteen years later, in Western & Atlantic R. Co. v. Henderson, 279 U.S. 639, 49 S. Ct. 445, 73 L. Ed. 884 (1929), the Court overturned a Georgia statute making railroads liable for damages done by trains, unless the railroad made it appear that reasonable care had been used, the presumption being against the railroad. The declaration alleged the death of plaintiff's husband from a grade crossing collision, due to specified acts of negligence by defendant. The jury were instructed that proof of the injury raised a presumption of negligence; the burden shifted to the railroad to prove ordinary care; and unless it did so, they should find for plaintiff. The instruction was held erroneous in an opinion stating (1) that there was no rational connection between the mere fact of collision and negligence on the part of anyone, and (2) that the statute was different from that in *Turnipseed* in imposing a burden upon the railroad. The reader is left in a state of some confusion. Is the difference between a derailment and a grade crossing collision of no significance? Would the *Turnipseed* presumption have been bad if it had imposed a burden of persuasion on defendant, although that would in nowise have impaired its "rational connection"? If *Henderson* forbids imposing a burden of persuasion on defendants, what happens to affirmative defenses?

Two factors serve to explain *Henderson.* The first was that it was common ground that negligence was indispensable to liability. Plaintiff thought so, drafted her complaint accordingly, and relied upon the presumption. But how in logic could the same presumption establish her alternative grounds of negligence that the engineer was so blind he could not see decedent's truck and that he failed to stop after he saw it? Second, take away the basic assumption of no liability without fault, as *Turnipseed* intimated might be done ("considerations of public policy arising out of the character of the business"), and the structure of the decision in *Henderson* fails. No question of logic would have arisen if the statute had simply said: a prima facie case of liability is made by proof of injury by a train; lack of negligence is an affirmative defense, to be pleaded and proved as other affirmative defenses. The problem would be one of economic due process only. While it seems likely that the Supreme Court of 1929 would have voted that due process was denied, that result today would be unlikely. *See, for example,* the shift in the direction of absolute liability in the consumer cases. Prosser, The Assault upon the Citadel (Strict Liability to the Consumer), 69 Yale L.J. 1099 (1960).

Any doubt as to the constitutional permissibility of a presumption imposing a burden of persuasion of the non-existence of the presumed fact in civil cases is laid at rest by Dick v. New York Life Ins. Co., 359 U.S. 437, 79 S. Ct. 921, 3 L. Ed. 2d 935 (1959). The Court unhesitatingly applied the North Dakota rule that the presumption against suicide imposed on defendant the burden of proving that the death of insured, under an accidental death clause, was due to suicide.

"Proof of coverage and of death by gunshot wound shifts the burden to the insurer to establish that the death of the insured was due to his suicide." 359 U.S. at 443, 79 S. Ct. at 925.

"In a case like this one, North Dakota presumes that death was accidental and places on the insurer the burden of proving that death resulted from suicide." *Id.* at 446, 79 S. Ct. at 927.

The rational connection requirement survives in criminal cases, Tot v. United States, 319 U.S. 463, 63 S. Ct. 1241, 87 L. Ed. 1519 (1943), because the Court has been unwilling to extend into that area the greater-includes-the-lesser theory of Ferry v. Ramsey, 277 U.S. 88, 48 S. Ct. 443, 72 L. Ed. 796 (1928). In that case the Court sustained a Kansas statute under which bank directors were personally liable for deposits made with their assent and with knowledge of insolvency, and the fact of insolvency was prima facie evidence of assent and knowledge of insolvency. Mr. Justice Holmes pointed out that the state legislature could have made the directors personally liable to depositors in every case. Since the statute imposed a less stringent liability, "the thing to be considered is the result reached, not the possibly inartificial or clumsy way of reaching it." *Id.* at 94, 48 S. Ct. at 444. Mr. Justice Sutherland dissented: though the state could have created an absolute liability, it did not purport to do so; a rational connection was necessary, but lacking, between the liability created and the prima facie evidence of it; the result might be different if the basis of the presumption were being open for business.

The Sutherland view has prevailed in criminal cases by virtue of the higher standard of notice there required. The fiction that everyone is presumed to know the law is applied to the substantive law of crimes as an alternative to complete unenforceability. But the need does not extend to criminal evidence and procedure, and the fiction does not encompass them. "Rational connection" is not fictional or artificial, and so it is reasonable to suppose that Gainey should have known that his presence at the site of an illicit still could convict him of being connected with (carrying on) the business, United States v. Gainey, 380 U.S. 63, 85 S. Ct. 754, 13 L. Ed. 2d 658 (1965), but not that Romano should have known that his presence at a still could convict him of possessing it, United States v. Romano, 382 U.S. 136, 86 S. Ct. 279, 15 L. Ed. 2d 210 (1965).

In his dissent in *Gainey*, Mr. Justice Black put it more artistically:

> "It might be argued, although the Court does not so argue or hold, that Congress if it wished could make presence at a still a crime in itself, and so Congress should be free to create crimes which are called 'possession' and 'carrying on an illegal distillery business' but which are defined in such a way that unexplained presence is sufficient and indisputable evidence in all cases to support conviction for those offenses. *See* Ferry v. Ramsey, 277 U.S. 88, 48 S. Ct. 443, 72 L. Ed. 796. Assuming for the sake of argument that Congress could make unexplained presence a criminal act, and ignoring also the refusal of this Court in other cases to uphold a statutory presumption on such a theory, *see* Heiner v. Donnan, 285 U.S. 312, 52 S. Ct. 358, 76 L. Ed. 772, there is no indication here that Congress intended to adopt such a misleading method of draftsmanship, nor in my judgement could the statutory provisions if so construed escape condemnation for vagueness, under the principles applied in Lanzetta v. New Jersey, 306 U.S. 451, 59 S. Ct. 618, 83 L. Ed. 888, and many other cases." 380 U.S. at 84, n.12, 85 S. Ct. at 766.

And the majority opinion in *Romano* agreed with him:

> "It may be, of course, that Congress has the power to make presence at an illegal still a punishable crime, but we find no clear indication that it intended to so exercise this power. The crime remains possession, not presence, and with all due deference to the judgement of Congress, the former may not constitutionally be inferred from the latter." 382 U.S. at 144, 86 S. Ct. at 284.

The rule does not spell out the procedural aspects of its application. Questions as to when the evidence warrants submission of a presumption and what instructions are proper under varying states of fact are believed to present no particular difficulties.

Rule 302.   Applying State Law to Presumptions in Civil Cases

In a civil case, state law governs the effect of a presumption regarding a claim or defense for which state law supplies the rule of decision.

(Pub. L. 93-595, § 1, Jan. 2, 1975, 88 Stat. 1931; Apr. 26, 2011, eff. Dec. 1, 2011.)

RESTYLED RULE 302 — ADVISORY COMMITTEE'S NOTE

The language of Rule 302 has been amended as part of the restyling of the Evidence Rules to make them more easily understood and to make style and terminology consistent throughout the rules. These changes are intended to be stylistic only. There is no intent to change any result in any ruling on evidence admissibility.

ADVISORY COMMITTEE'S NOTE
56 F.R.D. 183, 211 (1973)

A series of Supreme Court decisions in diversity cases leaves no doubt of the relevance of Erie Railroad Co. v. Tompkins, 304 U.S. 64, 58 S. Ct. 817, 82 L. Ed. 1188 (1938), to

questions of burden of proof. These decisions are Cities Service Oil Co. v. Dunlap, 308
U.S. 208, 60 S. Ct. 201, 84 L. Ed. 196 (1939), Palmer v. Hoffman, 318 U.S. 109, 63 S. Ct.
477, 87 L. Ed. 645 (1943), and Dick v. New York Life Ins. Co., 359 U.S. 437, 79 S. Ct. 921, 3
L. Ed. 2d 935 (1959). They involved burden of proof, respectively, as to status as bona
fide purchasers, contributory negligence, and non-accidental death (suicide) of an
insured. In each instance the state rule was held to be applicable. It does not follow,
however, that all presumptions in diversity cases are governed by state law. In each case
cited, the burden of proof question had to do with a substantive element of the claim or
defense. Application of the state law is called for only when the presumption operates
upon such an element. Accordingly the rule does not apply state law when the presumption operates upon a lesser aspect of the case, i.e., "tactical" presumptions.

The situations in which the state law is applied have been tagged for convenience in
the preceding discussion as "diversity cases." The designation is not a completely accurate one since *Erie* applies to any claim or issue having its source in state law, regardless of
the basis of federal jurisdiction, and does not apply to a federal claim or issue, even
though jurisdiction is based on diversity. Vestal, Erie R.R. v. Tompkins: A Projection, 48
Iowa L. Rev. 248, 257 (1963); Hart and Wechsler, The Federal Courts and the Federal
System, 697 (1953); 1A Moore, Federal Practice § 0.305[3] (2d ed. 1965); Wright, Federal
Courts, 217-218 (1963). Hence the rule employs, as appropriately descriptive, the phrase
"as to which state law supplies the rule of decision." *See* A.L.I. Study of the Division of
Jurisdiction Between State and Federal Courts, § 2344(c), p.40, P.F.D. No. 1 (1965).

ARTICLE IV.   RELEVANCY AND ITS LIMITS

Rule 401.   Test for Relevant Evidence

Evidence is relevant if:
  (a) it has any tendency to make a fact more or less probable than it
would be without the evidence; and
  (b) the fact is of consequence in determining the action.

(Pub. L. 93-595, § 1, Jan. 2, 1975, 88 Stat. 1931; Apr. 26, 2011, eff. Dec. 1, 2011.)

RESTYLED RULE 401 — ADVISORY COMMITTEE'S NOTE

The language of Rule 401 has been amended as part of the restyling of the Evidence
Rules to make them more easily understood and to make style and terminology consistent throughout the rules. These changes are intended to be stylistic only. There is no
intent to change any result in any ruling on evidence admissibility.

ADVISORY COMMITTEE'S NOTE
56 F.R.D. 183, 215 (1973)

Problems of relevancy call for an answer to the question whether an item of evidence,
when tested by the processes of legal reasoning, possesses sufficient probative value to
justify receiving it in evidence. Thus, assessment of the probative value of evidence that a
person purchased a revolver shortly prior to a fatal shooting with which he is charged is a
matter of analysis and reasoning.

The variety of relevancy problems is coextensive with the ingenuity of counsel in using circumstantial evidence as a means of proof. An enormous number of cases fall in no set pattern, and this rule is designed as a guide for handling them. On the other hand, some situations recur with sufficient frequency to create patterns susceptible of treatment by specific rules. Rule 404 and those following it are of that variety; they also serve as illustrations of the application of the present rule as limited by the exclusionary principles of Rule 403.

Passing mention should be made of so-called "conditional" relevancy. Morgan, Basic Problems of Evidence 45-46 (1962). In this situation, probative value depends not only upon satisfying the basic requirement of relevancy as described above but also upon the existence of some matter of fact. For example, if evidence of a spoken statement is relied upon to prove notice, probative value is lacking unless the person sought to be charged heard the statement. The problem is one of fact, and the only rules needed are for the purpose of determining the respective functions of judge and jury. *See* Rules 104(b) and 901. The discussion which follows in the present note is concerned with relevancy generally, not with any particular problem of conditional relevancy.

Relevancy is not an inherent characteristic of any item of evidence but exists only as a relation between an item of evidence and a matter properly provable in the case. Does the item of evidence tend to prove the matter sought to be proved? Whether the relationship exists depends upon principles evolved by experience or science, applied logically to the situation at hand. James, Relevancy, Probability and the Law, 29 Cal. L. Rev. 689, 696, n.15 (1941), in Selected Writings on Evidence and Trial 610, 615, n.15 (Fryer ed. 1957). The rule summarizes this relationship as a "tendency to make the existence" of the fact to be proved "more probable or less probable." *Compare* Uniform Rule 1(2) which states the crux of relevancy as "a tendency in reason," thus perhaps emphasizing unduly the logical process and ignoring the need to draw upon experience or science to validate the general principle upon which relevancy in a particular situation depends.

The standard of probability under the rule is "more . . . probable than it would be without the evidence." Any more stringent requirement is unworkable and unrealistic. As McCormick § 152, p.317, says, "A brick is not a wall," or, as Falknor, Extrinsic Policies Affecting Admissibility, 10 Rutgers L. Rev. 574, 576 (1956), quotes Professor McBaine, ". . . [I]t is not to be supposed that every witness can make a home run." Dealing with probability in the language of the rule has the added virtue of avoiding confusion between questions of admissibility and questions of the sufficiency of the evidence.

The rule uses the phrase "fact that is of consequence to the determination of the action" to describe the kind of fact to which proof may properly be directed. The language is that of California Evidence Code § 210; it has the advantage of avoiding the loosely used and ambiguous word "material." Tentative Recommendation and a Study Relating to the Uniform Rules of Evidence (Art. I. General Provisions), Cal. Law Revision Comm'n, Rep., Rec. & Studies, 10-11 (1964). The fact to be proved may be ultimate, intermediate, or evidentiary; it matters not, so long as it is of consequence in the determination of the action. *Cf.* Uniform Rule 1(2) which requires that the evidence relate to a "material" fact.

The fact to which the evidence is directed need not be in dispute. While situations will arise which call for the exclusion of evidence offered to prove a point conceded by the opponent, the ruling should be made on the basis of such considerations as waste of time and undue prejudice (*see* Rule 403), rather than under any general requirement that evidence is admissible only if directed to matters in dispute. Evidence which is essentially background in nature can scarcely be said to involve disputed matter, yet it is universally offered and admitted as an aid to understanding. Charts, photographs, views of real estate, murder weapons, and many other items of evidence fall in this category. A rule limiting admissibility to evidence directed to a controversial point would invite the exclusion of this helpful evidence, or at least the raising of endless questions over its admission. *Cf.* California Evidence Code § 210, defining relevant evidence in terms of tendency to prove a disputed fact.

Rule 402. General Admissibility of Relevant Evidence

Relevant evidence is admissible unless any of the following provides otherwise:

- the United States Constitution;
- a federal statute;
- these rules; or
- other rules prescribed by the Supreme Court.

Irrelevant evidence is not admissible.

(Pub. L. 93-595, § 1, Jan. 2, 1975, 88 Stat. 1931; Apr. 26, 2011, eff. Dec. 1, 2011.)

RESTYLED RULE 402 — ADVISORY COMMITTEE'S NOTE

The language of Rule 402 has been amended as part of the restyling of the Evidence Rules to make them more easily understood and to make style and terminology consistent throughout the rules. These changes are intended to be stylistic only. There is no intent to change any result in any ruling on evidence admissibility.

ADVISORY COMMITTEE'S NOTE
56 F.R.D. 183, 216 (1973)

The provisions that all relevant evidence is admissible, with certain exceptions, and that evidence which is not relevant is not admissible are "a presupposition involved in the very conception of a rational system of evidence." Thayer, Preliminary Treatise on Evidence 264 (1898). They constitute the foundation upon which the structure of admission and exclusion rests. For similar provisions *see* California Evidence Code § 350, 351. Provisions that all relevant evidence is admissible are found in Uniform Rule 7(f); Kansas Code of Civil Procedure § 60-407(f); and New Jersey Evidence Rule 7(f); but the exclusion of evidence which is not relevant is left to implication.

Not all relevant evidence is admissible. The exclusion of relevant evidence occurs in a variety of situations and may be called for by these rules, by the Rules of Civil and Criminal Procedure, by Bankruptcy Rules, by Act of Congress, or by constitutional considerations.

Succeeding rules in the present article, in response to the demands of particular policies, require the exclusion of evidence despite its relevancy. In addition, Article V recognizes a number of privileges; Article VI imposes limitations upon witnesses and the manner of dealing with them; Article VII specifies requirements with respect to opinions and expert testimony; Article VIII excludes hearsay not falling within an exception; Article IX spells out the handling of authentication and identification; and Article X restricts the manner of proving the contents of writings and recordings.

The Rules of Civil and Criminal Procedure in some instances require the exclusion of relevant evidence. For example, Rules 30(b) and 32(a)(3) of the Rules of Civil

Procedure, by imposing requirements of notice and unavailability of the deponent, place limits on the use of relevant depositions. Similarly, Rule 15 of the Rules of Criminal Procedure restricts the use of depositions in criminal cases, even though relevant. And the effective enforcement of the command, originally statutory and now found in Rule 5(a) of the Rules of Criminal Procedure, that an arrested person be taken without unnecessary delay before a commissioner or other similar officer is held to require the exclusion of statements elicited during detention in violation thereof. Mallory v. United States, 354 U.S. 449, 77 S. Ct. 1356, 1 L. Ed. 2d 1479 (1957); 18 U.S.C. § 3501(c).

While congressional enactments in the field of evidence have generally tended to expand admissibility beyond the scope of the common law rules, in some particular situations they have restricted the admissibility of relevant evidence. Most of this legislation has consisted of the formulation of a privilege or of a prohibition against disclosure. 8 U.S.C. § 1202(f), records of refusal of visas or permits to enter United States confidential, subject to discretion of Secretary of State to make available to court upon certification of need; 10 U.S.C. § 3693, replacement certificate of honorable discharge from Army not admissible in evidence; 10 U.S.C. § 8693, same as to Air Force; 11 U.S.C. § 25(a)(10), testimony given by bankrupt on his examination not admissible in criminal proceedings against him, except that given in hearing upon objection to discharge; 11 U.S.C. § 205(a), railroad reorganization petition, if dismissed, not admissible in evidence; 11 U.S.C. § 403(a), list of creditors filed with municipal composition plan not an admission; 13 U.S.C. § 9(a), census information confidential, retained copies of reports privileged; 47 U.S.C. § 605, interception and divulgence of wire or radio communications prohibited unless authorized by sender. These statutory provisions would remain undisturbed by the rules.

The rule recognizes but makes no attempt to spell out the constitutional considerations which impose basic limitations upon the admissibility of relevant evidence. Examples are evidence obtained by unlawful search and seizure, Weeks v. United States, 232 U.S. 383, 34 S. Ct. 341, 58 L. Ed. 652 (1914); Katz v. United States, 389 U.S. 347, 88 S. Ct. 507, 19 L. Ed. 2d 576 (1967); incriminating statement elicited from an accused in violation of right to counsel, Massiah v. United States, 377 U.S. 201, 84 S. Ct. 1199, 12 L. Ed. 2d 246 (1964).

Rule 403.   Excluding Relevant Evidence for Prejudice, Confusion, Waste of Time, or Other Reasons

The court may exclude relevant evidence if its probative value is substantially outweighed by a danger of one or more of the following: unfair prejudice, confusing the issues, misleading the jury, undue delay, wasting time, or needlessly presenting cumulative evidence.

(Pub. L. 93-595, § 1, Jan. 2, 1975, 88 Stat. 1932; Apr. 26, 2011, eff. Dec. 1, 2011.)

RESTLYED RULE 403 — ADVISORY COMMITTEE'S NOTE

The language of Rule 403 has been amended as part of the restyling of the Evidence Rules to make them more easily understood and to make style and terminology consistent throughout the rules. These changes are intended to be stylistic only. There is no intent to change any result in any ruling on evidence admissibility.

ADVISORY COMMITTEE'S NOTE
56 F.R.D. 183, 218 (1973)

The case law recognizes that certain circumstances call for the exclusion of evidence which is of unquestioned relevance. These circumstances entail risks which range all the way from inducing decision on a purely emotional basis, at one extreme, to nothing more harmful than merely wasting time, at the other extreme. Situations in this area call for balancing the probative value of and need for the evidence against the harm likely to result from its admission. Slough, Relevancy Unraveled, 5 Kan. L. Rev. 1, 12-15 (1956); Trautman, Logical or Legal Relevancy — A Conflict in Theory, 5 Vand. L. Rev. 385, 392 (1952); McCormick § 152, pp.319-321. The rules which follow in this Article are concrete applications evolved for particular situations. However, they reflect the policies under-lying the present rule, which is designed as a guide for the handling of situations for which no specific rules have been formulated.

Exclusion for risk of unfair prejudice, confusion of issues, misleading the jury, or waste of time, all find ample support in the authorities. "Unfair prejudice" within its context means an undue tendency to suggest decision on an improper basis, commonly, though not necessarily, an emotional one.

The rule does not enumerate surprise as a ground for exclusion, in this respect following Wigmore's view of the common law. 6 Wigmore § 1849. *Cf.* McCormick § 152, p.320, n.29, listing unfair surprise as a ground for exclusion but stating that it is usually "coupled with the danger of prejudice and confusion of issues." While Uniform Rule 45 incorporates surprise as a ground and is followed in Kansas Code of Civil Procedure § 60-445, surprise is not included in California Evidence Code § 352 or New Jersey Rule 4, though both the latter otherwise substantially embody Uniform Rule 45. While it can scarcely be doubted that claims of unfair surprise may still be justified despite procedural requirements of notice and instrumentalities of discovery, the grant-ing of a continuance is a more appropriate remedy than exclusion of the evidence. Tentative Recommendation and a Study Relating to the Uniform Rules of Evidence (Art. VI. Extrinsic Policies Affecting Admissibility), Cal. Law Revision Comm'n, Rep., Rec. & Studies, 612 (1964). Moreover, the impact of a rule excluding evidence on the ground of surprise would be difficult to estimate.

In reaching a decision whether to exclude on grounds of unfair prejudice, consider-ation should be given to the probable effectiveness or lack of effectiveness of a limiting instruction. *See* Rule 106 [now 105] and Advisory Committee's Note thereunder. The availability of other means of proof may also be an appropriate factor.

Rule 404.   Character Evidence; Crimes or Other Acts

(a) Character Evidence.

(1) *Prohibited Uses.* Evidence of a person's character or character trait is not admissible to prove that on a particular occasion the person acted in accordance with the character or trait.

(2) *Exceptions for a Defendant or Victim in a Criminal Case.* The following exceptions apply in a criminal case:

(A) a defendant may offer evidence of the defendant's pertinent trait, and if the evidence is admitted, the prosecutor may offer evidence to rebut it;

(B) subject to the limitations in Rule 412, a defendant may offer evidence of an alleged victim's pertinent trait, and if the evidence is admitted, the prosecutor may:

(i) offer evidence to rebut it; and

(ii) offer evidence of the defendant's same trait; and

(C) in a homicide case, the prosecutor may offer evidence of the alleged victim's trait of peacefulness to rebut evidence that the victim was the first aggressor.

(3) *Exceptions for a Witness.* Evidence of a witness's character may be admitted under Rules 607, 608, and 609.

(b) Crimes, Wrongs, or Other Acts.

(1) *Prohibited Uses.* Evidence of a crime, wrong or other act is not admissible to prove a person's character in order to show that on a particular occasion the person acted in accordance with the character.

(2) *Permitted Uses; Notice in a Criminal Case.* This evidence may be admissible for another purpose, such as proving motive, opportunity, intent, preparation, plan, knowledge, identity, absence of mistake, or lack of accident. On request by a defendant in a criminal case, the prosecutor must:

(A) provide reasonable notice of the general nature of any such evidence that the prosecutor intends to offer at trial; and

(B) do so before trial — or during trial if the court, for good cause, excuses lack of pretrial notice.

(Pub. L. 93-595, § 1, Jan. 2, 1975, 88 Stat. 1932; Mar. 2, 1987, eff. Oct. 1, 1987; Apr. 30, 1991, eff. Dec. 1, 1991; Apr. 17, 2000, eff. Dec. 1, 2000; Apr. 26, 2011, eff. Dec. 1, 2011.)

RESTYLED RULE 404 — ADVISORY COMMITTEE'S NOTE

The language of Rule 404 has been amended as part of the restyling of the Evidence Rules to make them more easily understood and to make style and terminology consistent throughout the rules. These changes are intended to be stylistic only. There is no intent to change any result in any ruling on evidence admissibility.

ADVISORY COMMITTEE'S NOTE
56 F.R.D. 183, 219 (1973)

Subdivision (a). This subdivision deals with the basic question whether character evidence should be admitted. Once the admissibility of character evidence in some form is established under this rule, reference must then be made to Rule 405, which follows, in order to determine the appropriate method of proof. If the character is that of a witness, *see* Rules 608 and 610 for methods of proof.

Character questions arise in two fundamentally different ways. (1) Character may itself be an element of a crime, claim, or defense. A situation of this kind is commonly referred to as "character in issue." Illustrations are: the chastity of the victim under a statute specifying her chastity as an element of the crime of seduction, or the competency of the driver in an action for negligently entrusting a motor vehicle to an incompetent driver. No problem of the general relevancy of character evidence is involved, and the present rule therefore has no provision on the subject. The only question relates to allowable methods of proof, as to which *see* Rule 405, immediately following. (2) Character evidence is susceptible of being used for the purpose of suggesting an inference that the person acted on the occasion in question consistently with his character. This use of character is often described as "circumstantial." Illustrations are: evidence of a violent disposition to prove that the person was the aggressor in an affray, or evidence of honesty in disproof of a charge of theft. This circumstantial use of character evidence raises questions of relevancy as well as questions of allowable methods of proof.

In most jurisdictions today, the circumstantial use of character is rejected but with important exceptions: (1) an accused may introduce pertinent evidence of good character (often misleadingly described as "putting his character in issue"), in which event the prosecution may rebut with evidence of bad character; (2) an accused may introduce pertinent evidence of the character of the victim, as in support of a claim of self-defense to a charge of homicide or consent in a case of rape, and the prosecution may introduce similar evidence in rebuttal of the character evidence, or, in a homicide case, to rebut a claim that deceased was the first aggressor, however proved; and (3) the character of a witness may be gone into as bearing on his credibility. McCormick § 155-161. This pattern is incorporated in the rule. While its basis lies more in history and experience than in logic as underlying justification can fairly be found in terms of the relative presence and absence of prejudice in the various situations. Falknor, Extrinsic Policies Affecting Admissibility, 10 Rutgers L. Rev. 574, 584 (1956); McCormick § 157. In any event, the criminal rule is so deeply imbedded in our jurisprudence as to assume almost constitutional proportions and to override doubts of the basic relevancy of the evidence.

The limitation to pertinent traits of character, rather than character generally, in paragraphs (1) and (2) is in accordance with the prevailing view. McCormick § 158, p.334. A similar provision in Rule 608, to which reference is made in paragraph (3), limits character evidence respecting witnesses to the trait of truthfulness or untruthfulness.

The argument is made that circumstantial use of character ought to be allowed in civil cases to the same extent as in criminal cases, i.e., evidence of good (nonprejudicial) character would be admissible in the first instance, subject to rebuttal by evidence of bad character. Falknor, Extrinsic Policies Affecting Admissibility, 10 Rutgers L. Rev. 574, 581-583 (1956); Tentative Recommendation and a Study Relating to the Uniform Rules of Evidence (Art. VI. Extrinsic Policies Affecting Admissibility), Cal. Law Revision Comm'n, Rep., Rec. & Studies, 657-658 (1964). Uniform Rule 47 goes farther, in that it assumes that character evidence in general satisfies the conditions of relevancy, except as provided in Uniform Rule 48. The difficulty with expanding the use of character evidence in civil cases is set forth by the California Law Revision Commission in its ultimate rejection of Uniform Rule 47, *Id.* 615:

> Character evidence is of slight probative value and may be very prejudicial. It tends to distract the trier of fact from the main question of what actually happened on the particular occasion. It subtly permits the trier of fact to reward the good man to punish the bad man because of their respective characters despite what the evidence in the case shows actually happened.

Much of the force of the position of those favoring greater use of character evidence in civil cases is dissipated by their support of Uniform Rule 48 which excludes the evidence in negligence cases, where it could be expected to achieve its maximum usefulness.

Moreover, expanding concepts of "character," which seem of necessity to extend into such areas as psychiatric evaluation and psychological testing, coupled with expanded admissibility, would open up such vistas of mental examinations as caused the Court concern in Schlagenhauf v. Holder, 379 U.S. 104, 85 S. Ct. 234, 13 L. Ed. 2d 152 (1964). It is believed that those espousing change have not met the burden of persuasion.

Subdivision (b) deals with a specialized but important application of the general rule excluding circumstantial use of character evidence. Consistently with that rule, evidence of other crimes, wrongs, or acts is not admissible to prove character as a basis for suggesting the inference that conduct on a particular occasion was in conformity with it. However, the evidence may be offered for another purpose, such as proof of motive, opportunity, and so on, which does not fall within the prohibition. In this situation the rule does not require that the evidence be excluded. No mechanical solution is offered. The determination must be made whether the danger of undue prejudice outweighs the probative value of the evidence in view of the availability of other means of proof and other factors appropriate for making decisions of this kind under Rule 403. Slough and Knightly, Other Vices, Other Crimes, 41 Iowa L. Rev. 325 (1956).

ADVISORY COMMITTEE'S NOTE — 1987 AMENDMENT

The amendments are technical. No substantive change is intended.

ADVISORY COMMITTEE'S NOTE — 1991 AMENDMENT

Rule 404(b) has emerged as one of the most cited Rules in the Rules of Evidence. And in many criminal cases evidence of an accused's extrinsic acts is viewed as an important asset in the prosecution's case against an accused. Although there are a few reported decisions on use of such evidence by the defense, *see, e.g.*, United States v. McClure, 546 F.2d 670 (5th Cir. 1990) (acts of informant offered in entrapment defense), the overwhelming number of cases involve introduction of that evidence by the prosecution.

The amendment to Rule 404(b) adds a pretrial notice requirement in criminal cases and is intended to reduce surprise and promote early resolution on the issue of admissibility. The notice requirement thus places Rule 404(b) in the mainstream with notice and disclosure provisions in other rules of evidence. *See, e.g.*, Rule 412 (written motion of intent to offer evidence under rule), Rule 609 (written notice of intent to offer conviction older than 10 years), Rule 803(24) and 804(b)(5) (notice of intent to use residual hearsay exceptions).

The Rule expects that counsel for both the defense and the prosecution will submit the necessary request and information in a reasonable and timely fashion. Other than requiring pretrial notice, no specific time limits are stated in recognition that what constitutes a reasonable request or disclosure will depend largely on the circumstances of each case. *Compare* Fla. Stat. Ann. § 90.404(2)(b) (notice must be given at least 10 days before trial) *with* Tex. R. Evid. 404(b) (no time limit).

Likewise, no specific form of notice is required. The Committee considered and rejected a requirement that the notice satisfy the particularity requirements normally required of language used in a charging instrument. *Cf.* Fla. Stat. Ann. § 90.404(2)(b) (written disclosure must describe uncharged misconduct with particularity required of an indictment or information). Instead, the Committee opted for a generalized notice provision which requires the prosecution to apprise the defense of the general nature of the evidence of extrinsic acts. The Committee does not intend that the amendment will supersede other rules of admissibility or disclosure, such as the Jencks Act, 18 U.S.C. § 3500, et seq. nor require the prosecution to disclose directly or indirectly the names and addresses of its witnesses, something it is currently not required to do under Federal Rule of Criminal Procedure 16.

The amendment requires the prosecution to provide notice, regardless of how it intends to use the extrinsic act evidence at trial, i.e., during its case-in-chief, for impeachment, or for possible rebuttal. The court in its discretion may, under the facts, decide that the particular request or notice was not reasonable, either because of the lack of timeliness or completeness. Because the notice requirement serves as condition precedent to admissibility of 404(b) evidence, the offered evidence is inadmissible if the court decides that the notice requirement has not been met.

Nothing in the amendment precludes the court from requiring the government to provide it with an opportunity to rule *in limine* on 404(b) evidence before it is offered or even mentioned during trial. When ruling *in limine*, the court may require the government to disclose to it the specifics of such evidence which the court must consider in determining admissibility.

The amendment does not extend to evidence of acts which are "intrinsic" to the charged offense, *see* United States v. Williams, 900 F.2d 823 (5th Cir. 1990) (noting distinction between 404(b) evidence and intrinsic offense evidence). Nor is the amendment intended to redefine what evidence would otherwise be admissible under Rule 404(b). Finally, the Committee does not intend through the amendment to affect the role of the court and the jury in considering such evidence. *See* United States v. Huddleston, 485 U.S. 681, 108 S. Ct. 1496 (1988).

ADVISORY COMMITTEE'S NOTE — 2000 AMENDMENT

Rule 404(a)(1) has been amended to provide that when the accused attacks the character of an alleged victim under subdivision (a)(2) of this Rule, the door is opened to an attack on the same character trait of the accused. Current law does not allow the government to introduce negative character evidence as to the accused unless the accused introduces evidence of good character. *See, e.g.*, United States v. Fountain, 768 F.2d 790 (7th Cir. 1985) (when the accused offers proof of self-defense, this permits proof of the alleged victim's character trait for peacefulness, but it does not permit proof of the accused's character trait for violence).

The amendment makes clear that the accused cannot attack the alleged victim's character and yet remain shielded from the disclosure of equally relevant evidence concerning the same character trait of the accused. For example, in a murder case with a claim of self-defense, the accused, to bolster this defense, might offer evidence of the alleged victim's violent disposition. If the government has evidence that the accused has a violent character, but is not allowed to offer this evidence as part of its rebuttal, the jury has only part of the information it needs for an informed assessment of the probabilities as to who was the initial aggressor. This may be the case even if evidence of the accused's prior violent acts is admitted under Rule 404(b), because such evidence can be admitted only for limited purposes and not to show action in conformity with the accused's character on a specific occasion. Thus, the amendment is designed to permit a more balanced presentation of character evidence when an accused chooses to attack the character of the alleged victim.

The amendment does not affect the admissibility of evidence of specific acts of uncharged misconduct offered for a purpose other than proving character under Rule 404(b). Nor does it affect the standards for proof of character by evidence of other sexual behavior or sexual offenses under Rules 412-415. By its placement in Rule 404(a)(1), the amendment covers only proof of character by way of reputation or opinion.

The amendment does not permit proof of the accused's character if the accused merely uses character evidence for a purpose other than to prove the alleged victim's propensity to act in a certain way. *See* United States v. Burks, 470 F.2d 432, 434-5 (D.C. Cir. 1972) (evidence of the alleged victim's violent character, when known by the accused, was admissible "on the issue of whether or not the defendant reasonably feared he was in danger of imminent great bodily harm"). Finally, the amendment does not permit proof of the accused's character when the accused attacks the alleged victim's character as a witness under Rule 608 or 609.

The term "alleged" is inserted before each reference to "victim" in the Rule, in order to provide consistency with Evidence Rule 412.

ADVISORY COMMITTEE'S NOTE — 2006 AMENDMENT

The Rule has been amended to clarify that in a civil case evidence of a person's character is never admissible to prove that the person acted in conformity with the character trait. The amendment resolves the dispute in the case law over whether the exceptions in subdivisions (a)(1) and (2) permit the circumstantial use of character evidence in civil cases. *Compare* Carson v. Polley, 689 F.2d 562, 576 (5th Cir. 1982) ("when a central issue in a case is close to one of a criminal nature, the exceptions to the Rule 404(a) ban on character evidence may be invoked"), *with* SEC v. Towers Financial Corp., 966 F. Supp. 203 (S.D.N.Y. 1997) (relying on the terms "accused" and "prosecution" in Rule 404(a) to conclude that the exceptions in subdivisions (a)(1) and (2) are inapplicable in civil cases). The amendment is consistent with the original intent of the Rule, which was to prohibit the circumstantial use of character evidence in civil cases, even where closely related to criminal charges. *See* Ginter v. Northwestern Mut. Life Ins. Co., 576 F. Supp. 627, 629-30 (D. Ky. 1984). ("It seems beyond peradventure of doubt that the drafters of F. R. Evi. 404(a) explicitly intended that all character evidence, except where 'character is at issue' was to be excluded" in civil cases.)

The circumstantial use of character evidence is generally discouraged because it carries serious risks of prejudice, confusion, and delay. *See* Michelson v. United States, 335 U.S. 469, 476 (1948) ("The overriding policy of excluding such evidence, despite its admitted probative value, is the practical experience that its disallowance tends to prevent confusion of issues, unfair surprise and undue prejudice."). In criminal cases, the so-called "mercy rule" permits a criminal defendant to introduce evidence of pertinent character traits of the defendant and the victim. But that is because the accused, whose liberty is at stake, may need "a counterweight against the strong investigative and prosecutorial resources of the government." C. Mueller & L. Kirkpatrick, Evidence: Practice Under the Rules, pp. 264-5 (2d ed. 1999). See also Richard Uviller, Evidence of Character to Prove Conduct: Illusion, Illogic, and Injustice in the Courtroom, 130 U. Pa. L. Rev. 845, 855 (1982) (the rule prohibiting circumstantial use of character evidence "was relaxed to allow the criminal defendant with so much at stake and so little available in the way of conventional proof to have special dispensation to tell the factfinder just what sort of person he really is"). Those concerns do not apply to parties in civil cases. . . .

Nothing in the amendment is intended to affect the scope of Rule 404(b). While Rule 404(b) refers to the "accused," the "prosecution," and a "criminal case," it does so only in the context of a notice requirement. The admissibility standards of Rule 404(b) remain fully applicable to both civil and criminal cases.

Rule 405.   Methods of Proving Character

(a) By Reputation or Opinion. When evidence of a person's character or character trait is admissible, it may be proved by testimony about the person's reputation or by testimony in the form of an opinion. On cross-examination of the character witness, the court may allow an inquiry into relevant specific instances of the person's conduct.

(b) By Specific Instances of Conduct. When a person's character or character trait is an essential element of a charge, claim, or defense, the character or trait may also be proved by relevant specific instances of the person's conduct.

(Pub. L. 93-595, §1, Jan. 2, 1975, 88 Stat. 1932; Mar. 2, 1987, eff. Oct. 1, 1987; Apr. 26, 2011, eff. Dec. 1, 2011.)

RESTLYED RULE 405 — ADVISORY COMMITTEE'S NOTE

The language of Rule 405 has been amended as part of the restyling of the Evidence Rules to make them more easily understood and to make style and terminology consistent throughout the rules. These changes are intended to be stylistic only. There is no intent to change any result in any ruling on evidence admissibility.

ADVISORY COMMITTEE'S NOTE
56 F.R.D. 183, 222 (1973)

The rule deals only with allowable methods of proving character, not with the admissibility of character evidence, which is covered in Rule 404.

Of the three methods of proving character provided by the rule, evidence of specific instances of conduct is the most convincing. At the same time it possesses the greatest capacity to arouse prejudice, to confuse, to surprise, and to consume time. Consequently the rule confines the use of evidence of this kind to cases in which character is, in the strict sense, in issue and hence deserving of a searching inquiry. When character is used circumstantially and hence occupies a lesser status in the case, proof may be only by reputation and opinion. These latter methods are also available when character is in issue. This treatment is, with respect to specific instances of conduct and reputation, conventional contemporary common law doctrine. McCormick § 153.

In recognizing opinion as a means of proving character, the rule departs from usual contemporary practice in favor of that of an earlier day. *See* 7 Wigmore § 1986, pointing out that the earlier practice permitted opinion and arguing strongly for evidence based on personal knowledge and belief as contrasted with "the secondhand, irresponsible product of multiplied guesses and gossip which we term 'reputation.'" It seems likely that the persistence of reputation evidence is due to its largely being opinion in disguise. Traditionally character has been regarded primarily in moral overtones of good and bad: chaste, peaceable, truthful, honest. Nevertheless, on occasion nonmoral considerations crop up, as in the case of the incompetent driver, and this seems bound to happen increasingly. If character is defined as the kind of person one is, then account must be taken of varying ways of arriving at the estimate. These may range from the opinion of the employer who has found the man honest to the opinion of the psychiatrist based upon examination and testing. No effective dividing line exists between character and mental capacity, and the latter traditionally has been provable by opinion.

According to the great majority of cases, on cross-examination inquiry is allowable as to whether the reputation witness has heard of particular instances of conduct pertinent to the trait in question. Michelson v. United States, 335 U.S. 469, 69 S. Ct. 213, 93 L. Ed. 168 (1948); Annot., 47 A.L.R.2d 1258. The theory is that, since the reputation witness relates what he has heard, the inquiry tends to shed light on the accuracy of his hearing and reporting. Accordingly, the opinion witness would be asked whether he knew, as well as whether he had heard. The fact is, of course, that these distinctions are of slight if any practical significance, and the second sentence of subdivision (a) eliminates them as a factor in formulating questions. This recognition of the propriety of inquiring into specific instances of conduct does not circumscribe inquiry otherwise into the bases of opinion and reputation testimony.

The express allowance of inquiry into specific instances of conduct on cross-examination in subdivision (a) and the express allowance of it as part of a case in chief when character is actually in issue in subdivision (b) contemplate that testimony of specific instances is not generally permissible on the direct examination of an ordinary opinion witness to character. Similarly as to witnesses to the character of witnesses under Rule 608(b). Opinion testimony on direct in these situations ought in general to correspond to reputation testimony as now given, i.e., be confined to the nature and extent of observation and acquaintance upon which the opinion is based. *See* Rule 701.

ADVISORY COMMITTEE'S NOTE — 1987 AMENDMENT

The amendment is technical. No substantive change is intended.

Rule 406.   Habit; Routine Practice

Evidence of a person's habit or an organization's routine practice may be admitted to prove that on a particular occasion the person or organization acted in accordance with the habit or routine practice. The court may admit this evidence regardless of whether it is corroborated or whether there was an eyewitness.

(Pub. L. 93-595, § 1, Jan. 2, 1975, 88 Stat. 1932; Apr. 26, 2011, eff. Dec. 1, 2011.)

RESTYLED RULE 406 — ADVISORY COMMITTEE'S NOTE

The language of Rule 406 has been amended as part of the restyling of the Evidence Rules to make them more easily understood and to make style and terminology consistent throughout the rules. These changes are intended to be stylistic only. There is no intent to change any result in any ruling on evidence admissibility.

ADVISORY COMMITTEE'S NOTE
56 F.R.D. 183, 223 (1973)

An oft-quoted paragraph, McCormick, § 162, p.340, describes habit in terms effectively contrasting it with character:

> Character and habit are close akin. Character is a generalized description of one's disposition, or of one's disposition in respect to a general trait, such as honesty, temperance, or peacefulness. "Habit," in modern usage, both lay and psychological, is more specific. It describes one's regular response to a repeated specific situation. If we speak of character for care, we think of the person's tendency to act prudently in all the varying situations of life, in business, family life, in handling automobiles and in walking across the street. A habit, on the other hand, is the person's regular practice of meeting a particular kind of situation with a specific type of conduct, such as the habit of going down a particular stairway two stairs at a time, or of giving the hand-signal for a left turn, or of alighting from railway cars while they are moving. The doing of the habitual acts may become semi-automatic.

Equivalent behavior on the part of a group is designated "routine practice of an organization" in the rule.

Agreement is general that habit evidence is highly persuasive as proof of conduct on a particular occasion. Again quoting McCormick § 162, p.341:

> Character may be thought of as the sum of one's habits though doubtless it is more than this. But unquestionably the uniformity of one's response to habit is far greater than the consistency with which one's conduct conforms to character or disposition. Even though character comes in only exceptionally as evidence of an act, surely any sensible man in investigating whether X did a particular act would be greatly helped in his inquiry by evidence as to whether he was in the habit of doing it.

When disagreement has appeared, its focus has been upon the question what constitutes habit, and the reason for this is readily apparent. The extent to which instances must be multiplied and consistency of behavior maintained in order to rise to the status of habit inevitably gives rise to differences of opinion. Lewan, Rationale of Habit Evidence, 16 Syracuse L. Rev. 39, 49 (1964). While adequacy of sampling and uniformity of response are key factors, precise standards for measuring their sufficiency for evidence purposes cannot be formulated.

The rule is consistent with prevailing views. Much evidence is excluded simply because of failure to achieve the status of habit. Thus, evidence of intemperate "habits" is generally excluded when offered as proof of drunkenness in accident cases, Annot., 46 A.L.R.2d 103, and evidence of other assaults is inadmissible to prove the instant one in a civil assault action, Annot., 66 A.L.R.2d 806. In Levin v. United States, 119 U.S. App. D.C. 156, 338 F.2d 265 (1964), testimony as to the religious "habits" of the accused, offered as tending to prove that he was at home observing the Sabbath rather than out obtaining money through larceny by trick, was held properly excluded;

> "It seems apparent to us that an individual's religious practices would not be the type of activities which would lend themselves to the characterization of 'invariable regularity.' [1 Wigmore 520.] Certainly the very volitional basis of the activity raises serious questions as to its invariable nature, and hence its probative value." *Id.* at 272.

These rulings are not inconsistent with the trend towards admitting evidence of business transactions between one of the parties and a third person as tending to prove that he made the same bargain or proposal in the litigated situation. Slough, Relevancy Unraveled, 6 Kan. L. Rev. 38-41 (1957). Nor are they inconsistent with such cases as Whittemore v. Lockheed Aircraft Corp., 65 Cal. App. 2d 737, 151 P.2d 670 (1944), upholding the admission of evidence that plaintiff's intestate had on four other occasions flown planes from defendant's factory for delivery to his employer airline, offered to prove that he was piloting rather than a guest on a plane which crashed and killed all on board while en route for delivery.

A considerable body of authority has required that evidence of the routine practice of an organization be corroborated as a condition precedent to its admission in evidence. Slough, Relevancy Unraveled, 5 Kan. L. Rev. 404, 449 (1957). This requirement is specifically rejected by the rule on the ground that it relates to the sufficiency of the evidence rather than admissibility. A similar position is taken in New Jersey Rule 49. The rule also rejects the requirement of the absence of eyewitnesses, sometimes encountered with respect to admitting habit evidence to prove freedom from contributory negligence in wrongful death cases. For comment critical of the requirements *see* Frank, J., in Cereste v. New York, N.H. & H.R. Co., 231 F.2d 50 (2d Cir. 1956), *cert. denied*, 351 U.S. 951, 76 S. Ct. 848, 100 L. Ed. 1475, 10 Vand. L. Rev. 447 (1957); McCormick §162, p.342. The omission of the requirement from the California Evidence Code is said to have effected its elimination. Comment, Cal. Ev. Code §1105.

Rule 407.   Subsequent Remedial Measures

When measures are taken that would have made an earlier injury or harm less likely to occur, evidence of the subsequent measures is not admissible to prove:

- negligence;
- culpable conduct;
- a defect in a product or its design; or
- a need for a warning or instruction.

But the court may admit this evidence for another purpose, such as impeachment or — if disputed — proving ownership, control, or the feasibility of precautionary measures.

(Pub. L. 93-595, §1, Jan. 2, 1975, 88 Stat. 1932; Apr. 11, 1997, eff. Dec. 1, 1997; Apr. 26, 2011, eff. Dec. 1, 2011.)

RESTYLED RULE 406 — ADVISORY COMMITTEE'S NOTE

The language of Rule 406 has been amended as part of the restyling of the Evidence Rules to make them more easily understood and to make style and terminology consistent throughout the rules. These changes are intended to be stylistic only. There is no intent to change any result in any ruling on evidence admissibility.

ADVISORY COMMITTEE'S NOTE
56 F.R.D. 183, 225 (1973)

The rule incorporates conventional doctrine which excludes evidence of subsequent remedial measures as proof of an admission of fault. The rule rests on two grounds. (1) The conduct is not in fact an admission, since the conduct is equally consistent with injury by mere accident or through contributory negligence. Or, as Baron Bramwell put it, the rule rejects the notion that "because the world gets wiser as it gets older, therefore it was foolish before." Hart v. Lancashire & Yorkshire Ry. Co., 21 L.T.R. N.S. 261, 263 (1869). Under a liberal theory of relevancy this ground alone would not support exclusion as the inference is still a possible one. (2) The other, and more impressive, ground for exclusion rests on a social policy of encouraging people to take, or at least not discouraging them from taking, steps in furtherance of added safety. The courts have applied this principle to exclude evidence of subsequent repairs, installation of safety devices, changes in company rules, and discharge of employees, and the language of the present rules is broad enough to encompass all of them. *See* Falknor, Extrinsic Policies Affecting Admissibility, 10 Rutgers L. Rev. 574, 590 (1956).

The second sentence of the rule directs attention to the limitations of the rule. Exclusion is called for only when the evidence of subsequent remedial measures is offered as proof of negligence or culpable conduct. In effect it rejects the suggested inference that fault is admitted. Other purposes are, however, allowable, including ownership or control, existence of duty, and feasibility of precautionary measures, if controverted, and impeachment. 2 Wigmore § 283; Annot., 64 A.L.R.2d 1296. Two recent federal cases are illustrative. Boeing Airplane Co. v. Brown, 291 F.2d 310 (9th Cir. 1961), an action against an airplane manufacturer for using an allegedly defectively designed alternator shaft which caused a plane crash, upheld the admission of evidence of subsequent design modification for the purpose of showing that design changes and safeguards were feasible. And Powers v. J. B. Michael & Co., 329 F.2d 674 (6th Cir. 1964), an action against a road contractor for negligent failure to put out warning signs, sustained the admission of evidence that defendant subsequently put out signs to show that the portion of the road in question was under defendant's control. The requirement that the other purpose be controverted calls for automatic exclusion unless a genuine issue be present and allows the opposing party to lay the groundwork for exclusion by making an admission. Otherwise the factors of undue prejudice, confusion of issues, misleading the jury, and waste of time remain for consideration under Rule 403.

For comparable rules, *see* Uniform Rule 51; California Evidence Code § 1151; Kansas Code of Civil Procedure § 60-451; New Jersey Evidence Rule 51.

ADVISORY COMMITTEE'S NOTE — 1997 AMENDMENT

The amendment to Rule 407 makes two changes in the rule. First, the words "an injury or harm allegedly caused by" were added to clarify that the rule applies only to changes made after the occurrence that produced the damages giving rise to the action. Evidence of measures taken by the defendant prior to the "event" causing "injury or harm" do not fall within the exclusionary scope of Rule 407 even if they occurred after the manufacture or design of the product. *See* Chase v. General Motors Corp., 856 F.2d 17, 21-22 (4th Cir. 1988).

Second, Rule 407 has been amended to provide that evidence of subsequent remedial measures may not be used to prove "a defect in a product or its design, or that a warning or instruction should have accompanied a product." This amendment adopts the view of a majority of the circuits that have interpreted Rule 407 to apply to products liability actions. *See* Raymond v. Raymond Corp., 938 F.2d 1518, 1522 (1st Cir. 1991); In re Joint

Eastern District and Southern District Asbestos Litigation v. Armstrong World Industries, Inc., 995 F.2d 343 (2d Cir. 1993); Cann v. Ford Motor Co., 658 F.2d 54, 60 (2d Cir. 1981), *cert. denied*, 456 U.S. 960 (1982); Kelly v. Crown Equipment Co., 970 F.2d 1273, 1275 (3d Cir. 1992); Werner v. Upjohn, Inc., 628 F.2d 848 (4th Cir. 1980), *cert. denied*, 449 U.S. 1080 (1981); Grenada Steel Industries, Inc. v. Alabama Oxygen Co., Inc., 695 F.2d 883 (5th Cir. 1983); Bauman v. Volkswagenwerk Aktiengesellschaft, 621 F.2d 230, 232 (6th Cir. 1980); Flaminio v. Honda Motor Company, Ltd., 733 F.2d 463, 469 (7th Cir. 1984); Gauthier v. AMF, Inc., 788 F.2d 634, 636-37 (9th Cir. 1986).

Although this amendment adopts a uniform federal rule, it should be noted that evidence of subsequent remedial measures may be admissible pursuant to the second sentence of Rule 407. Evidence of subsequent measures that is not barred by Rule 407 may still be subject to exclusion on Rule 403 grounds when the dangers of prejudice or confusion substantially outweigh the probative value of the evidence.

RESTYLED RULE 407 — ADVISORY COMMITTEE'S NOTE

The language of Rule 407 has been amended as part of the general restyling of the Evidence Rules to make them more easily understood and to make style and terminology consistent throughout the rules. These changes are intended to be stylistic only. There is no intent to change any result in any ruling on evidence admissibility.

Rule 407 previously provided that evidence was not excluded if offered for a purpose not explicitly prohibited by the Rule. To improve the language of the Rule, it now provides that the court may admit evidence if offered for a permissible purpose. There is no intent to change the process for admitting evidence covered by the Rule. It remains the case that if offered for an impermissible purpose, it must be excluded, and if offered for a purpose not barred by the Rule, its admissibility remains governed by the general principles of Rules 402, 403, 801, etc.

Rule 408. Compromise Offers and Negotiations

(a) Prohibited Uses. Evidence of the following is not admissible — on behalf of any party — either to prove or disprove the validity or amount of a disputed claim or to impeach by a prior inconsistent statement or a contradiction:

(1) furnishing, promising, or offering — or accepting, promising to accept, or offering to accept — a valuable consideration in compromising or attempting to compromise the claim; and

(2) conduct or a statement made during compromise negotiations about the claim — except when offered in a criminal case and when the negotiations related to a claim by a public office in the exercise of its regulatory, investigative, or enforcement authority.

(b) Exceptions. The court may admit this evidence for another purpose, such as proving a witness's bias or prejudice, negating a contention of undue delay, or proving an effort to obstruct a criminal investigation or prosecution.

(Pub. L. 93-595, § 1, Jan. 2, 1975, 88 Stat. 1933; Apr. 26, 2011, eff. Dec. 1, 2011.)

RESTYLED RULE 408 — ADVISORY COMMITTEE'S NOTE

The language of Rule 408 has been amended as part of the general restyling of the Evidence Rules to make them more easily understood and to make style and terminology consistent throughout the rules. These changes are intended to be stylistic only. There is no intent to change any result in any ruling on evidence admissibility.

Rule 408 previously provided that evidence was not excluded if offered for a purpose not explicitly prohibited by the Rule. To improve the language of the Rule, it now provides that the court may admit evidence if offered for a permissible purpose. There is no intent to change the process for admitting evidence covered by the Rule. It remains the case that if offered for an impermissible purpose, it must be excluded, and if offered for a purpose not barred by the Rule, its admissibility remains governed by the general principles of Rules 402, 403, 801, etc.

ADVISORY COMMITTEE'S NOTE
56 F.R.D. 183, 226 (1973)

As a matter of general agreement, evidence of an offer to compromise a claim is not receivable in evidence as an admission of, as the case may be, the validity or invalidity of the claim. As with evidence of subsequent remedial measures, dealt with in Rule 407, exclusion may be based on two grounds. (1) The evidence is irrelevant, since the offer may be motivated by a desire for peace rather than from any concession of weakness of position. The validity of this position will vary as the amount of the offer varies in relation to the size of the claim and may also be influenced by other circumstances. (2) A more consistently impressive ground is promotion of the public policy favoring the compromise and settlement of disputes. McCormick § 76, 251. While the rule is ordinarily phrased in terms of offers of compromise, it is apparent that a similar attitude must be taken with respect to completed compromises when offered against a party thereto. This latter situation will not, of course, ordinarily occur except when a party to the present litigation has compromised with a third person.

The same policy underlies the provision of Rule 68 of the Federal Rules of Civil Procedure that evidence of an unaccepted offer of judgment is not admissible except in a proceeding to determine costs.

The practical value of the common law rule has been greatly diminished by its inapplicability to admissions of fact, even though made in the course of compromise negotiations, unless hypothetical, stated to be "without prejudice," or so connected with the offer as to be inseparable from it. McCormick § 251, pp.540-541. An inevitable effect is to inhibit freedom of communication with respect to compromise, even among lawyers. Another effect is the generation of controversy over whether a given statement falls within or without the protected area. These considerations account for the expansion of the rule herewith to include evidence of conduct or statements made in compromise negotiations, as well as the offer or completed compromise itself. For similar provisions *see* California Evidence Code § 1152, 1154.

The policy considerations which underlie the rule do not come into play when the effort is to induce a creditor to settle an admittedly due amount for a lessor sum. McCormick § 251, p.540. Hence the rule requires that the claim be disputed as to either validity or amount.

The final sentence of the rule serves to point out some limitations upon its applicability. Since the rule excludes only when the purpose is proving the validity or invalidity of the claim or its amount, an offer for another purpose is not within the rule. The illustrative situations mentioned in the rule are supported by the authorities. As to proving bias or prejudice of a witness, *see* Annot., 161 A.L.R. 395, *contra*, Fenberg v.

Rosenthal, 348 Ill. App. 510, 109 N.E.2d 402 (1952), and negativing a contention of lack of due diligence in presenting a claim, 4 Wigmore § 1061. An effort to "buy off" the prosecution or a prosecuting witness in a criminal case is not within the policy of the rule of exclusion. McCormick § 251, p.542.

For other rules of similar import, *see* Uniform Rules 52 and 53; California Evidence Code § 1152, 1154; Kansas Code of Civil Procedure § 60-452, 60-453; New Jersey Evidence Rules 52 and 53.

ADVISORY COMMITTEE'S NOTE — 2006 AMENDMENT

Rule 408 has been amended to settle some questions in the courts about the scope of the Rule and to make it easier to read and apply. First, the amendment provides that Rule 408 does not prohibit the government from introducing statements or conduct of an accused made during compromise negotiations of a prior civil dispute between the accused and a government regulatory agency. *See, e.g.*, United States v. Prewitt, 34 F.3d 436, 439 (7th Cir. 1994) (admissions of fault made in compromise of a civil securities enforcement action were admissible against the accused in a subsequent criminal action for mail fraud). When an individual makes a statement in the presence of government agents, its subsequent admission in a criminal case should not be unexpected. The individual can seek to protect against subsequent disclosure through negotiation and agreement with the civil regulator, or even in certain circumstances with an attorney for the government under Rule 410.

Statements made in compromise negotiations of a government enforcement action may be excluded in criminal cases where the circumstances so warrant under Rule 403. For example, if an individual was unrepresented at the time the statement was made in a civil enforcement proceeding, its probative value in a subsequent criminal case may be minimal. But there is no absolute exclusion imposed by Rule 408.

In contrast, statements made during compromise negotiations of other disputed claims are not admissible in subsequent criminal litigation, when offered as an admission of the validity or amount of that claim. Where private parties enter into compromise negotiations they cannot protect against the subsequent use of statements in criminal cases by way of private ordering. The inability to guarantee protection against subsequent use could lead to parties refusing to admit fault, even if by doing so they could favorably settle the private matter. Such a chill on settlement negotiations would be contrary to the policy of Rule 408.

The amendment distinguishes statements and conduct (such as a direct admission of fault) made in compromise negotiations of a claim by a government agency from an offer or acceptance of a compromise of such a claim. An offer or acceptance of a compromise of any civil claim is excluded under the Rule if offered against a criminal defendant as an admission of fault. In that case, the predicate for the evidence would be that the defendant, by compromising with the government regulator, has admitted the validity and amount of the civil claim, and that this admission has sufficient probative value to be considered as proof of guilt. But unlike a direct statement of fault, an offer or acceptance of a compromise is not very probative of the defendant's guilt. Moreover, admitting such an offer or acceptance could deter defendants from settling a civil regulatory action for fear of evidentiary use in a subsequent criminal action. *See, e.g.*, Fishman, Jones on Evidence, Civil and Criminal, § 22:16 at 199, n.83 (7th ed. 2000) ("A target of a potential criminal investigation may be unwilling to settle civil claims against him if by doing so he increases the risk of prosecution and conviction.").

The amendment retains the language of the original rule that bars compromise evidence only when offered as evidence of the "validity," "invalidity," or "amount" of the disputed claim. The intent is to retain the extensive case law, finding Rule 408 inapplicable when compromise evidence is offered for a purpose other than to prove the validity, invalidity, or amount of a disputed claim. *See, e.g.*, Athey v. Farmers Ins. Exchange, 234 F.3d 357 (8th Cir. 2000) (evidence of settlement offer by insurer was properly admitted to prove insurer's bad faith); Coakley & Williams v. Structural Concrete Equip., 973 F.2d 349 (4th Cir. 1992) (evidence of settlement is not precluded by Rule 408 where offered to prove a party's intent with respect to the scope of a release); Cates v. Morgan Portable Bldg. Corp., 708 F.2d 683 (7th Cir. 1985) (Rule 408 does not bar evidence of a settlement when offered to prove a breach of the settlement agreement, as the purpose of the evidence is to prove the fact of settlement as opposed to the validity or amount of the underlying claim); Uforma/Shelby Bus. Forms, Inc. v. NLRB, 111 F.3d 1284 (6th Cir. 1997) (threats made in settlement negotiations were admissible; Rule 408 is inapplicable when the claim is based upon a wrong that is committed during the course of settlement negotiations). So, for example, Rule 408 is inapplicable if offered to show that a party made fraudulent statements in order to settle a litigation.

The amendment does not affect the case law providing that Rule 408 is inapplicable when evidence of the compromise is offered to prove notice. *See, e.g.*, United States v. Austin, 54 F.3d 394 (7th Cir. 1995) (no error to admit evidence of the defendant's settlement with the FTC, because it was offered to prove that the defendant was on notice that subsequent similar conduct was wrongful); Spell v. McDaniel, 824 F.2d 1380 (4th Cir. 1987) (in a civil rights action alleging that an officer used excessive force, a prior settlement by the City of another brutality claim was properly admitted to prove that the City was on notice of aggressive behavior by police officers).

The amendment prohibits the use of statements made in settlement negotiations when offered to impeach by prior inconsistent statement or through contradiction. Such broad impeachment would tend to swallow the exclusionary rule and would impair the public policy of promoting settlements. *See* McCormick on Evidence at 186 (5th ed. 1999) ("Use of statements made in compromise negotiations to impeach the testimony of a party, which is not specifically treated in Rule 408, is fraught with danger of misuse of the statements to prove liability, threatens frank interchange of information during negotiations, and generally should not be permitted."). *See also* EEOC v. Gear Petroleum, Inc., 948 F.2d 1542 (10th Cir. 1991) (letter sent as part of settlement negotiation cannot be used to impeach defense witnesses by way of contradiction or prior inconsistent statement; such broad impeachment would undermine the policy of encouraging uninhibited settlement negotiations).

The amendment makes clear that Rule 408 excludes compromise evidence even when a party seeks to admit its own settlement offer or statements made in settlement negotiations. If a party were to reveal its own statement or offer, this could itself reveal the fact that the adversary entered into settlement negotiations. The protections of Rule 408 cannot be waived unilaterally because the Rule, by definition, protects both parties from having the fact of negotiation disclosed to the jury. Moreover, proof of statements and offers made in settlement would often have to be made through the testimony of attorneys, leading to the risks and costs of disqualification. *See generally* Pierce v. F.R. Tripler & Co., 955 F.2d 820, 828 (2d Cir. 1992) (settlement offers are excluded under Rule 408 even if it is the offeror who seeks to admit them, noting that the "widespread admissibility of the substance of settlement offers could bring with it a rash of motions for disqualification of a party's chosen counsel who would likely become a witness at trial").

The sentence of the Rule referring to evidence "otherwise discoverable" has been deleted as superfluous. *See, e.g.*, Advisory Committee Note to Maine Rule of Evidence 408 (refusing to include the sentence in the Maine version of Rule 408 and noting that the sentence "seems to state what the law would be if it were omitted"); Advisory Committee Note to Wyoming Rule of Evidence 408 (refusing to include the sentence in Wyoming Rule 408 on the ground that it was "superfluous"). The intent of the sentence was to prevent a party from trying to immunize admissible information, such as a pre-existing document, through the pretense of disclosing it during compromise negotiations. *See* Ramada Development Co. v. Rauch, 644 F.2d 1097 (5th Cir. 1981). But even without the sentence, the Rule cannot be read to protect pre-existing information simply because it was presented to the adversary in compromise negotiations.

CHANGES MADE AFTER PUBLICATION AND COMMENTS

In response to public comment, the proposed amendment was changed to provide that statements and conduct during settlement negotiations are to be admissible in subsequent criminal litigation only when made during settlement discussions of a claim brought by a government regulatory agency. Stylistic changes were made in accordance with suggestions from the Style Subcommittee of the Standing Committee. The Committee Note was altered to accord with the change in the text, and also to clarify that fraudulent statements made during settlement negotiations are not protected by the Rule.

Rule 409.   Offers to Pay Medical and Similar Expenses

Evidence of furnishing, promising to pay, or offering to pay medical, hospital, or similar expenses resulting from an injury is not admissible to prove liability for the injury.

(Pub. L. 93-595, § 1, Jan. 2, 1975, 88 Stat. 1933; Apr. 26, 2011, eff. Dec. 1, 2011.)

RESTYLED RULE 409 — ADVISORY COMMITTEE'S NOTE

The language of Rule 409 has been amended as part of the restyling of the Evidence Rules to make them more easily understood and to make style and terminology consistent throughout the rules. These changes are intended to be stylistic only. There is no intent to change any result in any ruling on evidence admissibility.

ADVISORY COMMITTEE'S NOTE
56 F.R.D. 183, 228 (1973)

The considerations underlying this rule parallel those underlying Rules 407 and 408, which deal respectively with subsequent remedial measures and offers of compromise. As stated in Annot., 20 A.L.R.2d 291, 293:

> [G]enerally, evidence of payment of medical, hospital, or similar expenses of an injured party by the opposing party, is not admissible, the reason often given being that such payment or offer is usually made from humane impulses and not from an admission of liability, and that to hold otherwise would tend to discourage assistance to the injured person.

Contrary to Rule 408, dealing with offers of compromise, the present rule does not extend to conduct or statements not a part of the act of furnishing or offering or promising to pay. This difference in treatment arises from fundamental differences in nature. Communication is essential if compromises are to be effected, and consequently broad protection of statements is needed. This is not so in cases of payments or offers or promises to pay medical expenses, where factual statements may be expected to be incidental in nature.

For rules on the same subject, but phrased in terms of "humanitarian motives," *see* Uniform Rule 52; California Evidence Code § 1152; Kansas Code of Civil Procedure § 60-452; New Jersey Evidence Rule 52.

Rule 410.   Pleas, Plea Discussions, and Related Statements

(a) Prohibited Uses. In a civil or criminal case, evidence of the following is not admissible against the defendant who made the plea or participated in the plea discussions:

(1) a guilty plea that was later withdrawn;

(2) a nolo contendere plea;

(3) a statement made during a proceeding on either of those pleas under Federal Rule of Criminal Procedure 11 or a comparable state procedure; or

(4) a statement made during plea discussions with an attorney for the prosecuting authority if the discussions did not result in a guilty plea or they resulted in a later-withdrawn guilty plea.

(b) Exceptions. The court may admit a statement described in Rule 410(a)(3) or (4):

(1) in any proceeding in which another statement made during the same plea or plea discussions has been introduced, if in fairness the statements ought to be considered together; or

(2) in a criminal proceeding for perjury or false statement, if the defendant made the statement under oath, on the record, and with counsel present.

(Pub. L. 93-595, § 1, Jan. 2, 1975, 88 Stat. 1933; Pub. L. 94-149, § 1(9), Dec. 12, 1975, 89 Stat. 805; Apr. 30, 1979, eff. Dec. 1, 1980; Apr. 26, 2011, eff. Dec. 1, 2011.)

RESTYLED RULE 410—ADVISORY COMMITTEE'S NOTE

The language of Rule 410 has been amended as part of the restyling of the Evidence Rules to make them more easily understood and to make style and terminology consistent throughout the rules. These changes are intended to be stylistic only. There is no intent to change any result in any ruling on evidence admissibility.

ADVISORY COMMITTEE'S NOTE
56 F.R.D. 183, 228 (1973)

Withdrawn pleas of guilty were held inadmissible in federal prosecutions in Kercheval v. United States, 274 U.S. 220, 47 S. Ct. 582, 71 L. Ed. 1009 (1927). The Court pointed out that to admit the withdrawn plea would effectively set at naught the allowance of withdrawal and place the accused in a dilemma utterly inconsistent with the decision to award him a trial. The New York Court of Appeals, in People v.

Spitaleri, 9 N.Y.2d 168, 212 N.Y.S.2d 53, 173 N.E.2d 35 (1961), reexamined and over-turned its earlier decisions which had allowed admission. In addition to the reasons set forth in *Kercheval*, which was quoted at length, the court pointed out that the effect of admitting the plea was to compel defendant to take the stand by way of explanation and to open the way for the prosecution to call the lawyer who had represented him at the time of entering the plea. State court decisions for and against admissibility are collected in Annot., 86 A.L.R.2d 326.

Pleas of nolo contendere are recognized by Rule 11 of the Rules of Criminal Proce-dure, although the law of numerous States is to the contrary. The present rule gives effect to the principal traditional characteristic of the nolo plea, i.e., avoiding the admission of guilt which is inherent in pleas of guilty. This position is consistent with the construction of Section 5 of the Clayton Act, 15 U.S.C. §16(a), recognizing the inconclusive and compromised nature of judgments based on nolo pleas. General Electric Co. v. City of San Antonio, 334 F.2d 480 (5th Cir. 1964); Commonwealth Edison Co. v. Allis-Chal-mers Mfg. Co., 323 F.2d 412 (7th Cir. 1963), *cert. denied*, 376 U.S. 939, 84 S. Ct. 794, 11 L. Ed. 2d 659; Armco Steel Corp. v. North Dakota, 376 F.2d 206 (8th Cir. 1967); City of Burbank v. General Electric Co., 329 F.2d 825 (9th Cir. 1964). *See also* state court deci-sions in Annot., 18 A.L.R.2d 1287, 1314.

Exclusion of offers to plead guilty or nolo has as its purpose the promotion of disposi-tion of criminal cases by compromise. As pointed out in McCormick §251, p.543:

> Effective criminal law administration in many localities would hardly be possible if a large proportion of the charges were not disposed of by such compromises.

See also People v. Hamilton, 60 Cal. 2d 105, 32 Cal. Rptr. 4, 383 P.2d 412 (1963), discuss-ing legislation designed to achieve this result. As with compromise offers generally, Rule 408, free communication is needed, and security against having an offer of compromise or related statement admitted in evidence effectively encourages it.

Limiting the exclusionary rule to use against the accused is consistent with the purpose of the rule, since the possibility of use for or against other persons will not impair the effectiveness of withdrawing pleas or the freedom of discussion which the rule is designed to foster. *See* A.B.A. Standards Relating to Pleas of Guilty §2.2 (1968). *See also* the narrower provisions of New Jersey Evidence Rule 52(2) and the unlimited exclu-sion provided in California Evidence Code §1153.

ADVISORY COMMITTEE'S NOTE — 1979 AMENDMENT

Present Rule 410 conforms to Rule 11(e)(6) of the Federal Rules of Criminal Proce-dure. A proposed amendment to Rule 11(e)(6) would clarify the circumstances in which pleas, plea discussions and related statements are inadmissible in evidence; *see* Advisory Committee Note thereto. The amendment proposed above would make comparable changes in Rule 410.

NOTES OF CRIMINAL PROCEDURE ADVISORY COMMITTEE
77 F.R.D. 507, 533 (1978)

The major objective of the amendment to Rule 11(e)(6) is to describe more precisely, consistent with the original purpose of the provision, what evidence relating to pleas or plea discussions is inadmissible. The present language is susceptible to interpretation which would make it applicable to a wide variety of statements made under various circumstances other than within the context of those plea discussions authorized by

Rule 11(e) and intended to be protected by subdivision (e)(6) of the rule. *See* United States v. Herman, 544 F.2d 791 (5th Cir. 1977), discussed herein.

Fed. R. Ev. 410, as originally adopted by Pub. L. 93-595, provided in part that

> evidence of a plea of guilty, later withdrawn, or a plea of nolo contendere, or of an offer to plead guilty or nolo contendere to the crime charged or any other crime, or of statements made in connection with any of the foregoing pleas or offers, is not admissible in any civil or criminal action, case, or proceeding against the person who made the plea or offer.

(This rule was adopted with the proviso that it "shall be superseded by any amendment to the Federal Rules of Criminal Procedure which is inconsistent with this rule.") As the Advisory Committee Note explained: "Exclusion of offers to plead guilty or nolo has as its purpose the promotion of disposition of criminal cases by compromise." The amendment of Fed. R. Crim. P. 11, transmitted to Congress by the Supreme Court in April 1974, contained a subdivision (e)(6) essentially identical to the Rule 410 language quoted above, as a part of a substantial revision of Rule 11. The most significant feature of this revision was the express recognition given to the fact that the "attorney for the government and the attorney for the defendant or the defendant when acting pro se may engage in discussions with a view toward reaching" a plea agreement. Subdivision (e)(6) was intended to encourage such discussions. As noted in H.R. Rep. No. 94-247, 94th Cong., 1st Sess. 7 (1975), the purpose of subdivision (e)(6) is to not "discourage defendants from being completely candid and open during plea negotiations." Similarly, H.R. Rep. No. 94-414, 94th Cong., 1st Sess. 10 (1975), states that "Rule 11e(6) deals with the use of statements made in connection with plea agreements." (Rule 11(e)(6) was thereafter enacted, with the addition of the proviso allowing use of statements in a prosecution for perjury, and with the qualification that the inadmissible statements must also be "relevant to" the inadmissible pleas or offers. Pub. L. 94-64; Fed. R. Ev. 410 was then amended to conform. Pub. L. 94-149.)

While this history shows that the purpose of Fed. R. Ev. 410 and Fed. R. Crim. P. 11(e)(6) is to permit the unrestrained candor which produces effective plea discussions between the "attorney for the government and the attorney for the defendant or the defendant when acting pro se," given visibility and sanction in Rule 11(e), a literal reading of the language of these two rules could reasonably lead to the conclusion that a broader rule of inadmissibility obtains. That is, because "statements" are generally inadmissible if "made in connection with, and relevant to" an "offer to plead guilty," it might be thought that an otherwise voluntary admission to law enforcement officials is rendered inadmissible merely because it was made in the hope of obtaining leniency by a plea. Some decisions interpreting Rule 11(e)(6) point in this direction. *See* United States v. Herman, 544 F.2d 791 (5th Cir. 1977) (defendant in custody of two postal inspectors during continuance of removal hearing instigated conversation with them and at some point said he would plead guilty to armed robbery if the murder charge was dropped; one inspector stated they were not "in position" to make any deals in this regard; held, defendant's statement inadmissible under Rule 11(e)(6) because the defendant "made the statements during the course of a conversation in which he sought concessions from the government in return for a guilty plea"); United States v. Brooks, 536 F.2d 1137 (6th Cir. 1976) (defendant telephoned postal inspector and offered to plead guilty if he got 2-year maximum; statement inadmissible).

The amendment makes inadmissible statements made "in the course of any proceedings under this rule regarding" either a plea of guilty later withdrawn or a plea of nolo contendere, and also statements "made in the course of plea discussions with an attorney for the government which do not result in a plea of guilty or which result in a plea of guilty later withdrawn." It is not limited to statements by the defendant himself, and thus would cover statements by defense counsel regarding defendant's incriminating admissions to him. It thus fully protects the plea discussion process authorized by Rule 11 without attempting to deal with confrontations between suspects and law enforcement agents, which involve problems of quite different dimensions. *See, e.g.*, ALI Model Code of Pre-Arraignment Procedure art. 140 and § 150.2(8) (Proposed Official Draft, 1975) (latter section requires exclusion if "a law enforcement officer induces any person to make a statement by promising leniency"). This change, it must be emphasized, does not compel the conclusion that statements made to law enforcement agents, especially when the agents purport to have authority to bargain, are inevitably admissible. Rather, the point is that such cases are not covered by the per se rule of 11(e)(6) and thus must be resolved by that body of law dealing with police interrogations.

If there has been a plea of guilty later withdrawn or a plea of nolo contendere, sub-division (e)(6)(C) makes inadmissible statements made "in the course of any proceedings under this rule" regarding such pleas. This includes, for example, admissions by the defendant when he makes his plea in court pursuant to Rule 11 and also admissions made to provide the factual basis pursuant to subdivision (f). However, subdivision (e)(6)(C) is not limited to statements made in court. If the court were to defer its decision on a plea agreement pending examination of the presentence report, as authorized by subdivision (e)(2), statements made to the probation officer in connection with the preparation of that report would come within this provision.

This amendment is fully consistent with all recent and major law reform efforts on this subject. ALI Model Code of Pre-Arraignment Procedure § 350.7 (Proposed Official Draft, 1975), and ABA Standards Relating to Pleas of Guilty § 3.4 (Approved Draft, 1968) both provide:

> Unless the defendant subsequently enters a plea of guilty or nolo contendere which is not withdrawn, the fact that the defendant or his counsel and the prosecuting attorney engaged in plea discussions or made a plea agreement should not be received in evidence against or in favor of the defendant in any criminal or civil action or administrative proceedings.

The Commentary to the latter states:

> The above standard is limited to discussions and agreements with the prosecuting attorney. Sometimes defendants will indicate to the police their willingness to bargain, and in such instances these statements are sometimes admitted in court against the defendant. State v. Christian, 245 S.W.2d 895 (Mo. 1952). If the police initiate this kind of discussion, this may have some bearing on the admissibility of the defendant's statement. However, the policy considerations relevant to this issue are better dealt with in the context of standards governing in-custody interrogation by the police.

Similarly, Unif. R. Crim. P. 441(d) (Approved Draft, 1974), provides that except under limited circumstances "no discussion between the parties or statement by the defendant or his lawyer under this Rule," i.e., the rule providing "the parties may meet to discuss the possibility of pretrial diversion . . . or of a plea agreement," are admissible. The amendment is likewise consistent with the typical state provision on this subject; *see, e.g.*, Ill. S. Ct. Rule 402(f).

The language of the amendment identifies with more precision than the present language the necessary relationship between the statements and the plea or discussion. *See* the dispute between the majority and concurring opinions in United States v. Herman, 544 F.2d 791 (5th Cir. 1977), concerning the meanings and effect of the phrases "connection to" and "relevant to" in the present rule. Moreover, by relating the statements to "plea discussions" rather than "an offer to plead," the amendment ensures "that even an attempt to open plea bargaining [is] covered under the same rule of inadmissibility." United States v. Brooks, 536 F.2d 1137 (6th Cir. 1976).

The last sentence of Rule 11(e)(6) is amended to provide a second exception to the general rule of nonadmissibility of the described statements. Under the amendment, such a statement is also admissible "in any proceeding wherein another statement made in the course of the same plea or plea discussions has been introduced and the statement ought in fairness be considered contemporaneously with it." This change is necessary so that, when evidence of statements made in the course of or as a consequence of a certain plea or plea discussions [is] introduced under circumstances not prohibited by this rule (e.g., not "against" the person who made the plea), other statements relating to the same plea or plea discussions may also be admitted when relevant to the matter at issue. For example, if a defendant upon a motion to dismiss a prosecution on some ground were able to admit certain statements made in aborted plea discussions in his favor, then other relevant statements made in the same plea discussions should be admissible against the defendant in the interest of determining the truth of the matter at issue. The language of the amendment follows closely that in Fed. R. Evid. 106, as the considerations involved are very similar.

The phrase "in any civil or criminal proceeding" has been moved from its present position, following the word "against," for purposes of clarity. An ambiguity presently exists because the word "against" may be read as referring either to the kind of proceeding in which the evidence is offered or the purpose for which it is offered. The change makes it clear that the latter construction is correct. No change is intended with respect to provisions making evidence rules inapplicable in certain situations. *See, e.g.,* Fed. R. Evid. 104(a) and 1101(d).

Unlike ABA Standards Relating to Pleas of Guilty § 3.4 (Approved Draft, 1968), and ALI Model Code of Pre-Arraignment Procedure § 350.7 (Proposed Official Draft, 1975), Rule 11(e)(6) does not also provide that the described evidence is inadmissible "in favor of" the defendant. This is not intended to suggest, however, that such evidence will inevitably be admissible in the defendant's favor. Specifically, no disapproval is intended of such decisions as United States v. Verdoorn, 528 F.2d 103 (8th Cir. 1976), holding that the trial judge properly refused to permit the defendants to put into evidence at their trial the fact the prosecution had attempted to plea bargain with them, as "meaningful dialogue between the parties would, as a practical matter, be impossible if either party had to assume the risk that plea offers would be admissible in evidence."

Rule 411.   Liability Insurance

Evidence that a person was or was not insured against liability is not admissible to prove whether the person acted negligently or otherwise wrongfully. But the court may admit this evidence for another purpose, such as proving a witness's bias or prejudice or proving agency, ownership, or control.

(Pub. L. 93-595, § 1, Jan. 2, 1975, 88 Stat. 1933; Mar. 2, 1987, eff. Oct. 1, 1987; Apr. 26, 2011, eff. Dec. 1, 2011.)

RESTYLED RULE 411 — ADVISORY COMMITTEE'S NOTE

The language of Rule 411 has been amended as part of the general restyling of the Evidence Rules to make them more easily understood and to make style and terminology consistent throughout the rules. These changes are intended to be stylistic only. There is no intent to change any result in any ruling on evidence admissibility.

Rule 411 previously provided that evidence was not excluded if offered for a purpose not explicitly prohibited by the Rule. To improve the language of the Rule, it now provides that the court may admit evidence if offered for a permissible purpose. There is no intent to change the process for admitting evidence covered by the Rule. It remains the case that if offered for an impermissible purpose, it must be excluded, and if offered for a purpose not barred by the Rule, its admissibility remains governed by the general principles of Rules 402, 403, 801, etc.

ADVISORY COMMITTEE'S NOTE
56 F.R.D. 183, 230 (1973)

The courts have with substantial unanimity rejected evidence of liability insurance for the purpose of proving fault, and absence of liability insurance as proof of lack of fault. At best the inference of fault from the fact of insurance coverage is a tenuous one, as is its converse. More important, no doubt, has been the feeling that knowledge of the presence or absence of liability insurance would induce juries to decide cases on improper grounds. McCormick § 168; Annot., 4 A.L.R.2d 761. The rule is drafted in broad terms so as to include contributory negligence or other fault of a plaintiff as well as fault of a defendant.

The second sentence points out the limits of the rule, using well established illustrations. *Id.*

For similar rules *see* Uniform Rule 54; California Evidence Code § 1155; Kansas Code of Civil Procedure § 60-454; New Jersey Evidence Rule 54.

ADVISORY COMMITTEE'S NOTE — 1987 AMENDMENT

The amendment is technical. No substantive change is intended.

Rule 412. Sex Offense Cases: The Victim's Sexual Behavior or Predisposition

(a) Prohibited Uses. The following evidence is not admissible in a civil or criminal proceeding involving alleged sexual misconduct:

(1) evidence offered to prove that a victim engaged in other sexual behavior; or

(2) evidence offered to prove a victim's sexual predisposition.

(b) Exceptions.

(1) *Criminal Cases.* The court may admit the following evidence in a criminal case:

(A) evidence of specific instances of a victim's sexual behavior, if offered to prove that someone other than the defendant was the source of semen, injury, or other physical evidence;

(B) evidence of specific instances of a victim's sexual behavior with respect to the person accused of the sexual misconduct, if offered by the defendant to prove consent or if offered by the prosecutor; and

---

(continued)

(C) evidence whose exclusion would violate the defendant's constitutional rights.

(2) *Civil Cases.* In a civil case, the court may admit evidence offered to prove a victim's sexual behavior or sexual predisposition if its probative value substantially outweighs the danger of harm to any victim and of unfair prejudice to any party. The court may admit evidence of a victim's reputation only if the victim has placed it in controversy.

(c) Procedure to Determine Admissibility.

(1) *Motion.* If a party intends to offer evidence under Rule 412(b), the party must:

(A) file a motion that specifically describes the evidence and states the purpose for which it is to be offered;

(B) do so at least 14 days before trial unless the court, for good cause, sets a different time;

(C) serve the motion on all parties; and

(D) notify the victim or, when appropriate, the victim's guardian or representative.

(2) *Hearing.* Before admitting evidence under this rule, the court must conduct an in-camera hearing and give the victim and parties a right to attend and be heard. Unless the court orders otherwise, the motion, related materials, and the record of the hearing must be and remain sealed.

(d) Definition of "Victim." In this rule, "victim" includes an alleged victim.

(Added Pub. L. 95-540, § 2(a), Oct. 28, 1978, 92 Stat. 2046; amended Pub. L. 100-690, title VII, § 7046(a), Nov. 18, 1988, 102 Stat. 4400; Apr. 29, 1994, eff. Dec. 1, 1994; Pub. L. 103-322, title IV, § 40141(b), Sept. 13, 1994, 108 Stat. 1919; Apr. 26, 2011, eff. Dec. 1, 2011.)

RESTYLED RULE 412 — ADVISORY COMMITTEE'S NOTE

The language of Rule 412 has been amended as part of the restyling of the Evidence Rules to make them more easily understood and to make style and terminology consistent throughout the rules. These changes are intended to be stylistic only. There is no intent to change any result in any ruling on evidence admissibility.

ADVISORY COMMITTEE'S NOTE — 1994 AMENDMENT

Rule 412 has been revised to diminish some of the confusion engendered by the original rule and to expand the protection afforded alleged victims of sexual misconduct. Rule 412 applies to both civil and criminal proceedings. The rule aims to safeguard the alleged victim against the invasion of privacy, potential embarrassment and sexual stereotyping that is associated with public disclosure of intimate sexual details and the infusion of sexual innuendo into the factfinding process. By affording victims protection in most instances, the rule also encourages victims of sexual misconduct to institute and to participate in legal proceedings against alleged offenders.

Rule 412 seeks to achieve these objectives by barring evidence relating to the alleged victim's sexual behavior or alleged sexual predisposition, whether offered as substantive evidence or for impeachment, except in designated circumstances in which the probative value of the evidence significantly outweighs possible harm to the victim.

The revised rule applies in all cases involving sexual misconduct without regard to whether the alleged victim or person accused is a party to the litigation. Rule 412 extends to "pattern" witnesses in both criminal and civil cases whose testimony about other instances of sexual misconduct by the person accused is otherwise admissible. When the case does not involve alleged sexual misconduct, evidence relating to a third-party witness' alleged sexual activities is not within the ambit of Rule 412. The witness will, however, be protected by other rules such as Rules 404 and 608, as well as Rule 403.

The terminology "alleged victim" is used because there will frequently be a factual dispute as to whether sexual misconduct occurred. It does not connote any requirement that the misconduct be alleged in the pleadings. Rule 412 does not, however, apply unless the person against whom the evidence is offered can reasonably be characterized as a "victim of alleged sexual misconduct." When this is not the case, as for instance in a defamation action involving statements concerning sexual misconduct in which the evidence is offered to show that the alleged defamatory statements were true or did not damage the plaintiff's reputation, neither Rule 404 nor this rule will operate to bar the evidence; Rules 401 and 403 will continue to control. Rule 412 will, however, apply in a Title VII action in which the plaintiff has alleged sexual harassment.

The reference to a person "accused" is also used in a non-technical sense. There is no requirement that there be a criminal charge pending against the person or even that the misconduct would constitute a criminal offense. Evidence offered to prove allegedly false prior claims by the victim is not barred by Rule 412. However, this evidence is subject to the requirements of Rule 404.

Subdivision (a). As amended, Rule 412 bars evidence offered to prove the victim's sexual behavior and alleged sexual predisposition. Evidence, which might otherwise be admissible under Rules 402, 404(b), 405, 607, 608, 609, or some other evidence rule, must be excluded if Rule 412 so requires. The word "other" is used to suggest some flexibility in admitting evidence "intrinsic" to the alleged sexual misconduct. *Cf.* Committee Note to 1991 amendment to Rule 404(b).

Past sexual behavior connotes all activities that involve actual physical conduct, i.e., sexual intercourse and sexual contact, or that imply sexual intercourse or sexual contact. *See, e.g.,* United States v. Galloway, 937 F.2d 542 (10th Cir. 1991), *cert. denied,* 113 S. Ct. 418 (1992) (use of contraceptives inadmissible since use implies sexual activity); United States v. One Feather, 702 F.2d 736 (8th Cir. 1983) (birth of an illegitimate child inadmissible); State v. Carmichael, 727 P.2d 918, 925 (Kan. 1986) (evidence of venereal disease inadmissible). In addition, the word "behavior" should be construed to include activities of the mind, such as fantasies or dreams. *See* 23 C. Wright & K. Graham, Jr., Federal Practice and Procedure, § 5384 at p.548 (1980) ("While there may be some doubt under statutes that require 'conduct,' it would seem that the language of Rule 412 is broad enough to encompass the behavior of the mind.").

The rule has been amended to also exclude all other evidence relating to an alleged victim of sexual misconduct that is offered to prove a sexual predisposition. This amendment is designed to exclude evidence that does not directly refer to sexual activities or thoughts but that the proponent believes may have a sexual connotation for the factfinder. Admission of such evidence would contravene Rule 412's objectives of shielding the alleged victim from potential embarrassment and safeguarding the victim against stereotypical thinking. Consequently, unless the (b)(2) exception is satisfied, evidence such as that relating to the alleged victim's mode of dress, speech, or life-style will not be admissible.

The introductory phrase in subdivision (a) was deleted because it lacked clarity and contained no explicit reference to the other provisions of law that were intended to be overridden. The conditional clause, "except as provided in subdivisions (b) and (c)" is intended to make clear that evidence of the types described in subdivision (a) is admissible only under the strictures of those sections.

The reason for extending the rule to all criminal cases is obvious. The strong social policy of protecting a victim's privacy and encouraging victims to come forward to report criminal acts is not confined to cases that involve a charge of sexual assault. The need to protect the victim is equally great when a defendant is charged with kidnapping, and evidence is offered, either to prove motive or as background, that the defendant sexually assaulted the victim.

The reason for extending Rule 412 to civil cases is equally obvious. The need to protect alleged victims against invasions of privacy, potential embarrassment, and unwarranted sexual stereotyping, and the wish to encourage victims to come forward when they have been sexually molested do not disappear because the context has shifted from a criminal prosecution to a claim for damages or injunctive relief. There is a strong social policy in not only punishing those who engage in sexual misconduct, but in also providing relief to the victim. Thus, Rule 412 applies in any civil case in which a person claims to be the victim of sexual misconduct, such as actions for sexual battery or sexual harassment.

Subdivision (b). Subdivision (b) spells out the specific circumstances in which some evidence may be admissible that would otherwise be barred by the general rule expressed in subdivision (a). As amended, Rule 412 will be virtually unchanged in criminal cases, but will provide protection to any person alleged to be a victim of sexual misconduct regardless of the charge actually brought against an accused. A new exception has been added for civil cases.

In a criminal case, evidence may be admitted under subdivision (b)(1) pursuant to three possible exceptions, provided the evidence also satisfies other requirements for admissibility specified in the Federal Rules of Evidence, including Rule 403. Subdivisions (b)(1)(A) and (b)(1)(B) require proof in the form of specific instances of sexual behavior in recognition of the limited probative value and dubious reliability of evidence of reputation or evidence in the form of an opinion.

Under subdivision (b)(1)(A), evidence of specific instances of sexual behavior with persons other than the person whose sexual misconduct is alleged may be admissible if it is offered to prove that another person was the source of semen, injury or other physical evidence. Where the prosecution has directly or indirectly asserted that the physical evidence originated with the accused, the defendant must be afforded an opportunity to prove that another person was responsible. *See* United States v. Begay, 937 F.2d 515, 523 n.10 (10th Cir. 1991). Evidence offered for the specific purpose identified in this subdivision may still be excluded if it does not satisfy Rules 401 or 403. *See, e.g.,* United States v. Azure, 845 F.2d 1503, 1505-06 (8th Cir. 1988) (10 year old victim's injuries indicated recent use of force; court excluded evidence of consensual sexual activities with witness who testified at in camera hearing that he had never hurt victim and failed to establish recent activities).

Under the exception in subdivision (b)(1)(B), evidence of specific instances of sexual behavior with respect to the person whose sexual misconduct is alleged is admissible if offered to prove consent, or offered by the prosecution. Admissible pursuant to this exception might be evidence of prior instances of sexual activities between the alleged victim and the accused, as well as statements in which the alleged victim expressed an intent to engage in sexual intercourse with the accused, or voiced sexual fantasies involving the specific accused. In a prosection [sic] for child sexual abuse, for example, evidence of uncharged sexual activity between the accused and the alleged victim offered by the prosecution may be admissible pursuant to Rule 404(b) to show a pattern of behavior. Evidence relating to the victim's alleged sexual predisposition is not admissible pursuant to this exception.

Under subdivision (b)(1)(C), evidence of specific instances of conduct may not be excluded if the result would be to deny a criminal defendant the protections afforded by the Constitution. For example, statements in which the victim has expressed an intent to have sex with the first person encountered on a particular occasion might not be excluded without violating the due process right of a rape defendant seeking to prove consent. Recognition of this basic principle was expressed in subdivision (b)(1) of the original rule. The United States Supreme Court has recognized that in various circumstances a defendant may have a right to introduce evidence otherwise precluded by an evidence rule under the Confrontation Clause. *See, e.g.,* Olden v. Kentucky, 488 U.S. 227 (1988) (defendant in rape cases had right to inquire into alleged victim's cohabitation with another man to show bias).

Subdivision (b)(2) governs the admissibility of otherwise proscribed evidence in civil cases. It employs a balancing test rather than the specific exceptions stated in subdivision (b)(1) in recognition of the difficulty of foreseeing future developments in the law. Greater flexibility is needed to accommodate evolving causes of action such as claims for sexual harassment.

The balancing test requires the proponent of the evidence, whether plaintiff or defendant, to convince the court that the probative value of the proffered evidence "substantially outweighs the danger of harm to any victim and of unfair prejudice of any party." This test for admitting evidence offered to prove sexual behavior or sexual propensity in civil cases differs in three respects from the general rule governing admissibility set forth in Rule 403. First, it reverses the usual procedure spelled out in Rule 403 by shifting the burden to the proponent to demonstrate admissibility rather than making the opponent justify exclusion of the evidence. Second, the standard expressed in subdivision (b)(2) is more stringent than in the original rule; it raises the threshold for admission by requiring that the probative value of the evidence *substantially* outweigh the specified dangers. Finally, the Rule 412 test puts "harm to the victim" on the scale in addition to prejudice to the parties.

Evidence of reputation may be received in a civil case only if the alleged victim has put his or her reputation into controversy. The victim may do so without making a specific allegation in a pleading. *Cf.* Fed. R. Civ. P. 35(a).

Subdivision (c). Amended subdivision (c) is more concise and understandable than the subdivision it replaces. The requirement of a motion before trial is continued in the amended rule, as is the provision that a late motion may be permitted for good cause shown. In deciding whether to permit late filing, the court may take into account the conditions previously included in the rule: namely whether the evidence is newly discovered and could not have been obtained earlier through the existence of due diligence, and whether the issue to which such evidence relates has newly arisen in the case. The rule recognizes that in some instances the circumstances that justify an application to introduce evidence otherwise barred by Rule 412 will not become apparent until trial.

The amended rule provides that before admitting evidence that falls within the prohibition of Rule 412(a), the court must hold a hearing in camera at which the alleged victim and any party must be afforded the right to be present and an opportunity to be heard. All papers connected with the motion and any record of a hearing on the motion must be kept and remain under seal during the course of trial and appellate proceedings unless otherwise ordered. This is to assure that the privacy of the alleged victim is preserved in all cases in which the court rules that proffered evidence is not admissible, and in which the hearing refers to matters that are not received, or are received in another form.

The procedures set forth in subdivision (c) do not apply to discovery of a victim's past sexual conduct or predisposition in civil cases, which will be continued to be governed by Fed. R. Civ. P. 26. In order not to undermine the rationale of Rule 412, however, courts should enter appropriate orders pursuant to Fed. R. Civ. P. 26(c) to protect the victim against unwarranted inquiries and to ensure confidentiality. Courts should presumptively issue protective orders barring discovery unless the party seeking discovery makes a showing that the evidence sought to be discovered would be relevant under the facts and theories of the particular case, and cannot be obtained except through discovery. In an action for sexual harassment, for instance, while some evidence of the alleged victim's sexual behavior and/or predisposition in the workplace may perhaps be relevant, non-work place conduct will usually be irrelevant. *Cf.* Burns v. McGregor Electronic Industries, Inc., 989 F.2d 959, 962-63 (8th Cir. 1993) (posing for a nude magazine outside work hours is irrelevant to issue of unwelcomeness of sexual advances at work). Confidentiality orders should be presumptively granted as well.

One substantive change made in subdivision (c) is the elimination of the following sentence: "Notwithstanding subdivision (b) of Rule 104, if the relevancy of the evidence which the accused seeks to offer in the trial depends upon the fulfillment of a condition of fact, the court, at the hearing in chambers or at a subsequent hearing in chambers scheduled for such purpose, shall accept evidence on the issue of whether such condition of fact is fulfilled and shall determine such issue." On its face, this language would appear to authorize a trial judge to exclude evidence of past sexual conduct between an alleged victim and an accused or a defendant in a civil case based upon the judge's belief that such past acts did not occur. Such an authorization raises questions of invasion of the right to a jury trial under the Sixth and Seventh Amendments. *See* 1 S. Saltzburg & M. Martin, Federal Rules of Evidence Manual, 396-97 (5th ed. 1990).

The Advisory Committee concluded that the amended rule provided adequate protection for all persons claiming to be the victims of sexual misconduct, and that it was inadvisable to continue to include a provision in the rule that has been confusing and that raises substantial constitutional issues.

[The Supreme Court withheld that portion of the proposed amendment to Rule 412 transmitted to the Court by the Judicial Conference of the United States that would apply that rule to civil cases. This Note was not revised to account for the Court's action, because the Note is the commentary of the advisory committee. The proposed amendment to Rule 412 was subsequently amended by § 40141(b) of Pub. L. 103-322.]

Rule 413.   Similar Crimes in Sexual-Assault Cases

(a) **Permitted Uses.** In a criminal case in which a defendant is accused of a sexual assault, the court may admit evidence that the defendant committed any other sexual assault. The evidence may be considered on any matter to which it is relevant.

(b) **Disclosure to the Defendant.** If the prosecutor intends to offer this evidence, the prosecutor must disclose it to the defendant, including witnesses' statements or a summary of the expected testimony. The prosecutor must do so at least 15 days before trial or at a later time that the court allows for good cause.

(c) **Effect on Other Rules.** This rule does not limit the admission or consideration of evidence under any other rule.

(d) **Definition of "Sexual Assault."** In this rule and Rule 415, "sexual assault" means a crime under federal law or under state law (as "state" is defined in 18 U.S.C. § 513) involving:

(1) any conduct prohibited by 18 U.S.C. chapter 109A;

(2) contact, without consent, between any part of the defendant's body — or an object — and another person's genitals or anus;

(3) contact, without consent, between the defendant's genitals or anus and any part of another person's body;

(4) deriving sexual pleasure or gratification from inflicting death, bodily injury, or physical pain on another person; or

(5) an attempt or conspiracy to engage in conduct described in paragraphs (1)-(4).

(Added Pub. L. 103-322, title XXXII, § 320935(a), Sept. 13, 1994, 108 Stat. 2135; Apr. 26, 2011, eff. Dec. 1, 2011.)

Rule 414.   Similar Crimes in ChildMolestation Cases

(a) **Permitted Uses.** In a criminal case in which a defendant is accused of child molestation, the court may admit evidence that the defendant committed any other child molestation. The evidence may be considered on any matter to which it is relevant.

(b) **Disclosure to the Defendant.** If the prosecutor intends to offer this evidence, the prosecutor must disclose it to the defendant, including witnesses' statements or a summary of the expected testimony. The prosecutor must do so at least 15 days before trial or at a later time that the court allows for good cause.

(c) **Effect on Other Rules.** This rule does not limit the admission or consideration of evidence under any other rule.

(d) **Definition of "Child" and "Child Molestation."** In this rule and Rule 415:

(1) "child" means a person below the age of 14; and

(2) "child molestation" means a crime under federal law or under state law (as "state" is defined in 18 U.S.C. §513) involving:

(A) any conduct prohibited by 18 U.S.C. chapter 109A and committed with a child;

(B) any conduct prohibited by 18 U.S.C. chapter 110;

(C) contact between any part of the defendant's body—or an object—and a child's genitals or anus;

(D) contact between the defendant's genitals or anus and any part of a child's body;

(E) deriving sexual pleasure or gratification from inflicting death, bodily injury, or physical pain on a child; or

(F) an attempt or conspiracy to engage in conduct described in subparagraphs (A)-(E).

(Added Pub. L. 103-322, title XXXII, §320935(a), Sept. 13, 1994, 108 Stat. 2136; Apr. 26, 2011, eff. Dec. 1, 2011.)

Rule 415.   Similar Acts in Civil Cases Involving Sexual Assault or Child Molestation

(a) **Permitted Uses.** In a civil case involving a claim for relief based on a party's alleged sexual assault or child molestation, the court may admit evidence that the party committed any other sexual assault or child molestation. The evidence may be considered as provided in Rules 413 and 414.

(b) **Disclosure to the Opponent.** If a party intends to offer this evidence, the party must disclose it to the party against whom it will be offered, including witnesses' statements or a summary of the expected testimony.

(continued)

The party must do so at least 15 days before trial or at a later time that the court allows for good cause.

(c) Effect on Other Rules. This rule does not limit the admission or consideration of evidence under any other rule.

(Added Pub. L. 103-322, title XXXII, § 320935(a), Sept. 13, 1994, 108 Stat. 2137; Apr. 26, 2011, eff. Dec. 1, 2011.)

[NOTE: Rules 413, 414, and 415 were enacted by Congress as part of major crime legislation. Because the rules were enacted without the usual process set forth in the Rules Enabling Act, there are no Advisory Committee Notes.]

RESTYLED RULES 413-415 — ADVISORY COMMITTEE'S NOTE

The language of [Rules 413, 414, and 415] has been amended as part of the restyling of the Evidence Rules to make them more easily understood and to make style and terminology consistent throughout the rules. These changes are intended to be stylistic only. There is no intent to change any result in any ruling on evidence admissibility.

ARTICLE V.   PRIVILEGES

Rule 501.   Privilege in General

The common law—as interpreted by United States courts in the light of reason and experience—governs a claim of privilege unless any of the following provides otherwise:

* the United States Constitution;
* a federal statute; or
* rules prescribed by the Supreme Court.

But in a civil case, state law governs privilege regarding a claim or defense for which state law supplies the rule of decision.

(Pub. L. 93-595, § 1, Jan. 2, 1975, 88 Stat. 1933; Apr. 26, 2011, eff. Dec. 1, 2011.)

[NOTE: Congress substituted Rule 501 for a series of specific privilege rules promulgated by the Supreme Court.]

RESTYLED RULE 501 — ADVISORY COMMITTEE'S NOTE

The language of Rule 501 has been amended as part of the restyling of the Evidence Rules to make them more easily understood and to make style and terminology consistent throughout the rules. These changes are intended to be stylistic only. There is no intent to change any result in any ruling on evidence admissibility.

Rule 502. Attorney-Client Privilege and Work Product; Limitations on Waiver

The following provisions apply, in the circumstances set out, to disclosure of a communication or information covered by the attorney-client privilege or work-product protection.

(a) Disclosure Made in a Federal Proceeding or to a Federal Office or Agency; Scope of a Waiver. When the disclosure is made in a federal proceeding or to a federal office or agency and waives the attorney-client privilege or work-product protection, the waiver extends to an undisclosed communication or information in a federal or state proceeding only if:

(1) the waiver is intentional;

(2) the disclosed and undisclosed communications or information concern the same subject matter; and

(3) they ought in fairness to be considered together.

(b) Inadvertent Disclosure. When made in a federal proceeding or to a federal office or agency, the disclosure does not operate as a waiver in a federal or state proceeding if:

(1) the disclosure is inadvertent;

(2) the holder of the privilege or protection took reasonable steps to prevent disclosure; and

(3) the holder promptly took reasonable steps to rectify the error, including (if applicable) following Federal Rule of Civil Procedure 26(b)(5)(B).

(c) Disclosure Made in a State Proceeding. When the disclosure is made in a state proceeding and is not the subject of a state-court order concerning waiver, the disclosure does not operate as a waiver in a federal proceeding if the disclosure:

(1) would not be a waiver under this rule if it had been made in a federal proceeding; or

(2) is not a waiver under the law of the state where the disclosure occurred.

(d) Controlling Effect of a Court Order. A federal court may order that the privilege or protection is not waived by disclosure connected with the litigation pending before the court — in which event the disclosure is also not a waiver in any other federal or state proceeding.

(e) Controlling Effect of a Party Agreement. An agreement on the effect of disclosure in a federal proceeding is binding only on the parties to the agreement, unless it is incorporated into a court order.

(f) Controlling Effect of this Rule. Notwithstanding Rules 101 and 1101, this rule applies to state proceedings and to federal court-annexed and federal court-mandated arbitration proceedings, in the circumstances set out in the rule. And notwithstanding Rule 501, this rule applies even if state law provides the rule of decision.

(g) Definitions. In this rule:

(1) "attorney-client privilege" means the protection that applicable law provides for confidential attorney-client communications; and

(continued)

> **(2)** "work-product protection" means the protection that applicable law provides for tangible material (or its intangible equivalent) prepared in anticipation of litigation or for trial.
>
> (Pub. L. 110–322, Sept. 19, 2008, 122 Stat. 3537)

RESTLYED RULE 502 — ADVISORY COMMITTEE'S NOTE

Rule 502 has been amended by changing the initial letter of a few words from uppercase to lowercase as part of the restyling of the Evidence Rules to make style and terminology consistent throughout the rules. There is no intent to change any result in any ruling on evidence admissibility.

ADVISORY COMMITTEE'S NOTE
(Nov. 28, 2007)

This new rule has two major purposes:

1) It resolves some longstanding disputes in the courts about the effect of certain disclosures of communications or information protected by the attorney-client privilege or as work product — specifically those disputes involving inadvertent disclosure and subject matter waiver.

2) It responds to the widespread complaint that litigation costs necessary to protect against waiver of attorney-client privilege or work product have become prohibitive due to the concern that any disclosure (however innocent or minimal) will operate as a subject matter waiver of all protected communications or information. This concern is especially troubling in cases involving electronic discovery. *See, e.g., Hopson v. City of Baltimore*, 232 F.R.D. 228, 244 (D.Md. 2005) (electronic discovery may encompass "millions of documents" and to insist upon "record-by-record pre-production privilege review, on pain of subject matter waiver, would impose upon parties costs of production that bear no proportionality to what is at stake in the litigation").

The rule seeks to provide a predictable, uniform set of standards under which parties can determine the consequences of a disclosure of a communication or information covered by the attorney-client privilege or work-product protection. Parties to litigation need to know, for example, that if they exchange privileged information pursuant to a confidentiality order, the court's order will be enforceable. Moreover, if a federal court's confidentiality order is not enforceable in a state court then the burdensome costs of privilege review and retention are unlikely to be reduced.

The rule makes no attempt to alter federal or state law on whether a communication or information is protected under the attorney-client privilege or work-product immunity as an initial matter. Moreover, while establishing some exceptions to waiver, the rule does not purport to supplant applicable waiver doctrine generally.

The rule governs only certain waivers by disclosure. Other common-law waiver doctrines may result in a finding of waiver even where there is no disclosure of privileged information or work product. *See, e.g., Nguyen v. Excel Corp.*, 197 F.3d 200 (5th Cir. 1999) (reliance on an advice of counsel defense waives the privilege with respect to attorney-client communications pertinent to that defense); *Ryers v. Burleson*, 100 F.R.D. 436 (D.D.C. 1983) (allegation of lawyer malpractice constituted a waiver of confidential communications under the circumstances). The rule is not intended to displace or modify federal common law concerning waiver of privilege or work product where no disclosure has been made.

Subdivision (a). The rule provides that a voluntary disclosure in a federal proceeding or to a federal office or agency, if a waiver, generally results in a waiver only of the communication or information disclosed; a subject matter waiver (of either privilege or work product) is reserved for those unusual situations in which fairness requires a further disclosure of related, protected information, in order to prevent a selective and misleading presentation of evidence to the disadvantage of the adversary. *See, e.g., In re United Mine Workers of America Employee Benefit Plans Litig.,* 159 F.R.D. 307, 312 (D.D.C. 1994) (waiver of work product limited to materials actually disclosed, because the party did not deliberately disclose documents in an attempt to gain a tactical advantage). Thus, subject matter waiver is limited to situations in which a party intentionally puts protected information into the litigation in a selective, misleading and unfair manner. It follows that an inadvertent disclosure of protected information can never result in a subject matter waiver. *See* Rule 502(b). The rule rejects the result in *In re Sealed Case,* 877 F.2d 976 (D.C. Cir. 1989), which held that inadvertent disclosure of documents during discovery automatically constituted a subject matter waiver.

The language concerning subject matter waiver — "ought in fairness" — is taken from Rule 106, because the animating principle is the same. Under both Rules, a party that makes a selective, misleading presentation that is unfair to the adversary opens itself to a more complete and accurate presentation.

To assure protection and predictability, the rule provides that if a disclosure is made at the federal level, the federal rule on subject matter waiver governs subsequent state court determinations on the scope of the waiver by that disclosure.

Subdivision (b). Courts are in conflict over whether an inadvertent disclosure of a communication or information protected as privileged or work product constitutes a waiver. A few courts find that a disclosure must be intentional to be a waiver. Most courts find a waiver only if the disclosing party acted carelessly in disclosing the communication or information and failed to request its return in a timely manner. And a few courts hold that any inadvertent disclosure of a communication or information protected under the attorney-client privilege or as work product constitutes a waiver without regard to the protections taken to avoid such a disclosure. *See generally Hopson v. City of Baltimore,* 232 F.R.D. 228 (D. Md. 2005), for a discussion of this case law.

The rule opts for the middle ground: inadvertent disclosure of protected communications or information in connection with a federal proceeding or to a federal office or agency does not constitute a waiver if the holder took reasonable steps to prevent disclosure and also promptly took reasonable steps to rectify the error. This position is in accord with the majority view on whether inadvertent disclosure is a waiver.

Cases such as *Lois Sportswear, U.S.A., Inc. v. Levi Strauss & Co.,* 104 F.R.D. 103, 105 (S.D.N.Y. 1985) and *Hartford Fire Ins. Co. v. Garvey,* 109 F.R.D. 323, 332 (N.D. Cal. 1985), set out a multifactor test for determining whether inadvertent disclosure is a waiver. The stated factors (none of which is dispositive) are the reasonableness of precautions taken, the time taken to rectify the error, the scope of discovery, the extent of disclosure and the overriding issue of fairness. The rule does not explicitly codify that test, because it is really a set of non-determinative guidelines that vary from case to case. The rule is flexible enough to accommodate any of those listed factors. Other considerations bearing on the reasonableness of a producing party's efforts include the number of documents to be reviewed and the time constraints for production. Depending on the circumstances, a party that uses advanced analytical software applications and linguistic tools in screening for privilege and work product may be found to have taken "reasonable steps" to prevent inadvertent disclosure. The implementation of an efficient system of records management before litigation may also be relevant.

The rule does not require the producing party to engage in a post-production review to determine whether any protected communication or information has been produced by mistake. But the rule does require the producing party to follow up on any obvious indications that a protected communication or information has been produced inadvertently.

The rule applies to inadvertent disclosures made to a federal office or agency, including but not limited to an office or agency that is acting in the course of its regulatory, investigative or enforcement authority. The consequences of waiver, and the concomitant costs of pre-production privilege review, can be as great with respect to disclosures to offices and agencies as they are in litigation.

Subdivision (c). Difficult questions can arise when 1) a disclosure of a communication or information protected by the attorney-client privilege or as work product is made in a state proceeding, 2) the communication or information is offered in a subsequent federal proceeding on the ground that the disclosure waived the privilege or protection, and 3) the state and federal laws are in conflict on the question of waiver. The Committee determined that the proper solution for the federal court is to apply the law that is most protective of privilege and work product. If the state law is more protective (such as where the state law is that an inadvertent disclosure can never be a waiver), the holder of the privilege or protection may well have relied on that law when making the disclosure in the state proceeding. Moreover, applying a more restrictive federal law of waiver could impair the state objective of preserving the privilege or work-product protection for disclosures made in state proceedings. On the other hand, if the federal law is more protective, applying the state law of waiver to determine admissibility in federal court is likely to undermine the federal objective of limiting the costs of production.

The rule does not address the enforceability of a state court confidentiality order in a federal proceeding, as that question is covered both by statutory law and principles of federalism and comity. *See* 28 U.S.C. § 1738 (providing that state judicial proceedings "shall have the same full faith and credit in every court within the United States . . . as they have by law or usage in the courts of such State . . . from which they are taken"). *See also Tucker v. Ohtsu Tire & Rubber Co.,* 191 F.R.D. 495, 499 (D. Md. 2000) (noting that a federal court considering the enforceability of a state confidentiality order is "constrained by principles of comity, courtesy, and . . . federalism"). Thus, a state court order finding no waiver in connection with a disclosure made in a state court proceeding is enforceable under existing law in subsequent federal proceedings.

Subdivision (d). Confidentiality orders are becoming increasingly important in limiting the costs of privilege review and retention, especially in cases involving electronic discovery. But the utility of a confidentiality order in reducing discovery costs is substantially diminished if it provides no protection outside the particular litigation in which the order is entered. Parties are unlikely to be able to reduce the costs of pre-production review for privilege and work product if the consequence of disclosure is that the communications or information could be used by non-parties to the litigation.

There is some dispute on whether a confidentiality order entered in one case is enforceable in other proceedings. *See generally Hopson v. City of Baltimore,* 232 F.R.D. 228 (D. Md. 2005), for a discussion of this case law. The rule provides that when a confidentiality order governing the consequences of disclosure in that case is entered in a federal proceeding, its terms are enforceable against non-parties in any federal or state proceeding. For example, the court order may provide for return of documents without waiver irrespective of the care taken by the disclosing party; the rule contemplates enforcement of "claw-back" and "quick peek" arrangements as a way to avoid the excessive costs of pre-production review for privilege and work product. *See Zubulake v. UBS Warburg LLC,* 216 F.R.D. 280, 290 (S.D.N.Y. 2003) (noting that parties may enter into "so-called 'claw-back' agreements that allow the parties to forego privilege review altogether in favor of an agreement to return inadvertently produced privilege documents"). The rule provides a party with a predictable protection from a court order — predictability that is needed to allow the party to plan in advance to limit the prohibitive costs of privilege and work product review and retention.

Under the rule, a confidentiality order is enforceable whether or not it memorializes an agreement among the parties to the litigation. Party agreement should not be a condition of enforceability of a federal court's order.

Under subdivision (d), a federal court may order that disclosure of privileged or protected information "in connection with" a federal proceeding does not result in waiver. But subdivision (d) does not allow the federal court to enter an order determining the waiver effects of a separate disclosure of the same information in other proceedings, state or federal. If a disclosure has been made in a state proceeding (and is not the subject of a state-court order on waiver), then subdivision (d) is inapplicable. Subdivision (c) would govern the federal court's determination whether the state-court disclosure waived the privilege or protection in the federal proceeding.

Subdivision (e). Subdivision (e) codifies the well-established proposition that parties can enter an agreement to limit the effect of waiver by disclosure between or among them. Of course such an agreement can bind only the parties to the agreement. The rule makes clear that if parties want protection against non-parties from a finding of waiver by disclosure, the agreement must be made part of a court order.

Subdivision (f). The protections against waiver provided by Rule 502 must be applicable when protected communications or information disclosed in federal proceedings are subsequently offered in state proceedings. Otherwise the holders of protected communications and information, and their lawyers, could not rely on the protections provided by the Rule, and the goal of limiting costs in discovery would be substantially undermined. Rule 502(f) is intended to resolve any potential tension between the provisions of Rule 502 that apply to state proceedings and the possible limitations on the applicability of the Federal Rules of Evidence otherwise provided by Rules 101 and 1101.

The rule is intended to apply in all federal court proceedings, including court-annexed and court-ordered arbitrations, without regard to any possible limitations of Rules 101 and 1101. This provision is not intended to raise an inference about the applicability of any other rule of evidence in arbitration proceedings more generally.

The costs of discovery can be equally high for state and federal causes of action, and the rule seeks to limit those costs in all federal proceedings, regardless of whether the claim arises under state or federal law. Accordingly, the rule applies to state law causes of action brought in federal court.

Subdivision (g). The rule's coverage is limited to attorney-client privilege and work product. The operation of waiver by disclosure, as applied to other evidentiary privileges, remains a question of federal common law. Nor does the rule purport to apply to the Fifth Amendment privilege against compelled self-incrimination.

The definition of work product "materials" is intended to include both tangible and intangible information. *See In re Cendant Corp. Sec. Litig.*, 343 F.3d 658, 662 (3d Cir. 2003) ("work product protection extends to both tangible and intangible work product").

[During the legislative process by which Congress enacted legislation adopting Rule 502 (Pub. L. 110–322, Sept. 19, 2008, 122 Stat. 3537), the Judicial Conference agreed to augment its note to the new rule with an addendum that contained a "Statement of Congressional Intent Regarding Rule 502 of the Federal Rules of Evidence." The Congressional statement can be found on pages H7818–H7819 of the Congressional Record, vol. 154 (September 8, 2008).]

Pub. L. 110–322, § 1(c), Sept. 19, 2008, 122 Stat. 3538, provided that: "The amendments made by this Act [enacting this rule] shall apply in all proceedings commenced after the date of enactment of this Act [Sept. 19, 2008] and, insofar as is just and practicable, in all proceedings pending on such date of enactment."

ARTICLE VI.   WITNESSES

Rule 601.   Competency to Testify in General

Every person is competent to be a witness unless these rules provide otherwise. But in a civil case, state law governs the witness's competency regarding a claim or defense for which state law supplies the rule of decision

(Pub. L. 93-595, § 1, Jan. 2, 1975, 88 Stat. 1934; Apr. 26, 2011, eff. Dec. 1, 2011.)

RESTYLED RULE 601 — ADVISORY COMMITTEE'S NOTE

The language of Rule 601 has been amended as part of the restyling of the Evidence Rules to make them more easily understood and to make style and terminology consistent throughout the rules. These changes are intended to be stylistic only. There is no intent to change any result in any ruling on evidence admissibility.

ADVISORY COMMITTEE'S NOTE
56 F.R.D. 183, 262 (1973)

This general ground-clearing eliminates all grounds of incompetency not specifically recognized in the succeeding rules of this Article. Included among the grounds thus abolished are religious belief, conviction of crime, and connection with the litigation as a party or interested person or spouse of a party or interested person. With the exception of the so-called Dead Man's Acts, American jurisdictions generally have ceased to recognize these grounds.

The Dead Man's Acts are surviving traces of the common law disqualification of parties and interested persons. They exist in variety too great to convey conviction of their wisdom and effectiveness. These rules contain no provision of this kind. For the reasoning underlying the decision not to give effect to state statutes in diversity cases, *see* the Advisory Committee's Note to Rule 501.

No mental or moral qualifications for testifying as a witness are specified. Standards of mental capacity have proved elusive in actual application. A leading commentator observes that few witnesses are disqualified on that ground. Weihofen, Testimonial Competence and Credibility, 34 Geo. Wash. L. Rev. 53 (1965). Discretion is regularly exercised in favor of allowing the testimony. A witness wholly without capacity is difficult to imagine. The question is one particularly suited to the jury as one of weight and credibility, subject to judicial authority to review the sufficiency of the evidence. 2 Wigmore § 501, 509. Standards of moral qualification in practice consist essentially of evaluating a person's truthfulness in terms of his own answers about it. Their principal utility is in affording an opportunity on voir dire examination to impress upon the witness his moral duty. This result may, however, be accomplished more directly, and without haggling in terms of legal standards, by the manner of administering the oath or affirmation under Rule 603.

Admissibility of religious belief as a ground of impeachment is treated in Rule 610. Conviction of crime as a ground of impeachment is the subject of Rule 609. Marital relationship is the basis for privilege under Rule 505. Interest in the outcome of litigation and mental capacity are, of course, highly relevant to credibility and require no special treatment to render them admissible along with other matters bearing upon the perception, memory, and narration of witnesses.

Rule 602.   Need for Personal Knowledge

A witness may testify to a matter only if evidence is introduced sufficient to support a finding that the witness has personal knowledge of the matter. Evidence to prove personal knowledge may consist of the witness's own testimony. This rule does not apply to a witness's expert testimony under Rule 703.

(Pub. L. 93-595, § 1, Jan. 2, 1975, 88 Stat. 1934; Mar. 2, 1987, eff. Oct. 1, 1987; Apr. 25, 1988, eff. Nov. 1, 1988; Apr. 26, 2011, eff. Dec. 1, 2011.)

RESTYLED RULE 602 — ADVISORY COMMITTEE'S NOTE

The language of Rule 602 has been amended as part of the restyling of the Evidence Rules to make them more easily understood and to make style and terminology consistent throughout the rules. These changes are intended to be stylistic only. There is no intent to change any result in any ruling on evidence admissibility.

ADVISORY COMMITTEE'S NOTE
56 F.R.D. 183, 263 (1973)

". . . [T]he rule requiring that a witness who testifies to a fact which can be perceived by the senses must have had an opportunity to observe, and must have actually observed the fact" is a "most pervasive manifestation" of the common law insistence upon "the most reliable sources of information." McCormick § 10, p.19. These foundation requirements may, of course, be furnished by the testimony of the witness himself; hence personal knowledge is not an absolute but may consist of what the witness thinks he knows from personal perception. 2 Wigmore § 650. It will be observed that the rule is in fact a specialized application of the provisions of Rule 104(b) on conditional relevancy.

This rule does not govern the situation of a witness who testifies to a hearsay statement as such, if he has personal knowledge of the making of the statement. Rules 801 and 805 would be applicable. This rule would, however, prevent him from testifying to the subject matter of the hearsay statement, as he has no personal knowledge of it.

The reference to Rule 703 is designed to avoid any question of conflict between the present rule and the provisions of that rule allowing an expert to express opinions based on facts of which he does not have personal knowledge.

ADVISORY COMMITTEE'S NOTE — 1987 AMENDMENT

The amendments are technical. No substantive change is intended.

ADVISORY COMMITTEE'S NOTE — 1988 AMENDMENT

The amendment is technical. No substantive change is intended.

Rule 603.   Oath or Affirmation to Testify Truthfully

Before testifying, a witness must give an oath or affirmation to testify truthfully. It must be in a form designed to impress that duty on the witness's conscience.

(Pub. L. 93-595, §1, Jan. 2, 1975, 88 Stat. 1934; Mar. 2, 1987, eff. Oct. 1, 1987; Apr. 26, 2011, eff. Dec. 1, 2011.)

RESTYLED RULE 603 — ADVISORY COMMITTEE'S NOTE

The language of Rule 603 has been amended as part of the restyling of the Evidence Rules to make them more easily understood and to make style and terminology consistent throughout the rules. These changes are intended to be stylistic only. There is no intent to change any result in any ruling on evidence admissibility.

ADVISORY COMMITTEE'S NOTE
56 F.R.D. 183, 263 (1973)

The rule is designed to afford the flexibility required in dealing with religious adults, atheists, conscientious objectors, mental defectives, and children. Affirmation is simply a solemn undertaking to tell the truth; no special verbal formula is required. As is true generally, affirmation is recognized by federal law. "Oath" includes affirmation, 1 U.S.C. §1; judges and clerks may administer oaths and affirmations, 28 U.S.C. §459, 953; and affirmations are acceptable in lieu of oaths under Rule 43(d) of the Federal Rules of Civil Procedure. Perjury by a witness is a crime, 18 U.S.C. §1621.

ADVISORY COMMITTEE'S NOTE — 1987 AMENDMENT

The amendments are technical. No substantive change is intended.

Rule 604.   Interpreter

An interpreter must be qualified and must give an oath or affirmation to make a true translation.

(Pub. L. 93-595, §1, Jan. 2, 1975, 88 Stat. 1934; Mar. 2, 1987, eff. Oct. 1, 1987; Apr. 26, 2011, eff. Dec. 1, 2011.)

RESTYLED RULE 604 — ADVISORY COMMITTEE'S NOTE

The language of Rule 604 has been amended as part of the restyling of the Evidence Rules to make them more easily understood and to make style and terminology consistent throughout the rules. These changes are intended to be stylistic only. There is no intent to change any result in any ruling on evidence admissibility.

ADVISORY COMMITTEE'S NOTE
56 F.R.D. 183, 264 (1973)

The rule implements Rule 43(f) of the Federal Rules of Civil Procedure and Rule 28(b) of the Federal Rules of Criminal Procedure, both of which contain provisions for the appointment and compensation of interpreters.

ADVISORY COMMITTEE'S NOTE — 1987 AMENDMENT

The amendment is technical. No substantive change is intended.

Rule 605.   Judge's Competency as a Witness

The presiding judge may not testify as a witness at the trial. A party need not object to preserve the issue.

(Pub. L. 93-595, § 1, Jan. 2, 1975, 88 Stat. 1934; Apr. 26, 2011, eff. Dec. 1, 2011.)

RESTYLED RULE 605 — ADVISORY COMMITTEE'S NOTE

The language of Rule 605 has been amended as part of the restyling of the Evidence Rules to make them more easily understood and to make style and terminology consistent throughout the rules. These changes are intended to be stylistic only. There is no intent to change any result in any ruling on evidence admissibility.

ADVISORY COMMITTEE'S NOTE
56 F.R.D. 183, 264 (1973)

In view of the mandate of 28 U.S.C. § 455 that a judge disqualify himself in "any case in which he . . . is or has been a material witness," the likelihood that the presiding judge in a federal court might be called to testify in the trial over which he is presiding is slight. Nevertheless the possibility is not totally eliminated.

The solution here presented is a broad rule of incompetency, rather than such alternatives as incompetency only as to material matters, leaving the matter to the discretion of the judge, or recognizing no incompetency. The choice is the result of inability to evolve satisfactory answers to questions which arise when the judge abandons the bench for the witness stand. Who rules on objections? Who compels him to answer? Can he rule impartially on the weight and admissibility of his own testimony? Can he be impeached or cross-examined effectively? Can he, in a jury trial, avoid conferring his seal of approval on one side in the eyes of the jury? Can he, in a bench trial, avoid an involvement destructive of impartiality? The rule of general incompetency has substantial support. *See* Report of the Special Committee on the Propriety of Judges Appearing as Witnesses, 36 A.B.A. J. 630 (1950); cases collected in Annot. 157 A.L.R. 311; McCormick § 68, p.147; Uniform Rule 42; California Evidence Code § 703; Kansas Code of Civil Procedure § 60-442; New Jersey Evidence Rule 42. *Cf.* 6 Wigmore § 1909, which advocates leaving the matter to the discretion of the judge, and statutes to that effect collected in Annot. 157 A.L.R. 311.

The rule provides an "automatic" objection. To require an actual objection would confront the opponent with a choice between not objecting, with the result of allowing the testimony, and objecting, with the probable result of excluding the testimony but at the price of continuing the trial before a judge likely to feel that his integrity had been attacked by the objector.

Rule 606.   Juror's Competency as a Witness

(a) At the Trial. A juror may not testify as a witness before the other jurors at the trial. If a juror is called to testify, the court must give a party an opportunity to object outside the jury's presence.

(b) During an Inquiry into the Validity of a Verdict or Indictment.

(1) *Prohibited Testimony or Other Evidence.* During an inquiry into the validity of a verdict or indictment, a juror may not testify about any statement made or incident that occurred during the jury's deliberations; the effect of anything on that juror's or another juror's vote; or any juror's mental processes concerning the verdict or indictment. The court may not receive a juror's affidavit or evidence of a juror's statement on these matters.

(2) *Exceptions.* A juror may testify about whether:

(A) extraneous prejudicial information was improperly brought to the jury's attention;

(B) an outside influence was improperly brought to bear on any juror; or

(C) a mistake was made in entering the verdict on the verdict form.

(Pub. L. 93-595, § 1, Jan. 2, 1975, 88 Stat. 1934; Pub. L. 94-149, § 1(10), Dec. 12, 1975, 89 Stat. 805; Mar. 2, 1987, eff. Oct. 1, 1987; Apr. 26, 2011, eff. Dec. 1, 2011.)

RESTYLED RULE 606—ADVISORY COMMITTEE'S NOTE

The language of Rule 606 has been amended as part of the restyling of the Evidence Rules to make them more easily understood and to make style and terminology consistent throughout the rules. These changes are intended to be stylistic only. There is no intent to change any result in any ruling on evidence admissibility.

ADVISORY COMMITTEE'S NOTE
56 F.R.D. 183, 265 (1973)

Subdivision (a). The considerations which bear upon the permissibility of testimony by a juror in the trial in which he is sitting as juror bear an obvious similarity to those evoked when the judge is called as a witness. *See* Advisory Committee's Note to Rule 605. The judge is not, however, in this instance so involved as to call for departure from usual principles requiring objection to be made; hence the only provision on objection is that opportunity be afforded for its making out of the presence of the jury. Compare Rules 605.

Subdivision (b). Whether testimony, affidavits, or statements of jurors should be received for the purpose of invalidating or supporting a verdict or indictment, and if so, under what circumstances, has given rise to substantial differences of opinion. The familiar rubric that a juror may not impeach his own verdict, dating from Lord Mansfield's time, is a gross oversimplification. The values sought to be promoted by excluding the evidence include freedom of deliberation, stability and finality of verdicts, and protection of jurors against annoyance and embarrassment. McDonald v. Pless, 238 U.S. 264, 35 S. Ct. 785, 59 L. Ed. 1300 (1915). On the other hand, simply putting verdicts beyond effective reach can only promote irregularity and injustice. The rule offers an accommodation between these competing considerations.

The mental operations and emotional reactions of jurors in arriving at a given result would, if allowed as a subject of inquiry, place every verdict at the mercy of jurors and invite tampering and harassment. *See* Grenz v. Werre, 129 N.W.2d 681 (N.D. 1964). The authorities are in virtually complete accord in excluding the evidence. Fryer, Note on Disqualification of Witnesses, Selected Writings on Evidence and Trial 345, 347 (Fryer ed. 1957); Maguire, Weinstein, et al., Cases on Evidence 887 (5th ed. 1965); 8 Wigmore § 2340 (McNaughton rev. 1961). As to matters other than mental operations and emotional reactions of jurors, substantial authority refuses to allow a juror to disclose irregularities which occur in the jury room, but allows his testimony as to irregularities occurring outside and allows outsiders to testify as to occurrences both inside and out. 8 Wigmore § 2354 (McNaughton rev. 1961). However, the door of the jury room is not necessarily a satisfactory dividing point, and the Supreme Court has refused to accept it for every situation. Mattox v. United States, 146 U.S. 140, 13 S. Ct. 50, 36 L. Ed. 917 (1892).

Under the federal decisions the central focus has been upon insulation of the manner in which the jury reached its verdict, and this protection extends to each of the components of deliberation, including arguments, statements, discussions, mental and emotional reactions, votes, and any other feature of the process. Thus testimony or affidavits of jurors have been held incompetent to show a compromise verdict, Hyde v. United States, 225 U.S. 347, 382 (1912); a quotient verdict, McDonald v. Pless, 238 U.S. 264 (1915); speculation as to insurance coverage, Holden v. Porter, 495 F.2d 878 (10th Cir. 1969), Farmers Coop. Elev. Ass'n v. Strand, 382 F.2d 224, 230 (8th Cir. 1967), *cert. denied*, 389 U.S. 1014; misinterpretations of instructions, Farmers Coop. Elev. Ass'n v. Strand, *supra;* mistake in returning verdict, United States v. Chereton, 309 F.2d 197 (6th Cir. 1962); interpretation of guilty plea by one defendant as implicating others, United States v. Crosby, 294 F.2d 928, 949 (2d Cir. 1961). The policy does not, however, foreclose testimony by jurors as to prejudicial extraneous information or influences injected into or brought to bear upon the deliberative process. Thus a juror is recognized as competent to testify to statements by the bailiff or the introduction of a prejudicial newspaper account into the jury room, Mattox v. United States, 146 U.S. 140 (1892). *See also* Parker v. Gladden, 385 U.S. 363 (1966).

This rule does not purport to specify the substantive grounds for setting aside verdicts for irregularity; it deals only with the competency of jurors to testify concerning those grounds. Allowing them to testify as to matters other than their own inner reactions involves no particular hazard to the values sought to be protected. The rule is based upon this conclusion. It makes no attempt to specify the substantive grounds for setting aside verdicts for irregularity.

See also Rule 6(e) of the Federal Rules of Criminal Procedure and 18 U.S.C. § 3500, governing the secrecy of grand jury proceedings. The present rule does not relate to secrecy and disclosure but to the competency of certain witnesses and evidence.

ADVISORY COMMITTEE'S NOTE — 1987 AMENDMENT

The amendments are technical. No substantive change is intended.

ADVISORY COMMITTEE'S NOTE — 2006 AMENDMENT

Rule 606(b) has been amended to provide that juror testimony may be used to prove that the verdict reported was the result of a mistake in entering the verdict on the verdict form. The amendment responds to a divergence between the text of the Rule and the case law that has established an exception for proof of clerical errors. *See, e.g.*, Plummer v. Springfield Term. Ry., 5 F.3d 1, 3 (1st Cir. 1993) ("A number of circuits hold, and we agree, that juror testimony regarding an alleged clerical error, such as announcing a verdict different than that agreed upon, does not challenge the validity of the verdict or the deliberation of mental processes, and therefore is not subject to Rule 606(b)."); Teevee Toons, Inc., v. MP3.Com, Inc., 148 F. Supp. 2d 276, 278 (S.D.N.Y. 2001) (noting that Rule 606(b) has been silent regarding inquiries designed to confirm the accuracy of a verdict).

In adopting the exception for proof of mistakes in entering the verdict on the verdict form, the amendment specifically rejects the broader exception, adopted by some courts, permitting the use of juror testimony to prove that the jurors were operating under a misunderstanding about the consequences of the result that they agreed upon. *See, e.g.*, Attridge v. Cencorp Div. of Dover Techs. Int'l, Inc., 836 F.2d 113, 116 (2d Cir. 1987); Eastridge Development Co., v. Halpert Associates, Inc., 853 F.2d 772 (10th Cir. 1988). The broader exception is rejected because an inquiry into whether the jury misunderstood or misapplied an instruction goes to the jurors' mental processes underlying the verdict, rather than the verdict's accuracy in capturing what the jurors had agreed upon. *See, e.g.*, Karl v. Burlington Northern R.R., 880 F.2d 68, 74 (8th Cir. 1989) (error to receive juror testimony on whether verdict was the result of jurors' misunderstanding of instructions: "The jurors did not state that the figure written by the foreman was different from that which they agreed upon, but indicated that the figure the foreman wrote down was intended to be a net figure, not a gross figure. Receiving such statements violates Rule 606(b) because the testimony relates to how the jury interpreted the court's instructions, and concerns the jurors' 'mental processes,' which is forbidden by the rule."); Robles v. Exxon Corp., 862 F.2d 1201, 1208 (5th Cir. 1989) ("the alleged error here goes to the substance of what the jury was asked to decide, necessarily implicating the jury's mental processes insofar as it questions the jury's understanding of the court's instructions and application of those instructions to the facts of the case"). Thus, the exception established by the amendment is limited to cases such as "where the jury foreperson wrote down, in response to an interrogatory, a number different from that agreed upon by the jury, or mistakenly stated that the defendant was 'guilty' when the jury had actually agreed that the defendant was not guilty." *Id.*

It should be noted that the possibility of errors in the verdict form will be reduced substantially by polling the jury. Rule 606(b) does not, of course, prevent this precaution. *See* 8 C. Wigmore, Evidence, § 2350 at 691 (McNaughten ed. 1961) (noting that the reasons for the rule barring juror testimony, "namely, the dangers of uncertainty and of tampering with the jurors to procure testimony, disappear in large part if such investigation as may be desired is made by the judge and takes place before the jurors' discharge and separation") (emphasis in original). Errors that come to light after polling the jury "may be corrected on the spot, or the jury may be sent out to continue deliberations, or, if necessary, a new trial may be ordered." C. Mueller & L. Kirkpatrick, Evidence Under the Rules at 671 (2d ed. 1999) (*citing* Sincox v. United States, 571 F.2d 876, 878-79 (5th Cir. 1978)).

Rule 607.   Who May Impeach a Witness

Any party, including the party that called the witness, may attack the witness's credibility.

(Pub. L. 93-595, § 1, Jan. 2, 1975, 88 Stat. 1934; Mar. 2, 1987, eff. Oct. 1, 1987; Apr. 26, 2011, eff. Dec. 1, 2011.)

RESTLYED RULE 607 — ADVISORY COMMITTEE'S NOTE

The language of Rule 607 has been amended as part of the restyling of the Evidence Rules to make them more easily understood and to make style and terminology consistent throughout the rules. These changes are intended to be stylistic only. There is no intent to change any result in any ruling on evidence admissibility.

ADVISORY COMMITTEE'S NOTE
56 F.R.D. 183, 266 (1973)

The traditional rule against impeaching one's own witness is abandoned as based on false premises. A party does not hold out his witnesses as worthy of belief, since he rarely has a free choice in selecting them. Denial of the right leaves the party at the mercy of the witness and the adversary. If the impeachment is by a prior statement, it is free from hearsay dangers and is excluded from the category of hearsay under Rule 801(d)(1). Ladd, Impeachment of One's Own Witness — New Developments 4 U. Chi. L. Rev. 69 (1936); McCormick § 38; 3 Wigmore § 896-918. The substantial inroads into the old rule made over the years by decisions, rules, and statutes are evidence of doubts as to its basic soundness and workability. Cases are collected in 3 Wigmore § 905. Revised Rule 32(a)(1) of the Federal Rules of Civil Procedure allows any party to impeach a witness by means of his deposition, and Rule 43(b) has allowed the calling and impeachment of an adverse party or person identified with him. Illustrative statutes allowing a party to impeach his own witness under varying circumstances are Ill. Rev. Stats. 1967, c. 110, § 60; Mass. Laws Annot. 1959, c. 233 § 23; 20 N.M. Stats. Annot. 1953, § 20-2-4; N.Y. CPLR § 4514 (McKinney 1963); 12 Vt. Stats. Annot. 1959, § 1641a, 1642. Complete judicial rejection of the old rule is found in United States v. Freeman, 302 F.2d 347 (2d Cir. 1962). The same result is reached in Uniform Rule 20; California Evidence Code § 785; Kansas Code of Civil Procedure § 60-420. *See also* New Jersey Evidence Rule 20.

ADVISORY COMMITTEE'S NOTE—1987 AMENDMENT

The amendment is technical. No substantive change is intended.

Rule 608.   A Witness's Character for Truthfulness or Untruthfulness

(a) Reputation or Opinion Evidence. A witness's credibility may be attacked or supported by testimony about the witness's reputation for having a character for truthfulness or untruthfulness, or by testimony in the form of an opinion about that character. But evidence of truthful character is admissible only after the witness's character for truthfulness has been attacked.

(b) Specific Instances of Conduct. Except for a criminal conviction under Rule 609, extrinsic evidence is not admissible to prove specific instances of a witness's conduct in order to attack or support the witness's character for truthfulness. But the court may, on cross-examination, allow them to be inquired into if they are probative of the character for truthfulness or untruthfulness of:

(1) the witness; or

(2) another witness whose character the witness being cross-examined has testified about.

By testifying on another matter, a witness does not waive any privilege against self-incrimination for testimony that relates only to the witness's character for truthfulness.

(Pub. L. 93-595, §1, Jan. 2, 1975, 88 Stat. 1935; Mar. 2, 1987, eff. Oct. 1, 1987; Apr. 25, 1988, eff. Nov. 1, 1988; Mar. 27, 2003, eff. Dec. 1, 2003; Apr. 26, 2011, eff. Dec. 1, 2011.)

RESTYLED RULE 608—ADVISORY COMMITTEE'S NOTE

The language of Rule 608 has been amended as part of the general restyling of the Evidence Rules to make them more easily understood and to make style and terminology consistent throughout the rules. These changes are intended to be stylistic only. There is no intent to change any result in any ruling on evidence admissibility.

The Committee is aware that the Rule's limitation of bad-act impeachment to "cross-examination" is trumped by Rule 607, which allows a party to impeach witnesses on direct examination. Courts have not relied on the term "on cross-examination" to limit impeachment that would otherwise be permissible under Rules 607 and 608. The Committee therefore concluded that no change to the language of the Rule was necessary in the context of a restyling project.

ADVISORY COMMITTEE'S NOTE
56 F.R.D. 183, 268 (1973)

Subdivision (a). In Rule 404(a) the general position is taken that character evidence is not admissible for the purpose of proving that the person acted in conformity therewith, subject, however, to several exceptions, one of which is character evidence of a witness as bearing upon his credibility. The present rule develops that exception.

In accordance with the bulk of judicial authority, the inquiry is strictly limited to character for veracity, rather than allowing evidence as to character generally. The result is to sharpen relevancy, to reduce surprise, waste of time, and confusion, and to make the lot of the witness somewhat less unattractive. McCormick § 44.

The use of opinion and reputation evidence as means of proving the character of witnesses is consistent with Rule 405(a). While the modern practice has purported to exclude opinion, witnesses who testify to reputation seem in fact often to be giving their opinions, disguised somewhat misleadingly as reputation. *See* McCormick § 44. And even under the modern practice, a common relaxation has allowed inquiry as to whether the witnesses would believe the principal witness under oath. United States v. Walker, 313 F.2d 236 (6th Cir. 1963), and cases cited therein; McCormick § 44, pp.94-95, n.3.

Character evidence in support of credibility is admissible under the rule only after the witness' character has first been attacked, as has been the case at common law. Maguire, Weinstein, et al., Cases on Evidence 295 (5th ed. 1965); McCormick § 49, p.105; 4 Wigmore § 1104. The enormous needless consumption of time which a contrary practice would entail justifies the limitation. Opinion or reputation that the witness is untruthful specifically qualifies as an attack under the rule, and evidence or misconduct, including conviction of crime, and of corruption also fall within this category. Evidence of bias or interest does not. McCormick § 49; 4 Wigmore § 1106, 1107. Whether evidence in the form of contradiction is an attack upon the character of the witness must depend upon the circumstances. McCormick § 49; *cf.* 4 Wigmore § 1108, 1109. As to the use of specific instances on direct by an opinion witness, *see* the Advisory Committee's Note to Rule 405, *supra*.

Subdivision (b). In conformity with Rule 405, which forecloses use of evidence of specific incidents as proof in chief of character unless character is an issue in the case, the present rule generally bars evidence of specific instances of conduct of a witness for the purpose of attacking or supporting his credibility. There are, however, two exceptions: (1) specific instances are provable when they have been the subject of criminal conviction, and (2) specific instances may be inquired into on cross-examination of the principal witness or of a witness giving an opinion of his character for truthfulness.

(1) Conviction of crime as a technique of impeachment is treated in detail in Rule 609, and here is merely recognized as an exception to the general rule excluding evidence of specific incidents for impeachment purposes.

(2) Particular instances of conduct, though not the subject of criminal conviction, may be inquired into on cross-examination of the principal witness himself or of a witness who testifies concerning his character for truthfulness. Effective cross-examination demands that some allowance be made for going into matters of this kind, but the possibilities of abuse are substantial. Consequently safeguards are erected in the form of specific requirements that the instances inquired into be probative of truthfulness or its opposite and not remote in time. Also, the overriding protection of Rule 403 requires that probative value not be outweighed by danger of unfair prejudice, confusion of issues, or misleading the jury, and that of Rule 611 bars harassment and undue embarrassment.

The final sentence constitutes a rejection of the doctrine of such cases as People v. Sorge, 301 N.Y. 198, 93 N.E.2d 637 (1950), that any past criminal act relevant to credibility may be inquired into on cross-examination, in apparent disregard of the privilege against self-incrimination. While it is clear that an ordinary witness cannot make a partial disclosure of incriminating matter and then invoke the privilege on cross-examination, no tenable contention can be made that merely by testifying he waives his right to foreclose inquiry on cross-examination into criminal activities for the purpose of attacking his credibility. So to hold would reduce the privilege to a nullity. While it is true that an accused, unlike an ordinary witness, has an option whether to testify, if the option can be exercised only at the price of opening up inquiry as to any and all criminal acts committed during his lifetime, the right to testify could scarcely be said to possess much vitality. In Griffin v. California, 380 U.S. 609, 85 S. Ct. 1229, 14 L. Ed. 2d 106 (1965), the Court held that allowing comment on the election of an accused not to testify exacted a constitutionally impermissible price, and so here. While no specific provision in terms confers constitutional status on the right of an accused to take the stand in his own defense, the existence of the right is so completely recognized that a denial of it or substantial infringement upon it would surely be of due process dimensions. *See* Ferguson v. Georgia, 365 U.S. 570, 81 S. Ct. 756, 5 L. Ed. 2d 783 (1961); McCormick § 131; 8 Wigmore § 2276 (McNaughton rev. 1961). In any event, wholly aside from constitutional considerations, the provision represents a sound policy.

ADVISORY COMMITTEE'S NOTE — 1987 AMENDMENT

The amendments are technical. No substantive change is intended.

ADVISORY COMMITTEE'S NOTE — 1988 AMENDMENT

The amendment is technical. No substantive change is intended.

ADVISORY COMMITTEE'S NOTE — 2003 AMENDMENT

The Rule has been amended to clarify that the absolute prohibition on extrinsic evidence applies only when the sole reason for proffering that evidence is to attack or support the witness' character for truthfulness. *See* United States v. Abel, 469 U.S. 45 (1984); United States v. Fusco, 748 F.2d 996 (5th Cir. 1984) (Rule 608(b) limits the use of evidence "designed to show that the witness has done things, unrelated to the suit being tried, that make him more or less believable per se"); Ohio R. Evid. 608(b). On occasion the Rule's use of the overbroad term "credibility" has been read "to bar extrinsic evidence for bias, competency and contradiction impeachment since they too deal with credibility." American Bar Association Section of Litigation, Emerging Problems Under the Federal Rules of Evidence at 161 (3d ed. 1998). The amendment conforms the language of the Rule to its original intent, which was to impose an absolute bar on extrinsic evidence only if the sole purpose for offering the evidence was to prove the witness' character for veracity. *See* Advisory Committee Note to Rule 608(b) (stating that the Rule is "[i]n conformity with Rule 405, which forecloses use of evidence of specific incidents as proof in chief of character unless character is in issue in the case . . .").

By limiting the application of the Rule to proof of a witness' character for truthfulness, the amendment leaves the admissibility of extrinsic evidence offered for other grounds of impeachment (such as contradiction, prior inconsistent statement, bias and mental capacity) to Rules 402 and 403. *See, e.g.,* United States v. Winchenbach, 197 F.3d 548 (1st Cir. 1999) (admissibility of a prior inconsistent statement offered for impeachment is governed by Rules 402 and 403, not Rule 608(b)); United States v. Tarantino, 846 F.2d 1384 (D.C. Cir. 1988) (admissibility of extrinsic evidence offered to contradict a witness is governed by Rules 402 and 403); United States v. Lindemann, 85 F.3d 1232 (7th Cir. 1996) (admissibility of extrinsic evidence of bias is governed by Rules 402 and 403).

It should be noted that the extrinsic evidence prohibition of Rule 608(b) bars any reference to the consequences that a witness might have suffered as a result of an alleged bad act. For example, Rule 608(b) prohibits counsel from mentioning that a witness was suspended or disciplined for the conduct that is the subject of impeachment, when that conduct is offered only to prove the character of the witness. *See* United States v. Davis,

183 F.3d 231, 257 n.12 (3d Cir. 1999) (emphasizing that in attacking the defendant's character for truthfulness "the government cannot make reference to Davis's forty-four day suspension or that Internal Affairs found that he lied about" an incident because "[s]uch evidence would not only be hearsay to the extent it contains assertion of fact, it would be inadmissible extrinsic evidence under Rule 608(b)"). *See also* Stephen A. Saltzburg, Impeaching the Witness: Prior Bad Acts and Extrinsic Evidence, 7 Crim. Just. 28, 31 (Winter 1993) ("counsel should not be permitted to circumvent the no-extrinsic-evidence provision by tucking a third person's opinion about prior acts into a question asked of the witness who has denied the act").

For purposes of consistency the term "credibility" has been replaced by the term "character for truthfulness" in the last sentence of subdivision (b). The term "credibility" is also used in subdivision (a). But the Committee found it unnecessary to substitute "character for truthfulness" for "credibility" in Rule 608(a), because subdivision (a)(1) already serves to limit impeachment to proof of such character.

Rules 609(a) and 610 also use the term "credibility" when the intent of those Rules is to regulate impeachment of a witness' character for truthfulness. No inference should be derived from the fact that the Committee proposed an amendment to Rule 608(b) but not to Rules 609 and 610.

Rule 609.   Impeachment by Evidence of a Criminal Conviction

(a) In General. The following rules apply to attacking a witness's character for truthfulness by evidence of a criminal conviction:

(1) for a crime that, in the convicting jurisdiction, was punishable by death or by imprisonment for more than one year, the evidence:

(A) must be admitted, subject to Rule 403, in a civil case or in a criminal case in which the witness is not a defendant; and

(B) must be admitted in a criminal case in which the witness is a defendant, if the probative value of the evidence outweighs its prejudicial effect to that defendant; and

(2) for any crime regardless of the punishment, the evidence must be admitted if the court can readily determine that establishing the elements of the crime required proving — or the witness's admitting — a dishonest act or false statement.

(b) Limit on Using the Evidence After 10 Years. This subdivision (b) applies if more than 10 years have passed since the witness's conviction or release from confinement for it, whichever is later. Evidence of the conviction is admissible only if:

(1) its probative value, supported by specific facts and circumstances, substantially outweighs its prejudicial effect; and

(2) the proponent gives an adverse party reasonable written notice of the intent to use it so that the party has a fair opportunity to contest its use.

(c) Effect of a Pardon, Annulment, or Certificate of Rehabilitation. Evidence of a conviction is not admissible if:

(1) the conviction has been the subject of a pardon, annulment, certificate of rehabilitation, or other equivalent procedure based on a finding that the person has been rehabilitated, and the person has not been convicted of a later crime punishable by death or by imprisonment for more than one year; or

(continued)

(2) the conviction has been the subject of a pardon, annulment, or other equivalent procedure based on a finding of innocence.

(d) Juvenile Adjudications. Evidence of a juvenile adjudication is admissible under this rule only if:

(1) it is offered in a criminal case;

(2) the adjudication was of a witness other than the defendant;

(3) an adult's conviction for that offense would be admissible to attack the adult's credibility; and

(4) admitting the evidence is necessary to fairly determine guilt or innocence.

(e) Pendency of an Appeal. A conviction that satisfies this rule is admissible even if an appeal is pending. Evidence of the pendency is also admissible.

(Pub. L. 93-595, § 1, Jan. 2, 1975, 88 Stat. 1935; Mar. 2, 1987, eff. Oct. 1, 1987; Jan. 26, 1990, eff. Dec. 1, 1990; Apr. 26, 2011, eff. Dec. 1, 2011.)

RESTYLED RULE 609 — ADVISORY COMMITTEE'S NOTE

The language of Rule 609 has been amended as part of the restyling of the Evidence Rules to make them more easily understood and to make style and terminology consistent throughout the rules. These changes are intended to be stylistic only. There is no intent to change any result in any ruling on evidence admissibility.

ADVISORY COMMITTEE'S NOTE
56 F.R.D. 183, 270 (1973)

As a means of impeachment, evidence of conviction of crime is significant only because it stands as proof of the commission of the underlying criminal act. There is little dissent from the general proposition that at least some crimes are relevant to credibility but much disagreement among the cases and commentators about which crimes are usable for this purpose. *See* McCormick § 43; 2 Wright, Federal Practice and Procedure; Criminal § 416 (1969). The weight of traditional authority has been to allow use of felonies generally, without regard to the nature of the particular offense, and of *crimen falsi* without regard to the grade of the offense. This is the view accepted by Congress in the 1970 amendment of § 14-305 of the District of Columbia Code, P.L. 91-358, 84 Stat. 473. Uniform Rule 21 and Model Code Rule 106 permit only crimes involving "dishonesty or false statement." Others have thought that the trial judge should have discretion to exclude convictions if the probative value of the evidence of the crime is substantially outweighed by the danger of unfair prejudice. Luck v. United States, 121 U.S. App. D.C. 151, 348 F.2d 763 (1965); McGowan, Impeachment of Criminal Defendants by Prior Convictions, 1970 Law & Soc. Order 1. Whatever may be the merits of those views, this rule is drafted to accord with the Congressional policy manifested in the 1970 legislation.

The proposed rule incorporates certain basic safeguards, in terms applicable to all witnesses but of particular significance to an accused who elects to testify. These protections include the imposition of definite time limitations, giving effect to demonstrated rehabilitation, and generally excluding juvenile adjudications.

Subdivision (a). For purposes of impeachment, crimes are divided into two categories by the rule: (1) those of what is generally regarded as felony grade, without particular regard to the nature of the offense, and (2) those involving dishonesty or false statement, without regard to the grade of the offense. Provable convictions are not limited to violations of federal law. By reason of our constitutional structure, the federal catalog of crimes is far from being a complete one, and resort must be had to the laws of the states for the specification of many crimes. For example, simple theft as compared with theft from interstate commerce. Other instances of borrowing are the Assimilative Crimes Act, making the state law of crimes applicable to the special territorial and maritime jurisdiction of the United States, 18 U.S.C. § 13, and the provision of the Judicial Code disqualifying persons as jurors on the grounds of state as well as federal convictions, 28 U.S.C. § 1865. For evaluation of the crime in terms of seriousness, reference is made to the congressional measurement of felony (subject to imprisonment in excess of one year) rather than adopting state definitions which vary considerably. *See* 28 U.S.C. § 1865, *supra*, disqualifying jurors for conviction in state or federal court of crime punishable by imprisonment for more than one year.

Subdivision (b). Few statutes recognize a time limit on impeachment by evidence of conviction. However, practical considerations of fairness and relevancy demand that some boundary be recognized. *See* Ladd, Credibility Tests — Current Trends, 89 U. Pa. L. Rev. 166, 176-177 (1940). This portion of the rule is derived from the proposal advanced in Recommendation Proposing in Evidence Code, § 788(5), p.142, Cal. Law Rev. Comm'n (1965), though not adopted. *See* California Evidence Code § 788.

Subdivision (c). A pardon or its equivalent granted solely for the purpose of restoring civil rights lost by virtue of a conviction has no relevance to an inquiry into character. If, however, the pardon or other proceeding is hinged upon a showing of rehabilitation the situation is otherwise. The result under the rule is to render the conviction inadmissible. The alternative of allowing in evidence both the conviction and the rehabilitation has not been adopted for reasons of policy, economy of time, and difficulties of evaluation.

A similar provision is contained in California Evidence Code § 788. *Cf.* A.L.I. Model Penal Code, Proposed Official Draft § 306.6(3)(e) (1962), and discussion in A.L.I. Proceedings 310 (1961).

Pardons based on innocence have the effect, of course, of nullifying the conviction *ab initio*.

Subdivision (d). The prevailing view has been that a juvenile adjudication is not usable for impeachment. Thomas v. United States, 74 App. D.C. 167, 121 F.2d 905 (1941); Cotton v. United States, 355 F.2d 480 (10th Cir. 1966). This conclusion was based upon a variety of circumstances. By virtue of its informality, frequently diminished quantum of required proof, and other departures from accepted standards for criminal trials under the theory of *parens patriae*, the juvenile adjudication was considered to lack the precision and general probative value of the criminal conviction. While In re Gault, 387 U.S. 1, 87 S. Ct. 1428, 18 L. Ed. 2d 527 (1967), no doubt eliminates these characteristics insofar as objectionable, other obstacles remain. Practical problems of administration are raised by the common provisions in juvenile legislation that records be kept confidential and that they be destroyed after a short time. While *Gault* was skeptical as to the realities of confidentiality of juvenile records, it also saw no constitutional obstacles to improvement. 387 U.S. at 25, 87 S. Ct. 1428. *See also* Note, Rights and Rehabilitation in the Juvenile Courts, 67 Colum. L. Rev. 281, 289 (1967). In addition, policy considerations much akin to those which dictate exclusion of adult convictions after rehabilitation has been established strongly suggest a rule of excluding juvenile adjudications. Admittedly, however, the rehabilitative process may in a given case be a demonstrated failure, or the strategic importance of a given witness may be so great as to require the overriding of general policy in the interests of particular justice. *See* Giles v. Maryland, 386 U.S. 66, 87 S. Ct. 793, 17 L. Ed. 2d 737 (1967). Wigmore was outspoken in his condemnation of the disallowance of juvenile adjudications to impeach, especially when the witness is the complainant in a case of molesting a minor. 1 Wigmore § 196; 3 *Id.* § 924a, 980.

The rule recognizes discretion in the judge to effect an accommodation among these various factors by departing from the general principle of exclusion. In deference to the general pattern and policy of juvenile statutes, however, no discretion is accorded when the witness is the accused in a criminal case.

Subdivision (e). The presumption of correctness which ought to attend judicial proceedings supports the position that pendency of an appeal does not preclude use of a conviction for impeachment. United States v. Empire Packing Co., 174 F.2d 16 (7th Cir. 1949), *cert. denied*, 337 U.S. 959, 69 S. Ct. 1534, 93 L. Ed. 1758; Bloch v. United States, 226 F.2d 185 (9th Cir. 1955), *cert. denied*, 350 U.S. 948, 76 S. Ct. 323, 100 L. Ed. 826 and 353 U.S. 959, 77 S. Ct. 868, 1 L. Ed. 2d 910; and *see* Newman v. United States, 331 F.2d 968 (8th Cir. 1964), *contra*, Campbell v. United States, 85 U.S. App. D.C. 133, 176 F.2d 45 (1949). The pendency of an appeal is, however, a qualifying circumstance properly considerable.

ADVISORY COMMITTEE'S NOTE — 1987 AMENDMENT

The amendments are technical. No substantive change is intended.

ADVISORY COMMITTEE'S NOTE — 1990 AMENDMENT

The amendment to Rule 609(a) makes two changes in the rule. The first change removes from the rule the limitation that the conviction may only be elicited during cross-examination, a limitation that virtually every circuit has found to be inapplicable. It is common for witnesses to reveal on direct examination their convictions to "remove the sting" of the impeachment. *See, e.g.,* United States v. Bad Cob, 560 F.2d 877 (8th Cir. 1977). The amendment does not contemplate that a court will necessarily permit proof of prior convictions through testimony, which might be time-consuming and more prejudicial than proof through a written record. Rules 403 and 611(a) provide sufficient authority for the court to protect against unfair or disruptive methods of proof.

The second change effected by the amendment resolves an ambiguity as to the relationship of Rules 609 and 403 with respect to impeachment of witnesses other than the criminal defendant. *See* Green v. Bock Laundry Machine Co., 109 S. Ct. 1981, 490 U.S. 504 (1989). The amendment does not disturb the special balancing test for the criminal defendant who chooses to testify. Thus, the rule recognizes that, in virtually every case in which prior convictions are used to impeach the testifying defendant, the defendant faces a unique risk of prejudice — i.e., the danger that convictions that would be excluded under Fed. R. Evid. 404 will be misused by a jury as propensity evidence despite their introduction solely for impeachment purposes. Although the rule does not forbid all use of convictions to impeach a defendant, it requires that the government show that the probative value of convictions as impeachment evidence outweighs their prejudicial effect.

Prior to the amendment, the rule appeared to give the defendant the benefit of the special balancing test when defense witnesses other than the defendant were called to testify. In practice, however, the concern about unfairness to the defendant is most acute when the defendant's own convictions are offered as evidence. Almost all of the decided cases concern this type of impeachment, and the amendment does not deprive the defendant of any meaningful protection, since Rule 403 now clearly protects against unfair impeachment of any defense witness other than the defendant. There are cases in which a defendant might be prejudiced when a defense witness is impeached. Such cases may arise, for example, when the witness bears a special relationship to the defendant such that the defendant is likely to suffer some spill-over effect from impeachment of the witness.

The amendment also protects other litigants from unfair impeachment of their witnesses. The danger of prejudice from the use of prior convictions is not confined to criminal defendants. Although the danger that prior convictions will be misused as character evidence is particularly acute when the defendant is impeached, the danger exists in other situations as well. The amendment reflects the view that it is desirable to protect all litigants from the unfair use of prior convictions, and that the ordinary balancing test of Rule 403, which provides that evidence shall not be excluded unless its prejudicial effect substantially outweighs its probative value, is appropriate for assessing the admissibility of prior convictions for impeachment of any witness other than a criminal defendant.

The amendment reflects a judgment that decisions interpreting Rule 609(a) as requiring a trial court to admit convictions in civil cases that have little, if anything, to do with credibility reach undesirable results. *See, e.g.*, Diggs v. Lyons, 741 F.2d 577 (3d Cir. 1984), *cert. denied*, 105 S. Ct. 2157 (1985). The amendment provides the same protection against unfair prejudice arising from prior convictions used for impeachment purposes as the rules provide for other evidence. The amendment finds support in decided cases. *See, e.g.*, Petty v. Ideco, 761 F.2d 1146 (5th Cir. 1985); Czaka v. Hickman, 703 F.2d 317 (8th Cir. 1983).

Fewer decided cases address the question whether Rule 609(a) provides any protection against unduly prejudicial prior convictions used to impeach government witnesses. Some courts have read Rule 609(a) as giving the government no protection for its witnesses. *See, e.g.*, United States v. Thorne, 547 F.2d 56 (8th Cir. 1976); United States v. Nevitt, 563 F.2d 406 (9th Cir. 1977), *cert. denied*, 444 U.S. 847 (1979). This approach also is rejected by the amendment. There are cases in which impeachment of government witnesses with prior convictions that have little, if anything, to do with credibility may result in unfair prejudice to the government's interest in a fair trial and unnecessary embarrassment to a witness. Fed. R. Evid. 412 already recognizes this and excluded certain evidence of past sexual behavior in the context of prosecutions for sexual assaults.

The amendment applies the general balancing test of Rule 403 to protect all litigants against unfair impeachment of witnesses. The balancing test protects civil litigants, the government in criminal cases, and the defendant in a criminal case who calls other witnesses. The amendment addresses prior convictions offered under Rule 609, not for other purposes, and does not run afoul, therefore, of Davis v. Alaska, 415 U.S. 308 (1974). *Davis* involved the use of a prior juvenile adjudication not to prove a past law violation, but to prove bias. The defendant in a criminal case has the right to demonstrate the bias of a witness and to be assured a fair trial, but not to unduly prejudice a trier of fact. *See generally* Rule 412. In any case in which the trial court believes that confrontation rights require admission of impeachment evidence, obviously the Constitution would take precedence over the rule.

The probability that prior convictions of an ordinary government witness will be unduly prejudicial is low in most criminal cases. Since the behavior of the witness is not the issue in dispute in most cases, there is little chance that the trier of fact will misuse the convictions offered as impeachment evidence as propensity evidence. Thus, trial courts will be skeptical when the government objects to impeachment of its witnesses with prior convictions. Only when the government is able to point to a real danger of prejudice that is sufficient to outweigh substantially the probative value of the conviction for impeachment purposes will the conviction be excluded.

The amendment continues to divide subdivision (a) into subsections (1) and (2) thus facilitating retrieval under current computerized research programs which distinguish the two provisions. The Committee recommended no substantive change in subdivision (a)(2), even though some cases raise a concern about the proper interpretation of the words "dishonesty or false statement." These words were used but not explained in the original Advisory Committee Note accompanying Rule 609. Congress extensively debated the rule, and the Report of the House and Senate Conference Committee states that "[b]y the phrase 'dishonesty and false statement,' the Conference means crimes such as perjury, subornation of perjury, false statement, criminal fraud, embezzlement, or false pretense, or any other offense in the nature of *crimen falsi*, commission of which involves some element of deceit, untruthfulness, or falsification bearing on the accused's propensity to testify truthfully." The Advisory Committee concluded that the Conference Report provides sufficient guidance to trial courts and that no amendment is necessary, notwithstanding some decisions that take an unduly broad view of "dishonesty," admitting convictions such as for bank robbery or bank larceny. Subsection (a)(2) continues to apply to any witness, including a criminal defendant.

Finally, the Committee determined that it was unnecessary to add to the rule language stating that, when a prior conviction is offered under Rule 609, the trial court is to consider the probative value of the prior conviction *for impeachment*, not for other purposes. The Committee concluded that the title of the rule, its first sentence, and its placement among the impeachment rules clearly establish that evidence offered under Rule 609 is offered only for purposes of impeachment.

ADVISORY COMMITTEE'S NOTE — 2006 AMENDMENT

The amendment provides that Rule 609(a)(2) mandates the admission of evidence of a conviction only when the conviction required the proof of (or in the case of a guilty plea, the admission of) an act of dishonesty or false statement. Evidence of all other convictions is inadmissible under this subsection, irrespective of whether the witness exhibited dishonesty or made a false statement in the process of the commission of the crime of conviction. Thus, evidence that a witness was convicted for a crime of violence, such as murder, is not admissible under Rule 609(a)(2), even if the witness acted deceitfully in the course of committing the crime.

The amendment is meant to give effect to the legislative intent to limit the convictions that are to be automatically admitted under subdivision (a)(2). The Conference Committee provided that by "dishonesty and false statement" it meant "crimes such as perjury, subornation of perjury, false statement, criminal fraud, embezzlement, or false pretense, or any other offense in the nature of *crimen falsi*, the commission of which involves some element of deceit, untruthfulness, or falsification bearing on the [witness's] propensity to testify truthfully." Historically, offenses classified as *crimina falsi* have included only those crimes in which the ultimate criminal act was itself an act of deceit. *See* Green, Deceit and the Classification of Crimes: Federal Rule of Evidence 609(a)(2) and the Origins of *Crimen Falsi*, 90 J. Crim. L. & Criminology 1087 (2000).

Evidence of crimes in the nature of *crimina falsi* must be admitted under Rule 609(a)(2), regardless of how such crimes are specifically charged. For example, evidence that a witness was convicted of making a false claim to a federal agent is admissible under this subdivision regardless of whether the crime was charged under a section that expressly references deceit (e.g., 18 U.S.C. § 1001, Material Misrepresentation to the Federal Government) or a section that does not (e.g., 18 U.S.C. § 1503, Obstruction of Justice).

The amendment requires that the proponent have ready proof that the conviction required the fact-finder to find, or the defendant to admit, an act of dishonesty or false statement. Ordinarily, the statutory elements of the crime will indicate whether it is one of dishonesty or false statement. Where the deceitful nature of the crime is not apparent from the statute and the face of the judgment — as, for example, where the conviction simply records a finding of guilt for a statutory offense that does not reference deceit expressly — a proponent may offer information such as an indictment, a statement of admitted facts, or jury instructions to show that the fact-finder had to find, or the defendant had to admit, an act of dishonesty or false statement in order for the witness to have been convicted. *Cf.* Taylor v. United States, 495 U.S. 575, 602 (1990) (providing that a trial court may look to a charging instrument or jury instructions to ascertain the nature of a prior offense where the statute is insufficiently clear on its face); Shepard v. United States, 125 S.Ct. 1254 (2005) (the inquiry to determine whether a guilty plea to a crime defined by a nongeneric statute necessarily admitted elements of the generic offense was limited to the charging document's terms, the terms of a plea agreement or transcript of colloquy between judge and defendant in which the factual basis for the plea was confirmed by the defendant, or a comparable judicial record). But the amendment does not contemplate a "mini-trial" in which the court plumbs the record of the previous proceeding to determine whether the crime was in the nature of *crimen falsi.*

The amendment also substitutes the term "character for truthfulness" for the term "credibility" in the first sentence of the Rule. The limitations of Rule 609 are not applicable if a conviction is admitted for a purpose other than to prove the witness's character for untruthfulness. *See, e.g.,* United States v. Lopez, 979 F.2d 1024 (5th Cir. 1992) (Rule 609 was not applicable where the conviction was offered for purposes of contradiction). The use of the term "credibility" in subdivision (d) is retained, however, as that subdivision is intended to govern the use of a juvenile adjudication for any type of impeachment.

Rule 610. Religious Beliefs or Opinions

Evidence of a witness's religious beliefs or opinions is not admissible to attack or support the witness's credibility.

(Pub. L. 93-595, § 1, Jan. 2, 1975, 88 Stat. 1936; Mar. 2, 1987, eff. Oct. 1, 1987; Apr. 26, 2011, eff. Dec. 1, 2011.)

RESTYLED RULE 610 — ADVISORY COMMITTEE'S NOTE

The language of Rule 610 has been amended as part of the restyling of the Evidence Rules to make them more easily understood and to make style and terminology consistent throughout the rules. These changes are intended to be stylistic only. There is no intent to change any result in any ruling on evidence admissibility.

ADVISORY COMMITTEE'S NOTE
56 F.R.D. 183, 272 (1973)

While the rule forecloses inquiry into the religious beliefs or opinions of a witness for the purpose of showing that his character for truthfulness is affected by their nature, an inquiry for the purpose of showing interest or bias because of them is not within the prohibition. Thus disclosure of affiliation with a church which is a party to the litigation would be allowable under the rule. *Cf.* Tucker v. Reil, 51 Ariz. 357, 77 P.2d 203 (1938). To the same effect, though less specifically worded, is California Evidence Code § 789. *See* 3 Wigmore § 936.

ADVISORY COMMITTEE'S NOTE—1987 AMENDMENT

The amendment is technical. No substantive change is intended.

Rule 611.   Mode and Order of Examining Witnesses and Presenting Evidence

(a) **Control by the Court; Purposes.** The court should exercise reasonable control over the mode and order of examining witnesses and presenting evidence so as to:

(1) make those procedures effective for determining the truth;

(2) avoid wasting time; and

(3) protect witnesses from harassment or undue embarrassment.

(b) **Scope of Cross-Examination.** Cross-examination should not go beyond the subject matter of the direct examination and matters affecting the witness's credibility. The court may allow inquiry into additional matters as if on direct examination.

(c) **Leading Questions.** Leading questions should not be used on direct examination except as necessary to develop the witness's testimony. Ordinarily, the court should allow leading questions:

(1) on cross-examination; and

(2) when a party calls a hostile witness, an adverse party, or a witness identified with an adverse party.

(Pub. L. 93-595, §1, Jan. 2, 1975, 88 Stat. 1936; Mar. 2, 1987, eff. Oct. 1, 1987; Apr. 26, 2011, eff. Dec. 1, 2011.)

RESTLYED RULE 611—ADVISORY COMMITTEE'S NOTE

The language of Rule 611 has been amended as part of the restyling of the Evidence Rules to make them more easily understood and to make style and terminology consistent throughout the rules. These changes are intended to be stylistic only. There is no intent to change any result in any ruling on evidence admissibility.

ADVISORY COMMITTEE'S NOTE
56 F.R.D. 183, 273 (1973)

Subdivision (a). Spelling out detailed rules to govern the mode and order of interrogating witnesses presenting evidence is neither desirable nor feasible. The ultimate responsibility for the effective working of the adversary system rests with the judge. The rule sets forth the objectives which he should seek to attain.

Item (1) restates in broad terms the power and obligation of the judge as developed under common law principles. It covers such concerns as whether testimony shall be in the form of a free narrative or responses to specific questions, McCormick §5, the order of calling witnesses and presenting evidence, 6 Wigmore §1867, the use of demonstrative evidence, McCormick §179, and the many other questions arising during the course of a trial which can be solved only by the judge's common sense and fairness in view of the particular circumstances.

Item (2) is addressed to avoidance of needless consumption of time, a matter of daily concern in the disposition of cases. A companion piece is found in the discretion vested in the judge to exclude evidence as a waste of time in Rule 403(b).

Item (3) calls for a judgement under the particular circumstances whether interrogation tactics entail harassment or undue embarrassment. Pertinent circumstances include the importance of the testimony, the nature of the inquiry, its relevance to credibility, waste of time, and confusion. McCormick § 42. In Alford v. United States, 282 U.S. 687, 694, 51 S. Ct. 218, 75 L. Ed. 624 (1931), the Court pointed out that, while the trial judge should protect the witness from questions which "go beyond the bounds of proper cross-examination merely to harass, annoy or humiliate," this protection by no means forecloses efforts to discredit the witness. Reference to the transcript of the prosecutor's cross-examination in Berger v. United States, 295 U.S. 78, 55 S. Ct. 629, 79 L. Ed. 1314 (1935), serves to lay at rest any doubts as to the need for judicial control in this area.

The inquiry into specific instances of conduct of a witness allowed under Rule 608(b) is, of course, subject to this rule.

Subdivision (b). The tradition in the federal courts and in numerous state courts has been to limit the scope of cross-examination to matters testified to on direct, plus matters bearing upon the credibility of the witness. Various reasons have been advanced to justify the rule of limited cross-examination. (1) A party vouches for his own witness but only to the extent of matters elicited on direct. Resurrection Gold Mining Co. v. Fortune Gold Mining Co., 129 F. 668, 675 (8th Cir. 1904), *quoted in* Maguire, Weinstein, et al., Cases on Evidence 277, n.38 (5th ed. 1965). But the concept of vouching is discredited, and Rule 607 rejects it. (2) A party cannot ask his own witness leading questions. This is a problem properly solved in terms of what is necessary for a proper development of the testimony rather than by a mechanistic formula similar to the vouching concept. *See* discussion under subdivision (c). (3) A practice of limited cross-examination promotes orderly presentation of the case. Finch v. Weiner, 109 Conn. 616, 145 A. 31 (1929). While this latter reason has merit, the matter is essentially one of the order of presentation and not one in which involvement at the appellate level is likely to prove fruitful. *See, for example,* Moyer v. Aetna Life Ins. Co., 126 F.2d 141 (3d Cir. 1942); Butler v. New York Central R. Co., 253 F.2d 281 (7th Cir. 1958); United States v. Johnson, 285 F.2d 35 (9th Cir. 1960); Union Automobile Indemnity Ass'n v. Capitol Indemnity Ins. Co., 310 F.2d 318 (7th Cir. 1962). In evaluating these considerations, McCormick says:

The foregoing considerations favoring the wide-open or restrictive rules may well be thought to be fairly evenly balanced. There is another factor, however, which seems to swing the balance overwhelmingly in favor of the wide-open rule. This is the consideration of economy of time and energy. Obviously, the wide-open rule presents little or no opportunity for dispute in its application. The restrictive practice in all its forms, on the other hand, is productive in many court rooms, of continual bickering over the choice of the numerous variations of the "scope of the direct" criterion, and of their application to particular cross-questions. These controversies are often reventilated on appeal, and reversals for error in their determination are frequent. Observance of these vague and ambiguous restrictions is a matter of constant and hampering concern to the cross-examiner. If these efforts, delays and misprisions were the necessary incidents to the guarding of substantive rights or the fundamentals of fair trial, they might be worth the cost. As the price of the choice of an obviously debatable regulation of the order of evidence, the sacrifice seems misguided. The American Bar Association's Committee for the Improvement of the Law of Evidence for the year 1937-38 said this:

> The rule limiting cross-examination to the precise subject of the direct examination is probably the most frequent rule (except the Opinion rule) leading in the trial practice today to refined and technical quibbles which obstruct the progress of the trial, confuse the jury, and give rise to appeal on technical grounds only. Some of the instances in which Supreme Courts have ordered new trials for the mere transgression of this rule about the order of evidence have been astounding.
>
> We recommend that the rule allowing questions upon any part of the issue known to the witness . . . be adopted. . . . McCormick, § 27, p.51. *See also* 5 Moore's Federal Practice § 43.10 (2d ed. 1964).

The provision of the second sentence, that the judge may in the interests of justice limit inquiry into new matters on cross-examination, is designed for those situations in which the result otherwise would be confusion, complication, or protraction of the case, not as a matter of rule but as demonstrable in the actual development of the particular case.

The rule does not purport to determine the extent to which an accused who elects to testify thereby waives his privilege against self-incrimination. The question is a constitutional one, rather than a mere matter of administering the trial. Under Simmons v. United States, 390 U.S. 377, 88 S. Ct. 967, 19 L. Ed. 2d 1247 (1968), no general waiver occurs when the accused testifies on such preliminary matters as the validity of a search and seizure or the admissibility of a confession. Rule 104(d), *supra.* When he testifies on the merits, however, can he foreclose inquiry into an aspect or element of the crime by avoiding it on direct? The affirmative answer given in Tucker v. United States, 5 F.2d 818 (8th Cir. 1925), is inconsistent with the description of the waiver as extending to "all other relevant facts" in Johnson v. United States, 318 U.S. 189, 195, 63 S. Ct. 549, 87 L. Ed. 704 (1943). *See also* Brown v. United States, 356 U.S. 148, 78 S. Ct. 622, 2 L. Ed. 2d 589 (1958). The situation of an accused who desires to testify on some but not all counts of a multiple-count indictment is one to be approached, in the first instance at least, as a problem of severance under Rule 14 of the Federal Rules of Criminal Procedure. Cross v. United States, 118 U.S. App. D.C. 324, 335 F.2d 987 (1964). *Cf.* United States v. Baker, 262 F. Supp. 657, 686 (D.D.C. 1966). In all events, the extent of the waiver of the privilege against self-incrimination ought not to be determined as a by-product of a rule on scope of cross-examination.

Subdivision (c). The rule continues the traditional view that the suggestive powers of the leading question are as a general proposition undesirable. Within this tradition, however, numerous exceptions have achieved recognition: The witness who is hostile, unwilling, or biased; the child witness or the adult with communication problems; the witness whose recollection is exhausted; and undisputed preliminary matters. 3 Wigmore §§ 774-778. An almost total unwillingness to reverse for infractions has been manifested by appellate courts. *See* cases cited in 3 Wigmore § 770. The matter clearly falls within the area of control by the judge over the mode and order of interrogation and presentation and accordingly is phrased in words of suggestion rather than command.

The rule also conforms to tradition in making the use of leading questions on cross-examination a matter of right. The purpose of the qualification "ordinarily" is to furnish a basis for denying the use of leading questions when the cross-examination is cross-examination in form only and not in fact, as for example the "cross-examination" of a party by his own counsel after being called by the opponent (savoring more of re-direct) or of an insured defendant who proves to be friendly to the plaintiff.

The final sentence deals with categories of witnesses automatically regarded and treated as hostile. Rule 43(b) of the Federal Rules of Civil Procedure has included only "an adverse party or an officer, director, or managing agent of a public or private corporation or of a partnership or association which is an adverse party." This limitation virtually to persons whose statements would stand as admissions is believed to be an unduly narrow concept of those who may safely be regarded as hostile without further demonstration.

See, for example, Maryland Casualty Co. v. Kador, 225 F.2d 120 (5th Cir. 1955), and Degelos v. Fidelity and Casualty Co., 313 F.2d 809 (5th Cir. 1963), holding despite the language of Rule 43(b) that an insured fell within it, though not a party in an action under the Louisiana direct action statute. The phrase of the rule, "witness identified with" an adverse party, is designed to enlarge the category of persons thus callable.

ADVISORY COMMITTEE'S NOTE — 1987 AMENDMENT

The amendment is technical. No substantive change is intended.

Rule 612.   Writing Used to Refresh a Witness's Memory

(a) Scope. This rule gives an adverse party certain options when a witness uses a writing to refresh memory:

(1) while testifying; or

(2) before testifying, if the court decides that justice requires a party to have those options.

(b) Adverse Party's Options; Deleting Unrelated Matter. Unless 18 U.S.C. § 3500 provides otherwise in a criminal case, an adverse party is entitled to have the writing produced at the hearing, to inspect it, to cross-examine the witness about it, and to introduce in evidence any portion that relates to the witness's testimony. If the producing party claims that the writing includes unrelated matter, the court must examine the writing in camera, delete any unrelated portion, and order that the rest be delivered to the adverse party. Any portion deleted over objection must be preserved for the record.

(c) Failure to Produce or Deliver the Writing. If a writing is not produced or is not delivered as ordered, the court may issue any appropriate order. But if the prosecution does not comply in a criminal case, the court must strike the witness's testimony or—if justice so requires—declare a mistrial.

(Pub. L. 93-595, § 1, Jan. 2, 1975, 88 Stat. 1936; Mar. 2, 1987, eff. Oct. 1, 1987; Apr. 26, 2011, eff. Dec. 1, 2011.)

RESTYLED RULE 612 — ADVISORY COMMITTEE'S NOTE

The language of Rule 612 has been amended as part of the restyling of the Evidence Rules to make them more easily understood and to make style and terminology consistent throughout the rules. These changes are intended to be stylistic only. There is no intent to change any result in any ruling on evidence admissibility.

ADVISORY COMMITTEE'S NOTE
56 F.R.D. 183, 277 (1973)

The treatment of writings used to refresh recollection while on the stand is in accord with settled doctrine. McCormick § 9, p.15. The bulk of the case law has, however, denied the existence of any right to access by the opponent when the writing is used prior to taking the stand, though the judge may have discretion in the matter. Goldman v. United States, 316 U.S. 129, 62 S. Ct. 993, 86 L. Ed. 1322 (1942); Needelman v. United States, 261 F.2d 802 (5th Cir. 1958), *cert. dismissed,* 362 U.S. 600, 80 S. Ct. 960, 4 L. Ed. 2d 980, *rehearing denied,* 363 U.S. 858, 80 S. Ct. 1606, 4 L. Ed. 2d 1739, Annot., 82 A.L.R.2d 473, 562 and 7 A.L.R.3d 181, 247. An increasing group of cases has repudiated the distinction, People v. Scott, 29 Ill. 2d 97, 193 N.E.2d 814 (1963); State v. Mucci, 25 N.J. 423, 136 A.2d 761 (1957); State v. Hunt, 25 N.J. 514, 138 A.2d 1 (1958); State v. Desolvers, 40 R.I. 89, 100, A. 64 (1917), and this position is believed to be correct. As Wigmore put it, "the risk of imposition and the need of safeguard is just as great" in both situations. 3 Wigmore § 762, p.111. To the same effect is McCormick § 9, p.17.

The purpose of the phrase "for the purpose of testifying" is to safeguard against using the rule as a pretext for wholesale exploration of an opposing party's files and to insure that access is limited only to those writings which may fairly be said in fact to have an impact upon the testimony of the witness.

The purpose of the rule is the same as that of the *Jencks* statute, 18 U.S.C. § 3500: to promote the search of credibility and memory. The same sensitivity to disclosure of government files may be involved; hence the rule is expressly made subject to the statute, subdivision (a) of which provides: "In any criminal prosecution brought by the United States, no statement or report in the possession of the United States which was made by a Government witness or prospective Government witness (other than the defendant) shall be the subject of a subpoena, discovery, or inspection until said witness has testified on direct examination in the trial of the case." Items falling within the purview of the statute are producible only as provided by its terms, Palermo v. United States, 360 U.S. 343, 351 (1959), and disclosure under the rule is limited similarly by the statutory conditions. With this limitation in mind, some differences of application may be noted. The *Jencks* statute applies only to statements of witnesses; the rule is not so limited. The statute applies only to criminal cases; the rule applies to all cases. The statute applies only to government witnesses; the rule applies to all witnesses. The statute contains no requirement that the statement be consulted for purposes of refreshment before or while testifying; the rule so requires. Since many writings would qualify under either statute or rule, a substantial overlap exists, but the identity of procedures makes this of no importance.

The consequences of nonproduction by the government in a criminal case are those of the *Jencks* statute, striking the testimony or in exceptional cases a mistrial. 18 U.S.C. § 3500(d). In other cases these alternatives are unduly limited, and such possibilities as contempt, dismissal, finding issues against the offender, and the like are available. *See* Rule 16(g) of the Federal Rules of Criminal Procedure and Rule 37(b) of the Federal Rules of Civil Procedure for appropriate sanctions.

ADVISORY COMMITTEE'S NOTE — 1987 AMENDMENT

The amendment is technical. No substantive change is intended.

Rule 613.   Witness's Prior Statement

(a) Showing or Disclosing the Statement During Examination. When examining a witness about the witness's prior statement, a party need not show it or disclose its contents to the witness. But the party must, on request, show it or disclose its contents to an adverse party's attorney.

> **(b) Extrinsic Evidence of a Prior Inconsistent Statement.** Extrinsic evidence of a witness's prior inconsistent statement is admissible only if the witness is given an opportunity to explain or deny the statement and an adverse party is given an opportunity to examine the witness about it, or if justice so requires. This subdivision (b) does not apply to an opposing party's statement under Rule 801(d)(2).
>
> (Pub. L. 93-595, §1, Jan. 2, 1975, 88 Stat. 1936; Mar. 2, 1987, eff. Oct. 1, 1987; Apr. 25, 1988, eff. Nov. 1, 1988; Apr. 26, 2011, eff. Dec. 1, 2011.)

RESTYLED RULE 613 — ADVISORY COMMITTEE'S NOTE

The language of Rule 613 has been amended as part of the restyling of the Evidence Rules to make them more easily understood and to make style and terminology consistent throughout the rules. These changes are intended to be stylistic only. There is no intent to change any result in any ruling on evidence admissibility.

ADVISORY COMMITTEE'S NOTE
56 F.R.D. 183, 278 (1973)

Subdivision (a). The Queen's Case, 2 Br. & B. 284, 129 Eng. Rep. 976 (1820), laid down the requirement that a cross-examiner, prior to questioning the witness about his own prior statement in writing, must first show it to the witness. Abolished by statute in the country of its origin, the requirement nevertheless gained currency in the United States. The rule abolishes this useless impediment to cross-examination. Ladd, Some Observations on Credibility: Impeachment of Witnesses, 52 Cornell L.Q. 239, 246-247 (1967); McCormick § 28; 4 Wigmore § 1259-1260. Both oral and written statements are included.

The provision for disclosure to counsel is designed to protect against unwarranted insinuations that a statement has been made when the fact is to the contrary.

The rule does not defeat the application of Rule 1002 relating to production of the original when the contents of a writing are sought to be proved. Nor does it defeat the application of Rule 26(b)(3) of the Rules of Civil Procedure, as revised, entitling a person on request to a copy of his own statement, though the operation of the latter may be suspended temporarily.

Subdivision (b). The familiar foundation requirement that an impeaching statement first be shown to the witness before it can be proved by extrinsic evidence is preserved but with some modifications. *See* Ladd, Some Observations on Credibility: Impeachment of Witnesses, 52 Cornell L.Q. 239, 247 (1967). The traditional insistence that the attention of the witness be directed to the statement on cross-examination is relaxed in favor of simply providing the witness an opportunity to explain and the opposite party an opportunity to examine on the statement, with no specification of any particular time or sequence. Under this procedure, several collusive witnesses can be examined before disclosure of a joint prior inconsistent statement. *See* Comment to California Evidence Code § 770. Also, dangers of oversight are reduced. *See* McCormick § 37, p.68.

In order to allow for such eventualities as the witness becoming unavailable by the time the statement is discovered, a measure of discretion is conferred upon the judge. Similar provisions are found in California Evidence Code § 770 and New Jersey Evidence Rule 22(b).

Under principles of *expression unius* the rule does not apply to impeachment by evidence of prior inconsistent conduct. The use of inconsistent statements to impeach a hearsay declaration is treated in Rule 806.

ADVISORY COMMITTEE'S NOTE — 1987 AMENDMENT

The amendments are technical. No substantive change is intended.

ADVISORY COMMITTEE'S NOTE — 1988 AMENDMENT

The amendment is technical. No substantive change is intended.

Rule 614.   Court's Calling or Examining a Witness

(a) Calling. The court may call a witness on its own or at a party's request. Each party is entitled to cross-examine the witness.

(b) Examining. The court may examine a witness regardless of who calls the witness.

(c) Objections. A party may object to the court's calling or examining a witness either at that time or at the next opportunity when the jury is not present.

(Pub. L. 93-595, §1, Jan. 2, 1975, 88 Stat. 1937; Apr. 26, 2011, eff. Dec. 1, 2011.)

RESTYLED RULE 614 — ADVISORY COMMITTEE'S NOTE

The language of Rule 614 has been amended as part of the restyling of the Evidence Rules to make them more easily understood and to make style and terminology consistent throughout the rules. These changes are intended to be stylistic only. There is no intent to change any result in any ruling on evidence admissibility.

ADVISORY COMMITTEE'S NOTE
56 F.R.D. 183, 279 (1973)

Subdivision (a). While exercised more frequently in criminal than in civil cases, the authority of the judge to call witnesses is well established. McCormick §8, p.14; Maguire, Weinstein, et al., Cases on Evidence 303-304 (5th ed. 1965); 9 Wigmore §2484. One reason for the practice, the old rule against impeaching one's own witness, no longer exists by virtue of Rule 607, *supra*. Other reasons remain, however, to justify the continuation of the practice of calling court's witnesses. The right to cross-examine, with all it implies, is assured. The tendency of juries to associate a witness with the party calling him, regardless of technical aspects of vouching, is avoided. And the judge is not imprisoned within the case as made by the parties.

Subdivision (b). The authority of the judge to question witnesses is also well established. McCormick § 8, pp.12-13; Maguire, Weinstein, et al., Cases on Evidence 737-739 (5th ed. 1965); 3 Wigmore § 784. The authority is, of course, abused when the judge abandons his proper role and assumes that of advocate, but the manner in which interrogation should be conducted and the proper extent of its exercise are not susceptible of formulation in a rule. The omission in no sense precludes courts of review from continuing to reverse for abuse.

Subdivision (c). The provision relating to objections is designed to relieve counsel of the embarrassment attendant upon objecting to questions by the judge in the presence of the jury, while at the same time assuring that objections are made in apt time to afford the opportunity to take possible corrective measures. Compare the "automatic" objection feature of Rule 605 when the judge is called as a witness.

Rule 615.   Excluding Witnesses

At a party's request, the court must order witnesses excluded so that they cannot hear other witnesses' testimony. Or the court may do so on its own. But this rule does not authorize excluding:

(a) a party who is a natural person;

(b) an officer or employee of a party that is not a natural person, after being designated as the party's representative by its attorney;

(c) a person whose presence a party shows to be essential to presenting the party's claim or defense; or

(d) a person authorized by statute to be present.

(Pub. L. 93-595, § 1, Jan. 2, 1975, 88 Stat. 1937; Mar. 2, 1987, eff. Oct. 1, 1987; Apr. 25, 1988, eff. Nov. 1, 1988; Pub. L. 100-690, title VII, § 7075(a), Nov. 18, 1988, 102 Stat. 4405; Apr. 24, 1998, eff. Dec. 1, 1998; Apr. 26, 2011, eff. Dec. 1, 2011.)

RESTYLED RULE 615 — ADVISORY COMMITTEE'S NOTE

The language of Rule 615 has been amended as part of the restyling of the Evidence Rules to make them more easily understood and to make style and terminology consistent throughout the rules. These changes are intended to be stylistic only. There is no intent to change any result in any ruling on evidence admissibility.

ADVISORY COMMITTEE'S NOTE
56 F.R.D. 183, 280 (1973)

The efficacy of excluding or sequestering witnesses has long been recognized as a means of discouraging and exposing fabrication, inaccuracy, and collusion. 6 Wigmore § 1837-1838. The authority of the judge is admitted, the only question being whether the matter is committed to his discretion or one of right. The rule takes the latter position. No time is specified for making the request.

Several categories of persons are excepted. (1) Exclusion of persons who are parties would raise serious problems of confrontation and due process. Under accepted practice they are not subject to exclusion. 6 Wigmore § 1841. (2) As the equivalent of the right of a natural-person party to be present, a party which is not a natural person is entitled to have a representative present. Most of the cases have involved allowing a police officer who has been in charge of an investigation to remain in court despite the fact that he will be a witness. United States v. Infanzon, 235 F.2d 318 (2d Cir. 1956); Portomene v. United States, 221 F.2d 582 (5th Cir. 1955); Powell v. United States, 208 F.2d 618 (6th Cir. 1953); Jones v. United States, 252 F. Supp. 781 (W.D. Okl. 1966). Designation of the representative by the attorney rather than by the client may at first glance appear to be an inversion of the attorney-client relationship, but it may be assumed that the attorney will follow the wishes of the client, and the solution is simple and workable. *See* California Evidence Code § 777. (3) The category contemplates such persons as an agent who handled the transaction being litigated or an expert needed to advise counsel in the management of the litigation. *See* 6 Wigmore § 1841, n.4.

ADVISORY COMMITTEE'S NOTE — 1987 AMENDMENT

The amendment is technical. No substantive change is intended.

ADVISORY COMMITTEE'S NOTE — 1988 AMENDMENT

The amendment is technical. No substantive change is intended.

ADVISORY COMMITTEE'S NOTE — 1998 AMENDMENT

The amendment is in response to: (1) the Victim's Rights and Restitution Act of 1990, 42 U.S.C. § 10606, which guarantees, within certain limits, the right of a crime victim to attend the trial; and (2) the Victim Rights Clarification Act of 1997 (18 U.S.C. § 3510).

ARTICLE VII.   OPINIONS AND EXPERT TESTIMONY

Rule 701.   Opinion Testimony by Lay Witnesses

If a witness is not testifying as an expert, testimony in the form of an opinion is limited to one that is:

(a) rationally based on the witness's perception;

(b) helpful to clearly understanding the witness's testimony or to determining a fact in issue; and

(c) not based on scientific, technical, or other specialized knowledge within the scope of Rule 702.

(Pub. L. 93-595, § 1, Jan. 2, 1975, 88 Stat. 1937; Mar. 2, 1987, eff. Oct. 1, 1987; Apr. 17, 2000, eff. Dec. 1, 2000; Apr. 26, 2011, eff. Dec. 1, 2011.)

RESTYLED RULE 701 — ADVISORY COMMITTEE'S NOTE

The language of Rule 701 has been amended as part of the general restyling of the Evidence Rules to make them more easily understood and to make style and terminology consistent throughout the rules. These changes are intended to be stylistic only. There is no intent to change any result in any ruling on evidence admissibility.

The Committee deleted all reference to an "inference" on the grounds that the deletion made the Rule flow better and easier to read, and because any "inference" is covered by the broader term "opinion." Courts have not made substantive decisions on the basis of any distinction between an opinion and an inference. No change in current practice is intended.

ADVISORY COMMITTEE'S NOTE
56 F.R.D. 183, 281 (1973)

The rule retains the traditional objective of putting the trier of fact in possession of an accurate reproduction of the event.

Limitation (a) is the familiar requirement of first-hand knowledge or observation.

Limitation (b) is phrased in terms of requiring testimony to be helpful in resolving issues. Witnesses often find difficulty in expressing themselves in language which is not that of an opinion or conclusion. While the courts have made concessions in certain recurring situations, necessity as a standard for permitting opinions and conclusions has proved too elusive and too unadaptable to particular situations for purposes of satisfactory judicial administration. McCormick § 11. Moreover, the practical impossibility of determining by rule what is a "fact," demonstrated by a century of litigation of the question of what is a fact for purposes of pleading under the Field Code, extends into evidence also. 7 Wigmore § 1919. The rule assumes that the natural characteristics of the adversary system will generally lead to an acceptable result, since the detailed account carries more conviction than the broad assertion, and a lawyer can be expected to display his witness to the best advantage. If he fails to do so, cross-examination and argument will point up the weakness. *See* Ladd, Expert Testimony, 5 Vand. L. Rev. 414, 415-417 (1952). If, despite these considerations, attempts are made to introduce meaningless assertions which amount to little more than choosing up sides, exclusion for lack of helpfulness is called for by the rule.

The language of the rule is substantially that of Uniform Rule 56(1). Similar provisions are California Evidence Code § 800; Kansas Code of Civil Procedure § 60-456(a); New Jersey Evidence Rule 56(1).

ADVISORY COMMITTEE'S NOTE — 1987 AMENDMENT

The amendments are technical. No substantive change is intended.

ADVISORY COMMITTEE'S NOTE — 2000 AMENDMENT

Rule 701 has been amended to eliminate the risk that the reliability requirements set forth in Rule 702 will be evaded through the simple expedient of proffering an expert in lay witness clothing. Under the amendment, a witness' testimony must be scrutinized under the rules regulating expert opinion to the extent that the witness is providing testimony based on scientific, technical, or other specialized knowledge within the scope of Rule 702. *See generally* Asplundh Mfg. Div. v. Benton Harbor Eng'g, 57 F.3d 1190 (3d Cir. 1995). By channeling testimony that is actually expert testimony to Rule 702, the amendment also ensures that a party will not evade the expert witness disclosure requirements set forth in Fed. R. Civ. P. 26 and Fed. R. Crim. P. 16 by simply calling an expert witness in the guise of a layperson. *See* Joseph, Emerging Expert Issues Under the 1993 Disclosure Amendments to the Federal Rules of Civil Procedure, 164 F.R.D. 97, 108 (1996) (noting that "there is no good reason to allow what is essentially surprise expert testimony," and that "the Court should be vigilant to preclude manipulative conduct designed to thwart the expert disclosure and discovery process"). *See also* United States v. Figueroa-Lopez, 125 F.3d 1241, 1246 (9th Cir. 1997) (law enforcement agents testifying that the defendant's conduct was consistent with that of a drug trafficker could not testify as lay witnesses; to permit such testimony under Rule 701 "subverts the requirements of Federal Rule of Criminal Procedure 16(a)(1)(E)").

The amendment does not distinguish between expert and lay *witnesses*, but rather between expert and lay *testimony*. Certainly it is possible for the same witness to provide both lay and expert testimony in a single case. *See, e.g.*, United States v. Figueroa-Lopez, 125 F.3d 1241, 1246 (9th Cir. 1997) (law enforcement agents could testify that the defendant was acting suspiciously, without being qualified as experts; however, the rules on experts were applicable where the agents testified on the basis of extensive experience that the defendant was using code words to refer to drug quantities and prices). The amendment makes clear that any part of a witness' testimony that is based upon scientific, technical, or other specialized knowledge within the scope of Rule 702 is governed by the standards of Rule 702 and the corresponding disclosure requirements of the Civil and Criminal Rules.

The amendment is not intended to affect the "prototypical example[s] of the type of evidence contemplated by the adoption of Rule 701 relat[ing] to the appearance of persons or things, identity, the manner of conduct, competency of a person, degrees of light or darkness, sound, size, weight, distance, and an endless number of items that cannot be described factually in words apart from inferences." Asplundh Mfg. Div. v. Benton Harbor Eng'g, 57 F.3d 1190, 1196 (3d Cir. 1995).

For example, most courts have permitted the owner or officer of a business to testify to the value or projected profits of the business, without the necessity of qualifying the witness as an accountant, appraiser, or similar expert. *See, e.g.*, Lightning Lube, Inc. v. Witco Corp., 4 F.3d 1153 (3d Cir. 1993) (no abuse of discretion in permitting the plaintiff's owner to give lay opinion testimony as to damages, as it was based on his knowledge and participation in the day-to-day affairs of the business). Such opinion testimony is admitted not because of experience, training or specialized knowledge within the realm of an expert, but because of the particularized knowledge that the witness has by virtue of his or her position in the business. The amendment does not purport to change this analysis. Similarly, courts have permitted lay witnesses to testify that a substance appeared to be a narcotic, so long as a foundation of familiarity with the substance is established. *See, e.g.*, United States v. Westbrook, 896 F.2d 330 (8th Cir. 1990) (two lay witnesses who were heavy amphetamine users were properly permitted to testify that a substance was amphetamine; but it was error to permit another witness to make such an identification where she had no experience with amphetamines). Such testimony is not based on specialized knowledge within the scope of Rule 702, but rather is based upon a layperson's personal knowledge. If, however, that witness were to describe how a narcotic was manufactured, or to describe the intricate workings of a narcotic distribution network, then the witness would have to qualify as an expert under Rule 702. United States v. Figueroa-Lopez, *supra*.

The amendment incorporates the distinctions set forth in State v. Brown, 836 S.W.2d 530, 549 (1992), a case involving former Tennessee Rule of Evidence 701, a rule that precluded lay witness testimony based on "special knowledge." In *Brown*, the court declared that the distinction between lay and expert witness testimony is that lay testimony "results from a process of reasoning familiar in everyday life," while expert testimony "results from a process of reasoning which can be mastered only by specialists in the field." The court in *Brown* noted that a lay witness with experience could testify that a substance appeared to be blood, but that a witness would have to qualify as an expert before he could testify that bruising around the eyes is indicative of skull trauma. That is the kind of distinction made by the amendment to this Rule.

Rule 702.   Testimony by Expert Witnesses

A witness who is qualified as an expert by knowledge, skill, experience, training, or education may testify in the form of an opinion or otherwise if:

(a) the expert's scientific, technical, or other specialized knowledge will help the trier of fact to understand the evidence or to determine a fact in issue;

(b) the testimony is based on sufficient facts or data;

(c) the testimony is the product of reliable principles and methods; and

(d) the expert has reliably applied the principles and methods to the facts of the case.

(Pub. L. 93-595, § 1, Jan. 2, 1975, 88 Stat. 1937; Apr. 17, 2000, eff. Dec. 1, 2000; Apr. 26, 2011, eff. Dec. 1, 2011.)

RESTYLED RULE 702 — ADVISORY COMMITTEE'S NOTE

The language of Rule 702 has been amended as part of the restyling of the Evidence Rules to make them more easily understood and to make style and terminology consistent throughout the rules. These changes are intended to be stylistic only. There is no intent to change any result in any ruling on evidence admissibility.

ADVISORY COMMITTEE'S NOTE
56 F.R.D. 183, 282 (1973)

An intelligent evaluation of facts is often difficult or impossible without the application of some scientific, technical, or other specialized knowledge. The most common source of this knowledge is the expert witness, although there are other techniques for supplying it.

Most of the literature assumes that experts testify only in the form of opinions. The assumption is logically unfounded. The rule accordingly recognizes that an expert on the stand may give a dissertation or exposition of scientific or other principles relevant to the case, leaving the trier of fact to apply them to the facts. Since much of the criticism of expert testimony has centered upon the hypothetical question, it seems wise to recognize that opinions are not indispensable and to encourage the use of expert testimony in non-opinion form when counsel believes the trier can itself draw the requisite inference. The use of opinions is not abolished by the rule, however. It will continue to be permissible for the experts to take the further step of suggesting the inference which should be drawn from applying the specialized knowledge to the facts. *See* Rules 703 to 705.

Whether the situation is a proper one for the use of expert testimony is to be determined on the basis of assisting the trier. "There is no more certain test for determining when experts may be used than the common sense inquiry whether the untrained layman would be qualified to determine intelligently and to the best possible degree the particular issue without enlightenment from those having a specialized understanding of the subject involved in the dispute." Ladd, Expert Testimony, 5 Vand. L. Rev. 414, 418 (1952). When opinions are excluded, it is because they are unhelpful and therefore superfluous and a waste of time. 7 Wigmore § 1918.

The rule is broadly phrased. The fields of knowledge which may be drawn upon are not limited merely to the "scientific" and "technical" but extend to all "specialized" knowledge. Similarly, the expert is viewed, not in a narrow sense, but as a person qualified by "knowledge, skill, experience, training or education." Thus within the scope of the rule are not only experts in the strictest sense of the word, e.g., physicians, physicists, and architects, but also the large group sometimes called "skilled" witnesses, such as bankers or landowners testifying to land values.

ADVISORY COMMITTEE'S NOTE — 2000 AMENDMENT

Rule 702 has been amended in response to Daubert v. Merrell Dow Pharmaceuticals, Inc., 509 U.S. 579 (1993), and to the many cases applying Daubert, including Kumho Tire Co. v. Carmichael, 119 S. Ct. 1167 (1999). In Daubert the Court charged trial judges with the responsibility of acting as gatekeepers to exclude unreliable expert testimony, and the Court in Kumho clarified that this gatekeeper function applies to all expert testimony, not just testimony based in science. See also Kumho, 119 S. Ct. at 1178 (citing the Committee Note to the proposed amendment to Rule 702, which had been released for public comment before the date of the Kumho decision). The amendment affirms the trial court's role as gatekeeper and provides some general standards that the trial court must use to assess the reliability and helpfulness of proffered expert testimony. Consistently with Kumho, the Rule as amended provides that all types of expert testimony present questions of admissibility for the trial court in deciding whether the evidence is reliable and helpful. Consequently, the admissibility of all expert testimony is governed by the principles of Rule 104(a). Under that Rule, the proponent has the burden of establishing that the pertinent admissibility requirements are met by a preponderance of the evidence. See Bourjaily v. United States, 483 U.S. 171 (1987).

Daubert set forth a non-exclusive checklist for trial courts to use in assessing the reliability of scientific expert testimony. The specific factors explicated by the Daubert Court are (1) whether the expert's technique or theory can be or has been tested — that is, whether the expert's theory can be challenged in some objective sense, or whether it is instead simply a subjective, conclusory approach that cannot reasonably be assessed for reliability; (2) whether the technique or theory has been subject to peer review and publication; (3) the known or potential rate of error of the technique or theory when applied; (4) the existence and maintenance of standards and controls; and (5) whether the technique or theory has been generally accepted in the scientific community. The Court in Kumho held that these factors might also be applicable in assessing the reliability of nonscientific expert testimony, depending upon "the particular circumstances of the particular case at issue." 119 S. Ct. at 1175.

No attempt has been made to "codify" these specific factors. Daubert itself emphasized that the factors were neither exclusive nor dispositive. Other cases have recognized that not all of the specific Daubert factors can apply to every type of expert testimony. In addition to Kumho, 119 S. Ct. at 1175, see Tyus v. Urban Search Management, 102 F.3d 256 (7th Cir. 1996) (noting that the factors mentioned by the Court in Daubert do not neatly apply to expert testimony from a sociologist). See also Kannankeril v. Terminix Int'l, Inc., 128 F.3d 802, 809 (3d Cir. 1997) (holding that lack of peer review or publication was not dispositive where the expert's opinion was supported by "widely accepted scientific knowledge"). The standards set forth in the amendment are broad enough to require consideration of any or all of the specific *Daubert* factors where appropriate.

Courts both before and after *Daubert* have found other factors relevant in determining whether expert testimony is sufficiently reliable to be considered by the trier of fact.

These factors include:

(1)   Whether experts are "proposing to testify about matters growing naturally and directly out of research they have conducted independent of the litigation, or whether they have developed their opinions expressly for purposes of testifying." Daubert v. Merrell Dow Pharmaceuticals, Inc., 43 F.3d 1311, 1317 (9th Cir. 1995).

(2)   Whether the expert has unjustifiably extrapolated from an accepted premise to an unfounded conclusion. *See* General Elec. Co. v. Joiner, 522 U.S. 136, 146 (1997) (noting that in some cases a trial court "may conclude that there is simply too great an analytical gap between the data and the opinion proffered").

(3)   Whether the expert has adequately accounted for obvious alternative explanations. *See* Claar v. Burlington N.R.R., 29 F.3d 499 (9th Cir. 1994) (testimony excluded where the expert failed to consider other obvious causes for the plaintiff's condition). *Compare* Ambrosini v. Labarraque, 101 F.3d 129 (D.C. Cir. 1996) (the possibility of some uneliminated causes presents a question of weight, so long as the most obvious causes have been considered and reasonably ruled out by the expert).

(4)   Whether the expert "is being as careful as he would be in his regular professional work outside his paid litigation consulting." Sheehan v. Daily Racing Form, Inc., 104 F.3d 940, 942 (7th Cir. 1997). *See* Kumho Tire Co. v. Carmichael, 119 S. Ct. 1167, 1176 (1999) (*Daubert* requires the trial court to assure itself that the expert "employs in the courtroom the same level of intellectual rigor that characterizes the practice of an expert in the relevant field").

(5)   Whether the field of expertise claimed by the expert is known to reach reliable results for the type of opinion the expert would give. *See* Kumho Tire Co. v. Carmichael, 119 S. Ct. 1167, 1175 (1999) (*Daubert*'s general acceptance factor does not "help show that an expert's testimony is reliable where the discipline itself lacks reliability, as, for example, do theories grounded in any so-called generally accepted principles of astrology or necromancy."); Moore v. Ashland Chemical, Inc., 151 F.3d 269 (5th Cir. 1998) (en banc) (clinical doctor was properly precluded from testifying to the toxicological cause of the plaintiff's respiratory problem, where the opinion was not sufficiently grounded in scientific methodology); Sterling v. Velsicol Chem. Corp., 855 F.2d 1188 (6th Cir. 1988) (rejecting testimony based on "clinical ecology" as unfounded and unreliable).

All of these factors remain relevant to the determination of the reliability of expert testimony under the Rule as amended. Other factors may also be relevant. *See Kumho*, 119 S. Ct. 1167, 1176 ("[w]e conclude that the trial judge must have considerable leeway in deciding in a particular case how to go about determining whether particular expert testimony is reliable."). Yet no single factor is necessarily dispositive of the reliability of a particular expert's testimony. *See, e.g.*, Heller v. Shaw Industries, Inc., 167 F.3d 146, 155 (3d Cir. 1999) ("not only must each stage of the expert's testimony be reliable, but each stage must be evaluated practically and flexibly without bright-line exclusionary (or inclusionary) rules"); Daubert v. Merrell Dow Pharmaceuticals, Inc., 43 F.3d 1311, 1317, n.5 (9th Cir. 1995) (noting that some expert disciplines "have the courtroom as a principal theatre of operations" and as to these disciplines "the fact that the expert has developed an expertise principally for purposes of litigation will obviously not be a substantial consideration").

A review of the caselaw after *Daubert* shows that the rejection of expert testimony is the exception rather than the rule. *Daubert* did not work a "seachange over federal evidence law," and "the trial court's role as gatekeeper is not intended to serve as a replacement for the adversary system." United States v. 14.38 Acres of Land Situated in Leflore County, Mississippi, 80 F.3d 1074, 1078 (5th Cir. 1996). As the Court in *Daubert* stated: "Vigorous cross-examination, presentation of contrary evidence, and careful instruction on the burden of proof are the traditional and appropriate means of attacking shaky but admissible evidence." 509 U.S. at 595. Likewise, this amendment is not intended to provide an excuse for an automatic challenge to the testimony of every expert. *See* Kumho Tire Co. v. Carmichael, 119 S. Ct. 1167, 1176 (1999) (noting that the trial judge has the discretion "both to avoid unnecessary 'reliability' proceedings in ordinary cases where the reliability of an expert's methods is properly taken for granted, and to require appropriate proceedings in the less usual or more complex cases where cause for questioning the expert's reliability arises").

When a trial court, applying this amendment, rules that an expert's testimony is reliable, this does not necessarily mean that contradictory expert testimony is unreliable. The amendment is broad enough to permit testimony that is the product of competing principles or methods in the same field of expertise. *See, e.g.,* Heller v. Shaw Industries, Inc., 167 F.3d 146, 160 (3d Cir. 1999) (expert testimony cannot be excluded simply because the expert uses one test rather than another, when both tests are accepted in the field and both reach reliable results). As the court stated in In re Paoli R.R. Yard PCB Litigation, 35 F.3d 717, 744 (3d Cir. 1994), proponents "do not have to demonstrate to the judge by a preponderance of the evidence that the assessments of their experts are correct, they only have to demonstrate by a preponderance of evidence that their opinions are reliable. . . . The evidentiary requirement of reliability is lower than the merits standard of correctness." *See also* Daubert v. Merrell Dow Pharmaceuticals, Inc., 43 F.3d 1311, 1318 (9th Cir. 1995) (scientific experts might be permitted to testify if they could show that the methods they used were also employed by "a recognized minority of scientists in their field"); Ruiz-Troche v. Pepsi Cola, 161 F.3d 77, 85 (1st Cir. 1998) ("*Daubert* neither requires nor empowers trial courts to determine which of several competing scientific theories has the best provenance.").

The Court in *Daubert* declared that the "focus, of course, must be solely on principles and methodology, not on the conclusions they generate." 509 U.S. at 595. Yet as the Court later recognized, "conclusions and methodology are not entirely distinct from one another." General Elec. Co. v. Joiner, 522 U.S. 136, 146 (1997). Under the amendment, as under *Daubert*, when an expert purports to apply principles and methods in accordance with professional standards, and yet reaches a conclusion that other experts in the field would not reach, the trial court may fairly suspect that the principles and methods have not been faithfully applied. *See* Lust v. Merrell Dow Pharmaceuticals, Inc., 89 F.3d 594, 598 (9th Cir. 1996). The amendment specifically provides that the trial court must scrutinize not only the principles and methods used by the expert, but also whether those principles and methods have been properly applied to the facts of the case. As the court noted in In re Paoli R.R. Yard PCB Litig., 35 F.3d 717, 745 (3d Cir. 1994), "*any* step that renders the analysis unreliable . . . renders the expert's testimony inadmissible. *This is true whether the step completely changes a reliable methodology or merely misapplies that methodology.*"

If the expert purports to apply principles and methods to the facts of the case, it is important that this application be conducted reliably. Yet it might also be important in some cases for an expert to educate the fact-finder about general principles, without ever attempting to apply these principles to the specific facts of the case. For example, experts might instruct the fact-finder on the principles of thermodynamics, or blood-clotting, or on how financial markets respond to corporate reports, without ever knowing about or trying to tie their testimony into the facts of the case. The amendment does not alter the venerable practice of using expert testimony to educate the fact-finder on general principles. For this kind of generalized testimony, Rule 702 simply requires that: (1) the expert be qualified; (2) the testimony address a subject matter on which the fact-finder can be assisted by an expert; (3) the testimony be reliable; and (4) the testimony "fit" the facts of the case.

As stated earlier, the amendment does not distinguish between scientific and other forms of expert testimony. The trial court's gatekeeping function applies to testimony by any expert. *See* Kumho Tire Co. v. Carmichael, 119 S. Ct. 1167, 1171 (1999) ("We conclude that *Daubert*'s general holding — setting forth the trial judge's general 'gatekeeping' obligation — applies not only to testimony based on 'scientific' knowledge, but also to testimony based on 'technical' and 'other specialized' knowledge."). While the relevant factors for determining reliability will vary from expertise to expertise, the amendment rejects the premise that an expert's testimony should be treated more permissively simply because it is outside the realm of science. An opinion from an expert who is not a scientist should receive the same degree of scrutiny for reliability as an opinion from an expert who purports to be a scientist. *See* Watkins v. Telsmith, Inc., 121 F.3d 984, 991 (5th Cir. 1997) ("[I]t seems exactly backwards that experts who purport to rely on general engineering principles and practical experience might escape screening by the district court simply by stating that their conclusions were not reached by any particular method or technique."). Some types of expert testimony will be more objectively verifiable, and subject to the expectations of falsifiability, peer review, and publication, than others. Some types of expert testimony will not rely on anything like a scientific method, and so will have to be evaluated by reference to other standard principles attendant to the particular area of expertise. The trial judge in all cases of proffered expert testimony must find that it is properly grounded, well-reasoned, and not speculative before it can be admitted. The expert's testimony must be grounded in an accepted body of learning or experience in the expert's field, and the expert must explain how the conclusion is so grounded. *See, e.g.*, American College of Trial Lawyers, Standards and Procedures for Determining the Admissibility of Expert Testimony after *Daubert*, 157 F.R.D. 571, 579 (1994) ("[W]hether the testimony concerns economic principles, accounting standards, property valuation or other non-scientific subjects, it should be evaluated by reference to the 'knowledge and experience' of that particular field.").

The amendment requires that the testimony must be the product of reliable principles and methods that are reliably applied to the facts of the case. While the terms "principles" and "methods" may convey a certain impression when applied to scientific knowledge, they remain relevant when applied to testimony based on technical or other specialized knowledge. For example, when a law enforcement agent testifies regarding the use of code words in a drug transaction, the principle used by the agent is that participants in such transactions regularly use code words to conceal the nature of their activities. The method used by the agent is the application of extensive experience to analyze the meaning of the conversations. So long as the principles and methods are reliable and applied reliably to the facts of the case, this type of testimony should be admitted.

Nothing in this amendment is intended to suggest that experience alone — or experience in conjunction with other knowledge, skill, training or education — may not provide a sufficient foundation for expert testimony. To the contrary, the text of Rule 702 expressly contemplates that an expert may be qualified on the basis of experience. In certain fields, experience is the predominant, if not sole, basis for a great deal of reliable expert testimony. *See, e.g.*, United States v. Jones, 107 F.3d 1147 (6th Cir. 1997) (no abuse of discretion in admitting the testimony of a handwriting examiner who had years of practical experience and extensive training, and who explained his methodology in detail); Tassin v. Sears Roebuck, 946 F. Supp. 1241, 1248 (M.D. La. 1996) (design engineer's testimony can be admissible when the expert's opinions "are based on facts, a reasonable investigation, and traditional technical/ mechanical expertise, and he provides a reasonable link between the information and procedures he uses and the conclusions he reaches"). *See also* Kumho Tire Co. v. Carmichael, 119 S. Ct. 1167, 1178 (1999) (stating that "no one denies that an expert might draw a conclusion from a set of observations based on extensive and specialized experience").

If the witness is relying solely or primarily on experience, then the witness must explain how that experience leads to the conclusion reached, why that experience is a sufficient basis for the opinion, and how that experience is reliably applied to the facts. The trial court's gatekeeping function requires more than simply "taking the expert's word for it." *See* Daubert v. Merrell Dow Pharmaceuticals, Inc., 43 F.3d 1311, 1319 (9th Cir. 1995) ("We've been presented with only the experts' qualifications, their conclusions and their assurances of reliability. Under *Daubert*, that's not enough."). The more subjective and controversial the expert's inquiry, the more likely the testimony should be excluded as unreliable. *See* O'Conner v. Commonwealth Edison Co., 13 F.3d 1090 (7th Cir. 1994) (expert testimony based on a completely subjective methodology held properly excluded). *See also* Kumho Tire Co. v. Carmichael, 119 S. Ct. 1167, 1176 (1999) ("[I]t will at times be useful to ask even of a witness whose expertise is based purely on experience, say, a perfume tester able to distinguish among 140 odors at a sniff, whether his preparation is of a kind that others in the field would recognize as acceptable.").

Subpart (1) of Rule 702 calls for a quantitative rather than qualitative analysis. The amendment requires that expert testimony be based on sufficient underlying "facts or data." The term "data" is intended to encompass the reliable opinions of other experts. *See* the original Advisory Committee Note to Rule 703. The language "facts or data" is broad enough to allow an expert to rely on hypothetical facts that are supported by the evidence. *Id.*

When facts are in dispute, experts sometimes reach different conclusions based on competing versions of the facts. The emphasis in the amendment on "sufficient facts or data" is not intended to authorize a trial court to exclude an expert's testimony on the ground that the court believes one version of the facts and not the other.

There has been some confusion over the relationship between Rules 702 and 703. The amendment makes clear that the sufficiency of the basis of an expert's testimony is to be decided under Rule 702. Rule 702 sets forth the overarching requirement of reliability, and an analysis of the sufficiency of the expert's basis cannot be divorced from the ultimate reliability of the expert's opinion. In contrast, the "reasonable reliance" requirement of Rule 703 is a relatively narrow inquiry. When an expert relies on inadmissible information, Rule 703 requires the trial court to determine whether that information is of a type reasonably relied on by other experts in the field. If so, the expert can rely on the information in reaching an opinion. However, the question whether the expert is relying on a *sufficient* basis of information — whether admissible information or not — is governed by the requirements of Rule 702.

The amendment makes no attempt to set forth procedural requirements for exercising the trial court's gatekeeping function over expert testimony. *See* Daniel J. Capra, The *Daubert* Puzzle, 38 Ga. L. Rev. 699, 766 (1998) ("Trial courts should be allowed substantial discretion in dealing with *Daubert* questions; any attempt to codify procedures will likely give rise to unnecessary changes in practice and create difficult questions for appellate review."). Courts have shown considerable ingenuity and flexibility in considering challenges to expert testimony under *Daubert*, and it is contemplated that this will continue under the amended Rule. *See, e.g.,* Cortes-Irizarry v. Corporacion Insular, 111 F.3d 184 (1st Cir. 1997) (discussing the application of *Daubert* in ruling on a motion for summary judgment); In re Paoli R.R. Yard PCB Litig., 35 F.3d 717, 736, 739 (3d Cir. 1994) (discussing the use of *in limine* hearings); Claar v. Burlington N.R.R., 29 F.3d 499, 502-05 (9th Cir. 1994) (discussing the trial court's technique of ordering experts to submit serial affidavits explaining the reasoning and methods underlying their conclusions).

The amendment continues the practice of the original Rule in referring to a qualified witness as an "expert." This was done to provide continuity and to minimize change. The use of the term "expert" in the Rule does not, however, mean that a jury should actually be informed that a qualified witness is testifying as an "expert." Indeed, there is much to be said for a practice that prohibits the use of the term "expert" by both the parties and the court at trial. Such a practice "ensures that trial courts do not inadvertently put their stamp of authority" on a witness's opinion, and protects against the jury's being "overwhelmed by the so-called 'experts.'" Hon. Charles Richey, Proposals to Eliminate the Prejudicial Effect of the Use of the Word "Expert" Under the Federal Rules of Evidence in Criminal and Civil Jury Trials, 154 F.R.D. 537, 559 (1994) (setting forth limiting instructions and a standing order employed to prohibit the use of the term "expert" in jury trials).

Rule 703. Bases of an Expert's Opinion Testimony

An expert may base an opinion on facts or data in the case that the expert has been made aware of or personally observed. If experts in the particular field would reasonably rely on those kinds of facts or data in forming an opinion on the subject, they need not be admissible for the opinion to be admitted. But if the facts or data would otherwise be inadmissible, the proponent of the opinion may disclose them to the jury only if their probative value in helping the jury evaluate the opinion substantially outweighs their prejudicial effect.

(Pub. L. 93-595, § 1, Jan. 2, 1975, 88 Stat. 1937; Mar. 2, 1987, eff. Oct. 1, 1987; Apr. 17, 2000, eff. Dec. 1, 2000; Apr. 26, 2011, eff. Dec. 1, 2011.)

RESTYLED RULE 703 — ADVISORY COMMITTEE'S NOTE

The language of Rule 703 has been amended as part of the general restyling of the Evidence Rules to make them more easily understood and to make style and terminology consistent throughout the rules. These changes are intended to be stylistic only. There is no intent to change any result in any ruling on evidence admissibility.

The Committee deleted all reference to an "inference" on the grounds that the deletion made the Rule flow better and easier to read, and because any "inference" is covered by the broader term "opinion." Courts have not made substantive decisions on the basis of any distinction between an opinion and an inference. No change in current practice is intended.

ADVISORY COMMITTEE'S NOTE
56 F.R.D. 183, 283 (1973)

Facts or data upon which expert opinions are based may, under the rule, be derived from three possible sources. The first is the firsthand observation of the witness, with opinions based thereon traditionally allowed. A treating physician affords an example. Rheingold, The Basis of Medical Testimony, 15 Vand. L. Rev. 473, 489 (1962). Whether he must first relate his observations is treated in Rule 705. The second source, presentation at the trial, also reflects existing practice. The technique may be the familiar hypothetical question or having the expert attend the trial and hear the testimony establishing the facts. Problems of determining what testimony the expert relied upon, when the latter technique is employed and the testimony is in conflict, may be resolved by resort to Rule 705. The third source contemplated by the rule consists of presentation of data to the expert outside of court and other than by his own perception. In this respect the rule is designed to broaden the basis for expert opinions beyond that current in many jurisdictions and to bring the judicial practice into line with the practice of the experts themselves when not in court. Thus a physician in his own practice bases his diagnosis on information from numerous sources and of considerable variety, including statements by patients and relatives, reports and opinions from nurses, technicians and other doctors, hospital records, and X-rays. Most of them are admissible in evidence, but only with the expenditure of substantial time in producing and examining various authenticating witnesses. The physician makes life-and-death decisions in reliance upon them. His validation, expertly performed and subject to cross-examination, ought to suffice for judicial purposes. Rheingold, *supra*, at 531; McCormick §15. A similar provision is California Evidence Code §801(b).

The rule also offers a more satisfactory basis for ruling upon the admissibility of public opinion poll evidence. Attention is directed to the validity of the techniques employed rather than to relatively fruitless inquiries whether hearsay is involved. *See* Judge Feinberg's careful analysis in Zippo Mfg. Co. v. Rogers Imports, Inc., 216 F. Supp. 670 (S.D.N.Y. 1963). *See also* Blum et al., The Art of Opinion Research: A Lawyer's Appraisal of an Emerging Service, 24 U. Chi. L. Rev. 1 (1956); Bonynge, Trademark Surveys and Techniques and Their Use in Litigation, 48 A.B.A. J. 329 (1962); Zeisel, The Uniqueness of Survey Evidence, 45 Cornell L.Q. 322 (1960); Annot., 76 A.L.R.2d 919.

If it be feared that enlargement of permissible data may tend to break down the rules of exclusion unduly, notice should be taken that the rule requires that the facts or data "be of a type reasonably relied upon by experts in the particular field." The language would not warrant admitting in evidence the opinion of an "accidentologist" as to the point of impact in an automobile collision based on statements of bystanders, since this requirement is not satisfied. *See* Comment, Cal. Law Rev. Comm'n, Recommendation Proposing an Evidence Code 148-150 (1965).

ADVISORY COMMITTEE'S NOTE — 1987 AMENDMENT

The amendment is technical. No substantive change is intended.

ADVISORY COMMITTEE'S NOTE — 2000 AMENDMENT

Rule 703 has been amended to emphasize that when an expert reasonably relies on inadmissible information to form an opinion or inference, the underlying information is not admissible simply because the opinion or inference is admitted. Courts have reached different results on how to treat inadmissible information when it is reasonably relied upon by an expert in forming an opinion or drawing an inference. *Compare* United States v. Rollins, 862 F.2d 1282 (7th Cir. 1988) (admitting, as part of the basis of an FBI agent's expert opinion on the meaning of code language, the hearsay statements of an informant), *with* United States v. 0.59 Acres of Land, 109 F.3d 1493 (9th Cir. 1997) (error to admit hearsay offered as the basis of an expert opinion, without a limiting instruction). Commentators have also taken differing views. *See, e.g.*, Ronald Carlson, Policing the Bases of Modern Expert Testimony, 39 Vand. L. Rev. 577 (1986) (advocating limits on the jury's consideration of otherwise inadmissible evidence used as the basis for an expert opinion); Paul Rice, Inadmissible Evidence as a Basis for Expert Testimony: A Response to Professor Carlson, 40 Vand. L. Rev. 583 (1987) (advocating unrestricted use of information reasonably relied upon by an expert).

When information is reasonably relied upon by an expert and yet is admissible only for the purpose of assisting the jury in evaluating an expert's opinion, a trial court applying this Rule must consider the information's probative value in assisting the jury to weigh the expert's opinion on the one hand, and the risk of prejudice resulting from the jury's potential misuse of the information for substantive purposes on the other. The information may be disclosed to the jury, upon objection, only if the trial court finds that the probative value of the information in assisting the jury to evaluate the expert's opinion substantially outweighs its prejudicial effect. If the otherwise inadmissible information is admitted under this balancing test, the trial judge must give a limiting instruction upon request, informing the jury that the underlying information must not be used for substantive purposes. *See* Rule 105. In determining the appropriate course, the trial court should consider the probable effectiveness or lack of effectiveness of a limiting instruction under the particular circumstances.

The amendment governs only the disclosure to the jury of information that is reasonably relied on by an expert, when that information is not admissible for substantive purposes. It is not intended to affect the admissibility of an expert's testimony. Nor does the amendment prevent an expert from relying on information that is inadmissible for substantive purposes.

Nothing in this Rule restricts the presentation of underlying expert facts or data when offered by an adverse party. *See* Rule 705. Of course, an adversary's attack on an expert's basis will often open the door to a proponent's rebuttal with information that was reasonably relied upon by the expert, even if that information would not have been disclosable initially under the balancing test provided by this amendment. Moreover, in some circumstances the proponent might wish to disclose information that is relied upon by the expert in order to "remove the sting" from the opponent's anticipated attack, and thereby prevent the jury from drawing an unfair negative inference. The trial court should take this consideration into account in applying the balancing test provided by this amendment.

This amendment covers facts or data that cannot be admitted for any purpose other than to assist the jury to evaluate the expert's opinion. The balancing test provided in this amendment is not applicable to facts or data that are admissible for any other purpose but have not yet been offered for such a purpose at the time the expert testifies.

The amendment provides a presumption against disclosure to the jury of information used as the basis of an expert's opinion and not admissible for any substantive purpose, when that information is offered by the proponent of the expert. In a multi-party case, where one party proffers an expert whose testimony is also beneficial to other parties, each such party should be deemed a "proponent" within the meaning of the amendment.

Rule 704.   Opinion on an Ultimate Issue

   (a) **In General — Not Automatically Objectionable.** An opinion is not objectionable just because it embraces an ultimate issue.

   (b) **Exception.** In a criminal case, an expert witness must not state an opinion about whether the defendant did or did not have a mental state or condition that constitutes an element of the crime charged or of a defense. Those matters are for the trier of fact alone.

   (Pub. L. 93-595, § 1, Jan. 2, 1975, 88 Stat. 1937; Pub. L. 98-473, title II, § 406, Oct. 12, 1984, 98 Stat. 2067; Apr. 26, 2011, eff. Dec. 1, 2011.)

RESTYLED RULE 704 — ADVISORY COMMITTEE'S NOTE

The language of Rule 704 has been amended as part of the general restyling of the Evidence Rules to make them more easily understood and to make style and terminology consistent throughout the rules. These changes are intended to be stylistic only. There is no intent to change any result in any ruling on evidence admissibility.

The Committee deleted all reference to an "inference" on the grounds that the deletion made the Rule flow better and easier to read, and because any "inference" is covered by the broader term "opinion." Courts have not made substantive decisions on the basis of any distinction between an opinion and an inference. No change in current practice is intended.

ADVISORY COMMITTEE'S NOTE
56 F.R.D. 183, 284 (1973)

Subdivision (a). The basic approach to opinions, lay and expert, in these rules is to admit them when helpful to the trier of fact. In order to render this approach fully effective and to allay any doubt on the subject, the so-called "ultimate issue" rule is specifically abolished by the instant rule.

The older cases often contained strictures against allowing witnesses to express opinions upon ultimate issues, as a particular aspect of the rule against opinions. The rule was unduly restrictive, difficult of application, and generally served only to deprive the trier of fact of useful information. 7 Wigmore § 1920, 1921; McCormick § 12. The basis usually assigned for the rule, to prevent the witness from "usurping the province of the jury," is aptly characterized as "empty rhetoric." 7 Wigmore § 1920, p.17. Efforts to meet the felt needs of particular situations led to odd verbal circumlocutions which were said not to violate the rule. Thus a witness could express his estimate of the criminal responsibility of an accused in terms of sanity or insanity, but not in terms of ability to tell right from wrong or other more modern standard. And in cases of medical causation, witnesses were sometimes required to couch their opinions in cautious phrases of "might or could," rather than "did," though the result was to deprive many opinions of the positiveness to which they were entitled, accompanied by the hazard of a ruling of insufficiency to support a verdict. In other instances the rule was simply disregarded, and, as concessions to need, opinions were allowed upon such matters as intoxication, speed, handwriting, and value, although more precise coincidence with an ultimate issue would scarcely be possible.

Many modern decisions illustrate the trend to abandon the rule completely. People v. Wilson, 25 Cal. 2d 341, 153 P.2d 720 (1944), whether abortion necessary to save life of patient; Clifford-Jacobs Forging Co. v. Industrial Comm., 19 Ill. 2d 236, 166 N.E.2d 582 (1960), medical causation; Dowling v. L. H. Shattuck, Inc., 91 N.H. 234, 17 A.2d 529 (1941), proper method of shoring ditch; Schweiger v. Solbeck, 191 Or. 454, 230 P.2d 195 (1951), cause of landslide. In each instance the opinion was allowed.

The abolition of the ultimate issue rule does not lower the bars so as to admit all opinions. Under Rules 701 and 702, opinions must be helpful to the trier of fact, and Rule 403 provides for exclusion of evidence which wastes time. These provisions afford ample assurances against the admission of opinions which would merely tell the jury what result to reach, somewhat in the manner of the oath-helpers of an earlier day. They also stand ready to exclude opinions phrased in terms of inadequately explored legal criteria. Thus the question, "Did T have capacity to make a will?" would be excluded, while the question, "Did T have sufficient mental capacity to know the nature and extent of his property and the natural objects of his bounty and to formulate a rational scheme of distribution?" would be allowed. McCormick § 12.

For similar provisions *see* Uniform Rule 56(4); California Evidence Code § 805; Kansas Code of Civil Procedures § 60-456(d); New Jersey Evidence Rule 56(3).

[NOTE: Congress added subdivision (b) to Rule 704 in response to concerns about the "battle of experts" in criminal cases over the question of the required mental state of the defendant.]

Rule 705.   Disclosing the Facts or Data Underlying an Expert's Opinion

Unless the court orders otherwise, an expert may state an opinion — and give the reasons for it — without first testifying to the underlying facts or data. But the expert may be required to disclose those facts or data on cross-examination.

(Pub. L. 93-595, § 1, Jan. 2, 1975, 88 Stat. 1938; Mar. 2, 1987, eff. Oct. 1, 1987; Apr. 22, 1993, eff. Dec. 1, 1993; Apr. 26, 2011, eff. Dec. 1, 2011.)

RESTYLED RULE 705 — ADVISORY COMMITTEE'S NOTE

The language of Rule 705 has been amended as part of the general restyling of the Evidence Rules to make them more easily understood and to make style and terminology consistent throughout the rules. These changes are intended to be stylistic only. There is no intent to change any result in any ruling on evidence admissibility.

The Committee deleted all reference to an "inference" on the grounds that the deletion made the Rule flow better and easier to read, and because any "inference" is covered by the broader term "opinion." Courts have not made substantive decisions on the basis of any distinction between an opinion and an inference. No change in current practice is intended.

ADVISORY COMMITTEE'S NOTE
56 F.R.D. 183, 285 (1973)

The hypothetical question has been the target of a great deal of criticism as encouraging partisan bias, affording an opportunity for summing up in the middle of the case, and as complex and time consuming. Ladd, Expert Testimony, 5 Vand. L. Rev. 414, 426-427 (1952). While the rule allows counsel to make disclosure of the underlying facts or data as a preliminary to the giving of an expert opinion, if he chooses, the instances in which he is required to do so are reduced. This is true whether the expert bases his opinion on data furnished him at secondhand or observed by him at firsthand.

The elimination of the requirement of preliminary disclosure at the trial of underlying facts or data has a long background of support. In 1937 the Commissioners on Uniform State Laws incorporated a provision to this effect in the Model Expert Testimony Act, which furnished the basis for Uniform Rules 57 and 58. Rule 4515, N.Y. CPLR (McKinney 1963), provides:

Unless the court orders otherwise, questions calling for the opinion of an expert witness need not be hypothetical in form, and the witness may state his opinion and reasons without first specifying the data upon which it is based. Upon cross-examination, he may be required to specify the data. . . .

See also California Evidence Code § 802; Kansas Code of Civil Procedure § 60-456, 60-457; New Jersey Evidence Rules 57, 58.

If the objection is made that leaving it to the cross-examiner to bring out the supporting data is essentially unfair, the answer is that he is under no compulsion to bring out any facts or data except those unfavorable to the opinion. The answer assumes that the cross-examiner has the advance knowledge which is essential for effective cross-examination. This advance knowledge has been afforded, though imperfectly, by the traditional foundation requirement. Rule 26(b)(4) of the Rules of Civil Procedure, as revised, provides for substantial discovery in this area, obviating in large measure the obstacles which have been raised in some instances to discovery of findings, underlying data, and even the identity of the experts. Friedenthal, Discovery and Use of an Adverse Party's Expert Information, 14 Stan. L. Rev. 455 (1962).

These safeguards are reinforced by the discretionary power of the judge to require preliminary disclosure in any event.

ADVISORY COMMITTEE'S NOTE — 1987 AMENDMENT

The amendment is technical. No substantive change is intended.

ADVISORY COMMITTEE'S NOTE — 1993 AMENDMENT

This rule, which relates to the manner of presenting testimony at trial, is revised to avoid an arguable conflict with revised Rules 26(a)(2)(B) and 26(e)(1) of the Federal Rules of Civil Procedure or with revised Rule 16 of the Federal Rules of Criminal Procedure, which require disclosure in advance of trial of the basis and reasons for an expert's opinions.

If a serious question is raised under Rule 702 or 703 as to the admissibility of expert testimony, disclosure of the underlying facts or data on which opinions are based may, of course, be needed by the court before deciding whether, and to what extent, the person should be allowed to testify. This rule does not preclude such an inquiry.

Rule 706.   Court-Appointed Expert Witnesses

(a) **Appointment Process.** On a party's motion or on its own, the court may order the parties to show cause why expert witnesses should not be appointed and may ask the parties to submit nominations. The court may appoint any expert witness that the parties agree on and any of its own choosing. But the court may only appoint someone who consents to act.

(b) **Expert's Role.** The court must inform the expert of the expert's duties. The court may do so in writing and have a copy filed with the clerk or may do so orally at a conference in which the parties have an opportunity to participate. The expert:

(1) must advise the parties of any findings the expert makes;

(2) may be deposed by any party;

(3) may be called to testify by the court or any party; and

(4) may be cross-examined by any party, including the party that called the expert.

> **(c) Compensation.** The expert is entitled to a reasonable compensation, as set by the court. The compensation is payable as follows:
>
> **(1)** in a criminal case or in a civil case involving just compensation under the Fifth Amendment, from any funds that are provided by law; and
>
> **(2)** in any other civil case, by the parties in the proportion and at the time that the court directs — and the compensation is then charged like other costs.
>
> **(d) Disclosing the Appointment to the Jury.** The court may authorize disclosure to the jury that the court appointed the expert.
>
> **(e) Parties' Choice of Their Own Experts.** This rule does not limit a party in calling its own experts.
>
> (Pub. L. 93-595, § 1, Jan. 2, 1975, 88 Stat. 1938; Mar. 2, 1987, eff. Oct. 1, 1987; Apr. 26, 2011, eff. Dec. 1, 2011.)

RESTYLED RULE 706 — ADVISORY COMMITTEE'S NOTE

The language of Rule 706 has been amended as part of the restyling of the Evidence Rules to make them more easily understood and to make style and terminology consistent throughout the rules. These changes are intended to be stylistic only. There is no intent to change any result in any ruling on evidence admissibility.

ADVISORY COMMITTEE'S NOTE
56 F.R.D. 183, 286 (1973)

The practice of shopping for experts, the venality of some experts, and the reluctance of many reputable experts to involve themselves in litigation, have been matters of deep concern. Though the contention is made that court appointed experts acquire an aura of infallibility to which they are not entitled, Levy, Impartial Medical Testimony — Revisited, 34 Temple L.Q. 416 (1961), the trend is increasingly to provide for their use. While experience indicates that actual appointment is a relatively infrequent occurrence, the assumption may be made that the availability of the procedure in itself decreases the need for resorting to it. The ever-present possibility that the judge may appoint an expert in a given case must inevitably exert a sobering effect on the expert witness of a party and upon the person utilizing his services.

The inherent power of a trial judge to appoint an expert of his own choosing is virtually unquestioned. Scott v. Spanjer Bros., Inc., 298 F.2d 928 (2d Cir. 1962); Danville Tobacco Assn. v. Bryant-Buckner Associates, Inc., 333 F.2d 202 (4th Cir. 1964); Sink, The Unused Power of a Federal Judge to Call His Own Expert Witnesses, 29 S. Cal. L. Rev. 195 (1956); 2 Wigmore § 563, 9 *Id.* § 2484; Annot., 95 A.L.R.2d 383. Hence the problem becomes largely one of detail.

The New York plan is well known and is described in Report by Special Committee of the Association of the Bar of the City of New York: Impartial Medical Testimony (1956).

On recommendation of the Section of Judicial Administration, local adoption of an impartial medical plan was endorsed by the American Bar Association. 82 A.B.A. Rep. 184-185 (1957). Descriptions and analyses of plans in effect in various parts of the country are found in Van Dusen, A United States District Judge's View of the Impartial

Medical Expert System, 322 F.R.D. 498 (1963); Wick and Kightlinger, Impartial Medical Testimony Under the Federal Civil Rules: A Tale of Three Doctors, 34 Ins. Counsel J. 115 (1967); and numerous articles collected in Klein, Judicial Administration and the Legal Profession 393 (1963). Statutes and rules include California Evidence Code § 730-733; Illinois Supreme Court Rule 215(d), Ill. Rev. Stat. 1969, c. 110A, § 215(d); Burns Indiana Stats. 1956, § 9-1702; Wisconsin Stats. Annot. 1958, § 957.27.

In the federal practice, a comprehensive scheme for court appointed experts was initiated with the adoption of Rule 28 of the Federal Rules of Criminal Procedure in 1946. The Judicial Conference of the United States in 1953 considered court appointed experts in civil cases, but only with respect to whether they should be compensated from public funds, a proposal which was rejected. Report of the Judicial Conference of the United States 23 (1953). The present rule expands the practice to include civil cases.

Subdivision (a) is based on Rule 28 of the Federal Rules of Criminal Procedure, with a few changes, mainly in the interest of clarity. Language has been added to provide specifically for the appointment either on motion of a party or on the judge's own motion. A provision subjecting the court appointed expert to deposition procedures has been incorporated. The rule has been revised to make definite the right of any party, including the party calling him, to cross-examine.

Subdivision (b) combines the present provision for compensation in criminal cases with what seems to be a fair and feasible handling of civil cases, originally found in the Model Act and carried from there into Uniform Rule 60. *See also* California Evidence Code § 730-731. The special provision for Fifth Amendment compensation cases is designed to guard against reducing constitutionally guaranteed just compensation by requiring the recipient to pay costs. *See* Rule 71A(*l*) of the Rules of Civil Procedure.

Subdivision (c) seems to be essential if the use of court appointed experts is to be fully effective. Uniform Rule 61 so provides.

Subdivision (d) is in essence the last sentence of Rule 28(a) of the Federal Rules of Criminal Procedure.

ADVISORY COMMITTEE'S NOTE — 1987 AMENDMENT

The amendments are technical. No substantive change is intended.

ARTICLE VIII.   HEARSAY

ADVISORY COMMITTEE'S INTRODUCTORY NOTE TO ARTICLE VIII

Introductory Note: The Hearsay Problem

The factors to be considered in evaluating the testimony of a witness are perception, memory, and narration. Morgan, Hearsay Dangers and the Application of the Hearsay Concept, 62 Harv. L. Rev. 177 (1948), Selected Writings on Evidence and Trial 764, 765 (Fryer ed. 1957); Shientag, Cross-Examination — A Judge's Viewpoint, 3 Record 12 (1948); Strahorn, A Reconsideration of the Hearsay Rule and Admissions, 85 U. Pa. L. Rev. 484, 485 (1937), Selected Writings, *supra*, 756, 757; Weinstein, Probative Force of Hearsay, 46 Iowa L. Rev. 331 (1961). Sometimes a fourth is added, sincerity, but in fact it seems merely to be an aspect of the three already mentioned.

In order to encourage the witness to do his best with respect to each of these factors, and to expose any inaccuracies which may enter in, the Anglo-American tradition has evolved three conditions under which witnesses will ideally be required to testify: (1)

under oath, (2) in the personal presence of the trier of fact, (3) subject to cross-examination.

(1) Standard procedure calls for the swearing of witnesses. While the practice is perhaps less effective than in an earlier time, no disposition to relax the requirement is apparent, other than to allow affirmation by persons with scruples against taking oaths.

(2) The demeanor of the witness traditionally has been believed to furnish trier and opponent with valuable clues. Universal Camera Corp. v. N.L.R.B., 340 U.S. 474, 495-496, 71 S. Ct. 456, 95 L. Ed. 456 (1951); Sahm, Demeanor Evidence: Elusive and Intangible Imponderables, 47 A.B.A. J. 580 (1961), quoting numerous authorities. The witness himself will probably be impressed with the solemnity of the occasion and the possibility of public disgrace. Willingness to falsify may reasonably become more difficult in the presence of the person against whom directed. Rules 26 and 43(a) of the Federal Rules of Criminal and Civil Procedure, respectively, include the general requirement that testimony be taken orally in open court. The Sixth Amendment right of confrontation is a manifestation of these beliefs and attitudes.

(3) Emphasis on the basis of the hearsay rule today tends to center upon the condition of cross-examination. All may not agree with Wigmore that cross-examination is "beyond doubt the greatest legal engine ever invented for the discovery of truth," but all will agree with his statement that it has become a "vital feature" of the Anglo-American system. 5 Wigmore § 1367, p.29. The belief, or perhaps hope, that cross-examination is effective in exposing imperfections of perception, memory, and narration is fundamental. Morgan, Foreword to Model Code of Evidence 37 (1942).

The logic of the preceding discussion might suggest that no testimony be received unless in full compliance with the three ideal conditions. No one advocates this position. Common sense tells that much evidence which is not given under the three conditions may be inherently superior to much that is. Moreover, when the choice is between evidence which is less than best and no evidence at all, only clear folly would dictate an across-the-board policy of doing without. The problem thus resolves itself into effecting a sensible accommodation between these considerations and the desirability of giving testimony under the ideal conditions.

The solution evolved by the common law has been a general rule excluding hearsay but subject to numerous exceptions under circumstances supposed to furnish guarantees of trustworthiness. Criticisms of this scheme are that it is bulky and complex, fails to screen good from bad hearsay realistically, and inhibits the growth of the law of evidence.

Since no one advocates excluding all hearsay, three possible solutions may be considered: (1) abolish the rule against hearsay and admit all hearsay; (2) admit hearsay possessing sufficient probative force, but with procedural safeguards; (3) revise the present system of class exceptions.

(1) Abolition of the hearsay rule would be the simplest solution. The effect would not be automatically to abolish the giving of testimony under ideal conditions. If the declarant were available, compliance with the ideal conditions would be optional with either party. Thus the proponent could call the declarant as a witness as a form of presentation more impressive than his hearsay statement. Or the opponent could call the declarant to be cross-examined upon his statement. This is the tenor of Uniform Rule 63(1), admitting the hearsay declaration of a person "who is present at the hearing and available for cross-examination." Compare the treatment of declarations of available declarants in Rule 801(d)(1) of the instant rules. If the declarant were unavailable, a rule of free admissibility would make no distinctions in terms of degrees of noncompliance with the ideal conditions and would exact no quid pro quo in the form of assurances of trustworthiness. Rule 503 of the Model Code did exactly that, providing for the admissibility of any hearsay declaration by an unavailable declarant, finding support in the Massachusetts act of 1898, enacted at the instance of Thayer, Mass. Gen. L. 1932, c. 233 § 65, and in the English act of 1938, St. 1938, c. 28, Evidence. Both are limited to civil cases. The draftsmen of the Uniform Rules chose a less advanced and more conventional

position. Comment, Uniform Rule 63. The present Advisory Committee has been unconvinced of the wisdom of abandoning the traditional requirement of some particular assurance of credibility as a condition precedent to admitting the hearsay declaration of an unavailable declarant.

In criminal cases, the Sixth Amendment requirement of confrontation would no doubt move into a large part of the area presently occupied by the hearsay rule in the event of the abolition of the latter. The resultant split between civil and criminal evidence is regarded as an undesirable development.

(2) Abandonment of the system of class exceptions in favor of individual treatment in the setting of the particular case, accompanied by procedural safeguards, has been impressively advocated. Weinstein, The Probative Force of Hearsay, 46 Iowa L. Rev. 331 (1961). Admissibility would be determined by weighing the probative force of the evidence against the possibility of prejudice, waste of time, and the availability of more satisfactory evidence. The bases of the traditional hearsay exceptions would be helpful in assessing probative force. Ladd, The Relationship of the Principles of Exclusionary Rules of Evidence to the Problem of Proof, 18 Minn. L. Rev. 506 (1934). Procedural safeguards would consist of notice of intention to use hearsay, free comment by the judge on the weight of the evidence, and a greater measure of authority in both trial and appellate judges to deal with evidence on the basis of weight. The Advisory Committee has rejected this approach to hearsay as involving too great a measure of judicial discretion, minimizing the predictability of rulings, enhancing the difficulties of preparation for trial, adding a further element to the already over-complicated congeries of pre-trial procedures, and requiring substantially different rules for civil and criminal cases. The only way in which the probative force of hearsay differs from the probative force of other testimony is in the absence of oath, demeanor, and cross-examination as aids in determining credibility. For a judge to exclude evidence because he does not believe it has been described as "altogether atypical, extraordinary. . . ." Chadbourn, Bentham and the Hearsay Rule—A Benthamic View of Rule 63(4)(c) of the Uniform Rules of Evidence, 75 Harv. L. Rev. 932, 947 (1962).

(3) The approach to hearsay in these rules is that of the common law, i.e., a general rule excluding hearsay, with exceptions under which evidence is not required to be excluded even though hearsay. The traditional hearsay exceptions are drawn upon for the exceptions, collected under two rules, one dealing with situations where availability of the declarant is regarded as immaterial and the other with those where unavailability is made a condition to the admission of the hearsay statement. Each of the two rules concludes with a provision for hearsay statements not within one of the specified exceptions "but having comparable circumstantial guarantees of trustworthiness." Rules 803(24) and 804(b)(6). This plan is submitted as calculated to encourage growth and development in this area of the law, while conserving the values and experience of the past as a guide to the future.

Confrontation and Due Process

Until very recently, decisions invoking the confrontation clause of the Sixth Amendment were surprisingly few, a fact probably explainable by the former inapplicability of the clause to the states and by the hearsay rule's occupancy of much the same ground. The pattern which emerges from the earlier cases invoking the clause is substantially that of the hearsay rule, applied to criminal cases: an accused is entitled to have the witnesses against him testify under oath, in the presence of himself and trier, subject to cross-examination; yet considerations of public policy and necessity require the recognition of such exceptions as dying declarations and former testimony of unavailable witnesses. Mattox v. United States, 156 U.S. 237, 15 S. Ct. 337, 39 L. Ed. 409 (1895); Motes v. United States, 178 U.S. 458, 20 S. Ct. 993, 44 L. Ed. 1150 (1900); Delaney v. United States, 263 U.S. 586, 44 S. Ct. 206, 68 L. Ed. 462 (1924). Beginning with Snyder v. Massachusetts, 291

U.S. 97, 54 S. Ct. 330, 78 L. Ed. 674 (1934), the Court began to speak of confrontation as an aspect of procedural due process, thus extending its applicability to state cases and to federal cases other than criminal. The language of *Snyder* was that of an elastic concept of hearsay. The deportation case of Bridges v. Wixon, 326 U.S. 135, 65 S. Ct. 1443, 89 L. Ed. 2103 (1945), may be read broadly as imposing a strictly construed right of confrontation in all kinds of cases or narrowly as the product of a failure of the Immigration and Naturalization Service to follow its own rules. In re Oliver, 333 U.S. 257, 68 S. Ct. 499, 92 L. Ed. 682 (1948), ruled that cross-examination was essential to due process in a state contempt proceeding, but in United States v. Nugent, 346 U.S. 1, 73 S. Ct. 991, 97 L. Ed. 1417 (1953), the court held that it was not an essential aspect of a "hearing" for a conscientious objector under the Selective Service Act. Stein v. New York, 346 U.S. 156, 196, 73 S. Ct. 1077, 97 L. Ed. 1522 (1953), disclaimed any purpose to read the hearsay rule into the Fourteenth Amendment, but in Greene v. McElroy, 360 U.S. 474, 79 S. Ct. 1400, 3 L. Ed. 2d 1377 (1959), revocation of security clearance without confrontation and cross-examination was held unauthorized, and a similar result was reached in Willner v. Committee on Character, 373 U.S. 96, 83 S. Ct. 1175, 10 L. Ed. 2d 224 (1963). Ascertaining the constitutional dimensions of the confrontation-hearsay aggregate against the background of these cases is a matter of some difficulty, yet the general pattern is at least not inconsistent with that of the hearsay rule.

In 1965 the confrontation clause was held applicable to the states. Pointer v. Texas, 380 U.S. 400, 85 S. Ct. 1065, 13 L. Ed. 2d 923 (1965). Prosecution use of former testimony given at a preliminary hearing where petitioner was not represented by counsel was a violation of the clause. The same result would have followed under conventional hearsay doctrine read in the light of a constitutional right to counsel, and nothing in the opinion suggests any difference in essential outline between the hearsay rule and the right of confrontation. In the companion case of Douglas v. Alabama, 380 U.S. 415, 85 S. Ct. 1074, 13 L. Ed. 2d 934 (1965), however, the result reached by applying the confrontation clause is one reached less readily via the hearsay rule. A confession implicating petitioner was put before the jury by reading it to the witness in portions and asking if he made that statement. The witness refused to answer on grounds of self-incrimination. The result, said the Court, was to deny cross-examination, and hence confrontation. True, it could broadly be said that the confession was a hearsay statement which for all practical purposes was put in evidence. Yet a more easily accepted explanation of the opinion is that its real thrust was in the direction of curbing undesirable prosecutorial behavior, rather than merely applying rules of exclusion, and that the confrontation clause was the means selected to achieve this end. Comparable facts and a like result appeared in Brookhart v. Janis, 384 U.S. 1, 86 S. Ct. 1245, 16 L. Ed. 2d 314 (1966).

The pattern suggested in *Douglas* was developed further and more distinctly in a pair of cases at the end of the 1966 term. United States v. Wade, 388 U.S. 218, 87 S. Ct. 1926, 18 L. Ed. 2d 1149 (1967), and Gilbert v. California, 388 U.S. 263, 87 S. Ct. 1951, 18 L. Ed. 2d 1178 (1967), hinged upon practices followed in identifying accused persons before trial. This pretrial identification was said to be so decisive an aspect of the case that accused was entitled to have counsel present; a pretrial identification made in the absence of counsel was not itself receivable in evidence and, in addition, might fatally infect a courtroom identification. The presence of counsel at the earlier identification was described as a necessary prerequisite for "a meaningful confrontation at trial." United States v. Wade, *supra*, 388 U.S. at p.236, 87 S. Ct. at p.1937. *Wade* involved no evidence of the fact of a prior identification and hence was not susceptible of being decided on hearsay grounds. In *Gilbert*, witnesses did testify to an earlier identification, readily classifiable as hearsay under a fairly strict view of what constitutes hearsay. The Court, however, carefully avoided basing the decision on the hearsay ground, choosing confrontation instead. 388 U.S. 263, 272, n.3, 87 S. Ct. 1951. *See also* Parker v. Gladden, 385 U.S. 363, 87 S. Ct. 468, 17 L. Ed. 2d 420 (1966), holding that the right of confrontation was violated when the bailiff made prejudicial statements to jurors, and Note, 75 Yale L.J. 1434 (1966).

Under the earlier cases, the confrontation clause may have been little more than a constitutional embodiment of the hearsay rule, even including traditional exceptions but with some room for expanding them along similar lines. But under the recent cases the impact of the clause clearly extends beyond the confines of the hearsay rule. These considerations have led the Advisory Committee to conclude that a hearsay rule can function usefully as an adjunct to the confrontation right in constitutional areas and independently in nonconstitutional areas. In recognition of the separateness of the confrontation clause and the hearsay rule, and to avoid inviting collisions between them or between the hearsay rule and other exclusionary principles, the exceptions set forth in Rules 803 and 804 are stated in terms of exemption from the general exclusionary mandate of the hearsay rule, rather than in positive terms of admissibility. *See* Uniform Rule 63(1) to (31) and California Evidence Code § 1200-1340.

Rule 801. Definitions That Apply to This Article; Exclusions from Hearsay

(a) Statement. "Statement" means a person's oral assertion, written assertion, or nonverbal conduct, if the person intended it as an assertion.

(b) Declarant. "Declarant" means the person who made the statement.

(c) Hearsay. "Hearsay" means a statement that:

(1) the declarant does not make while testifying at the current trial or hearing; and

(2) a party offers in evidence to prove the truth of the matter asserted in the statement.

(d) Statements That Are Not Hearsay. A statement that meets the following conditions is not hearsay:

(1) *A Declarant-Witness's Prior Statement.* The declarant testifies and is subject to cross-examination about a prior statement, and the statement:

(A) is inconsistent with the declarant's testimony and was given under penalty of perjury at a trial, hearing, or other proceeding or in a deposition;

(B) is consistent with the declarant's testimony and is offered to rebut an express or implied charge that the declarant recently fabricated it or acted from a recent improper influence or motive in so testifying; or

(C) identifies a person as someone the declarant perceived earlier.

(2) *An Opposing Party's Statement.* The statement is offered against an opposing party and:

(A) was made by the party in an individual or representative capacity;

(B) is one the party manifested that it adopted or believed to be true;

(C) was made by a person whom the party authorized to make a statement on the subject;

(D) was made by the party's agent or employee on a matter within the scope of that relationship and while it existed; or

(E) was made by the party's coconspirator during and in furtherance of the conspiracy.

> The statement must be considered but does not by itself establish the declarant's authority under (C); the existence or scope of the relationship under (D); or the existence of the conspiracy or participation in it under (E).
>
>
> (Pub. L. 93-595, § 1, Jan. 2, 1975, 88 Stat. 1938; Pub. L. 94-113, § 1, Oct. 16, 1975, 89 Stat. 576; Mar. 2, 1987, eff. Oct. 1, 1987; Apr. 11, 1997, eff. Dec. 1, 1997; Apr. 26, 2011, eff. Dec. 1, 2011.)

RESTYLED RULE 801 — ADVISORY COMMITTEE'S NOTE

The language of Rule 801 has been amended as part of the general restyling of the Evidence Rules to make them more easily understood and to make style and terminology consistent throughout the rules. These changes are intended to be stylistic only. There is no intent to change any result in any ruling on evidence admissibility.

Statements falling under the hearsay exclusion provided by Rule 801(d)(2) are no longer referred to as "admissions" in the title to the subdivision. The term "admissions" is confusing because not all statements covered by the exclusion are admissions in the colloquial sense — a statement can be within the exclusion even if it "admitted" nothing and was not against the party's interest when made. The term "admissions" also raises confusion in comparison with the Rule 804(b)(3) exception for declarations against interest. No change in application of the exclusion is intended.

ADVISORY COMMITTEE'S NOTE
56 F.R.D. 183, 293 (1973)

Subdivision (a). The definition of "statement" assumes importance because the term is used in the definition of hearsay in subdivision (c). The effect of the definition of "statement" is to exclude from the operation of the hearsay rule all evidence of conduct, verbal or nonverbal, not intended as an assertion. The key to the definition is that nothing is an assertion unless intended to be one.

It can scarcely be doubted that an assertion made in words is intended by the declarant to be an assertion. Hence verbal assertions readily fall into the category of "statement." Whether nonverbal conduct should be regarded as a statement for purposes of defining hearsay requires further consideration. Some nonverbal conduct, such as the act of pointing to identify a suspect in a lineup, is clearly the equivalent of words, assertive in nature, and to be regarded as a statement. Other nonverbal conduct, however, may be offered as evidence that the person acted as he did because of his belief in the existence of the condition sought to be proved, from which belief the existence of the condition may be inferred. This sequence is, arguably, in effect an assertion of the existence of the condition and hence properly includable within the hearsay concept. *See* Morgan, Hearsay Dangers and the Application of the Hearsay Concept, 62 Harv. L. Rev. 177, 214, 217 (1948), and the elaboration in Finman, Implied Assertions as Hearsay: Some Criticisms of the Uniform Rules of Evidence, 14 Stan. L. Rev. 682 (1962). Admittedly evidence of this character is untested with respect to the perception, memory, and narration (or their equivalents) of the actor, but the Advisory Committee is of the view that these dangers are minimal in the absence of an intent to assert and do not justify the loss of the evidence on hearsay grounds. No class of evidence is free of the possibility of fabrication, but the likelihood is less with nonverbal than with assertive verbal conduct. The situations giving rise to the nonverbal conduct are such as virtually to eliminate questions of sincerity. Motivation, the nature of the conduct, and the presence or absence of reliance will bear heavily upon the weight to be given the evidence. Falknor, The "Hear-Say" Rule as a "See-Do" Rule: Evidence of Conduct, 33 Rocky Mt. L. Rev. 133 (1961). Similar considerations govern nonassertive verbal conduct and verbal conduct which is assertive but offered as a basis for inferring something other than the matter asserted, also excluded from the definition of hearsay by the language of subdivision (c).

When evidence of conduct is offered on the theory that it is not a statement, and hence not hearsay, a preliminary determination will be required to determine whether an assertion is intended. The rule is so worded as to place the burden upon the party claiming that the intention existed; ambiguous and doubtful cases will be resolved against him and in favor of admissibility. The determination involves no greater difficulty than many other preliminary questions of fact. Maguire, The Hearsay System: Around and Through the Thicket, 14 Vand. L. Rev. 741, 765-767 (1961).

For similar approaches, *see* Uniform Rule 62(1); California Evidence Code § 225, 1200; Kansas Code of Civil Procedure § 60-459(a); New Jersey Evidence Rule 62(1).

Subdivision (c). The definition follows along familiar lines in including only statements offered to prove the truth of the matter asserted. McCormick § 225; 5 Wigmore § 1361, 6 *id.* § 1766. If the significance of an offered statement lies solely in the fact that it was made, no issue is raised as to the truth of anything asserted, and the statement is not hearsay. Emich Motors Corp. v. General Motors Corp., 181 F.2d 70 (7th Cir. 1950), *rev'd on other grounds*, 340 U.S. 558, 71 S. Ct. 408, 95 L. Ed. 534, letters of complaint from customers offered as a reason for cancellation of dealer's franchise, to rebut contention that franchise was revoked for refusal to finance sales through affiliated finance company. The effect is to exclude from hearsay the entire category of "verbal acts" and "verbal parts of an act," in which the statement itself affects the legal rights of the parties or is a circumstance bearing on conduct affecting their rights.

The definition of hearsay must, of course, be read with reference to the definition of statement set forth in subdivision (a).

Testimony given by a witness in the course of court proceedings is excluded since there is compliance with all the ideal conditions for testifying.

Subdivision (d). Several types of statements which would otherwise literally fall within the definition are expressly excluded from it:

(1) *Prior statement by witness.* Considerable controversy has attended the question whether a prior out-of-court statement by a person now available for cross-examination concerning it, under oath and in the presence of the trier of fact, should be classed as hearsay. If the witness admits on the stand that he made the statement and that it was true, he adopts the statement and there is no hearsay problem. The hearsay problem arises when the witness on the stand denies having made the statement or admits having made it but denies its truth. The argument in favor of treating these latter statements as hearsay is based upon the ground that the conditions of oath, cross-examination, and demeanor observation did not prevail at the time the statement was made and cannot adequately be supplied by the later examination. The logic of the situation is troublesome. So far as concerns the oath, its mere presence has never been regarded as sufficient to remove a statement from the hearsay category, and it receives much less emphasis than cross-examination as a truth-compelling device. While strong expressions are found to the effect that no conviction can be had or important right taken away on the basis of statements not made under fear of prosecution for perjury, Bridges v. Wixon, 326 U.S. 135, 65 S. Ct. 1443, 89 L. Ed. 2103 (1945), the fact is that, of the many common law exceptions to the hearsay rule, only that for reported testimony has required the statement to have been made under oath. Nor is it satisfactorily explained why cross-examination cannot be conducted subsequently with success. The decisions contending most vigorously for its inadequacy in fact demonstrate quite thorough exploration of the weaknesses and doubts attending the earlier statement. State v. Saporen, 205 Minn. 358, 285 N.W. 898 (1939); Ruhala v. Roby, 379 Mich. 102, 150 N.W.2d 146 (1967); People v. Johnson, 68 Cal. 2d 646, 68 Cal. Rptr. 599, 441 P.2d 111 (1968). In respect to demeanor,

as Judge Learned Hand observed in Di Carlo v. United States, 6 F.2d 364 (2d Cir. 1925), when the jury decides that the truth is not what the witness says now, but what he said before, they are still deciding from what they see and hear in court. The bulk of the case law nevertheless has been against allowing prior statements of witnesses to be used generally as substantive evidence. Most of the writers and Uniform Rule 63(1) have taken the opposite position.

The position taken by the Advisory Committee in formulating this part of the rule is founded upon an unwillingness to countenance the general use of prior prepared statements as substantive evidence, but with a recognition that particular circumstances call for a contrary result. The judgment is one more of experience than of logic. The rule requires in each instance, as a general safeguard, that the declarant actually testify as a witness, and it then enumerates three situations in which the statement is excepted from the category of hearsay. Compare Uniform Rule 63(1) which allows any out-of-court statement of a declarant who is present at the trial and available for cross-examination.

Subdivision (d)(1)(A). Prior inconsistent statements traditionally have been admissible to impeach but not as substantive evidence. Under the rule they are substantive evidence. As has been said by the California Law Revision Commission with respect to a similar provision:

> "Section 1235 admits inconsistent statements of witnesses because the dangers against which the hearsay rule is designed to protect are largely nonexistent. The declarant is in court and may be examined and cross-examined in regard to his statements and their subject matter. In many cases, the inconsistent statement is more likely to be true than the testimony of the witness at the trial because it was made nearer in time to the matter to which it relates and is less likely to be influenced by the controversy that gave rise to the litigation. The trier of fact has the declarant before it and can observe his demeanor and the nature of his testimony as he denies or tries to explain away the inconsistency. Hence, it is in as good a position to determine the truth or falsity of the prior statement as it is to determine the truth or falsity of the inconsistent testimony given in court. Moreover, Section 1235 will provide a party with desirable protection against the 'turncoat' witness who changes his story on the stand and deprives the party calling him of evidence essential to his case." Comment, California Evidence Code § 1235.

See also McCormick § 39. The Advisory Committee finds these views more convincing than those expressed in People v. Johnson, 68 Cal. 2d 646, 68 Cal. Rptr. 599, 441 P.2d 111 (1968). The constitutionality of the Advisory Committee's view was upheld in California v. Green, 399 U.S. 149, 90 S. Ct. 1930, 26 L. Ed. 2d 489 (1970). Moreover, the requirement that the statement be inconsistent with the testimony given assures a thorough exploration of both versions while the witness is on the stand and bars any general and indiscriminate use of previously prepared statements.

Subdivision (d)(1)(B). Prior consistent statements traditionally have been admissible to rebut charges of recent fabrication or improper influence or motive but not as substantive evidence. Under the rule they are substantive evidence. The prior statement is consistent with the testimony given on the stand, and, if the opposite party wishes to open the door for its admission in evidence, no sound reason is apparent why it should not be received generally.

Subdivision (d)(1)(C). The admission of evidence of identification finds substantial support, although it falls beyond a doubt in the category of prior out-of-court statements. Illustrative are People v. Gould, 54 Cal. 2d 621, 7 Cal. Rptr. 273, 354 P.2d 865 (1960); Judy v. State, 218 Md. 168, 146 A.2d 29 (1958); State v. Simmons, 63 Wash. 2d 17, 385 P.2d 389 (1963); California Evidence Code § 1238; New Jersey Evidence Rule 63(1)(c); N.Y. Code of Criminal Procedure § 393-b. Further cases are found in 4 Wigmore § 1130. The basis is the generally unsatisfactory and inconclusive nature of courtroom identifications as compared with those made at an earlier time under less suggestive conditions. The Supreme Court considered the admissibility of evidence of prior identification in Gilbert v. California, 388 U.S. 263, 87 S. Ct. 1951, 18 L. Ed. 2d 1178 (1967). Exclusion of lineup identification was held to be required because the accused did not then have the assistance of counsel. Significantly, the Court carefully refrained from placing its decision on the ground that testimony as to the making of a prior out-of-court identification ("That's the man") violated either the hearsay rule or the right of confrontation because not made under oath, subject to immediate cross-examination, in the presence of the trier. Instead the Court observed:

> "There is a split among the States concerning the admissibility of prior extrajudicial identifications, as independent evidence of identity, both by the witness and third parties present at the prior identification. *See* 71 ALR2d 449. It has been held that the prior identification is hearsay, and, when admitted through the testimony of the identifier, is merely a prior consistent statement. The recent trend, however, is to admit the prior identification under the exception that admits as substantive evidence a prior communication by a witness who is available for cross-examination at the trial. *See* 5 ALR2d Later Case Service 1225-1228. . . ." 388 U.S. at 272, n.3, 87 S. Ct. at 1956.

Subdivision (d)(2). Admissions by a party-opponent are excluded from the category of hearsay on the theory that their admissibility in evidence is the result of the adversary system rather than satisfaction of the conditions of the hearsay rule. Strahorn, A Reconsideration of the Hearsay Rule and Admissions, 85 U. Pa. L. Rev. 484, 564 (1937); Morgan, Basic Problems of Evidence 265 (1962); 4 Wigmore § 1048. No guarantee of trustworthiness is required in the case of an admission. The freedom which admissions have enjoyed from technical demands of searching for an assurance of trustworthiness in some against-interest circumstance, and from the restrictive influences of the opinion rule and the rule requiring firsthand knowledge, when taken with the apparently prevalent satisfaction with the results, calls for generous treatment of this avenue to admissibility.

The rule specifies five categories of statements for which the responsibility of a party is considered sufficient to justify reception in evidence against him:

(A) A party's own statement is the classic example of an admission. If he has a representative capacity and the statement is offered against him in that capacity, no inquiry whether he was acting in the representative capacity in making the statement is required; the statement need only be relevant to represent affairs. To the same effect in California Evidence Code § 1220. Compare Uniform Rule 63(7), requiring a statement to be made in a representative capacity to be admissible against a party in a representative capacity.

(B) Under established principles an admission may be made by adopting or acquiescing in the statement of another. While knowledge of contents would ordinarily be essential, this is not inevitably so: "X is a reliable person and knows what he is talking about." *See* McCormick § 246, p.527, n.15. Adoption or acquiescence may be manifested in any appropriate manner. When silence is relied upon, the theory is that the person would, under the circumstances, protest the statement made in his presence, if untrue. The decision in each case calls for an evaluation in terms of probable human behavior. In civil cases, the results have generally been satisfactory. In criminal cases, however, troublesome questions have been raised by decisions holding that failure to deny is an admission: the inference is a fairly weak one, to begin with; silence may be motivated by advice of counsel or realization that "anything you say may be used against you"; unusual opportunity is afforded to manufacture evidence; and encroachment upon the privilege against self-incrimination seems inescapably to be involved. However, recent decisions of the Supreme Court relating to custodial interrogation and the right to counsel appear to resolve these difficulties. Hence the rule contains no special provisions concerning failure to deny in criminal cases.

(C) No authority is required for the general proposition that a statement authorized by a party to be made should have the status of an admission by the party. However, the question arises whether only statements to third persons should be so regarded, to the exclusion of statements by the agent to the principal. The rule is phrased broadly so as to encompass both. While it may be argued that the agent authorized to make statements to his principal does not speak for him, Morgan, Basic Problems of Evidence 273 (1962), communication to an outsider has not generally been thought to be an essential characteristic of an admission. Thus a party's books or records are usable against him, without regard to any intent to disclose to third persons. 5 Wigmore § 1557. *See also* McCormick § 78, pp.159-161. In accord is New Jersey Evidence Rule 63(8)(a). *Cf.* Uniform Rule 63(8)(a) and California Evidence Code § 1222 which limit status as an admission in this regard to statements authorized by the party to be made "for" him, which is perhaps an ambiguous limitation to statements to third persons. Falknor, Vicarious Admissions and the Uniform Rules, 14 Vand. L. Rev. 855, 860-861 (1961).

(D) The tradition has been to test the admissibility of statements by agents, as admissions, by applying the usual test of agency. Was the admission made by the agent acting in the scope of his employment? Since few principals employ agents for the purpose of making damaging statements, the usual result was exclusion of the statement. Dissatisfaction with this loss of valuable and helpful evidence has been increasing. A substantial trend favors admitting statements related to a matter within the scope of the agency or employment. Grayson v. Williams, 256 F.2d 61 (10th Cir. 1958); Koninklijke Luchtvaart Maatschappij N.V. KLM Royal Dutch Airlines v. Tuller, 110 U.S. App. D.C. 282, 292 F.2d 775, 784 (1961); Martin v. Savage Truck Lines, Inc., 121 F. Supp. 417 (D.D.C. 1054), and numerous state court decisions collected in 4 Wigmore, 1964 Supp., pp.66-73, with comments by the editor that the statements should have been excluded as not within scope of agency. For the traditional view *see* Northern Oil Co. v. Socony Mobile Oil Co., 347 F.2d 81, 85 (2d Cir. 1965) and cases cited therein. Similar provisions are found in Uniform Rule 63(9)(a), Kansas Code of Civil Procedure § 60-460(i)(1), and New Jersey Evidence Rule 63(9)(a).

(E) The limitation upon the admissibility of statements of co-conspirators to those made "during the course and in furtherance of the conspiracy" is in the accepted pattern. While the broadened view of agency taken in item (iv) might suggest wider admissibility of statements of co-conspirators, the agency theory of conspiracy is at best a fiction and ought not to serve as a basis for admissibility beyond that already established. *See* Levie, Hearsay and Conspiracy, 52 Mich. L. Rev. 1159 (1954); Comment, 25 U. Chi. L. Rev. 530 (1958). The rule is consistent with the position of the Supreme Court in denying admissibility to statements made after the objectives of the conspiracy have either failed or been achieved. Krulewitch v. United States, 336 U.S. 440, 69 S. Ct. 716, 93 L. Ed. 790 (1949); Wong Sun v. United States, 371 U.S. 471, 490, 83 S. Ct. 407, 9 L. Ed. 2d 441 (1963). For similarly limited provisions *see* California Evidence Code § 1223 and New Jersey Rule 63(9)(b). *Cf.* Uniform Rule 63(9)(b).

ADVISORY COMMITTEE'S NOTE — 1987 AMENDMENT

The amendments are technical. No substantive change is intended.

ADVISORY COMMITTEE'S NOTE — 1997 AMENDMENT

Rule 801(d)(2) has been amended in order to respond to three issues raised by Bourjaily v. United States, 483 U.S. 171 (1987). First, the amendment codifies the holding in *Bourjaily* by stating expressly that a court shall consider the contents of a coconspirator's statement in determining "the existence of the conspiracy and the participation therein of the declarant and the party against whom the statement is offered." According to *Bourjaily*, Rule 104(a) requires these preliminary questions to be established by a preponderance of the evidence.

Second, the amendment resolves an issue on which the Court had reserved decision. It provides that the contents of the declarant's statement do not alone suffice to establish a conspiracy in which the declarant and the defendant participated. The court must consider in addition the circumstances surrounding the statement, such as the identity of the speaker, the context in which the statement was made, or evidence corroborating the contents of the statement in making its determination as to each preliminary question. This amendment is in accordance with existing practice. Every court of appeals that has resolved this issue requires some evidence in addition to the contents of the statement. *See, e.g.*, United States v. Beckham, 968 F.2d 47, 51 (D.C. Cir. 1992); United States v. Sepulveda, 15 F.3d 1161, 1181-82 (1st Cir. 1993), *cert. denied*, 114 S. Ct. 2714 (1994); United States v. Daly, 842 F.2d 1380, 1386 (2d Cir.), *cert. denied*, 488 U.S. 821 (1988); United States v. Clark, 18 F.3d 1337, 1341-42 (6th Cir.), *cert. denied*, 115 S. Ct. 152 (1994); United States v. Zambrana, 841 F.2d 1320, 1344-45 (7th Cir. 1988); United States v. Silverman, 861 F.2d 571, 577 (9th Cir. 1988); United States v. Gordon, 844 F.2d 1397, 1402 (9th Cir. 1988); United States v. Hernandez, 829 F.2d 988, 993 (10th Cir. 1987), *cert. denied*, 485 U.S. 1013 (1988); United States v. Byrom, 910 F.2d 725, 736 (11th Cir. 1990).

Third, the amendment extends the reasoning of *Bourjaily* to statements offered under subdivisions (C) and (D) of Rule 801(d)(2). In *Bourjaily*, the Court rejected treating foundational facts pursuant to the law of agency in favor of an evidentiary approach governed by Rule 104(a). The Advisory Committee believes it appropriate to treat analogously preliminary questions relating to the declarant's authority under subdivision (C), and the agency or employment relationship and scope thereof under subdivision (D).

Rule 802.   The Rule Against Hearsay

Hearsay is not admissible unless any of the following provides otherwise:

- a federal statute;
- these rules; or
- other rules prescribed by the Supreme Court.

(Pub. L. 93-595, § 1, Jan. 2, 1975, 88 Stat. 1939; Apr. 26, 2011, eff. Dec. 1, 2011.)

RESTLYED RULE 802 — ADVISORY COMMITTEE'S NOTE

The language of Rule 802 has been amended as part of the restyling of the Evidence Rules to make them more easily understood and to make style and terminology consistent throughout the rules. These changes are intended to be stylistic only. There is no intent to change any result in any ruling on evidence admissibility.

ADVISORY COMMITTEE'S NOTE
56 F.R.D. 183, 299 (1973)

The provision excepting from the operation of the rule hearsay which is made admissible by other rules adopted by the Supreme Court or by Act of Congress continues the admissibility thereunder of hearsay which would not qualify under these Evidence Rules. The following examples illustrate the working of the exception:

Federal Rules of Civil Procedure

Rule 4(g): proof of service by affidavit.
Rule 32: admissibility of depositions.
Rule 43(e): affidavits when motion based on facts not appearing of record.
Rule 56: affidavits in summary judgment proceedings.
Rule 65(b): showing by affidavit for temporary restraining order.

Federal Rules of Criminal Procedure

Rule 4(a): affidavits to show grounds for issuing warrants.
Rule 12(b)(4): affidavits to determine issues of fact in connection with motions.

Acts of Congress

10 U.S.C. § 7730: affidavits of unavailable witnesses in actions for damages caused by vessel in naval service, or towage or salvage of same, when taking of testimony or bringing of action delayed or stayed on security grounds.
29 U.S.C. § 161(4): affidavit as proof of service in NLRB proceedings.
38 U.S.C. § 5206: affidavit as proof of posting notice of sale of unclaimed property by Veterans Administration.

Rule 803.   Exceptions to the Rule Against Hearsay — Regardless of Whether the Declarant Is Available as a Witness

The following are not excluded by the rule against hearsay, regardless of whether the declarant is available as a witness:

(1) *Present Sense Impression.* A statement describing or explaining an event or condition, made while or immediately after the declarant perceived it.

(2) *Excited Utterance.* A statement relating to a startling event or condition, made while the declarant was under the stress of excitement that it caused.

(3) *Then-Existing Mental, Emotional, or Physical Condition.* A statement of the declarant's then-existing state of mind (such as motive, intent, or plan) or emotional, sensory, or physical condition (such as mental feeling, pain, or bodily health), but not including a statement of memory or belief to prove the fact remembered or believed unless it relates to the validity or terms of the declarant's will.

(4) *Statement Made for Medical Diagnosis or Treatment.* A statement that:

(continued)

(A) is made for — and is reasonably pertinent to — medical diagnosis or treatment; and

(B) describes medical history; past or present symptoms or sensations; their inception; or their general cause.

(5) *Recorded Recollection.* A record that:

(A) is on a matter the witness once knew about but now cannot recall well enough to testify fully and accurately;

(B) was made or adopted by the witness when the matter was fresh in the witness's memory; and

(C) accurately reflects the witness's knowledge.

If admitted, the record may be read into evidence but may be received as an exhibit only if offered by an adverse party.

(6) *Records of a Regularly Conducted Activity.* A record of an act, event, condition, opinion, or diagnosis if:

(A) the record was made at or near the time by — or from information transmitted by — someone with knowledge;

(B) the record was kept in the course of a regularly conducted activity of a business, organization, occupation, or calling, whether or not for profit;

(C) making the record was a regular practice of that activity;

(D) all these conditions are shown by the testimony of the custodian or another qualified witness, or by a certification that complies with Rule 902(11) or (12) or with a statute permitting certification; and

(E) neither the source of information nor the method or circumstances of preparation indicate a lack of trustworthiness.

(7) *Absence of a Record of a Regularly Conducted Activity.* Evidence that a matter is not included in a record described in paragraph (6) if:

(A) the evidence is admitted to prove that the matter did not occur or exist;

(B) a record was regularly kept for a matter of that kind; and

(C) neither the possible source of the information nor other circumstances indicate a lack of trustworthiness.

(8) *Public Records.* A record or statement of a public office if:

(A) it sets out

(i) the office's activities;

(ii) a matter observed while under a legal duty to report, but not including, in a criminal case, a matter observed by law-enforcement personnel; or

(iii) in a civil case or against the government in a criminal case, factual findings from a legally authorized investigation; and

(B) neither the source of information nor other circumstances indicate a lack of trustworthiness.

(9) *Public Records of Vital Statistics.* A record of a birth, death, or marriage, if reported to a public office in accordance with a legal duty.

(10) *Absence of a Public Record.* Testimony — or a certification under Rule 902 — that a diligent search failed to disclose a public record or statement if the testimony or certification is admitted to prove that:

(A) the record or statement does not exist; or

(B) a matter did not occur or exist, if a public office regularly kept a record for a matter of that kind.

(11) *Records of Religious Organizations Concerning Personal or Family History.* A statement of birth, legitimacy, ancestry, marriage, divorce, death, relationship by blood or marriage, or similar facts of personal or family history, contained in a regularly kept record of a religious organization.

(12) *Certificates of Marriage, Baptism, and Similar Ceremonies.* A statement of fact contained in a certificate:

(A) made by a person who is authorized by a religious organization or by law to perform the act certified;

(B) attesting that the person performed a marriage or similar ceremony or administered a sacrament; and

(C) purporting to have been issued at the time of the act or within a reasonable time after it.

(13) *Family Records.* A statement of fact about personal or family history contained in a family record, such as a Bible, genealogy, chart, engraving on a ring, inscription on a portrait, or engraving on an urn or burial marker.

(14) *Records of Documents That Affect an Interest in Property.* The record of a document that purports to establish or affect an interest in property if:

(A) the record is admitted to prove the content of the original recorded document, along with its signing and its delivery by each person who purports to have signed it;

(B) the record is kept in a public office; and

(C) a statute authorizes recording documents of that kind in that office.

(15) *Statements in Documents That Affect an Interest in Property.* A statement contained in a document that purports to establish or affect an interest in property if the matter stated was relevant to the document's purpose—unless later dealings with the property are inconsistent with the truth of the statement or the purport of the document.

(16) *Statements in Ancient Documents.* A statement in a document that is at least 20 years old and whose authenticity is established.

(17) *Market Reports and Similar Commercial Publications.* Market quotations, lists, directories, or other compilations that are generally relied on by the public or by persons in particular occupations.

(18) *Statements in Learned Treatises, Periodicals, or Pamphlets.* A statement contained in a treatise, periodical, or pamphlet if:

(A) the statement is called to the attention of an expert witness on cross-examination or relied on by the expert on direct examination; and

(B) the publication is established as a reliable authority by the expert's admission or testimony, by another expert's testimony, or by judicial notice.

(continued)

If admitted, the statement may be read into evidence but not received as an exhibit.

(19) *Reputation Concerning Personal or Family History.* A reputation among a person's family by blood, adoption, or marriage — or among a person's associates or in the community — concerning the person's birth, adoption, legitimacy, ancestry, marriage, divorce, death, relationship by blood, adoption, or marriage, or similar facts of personal or family history.

(20) *Reputation Concerning Boundaries or General History.* A reputation in a community — arising before the controversy — concerning boundaries of land in the community or customs that affect the land, or concerning general historical events important to that community, state, or nation.

(21) *Reputation Concerning Character.* A reputation among a person's associates or in the community concerning the person's character.

(22) *Judgment of a Previous Conviction.* Evidence of a final judgment of conviction if:

  (A) the judgment was entered after a trial or guilty plea, but not a nolo contendere plea;

  (B) the conviction was for a crime punishable by death or by imprisonment for more than a year;

  (C) the evidence is admitted to prove any fact essential to the judgment; and

  (D) when offered by the prosecutor in a criminal case for a purpose other than impeachment, the judgment was against the defendant.

The pendency of an appeal may be shown but does not affect admissibility.

(23) *Judgments Involving Personal, Family, or General History or a Boundary.* A judgment that is admitted to prove a matter of personal, family, or general history, or boundaries, if the matter:

  (A) was essential to the judgment; and

  (B) could be proved by evidence of reputation.

(24) [*Other Exceptions.*][Transferred to Rule 807]

(Pub. L. 93-595, § 1, Jan. 2, 1975, 88 Stat. 1939; Pub. L. 94-149, § 1(11), Dec. 12, 1975, 89 Stat. 805; Mar. 2, 1987, eff. Oct. 1, 1987; Apr. 11, 1997, eff. Dec. 1, 1997; Apr. 17, 2000, eff. Dec. 1, 2000; Apr. 26, 2011, eff. Dec. 1, 2011.)

RESTLYED RULE 803 — ADVISORY COMMITTEE'S NOTE

The language of Rule 803 has been amended as part of the restyling of the Evidence Rules to make them more easily understood and to make style and terminology consistent throughout the rules. These changes are intended to be stylistic only. There is no intent to change any result in any ruling on evidence admissibility.

ADVISORY COMMITTEE'S NOTE
56 F.R.D. 183, 303 (1973)

The exceptions are phrased in terms of nonapplication of the hearsay rule, rather than in positive terms of admissibility, in order to repel any implication that other possible grounds for exclusion are eliminated from consideration.

The present rule proceeds upon the theory that under appropriate circumstances a hearsay statement may possess circumstantial guarantees of trustworthiness sufficient to justify nonproduction of the declarant in person at the trial even though he may be available. The theory finds vast support in the many exceptions to the hearsay rule developed by the common law in which unavailability of the declarant is not a relevant factor. The present rule is a synthesis of them, with revision where modern developments and conditions are believed to make that course appropriate.

In a hearsay situation, the declarant is, of course, a witness, and neither this rule nor Rule 804 dispenses with the requirement of firsthand knowledge. It may appear from his statement or be inferable from circumstances. *See* Rule 602.

Exceptions (1) and (2). In considerable measure these two examples overlap, though based on somewhat different theories. The most significant practical difference will lie in the time lapse allowable between event and statement.

The underlying theory of Exception [paragraph] (1) is that substantial contemporaneity of event and statement negative the likelihood of deliberate or conscious misrepresentation. Moreover, if the witness is the declarant, he may be examined on the statement. If the witness is not the declarant, he may be examined as to the circumstances as an aid in evaluating the statement. Morgan, Basic Problems of Evidence 340-341 (1962).

The theory of Exception [paragraph] (2) is simply that circumstances may produce a condition of excitement which temporarily stills the capacity of reflection and produces utterances free of conscious fabrication. 6 Wigmore § 1747, p.135. Spontaneity is the key factor in each instance, though arrived at by somewhat different routes. Both are needed in order to avoid needless niggling.

While the theory of Exception [paragraph] (2) has been criticized on the ground that excitement impairs accuracy of observation as well as eliminating conscious fabrication, Hutchins and Slesinger, Some Observations on the Law of Evidence: Spontaneous Exclamations, 28 Colum. L. Rev. 432 (1928), it finds support in cases without number. *See* cases in 6 Wigmore § 1750; Annot., 53 A.L.R.2d 1245 (statements as to cause of or responsibility for motor vehicle accident); Annot., 4 A.L.R.3d 149 (accusatory statements by homicide victims). Since unexciting events are less likely to evoke comment, decisions involving Exception [paragraph] (1) are far less numerous. Illustrative are Tampa Elec. Co. v. Getrost, 151 Fla. 558, 10 So. 2d 83 (1942); Houston Oxygen Co. v. Davis, 139 Tex. 1, 161 S.W.2d 474 (1942); and cases cited in McCormick § 273, p.585, n.4.

With respect to the *time element*, Exception [paragraph] (1) recognizes that in many, if not most, instances precise contemporaneity is not possible, and hence a slight lapse is allowable. Under Exception [paragraph] (2) the standard of measurement is the duration of the state of excitement. "How long can excitement prevail? Obviously there are no pat answers and the character of the transaction or event will largely determine the significance of the time factor." Slough, Spontaneous Statements and State of Mind, 46 Iowa L. Rev. 224, 243 (1961); McCormick § 272, p.580.

Participation by the declarant is not required: a nonparticipant may be moved to describe what he perceives, and one may be startled by an event in which he is not an actor. Slough, *supra*; McCormick, *supra*; 6 Wigmore § 1755; Annot., 78 A.L.R.2d 300.

Whether *proof of the startling event* may be made by the statement itself is largely an academic question, since in most cases there is present at least circumstantial evidence that something of a startling nature must have occurred. For cases in which the evidence consists of the condition of the declarant (injuries, state of shock), *see* Insurance Co. v.

Mosely, 75 U.S. (8 Wall.), 397, 19 L. Ed. 437 (1869); Wheeler v. United States, 93 U.S. App. D.C. 159, 211 F.2d 19 (1953); *cert. denied,* 347 U.S. 1019, 74 S. Ct. 876, 98 L. Ed. 1140; Wetherbee v. Safety Casualty Co., 219 F.2d 274 (5th Cir. 1955); Lampe v. United States, 97 U.S. App. D.C. 160, 229 F.2d 43 (1956). Nevertheless, on occasion the only evidence may be the content of the statement itself, and rulings that it may be sufficient are described as "increasing," Slough, *supra* at 246, and as the "prevailing practice," McCormick § 272, p.579. Illustrative are Armour & Co. v. Industrial Commission, 78 Colo. 569, 243 P. 546 (1926); Young v. Stewart, 191 N.C. 297, 131 S.E. 735 (1926). Moreover, under Rule 104(a) the judge is not limited by the hearsay rule in passing upon preliminary questions of fact.

Proof of declarant's perception by his statement presents similar considerations when declarant is identified. People v. Poland, 22 Ill. 2d 175, 174 N.E.2d 804 (1961). However, when declarant is an unidentified bystander, the cases indicate hesitancy in upholding the statement alone as sufficient, Garrett v. Howden, 73 N.M. 307, 387 P.2d 874 (1963); Beck v. Dye, 200 Wash. 1, 92 P.2d 1113 (1939), a result which would under appropriate circumstances be consistent with the rule.

Permissible *subject matter* of the statement is limited under Exception [paragraph] (1) to description or explanation of the event or condition, the assumption being that spontaneity, in the absence of a startling event, may extend no farther. In Exception [paragraph] (2), however, the statement need only "relate" to the startling event or condition, thus affording a broader scope of subject matter coverage. 6 Wigmore § 1750, 1754. *See* Sanitary Grocery Co. v. Snead, 67 App. D.C. 129, 90 F.2d 374 (1937), slip-and-fall case sustaining admissibility of clerk's statement, "That has been on the floor for a couple of hours," and Murphy Auto Parts Co., Inc. v. Ball, 101 U.S. App. D.C. 416, 249 F.2d 508 (1957), upholding admission, on issue of driver's agency, of his statement that he had to call on a customer and was in a hurry to get home. Quick, Hearsay, Excitement, Necessity and the Uniform Rules: A Reappraisal of Rule 63(4), 6 Wayne L. Rev. 204, 206-209 (1960).

Similar provisions are found in Uniform Rule 63(4)(a) and (b); California Evidence Code § 1240 (as to Exception (2) only); Kansas Code of Civil Procedure § 60-460(d)(1) and (2); New Jersey Evidence Rule 63(4).

Exception (3) is essentially a specialized application of Exception [paragraph] (1), presented separately to enhance its usefulness and accessibility. *See* McCormick § 265, 268.

The exclusion of "statements of memory or belief to prove the fact remembered or believed" is necessary to avoid the virtual destruction of the hearsay rule which would otherwise result from allowing state of mind, provable by a hearsay statement, to serve as the basis for an inference of the happening of the event which produced the state of mind. Shepard v. United States, 290 U.S. 96, 54 S. Ct. 22, 78 L. Ed. 196 (1933); Maguire, The Hillmon Case — Thirty-three Years After, 38 Harv. L. Rev. 709, 719-731 (1925); Hinton, States of Mind and the Hearsay Rule, 1 U. Chi. L. Rev. 394, 421-423 (1934). The rule of Mutual Life Ins. Co. v. Hillman, 145 U.S. 285, 12 S. Ct. 909, 36 L. Ed. 706 (1892), allowing evidence of intention as tending to prove the doing of the act intended, is of course, left undisturbed.

The carving out, from the exclusion mentioned in the preceding paragraph, of declarations relating to the execution, revocation, identification, or terms of declarant's will represents an *ad hoc* judgment which finds ample reinforcement in the decisions, resting on practical grounds of necessity and expediency rather than logic. McCormick § 271, pp.577-578; Annot., 34 A.L.R.2d 588, 62 A.L.R.2d 855. A similar recognition of the need for and practical value of this kind of evidence is found in California Evidence Code § 1260.

Exception (4). Even those few jurisdictions which have shied away from generally admitting statements of present condition have allowed them if made to a physician for purposes of diagnosis and treatment in view of the patient's strong motivation to be truthful. McCormick § 266, p.563. The same guarantee of trustworthiness extends to statements of past conditions and medical history, made for purposes of diagnosis or treatment. It also extends to statements as to causation, reasonably pertinent to the same purposes, in accord with the current trend, Shell Oil Co. v. Industrial Commission, 2 Ill. 2d 590, 119 N.E.2d 224 (1954); McCormick § 266, p.564; New Jersey Evidence Rule 63(12)(c). Statements as to fault would not ordinarily qualify under this latter language. Thus a patient's statement that he was struck by an automobile would qualify but not his statement that the car was driven through a red light. Under the exception the statement need not have been made to a physician. Statements to hospital attendants, ambulance drivers, or even members of the family might be included.

Conventional doctrine has excluded from the hearsay exception, as not within its guarantee of truthfulness, statements to a physician consulted only for the purpose of enabling him to testify. While these statements were not admissible as substantive evidence, the expert was allowed to state the basis of his opinion, including statements of this kind. The distinction thus called for was one most unlikely to be made by juries. The rule accordingly rejects the limitation. This position is consistent with the provision of Rule 703 that the facts on which expert testimony is based need not be admissible in evidence if of a kind ordinarily relied upon by experts in the field.

Exception (5). A hearsay exception for recorded recollection is generally recognized and has been described as having "long been favored by the federal and practically all the state courts that have had occasion to decide the question." United States v. Kelly, 349 F.2d 720, 770 (2d Cir. 1965), citing numerous cases and sustaining the exception against a claimed denial of the right of confrontation. Many additional cases are cited in Annot., 82 A.L.R.2d 473, 520. The guarantee of trustworthiness is found in the reliability inherent in a record made while events were still fresh in mind and accurately reflecting them. Owens v. State, 67 Md. 307, 316, 10 A. 210, 212 (1887).

The principal controversy attending the exception has centered, not upon the propriety of the exception itself, but upon the question whether a preliminary requirement of impaired memory on the part of the witness should be imposed. The authorities are divided. If regard be had only to the accuracy of the evidence, admittedly impairment of the memory of the witness adds nothing to it and should not be required. McCormick § 277, p.593; 3 Wigmore § 738, p.76; Jordan v. People, 151 Colo. 133, 376 P.2d 699 (1962), *cert. denied*, 373 U.S. 944, 83 S. Ct. 1553, 10 L. Ed. 2d 699; Hall v. State, 223 Md. 158, 162 A.2d 751 (1960); State v. Bindhammer, 44 N.J. 372, 209 A.2d 124 (1965). Nevertheless, the absence of the requirement, it is believed, would encourage the use of statements carefully prepared for purposes of litigation under the supervision of attorneys, investigators, or claim adjusters. Hence the example includes a requirement that the witness not have "sufficient recollection to enable him to testify fully and accurately." To the same effect are California Evidence Code § 1237 and New Jersey Rule 63(1)(b), and this has been the position of the federal courts. Vicksburg & Meridian R.R. v. O'Brien, 119 U.S. 99, 7 S. Ct. 118, 30 L. Ed. 299 (1886); Ahern v. Webb, 268 F.2d 45 (10th Cir. 1959); and *see* N.L.R.B. v. Hudson Pulp and Paper Corp., 273 F.2d 660, 665 (5th Cir. 1960); N.L.R.B. v. Federal Dairy Co., 297 F.2d 487 (1st Cir. 1962). But *cf.* United States v. Adams, 385 F.2d 548 (2d Cir. 1967).

No attempt is made in the exception to spell out the method of establishing the initial knowledge or the contemporaneity and accuracy of the record, leaving them to be dealt with as the circumstances of the particular case might indicate. Multiple person involvement in the process of observing and recording, as in Rathbun v. Brancatella, 93 N.J.L. 222, 107 A. 279 (1919), is entirely consistent with the exception.

Locating the exception at this place in the scheme of the rules is a matter of choice. There were two other possibilities. The first was to regard the statement as one of the group of prior statements of a testifying witness which are excluded entirely from the category of hearsay by Rule 801(d)(1). That category, however, requires that declarant be "subject to cross-examination," as to which the impaired memory aspect of the exception raises doubts. The other possibility was to include the exception among those covered by Rule 804. Since unavailability is required by that rule and lack of memory is listed as a species of unavailability by the definition of the term in Rule 804(a)(3), that treatment at first impression would seem appropriate. The fact is, however, that the unavailability requirement of the exception is of a limited and peculiar nature. Accordingly, the exception is located at this point rather than in the context of a rule where unavailability is conceived of more broadly.

Exception (6) represents an area which has received much attention from those seeking to improve the law of evidence. The Commonwealth Fund Act was the result of a study completed in 1927 by a distinguished committee under the chairmanship of Professor Morgan. Morgan et al., The Law of Evidence: Some Proposals for Its Reform 63 (1927). With changes too minor to mention, it was adopted by Congress in 1936 as the rule for federal courts. 28 U.S.C. § 1732. A number of states took similar action. The Commissioners on Uniform State Laws in 1936 promulgated the Uniform Business Records as Evidence Act, 9A U.L.A. 506, which has acquired a substantial following in the states. Model Code Rule 514 and Uniform Rule 63(13) also deal with the subject. Difference of varying degrees of importance exist among these various treatments.

These reform efforts were largely within the context of business and commercial records, as the kind usually encountered, and concentrated considerable attention upon relaxing the requirement of producing as witnesses, or accounting for the nonproduction of, all participants in the process of gathering, transmitting, and recording information which the common law had evolved as a burdensome and crippling aspect of using records of this type. In their areas of primary emphasis on witnesses to be called and the general admissibility of ordinary business and commercial records, the Commonwealth Fund Act and the Uniform Act appear to have worked well. The exception seeks to preserve their advantages.

On the subject of what witnesses must be called, the Commonwealth Fund Act eliminated the common law requirement of calling or accounting for all participants by failing to mention it. United States v. Mortimer, 118 F.2d 266 (2d Cir. 1941); La Porte v. United States, 300 F.2d 878 (9th Cir. 1962); McCormick § 290, p.608. Model Code Rule 514 and Uniform Rule 63(13) did likewise. The Uniform Act, however, abolished the common law requirement in express terms, providing that the requisite foundation testimony might be furnished by "the custodian or other qualified witness." Uniform Business Records as Evidence Act, § 2; 9A U.L.A. 506. The exception follows the Uniform Act in this respect.

The element of unusual reliability of business records is said variously to be supplied by systematic checking, by regularity and continuity which produce habits of precision, by actual experience of business in relying upon them, or by a duty to make an accurate record as part of a continuing job or occupation. McCormick § 281, 286, 287; Laughlin, Business Entries and the Like, 46 Iowa L. Rev. 276 (1961). The model statutes and rules have sought to capture these factors and to extend their impact by employing the phrase "regular course of business," in conjunction with a definition of "business" far broader than its ordinarily accepted meaning. The result is a tendency unduly to emphasize a requirement of routineness and repetitiveness and an insistence that other types of records be squeezed into the fact patterns which give rise to traditional business records. The rule therefore adopts the phrase "the course of a regularly conducted activity" as capturing the essential basis of the hearsay exception as it has evolved and the essential element which can be abstracted from the various specifications of what is a "business."

Amplification of the kinds of activities producing admissible records has given rise to problems which conventional business records by their nature avoid. They are problems of the source of the recorded information, of entries in opinion form, of motivation, and of involvement as participant in the matters recorded.

Sources of information presented no substantial problem with ordinary business records. All participants, including the observer or participant furnishing the information to be recorded, were acting routinely, under a duty of accuracy, with employer reliance on the result, or in short "in the regular course of business." If, however, the supplier of the information does not act in the regular course, an essential link is broken; the assurance of accuracy does not extend to the information itself, and the fact that it may be recorded with scrupulous accuracy is of no avail. An illustration is the police report incorporating information obtained from a bystander: the officer qualifies as acting in the regular course but the informant does not. The leading case, Johnson v. Lutz, 253 N.Y. 124, 170 N.E. 517 (1930), held that a report thus prepared was inadmissible. Most of the authorities have agreed with the decision. Gencarella v. Fyfe, 171 F.2d 419 (1st Cir. 1948); Gordon v. Robinson, 210 F.2d 192 (3d Cir. 1954); Standard Oil Co. of California v. Moore, 251 F.2d 188, 214 (9th Cir. 1957), *cert. denied*, 356 U.S. 975, 78 S. Ct. 1139, 2 L. Ed. 2d 1148; Yates v. Bair Transport, Inc., 249 F. Supp. 681 (S.D.N.Y. 1965); Annot., 69 A.L.R.2d 1148. *Cf.* Hawkins v. Gorea Motor Express, Inc., 360 F.2d 933 (2d Cir 1966). *Contra*, 5 Wigmore § 1530a, n.1, pp.391-392. The point is not dealt with specifically in the Commonwealth Fund Act, the Uniform Act, or Uniform Rule 63(13). However, Model Code Rule 514 contains the requirement "that it was the regular course of that business for one with personal knowledge . . . to make such a memorandum or record or to transmit information thereof to be included in such a memorandum or record . . ." The rule follows this lead in requiring an informant with knowledge acting in the course of the regularly conducted activity.

Entries in the form of opinions were not encountered in traditional business records in view of the purely factual nature of the items recorded, but they are now commonly encountered with respect to medical diagnoses, prognoses, and test results, as well as occasionally in other areas. The Commonwealth Fund Act provided only for records of an "act, transaction, occurrence, or event," while the Uniform Act, Model Code Rule 514, and Uniform Rule 63(13) merely added the ambiguous term "condition." The limited phrasing of the Commonwealth Fund Act, 28 U.S.C. § 1732, may account for the reluctance of some federal decisions to admit diagnostic entries. New York Life Ins. Co. v. Taylor, 79 U.S. App. D.C. 66, 147 F.2d 297 (1945); Lyles v. United States, 103 U.S. App. D.C. 22, 254 F.2d 725 (1957), *cert. denied*, 356 U.S. 961, 78 S. Ct. 997, 2 L. Ed. 2d 1067; England v. United States, 174 F.2d 466 (5th Cir. 1949); Skogen v. Dow Chemical Co., 375 F.2d 692 (8th Cir. 1967). Other federal decisions, however, experienced no difficulty in freely admitting diagnostic entries. Reed v. Order of United Commercial Travelers, 123 F.2d 252 (2d Cir. 1941); Buckminster's Estate v. Commissioner of Internal Revenue, 147 F.2d 331 (2d Cir. 1944); Medina v. Erickson, 226 F.2d 475 (9th Cir. 1955); Thomas v. Hogan, 308 F.2d 355 (4th Cir. 1962); Glawe v. Rulon, 284 F.2d 495 (8th Cir. 1960). In the state courts, the trend favors admissibility. Borucki v. MacKenzie Bros. Co., 125 Conn. 92, 3 A.2d 224 (1938); Allen v. St. Louis Public Service Co., 365 Mo. 677, 285 S.W.2d 663, 55 A.L.R.2d 1022 (1956); People v. Kohlmeyer, 284 N.Y. 366, 31 N.E.2d 490 (1940); Weis v. Weis, 147 Ohio St. 416, 72 N.E.2d 245 (1947). In order to make clear its adherence to the latter position, the rule specifically includes both diagnoses and opinions, in addition to acts, events, and conditions, as proper subjects of admissible entries.

Problems of the motivation of the informant have been a source of difficulty and disagreement. In Palmer v. Hoffman, 318 U.S. 109, 63 S. Ct. 477, 87 L. Ed. 645 (1943), exclusion of an accident report made by the since deceased engineer, offered by defendant railroad trustees in a grade crossing collision case, was upheld. The report was not "in the regular course of business," not a record of the systematic conduct of the business as a business, said the Court. The report was prepared for use in litigating, not railroading. While the opinion mentions the motivation of the engineer only obliquely, the emphasis on records of routine operations is significant only by virtue of impact on motivation to be accurate. Absence of routineness raises lack of motivation to be accurate. The opinion of the Court of Appeals had gone beyond mere lack of motive to be accurate: the engineer's statement was "dripping with motivations to misrepresent." Hoffman v. Palmer, 129 F.2d 976, 991 (2d Cir. 1942). The direct introduction of motivation is a disturbing factor, since absence of motivation to misrepresent has not traditionally been a requirement of the rule; that records might be self-serving has not been a ground for exclusion. Laughlin, Business Records and the Like, 46 Iowa L. Rev. 276, 285 (1961). As Judge Clark said in his dissent, "I submit that there is hardly a grocer's account book which could not be excluded on that basis." 129 F.2d at 1002. A physician's evaluation report of a personal injury litigant would appear to be in the routine of his business. If the report is offered by the party at whose instance it was made, however, it has been held inadmissible, Yates v. Bair Transport, Inc., 249 F. Supp. 681 (S.D.N.Y. 1965), otherwise if offered by the opposite party, Korte v. New York, N.H. & H.R. Co., 191 F.2d 86 (2d Cir. 1951), *cert. denied*, 342 U.S. 868, 72 S. Ct. 108, 96 L. Ed. 652.

The decisions hinge on motivation and which party is entitled to be concerned about it. Professor McCormick believed that the doctor's report or the accident report were sufficiently routine to justify admissibility. McCormick § 287, p.604. Yet hesitation must be experienced in admitting everything which is observed and recorded in the course of a regularly conducted activity. Efforts to set a limit are illustrated by Hartzog v. United States, 217 F.2d 706 (4th Cir. 1954), error to admit worksheets made by since deceased deputy collector in preparation for the instant income tax evasion prosecution, and United States v. Ware, 247 F.2d 698 (7th Cir. 1957), error to admit narcotics agents' records of purchases. *See also* Exception [paragraph] (8), *infra*, as to the public record aspects of records of this nature. Some decisions have been satisfied as to motivation of an accident report if made pursuant to statutory duty, United States v. New York Foreign Trade Zone Operators, 304 F.2d 792 (2d Cir. 1962); Taylor v. Baltimore & O. R. Co., 344 F.2d 281 (2d Cir. 1965), since the report was oriented in a direction other than the litigation which ensued. *Cf.* Matthews v. United States, 217 F.2d 409 (5th Cir. 1954). The formulation of specific terms which would assure satisfactory results in all cases is not possible. Consequently the rule proceeds from the base that records made in the course of a regularly conducted activity will be taken as admissible but subject to authority to exclude if "the sources of information or other circumstances indicate lack of trustworthiness."

Occasional decisions have reached for enhanced accuracy by requiring involvement as a participant in matters reported. *Clainos v. United States*, 82 U.S. App. D.C. 278, 163 F.2d 593 (1947), error to admit police records of convictions; Standard Oil Co. of California v. Moore, 251 F.2d 188 (9th Cir. 1957), *cert. denied*, 356 U.S. 975, 78 S. Ct. 1139, 2 L. Ed. 2d 1148, error to admit employees' records of observed business practices of others. The rule includes no requirement of this nature. Wholly acceptable records may involve matters merely observed, e.g., the weather.

The form which the "record" may assume under the rule is described broadly as a "memorandum, report, record, or data compilation, in any form." The expression "data compilation" is used as broadly descriptive of any means of storing information other than the conventional words and figures in written or documentary form. It includes, but is by no means limited to, electronic computer storage. The term is borrowed from revised Rule 34(a) of the Rules of Civil Procedure.

Exception (7). Failure of a record to mention a matter which would ordinarily be mentioned is satisfactory evidence of its nonexistence. Uniform Rule 63(14), Comment. While probably not hearsay as defined in Rule 801, *supra*, decisions may be found which class the evidence not only as hearsay but also as not within any exception. In order to set the question at rest in favor of admissibility, it is specifically treated here. McCormick § 289, p.609; Morgan, Basic Problems of Evidence 314 (1962); 5 Wigmore § 1531; Uniform Rule 63(14); California Evidence Code § 1272; Kansas Code of Civil Procedure § 60-460(n); New Jersey Evidence Rule 63(14).

Exception (8). Public records are a recognized hearsay exception at common law and have been the subject of statutes without number. McCormick § 291. *See, for example*, 28 U.S.C. § 1733, the relative narrowness of which is illustrated by its nonapplicability to nonfederal public agencies, thus necessitating report to the less appropriate business record exception to the hearsay rule. Kay v. United States, 255 F.2d 476 (4th Cir. 1958). The rule makes no distinction between federal and nonfederal offices and agencies.

Justification for the exception is the assumption that a public official will perform his duty properly and the unlikelihood that he will remember details independently of the record. Wong Wing Foo v. McGrath, 196 F.2d 120 (9th Cir. 1952), and *see* Chesapeake & Delaware Canal Co. v. United States, 250 U.S. 123, 39 S. Ct. 407, 63 L. Ed. 889 (1919). As to items (a) and (b), further support is found in the reliability factors underlying records of regularly conducted activities generally. *See* Exception [paragraph] (6), *supra.*

(a) Cases illustrating the admissibility of records of the office's or agency's own activities are numerous. Chesapeake & Delaware Canal Co. v. United States, 250 U.S. 123, 39 S. Ct. 407, 63 L. Ed. 889 (1919), Treasury records of miscellaneous receipts and disbursements; Howard v. Perrin, 200 U.S. 71, 26 S. Ct. 195, 50 L. Ed. 374 (1906), General Land Office records; Ballew v. United States, 160 U.S. 187, 16 S. Ct. 263, 40 L. Ed. 388 (1895), Pension Office records.

(b) Cases sustaining admissibility of records of matters observed are also numerous. United States v. Van Hook, 284 F.2d 489 (7th Cir. 1960), *remanded for resentencing,* 365 U.S. 609, 81 S. Ct. 823, 5 L. Ed. 2d 821, letter from induction officer to District Attorney, pursuant to army regulations, stating fact and circumstances of refusal to be inducted; T'Kach v. United States, 242 F.2d 937 (5th Cir. 1957), affidavit of White House personnel officer that search of records showed no employment of accused, charged with fraudulently representing himself as an envoy of the President; Minnehaha County v. Kelley, 150 F.2d 356 (8th Cir. 1945); Weather Bureau records of rainfall; United States v. Meyer, 113 F.2d 387 (7th Cir. 1940), *cert. denied,* 311 U.S. 706, 61 S. Ct. 174, 85 L. Ed. 459, map prepared by government engineer from information furnished by men working under his supervision.

(c) The more controversial area of public records is that of the so-called "evaluative" report. The disagreement among the decisions has been due in part, no doubt, to the variety of situations encountered, as well as to differences in principle. Sustaining admissibility are such cases as United States v. Dumas, 149 U.S. 278, 13 S. Ct. 872, 37 L. Ed. 734 (1893), statement of account certified by Postmaster General in action against postmaster; McCarty v. United States, 185 F.2d 520 (5th Cir. 1950), *reh. denied,* 187 F.2d 234, Certificate of Settlement of General Accounting Office showing indebtedness and letter from Army official stating Government had performed, in action on contract to purchase and remove waste food from Army camp; Moran v. Pittsburgh-Des Moines Steel Co., 183 F.2d 467 (3d Cir. 1950), report of Bureau of Mines as to cause of gas tank explosion; Petition of W—, 164 F. Supp. 659 (E.D. Pa. 1958), report by Immigration and Naturalization Service investigator that petitioner was known in community as wife of man to whom she was not married. To the opposite effect and denying admissibility are Franklin v. Skelly Oil Co., 141 F.2d 568 (10th Cir. 1944), State Fire Marshal's report of cause of gas explosion; Lomax Transp. Co. v. United States, 183 F.2d 331 (9th Cir. 1950), Certificate of Settlement from General Accounting Office in action for naval supplies lost in warehouse fire; Yung Jin Teung v. Dulles, 229 F.2d 244 (2d Cir. 1956), "Status Reports" offered to justify delay in processing passport applications. Police reports have generally been excluded except to the extent to which they incorporate firsthand observations of the officer. Annot., 69 A.L.R.2d 1148. Various kinds of evaluative reports are admissible under federal statutes: 7 U.S.C. § 78, findings of Secretary of Agriculture prima facie evidence of true grade of grain; 7 U.S.C. § 210(f), findings of Secretary of Agriculture prima facie evidence in action for damages against stockyard owner; 7 U.S.C. § 292, order by Secretary of Agriculture prima facie evidence in judicial enforcement proceedings against producers association monopoly; 7 U.S.C. § 1622(h), Department of Agriculture inspection certificates of products shipped in interstate commerce prima facie evidence; 8 U.S.C. § 1440(c), separation of alien from military service on conditions other than honorable provable by certificate from department in proceedings to revoke citizenship; 18 U.S.C. § 4245, certificate of Director of Prisons that convicted person has been examined and found probably incompetent at time of trial prima facie evidence in court hearing on competency; 42 U.S.C. § 269(b), bill of health by appropriate official prima facie evidence of vessel's sanitary history and condition and compliance with regulations; 46 U.S.C. § 679, certificate of consul presumptive evidence of refusal of master to transport destitute seamen to United States. While these statutory exceptions to the hearsay rule are left undisturbed, Rule 802, the willingness of Congress to recognize a substantial measure of admissibility for evaluative reports is a helpful guide.

Factors which may be of assistance in passing upon the admissibility of evaluative reports include; (1) the timeliness of the investigation, McCormack, Can the Courts Make Wider Use of Reports of Official Investigations? 42 Iowa L. Rev. 363 (1957); (2) the special skill or experience of the official, *id.*; (3) whether a hearing was held and the level at which conducted, Franklin v. Skelly Oil Co., 141 F.2d 568 (10th Cir. 1944); (4) possible motivation problems suggested by Palmer v. Hoffman, 318 U.S. 109, 63 S. Ct. 477, 87 L. Ed. 645 (1943). Others no doubt could be added.

The formulation of an approach which would give appropriate weight to all possible factors in every situation is an obvious impossibility. Hence the rule, as in Exception [paragraph] (6), assumes admissibility in the first instance but with ample provision for escape if sufficient negative factors are present. In one respect, however, the rule with respect to evaluate reports under item (c) is very specific; they are admissible only in civil cases and against the government in criminal cases in view of the almost certain collision with confrontation rights which would result from their use against the accused in a criminal case.

Exception (9). Records of vital statistics are commonly the subject of particular statutes making them admissible in evidence. Uniform Vital Statistics Act, 9C U.L.A. 350 (1957). The rule is in principle narrower than Uniform Rule 63(16) which includes reports required of persons performing functions authorized by statute, yet in practical effect the two are substantially the same. Comment Uniform Rule 63(16). The exception as drafted is in the pattern of California Evidence Code § 1281.

Exception (10). The principle of proving nonoccurrence of an event by evidence of the absence of a record which would regularly be made of its occurrence, developed in Exception [paragraph] (7) with respect to regularly conducted activities, is here extended to public records of the kind mentioned in Exceptions [paragraphs] (8) and (9). 5 Wigmore § 1633(6), p.519. Some harmless duplication no doubt exists with Exception [paragraph] (7). For instances of federal statutes recognizing this method of proof, *see* 8 U.S.C. § 1284(b), proof of absence of alien crewman's name from outgoing manifest prima facie evidence of failure to detain or deport, and 42 U.S.C. § 405(c)(3), (4)(B), (4)(C), absence of HEW [Department of Health, Education, and Welfare] record prima facie evidence of no wages or self-employment income.

The rule includes situations in which absence of a record may itself be the ultimate focal point of inquiry, e.g., People v. Love, 310 Ill. 558, 142 N.E. 204 (1923), certificate of Secretary of State admitted to show failure to file documents required by Securities Law, as well as cases where the absence of a record is offered as proof of the nonoccurrence of an event ordinarily recorded.

The refusal of the common law to allow proof by certificate of the lack of a record or entry has no apparent justification, 5 Wigmore § 1678(7), p.752. The rule takes the opposite position, as do Uniform Rule 63(17); California Evidence Code § 1284; Kansas Code of Civil Procedure § 60-460(*c*); New Jersey Evidence Rule 63(17). Congress has recognized certification as evidence of the lack of a record. 8 U.S.C. § 1360(d), certificate of Attorney General or other designated officer that no record of Immigration and Naturalization Service of specified nature or entry therein is found, admissible in alien cases.

Exception (11). Records of activities of religious organizations are currently recognized as admissible at least to the extent of the business records exception to the hearsay rule, 5 Wigmore § 1523, p.371, and Exception [paragraph] (6) would be applicable. However, both the business record doctrine and Exception [paragraph] (6) require that the person furnishing the information be one in the business or activity. The result is such decisions as Daily v. Grand Lodge, 311 Ill. 184, 142 N.E. 478 (1924), holding a church record admissible to prove fact, date, and place of baptism, but not age of child except that he had at least been born at the time. In view of the unlikelihood that false information would be furnished on occasions of this kind, the rule contains no requirement that the informant be in the course of the activity. *See* California Evidence Code § 1315 and Comment.

Exception (12). The principle of proof by certification is recognized as to public officials in Exceptions [paragraphs] (8) and (10), and with respect to authentication in Rule 902. The present exception is a duplication to the extent that it deals with a certificate by a public official, as in the case of a judge who performs a marriage ceremony. The area covered by the rule is, however, substantially larger and extends the certification procedure to clergymen and the like who perform marriages and other ceremonies or administer sacraments. Thus certificates of such matters as baptism or confirmation, as well as marriage, are included. In principle they are as acceptable evidence as certificates of public officers. *See* 5 Wigmore § 1645, as to marriage certificates. When the person executing the certificate is not a public official, the self-authenticating character of documents purporting to emanate from public officials, *see* Rule 902, is lacking and proof is required that the person was authorized and did make the certificate. The time element, however, may safely be taken as supplied by the certificate, once authority and authenticity are established, particularly in view of the presumption that a document was executed on the date it bears.

For similar rules, some limited to certificates of marriage, with variations in foundation requirements, *see* Uniform Rule 63(18); California Evidence Code § 1316; Kansas Code of Civil Procedure § 60-460(p); New Jersey Evidence Rule 63(18).

Exception (13). Records of family history kept in family Bibles have by long tradition been received in evidence. 5 Wigmore § 1495, 1496, citing numerous statutes and decisions. *See also* Regulations, Social Security Administration, 20 C.F.R. § 404.703(c), recognizing family Bible entries as proof of age in the absence of public or church records. Opinions in the area also include inscriptions on tombstones, publicly displayed pedigrees, and engravings on rings. Wigmore, *supra*. The rule is substantially identical in coverage with California Evidence Code § 1312.

Exception (14). The recording of title documents is a purely statutory development. Under any theory of the admissibility of public records, the records would be receivable as evidence of the contents of the recorded document, else the recording process would be reduced to a nullity. When, however, the record is offered for the further purpose of proving execution and delivery, a problem of lack of first-hand knowledge by the recorder, not present as to contents, is presented. This problem is solved, seemingly in all jurisdictions, by qualifying for recording only those documents shown by a specified procedure, either acknowledgement or a form of probate, to have been executed and delivered. 5 Wigmore § 1647-1651. Thus what may appear in the rule, at first glance, as endowing the record with an effect independently of local law and inviting difficulties of an *Erie* nature under Cities Service Oil Co. v. Dunlap, 308 U.S. 208, 60 S. Ct. 201, 84 L. Ed. 196 (1939), is not present, since the local law in fact governs under the example.

Exception (15). Dispositive documents often contain recitals of fact. Thus a deed purporting to have been executed by an attorney in fact may recite the existence of the power of attorney, or a deed may recite that the grantors are all the heirs of the last record owner. Under the rule, these recitals are exempted from the hearsay rule. The circumstances under which dispositive documents are executed and the requirement that the recital be germane to the purpose of the document are believed to be adequate guarantees of trustworthiness, particularly in view of the nonapplicability of the rule if dealings with the property have been inconsistent with the document. The age of the document is of no significance, though in practical application the document will most often be an ancient one. *See* Uniform Rule 63(29), Comment.

Similar provisions are contained in Uniform Rule 63(29); California Evidence Code §1330; Kansas Code of Civil Procedure §60-460(aa); New Jersey Evidence Rule 63(29).

Exception (16). Authenticating a document as ancient, essentially in the pattern of the common law, as provided in Rule 901(b)(8), leaves open as a separate question the admissibility of assertive statements contained therein as against a hearsay objection. 7 Wigmore §2145a. Wigmore further states that the ancient document technique of authentication is universally conceded to apply to all sorts of documents, including letters, records, contracts, maps, and certificates, in addition to title documents, citing numerous decisions. *Id.* §2145. Since most of these items are significant evidentially only insofar as they are assertive, their admission in evidence must be as a hearsay exception. *But see* 5 *id.* §1573, p.429, referring to recitals in ancient deeds as a "limited" hearsay exception. The former position is believed to be the correct one in reason and authority. As pointed out in McCormick §298, danger of mistake is minimized by authentication requirements, and age affords assurance that the writing antedates the present controversy. *See* Dallas County v. Commercial Union Assurance Co., 286 F.2d 388 (5th Cir. 1961), upholding admissibility of 58-year-old newspaper story. *Cf.* Morgan, Basic Problems of Evidence 364 (1962), *but see id.* 254.

For a similar provision, but with the added requirement that "the statement has since generally been acted upon as true by persons having an interest in the matter," *see* California Evidence Code §1331.

Exception (17). Ample authority at common law supported the admission in evidence of items falling in this category. While Wigmore's text is narrowly oriented to lists, etc., prepared for the use of a trade or profession, 6 Wigmore §1702, authorities are cited which include other kinds of publications, for example, newspaper market reports, telephone directories, and city directories. *Id.* §1702-1706. The basis of trustworthiness is general reliance by the public or by a particular segment of it, and the motivation of the compiler to foster reliance by being accurate.

For similar provisions, *see* Uniform Rule 63(30); California Evidence Code §1340; Kansas Code of Civil Procedure §60-460(bb); New Jersey Evidence Rule 63(30). Uniform Commercial Code §2-724 provides for admissibility in evidence of "reports in official publications or trade journals or in newspapers or periodicals of general circulation published as the reports of such [established commodity] market."

Exception (18). The writers have generally favored the admissibility of learned treatises, McCormick §296, p.621; Morgan, Basic Problems of Evidence 366 (1962); 6 Wigmore §1692, with the support of occasional decisions and rules, City of Dothan v. Hardy, 237 Ala. 603, 188 So. 264 (1939); Lewandowski v. Preferred Risk Mut. Ins. Co., 33 Wis. 2d 69, 146 N.W.2d 505 (1966), 66 Mich. L. Rev. 183 (1967); Uniform Rule 63(31); Kansas Code of Civil Procedure §60-460(ce), but the great weight of authority has been that learned treatises are not admissible as substantive evidence though usable in the cross-examination of experts. The foundation of the minority view is that the hearsay objection must be regarded as unimpressive when directed against treatises since a high standard of accuracy is engendered by various factors: the treatise is written primarily and impartially for professionals, subject to scrutiny and exposure for inaccuracy, with the reputation of the writer at stake. 6 Wigmore §1692. Sound as this position may be with respect to trustworthiness, there is, nevertheless, an additional difficulty in the likelihood that the treatise will be misunderstood and misapplied without expert assistance and supervision. This difficulty is recognized in the cases demonstrating unwillingness to sustain findings relative to disability on the basis of judicially noticed medical texts. Ross v. Gardner, 365 F.2d 554 (6th Cir. 1966); Sayers v. Gardner, 380 F.2d 940 (6th Cir. 1967); Colwell v. Gardner, 386 F.2d 56 (6th Cir. 1967); Glendenning v. Ribicoff, 213 F. Supp. 301 (W.D. Mo. 1962); Cook v. Celebrezze, 217 F. Supp. 366 (W.D. Mo. 1963); Sosna v. Celebrezze, 234 F. Supp. 289 (E.D. Pa. 1964); and *see* McDaniel v. Celebrezze,

331 F.2d 426 (4th Cir. 1964). The rule avoids the danger of misunderstanding and misapplication by limiting the use of treatises as substantive evidence to situations in which an expert is on the stand and available to explain and assist in the application of the treatise if declared. The limitation upon receiving the publication itself physically in evidence, contained in the last sentence, is designed to further this policy.

The relevance of the use of treatises on cross-examination is evident. This use of treatises has been the subject of varied views. The most restrictive position is that the witness must have stated expressly on direct his reliance upon the treatise. A slightly more liberal approach still insists upon reliance but allows it to be developed on cross-examination. Further relaxation dispenses with reliance but requires recognition as an authority by the witness, developable on cross-examination. The greatest liberality is found in decisions allowing use of the treatise on cross-examination when its status as an authority is established by any means. Annot., 60 A.L.R.2d 77. The exception is hinged upon this last position, which is that of the Supreme Court, Reilly v. Pinkus, 338 U.S. 269, 70 S. Ct. 110, 94 L. Ed. 63 (1949), and of recent well considered state court decisions, City of St. Petersburg v. Ferguson, 193 So. 2d 648 (Fla. App. 1967), *cert. denied*, Fla., 201 So. 2d 556; Darling v. Charleston Memorial Community Hospital, 33 Ill. 2d 326, 211 N.E.2d 253 (1965); Dabroe v. Rhodes Co., 64 Wash. 2d 431, 392 P.2d 317 (1964).

In Reilly v. Pinkus, *supra*, the Court pointed out that testing of professional knowledge was incomplete without exploration of the witness' knowledge of and attitude toward established treatises in the field. The process works equally well in reverse and furnishes the basis of the rule.

The rule does not require that the witness rely upon or recognize the treatise as authoritative, thus avoiding the possibility that the expert may at the outset block cross-examination by refusing to concede reliance or authoritativeness. Dabroe v. Rhodes Co., *supra*. Moreover, the rule avoids the unreality of admitting evidence for the purpose of impeachment only, with an instruction to the jury not to consider it otherwise. The parallel to the treatment of prior inconsistent statements will be apparent. *See* Rules 6130(b) and 801(d)(1).

Exceptions (19), (20), and (21). Trustworthiness in reputation evidence is found "when the topic is such that the facts are likely to have been inquired about and that persons having personal knowledge have disclosed facts which have thus been discussed in the community; and thus the community's conclusion, if any has been formed, is likely to be a trustworthy one." 5 Wigmore § 1580, p.444, and *see also* § 1583. On this common foundation, reputation as to land boundaries, customs, general history, character, and marriage have come to be regarded as admissible. The breadth of the underlying principle suggests the formulation of an equally broad exception, but tradition has in fact been much narrower and more particularized, and this is the pattern of these exceptions in the rule.

Exception [paragraph] (19) is concerned with matters of personal and family history. Marriage is universally conceded to be a proper subject of proof by evidence of reputation in the community. 5 Wigmore § 1602. As to such items as legitimacy, relationship, adoption, birth, and death, the decisions are divided. *Id.* § 1605. All seem to be susceptible to being the subject of well founded repute. The "world" in which the reputation may exist may be family, associates, or community. This world has proved capable of expanding with changing times from the single uncomplicated neighborhood, in which all activities take place, to the multiple and unrelated worlds of work, religious affiliation, and social activity, in each of which a reputation may be generated. People v. Reeves, 360 Ill. 55, 195 N.E. 443 (1935); State v. Axilrod, 248 Minn. 204, 79 N.W.2d 677 (1956); Mass. Stat. 1947, c. 410, M.G.L.A. c. 233 § 21A; 5 Wigmore § 1616. The family has often served as the point of beginning for allowing community reputation. 5 Wigmore § 1488. For comparable provisions *see* Uniform Rule 63(26), (27)(c); California Evidence Code § 1313, 1314; Kansas Code of Civil Procedure § 60-460(x), (y)(3); New Jersey Evidence Rule 63(26), (27)(c).

The first portion of Exception [paragraph] (20) is based upon the general admissibility of evidence of reputation as to land boundaries and land customs, expanded in this country to include private as well as public boundaries. McCormick § 299, p.625. The reputation is required to antedate the controversy, though not to be ancient. The second portion is likewise supported by authority, *id.*, and is designed to facilitate proof of events when judicial notice is not available The historical character of the subject matter dispenses with any need that the reputation antedate the controversy with respect to which it is offered. For similar provisions *see* Uniform Rule 63(27)(a), (b); California Evidence Code § 1320-1322; Kansas Code of Civil Procedure § 60-460(y), (1), (2); New Jersey Evidence Rule 63(27)(a), (b).

Exception [paragraph] (21) recognizes the traditional acceptance of reputation evidence as a means of proving human character. McCormick § 44, 158. The exception deals only with the hearsay aspect of this kind of evidence. Limitations upon admissibility based on other grounds will be found in Rules 404, relevancy of character evidence generally, and 608, character of witness. The exception is in effect a reiteration, in the context of hearsay, of Rule 405(a). Similar provisions are contained in Uniform Rule 63(28); California Evidence Code § 1324; Kansas Code of Civil Procedure § 60-460(z); New Jersey Evidence Rule 63(28).

Exception (22). When the status of a former judgment is under consideration in subsequent litigation, three possibilities must be noted: (1) the former judgment is conclusive under the doctrine of res judicata, either as a bar or a collateral estoppel; or (2) it is admissible in evidence for what it is worth; or (3) it may be of no effect at all. The first situation does not involve any problem of evidence except in the way that principles of substantive law generally bear upon the relevancy and materiality of evidence. The rule does not deal with the substantive effect of the judgment as a bar or collateral estoppel. When, however, the doctrine of res judicata does not apply to make the judgment either a bar or a collateral estoppel, a choice is presented between the second and third alternatives. The rule adopts the second for judgments of criminal conviction of felony grade. This is the direction of the decisions, Annot., 18 A.L.R.2d 1287, 1299, which manifest an increasing reluctance to reject *in toto* the validity of the law's factfinding processes outside the confines of res judicata and collateral estoppel. While this may leave a jury with the evidence of conviction but without means to evaluate it, as suggested by Judge Hinton, Note 27 Ill. L. Rev. 195 (1932), it seems safe to assume that the jury will give it substantial effect unless defendant offers a satisfactory explanation, a possibility not foreclosed by the provision. *But see* North River Ins. Co. v. Militello, 104 Colo. 28, 88 P.2d 567 (1939), in which the jury found for plaintiff on a fire policy despite the introduction of his conviction for arson. For supporting federal decisions *see* Clark, J., in New York & Cuba Mail S.S. Co. v. Continental Cas. Co., 117 F.2d 404, 411 (2d Cir. 1941); Connecticut Fire Ins. Co. v. Farrara, 277 F.2d 388 (8th Cir. 1960).

Practical considerations require exclusion of convictions of minor offenses, not because the administration of justice in its lower echelons must be inferior, but because motivation to defend at this level is often minimal or nonexistent. Cope v. Goble, 39 Cal. App. 2d 448, 103 P.2d 598 (1940); Jones v. Talbot, 87 Idaho 498, 394 P.2d 316 (1964); Warren v. Marsh, 215 Minn. 615, 11 N.W.2d 528 (1943); Annot., 18 A.L.R.2d 1287, 1295-1297; 16 Brooklyn L. Rev. 286 (1950); 50 Colum. L. Rev. 529 (1950); 35 Cornell L.Q. 872 (1950). Hence the rule includes only convictions of felony grade, measured by federal standards.

Judgments of conviction based upon pleas of nolo contendere are not included. This position is consistent with the treatment of nolo pleas in Rule 410 and the authorities cited in the Advisory Committee's Note in support thereof.

While these rules do not in general purport to resolve constitutional issues, they have in general been drafted with a view to avoiding collision with constitutional principles. Consequently the exception does not include evidence of the conviction of a third person, offered against the accused in a criminal prosecution to prove any fact essential to sustain the judgment of conviction. A contrary position would seem clearly to violate the right of confrontation. Kirby v. United States, 174 U.S. 47, 19 S. Ct. 574, 43 L. Ed. 890 (1899), error to convict of possessing stolen postage stamps with the only evidence of theft being the record of conviction of the thieves. The situation is to be distinguished from cases in which conviction of another person is an element of the crime, e.g., 15 U.S.C. § 902(d), interstate shipment of firearms to a known convicted felon, and, as specifically provided, from impeachment.

For comparable provisions *see* Uniform Rule 63(20); California Evidence Code § 1300; Kansas Code of Civil Procedure § 60-460(r); New Jersey Evidence Rule 63(20).

Exception (23). A hearsay exception in this area was originally justified on the ground that verdicts were evidence of reputation. As trial by jury graduated from the category of neighborhood inquests, this theory lost its validity. It was never valid as to chancery decrees. Nevertheless the rule persisted, though the judges and writers shifted ground and began saying that the judgment or decree was as good evidence as reputation. *See* City of London v. Clerke, Carth. 181, 90 Eng. Rep. 710 (K.B. 1691); Neill v. Duke of Devonshire, 8 App. Cas. 135 (1882). The shift appears to be correct, since the process of inquiry, sifting, and scrutiny which is relied upon to render reputation reliable is present in perhaps greater measure in the process of litigation. While this might suggest a broader area of application, the affinity to reputation is strong, and paragraph (23) goes no further, not even including character.

The leading case in the United States, Patterson v. Gaines, 47 U.S. (6 How.) 550, 599, 12 L. Ed. 553 (1847), follows in the pattern of the English decisions, mentioning as illustrative matters thus provable: manorial rights, public rights of way, immemorial custom, disputed boundary, and pedigree. More recent recognition of the principle is found in Grant Bros. Construction Co. v. United States, 232 U.S. 647, 34 S. Ct. 452, 58 L. Ed. 776 (1914), in action for penalties under Alien Contract Labor Law, decision of board of inquiry of Immigration Service admissible to prove alienage of laborers, as a matter of pedigree; United States v. Mid-Continent Petroleum Corp., 67 F.2d 37 (10th Cir. 1933), records of commission enrolling Indians admissible on pedigree; Jung Yen Loy v. Cahill, 81 F.2d 809 (9th Cir. 1936), board decisions as to citizenship of plaintiff's father admissible in proceeding for declaration of citizenship. *Contra*, In re Estate of Cunha, 49 Haw. 273, 414 P.2d 925 (1966).

ADVISORY COMMITTEE'S NOTE — 1987 AMENDMENT

The amendments are technical. No substantive change is intended.

ADVISORY COMMITTEE'S NOTE — 1997 AMENDMENT

The contents of Rule 803(24) and Rule 804(b)(5) have been combined and transferred to a new Rule 807. This was done to facilitate additions to Rules 803 and 804. No change in meaning is intended.

ADVISORY COMMITTEE'S NOTE — 2000 AMENDMENT

The amendment provides that the foundation requirements of Rule 803(6) can be satisfied under certain circumstances without the expense and inconvenience of producing time-consuming foundation witnesses. Under current law, courts have generally required foundation witnesses to testify. *See, e.g.*, Tongil Co., Ltd. v. Hyundai Merchant Marine Corp., 968 F.2d 999 (9th Cir. 1992) (reversing a judgment based on business records where a qualified person filed an affidavit but did not testify). Protections are provided by the authentication requirements of Rule 902(11) for domestic records, Rule 902(12) for foreign records in civil cases, and 18 U.S.C. §3505 for foreign records in criminal cases.

Rule 804.   Exceptions to the Rule Against Hearsay — When the Declarant Is Unavailable as a Witness

(a) Criteria for Being Unavailable. A declarant is considered to be unavailable as a witness if the declarant:

(1) is exempted from testifying about the subject matter of the declarant's statement because the court rules that a privilege applies;

(2) refuses to testify about the subject matter despite a court order to do so;

(3) testifies to not remembering the subject matter;

(4) cannot be present or testify at the trial or hearing because of death or a then-existing infirmity, physical illness, or mental illness; or

(5) is absent from the trial or hearing and the statement's proponent has not been able, by process or other reasonable means, to procure:

(A) the declarant's attendance, in the case of a hearsay exception under Rule 804(b)(1) or (6); or

(B) the declarant's attendance or testimony, in the case of a hearsay exception under Rule 804(b)(2), (3), or (4).

But this subdivision (a) does not apply if the statement's proponent procured or wrongfully caused the declarant's unavailability as a witness in order to prevent the declarant from attending or testifying.

(b) The Exceptions. The following are not excluded by the rule against hearsay if the declarant is unavailable as a witness:

(1) *Former Testimony.* Testimony that:

(A) was given as a witness at a trial, hearing, or lawful deposition, whether given during the current proceeding or a different one; and

(B) is now offered against a party who had — or, in a civil case, whose predecessor in interest had — an opportunity and similar motive to develop it by direct, cross-, or redirect examination.

(2) *Statement Under the Belief of Imminent Death.* In a prosecution for homicide or in a civil case, a statement that the declarant, while believing the declarant's death to be imminent, made about its cause or circumstances.

(3) *Statement Against Interest.* A statement that:

(A) a reasonable person in the declarant's position would have made only if the person believed it to be true because, when made, it was so contrary to the declarant's proprietary or pecuniary interest or had so great a tendency to invalidate the declarant's claim against someone else or to expose the declarant to civil or criminal liability; and

(B) is supported by corroborating circumstances that clearly indicate its trustworthiness, if it is offered in a criminal case as one that tends to expose the declarant to criminal liability.

(4) *Statement of Personal or Family History.* A statement about:

(A) the declarant's own birth, adoption, legitimacy, ancestry, marriage, divorce, relationship by blood, adoption or marriage, or similar facts of personal or family history, even though the declarant had no way of acquiring personal knowledge about that fact; or

(B) another person concerning any of these facts, as well as death, if the declarant was related to the person by blood, adoption, or marriage or was so intimately associated with the person's family that the declarant's information is likely to be accurate.

(5) [*Other Exceptions.*] [**Transferred to Rule 807.**]

(6) *Statement Offered Against a Party That Wrongfully Caused the Declarant's Unavailability.* A statement offered against the party that wrongfully caused — or acquiesced in wrongfully causing — the declarant's unavailability as a witness, and did so intending that result.

(Pub. L. 93-595, § 1, Jan. 2, 1975, 88 Stat. 1942; Pub. L. 94-149, § 1(12), (13), Dec. 12, 1975, 89 Stat. 806; Mar. 2, 1987, eff. Oct. 1, 1987; Pub. L. 100-690, title VII, § 7075(b), Nov. 18, 1988, 102 Stat. 4405; Apr. 11, 1997, eff. Dec. 1, 1997; Apr. 26, 2011, eff. Dec. 1, 2011.)

RESTYLED RULE 804 — ADVISORY COMMITTEE'S NOTE

The language of Rule 804 has been amended as part of the general restyling of the Evidence Rules to make them more easily understood and to make style and terminology consistent throughout the rules. These changes are intended to be stylistic only. There is no intent to change any result in any ruling on evidence admissibility.

The amendment to Rule 804(b)(3) provides that the corroborating circumstances requirement applies not only to declarations against penal interest offered by the defendant in a criminal case, but also to such statements offered by the government. The language in the original rule does not so provide, but a proposed amendment to Rule 804(b)(3) — released for public comment in 2008 and scheduled to be enacted before the restyled rules — explicitly extends the corroborating circumstances requirement to statements offered by the government.

Rule 804(b)(6) has been renumbered to fill a gap left when the original Rule 804(b)(5) was transferred to Rule 807.

ADVISORY COMMITTEE'S NOTE
56 F.R.D. 183, 322 (1973)

As to firsthand knowledge on the part of hearsay declarants, *see* the introductory portion of the Advisory Committee's Note to Rule 803.

Subdivision (a). The definition of unavailability implements the division of hearsay exceptions into two categories by Rules 803 and 804(b).

At common law the unavailability requirement was evolved in connection with particular hearsay exceptions rather than along general lines. For example, *see* the separate explication of unavailability in relation to former testimony, declarations against interest, and statements of pedigree, separately developed in McCormick § 234, 257, and 297. However, no reason is apparent for making distinctions as to what satisfies unavailability for the different exceptions. The treatment in the rule is therefore uniform although differences in the range of process for witnesses between civil and criminal cases will lead to a less exacting requirement under item (5). *See* Rule 45(e) of the Federal Rules of Civil Procedure and Rule 17(e) of the Federal Rules of Criminal Procedure.

Five instances of unavailability are specified:

(1)   Substantial authority supports the position that exercise of a claim of privilege by the declarant satisfies the requirement of unavailability (usually in connection with former testimony). Wyatt v. State, 35 Ala. App.147, 46 So. 2d 837 (1950); State v. Stewart, 85 Kan. 404, 116 P. 489 (1911); Annot., 45 A.L.R.2d 1354; Uniform Rule 62(7)(a); California Evidence Code § 240(a)(1); Kansas Code of Civil Procedure § 60-459(g) (1). A ruling by the judge is required, which clearly implies that an actual claim of privilege must be made.

(2)   A witness is rendered unavailable if he simply refuses to testify concerning the subject matter of his statement despite judicial pressures to do so, a position supported by similar considerations of practicality. Johnson v. People, 152 Colo. 586, 384 P.2d 454 (1963); People v. Pickett, 339 Mich. 294, 63 N.W.2d 681, 45 A.L.R.2d 1341 (1954). *Contra,* Pleau v. State, 255 Wis. 362, 38 N.W.2d 496 (1949).

(3)   The position that a claimed lack of memory by the witness of the subject matter of his statement constitutes unavailability likewise finds support in the cases, though not without dissent. McCormick § 234, p.494. If the claim is successful, the practical effect is to put the testimony beyond reach, as in the other instances. In this instance, however, it will be noted that the lack of memory must be established by the testimony of the witness himself, which clearly contemplates his production and subjection to cross-examination.

(4)   Death and infirmity find general recognition as ground. McCormick § 234, 257, 297; Uniform Rule 62(7)(c); California Evidence Code § 240(a)(3); Kansas Code of Civil Procedure § 60-459(g)(3); New Jersey Evidence Rule 62(6)(c). *See also* the provisions on use of depositions in Rule 32(a)(3) of the Federal Rules of Civil Procedure and Rule 15(e) of the Federal Rules of Criminal Procedure.

(5)   Absence from the hearing coupled with inability to compel attendance by process or other reasonable means also satisfies the requirement. McCormick § 234; Uniform Rule 62(7)(d) and (e); California Evidence Code § 240(a)(4) and (5); Kansas Code of Civil Procedure § 60-459(g)(4) and (5); New Jersey Rule 62(6)(b) and (d). *See* the discussion of procuring attendance of witnesses who are nonresidents or in custody in Barber v. Page, 390 U.S. 719, 88 S. Ct. 1318, 20 L. Ed. 2d 255 (1968).

If the conditions otherwise constituting unavailability result from the procurement or wrongdoing of the proponent of the statement, the requirement is not satisfied. The rule contains no requirement that an attempt be made to take the deposition of a declarant.

Subdivision (b). Rule 803 *supra* is based upon the assumption that a hearsay statement falling within one of its exceptions possesses qualities which justify the conclusion that whether the declarant is available or unavailable is not a relevant factor in determining admissibility. The instant rule proceeds upon a different theory: hearsay which admittedly is not equal in quality to testimony of the declarant on the stand may nevertheless be admitted if the declarant is unavailable and if his statement meets a specified standard. The rule expresses preferences: testimony given on the stand in person is preferred over hearsay, and hearsay, if of the specified quality, is preferred over complete loss of the evidence of the declarant. The exceptions evolved at common law with respect to declarations of unavailable declarants furnish the basis for the exceptions enumerated in the proposal. The term "unavailable" is defined in subdivision (a).

Exception (1). Former testimony does not rely upon some set of circumstances to substitute for oath and cross-examination, since both oath and opportunity to cross-examine were present in fact. The only missing one of the ideal conditions for the giving of testimony is the presence of trier and opponent ("demeanor evidence"). This is lacking with all hearsay exceptions. Hence it may be argued that former testimony is the strongest hearsay and should be included under Rule 803 *supra*. However, opportunity to observe demeanor is what in a large measure confers depth and meaning upon oath and cross-examination. Thus in cases under Rule 803 demeanor lacks the significance which it possesses with respect to testimony. In any event, the tradition, founded in experience, uniformly favors production of the witness if he is available. The exception indicates continuation of the policy. This preference for the presence of the witness is apparent also in rules and statutes on the use of depositions, which deal with substantially the same problem.

Under the exception, the testimony may be offered (1) against the party *against* whom it was previously offered or (2) against the party *by* whom it was previously offered. In each instance the question resolves itself into whether fairness allows imposing, upon the party against whom now offered, the handling of the witness on the earlier occasion. (1) If the party against whom now offered is the one against whom the testimony was offered previously, no unfairness is apparent in requiring him to accept his own prior conduct of cross-examination or decision not to cross-examine. Only demeanor has been lost, and that is inherent in the situation. (2) If the party against whom now offered is the one *by* whom the testimony was offered previously, a satisfactory answer becomes somewhat more difficult. One possibility is to proceed somewhat along the line of an adoptive admission, i.e., by offering the testimony proponent in effect adopts it. However, this theory savors of discarded concepts of witnesses' belonging to a party, of litigants' ability to pick and choose witnesses, and of vouching for one's own witnesses. *Cf.* McCormick § 246, pp.526-527; 4 Wigmore § 1075. A more direct and acceptable approach is simply to recognize direct and redirect examination of one's own witness as the equivalent of cross-examining an opponent's witness. Falknor, Former Testimony and the Uniform Rules: A Comment, 38 N.Y.U. L. Rev. 651, n.1 (1963); McCormick § 231, p.483. *See also* 5 Wigmore § 1389. Allowable techniques for dealing with hostile, doublecrossing, forgetful, and mentally deficient witnesses leave no substance to a claim that one could not adequately develop his own witness at the former hearing. An even less appealing argument is presented when failure to develop fully was the result of a deliberate choice.

The common law did not limit the admissibility of former testimony to that given in an earlier trial of the same case, although it did require identity of issues as a means of insuring that the former handling of the witness was the equivalent of what would now be done if the opportunity were presented. Modern decisions reduce the requirement to "substantial" identity. McCormick § 233. Since identity of issues is significant only in that it bears on motive and interest in developing fully the testimony of the witness, expressing the matter in the latter terms is preferable. *Id.* Testimony given at a preliminary hearing was held in California v. Green, 399 U.S. 149, 90 S. Ct. 1930, 26 L. Ed. 2d 489 (1970), to satisfy confrontation requirements in this respect.

As a further assurance of fairness in thrusting upon a party the prior handling of the witness, the common law also insisted upon identity of parties, deviating only to the extent of allowing substitution of successors in a narrowly construed privity. Mutuality as an aspect of identity is now generally discredited, and the requirement of identity of the offering party disappears except as it might affect motive to develop the testimony. Falknor, *supra*, at 652; McCormick § 232, pp.487-488. The question remains whether strict identity, or privity, should continue as a requirement with respect to the party against whom offered. The rule departs to the extent of allowing substitution of one with the right and opportunity to develop the testimony with similar motive and interest. This position is supported by modern decisions. McCormick § 232, pp.489-490; 5 Wigmore § 1388.

Provisions of the same tenor will be found in Uniform Rule 63(3)(b); California Evidence Code § 1290-1292; Kansas Code of Civil Procedure § 60-460(c)(2); New Jersey

Evidence Rule 63(3). Unlike the rule, the latter three provide either that former testimony is not admissible if the right of confrontation is denied or that it is not admissible if the accused was not a party to the prior hearing. The genesis of these limitations is a caveat in Uniform Rule 63(3) Comment that use of former testimony against an accused may violate his right of confrontation. Mattox v. United States, 156 U.S. 237, 15 S. Ct. 337, 39 L. Ed. 409 (1895), held that the right was not violated by the Government's use, on a retrial of the same case, of testimony given at the first trial by two witnesses since deceased. The decision leaves open the questions (1) whether direct and redirect are equivalent to cross-examination for purposes of confrontation, (2) whether testimony given in a different proceeding is acceptable, and (3) whether the accused must himself have been a party to the earlier proceeding or whether a similarly situated person will serve the purpose. Professor Falknor concluded that, if a dying declaration untested by cross-examination is constitutionally admissible, former testimony tested by the cross-examination of one similarly situated does not offend against confrontation. Falknor, *supra*, at 659-660. The constitutional acceptability of dying declarations has often been conceded. Mattox v. United States, 156 U.S. 237, 243, 15 S. Ct. 337, 39 L. Ed. 409 (1895); Kirby v. United States, 174 U.S. 47, 61, 19 S. Ct. 574, 43 L. Ed. 890 (1899); Pointer v. Texas, 380 U.S. 400, 407, 85 S. Ct. 1065, 13 L. Ed. 2d 923 (1965).

Exception (2). The exception is the familiar dying declaration of the common law, expanded somewhat beyond its traditionally narrow limits. While the original religious justification for the exception may have lost its conviction for some persons over the years, it can scarcely be doubted that powerful psychological pressures are present. *See* 5 Wigmore §1443 and the classic statement of Chief Baron Eyre in Rex v. Woodcock, 1 Leach 500, 502, 168 Eng. Rep. 352, 353 (K.B. 1789).

The common law required that the statement be that of the victim, offered in a prosecution for criminal homicide. Thus declarations by victims in prosecutions for other crimes, e.g., a declaration by a rape victim who dies in childbirth, and all declarations in civil cases were outside the scope of the exception. An occasional statute has removed these restrictions, as in Colo. R.S. §52-1-20, or has expanded the area of offenses to include abortions, 5 Wigmore §1432, p.224, n.4. Kansas by decision extended the exception to civil cases. Thurston v. Fritz, 91 Kan. 468, 138 P.625 (1914). While the common law exception no doubt originated as a result of the exceptional need for the evidence in homicide cases, the theory of admissibility applies equally in civil cases and in prosecutions for crimes other than homicide. The same considerations suggest abandonment of the limitation to circumstances attending the event in question, yet when the statement deals with matters other than the supposed death, its influence is believed to be sufficiently attenuated to justify the limitation. Unavailability is not limited to death. *See* subdivision (a) of this rule. Any problem as to declarations phrased in terms of opinion is laid at rest by Rule 701, and continuation of a requirement of first-hand knowledge is assured by Rule 602.

Comparable provisions are found in Uniform Rule 63 (5); California Evidence Code §1242; Kansas Code of Civil Procedure §60-460(e); New Jersey Evidence Rule 63(5).

Exception (3). The circumstantial guaranty of reliability for declarations against interest is the assumption that persons do not make statements which are damaging to themselves unless satisfied for good reason that they are true. Hileman v. Northwest Engineering Co., 346 F.2d 668 (6th Cir. 1965). If the statement is that of a party, offered by his opponent, it comes in as an admission, Rule 803(d)(2), and there is no occasion to inquire whether it is against interest, this not being a condition precedent to admissibility of admissions by opponents.

The common law required that the interest declared against be pecuniary or proprietary but within this limitation demonstrated striking ingenuity in discovering an against-interest aspect. Higham v. Ridgeway, 10 East 109, 103 Eng. Rep. 717 (K.B. 1808); Reg. v. Overseers of Birmingham, 1 B. & S. 763, 121 Eng. Rep. 897 (Q.B. 1861); McCormick, §256, p.551, nn.2 and 3.

The exception discards the common law limitation and expands to the full logical limit. One result is to remove doubt as to the admissibility of declarations tending to establish a tort liability against the declarant or to extinguish one which might be asserted by him, in accordance with the trend of the decisions in this country. McCormick § 254, pp.548-549. Another is to allow statements tending to expose declarant to hatred, ridicule, or disgrace, the motivation here being considered to be as strong as when financial interests are at stake. McCormick § 255, p.551. And finally, exposure to criminal liability satisfies the against-interest requirement. The refusal of the common law to concede the adequacy of a penal interest was no doubt indefensible in logic, *see* the dissent of Mr. Justice Holmes in Donnelly v. United States, 228 U.S. 243, 33 S. Ct. 449, 57 L. Ed. 820 (1913), but one senses in the decisions a distrust of evidence of confessions by third persons offered to exculpate the accused arising from suspicions of fabrication either of the fact of the making of the confession or in its contents, enhanced in either instance by the required unavailability of the declarant. Nevertheless, an increasing amount of decisional law recognizes exposure to punishment for crime as a sufficient stake. People v. Spriggs, 60 Cal. 2d 868, 36 Cal. Rptr. 841, 389 P.2d 377 (1964); Sutter v. Easterly, 354 Mo. 282, 189 S.W.2d 284 (1945); Band's Refuse Removal, Inc. v. Fairlawn Borough, 62 N.J. Super. 552, 163 A.2d 465 (1960); Newberry v. Commonwealth, 191 Va. 445, 61 S.E.2d 318 (1950); Annot., 162 A.L.R. 446. The requirement of corroboration is included in the rule in order to effect an accommodation between these competing considerations. When the statement is offered by the accused by way of exculpation, the resulting situation is not adapted to control by rulings as to the weight of the evidence and, hence the provision is cast in terms of a requirement preliminary to admissibility. *Cf.* Rule 406(a). The requirement of corroboration should be construed in such a manner as to effectuate its purpose of circumventing fabrication.

Ordinarily the third-party confession is thought of in terms of exculpating the accused, but this is by no means always or necessarily the case: it may include statements implicating him, and under the general theory of declarations against interest they would be admissible as related statements. Douglas v. Alabama, 380 U.S. 415, 85 S. Ct. 1074, 13 L. Ed. 2d 934 (1965), and Bruton v. United States, 389 U.S. 818, 88 S. Ct. 126, 19 L. Ed. 2d 70 (1968), both involved confessions by codefendants which implicated the accused. While the confession was not actually offered in evidence in *Douglas,* the procedure followed effectively put it before the jury, which the Court ruled to be in error. Whether the confession might have been admissible as a declaration against penal interest was not considered or discussed. *Bruton* assumed the inadmissibility, as against the accused, of the implicating confession of his codefendant, and centered upon the question of the effectiveness of a limiting instruction. These decisions, however, by no means require that all statements implicating another person be excluded from the category of declarations against interest. Whether a statement is in fact against interest must be determined from the circumstances of each case. Thus a statement admitting guilt and implicating another person, made while in custody, may well be motivated by a desire to curry favor with the authorities and hence fail to qualify as against interest. *See* the dissenting opinion of Mr. Justice White in *Bruton.* On the other hand, the same words spoken under different circumstances, e.g., to an acquaintance, would have no difficulty in qualifying. The rule does not purport to deal with questions of the right of confrontation.

The balancing of self-serving against dissenting aspects of a declaration is discussed in McCormick § 256.

For comparable provisions, *see* Uniform Rule 63(10): California Evidence Code § 1230; Kansas Code of Civil Procedure § 60-460(j); New Jersey Evidence Rule 63(10).

Exception (4). The general common law requirement that a declaration in this area must have been made *ante litem motam* has been dropped, as bearing more appropriately on weight than admissibility. *See* 5 Wigmore § 1483. Item (i)[(A)] specifically disclaims any need of firsthand knowledge respecting declarant's own personal history. In some instances it is self-evident (marriage) and in others impossible and traditionally not required (date of birth). Item (ii) [(B)] deals with declarations concerning the history of another person. As at common law, declarant is qualified if related by blood or marriage. 5 Wigmore § 1489. In addition, and contrary to the common law, declarant qualifies by virtue of intimate association with the family. *Id.*, § 1487. The requirement sometimes encountered that when the subject of the statement is the relationship between two other persons the declarant must qualify as to both is omitted. Relationship is reciprocal. *Id.*, § 1491.

For comparable provisions, *see* Uniform Rule 63 (23), (24), (25); California Evidence Code § 1310, 1311; Kansas Code of Civil Procedure § 60-460(u), (v), (w); New Jersey Evidence Rules 63(23), 63(24), 63(25).

ADVISORY COMMITTEE'S NOTE — 1987 AMENDMENT

The amendments are technical. No substantive change is intended.

ADVISORY COMMITTEE'S NOTE — 1997 AMENDMENT

Subdivision (b)(5). The contents of Rule 803(24) and Rule 804(b)(5) have been combined and transferred to a new Rule 807. This was done to facilitate additions to Rules 803 and 804. No change in meaning is intended.

Subdivision (b)(6). Rule 804(b)(6) has been added to provide that a party forfeits the right to object on hearsay grounds to the admission of a declarant's prior statement when the party's deliberate wrongdoing or acquiescence therein procured the unavailability of the declarant as a witness. This recognizes the need for a prophylactic rule to deal with abhorrent behavior "which strikes at the heart of the system of justice itself." United States v. Mastrangelo, 693 F.2d 269, 273 (2d Cir. 1982), *cert. denied*, 467 U.S. 1204 (1984). The wrongdoing need not consist of a criminal act. The rule applies to all parties, including the government.

Every circuit that has resolved the question has recognized the principle of forfeiture by misconduct, although the tests for determining whether there is a forfeiture have varied. *See, e.g.*, United States v. Aguiar, 975 F.2d 45, 47 (2d Cir. 1992); United States v. Potamitis, 739 F.2d 784, 789 (2d Cir.), *cert. denied*, 469 U.S. 918 (1984); Steele v. Taylor, 684 F.2d 1193, 1199 (6th Cir. 1982), *cert. denied*, 460 U.S. 1053 (1983); United States v. Balano, 618 F.2d 624, 629 (10th Cir. 1979), *cert. denied*, 449 U.S. 840 (1980); United States v. Carlson, 547 F.2d 1346, 1358-59 (8th Cir.), *cert. denied*, 431 U.S. 914 (1977). The foregoing cases apply a preponderance of the evidence standard. *Contra* United States v. Thevis, 665 F.2d 616, 631 (5th Cir.) (clear and convincing standard), *cert. denied*, 459 U.S. 825 (1982). The usual Rule 104(a) preponderance of the evidence standard has been adopted in light of the behavior the new Rule 804(b)(6) seeks to discourage.

Rule 805.   Hearsay within Hearsay

Hearsay within hearsay is not excluded by the rule against hearsay if each part of the combined statements conforms with an exception to the rule.

(Pub. L. 93-595, § 1, Jan. 2, 1975, 88 Stat. 1943; Apr. 26, 2011, eff. Dec. 1, 2011.)

RESTYLED RULE 805 — ADVISORY COMMITTEE'S NOTE

The language of Rule 805 has been amended as part of the restyling of the Evidence Rules to make them more easily understood and to make style and terminology consistent throughout the rules. These changes are intended to be stylistic only. There is no intent to change any result in any ruling on evidence admissibility.

ADVISORY COMMITTEE'S NOTE
56 F.R.D. 183, 329 (1973)

On principle it scarcely seems open to doubt that the hearsay rule should not call for exclusion of a hearsay statement which includes a further hearsay statement when both conform to the requirements of a hearsay exception. Thus a hospital record might contain an entry of the patient's age based on information furnished by his wife. The hospital record would qualify as a regular entry except that the person who furnished the information was not acting in the routine of the business. However, her statement independently qualifies as a statement of pedigree (if she is unavailable) or as a statement made for purposes of diagnosis or treatment, and hence each link in the chain falls under sufficient assurances. Or, further to illustrate, a dying declaration may incorporate a declaration against interest by another declarant. *See* McCormick § 290, p.611.

Rule 806.   Attacking and Supporting the Declarant's Credibility

When a hearsay statement — or a statement described in Rule 801(d)(2)(C), (D), or (E) — has been admitted in evidence, the declarant's credibility may be attacked, and then supported, by any evidence that would be admissible for those purposes if the declarant had testified as a witness. The court may admit evidence of the declarant's inconsistent statement or conduct, regardless of when it occurred or whether the declarant had an opportunity to explain or deny it. If the party against whom the statement was admitted calls the declarant as a witness, the party may examine the declarant on the statement as if on cross-examination.

(Pub. L. 93-595, § 1, Jan. 2, 1975, 88 Stat. 1943; Mar. 2, 1987, eff. Oct. 1, 1987; Apr. 11, 1997, eff. Dec. 1, 1997; Apr. 26, 2011, eff. Dec. 1, 2011.)

RESTYLED RULE 806 — ADVISORY COMMITTEE'S NOTE

The language of Rule 806 has been amended as part of the restyling of the Evidence Rules to make them more easily understood and to make style and terminology consistent throughout the rules. These changes are intended to be stylistic only. There is no intent to change any result in any ruling on evidence admissibility.

ADVISORY COMMITTEE'S NOTE
56 F.R.D. 183, 329 (1973)

The declarant of a hearsay statement which is admitted in evidence is in effect a witness. His credibility should in fairness be subject to impeachment and support as though he had in fact testified. *See* Rules 608 and 609. There are, however, some special aspects of the impeaching of a hearsay declarant which require consideration. These special aspects center upon impeachment by inconsistent statement, arise from factual differences which exist between the use of hearsay and an actual witness and also between various kinds of hearsay, and involve the question of applying to declarants the general rule disallowing evidence of an inconsistent statement to impeach a witness unless he is afforded an opportunity to deny or explain. *See* Rule 613(b).

The principal difference between using hearsay and an actual witness is that the inconsistent statement will in the case of the witness almost inevitably of necessity in the nature of things be a *prior* statement, which it is entirely possible and feasible to call to his attention, while in the case of hearsay the inconsistent statement may well be a *subsequent* one, which practically precludes calling it to the attention of the declarant. The result of insisting upon observation of this impossible requirement in the hearsay situation is to deny the opponent, already barred from cross-examination, any benefit of this important technique of impeachment. The writers favor allowing the subsequent statement. McCormick § 37, p.69; 3 Wigmore § 1033. The cases, however, are divided. Cases allowing the impeachment include People v. Collup, 27 Cal. 2d 829, 167 P.2d 714 (1946); People v. Rosoto, 58 Cal. 2d 304, 23 Cal. Rptr. 779, 373 P.2d 867 (1962); Carver v. United States, 164 U.S. 694, 17 S. Ct. 228, 41 L. Ed. 602 (1897). *Contra*, Mattox v. United States, 156 U.S. 237, 15 S. Ct. 337, 39 L. Ed. 409 (1895); People v. Hines, 284 N.Y. 93, 29 N.E.2d 483 (1940). The force of *Mattox*, where the hearsay was the former testimony of a deceased witness and the denial of use of a subsequent inconsistent statement was upheld, is much diminished by *Carver*, where the hearsay was a dying declaration and denial of use of a subsequent inconsistent statement resulted in reversal. The difference in the particular brand of hearsay seems unimportant when the inconsistent statement is a *subsequent* one. True, the opponent is not totally deprived of cross-examination when the hearsay is former testimony or a deposition but he is deprived of cross-examining on the statement or along lines suggested by it. Mr. Justice Shiras, with two justices joining him, dissented vigorously in *Mattox*.

When the impeaching statement was made *prior* to the hearsay statement, differences in the kinds of hearsay appear which arguably may justify differences in treatment. If the hearsay consisted of a simple statement by the witness, e.g., a dying declaration or a declaration against interest, the feasibility of affording him an opportunity to deny or explain encounters the same practical impossibility as where the statement is a subsequent one, just discussed, although here the impossibility arises from the total absence of anything resembling a hearing at which the matter could be put to him. The courts by a large majority have ruled in favor of allowing the statement to be used under these circumstances. McCormick § 37, p.69; 3 Wigmore § 1033. If, however, the hearsay consists of former testimony or a deposition, the possibility of calling the prior statement to the attention of the witness or deponent is not ruled out, since the opportunity to cross-examine was available. It might thus be concluded that with former testimony or depositions the conventional foundation should be insisted upon. Most of the cases involve depositions, and Wigmore describes them as divided. 3 Wigmore § 1031. Deposition procedures at best are cumbersome and expensive, and to require the laying of the foundation may impose an undue burden. Under the federal practice, there is no way of knowing with certainty at the time of taking a deposition whether it is merely for discovery or will ultimately end up in evidence. With respect to both former testimony and depositions the possibility exists that knowledge of the statement might not be acquired until after the time of the cross-examination. Moreover, the expanded admissibility of former testimony and depositions under Rule 804(b)(1) calls for a correspondingly expanded approach to impeachment. The rule dispenses with the requirement in all hearsay situations, which is readily administered and best calculated to lead to fair results.

Notice should be taken that Rule 26(f) of the Federal Rules of Civil Procedure, as originally submitted by the Advisory Committee, ended with the following:

> . . . and, without having first called them to the deponent's attention, may show statements contradictory thereto made at any time by the deponent.

This language did not appear in the rule as promulgated in December, 1937. *See* 4 Moore's Federal Practice § 26.01[9], 26.35 (2d ed. 1967). In 1951, Nebraska adopted a provision strongly resembling the one stricken from the federal rule:

> "Any party may impeach any adverse deponent by self-contradiction without having laid foundation for such impeachment at the time such deposition was taken." R.S. Neb. § 25-1267.07.

For similar provisions, *see* Uniform Rule 65; California Evidence Code § 1202; Kansas Code of Civil Procedure § 60-462; New Jersey Evidence Rule 65.

The provision for cross-examination of a declarant upon his hearsay statement is a corollary of general principles of cross-examination. A similar provision is found in California Evidence Code § 1203.

ADVISORY COMMITTEE'S NOTE — 1987 AMENDMENT

The amendments are technical. No substantive change is intended.

ADVISORY COMMITTEE'S NOTE — 1997 AMENDMENT

The amendment is technical. No substantive change is intended.

Rule 807.   Residual Exception

(a) In General. Under the following circumstances, a hearsay statement is not excluded by the rule against hearsay even if the statement is not specifically covered by a hearsay exception in Rule 803 or 804:

(1) the statement has equivalent circumstantial guarantees of trustworthiness;

(2) it is offered as evidence of a material fact;

(3) it is more probative on the point for which it is offered than any other evidence that the proponent can obtain through reasonable efforts; and

---

(continued)

(4) admitting it will best serve the purposes of these rules and the interests of justice.

(b) Notice. The statement is admissible only if, before the trial or hearing, the proponent gives an adverse party reasonable notice of the intent to offer the statement and its particulars, including the declarant's name and address, so that the party has a fair opportunity to meet it.

(Added Apr. 11, 1997, eff. Dec. 1, 1997; Apr. 26, 2011, eff. Dec. 1, 2011.)

RESTYLED RULE 807 — ADVISORY COMMITTEE'S NOTE

The language of Rule 807 has been amended as part of the restyling of the Evidence Rules to make them more easily understood and to make style and terminology consistent throughout the rules. These changes are intended to be stylistic only. There is no intent to change any result in any ruling on evidence admissibility.

ADVISORY COMMITTEE'S NOTE — 1997 AMENDMENT

The contents of Rule 803(24) and Rule 804(b)(5) have been combined and transferred to a new Rule 807. This was done to facilitate additions to Rules 803 and 804. No change in meaning is intended.

ADVISORY COMMITTEE'S NOTE — ORIGINAL RULE 803(24)
56 F.R.D. 183, 320 (1973)

Exception (24). The preceding 23 exceptions of Rule 803 and the first five exceptions of Rule 804(b), *infra*, are designed to take full advantage of the accumulated wisdom and experience of the past in dealing with hearsay. It would, however, be presumptuous to assume that all possible desirable exceptions to the hearsay rule have been catalogued and to pass the hearsay rule to oncoming generations as a closed system. Exception (24) and its companion provision in Rule 804(b)(6) are accordingly included. They do not contemplate an unfettered exercise of judicial discretion, but they do provide for treating new and presently unanticipated situations which demonstrate a trustworthiness within the spirit of the specifically stated exceptions. Within this framework, room is left for growth and development of the law of evidence in the hearsay area, consistently with the broad purposes expressed in Rule 102. *See* Dallas County v. Commercial Union Assur. Co., 286 F.2d 388 (5th Cir. 1961).

ADVISORY COMMITTEE'S NOTE — ORIGINAL RULE 804(B)(6)
56 F.R.D. 183, 328 (1973)

Exception (6). In language and purpose, this exception is identical with Rule 803(24). *See* the Advisory Committee's Note to that provision.

[NOTE: The rule that became number 804(b)(5) was originally proposed as Rule 804(b)(6).]

ARTICLE IX.   AUTHENTICATION AND IDENTIFICATION

Rule 901.   Authenticating or Identifying Evidence

(a) In General. To satisfy the requirement of authenticating or identifying an item of evidence, the proponent must produce evidence sufficient to support a finding that the item is what the proponent claims it is.

(b) Examples. The following are examples only — not a complete list — of evidence that satisfies the requirement:

(1) *Testimony of a Witness with Knowledge.* Testimony that an item is what it is claimed to be.

(2) *Nonexpert Opinion About Handwriting.* A nonexpert's opinion that handwriting is genuine, based on a familiarity with it that was not acquired for the current litigation.

(3) *Comparison by an Expert Witness or the Trier of Fact.* A comparison with an authenticated specimen by an expert witness or the trier of fact.

(4) *Distinctive Characteristics and the Like.* The appearance, contents, substance, internal patterns, or other distinctive characteristics of the item, taken together with all the circumstances.

(5) *Opinion About a Voice.* An opinion identifying a person's voice — whether heard firsthand or through mechanical or electronic transmission or recording — based on hearing the voice at any time under circumstances that connect it with the alleged speaker.

(6) *Evidence About a Telephone Conversation.* For a telephone conversation, evidence that a call was made to the number assigned at the time to:

(A) a particular person, if circumstances, including self-identification, show that the person answering was the one called; or

(B) a particular business, if the call was made to a business and the call related to business reasonably transacted over the telephone.

(7) *Evidence About Public Records.* Evidence that:

(A) a document was recorded or filed in a public office as authorized by law; or

(B) a purported public record or statement is from the office where items of this kind are kept.

(8) *Evidence About Ancient Documents or Data Compilations.* For a document or data compilation, evidence that it:

(A) is in a condition that creates no suspicion about its authenticity;

(B) was in a place where, if authentic, it would likely be; and

(C) is at least 20 years old when offered.

(9) *Evidence About a Process or System.* Evidence describing a process or system and showing that it produces an accurate result.

(continued)

---

(10) *Methods Provided by a Statute or Rule.* Any method of authentication or identification allowed by a federal statute or a rule prescribed by the Supreme Court.

(Pub. L. 93-595, § 1, Jan. 2, 1975, 88 Stat. 1943; Apr. 26, 2011, eff. Dec. 1, 2011.)

RESTYLED RULE 901 — ADVISORY COMMITTEE'S NOTE

The language of Rule 901 has been amended as part of the restyling of the Evidence Rules to make them more easily understood and to make style and terminology consistent throughout the rules. These changes are intended to be stylistic only. There is no intent to change any result in any ruling on evidence admissibility.

ADVISORY COMMITTEE'S NOTE
56 F.R.D. 183, 332 (1973)

Subdivision (a). Authentication and identification represent a special aspect of relevancy. Michael and Adler, Real Proof, 5 Vand. L. Rev. 344, 362 (1952); McCormick § 179, 185; Morgan, Basic Problems of Evidence 378 (1962). Thus a telephone conversation may be irrelevant because on an unrelated topic or because the speaker is not identified. The latter aspect is the one here involved. Wigmore describes the need for authentication as "an inherent logical necessity." 7 Wigmore § 2129, p.564.

This requirement of showing authenticity or identity falls in the category of relevancy dependent upon fulfillment of a condition of fact and is governed by the procedure set forth in Rule 104(b).

The common law approach to authentication of documents has been criticized as an "attitude of agnosticism," McCormick, Cases on Evidence 388, n.4 (3d ed. 1956), as one which "departs sharply from men's customs in ordinary affairs," and as presenting only a slight obstacle to the introduction of forgeries in comparison to the time and expense devoted to proving genuine writings which correctly show their origin on their face, McCormick § 185, pp.395, 396. Today, such available procedures as requests to admit and pretrial conference afford the means of eliminating much of the need for authentication or identification. Also, significant inroads upon the traditional insistence on authentication and identification have been made by accepting as at least prima facie genuine items of the kind treated in Rule 902, *infra.* However, the need for suitable methods of proof still remains, since criminal cases pose their own obstacles to the use of preliminary procedures, unforeseen contingencies may arise, and cases of genuine controversy will still occur.

Subdivision (b). The treatment of authentication and identification draws largely upon the experience embodied in the common law and in statutes to furnish illustrative applications of the general principle set forth in subdivision (a). The examples are not intended as an exclusive enumeration of allowable methods but are meant to guide and suggest, leaving room for growth and development in this area of the law.

The examples relate for the most part to documents, with some attention given to voice communications and computer print-outs. As Wigmore noted, no special rules have been developed for authenticating chattels. Wigmore, Code of Evidence § 2086 (3d ed. 1942).

It should be observed that compliance with requirements of authentication or identification by no means assures admission of an item into evidence, as other bars, hearsay for example, may remain.

Example (1). Example (1) contemplates a broad spectrum ranging from testimony of a witness who was present at the signing of a document to testimony establishing narcotics as taken from an accused and accounting for custody through the period until trial, including laboratory analysis. *See* California Evidence Code § 1413, eyewitness to signing.

Example (2). Example (2) states conventional doctrine as to lay identification of handwriting, which recognizes that a sufficient familiarity with the handwriting of another person may be acquired by seeing him write, by exchanging correspondence, or by other means, to afford a basis for identifying it on subsequent occasions. McCormick § 189. *See also* California Evidence Code § 1416. Testimony based upon familiarity acquired for purposes of the litigation is reserved to the expert under the example which follows.

Example (3). The history of common law restrictions upon the technique of proving or disproving the genuineness of a disputed specimen of handwriting through comparison with a genuine specimen, by either the testimony of expert witnesses or direct viewing by the triers themselves, is detailed in 7 Wigmore § 1991-1994. In breaking away, the English Common Law Procedure Act of 1854, 17 and 18 Viet., c. 125, § 27, cautiously allowed expert or trier to use exemplars "proved to the satisfaction of the judge to be genuine" for purposes of comparison. The language found its way into numerous statutes in this country, e.g., California Evidence Code § 1417, 1418. While explainable as a measure of prudence in the process of breaking with precedent in the handwriting situation, the reservation to the judge of the question of the genuineness of exemplars and the imposition of an unusually high standard of persuasion are at variance with the general treatment of relevancy which depends upon fulfillment of a condition of fact. Rule 104(b). No similar attitude is found in other comparison situations, e.g., ballistics comparison by jury, as in Evans v. Commonwealth, 230 Ky. 411, 19 S.W.2d 1091 (1929), or by experts, Annot. 26 A.L.R.2d 892, and no reason appears for its continued existence in handwriting cases. Consequently Example (3) sets no higher standard for handwriting specimens and treats all comparison situations alike, to be governed by Rule 104(b). This approach is consistent with 28 U.S.C. § 1731: "The admitted or proved handwriting of any person shall be admissible, for purposes of comparison, to determine genuineness of other handwriting attributed to such person."

Precedent supports the acceptance of visual comparison as sufficiently satisfying preliminary authentication requirements for admission in evidence. Brandon v. Collins, 267 F.2d 731 (2d Cir. 1959); Wausau Sulphate Fibre Co. v. Commissioner of Internal Revenue, 61 F.2d 879 (7th Cir. 1932); Desimone v. United States, 227 F.2d 864 (9th Cir. 1955).

Example (4). The characteristics of the offered item itself, considered in the light of circumstances, afford authentication techniques in great variety. Thus a document or telephone conversation may be shown to have emanated from a particular person by virtue of its disclosing knowledge of facts known peculiarly to him; Globe Automatic Sprinkler Co. v. Braniff, 89 Okl. 105, 214 P. 127 (1923); California Evidence Code § 1421; similarly, a letter may be authenticated by content and circumstances indicating it was in reply to a duly authenticated one. McCormick § 192; California Evidence Code § 1420. Language patterns may indicate authenticity or its opposite. Magnuson v. State, 187 Wis. 122, 203 N.W. 749 (1925); Arens and Meadow, Psycholinguistics and the Confession Dilemma, 56 Colum. L. Rev. 19 (1956).

Example (5). Since aural voice identification is not a subject of expert testimony, the requisite familiarity may be acquired either before or after the particular speaking which is the subject of the identification, in this respect resembling visual identification of a person rather than identification of handwriting. *Cf.* Example (2), *supra*, People v. Nichols, 378 Ill. 487, 38 N.E.2d 766 (1942); McGuire v. State, 200 Md. 601, 92 A.2d 582 (1952); State v. McGee, 336 Mo. 1082, 83 S.W.2d 98 (1935).

Example (6). The cases are in agreement that a mere assertion of his identity by a person talking on the telephone is not sufficient evidence of the authenticity of the conversation and that additional evidence of his identity is required. The additional evidence need not fall in any set pattern. Thus the content of his statements or the reply technique, under Example (4), *supra,* or voice identification under Example (5), may furnish the necessary foundation. Outgoing calls made by the witness involve additional factors bearing upon authenticity. The calling of a number assigned by the telephone company reasonably supports the assumption that the listing is correct and that the number is the one reached. If the number is that of a place of business, the mass of authority allows an ensuing conversation if it relates to business reasonably transacted over the telephone, on the theory that the maintenance of the telephone connection is an invitation to do business without further identification. Matton v. Hoover Co., 350 Mo. 506, 166 S.W.2d 557 (1942); City of Pawhuska v. Crutchfield, 147 Okl. 4. 293 P. 1095 (1930); Zurich General Acc. & Liability Ins. Co. v. Baum, 159 Va. 404, 165 S.E. 518 (1932). Otherwise, some additional circumstance of identification of the speaker is required. The authorities divide on the question whether the self-identifying statement of the person answering suffices. Example (6) answers in the affirmative on the assumption that usual conduct respecting telephone calls furnish adequate assurances of regularity, bearing in mind that the entire matter is open to exploration before the trier of fact. In general, *see* McCormick § 193; 7 Wigmore § 2155; Annot., 71 A.L.R. 5, 105 *id.* 326.

Example (7). Public records are regularly authenticated by proof of custody, without more. McCormick § 191; 7 Wigmore § 2158, 2159. The example extends the principle to include data stored in computers and similar methods, of which increasing use in the public records area may be expected. *See* California Evidence Code § 1532, 1600.

Example (8). The familiar ancient document rule of the common law is extended to include data stored electronically or by other similar means. Since the importance of appearance diminishes in this situation, the importance of custody or place where found increases correspondingly. This expansion is necessary in view of the widespread use of methods of storing data in forms other than conventional written records.

Any time period selected is bound to be arbitrary. The common law period of 30 years is here reduced to 20 years, with some shift of emphasis from the probable unavailability of witnesses to the unlikeliness of a still viable fraud after the lapse of time. The shorter period is specified in the English Evidence Act of 1938, 1 & 2 Geo. 6, c. 28, and in Oregon R.S. 1963, § 41.360(34). *See also* the numerous statutes prescribing periods of less than 30 years in the case of recorded documents. 7 Wigmore § 2143.

The application of Example (8) is not subject to any limitation to title documents or to any requirement that possession, in the case of a title document, has been consistent with the document. *See* McCormick § 190.

Example (9). Example (9) is designed for situations in which the accuracy of a result is dependent upon a process or system which produces it. X-rays afford a familiar instance. Among more recent developments is the computer, as to which *see* Transport Indemnity Co. v. Seib, 178 Neb. 253, 132 N.W.2d 871 (1965); State v. Veres, 7 Ariz. App. 117, 436 P.2d 629 (1968); Merrick v. United States Rubber Co., 7 Ariz. App. 433, 440 P.2d 314 (1968); Freed, Computer Print-Outs as Evidence, 16 Am. Jur. Proof of Facts 273; Symposium, Law and Computers in the Mid-Sixties, ALI-ABA (1966); 37 Albany L. Rev. 61 (1967). Example (9) does not, of course, foreclose taking judicial notice of the accuracy of the process or system.

Example (10). The example makes clear that methods of authentication provided by Act of Congress and by the Rules of Civil and Criminal Procedure or by Bankruptcy Rules are not intended to be superseded. Illustrative are the provisions for authentication of official records in Civil Procedure Rule 44 and Criminal Procedure Rule 27, for authentication of records of proceedings by court reporters in 28 U.S.C. §753(b) and Civil Procedure Rule 80(c), and for authentication of depositions in Civil Procedure Rule 30(f).

Rule 902.   Evidence That Is Self-Authenticating

The following items of evidence are self-authenticating; they require no extrinsic evidence of authenticity in order to be admitted:

(1) *Domestic Public Documents That Are Sealed and Signed.* A document that bears:

(A) a seal purporting to be that of the United States; any state, district, commonwealth, territory, or insular possession of the United States; the former Panama Canal Zone; the Trust Territory of the Pacific Islands; a political subdivision of any of these entities; or a department, agency, or officer of any entity named above: and

(B) a signature purporting to be an execution or attestation.

(2) *Domestic Public Documents That Are Not Sealed but are Signed and Certified.* A document that bears no seal if:

(A) it bears the signature of an officer or employee of an entity named in Rule 902(1)(A); and

(B) another public officer who has a seal and official duties within that same entity certifies under seal — or its equivalent — that the signer has the official capacity and that the signature is genuine.

(3) *Foreign Public Documents.* A document that purports to be signed or attested by a person who is authorized by a foreign country's law to do so. The document must be accompanied by a final certification that certifies the genuineness of the signature and official position of the signer or attester — or of any foreign official whose certificate of genuineness relates to the signature or attestation or is in a chain of certificates of genuineness relating to the signature or attestation. The certification may be made by a secretary of a United States embassy or legation; by a consul general, vice consul, or consular agent of the United States; or by a diplomatic or consular official of the foreign country assigned or accredited to the United States. If all parties have been given a reasonable opportunity to investigate the document's authenticity and accuracy, the court may, for good cause, either:

(A) order that it be treated as presumptively authentic without final certification; or

(B) allow it to be evidenced by an attested summary with or without final certification.

(4) *Certified Copies of Public Records.* A copy of an official record — or a copy of a document that was recorded or filed in a public office as authorized by law — if the copy is certified as correct by:

(A) the custodian or another person authorized to make the certification; or

(B) a certificate that complies with Rule 902(1), (2), or (3), a federal statute, or a rule prescribed by the Supreme Court.

(continued)

(5) *Official Publications.* A book, pamphlet, or other publication purporting to be issued by a public authority.

(6) *Newspapers and Periodicals.* Printed material purporting to be a newspaper or periodical.

(7) *Trade Inscriptions and the Like.* An inscription, sign, tag, or label purporting to have been affixed in the course of business and indicating origin, ownership, or control.

(8) *Acknowledged Documents.* A document accompanied by a certificate of acknowledgment that is lawfully executed by a notary public or another officer who is authorized to take acknowledgments.

(9) *Commercial Paper and Related Documents.* Commercial paper, a signature on it, and related documents, to the extent allowed by general commercial law.

(10) *Presumptions Under a Federal Statute.* A signature, document, or anything else that a federal statute declares to be presumptively or prima facie genuine or authentic.

(11) *Certified Domestic Records of a Regularly Conducted Activity.* The original or a copy of a domestic record that meets the requirements of Rule 803(6) (A)-(C), as shown by a certification of the custodian or another qualified person that complies with a federal statute or a rule prescribed by the Supreme Court. Before the trial or hearing, the proponent must give an adverse party reasonable written notice of the intent to offer the record—and must make the record and certification available for inspection—so that the party has a fair opportunity to challenge them.

(12) *Certified Foreign Records of a Regularly Conducted Activity.* In a civil case, the original or a copy of a foreign record that meets the requirements of Rule 902(11), modified as follows: the certification, rather than complying with a federal statute or Supreme Court rule, must be signed in a manner that, if falsely made, would subject the maker to a criminal penalty in the country where the certification is signed. The proponent must also meet the notice requirements of Rule 902(11).

(Pub. L. 93-595, § 1, Jan. 2, 1975, 88 Stat. 1944; Mar. 2, 1987, eff. Oct. 1, 1987; Apr. 25, 1988, eff. Nov. 1, 1988; Apr. 17, 2000, eff. Dec. 1, 2000; Apr. 26, 2011, eff. Dec. 1, 2011.)

RESTYLED RULE 902 — ADVISORY COMMITTEE'S NOTE

The language of Rule 902 has been amended as part of the restyling of the Evidence Rules to make them more easily understood and to make style and terminology consistent throughout the rules. These changes are intended to be stylistic only. There is no intent to change any result in any ruling on evidence admissibility.

ADVISORY COMMITTEE'S NOTE
56 F.R.D. 183, 337 (1973)

Case law and statutes have, over the years, developed a substantial body of instances in which authenticity is taken as sufficiently established for purposes of admissibility without extrinsic evidence to that effect, sometimes for reasons of policy but perhaps more often because practical considerations reduce the possibility of unauthenticity to a very small dimension. The present rule collects and incorporates these situations, in some instances expanding them to occupy a larger area which their underlying considerations justify. In no instance is the opposite party foreclosed from disputing authenticity.

Paragraph (1). The acceptance of documents bearing a public seal and signature, most often encountered in practice in the form of acknowledgments or certificates authenticating copies of public records, is actually of broad application. Whether theoretically based in whole or in part upon judicial notice, the practical underlying considerations are that forgery is a crime and detection is fairly easy and certain. 7 Wigmore § 2161, p.638; California Evidence Code § 1452. More than 50 provisions for judicial notice of official seals are contained in the United States Code.

Paragraph (2). While statutes are found which raise a presumption of genuineness of purported official signatures in the absence of an official seal, 7 Wigmore § 2167; California Evidence Code § 1453, the greater ease of effecting a forgery under these circumstances is apparent. Hence this paragraph of the rule calls for authentication by an officer who has a seal. Notarial acts by members of the armed forces and other special situations are covered in paragraph (10).

Paragraph (3) provides a method for extending the presumption of authenticity to foreign official documents by a procedure of certification. It is derived from Rule 44(a)(2) of the Rules of Civil Procedure but is broader in applying to public documents rather than being limited to public records.

Paragraph (4). The common law and innumerable statutes have recognized the procedure of authenticating copies of public records by certificate. The certificate qualifies as a public document, receivable as authentic when in conformity with paragraph (1), (2), or (3). Rule 44(a) of the Rules of Civil Procedure and Rule 27 of the Rules of Criminal Procedure have provided authentication procedures of this nature for both domestic and foreign public records. It will be observed that the certification procedure here provided extends only to public records, reports, and recorded documents, all including data compilations, and does not apply to public documents generally. Hence documents provable when presented in original form under paragraphs (1), (2), or (3) may not be provable by certified copy under paragraph (4).

Paragraph (5). Dispensing with preliminary proof of the genuineness of purportedly official publications, most commonly encountered in connection with statutes, court reports, rules, and regulations, has been greatly enlarged by statutes and decisions. 5 Wigmore § 1684. Paragraph (5), it will be noted, does not confer admissibility upon all official publications; it merely provides a means whereby their authenticity may be taken as established for purposes of admissibility. Rule 44(a) of the Rules of Civil Procedure has been to the same effect.

Paragraph (6). The likelihood of forgery of newspapers or periodicals is slight indeed. Hence no danger is apparent in receiving them. Establishing the authenticity of the publication may, of course, leave still open questions of authority and responsibility for items therein contained. *See* 7 Wigmore § 2150. *Cf.* 39 U.S.C. § 4005(b), public advertisement prima facie evidence of agency of person named, in postal fraud order proceeding; Canadian Uniform Evidence Act, Draft of 1936, printed copy of newspaper prima facie evidence that notices or advertisements were authorized.

Paragraph (7). Several factors justify dispensing with preliminary proof of genuineness of commercial and mercantile labels and the like. The risk of forgery is minimal. Trademark infringement involves serious penalties. Great efforts are devoted to inducing the public to buy in reliance on brand names, and substantial protection is given them. Hence the fairness of this treatment finds recognition in the cases. Curtiss Candy Co. v. Johnson, 163 Miss. 426, 141 So. 762 (1932), Baby Ruth candy bar; Doyle v. Continental Baking Co., 262 Mass. 516, 160 N.E. 325 (1928), loaf of bread; Weiner v. Mager & Throne, Inc., 167 Misc. 338, 3 N.Y.S.2d 918 (1938), same. *And see* W. Va. Code 1966, § 47-

3-5, trademark on bottle prima facie evidence of ownership. *Contra,* Keegan v. Green Giant Co., 150 Me. 283, 110 A.2d 599 (1954); Murphy v. Campbell Soup Co., 62 F.2d 564 (1st Cir. 1933). Cattle brands have received similar acceptance in the western states. Rev. Code Mont. 1947, §46-606; State v. Wolfley, 75 Kan. 406, 89 P. 1046 (1907); Annot., 11 L.R.A. (N.S.) 87. Inscriptions on trains and vehicles are held to be prima facie evidence of ownership or control. Pittsburgh, Ft. W. & C. Ry. v. Callaghan, 157 Ill. 406, 41 N.E. 909 (1895); 9 Wigmore §2510a. *See also* the provision of 19 U.S.C.§1615(2) that marks, labels, brands, or stamps indicating foreign origin are prima facie evidence of foreign origin of merchandise.

Paragraph (8). In virtually every state, acknowledged title documents are receivable in evidence without further proof. Statutes are collected in 5 Wigmore §1676. If this authentication suffices for documents of the importance of those affecting titles, logic scarcely permits denying this method when other kinds of documents are involved. Instances of broadly inclusive statutes are California Evidence Code §1451 and N.Y. CPLR 4538, McKinney's Consol. Laws 1963.

Paragraph (9). Issues of the authenticity of commercial paper in federal courts will usually arise in diversity cases, will involve an element of a cause of action or defense, and with respect to presumptions and burden of proof will be controlled by Erie Railroad Co. v. Tompkins, 304 U.S. 64, 58 S. Ct. 817, 82 L. Ed. 1188 (1938). Rule 302, *supra.* There may, however, be questions of authenticity involving lesser segments of a case or the case may be one governed by federal common law. Clearfield Trust Co. v. United States, 318 U.S. 363, 63 S. Ct. 573, 87 L. Ed. 838 (1943). *Cf.* United States v. Yazell, 382 U.S. 341, 86 S. Ct. 500, 15 L. Ed. 2d 404 (1966). In these situations, resort to the useful authentication provisions of the Uniform Commercial Code is provided for. While the phrasing is in terms of "general commercial law," in order to avoid the potential complication inherent in borrowing local statutes, today one would have difficulty in determining the general commercial law without referring to the Code. *See* Williams v. Walker-Thomas-Furniture Co., 121 U.S. App. D.C. 315, 350 F.2d 445 (1965). Pertinent Code provisions are sections 1-202, 3-307, and 3-510, dealing with third-party documents, signatures on negotiable instruments, protests, and statements of dishonor.

Paragraph (10). The paragraph continues in effect dispensations with preliminary proof of genuineness provided in various Acts of Congress. *See, for example,* 10 U.S.C. §936, signature, without seal, together with title, prima facie evidence of authenticity of acts of certain military personnel who are given notarial power; 15 U.S.C. §77f(a), signature on SEC registration presumed genuine; 26 U.S.C. §6064, signature to tax return prima facie genuine.

ADVISORY COMMITTEE'S NOTE — 1987 AMENDMENT

The amendments are technical. No substantive change is intended.

ADVISORY COMMITTEE'S NOTE — 1988 AMENDMENT

These two sentences were inadvertently eliminated from the 1987 amendments. The amendment is technical. No substantive change is intended.

ADVISORY COMMITTEE'S NOTE — 2000 AMENDMENT

The amendment adds two new paragraphs to the rule on self-authentication. It sets forth a procedure by which parties can authenticate certain records of regularly conducted activity, other than through the testimony of a foundation witness. *See* the amendment to Rule 803(6). 18 U.S.C. § 3505 currently provides a means for certifying foreign records of regularly conducted activity in criminal cases, and this amendment is intended to establish a similar procedure for domestic records, and for foreign records offered in civil cases.

A declaration that satisfies 28 U.S.C. § 1746 would satisfy the declaration requirement of Rule 902(11), as would any comparable certification under oath.

The notice requirement in Rules 902(11) and (12) is intended to give the opponent of the evidence a full opportunity to test the adequacy of the foundation set forth in the declaration.

Rule 903.   Subscribing Witness's Testimony

A subscribing witness's testimony is necessary to authenticate a writing only if required by the law of the jurisdiction that governs its validity.

(Pub. L. 93-595, § 1, Jan. 2, 1975, 88 Stat. 1945; Apr. 26, 2011, eff. Dec. 1, 2011.)

RESTYLED RULE 903 — ADVISORY COMMITTEE'S NOTE

The language of Rule 903 has been amended as part of the restyling of the Evidence Rules to make them more easily understood and to make style and terminology consistent throughout the rules. These changes are intended to be stylistic only. There is no intent to change any result in any ruling on evidence admissibility.

ADVISORY COMMITTEE'S NOTE
56 F.R.D. 183, 340 (1973)

The common law required that attesting witnesses be produced or accounted for. Today the requirement has generally been abolished except with respect to documents which must be attested to be valid, e.g., wills in some states. McCormick § 188. Uniform Rule 71; California Evidence Code § 1411; Kansas Code of Civil Procedure § 60-468; New Jersey Evidence Rule 71; New York CPLR Rule 4537.

ARTICLE X.   CONTENTS OF WRITINGS, RECORDINGS, AND PHOTOGRAPHS

Rule 1001.   Definitions That Apply to This Article

In this article:
    (a) A "writing" consists of letters, words, numbers, or their equivalent set down in any form.

(continued)

(b) A "recording" consists of letters, words, numbers, or their equivalent recorded in any manner.

(c) A "photograph" means a photographic image or its equivalent stored in any form.

(d) An "original" of a writing or recording means the writing or recording itself or any counterpart intended to have the same effect by the person who executed or issued it. For electronically stored information, "original" means any printout—or other output readable by sight—if it accurately reflects the information. An "original" of a photograph includes the negative or a print from it.

(e) A "duplicate" means a counterpart produced by a mechanical, photographic, chemical, electronic, or other equivalent process or technique that accurately reproduces the original.

(Pub. L. 93-595, § 1, Jan. 2, 1975, 88 Stat. 1945; Apr. 26, 2011, eff. Dec. 1, 2011.)

RESTYLED RULE 1001 — ADVISORY COMMITTEE'S NOTE

The language of Rule 1001 has been amended as part of the restyling of the Evidence Rules to make them more easily understood and to make style and terminology consistent throughout the rules. These changes are intended to be stylistic only. There is no intent to change any result in any ruling on evidence admissibility.

ADVISORY COMMITTEE'S NOTE
56 F.R.D. 183, 341 (1973)

In an earlier day, when discovery and other related procedures were strictly limited, the misleading named "best evidence rule" afforded substantial guarantees against inaccuracies and fraud by its insistence upon production of original documents. The great enlargement of the scope of discovery and related procedures in recent times has measurably reduced the need for the rule. Nevertheless important areas of usefulness persist: discovery of documents outside the jurisdiction may require substantial outlay of time and money; the unanticipated document may not practically be discoverable; criminal cases have built-in limitations on discovery. Cleary and Strong, The Best Evidence Rule: An Evaluation in Context, 51 Iowa L. Rev. 825 (1966).

Paragraph (1). Traditionally the rule requiring the original centered upon accumulations of data and expressions affecting legal relations set forth in words and figures. This meant that the rule was one essentially related to writings. Present day techniques have expanded methods of storing data, yet the essential form which the information ultimately assumes for usable purposes is words and figures. Hence the considerations underlying the rule dictate its expansion to include computers, photographic systems, and other modern developments.

Paragraph (3). In most instances, what is an original will be self-evident and further refinement will be unnecessary. However, in some instances particularized definition is required. A carbon copy of a contract executed in duplicate becomes an original, as does a sales ticket carbon copy given to a customer. While strictly speaking the original of a photograph might be thought to be only the negative, practicality and common usage require that any print from the negative be regarded as an original. Similarly, practicality and usage confer the status of original upon any computer printout. Transport Indemnity Co. v. Seib, 178 Neb. 253, 132 N.W.2d 871 (1965).

Paragraph (4). The definition describes "copies" produced by methods possessing an accuracy which virtually eliminates the possibility of error. Copies thus produced are given the status of originals in large measure by Rule 1003, *infra.* Copies subsequently produced manually, whether handwritten or typed, are not within the definition. It should be noted that what is an original for some purposes may be a duplicate for others. Thus a bank's microfilm record of checks cleared is the original as a record. However, a print offered as a copy of a check whose contents are in controversy is a duplicate. This result is substantially consistent with 28 U.S.C. § 1732(b). *Compare* 26 U.S.C. § 7513(c), giving full status as originals to photographic reproductions of tax returns and other documents, made by authority of the Secretary of the Treasury, and 44 U.S.C. § 399(a), giving original status to photographic copies in the National Archives.

Rule 1002. Requirement of the Original

An original writing, recording, or photograph is required in order to prove its content unless these rules or a federal statute provides otherwise.

(Pub. L. 93-595, § 1, Jan. 2, 1975, 88 Stat. 1946; Apr. 26, 2011, eff. Dec. 1, 2011.)

RESTYLED RULE 1002 — ADVISORY COMMITTEE'S NOTE

The language of Rule 1002 has been amended as part of the restyling of the Evidence Rules to make them more easily understood and to make style and terminology consistent throughout the rules. These changes are intended to be stylistic only. There is no intent to change any result in any ruling on evidence admissibility.

ADVISORY COMMITTEE'S NOTE
56 F.R.D. 183, 342 (1973)

The rule is the familiar one requiring production of the original of a document to prove its contents, expanded to include writings, recordings, and photographs, as defined in Rule 1001(1) and (2), *supra.*

Application of the rule requires a resolution of the question whether contents are sought to be proved. Thus an event may be proved by nondocumentary evidence, even though a written record of it was made. If, however, the event is sought to be proved by the written record, the rule applies. For example, payment may be proved without producing the written receipt which was given. Earnings may be proved without producing books of account in which they are entered. McCormick § 198; 4 Wigmore § 1245. Nor does the rule apply to testimony that books or records have been examined and found not to contain any reference to a designated matter.

The assumption should not be made that the rule will come into operation on every occasion when use is made of a photograph in evidence. On the contrary, the rule will seldom apply to ordinary photographs. In most instances a party *wishes* to introduce the item and the question raised is the propriety of receiving it in evidence. Cases in which an offer is made of the testimony of a witness as to what he saw in a photograph or motion picture, without producing the same, are most unusual. The usual course is for a witness on the stand to identify the photograph or motion picture as a correct representation of events which he saw or of a scene with which he is familiar. In fact he adopts the picture as his testimony, or, in common parlance, uses the picture to illustrate his testimony. Under these circumstances, no effort is made to prove the contents of the picture, and the rule is inapplicable. Paradis, The Celluloid Witness, 37 U. Colo. L. Rev. 235, 249-251 (1965).

On occasion, however, situations arise in which contents are sought to be proved. Copyright, defamation, and invasion of privacy by photograph or motion picture falls in this category. Similarly as to situations in which the picture is offered as having independent probative value, e.g., automatic photograph of bank robber. *See* People v. Doggett, 83 Cal. App. 2d 405, 188 P.2d 792 (1948), photograph of defendants engaged in indecent act; Mouser and Philbin, Photographic Evidence — Is There a Recognized Basis for Admissibility? 8 Hastings L.J. 310 (1957). The most commonly encountered of this latter group is of course, the X-ray, with substantial authority calling for production of the original. Daniels v. Iowa City, 191 Iowa 811, 183 N.W. 415 (1921); Cellamare v. Third Acc. Transit Corp., 273 App. Div. 260, 77 N.Y.S.2d 91 (1948); Patrick & Tilman v. Matkin, 154 Okl. 232, 7 P.2d 414 (1932); Mendoza v. Rivera, 78 P.R.R. 569 (1955).

It should be noted, however, that Rule 703, *supra*, allows an expert to give an opinion based on matters not in evidence, and the present rule must be read as being limited accordingly in its application. Hospital records which may be admitted as business records under Rule 803(6) commonly contain reports interpreting X-rays by the staff radiologist, who qualifies as an expert, and these reports need not be excluded from the records by the instant rule.

The reference to Acts of Congress is made in view of such statutory provisions as 26 U.S.C. § 7513, photographic reproductions of tax returns and documents, made by authority of the Secretary of the Treasury, treated as originals, and 44 U.S.C. § 399(a), photographic copies in National Archives treated as originals.

Rule 1003.   Admissibility of Duplicates

A duplicate is admissible to the same extent as the original unless a genuine question is raised about the original's authenticity or the circumstances make it unfair to admit the duplicate.

(Pub. L. 93-595, § 1, Jan. 2, 1975, 88 Stat. 1946; Apr. 26, 2011, eff. Dec. 1, 2011.)

RESTYLED RULE 1003 — ADVISORY COMMITTEE'S NOTE

The language of Rule 1003 has been amended as part of the restyling of the Evidence Rules to make them more easily understood and to make style and terminology consistent throughout the rules. These changes are intended to be stylistic only. There is no intent to change any result in any ruling on evidence admissibility.

ADVISORY COMMITTEE'S NOTE
56 F.R.D. 183, 343 (1973)

When the only concern is with getting the words or other contents before the court with accuracy and precision, then a counterpart serves equally as well as the original, if the counterpart is the product of a method which insures accuracy and genuineness. By definition in Rule 1001(4), *supra,* a "duplicate" possesses this character.

Therefore, if no genuine issue exists as to authenticity and no other reason exists for requiring the original, a duplicate is admissible under the rule. This position finds support in the decisions, Myrick v. United States, 332 F.2d 279 (5th Cir. 1964), no error in admitting photostatic copies of checks instead of original microfilm in absence of suggestion to trial judge that photostats were incorrect; Johns v. United States, 323 F.2d 421 (5th Cir. 1963), not error to admit concededly accurate tape recording made from original wire recording; Sauget v. Johnston, 315 F.2d 816 (9th Cir. 1963), not error to admit copy of agreement when opponent had original and did not on appeal claim any discrepancy. Other reasons for requiring the original may be present when only a part of the original is reproduced and the remainder is needed for cross-examination or may disclose matters qualifying the part offered or otherwise useful to the opposing party. United States v. Alexander, 326 F.2d 736 (4th Cir. 1964). *And see* Toho Bussan Kaisha, Ltd. v. American President Lines, Ltd., 265 F.2d 418, 76 A.L.R.2d 1344 (2d Cir. 1959).

Rule 1004. Admissibility of Other Evidence of Content

An original is not required and other evidence of the content of a writing, recording, or photograph is admissible if:

(a) all the originals are lost or destroyed, and not by the proponent acting in bad faith;

(b) an original cannot be obtained by any available judicial process;

(c) the party against whom the original would be offered had control of the original; was at that time put on notice, by pleadings or otherwise, that the original would be a subject of proof at the trial or hearing; and fails to produce it at the trial or hearing; or

(d) the writing, recording, or photograph is not closely related to a controlling issue.

(Pub. L. 93-595, § 1, Jan. 2, 1975, 88 Stat. 1946; Mar. 2, 1987, eff. Oct. 1, 1987; Apr. 26, 2011, eff. Dec. 1, 2011.)

The amendments are technical. No substantive change is intended.

RESTYLED RULE 1004 — ADVISORY COMMITTEE'S NOTE

The language of Rule 1004 has been amended as part of the restyling of the Evidence Rules to make them more easily understood and to make style and terminology consistent throughout the rules. These changes are intended to be stylistic only. There is no intent to change any result in any ruling on evidence admissibility.

ADVISORY COMMITTEE'S NOTE
56 F.R.D. 183, 344 (1973)

Basically the rule requiring the production of the original as proof of contents has developed as a rule of preference: if failure to produce the original is satisfactorily explained, secondary evidence is admissible. The instant rule specifies the circumstances under which production of the original is excused.

The rule recognizes no "degrees" of secondary evidence. While strict logic might call for extending the principle of preference beyond simply preferring the original, the formulation of a hierarchy of preferences and a procedure for making it effective is believed to involve unwarranted complexities. Most, if not all, that would be accomplished by an extended scheme of preferences will, in any event, be achieved through the normal motivation of a party to present the most convincing evidence possible and the arguments and procedures available to his opponent if he does not. *Compare* McCormick § 207.

Paragraph (1). Loss or destruction of the original, unless due to bad faith of the proponent, is a satisfactory explanation of nonproduction. McCormick § 201.

Paragraph (2). When the original is in the possession of a third person, inability to procure it from him by resort to process or other judicial procedure is sufficient explanation of nonproduction. Judicial procedure includes subpoena duces tecum as an incident to the taking of a deposition in another jurisdiction. No further showing is required. *See* McCormick § 202.

Paragraph (3). A party who has an original in his control has no need for the protection of the rule if put on notice that proof of contents will be made. He can ward off secondary evidence by offering the original. The notice procedure here provided is not to be confused with orders to produce or other discovery procedures, as the purpose of the procedure under this rule is to afford the opposite party an opportunity to produce the original, not to compel him to do so. McCormick § 203.

Paragraph (4). While difficult to define with precision, situations arise in which no good purpose is served by production of the original. Examples are the newspaper in an action for the price of publishing defendant's advertisement, Foster-Holcomb Investment Co. v. Little Rock Publishing Co., 151 Ark. 449, 236 S.W. 597 (1922), and the streetcar transfer of plaintiff claiming status as a passenger, Chicago City Ry. Co. v. Carroll, 206 Ill. 318, 68 N.E. 1087 (1903). Numerous cases are collected in McCormick § 200, p.412, n.1.

Rule 1005.   Copies of Public Records to Prove Content

The proponent may use a copy to prove the content of an official record—or of a document that was recorded or filed in a public office as authorized by law—if these conditions are met: the record or document is otherwise admissible; and the copy is certified as correct in accordance with Rule 902(4) or is testified to be correct by a witness who has compared it with the original. If no such copy can be obtained by reasonable diligence, then the proponent may use other evidence to prove the content.

(Pub. L. 93-595, § 1, Jan. 2, 1975, 88 Stat. 1946; Apr. 26, 2011, eff. Dec. 1, 2011.)

RESTYLED RULE 1005—ADVISORY COMMITTEE'S NOTE

The language of Rule 1005 has been amended as part of the restyling of the Evidence Rules to make them more easily understood and to make style and terminology consistent throughout the rules. These changes are intended to be stylistic only. There is no intent to change any result in any ruling on evidence admissibility.

ADVISORY COMMITTEE'S NOTE
56 F.R.D. 183, 345 (1973)

Public records call for somewhat different treatment. Removing them from their usual place of keeping would be attended by serious inconvenience to the public and to the custodian. As a consequence judicial decisions and statutes commonly hold that no explanation need be given for failure to produce the original of a public record. McCormick § 204; 4 Wigmore § 1215-1228. This blanket dispensation from producing or accounting for the original would open the door to the introduction of every kind of secondary evidence of contents of public records were it not for the preference given certified or compared copies. Recognition of degrees of secondary evidence in this situation is an appropriate *quid pro quo* for not applying the requirement of producing the original.

The provisions of 28 U.S.C. § 1733(b) apply only to departments or agencies of the United States. The rule, however, applies to public records generally and is comparable in scope in this respect to Rule 44(a) of the Rules of Civil Procedure.

Rule 1006.   Summaries to Prove Content

The proponent may use a summary, chart, or calculation to prove the content of voluminous writings, recordings, or photographs that cannot be conveniently examined in court. The proponent must make the originals or duplicates available for examination or copying, or both, by other parties at a reasonable time and place. And the court may order the proponent to produce them in court.

(Pub. L. 93-595, § 1, Jan. 2, 1975, 88 Stat. 1946; Apr. 26, 2011, eff. Dec. 1, 2011.)

RESTYLED RULE 1006 — ADVISORY COMMITTEE'S NOTE

The language of Rule 1006 has been amended as part of the restyling of the Evidence Rules to make them more easily understood and to make style and terminology consistent throughout the rules. These changes are intended to be stylistic only. There is no intent to change any result in any ruling on evidence admissibility.

ADVISORY COMMITTEE'S NOTE
56 F.R.D. 183, 346 (1973)

The admission of summaries of voluminous books, records, or documents offers the only practicable means of making their contents available to judge and jury. The rule recognizes this practice, with appropriate safeguards. 4 Wigmore § 1230.

Rule 1007.   Testimony or Statement of a Party to Prove Content

The proponent may prove the content of a writing, recording, or photograph by the testimony, deposition, or written statement of the party against whom the evidence is offered. The proponent need not account for the original.

(Pub. L. 93-595, §1, Jan. 2, 1975, 88 Stat. 1947; Mar. 2, 1987, eff. Oct. 1, 1987; Apr. 26, 2011, eff. Dec. 1, 2011.)

RESTYLED RULE 1007—ADVISORY COMMITTEE'S NOTE

The language of Rule 1007 has been amended as part of the restyling of the Evidence Rules to make them more easily understood and to make style and terminology consistent throughout the rules. These changes are intended to be stylistic only. There is no intent to change any result in any ruling on evidence admissibility.

ADVISORY COMMITTEE'S NOTE
56 F.R.D. 183, 356 (1973)

While the parent case, Slatterie v. Pooley, 6 M. & W. 664, 151 Eng. Rep. 579 (Exch. 1840), allows proof of contents by evidence of an oral admission by the party against whom offered, without accounting for nonproduction of the original, the risk of inaccuracy is substantial and the decision is at odds with the purpose of the rule giving preference to the original. *See* 4 Wigmore § 1255. The instant rule follows Professor McCormick's suggestion of limiting this use of admissions to those made in the course of giving testimony or in writing. McCormick § 208, p.424. The limitation, of course, does not call for excluding evidence of an oral admission when nonproduction of the original has been accounted for and secondary evidence generally has become admissible. Rule 1004, *supra*.

A similar provision is contained in New Jersey Evidence Rule 70(1)(h).

ADVISORY COMMITTEE'S NOTE—1987 AMENDMENT

The amendment is technical. No substantive change is intended.

Rule 1008.   Functions of Court and Jury

Ordinarily, the court determines whether the proponent has fulfilled the factual conditions for admitting other evidence of the content of a writing, recording, or photograph under Rule 1004 or 1005. But in a jury trial, the jury determines—in accordance with Rule 104(b)—any issue about whether:

   (a) an asserted writing, recording, or photograph ever existed;
   (b) another one produced at the trial or hearing is the original; or
   (c) other evidence of content accurately reflects the content.

(Pub. L. 93-595, §1, Jan. 2, 1975, 88 Stat. 1947; Apr. 26, 2011, eff. Dec. 1, 2011.)

RESTYLED RULE 1008 — ADVISORY COMMITTEE'S NOTE

The language of Rule 1008 has been amended as part of the restyling of the Evidence Rules to make them more easily understood and to make style and terminology consistent throughout the rules. These changes are intended to be stylistic only. There is no intent to change any result in any ruling on evidence admissibility.

ADVISORY COMMITTEE'S NOTE
56 F.R.D. 183, 347 (1973)

Most preliminary questions of fact in connection with applying the rule preferring the original as evidence of contents are for the judge, under the general principles announced in Rule 104, *supra*. Thus, the question whether the loss of the originals has been established, or of the fulfillment of other conditions specified in Rule 1004, *supra*, is for the judge. However, questions may arise which go beyond the mere administration of the rule preferring the original and into the merits of the controversy. For example, plaintiff offers secondary evidence of the contents of an alleged contract, after first introducing evidence of loss of the original, and defendant counters with evidence that no such contract was ever executed. If the judge decides that the contract was never executed and excludes the secondary evidence, the case is at an end without ever going to the jury on a central issue. Levin, Authentication and Content of Writings, 10 Rutgers L. Rev. 632, 644 (1956). The latter portion of the instant rule is designed to insure treatment of these situations as raising jury questions. The decision is not one for uncontrolled discretion of the jury but is subject to the control exercised generally by the judge over jury determinations. *See* Rule 104(b), *supra*.

For similar provisions, *see* Uniform Rule 70(2); Kansas Code of Civil Procedure § 60-467(b); New Jersey Evidence Rule 70(2), (3).

ARTICLE XI.   MISCELLANEOUS RULES

Rule 1101.   Applicability of the Rules

(a) To Courts and Judges. These rules apply to proceedings before:

- United States district courts;
- United States bankruptcy and magistrate judges;
- United States courts of appeals;
- the United States Court of Federal Claims; and
- the district courts of Guam, the Virgin Islands, and the Northern Mariana Islands.

(b) To Cases and Proceedings. These rules apply in:

- civil cases and proceedings, including bankruptcy, admiralty and maritime cases;
- criminal cases and proceedings; and
- contempt proceedings, except those in which the court may act summarily.

(continued)

(c) Rules on Privilege. The rules on privilege apply to all stages of a case or proceeding.

(d) Exceptions. These rules — except for those on privilege — do not apply to the following:

(1) the court's determination, under Rule 104(a), on a preliminary question of fact governing admissibility;

(2) grand-jury proceedings; and

(3) miscellaneous proceedings such as:

- extradition or rendition;
- issuing an arrest warrant, criminal summons, or search warrant;
- a preliminary examination in a criminal case;
- sentencing;
- granting or revoking probation or supervised release; and
- considering whether to release on bail or otherwise.

(e) Other Statutes and Rules. A federal statute or a rule prescribed by the Supreme Court may provide for admitting or excluding evidence independently from these rules.

(Pub. L. 93-595, § 1, Jan. 2, 1975, 88 Stat. 1947; Pub. L. 94-149, § 1(14), Dec. 12, 1975, 89 Stat. 806; Pub. L. 95-598, title II, § 251, 252, Nov. 6, 1978, 92 Stat. 2673; Pub. L. 97-164, title I, § 142, Apr. 2, 1982, 96 Stat. 45; Mar. 2, 1987, eff. Oct. 1, 1987; Apr. 25, 1988, eff. Nov. 1, 1988; Pub. L. 100-690, title VII, § 7075(c), Nov. 18, 1988, 102 Stat. 4405; Apr. 22, 1993, eff. Dec. 1, 1993; Apr. 26, 2011, eff. Dec. 1, 2011.)

RESTYLED RULE 1101 — ADVISORY COMMITTEE'S NOTE

The language of Rule 1101 has been amended as part of the restyling of the Evidence Rules to make them more easily understood and to make style and terminology consistent throughout the rules. These changes are intended to be stylistic only. There is no intent to change any result in any ruling on evidence admissibility.

ADVISORY COMMITTEE'S NOTE
56 F.R.D. 183, 348 (1973)

Subdivision (a). The various enabling acts contain differences in phraseology in their descriptions of the courts over which the Supreme Court's power to make rules of practice and procedure extends. The act concerning civil actions, as amended in 1966, refers to "the district courts . . . of the United States in civil actions, including admiralty and maritime cases. . . ." 28 U.S.C. § 2072, Pub. L. 89-773, § 1, 80 Stat. 1323. The bankruptcy authorization is for rules of practice and procedure "under the Bankruptcy Act." 28 U.S.C. § 2075, Pub. L. 88-623, § 1, 78 Stat. 1001. The Bankruptcy Act in turn creates bankruptcy courts of "the United States district courts and the district courts of the Territories and possessions to which this title is or may hereafter be applicable." 11 U.S.C. § 1(10), 11(a). The provision as to criminal rules up to and including verdicts applies to "criminal cases and proceedings to punish for criminal contempt of court in the United States district courts, in the district courts for the districts of the Canal Zone and Virgin Islands, in the Supreme Court of Puerto Rico, and in proceedings before United States magistrates." 18 U.S.C. § 3771.

These various provisions do not in terms describe the same courts. In congressional usage the phrase "district courts of the United States," without further qualification, traditionally has included the district courts established by Congress in the states under Article III of the Constitution, which are "constitutional" courts, and has not included the territorial courts created under Article IV, Section 3, Clause 2, which are "legislative" courts. Hornbuckle v. Toombs, 85 U.S. 648, 21 L. Ed. 966 (1873). However, any doubt as to the inclusion of the District Court for the District of Columbia in the phrase is laid at rest by the provisions of the Judicial Code constituting the judicial districts, 28 U.S.C. § 81 et seq. creating district courts therein, *Id.* § 132, and specifically providing that the term "district court of the United States" means the courts so constituted. *Id.* § 451. The District of Columbia is included. *Id.* § 88. Moreover, when these provisions were enacted, reference to the District of Columbia was deleted from the original civil rules enabling act. 28 U.S.C. § 2072. Likewise Puerto Rico is made a district, with a district court, and included in the term. *Id.* § 119. The question is simply one of the extent of the authority conferred by Congress. With respect to civil rules it seems clearly to include the district courts in the states, the District Court for the District of Columbia, and the District Court for the District of Puerto Rico.

The bankruptcy coverage is broader. The bankruptcy courts include "the United States district courts," which includes those enumerated above. Bankruptcy courts also include "the district courts of the Territories and possessions to which this title is or may hereafter be applicable." 11 U.S.C. § 1(10), 11(a). These courts include the district courts of Guam and the Virgin Islands. 48 U.S.C. § 1424(b), 1615. Professor Moore points out that whether the District Court for the District of the Canal Zone is a court of bankruptcy "is not free from doubt in view of the fact that no other statute expressly or inferentially provides for the applicability of the Bankruptcy Act in the Zone." He further observes that while there seems to be little doubt that the Zone is a territory or possession within the meaning of the Bankruptcy Act, 11 U.S.C. § 1(10), it must be noted that the appendix to the Canal Zone Code of 1934 did not list the Act among the laws of the United States applicable to the Zone. 1 Moore's Collier on Bankruptcy § 1.10, pp.67, 72, n.25 (14th ed. 1967). The Code of 1962 confers on the district court jurisdiction of:

> "(4) actions and proceedings involving laws of the United States applicable to the Canal Zone; and

> "(5) other matters and proceedings wherein jurisdiction is conferred by this Code or any other law." Canal Zone Code, 1962, Title 3, § 141.

Admiralty jurisdiction is expressly conferred. *Id.* § 142. General powers are conferred on the district court, "if the course of proceeding is not specifically prescribed by this Code, by the statute, or by applicable rule of the Supreme Court of the United States. . . ." *Id.* § 279. Neither these provisions nor § 1(10) of the Bankruptcy Act ("district courts of the Territories and possessions to which this title is or may hereafter be applicable") furnishes a satisfactory answer as to the status of the District Court for the District of the Canal Zone as a court of bankruptcy. However, the fact is that this court exercises no bankruptcy jurisdiction in practice.

The criminal rules enabling act specifies United States district courts, district courts for the districts of the Canal Zone and the Virgin Islands, the Supreme Court of the Commonwealth of Puerto Rico, and proceedings before United States commissioners. Aside from the addition of commissioners, now magistrates, this scheme differs from the bankruptcy pattern in that it makes no mention of the District Court of Guam but by specific mention removes the Canal Zone from the doubtful list.

The further difference in including the Supreme Court of the Commonwealth of Puerto Rico seems not to be significant for present purposes, since the Supreme

Court of the Commonwealth of Puerto Rico is an appellate court. The Rules of Criminal Procedure have not been made applicable to it, as being unneeded and inappropriate, Rule 54(a) of the Federal Rules of Criminal Procedure, and the same approach is indicated with respect to rules of evidence.

If one were to stop at this point and frame a rule governing the applicability of the proposed rules of evidence in terms of the authority conferred by the three enabling acts, an irregular pattern would emerge as follows:

Civil actions, including admiralty and maritime cases—district courts in the states, District of Columbia, and Puerto Rico.

Bankruptcy—same as civil actions, plus Guam and Virgin Islands.

Criminal cases—same as civil actions, plus Canal Zone and Virgin Islands (but not Guam).

This irregular pattern need not, however, be accepted. Originally the Advisory Committee on the Rules of Civil Procedure took the position that, although the phrase "district courts of the United States" did not include territorial courts, provisions in the organic laws of Puerto Rico and Hawaii would make the rules applicable to the district courts thereof, though this would not be so as to Alaska, the Virgin Islands, or the Canal Zone, whose organic acts contained no corresponding provisions. At the suggestion of the Court, however, the Advisory Committee struck from its notes a statement to the above effect. 2 Moore's Federal Practice § 1.07 (2d ed. 1967); 1 Barron and Holtzoff, Federal Practice and Procedure § 121 (Wright ed. 1960). Congress thereafter by various enactments provided that the rules and future amendments thereto should apply to the district courts of Hawaii, 53 Stat. 841 (1939), Puerto Rico, 54 Stat. 22 (1940), Alaska, 63 Stat. 445 (1949), Guam, 64 Stat. 384-390 (1950), and the Virgin Islands, 68 Stat. 497, 507 (1954). The original enabling act for rules of criminal procedure specifically mentioned the district courts of the Canal Zone and the Virgin Islands. The Commonwealth of Puerto Rico was blanketed in by creating its court a "district court of the United States" as previously described. Although Guam is not mentioned in either the enabling act or in the expanded definition of "district court of the United States," the Supreme Court in 1956 amended Rule 54(a) to state that the Rules of Criminal Procedure are applicable in Guam. The Court took this step following the enactment of legislation by Congress in 1950 that rules theretofore or thereafter promulgated by the Court in civil cases, admiralty, criminal cases and bankruptcy should apply to the District Court of Guam, 48 U.S.C. § 1424(b), and two Ninth Circuit decisions upholding the applicability of the Rules of Criminal Procedure to Guam. Pugh v. United States, 212 F.2d 761 (9th Cir. 1954); Hatchett v. Guam, 212 F.2d 767 (9th Cir. 1954); Orfield, The Scope of the Federal Rules of Criminal Procedure, 38 U. of Det. L.J. 173, 187 (1960).

From this history, the reasonable conclusion is that Congressional enactment of a provision that rules and future amendments shall apply in the courts of a territory or possession is the equivalent of mention in an enabling act and that a rule on scope and applicability may properly be drafted accordingly. Therefore the pattern set by Rule 54 of the Federal Rules of Criminal Procedure is here followed.

The substitution of magistrates in lieu of commissioners is made in pursuance of the Federal Magistrates Act, P.L. 90-578, approved October 17, 1968, 82 Stat. 1107.

Subdivision (b) is a combination of the language of the enabling acts, *supra,* with respect to the kinds of proceedings in which the making of rules is authorized. It is subject to the qualifications expressed in the subdivisions which follow.

Subdivision (c), singling out the rules of privilege for special treatment, is made necessary by the limited applicability of the remaining rules.

Subdivision (d). The rule is not intended as an expression as to when due process or other constitutional provisions may require an evidentiary hearing. Paragraph

(1) restates, for convenience, the provisions of the second sentence of Rule 104(a), *supra. See* Advisory Committee's Note to that rule.

(2) While some states have statutory requirements that indictments be based on "legal evidence," and there is some case law to the effect that the rules of evidence apply to grand jury proceedings, 1 Wigmore § 4(5), the Supreme Court has not accepted this view. In Costello v. United States, 350 U.S. 359, 76 S. Ct. 406, 100 L. Ed. 397 (1965), the Court refused to allow an indictment to be attacked, for either constitutional or policy reasons, on the ground that only hearsay evidence was presented.

> "It would run counter to the whole history of the grand jury institution, in which laymen conduct their inquiries unfettered by technical rules. Neither justice nor the concept of a fair trial requires such a change." *Id.* at 364.

The rule as drafted does not deal with the evidence required to support an indictment.

(3) The rule exempts preliminary examinations in criminal cases. Authority as to the applicability of the rules of evidence to preliminary examinations has been meagre and conflicting. Goldstein, The State and the Accused: Balance of Advantage in Criminal Procedure, 69 Yale L.J. 1149, 1168, n.53 (1960); Comment, Preliminary Hearings on Indictable Offenses in Philadelphia, 106 U. Pa. L. Rev. 589, 592-593 (1958). Hearsay testimony is, however, customarily received in such examinations. Thus in a Dyer Act case, for example, an affidavit may properly be used in a preliminary examination to prove ownership of the stolen vehicle, thus saving the victim of the crime the hardship of having to travel twice to a distant district for the sole purpose of testifying as to owner-ship. It is believed that the extent of the applicability of the Rules of Evidence to preliminary examinations should be appropriately dealt with by the Federal Rules of Criminal Procedure which regulate those proceedings.

Extradition and rendition proceedings are governed in detail by statute. 18 U.S.C. § 3181-3195. They are essentially administrative in character. Traditionally the rules of evidence have not applied. 1 Wigmore § 4(6). Extradition proceedings are accepted from the operation of the Rules of Criminal Procedure. Rule 54(b)(5) of Federal Rules of Criminal Procedure.

The rules of evidence have not been regarded as applicable to sentencing or probation proceedings, where great reliance is placed upon the presentence investigation and report. Rule 32(c) of the Federal Rules of Criminal Procedure requires a presentence investigation and report in every case unless the court otherwise directs. In Williams v. New York, 337 U.S. 241, 69 S. Ct. 1079, 93 L. Ed. 1337 (1949), in which the judge overruled a jury recommendation of life imprisonment and imposed a death sentence, the Court said that due process does not require confrontation or cross-examination in sentencing or passing on probation, and that the judge has broad discretion as to the sources and types of information relied upon. Compare the recommendation that the substance of all derogatory information be disclosed to the defendant, in A.B.A. Project on Minimum Standards for Criminal Justice, Sentencing Alternatives and Procedures § 4.4, Tentative Draft (1967, Sobeloff, Chm.). Williams was adhered to in Specht v. Patterson, 386 U.S. 605, 87 S. Ct. 1209, 18 L. Ed. 2d 326 (1967), but not extended to a proceeding under the Colorado Sex Offenders Act, which was said to be a new charge leading in effect to punishment, more like the recidivist statutes where opportunity must be given to be heard on the habitual criminal issue.

Warrants for arrest, criminal summonses, and search warrants are issued upon complaint or affidavit showing probable cause. Rules 4(a) and 41(c) of the Federal Rules of Criminal Procedure. The nature of the proceedings makes application of the formal rules of evidence inappropriate and impracticable.

Criminal contempts are punishable summarily if the judge certifies that he saw or heard the contempt and that it was committed in the presence of the court. Rule 42(a) of the Federal Rules of Criminal Procedure. The circumstances which preclude application of the rules of evidence in this situation are not present, however, in other cases of criminal contempt.

Proceedings with respect to release on bail or otherwise do not call for application of the rules of evidence. The governing statute specifically provides:

"Information stated in, or offered in connection with, any order entered pursuant to this section need not conform to the rules pertaining to the admissibility of evidence in a court of law." 18 U.S.C.A. § 3146(f).

This provision is consistent with the type of inquiry contemplated in A.B.A. Project on Minimum Standards for Criminal Justice, Standards Relating to Pretrial Release, § 4.5(b), (c), p.16 (1968). The references to the weight of the evidence against the accused, in Rule 46(a)(1), (c) of the Federal Rules of Criminal Procedure and in 18 U.S.C.A. § 3146(b), as a factor to be considered, clearly do not have in view evidence introduced at a hearing.

The rule does not exempt habeas corpus proceedings. The Supreme Court held in Walker v. Johnston, 312 U.S. 275, 61 S. Ct. 574, 85 L. Ed. 830 (1941), that the practice of disposing of matters of fact on affidavit, which prevailed in some circuits, did not "satisfy the command of the statute that the judge shall proceed 'to determine the facts of the case, by hearing the testimony and arguments.'" This view accords with the emphasis in Townsend v. Sain, 372 U.S. 293, 83 S. Ct. 745, 9 L. Ed. 2d 770 (1963), upon trial-type proceedings, *Id.* 311, 83 S. Ct. 745, with demeanor evidence as a significant factor, *Id.* 322, 83 S. Ct. 745, in applications by state prisoners aggrieved by unconstitutional detentions. Hence subdivision (e) applies the rules to habeas corpus proceedings to the extent not inconsistent with the statute.

Subdivision (e). In a substantial number of special proceedings, *ad hoc* evaluation has resulted in the promulgation of particularized evidentiary provisions, by Act of Congress or by rule adopted by the Supreme Court. Well adapted to the particular proceedings, though not apt candidates for inclusion in a set of general rules, they are left undisturbed. Otherwise, however, the rules of evidence are applicable to the proceedings enumerated in the subdivision.

ADVISORY COMMITTEE'S NOTE — 1987 AMENDMENT

Subdivision (a) is amended to delete the reference to the District Court for the District of the Canal Zone, which no longer exists, and to add the District Court for the Northern Mariana Islands. The United States bankruptcy judges are added to conform the subdivision with Rule 1101(b) and Bankruptcy Rule 9017.

ADVISORY COMMITTEE'S NOTE — 1988 AMENDMENT

The amendments are technical. No substantive change is intended.

ADVISORY COMMITTEE'S NOTE — 1993 AMENDMENT

This revision is made to conform the rule to changes in terminology made by Rule 58 of the Federal Rules of Criminal Procedure and to the changes in the title of United States magistrates made by the Judicial Improvements Act of 1990.

Rule 1102.   Amendments

These rules may be amended as provided in 28 U.S.C. § 2072.

(Pub. L. 93-595, § 1, Jan. 2, 1975, 88 Stat. 1948; Apr. 30, 1991, eff. Dec. 1, 1991; Apr. 26, 2011, eff. Dec. 1, 2011.)

RESTYLED RULE 1102 — ADVISORY COMMITTEE'S NOTE

The language of Rule 1102 has been amended as part of the restyling of the Evidence Rules to make them more easily understood and to make style and terminology consistent throughout the rules. These changes are intended to be stylistic only. There is no intent to change any result in any ruling on evidence admissibility.

ADVISORY COMMITTEE'S NOTE — 1991 AMENDMENT

The amendment is technical. No substantive change is intended.

Rule 1103.   Title

These rules may be cited as the Federal Rules of Evidence.

(Pub. L. 93-595, § 1, Jan. 2, 1975, 88 Stat. 1948; Apr. 26, 2011, eff. Dec. 1, 2011.)

RESTYLED RULE 1103 — ADVISORY COMMITTEE'S NOTE

The language of Rule 1103 has been amended as part of the restyling of the Evidence Rules to make them more easily understood and to make style and terminology consistent throughout the rules. These changes are intended to be stylistic only. There is no intent to change any result in any ruling on evidence admissibility.

APPENDIX B

Unadopted Federal Rules of Evidence

ARTICLE I.   GENERAL PROVISIONS

Rule 105.   Summing Up and Comment by Judge

After the close of the evidence and arguments of counsel, the judge may fairly and impartially sum up the evidence and comment to the jury upon the weight of the evidence and the credibility of the witnesses, if he also instructs the jury that they are to determine for themselves the weight of the evidence and the credit to be given to the witnesses and that they are not bound by the judge's summation or comment.

ARTICLE III.   PRESUMPTIONS

Rule 303.   Presumptions in Criminal Cases

(a) Scope. Except as otherwise provided by Act of Congress, in criminal cases, presumptions against an accused, recognized at common law or created by statute, including statutory provisions that certain facts are prima facie evidence of other facts or of guilt, are governed by this rule.

(b) Submission to jury. The judge is not authorized to direct the jury to find a presumed fact against the accused. When the presumed fact establishes guilt or is an element of the offense or negatives a defense, the judge may submit the question of guilt or of the existence of the presumed fact to the jury, if, but only if, a reasonable juror on the evidence as a whole, including the evidence of the basic facts, could find guilt or the presumed fact beyond a reasonable doubt. When the presumed fact has a lesser effect, its existence may be submitted to the jury if the basic facts are supported by substantial evidence, or are otherwise established, unless the evidence as a whole negatives the existence of the presumed fact.

(c) Instructing the jury. Whenever the existence of a presumed fact against the accused is submitted to the jury, the judge shall give an instruction that the law declares that the jury may regard the basic facts as

(continued)

sufficient evidence of the presumed fact but does not require it to do so. In addition, if the presumed fact establishes guilt or is an element of the offense or negatives a defense, the judge shall instruct the jury that its existence must, on all the evidence, be proved beyond a reasonable doubt.

ARTICLE V.   PRIVILEGES

Rule 501.   Privileges Recognized Only as Provided

Except as otherwise required by the Constitution of the United States or provided by Act of Congress, and except as provided in these rules or in other rules adopted by the Supreme Court, no person has a privilege to:

(1) Refuse to be a witness; or

(2) Refuse to disclose any matter; or

(3) Refuse to produce any object or writing; or

(4) Prevent another from being a witness or disclosing any matter or producing any object or writing.

Rule 502.   Required Reports Privileged by Statute

A person, corporation, association, or other organization or entity, either public or private, making a return or report required by law to be made has a privilege to refuse to disclose and to prevent any other person from disclosing the return or report, if the law requiring it to be made so provides. A public officer or agency to whom a return or report is required by law to be made has a privilege to refuse to disclose the return or report if the law requiring it to be made so provides. No privilege exists under this rule in actions involving perjury, false statements, fraud in the return or report, or other failure to comply with the law in question.

Rule 503.   Lawyer-Client Privilege

(a) **Definitions.** As used in this rule:

(1) A "client" is a person, public officer, or corporation, association, or other organization or entity, either public or private, who is rendered professional legal services by a lawyer, or who consults a lawyer with a view to obtaining professional legal services from him.

(2) A "lawyer" is a person authorized, or reasonably believed by the client to be authorized, to practice law in any state or nation.

(3) A "representative of the lawyer" is one employed to assist the lawyer in the rendition of professional legal services.

(4) A communication is "confidential" if not intended to be disclosed to third persons other than those to whom disclosure is in furtherance of the rendition of professional legal services to the client or those reasonably necessary for the transmission of the communication.

(b) General rule of privilege. A client has a privilege to refuse to disclose and to prevent any other person from disclosing confidential communications made for the purpose of facilitating the rendition of professional legal services to the client, (1) between himself or his representative and his lawyer or his lawyer's representative, or (2) between his lawyer and the lawyer's representative, or (3) by him or his lawyer to a lawyer representing another in a matter of common interest, or (4) between representatives of the client or between the client and a representative of the client, or (5) between lawyers representing the client.

(c) Who may claim the privilege. The privilege may be claimed by the client, his guardian or conservator, the personal representative of a deceased client, or the successor, trustee, or similar representative of a corporation, association, or other organization, whether or not in existence. The person who was the lawyer at the time of the communication may claim the privilege but only on behalf of the client. His authority to do so is presumed in the absence of evidence to the contrary.

(d) Exceptions. There is no privilege under this rule:

(1) Furtherance of crime or fraud. If the services of the lawyer were sought or obtained to enable or aid anyone to commit or plan to commit what the client knew or reasonably should have known to be a crime or fraud; or

(2) Claimants through same deceased client. As to a communication relevant to an issue between parties who claim through the same deceased client, regardless of whether the claims are by testate or intestate succession or by inter vivos transaction; or

(3) Breach of duty by lawyer or client. As to a communication relevant to an issue of breach of duty by the lawyer to his client or by the client to his lawyer; or

(4) Document attested by lawyer. As to a communication relevant to an issue concerning an attested document to which the lawyer is an attesting witness; or

(5) Joint clients. As to a communication relevant to a matter of common interest between two or more clients if the communication was made by any of them to a lawyer retained or consulted in common, when offered in an action between any of the clients.

Rule 504.   Psychotherapist-Patient Privilege

(a) Definitions.

(1) A "patient" is a person who consults or is examined or interviewed by a psychotherapist.

(2) A "psychotherapist" is (A) a person authorized to practice medicine in any state or nation, or reasonably believed by the patient so to be, while engaged in the diagnosis or treatment of a mental or emotional condition, including drug addiction, or (B) a person licensed or certified as a psychologist under the laws of any state or nation, while similarly engaged.

(3) A communication is "confidential" if not intended to be disclosed to third persons other than those present to further the interest of the patient in the consultation, examination, or interview, or persons reasonably necessary for the transmission of the communication, or persons who are participating in the diagnosis and treatment under the direction of the psychotherapist, including members of the patient's family.

(b) General rule of privilege. A patient has a privilege to refuse to disclose and to prevent any other person from disclosing confidential communications, made for the purposes of diagnosis or treatment of his mental or emotional condition, including drug addiction, among himself, his psychotherapist, or persons who are participating in the diagnosis or treatment under the direction of the psychotherapist, including members of the patient's family.

(c) Who may claim the privilege. The privilege may be claimed by the patient, by his guardian or conservator, or by the personal representative of a deceased patient. The person who was the psychotherapist may claim the privilege but only on behalf of the patient. His authority so to do is presumed in the absence of evidence to the contrary.

(d) Exceptions.

(1) **Proceedings for hospitalization.** There is no privilege under this rule for communications relevant to an issue in proceedings to hospitalize the patient for mental illness, if the psychotherapist in the course of diagnosis or treatment has determined that the patient is in need of hospitalization.

(2) **Examination by order of judge.** If the judge orders an examination of the mental or emotional condition of the patient, communications made in the course thereof are not privileged under this rule with respect to the particular purpose for which the examination is ordered unless the judge orders otherwise.

(3) **Condition an element of claim or defense.** There is no privilege under this rule as to communications relevant to an issue of the mental or emotional condition of the patient in any proceeding in which he relies upon the condition as an element of his claim or defense, or, after the patient's death, in any proceeding in which any party relies upon the condition as an element of his claim or defense.

Rule 505.   Husband-Wife Privilege

(a) General rule of privilege. An accused in a criminal proceeding has a privilege to prevent his spouse from testifying against him.

(b) Who may claim the privilege. The privilege may be claimed by the accused or by the spouse on his behalf. The authority of the spouse to do so is presumed in the absence of evidence to the contrary.

(c) Exceptions. There is no privilege under this rule (1) in proceedings in which one spouse is charged with a crime against the person or property of the other or of a child of either, or with a crime against the person or property of a third person committed in the course of committing a crime against the other, or (2) as to matters occurring prior to the marriage, or (3) in proceedings in which a spouse is charged with importing an alien for prostitution or other immoral purpose in violation of 8 U.S.C § 1328, with transporting a female in interstate commerce for immoral purposes or other offense in violation of 18 U.S.C. §§ 2421-2424, or with violation of other similar statutes.

Rule 506.   Communications to Clergymen

(a) Definitions. As used in this rule:

(1) A "clergyman" is a minister, priest, rabbi, or other similar functionary of a religious organization, or an individual reasonably believed so to be by the person consulting him.

(2) A communication is "confidential" if made privately and not intended for further disclosure except to other persons present in furtherance of the purpose of the communication.

(b) General rule of privilege. A person has a privilege to refuse to disclose and to prevent another from disclosing a confidential communication by the person to a clergyman in his professional character as spiritual adviser.

(c) Who may claim the privilege. The privilege may be claimed by the person, by his guardian or conservator, or by his personal representative if he is deceased. The clergyman may claim the privilege on behalf of the person. His authority so to do is presumed in the absence of evidence to the contrary.

Rule 507.   Political Vote

Every person has a privilege to refuse to disclose the tenor of his vote at a political election conducted by secret ballot unless the vote was cast illegally.

Rule 508.   Trade Secrets

A person has a privilege, which may be claimed by him or his agent or employee, to refuse to disclose and to prevent other persons from disclosing a trade secret owned by him, if the allowance of the privilege will not tend to conceal fraud or otherwise work injustice. When disclosure is directed, the judge shall take such protective measure as the interests of the holder of the privilege and of the parties and the furtherance of justice may require.

Rule 509.   Secrets of State and Other Official Information

(a) Definitions.

(1) Secret of state. A "secret of state" is a governmental secret relating to the national defense or the international relations of the United States.

(2) Official information. "Official information" is information within the custody or control of a department or agency of the government the disclosure of which is shown to be contrary to the public interest and which consists of: (A) intragovernmental opinions or recommendations submitted for consideration in the performance of decisional or policy-making functions, or (B) subject to the provisions of 18 U.S.C. § 3500, investigatory files compiled for law enforcement purposes and not otherwise available, or (C) information within the custody or control of a governmental department or agency whether initiated within the department or agency or acquired by it in its exercise of its official responsibilities and not otherwise available to the public pursuant to 5 U.S.C. § 552.

(b) General rule of privilege. The government has a privilege to refuse to give evidence and to prevent any person from giving evidence upon a showing of reasonable likelihood of danger that the evidence will disclose a secret of state or official information, as defined in this rule.

(c) Procedures. The privilege for secrets of state may be claimed only by the chief officer of the government agency or department administering the subject matter which the secret information sought concerns, but the privilege for official information may be asserted by any attorney representing the government. The required showing may be made in whole or in part in the form of a written statement. The judge may hear the matter in chambers, but all counsel are entitled to inspect the claim and showing and to be heard thereon, except that, in the case of secrets of state, the judge upon motion of the government, may permit the government to make the required showing in the above form in camera. If the judge sustains the privilege upon a showing in camera, the entire text of the government's statements shall be sealed and preserved in the court's records in the event of appeal. In the case of privilege claimed for official information the court may require examination in camera of the information itself. The judge may take any protective measure which the interests of the government and the furtherance of justice may require.

(d) Notice to government. If the circumstances of the case indicate a substantial possibility that a claim of privilege would be appropriate but has not been made because of oversight or lack of knowledge, the judge shall give or cause notice to be given to the officer entitled to claim the privilege and shall stay further proceedings a reasonable time to afford opportunity to assert a claim of privilege.

(e) Effect of sustaining claim. If a claim of privilege is sustained in a proceeding to which the government is a party and it appears that another party is thereby deprived of material evidence, the judge shall make any further orders which the interests of justice require, including striking the testimony of a witness, declaring a mistrial, finding against the government upon an issue as to which the evidence is relevant, or dismissing the action.

Rule 510. Identity of Informer

(a) Rule of privilege. The government or a state or subdivision thereof has a privilege to refuse to disclose the identity of a person who has furnished information relating to or assisting in an investigation of a possible violation of law to a law enforcement officer or member of a legislative committee or its staff conducting an investigation.

(b) Who may claim. The privilege may be claimed by an appropriate representative of the government, regardless of whether the information was furnished to an officer of the government or of a state or subdivision thereof. The privilege may be claimed by an appropriate representative of a state or subdivision if the information was furnished to an officer thereof, except that in criminal cases the privilege shall not be allowed if the government objects.

(c) Exceptions.

(1) Voluntary disclosure; informer a witness. No privilege exists under this rule if the identity of the informer or his interest in the subject matter of his communication has been disclosed to those who would have cause to resent the communication by a holder of the privilege or by the informer's own action, or if the informer appears as a witness for the government.

(2) Testimony on merits. If it appears from the evidence in the case or from other showing by a party that an informer may be able to give testimony necessary to a fair determination of the issue of guilt or innocence in a criminal case or of a material issue on the merits in a civil case to which the government is a party, and the government invokes the

(continued)

privilege, the judge shall give the government an opportunity to show in camera facts relevant to determining whether the informer can, in fact, supply that testimony. The showing will ordinarily be in the form of affidavits, but the judge may direct that testimony be taken if he finds that the matter cannot be resolved satisfactorily upon affidavit. If the judge finds that there is a reasonable probability that the informer can give the testimony, and the government elects not to disclose his identity, the judge on motion of the defendant in a criminal case shall dismiss the charges to which the testimony would relate, and the judge may do so on his own motion. In civil cases, he may make any order that justice requires. Evidence submitted to the judge shall be sealed and preserved to be made available to the appellate court in the event of an appeal, and the contents shall not otherwise be revealed without consent of the government. All counsel and parties shall be permitted to be present at every stage of proceedings under this subdivision except a showing in camera, at which no counsel or party shall be permitted to be present.

(3) **Legality of obtaining evidence.** If information from an informer is relied upon to establish the legality of the means by which evidence was obtained and the judge is not satisfied that the information was received from an informer reasonably believed to be reliable or credible, he may require the identity of the informer to be disclosed. The judge shall, on request of the government, direct that the disclosure be made in camera. All counsel and parties concerned with the issue of legality shall be permitted to be present at every stage of proceedings under this subdivision except a disclosure in camera, at which no counsel or party shall be permitted to be present. If disclosure of the identity of the informer is made in camera, the record thereof shall be sealed and preserved to be made available to the appellate court in the event of an appeal, and the contents shall not otherwise be revealed without consent of the government.

Rule 511.   Waiver of Privilege by Voluntary Disclosure

A person upon whom these rules confer a privilege against disclosure of the confidential matter or communication waives the privilege if he or his predecessor while holder of the privilege voluntarily discloses or consents to disclosure of any significant part of the matter or communication. This rule does not apply if the disclosure is itself a privileged communication.

Rule 512.   Privileged Matter Disclosed under Compulsion or without Opportunity to Claim Privilege

Evidence of a statement or other disclosure of privileged matter is not admissible against the holder of the privilege if the disclosure was (a) compelled erroneously or (b) made without opportunity to claim the privilege.

Rule 513.   Comment upon or Inference from Claim of Privilege; Instruction

(a) Comment or inference not permitted. The claim of a privilege, whether in the present proceeding or upon a prior occasion, is not a proper subject of comment by judge or counsel. No inference may be drawn therefrom.

(b) Claiming privilege without knowledge of jury. In jury cases, proceedings shall be conducted, to the extent practicable, so as to facilitate the making of claims of privilege without the knowledge of the jury.

(c) Jury instruction. Upon request, any party against whom the jury might draw an adverse inference from a claim of privilege is entitled to an instruction that no inference may be drawn therefrom.

ARTICLE VIII.   HEARSAY

Rule 804.   Hearsay Exceptions: Declarant Unavailable . . .

(b) Hearsay exceptions. — The following are not excluded by the hearsay rule if the declarant is unavailable as a witness: . . .

(2) Statement of recent perception. A statement, not in response to the instigation of a person engaged in investigating, litigating, or settling a claim, which narrates, describes, or explains an event or condition recently perceived by the declarant, made in good faith, not in contemplation of pending or anticipated litigation in which he was interested, and while his recollection was clear.

TABLE OF CASES

Principal cases are italicized.

TABLE OF FEDERAL RULES
OF EVIDENCE

TABLE OF AUTHORITIES

Berger, M., *The Deconstitutionalization of the Confrontation Clause: The Fallacy That Hearsay Rules and the Confrontation Clause Protect Similar Values*, 76 Minn. L. Rev. 557 (1992), 316

Berger, V., *Man's Trial, Woman's Tribulation: Rape Cases in the Courtroom*, 77 Colum. L. Rev. 1 (1977), 364

Birdsong, *The Exclusion of Hearsay Through Forfeiture by Wrongdoing — Old Wine in a New Bottle — Solving the Mystery of the Codification of the Concept into Federal Rule 804(b)(6)*, 80 Neb. L. Rev. 891 (2001), 283

Blakely, *Article IV: Relevancy and Its Limits*, 20 Hous. L. Rev. 151 (1983), 427

Broeder, *The University of Chicago Jury Project*, 38 Neb. L. Rev. 744 (1959), 443

Broun, *Authentication and Contents of Writings*, 1969 Law & Soc. Ord. 611, 62

_____, *Giving Codification a Second Chance — Testimonial Privileges and the Federal Rules of Evidence*, 53 Hastings L.J. 769-815 (2002), 593

Bryden & Park, *"Other Crimes" Evidence in Sex Offense Cases*, 78 Minn. L. Rev. 529 (1994), 368

Bullock & Gardner, *Prior Consistent Statements and the Premotive Rule*, 24 Fla. St. U. L. Rev. 509 (1997), 504

Callen, *Hearsay and Informal Reasoning*, 47 Vand. L. Rev. 43 (1994), 170

_____, *Othello Could Not Optimize: Economics, Hearsay, and Less Adversary Systems*, 22 Cardozo L. Rev. 1791 (2001), 170

Calnan, *The Insurance Exclusionary Rule Revisited: Are Reports of Its Demise Exaggerated?*, 52 Ohio St. L.J. 1177 (1991), 443

Cammack, *The Jurisprudence of Jury Trials: The No Impeachment Rule and the Conditions for Legitimate Decisionmaking*, 64 U. Colo. L. Rev. 57 (1993), 33

Carlson, *Collision Course in Expert Testimony: Limitations on Affirmative Introduction of Underlying Data*, 36 Fla. L. Rev. 234 (1984), 570

_____, *Policing the Bases of Modern Expert Testimony*, 39 Vand. L. Rev. 577 (1986), 570

_____, *Scope of Cross-Examination and the Proposed Federal Rules*, 32 Fed. B.J. 244 (1973), 452

Carr, *Voices, Texts, and Technology: Evidence Law Confronts Tapes and Their Transcriptions*, 35 St. Louis U. L.J. 289 (1991), 62

Cecil et al., *Citizen Comprehension of Difficult Issues: Lessons from Civil Jury Trials*, 40 Am. U. L. Rev. 727 (1991), 14

Chafee, *Privileged Communications: Is Justice Served or Obstructed by Closing the Doctor's Mouth on the Witness Stand?*, 52 Yale L.J. 607 (1943), 630

Cleary & Strong, *The Best Evidence Rule: An Evaluation in Context*, 51 Iowa L. Rev. 825 (1966), 67

Clinton, *The Right to Present a Defense: An Emergent Constitutional Guarantee in Criminal Trials*, 9 Ind. L. Rev. 711 (1976), 325

Cohen, *Subjective Probability and the Paradox of the Gatecrasher*, 1981 Ariz. St. L.J. 635, 121

Comment, *The Spousal Testimonial Privilege After Trammel v. United States*, 58 Den. L.J. 357 (1981), 645

Conley et al., *The Power of Language: Presentation Style in the Courtroom*, 1978 Duke L.J. 1375, 452

Cordray, *Evidence Rule 806 and the Problem of Impeaching the Nontestifying Declarant*, 56 Ohio St. L.J. 495 (1995), 509

Crump, *On the Uses of Irrelevant Evidence*, 34 Hous. L. Rev. 1 (1997), 93

Rapoport, Note, *Evidence: Proper Disclosure During Trial That Defendant Is Insured*, 26 Cornell L.Q. 137 (1940), 443

Rasmusen, *Mezzanatto and the Economics of Self-Incrimination*, 19 Cardozo L. Rev. 1541 (1998), 428

Report No. 45, Group for the Advancement of Psychiatry 92 (1960), 599

Rice, *Inadmissible Evidence as a Basis for Expert Testimony: A Response to Professor Carlson*, 40 Vand. L. Rev. 583 (1987), 570

Richman, *Bargaining About Future Jeopardy*, 48 Vand. L. Rev. 1181 (1996), 438

Risinger et al., *The Daubert/Kumho Implications of Observer Effects in Forensic Science: Hidden Problems of Expectation and Suggestion*, 90 Cal. L. Rev. 1 (2002), 566

_____ & Saks, *Science and Nonscience in the Courts: Daubert Meets Handwriting Identification Expertise*, 82 Iowa L. Rev. 21 (1996), 566

Robinson, *From Fat Tony and Matty the Horse to the Sad Case of A.A.: Defensive and Offensive Use of Hearsay Evidence in Criminal Cases*, 32 Hous. L. Rev. 895 (1995), 325

Rosenberg, *Judicial Discretion of the Trial Court, Viewed from Above*, 22 Syracuse L. Rev. 635 (1971), 101

Roth, *Understanding Admissibility of Prior Bad Acts: A Diagrammatic Approach*, 9 Pepp. L. Rev. 297 (1982), 394

Saltzburg, *Communications Falling Within the Attorney-Client Privilege*, 66 Iowa L. Rev. 811 (1981), 620

_____, *The Harm of Harmless Error*, 59 Va. L. Rev. 988 (1973), 23

_____, *Offers of Proof: The Basic Requirement*, 17 Crim. Just. 50 (2002), 23

_____, *Standards of Proof and Preliminary Questions of Fact*, 27 Stan. L. Rev. 271 (1975), 670

Sanchirico, *Character Evidence and the Object of Trial*, 101 Colum. L. Rev. 1227 (2001), 368

Scallen, *Classical Rhetoric, Practical Reasoning, and the Law of Evidence*, 44 Am.U.L. Rev. 101 (1995), 7

Schmertz, *Relevancy and Its Policy Counterweights: A Brief Excursion Through Article IV of the Proposed Federal Rules of Evidence*, 33 Fed. B.J. 1 (1974), 419

Schwartz, *The Exclusionary Rule on Subsequent Repairs — A Rule in Need of Repair*, 7 Forum 1 (1971), 419

Seidelson, *Extrinsic Evidence on a Collateral Matter May Note Be Used to Impeach Credibility: What Constitutes "Collateral Matter"?*, 9 Rev. Litig. 203 (1990), 509

_____, *Implied Assertions and Federal Rule of Evidence 801: A Quandary for Federal Courts*, 24 Duq. L. Rev. 251 (1974), 168

_____, *The State of Mind Exception to the Hearsay Rule*, 13 Duq. L. Rev. 251 (1974), 222

Sexton, *A Post-Upjohn Consideration of the Corporate Attorney-Client Privilege*, 57 N.Y.U. L. Rev. 443 (1982), 620

Sharpe, *Two-Step Balancing and the Admissibility of Other Crimes Evidence: A Sliding Scale of Proof*, 55 Notre Dame L. Rev. 556 (1984), 394

Sheppard, Commentary, *Subterfuge: Improper Impeachment of a Party's Own Witness in Alabama*, 53 Ala. L. Rev. 1003 (2002), 459

Shuman, *The Origins of the Physician-Patient Privilege and Professional Secret*, 39 Sw. L.J. 661 (1985), 630

_____ & Weiner, *The Privilege Study: An Empirical Examination of the Psychotherapist-Patient Privilege*, 60 N.C. L. Rev. 893 (1982), 630

INDEX